# YEARBOOK OF
# EUROPEAN ENVIRONMENTAL LAW

## Vol. 2

# YEARBOOK OF EUROPEAN ENVIRONMENTAL LAW

## Volume 2

H. SOMSEN
*Lecturer at Nijmegen University*
*Editor-in-Chief*

H. SEVENSTER
*Professor at the University*
*of Amsterdam*
CURRENT SURVEY
EDITOR

J. SCOTT
*Lecturer at the University*
*of Cambridge*
BOOK REVIEW
EDITOR

L. KRÄMER
*DG Environment,*
*Commission of the*
*European Communities*
DOCUMENTS
EDITOR

T. F. M. ETTY
ASSISTANT EDITOR

OXFORD
UNIVERSITY PRESS

# OXFORD
UNIVERSITY PRESS

Great Clarendon Street, Oxford ox2 6DP

Oxford University Press is a department of the University of Oxford.
It furthers the University's objective of excellence in research, scholarship,
and education by publishing worldwide in

Oxford  New York

Athens Auckland Bangkok Bogotá Buenos Aires Cape Town
Chennai Dar es Salaam Delhi Florence Hong Kong Istanbul Karachi
Kolkata Kuala Lumpur Madrid Melbourne Mexico City Mumbai Nairobi
Paris São Paulo Shanghai Singapore Taipei Tokyo Toronto Warsaw
with associated companies in Berlin Ibadan

British Library Cataloguing in Publication Data
Data available

Library of Congress Cataloging in Publication Data
Data available
ISBN 0–19–924778–1

1 3 5 7 9 10 8 6 4 2

Typeset by Hope Services (Abingdon) Ltd.
Printed in Great Britain
on acid-free paper by
Biddles Ltd., Guildford and King's Lynn

# Editorial Committee

# Editor's Preface

Dictated by political reality rather than by design, European environmental policy has entered a crucial phase. Two recent developments, in particular, have forced the European Union in a position where, more than ever before, it bears primary responsibility for the global environment. First, in the face of growing evidence that a new introspective Bush administration is not prepared to lead by example, and to make sacrifices which have become inevitable to combat climate change, such global leadership at present is not to be anticipated from the United States of America. Loibl's chapter shows that, despite intricate and serious institutional obstacles, the role of the European Union in the formation of international environmental law indeed can be constructive and exemplary, but that this requires high degrees of inter-institutional coordination.

Second, and closer to home, sooner or later an enlarged European Union will need to dispose radical and innovative environmental policies and laws for new Member States which have little or no tradition in environmental management. Initially, it may appear questionable whether the as yet untested instrument of Enhanced Cooperation, designed to allow a core of Member States to accelerate European integration within the framework of existing institutional arrangements and procedures, necessarily at the expense of laggards, is the proper response to enlargement. However, on the basis of an analysis of the wider dynamics of integration, Bär *et al.* convincingly argue that Enhanced Cooperation does not need to lead to a rift in regulatory intensity between 'ins' and 'outs', but instead may serve as an incentive for the latter to catch up.

Political developments and realities ultimately must also affect legal scholarship. Scholars too often still treat EC environmental law as an exponent of a 'new' policy, which therefore to a large extent is approached as a species of more established goals associated with the establishment of the internal market. Consequently, the parameters for such a policy are also obtained with reference to the same instruments and processes as those developed in the context of EC trade law. What is increasingly called for, however, is an autonomous and innovative set of legal tools, offering effective solutions to growing environmental decline, which therefore often may not neatly fit preconceived ideas.

One important lesson nonetheless may be learned from internal market policy. After thirty years of sustained efforts to establish an internal market, the Commission finally decided to force progress in 1985 by publishing its revolutionary White Paper on the Completion of the Internal Market. Thirty years have also passed since the Paris Summit of 1972, in which the Heads of State and Government called upon the institutions of the Community to develop an environmental policy. Although the prevailing political climate is different and the problems faced are more complex, in the light of an assessment of past achievements there is every reason to be similarly creative and radical in the formulation of appropriate new initiatives. Krämer courageously undertakes such a self-critical and constructive assessment in this volume.

If it is agreed that, in this period of flux, radical policy innovation is what is needed, then perhaps so is constitutionalization of environmental imperatives. Such a constitution would serve to instruct the EC to act, to provide the necessary competencies and substantive guidance for such action, and to protect citizens against breaches of fundamental rights. In his chapter, Winter outlines 'a pragmatic approach, which may help to avoid the present stalemate where, on the basis of a state-centred definition of constitution, creative reformatory design is often deemed proof of a European federal state'.

Some current principles of EC environmental law already enjoy quasi-constitutional status. Among these, the principle of integration of Article 6 EC features prominently. It instructs the EC to incorporate environmental goals in all its policies, and hence emancipates environmental law from the straitjacket of internal market principles. It is a measure of the complexity of the principle, that such a large proportion of the policy papers reviewed by Krämer in the Documents Section of this volume struggle with the question as to how it may be implemented in practice, and how indicators may be developed by which progress in the integration of environmental imperatives in other policy areas may be measured.

A case study by Geradin focuses on a similar balancing exercise in the key policy area of competition and suggests that, currently, the Commission applies an established and, one could be forgiven for suggesting, relatively inadventurous set of tests. It remains to be seen whether the principle of integration can affect the operationalization of, in particular, the principle of proportionality in this field in a way similar to which the principle of proximity of Article 175 EC has affected the fundamentals of the free movement of goods provisions of Articles 28 to 30 EC.

Intrinsically connected with these constitutional issues are questions pertaining to the nature and significance of the concept of 'individual environmental rights'. Originally and somewhat erratically developed in relation to market participants, Prechal and Hancher disentangle the many ambiguities which undermine the legal significance of this concept, while proposing alternative doctrinal and institutional directions.

Another important aspect of the wider constitutional debate relates to the accountability of the Commission in the context of its different responsibilities as enforcer of EC environmental law. Williams shows that, as it stands, Community law allows the Commission to remain almost entirely unaccountable. Treaty reform being an unlikely prospect, and the ratification of the Aarhus Convention merely a distant possibility, it appears that in the short term any innovation will have to come from the Court of First Instance and the European Court of Justice.

Calls for the constitutionalization of EC environmental law may not appear readily compatible with the growing recourse to Law and Economics methodology in the search for EC policy responses to environmental decline.

After all, employing terminology that appears to forebode President Bush's bluntly worded rejection of the Kyoto protocol, Stewart readily concedes that this legal discipline has a normative component, in that:

> the normative criterion that Law and Economics generally adopts . . . to determine which laws and arrangements should be adopted in practice is maximization of aggregate individual welfare, where welfare is defined in terms of satisfaction of individual preferences, and preference-satisfaction is measured quantitatively in terms of how much individuals would pay in order to satisfy their preferences.

Yet, it would be folly to underplay the force of economic analyses in the design of environmental instruments, which in turn may be based on other, non-economical values. The methodology of Law and Economics, arguably, should in fact be afforded a role of increased importance in the light of the future accession by new Member States which simply do not possess bureaucracies realistically capable of administering and subsequently enforcing command and control regulation.

This being as it may, the appeal of Law and Economics as a tool to develop environmental instruments largely stems from the rational, relatively value-free methodology it appears to represent. Interestingly, adopting an innovative microsociological approach to examine the roots of the shift from command and control regulation towards the use of the 'new instruments' developed by proponents of this methodology, Dezalay focuses on the internal dynamics of this revolution. Some 150 interviews in Brussels and four European countries with professionals, bureaucrats, managers, and interest groups, provide persuasive evidence that the rise of new instruments also is the outcome of internal power struggles. This conclusion significantly undermines the *prima facie* legitimacy of the case for new instruments.

Although certainly fully compatible with the logic of new instruments, in particular the principle that the polluter must pay, such power struggles appear to explain the excessive delays, even by the standards of the European Union, in adopting let alone agreeing, a Directive on Civil Liability for Environmental Damage. Betlem and Brans show that, even when ultimately adopted, the Directive will merely bring about a liability regime for a limited category of environmental damage. Nonetheless, the White Paper on Civil Liability for Environmental Damage contains a number of positive innovations, in particular as regards *locus standi* and the amount of damages. These innovations may more generally serve as examples of the way in which the European Union should discharge its global environmental responsibility.

In the light of the changing political climate, the European Union now has the opportunity to show its capacity to lead the way in the development of constitutional arrangements, accommodating the environment in a trade-driven world, as well as in the design of operational environmental instruments, both 'new' and 'old', to fulfil these constitutional duties.

HAN SOMSEN
*Editor-in-Chief*

# Acknowledgements

This volume of the *Yearbook of European Environmental Law* is the result of the combined efforts of a growing number of individuals and organizations. Even though it will be impossible to do justice to all of them, I first of all wish to express my sincere thanks for the substantial specialized assistance provided by the Centre for Environmental Law of the University of Amsterdam. The Law Faculty of Nijmegen University also provided crucial financial support for a student-assistant. This volume benefited significantly from the expertise and professionalism of the Pallas Consortium of Nijmegen University which, sponsored by the European Commission, organized a stimulating conference that served to discuss ideas for many of the chapters published in this volume. I wish to thank Anne-Marie Van den Bossche for so unselfishly allowing her assistant, Floris Van Laanen to devote a considerable part of his time and boundless energy to this volume.

I am particularly fortunate that Joanne Scott agreed to take responsibility for the Book Review Section, and provide regular advice and assistance on many other matters. Ludwig Krämer's first-hand knowledge of environmental and institutional affairs once more proved an invaluable asset, which is reflected in a comprehensive, informative, and critical Documents Section. The Annual Survey of this volume continues to benefit from Hanna Sevenster's expertise and leadership. Joseph McCahery's creative mind on many occasions has come to the rescue when my own was letting me down. During what at times has been a difficult year, David Freestone never failed to offer his support and encouragement. I am deeply indebted to Anne Marie Sprokkereef who, after returning from work, voluntarily spent many late hours checking the typescript, yet never allowed fatigue to dampen her enthusiasm for the project.

All these efforts, however, would not have sufficed had it not been for the unqualified dedication and natural talents of Thijs Etty. I am conscious that the demands I made on him sometimes were unreasonable, and often impossible.

Finally, I have been privileged to be entrused with the work of the lawyers, political scientists, economists, and sociologists, who as referees and authors have all contributed to the realization of this volume.

HAN SOMSEN
*Editor-in-Chief*

# Contents

# List of Contributors

**Stefani Bär** is a solicitor and Senior Research Fellow at Ecologic, Centre for International and European Environmental Research in Berlin (*Federal Republic of Germany*). She published on the role of environmental interest groups in European Community environmental policy-making, and currently researches the environmental impact of future enlargements of the European Union.

**Gerrit Betlem** is Senior Lecturer at the University of Exeter (England), where he teaches European Community law and international business law. His research interests and numerous publications focus on comparative tort law, in particular environmental liability, and more generally European private (international) law, with an emphasis on the private enforcement of European Community law. It is also in this area that he published his monograph *Civil Liability for Transfrontier Pollution* (Graham & Trotman: London, 1994).

**Edward Brans** is Lecturer in Law at the Free University of Amsterdam (the Netherlands). He has published on issues concerning environmental liability and assessment of damages for injury to natural resources. He undertook one of the background studies for the European Commission in preparation of the White Paper on Environmental Liability, and was involved in a study for the follow-up of the White Paper. His forthcoming monograph *Liability for Damage to Public Natural Resources* will be published with Kluwer Law International.

**Yves Dezalay** is *Directeur de Recherches* at the CNRS (Centre National de la Recherche Scientifique), (France) and an affiliated scholar of the American Bar Foundation where he works with Bryant Garth on the emergence of an international legal field, and the restructuring of state and political elites. For more than twenty years, his work has focused on corporate professionals such as lawyers, consultants, and economists whose transformation has been analysed from a comparativist and multi-disciplinary perspective. He has published countless articles in books, journals, and newspapers. His most recent book is entitled *Global Palace Wars: Lawyers, Economists and the Destructive Creation of the State in Latin America* (Paris: Editions du Seuil, 2001).

**Damien Geradin** is an Associate Professor of Law at the University of Liège (Belgium) and a Professor at the College of Europe in Bruges (Belgium). He has also held visiting appointments at King's College London, the University of Paris II, Yale Law School, Peking University, and UCLA School of Law. His research interests include European, international, and comparative law. He holds a Ph.D. in law from Cambridge University, and was a Fulbright Research Scholar at Yale Law School.

**Leigh Hancher** is Professor of European Law at Tilburg University (the Netherlands). She co-authored *EC State Aids Law* (Carswell: Toronto, 1999), and has published numerous articles dealing with many aspects of European competition law, state aids law, and utility law. She is general editor of *Utilities Law Review* (Wiley) and a member of the editorial boards of *Utilities Policy* (Elsevier), the *European Law Journal* (Blackwell), and the *Netherlands Yearbook of International Law* (Martinus Nijhoff).

**Ingmar von Hoymeyer** is Research Fellow at Ecologic, Centre for International and European Environmental Research in Berlin (Germany). Previously, he has worked in the European Parliament in different capacities. At present, his research concentrates on issues of European environmental policy, in particular the implications of future enlargements. He is preparing a doctoral thesis on the regulation of biotechnology in Europe at the European University Institute (Florence, Italy).

**Anneke Klasing** is Research Fellow at Ecologic, Centre for International and European Environmental Research (*Berlin, Federal Republic of Germany*). Her research focuses on European Communty environmental policy, in particular its integration in other policies of the European Union, and the environmental impact of enlargement.

**Ludwig Krämer** has since long held a wide range of responsibilities in the European Commission. He also is Professor at the Faculty of Law at the University of Bremen (*Federal Republic of Germany*). His numerous publications in the field of European Community environmental law include *European Environmental Law* (London: Sweet & Maxwell, 1993), *Focus on European Environmental Law* (2nd edn., London: Sweet & Maxwell, 1997), and *EC Treaty and Environmental Law* (4th edn., London: Sweet & Maxwell, 2000). His most recent co-authored book is *Economic Development and Environmental Gain: European Integration and Regional Competitiveness* (Earthscan: London, 2001).

**Gerhard Loibl** is Professor of Public International Law at the University of Vienna (Austria), and member of the Faculty of the Diplomatic Academy in Vienna. He also teaches in the LL.M. programme of the University of London. He is currently chairman of the Water Resources Committee of the International Law Association, and editor-in-chief of the *Austrian Review of International and European Law*. He has widely published on a wide range of issues of public international law, law of international organizations, European law, and international environmental law.

**Sacha Prechal** is Professor of European Law at Tilburg University (the Netherlands). She has published extensively in the area of European law, in particular on various aspects of the relationship between European Community law and national law, and on issues related to directives. Apart from various articles on these questions, she has published a monograph entitled *Directives in European Community Law* (Oxford: Oxford University Press, 1995).

**Rhiannon Williams** is a solicitor specializing in environmental law with Renouf & Co. in Brussels (Belgium). She previously worked in the Legal Affairs Unit of DG Environment of the European Commission. She graduated in law from the University of Cambridge, and has a *Licence Spéciale en Droit Européen*, and a Master's degree in environmental law. She has published various articles on substantive European environmental law, and has focused on issues of enforcement.

**Richard B. Stewart** is Emily Kempin Professor of Law and Director of the Centre on Environmental and Land Use Law at New York University (USA). He teaches on environmental law, international environmental law, torts, and comparative environmental law. He has published books and articles on numerous issues of environmental law related to the use of economic incentives, trade and investment, administrative law and regulation, and international and comparative law. His most recent co-edited book is *Environmental Law, the Economy, and Sustainable Development: Europe, the United States and the Global Regime* (Cambridge: Cambridge University Press, 2000). He co-authored the fourth edition of *Administrative Law and Regulatory Policy* (Little, Brown & Co., 1998).

**Gerd Winter** is Professor of Public Law, European Law and Legal Sociology at the University of Bremen (*Federal Republic of Germany*). He is head of the *Forschungsstelle für Europäisches Umweltrecht* at the same university. He acts as a legal adviser to various bodies and institutions outside the university. His edited work includes *European Environmental Law—A Comparative Perspective* (Aldershot: London, 1996) and *Sources and Categories of European Union Law* (Nomos: Badean-Baden, 1996). His most recent publication is his edited book *Risk Assessment and Risk Management of Toxic Chemicals in the European Community* (Nomos: Baden-Baden, 2000).

# Table of Cases

**United States of America**

# Table of Legislation

*Directives*

**France**

**Germany**

# The Importance of Law and Economics for European Environmental Law

## I. Introduction

The discipline of Law and Economics has made important contributions to our understanding of environmental problems that arise as a result of human activity and the role of law in promoting environmental protection. It has also contributed significantly to improving environmental law and policy in the USA. These contributions can be beneficially applied to the future development of environmental law in Europe.

Although Law and Economics traces its roots back to Jeremy Bentham, it emerged as a distinct intellectual movement about thirty years ago in the USA. The discipline of Law and Economics has since attained wide currency in US universities and research institutes, and has spawned an enormous output of research and publications in law, public policy studies, political science, and economics. It is beginning to become established in European academic circles and research centres. Originally focused primarily on competition law and economic regulation, Law and Economics research now aspires to provide a comprehensive account of legal rules and institutions. It has examined an extraordinarily broad range of public and private law and institutional topics, including environmental law and regulation.[1]

Law and Economics methodology and research has made important contributions to our understanding of the anthropogenic sources of and potential remedies for environmental problems.[2] Its contributions, moreover, are not

* Emily Kempin, Professor, New York University School of Law, New York City, NY. I am grateful to Richard Revesz for helpful comments and Brian Wheeler for research assistance. Research for this article was supported by the Filomen D'Agostino and Max E. Greenberg Research Fund of New York University School of Law.

[1] For an overview of Law and Economics and relevant literature, see R. Posner, *Economic Analysis of Law* (New York: Aspen Publishing, 1998); R. Cooter, *Law and Economics* (Reading, Mass.: Addison-Wesley, 2000). A comparative perspective is provided in U. Mattei, *Comparative Law and Economics* (Ann Arbor: University of Michigan Press, 1997). Leading Law and Economics journals include the *Journal of Law and Economics* and the *Journal of Legal Studies*, both published by the University of Chicago Press.

[2] See the literature excerpted, discussed, and referenced in R. L. Revesz, *Foundations of Environmental Law and Policy* (New York: Oxford University Press, 1997). Excellent basic expositions of the economic approach to environmental problems and their solution are presented in W. J. Baumol and W. C. Oates, *The Theory of Environmental Policy* (New York: Cambridge University Press, 1988); R. N. Stavins, *Economics of the Environment: Selected Readings* (New York: W. W. Norton, 2000) (hereinafter Stavins, *Economics of the Environment*).

solely academic. Law and Economics has had a major practical impact on environmental law and policy in the USA. It has promoted systematic analysis of the costs and benefits of environmental regulatory measures, most notably through procedures for regulatory analysis and review of the costs and benefits of major new federal environmental regulations. Law and Economics has also stimulated attention to more cost-effective means of achieving environmental goals, including use of market-based regulatory instruments in lieu of command and control regulation. It has stimulated reconsideration of how responsibility for environmental regulation should be allocated among different levels of government. Perhaps most important, the application of Law and Economics techniques to government decisions about environmental regulation has helped to bring a greater degree of transparency, discipline, and accountability to these decisions. These several contributions have been fostered by hospitable changes in social, economic, and political circumstances:

— the emergence of a political consensus that sustained economic growth requires firm limits on government spending;
— recognition that environmental regulation 'spends' massive amounts of society's economic resources, and must accordingly be carefully examined and wisely designed;
— the demise of state socialism and central economic planning, and the overall success of market-oriented economic deregulation and privatization throughout the world;
— recognition that traditional command regulatory approaches are often unduly costly, penalize investment and innovation, and are ill-suited to meet the public's demand for continued improvements in environmental quality;
— demand for greater discipline and accountability for decision-making by remote, centralized regulatory bureaucracies.

These same circumstances are increasingly found in Europe. Accordingly, there is a good reason to suppose that Law and Economics can make contributions to EC environmental law and policy similar to those that it has made in the USA.

## II. Law and Economics

As a discipline, Law and Economics has two analytically distinct aims and methods.[3] First, it has a positive component that seeks to determine what effects legal rules and institutions have on behaviour. Law and Economics researchers seek to answer this question by positing that individuals act as rational maximizers of their welfare and by developing models, based on this assumption, to examine the behavioural incentives created by different legal

[3] M. J. Trebilcock, 'An Introduction to Law and Economics' (1997) 23 *Monash University Law Review*, 123.

rules and their effects on conduct. They study how individuals (and, by extension, business firms and other organizations) will respond to the incentives created by legal rules and institutions in different settings, including market settings. They also gather and analyse empirical data on behaviour under legal rules in order to test hypotheses generated by the models, and determine the effects of legal arrangements. Public choice theory, developed primarily by political scientists and economists, seeks to apply the assumptions and methods of economics to study political institutions.[4]

Second, Law and Economics has a normative component. It seeks to evaluate whether the effects of different legal rules and institutional arrangements are desirable or not, and on that basis to determine which laws and arrangements should be adopted. The normative criterion that Law and Economics generally adopts in making these evaluations in practice is maximization of aggregate individual welfare, where welfare is defined in terms of satisfaction of individual preferences, and preference-satisfaction is measured quantitatively in terms of how much individuals would pay in order to satisfy their preferences. In order to apply this criterion of value to evaluate alternative legal rules and institutions, researchers must systematically account for the benefits provided and the costs entailed by the alternatives. They then add the various costs and benefits through use of a common metric—money—in order to determine the net value (benefits minus costs) of each alternative, and identify the one that generates the highest net value and thereby maximizes societal welfare.[5] This is the alternative that should be selected. The ultimate normative objective of Law and Economics is to maximize collective individual welfare within existing resource constraints. Legal rules and institutions are regarded as a form of social capital which, if properly designed, can enhance societal welfare by providing actors in ways that benefit society. Property law, for example, can create desirable incentives for persons to conserve and enhance the value of natural and other resources by ensuring that they reap the fruits of their investments. Contract law can help ensure that resources are allocated to those that can use them most productively, and provide the legal and institutional foundation for cooperative ventures for mutual gain.

The assumption that individuals act rationally to maximize their individual preference satisfaction has been challenged as unrealistic in many situations. Law and Economics proponents reply, with considerable force, that it is a useful simplifying assumption for purposes of analysis, and that it has considerable realism in many settings, especially market settings. The norm of social welfare maximization, defined in terms of individual preference-satisfaction

---

[4] D. Farber and P. Frickey, *Law and Public Choice* (Chicago: University of Chicago Press, 1991).
[5] This and other normative criteria that have been developed by welfare economics are discussed in R. Dorfman, 'An Introduction to Cost-Benefit Analysis' in R. Dorfman and N. S. Dorfman, *Economics of the Environment: Selected Readings* (New York: W. W. Norton, 1993), 297; K. J. Arrow, 'Criteria for Social Investment' (1965) 1 *Water Resources Research*, 1. See also Trebilcock, n. 3 above (criticizing normative criterion of wealth maximization).

based on willingness to pay and monetized costs and benefits, has been attacked as one-sided and impoverished in its assumption that all questions of value are a function of whatever preferences individuals may happen to have, disregarding the collective or communitarian elements of norms and other ethical concerns and considerations of justice. The normative limitations of Law and Economics appear to be especially pronounced in the context of environmental law and policy, which is informed by a wide range of non-utilitarian ethical considerations and values.[6] Criticisms have also been levied at the use of discount rates, especially market rates, to discount the future environmental benefits of measures taken today.[7]

On the other hand, the perspective and methodology of Law and Economics is in many respects well suited for understanding environmental concerns and advancing environmental objectives. The focus of Law and Economics is on how best to address resource scarcity, which is also the fundamental problem of environmental policy. The question for both enterprises is how to arrange laws and institutions so as to facilitate and promote beneficial human activity without causing environmental harm and impairing the ecological resource base that supports and sustains all life. Thus, the orientation and the concerns of Law and Economics are in many respects similar to those of sustainable development.[8] Law and Economics can also provide significant assistance in diagnosing how laws may be redesigned to provide incentives for conduct in order to prevent such degradation and promote sustainable use of natural resources.

Law and Economics has developed an extremely powerful conceptual structure and a rich body of research that has made profound contributions to our understanding of how environmental problems arise, and how they can be most effectively addressed. One need not accept the Law and Economics system of normative value in order to appreciate these contributions, and use them in order to improve environmental law and policy. Even if one rejects welfare maximization as the sole goal of social policy, one can use the insights of economic analysis instrumentally to design laws and measures as a means to promote goals based on justice and other moral and ethical values that are non-economic in character. Moreover, the normative element of Law and Economics cannot be disregarded. Trade-offs between environmental goals and other societal goals and values are inevitable and pervasive. Economic cost-benefit analysis illuminates these trade-offs and provides valuable insight into the societal implications of different environmental laws and policies, even if it is not accepted as the sole criterion of decision.

---

[6] R. Stewart, 'Regulation in a Liberal State: The Role of Non-Commodity Values' (1983) 92 *Yale Law Journal*, 1537.

[7] For discussion, see R. L. Revesz, 'Environmental Regulation, Cost-Benefit Analysis, and the Discounting of Human Lives' (1999) 99 *Columbia Law Review*, 941; R. M. Solow, 'The Economics of Resources or the Resources of Economics' (1974) 64 *American Economic Review*, 1.

[8] Revesz, n. 7 above; R. M. Solow, 'Sustainability: An Economist's Perspective' in Stavins, *Economics of the Environment*, n. 2 above, 179.

### III.  Potential Contributions of Law and Economics to Environmental Law

What is the relevance, analytical utility, and normative contribution of economic analysis in understanding and evaluating environmental regulatory issues? Law and Economics generally views environmental problems as instances of market failures.[9] This insight can inform the design of legal measures to solve environmental problems by redressing such failures, and providing incentives for actors to change their conduct in ways that will reduce environmental problems. Economic analysis can be used to analyse the incentives provided by different types of laws and institutions and their consequences, both positive and negative, in market as well as non-market settings. Such analysis can help improve the design and performance of environmental law and regulations and the choice of regulatory instruments and institutional designs, including decisions about which level of government should be responsible for dealing with particular types of environmental problems in multi-jurisdictional legal and political systems, such as the European Union (EU), the USA, or the global community.[10]

Researchers that rely on Law and Economics to illumine environmental legal and regulatory issues use various methodological approaches. For example, studies of the effects of assigning primary responsibility for environmental regulation to lower-level jurisdictions, such as states in the USA or the Member States in the EU, have used economic theory and models of industry investment and location decisions to examine whether competition in environmental regulation among lower-level jurisdictions will lead to a 'race to the bottom', resulting in inadequate environmental protection. Those researching this question have also relied on game theory to analyse strategic interactions between jurisdictions competing for industrial investment. Researchers have also conducted empirical studies, which tend to show that environmental regulatory compliance costs are generally a very small fraction of total production costs, and that environmental regulation is not a significant factor in locational decisions by industry. This evidence tends to confirm the conclusion, reached by analysis based on economic theory and formal models, that decentralized environmental regulation will not lead to a welfare-diminishing 'race to the bottom'.[11]

---

[9] This analysis, of course, is most pertinent for market economies. The analysis of environmental degradation under state socialist regimes is somewhat different, based principally on public choice methodology.

[10] R. L. Revesz, P. Sands, and R. B. Stewart, *Environmental Law, the Economy, and Sustainable Development: Europe, the United States, and the Global Regime* (Cambridge: Cambridge University Press, 2000) (hereinafter Revesz, Sands, and Stewart, *Environmental Law and Economy*).

[11] R. L. Revesz, 'Federalism and Environmental Regulation: An Overview' in Revesz, Sands, and Stewart, *Environmental Law and Economy*, n. 10 above, 37 (and sources there cited); R. van den Bergh, 'Economic Criteria for Applying the Subsidiarity Principle in European Environmental Law' in Revesz, Sands, and Stewart, *Environmental Law and Economy*, n. 10 above, 80.

Researchers with legal training who are not economists generally do not use formal economic models, but draw in a more eclectic fashion on economic theory and insights on issues such as market failures, incentive effects, cost-effectiveness, allocational consequences, cost-benefit analysis, discount rates, collective good and free-rider problems, scale economies, comparative advantage, and property rights and contract regimes. They seek to use these insights to examine the consequences of different environmental regulatory arrangements and measures, and to draw conclusions about their appropriate design. Political scientists and others use public choice analysis to apply economic axioms to environmental regulatory politics and decision-making. For example, researchers have shown that the political and institutional interests that shape environmental law and policy are far more complex than the 'polluters *versus* environmentalists' stereotype, and have explained how many elements of environmental law are the product of conflicts among business, regional, and other organized economic instruments.[12] They have used collective action analysis to challenge the claim that centralization of environmental regulation at the federal or EU level is needed to offset organizational disadvantages that environmental interests assertedly incur relative to production interests when regulatory decisions are made by lower-level jurisdictions.[13]

As a result of such research, there is increasingly widespread recognition of the relevance and value of economic analysis to understanding environmental legal and regulatory issues. Economic analysis, in both positive and normative modes, is now a staple of environmental legal and policy analysis and discourse in the USA by academics, government authorities, industry, and environmental and consumer groups. At the same time, those who use Law and Economic approaches are generally well aware of the non-economic dimensions of environmental regulatory issues, including considerations of justice and equity. Many Law and Economics practitioners, however, do not view the welfare economic and non-economic dimensions of environmental policy as in fundamental conflict. Indeed, they tend to view them as mutually reinforcing, believing that well-crafted environmental regulatory institutions and instruments can advance both types of goals. Whether this view is unduly optimistic must await the lessons of further experience.

[12] B. Ackerman and W. Hassler, *Clean Coal and Dirty Air, or How the Clean Air Act Became a Multibillion-Dollar Bail-Out for High-Sulfur Coal Producers and What Should Be Done About It* (New Haven: Yale University Press, 1981); M. T. Maloney and R. E. McCormick, 'A Positive Theory of Political Economy' (1982) 25 *Journal of Law Economics and Organization*, 99; B. P. Pashigian, 'Environmental Regulation: Whose Self-Interests Are Being Protected?' (1985) 23 *Economic Inquiry*, 651.

[13] R. L. Revesz, 'The Race to the Bottom and Environmental Regulation: A Response to Critics' (1997) 82 *Minnesota Law Review*, 535, 542–3, 558–61; R. L. Revesz, 'Federalism and Environmental Regulation: A Public Choice Perspective' (forthcoming); R. L. Revesz, 'Environmental Regulation in Federal Systems' (2000) 1 *Yearbook of European Environmental Law*, 1–35.

## IV. Institutional Origins of and Remedies for Environmental Problems

In its positive aspect, Law and Economics provides a powerful conceptual framework for analysing how environmental problems arise, and how different types of legal rules and instruments perform in redressing those problems by providing different types of incentives for actors. In the context of a market economy, many environmental problems arise as a result of market failures. One perspective on market failure emphasizes externalities; excessive environmental degradation occurs because firms and other actors do not have to pay for the social costs imposed on others by the pollution and other forms of environmental degradation that they cause.[14] A related perspective emphasizes the lack of effective, well-defined property rights in common resources, which results in a lack of incentives for actors to protect those resources, and the inability of contractual arrangements to ensure that such resources are allocated to their socially most valuable uses.[15]

These failures result in a systematic divergence between the social costs (the costs imposed on society) that result from pollution and other by-products of human activity, including destruction or alternation of natural resources, and private costs (the costs faced by those undertaking such activities); private costs are generally lower than social costs.[16] As a result, actors do not bear the full costs imposed on society by their use of environmental resources, resulting in over-exploitation of natural resources, and excessive pollution and ecological destruction and degradation.[17] These failures of markets can also be regarded as failures of private law, ultimately attributable to high transaction costs.[18] If, for example, private law could effectively impose liability for all of the external harms caused by pollution, polluters would bear the cost of those externalities, and invest in pollution reduction up to the point where the additional costs of further reductions exceeded the benefits to the polluter of reduced liability. Alternatively, if private law could create effective individual property rights in environmental resources such as airsheds, polluters would have to contract with the owners of such rights for an easement or lease of the right at a price that would reflect the diminution in the value of those rights due to the pollution. Through these mechanisms, an ideally effective system of private law would mobilize the price system, either in the form of damages liabilities or contract payments in connection with property transactions, to internalize to polluters the social costs imposed on others by pollution and

[14] This insight was first formulated in the 1920s by the English economist A. C. Pigou. See A. C. Pigou, *The Economics of Welfare* (London: Macmillan & Co., 1932), 183.

[15] G. Hardin, 'The Tragedy of the Commons' (1968) 162 *Science*, 1243; H. S. Gordon, 'The Economic Theory of a Common-Property Resource: The Fishery' (1954) 62 *Journal of Political Economy*, 124.

[16] R. Turvey, 'On Divergences between Social Cost and Private Cost' in Dorfman and Dorfman, n. 5 above, 139 (first published in *Economica* in August 1963); A. Randall, 'The Problem of Market Failure', (1983) 23 *National Resources Journal*, 131.

[17] Ibid.

[18] R. H. Coase, 'The Problems of Social Cost' (1960) 3 *Journal of Law and Economics*, 1.

thereby provide them with economic incentives to reduce pollution. Such incentives would not result in elimination of pollution. Residuals are an inevitable by-product of human activity. Rather, the threat of damages liability or the need to pay others for using their property interests in environmental resources would lead polluters to reduce the generation of residuals to the point where the additional costs to the polluter of achieving additional reductions (through pollution control, resource efficiency measures, or reducing the level of the activity in question) would exceed the additional benefits to the polluter (in the form of reduced liabilities or contractual payments) and to society as a whole (in the form of enhanced environmental quality).

Analysis and experience show, however, that private law is incapable of dealing effectively with many environmental problems, such as widespread pollution, caused by many actors and affecting many individuals, because of the high transactions costs involved.[19] Such circumstances make it too difficult and costly to sort out causal responsibility for individual harm and impose liability on the responsible actors through case-by-case court litigation. Also, individuals generally lack information about the impacts on them of pollution; such information would be costly to acquire. Further, the harm suffered by or risk of harm posed to most individuals is too small to justify the costs of litigation. For similar reasons, it would be enormously difficult and transactionally costly to develop, through private law, a system of well-defined individual property rights in what are currently common resources, such as the atmosphere, that would enable holders of such rights effectively to exclude others from infringing them without permission.

For similar reasons, failures of markets and private law also lead to destruction or degradation of natural resources that provide valuable ecological services and are prized for their beauty, rarity, or ecological uniqueness. These ecosystem and preservation benefits are a positive environmental spillover, which are analogous to negative environmental spillovers such as pollution. In many instances they are not effectively recognized and protected as property rights by the legal system, and are therefore ignored by markets. The result is that those who own or manage such natural resources lack adequate market incentives to preserve them. Consider the example of rain forest preservation; the costs of preservation are borne by local populations, while the benefits are regional and global. Yet, there are no mechanisms for charging the beneficiaries, and using the proceeds to compensate local populations for preserving the resource.[20] It would be far too transactionally costly to develop and implement such compensation arrangements through private law; new legal and institutional structures must be developed.

Because of these twinned failures of markets and private law, environmental problems must often be addressed through administrative regulatory pro-

---

[19] P. S. Menell, 'Institutional Fantasylands; From Scientific Management to Free Market Environmentalism' (1992) 15 *Harvard Journal of Law and Public Policy*, 489.

[20] G. Heal, 'Markets and Sustainability' in Revesz, Sands, and Stewart, *Environmental Law and Economy*, n. 10 above, 410.

grammes. Command and control regulation, specifying the conduct of each pollution source or other regulated entity, has been the regulatory instrument of choice. Command regulation is a form of central planning of economic activity.[21] Law and Economics analysis reveals the inherent inefficiencies of such an approach in many applications. The defects of central economic planning in state socialist regimes, including excessive rigidity and cost, and inadequate incentives for innovation, are now well known. The interdependencies between economic and environmental issues have confronted regulatory decision makers with the challenge of meeting public demands for higher levels of environmental, health, and safety protection in an era in which there is increasing concern about regulatory costs and competitiveness, and a trend towards privatization of many previously entrenched governmental functions. Yet, laissez-faire is not an acceptable solution to environmental problems because of the existence of pervasive market and private law failures. In these circumstances, Law and Economics has made an important contribution by focusing attention on alternative, market-based regulatory instruments, which in many applications provide incentives for cost-effective environmental protection that are superior to those of command regulation, and far less transactionally costly than private law arrangements. Governments can mobilize the price system to internalize environmental costs and reward environmental resource preservation by imposing taxes or fees on pollution or by creating new forms of property rights in environmental resources in the form of tradable pollution quotas or credits or legally protected rights in watershed protection services, genetic resources, and atmospheric quality. Economic analysis can also provide useful guidance to government decision- makers in determining the substantive objectives of environmental laws through systematic consideration of the costs and benefits of alternative measures in order to target societal resources in such a way as to enhance the environmental benefit achieved.

## V. Alternative Regulatory Instruments for Environmental Protection

### A. THE INHERENT LIMITATIONS OF COMMAND AND CONTROL REGULATION

Command and control environmental regulation dictates specific conduct by each of many regulated actors, backed up by punitive sanctions for non-compliance, in order to produce environmental quality. When carried on a centralized basis, through US federal regulation or European Community (EC) legislation, such regulation must address staggering complexities.[22] For

---

[21] R. Stewart, *Markets v. Environment?* (Florence: Robert Schuman Centre, European University Institute, 1995).

[22] P. Caulkins and S. Sessions, 'Water Pollution and the Organic Chemicals Industry' in R. D. Morgenstern (ed.), *Economic Analysis at EPA* (Washington, DC.: Resources for the Future, 1997) (hereinafter *Economic Analysis at EPA*), 87. Caulkins and Sessions describe complexities encountered by EPA in devising technology-based discharge standards for water pollution discharges by US organic chemicals industry.

example, a command system of air pollution regulation in Europe or the USA requires detailed specifications of conduct for hundreds or thousands of different types of industrial and commercial stationary sources of air pollution that vary widely in character, as well as tens of millions of motor vehicles. Such regulation is a form of central economic planning that shares the inherent inefficiencies of all such systems. Throughout the world, central planning of economic activity has deservedly collapsed because of its built-in inefficiencies. Central planners are unable to gather and process the information needed to write directives that respond appropriately to the diverse and changing conditions of a dynamic economy composed of millions of firms and individuals. They cannot tap the 'local knowledge' of managers and other economic actors whose mobilization is vital to the workings of an innovative and efficient economy.[23] Rigid central planning blueprints cannot provide the necessary incentives and flexibility to meet changing social needs and spur innovation. Command and control environmental regulation is plagued by these same fundamental and irreparable defects.

Research inspired by Law and Economics has shown that, because of the need to economize on information and decision-making costs, central regulators tend to favour regulatory standards based on the level of pollution or waste control that can be achieved by Best Available Technology (BAT), as opposed to measures based, for example, on the degree of residuals limitation needed to achieve environmental quality goals. For the same reasons, they tend to adopt uniform requirements for all sources within a given industry or other category and do not attempt to coordinate regulations for different types of sources, and the discharge of different residuals, to different environmental media. As a result, requirements are not systematically tailored to variations among plants, industries, and economic sectors in the costs of limiting residuals. Sources with high costs of pollution or waste control tend to be held to the same requirements as those with lower costs. The total costs to society of achieving a given overall level of limitation of a given pollutant would be significantly reduced by shifting limitations from sources with high marginal control costs to those with low costs, to the point where marginal control costs for all sources of the same residual were equal. It would, however, neither be practicable nor equitable to achieve this goal within a command regulatory system. As a result, the costs of achieving a given overall level of pollution control under such a system can be twice or more what they would be under more flexible market-based regulatory instruments such as pollution fees or tradable pollution permits, which can achieve a far more cost-effective allocation of limitations burdens.[24]

In order to improve environmental quality while maintaining economic growth, enterprises must be given both the incentive and the flexibility to

---

[23] F. A. Hayek, 'The Use of Knowledge in Society' (1945) 35 *American Economic Review*, 519.

[24] B. Ackerman and R. Stewart, 'Reforming Environmental Law' (1985) 37 *Stanford Law Review*, 301 (and sources there cited); T. H. Tietenberg, *Emissions Trading: An Exercise in Reforming Pollution Policy* (Washington, DC.: Resources for the Future, 1985).

devise and adopt innovative, resource-efficient methods of production that reduce the amount of residuals generated per unit of output.[25] While command regulation can ensure adoption of existing technologies, the incentives that it provides for innovation are at best uneven and often counter-productive. The detailed requirements and short deadlines for compliance that are characteristic of command regulation tend to deny firms the lead time and flexibility necessary to make the investments and undertake the research and development needed to develop fundamentally new resource-efficient production processes and products. Centralized command regulation also inhibits innovation because uniform regulatory requirements are generally adopted on a piecemeal basis to regulate specific pollutants discharged into specific media from different types of discharge sources in all facilities of a given general type, without any consideration of the compatibility of all of these myriad different requirements in the practical circumstances of operating individual facilities. Among the important innovations needed to meet environmental as well as economic goals is the development and adoption of integrated pollution and waste prevention and resource efficiency measures, taking into account the specific characteristics, production methods, products, and markets of each facility. Inflexible uniform command requirements that have been adopted piecemeal for different residuals from different waste streams not only fail to encourage such innovations but often preclude them. Efforts to develop integrated pollution control approaches within the command structure in order to address this problem have met with only limited success.[26]

Command regulation also presents inherent problems of governance. It requires the government regulators to decide complex scientific, engineering, and economic issues in order to specify a myriad of control requirements for many hundreds of thousands of facilities. The sheer magnitude of the task inevitably requires the delegation of very large discretionary powers to specialized administrative bodies. Accordingly, the use of command regulation inexorably shifts decision-making power to centralized regulatory bureaucracies, such as the Environmental Protection Agency (EPA) in Washington and the European Commission in Brussels, creating serious problems of democratic accountability.[27]

In the past, command regulation has made important contributions to environmental protection. It is not, however, well suited to meeting the current and future regulatory challenge posed by many environmental problems. In the early stages of environmental regulation, command regulation was targeted on major facilities. The inherent inefficiencies of the command sys-

---

[25] R. B. Stewart, 'Regulation, Innovation and Administrative Law: A Conceptual Framework' (1981) 69 *California Law Review*, 1259.

[26] J. E. Krier and M. Brownstein, 'On Integrated Pollution Control' (1992) 22 *Environmental Law*, 119; D. Chalmers, 'Inhabitants in the Field of European Community Environmental Law' (1999) 5 *Columbia Journal of European Law*, 39 and 71 (describing experience under the UK's integrated pollution prevention and control programme).

[27] R. B. Stewart, 'Madison's Nightmare' (1990) 57 *University of Chicago Law Review*, 335; R. B. Stewart, 'Antidotes to the American Disease' (1993) 20 *Ecology Law Quarterly*, 85.

tem were not of much consequence because the means of reducing pollution and waste were obvious and controls were relatively cheap to implement. The situation that post-industrial economies now face is quite different. Major sources of pollution and wastes are already tightly controlled. Further reductions will be quite costly and require significant advances in technologies and in the character and organization of production and consumption. In order to sustain further environmental progress, not only must additional reductions be obtained from major sources, but discharges from small, non-point or area sources must be significantly curtailed, residuals created by consumers addressed, and resource efficiency enhanced throughout all sectors of production and consumption. The proliferation of ever more detailed regulations in an effort to meet these demands within the established command and control paradigm has accentuated the problems characteristic of central economic planning: information overload, rigidity, lack of coordination and consistency among different requirements, economic inefficiency, limited efficacy, and excessive accretion of centralized bureaucratic power. A fundamental shift in the regulatory paradigm is required.

### B. ECONOMIC INCENTIVE SYSTEMS FOR ENVIRONMENTAL PROTECTION

Law and Economics analysis has served to focus and document the important advantages of using economic regulatory instruments in lieu of command and control directives to achieve environmental objectives. It has played a significant role in promoting the growing interest in and use of such instruments.[28]

Economic Incentive Systems (EIS) use a set of behavioural incentives in order to promote environmental goals that is fundamentally different from that used by command regulation. Command regulation fixes, directly or indirectly, the quantity or rate of pollution or waste generated by each source, and often dictates or constrains the choice of means for achieving that limitation. Sources pay nothing for the pollution that they are allowed to discharge. EIS establish, directly or indirectly, a price that must be paid for each unit of residuals generated, but leave each actor free to decide on the level of residuals that it generates and how to achieve it.

There are many different types of EIS. Four different types of EIS have the greatest potential to serve as alternatives to command techniques for addressing environmental problems that cannot be adequately addressed by private law.[29]

---

[28] For an overview, see R. B. Stewart, 'Economic Incentives for Environmental Protection: Opportunities and Obstacles' in Revesz, Sands, and Stewart, *Environmental Law and Economy*, n. 10 above, 171.

[29] Other types of EIS include the following:

*Market-based information strategies* involve government measures—such as imposing disclosure requirements on firms or instituting ecolabel programmes—to provide consumers and investors with information regarding the environmental performance of products and firms. To the extent that consumers or investors value superior environmental performance in their purchasing or investing decisions, the market will penalize firms with inferior performance through diminished sales and higher capital costs.

*Liability for environmental damage* imposed by statutory schemes of liability such as the US Superfund programme for hazardous waste clean-up can be viewed as a form of EIS, because it

*i. Fees or taxes* on pollution, wastes, and other residuals directly impose a price on each unit of residuals generated or discharged by a source.

*ii. Tradable residuals quota or credit systems* create new forms of property rights in the use of environmental resources such as the atmosphere, water bodies, or the ground to dispose of pollution and other residuals. By limiting the total number of such rights, requiring sources to hold rights equal to the discharges that they generate, and making the rights transferable, these systems effectively impose a price on residuals. Thus, under a tradable quota system, the government issues a fixed number of pollution permits or allowances, limiting the aggregate amount of residuals that may be generated by all of the sources subject to the system. Quotas are distributed by government to individual sources by auction or by legislative or administrative allocation. A source may not emit residuals in excess of the number of quotas that it holds. Quotas may be bought, sold, and traded by anyone. Because the demand for quota permits exceeds the supply, they carry a positive price. A tradable quota system effectively imposes a cost on a source for each additional unit of pollution that it generates; the source must either purchase an additional quota or incur the opportunity cost of forgoing sale of a surplus quota that it already holds. In contrast to an environmental tax, under a tradable quota system the price on residuals is set by market supply and demand for quotas rather than directly by the government, and the aggregate quantity of pollution is fixed.[30] A variant of tradable quotas is a system of Emission Reduction Credits (ERC); a source that reduces pollution below the levels fixed by command regulations can obtain a credit which it can sell to other sources which they can use to help meet their regulatory obligations.[31]

---

imposes a price on conduct that causes environmental harm or loss. Liability systems generally operate *ex post*, and require a showing that harm or loss was caused by a given actor; these characteristics limit its effectiveness in dealing with some types of environmental harms. On the other hand, the general and pervasive applicability of the incentives provided by the threat of damages liability are an important advantage of liability systems as compared to regulatory measures that must be designed and targeted at particular risks *ex ante*.

[30] The implications for regulatory performance of this difference between environmental tax and quota trading systems is examined in L. Ruff, 'The Economic Common Sense of Pollution' (1970) 19 *The Public Interest*, 69; A. M. Spence and M. L. Weitzman, 'Regulatory Strategies for Pollution Control' in A. Friendlander (ed.), *Approaches to Controlling Air Pollution* (Cambridge, Mass.: MIT Press, 1979), 199.

[31] Under a tradable quota system, the government sets a limit on aggregate residuals. Under an ERC system, government initially sets required residuals limitations for each source through command requirements. Unlike pollution fee systems, residuals trading systems require development of a well-functioning market to establish an accurate price for residuals and ensure that sources can readily buy or sell quota permits or credits. The system must be designed to minimize transaction costs which would otherwise impede trading. See R. N. Stavins, 'Transaction Costs and Tradable Permits' (1995) 21 *Journal of Environmental Economics and Management*, 133. In order for a well-functioning market to develop, there must be a large number of sources; accordingly, a trading system must generally cover a relatively wide geographic area. In order to keep track of the new property rights that it has created, and ensuring that sources residuals levels do not exceed the number of quota permits or credits that they hold, the government must establish a system for recording trades and keeping accounts of holdings; the costs of doing so, however, are modest. Steps may also be necessary to address potential problems of market power with respect to quotas. See R. W. Hahn, 'Market Power and Transferable Property Rights' (1984) 99 *Quarterly Journal of Law and Economics*, 755.

*iii. Mitigation banking and transferable resource development and use rights* are forms of trading systems that can be used to implement land use controls and natural resource preservation schemes with environmental objectives. Under mitigation banking programmes, those who fund government acquisition and make binding legal commitments to preserve wildlife habitat or wetlands receive credits that they can use or sell to others in order to proceed with projects that will alter other habitat areas or wetlands.[32] Developers can invest in such mitigation projects directly or purchase credits from others who do so. This system limits the extent of development projects that alter the environment in potentially harmful ways by imposing a price (in the form of the cost of mitigation credits) based on the extent and intensity of the environmental stresses imposed by an activity as well as offsetting their impact through preservation of substitute resources.[33] Under Transferable Development Rights (TDR) programmes, landowners whose development rights are restricted for environmental reasons are given development rights that can be transferred and used for more intensive residential or commercial development in adjacent areas.[34] These techniques respond to the equity claims of the landowners subject to environmental regulation, help to defuse political opposition to land use restrictions, and encourage a regional approach to preservation and development planning.

*iv.* Under *Risk Bubbles*, a facility operates under an aggregative, multimedia 'umbrella' of residuals limitations on pollution and wastes for the facility as a whole. This 'risk cap' creates economic incentives because higher levels of discharges by the facility of a given residual in a given medium carry an opportunity cost in the form of the resources that must be devoted to reducing other residuals in order to stay within the cap. In effect, the cap creates an implicit internal residuals trading market. The risk bubble can be extended 'upstream' to include residuals generated by a facility's suppliers, and 'downstream' to include residuals generated by distributors and the ultimate consumers of its products and services. Such an approach could be a more effective means of controlling small, diffuse sources of pollution and wastes than proliferation of command regulations.

These systems, established by legislation and by administrative initiative, create new forms of property rights in environmental resources in order to advance both environmental and economic objectives.[35] A similar initiative

---

[32] R. C. Gardner, 'Banking on Entrepreneurs: Wetlands, Litigation Banking, and Takings' (1996) 81 *Iowa Law Review*, 527.

[33] There are, however, conflicts and trade-offs in designing a trading system that both takes into appropriate account the relevant specific features of and the environmental services performed by different parcels of wetlands or habitats and developing a well-functioning trading market based on a uniform community and unconstrained trading. See J. Salzman and J. B. Ruhl, 'Currencies and the Commodifications of Environmental Law' (forthcoming in *Stanford Law Review*).

[34] J. T. B. Tripp and D. J. Dudek, 'Institutional Guidelines for Designing Successful Transferable Rights Programs' (1989) 6 *Yale Journal on Regulation*, 369.

[35] See generally C. M. Rose, 'The Several Futures of Property: Of Cyberspace and Folk Tales, Emission Trades and Ecosystems' (1998) 83 *Minnesota Law Review*, 129.

is the creation of Individual Transferable Quotas (ITFQs) to harvest fishing stocks.[36]

Imposing a price on pollution and other environmental stresses creates powerful incentives for sources to minimize these externalities and promotes more efficient and sustainable use of environmental resources. Sources that do a better job in limiting the residuals and other environmental stresses that they generate will save money and enjoy a competitive advantage. Furthermore, competition among firms in developing and adopting less costly means of reducing environmental impacts will create benefits for society as a whole by reducing significantly the overall resource costs to society of achieving its environmental objectives. Each source will tend to limit residuals or other environmental stresses to the level where its marginal cost of limitation equals the price that it must pay on its remaining residuals. Sources with low marginal control costs will control to relatively high levels, and pay less in fees or for quotas than sources with high marginal costs, who will control less. Since all sources of the same residual or stress face the same price, the marginal control costs of all sources tend to converge. The resultant cost savings, relative to a command and control system, can be very large, running to 50 per cent or more.[37] Because the costs of complying with existing command regulatory requirements in the EU and the USA currently run to hundreds of billions of dollars annually, the cost savings from switching to EIS to address many environmental problems would be enormous. Further cost savings will accrue by reason of the fact that price-based regulatory instruments leave firms with broad flexibility to reduce discharges through any and all available means, including process and product changes and resource efficiency, in contrast with technology-based command regulation, which tends to be based on 'end of pipe' and other standardized technology controls. In these ways, well-designed EIS achieve strategic coupling between the decisions of myriad market actors and society's environmental goals, precisely because they do not attempt to dictate specific conduct. Through the price system, they can take advantage of the 'local knowledge' of a myriad of actors throughout the diverse and fast-changing market economy, who have a far better understanding of the opportunities for and means of cost-effectively reducing pollution and other environmental stresses than centralized regulators can ever have.

Economic incentives can also be an effective way of addressing the environmental problems associated with the growing services sectors of the economy.[38] They can steer the conduct of small businesses, farmers, and individual consumers in directions that are environmentally protective, through mechanisms such as pollution taxes on motor vehicle emissions, tradable risk permits for chemical and biological methods of addressing agricultural pests,

---

[36] P. A. Neber *et al.* (eds.), *Rights-Based Fishing* (Dordrecht: Kluwer Academic Publishers, 1988).

[37] Ackerman and Stewart, n. 24 above.

[38] For an analysis of the challenges and opportunities posed by extending environmental regulation to the services sector of the economy, see J. Salzman, 'Beyond the Smokestack: Environmental Protection in the Service Economy' (1999) 47 *University of California at Los Angeles Law Review*, 411.

and risk bubbles targeted on upstream manufacturers and distributors that include downstream impacts of the goods and services that they provide. Deposit/refund systems, which have already been used to promote recycling of beverage containers, can be extended to deal with post-consumer wastes generally or problems such as hazardous wastes generated by small sources and service establishments.

Moreover, EIS result in increases in the relative prices of goods and services that cause environmental problems or are produced by processes that are more highly polluting or otherwise impose higher levels of environmental stress, causing a systematic shift of consumer demand to more environment-friendly patterns of consumption and production.

EIS also have advantages in governance. Through use of price-based regulatory instruments, detailed engineering and economic decisions about the appropriate level and method of pollution control for particular sources are decentralized, via the price system, to managers of firms, who are generally far better equipped to make such decisions than are government officials (although this may not be the case for very small firms). Unlike government officials, they also have strong incentives to achieve residuals limitations at least cost. EIS limit the role of government to basic 'wholesale' decisions such as on the level of pollution taxes or the aggregate amount of pollution quotas. In doing so, these EIS can promote political accountability because the decisions that the government must make are decisions about the overall level of pollution to be allowed. Such macro-level decisions are more visible and comprehensible to the public than the myriad of micro-decisions about complex, facility-specific technology, and cost issues that must be made under a command system.[39] By invoking the price system, these EIS also generate current, accurate, and public information as to the cost of environmental protection measures—an important consideration in any democratic decision-making process. Also, as is illustrated by the history of the US $SO_2$ trading programme, EIS can often be established and implemented more rapidly than command systems, which require many detailed rules of conduct to be established through the adoption of regulations and the incorporation of regulatory requirements in permits for individual sources before they become operational.[40]

In all of these EIS programmes, the political process and the government establish, through the normal processes of public debate and deliberation, the environmental objectives to be achieved and use economic instruments as the means for achieving them. Accordingly, regulatory systems that use these instruments are not properly subject to the criticisms that they treat the environment as a mere commodity or ignore broader non-market ethical and collective values.[41]

---

[39] Ackerman and Stewart, n. 24 above.
[40] The US $SO_2$ trading programme is discussed below.
[41] R. B. Stewart, 'Ethical Objections to the Use of Economic Incentives for Environmental Protection' (forthcoming).

EIS systems, like command regulations, require effective government systems of monitoring and enforcement, backed by adequate sanctions, to ensure compliance with regulatory requirements. Thus, under a pollution tax system, government must ensure that sources pay taxes on all of their discharges, while under a quota trading system it must ensure that sources have quotas equal to their discharges. The flexibility which EIS affords may require greater investment in monitoring of residuals, particularly if sources take advantage of such flexibility to change frequently residuals limitations levels and/or methods, than in the case of command regulation. The added costs of additional or more intensive monitoring under EIS are, however, generally only a fraction of the overall cost savings achieved by EIS.

EIS, such as tax and trading systems, are extremely well suited for addressing environmental problems that can be solved by limiting the total amount of pollution or other environmental stresses generated. Additional steps must be taken to adapt them for dealing with environmental problems involving damage functions that are non-linear, so that serious harm will, for example, result if local residuals concentrations increase beyond a certain point. Typically, tradable quota systems establish an aggregate limitation on the total quantity of residuals discharges throughout a nation or region, but do not provide assurances about local residuals concentrations. Accordingly, one of such instruments may, in some circumstances, result in local pollution 'hot spots'. Command regulation can in principle prevent hot spots from occurring by dictating the level of residuals generated by each source as well as controlling source locations. The contrast between the two types of instruments in this respect should not, however, be overdrawn. In practice, command systems may be less than fully effective or efficient in avoiding locally harmful pollution concentrations. Also, steps can be taken to design EIS in order to deal with the risk of local residuals hot spots by imposing limitations on sources' flexibility with respect to emissions levels, adopting different residual tax levels or quota trading ratios for different geographic areas, or basing taxes or quotas on the environmental quality impacts of residuals generated rather than on the physical quantity of residuals generated.[42] Moreover, serious hot spot problems are by no means ubiquitous. Many important pollution problems, including local exposures to carcinogen residuals and regional or global air pollution, are not characterized by sharp damage function thresholds; the damage function appears to be more linear in character. Higher residuals levels pose somewhat greater risks, lower levels pose somewhat lesser risks. There is no clear 'safe' level. In these circumstances, the central objective is to limit environmental damage by reducing total residuals, rather than to achieve

[42] T. Tietenberg, 'Tradable Permits For Pollution Control When Emission Location Matters: What Have We Learned?' (1995) 5 *Environmental & Resource Economics*, 95; R. L. Revesz, 'Federalism and Interstate Environmental Externalities' (1996) 114 *University of Pennsylvania Law Review*, 2341; J. R. Nash and R. L. Revesz, 'Markets and Geography: Designing Marketable Permit Schemes to Control Local and Regional Pollutants' (forthcoming). See also Salzman and Ruhl, n. 33 above (discussing trade-offs presented in designing a quota trading system that takes appropriate account of local environmental quality variables and also ensures a robust trading market).

a particular quantitative limitation in a specific location. EIS are well adapted to deal with such situations. For example, by using nationwide quota trading, the US 1990 Clean Air Act Amendments have succeeded in reducing $SO_2$-based pollution levels dramatically and provided significant health and ecological benefits for all regions of the country, although some regions have benefited more than others.

### C. ENVIRONMENTAL COVENANTS AND CONTRACTS

An alternative approach to environmental regulation, widely used in Europe, relies on environmental contracts and covenants between government and industry.[43] A given industry (through its trade association) or in some cases an individual firm agrees to make a given reduction in overall discharges of pollution or wastes over a period of years. The government agrees to accept the provisions of the agreement as a substitute for detailed command regulatory requirements that the government has already adopted or that it might adopt if such an agreement had not been reached. Such agreements may serve as a means of implementing regulatory laws, including EU legislation, framed in general terms. In some cases, industry makes a 'voluntary' commitment to achieve designated reductions without a formal agreement with the government.

These techniques are sometimes spoken of as 'market based' or involving the use of economic incentives. Such arrangements, however, are not EIS because they generally impose quantitative limitations on residual discharges rather than prices. Thus, they can appropriately be regarded as a form of 'negotiated command and control'. These arrangements do, however, mitigate many of the disadvantages of detailed command requirements unilaterally imposed by government, and have some of the advantages of EIS. Because they are designed to be responsive to the conditions of specific industries, are generally framed in terms of aggregate residuals discharges, and allow industry a substantial number of years to comply, they afford industry with considerable flexibility in determining the means and timing of reductions, permitting use of innovative approaches to promoting resource efficiency and substantial cost savings. They also do not involve the long delays needed to adopt and implement detailed command regulatory requirements. Environmental covenants and contracts, however, suffer from disadvantages. Their legal status is often doubtful, especially where they function as substitutes for administrative regulations that the government has already adopted. Concerns have been raised about the lack of transparency and the effective exclusion of environmental and other public interests in the negotiation of such arrangements. Effective monitoring and enforcement of industry com-

---

[43] J. M. van Dunne (ed.), *Environmental Contracts and Covenants: New Instruments For a Realistic Environmental Policy?* (Lelystad: Koninklijke Vermande, 1993); The Environmental Law Network (ed.), *Environmental Agreements: The Role and Effect of Environmental Agreements in Environmental Policies, Final Report Summary* (London: Cameron May, 1998).

mitments may not be assured. Because of such concerns, and also because of the US system of congressional rather than parliamentary government, the characteristics of the US legal system, and the general suspicion in the USA towards corporatist approaches, there has been no use in the USA of industry-wide covenants or contracts. EPA, however, has instituted a series of programmes whereby business firms have made voluntary commitments to reduce the discharges of toxic chemicals and promote energy efficiency.[44]

### D. EXPERIENCE WITH ECONOMIC INCENTIVE SYSTEMS

The virtues of economic instruments for environmental protection are not merely theoretical; they have been and are being confirmed by experience. In the USA substantial use has been made of residuals trading systems to control air pollution and of transferable development right and mitigation banking programmes. In Europe, environmental taxes have been widely used. Public choice research has shown how vested stake of regulators, politicians, and many industry and environmental group interests in the command regulatory *status quo* has been a barrier to expanded use of EIS.[45] On the other hand, the growing limitations of the command system in meeting contemporary environmental regulatory challenges is creating increasingly urgent demands for deployment of alternative regulatory strategies. Thus, the rather limited use of EIS to date may be the harbinger of far more extensive applications in the future.

### i. Residuals Trading Systems

In the USA, there has been substantial use of tradable quota and credit systems to provide flexibility within the general federal air pollution control regulatory system, phase out lead additives in petrol, central emissions of ozone-depleting chemicals, and reduce sulphur dioxide emissions by 50 per cent over a ten-year period. These programmes have tended to follow a strategy of allocating quotas or credits by 'grandfathering' existing sources in order to lessen political opposition to their use.[46] These trading programmes have delivered effective environmental protection at costs that are generally far less than those of the command regulatory system.

---

[44] As discussed below, EPA has also experimented, through its Project XL, with the use of environmental contracts at the level of individual facilities.

[45] N. O. Keohane, R. L. Revesz, and R. N. Stavins, 'The Choice of Regulatory Instruments in Environmental Policy' (1998) 22 *Harvard Environmental Law Review*, 613.

[46] Law and Economics analysis shows that if there are efficient markets for quotas and for the commodities produced by sources, allocating quotas by 'grandfathering' existing sources should not impair the environmental and economic performance of the trading system and should not impede entry by new sources that must buy quotas from existing sources. Under such conditions, existing sources will have neither the incentive nor the ability to discriminate against newcomers. Entrants will only enter the market if they are more efficient than an incumbent; this is the case under both quota auction and 'grandfathering' schemes. See, e.g. C. Fischer, S. Kerr, and M. Toman, *Using Emissions Trading to Regulate US Greenhouse Gas Emissions: An Overview of Policy Design and Implementation Issues* (Washington, DC.: Resources for the Future, 1998).

The US EPA has authorized, by regulation, various emissions credit trading programmes to introduce a degree of flexibility in the intricate command regulatory system for air pollution regulation imposed by the Clean Air Act.[47] Under these programmes, many internal trades of emissions reduction credits have occurred within facilities and inside firms, resulting in significant cost savings estimated to run to billions of dollars.[48] External trades between sources have been much more limited because such trades are often subject to stringent regulatory oversight and control on a case-by-case basis.

California has adopted a quota trading programme (RECLAIM) to reduce emissions of sulphur dioxide, nitrogen oxides, and hydrocarbons in the Los Angeles basin.[49] The programme was endorsed by regulators, industry, and many environmental groups out of a belief that it would be too costly and administratively infeasible to achieve significant additional pollution reductions through further intensification of existing command regulations. Despite various programme impediments to trading, RECLAIM has achieved significant pollution reductions at compliance costs below what they would have been under an equivalent command regulatory system. A number of other US states have developed or are developing state and regional programmes for trading nitrogen oxide and hydrocarbon emissions.

EPA's programme to phase out lead additives in petrol during the 1980s used an emissions reduction credit system under which refiners that phased out lead faster or to a greater extent than required by the regulatory schedule could sell credits to other refiners who found it more costly or difficult to meet the schedule. This programme was highly successful and accomplished compliance cost savings running to several hundreds of millions of dollars.[50] Significantly, the cost savings and flexibility afforded by trading and banking secured industry agreement to a faster and deeper phase-out schedule than would have been possible under a command system.

The most far-reaching and successful US trading programme is the sulphur dioxide quota trading system adopted by the 1990 Amendments to the Clean Air Act. This programme is reducing $SO_2$ emissions nationwide by 50 per cent within ten years. Existing fossil fuel electric-generating plants are given $SO_2$ allowances based on sources energy input. New sources are not given allowances but must purchase them. Allowances are issued annually. Each allowance entitles the holder to emit 1 tonne of $SO_2$ in the year of

[47] R. Liroff, *Reforming Air Pollution Regulations: The Toil and Trouble of EPA's Bubble* (Washington, DC.: Conservation Foundation, 1986); T. Tietenberg, *Emissions Trading: An Exercise in Reforming Pollution Policy* (Washington, DC.: Resources for the Future, 1985).

[48] V. Foster and R. W. Hahn, 'Efficient Markets and Smog Control' (1995) 38 *Journal of Law and Economics*, 19 and 21 (estimating cost-savings of $0.5 to $12 billion, in mid-1980s dollars, mainly from intra-firm trading).

[49] T. Klier *et al.*, 'A Mixed Bag: Assessments of Market Performance and Firm Trading Behavior in the $NO_x$ RECLAIM Program' (1997) 40 *Journal of Environmental Planning and Management*, 751.

[50] R. W. Hahn and G. Hester, 'Marketable Permits: Lessons For Theory and Practice' (1989) 16 *Ecology Law Quarterly*, 361, 380–91; R. W. Hahn and R. N. Stavins, 'Incentive-Based Environmental Regulation: A New Era For an Old Idea?' (1991) 18 *Ecology Law Quarterly*, 1, 17.

issuance or a subsequent year. The number of allowances issued to sources is capped, and the cap is lowered over time in order to achieve the programme's overall reduction target. Sources that reduce emissions more quickly or by greater amounts than required by the phase-down schedule can sell their excess allowances to others, or bank them for future use or sale.[51] By reducing compliance costs and giving existing sources valuable property rights, the use of a trading programme in lieu of command regulation broke a decade-long political deadlock on legislation to reduce sulphur emissions in order to curb acid deposition, providing another example of how use of EIS can pay environmental dividends. A commodity market in $SO_2$ allowances has been successfully established. In 1996 over 4 million tonnes of allowances were traded. But most cost savings have come from internal trades within utilities, and the flexibility which the programme has afforded utilities to reduce emissions in the most cost-effective way, including through fuel switching, use of low sulphur or washed coal, energy conservation measures, and development of alternative forms of flue gas desulphurization 'scrubbers', alternatives that would not have been feasible under 'one size fits all' BAT controls. Overall, control costs under the programme are billions of dollars below what they would be under the command and control alternative of requiring universal stack gas scrubbing.[52] The programme has also been a success from an environmental perspective. For example, 1996 emissions, at 5.43 million tonnes, were well below the applicable regulatory cap of 8.12 million tonnes.[53] Requirements that sources participating in the programme install and report data from continuous emissions monitors and a strong system of sanctions has resulted in 100 per cent compliance with the programme's regulatory requirements. By relying on the market to promote environmental objectives, the programme has also provided impressive administrative efficiencies as well. It has achieved well over half of the total reductions in pollution obtained as a result of US environmental regulation during the past decade, yet it is administered by an EPA staff of only twenty.

The USA has also successfully implemented a system of tradable emissions quotas in CFCs and other ozone-depleting substances in order to phase out

---

[51] For detailed discussion of the $SO_2$ programme, see R. Schmalensee *et al.*, 'An Interim Evaluation of Sulfur Dioxide Emissions Trading' (1998) 12 *Journal of Economic Perspectives*, 53 (summarizing empirical analysis of compliance costs and allowance market performance); P. L. Joskow *et al.*, 'The Market for Sulfur Dioxide Emissions' (1998) 88 *American Economic Review*, 669 (finding that the $SO_2$ trading market had become efficient by 1994).

[52] R. N. Stavins, 'What Can We Learn from the Grand Policy Experiment? Lessons from $SO_2$ Allowance Trading' (1998) 12 *Journal of Economic Perspectives*, 69–70 (estimating savings of up to $1 billion per year as compared to command-and-control baseline); D. Burtow, 'The $SO_2$ Emissions Trading Program: Cost Savings Without Allowance Trades' (1996) 14 *Contemporary Economic Policy*, 79 (noting that estimated costs of $1 billion in 1997, $1.3 billion in 2000, and $2.2 billion in 2010 represent savings of 40% from command and control baseline, with promise of substantially more savings as allowance trading increases).

[53] A. D. Ellermann *et al.*, *Emissions Trading Under the U.S. Acid Rain Program: Evaluation of Compliance Costs and Allowance Market Performance* (Cambridge, Mass.: MIT Center for Energy and Environmental Policy Research, 1997). This text has been superceded by A. D. Ellermann *et al.*, *Markets for Clean Air: The U.S. Acid Rain Program* (New York: Cambridge University Press, 2000).

use of these chemicals pursuant to the requirements of the Montreal Protocol and the London Agreement, implemented domestically through the Clean Air Act.[54]

There is also developing interest in the use of tradable effluent credits to deal with water pollution. There have been experimental uses of this technique in the USA and a number of other countries, including China.[55]

At the international level, the Kyoto Protocol to the Framework Convention on Climate Change authorizes a variety of greenhouse gas (GHG) emissions trading arrangements, including several GHG trading systems among developed countries and another GHG trading system that includes developed and developing countries, and provides for participation by private sector entities. Criteria and procedures for implementing these arrangements are under active deliberation. The European Commission has recently issued a Green Paper on Greenhouse Gas Emissions Trading within the EU as a means of contributing to EU compliance with its Kyoto obligations. Denmark has adopted a domestic $CO_2$ trading system, and other nations, including the UK, Sweden, Australia, and Canada are actively considering the adoption of such systems. Trading systems are especially well suited to address GHG because they mix globally, with the result that all GHG reductions provide the same environmental benefit, regardless of where they occur. Also, the marginal costs of GHG reductions vary enormously among sectors and among nations; accordingly, the costs savings achieved by use of trading in lieu of traditional command regulation are dramatic, amounting to 75 per cent or more. Further, GHG trading between developed and developing countries can provide significant amounts of private capital to promote environmental modernization and energy efficiency in developing countries, creating local as well as global environmental benefits.[56]

## ii. *Environmental Taxes*

Environmental taxes or fees are increasingly being used to address a variety of environmental problems in Western Europe, countries with economies in transition, and a number of developing countries. Charges may be imposed directly on residuals based on the amount of pollution discharged or waste generated. Alternatively, charges may be imposed on inputs to a polluting activity (such as a tax on motor vehicle fuels), or on polluting substances in an input (such as a tax on the carbon or sulphur content of fuels), or on a final product (such as sales of motor vehicles or disposable products); in the latter case, the relation between the charge and residuals generated is more indirect.

[54] R. W. Hahn and A. M. McGartland, 'The Political Economy of Instrument Choice: An Examination of the US Role in Implementing the Montreal Protocol' (1989) 83 *Northwestern University Law Review*, 592.

[55] See US Environmental Protection Agency, Executive Summary, Draft Framework for Watershed-Based Trading, published on the Internet at: http://www.epa.gov/owow/watershed/summary.html.

[56] See generally J. B. Wiener, 'Global Environmental Regulation: Instrument Choice in Legal Context' (1999) 108 *Yale Law Journal*, 622.

User charges for services, such as waste collection, can also be structured in order to promote environmental objectives.

Until recently, environmental taxes or fees were used primarily for revenue-raising purposes; they were generally set at levels too low to produce appreciable reductions in residuals levels.[57] For example, between 1980 and 1994, the use in OECD countries of environmental taxes, as measured in tax revenues as a percentage of GDP, rose only negligibly.[58] In recent years, however, a number of European countries have adopted significantly higher environmental taxes with the aim of reducing pollution and other residuals.

One successful example of the use of environmental taxes for incentives programmes is Sweden's tax on the sulphur content of fuel oil, which led to a 30 per cent reduction in sulphur content between 1990 and 1992; administrative charges were reported at only 1 per cent of revenue. Sweden has also instituted a significant tax on nitrogen oxide emissions, which resulted in a 40 per cent reduction in emissions within two years.[59] The Netherlands has implemented levies on noise, air, and water pollution as well as taxes on motor vehicles,[60] and recently issued a White Paper calling for further 'greening taxes'.[61] Denmark subjects CFCs and halons to environmental taxes, and has shifted taxes from wages to taxes on extraction of ground and surface waters, wastewater discharges, generation of solid waste, and shopping bags. Several European countries have instituted taxes on $CO_2$ emissions or the carbon content of fuels at levels that are likely to have appreciable incentive effects.

There has been no significant use of environmental taxes or fees in the USA, with the exception of taxes on CFCs and other ozone-depleting substances (ODS).[62]

### iii. *Transferable Development Rights and Mitigation Banking*

Transferable development right programmes have been used successfully in a variety of localities in the USA to preserve farmlands and protect nature preserves. Mitigation banking is also beginning to be widely used in the implementation of the Clean Water Act to limit and regulate development activities in wetlands. Development projects that are allowed to proceed in wetlands must obtain and dedicate to public use and preservation other wetlands

---

[57] See National Academy of Public Administration, *The Environment Goes to Market* (Washington, DC.: National Academy of Public Administration, 1994); OECD, *Environmental Taxes in OECD Countries* (Paris: OECD, 1995); OECD, *Managing the Environment: The Role of Economic Instruments* (Paris: OECD, 1994).

[58] See (1997) 25 *INTERTAX*, 28.

[59] OECD, *Evaluating Economic Instruments for Environmental Policy* (Paris: OECD, 1997); K. Lovgren, 'Instruments For Air Pollution Control in Sweden' in G. Klaassen and F. Forsund (eds.), *Economic Instruments for Air Pollution Control* (Boston: Kluwer Academic Publishers, 1994); T. Sterner and L. Hoglund, *Refunded Emission Payments: A Hybrid Instrument With Some Attractive Properties* (Washington, DC.: Resources for the Future, Working Paper, 1998).

[60] OECD, *Environmental Taxes in OECD Countries*, n. 57 above, 10–11.

[61] (1998) 27 *Financial Times World Tax Report*, 21.

[62] These taxes were adopted not for incentive purposes, but to recoup the economic rents enjoyed by ODS producers as a result of the regulatory phase-out (through use of a tradable quota system) of ozone-depleting substances; nonetheless, the taxes have had incentive effects.

greater in amount and/or ecological value than those affected by the development project. A form of trading is also emerging in connection with the
habitat conservation plans under the Endangered Species Act. Federal regulators may allow a development that will disturb habitat of endangered or
threatened species to proceed if the project sponsor agrees to acquire or fund
the acquisition of an alternative habitat that will be preserved for the benefit
of the species. This approach is environmentally advantageous because it
enables the government to assemble large tracts of integral habitat areas that
have greater ecological value than the patchwork of habitat that might be preserved by prohibiting specific developments.[63] Until recently, these trading
arrangements have been negotiated case-by-case under close regulatory control; these arrangements represent a form of barter. Markets in substitute
resources are, however, beginning to emerge. Sponsors of development projects may obtain substitute wetlands or habitat resources from resource
'banks' established by private firms or non-governmental organizations
(NGOs) that have preserved or restored wetlands or other habitats at other
sites.

One of the problems that has emerged in these various natural-resources
trading programmes has been the problem of fungibility. Because of local
variations in the character of ecosystems and the habitat that they provide,
and the needs of particular species (including the need for certain patterns of
habitat continuity), one-acre of wetlands or habitat is often not equivalent to
another. This problem can to some extent be addressed through use of conservative ratios in crediting substitute resources. But in order to solve the
problem fully, more sophisticated, science-based methods must be developed
to index the functional value of wetlands and other habitat. Such a step could
open the way to far greater use of these techniques as a means of achieving
environmental regulatory objectives.[64]

### iv. Risk Bubbles

In the USA, EPA has initiated an administrative programme, Project XL, to promote adoption of facility-specific agreements between businesses and federal
and state environmental regulators that would provide greater flexibility in
pollution and waste-control strategies than currently applicable command
and control requirements, thereby reducing compliance costs and burdens,
and promoting innovation.[65] EPA requires that these agreements provide
new and additional environmental benefits, in the form of higher levels of
local environmental quality than would be achieved by current requirements
and/or development of innovative pollution prevention and other strategies

[63] See Gardner, n. 32 above.      [64] See Salzman and Ruhl, n. 33 above
[65] For discussion of the Project XL programme, see D. D. Hirsch, 'Bill and Al's XL-Ent Adventure:
An Analysis of the EPA's Legal Authority to Implement the Clinton Administration's Project XL'
(1998) *University of Illinois Law Review*, 129; C. C. Caldart and N. A. Ashford, 'Negotiation as a
Means of Developing and Implementing Environmental and Occupational Health and Safety
Policy' (1999) 23 *Harvard Environmental Law Review*, 141.

that can be widely replicated at other facilities. Project XL agreements represent a form of negotiated command and control regulation at the level of individual facilities; these agreements bear a family resemblance to the environmental contracts or covenants used in many European countries, which are generally negotiated at the industry or firm level. Incorporation of the risk-bubble concept into such agreements would make them into true economic incentive systems. In some of the XL agreements that have been concluded, the facility is allowed to increase discharges of a given pollutant from some of its sources if it reduces discharges of the same pollutant from other sources. This approach, however, has not yet been extended to include intra-pollutant trading. Sources have also been exempted from waste treatment requirements in exchange for adoption of waste prevention measures. Sources may also be relieved of the need to make frequent permit modification applications that would otherwise be required in order to reflect changes in production levels or methods.

The Project XL programme's performance to date has been relatively disappointing. Only a small number of agreements have been concluded. Efforts at negotiating others have floundered in stalemate. One problem that hinders wider use of XL is uncertainty about the legality of allowing alternatives to applicable command regulations. If these and other problems with the programme, including suspicion by national environmental groups (who would lose power due to the decentralization of regulatory decision-making involved in a facility-specific approach to establishing environmental requirements), such a programme could be a means of developing full-fledged risk bubbles by affording wide flexibility into facilities to shift different residuals levels within a governing overall risk cap, and by extending the risk-bubble to upstream and downstream residual sources that are functionally linked to the facility. In order to accommodate the extensive flexibility involved in a risk-bubble approach, it would be necessary to develop improved monitoring techniques, as well as a sound scientific basis for indexing trades and offsets among different residuals in different waste streams at a facility and its associated upstream or downstream residuals sources in order to determine and appropriately control overall risk levels.

### v. New Property and Contract Regimes to Preserve Natural Resources

Insights based on Law and Economics analysis have also contributed to the identification and development of new forms of property rights and contract arrangements to preserve natural resources, while fostering sustainable patterns of economic growth. For example, emerging greenhouse gas emissions trading schemes are providing incentives for forest preservation. Costa Rica has, as part of an ambitious national programme of reforestation and sustainable forest use and preservation, obtained certification of the carbon stored in the forests and is offering $CO_2$ offset credits for sale. New York City is investing $1 billion in upstate watershed preservation in order to protect the purity of its drinking water; such preservation is far less costly than the alternative of

installing technologies to filter the water, and will, like the Costa Rican programme, provide a broad range of additional environmental benefits. South
African entrepreneurs have developed franchising arrangements under which
local communities that preserve wild animal habitats receive a portion of the
revenues paid by game hunters to hunt the animals supported by the habitat.
Pharmaceutical companies have entered into bioprospecting arrangements
with developing country government authorities or other entities, under
which the companies make payments in exchange for being granted access to
biologically rich rain forests containing species that may provide genetic tem-
plates for new drugs and other products.[66]

## VI. Level-of-Government Issues in Environmental Law

Law and Economics can also illuminate important questions as to which level
of government should have responsibility for dealing with different types of
environmental problems in multi-jurisdictional political systems that are economically integrated, such as the USA and the EU. The USA has a relatively
highly centralized environmental regulatory system, dominated by federal
statutes and administrative regulations. EU environmental law is also substantially centralized, although not as pervasively as in the USA. In both systems, however, there have recently been criticisms of the current degree
of central control, and of the attendant rigidity and bureaucratization of environmental law. The critics have invoked principles of subsidiarity to justify
devolution of greater law-making authority to the states and Member States,
claiming that more localized decision-making is more responsive and
accountable. The defenders of centralization assert that it is necessary in order
to ensure effective environmental protection and market integration. Similar
issues are posed in the international context.

What issues should be addressed at the local level (state or Member State)
and which at the higher or more centralized level (US federal government, EU
authorities)? Does the answer turn on the nature of the environmental problem
at stake? Is the problem generated by products, for example, the health risks of
genetically modified foods or air pollution from automobiles? Is the problem
one of production and process methods, such as pollution from factories? To
what extent does the problem involve pollution or wastes that cross state or
Member State jurisdictional boundaries? To what extent does the problem
involve threats to rare or treasured ecosystems, natural resources, or endangered species, which may be of concern to persons outside the state or Member
State in which they are located? To what extent and how does the relation
between market-based economic factors—investment and trade flows and
competitiveness concerns—and environmental regulation affect the level of
government issue? Do stringent environmental regulations cause significant

---

[66] Heal, n. 20 above.

competitive disadvantage for industry? Is there a real prospect of competition in environmental regulatory laxity if primary responsibility for environmental protection were vested in the states or Member States? Would market integration be threatened? [67]

Law and Economics scholarship is engaged in systematic research on these questions. It generally concludes that decentralized regulation by state or Member State governments has the advantage of being more responsive to local variations in environmental conditions and citizens' environmental preferences, whereas regulation at the federal or European level involves many of the drawbacks of centralized economic planning including information-processing costs and distortions, and the tendency to adopt inappropriately uniform and therefore excessively costly or ecologically inappropriate requirements. On the other hand, regulation at the state or Member State level may be prone to various forms of 'decentralization failure'. One claim that has been widely invoked in the USA to justify federal regulation is that state-level environmental regulation will be inadequate because states will compete in regulatory laxity in order to attract industry. Law and Economic scholars have, however, shown that this claim lacks substantial justification, either theoretically or empirically. [68] Analysis based on economic models and game theory have not established that independent environmental standard-setting by local jurisdictions will result in unduly lax levels of environmental regulation. [69] Empirical studies show that, in most instances, the costs of complying with environmental regulatory requirements are too minor a percentage of total production costs to cause industry to migrate to jurisdictions with less stringent environmental regulations, and that industry location decisions are not significantly influenced by environmental regulatory considerations. [70] In Europe, it has been claimed that environmental regulation at the EC level is necessary in order to ensure market integration. Research has shown that, although this claim may justify some forms of centralized product regulation, it provides no justification for regulation of production methods and processes. [71] Local differences in product regulation may hinder achievement of scale economies in production, increase transaction costs, and serve as a means of unjustifiedly protecting local industry against import competition. Harmonized product standards may in some cases be needed to address these problems, and ensure broad market integration. Differences in local process standards, however, only

[67] These questions can arise with respect to various forms of regulation in addition to environmental regulation. See generally D. C. Esty and D. Geradin, *Regulatory Competition and Economic Integration* (Oxford: Oxford University Press, 2001).

[68] Revesz, 'Federalism and Environmental Regulation: An Overview' and Van den Bergh, n. 11 above.

[69] Revesz, ibid.

[70] R. B. Stewart, 'Environmental Regulation and International Competitiveness' (1993) 102 *Yale Law Journal*, 2039.

[71] R. B. Stewart, 'International Trade and Environment: Lessons from the Federal Experience' (1992) 49 *Washington and Lee Law Review*, 1329.

affect local production costs, and do not hinder market integration. Market integration goals accordingly do not justify harmonization of local process regulations in order to 'equalize the condition of competition'. The principle of imposing uniform requirements or production processes in order to equalize production costs would, if carried to its logical conclusion, include wage rates, raw material prices, and all other production costs, eliminating comparative advantage and trade altogether.

Experience also shows that centralized environmental regulation does not necessarily mean stronger regulation. For example, central measures have been enacted with industry support in order to prevent adoption of more stringent regulation by local jurisdictions.[72] Analysts have also shown that centralized regulation tends to produce uniform standards that ignore relevant differences in local circumstances and the characteristics of regulated activities, imposing excessive costs and other burdens on society as a result.[73] Law and Economics scholarship shows that the strongest potential justification for centralized regulation is the presence of significant transjurisdictional spillovers among local jurisdictions, but that centralized environmental regulations often do not effectively control such spillovers.[74] These conclusions are especially striking in light of the growing concern in the USA and Europe with the drawbacks of regulatory centralization. A final potential justification for centralized regulation rests on the claim that lower-level jurisdictions are more likely to be dominated by short-term development interests, and will slight environmental concerns, whereas centralized decision-making gives greater and more appropriate weight to environmental values. Thus far, however, the support for this claim has been largely anecdotal; public choice research has thus far failed to vindicate this thesis.

## VII. Improving Environmental Laws and Regulations through Cost-Effectiveness and Cost-Benefit Analysis

The public demand for higher levels of environmental protection in the face of equally insistent concerns over economic competitiveness and excessive centralized government requires not only the use of more efficient instruments of environmental protection, but also careful assessments of the magnitude of

---

[72] E. D. Elliott, B. A. Ackerman, and J. C. Millian, 'Toward a Theory of Statutory Evolution: The Federalization of Environmental Law' (1985) 1 *Journal of Law Economics and Organization*, 313 (analysing how provisions for federal regulation of automobile emissions in the 1970 US Clean Air Act were enacted in part in response to industry pressure for federal legislation to pre-empt more stringent state regulation).

[73] T. M. Dinan, M. L. Cropper, and P. R. Portney, 'Environmental Federalism: Welfare Losses from Uniform National Drinking Water Standards' in P. R. Portney and R. M. Schwab (eds.), *Environmental and Public Economics: Essays in Honor of Wallace E. Oates* (Northampton, Mass.: Edward Elgar, 1999); J. E. Krier, 'The Irrational National Air Quality Standards: Macro- and Micro-Mistakes' (1974) 22 *University of California at Los Angeles Law Review*, 323.

[74] R. L. Revesz, 'Federalism and Control of Interstate Externalities' (1996) 144 *University of Pennsylvania Law Review*, 2341.

different environmental risks, and better risk prioritization in order to target limited societal resources, including governmental resources, on the most significant resolved risks, and those that can be controlled more readily and at less cost. Law and Economics can help to meet this need, and improve the policy choices embedded in environmental law through the use of cost-effectiveness and cost-benefit analysis. These decision-making tools seek, respectively, to identify the least costly means of achieving a given environmental objective, and to inform the choice of the objective by weighing the environmental benefits provided and the economic and social burdens imposed by regulatory requirements of differing ambition or character.[75] There has been extensive use of these tools in environmental decision-making by the US federal government in order to improve risk management. They have, overall, made a substantial positive contribution to environmental law and policy by promoting more rational and informed decisions and wiser use of societal resources.

A. COST EFFECTIVENESS

The principle of cost effectiveness holds that government should choose the least costly means of achieving societal objectives, such as environmental protection. Cost effectiveness focuses on the means of achieving environmental objectives, rather than the determination of the objectives themselves. Those objectives could be chosen through procedures or principles that are wholly non-economic in character. For example, the government may adopt a given environmental protection objective based on the right of citizens to a healthy environment, or on ethical duties to nature, or on conceptions of structural diversity in the opportunities for human experience. However, once such goals are defined, government should avoid wasting scarce societal resources in achieving them. If a given environment protection objective can be achieved at less cost, more resources will be available to fulfil other societal objectives, including other environmental objectives. On the other hand, if a decision is made to devote a given amount of societal resources to achieving a given environmental objective, cost-effectiveness can allow a higher level of protection to be achieved with the same resource commitment. The cost-effectiveness criterion can thus be used to minimize costs or maximize benefits, depending on whether benefits or costs are regarded as fixed.

Implementing the principle of cost effectiveness in environmental decision-making—in the context, for example, of drafting a law or regulation—requires a clear specification of the objective to be achieved, a consideration of various alternative means for achieving those objectives, and a systematic accounting of the costs of those measures, all in order to determine which alternative will

---

[75] See generally E. J. Mishan, *Cost Benefit Analysis: An Introduction* (New York: Praeger Publishers, 1971); R. Zeckhauser and E. Stokey, *A Primer for Policy Analysis* (New York: W. W. Norton, 1976).

achieve the objective at least total cost. The costs of various regulatory measures include the following:

— *Compliance outlays.* The amounts spent by regulated entities to comply
  with regulatory programmes through capital investments and increased
  operating costs are a major component of regulatory costs. In many
  cases, it is the only component that receives attention, even though regulatory requirements typically impose other types of costs.
— *Indirect opportunity costs.* Another important component of regulatory
  costs is indirect. These costs consist, for example, of investments in new
  plants and products, and other productive activities that are never
  undertaken because of regulatory constraints, delays, and uncertainties
  in the regulatory process, and the threat of potentially large liabilities for
  potential risks that may be created by new technologies, new products,
  and other new activities but cannot be foreseen by those undertaking
  them. These costs are difficult to quantify, but may nonetheless be very
  large and have a significant adverse impact on innovation and investment.[76]
— *Environmental costs.* Fairly frequently, regulatory measures that reduce
  one environmental risk have the effect of increasing other environmental risks. Thus, a decision to ban all uses of asbestos may have the effect
  of increasing automobile injuries because of reduced brake efficacy.
  These adverse effects must be considered a cost of the measure in question.[77]
— *Administrative costs.* The costs of regulation also include the costs
  incurred by governments and by regulated entities in implementing
  regulatory programmes: gathering information, issuing and understanding regulations and permits, filing reports, and so on.

Many of these costs are often difficult to determine or quantify. Applying the
cost-effectiveness criterion involves a considerable degree of judgement and
is by no means a mechanical exercise. Nonetheless, systematic attention to
cost effectiveness in the design of regulatory measures can help to identify and
select alternative approaches to achieving regulatory objectives that result in
large cost savings relative to traditional approaches. Cost-effectiveness analysis can be used to assess which type of regulatory instrument—for example,
command regulation or EIS—should be chosen to implement a given environmental objective, as well as to assess which particular measure should be
adopted within a given instrument category. The cost-effectiveness heuristic

[76] R. B. Stewart, 'Regulation, Innovation and Administrative Law: A Conceptual Framework'
(1981) 69 *California Law Review*, 1259.
[77] Introducing environmental costs into the analysis requires that the environmental benefits
considered in the cost-effectiveness analysis be reduced by the amount of such costs; in order to
make this adjustment in cost-effective analysis, the relevant environmental cost and benefits
must be capable of measurement through a common metric. To the extent that this is not possible,
the environmental benefits must be balanced against the environmental costs (as well as other
costs) of a measure, transforming the analysis into a form of cost-benefit analysis.

has served to focus attention on the advantage of market-based regulatory instruments, such as environmental taxes and emissions trading, for achieving environmental protection objectives. As previously described, these alternatives can achieve environmental objectives at significantly lower cost than command approaches.

### B.  COST-BENEFIT BALANCING (HEREIN OF PROPORTIONALITY)

Environmental regulation today has, especially in the USA, increasingly focused on cost/benefit trade-offs. It is widely recognized—by analysts of risk regulation, by regulators, and by the political system generally—that societal resources are limited, and that a balance must be struck, at the margin, between regulatory benefits and costs.[78] Conceptually, cost-benefit analysis is distinct from, and goes a step beyond, cost-effectiveness analysis. It involves analysis of and choice among different objectives—for example, different levels of environmental protection, achieved through regulatory requirements of differing stringency. In applying cost-benefit analysis, the most cost-effective means of achieving each alternative protection level should first be determined. The environmental benefits of each alternative must also be determined. In a full-fledged Law and Economics approach, all costs and benefits must be quantified by reference to a common metric, generally money, and a monetized net benefit (or cost) determined for each alternative assessed. The alternative providing the highest net benefit should be selected.

Some environmental benefits have a market value; for example, the benefits of environmental regulation can include reduced health-care costs for illnesses caused by pollution, or increased fisheries harvests. Other benefits can be given a monetary value by using surrogate or benchmark measures. For example, the recreational benefits due to environmental regulations that enhance recreational fishing or hiking opportunities can be estimated by reference to the travel costs that resource users incur to visit the sites in question.[79] In the USA, EPA, in conducting cost-benefit analysis of regulatory requirements that will reduce the risk of mortality, assigns a value of around $5 million per life saved, derived in part from evidence regarding the amount of wage premium that workers demand for exposure to higher workplace risks.[80] In the case of preservation or 'non-use' values, such as the value of preserving the Arctic National Wildlife Refuge in Alaska against oil development to persons who will never visit the Refuge, no direct or indirect market measures of value are available. The Department of Interior and the National Oceanic and Atmospheric Administration are seeking to develop values for resource preservation through contingent valuation surveys that seek to determine the

---

[78] R. Pildes and C. Sunstein, 'Reinventing the Regulatory State' (1995) 62 *University of Chicago Law Review*, 1; 'Symposium, Cost-Benefit Analysis: Legal, Economic, and Philosophical Perspectives', 29 *Journal of Legal Studies*, 837.

[79] Ibid.

[80] Revesz, n. 7 above (discussing issues presented in deriving an economic value for reductions in the risk of death based on market data on risk premia paid to workers in riskier occupations).

economic value that individuals place on 'non-use' resource values through hypothetical scenarios that seek to elicit the amount that they would be willing to pay for such preservation.[81] Such approaches are sometimes criticized as improperly commodifying values that are inherently non-monetary in character.[82] The rejoinder, however, is that all regulatory decisions implicitly place a value on avoiding a statistical death or avoiding the risk of ecological injury. Although life and the nature may be 'priceless', we do not commit infinite societal resources to preventing such losses. In order to promote more rational decision-making and better target-limited societal resources for risk-reduction in making risk management trade-offs, it is generally better to make the value that we place on avoiding such harms explicit in making risk management trade-offs, by whatever processes (market-based or otherwise) are judged appropriate, than to make the trade-offs intuitively, haphazardly, or covertly.

If monetization of all environmental benefits (as well as environmental costs) is judged infeasible or inappropriate, one can still undertake a qualitative form of cost–benefit analysis that compares benefits (both monetizable and non-monetizable) against costs (both monetizable and non-monetizable). Even this limited type of cost–benefit analysis can be extremely useful in disciplining the decisional process by focusing attention on the various costs and benefits involved, their character and magnitude, and the trade-offs involved in deciding what level of protection we should aim for. In this regard, an incremental application of qualitative cost–benefit analysis is often very useful. If the choice is between spending nothing and incurring serious environmental harm on the one hand, and eliminating 99 per cent of the harm at a cost of $100 million on the other, we may well choose the latter alternative. But suppose, as is frequently the case, that there is a third alternative of spending $10 million and eliminating 98 per cent of the harm. We may well judge that spending an additional $90 million to reduce harm by one additional percentage point is not justified. Thus, incremental application of cost–benefit analysis can help focus our judgements on proportionality.[83]

It is often claimed that use of cost–benefit analysis inevitably tends to produce unduly weak environmental policies because, for example, it tends to 'dwarf' environmental values that cannot readily be quantified. There is considerable experience to the contrary. For example, in the USA EPA regularly uses cost–benefit analysis to evaluate new regulatory measures, yet adopts regulations that are, on the whole, quite strong. Indeed, cost–benefit analysis can help to focus attention on neglected environmental protection measures that are eminently desirable. As a striking example, during the early 1980s, the Reagan EPA adopted a programme to phase out use of lead additives in

[81] R. B. Stewart, 'Natural Resource Damages' in R. L. Revesz and R. B. Stewart, *Analyzing Superfund* (Washington, DC.: Resources for the Future, 1995).

[82] S. Kelman, *What Price Incentives?* (Boston: Auburn House Publishing Co., 1981).

[83] R. W. Crandall, F. H. Rueber, and W. A. Steger, *Clearing the Air: EPA's Self-Assessment of Clean Air Policy* (1996) *Regulation*, no. 435 (emphasizing importance of marginal analysis of regulatory costs and benefits in assessing EPA's implementation of US Clean Air Act).

petrol for health reasons, far in advance of other nations. It did so on the basis of cost–benefit studies showing that the monetizable health benefits of such a measure would be enormous, while the costs would be negative because of reduced engine wear and maintenance.[84] Other regulatory cost–benefit studies have provided empirical support for and furthered the adoption of more stringent regulatory controls for lead in drinking water, reformulated petrol to control automobile air pollution, and air pollution controls to protect visibility at the Grand Canyon.[85]

Cost–benefit analysis is not a mechanical exercise. It requires judgement and considerations of practicality in design and application. Also, cost–benefit analysis can only be as good as the data on which it is based. In many cases, data on the health and ecological benefits that would be achieved by regulatory measures are quite poor, and data regarding costs are also problematic in some cases. There may be significant difficulties in monetizing some benefits and costs. Account must be taken of distributional and equity issues, and of potential environmental irreversibilities. The costs and potential delays involved with the use of cost–benefit analysis in regulatory decision-making must also be taken into account.[86] Recognizing these limitations, however, cost–benefit analysis can make important contributions to improving the quality of environmental regulatory decisions, and enhance the transparency and accountability of the decision process.[87]

### C. ISSUES OF RISK ASSESSMENT AND MANAGEMENT

Sound risk regulatory policy requires that environmental risks rules should, to the extent feasible, be quantified in order to determine their absolute and relative magnitude and to determine the extent to which such risks would be reduced by alternative regulatory measures. It also provides an empirical foundation for risk prioritization. Quantitative risk assessment provides the basis for specifying the benefits and the environmental costs of regulatory measures for purposes of applying cost effectiveness and cost–benefit analysis to regulatory risk management. Quantitative risk assessment, including comparative risk assessment, has been more widely adopted in the USA than in Europe. There appears, however, to be increasing pressures for more systematic risk assessment and prioritization in Europe.[88]

Quantitative risk analysis is a complex exercise. It requires the identification of potential hazards; the collection of information about and analysis, based on

[84] *Economic Analysis at EPA*, n. 22 above, 49–86, 458.

[85] Crandall, Rueber, and Steger, n. 83 above, 205–32, 267–302, 391–418, 458.

[86] R. D. Morgenstern, 'Conducting an Economic Analysis: Rationale, Issues, and Requirements' in *Economic Analysis at EPA*, n. 22 above, 25.

[87] R. L. Revesz, P. Sands, and R. B. Stewart (eds.), *Environmental Law, the Economy, and Sustainable Development: the United States, the European Union, and the International Community* (New York: Cambridge University Press, 2000).

[88] S. Breyer and V. Heyvaert, 'Institutions for Regulating Risk' in Revesz, Sands, and Stewart, *Environmental Law and Economy*, n. 10 above.

relevant science, of the adverse impacts of residuals or other stresses on human health and the environment, and the development of a dose–response relation; the collection of information about the extent of exposures of humans or the environment to harmful residuals or stresses; and characterization risks in accordance with the estimated nature and extent of the adverse effects. The results of risk analysis form the basis for risk management through regulatory or other measures.[89] Like cost–benefit analysis, quantitative risk assessment involves the application of considerable judgement. A quantitative risk assessment can only be as good as the science and data on which it is based. In many cases, scientific understanding of the mechanisms by which a substance or stress produces an adverse effect, as in the case of cancers, is quite limited. Extrapolating from *in vitro* or animal studies to human effects poses many difficulties. Relevant data are often incomplete or poor. Epidemiological studies are costly, and any single study can generally provide only limited insight. Default assumptions or other techniques must be used to deal with the resulting uncertainties, which in some cases are very large. The costs and delays involved in conducting quantitative risk assessments must also be considered. In some cases, precautionary considerations justify adoption of regulatory measures to address situations where risks remain uncertain and significant adverse impacts are not established. Nonetheless, meaningful risk assessment is a key element in rational and democratic environmental regulatory policy. It serves to identify regulatory priorities, inform the nature and extent of regulatory measures, and enhances the transparency and accountability of regulatory decision-making.

It is increasingly recognized that regulatory decisions must often confront risk/risk trade-offs. A decision to regulate or ban a product or a process in order to address environmental, health, and safety risks that it poses may have the effect of increasing other environmental, health, and safety risks.[90] For example, as previously noted, a decision to ban all uses of asbestos may create more traffic accidents because brakes without asbestos linings are not as effective as those with such linings.[91] These risk/risk trade-offs, which can most completely be assessed if risks can be quantified and, to the extent that

[89] Introductions to quantitative risk assessment are provided in J. J. Cohrssen and V. T. Covello, *Risk Analysis: A Guide to Principles and Methods for Analyzing Health and Environmental Risks* (Washington, DC.: US Council on Environmental Quality, 1989); Committee on Risk Characterization, Commission on Behavioral and Social Sciences and Education, National Research Council, *Understanding Risk: Informing Decisions in Democratic Society* (Washington, DC.: Natural Academy Press, 1996).

[90] J. B. Graham and J. B. Wiener, *Risk-Risk Tradeoffs* (Cambridge, Mass.: Harvard University Press, 1995); C. R. Sunstein, 'Health-Health Tradeoffs' (1996) 63 *University of Chicago Law Review*, 1533.

[91] See *Corrosion Proof Fittings* v. *EPA*, 947 F.2d 1201 (5th Cir. 1991). Some policy analysts argue that almost all decisions present risk/risk trade-offs. They argue that even if a regulatory requirement does not directly result in increased environmental health and safety risks, excessive regulatory stringency will deter the introduction of new technologies that are safer than old ones. They also argue that 'wealthier is healthier', relying on aggregate data which indicate higher levels of health in more prosperous societies and among wealthier sectors of the population. Accordingly, they argue, excessively stringent regulation will reduce society's health by reducing its wealth. See P. W. Huber and R. E. Litan (eds.), *The Liability Maze: The Impact of Liability Law on Safety and Innovation* (Washington, DC.: Brookings Institution, 1991); P. W. Huber, 'Safety and the Second Best: The Hazards of Public Risk Management in the Courts' (1985) 185 *Columbia Law Review*, 277.

different types of risks are involved, compared on the basis of a common metric, are often an important part of cost-effectiveness analysis (counting the increased risks due to regulation as a cost) and cost–benefit analysis (in determining net environmental benefits).

Risk management also often involves benefit/benefit trade-offs that occur in the allocation of compliance resources among different regulatory programmes and requirements.[92] These trade-offs can also best be assessed if the risks involved can be quantified and compared. There are significant disparities among different regulatory programmes and requirements in the level of environmental health and safety benefits provided in relation to the resource costs devoted to achieving compliance with them. For example, studies of US environmental regulation show that there are great variations among regulatory programmes and requirements in the cost per statistical death avoided. For example, some requirements save statistical lives at a marginal cost of as little as $100,000 or less per life saved, while others spend tens of millions of dollars or more to save a life.[93] Similar variations are undoubtedly found in environmental regulations in Europe at both the EC and Member State level. By readjusting the relative stringency of different regulatory programmes and requirements so as to redirect societal resources away from those programmes with high marginal costs per unit of benefit provided to those with lower marginal costs, significant increases in overall health, safety, and environmental benefits can be achieved with the same expenditure of societal resources. The ultimate objective is to optimize the benefits provided by different programmes in relation to the societal resources committed to environmental protection.[94] There are, of course, significant institutional and other obstacles to achieving an improved benefit/benefit trade-off among regulatory programmes, but the importance of the objective is increasingly recognized.

## VIII. US Experience with Economic Analysis of Environmental Regulations and Risk Assessment

In the USA, a number of steps have been taken to apply and implement the decision-making tools summarized in the previous section. They include a well-developed system of cost–benefit analysis of new federal regulations, and steps to improve risk analysis and management.

---

[92] S. G. Breyer, *Breaking the Vicious Cycle: Toward Effective Risk Regulation* (Cambridge, Mass.: Harvard University Press, 1993); J. C. Davies (ed.), *Comparing Environmental Risks: Tools for Setting Government Priorities* (Washington, DC.: Resources for the Future, 1996); A. M. Finkel and D. Golding (eds.), *Worst Things First? The Debate over Risk-Based National Environmental Policies* (Washington, DC.: Resources for the Future, 1994).

[93] S. Breyer, R. Stewart, C. Sunstein, and M. Spitzer, *Administrative Law and Regulatory Policy* (Boston: Little, Brown & Co., 1998), 30–1.

[94] If it were assumed that compliance resource inputs were fixed, this optimization process could be analysed in risk/risk terms, because a decision to devote more resources to one regulatory programme in order to reduce the risks that it addresses would result in a corresponding increase in the risks addressed by other programmes.

## A. OMB SUPERVISION OF REGULATORY AGENCY ECONOMIC ANALYSIS

Beginning with President Nixon, every President has maintained a system of centralized review by the Office of Management and Budget (OMB) of new administrative regulations that have a significant impact on the economy. The system was established in essentially its current form by President Reagan. President Clinton continued it with minor modifications.[95] The review system has been primarily applied to environmental regulations. It has been adopted and maintained by Presidents of both parties because of concern that EPA and other environmental, health, and safety regulatory agencies often fail to pay adequate attention to the costs and burdens imposed by their regulations, to balance appropriately regulatory costs and environmental benefits, and to heed the adverse impact of unjustifiedly burdensome costs on the health of the economy and international competitiveness.

The essentials of the system, which are carried out under the supervision of the White House OMB, are as follows. Federal regulatory agencies are required to conduct a Regulatory Impact Analysis (RIA) of the costs and benefits of pro-posed and final 'major' rules with a significant impact on the US economy. The analysis must consider alternative means of accomplishing the regulatory objective as well as the alternative of 'no action'. In making its decision, an agency must, 'to the extent permitted by law', consider costs and benefits of a proposed rule and alternatives, and adopt the alternative that maximizes net benefits, although in doing so agencies must consider qualitative costs and benefits and distributional impacts and equity. Drafts of the proposed and final rule and the accompanying RIA must be submitted to OMB prior to pub-lication of the proposed or final rules for review by OMB for compliance with RIA requirements. If OMB concludes that an agency regulatory analysis fails to comply with these requirements, it will submit comments to the agency or return the rule and analysis to it. OMB has no formal authority to veto a pro-posed or final rule, but it can sometimes use the review system to obtain modi-fications in the agency's original version of a rule. In case of unresolved disagreement between OMB and the agency, OMB can refer the matter to the President for resolution; this has occurred in only a few instances.

Members of Congress and environmental groups voiced strident objections to this procedure in the early days of its implementation following the Reagan Executive Order. Today, however, the OMB review process has become firmly established and is widely accepted as a permanent and valuable part of the federal administrative regulatory system. Many thoughtful observers have

---

[95] Breyer, Stewart, Sunstein and Spitzer, n. 93 above, 102–23. Under the executive orders, agen-cies are required to conduct cost–benefit analysis of proposed regulations and consider the results of the analysis in making decisions, 'to the extent permitted by law'. Some environmental regula-tory statutes have been held by the courts to preclude EPA consideration of costs in establishing certain environmental standards. *Whitman v. American Trucking Associations, Inc.*, 531 U.S. 457 (2001) (EPA may not consider costs in establishing National Ambient Air Quality Standards under Clean Act). EPA, however, still conducts RIA in the course of the proceedings to establish such standards.

concluded that such a system of centralized review of regulations under the direct supervision of the President is necessary to counteract the powerful dispersion of power and accountability that results from a congressional form of government, and the creation of a vast and many-headed federal bureaucracy exercising significant regulatory discretion. They also believe that the OMB review process has, on balance, improved agency decisions by promoting more careful identification and consideration of the benefits and the various costs of alternative regulatory measures, and reducing the number of regulations adopted that involve costs that are wholly disproportionate to benefits.[96] Some would like to see the OMB review process become even more systematic and professionalized, drawing on science as well as economics to promote better risk analysis and management by environmental regulatory agencies. Proposals in Congress to adopt legislation codifying the RIA process and providing for judicial review of agency compliance with these requirements have not, however, been enacted, in part because of concerns about delays resulting from court litigation and concerns over judicial competence to evaluate controversies over cost–benefit analyses.

The impact on environmental regulatory decision-making of the RIA system established by Executive Order has been thoroughly studied in a project sponsored by Resources for the Future (RFF), a respected research institute.[97] The research project found, based on twelve intensive case studies of a wide range of EPA regulatory decisions, that the extent of EPA compliance with RIA requirements varied, as did the influence of the analyses on regulatory outcomes, but that on the whole the impact of the regulatory impact assessment system was quite beneficial. In five of the case studies, involving visibility protection for the Grand Canyon, emissions of organic chemicals, lead in petrol, reformulated petrol, and lead in drinking water, the cost–benefit analysis provided strong support for environmental protection measures more stringent than those originally contemplated by EPA, and contributed, in varying degrees, to the eventual adoption by EPA of more stringent regulations. In a sixth, regulation of CFCs, the cost–benefit analysis provided support for US ratification of the Montreal Protocol for International Control of Ozone-Depleting Substances. In all of the twelve case studies, the data and analyses in the RIAs identified ways in which the regulations initially proposed by EOA could be modified to reduce compliance costs without significant loss of environmental benefits and contributed to the adoption of such modifications.[98] The RFF studies also found that RIAs made important contributions to the quality of the overall regulatory decision-making process by providing a framework for collecting and organizing information and determining what information was missing, encouraging systemic analysis of potential alternatives to

---

[96] R. W. Hahn and R. E. Litan, *Improving Regulatory Accountability* (Washington, DC: American Enterprise Institute for Public Policy Research, 1997).

[97] *Economic Analysis at EPA*, n. 22 above.

[98] Ibid. 458 (summarizing results of case studies described in detail in earlier portions of the book).

the proposed action, and making the policy trade-offs involved more explicit and the decision process more transparent.[99] These conclusions were similar to those of an earlier study on the RIA process conducted by EPA, which found that it had contributed to the identification of new regulatory alternatives, helped to eliminate proposed measures that were found not to be cost-effective, and had led to adjustments in proposed regulations to take appropriate account of differences among industries or industry segments.[100]

The RFF study found that the cost of preparing RIAs averaged around $1 million per regulation; if also found that this cost was far less than the cost savings achieved through improvements in the regulations achieved with the assistance of the information and analysis assembled by the RIAs. It acknowledged that the RIA process had contributed in some cases to delays in adopting final regulations, but noted that in many cases such delays contributed to improved regulations, including many that were more environmentally protective. The RFF studies also found that the quality of the RIAs and the contributions that they made to the regulatory decision process were limited (1) by certain weaknesses in the analysis itself and, more importantly, (2) inadequacies in the underlying risk assessment data that form the basis for estimating the benefits of regulatory measures, and (3) the tendency of EPA, for political and administrative reasons, not to pursue promising alternatives to proposed measures or to examine adequately cost–benefit trade-offs in some cases.[101] Overall, however, the studies provide strong support for the conclusion that systematized cost–benefit analyses produced better regulations that were more cost-effective and in many cases environmentally more protective, and also improved the quality and accountability of the decision process.

Law and Economics researchers, policy analysts, and economists in universities, research institutes, and non-governmental organizations devoted to policy analysis and advocacy analyse and criticize federal environmental regulations and policies on a regular basis, enriching the policy dialogue.[102] Many national environmental groups have several Ph.D. economists on their staffs in order to ensure that they can participate effectively in this dialogue, and develop economic data and analysis to support their proposals for environmental regulatory initiatives.

In the USA, courts review cost–benefit analyses prepared by environmental regulatory agencies as a part of the overall administrative record of an agency rule or decision. Such review is generally highly deferential; although in a few instances judges have pushed deeply the assumptions and methodologies used by regulators, and set aside their decisions because of deficiencies in

[99] *Economic Analysis at EPA*, n. 22 above 459–76.

[100] US Environmental Protection Agency, *EPA's Use of Cost–Benefit Analysis 1981–1986* (Washington, DC.: EPA Publication nos. 230–05–87–028, 1987).

[101] *Economic Analysis at EPA*, n. 22 above, 460–72.

[102] Crandall, Rueter, and Steger, n. 83 above; A. J. Krupnick and P. A. Portney, 'Controlling Urban Air Pollution: A Benefit-Cost Assessment' (1991) 252 *Science*, 522 (assessing national and regional costs and benefits of EPA ambient air-quality standards for ozone pollution).

their cost–benefit analysis.[103] Overall, however, the impact of the OMB review process has been by far the more important influence on agency decision-making.

The role of cost–benefit analysis should not be overstated. Regulatory decisions are driven to a considerable extent by political and bureaucratic forces and other considerations. Nonetheless, systematic use of economic analysis has had a significant and beneficial influence.

### B. RISK ANALYSIS AND MANAGEMENT

Several steps have already been taken to promote improved risk analysis and management by environmental regulatory agencies. Courts have sometimes set aside agency decisions because of inadequate or faulty risk or risk management analysis.[104] The more important initiatives, however, have been administrative. EPA has established a Science Advisory Board, a Clean Air Act Science Advisory Board, and other advisory committees composed of independent scientists to promote the use of improved analytical methods and procedures, and provide peer review of the quality of the risk analyses underlying important regulatory decisions.[105] The President's Office of Science and Technology Policy has taken steps to promote improved and more consistent risk analysis and management methods across as well as within federal regulatory agencies. The National Academy of Sciences and outside research institutes have from time to time been engaged to review the science and the risk analyses relevant to especially controversial regulatory decisions. These arrangements have substantially improved the quality of risk analysis, especially at EPA, which has issued Risk Assessment Guidelines, compiled data bases on the results of risk analyses, and conducted studies of comparative health and environmental risks in order to evaluate the agency's regulatory priorities.[106] Critics, however, contend that more improvement is needed and that lack of consistency in risk-analytic procedures and methods among regulatory programmes and agencies remains a serious problem. Proposals for legislation to impose statutory risk assessment procedures and standards on regulatory agencies and provide for judicial review of agency compliance have not, however, been enacted. Also, EPA regulatory priorities remain largely driven by public perceptions of relative risks and congressional demands, which are often inconsistent with scientific assessments of comparative risks. There is reluctance, based on fear of exposure to political controversy, within many parts of EPA to make officially explicit uncertainties regarding environmental risks and the trade-offs involved in risk management decisions.[107]

---

[103] See, e.g. *Corrosion Proof Fittings* v. *EPA*, n. 91 above.

[104] See, e.g. *Industrial Union Dep't, AFL-CIO* v. *American Petroleum Institute*, 448 US 607 (1980).

[105] M. R. Powell, *Science at EPA: Information in the Regulatory Process* (Washington, D.C.: Resources for the Future, 1999), 38–43.

[106] Ibid.

[107] M. K. Landy and M. J. Roberts, *The Environmental Protection Agency: Asking the Wrong Questions: From Nixon to Clinton* (New York: Oxford University Press, 1994).

Steps have also been taken in the USA to promote greater agency attention to risk/risk trade-offs. A few court decisions have held that an agency's failure to consider such trade-offs and take them into account in their decisions is arbitrary and capricious.[108] But the major impetus for greater consideration of risk/risk trade-offs has come through the OMB regulatory impact analysis process. If a new environmental regulation will result in increases in environmental risks, that represents a regulatory cost that must be included in the cost–benefit analysis and the consideration of alternative measures.

Benefit/benefit trade-offs present a far more difficult problem. Analysis of risk/risk trade-offs can be conducted on a regulation-by-regulation basis within the existing structure of regulatory statutes. The aim of such analysis, like RIA of proposed regulations generally, is to promote more rational regulation on a 'retail' basis, focusing on individual regulatory decisions without attempting to relate one to another. By contrast, benefit/benefit trade-offs can only be assessed and made through a 'wholesale' approach, considering the comparative cost effectiveness of a large number of different individual regulations and adjusting them in a coordinated fashion in order to promote a greater degree of aggregate cost-effectiveness. The aim is synoptic rather than regulation-specific rationality. The regulatory structure established by existing US and EC environmental statutes creates many barriers to achieving this goal. The statutes create a series of independent and uncoordinated regulatory programmes. Furthermore, existing statutes often constrain regulatory discretion in ways that limit an agency's ability to adjust the relative stringency of different regulatory requirements in order to promote greater overall cost-effectiveness.[109] US Supreme Court Justice Stephen Breyer proposed an ambitious approach that would establish a regulatory 'super agency' within the Executive that would have authority to establish risk assessment criteria and procedures for all environmental health and safety regulatory agencies; review agency compliance with these requirements in a manner analogous to OMB RIA review; and exercise authority, under the President, to assess benefit/benefit trade-offs and modify regulatory programmes and measures in order to promote aggregate cost effectiveness.[110] Serious political support for this proposal has yet to materialize.

---

[108] See *Corrosion Proof Fittings*, n. 91 above; *American Trucking Ass'ns* v. *EPA*, 195 F.3d 4, 9 (D.C. Cir. 1999).

[109] An even more comprehensive approach would consider not only the health and environmental benefits provided by different regulatory measures but also those provided by government-funded medical, public health, and resource conservation and protection programmes. The legal and institutional barriers to implementing such an approach are greater still.

[110] S. G. Breyer, *Breaking the Vicious Circle* (Cambridge, Mass.: Harvard University Press, 1993). This book was written prior to the author becoming a Justice.

## IX.  Promoting Discipline and Accountability in Regulatory Decision-making

The US developments summarized above have been beneficial in promoting greater transparency and accountability in regulatory decision-making. The system of OMB regulatory review was instituted and has been maintained by Presidents in order to exert greater control over regulatory agencies, especially EPA, and prevent adoption of disproportionately costly regulations. But it has, as a side effect, promoted collection and dissemination of substantial information about the costs and benefits of regulatory measures and promoted healthy discussion over appropriate regulatory policy within and among the EPA, the Executive, Congress, the regulatory policy community, and the public.

Cost effectiveness and cost–benefit analysis serve to help discipline the process of governmental decision-making and make it more transparent and accountable. They do so by requiring that the benefits to be achieved and the costs imposed by regulatory measures be explicitly identified, and that such measures be openly evaluated against reasonable alternatives. These steps tend to prevent decisions that are inadequately informed or considered. They also require government officials to provide explicit justifications for adopting measures that are more costly than alternative ways of achieving environment objectives, or that appear to involve costs that are highly disproportionate to benefits. Such measures may in fact be justified. But the justifications must be stated, and can be evaluated against the record of facts and analysis regarding the benefits and costs of the chosen measure, and of alternatives to it that are generated by the RIA process. In other cases, costly and inefficient regulations may not be justified, reflecting parochial or partisan interests or bureaucratic 'tunnel vision'. The need to justify such decisions openly against the background of facts and analysis which discredit them may have a salutary prophylactic effect.

There has not been, as some critics of cost–benefit analysis have feared, a massive rollback of environmental protection regulation as a result of the institutionalization of cost effectiveness and cost–benefit analysis and quantitative risk assessment in the USA. The general effect has been to weed out unwise regulatory measures and, in many instances, to provide factual and analytic justification for and help build political support for more environmentally protective regulations. The debate over environmental law and policy has become more informed and better anchored in facts and analysis.[111] Similar benefits, although more modest in scale, have been generated by the efforts to improve risk analysis and management. The use of more flexible economic incentive system in lieu of command and control regulation has similarly stimulated enriched professional and public discourse regarding

---

[111] *Economic Analysis at EPA*, n. 22 above.

regulatory ends and means, and has led to the development of emissions trading and other programmes that have produced environmental and economic
dividends while also defusing some of the sharp and divisive conflicts generated within the command regulatory framework.

One cannot make a fetish out of formal analysis. There are a range of legitimate considerations, including equitable and distributional concerns and
structural environmental values which may not be captured, or captured only
quite imperfectly, by cost effectiveness and cost–benefit analysis and by quantitative risk assessment. Also, it takes time and resources to gather and sift the
relevant facts, identify and select a reasonable number of alternatives, and
conduct analysis. Such techniques will not automatically generate the 'correct'
solution. Analyses relying on different assumptions and data can reach quite
different results. Their application, and the ultimate decision on the appropriate course of action, require considerable judgement. Nonetheless, economic
analysis and risk analysis are valuable tools that deserve wide use in the complex field of environmental protection.[112] Environmental impact assessment
(EIA) of proposed projects and activities that will have significant environmental impacts, and of alternatives to such projects and activities is now
widely accepted throughout the world. Regulatory cost–benefit analysis and
risk analysis uses the same logic and many of the same tools to examine the
economic and other societal impacts of proposed regulatory measures and
alternatives. It is recognized that EIA involves costs and delays and that its
contributions are limited by political and institutional factors. Yet, the judgement has been made that its contributions are quite positive, and that EIAs
should be conducted for all environmentally significant new projects and
activities. Widespread use of cost-benefit analysis and risk analysis for significant new environmental regulations is likewise justified.

## X. Potential Implications of Law and Economics and the US Experience for European Environmental Law

The EU and the USA are characterized, of course, by significant differences in
the traditions and structures of law and governance. On the whole, Europeans
have been less willing than Americans to rely on market arrangements to
achieve societal goals, and more inclined to rely on the state (it is striking that
the concept of the 'state' barely exists in the USA). Europeans have also been
more receptive to corporatist approaches to making and implementing public
policy, and have had a higher regard for the bureaucratic elite. In European
universities and research centres, there is, on the whole, less interest in and
use of cross-disciplinary approaches and problem-solving orientations in the
social sciences than in the USA. These are among the factors that may explain
why Law and Economics has not found the same degree of rapid and broad
acceptance in Europe as in the USA.

[112] M. D. Adler and E. A. Posner, 'Rethinking Cost–Benefit Analysis' (1999) 106 *Yale Law Journal*, 165.

While these differences remain significant, they are narrowing. The collapse of state socialism abroad, the enormous success of EC market integration, and the recent steps towards privatization and deregulation in the Member States have promoted a new respect for the virtues of market competition. This development has undermined deference to bureaucratic governance and corporatist arrangements. Accelerating global economic integration has made international competitiveness and economic efficiency major concerns in Europe. These developments have promoted fiscal restraint, and recognition that government regulation as well as direct government spending must be carefully watched in order to ensure the viability of the euro and ever closer European integration. Within the specific context of the EC, there is concern over excessive regulatory centralization in Brussels, and the lack of transparency and accountability in the present processes of EC decision-making. There is also growing interest in the use of economic incentive systems as alternatives to traditional command and control environmental regulation.[113] At the same time, Law and Economics is gaining a substantial footing among younger researchers in European universities and research centres. These circumstances create a hospitable environment for the emergence, in a form appropriate for Europe, of some of the legal and policy innovations that have been engendered by Law and Economics in the USA.

One potential European innovation derived from US experience could be the adoption of a system of cost–benefit analysis of new EC environmental legislation similar to the OMB RIA programme in the USA. The Commission is increasingly using economic tools to analyse proposals for new legislation, but there is no systematic programme, nor is there a routine process for publicly disclosing the results of cost–benefit analysis of new proposals, and inviting public comment thereon as part of the legislative process, as is the case with administrative rule-making in the USA. Establishing such a system could not only help to further improve Commission proposals but, perhaps more important, promote a greater degree of transparency and accountability in the EC legislative process. A systemic identification of the costs and benefits of proposed measures and of alternatives could help inform debate in the Parliament, the media, and the public over EC environmental policy and specific legislation, and help promote greater accountability with respect to the decisions of the Commission, Parliament, and Council.

Such a programme of systemic regulatory analysis could require, as in the USA, a discussion of alternative regulatory instruments for achieving environmental objectives. The Commission (as well as many Member States) has in recent years paid greater attention to economic incentives systems, including

---

[113] B. Deute (ed.), *Environmental Policy in Search of New Instruments* (Dordrecht: Kluwer Academic Publishers, 1995); F. J. Dietz, H. R. J. Vollebergh, and J. L. de Vries (eds.), *Environment, Incentives and Common Market* (Dordrecht: Kluwer Academic Publishers, 1995); J. Golub (ed.), *New Instruments for Environmental Policy in the EU* (London and New York: Routledge, 1998); T. O'Riordan (ed.), *Ecotaxation* (New York: St Martins Press, 1997); H. Opschoor and K. Turner (eds.), *Economic Incentives and Environmental Policies: Principles and Practice* (Dordrecht: Kluwer Academic Publishers, 1994).

environmental taxes, pollution trading, and other flexibility mechanisms. There have been political obstacles to harmonization of environmental taxes, as illustrated by the Commission's lack of success in promoting adoption of EC legislation to impose a tax on GHG emissions. Recently, the Commission has proposed the use instead of an EU GHG emissions trading system. A number of Member States may adopt such a system at the domestic level. These are notable developments in light of the general lack of interest in Europe in trading programmes, which have the advantage, relative to taxes, of lessening industry resistance to new regulatory programmes based on EIS by allocating quotas or credits by allocating quotas *gratis* to existing firms, thereby substantially reducing the net economic impact of new regulatory initiatives on existing industry. A regulatory analysis programme for new EU environmental legislation would encourage wider use of EIS by documenting their advantages relative to command approaches in dealing with many environmental problems.

The analytical and decision-making techniques for risk analysis and management that have been generated through from Law and Economics thinking and used in the USA may also be of growing interest and importance for Europe. The World Trade Organization (WTO) *Beef Hormones* case, European concerns about food safety, the international controversies over GM technologies, and the European Commission's recent paper on the Precautionary Principle all reflect a growing interest and concern in Europe with issues of risk assessment and risk management.[114] As a result of the WTO *Beef Hormones* case, systematic risk assessment will be required for EC regulatory determinations with international trade consequences. The economic and global competitive factors, discussed above, favouring greater attention to regulatory costs and benefits and cost-effectiveness in environmental health and safety regulatory policy will focus increasing attention on risk/risk and benefit/benefit trade-offs. These developments favour more systematic use of quantitative and comparative risk assessment and economic analysis to promote systemic rationality in European risk management, especially at the EC level, consonant with the Law and Economics approach.

Law and Economics research can help inform the current debate in Europe over environmental regulatory centralization, and the principle of subsidiarity. That research casts grave doubt on the validity of the 'race to the bottom' rationale for centralized regulation, and demonstrates that market integration goals provide no justification for centralized adoption of uniform or harmonized environmental regulations for production methods and processes. As a result of amendments to the Rome Treaty, environmental legislation in the EU is no longer constitutionally dependent on a market integration rationales, and its justification and scope can be examined afresh and on its own terms. Law and Economics research indicates that the strongest justification for centralized measures is to address transjurisdictional environmental externalities, in

---

[114] See Breyer and Heyvaert, n. 88 above.

the form of pollution spillovers or the value that many in Europe place on preservation of ecological resources that are located in other Member States. Consideration of the current and future character of EC environmental law might usefully focus on the question of how effectively it deals with such externalities.

To the extent that EC-level environmental regulation is justified, EIS have important governance as well as performance advantages over detailed command-and-control measures and over other alternative approaches, including environmental and covenants and EC framework legislation, for carrying out such regulation. Because environmental taxes and trading systems and other EIS would afford regulated entities wide flexibility in the nature and means of implementing EC-level regulatory legislation that incorporates these instruments, they avoid the excessive rigidity, cost, and bureaucratic centralization that are produced by the command-and-control regulatory approach that currently dominates EC environmental legislation. EIS also have important advantages over other regulatory approaches for avoiding the defects of detailed EC-level command and control regulation. Relative to environmental covenants and contracts and EC framework legislation, environmental taxes and trading programmes provide stronger assurances of effective implementation, especially if adequate discharge monitoring and reporting requirements are imposed on all regulated entities. EIS also provide greater transparency in government decision-making and accountability to the European public than environmental covenants, where decisions about aggregate residuals levels are generally negotiated between government and industry behind closed doors, or than EC-level framework legislation that leaves considerable discretion to the Member States in framing detailed implementing measures.

For these reasons, US regulatory experience with Law and Economics methodologies, decision-making techniques, and regulatory instruments informed by Law and Economics approaches can make valuable contributions to both the substance and the process of European environmental regulation in the years ahead.

# From a Golden Age to an Uncertain Future: Lawyers and the Battles around the German Environmental State

YVES DEZALAY*

## I. Introduction

This chapter aims to contribute to a better understanding of the dynamics of the transformation of the practices of environmental regulation. This development is often misleadingly summarized in terms, which we will challenge, of the opposition between a bureaucratic model of 'command-and-control', and a new generation of 'market instruments'.[1] By putting forward an outline of the structural history of environmental policies, their transformation, through the recompositions of the field of environmental practitioners and professionals from which they flow, will be clarified.

In this respect, law provides a privileged field. Conceived according to the command-state model, legal practices in relation to the environment are directly affected by the reorientation of these policies to favour 'new instruments', especially economic ones, serving a form of regulation which claims to be negotiated, rather than imposed.[2] Further, many environmental lawyers express, if not criticisms, at least some reservations towards changes which undermine the utility and social legitimacy of abilities and skills largely derived from administrative law. For their part, the champions of these new policies, in line with neoliberal ideology, do not hesitate to denounce the inefficiency of bureaucratic administrative frameworks which they (dis)qualify as anachronistic vestiges of a 'command-and-control economy'.

If environmental policies can readily be seen to help structure this new field of expertise, it must also be conceded that they in turn are strongly influenced by the strategies of alliance and competition played out between the different groups of environmental specialists. What is at stake, is the redefinition and reallocation of tasks, and of hierarchical positions between agents who often wear different or several hats: switching from militant to expert, from bureaucrat to manager, or even from researcher to consultant.

* Professor of Sociology, Director of Research at the Centre National de la Recherche Scientifique (CNRS), Paris, France. Translated from the French by Professor Sol Picciotto, University of Lancaster, Lancaster, UK.
  [1] J. Golub (ed.), *New Instruments for Environmental Policy in the EU* (London: Routledge, 1998).
  [2] N. Gunningham, P. Grabosky, and D. Sinclair, *Smart Regulation—Designing Environmental Policy* (Oxford: Clarendon Press, 1998).

This fundamental shift is linked to the arrival on the scene of multinationals, whose investments upset the power relations in this field of practice, while at the same time opening up new opportunities, both for the modes of environmental protection, and for the careers of the professionals devoted to it.[3] The arrival of industrialists, and of environmental managers, is thus a major factor which enables us to understand a transformation of the practices of environmental regulation which develops in a much more gradual and complex way than is suggested by the opposition between 'market' and 'command-and-control'.

To implement this approach in full, we would need to take into account the interaction, or competition, between national logics played out at the European level.[4] For Brussels is the scene of the main political and ideological assault against an approach to environmental regulation which was in the interventionist tradition of the welfare state. Since it is not possible to do this in the context of this chapter without sacrificing the level of detail, and above all the continuity of the trajectories which are essential for such a structural history, we will instead focus on the German case to illustrate this problem. After all, German lawyers played a key role in establishing a system of environmental regulation seen—rightly—as one of the most developed examples of the command-state model.[5] Yet, it is also one of the countries where firms have made substantial investments in the environmental field, going back to the 1980s.

Therefore, the legal field provides a kind of prism through which to observe concretely the social and professional stakes which help to restructure the arena of environmental regulation, first in the '*Bürgerinitiativ*' mobilization, then with the 'conversion' of business under the pressure of public opinion. As we will see through the trajectories of different types of environmental lawyers, from academic pioneers to business lawyers to anti-nuclear militants, this field of practice is a long way from the (theoretical) model of the command-state.

Yet, for all that, nor does it resemble the (programmatic) model advocated by the proponents of 'new instruments'. Professionals who go into the service of corporations evidently have little interest in upsetting the institutional arrangements and the gamut of relationships which constitute the essence of their social capital, when they only have to mobilize these resources to ensure themselves a dominant position in this new configuration of the field of regulation. This is likely to remain so until the internationalization of the regulatory game forces them to revise their strategy, and to invest in the new abilities and skills which have become prevalent in these new spaces of state power. Before analysing these transformations, it is therefore necessary first to deconstruct

[3] L. Sklair, *The Transnational Capitalist Class* (Oxford: Blackwell, 2001), 210.

[4] A. Heritier, C. Knill, and S. Mingers, *Ringing the Changes in Europe—Regulatory Competition and Redefinition of the State—Britain, France, Germany* (Berlin: De Gruyter, 1996).

[5] H. Weidner, *25 Years of Modern Environmental Policy in Germany: Treading a Well-Worn Path to the Top of the International Field—Working Papers NFS II 95–301* (Berlin: Wissenschaftszentrum Berlin, 1995).

these learned representations, which are as much rhetorical arguments produced by and for the struggles through which the field becomes transformed.

One of the main advantages of this structural approach is to provide us with a research methodology. Thus, this attempt to reconstruct an evolving map of the European social circle of specialists in environmental policy was based on interviews with a very diverse range of subjects—professionals, militants, managers, or bureaucrats. For this study, over 150 interviews were conducted in Brussels and four European countries throughout 1999 and 2000.[6] Generally used to analyse scientists, this concept has not been much applied to environmental lawyers.[7] Several interpretations of this omission are possible: either as an indication of the minor importance of legal professionals in a field of practices dominated by scientists or militants; or as the result of a strategy of discretion resulting from skills which emerge as an instrument of power in the world of the dominant. Thus, while the different environmental actors, and especially green militants, have been the object of many studies in political sociology, the legal practitioners I interviewed seemed surprised to be selected as an object for research. As if they viewed their role as that of a perfectly neutral technician, happy to translate into legal language the policy choices over which they have no control.

This approach leads me to challenge some of the concepts, such as that of 'epistemic communities', which have been elaborated to theorize environmental institutions and policies. This notion may be helpful to emphasize that the success of these policies greatly depends on the social characteristics of the actors, but it is also quite idealist in concealing the rifts and competitive struggles, as well as the relations of domination. This blindness is particularly troublesome since these power games are essential to an understanding of both the origin of these fields of social practice, and the internal dynamics of their transformation. By focusing on the tactical alliance between dominated bureaucrats and marginalized scientists, this idealized representation of strategies of emergence gives a rather poor account of the competitive struggles which have helped to restructure these initial alliances within the market for expertise, the economic logic of which is then imposed as much on the activist enterprises as on the expert consultants.

A microsociological approach can help illuminate this black box of political science analysis by describing by what mechanisms a field of practice becomes transformed to stay in step with new ideological perspectives which in turn are the product of macrosocial transformations. In this instance, we need to understand how a whole complex of institutions and bodies of knowledge, conceived according to the command-state model of the environment, can be recomposed according to a quite different logic, which represents itself,

---

[6] For a more complete explanation of this methodology applied to other fields of legal practice, see Y. Dezalay and B. Garth, *Dealing in Virtue: International Commercial Arbitration and the Emergence of a New International Legal Order* (Chicago: University of Chicago Press, 1996).

[7] M. Keck and K. Sikkink, *Activists beyond Borders: Advocacy Networks in International Politics* (New York: Cornell University Press, 1998).

perhaps falsely, as the opposite of its predecessor. In brief, we need to understand the internal dynamics of this 'revolution', described by some as having been imposed, and by others as a natural and self-evident development.

The very simplicity of this schematic opposition between two regulatory models, which are said to correspond to two periods—and two philosophies—is perfectly suited to the tactical argumentations confronting each other in the field of environmental policies. On the other hand, this simplistic dichotomy is of little use in understanding the dynamics of this 'revolution', if indeed that is what it is. In fact, the term 'command-and-control' is all the more unwarranted since the model of the guardian state supervising the environment hardly ever existed—except in a programmatic way, as a sort of ideal label for a strategy which derives from 'symbolic politics'.

This bureaucratic system of supervision, once it had been established in texts, policy, and doctrinal debates, found itself immediately overshadowed by the soaring rise of neoliberal policies in the Reagan years. From that moment, everything was allied against it. Although intended to demonstrate the efforts to be made, studies of the 'implementation deficit' provide arguments for denouncing the inefficiency of bureaucratic arrangements, destined by definition to powerlessness.[8] Similarly, the intensity of activist struggles, pursued even into the courts (notably in the case of nuclear power or industrial projects), stimulates the establishment of mediation arrangements capable of preventing the violence of public confrontations which the rostrum of the courts only serves to amplify.

The mobilization of public opinion, accelerated by media representations of ecological catastrophes, only increases the dissuasive effects of the first attempts to operationalize state regulation of the environment. This applies in particular to directors of multinationals, especially chemicals firms, who ultimately decide to invest in environmental protection. One might have expected that these developments served to justify these policies, retrospectively, as well founded, by facilitating the realization of aims which, until then, tended to belong to symbolic politics. On the contrary, they sound the death-knell of this highly legalized form of state interventionism. For these managers are above all concerned to avoid the negative publicity of militant actions or of administrative sanctions, especially when they are amplified by the rostrum of the courts.

This change of strategy is due not only to preventive tactics, it is also part of the neoliberal counter-offensive aiming to dismantle the interventionism of the welfare state. In this case, it is a matter of diluting supervision by state agencies, and even bypassing it. Managers make the most of the opportunity of their firms to achieve much better results in terms of the environment, as long as they have the freedom to choose a timetable and the methods which suit their industrial strategies. The promotion of self-regulation is of course

---

[8] R. Mayntz (ed.), *Implementation Politischer Programme: Empirische Forschungsberichte* (Königstein: Athenäum, 1980).

aimed at the media, but also tries to seduce the non-governmental organizations (NGOs). So as to deflect their criticisms, they are incited to bypass state agencies, and negotiate directly with corporations. In this rather unfavourable context, the command-state model could only be stillborn. Arriving too late, it served above all as a target for its detractors.

It is not enough to understand that the concept of 'command-and-control' was a tactical construction. It is also necessary to emphasize that the promotion of 'new instruments' is just as much part of the programmatic discourse as the appeals for an 'environmental welfare state'. Multinationals, which make massive investments in the field of the environment—and its institutions—have little interest in inventing or developing new instruments for as long as they only have to deploy their economic and symbolic resources to be in a powerful position in the game of state-style regulation. Thus, instead of referring to market-style regulation as opposed to bureaucratic supervision, it is the entire machinery, including activist mobilization and state intervention, which becomes permeated by the logic of competition. The dominant economic operators are all the more comfortable with this new market for expertise in environmental matters, because the resources they invest in it, both financial and symbolic, allow them to obtain official approval and legitimacy for their industrial strategies from state agencies.

This scenario is played out in broad terms in the countries considered to be pioneers of the environment.[9] But it unfolds in different ways according to the national histories which determine where and how the political confrontation occurs. In Germany, this strategy of self-regulation by the big corporations ends in neocorporatist-type regulatory arrangements, facilitated by the homogeneity of a small elite of professionals who act as intermediaries between big firms and state institutions. To understand the origins of this arrangement, one must go back to the social conflicts of the late 1970s. Paradoxically, although intending to denounce such collusion, the mobilization of the greens against state nuclear power stimulated the growth of neocorporatist regulation in the environmental field. For the violence of the clashes not only accelerated the construction and diffusion of a new expertise, it also emphasized the benefits of mediation between experts to avoid the risks of social conflicts.

## II. Doctrinal Strategies and 'Symbolic Politics'

In Germany, lawyers are well represented in the entourage of politicians, such as Brandt and Genscher, who in the early1970s initiated environmental policies. Many of them consider that these professionals were influenced by trips to or contacts with North America. Thus, the International Union for Conservation of Nature and Natural Resources (IUCN) for long was one of the

---

[9] M. S. Andersen and D. Liefferink (eds.), *European Environmental Policy: the Pioneers* (Manchester: Manchester University Press, 1997).

main centres for meetings between American environmental lawyers and their European colleagues.[10] Wolfgang Burhenne thus seems to be the link between various networks which he built. Apart from the IUCN Legal Committee, and more recently the International Centre for Environmental Law (ICEL), this promoter of environmental law also helped launch two associations by finding them funds through foundations with which he is well connected: the *Arbeitskreis für Umweltrecht* (AKUR) and the *Centre Européen du Droit de l'Environnement* (CEDE). The latter brings together academic lawyers, mostly French and German, to carry out comparative legal studies or seminars. In the circumstances, the international and the national are mutually supportive: the promotion internationally of environmental law is in step with the interests of the young academics who have to struggle to gain recognition by their national hierarchies. Yet these symbolic importations were successful because they were carried by local agents, in particular the Protestant churches, which concretized their social commitment by organizing 'academies', which brought together people of various backgrounds ready to mobilize around collective social issues such as the environment.

The *Arbeitskreis für Umweltsrecht* (AKUR), the German association for environmental law, provides a good illustration of this intermingling of law and politics. Academic recognition of environmental law is obtained by making an investment—discreet but influential—in the field of environmental policies. This elitist association (voluntarily limited to twelve members) brings together eminent lawyers, mainly professors and senior administrative court judges, who use their authority with lawyers in the civil service—some of whom are indeed their former students—to provide advice in the process of elaborating of environmental norms, in the name of the rigour and coherence necessary for legal measures.[11] Adopting the role of guardian of the law allows them to be present in the corridors of the political arena, while proclaiming their neutrality in relation to partisan disputes.

This strategy is therefore perfectly compatible with the rules of the university arena, which must be respected to obtain the recognition of their peers for the autonomy of this new branch of administrative law. In turn, this academic reputation, expressed in the form of manuals, lectures, and even professorial chairs, only increases the size of their audience in the arena of the budding bureaucracies of the environment, which themselves are in search of recognition and legitimacy. This elitist strategy is therefore very successful, especially for the privileged few who may benefit from this scarcity-rent to build prestigious academic careers. In other European countries, academic lawyers attempted similar strategies, but with much less success. Lacking the support of a juridical culture, which is specific to the German administrative system,

---

[10] Cf. M. Holdgate, *The Green Web: a Union for World Conservation* (London: Earthscan, 1999).

[11] One of these founding fathers defines his role as that of a 'respected lobbyist on legal issues'. He adds that both he and his colleagues are frequently called upon to intervene, due to the numerous hearings resulting from the complexity of the normative processes in a federal system. In addition, the civil servants write to ask the advice of academics whom they treat rather like mentors.

academic lawyers of other European countries could not achieve a significant position in either state environmental agencies or the academic hierarchy. This marginalization in the field of power is reinforced by their distance from, and even mistrust of, militant activities, which they share with their German colleagues.

On the other hand, to the extent that it privileges the values cultivated by the hierarchy of 'pure lawyers', such as neutrality and distance, this strategy disqualifies practitioners. It is true that, in the first stage, the problem barely arises: the first pieces of environmental legislation are the product of social consensus, which bureaucrat lawyers merely formalize, leaving to engineers the task of agreeing technical standards to be met. The priority is to draw up the texts, whilst the problem of subsequently applying them is hardly raised. As one interviewer observed: 'in the early 1970s everybody agreed that there was urgent need for environmental legislation, and nobody thought about costs. Implementation was not a real issue. What mattered was to put the new laws in place.' Pehl even considers that the 'implementation deficits of the 1970s, as they were revealed by the implementation research projects (e.g. Hucke and Ullmann),[12] were to a certain extent pre-programmed by the legislation'.[13]

This symbolic management of environmental politics is undermined by the social and ideological struggles which crystallize around nuclear power. As these conflicts become legalized and shift to the courts, a refocusing occurs with an increased role for practitioners. In a second phase, it stimulates the development of preventive strategies, by discreet arrangements of a neo-corporatist type which will be discussed below. Hence, theoreticians of 'symbolic politics' advocate a more nuanced view. While admitting that the first environmental texts are mostly 'empty shells', they defend them as representing a first step in the right direction, waiting for a next catastrophe for the purpose of reinforcing existing regimes. These successes, however, at the same time incite the business firms to establish counter-strategies, which displace these regulatory arrangements and mechanisms.

After the oil crises, industrialists and trade unions pressured politicians by denouncing the environment as an 'obstacle to economic growth', and a 'job killer'.[14] At Gymnich in 1975, the new Chancellor Schmidt gave in to their demands, and proposed a kind of moratorium on legislation,[15] as well as on the enforcement of legislation on pollution, and on waste disposal. The bureaucracy resisted, by retreating behind administrative rules. But a massive mobilization at local level, the *Bürgerinitiative*, has become a new element, often indeed with the connivance, if not the support, of officials of the

---

[12] J. Hucke and A. A. Ullmann, *Konfliktregelung zwischen Industriebetrieb und Vollzugsbehörde bei der Durchsetzung Regulativer Politik* in Mayntz, n. 8 above, 105–26.

[13] H. Pehle, 'Germany: Domestic Obstacles to an International Forerunner', in Andersen and Liefferink, n. 9 above, 163.

[14] Pehle, n. 13 above, 164.

[15] In fact, no new legislation was enacted between 1975 and 1978, a period commentators have called 'the first Ice Age of Environmental Policy'.

environment agencies. The immediate assistant of Genscher, the head of the environment office and spokesperson on environmental questions of the *Freie Demokratische Partei* (FDP), was one of the founders of the *Bundesverband Bürgerinitiative Umweltschutz* (BBU), the coordinating organ of the *Bürgerinitiative*: 'We were always in contact. . . . They were my best advocates,' he says. These groups are not content to pressurize public opinion by demonstrations or recourse to the media. They make full use of the opportunities presented by the plethora of public hearings required by licensing procedures, especially for anything relating to industries involving risk, such as nuclear power. From that moment, environmental law is no longer merely a legislative or academic matter, it becomes the object of a professional practice, for barristers, business lawyers, or the administrative agencies, which are often mobilized full-time on these cases.[16]

From the perspective of professional circles, the effects of this very conflictual period are contradictory. Since administrative procedures are one of the main fields of confrontation, this can only reinforce the administrative roots of this new law and of its practitioners. Yet these newcomers, not well recognized in their professional world,[17] are still marked by the ideal of distance and neutrality imposed by—and for—the small elite of founding fathers of the AKUR. The spectacular rise of environmental law is accompanied by a marked hierarchization, which benefits the pioneers, whose reputation and networks of influence continue to grow. On the other hand, this hierarchical division of legal labour does not facilitate the incorporation of these new forms of practice, which are more diverse and conflictual, but are nevertheless the key to its evolution and renewal.[18] On the contrary, environmental law tends to retreat into administrative doctrine, where it was rooted and constituted. In this respect, it is revealing to note that the mobilization of the greens against

---

[16] Thus, one of these lawyers reported to us of having spent over ten years working full-time on various aspects of the defence of militants mobilizing against the proposed Backersdorf power station. Business lawyers and barristers also take advantage of this move into the courts. For the licensing procedures are complex and lengthy: they take one to three years, even longer when there is an appeal.

[17] This gap is ultimately filled on initiative of a judge, who was the first president of AKUR. Disagreeing with his peers, who want the presidency to rotate, he founds a new association aiming to be more open to barristers, but also to civil servants and business lawyers. As for the lawyers who are activists or close to the associations, they remain very much in the minority and marginalized.

[18] Several of our interviewees report a kind of 'disenchantment'. According to one of the founding fathers:

We have grown older. We are no longer seen as progressive. Particularly since the emergence of a very active environmental movement. . . . It is true that, as a group, we are less interested in the new developments, like soft law or pollution rights. Lawyers are not involved in the debate on sustainability. That debate is conducted outside of legal fora. . . . Maybe we are not made to deal with big social issues. . . . Environmental law has lost its extraordinary status. It has been normalized as part of the accepted body of laws. It is no longer something new. It is the usual story of the modernists caught up by traditionalists, the domestication of a young discipline by the more traditional branches. Even if we are still more innovative, we have been reintegrated, we have become mainstream administrative law.

nuclear power has had little impact on the legal domain, while it stimulated the emergence and recognition of an alternative expertise in the scientific disciplines.

### III. Conflicts and Professionalization

The *Öko Institut* is the prototypical organization of this new period of the late 1970s, when pressures and initiatives on behalf of the environment no longer come from above but from below. After the departure of Brandt and Genscher, and the U-turn of Schmidt on environmental questions, an entire network of local groups mobilized to put pressure on public authorities to force them to fulfil all the commitments of their predecessors. Yet, although the forms of organization and the strategy are very different, one finds the same components as before: the influence of the North American model, and the support of the Churches. Thus, it is after a trip to the USA on the invitation of Jacob Sherman, director of the National Research Defence Council (NRDC), that the founders of the *Öko Institut* formulated their project, which is explicitly inspired by the strategy of the Environmental Defence Fund (EDF): to put a network of lawyers and experts at the disposal of the activist groups, to ensure that cases are well prepared when they are put to the administration or the courts. It is the German Marshall Fund, which provides the initial funding for the development of an alternative scenario for nuclear power. The new institution itself also benefits from the support of the Protestant Churches. The presence of a professor of theology on the board of the *Öko* demonstrates these close links with the network of the 'academies', which contribute to the publicization and credibility of this alternative discourse.

This conjunction of influence which, as was already noted, one finds at other points of the story, is not just a coincidence. In many ways, the reformist strategy of the Protestant elites is very close to that of the big North American philanthropic foundations such as Ford, which godfathered the emergence of an environmental expertise around organizations such as the NRDC or the EDF.[19] Giving greater political credibility to ecological demands also reinforces the more responsible—or moderate—fraction of this movement, against the more radical fringes which prefer direct or even violent action. The valorization of expertise helps to structure these groups of marginals around 'responsible' organizations, which are capable of building an 'alternative' definition of the public interest. These are more willing to enter into dialogue the more they consider themselves to have experts capable of replying to their opponents on their own ground, with arguments which are just as legitimate. In the USA, the law plays a key role in this strategy. Organizations such as the NRDC or the EDF bring together lawyers and scientists to combine the resources of legal procedure and substantive arguments.

[19] R. Gottlieb, *Forcing the Spring—The Transformation of the American Environmental Movement* (Washington, DC.: Island Press, 1993).

It is this type of mechanism that the founders of the *Öko Institut* had the ambition to establish in 1977, to bring this dual expertise to the aid of militants fighting against the plans to establish nuclear generators, especially the one at Wyhl, near Freiburg. A group of young lawyers from Freiburg invested their efforts into this enterprise, alongside scientists, members of associations, and representatives of the evangelical academies.[20] This professionalization of confrontation occurs in a climate of very violent clashes around nuclear power, such as at Backersdorf, where the police and army were mobilized to intimidate, expel, or imprison not only the demonstrators occupying the site, but also the local sympathizers who supported or fed them.[21] Here again, we find the support of the Churches, notably the Catholic Church, which is very powerful in Bavaria, and whose caution helps to widen the social base of this protest movement. Hence, masses were held on the site, and not infrequently, demonstrations were led by crosses. As often happens in times of political crisis or of institutional conflict, the Churches became a sort of substitute for the state. In this instance, they incarnated a general interest in the face of a state under attack for being subordinated to the nuclear industry.

The strategy of professionalization of the anti-nuclear confrontation seems, in many respects, a success. As had been the case in the USA, the pooling of scientific and legal skills permitted opponents of nuclear power to gain unexpected victories in a field, that of the courts, considered to be conquered by the adversary. They felt that state justice accepted their arguments against the state. And these victories, even if they were only partial or temporary, encourage further investments in this field. [22]

Yet, despite these court victories, the lawyer-militants gain little from this process of professionalization. Despite participating actively from the start in

[20] Several of the founding members indeed have both these qualifications, such as Günther Altner, who describes himself as both a biologist and a theologian, or Karl Müller-Reissman, information-technologist and theologian.

[21] In this instance, the confrontation was heightened by the obstinacy of the political powers, notably of Strauss, who took personal charge of the matter. He succeeded in creating a united front of opponents, in which activists of all political stripes combined to denounce the 'totalitarianism' of the nuclear-state' which, in their eyes, threatened constitutional freedoms. At least this is how their defender puts it:

> These were people who trusted the state. And here, they felt that a group of politicians linked to unscrupulous entrepreneurs were undermining the very foundations of our constitutional system, that the new technologies would give them an enormous concentration of power, at the expense of ordinary people. Constitutional freedoms, such as the right to demonstrate, were constantly violated by police brutality, which was simply intended to intimidate.

[22] One of these activist lawyers gives this description of the 'step-by-step' strategy:

> We were the underdog, David against Goliath. When we won our first case we were really astonished. . . . It was very helpful. It made the whole group realize that participating in legal proceedings was a worthwhile strategy. Because we were there at the hearings with scientific advisers who had worked on the files and brought forward solid arguments, the other side had to provide good answers in terms of risks and security measures. As a result the security level increased after every round of approval. Our group of technical experts took part in every public hearing. They knew the debate and the results of the last hearing. So they could improve their argument, push one step further. Now, because of that strategy, the security standards in Germany are certainly the highest in the world.

projects such as the *Öko Institut*, their position in it remains ambiguous, if not marginal, due to their lack of recognition in the legal hierarchy. They are for the most part younger practitioners, still untried, who limit themselves to supplying tactical advice on how best to present the scientific arguments, during the multiple hearings or administrative procedures in which the *Öko Institut* offers help.[23]

One reason for this retreat may be the fact that these young activist lawyers feel caught between two social spaces driven by different logics. How can they reconcile this commitment with a professional *habitus*—and a hierarchy—which value neutrality and distance? All the more so when these activist practices claim to challenge the state order and a market logic embedded in the law. Caught in the crossfire of these two imperatives, which are difficult to reconcile, the lawyer-activist can hardly escape being doubly marginalized: 'I feel remote from both positions, the mainstream lawyers as well as the militants.'[24]

It is in any case significant that, during the years when the multiplying hearings and procedures mobilized numerous legal professionals, the latter did not form any networks. A few meetings were organized, but differences were too big to allow a collective identity to be built, or even simply to pool the capital derived from experience. Around the *Öko Institut*, the small group of lawyers made its contribution to the different teams without really developing a holistic legal project. They were, for the most part, independent practitioners collaborating more or less regularly. In addition, two or three permanent staff worked on building a database from the range of cases involving licensing applications in Germany for industrial establishments. This substantial archival work is very helpful for the associations and collectivities, giving them a bank of precedents they could use. But this is not, strictly speaking, legal research. Only later, in the early 1990s, did the idea emerge of combining the experience or research of the lawyers close to the movements for the defence of the environment. And it is significant that this network, the Environmental Law Network International (ELNI), for which the *Öko Institut* provides the secretariat and the newsletter, from the start has been European, with a rather low German membership.[25] The aim is to combine legal

---

[23] One of our interviewees noted:

The key aspect of that strategy was not legal but scientific. What was important was to build a strong file of scientific opinions. Our role as lawyers was to say when and how to use it, tell them at what point we had to produce our evidence, or whose burden of proof it was. I never took part in these cases as the strategic leader. The various groups had their own leaders who followed their own tactics.

[24] One of these academic lawyers, although very committed, remembers that at first those who considered themselves as 'true' militants were rather mistrustful of these intellectual 'fellow-travellers' who they described as '*scheisse*-liberals'. He himself admits that he always felt

a bit remote from those I represented. I always believed in the importance of reason. I always try to keep up my scientific standards, and I refuse to take cheap leftist environmental positions.... Yet, for a long time, we were considered as leftist outsiders, both by the academic world of AKUR, and by the mainstream environmental practitioners of the association.

[25] The initiative came from a former assistant to Rehbinder, who was able to make contacts with other young lawyers close to the movement, notably those of *Stichting Natuur en Milieu* (SNM), due to a placement at the *Bureau Européen de l'Environnement* (BEE).

skills with a commitment to environmental protection. While manifesting themselves as lawyers, these professionals wish to distinguish themselves from the national environmental law associations, which are increasingly dominated by business lawyers, far removed from activist preoccupations. The virtual somnolence of this European network emphasizes the difficulty of lawyers involved in the defence of the environment in gaining recognition both from the militants and from professional circles. Organizing at the European level exacerbated the problems of coordination and finance, without thereby compensating for their weak positions in the national fields. The first conference, which brought together some fifty participants in Frankfurt in 1990, with the financial support of Directorate-General (DG) XI of the European Commission, had as its theme the participation of citizens and associations in the administrative procedures, and the prospects for legal actions. Apart from the Newsletter and a few occasional studies for DG XI on access to justice, the main activity of this network was the exchange of experiences during conferences on themes such as licensing procedures, eco-audit, dangerous products and substances, and environmental impact assessments. At first, these meetings were held annually, but the lack of resources—specially after the reorientation of policy at DG XI—resulted in longer gaps between them, and finally in their suspension. Combining marginalized elements is not an adequate strategy to obtain recognition. In this respect, German activist lawyers are hardly better off than their neighbours. Thus, in the UK, the few activist lawyers come up against the suspicion of a movement for whom the judges—and by extension the law—'cannot be the solution because they are the enemy'. The precariousness of their position is exacerbated by the prosperity and professional recognition achieved by this field of practice, which is little inclined to recognize the originality of their contribution.[26]

## IV. Business Strategies and Neo-corporatist Arrangements

Without enjoying the authority of the top professors, business barristers and corporate lawyers are recognized in the world of the environment as respected experts defending the interests of the enterprises. All freely admit to having first chosen this specialism more for opportunistic reasons than out of personal motivation: it was a gap which opened as their career began. But they knew how to make the intellectual investments vital to building a legitimate reputation and authority. They publish articles or manuals to commentate on this new law, and to emphasize their abilities.[27] While this strategy valorizes

[26] Far from being able to use this exemplary experience as a springboard into a career, *Öko Institut* lawyers, it seems, have considerable difficulty in re-entering university or professional circles.

[27] As one of these pioneers emphasizes: 'I was lucky to be already in this field when it got its fantastic development. I just had one of the first big cases; so I decided to go into a theoretical mode and wrote a small book which was one of the first books in this field.'

This practitioner stresses the fact that those of his generation were trained on the job, while their successors only had an array of options among the various specialisms in environmental law. In turn, the latter contribute to the demand in a rising market for publications.

them by reinforcing their autonomy in relation to the demands of their clients or employers, it also serves the interests of the latter. For it permits these large firms to defend their positions by playing the card of the law, a field in which they can count on the capital of authority and the image of professional neutrality, built by their representatives.

In their comments, many of our interviewees referred to a 'golden age' of environmental law, at the turn of the 1980s, when the firms began to invest in this field. A series of ecological catastrophes such as the pollution of the Rhine and the *Waldsterben* considerably increased the audience for the greens, which allowed them to extend their activist demands well beyond the issue of nuclear power stations. With each new catastrophe, under the pressure of public opinion, the government imposed new and more stringent rules,[28] which industry could merely oppose by delaying tactics, notably by establishing self-regulatory arrangements. However, this strategy has a limited impact because it comes up against the juridical culture of a bureaucracy which is 'highly suspicious of self-regulation'.[29]

The legal representatives of the corporate world have close links with this normative process. They share these tasks with other directors more specifically responsible for *Umweltpolitik*. The lawyers are resoundingly unanimous in denying involvement in 'lobbying': 'if we intervene, it is in the name of the law, to improve the legal quality of the proposed texts.' Thus, one of these top lawyers, who built his reputation as one of the main defenders of the nuclear power industry, is regularly asked to give advice on proposed laws affecting the environment. But he does this in the name of the Bar's environment committee, which he has chaired for over twenty years. And he emphasizes the fact that he does not intervene in the name of this or that client, but 'to defend the interests of the entire community of environmental lawyers', by pointing to the problems which could be created by the application of any provision. Nevertheless, this concern for neutrality has not prevented him from developing over the past few years a practice including lobbying—which he describes as 'legislative'—on behalf of a few big clients. The latter no doubt appreciate the full value of the legitimate authority and the social capital built in the name of the law. Similarly, legal directors of the big firms—and of employers' organizations—emphasize the technical aspects of their contributions. According to them, their role is limited to exposing the technical imperfections of a proposed text, or perhaps to explaining to an administrator the specific constraints of any given industry.

---

[28] According to the legal director of one of the large chemical groups: 'After each catastrophe, the government's first reaction is to take advantage of it to pass new laws and establish new and more interventionist enforcement procedures.'

[29] As one of these representatives acknowledges:

the German civil servant is brought up in a legal culture. For him, an industry code of good conduct makes no sense, unless it is inscribed in the tablets of the law. Self-regulation he can hardly believe in, so long as there are no texts which allow him to supervise and penalize. He does not see self-regulation as an alternative, but as a provision that is additional to and a reinforcement of the regulatory mechanism. Here, one thinks always in terms of addition, not of substitution.

All parties involved therefore avoid a too overt defence of the interests of their employers—or clients—in order to preserve their credibility in the eyes of the persons with whom they are speaking.[30] To understand this code of good conduct, we need to take account of the complexity of the corporatist apparatus, which frames and institutionalizes this game of influences. Most of these corporate lawyers are also members of many employers' committees, or public committees. This brings them into regular contact, not only with their peers, but also with the officials and elected representatives in charge of environmental policies. This implicit ethical principle is imposed by the social group to permit the emergence of a collective consensus which can take account of the interests of all concerned. In turn, the appearance of professional objectivity facilitates the circulation of information in both directions. The discreet contacts cultivated in many forums permit politicians as well as directors of enterprises to make a continuous evaluation of their room for manoeuvre. If they cannot influence policies, entrepreneurs can at least make preparations, or negotiate the mechanisms and timetable of application of these new measures.[31]

## V. From Courtroom Confrontations to Accommodation between Experts

The social construction of such an institutionalized machinery of collective mediation, as efficient as it is discreet, does not happen spontaneously. Certainly, German companies have a long experience of partnership with public

[30] 'People you talk to need to think of you as a partner. They want you to provide them only with objective information that they can check with others. Those are the only acceptable arguments. As soon as they suspect that you are defending the interests of your enterprise, you completely lose influence.'

[31] The importance of these compromises was revealed as early as the mid-1970s by a series of studies, inspired by Anglo-American work, on the 'implementation deficit'. However, as indicated by the term 'the informal *Rechtstaat*', this deficit takes a paradoxical form in Germany:

> This bargaining takes place at every level. Usually a company never starts filing officially for a permit without first having negotiated its content with the administration, sometimes for one or two years. The same happens when a company needs to upgrade an existing plant in order to keep up with new standards. Rather than issuing an order, the administration negotiates until they reach a sort of gentleman's agreement. Even if it is not legally binding, it is in their interest. They know that if they issue an order, the company will challenge it in court, just to buy time. And the company prefers it also: their technicians know the administration, they speak the same language, they get along. Also, non-governmental organizations are kept outside of these bilateral negotiations. Usually they're not even aware of what's going on. . . . The same sort of bargaining takes place at the law-making level. It is symbolic politics. A new law is passed with lots of publicity. Then the administration negotiates with the industry the executive orders which say how it is going to be applied. And there it all depends on the bargaining power of each side. Industry can always go to the Ministry of Economic Affairs in order to block a new regulation. On the other hand, when you have a powerful minister like Genscher, he can put pressure on industry by giving them something in exchange. That is how Zimmerman, who was a cornerstone in Kohl's coalition, managed to introduce the catalytic converter almost single-handedly. . . . Politicians love to negotiate this kind of agreement. It is like a drug for them. They can go to the media with the industry Chief Executive Officer, and present themselves as the great protectors of environment. This is certainly not market regulation, it's corporatism at its best.

authorities, and they are involved from the start in the elaboration of pollution standards. This, by itself, does not justify talk of corporatist management of environmental regulation, because this requires diffusion of experiences and skills between the different social groups involved in various aspects of regulation. The accommodation of divergent interests or the negotiating of compromises requires a minimum of common discourse. In this regard, we may wonder whether the conflicts in the legal and judicial fields which marked the 1970s have acted as an accelerator. Since, particularly in the legal field, the strong mobilization allowed a small group of practitioners to accumulate a substantial social capital of expertise and of social networks, indispensable for the efficient operation of a regulatory mechanism of the neocorporatist type.

This crisis period therefore constituted a decisive moment in the birth of a new field of practice. On each side, the adversaries invest in the law; they spark off a fierce competition which helps to lay the foundation of a new discipline. Thus, when a small group of young lawyers decided to bring a legal action to try to stop a project to extend a nuclear power plant, it formulated a very sophisticated legal strategy which even included, we were told, the publication of an article on constitutional law in the main environmental law review, to enhance the legal authority and visibility of the principles they put forward. On the other side, the corporations' lawyers mobilized major resources to prepare for the many hearings required by the licensing procedures, which are both complex[32] and long: on average between one and three years, if not more, in cases where there is an appeal in the administrative courts. Pitched against lawyers who are often less well prepared, many use all the tricks in the procedural book.[33] The stakes are important, and even if the associations rarely win a case on the substantive issue, the delays involve substantial costs which could even cancel out the profitability of these investments. The symbolic stakes are equally high, for the media loudly trumpet the details of these procedural battles, which are carried right up to the highest administrative tribunals, raising fundamental questions about the constitutional balance of powers.[34] It is easy to understand the nostalgia for this 'golden age' of a young discipline which, when hardly established, enjoyed such high visibility, both political and professional.[35]

[32] According to one of our interviewees, the thickness of the case-files on the licensing applications illustrates this growing complexity in administrative requirements: from a dozen or so pages in the early 1970s, today they exceed 100 pages.

[33] 'Sometimes, I had to give some legal advice to the person who represented the licensing authority in order to prevent some procedural mistake.'

[34] It was an immense debate. Our jurisdictions developed a fantastic influence during that whole decade. They had a huge case load, somewhere between 100 and 150 cases. All sorts of fundamental questions were raised, and discussed at length. How deeply can the courts go into such affairs? How far should they control the licensing done by various state authorities? In the end, the highest court decided to observe some political restraints. They wrote that the courts had no right to decide on the basis of their own judgement of risk; that it remained the responsibility of the government.

[35] 'The public interest in environment law has decreased. There is a general feeling that all the big fights have been settled. The big companies are very careful. Anyway they have managed to export their problems elsewhere, by building new production sites in Asia or China.'

This exceptional period caused a rift between the pioneers and their juniors. The former continued to prosper thanks to the capital of reputation and contacts they had accumulated. Several of them occupy key positions, in the twilight between politics and law. In addition, their sphere of influence was extended with the 'normalization' of environmental preoccupations, which had become inseparable from decisions about industrial or commercial strategy. Thus, one of these pioneers—now vice-president responsible for environmental policy for a big employers' organization—considers that these matters comprise over two-thirds of the agenda for his board: 'environmental issues are certainly not decreasing in importance. Quite the contrary. Now they are really at the core of industrial strategy. They're moving from narrow technical problems to complex political issues.' In contrast, the successive generation finds it more difficult to get to grips with the relative tedium and routine which follows the crisis period. One of these corporate lawyers—who is referred to by his peers as one of the 'best representatives of the second generation'—stresses his marginalization within the big firm in which he has been working for ten years:

I am not the person who decides on environmental policy. This is in the hands of the management for environmental affairs, which is a huge division. If they ask my advice, which happens sometimes, I can only influence at a low level, by giving my interpretation of the law. . . . Chemists have their own way of thinking, including about the law, which they have learned on the job. For instance, there is a whole department in charge of licensing and approvals. They have forty people, but no lawyers, and in the legal department we are the only two specialized in the environment. It shows very well the little influence of lawyers: two against forty. In a big company like this, law is used and produced by non-lawyers. They have daily contacts with various administrations, but 99 per cent of the time they do it without lawyers. Sometimes, they call me to ask a specific question, but I almost never go to a meeting with them.

This routinization of administrative procedures is undoubtedly only one aspect of a more general strategy of avoidance of the courts. The big firms have learned, to their cost, to be wary of falling into the litigation trap: 'won in court but lost in the eyes of public opinion.' 'Avoid litigation at all costs': in environmental matters, this new rule imposed by those responsible for public relations must be obeyed without exception.[36]

Excluded or sidelined from the practices around which environmental law was constructed, these business lawyers made hardly any investment in the new arrangements of self-regulation. Although they do not go so far as the total rejection of some of their colleagues, especially in university or administrative circles, who see it as an 'anti-law movement', business lawyers are suspicious of these 'hybrid' instruments with unclear legal status.[37]

[36] 'In the Case of Sandoz, there was not a single court case. They decided to pay for every single fish without bargaining. And that is true for every big company. They are so afraid of adverse publicity, they are willing to settle at any cost. . . . The chemical industry has learned this lesson from the nuclear cases. They do not want to get into the same kind of public exposure.'

[37] 'Responsive Care, EMASS and all these sort of things . . . lawyers hardly look at it. These agreements have no legal base, thus no legal force. They're usually negotiated by non-lawyers who fear contracts, fear the legal instrument.'

As it happens, the object of the suspicion, this 'non-law', is above all another law, another model of regulation of the environment, which everyone is in agreement in finding less efficient than the German model. In this regard there exists virtual unanimity. Mostly brought up in this 'golden age' of environmental law, German lawyers are still firmly convinced[38] that these new 'imported' arrangements represent a regression compared to the high quality of a 'German model' of environmental protection, which they consider to be well ahead of its neighbours and rivals.[39] Since the EC is the most important source of these new approaches, this 'teacher's complex' is mainly expressed in that direction.

It seems we did not do enough to influence the European process. We felt that we were so much ahead, that we did not bother to push our ideas in Brussels. We thought that our environmental legislation was so good, that no other European countries could compete. They just had to follow our lead. . . . We had completely misunderstood the politics of the European construction. Then, too late, we started to realize that, more and more, environmental protection was being driven by Europe, not by the nation-states. And all these directives came, on Environmental Impact Assessment, EMASS, IPPC . . . , and they did not fit into German culture. Partly because it was constructed by the British, for the British. Yet, even if we did not need it, we could not avoid it; and we still have big problems of implementation. Now, of course we have learned our lesson and we do have an office in Brussels.

Paradoxically, it is the pioneers of environmental law who often demonstrate most receptiveness in response to these imported innovations. For some, this opening leads to the straight road of a cosmopolitan career, which had already been taken by the first importers of environmental law, inspired by the American example. One of the few lawyers who publicly supported these 'new instruments' explains his choice as due to his training at the University of Madison in public administration. 'I have not been socialized in the regulatory system. I have always seen through the eyes of a foreign system. It helps me to "relativate" the German model. Also, I knew that these tools worked elsewhere.' For others, especially in the world of big business, this cosmopolitan attitude entails a pragmatic choice. 'Euro law is a fact. We should be more pragmatic in Germany and just accept it.' This conversion also fits into the globalization strategy pursued by large German firms since the mid-1990s. This is why, after initially opposing it, German entrepreneurs played the Environmental Management Schemes (EMASS) card much more quickly than their European counterparts. This tactical choice is part of a communication strategy aimed at Anglo-American consumers or shareholders. For these firms it is also a very useful bargaining chip in the regulatory negotiations played out at many levels, from the local to the international.

[38] Indeed, many of them say so explicitly.
[39] 'When Responsive Care came from the USA and Canada, we already had very elaborate and thorough legislation. Our first reaction was to say: "What do we need that for? We already have effective laws, and we have very powerful courts that make sure it is implemented. This is OK for countries with weak laws, or 'Roman implementation' . . . Not for us!" '

These new strategies of avoidance also serve to avoid the need for the law. More precisely, they try to avoid the visibility of court procedures, preferring informal agreements based on personalized relations, in order to reach arrangements in the margins of the law.[40] This raises the question of the place of lawyers in this new mechanism, in which the key moves take place outside the law, and legal procedures are relegated to symbolic, or even virtual uses. Certainly, as we have seen, a number of the legal pioneers are much in demand as mediators. But they owe this to their reputation and the extensive network of relationships they have managed to build.[41] These very visible exceptions should not obscure the fact that, in general, in this new market for expertise in matters of legal regulation, the position of legal professionals is in retreat. This phenomenon is not specific to countries with an administrative culture. Thus, having placed great hopes in the development of a market for environmental law, the big city solicitors' firms carried out a strategic retreat, described by one of our interviewees as the 'boom and bust of environmental law'. Rather than blaming their background in administrative law, it is probably necessary to examine other features of this field of practice. Notably, the suspicion of activist practices, especially when combined with a highly inward-looking attitude,[42] make it hard for legal professionals to acquire these networks of very diverse relationships, both in the associations and in business circles, which are essential to fulfil with any success the functions of mediation.

## VI. Conclusion

My relatively pessimistic prognosis for the place of legal professionals in the market for expertise in the law indeed is confirmed by practitioners themselves. This is as much so in Germany where, as we have said, many administrative law specialists denounce the 'anti-law movement', as in the UK, where the corporate lawyers of the City law firms are virtually unanimous in deploring the 'boom and bust' of environmental law. These feelings of bitter deception are sufficiently widespread for one to ask what possibly could have caused them. The question is the more pressing since these impressions of a degeneration into 'routine', if not the complete decline, of the field of environmental legal practice, are in contrast with its rapid growth across the Atlantic

---

[40] This theme of 'bargaining in the shadow of the law' has been the subject of important Anglo-Saxon literature; see Y. Dezalay, 'Negotiated Justice within the Field of Law' in C. Meschievitz and K. Plett (eds.), *Beyond Disputing: Exploring Legal Culture in Five European Countries* (Baden-Baden: Nomos, 1991).

[41] On this question of the social capital of relationships of legal practitioners, see Y. Dezalay and B. Garth, 'Law, Lawyers and Social Capital: Rule of Law versus Relational Capitalism or Lawyers as Professional Brokers in Social and Relational Capital' (1997) 6 *Social & Legal Studies*, 109.

[42] On these two points there is a stark difference with the world of North American lawyers. See Y. Dezalay, 'Between the State, Law and the Market: The Social and Professional Stakes in the Construction and Definition of a Regulatory Arena' in J. McCahery and S. Picciotto (eds.), *International Regulatory Competition and Coordination* (Oxford: Oxford University Press, 1996).

and the hopes placed on it in Europe. These 'failures' therefore directly lead to the classic legal question of the difficulties of 'legal transplants'.

In this respect, the misfortunes of environmental law are evidence not only of the inherent contradictions of environmental policies. They also reveal structural weaknesses which in Europe contributed to the marginalization of the role of legal professionals in the field of the environment.[43] For this marginalization is not new. Certainly, the environmental policies of the 1970s made great use of legal forms. Because this legislative production results, above all, from a strategy of symbolic advertising on the part of both young environmental bureaucracies, and the most institutionalized—or 'responsible'—fraction of the environmental movement. Recourse to law rarely extends beyond a simple 'instrumentalization' of legal forms. This is because the promoters of these policies, whether they are bureaucrats, technicians, or militants, are suspicious of lawyers, and have little interest in formalizing an alliance which could succeed only on the basis of discretion and connivance. Hence, lawyers stayed in the corridors, acting as producers of learned commentaries or programmatic lectures. This reserve in any case perfectly fits with the needs of the European academic *habitus*,[44] which conditions scientific legitimacy on keeping social interests at arm's length.

Paradoxically, after a phase of intense mobilization, the juridification of struggles over the environment only serves to reinforce this sidelining of law and its professionals. Certainly, it is due to these confrontations—especially around nuclear power—that the beginnings of a field of environmental law emerges. But the beneficiaries of the rise of this new market are above all practitioners working for enterprises, both to defend their clients and to help them elaborate preventive or reactive counter-attack strategies. In contrast, the few lawyers who tried to put their skills at the service of the world of social organizations see themselves doubly marginalized due to the growing gap between these activist engagements, and the interests of their professional groups. Unless they can choose between these two, they run the risk of losing credibility on both sides. In short, as soon as environmental law no longer consists of learned commentaries on symbolic policies, and enters the field of practice, market logic succeeds in turning it into a law for entrepreneurs, if not for polluters.

Such a development can merely reinforce the distrust of activists towards a juridical terrain, which they will therefore prefer to instrumentalize by way of essentially media-oriented strategies. Judicial findings of guilt provide arguments to mobilize public opinion. Company directors have learned to their

[43] This diagnosis, which applies to most of the European countries, also applies to Germany, even if it is there that environmental lawyers became the most involved in environmental policies and conflicts. The arguments summarized in this conclusion are developed in the last chapter of our research report for the Environment Ministry (Y. Dezalay, *De la Genèse d'une Politique Symbolique a un Marché de Consultants et Médiateurs: Stratégies Juridiques et Enjeux Politiques dans le Champ Européen de l'Expertise sur l'Environnement—Rapport de Recherche au Ministère de l'Aménagement du Territoire et de l'Environnement* (Paris: Maison des Sciences de l'Homme, 2000).

[44] P. Bourdieu and L. Wacquant, *An Invitation to Reflexive Sociology* (Chicago: University of Chicago Press, 1992), 120; P. Bourdieu, *Homo Academicus* (Paris: Editions de Minuit, 1984), 72.

costs the dangers of court actions 'won in court, but catastrophic in terms of marketing'. These spectacular court cases, whose reverberations in the media ultimately have more impact than legal arguments, therefore lead to a strategy of avoidance. The new generation of environmental managers, often indeed trained in the school of public relations, more recently abide by the rule: 'avoid litigation at all costs!'

This strategic redirection explains the disarray of the bulk of practitioners of environmental law, who lament a drastic fall in this market, all the more dramatic since it follows the great hopes placed in it. The realization of this crisis is simply a reminder that legal skills are symbolic assets, the value of which is linked to the capital of social legitimacy which they embody. The takeover by business law firms of academics in the still tentative market for environmental law quickly uses up the little social credibility of this new legal discipline by reducing it to little more than a sort of 'bargaining chip' in the grand negotiations through which the big international merger and acquisition deals are handled.

In losing its neutral image to become no more than a supplementary technical argument at the disposal of directors of the economy and their 'hired guns', environmental law has lost what gave it a market value for these 'mercenaries', even in the eyes of their paymasters. In allowing themselves to be seduced by the financial offers of the legal tradesmen, these academic turncoats have sold the 'goose that lays the golden eggs'. They have also forgotten the lesson learned by their transatlantic exemplars who, while following the same route,[45] were careful to save some resources to provide moral (and even financial) support, as well as their help (or, more precisely, that of their juniors), to the militant organizations which, by investing in the legal field, contribute to the reproduction of its legitimacy—and of its market value. The activism of the militants of environmental law is perhaps indeed the best argument for firms who sell this expertise to entrepreneurs who are under attack or threat. According to one American saying, which was forgotten by their imitators in their haste: 'One lawyer in town starves, two will thrive.'

[45] M. Dowie, *Losing Ground: American Environmentalism at the Close of the Twentieth Century* (Cambridge: MIT Press, 1995).

# Constitutionalizing Environmental Protection in the European Union

GERD WINTER*

## I. Does the European Union have a Constitution?

Any inquiry into the place of the environment in the constitution of the European Union presupposes the existence of such a constitution. This, however, is not self-evident. Especially British authors have often warned against such a premise, arguing that only states can have constitutions. We therefore first have to come to grips with the more general issue of an EU constitution, before we can turn to the more specific question of the constitutional status of the environment.

Since the term has been used in relation with human society,[1] 'constitution' has been understood as the basic political structure of a society. For a long time the understanding of the concept was material, in the sense that the constitution carries a dignity beyond human rule-making, which does not need to be written down. Only with the rise of social contract theories in the seventeenth century, did 'constitution' come to mean a man-made order, often in the form of a written document, forming the basic rules of state and society.

This document was to contain, in modern terms, second-order law, which regulates the formation and application of first-order law.[2] It should contain, so to speak, the law of laws, or, as Dicey put it: 'Constitutional law, as the term is used in England, appears to include all rules which directly or indirectly affect the distribution or the exercise of the sovereign power of the state.'[3] The essential components of such second-order law are the allocation of different tasks to different state institutions, structures of cooperation and mutual checking of those institutions, the basis of their legitimacy (which in a democratic constitution is the people), a mechanism for the adaptation of the constitution to new circumstances, and fundamental rights of the citizen.[4] In a growing

* Professor, Director of the Research Unit for European Environmental Law, University of Bremen, Germany.

[1] Cicero was probably the first, although he relied on the Greek concept of the *politeia* as developed by Plato and Aristotle. See K. Löwenstein, *Verfassungslehre* (Tübingen: J. C. B. Mohr, 1959), 129.

[2] See H. L. A. Hart, *The Concept of Law* (Oxford: Clarendon Press, 1961, repr. 1993), 77 ff. who proposes to distinguish between ('secondary') rules of recognition, of change, and of adjudication of 'primary' rules.

[3] A. V. Dicey, *Introduction to the Study of the Law of the Constitution (1885)* (London: Macmillan 1965), 23.

[4] Löwenstein, n. 1 above, 131.

number of legal systems, second-order law also came to mean that first-order rules violating the constitution were to be considered null and void.

Throughout European history, the making of a constitution has served to domesticate the power of the sovereign. Tradition or charisma, which were the basis of his or her legitimacy, was replaced by legality.[5] His power was subsumed under a number of higher substantial and organizational rules.

The history of constitutionalism is nothing else but the search of political man for the limitation of the absolute power of the Sovereign, and an attempt to replace blind submission to the existing authority by a spiritual, moral or ethical legitimation of that authority. The legitimation was found in the consent to the exercise of social control by the addressees of power, and in correspondence with this their active participation in the political process.[6]

Can it be maintained that, in the EU, we have a similar situation of pre-state power which must be constitutionalized? Quite obviously the answer is no; there are no sovereign powers to be domesticated, since the powers acquired, and the institutions created, flow from the legal transfer of sovereign rights. In this context of the creation (rather than the control) of government, the term 'constitution' has another connotation, i.e. that of constructing a state-like entity, as opposed to a looser form of international organization.

This manifestation of constitutionalism has acquired particular importance in the context of the evolution of federations out of existing states. An important example is the formation of the 'Constitution' of the 'United States', which was specifically designed to overcome the disastrous experiences associated with its predecessor, the 'Federal Convention' of the Confederation.[7] Another example is the formation of the *German Reich* and its *Reichsverfassung* of 1871, which is earlier proof that the new entity can be based on concepts of shared sovereignty and double legitimacy.[8]

Although in post-war Western Europe, sovereign rights shifted from the national to the supranational level, the European integration process has been profoundly different from that of the USA. Unlike in the case of the USA, in Europe there has never been an intentional decision to create a federation. The 'Communities' were based on international treaties, and these were not replaced by, or did not develop into a clear-cut constitution, but slowly evolved into a *sui generis* legal order, floating somewhere between a federal state and a union of states. The development is fed by the mutual reinforcement of *sui generis* innovations at EU-level, and supporting and complementary action by the Member States. The result is a highly complex polyarchical regime, an

---

[5] M. Weber, *Wirtschaft und Gesellschaft* (Köln/Berlin: Kiepenheuer & Witsch, 1964), 159.

[6] Löwenstein, n. 1 above, 128 (trans. from the German).

[7] See the discussion in R. H. Gabriel (ed.), *Hamilton, Madison and Jay on the Constitution: Selections from the Federalist Papers* (New York: The Liberal Arts Press, 1954), in particular no. 39 (Madison).

[8] For a comparative analysis of the formation of the Deutsches Reich and the EU, see St. Oeter, 'Souveränität und Demokratie als Probleme in der "Verfassungsentwicklung" der Europäischen Union' (1995) 5 *Zeitschrift für Ausländisches Öffentliches Recht und Völkerrecht*, 659–707.

*irregulare aliquod corpus et monstro simile*,[9] to use Samuel Pufendorf's earlier characterization of 'das Heilige Römische Reich Deutscher Nation' in the aftermath of the Westphalian peace of 1648, where constitutional theorists struggled with the structure of the *Reich* in a way similar to today's theorizing about the nature of the EU.[10]

This *irregulare aliquod corpus* may be characterized as a multifaceted regime, where internal and external sovereignty is shared between the Union and the Member States; supranational structures are supplemented by intergovernmental structures; legitimacy of supranational power is derived not from one but from two fundamentally different sources; the main legislative body (the Council of Ministers) also functions as an executive body; the formal executive body (the Commission) in fact is a clearing mechanism for national bureaucracies; the judiciary is not only the mouth of the law but also its creator and even a constitution builder;[11] the formal structures are intricately interspersed with informal networks; and where networks aiming at economic expansion constantly clash with opposing networks defending social and ecological goals.

Although it is both unlikely and undesirable that this polyarchial regime is turned into a federal state, this does not necessarily imply that it should not have a constitution. A different notion of constitution and constitutionalism is demanded in order to understand why there indeed is a need for a constitution, this despite the fact that there exists neither a pre-legal power centre to be transformed into a state, nor a new state to be carved out of existing states. In this third, and more pragmatic conception, the connotation is abandoned that what is constitutionalized must be a state. Rather, constitutionalization can be the object of any organization (which has been defined as a large grouping of people, structured along impersonal lines, and set up to achieve specific objectives).[12] 'Constitutionalization', in this understanding, means to consolidate the basic structures of the organization, and to generate a corporate identity. Such 'concept of law', where no single sovereign power is assumed, but rather where secondary rules gradually evolve out of primary rules,[13] is more apt to cope with informal and piecemeal institution-building as in the EU. It is a pragmatic approach,[14] which may help to avoid the present stalemate where, on the basis of a state-centred definition of constitution, cre-

---

[9] 'Some irregular corpse, similar to a monster.'

[10] Severinus de Monzambano (pseudonym for Samuel Pufendorf), *De Statu Imperii Germanici* (1667), cited in B. Gebhardt, *Handbuch der Deutschen Geschichte*, i (Stuttgart: Union Deutsche Verlagsgesellschaft, 1930), 786.

[11] F. G. Jacobs, 'Is the Court of Justice of the European Communities a Constitutional Court?' in D. Curtin and D. O'Keefe (eds.), *Constitutional Adjudication in European Community and National Law* (Dublin: Butterworths, 1992), 29. On the methodological implications see K. H. Ladeur, 'Richterrecht und Dogmatik-eine verfehlte Konfrontaion? Eine Untersuchung am Beispiel der Rechtsprechung des Europäischen Gerichtshofs' (1996) 1 *Kritische Vierteljahresschrift für Gesetzgebung und Rechtswissenschaft*, 77 ff.

[12] A. Giddens, *Sociology* (Cambridge: Polity Press, 1998), 284.       [13] Hart, n. 2 above, 107.

[14] E. U. Petersmann, 'Proposals for a New Constitution for the European Union' (1995) 32 *Common Market Law Review*, 1123.

ative reformatory design is often deemed proof of laying the bricks for a European federal state. On the other hand, the wealth of formal and informal patterns, helpful as they may be as a vehicle for flexibility, can lead to anomy and mistrust. Besides the EU, many other international regimes suffer from this disease. The trade and environment' complex (WTO and environmental regimes) is a case in point, where debates about constitutionalization have also emerged.[15]

The omens for gradual constitution-building for the EU are, however, not all that good. There are different philosophies—*fallacies*, I believe—which frustrate the process.

The first is the fallacy of the technical nature of the EU.[16] It assumes that the Union is a *Zweckverband*, whose tasks are mostly apolitical, and could therefore be adequately discharged by a European executive as it stands. As a corollary, legitimacy is localized more in the chain leading to national parliaments, than in the European Parliament (EP). In reality, in many policy areas, the EU has shouldered responsibility for substantive political tasks, rather than mere technical management. As it has taken up genuine political functions, it must be organized as a polity of its own. To deny this may be a sign of short-sightedness, but more often is a strategic attempt to conceal policy behind a veil of technicality.

The second fallacy is the mediation hypothesis,[17] which presents the EU as a forum for informal and flexible negotiation and cooperation. Its proponents tend to focus on emerging innovative organizational forms, and regard them as close to the best of all possible worlds. This panglossian perspective is not conducive to an organizing normative idea. It sees flexibility, expertise, cooperation, autonomous control, deliberation, etc., as a self-organized process of rationalization,[18] making constitution-building superfluous. Quite obviously, however, it cannot be taken for granted that the enlightened benevolence of polyarchy will necessarily also endure in times of clashing conflicts or inertia, at least if it is not fettered within a clear and formal framework.

The third fallacy is represented by the analogy with the state. Over the years, several ambitious constitutions for Europe were drafted, drawing on the model of a European federal state. Such initiatives were bound to fail, because principles and institutions derived from the state model, such as the separation

[15] Cf. E. U. Petersmann, 'The Dispute Settlement System of the World Trade Organization and the Evolution of the GATT Dispute Settlement System since 1948' (1994) 31 *Common Market Law Review*, 1157 ff.

[16] This theory has most forcefully been proposed by H. P. Ipsen, 'Zur Exekutivrechtssetzung in der Europäischen Gemeinschaft', in P. Badura and R. Scholz (eds.), *Wege und Verfahren des Verfassungslebens: Festschrift für Peter Lerche zum 65. Geburtstag* (München: Beck, 1993), 425 ff. Another influential author of this school is G. Majone, 'The European Community: An "Independent Fourth Branch of Government"?' in G. Brüggemeier (ed.), *Verfassungen für ein Ziviles Europa* (Baden-Baden: Nomos, 1994).

[17] See R. O. Keohane and S. Hoffmann, 'Conclusions: Community Politics and Institutional Change' in W. Wallace (ed.), *The Dynamics of European Integration* (London: Pinter for the Royal Institute of International Affairs, 1990), 276 ff.

[18] See the contributions by C. Joerges and J. Neyer in C. Joerges and J. Falke (ed.), *Das Ausschusswesen der Europäischen Union* (Baden-Baden: Nomos, 1999).

of powers, distribution of legislative competences, hierarchy of norms and administrative levels, fundamental rights, judicial review, etc., cannot be made operational in the context of EU law without a process of prior adaptation to its *sui generis* nature.

Consequently, the search for a European constitution must start with an inventory of existing legal and factual forms, goals, and principles, which may subsequently be reorganized along more simple and transparent lines and visions of identity, falling short of the model of a state.

## II. Constitutionalizing Environmental Protection

It is already difficult enough to find ways to mould the core structures of the European polity in an acceptable constitutional form. This task is even more intricate with regard to the place of the environment, because environmental concern has only recently entered into constitutions in general. Therefore, its proper place has not yet been determined, either on the national or on the supranational level.

On the other hand, we can approach the question more creatively, because the *sui generis* character of the Union also extends to environmental issues. We do not need first to clarify the role of environmental protection in state constitutions, before discussing the same issue in regard of the European polity. Whilst states must find an equilibrium of all interests concerned, the 'irregular' European polity is given special and even unbalanced tasks. Among these may figure an especially important task and, indeed, identity of protecting the environment. This is because the larger the geographic scope of a regime, the more the environment appears as an exhaustible resource. States will not usually see the environment as a highly vulnerable part of the biosphere. Such a perception is more likely to be triggered from a position transcending the states.

No matter if related to a state or a *sui generis* polity, constitutions organize *societal* relationships, including relationships between citizens and governments. As to the question of the place of nature in such a constitution, the answer *prima facie* might appear that protection of the environment should be framed and represented analogous to other interests like the protection of economic enterpreneurship, human health, social security, or consumer interests.

However, this would assume that nature is a concern comparable to any other. Yet it is the very precondition of survival for human society. While the biosphere can exist without human society, the reverse is not true. Human society has developed the potential to destroy earth as a habitat, and despite efforts of conservation, it is still progressively exhausting natural resources and damaging the environment. Approached from the perspective of the habitable biosphere, it would therefore be a misconception if in the European floating polyarchy the environment were represented as an interest on an equal footing with any other interest.

Once we accept that a balanced biosphere is a physical precondition of life, its preservation must be afforded essential and priviledged constitutional status. This reorientation will affect all the core elements of the constitution: the overall objectives of the polity, fundamental rights, and the institutions. The objective of government must be extended from economic and social, to ecological welfare, fundamental rights must be complemented by fundamental duties and ecological rights, and the institutions must be made accessible to allow for the representation of ecological interests.

We now proceed to examining if these requirements are reflected in the process of European constitutionalization.

## III. The Environmental Objectives of the European Union

Ecological thinking indeed has been written into the proclamation of objectives of the Union, both by the Maastricht and Amsterdam treaties. In the Maastricht version of the treaties, the preamble of the Treaty on European Union (TEU) mentions environmental protection, Article B TEU refers to 'economic and social progress which is ... sustainable', and Article 2 EC appeals for 'sustainable ... growth respecting the environment'. The preamble of the TEU in the Amsterdam version once again mentions environmental protection but cites, in addition, 'the principle of sustainable development', Article 2 TEU repeats the need for 'balanced and sustainable development', and Article 2 EC combines the 'balanced and sustainable development' with 'a high level of protection and improvement of the quality of the environment'.

In sum, the objectives apparently adopt a double approach: environmental protection and sustainability. The older concept of protection has been flanked by the more recent of sustainability. This does not mean that the former concept has become obsolete. Both objectives can be understood to be complementary. In what precise sense needs to be clarified, however.

One suggestion is to understand sustainability as concerned with the consumption of natural resources (such as forests, water, minerals, or arable land), whilst the focus of protection is concerned with the utilization of environmental media (such as the atmosphere, soil, or inland waters and the sea) as absorption potential for many kinds of residues (such as exhaust, sewage, or waste). The fact that Article 174(1) EC distinguishes between protection of the environment and utilization of natural resources speaks in favour of this interpretation.[19]

Another and more profound interpretation would be based on a shift of paradigm. Protection, more traditionally, involves the shielding of the environment against overexploitation, inferring from what the environment can tolerate what the economy must refrain from, whereas sustainability concerns the inner logic of the economy, demanding that environmental protection is

[19] Cf. J. Jans, *European Environmental Law* (Groningen: Europa Law Publishing, 2000), 28.

perceived as a (long-term) self-interest of the economic actor. In this instrumental perspective, whereas for protection it would suffice that production processes are subjected to 'external' threshold values, sustainability would necessitate that environmental concerns be part of the management structure of firms.

The EU objectives might be expressed more clearly in the future. A concept integrating protection and sustainability should be developed. The notion of the liveable biosphere of which man is at the same time subject and object, may be considered as appropriate. Reference can be made to the UNESCO concept 'man and the biosphere'.[20] However, the double approach is also valuable as it stands, no matter what interpretation prevails. It serves as a point of reference for more detailed principles, the allocation of competencies, and institutional design.

## IV. Basic Obligations and EC Action

Normal constitutions usually accept the *Kompetenz Kompetenz* of the state as an implicit basis, and seek to define those powers in the context of, *inter alia*, fundamental rights which limit state action. Such constitutions have traditionally been reserved about incorporating programmatic proclamations, driving the state to act. One of the characteristics of the EU, which distinguishes it from a state, is that the Union is driven by a programme of action, and that the bases for competence, for secondary law-making, are framed as means for fulfilling that programme, or even as obligations to do so. This dynamic feature could be particularly useful as regards a specific policy focusing upon the preservation of the biosphere.

Numerous programmatic principles on environmental matters are found in the EC treaty. They are contained in:

— the integration principle (Article 6 EC),[21]
— the objectives of preservation of the environment, protection of human health, rational utilization of natural resources, and promotion of measures at international level (Article 174 (1) EC),
— the principles of aiming at a high level of protection, precaution, and prevention, of rectification at source and of making the polluter pay (Article 95(3) and Article 174(2) EC), and
— circumstances to be taken into account such as the available scientific data, diverging regional conditions, potential advantages and drawbacks of action, and the balanced development of the regions (Article 174(3) EC).

[20] See Resolution 28 C/2.4 of the UNESCO General Assembly. See also G. Winter, 'Umwelt-Ressource-Biosphäre. Ansichten von Natur im Recht' (2000) 3 *GAIA*, 200 ff.
[21] The integration principle, in combination with the principles of high levels of environmental protection and of sustainable development, was also adopted by Art. 37 of the Charter of Fundamental Rights.

Most of these provisions are relatively vague. Some guidance may be derived from the terminology employed in the Treaty in Article 174 EC, distinguishing between objectives (para. 1), principles (para. 2, sentence 2), and criteria to be taken into account (para. 3). Although some of these requirements conflict, they are not unfit for case-related concretization and compromise. For instance, the apparent contradiction between precaution and respect for scientific data may be solved by understanding this to mean that beyond scientific proof there is room for extrapolations from the known to the uncertain.[22]

Since the meaning of the provisions cited clearly can be concretized, the question poses itself as to what extent they have legal effect. Are they perhaps merely unenforceable programmatic policy guidelines without any such effect? The question remains controversial among commentators.[23] Whether these provisions have binding force, and if so, what the substance of the obligation is, should be answered differently depending on the context where the requirements are to be applied. Four different contexts may be distinguished:

— the framing of EC competencies,
— the justification of incursions, by EC action, of fundamental rights,
— the obligation of the EC institutions to act, and
— the directions for EC action.

In the first and second contexts, i.e. competencies for action and justifications of restrictions of fundamental rights, the requirements have an *enabling* character, which without doubt entail legal effects.

With regard to competencies, this legal effect of the objectives is expressed by the reference made to them in Article 175(1) EC, whilst the principles and criteria have been given legal value by the case law of the ECJ. For instance, in the *BSE* case, the Court of Justice, referring to the principles of high level of protection, prevention, and integration, held that 'where there is uncertainty as to the existence or extent of risks to human health, the institutions may take protective measures without having to wait until the reality and seriousness of those risks become fully apparent'.[24] In the *Bettati* case the court has even given the criterion of taking account of available scientific and technical data legal effect.[25]

As to encroachments upon fundamental rights, the European courts have very rarely invoked the objectives and principles of Article 174 EC as a source for justification. It seems that the national plaintiffs challenging action based on EC environmental legal acts seldom allege that these laws violate European fundamental rights. One rare example is *Standley*.[26] This is interesting from a

---

[22] Jans, n. 19 above, 33.
[23] *Pro*: A. Epiney, *Umweltrecht in der Europäischen Union* (Köln: Heymanns Verlag, 1997), 108. *Contra*: L. Krämer, *EC Environmental Law* (London: Sweet & Maxwell, 2000), 8; Jans, n. 19 above, 32; both authors referring to the principle of a high level of protection.
[24] Case C–180/96, *United Kingdom* v. *Commission* [1998] ECR I–2265, para. 99.
[25] Case C–341/95, *Gianni Bettati* v. *Safety High-Tech Srl* [1998] ECR I–4355, para. 48 ff.
[26] Case C–293/97, *R.* v. *Minister of Agriculture, Fisheries and Food, ex p. Standley and others* [1999] ECR I–2603. The relevant passage is found in paras. 55 and 56 which read: 'It is true that the

German perspective, because German environmental laws have often been challenged on the basis of fundamental rights, such as the right of free enterprise or private property. It is true, however, that the European courts have sometimes referred to environmental protection principles as a yardstick for a proportionality test (which, although being an element of a more comprehensive examination of violations of basic rights, is sometimes used as a separate yardstick). For instance, in the *Bettati* case the Court of Justice ruled that the regulation restricting the use of a chemical was proportional in relation to its environmental protection goal.[27]

As to the substance of the requirements of Article 174 EC, their full meaning should be appreciated in the enabling context. For instance, in the *Safety Hi-Tech* judgment the Court applied the principle of a high level of protection, but did not find it had been violated in the present instance, because the principle did not require the 'technically highest level'.[28] The Court was further asked to decide whether a marketing restriction of a chemical substance always requires a comprehensive assessment of its effects on all of the relevant environmental compartments. The Court ruled that it was sufficient to show negative effects on just one compartment, which in the given case was the ozone layer, whilst it did not find it necessary also to assess effects on the warming up of the atmosphere.[29] This example shows that the Court does explore the full meaning of Article 174 EC.

It should be added that, by implication, in the enabling context, there is room for reasoning *a maiore ad minus*. Article 174 EC sets out the minimum standards for action, and does obviously not exclude that, if even more compelling reasons exist the measure may also be taken. For instance, since a Community measure can be based on the precaution principle, it can of course also be taken if there is an imminent danger of environmental damage. Similarly, because a Community act pursuing a high level of protection may have restrictive effects for the relevant actors, it can all the more be adopted if the measure envisaged is less restrictive. Another implication of the enabling character is that even one ground for action suffices, in other words not all of the imperatives need to have been fulfilled. This was the dominant message of the *Safety Hi-Tech* judgment.

In the third and fourth contexts, EC action is mandated and directed. It is of the utmost importance to know if and to what extent the EC institutions (and,

---

action programmes which are provided for in Art. 5 of the Directive and are to contain the mandatory measures referred to in Annex III impose certain conditions on the spreading of fertilizer and livestock manure, so that those programmes are liable to restrict the exercise by the farmers concerned of the right to property. However, the system laid down in Art. 5 reflects requirements relating to the protection of public health, and thus pursues an objective of general interest without the substance of the right to property being impaired.'

[27] Case C–341/95, n. 25 above, para. 54 ff.

[28] Case C–284/95, *Safety Hi-Tech Srl* v. *S & T Srl* [1998] ECR I–4301, para. 49. See also Case C–233/94, *Germany* v. *European Parliament and Council* [1997] ECR I–2405, para. 48 for the respective clause in Art. 95, para. 3.

[29] Ibid., para. 45.

as will be seen, also Member States) are pushed to take environmental protection measures. The environment, although recognized as a reason for justifying encroachments upon competencies and freedoms, will normally bear the burden of proof in these contexts. By contrast, if there is an obligation to act, the burden of proof that some environment protection measure is unsound is shifted to the other (the economic) side.

Unfortunately, as yet no case law exists as to the legal effect of environmental obligations. However, to deny legal effect from the outset would contradict the general approach the ECJ pursued as regards programmatic clauses since its judgment of 1985, when it held that the obligation under Article 75 (now 71) EC to take action towards a common transport policy, although allowing for a margin of discretion, binds the Council.[30] It is true, however, that those measures are more exactly circumscribed in Article 71 EC than in Article 174 EC. The nature of the obligation here is to establish a 'Community policy on the environment', whereas Articles 71 and 72 EC require a number of specific legal acts. Interestingly, however, the integration principle of Article 6 EC refers to policies, and also to 'activities'.[31]

Assuming the mandatory legal effect of such obligations, their content differs from the enabling context. Not every single objective, principle, or criterion can be said to amount to an obligation to act or instruction to be followed. Given the comprehensiveness of the programme contained in Articles 2 and 174 EC, the political process of legislation would otherwise be strangled, and ultimately handed over to the discretion of the courts. Therefore, only some fundamental and indispensable requirements should be afforded binding effect.[32]

The methodology of distilling those binding principles, however, remains to be developed. For the purpose of laying bare the envisaged core, it would be useful to 'mirror' the design previously discussed in the enabling context. This would give rise to the following kind of reasoning:

— if *precautionary* measures are admissible, measures which abate *imminent and severe dangers* should be obligatory;
— if measures aiming at a *high level* of protection are admissible, measures aiming at a *minimum level* of protection should be obligatory;
— if measures *improving* environmental conditions are admissible, measures *preserving* a given environment should be obligatory;
— if measures which *substantially integrate* environmental requirements into any other policy are admissible, a *reasoned and public statement* about the environmental consequences of a measure must be obligatory.

An alternative to mandating protective action is to prohibit detrimental action. It is more modest and realistic but would nevertheless be a significant

---

[30] Case 13/83, *European Parliament* v. *Council* [1985] ECR I–1513, para. 49.　　　[31] Art. 6 EC.
[32] Alternatively, one might postulate that the requirements are indeed binding in all respects, but that the relevant regulators have a wide margin of appreciation. But this approach to the problem is less suggestive for the purpose of elaborating the core of indispensable duties.

step forward. Such a proposal was made by the newly founded Avosetta Group. A new paragraph to be inserted into Article 6 EC was suggested, which would read: 'Subject to imperative reasons of overriding public interests, significantly impairing the environment or human health shall be prohibited.'[33]

## V. Basic Rights to EC Action?

From a radical democratic perspective, it may be argued that EC decision-making should not be bound by basic environmental rights. In this view, policies should be an outcome of democratic political processes which contain sufficient safeguards against unresponsive attitudes. But even if we (unrealistically) assume that a democratic polity exists at EC level, the crucial problem is that fundamental rights have already been developed that bind the legislature, and that economic and ecological stakes are unevenly represented. A simple example may illustrate this imbalance. Let us assume that a German enterprise encounters difficulties exporting goods to Spain. Numerous basic rights may be invoked by the undertaking to challenge this obstacle, such as:

— the German basic right to free enterprise (Article 12 of the German Federal Constitution), if the restriction is German;
— the Spanish basic right to free enterprise (Article 38 of the Spanish Constitution), if the restriction is Spanish;
— the basic EC freedom of trade (Article 28 EC), if the restriction is German or Spanish;
— the basic EC right to free enterprise as developed by the ECJ, if the restriction is European;
— the basic EC right to free enterprise if the restriction is German or Spanish, but based on EC law;
— the basic right to property guaranteed by the European Convention on Human Rights (ECHR), if the restriction is German or Spanish (Article 1 of the 1st Additional Protocol to the ECHR);[34]
— in future possibly a basic right to free enterprise as provided by the General Agreement on Tarifs and Trade (GATT).

Of course, these basic rights are not absolute, and the restriction therefore could well be found constitutional. What this example shows, however, is that *homo oeconomicus* is privileged by virtue of the possibility to invoke judicial review, as well as by the shift of the burden of proof from the necessity to protect economic freedom, to the necessity to protect the environment or other social goods.

---

[33] For a commentary on this draft, see on the Internet at: http://www.uni-bremen.de/~avosetta.

[34] The ECHR guarantee of property has been interpreted broadly by the European Court of Human Rights (beginning with ECHR 23 Sept. 1982, A52, *Sporrong and Lönnroth* v. *Sweden*). Also, know-how and its usage is protected against unjustified state intrusion. Therefore, in our case, Art. 1 indeed may be invoked. See L. Condorelli in L. E. Pettiti, E. Decaux, and P. H. Imbert (eds.), *La Convention Européenne des Droits de l´Homme* (Paris: Economica, 1995), 977 and 994.

In stark contrast, constitutional environmental rights are generally lacking. This becomes also apparent from a survey of national constitutions. Article 45 of the Spanish constitution and Article 66 of the Portuguese constitution[35] *prima facie* seem to be exceptions in this regard, but closer analysis shows that, as for the Spanish provision, this is regarded as a mere guiding principle which does not provide access to the Constitutional Court.[36] Nevertheless, basic rights of other content do have environmental implications.[37] In so far as human health is dependent on environmental conditions, the right to human health found in many constitutions may serve as a vehicle upon the back of which some environmental protection may also be carried.[38] The same kind of reasoning applies with regard to the protection of private property. For example, to the extent that polluted air impairs the growing of crops, the fundamental right to property also touches upon environmental conditions. However, beyond this overlap with immediate human health or property, the environment is normally not framed in terms of a subjective right in national constitutions.

At the level of EU constitutional law the situation is similar. Case law has established the fundamental right to private property, which also covers environmental dimensions in appropriate cases. Although a right to personal health has not yet been formally introduced,[39] at least the Fundamental Rights Charter proposes, in Article 3, everybody's 'right to respect for his or her physical and mental integrity'.[40] Subsequent case law may develop which holds (along the lines of the judgments of the European Court of Human Rights in relation to Article 8 ECHR)[41] that the right is breached where the Community

[35] See Art. 45, para 1 of the Spanish constitution: 'Everyone has the right to enjoy an adequate environment for the development of the person, as well as the duty to preserve it', and Art. 66, para. 1 of the Portuguese Constitution: 'Everyone shall have the right to a healthy and ecologically balanced human environment and the duty to defend it.'

[36] A. M. Moreno, *The Right to Environmental Protection in the Spanish Constitutional System* (paper presented to the Avosetta Group, 12/13 Jan. 2001; published on the Internet at: http://www. uni-bremen.de/~avosetta).

[37] For a comparative analysis, see M. Ruffert, *Subjektive Rechte im Umweltrecht der Europäischen Gemeinschaft* (Heidelberg: R. v. Decker's Verlag, 1996), 50 ff.

[38] For instance, in a judgment concerning a fast breeder reactor, the German Constitutional Court held that the individual has a right to demand health protection against possible damages caused by the reactor. The Court, however, found that this right was not violated in the particular case (*Bundesverfassungsgericht* (Federal Constitutional Court) 8 Aug. 1978, (1979) 49 *Entscheidungen des Bundesverfassungsgerichts*, 140 (*Kalkar*)).

[39] Cf. B. Beutler in H. von der Groeben, J. Thiesing, and C. D. Ehlermann (eds.), *EG-Vertrag. Kommentar* (Baden-Baden: Nomos 1997), Art. F nos. 55–62.

[40] [2000] OJ C364/1

[41] See ECtHR 9 Dec. 1994, A303-C, *Lopez Ostra* v. *Spain*:

Naturally, severe environmental pollution may affect individuals' well-being and prevent them from enjoying their homes in such a way as to affect their private and family life adversely, without, however, seriously endangering their health. Whether the question is analysed in terms of a positive duty on the State—to take reasonable and appropriate measures to secure the applicant's rights under paragraph 1 of Art. 8 (Art. 8-1)—, as the applicant wishes in her case, or in terms of an 'interference by a public authority' to be justified in accordance with paragraph 2 (Art. 8-2), the applicable principles are broadly similar. In both contexts regard must be had to the fair balance that has to be struck between the competing interests of the individual and of the community as a whole, and in any case the State enjoys a certain margin

fails to take protective action in the case of severe environmental degradation.[42] As a procedural safeguard, the Fundamental Rights Charter establishes, in Article 42, every citizen's right of access to official documents, including those concerning the environment. One may also mention the fundamental right, proposed in Article 41(2), of every person to be heard before any individual measure which would affect him or her adversely, is taken, which might be extended to third parties affected. However, a genuine substantive right to appropriate environmental conditions or a procedural right of public participation has not been recognized. The Charter confines itself to laying down an objective principle of environmental protection, not a subjective right of the individual or collectives.[43]

This is especially striking, because at the level of secondary EC law a number of subjective rights have been introduced.[44] In particular, procedural rights have been provided, such as the right of access to information, the right to be informed, and the right to comment on certain projects.[45] There are also rights of a more substantive character, where environmental quality standards are set with a view to protect human health.[46]

Of course, it is difficult to frame a fundamental right with sufficient specificity so as to allow for its judicial protection.[47] Indeed, the phrasing to be found in many texts is vague, both in national and international legal documents.[48] For instance, according to the Stockholm Declaration of 1972 'man has the fundamental right of . . . adequate conditions of life, in an environment of quality that permits a life of dignity and well-being'; according to the Rio Declaration of 1992, 'human beings . . . are entitled to a healthy and productive life in harmony with nature'.

of appreciation. Furthermore, even in relation to the positive obligations flowing from the first paragraph of Art. 8 (Art. 8-1), in striking the required balance the aims mentioned in the second paragraph (Art. 8-2) may be of a certain relevance.

See also ECtHR 19 Feb. 1998, Reports 1998–I, *Guerra* v. *Italy*, para. 60. For a comprehensive account of the environmental case law of the European Convention of Human Rights, see P. Szczekella, 'Grundrechte' in H. W. Rengeling (ed.), *Handbuch zum Europäischen und Deutschen Umweltrecht—i* (Köln: Carl Heymanns Verlag, 1998).

[42] R. Macrory, *Environmental Integration and the European Charter of Fundamental Rights* (paper presented to the Avosetta Group, 12/13 Jan. 2001; published on the Internet at: http://www.uni-bremen.de/~avosetta). For the problems of doctrinal construction of negative rights and protection obligations, see Szczekella, n. 41 above, nos. 20–6, 38.

[43] Art. 37 of the Charter.

[44] See for a wealth of examples including consumer rights N. Reich, *Bürgerrechte in der Europäischen Union* (Baden-Baden: Nomos, 1999); C. Hilson, 'Implementing EC Environmental Law in the UK' in J. Holder (ed.) *The Impact of EC Environmental Law in the United Kingdom* (New York/Chichester: John Wiley, 1997).

[45] See Case 131/88, *Commission* v. *Germany* [1991] ECR I–825 for a right that certain investigations required by Council Dir. 80/68/EEC on the Protection of Groundwater Against Pollution Caused by Certain Dangerous Substances ([1980] OJ L20/43) are implemented.

[46] See Case 361/88 *Commission* v. *Germany* [1991] ECR I–2567 for a right that certain air quality standards set up by Council Dir. 80/779/EEC on Air Quality Limit Values and Guide Values for Sulphur Dioxide and Suspended Particulates ([1980] OJ L229/30) are respected.

[47] This concern leads even 'subjectivists' to warn against the introduction of a basic right. See, e.g., Ruffert, n. 37 above, 43.

[48] L. Krämer, 'The Citizen and the Environment' (1999) 3 *Resource Management Journal*, 1 ff.

But this difficulty is associated with any fundamental right, including economic rights. No constitution specifies the precise content of the right to economic activity, the rationale of which is, as was observed, predominantly to reallocate burdens of proof, and instigate judicial review. The judiciary is familiar with, and has developed techniques to gradually concretize, vague formulas through case law. Initially, rights may be constructed merely as procedural safeguards and a check against arbitrary action, whilst the substantive content may be confined to an indispensable core.

In addition, there is the substantive objection of the difference between individual and collective environmental interests. The interests of individuals do not necessarily coincide with those of the environment. For instance, a landowner claiming liability for damage caused to crops may be satisfied if economic loss is compensated, and hence refrain from insisting on the return of the biotope in its original state. It would need an unrealistic measure of altruism for any individual also to defend the collective interest of environmental preservation, all the more so because legal action involves the risk of costs in the case of failure. This remains true even if some progress may be expected from the emergence of a more broadly concerned *homo oeconomicus*, such as in the concept of green consumerism.[49]

Scepticism is therefore appropriate with regard to an over-extensive citizen suit, as envisaged by Article 9(3) of the Aarhus Convention.[50] Environmental associations should step in, and be given rights and standing, as has often been proposed,[51] and recently once more been brought on the agenda by the said Aarhus Convention.[52] It is to be hoped that the European Commission will propose a horizontal directive in this regard, covering public participation and access to justice.[53] What is emphasized here is that it is now necessary to provide environmental organizations with a constitutional position. The model which may be followed is that of Article 139 EC, which institutes an EC-wide dialogue and contractual status of management and labour.

---

[49] T. Wilhelmsson, 'Consumer law and the environment: from consumer to citizen' (1998) 21 *Journal of Consumer Policy*, 45 ff.

[50] Convention on Access to Information, Public Participation in Decision-Making and Access to Justice in Environmental Matters (Aarhus, 25 June 1998), published on the Internet at: http://www.unece.org/env/ (not yet in force). Art. 9 (3) reads:

> In addition and without prejudice to the review procedures referred to in paragraphs 1 and 2 above, each party shall ensure that, where they meet the criteria, if any, laid down in its national law, members of the public have access to administrative and judicial procedures to challenge actions and omissions by private persons and public authorities which contravene provisions of its national law relating to the environment.

On the question whether the 'if any' makes the provision void or, on the contrary, allows for a limitless citizen suit, see J. Jendroska, *Aarhus Convention: Towards New Era in Granting Individual Rights in International Environmental Law* (paper presented to the Avosetta Group, 12/13 Jan. 2001; published on the Internet at: http://www.uni-bremen.de/~avosetta).

[51] See for a recent summary account including further references Krämer, n. 48 above, 12.

[52] See Art. 9 (2), subpara. 2, sentence 2.

[53] Unfortunately, this widely discussed project is not listed as a measure in the draft 6th Environment Action Programme (COM(2001)31, 24 Jan. 2001).

## VI. Basic Obligations and Member State Action

Principles of EC environmental law not only bind the EC institutions but possibly also the Member States. Two kinds of influence may be distinguished.

First the objectives, principles, and criteria laid down in Article 174 EC can be invoked for the purpose of justifying national market regulation intruding into basic Community freedoms. As with the case where Community action is backed by the principles of Article 174 EC, we may term this an enabling function.

Environmental protection has been accepted as a reason for domestic regulation since the *Danish Bottle* case.[54] The same is true with regard to the protection of human health, if only because human health already figures among the interests mentioned in Article 30 EC.[55] But the rational utilization of resources also should be accepted as a valid justification for trade restrictions. For instance, under this justification a Member State could hinder shipments of waste for recovery to another Member State, arguing that national technology of recovery is more effective.[56]

As to the principles in Article 174(2) EC, which concretize those environmental objectives, the ECJ in *Wallonian Waste* regarded the principle of rectification of damage at source a legitimate ground for Member State waste regulation incorporating the principle of self-sufficiency.[57] The principle of abatement of pollution at source consequently is a legitimate general interest in the sense discussed here. We may infer from this that the same applies to other principles, such as precaution and prevention.

The second kind of influence exerted by EC principles on national measures is not related to their enabling, but to their obliging potential. Member States are certainly not obliged to respect EC environmental protection principles in the pursuit of normal national political business. But to the extent they do apply EC law, notably in transposing EC directives, arguably they then also have to abide by those principles. This indirect obligation finds its precedent in the reasoning of the ECJ in *Wachauf*. The Court held that national authorities, when implementing EC milk quota regulations, must respect the EC

[54] Case 302/86, *Commission* v. *Denmark* [1988] ECR–4607, para. 9. For a full account of the case law see H. Temmink, 'From Danish Bottles to Danish Bees: the Dynamics of Free Movement of Goods and Environmental Protection. A Case Law Analysis' (2000) 1 *Yearbook of European Environmental Law*, 61–102.

[55] Case C–473/98, *Kemikalieinspektionen* v. *Toolex Alpha AB* [2000] ECR I–5681, para. 38. On differences of terminology in Art. 174 EC and Art. 30 EC, see Jans, n. 19 above, 27.

[56] In the *Dusseldorp* case (Case C–203/96, *Chemische Afvalstoffen Dusseldorp and others* v. *Minister van Volkshuisvesting, Ruimtelijke Ordening en Milieubeheer* [1998] ECR I–4075), where Dutch export restrictions for waste for recovery were at stake, the ECJ could have invoked the general interest in prudent resource utilization. But the Court was not asked to express itself on this matter, and the case itself did not necessitate such a ruling, because recovery technology in the country of destination was not less effective than the one in the country of origin. See G. Winter, 'Die Steuerung Grenzüberschreitender Abfallströme' (2000) 10 *Deutsches Verwaltungsblatt*, 657 ff.

[57] Case C–2/90, *Commission* v. *Belgium* [1992] ECR I–4431, para. 34.

fundamental right of private property.[58] Although this reasoning concerns fundamental rights,[59] there is no reason why it should not also be applicable to fundamental environmental principles framed in more objective terms.

In line with the distinction between enabling and obliging contexts, it is understood that we are dealing with an obliging context here. Therefore, only indispensable core principles will produce such binding effects.

Assuming that Member States' legislation pursues a respectable level of environmental protection, the principle of an indirect impact of EU principles may not appear of much practical significance. One crucial exception, however, is formed by the integration principle. This principle is a novelty in almost all Member States. For instance, according to this principle, an EC directive on the liberalization of the energy market must be transposed into national law by Member States in a way that takes into consideration the environmental implications.[60]

One further element of the relationship between national and EC law should be considered in connection with the foregoing. EC primary and secondary law also impacts on national constitutions, which has become most visible in the arena of human rights. The basic freedoms established by the treaties have led national constitutional courts to reinterpret national constitutional freedoms. For instance, the German freedom of enterprise (Article 12 of the German Federal Constitution) was reconstructed so as to apply not only to Germans, but also to other EU citizens.[61] In the environmental field, the basic freedoms of manifestation and association (Articles 8 and 9 of the German Federal Constitution) must similarly be extended to any EU-citizens.[62] The objectives of environmental protection of the former Article 130r EC have influenced the introduction of a similar objective into Article 20a of the German federal constitution. Likewise, it could be argued that the EC concepts of 'integrated pollution control' and 'river basin management' necessitate a shift of competencies for water legislation from the *Länder* to the *Bund*, turning the present framework competence into a concurrent competence of the *Bund*. This would facilitate the task of the federal legislature to preside over integrated air, water, and nature-related licensing, and to organize water management in river basins where they transcend the jurisdictions of the *Länder*.

[58] Case 5/88, *Hubert Wachauf* v. *Bundesamt für Ernährung und Forstwirtschaft* [1989] ECR–2609, para. 19.
[59] See for a fuller account M. Ruffert, 'Die Mitgliedstaaten der Europäischen Gemeinschaft als Verpflichtete der Gemeinschaftsgrundrechte' (1995) 22 *Europäische Grundrechte Zeitschrift*, 518 ff.
[60] R. Macrory, *Environmental Integration and the European Charter of Fundamental Rights* (paper presented to the Avosetta Group, 12/13 Jan. 2001, 8; published on the Internet at: http://www.uni-bremen.de/~avosetta); N. de Sadeleer, 'Les Fondements de l'Action Communautaire en Matière d'Environnement' in L. le Hardy de Beaulieu (ed.), *L' Europe et Ses Citoyens* (Frankfurt am Main: Peter Lang, 2000), 112; both authors discussing more examples.
[61] For the related doctrinal controversy see H. Bauer, 'Europäisierung des Verfassungsrechts' (2000) 122 *Juristische Blätter* 750, 758.
[62] Ibid.

## VII. Subsidiarity

EC environmental policy is, pursuant to the principle of subsidiarity, 'subsidiary' to Member State environmental policy. Although the debate of the early 1990s about the precise meaning of the principle of subsidiarity as expressed in Article 5(2) EC has now settled down, four important points of controversy remain, which have also a bearing on environmental action.

The first such question is whether the subsidiarity principle *a priori* aims at minimizing EC measures, or concerns the optimal level of regulating any given problem. The 1987 Treaty had adopted the second approach,[63] which was, in this respect, confirmed by the 5th Environment Action Programme. The Commission used to pursue this approach in its practice of motivating legislative proposals.[64] However, by introducing a two-step test (insufficiency of Member State action, and better achievement by Community action), the wording of Article 3b(2) of 1993 and Article 5(2) of 1997 seem to support the first interpretation. Such a reading would imply that, once it is concluded from the first test that Member State action sufficiently achieves the objective, the question of whether EC action could not be still more effective becomes obsolete. Such an outcome is highly undesirable. It is even logically unfeasible. For, how could the adequacy of national measures be assessed without prior consideration of the alternative at EC level? Therefore, it is submitted that the two steps proposed by the principle of subsidiarity are rearranged, so that as a first step the national and EC alternatives are identified, and subsequently assessed in the light of criteria of the kind listed in the Protocol on subsidiarity[65] and other documents[66] and publications[67] (transnational effect, conflict with requirements of the Treaty, economies of scale, effects on investment and quality of life, scale of the problem, etc.).

The second problem relates to the question whether, once the competent level has been determined, the relevant organs are obliged rather than permitted to use their powers. Those who argue that this is indeed the case understand 'subsidiarity' literally as 'providing assistance'.[68] Whereas in a political discourse about subsidiarity this may be considered, it would be to overstate

---

[63] Art. 130r read: 'The Community shall take action relating to the environment to the extent to which the objectives referred to in paragraph 1 can be attained better at Community level than at the level of the individual Member State.'

[64] e.g. Proposal for a Council Directive on Integrated Pollution Prevention and Control, COM(93)423, 14 Sept. 1993, 11.

[65] Protocol on the Application of the Principles of Subsidiarity and Proportionality (Annex to the Treaty of Amsterdam), para. 5. For an interpretation of the Protocol, see Jans, n. 19 above, 12.

[66] Earlier lists of the Council and the Commission as well as the German and even the Bavarian Government are reproduced in D. Mertens (ed.), *Die Subsidiarität Europas* (Berlin: Duncker & Humblot, 1993).

[67] L. Krämer, *EC Treaty and Environmental Law* (London: Sweet & Maxwell, 1998), 76, citing H. Sevenster.

[68] Cf. V. Constantinesco, '"Subsidiarität": Magisches Wort oder Handlungsprinzip der Europäischen Union?' (1991) *Europäisches Wirtschaftsrecht*, 561.

the force of subsidiarity as a legal principle.[69] If one accepts the notion of a constitutional duty to act, then this should be derived from the specific policy-related provisions of the Treaty (such as those discussed earlier), rather than from a general understanding of subsidiarity.

The third point of controversy is whether subsidiarity merely requires a comparison of Member State action with EC alternatives or, in addition, a comparison of public action with private forms of self-regulation. Although subsidiarity in the Catholic tradition extends to the government–society comparison, according to the clear wording of Article 5 EC the principle is exclusively related to the Member State–EC dimension. The question whether the goal could be better attained by self-regulation, is a matter to be judged in the light of the proportionality principle. To be sure, in this instance we should apply the unwritten version, associated with the justification of encroachments on basic rights, rather than the one contained in Article 5(3) EC, the latter, in common with the other sections of Article 5 EC, exclusively concerning the Member State–EC dimension.[70] In its proposals for legal acts, the Commission not always separately identifies these two dimensions, even though it would contribute to transparency if it were to do so.

This applies in particular to instances where legal acts operate to deregulate a policy area. Often, deregulation has been confused with subsidiarity[71] and even 'promoted' by using the rhetorics of subsidiarity.[72] Deregulation, however, is a matter of political discretion rather than imperative command. A genuine enquiry into the necessity of any measure, if compared with self-regulation, would require the Commission to prove that the problem can equally well be resolved by self-regulation. Mere reference to subsidiarity should not free the Commission from this enquiry.

A fourth point relates to the fact that the Commission often provides a quantified account of the costs and benefits of Community action measured against lower degrees of integration or inaction. This has occasionally provoked bizarre calculations of the gains of avoided fatalities valued in euros as opposed to costs of pollution abatement. For instance, in the Proposal for a Council Directive Relating to Limit Values for Sulphur Dioxide, Oxides of Nitrogen, Particulate Matter and Lead in Ambient Air, the Commission estimated the expected additional costs at 48 million ecu, and the expected gain in avoided mortality at up to 3.784 million ecu per year, human life being valued as up to 4.2 million ecu.[73] Whereas it is perfectly reasonable, and even required by the Protocol on subsidiarity, to consider financial burdens which actually fall upon public and private actors,[74] an exercise of artificial monetization of intangible goods is unsound and also not required by subsidiarity as a legal principle. Even if the instance cited may appeal to environmentalists,

---

[69] G. Winter, 'Subsidiarität und Deregulierung im Gemeinschaftsrecht' (1996) *Europarecht*, 259.
[70] *Contra*: Jans, n. 19 above, 14 ff.     [71] Krämer, n. 67 above, 73.
[72] Winter, n. 69 above, 263.     [73] COM(97)500, 14 Jan. 1998, 18 ff.
[74] Protocol on the Application of the Principles of Subsidiarity and Proportionality, n. 67 above, para. 9, 3rd indent.

this should not excuse poor methodology.[75] Obversely, in the case of benzene standards, the Commission's assessment of costs and benefits found that the abatements costs were excessive compared to the benefits. The Commission made some effort to correct this undesirable outcome with some qualitative arguments, which had the taste of *corriger la fortune*. More realistic is the Commission's approach in the Proposal for a Council Directive Establishing a Framework for Community Action in the Field of Water Policy, where it stated:

Given the said difficulties, the Commission concludes that any assembling of figures or estimations concerning a financial cost/benefit analysis would at best be unreliable and at worst misleading or quite simply wrong. Therefore, in the following analysis mainly the kind of cost/benefit factors involved by the proposal are given. Figures are only submitted in order to convey an idea of the order of magnitude of the costs of monitoring and management.[76]

## VIII. The Making of Tertiary Law

The term 'tertiary law' refers to regulations, directives, and decisions giving EC secondary law concrete significance. Tertiary law is of particular importance in environmental policy, because it is an important tool for fixing technical standards. The immense multitude of processes and products putting stress on nature requires fast-track procedures. However, this conflicts with the need for scientific proof and stakeholder participation, which makes standard-setting a time-consuming business.

Instruments therefore must be found at the EC level allowing for the process of tertiary rule-making to be accelerated. Four manifestations currently employed deserve brief consideration:

— The Council acts, be it alone or jointly with the EP. This is the case with for instance market restrictions for toxic chemicals.[77]
— The Commission acts in the context of one of the structures pursuant to comitology. This procedure is usually employed for process and environmental quality standards.[78]
— Standards may be elaborated by standardization institutions made up of representatives of the relevant industry, directed by general secondary law criteria, exposed to third-party comments, and supervised by the

---

[75] See COM(98)591, 24 Feb. 1999, 15. On efficiency analysis in environmental regulation in general, see G. Winter, 'Nutzen und Kosten der Effizienzregel im Öffentlichen Recht' in E. Gawel (ed.), *Effizienz im Umweltrecht. Grundsatzfragen Wirtschaftlicher Umweltnutzung aus Rechts-, Wirtschafts- und Sozialwissenschaftlicher Sicht* (Baden-Baden: Nomos, 2000).

[76] COM(97)49, 17 June 1997, 22 (my translation).

[77] L. Krämer, 'Introduction into the European Chemicals Regulation: Basic Structures and Performance' in G. Winter (ed.), *Risk Assessment and Risk Management of Toxic Chemicals in the European Community* (Baden-Baden: Nomos, 2000)

[78] See J. Falke and G. Winter, 'Management and Regulatory Committees in Executive Rule-Making' in G. Winter (ed.), *Sources and Categories of European Union Law* (Baden-Baden: Nomos, 1996), 541–82; Joerges and Falke (eds.), n. 18 above.

Commission. This so-called 'New Approach' has been employed in the area of product harmonization and consumer safety.[79]

— Specialized tests may be performed by Community administrative agencies existing autonomously from the administrative structures of the General Directorates, and which have been set up for the purpose of streamlining information gathering. The European Environment Agency (EEA) is a case in point. A similar agency is projected in the field of chemicals regulation. In some exceptional cases, where no discretionary powers are involved, decision-making powers were even delegated to these agencies, such as in the case of the Trademark Agency.[80]

The present discussion on this matter is conducted in terms of 'either/or'. Natural allies of the first variant (the preservation of a ministerial reserve) are Member States and national ministries. Comitology is favoured by the Commission, and—with certain reservations—the EP. Self-regulatory agencies are pushed by industry, whilst independent agencies are promoted by national sectoral bureaucracies. In reality, all of these structures have a proper role to play, the intricate question being which instrument suits what particular task.[81]

It is a misconception to hold that standard-setting is a mere cognitive operation, based on established scientific facts, and consequently to opt for independent scientific committees as standardization bodies. There is significant scope for variety in precautionary reasoning, balancing of environmental protection gains against economic drawbacks, or the influence of risk perception cultures, etc. Therefore, a line should be drawn between risk assessment and risk management, scientific committees having their role to play only in the risk-assessment phase of standard-setting.

A useful distinction can be made between economic and social regulation. Economic regulation aims at harmonizing product design in order to facilitate trade. One example is the DIN-standard for paper, which allows for the standardization of copying machines. The most appropriate tool for economic standardization is self-regulation by industry. To the extent the standards incite consumer preferences, this can be left to market mechanisms. Should there be implications for consumer safety, the 'New Approach' still may function well if combined with a strict product liability scheme.

By contrast, social regulation aims at the protection of diffuse interests, which usually have no purchasing power, and cannot be protected sufficiently by strict liability schemes. One major case in point is the environment. The appropriate forum for such externalized interests is fundamentally public.

---

[79] See J. Falke, 'Standardisation by Professional Organisations', in Winter (ed.), n. 78 above.

[80] See Majone, n. 16 above; M. Everson, 'Independent Agencies', in Winter (ed.), n. 78 above; D. Fischer-Appelt, *Agenturen der Europäischen Gemeinschaft* (Berlin: Duncker & Humblot, 1999).

[81] See for a description of the criteria emerging in the EU practice, M. Everson, 'The Constitutionalisation of European Administrative Law: Legal Oversight of a Stateless Internal Market' in C. Joerges and E. Vos (eds.), *EU Committees: Social Regulation, Law and Politics* (Oxford: Hart, 1999), 281, 298 ff.

Most appropriate is the Commission-comitology structure, because scientific, economic, and cultural interests meet in a procedure which allows for the issue to be returned to the legislature, should it prove too controversial.

Because this kind of deliberative procedure is very slow, however, it is intolerable in cases where hundreds or even thousands of standards need to be considered, such as in the case of waste-water emission norms or standards for dangerous substances and preparations. Where time is a major factor, regulatory agencies appear to offer the most suitable solution. Experience with independent agencies in the USA have shown that problems of unresponsiveness of new bureaucracies could be solved by a mixture of substantial criteria, procedural rules, organizational safeguards, political checks, and judicial review mechanisms.[82] The comitology structure could be integrated into a European type of regulatory agency. This would require a change in the constitutional principle articulated in the *Meroni* case law, which holds that decision-making powers may only be delegated to separate entities if no discretion is involved.[83]

## IX. Representing the Environment

The final issue of this chapter also concerns institutions. If interaction between humans and the environment is to be constitutionalized, the question which institutions should represent the environment becomes a crucial one. The EC has specialized structures in this respect, which are embedded in the general institutions, such as the Environment Committee of the EP, the Council of Environment Ministers, and the Commissioner and Directorate General for the Environment. They represent the environment as a concern which may be traded against gains in other policy areas.

Of course, this is normal and unavoidable political practice. In the case of the environment, however, the fact that this is an actor which does not trade must be taken into account. Rather, the environment supplies and uses resources according to its autonomous laws, which should be objectively ascertained. For this task, an independent watch-dog institution is needed at arm's length from the bargaining systems, determining as objectively as possible the state and development of the environment, and the likely impact of EC action. What is envisioned is a kind of independent Public Auditor of the Budget of the European Environment, which combines the more general observatory functions of the EEA, with the power to evaluate past and new EU policies.[84] Arguably the EEA should be developed in that direction.

---

[82]  Majone, n. 16 above.

[83]  Case 9/56, *Meroni & Co., Industrie Metallurgiche, SpA* v. *High Authority of the European Coal and Steel Community* [1958] ECR 11, at 43.

[84]  See Everson, n. 80 above.

## X. Conclusion

In this chapter, I have endeavoured to investigate how the horizon of EC law can be broadened so as to allow for increased substantial and organizational interaction between humans and the environment. Objectives, principles, basic rights, and institutional safeguards afford environmental protection undeniable constitutional status, which however needs to be consolidated and developed further. It is hoped that the EU will engage proactively in this process, instead of having to react to ecological reality at a later stage. What must be avoided at all costs is that the achievements of decades are somehow wasted because we failed to take heed of the bare essentials of human life.

# Individual Environmental Rights: Conceptual Pollution in EU Environmental Law?

SACHA PRECHAL and LEIGH HANCHER[*]

## I. Introduction

The past few decades have witnessed various efforts to recognize a right to a clean environment at national constitutional,[1] international,[2] and Community level. Recently, a number of European environmental organizations, in their proposal for 'Greening the Treaty', have demanded to include a right to a clean and healthy environment in the Charter of Fundamental Rights.[3] The importance of constitutional recognition of environmental rights[4] can hardly be contested, given the implications for legislators and the administration. As a result of their constitutional entrenchment, environmental interests become an important factor in the decision-making process, and acquire considerable weight in the process of balancing competing interests, in particular economic and environmental considerations. Moreover, the right to a clean environment competes with other fundamental rights, such as the right to property or the freedom of access to information.

However, constitutionalizing environmental interests does not necessarily imply the creation of automatically enforceable and justifiable rights.[5] Similarly, associated attempts to 'construe' individual environmental rights out of constitutional guarantees also raise problems. In certain jurisdictions, attempts to formulate individual environmental rights are based on the private

---

[*] Both Professor, Tilburg University, the Netherlands. The authors thank Famke Phoqué for her stimulating comments on earlier drafts of this contribution.

[1] Cf., e.g., Art. 45 of the Spanish constitution and Art. 23(3)(4) of the Belgian constitution. Art. 21 of the Dutch constitution is less explicit in that it formulates a duty for the state to care for, *inter alia*, the protection and improvement of the human environment.

[2] Cf. the recent Convention on Access to Information, Public Participation in Decision-Making and Access to Justice in Environmental Matters (Aarhus Convention of 25 June 1998), published on the Internet at: http://www.unece.org/env/.

[3] Greening the Treaty III: Institutional Reform, Citizen's Rights and Sustainable Development—Proposals for the 2000 Intergovernmental Conference; published on the Internet at: http://www.eeb.org/press/greening_the_treaty_iii_.htm. The Charter of Fundamental Rights of the EU contains a number of Articles which (may) relate to environmental protection, but does not recognize a right to environmental protection as such. See Winter, elsewhere in this volume.

[4] Including the EU constitutional level, i.e. the Treaty or the Charter, provided the latter becomes a binding instrument.

[5] The same problems apply in relation to other economic, social, and cultural rights.

law concept of 'subjective rights',[6] or may be cast in the context of the theory of 'subjective public rights' (*subjektive öffentliche Rechte*), which was developed in Germany in the nineteenth century, and still appears to permeate German public law thinking.[7]

One of the main concerns of theories of 'subjective rights',[8] whether public or private, is to transform legal provisions into legally enforceable entitlements. Rights are thus accompanied by the power to institute legal proceedings for their enforcement. If a breach of an individual right is claimed, in many legal systems the individual concerned will enjoy a guaranteed access to the courts. Furthermore, in relation to the consideration of the merits of a case and the possible remedies, a 'bearer of rights' will often be in a more advantageous position than a person who merely claims the protection of (legitimate) interests.[9]

Individual rights therefore appear to possess a special, almost mystical normative force. At the level of a concrete dispute, where courts often are required to balance conflicting interests, rights may also override other general welfare considerations, and, indeed, considerations of a more general economic character. The position of a person claiming breach of mere interests will usually be weaker.

Because rights are usually inextricably associated with effective judicial protection, at first sight it is attractive to link the concept of individual environmental rights to the protection of the environment. This tendency is becoming apparent in EC environmental law, not least because it is widely recognized that private individuals play a crucial role in its effective enforcement, by relying on 'their Community law rights' in their national courts. Reich has argued that European environmental law should be subjectivized, in the same way as economic law, i.e. market subjects should have enforceable rights to enter another Member State and pursue a professional activity there.[10] With the exception of certain explicit provisions in EC environmental legislation,[11] however, the case law of the European Court of Justice (ECJ) provides relatively

---

[6] A. Carette, 'Een Subjectief Recht op een Volwaardig Leefmilieu?' (1998) 35 *Tijdschrift voor Privaatrecht*, 821.

[7] Indeed, this is more generally the philosophy in Member States which follow the German model, such as Austria. For the significance of this concept in EU law, see N. Reich, *'System der Subjektiven Öffentlichen Rechte' in the Union: A European Constitution for Citizens of Bits and Pieces—Collected Courses of the Academy of European Law*, i: bk. I (The Hague: Martinus Nijhoff Publishers, 1995), 163 ff.

[8] Because of the distinction between 'law' and 'rights', in English law the phrase 'subjective rights' does not make much sense. We shall therefore use the term 'individual rights'.

[9] This holds true in particular for legal systems where this somewhat nebulous distinction is maintained. In Italian law, for instance, an infringement of a rule, which generates 'merely a legitimate interest', can give rise to damages. In Belgium, this distinction is also common and, as in Italy, determines the jurisdiction of ordinary and administrative courts. See Carette, n. 6 above, and M. Pâques, 'Trois Remèdes à l'Inexécution du Droit Communautaire: Utilité Pour l'Environnement?' (1996) 73 *Revue de Droit International et de Droit Comparé*, 135 (in particular 199–200).

[10] See Reich, n. 7 above, 167.    [11] e.g. access to environmental information.

few indications that the Court has recognized the existence of individual rights in the area of environmental law.[12]

In this chapter, we will briefly address three different problem areas in the ECJ's case law with a view to clarifying the most important issues in more concrete terms. We will endeavour to expose the problem of conceptual ambiguity in the environmental context through a critical analysis of the case law in which the Court has deployed the language of 'rights' and which, therefore, provides some indications on the issue under discussion. For this purpose we shall first examine the relationship between the concept of a 'right' and the direct effect of a Community norm. As will become evident, the existence of an individual right is often equated—in our view wrongly—with the direct effect of the norm at issue (Section III). Second, we shall examine what parameters the Court relies on in its case law on state liability in order to establish whether the provision breached confers rights upon individuals (Section IV). Third, we shall turn to the use of 'rights' language in the case law concerning the implementation of directives, and the link between an individual right and infringement proceedings against Member States for non-compliance with the provisions of such directives (Section V). Section VI lays bear the inherent dangers associated with a narrowly construed concept of rights. Alternatives to prevailing approaches are discussed in Section VII, which entails a shift from 'rights' to 'wrongs'. This section concludes with some suggestions aimed at a refashioning of procedures. Finally, a caveat: for the reasons discussed above, when we employ the notion of rights in the present contribution, in principle we use it as an umbrella term, without any specific meaning.

## II. Rights in the Case Law of the ECJ

Despite the many learned treatises on the notion of 'rights' in national law, the concept as such remains difficult to pin down and define. In EC law, the concept is even more ambiguous:

> It refers to the general right, and accompanying remedy concept, to have a court set aside national measures which conflict with the requirements of a directive, but may also refer to a specific right which a directive grants to private parties, and which, together with other conditions, gives rise . . . to a right and an accompanying remedy for compensation.[13]

The term 'right' employed here has various meanings, depending on the context in which the term is used. Van Gerven also provides us with a very general and, in his words, 'tentative' definition: 'the concept of rights refers to a legal

---

[12] For an analysis see H. Somsen, 'The Private Enforcement of Member State Compliance with EC Environmental Law: An Unfulfilled Promise?' in (2000) 1 *Yearbook of European Environmental Law*, 326 ff.

[13] W. van Gerven, 'Of Rights, Remedies and Procedures' (2000) 37 *Common Market Law Review*, 507, referring to the famous para. 25 of the *Becker* judgment, Case 8/81, *Ursula Becker* v. *Finanzamt Münster Innenstadt* [1982] ECR 53.

position which a person recognized as such by the law . . . may have and which in its normal state can be enforced by that person against . . . others before a court of law by means of one or more remedies.'[14]

The indiscriminate rights language of the ECJ, and subsequent analyses in legal writing, have hardly contributed to a clarification of the matter. This is due not only to purely doctrinal differences, but also a reflection of national perceptions and divergent legal traditions. It would seem that the catalyst for this confusion lies in the ECJ's case law on state liability, and it is this case law which has triggered a discussion on the concept of right in EC law, although the term has been employed regularly by the ECJ even prior to the development of this particular line of case law. Interestingly, the intensity of the debate in the Member States varies. In Germany, for instance, numerous studies have been devoted to the question of the necessity to rethink traditional national law concepts of 'subjective public rights' and the foundation for *Individual-rechtsschutz*.[15] Writers with roots in other legal traditions, appear to focus their enquiries on the inherent ambiguity of the terms employed by the ECJ, for example, whether it adopts a strict or narrow concept of a *droit subjectif*, or whether protection of a legitimate interest in the Community context would suffice for a 'right' to emerge.[16] Others have used a Hohfeldian analytical framework in order to clarify the ECJ's rights-language and describe more precisely the legal relationships and the specific legal effects involved.[17] In Hohfeld's analysis, there are in fact four kinds of rights with four kinds of correlatives:

— *claim* (or *right strictly speaking*), which has implications for the existence of duties of others;
— *privilege*, having implications for the existence of the duties of the person enjoying the 'right';

---

[14] Ibid. at 502.

[15] T. Eilmansberger, *Rechtsfolgen und Subjektives Recht im Gemeinschaftsrecht: Zugleich ein Beitrag zur Dogmatik der Staathaftungsdoktrin des EuGH* (Baden-Baden: Nomos, 1997); M. Ruffert, *Subjektive Rechte im Umweltrecht der Europäischen Gemeinschaft: Unter Besonderer Berücksichtigung Ihrer Prozessualen Durchsetzung* (Heidelberg: Decker, 1996); G. Winter, 'Individualrechtsschutz im Deutschen Umweltrecht Unter dem Einfluss des Gemeinschaftsrechts' (1999) 18 *Neue Zeitschrift für Verwaltungsrecht*, 467; D. Triantafyllou, 'Zur Europäisierung des Subjektiven Öffentlichen Rechts' (1997) 50 *Die Öffentliche Verwaltung: Zeitschrift für Verwaltungsrecht und Verwaltungspolitik*, 192; M. Ruffert, 'Dogmatik und Praxis des Subjektiv-Öffentlichen Rechts Unter dem Einfluss des Gemeinschaftsrechts' (1998) 113 *Deutsches Verwaltungsblatt*, 69; F. Schoch, 'Individualrechtsschutz im Deutschen Umweltrecht Unter dem Einfluss des Gemeinschaftsrechts' (1999) 18 *Neue Zeitschrift für Verwaltungsrecht*, 457.

[16] Often without explaining what the difference between a right and a (legitimate or mere) interest is. Cf. Pâques, n. 9 above; M. P. Léger, 'Libres Propos sur l'Application Effective du Droit Communautaire de l'Environnement' in G. C. Rodriguez Iglesias (ed.), *Mélanges en Hommage à Fernand Schockweiler* (Baden-Baden: Nomos, 1999), 299 (in particular 328). On the Community law implications for the 'Italian' distinction between (subjective) rights and legitimate interests, see R. Caranta, 'Government Liability after Francovich' (1993) 52 *Cambridge Law Journal*, 286–91.

[17] See, in particular, C. Hilson and T. Downes, 'Making Sense of Rights: Community Rights in EC Law' (1999) 24 *European Law Review*, 121; H. Gilliams, 'Horizontale Werking van Richtlijnen: Dogma's en Realiteit' in H. Cousy *et al.* (eds.), *Liber Amicorum Walter van Gerven* (Deurne: Kluwer, 2000), and partly also J. Coppel, 'Rights, Duties and the End of Marshall' (1994) 57 *Modern Law Review*, 859.

— *power*, which affects the possible alteration of the duties of the persons involved in the relationship; and,

— *immunity*, which has ramifications for the freedom from possible alteration of the duties of the person in which the 'right' is vested. Thus, for instance, Ms Becker's right to exemption from VAT in this approach is a *privilege*: she was under no obligation to pay VAT.[18] Faccini Dori had a *power* to revoke a contract,[19] and Francovich had a wage *claim*.[20]

However, as an *analytical* approach, the Hohfeldian framework is by no means exhaustive, and, in any event, only one way of approaching the problem. Attempts have been made in German literature to define criteria to discern whether a Community norm implies a right.[21] It must of course be acknowledged that the doctrine of the ECJ is only in its infant phase.[22] As long as there exists no clear doctrine, debates on the nature and scope of the concept of a right in Community law will continue. Obviously, there is an undeniable (and absolutely comprehensible) tendency to approach the problem from within the legal tradition in which one has been educated. These national perspectives and approaches not only influence the interpretation of EC law in legal writing, they also exert a certain influence on the judgments of the ECJ itself. After all, the Court's judges are also drawn from a specific national legal background. An open-minded attitude and comparative law insights may save us from the tower of Babel.[23]

A comparative study would therefore seem necessary to serve as a basis for a working definition of 'rights'.[24] Nevertheless, if indeed such a working definition could be produced, this would not offer a solution to all problems. Any definition must be further understood and operationalized within a specific conceptual framework, which may differ from Member State to Member State. Insights into how rights operate in other legal systems are necessary to avoid misunderstandings between lawyers from different legal backgrounds, which meet in the context of Community law. Such a comparative exercise is not viable in the context of this chapter, however.

[18] Case 8/81, *Ursula Becker* v. *Finanzamt Münster-Innenstadt* [1982] ECR 53.
[19] Case C–91/92, *Paola Faccini Dori* v. *Recreb Srl* [1994] ECR I–3325
[20] Joined Cases C–6/90 and 9/90, *Andrea Francovich and Danila Bonifaci and others* v. *Italian Republic* [1991] ECR I–5357.
[21] Cf. M. Ruffert, 'Rights and Remedies in European Community Law: a Comparative View' (1997) 34 *Common Market Law Review*, 307; Ruffert, n. 15 above; Schoch, n. 15 above. Another attempt has been undertaken by S. Prechal, *Directives in European Community Law: a Study of Directives and Their Enforcement by National Courts* (Oxford: Clarendon Press, 1995), ch. 7.
[22] Cf. Winter, n. 15 above.
[23] Cf. German literature and emphasis there on the fact that Community law is under a strong influence of French legal thought.
[24] Cf. the definition by W. van Gerven, which is based on certain findings made in the context of the *ius commune* project on tort law. See W. van Gerven, J. Lever, P. Larouche, Ch. von Bär, and G. Viney, *Cases, Materials and Text on National, Supranational and International Tort Law, Scope of Protection* (Oxford: Hart Publishing, 1998)

## III.  Rights and Direct Effect

The existence of an individual right is often equated with direct effect. Indeed, in the slipstream of the landmark *Van Gend & Loos* judgment, direct effect was often defined as the creation of rights which the courts must protect.[25] Gradually, a broader concept revolving around the 'invocability' of a Community norm has emerged in subsequent case law, based on the conception that the particular significance of the Community law provision at issue depends on the nature and subject matter of the proceedings before national courts. The concept of invocability is broader, because it allows a Community provision to be relied upon or invoked for a wide variety of purposes, for example, as a defence in criminal proceedings, or as a standard for review of the legality of Member States' action in administrative proceedings.[26] The question whether any provision confers an individual right therefore is not necessarily relevant, and to equate the concept of direct effect with the creation of rights does no justice to the diversity of the effects which directly effective provisions may produce.

Although the debate on direct effect and the nature of the rights created by directly effective provisions of Community law is an established one, *Kraaijeveld* appears to have triggered a revival of the discussion on the concept of direct effect. The central issue in this discussion is whether a 'legality review' *à la Kraaijeveld* is a form of direct effect.[27]

In *Kraaijeveld* the Court recalled that:

[W]here the Community authorities have, by a directive, imposed on Member States the obligation to pursue a particular course of conduct, the useful effect of such an act would be weakened if individuals were prevented from relying on it before their national courts, and if the latter were prevented from taking it into consideration as an element of Community law in order to rule whether the national legislature, in exercising the choice open to it as to the form and methods for implementation, has kept within the limits of its discretion set out in the directive.[28]

More concretely, the obligation of the Member States at issue was conditioned by the discretion allowed to them under Article 4(2) of Directive

---

[25] Case 26/62, *N.V. Algemene Transport – en Expeditie-onderneming Van Gend & Loos* v. *Nederlandse Administratie der Belastingen* [1963] ECR 1.

[26] For a more detailed discussion see Prechal, n. 21 above, sects. 7.2.2 and 11.3.3.

[27] Cf., e.g., J. Scott, *EC Environmental Law* (London: Longman, 1998), 123–4; D. Wyatt, 'Litigating Community Environmental Law—Thoughts on the Direct Effect Doctrine' (1998) 10 *Journal of Environmental Law*, 9, who has obvious doubts as to the extension of direct effect beyond the concept of 'self-standing source of rights'. For a brief overview of the 'old' discussion on this issue, see Prechal, n. 21 above, sect. 11.3.6.

[28] Case C–72/95, *Aannemersbedrijf P.K. Kraaijeveld BV e.a.* v. *Gedeputeerde Staten van Zuid-Holland* [1996] ECR I–5403, para. 56. This type of review had already been applied in Case 51/76, *Verbond van Nederlandse Ondernemingen* v. *Inspecteur der Invoerrechten en Accijnzen* [1977] ECR 133. See on this C. W. A. Timmermans, 'Directives: Their Effects within the National Legal System' (1979) 16 *Common Market Law Review*, 533. See also Case C–435/97, *World Wildlife Fund (WWF) and others* v. *Autonome Provinz Bozen and others* [1999] ECR I–5613.

85/337/EEC on the Assessment of the Effects of Certain Public and Private Projects on the Environment (EIA Directive).[29] The limits of this discretion were to be found in Article 2(1), which requires assessment of projects having significant effects on the environment.

It is sometimes observed that since the relevant provisions of the Directive do not necessarily confer rights upon individuals, *Kraaijeveld* is not concerned with direct effect. This reasoning is somewhat perplexing. For, if one looks closely at the Court's case law, it becomes obvious that Community law has long recognized that there exist various degrees of discretion regarding implementation by the Member States, the exercise of which has been already for a long time subject to judicial control by national courts.[30] *Kraaijeveld*, as such, represents nothing new under the sun. Rather it is the language and the *explicit* extension of the review of legality to the national implementing measures in the light of the objectives of the Directive, that seems to have provoked this response.

More recently, the approach pursued in *Kraaijeveld* was reconfirmed in *Linster*.[31] In relation to the latter case, it is interesting to note that Advocate General Léger proposed, in his Opinion of 11 January 2000, to draw a clear distinction between 'invocability for the purposes of substitution' of the national provisions at issue and 'invocability for the purposes of exclusion' of the national provisions. In accordance with this traditional French distinction, the first type of invocability corresponds more or less with 'direct effect as creation of rights', while the second type may to an extent be equated to the 'mere' review of legality. In the Advocate's General opinion, if EC law provisions are relied upon for the purposes of exclusion, or the review of legality of the national measures at issue, there is no need to verify whether the traditional conditions for direct effect were satisfied.[32] However, the ECJ did not adopt the distinction, and simply resorted to the said formulation in *Kraaijeveld*. It is, of course, dangerous to speculate why the ECJ did not follow the Advocate General. One of the explanations could be that, according to the ECJ, too, there is no reason to draw such a distinction, since the concept of direct effect already covers both notions of invocability.

Nevertheless, the fact remains that the ECJ occasionally still employs the language of 'creating rights' in order to determine direct effect. It is often induced to do so by the formulation of the preliminary question(s) referred to it. This may, however, mean different things, and lead to different results. It may indicate that the person is entitled to invoke the provision at issue, for whatever purpose. In several cases the ECJ has labelled direct effect as the right to rely on Community law provisions,[33] and hence as a kind of 'procedural

---

[29]  [1985] OJ L175/40.

[30]  Cf. S. Prechal, 'Does Direct Effect Still Matter?' (2000) 37 *Common Market Law Review*, 1047 (in particular 1059–62).

[31]  Case C–287/98, *Grand Duchy of Luxemburg* v. *Berthe Linster, Aloyse Linster and Yvonne Linster* [2000] ECR I–6917. See also C–435/97, n. 28 above.

[32]  i.e. whether the provision is sufficiently precise and unconditional.

[33]  See, e.g., Case C–431/92, *Commission* v. *Germany* [1995] ECR I–2189, para. 26.

right'.[34] However, in other cases, it is less clear what the implications of direct effect are. Indeed, the consequence may well be that a substantive individual right is created. Ultimately this is a question of substantive law, and directly related to the concept of invocability as such. In certain cases, direct effect and the creation of substantive rights may coincide, but this is not always necessarily so.

Arguably, this latter proposition is explicitly confirmed in the recent *Unilever* case.[35] In this case, Unilever contended, in a dispute with another firm, that an Italian law on the labelling of olive oil should not be applied. Italy failed to comply with Article 9 of Directive 83/189/EEC Laying Down a Procedure for the Provision of Information in the Field of Technical Standards and Regulations,[36] which provides for an obligation to observe a certain period of delay after the national measures are notified to the Commission, giving the latter the opportunity to form an opinion on their compatibility with Community law. On the basis of the judgment in *CIA Security*,[37] Unilever argued that such a failure to observe the requisite procedure rendered the Italian law inapplicable. After having found that this was indeed the case, and such procedures should have been observed, the ECJ addressed the arguments submitted by several Member States who had claimed that if the ECJ recognized the inapplicability of a national measure in the case at issue, this would amount to an implicit recognition of horizontal direct effect. It is established law that directives cannot directly impose obligations on individuals and cannot, therefore, be relied upon in a dispute concerning contractual rights and obligations between private parties.[38] The Court countered this argument by pointing out that Directive 83/189/EEC did not 'define the substantive scope of the legal rule on the basis of which the national court must decide the case before it. It creates neither rights nor obligations for individuals.'[39] Nonetheless, Unilever was allowed to rely on the Directive but only for the purpose of having the Italian law at issue set aside.

In addition, the discussion on the creation of rights and direct effect is complicated by national factors. In some legal systems, individual rights play a pivotal role, and in that context have a specific meaning, as for example in Germany or Italy. In other legal systems, the term 'right' may be used as shorthand for a person's legal position, without any specific consequences being attributed to it. Still in other jurisdictions, the concept may play a particular role in private law procedures, while in administrative law procedures different concepts apply, as for example in France or the Netherlands.

---

[34] The term 'procedural right' is used here in contrast to 'substantive right', which reflects the content of the provision, and which seems to correspond with what van Gerven, n. 13 above, 507, calls 'specific rights'.

[35] Case C–443/98, *Unilever Italia SpA* v. *Central Food SpA* [2000] ECR I–7535.

[36] [1983] OJ L109/8, as amended by Dir. 88/182/EEC, [1988] OJ L81/75.

[37] Case C–194/94, *CIA Security International SA* v. *Signalson SA and Securitel SPRL* [1996] ECR I–2201.

[38] Cf. Case 152/84, *M. H. Marshall* v. *Southampton and South-West Hampshire Area Health Authority (Teaching)* [1986] ECR I–723 and, in particular, Case C–91/92, n. 19 above.

[39] See n. 35 above, para. 51 of the judgment.

In German administrative law literature concerning EC law, it is not unusual, at least until recently, to find arguments to the effect that the creation of an individual right is another (implicit) condition for direct effect. This approach is closely linked with the focus in German law on *Individual-rechtsschutz*, the protection of individual rights. This protection implies a three-step scrutiny of the provisions at issue:

— there must be a generally binding (statutory) provision (*ein zwingender Rechtssatz des objektiven Rechts*);
— the provisions must aim at the protection of individual interests (only those who can avail themselves of such a *Schutznorm* can claim individual rights); and,
— the persons concerned must be given the *Rechtsmacht zur Durchsetzung* (power to effectuate/enforce) their legally protected interests.

Only when a person can claim an individual right,[40] can an action before an administrative court be instigated, for example. This also is the direct background to the fierce debate in German legal literature on the nature and impact of ECJ case law, which in turn has caused significant conceptual problems. In particular, it has resulted in a distinction between 'subjective direct effect', which remains conditional upon the existence of an individual right, and 'objective direct effect', a new form of direct effect which is not conditional upon the existence of an individual right.[41]

In common law systems, the language of rights does not seem to have any particular dogmatic meaning. Usage of the term, as one writer put it, is 'popular'.[42] This is understandable, since in those systems, emphasis is placed on remedies. It is not rights, which give rise to a remedy, but a cause of action, in other words, the facts that entitle a person to sue. The focus of judicial proceedings is not directed towards the specific interpretation of the provision at issue in order to establish whether an individual right has been granted or not. It is therefore not surprising that English lawyers have approached the creation of rights as a corollary of direct effect. *Ubi ius, ibi remedium* and, after all, does direct effect not imply that there *must* be a remedy available?[43]

Neither do the French appear overly concerned about the concept, because in French administrative law the focus is not on the creation of rights, but on the question whether state or public authority behaviour is compatible with EC law. Hence, EC law provisions are often used in the context of the *contrôle de légalité*.[44] In France, direct effect is usually approached from the perspective of either *l'invocabilité d'exclusion* or *l'invocabilité de substitution*. The first

---

[40] In so far as this term can serve as an appropriate translation for the German *subjektives Recht*.

[41] Cf. Ruffert, n. 21 above, in particular at 320, with further references.

[42] P. Legrand, 'European Legal Systems Are not Converging' (1996) 45 *International and Comparative Law Quarterly*, 70.

[43] Cf. also Art. 2(1) of the European Communities Act 1972, which stresses the enforceability of EC law provisions.

[44] In the context of an action for damages, however, the main concern is the protection of rights.

form of invocability occurs when EC law is used as a standard for review and, if there is incompatibility, the national rules are disapplied or set aside. Often, depending on a number of factors, this may lead to satisfactory outcomes. The second form is resorted to in certain cases where it is necessary to apply EC law provisions instead of national rules incompatible with EC law.[45]

It is therefore submitted that it is crucial, certainly in the environmental law context, to understand that direct effect as a concept is broader than merely that of the creation of rights. Therefore it is of singular importance to appreciate the kind of conceptual pitfalls which may be hidden in ECJ rulings. A case such as *Comitato*[46] clearly illustrates this point. To start with, the national court had asked the wrong question (does Article 4 of the Waste Directive grant individuals 'subjective rights'?),[47] which inevitably led to the Court's finding that that provision, which 'indicates a programme to be followed and sets out the objectives which the Member States must observe in their performance of the more specific obligations imposed on them [by the Directive]',[48] does not require, in itself, the adoption of specific measures or a particular method of waste disposal. Therefore, the ECJ held that Article 4 is 'neither unconditional nor sufficiently precise and thus is not capable of conferring rights on which individuals may rely as against the State.'[49] As long as this case is understood as denying individuals the right to claim the adoption of specific measures, or a particular method of waste disposal from the competent authorities, there is no problem. Yet, this case has not decided for once and for ever that Article 4 of the Waste Directive has no direct effect in the sense that it may not be relied upon, and that it is, therefore, absolutely unenforceable. The Court's finding does not exclude that a national court may be called upon to review whether

[45] An intermediate position can be found in Belgium, where a distinction is made between direct effect *senso stricto*, and direct effect *senso lato*. The latter encompasses the control of legality, without addressing the question whether the provision at issue creates individual rights. Cf. H. Bribosia, 'Report on Belgium' in A. Slaughter *et al.* (eds.), *The European Courts and National Courts—Doctrine and Jurisprudence: Legal Change in its Social Context* (Oxford: Hart Publishing, 1998), 6–10. On the issue of direct effect of environmental directives without individual rights being created, see M. Wathelet and S. van Raepenbusch, 'La Responsabilité des États Membres en cas de Violation du Droit Communautaire. Vers un Alignement de la Responsabilité de l'État sur Celle de la Communauté ou l'Inverse?' (1997) 33 *Cahiers de Droit Européen*, 44. For a 'traditional' French administrative law approach (review or control of legality and disapplication of the provisions which are contrary to EC law), see Y. Galmot and J. Bonichot, 'La Cour de Justice des Communautés Européennes et la Transposition des Directives en Droit National' (1988) 4 *RFDA*, 1. For an (not entirely up-to-date) overview in English of the particular problems in France, see A. F. T. Tatham, 'Effect of European Community Directives in France: The Development of the Cohn-Bendit Jurisprudence' (1991) 40 *International and Comparative Law Quarterly*, 907. Equally instructive is the case note on *Rothmans* by J. Dutheil de la Rochère, in (1993) 30 *Common Market Law Review*, 187.

[46] Case C–236/92, *Comitato di Coordinamento per la Difesa della Cava and others* v. *Regione Lombardia and others* [1994] ECR I–483, which is often considered as authority for denying direct effect to the Waste Directive, in particular by those who equate direct effect with the creation of rights. Cf. J. Holder, 'A Dead End for Direct Effect?: Prospects for Enforcement of European Community Environmental Law by Individuals' (1996) 8 *Journal of Environmental Law*, 321.

[47] Apparently the reference to the ECJ was anything but clear. See the Opinion of AG Darmon, ibid., para. 3.

[48] See n. 46 above, para. 12 of the judgment.          [49] Ibid., para. 14 of the judgment.

the measures taken by the authorities are in conformity with the objectives and of the Direicitve. This, after all, was the approach followed in *Kraaijeveld*.[50]

A more recent judgment in the context of infringement proceedings has confirmed this approach. In *San Rocco*,[51] the Court established, on the basis of evidence submitted to it, that in respect of biological and chemical waste from a hospital discharged in the San Rocco valley, that the competent authorities had failed to act over a protracted period of time and, therefore, that no measures necessary to ensure that the waste was disposed without endangering human health or harming the environment were taken. Although, according to the ECJ, the provision at issue did not specify the substantive content of the measures to be taken, and left Member States a margin of discretion to assess the need for such measures, it nevertheless indicated that the Member State *in casu* has probably exceeded that discretion. The same assessment evidently can be made by a national court.[52]

It should be pointed out that the acceptance of the 'broader view' of direct effect, which is less closely tied to the creation of individual rights, may have important consequences for EC environmental law. In particular, it could result in direct effect of provisions such as Article 174 EC and the principles enshrined therein, such as the principles of precaution and prevention. This type of direct effect would imply that Member States' action should be reviewed against these principles, at least in the sense that national authorities are obliged to act within the limits of these principles. Taking the comparison with *San Rocco* further, there are no obvious reasons why, for example, a Member State measure to fight mad cow disease could not be reviewed in the light of Article 174 EC, in the same way as the ECJ reviews the Commission's action.[53] Although in situations where the authorities enjoy a wide measure of

[50] Cf. the approach pursued in the earlier Case 14/83, *Sabine von Colson and Elisabeth Kamann v. Land Nordrhein-Westfalen* [1984] ECR 1891. On this issue see also Ch. Boch, 'The Iroquois at the Kirchberg; or Some Naïve Remarks on the Status and the Relevance of Direct Effect' in J. Usher (ed.), *The State of the European Union: Structure, Enlargement and Economic Union* (Harlow: Longman, 2000), 21 (in particular 36); Somsen, n. 12 above, 345.

[51] Case C–365/97, *Commission v. Italy* [1999] ECR I–7773.

[52] Similar and instructive cases are Cases C–392/96, *Commission v. Ireland* [1999] ECR I–5901 and C–72/95, n. 24 above, and the cases C–355/90, *Commission v. Spain* [1993] ECR I–4221 and C–44/95, *R. v. Secretary of State for the Environment, ex p. Royal Society for the Protection of Birds* [1996] ECR I–3843.

[53] Cf. Case C–180/96, *United Kingdom v. Commission* [1999] ECR I–2265. See also Case C–94/98, *The Queen, ex p. Rhône-Poulenc Rorer Ltd and May & Baker Ltd v. The Licensing Authority established by the Medicines Act 1968 (represented by the Medicines Control Agency)* [1999] ECR I–8789. In this respect, we would suggest developing the argument of Winter on the 'obliging potential' of the EC Treaty environmental principles (in his chapter published elsewhere in this volume). In particular, it is not only when the Member States apply or implement EC law that they should abide by fundamental rights and, in his perspective, all other fundamental principles of the Treaty, but also where the measure which the Member States takes does not as such implement or apply EC law, but nevertheless falls within the scope of Community law. Cf. Case C–260/89, *Elliniki Radiophonia Tiléorassi AE and Panellinia Omospondia Syllogon Prossopikou v. Dimotiki Etairia Pliroforissis and Sotirios Kouvelas and Nicolaos Avdellas and others* [1991] ECR I–2925.

discretion the scope for judicial review can be very limited,[54] it may nevertheless allow for some degree of control by the courts.[55]

In summary, ECJ case law linking the concept of direct effect with the creation of rights must, for reasons set out above, be employed with a good deal of
caution. The Court's 'rights' language appears to vary from one case to the
next.

## IV. Rights and State Liability

Although the language of rights is certainly present in the ECJ case law on state
liability, this has not been particularly helpful in providing the necessary criteria for identifying the existence of an individual right. To a certain extent, the
issue seems unproblematic. In *Francovich*,[56] the Court acknowledged that
the result required by Directive 80/987/EEC Relating to the Protection of
Employees in the Event of the Insolvency of their Employer, entailed the grant
of a right to the employees concerned 'to a guarantee of payment of their
unpaid wage claims'.[57] Perhaps because the issue was so obvious, the ECJ did
not explain the grounds for its conclusion.

In other cases, the ECJ relies on the terms and/or the aim of the provisions
at issue, or on the preamble, or both. The preamble of Directive 85/577/EEC to
Protect the Consumer in Respect of Contracts Negotiated away from Business
Premises,[58] at issue in *Faccini Dori*,[59] made clear, according to the ECJ, that the
Directive intended to improve consumer protection. Since the Directive was
'undeniably intended to confer rights on individuals', the first condition for liability, namely that the purpose of the directive grant of rights to individuals,
was fulfilled.

In *Dillenkofer*,[60] it was submitted that the main aim of Directive,
90/314/EEC on Package Travel, Package Holidays and Package Tours was to
guarantee freedom to provide services and fair competition.[61] However, the
ECJ stressed that the preamble repeatedly refers to the purpose of protecting
consumers, which also followed from the aim and wording of Article 7 of the
Directive. The fact that the Directive intended to ensure other additional
objectives could not detract from this conclusion. Therefore, the purpose of
the pertinent provision was 'to grant to individuals rights'.

---

[54] Cf. Case C–120/97, *Upjohn Ltd* v. *The Licensing Authority established by the Medicines Act 1968 and others* [1999] ECR I–223.

[55] For another interesting attempt to give effect to Art. 174 EC, along comparable lines as EC competition law operates, see A. Doyle and T. Carney, 'Precaution and Prevention: Giving Effect to Art. 130r without Direct Effect' (1999) 8 *European Environmental Law Review*, 44.

[56] Joined Cases C–6/90 and 9/90, n. 20 above.     [57] [1980] OJ L283/23.

[58] [1985] OJ L375/31.     [59] Case C–91/92, n. 19 above.

[60] Joined Cases C–178/94, C–179/94, C–188/94, and C–190/94, *Dillenkofer and others* v. *Bundesrepublik Deutschland* [1996] ECR I–4845.

[61] [1990] OJ L158/59.

In *Norbrook*,[62] where a licensing authority imposed requirements which allegedly were incompatible with the directives at issue, the ECJ found that Directive 81/851/EEC on Veterinary Medicinal products provides that an application for marketing authorization may be refused only for the reasons set out in the Directive.[63] Therefore, according to the ECJ, the Directive gives individuals the right to obtain an authorization if certain conditions are fulfilled. These conditions are laid down precisely and exhaustively in Directives 81/851/EEC and 81/852/EEC on Testing of Veterinary Medicinal Products.[64] These Directives also provide a basis to identify the scope of the right to obtain a marketing authorization.

In the case law involving state liability for failed or incorrect implementation of directives, an additional uncertainty should be taken into account. In *Francovich*, the ECJ stated that the *result* of the directive must entail the grant of a right, but in *Faccini* it required that it should be the *purpose* of the directive to grant rights.[65] There is of course a difference between these conditions. The first may be understood broadly, namely that even in cases where a directive does not intend to create rights as such, an individual provision in the directive still may do so.[66] Put differently, under the first formulation, it is not the objective pursued by the Directive, but the result that counts. In later cases, the ECJ, in the light of *Brasserie du Pêcheur*, has reformulated the first condition for liability, so that the rule of law infringed must have been intended to confer rights.[67] It would seem to follow that it is sufficient that a provision confers or intends to confer rights.

In other cases, the ECJ merely stated that the relevant provision created rights for the purposes of establishing state liability, because it had previously found that the provision at issue created rights in the sense of having direct effect.[68] In the light of what was said in the previous section it may be clear that this link is not necessarily always present: the fact that a provision of Community law is directly effective does not automatically imply that it confers individual rights. On the other hand, it cannot be denied that there is a link between direct effect and individual rights. This link resides in the traditional conditions for direct effect, namely that such provisions must be clear, sufficiently precise, and unconditional. These conditions are still valid in situations where a person asserts a positive claim, often a right,[69] so that the creation of

---

[62] Case C–127/95, *Norbrook Laboratories Ltd* v. *Ministry of Agriculture, Fisheries and Food* [1998] ECR I–1531.

[63] [1981] OJ L317/1.     [64] [1981] OJ L17/16.

[65] Reiterated in Case C–192/94, *El Corte Inglés SA* v. *Cristina Blázquez Rivero* [1996] ECR I–1281.

[66] Cf. S. Prechal, n. 21 above, sect. 12.4.3.

[67] Cf. Case C–127/95, n. 57 above; C–66/95, *The Queen* v. *Secretary of State for Social Security, ex p. Eunice Sutton* [1997] ECR I–2163; and C–94/95 and C–95/95, *Danila Bonifaci and others and Wanda Berto and others* v. *Istituto nazionale della previdenza sociale (INPS)* [1997] ECR I–3969.

[68] Cf. Case C–5/94, *The Queen* v. *Ministry of Agriculture, Fisheries and Food, ex p. Hedley Lomas (Ireland) Ltd.* [1996] ECR I–2553.

[69] The situation may be different where a person uses EC law provisions in the context of legality review. Cf. the Opinion of Advocate-General Léger of 11 January 2000 in Case C–287/98, n. 31 above.

rights is a consequence of, but not a condition for, direct effect. In the context of state liability, the ECJ also requires that the right allegedly violated must be 'determinable with sufficient precision'. In this respect, the Court seems to pursue a general line of thinking, which also prevails in national law, namely that the ascertainability of the scope of the right is a criterion which helps to decide whether a provision confers rights as such. The content of the alleged right must be sufficiently concrete or delineated. Hence, provisions involving discretion may not give rise to rights.[70]

## V. Rights and the Implementation of Directives

In well-established case law on the requirements which national measures implementing directives must satisfy, the ECJ has made plain that where directives are intended to create rights and duties for individuals, they must be implemented by legally binding measures. This case law also reveals that for individuals the binding quality of the implementing measures is significant in at least two respects. First, from the perspective of legal certainty, since it enables individuals to ascertain in a sufficiently predictable way the extent of their rights and duties. Second, from the perspective of effective judicial protection, since it defines a legal position upon which individuals may rely in national courts.

In the context of infringement proceedings, the ECJ has frequently addressed the question whether a particular directive intends to create rights (and duties) for individuals. In several cases relating to environmental directives, it ruled that the latter were intended to create rights and obligations for individuals, because the directives at issue were enacted, *inter alia*, with a view to protect human health.[71] If human health is endangered as a result of non-compliance, the persons concerned must be able to rely on mandatory rules, and assert their rights. Such reasoning could suggest that the objective of the protection of human health as such is sufficient to give rise to individual rights. In one such case, the ECJ did not focus on the objective of the directive, but analysed specific provisions. These provisions required the Member States to adopt a series of prohibitions, authorization schemes, and monitoring procedures 'in order to prevent or limit discharges of certain substances'. The

---

[70] Cf. Prechal, n. 21 above, ch. 7.

[71] Cf. Cases C–361/88, *Commission* v. *Germany* [1991] ECR I–2567; C–58/89, *Commission* v. *Germany* [1991] ECR I–4983; C–59/89, *Commission* v. *Germany* [1991] ECR I–2607; C–13/90, *Commission* v. *France* [1991] ECR I–4327; C–14/90, *Commission* v. *France* [1991] ECR I–4331; C–64/90, *Commission* v. *France* [1991] ECR I–4335; and C–298/95, *Commission* v. *Germany* [1996] ECR I–6747. These cases concerned water- and air-quality legislation. Since, by setting environmental quality standards, the directives aim at protecting, *inter alia*, human health, other directives could be relevant in this respect too. For instance, Council Dir. 90/219/EEC on the Contained Use of Genetically Modified Micro-Organisms [1990] OJ L117/1, and Council Dir. 90/220/EEC on the Deliberate Release into the Environment of Genetically Modified Organisms [1990] OJ L117/15.

Court concluded that '[t]he purpose of the directive is . . . to create rights and obligations for individuals'.[72]

The first question is what the ECJ has in mind when it refers, in this context, to rights. Once more, there remains uncertainty in this respect. This is illustrated by the approach adopted by AG Jacobs who opined, on the basis of this case law, that Directive 80/788/EEC on Drinking Water confers rights, and that incorrect implementation may give rise to liability pursuant to *Francovich*-type principles. Zuleeg, on the other hand, failed to see how an individual right could be construed on the basis of the mere fact that a directive aims at protecting human health.[73] In addition, Schockweiler has pointed out that the requirement of 'rights' in *Francovich* implies that state liability is not concerned with breaches where mere 'interests' are protected by the directive at issue, such as is the case with numerous environmental directives.[74] It would appear that each of these authors entertains a slightly different meaning of the concept of right.

Moreover, if the objective of a directive is the protection of human health, and this in turn determines whether a directive gives rise to rights, then it is not readily apparent why, in *Comitato*,[75] no such rights were found to exist. The Directive at issue after all was aimed at the protection of human health.

It is submitted that ECJ case law in infringement proceedings should not be interpreted as meaning that the directives give rise to *concrete* individual environmental rights. Directives, and environmental directives in particular, usually aim to produce a certain degree of external effect, in that they are designed to regulate relations between individuals, and between individuals and public authorities. They require Member States to provide at the national level, through the process of implementation, for legally sufficiently defined positions which, if necessary, may be relied upon in the courts. These may take the shape of rights, which are then in some way implied in the directive, but they must be given their *final* shape through the process of implementation,[76] or perhaps even require the intervention of the national administration, for instance where a licence or authorization should be issued.[77]

However, this is not necessarily the only way in which the provisions may be implemented and further concretized. Much depends on how the individual's position is perceived and translated in national legal systems. A case in which the ECJ did *not* use the language of rights clarifies this further. In *Commission* v. *Germany*[78] the ECJ held that the rules regarding participation and advertising in

---

[72] Case C–131/88, *Commission* v. *Germany* [1991] ECR I–825.
[73] M. Zuleeg, 'Umweltschutz in der Rechtsprechung des Europäischen Gerichtshofs' (1993) 46 *Neue Juristische Wochenschrift*, 31.
[74] F. Schockweiler, 'La Responsabilité de l'Autorité Nationale en cas de Violation du Droit Communautaire' (1992) 28 *Revue Trimestrielle de Droit Européen*, 44. Cf. also W. van Gerven, 'The ECJ's Recent Case-Law in the Field of Tort Liability, towards a European *Ius Commune*?', in N. Reich and R. Heinz-Marnik (eds.), *Umweltverfassung und Nachhaltige Entwicklung in der Europäischen Union* (Baden-Baden: Nomos, 1997), 187.
[75] Case C–236/92, n. 46 above.       [76] Cf. Winter, n. 15 above, 470.
[77] Cf. Case C–127/95, n. 67 above.
[78] Case C–433/93, *Commission* v. *Germany* [1995] ECR I–2303.

public procurement directives[79] are intended to protect tenderers against arbitrariness on the part of the contract-awarding authority. Effective protection implies that a tenderer must be able to rely on those rules as against the procuring authority and, if necessary, to plead a breach of those rules before national courts. This case may be defined in terms of the protection of the bidder's rights. It may, however, also be couched in a system of control of administrative action.

In brief, the main concern of the ECJ seems to be that the legal position of individuals must be safeguarded and, perhaps even more importantly, that EC law is simply applied. How this position is further qualified under national law (for example, as one of individual rights or protected interests) is primarily a matter for the national legal order. If this is true, the implication is that, where the ECJ uses the term 'right' in the context of its 'implementation case law', no particular significance should be afforded to the concept.

Comparable concerns also seem to lurk behind the notion of the effective protection of rights (and its equivalents), which Member States and, in particular, national courts must guarantee. This principle is derived from another line of case law in which the ECJ requires, on the basis of Article 10 EC, that national courts must protect the rights individuals derive from Community law.[80] Usually, it is the full application of EC law as such that matters, rather than the protection of any specific rights. Although, for the purposes of the principle of effective judicial protection, the Court may refer to the principles enshrined in Articles 6 and 13 of the European Convention on Human Rights (ECHR), the scope of the protection required is much broader than (civil) rights.

## A. PRELIMINARY CONCLUSIONS

In the case law on implementation as well as that on state liability, either the objective or the terms of the provisions at issue can play a pivotal role in relation to the question whether rights are (intended to be) created.

There seem two possibilities: the directive at issue may indicate that rights should be created at the national level (implementation/liability case law) or, alternatively, it may be that the rights are directly created by the directive, namely as a result of direct effect (direct effect/liability case law). Unfortunately, the case law does not bring us much further than this: it neither defines or delineates, *a priori*, when rights exist, nor what their nature or scope should be.

It may well be that by invoking the language of individual rights, the ECJ tries to benefit from the mystique of the term in order to ensure that the requirements

---

[79] Council Dir. 88/295/EEC Amending Dir. 77/62/EEC Relating to the Coordination of Procedures on the Award of Public Supply Contracts and Repealing Certain Provisions of Dir. 80/767/EEC, [1988] OJ L127/1 and Council Dir. 89/440/EEC Amending Dir. 71/305/EEC Concerning Coordination of Procedures for the Award of Public Works Contracts, [1989] OJ L210/1.

[80] Cf. the case law that started with Cases 33/76, *Rewe-Zentralfinanz eG and Rewe-Zentral AG v. Landwirtschaftskammer für das Saarland* [1976] ECR 1989 and 45/76, *Comet BV v. Produktschap voor Siergewassen* [1976] ECR 2043.

which it formulates are more readily accepted in the national legal orders. After all, in the supranational context the protection of individual citizens' rights seems a much more laudable project than merely stipulating that Member States must be controlled. However, it is also a dangerous approach. It may be clear that in the light of all the speculations set out above, considerable uncertainty surrounds the concept of rights in Community law. It is submitted that, as long as this concept is not clarified, it is not suitable as a tool for legal analysis. It may even be perilous, as it may result in fictive rights, as opposed to real rights.

## VI. The 'Tunnel' of Individual Rights

An important concern, or perhaps problem, in relation to a narrow rights-based approach to environmental protection, is the role which the concept of standing plays in the process of the enforcement of such rights. In this section, we shall attempt to draw attention to the dangers of what may be termed a 'tunnel' of rights. In brief, environmental groups or other non-governmental organizations (NGOs) could find themselves left out in the cold. Furthermore, even within the constraints of this tunnel, the individual rights-based approach exerts a strong influence on crucial issues, such as the pleas which may be invoked and remedies which may be sought. An important drawback of an individual rights centred approach is that the enforcement of EC environmental law remains linked to 'individual interests'. In legal writings it has often been observed that environmental concerns are public matters of interest, which do not translate easily into individual rights, since the protection of an individual interest is part and parcel of the latter concept.

### A. STANDING

We have briefly referred to the German requirement of a *Schutznorm*, which implies an enquiry as to whether the provision at issue aims at the protection of individual interests. Only if the answer is in the affirmative can the person concerned claim to enjoy an individual right. This *Schutznorm* requirement may be interpreted in an onerous way, while in other legal systems it may be much less restrictive. Yet, the view which links a right to an interest has permanently marked the general thinking about rights, which are thus considered as serving the protection of individual interests.[81] This is certainly not only the case in Germany, or even other Continental legal traditions. For instance, when Hilson and Downes deal with the question of who enjoys a right in the context of a Hohfeldian analytical exercise, they have recourse to the interest theory.[82] One of the most crucial problems indeed is the fact that the distinction

---

[81] Cf. Prechal, n. 21 above, sect. 7.3.4.

[82] And next, because there is no 'traditional' (protected) individual interest ascertainable in *Kraaijeveld*, they submit that it is not a direct effect case. The point is that they seem to equate direct effect to rights. See Hilson and Downes, n. 17 above.

between a public interest, and an individual interest is not always easy to draw. Often, this is a matter of interpretation and, to an extent, of legal policy choices. Thus, while the ECJ has ruled that the aim of the protection of human health implied that a directive intended to create rights, others have strongly disagreed with this view.[83]

As already observed, in Germany the existence of an individual right is a prerequisite for bringing an action in a national administrative court. However, even in legal systems where access to the courts is not dependent upon the existence of an individual right, 'individual interests' still often underpin standing rules. Much depends on the function of legal protection that prevails, the subjective, or the general legality view. As is well known, in terms of the former, judges are primarily responsible for the protection of individual citizens. Judicial intervention then serves primarily to protect individual rights, or at least individual interests. In the latter view, judges have a wider responsibility for controlling the legality of government action. Hence, judicial review is perceived as a matter of public interest. Obviously, in environmental law disputes focusing on the protection of collective interests, effective access to the courts may well be denied in Member States with restricted 'subjective' standing rules.

In legal literature, it has been pointed out that Community law is developing along lines which are much closer to the French system of administrative law (*recours objectif*), in particular where the ECJ relies on the *effet utile* principle, than that of Germany and the United Kingdom (*recours subjectif*).[84] This is despite the individual rights language deployed by the ECJ.[85] It is submitted that a narrow focus on the individual rights approach may reinforce the individual interest requirement for standing, with the result that environmental groups may be excluded.

### B. ADMISSIBILITY OF PLEAS

The individual interest requirement may be further relevant for other procedural issues, for example, in relation to what in French law is referred to as *recevabilité des moyens*, i.e. the admissibility of submissions or pleas. For the purposes of this contribution, this aspect should be understood, very broadly, as relating to the requirement that, where a party to a proceeding relies on a provision in order, for instance, to defend himself, the provision at issue should also aim at protecting his interests. Or, to phrase the question differently: could a purely 'objective' plea of illegality based on the incompatibility of the relevant national rules with a Community law provision suffice? We are in no position to answer this question, since this would require a comparative study of the vari-

---

[83] Hilson and Downes, n. 17 above.

[84] Cf. J. H. Jans, *European Environmental Law* (The Hague: Kluwer Law International, 1995), 187.

[85] *Effet utile* and protection of individual rights will often coincide, which results in 'double legitimization' of the requirements imposed by the ECJ.

ous legal systems and, moreover, also an analysis of the proceedings in which the provisions of Community law are invoked, i.e. administrative, criminal, civil, etc. In criminal proceedings, for instance, mere illegality may often suffice, when invoked by way of defence. Things may be different, however, in civil proceedings.

Even at Community level, there are instances where the individual interest orientation may determine the course of legal reasoning in this respect, even where this is not strictly necessary. In the aftermath of the *CIA-Security* judgment,[86] a type of *Schutznorm* requirement has slipped into the discussion on direct effect. In that judgment, the ECJ ruled that national measures on technical standards, which had been enacted in a Member State without respecting the notification requirement pursuant to Directive 83/189/EEC, were inapplicable. The associated question was *who* is allowed to rely on this inapplicability.[87] Does this include a drunken driver who was prosecuted for driving under influence, and who had been tested by means of certain equipment manufactured on the basis of technical standards which had not been notified to the Commission? According to the Dutch Government before the ECJ, and Advocate General Fennely in the *Lemmens* case,[88] only those persons whose interests are intended to be protected by a directive's provisions may invoke those provisions before national courts. Both therefore contended that the invocability of the Directive was reserved to those persons who have an interest in the free movement of goods. Unfortunately, the ECJ did not settle this issue in *Lemmens*. The judgment is particularly obscure on this point, and can be interpreted in different ways. While some read it as evidence of a linkage of invocability to an interest requirement,[89] others find that the Court's judgment is not conclusive in this respect.[90]

An interesting, and related problem may arise where direct effect is equated to the creation of rights, and the conditions for direct effect determine the admissibility of the claim. In Belgium,[91] for instance, when parties seek to vindicate individual rights,[92] the relevant provisions should be directly effective. The *Conseil d'Etat* subordinates the review of the question whether the claim is

---

[86] Case C–194/94, n. 37 above.

[87] Note this is not an issue of standing, but a question of what pleas may validly be submitted.

[88] Case C–226/97, *Criminal proceedings against Johannes Martinus Lemmens* [1998] ECR I–3711; see also Hilson and Downes, n. 17 above, 131 ff., who are also introducing an interest requirement into the concept of direct effect.

[89] Cf. W. van Gerven, n. 13 above, 508; K. Lenaerts, 'Redactionele Signalen' (1998) 46 *Sociaal-Economische Wetgeving*, 269. On the lack of clarity of this judgment see also the comment by R. Streinz, (1999) 39 *Juristische Schulung*, 599–600 and R. Abele, (1998) 9 *Europäisches Zeitschrift für Wirtschaftsrecht*, 571–2.

[90] Cf. T. Koopmans (case note on *Lemmens*), (1999) 47 *Sociaal-Economische Wetgeving*, 338; J. H. Jans *et al.*, *Inleiding tot het Europees Bestuursrecht* (Nijmegen: Ars Aequi Libri, 1999), 56. In my view, the ECJ ruled on the consequences of the violation at issue, i.e. the non-applicability, rather than on the circle of persons who may rely on the Directive. Cf. also S. Prechal, n. 30 above, 1056.

[91] Cf. P. Gilliaux, 'Rapport Belge: Les directives communautaires: effets, efficacité, justitiabilité ' in XVIII congrès FIDE, Stockholm 3–6 juin 1998, Congrès FIDE. 18 (Stockholm: FIDE, 1998).

[92] In the original version: 'requêtes ayant pour objet de préserver ou de mettre en cause des situations subjectives ou indirectement des droits.' Rapport Delge, ibid. 104.

well founded to the preliminary question as to whether the provisions relied upon are unconditional and sufficiently precise. Where, however, an environmental association brings an action, the *Conseil d'Etat* does not seem to require that the provisions relied upon are directly effective. An explanation may be found in the fact that, where an NGO brings a case, it is usually a priori acting in the general interest. Since these type of actions are considered to aim at the maintenance of 'objective legality', and thus to focus on the control of legality as such, they are no longer linked to any individual interest, and the conditions for direct effect, which apply in more individual-oriented cases, are dropped.

C. REMEDIES

The dichotomy between the protection of individual rights and the control of legality (the *effet utile* school of thought) is not only at the root of the debate as to who is entitled to bring an action and the admissibility of pleas. It may also influence eventual outcomes, determine the consequences of a breach, and the types of remedies which may be available. Where the protection of individual rights or direct interests is at stake, any compensation is likely to come in the form of 'traditional' compensation in damages. In actions brought for the protection of a general interest, the appropriate remedy may be different. Injunctions, orders to compel action in conformity with EC law, or to restore the *status quo*, may be more appropriate. For environmental organizations, for instance, compensation often makes little sense. In the first place, they are not suffering any material loss themselves, which is a prerequisite for traditional damages. In the second place, damages may often be a poor alternative for measures securing the immediate protection of the environment. A more useful alternative would be to strengthen the obligation to award interim measures, possibly in combination with another action.[93] Interim safeguard measures correspond with the preventive and precautionary approach to environmental protection.

It is conceivable that measures aimed at increased legal protection along the lines of *Francovich* could be developed so as to include (interim) injunctions alongside the action for damages. The problem remains, however, that as long as liability and injunctions are linked to the issue of infringement of an individual right,[94] and access to interim measures depends on proof that the applicant will personally suffer serious and irreparable damage, these remedies will not necessarily work for directives which seek to protect general environmental interest, as for example in the field of habitat protection.

The Commission's White Paper on Environmental Liability[95] introduces a welcome change in conceptual approaches. By introducing a liability regime

[93] For instance, pending the preliminary procedure, the Lappel Bank (an important area of habitats for wild birds, near to the Port of Sheerness) was allowed to be destroyed.

[94] In general, in systems of administrative law aiming at the protection of individual rights or interests, it is easier to obtain interim measures, provided those rights or interests are imperilled.

[95] COM (2000)66 final, 9 Feb. 2000, discussed in detail by Betlem and Brans, elsewhere in this volume.

which not only covers damage to persons, goods, and soil in case of contaminated sites, but also damage to nature as such, it divorces liability from a right
to damages arising from an individual interest. The focus is no longer
restricted to other people's health or property, but is expanded to damage to
the wider environment, the 'public good'. Moreover, by proposing that the
funds recovered by the plaintiff should be spent on restoring the environment,
the White Paper limits the freedom of the individual concerned, and forces
that any compensation is used to benefit the general interest. It is also proposed that in certain circumstances, NGOs should have the right to apply for
injunctive measures where there exists a risk of significant damage to the
environment.

### D. NEED FOR ALTERNATIVES

Summing up, environmental law is different from other areas of law. The
diffuse interests which environmental law often represents cannot easily be
captured in the language of individual rights. Therefore, the category of environmental rules which may be potentially enforced through the concept of
protection of individual rights is limited.[96] The underlying problem remains
that any thinking in terms of individual rights remains inextricably linked to
the protection of individual interest. Both concepts play an extremely influential role in national systems of judicial protection but, at the same time, they
mark the boundaries. By translating environmental concerns into individual
rights, actions aiming primarily at the protection of environment are sucked
into the tunnel of protection of individual rights and interests. Yet, since for
many of these actions the tunnel is a dead end, the individual rights approach
should not divert attention from the possibilities and need to develop realistic
alternatives for the sake of effective environmental protection.

## VII. Concluding Observations: From Rights to Wrongs?

### A. JUDICIAL CONTROL

If effective protection of the environment cannot be evaluated solely from the
perspective of individual rights, individual interest thinking should perhaps
be set aside altogether, and innovative concepts, based on the notion of public interest, should be developed and made operational. One may, indeed, look
for new solutions within the concept of rights. For instance, Reich has proposed developing a Euro-specific theory of subjective rights, which must not
only go beyond the economic component, but which should also be extended
to collective and diffuse rights, especially in social and ecological matters, and

---

[96] To this one may add that many of the more recent forms of environmental regulation, such
as soft-law instruments, environmental covenants, and negotiated administration, seem unsuitable for the individual-rights-based approach. Yet, also in relation to these forms of regulation,
mechanisms should be developed to secure compliance. See Somsen, n. 12 above.

thus include consumer rights, social rights, ecological rights, and citizen's rights.[97] In the same line lie proposals to widen the scope of domestic tort law so as to include general interests of environmental protection amongst the interests protected by tortuous liability.[98]

We suggest another shift in perspective. An important first step obviously is to accept fully the broader approach to the doctrine of direct effect, including the legality review approach. A proposal which takes this line of thought one stage further has been proposed by Boch.[99] In her view, individuals also have an interest that Member States apply EC law. She suggests that individuals, too, should be regarded as guardians of the Community interest 'in so far as overseeing actions by Member States, ensuring that Member States comply with their Community obligations and fulfil their duties, in turn guarantees that individuals are not deprived of the benefits that would accrue to them if Member States complied with their Community obligations'.[100] By giving a new meaning to the concept of individuals' vigilance, she turns the paradigm from protection of individual Community law rights into one of protection of EC law by individuals. Where individuals bring cases, courts could then approach them as exercising judicial control of discretionary power. Member States will be kept in line 'in the same way as judicial review of administrative action kept the executive under proper control'.[101] This, according to Boch, also has implications for questions of title and standing, since such review does not primarily concentrate on private law rights, but rather on public law wrongs.

The use of a legality review, even in a less ambitious form, implies that private enforcement does not need to be linked to individual rights. In many instances, where a perceived lack of direct effect has been used to deny the application of a Community measure, for example, on account of the discretion left to Member State authorities, the provision at issue may still be treated as justiciable. As already pointed out, this approach might offer another additional but important advantage in that it involves policing the boundaries of Member States or national authorities' discretion in the performance of their functions, and as such could imply that environmental principles, such as the precautionary principle may become at least partially and gradually, justiciable. As Winter points out, courts may gradually concretize vague terms, which often will imply discretion, and at least check 'arbitrary action and core minimal contents'.[102] The tension, discussed above, between the ECJ's approach in *Comitato* and *San Rocco* illustrates this point clearly.

The shift in perspective from the protection of rights to responding adequately to wrongs may also provide a better explanation of those rulings involving purely 'procedural cases', where the failure of national authorities to

---

[97]  Cf. Reich, n. 7 above (in particular at 164).
[98]  See Betlem and Brans, elsewhere in this volume.
[99]  See n. 50 above.              [100] See Boch, n. 45 above, 32.              [101] Ibid. 37.
[102]  See Winter, elsewhere in this volume. Note that Winter discusses these activities from the perspective of 'constructing the right' at issue. In our analysis this is not necessary.

follow a certain procedure as such is sufficient to result in inapplicability of the relevant national rules. Such failures were at issue in several cases concerning environmental impact assessment, and in relation to the notification of technical standards. In *Unilever*[103] the mere 'procedural wrong'[104] of Italy resulted in the harsh sanction of inapplicability, in fact to the detriment of another private firm.

## B. PUBLIC INTEREST LITIGATION

The 'wrongs-perspective' also makes more readily acceptable that the mere breach of the relevant EC law provisions, whether they lay down individual rights or just a standard, or a certain procedure, or where they result in imposing conditions upon others, may result in a very broad circle of persons having standing. The separation from protection of individual rights/interest and the related standing possibilities stimulates measures which should improve national standing rules, or even introduce standing for those who bring actions in the public interest, and who were previously excluded, in particular environmental interest groups.[105]

It is probably a platitude to stress the role environmental groups and NGOs play in the field of environmental protection. At the same time, doubts as to the validity of their claims to assert a role as environmental watchdogs cannot be ruled out.[106] Yet, the same can be said *a fortiori* in relation to private individuals. No doubt there is a serious lack of private interest as driving force behind enforcement of (EC) environmental law. A considerable number of preliminary judgments relating to environmental law are 'market interest driven', in particular relating to issues where environmental standards have curtailed economic activities, etc. Although the individuals' reluctance may to an extent be explained by factors relating to procedural and other limitations, the general impression is that individuals are not eager to litigate for the sake of the environment.[107] In this respect, the White Paper on Environmental Liability contains a number of interesting proposals; in particular the two-tier regime of access to justice, under which public interest groups are given a right to step into the shoes of public authorities, where these are responsible for tackling environmental damage but have not acted. The groups are also allowed to take action in urgent cases where there is need to prevent damage, without waiting whether the state authorities act.[108] It is submitted that such

[103] See n. 35 above.

[104] On purpose we say the mere 'procedural wrong', since it was not clear that, upon substantive analysis, the law at issue would amount to a restriction on the free movement of goods.

[105] See Betlem and Brans, elsewhere in this volume, who point out, that the EU seems to be in a process of granting NGOs and individuals more extensive rights of legal standing. About the choices to be made, their implications, etc., see E. Rehbinder, 'Locus Standi. Community Law and the Case for Harmonization' in H. Somsen (ed.), *Protecting the European Environment* (London: Blackstone Press, 1996), 151.

[106] See Betlem and Brans, elsewhere in this volume.

[107] Cf. on this issue Somsen, n. 12 above (in particular 326 ff.).

[108] Cf. Betlem and Brans, elsewhere in this volume.

a regime should be extended to a situation where there is a private individual with standing, but who does not act for whatever reason.

Another important innovation would be, in our view, the setting up of public but independent environmental watchdogs, a kind of environmental 'defender', which should have the powers to act, if necessary through the courts, if 'their' Member State has not complied with EC environmental law provisions, and could be allowed to be, unlike national administrations in general, rather 'monomaniac' in persecuting the 'wrongs'.

### C. EXTRA-JUDICIAL MEANS OF ENFORCEMENT

There are many extra-judicial means of enforcement of environmental law, including the operation of environmental complaints and investigations procedures within Member States, and bodies such as an environmental ombudsman. Although these are, in practical terms, important alternatives, we are not addressing any of these methods except one. In our view, greater attention could and should be paid to the role of 'spotlighting' and related 'sunshine' methods of ensuring effective enforcement of environmental law. One of the most well-known and widely commented upon approaches to 'spotlighting' is the Citizens Submission Process, set up in the context of the side agreement on environment cooperation (NAAEC) to the North American Free Trade Agreement (NAFTA).[109] The NAAEC has created a Commission for Environmental Cooperation (CEC) to advance its objectives. The CEC has a tripartite structure. It is governed by a Council, and has a permanent Secretariat. The Council is advised by a Joint Public Advisory Committee (JPAC) comprised of fifteen citizens, five from each of the three countries. The CEC itself carries out a wide range of activities with a view to realizing the lengthy menu of objectives set out in Article 1 of the NAAEC. A significant CEC responsibility is to implement a 'citizen submission' process, in which citizens may file 'submissions', asserting that any of the three signatory countries is not enforcing its environmental laws effectively. To quote from the CEC's home page:

The Citizen Submissions on Enforcement Matters mechanism enables the public to play an active whistle-blower role when a government appears to be failing to enforce its environmental laws effectively. Members of the public trigger the process by submitting to NACEC a claim alleging such a failure on the part of any of the NAFTA partners. Following a review of the submission, NACEC may investigate the matter and publish a factual record of its findings, subject to approval by the NACEC Council.[110]

Articles 14 and 15 of the NAAEC establish a citizen submission process through which NGOs and individuals can file a submission to the CEC. The comparatively straightforward procedures governing such submissions are set

[109] North American Free Trade Agreement (NAFTA) (signed at Washington, DC., 8 Dec. 1992), (1993) 32 *International Legal Materials*, 296.

[110] For further information on all aspects of the citizens submission process, the role of the Council, and a registry of submissions filed, see the home page of the CEC published on the Internet at: http://www.cec.org.

out in Article 14(1) NAAEC, and have been further developed by Guidelines adopted by the Council in 1995 and revised in 1999. While it is beyond the scope of this article to explore the nature of this innovative procedure in any great detail, it is worth noting that its primary aim is to ensure the effective enforcement of environmental laws. As such, any NGO or individual can file a submission alleging that one of the three NAFTA parties has failed to enforce their national rules on environmental protection. The concept of failure has been recognized to include not only violations by national administrations of existing legislation and related regulations and relevant statutory requirements, but also inaction such as inadequate inspection procedures or prosecution-related efforts.

No particular standing requirements attend the procedures with regard to these citizens' submissions. The submitter must merely provide sufficient information to identify the measure which is not being properly enforced, and such evidence should be focused on the relevant acts or omissions. The CEC has established at an early stage that the production of sufficient information should not place an undue burden on submitters, and that this requirement, as laid down in Article 14(1) NAAEC, should be given a liberal interpretation. If the submission is determined to satisfy a number of criteria and factors (identified in paragraphs 1 and 2 of Article 14), a response will be requested from the Party named in the submission. In light of that response, the Commission may proceed with the development of a factual record on the matter, as provided by Article 15.

A factual record outlines, in as objective a manner as possible, the history of the issue, the obligations of the Party under the law in question, the actions of the Party in fulfilling those obligations, and the facts relevant to the assertions made in the submission of a failure to enforce environmental law effectively. Its development is a process that can take months and has, in some cases, taken over a year. Once complete, the Council may, by a two-thirds vote, make the final factual record publicly available.

A factual record provides information regarding enforcement practices that may prove useful to governments, and to the submitters and other members of the interested public. It should be observed that the citizens' submission process does not involve the imposition of any specific sanctions. Its aim, through the production of the factual record, is solely to enhance compliance through casting a 'spotlight' on failure to enforce national environmental protection regulations. The CEC may take upon itself in developing the factual record the responsibility to commission scientific and technical reports, to seek expert opinions as well as to engage in its own research.[111] Although originally criticized as a weak palliative to the concerns of those who feared that environmental protection would be threatened by the singular focus of

---

[111] Some 29 submissions had been received by the end of 2000, of which 18 have been closed, and 2 factual records have been prepared and made public (SEM-96–001 and SEM–97–001) while the remainder are still pending. Full details are available on the CEC home page, n. 110 above.

the NAFTA itself on free trade goals, the citizens' submission process is now welcomed as a creative initiative, which not only enhances domestic enforcement through the promotion of compliance, but contributes to the emergence of a more global civil society through the creation of new mechanisms, which enhance the interaction of citizens with governments and others on the North American continent.[112]

### D. BETTER INPUT IN REFASHIONED PROCEDURES

Returning to Europe, and as has been pointed out above, apart from limited access of environmental groups and some 'altruistic' individuals, there are often no appropriate forms of action or remedies for environmental problems, which, for instance, do justice to preventive and precautionary principles. The national legal systems and court procedures are still designed to protect economic interests (property rights, rights to free enterprise) or personal interests, related to the person such as health, freedom of expression, non-discrimination, and comparable types of personal integrity rights. This begs the question in how far the remedies and procedures available should be refashioned to reflect creative initiatives such as the citizens' submission procedure. Betlem and Brans have pointed to a number of EC directives which, in other areas, either introduce a specific standard of action, or set standards to the already available ones.[113] Their suggestion should, in our view, be further explored, while taking into account the 'wrongs-character' of non-compliance with EC environmental law.

Another aspect that merits more attention is, in our view, the possibility of wider input into judicial procedures. Environmental litigation often entails an individual or private party against public authorities or, in some cases, two opposed individuals or parties. The parties involved will litigate with the primary aim of protecting their own rights and interests. If one of the parties is an idealistic individual or environmental interest group, which pursues primarily the general environmental interest, costly studies may be required to adduce evidence to support their contentions. Yet the impact of the resulting judgment may be very broad, in the sense that it may contribute to the general interest in environmental protection. In such circumstances, the courts should be informed sufficiently about all the relevant dimensions and the possible implications of their judgment. In this respect, their decision should not depend on information which the parties submit. Procedural openings for *amicus curiae* briefs, the introduction of a right to be heard in such a procedure involving 'general environmental interests' may be important steps forward. And last but not least: the involvement of EC lawyers who are familiar with the pitfalls of the transnational character of Community law, and who do

---

[112] For a good introduction to and thorough evaluation of the procedure, see, D. L. Markell, 'The Commission for Environmental Co-operation's Citizen Submission Process' (2000) 12 *Georgetown International Environmental Law Review*, 545–74.

[113] See in this volume: Betlem and Brans.

not solely argue the case at hand on the basis of their national law background, may be a necessary condition to ensure the proper translation of the ECJ's rulings into national law. In this way, debacles such as *Comitato* could be avoided.

# EC Competition Law and Environmental Protection: Conflict or Compatibility?

DAMIEN GERADIN*

## I. Introduction

This chapter discusses the relationship between two key policies of the European Community (EC): competition policy and environmental policy.

From the very beginning, competition policy has of been one of the EC's core policies. Indeed, the original Treaty of Rome contained several provisions designed to protect competition in the Common Market.[1] These provisions seek to prohibit restrictive agreements between competitors (Article 81 EC), abuse of a dominant position (Article 82 EC), ensure the application of competition law principles to public undertakings and undertakings holding special or exclusive rights (Article 86 EC), and prevent the granting of illegal state aids (Articles 87–9 EC). The objectives of EC competition policy are well known: first, to promote economic efficiency through the maintenance of a competitive market structure and, second, to promote the creation of an integrated European market by preventing certain forms of restrictive trade behaviour.[2]

By contrast, environmental protection was not even mentioned in the Treaty of Rome.[3] In the aftermath of the Second World War, the drafters of the Treaty were preoccupied more with economic, rather than environmental or social protection concerns. From the beginning of the 1970s, however, the EC started to intervene in environmental policy so as to harmonize product and process standards.[4] The EC authorities were concerned that variety in standards would

---

* Associate Professor, University of Liège, and Professor, College of Europe, Bruges, Belgium. This article was originally prepared for the Brodies lecture at the University of Edinburgh on 18 Feb. 2000.

[1] On EC competition policy in general, see V. Rose (ed.), *Bellamy and Child Common Market Law of Competition* (London: Sweet & Maxwell, 1993).

[2] S. Bishop and M. Walker, *The Economics of EC Competition Law* (London: Sweet & Maxwell, 1999), 3.

[3] See C. Blumann, 'Historique de la Politique Communautaire de l'Environnement' in J. Dutheil de la Rochère (ed.), *Le Droit Communautaire de l'Environnement: Mise en Oeuvre et Perspectives* (Paris: La Documentation Française, 1998), 17.

[4] For examples of directives harmonizing product standards, see Council Dir. 70/220/EEC on Measures to be Taken against Air Pollution by Gases from Positive-Ignition Engines of Motor Vehicles [1970] OJ L76/1; Council Dir. 85/210/EEC on Lead Content of Petrol [1985] OJ L96/25. For an example of a directive harmonizing process standards, see Council Dir. 89/428/EEC on Procedures for Harmonizing the Programmes for the Reduction and Eventual Elimination of Pollution Caused by Waste from the Titanium Dioxide Industry [1989] OJ L201/59.

create barriers to trade or distortions of competition between Member States.[5] Community action in this field thus was initially predominantly motivated by economic reasons.

A turning point was the adoption of the Single European Act (SEA) in 1987.[6] The SEA increased the importance and autonomy of Community action in the field of the environment by inserting a specific legal basis in the Treaty: Article 130s (now Article 175 EC). The SEA also introduced a principle pursuant to which '[e]nvironmental protection requirements shall be a component of the Community's other policies'. This principle, which was criticized for its vagueness, was successively modified by the Maastricht[7] and Amsterdam Treaties.[8] Article 6 EC, as inserted by the Amsterdam Treaty, provides that 'Environmental Protection requirements must be integrated into the definition and implementation of the Community policies and activities referred to in Article 3, in particular with a view to promoting sustainable development.' This principle of integration takes on particular significance in the context of the relationship between environmental policy and other Community policies, such as competition policy. The question arises whether this principle implies that environmental protection should take precedence over other EC policies, and thus that competition rules and principles should in no case lead to restrictions on environmental protection measures.

In its XXIIIrd Competition Report, the European Commission dealt with that question.[9] At the time, the Commission was confronted with several cases cutting across its competition and environmental protection policies. In the report, the Commission recognizes that competition policy, like any other EC policy, must take the environmental dimension into account. However, the Commission denies the existence of any fundamental conflict between these Community policies. On the contrary, it argues that competition policy has a very important role to play for the realization of environmental protection objectives. Pursuant to the polluter-pays principle, undertakings must internalize environmental costs generated by their activities.[10] Since market pressure

---

[5] See D. Geradin, 'Trade and Environmental Protection: Community Harmonization and National Environmental Standards' (1994) 13 *Yearbook of European Law*, 162 ff.

[6] For a discussion of the impact of the Single European Act on environmental policy, see D. Vandermeersch, 'The Single European Act and the Environmental Policy of the European Community' (1987) 12 *European Law Review*, 407; L. Krämer, 'The Single European Act and Environment Protection: Reflections on Several New Provisions Community Law' (1987) 24 *Common Market Law Review*, 659.

[7] For a discussion of the impact of the Maastricht Treaty on environmental policy, see D. Wilkinson, 'Maastricht and the Environment: The Implications for the EC's Environmental Policy of the Treaty on European Union' (1994) 6 *Journal of Environmental Law*, 221.

[8] For a discussion of the impact of the Amsterdam Treaty on environmental policy, see S. Bär and R. A. Krämer, 'European Environmental Policy after Maastricht' (1998) 10 *Journal of Environmental Law*, 315; G. Van Calster and K. Deketeleare, 'Amsterdam, the IGC and the EU Treaty' (1998) 7 *European Environmental Law Review*, 12.

[9] See points 164–5 of the report.

[10] The principle, which is now found in Art. 174(2) EC, was originally introduced by the OECD in 1972. See Council Rec. on Guiding Principles Concerning International Economic Aspects on Environmental Policies, OECD, Doc. C(72)128, 26 May 1972 (reprinted in OECD (ed.), *Polluter Pays Principle: Definition, Analysis, Implementation* (Paris: OECD, 1975), 11. The 'polluter pays

forces undertakings to reduce costs, competition is one of the mechanisms which will prompt undertakings to reduce emissions, by using less polluting production and disposal techniques. According to the Commission, the effectiveness of environmental protection measures would be increased, and not undermined, by competition and market mechanisms.

Experience, however, reveals that the relationship between competition and environmental protection is not as straightforward as presented by the Commission,[11] but indeed can be a source of conflict.[12] Four sources of tension can easily be identified.

A first source of conflict stems from the increased use of environmental agreements.[13] The past few years have witnessed the adoption of a large number of agreements between private undertakings *inter se*, or between private undertakings and public authorities, to achieve environmental protection goals. This flurry of agreements may be explained with reference to different factors. First, from the point of view of producers, the increasing stringency of environmental rules and the spiralling costs associated with their implementation, provide a strong incentive to pool resources to develop less polluting technologies and cleaner products.

Often, it may also be more attractive for undertakings in a specific sector to self-regulate their practices, than to wait until government imposes binding legislation.[14] Moreover, from the perspective of public authorities, resort to

principle' is generally interpreted as a non-subsidization principle, meaning the governments should not as a general principle grant subsidies to their companies for pollution-control purposes.

[11] On the relationship between competition policy and environmental protection, see generally R. Jacobs, 'EEC Competition Law and the Protection of the Environment' (1993) 20 *Legal Issues of European Integration*, 2, 37; T. Portwood, *Competition Law and the Environment* (London: Cameron & May, 1994); F. Vogelaar, 'Towards an Improved Integration of EC Environmental Policy and EC Competition Policy: An Interim Report' in B. Hawk (ed.), *International Antitrust Law and Policy 1994* (The Hague: Kluwer Law International, 1995), 552; L. Gyselen, 'The Emerging Interface between Competition Policy and Environmental Policy in the EC' in J. Cameron *et al.* (eds.), *Trade and the Environment: The Search for Balance* (London: Cameron & May, 1994), 250; L. Idot, 'Environnement et Droit Communautaire de la Concurrence' (1995) 24 *La Semaine Juridique*, 257; D. Vandermeersch, 'The Interaction between Environmental Policy and EC Competition Law' in D. Geradin (ed.), *Recent Developments in European Environmental Law* (The Hague: Kluwer Law International, 1997), 79; H. Vedder, 'Competition Law and the Use of Environmental Agreements' in E. W. Orts and K. Deketelaere (eds.), *Environmental Contracts: Comparative Approaches to Regulatory Innovation in the United States and Europe* (The Hague: Kluwer Law International, 2001).

[12] See Competition Policy and Environment, OECD/GD(96)22, 1996, published on the Internet at: http://www.oecd.org//daf/clp/ Roundtables/ENVR00.HTM.

[13] For a discussion of the different types of environmental agreements see Communication from the Commission to the Council and the European Parliament on Environmental Agreements, COM(96)561 final, 27 Nov. 1996. See also R. Khalastchi and H. Ward, 'New Instruments for Sustainability: An Assessment of Environmental Agreements under Community Law' (1998) 10 *Journal of Environmental Law*, 257; J. Verschuuren, 'EC Environmental Law and Self-Regulation in the Member States: In Search for a Legislative Framework' (2000) 1 *Yearbook of European Environmental Law*, 103; G. Van Calster and K. Deketelaere, 'The Use of Environmental Agreements in the European Community's Environmental Policy' in Deketelaere and Orts (eds.), n. 11 above.

[14] J. Jans, *European Environmental Law* (The Hague: Kluwer Law International, 1995), 238.

environmental agreements is explained by the fact that the effectiveness of traditional regulatory instruments is increasingly questioned,[15] as well as more generally by the tendency to opt for flexible solutions in which industry plays a proactive role.[16] Since such agreements involve some degree of cooperation or a coordination of behaviour between actual or potential competitors, they might, however, present serious risks from the perspective of competition. As will be seen, such agreements may facilitate collusion between competitors, or allow them to erect barriers against entry of new operators on the market.

A second source of tension may stem from the discipline imposed by Article 82 EC on the behaviour of undertakings carrying out environmental activities, and which hold a dominant position (because they have large market shares or are in a monopolistic position). For instance, many waste collection/ recycling systems are organized on a collective basis and, thus, face little or no competition.[17] Article 82 EC prevents such undertakings from abusing their market power by fixing excessive or predatory prices, adopting lax management practices, or imposing discriminatory conditions to consumers. In general, the discipline imposed by Article 82 EC on such undertakings should benefit the environment. Indeed, it is in the interest of environmental protection that waste producers have access to reasonably priced and efficient waste-collection, recycling, and disposal services. A tension could occur between Article 82 EC and environmental protection, however, if this provision were to be interpreted as preventing dominant undertakings from requiring suppliers to supply products that meet certain environmental criteria. Another interesting question is whether an infrastructure owned by a dominant undertaking (for example a pool of reusable bottles) which is essential to one or several of its competitor(s) on an upstream market (for example undertakings selling beverages) must be considered an 'essential facility', access to which must be granted in exchange for adequate compensation.

A third controversy relates to the granting by public authorities of special or exclusive rights to undertakings entrusted with the accomplishment of environmental protection duties.[18] Such undertakings may be granted, for instance,

---

[15] See E. Rehbinder, Jean Monnet Chair Paper RSC 97/45, *Environmental Agreements: A New Instrument for Environmental Policy* (Florence: European University Institute, 1997).

[16] For instance, the Commission justified its strategy of negotiating agreements with car manufacturers' associations to reduce $CO_2$ emissions on the ground that such agreements 'as compared to legislation, allowed taking the necessary action in the quickest way possible. At the same time, it provides great flexibility to the automobile manufacturers with regard to achievement of the targets.' See Commission's Press Release IP/00/381, published on the Internet at: http://www.europa.eu.int (RAPID database).

[17] In recent years, waste collection/recycling schemes have been set up as responses to regulations that render producers or distributors responsible for the packaging waste they place on the market. The best-known scheme is the 'Green Dot' system that was set up in Germany in the early 1990s. Comparable systems now exist in most Member States in response to Dir. 94/62/EC on Packaging and Packaging Waste [1994] OJ L365/10.

[18] It is generally agreed that 'exclusive rights' exist where a single undertaking has been granted the right to carry out a certain activity throughout the territory. See, e.g., Case C–323/93, *Société Civile Agricole du Centre d'Insémination de la Crespelle* v. *Coopérative d'Elevage et d'Insémination*

exclusive rights to collect, sort, and eliminate or recycle certain categories of waste. The granting of exclusive rights is sometimes justified by considerable economies of scale, rendering one operator more efficient than two or several operators. Such rights may also be justified as counterpart for the accomplishment of public service tasks.[19] From the perspective of competition, special or exclusive rights are problematic, since they lead to the creation of monopolies or quasi-monopolies, whose compatibility with the rules of the Treaty may be doubtful.

The granting of state aids for environmental protection represents a fourth source of tension between competition and environmental protection policies. Such aids indeed may introduce distortions of competition by unduly assisting subsidized undertakings. Environmental state aids have been subject to Commission scrutiny for a long time. As early as 1974, the Commission adopted guidelines designed to control the granting of state aids for environmental protection reasons.[20] These guidelines, which allowed the use of environmental state aids for a limited number of years, were prolonged on several occasions. A new set of guidelines was adopted in 1994.[21]

In this chapter, I will attempt to review these areas of conflict between competition and environmental protection. First, I will examine the compatibility of EC competition rules with environmental agreements (Section II). Section III focuses on certain behaviour of dominant undertakings carrying out environmental activities. Exclusive rights granted to undertakings entrusted with environmental protection tasks is the subject of analysis in Section IV. Finally, state aids granted for environmental protection are examined in Section V. This paper will draw a short conclusion in which it is argued that the Commission, entrusted with the application of competition rules, generally has succeeded in finding a balance between environmental protection and competition policy objectives.

## II. Environmental Agreements in Light of Article 81 EC

As noted, environmental agreements represent an increasingly important tool for environmental policy. They may take different forms. For instance, such

---

*Artificielle du Département de la Mayenne* [1994] ECR I–5077. By contrast, 'special rights' exist when the right to carry out a certain activity throughout a territory has been granted to a limited number of undertakings. See Case C–302/94, *The Queen v. Secretary of State for Trade and Industry, ex p. British Telecommunications plc.* [1996] ECR I–6417. See generally: F. Blum and A. Logue, *State Monopolies Under EC Law* (Chichester: John Wiley & Sons, 1998), 9.

[19] Such public service obligations will, for instance, comprise the obligation to provide the service over the entirety of a given territory, without interruption, and at a non-discriminatory and affordable price. See Communication from the Commission—Services of General Interest in Europe, COM(96)443 final, 11 Sept. 1996.

[20] Fourth Competition Report (1974), paras. 175 ff.

[21] Commission Guidelines on State Aid for Environmental Protection [1994] OJ C72/3. Since the submission of this chapter, these have been replaced by Commission Guidelines on State Aid for Environmental Protection, [2001] OJ L10/30.

agreements may be adopted at the regional, national, or Community level, compulsory or merely optional, horizontal (concluded by undertakings situated at the same level in the production or distribution chain) or vertical (concluded between undertakings situated at different levels in the production or distribution chain), have general or specific objectives, and, finally, involve the participation of public authorities or not.[22]

In spite of their diversity, these agreements share the common characteristic of raising competition law problems. First, they may amount to restrictive practices prohibited by Article 81(1) EC (Section A). When such agreements are imposed or encouraged by public authorities, they may also be contrary to Article 81 EC read in conjunction with Articles 3(g) and 10 EC (Section B).

### A. COMPATIBILITY OF ENVIRONMENTAL AGREEMENTS WITH ARTICLE 81 EC

#### i. Article 81(1) EC: the Prohibition of Restrictive Practices

Article 81(1) EC provides that all agreements between undertakings which may affect trade between Member States and which have as their object or effect the prevention, restriction, or distortion of competition are incompatible with the Common Market.[23] Pursuant to Article 81(2) EC such agreements are automatically void.

Article 81(1) EC has been interpreted broadly, and may apply to environmental agreements that have a restrictive impact on competition. As indicated by the Commission in its XXIInd Competition Report, the fact that an agreement is justified by environmental protection reasons does not rule out the application of this provision.[24] Thus, it appears that Article 81(1) EC can be applied to a variety of environmental agreements, including:

— agreements aiming at the development of common technical standards, or labels certifying conformity of labelled products with certain environmental norms;[25]

— agreements aiming at the joint development (for instance through the creation of joint ventures or cooperation agreements) of new, less polluting production methods or products;[26]

— agreements pursuant to which competitors agree to reduce by a certain margin, energy consumption of their products;[27]

— agreements between undertakings pursuant to which they decide to set up common waste-collection and recycling schemes;[28] and,

---

[22] See Rehbinder, n. 15 above.

[23] For an analysis of Art. 81(1)EC, see Rose, n. 1 above, paras. 2.001.

[24] Point 77 of the report.

[25] See e.g. Commission Decision 82/731/EEC, *Navewa-Anseau* [1982] OJ L167/39.

[26] See e.g. Commission Decision 94/986/EC, *Philips-Osram* [1994] OJ L378/37; Commission Decision 88/541/EEC, *BBC Brown Boveri* [1988] OJ L301/68; Commission Decision 88/669/EEC, *Carbon Gas Technologie* [1983] OJ L376/17.

[27] See EACEM; XXVIIIth Competition Report (1998), para. 130.

[28] See Valpack; XXVIIIth Competition Report (1998), paras. 133–4.

— agreements in which competitors agree to pass on to consumers the costs of compliance with certain environmental measures through a uniform price increase.[29]

While such agreements, when concluded for genuine environmental reasons, may not have as their object a restraint of competition, they may nevertheless produce such effects.[30] For instance, agreements by which undertakings develop conformity labels may have the effect of rendering imports of foreign products more difficult. Similarly, agreements on technical standards may prevent parties from selling differentiated products, or impede entry of new competitors using innovative technologies.[31]

### ii. Article 81(3) EC: Exemptions to the Prohibition

The prohibition of Article 81(1) EC is not absolute. Article 81(3) EC authorizes the Commission to exempt agreements whose advantages for the realization of the internal market would outweigh the negative impact they may have on competition. Pursuant to Article 81(3) EC, a restrictive agreement may benefit from an exemption when four conditions are fulfilled. The agreement must: (i) contribute to improving the production or distribution of goods or to promote technical or economic progress, while (ii) allowing consumers a fair share of the resulting benefit (positive conditions). It cannot, however: (iii) impose on the undertakings concerned restrictions that are not indispensable to achieve the above objectives, and (iv) afford such undertakings the possibility of eliminating competition in respect of a substantial part of the products in question (negative conditions).[32]

Environmental protection does not figure among the positive conditions, allowing the granting of an exemption. In its practice, however, the Commission has considered that environmental protection was one of the factors contributing to 'technical or economic progress'. In the *Assurpol* decision, which concerned a reinsurance agreement for covering certain environmental risks, the Commission considered that this agreement facilitated 'the introduction of risk prevention measures which lead to the development of industrial production techniques less hazardous to the environment and

---

[29] See VOTOB; XXIInd Competition Report (1992), para. 177.

[30] Environmental agreements may also have a restrictive effect on trade between Member States in breach of Art. 28 EC. Trade-related aspects will not be covered in this chapter. For a discussion on such aspects, see Khalastchi and Ward, n. 13 above, 275 ff.

[31] On the compatibility of agreements on technical standards with Art. 81(1), see Rose, n. 1 above, paras. 4-047 ff.

[32] Some authors have suggested the introduction of the principle of integration in the Treaty has had the effect of adding a third negative condition to Art. 81(3) EC pursuant to which no agreement can be exempted unless it is proved it has no negative impact on the environment. See Jacobs, n. 11 above. In addition to the fact that such a test would be extremely difficult to apply in practice (it would require an environmental impact assessment of all notified agreements), it seems more logical to integrate this dimension in the analysis of proportionality which, as will be seen below, Art. 81(3) EC requires.

conducive to technical and economic progress'.[33] This flexible interpretation of the concept of 'technical and economic progress', which takes into account environmental considerations, appears to be in conformity with the principle of integration found in Article 6 EC.[34]

Similarly, the Commission has taken environmental considerations into account in its assessment of whether consumers have obtained a fair share of the benefits resulting from the agreement. An illustration is found in the *Exxon/Shell* decision, which concerned a set of agreements between Exxon and Shell relating to the establishment of a joint venture specializing in the production of linear low-density polyethylene (LLDPE) and high-density polyethylene (HDPE).[35] In considering whether this agreement would allow a fair share of its benefits to benefit consumers, the Commission observed that the creation of the production joint venture would permit a reduction in the use of raw materials and plastic waste, and the avoidance of certain environmental risks, something which 'will be perceived as beneficial by many customers at a time when the limitation of natural resources and threats to the environment are of increasing public concern'.[36]

The Commission, however, has been generally strict in its interpretation of the requirement of 'necessity' that is imposed by Article 81(3) EC. The Commission summarized its position in its XXIIIrd Competition Report, in which it indicated that it 'will examine carefully all agreements between companies, to see if they are *indispensable* to attain environmental objectives'.[37] The Commission also indicated that in its analysis of individual cases, it will 'have to weigh the restrictions of competition in the agreement against the environmental objectives that the agreement will help to attain, in order to determine whether, under the *proportionality analysis*, it can approve the agreement'.[38]

### iii. Practice of the Commission

We will now briefly examine several Article 81 EC decisions dealing with environmental agreements. The objective of this section is to illustrate the

---

[33] See Commission Decision 92/96/EC, *Assurpol* [1992] OJ L37/16, para. 38. Other Commission decisions tend to support this interpretation. See Commission Decision 88/541/EC, n. 26 above (where the Commission indicated, in considering whether a cooperation agreement between BBC Brown Boveri and NGK regarding the development of high-performance batteries primarily intended for use in electrically driven vehicles, that 'an electrically driven vehicle causes no damage to the environment through harmful exhaust emissions or loud engine noise. There is therefore much to be said for the cooperation agreement in terms of improvement of the quality of life of consumers through the development of batteries for vehicles'). See Commission Decision 83/669/EC, n. 26 above (where the Commission exempted an agreement between a number of German companies aimed at developing a process of coal gasification. The fact that the process 'was less harmful to the environment than direct combustion of coal' was one of the factors taken into account by the Commission to decide that the agreement contributed to the promotion of technical and economic progress).

[34] A. Ziegler, *Trade and Environmental Law in the European Community* (Oxford: Clarendon Press, 1996), 112.

[35] Commission Decision 94/322/EC, *Exxon/Shell* [1994] OJ L144/20.

[36] Commission Decision 94/322/EC, n. 35 above, para. 81.

[37] XXIIIrd Competition Report (1993), para. 170.             [38] Ibid.

Commission's attempts to balance competition law principles with environmental protection objectives rather than to provide an exhaustive review of the Commission's decisional practice.

In *Anseau-Navewa*, the Belgian manufacturers and sole importers of washing-machines and dishwashers had adopted an agreement with the national association of water-supply companies (Anseau), seeking to make compulsory the attachment of a conformity label to washing-machines and dishwashers intended for the Belgian market. Such labels indicate that products conform to the general safety requirements laid down by water companies for the avoidance of contamination of publicly supplied drinking water.[39] The official purpose of the agreement was thus 'to prevent, in the interest of public health, any deterioration of the water supplied due to contamination or pollution, particularly when washing-machines or dishwashers are connected to the drinking-water supply'.[40]

The Commission declared this agreement incompatible with Article 81 EC. It considered the agreement discriminatory in essence, since only manufacturers or sole importers could obtain the label from Anseau. The existence of such discrimination suggested that, in addition to the objectives of preventing water contamination and reducing compliance costs, by preventing parallel imports, the system put in place sought to prevent entry on the Belgian market. The Commission adopted a negative decision, and imposed a fine on the parties to the agreement.

In *VOTOB*, an association of undertakings offering tank storage facilities to third parties in the Netherlands (VOTOB) decided to increase prices charged by its members to customers by a uniform, fixed amount called 'environmental charge'.[41] This uniform charge was to cover the costs of investments required to reduce vapour emissions from members' storage tanks. The VOTOB decision aimed to implement an agreement concluded with the Dutch Government to improve environmental standards.

The Commission objected to the charge as being incompatible with Article 81 EC for several reasons. First, because it was a fixed charge, all members were required to apply it, regardless of their circumstances. Where a price or an element of the price is fixed, competition on that price element obviously is excluded. By fixing the charge, VOTOB members had few incentives to invest efficiently. Second, due to the uniform character of the charge, differences amongst members' individual circumstances were ignored. The Commission argued that, absent the VOTOB agreement, each individual member could have calculated the necessary investment, decided whether to meet it from its own profit or to pass it on the customers. This then would have been decided by the companies autonomously, having regard to prevailing market conditions and according to their own competitive conditions.

The Commission insisted that it does not oppose the passing on to customers of 'polluter pays' investment costs, since it makes them more aware of

---

[39] See Commission Decision 82/731/EEC, n. 25 above.     [40] Ibid., para. 6.
[41] XXIInd Competition Report (1992), paras. 177–86.

environmental problems and their implications. However, customers should not be prevented from challenging price increases and shopping around for the smallest increase.

In *VOTOB*, the Commission sought to protect two well-recognized benefits of free, unimpeded competition between firms: efficiency (competitive pressures inducing firms to make more efficient investments) and consumer benefits (competition giving customers the opportunity to bargain with a view to obtaining the lowest possible price or, in the present case, the lowest possible price increase).

*Oliebranches Faelleråd* concerned the decision by a Danish association of oil companies to create an 'Environmental Pool' to finance the clean-up of polluted petrol station sites.[42] This Pool would be financed by a charge payable on oil sales by participating companies. Under the Pool's rules, whenever the Danish authorities ordered the clean-up of a polluted petrol station, and the owner of the station does not have the necessary funds to pay for the clean-up, the Pool would pay for the clean-up, provided that the site would be closed after the end of the operations. If the site owner wants to reopen the station within ten years after the clean-up, it must reimburse the Pool the clean-up costs, and also pay an additional sum of DKR250,000 (33,616 euro). This sum aimed to prevent speculative applications to the Pool.

The Commission took the view that the restrictions regarding the reopening of a station were contrary to competition rules. Apparently, the Commission was concerned that the above system would be used to regulate aspects that are unrelated to environmental protection, such as the number of stations on the market. The Commission was also concerned that the system would be operated in such as way as to encourage independent station operators to withdraw from the market. Under Commission pressure, the Pool's rules were amended so as to abolish the DKR250,000 reopening penalty. The only obligations currently imposed on station owners wishing to continue operations are to reimburse the Pool for administration and clean-up costs and interests, to take out adequate insurance covering the risk of future pollution, and to notify the Pool that they have such an insurance.

*EUCAR* and *ACEA* are recent cases, which relate to efforts undertaken by automobile manufacturers to reduce nuisances created by vehicles they place on the market.

In *EUCAR*, the Commission adopted a favourable decision on a cooperation agreement signed between Europe's leading motor manufacturers, which is designed to stimulate research within the motor industry, particularly on environmental issues.[43] Most of the projects that will be developed involve experimental research on, for example, limiting noise or exhaust emissions caused by automobiles. The results obtained from this research may not be directly usable for any specific type of vehicle. The Commission therefore took

---

[42] XXIVth Competition Report (1994), 368.    [43] Commission, n. 27 above, para. 131.

the view that the research was at the pre-competitive stage, and that the agreements did not infringe Community law.

The second decision concerns the commitment made by the Association of European Automobile Manufacturers (ACEA) on behalf of its members to reduce $CO_2$ emissions from new passenger cars by a target of 25 per cent by 2008.[44] The Commission took the view that this agreement did not infringe competition rules. Pursuant to the agreement, ACEA determines an average reduction target for all its members, but each of them is free to set its own level, which will encourage them to develop and introduce new $CO_2$-efficient technologies independently and in competition with one another. Accordingly, the Commission considered that ACEA's agreement does not constitute a restriction on competition and is not caught by Article 81(1) EC.

Both agreements were accepted by the Commission, because they would not prevent manufacturers developing their vehicles independently. In the author's opinion, however, these agreements are not free from risks from the perspective of competition policy. The second agreement, in particular, over time will inevitably lead to a significant degree of cooperation between market participants. The 25 per cent cut in emissions indeed does not apply to individual manufacturers, but to the industry as a whole. Unless all manufacturers unilaterally improve their vehicles' fuel efficiency, they will have to negotiate between themselves, and probably bargain hard, how to meet the 25 per cent target. Such negotiations over a highly sensitive issue could provide a fertile ground for collusive behaviour. Moreover, it could be argued that the existence of a bundle of agreements designed to control or reduce $CO_2$ emissions from automobiles (the EUCAR and ACEA agreements, as well as other present or future agreements in this field) could strengthen the anti-competitive effect of each individual agreement.[45]

In fact, the analysis of the Commission was probably influenced by its desire to achieve a quick and flexible solution to the problem of emission reductions.[46] Experience shows that the control of vehicle emissions is an area where the negotiation of EC legislation is particularly difficult due to competing national interests.[47] Hence, the Commission decided that a voluntary agreement was the best approach to obtain rapid results. Competitiveness may also have played a role. The European automobile industry is facing tough competition from third-country producers. This may help to understand why the Commission judged positively agreements that may help producers to reduce, or at least share, the costs of emission reductions.[48]

[44] Ibid., para. 132. See also the Commission's Press Release IP/98/865, published on the Internet at: http://www.europa.eu.int (RAPID database).

[45] On this aspect, see Commission Decision 94/594/EC, *ACI* [1994] OJ L224/28, paras 37–42.

[46] See the Commission's declaration in Press Release IP/00/381, n. 16 above.

[47] See O. Lomas, 'Environmental Protection, Economic Conflict and the European Community' (1988) 33 *McGill Law Journal*, 506.

[48] On the other hand, in some areas, the Commission has not hesitated to propose environmental measures that will impose heavy costs on automobile manufacturers. See, e.g., the Commission's proposal for a Council Directive on End of Life Vehicles, COM(97)358, 9 July 1997 (amended by COM(99)176, 28 Apr. 1999) and M. Onida, 'Challenges and Opportunities in EC

The *Valpak* case concerned the membership agreements of Valpak, an industry-led scheme operating in the UK set up to discharge packaging waste recovery and recycling obligations of its members.[49] The legal framework set up in the UK to implement Directive 94/62 EC on Packaging and Packaging Waste provides scope for competition in the framework of these compliance schemes. While Valpak is currently the largest compliance scheme operating in the United Kingdom, other schemes exist with which Valpack could enter into competition.

The Commission considered that Valpak's membership agreements restricted competition within the meaning of Article 81(1) EC, because they obliged businesses wishing to join the scheme to transfer the totality of their obligations in all packaging materials. For the Commission, this 'all or nothing' approach restricts the extent to which Valpak and other schemes will be able to compete against one another on a substance-specific basis. The Commission, however, considered that the agreements could benefit from an Article 81(3) EC exemption. In the short term, an 'all or nothing' approach was necessary if schemes such as Valpak were to succeed in securing sufficient funding to allow the necessary investment to meet the collection and recycling obligations of their members. The Commission, however, indicated that it reserved the right to re-examine the case after three years.

This summary allows us to draw some conclusions regarding the way the Commission attempts to reconcile competition principles with environmental objectives in its treatment of environmental agreements.

First, it should be observed that the Commission will not tolerate that environmental protection is used as an excuse to justify an agreement whose primary objective is to restrict competition (see *Navewa-Anseau*). In such a case, the Commission will adopt a negative decision and impose a fine. By contrast, the Commission has taken a more favourable position towards agreements whose primary aim is to protect the environment but which have, as a side-effect, some impact on competition. In such cases, the Commission generally requires amendments to the agreement, so as to minimize its impact on competition, while ensuring that it meets its environmental objective (see *VOTOB* and *Oliebranches Faelleråd*). Some restrictions of competition will, however, never be tolerated by the Commission. This is, for instance, the case when agreements seek to partition national markets or eliminate price competition (see *Navewa-Anseau* and *VOTOB*). By contrast, certain restrictions of competition, which are less important or only temporary, will be accepted, provided they are essential to achieve the environmental objective (see *Valpak*).

The position of the Commission in *Valpak*, *EUCAR*, and *ACEA* suggests that it will generally adopt a favourable position with respect to agreements seeking to implement environmental objectives defined at Community level. This will be especially the case in sectors (such as packaging waste recycling or the

---

Waste Management: Perspectives on the Problem of End of Life Vehicles' (2000) 1 *Yearbook of European Environmental Law*, 253–89.

[49] See n. 28 above.

control of air pollution and greenhouse gases) where the Commission itself has explicitly or implicitly indicated that it was favourable to agreements concluded with industry. The Commission will not accept, however, that such agreements eliminate all forms of competition between the parties.

### iv. Draft Guidelines on the Applicability of Article 81 EC to Horizontal Agreements

Reference should be made to the draft guidelines on the applicability of Article 81 EC to horizontal cooperation, since these guidelines expressly refer to environmental agreements.[50] The purpose of these draft guidelines is to provide an analytical framework for the most common forms of horizontal cooperation.[51] This framework is primarily based on criteria that help to analyse the economic context of a cooperation agreement.[52] The guidelines provide that the market power of the parties and other factors relating to market structure will be taken into account by the Commission in assessing whether an agreement falls within the scope of Article 81(1) EC. Economic factors will also be taken into account in the application of Article 81(3) EC.

The section of the draft guidelines, which deals specifically with environmental agreements, is discussed later. Some references will also be made to the recent *CECED* Decision, in which the Commission seems to apply some of the draft guidelines' criteria.[53] This decision, adopted in January 2000, concerns an agreement between the major manufacturers and importers of washing-machines, together holding 90 per cent of the market, to cease the production or importation of machines which do not comply with certain energy-efficiency criteria. These machines have to be replaced with more environmentally friendly, but also more expensive, products.

As far as the assessment under Article 81(1) EC is concerned, the draft guidelines draw a distinction between environmental agreements that do not fall under Article 81(1) EC,[54] environmental agreements that almost always come under Article 81(1) EC,[55] and environmental agreements that may fall under Article 81(1) EC.[56]

First, the Commission indicates that some agreements are not likely to fall within the scope of Article 81(1) EC, irrespective of the aggregated market share of the parties. This may be the case where an agreement places 'no precise obligation upon the parties or if they are loosely committed to contributing to the attainment of a sector-wide environmental target'.[57] Thus, agreements

---

[50] Competition Rules Relating to Horizontal Cooperation Agreements—Communication pursuant to Art. 5 of Council Reg. (EEC) no. 2821/71 on the Application of Art. 81(3) EC to Categories of Agreements, Decisions and Concerted Practices Modified by Reg. (EEC) No. 2743/72, [1972] OJ C118/3. Guidelines have no binding force. They are designed to provide guidance on the Commission's views on some competition law issues. Since submission of the text of this article, the guidelines have been published in a definitive version [2000] OJ C3.

[51] These include not only environmental agreements, but also other types of cooperation agreements which potentially generate efficiency gains, i.e. Research & Development, production, purchasing, commercialization, and standardization agreements.

[52] Draft Guidelines, n. 50 above, para. 7.

[53] Commission Decision 2000/475/EC, *CECED* [2000] OJ L47/54.

[54] Draft Guidelines, n. 50 above, paras. 176–9.

[55] Ibid., para. 180.      [56] Ibid., paras. 181–3.      [57] Ibid., para. 177.

leaving a large degree of discretion to the parties as to the means of achieving the environmental objective agreed upon are unlikely to fall under Article 81(1) EC. Similarly, the prohibition included in Article 81(1) EC will not apply to 'agreements setting the environmental performance of products or processes that do not appreciably affect product or production diversity in the relevant market'.[58] On the other hand, agreements limiting product or production method diversity will breach Article 81(1) EC, unless the share of the products involved in the relevant geographic market is minor.[59]

By contrast, the Commission notes that environmental agreements will automatically breach Article 81(1) EC when 'the cooperation does not truly concern environmental objectives, but serves as a tool to engage in a disguised cartel, i.e. otherwise prohibited price-fixing, output limitation, or market allocation, or if the cooperation is used as a means amongst other parts of a broader restrictive agreement which aims at excluding actual or potential competitors'.[60] As we have seen, the Commission thus will not tolerate that environmental protection be used as an excuse to an agreement whose real objective is to restrict competition.

Finally, the draft guidelines provide that environmental agreements covering a major share of an industry at national or EC level are likely to breach Article 81(1) EC 'where they appreciably restrict the parties' ability to devise the characteristics of their products or the way in which they produce them, thereby granting them influence over each others production or sales'.[61] The guidelines also note that, in addition to restrictions between parties, an environmental agreement may also reduce or substantially affect the output of third parties, either as suppliers or buyers.

The agreement in question in *CECED* belongs to this third category of agreement, which the Commission considers likely to breach Article 81(1) EC. This agreement concerns a very large share (i.e. more than 90 per cent) of the relevant market. By restricting the parties' autonomy in producing or importing the machines of their choice, it has the object of controlling one important product characteristic (i.e. the degree of energy efficiency) on which there is competition in the relevant market, thereby restricting competition between the parties.[62] Moreover, this agreement will have the effect of reducing electricity demand, thereby reducing third parties' output.[63] As a result, the Commission decided that this agreement violated Article 81(1) EC.

The draft guidelines also give some indications as to how the Commission intends to assess environmental agreements under Article 81(3) EC. First, the guidelines provide that, in order to achieve the 'contribution to economic and technical progress' and the 'conferment of benefits to consumers' criteria set in Article 81(3) EC, the environmental agreement must achieve 'economic benefits which, either at individual or aggregate consumer level, outweigh their negative effect on competition'.[64] The benefits of an agreement might be

---

[58] Draft Guidelines, n. 50 above, para. 178.          [59] Ibid.          [60] Ibid., para. 180.
[61] Ibid., para. 181.          [62] Commission Decision 2000/475/EC, n. 53 above, para. 33.
[63] Ibid., para. 36.                              [64] Draft Guidelines, n. 50 above, para. 185.

assessed in two stages.[65] Where consumers individually have a positive rate of return from the agreement during reasonable payback periods, there is no need for the aggregate environmental benefits to be objectively established. Alternatively, a cost–benefit analysis must be carried out to determine whether net benefits for consumers in general are likely under reasonable assumptions.

The *CECED* decision provides a good illustration of this two-stage proportionality test. Although the agreement in question restricted competition, the Commission identified both individual economic benefits and collective environmental benefits. As far as individual consumers are concerned, higher initial purchase costs derived from stringent energy efficiency standards will be recouped within nine to forty months (depending on several factors, such as frequency use and the price of electricity) because of the machines' lower running costs.[66] As far as the collective environmental benefits are concerned, the Commission balances the increased purchase costs of more energy-efficient machines with the saving in marginal damage from avoided carbon dioxide, sulphur dioxide, and nitrous oxide emissions.[67] On the basis of its calculations,[68] the Commission considers that the benefits to society brought about by the agreement are more than seven times the increase in purchase costs. For the Commission, such societal gains adequately allow consumers a fair share of these benefits, even if no benefits accrued to individual purchasers of machines.

With respect to the 'indispensability of the restrictions' criterion found in Article 81(3) EC, the draft guidelines provide that 'an objective evaluation of provisions which "*prima facie*" might be deemed not indispensable must be supported with a cost-effectiveness analysis showing that alternative means of attaining the expected environmental benefits, would be more economically or financially costly, under reasonable assumptions'.[69]

In *CECED*, the Commission analysed the cost-effectiveness of any alternative means (i.e. an agreement limited to an undertaking of the parties to contribute to an industry-wide target, information campaigns or eco-labelling) that could be used by manufacturers of washing-machines to achieve comparable environmental benefits.[70] For instance, the Commission considered that, while the setting of a more stringent industry-wide target could in theory lead to more indirect pollution abatement, and allow manufacturers and importers more flexibility than the application of a mandatory standard, such an agreement would have higher transaction and monitoring costs, and could even be more restrictive.[71]

---

[65] Ibid., para. 186.        [66] Commission Decision 2000/475/EC, n. 50 above, para. 52.
[67] Ibid., para. 56.
[68] The Commission estimates the savings in avoided damage from carbon dioxide emissions at 41 to 61 euro per tonne, from sulphur dioxide emissions at 4,000 to 7,000 euro per tonne, and from nitrous oxide at 3,000 to 5,000 euro per tonne.
[69] Para. 188 of the Draft Guidelines, n. 50 above.
[70] Commission Decision 2000/475/EC, n. 53 above, para. 59.        [71] Ibid., para. 61.

In summary, the draft guidelines on horizontal cooperation essentially confirm the approach taken by the Commission in the cases discussed in the previous section. The Commission takes a positive stance on the use of environmental agreements as a policy instrument to achieve environmental objectives. However, the fact that an agreement seeks to achieve environmental objectives does not exempt it from the application of competition rules.[72] Interestingly, the guidelines do not explicitly refer to the integration principle contained in Article 6 EC.

The most innovative part of the draft guidelines stems from the increased emphasis placed on economic criteria in the assessment of environmental agreements under Article 81 EC. This is, of course, not surprising since, as noted above, placing greater emphasis on the economic circumstances in which agreements are adopted is one of the central objectives of the guidelines. For instance, the market shares of the parties will be one of the factors taken into account by the Commission to determine whether an environmental agreement falls under Article 81(1) EC.

Cost–benefit and cost-effectiveness analyses will also be employed by the Commission to assess whether environmental agreements falling under Article 81(1) EC can be exempted by Article 81(3) EC. An important aspect of the draft guidelines and the *CECED* decision is that they make clear that collective environmental benefits, such as, for example, reduction in air or water pollution, will be taken into account to assess the proportionality of an agreement. More generally, a positive aspect of cost–benefit analysis and cost-effectiveness analysis is that, if used properly, they will bring more objectivity to the assessment of environmental agreements made by the Commission under Article 81(3) EC.

### B. COMPATIBILITY OF ENVIRONMENTAL AGREEMENTS ENCOURAGED OR IMPOSED BY PUBLIC AUTHORITIES WITH ARTICLES 3(1)(G), 10, AND 81 EC

In the previous section, we have observed that environmental agreements between undertakings may fall under the prohibition contained in Article 81(1) EC. But what happens when these agreements are encouraged, or even imposed by public authorities? Two questions arise. Does such an intervention absolve such agreements from the prohibition contained in Article 81(1) EC? Alternatively, does it trigger the application of Article 81(1) EC to the measure adopted by the public authorities?

As far as the first question is concerned, there is no doubt that, when government compels private undertakings to engage in anti-competitive practices, Article 81(1) EC does not apply, since the restriction of competition does not find its cause in a freely concluded agreement.[73] Similarly, in its *Suiker Unie* and *Fedetab* cases the European Court of Justice (ECJ) confirmed that

---

[72] Para. 184 of the Draft Guidelines, n. 50 above.
[73] Commission Decision 74/634/EEC, *Franco-Japanese Ball Bearings Agreement* [1974] OJ L343/19.

Article 81 EC could not be applied when state intervention, even if it does not translate into a legally binding measure, exerts a *decisive influence* on the undertakings' behaviour.[74] This justification only applies, however, when all possibilities of competition have been eliminated by state intervention. When some possibilities of competition continue to exist, even if they are very limited, Article 81 EC remains applicable to the undertakings.[75]

As far as the second question is concerned, the Commission observed in its IInd Competition Report that:

Another problem arises where measures are taken by public authorities which might compromise the effect of the competition rules, for example by requiring firms to engage in behaviour which restricts competition. Such measures can have a very appreciable effect on competition and trade between Member States. In such cases the Court has held that Article 85 may apply, in conjunction with Articles 3(f) and 5 of the Treaty.[76]

It results from the case law of the ECJ that, read in combination with Articles 3(1)(g) EC and 10 EC, Article 81 EC requires that Member States refrain from adopting or maintaining measures, even of a legislative or regulatory nature, that eliminate the *effet utile* of the competition rules applicable to undertakings.[77] According to the same case law, this is the case in two different sets of circumstances, namely first when a Member State requires or favours the conclusion of agreements contrary to Article 81 EC or strengthens their effects and, second, deprives its own legislation of its official character by delegating to private companies the responsibility to make decisions in the economic sphere leading to restrictions of competition.

Placed in an environmental context, the above case law suggests that state regulation compelling private firms to conclude an environmental agreement that restricts competition would be contrary to Articles 3(1)(g), 10, and 81 EC.[78] The same provisions would prohibit a Member State to strengthen the

---

[74] Joined Cases 40 to 48, 50, 54 to 56, 111, 113, and 114/73, *Coöperatieve Vereniging 'Suiker Unie' UA and others* v. *Commission* [1975] ECR 1663; Joined Cases 209 to 215 and 218/78, *Heintz van Landewyck SARL and others* v. *Commission* [1980] ECR 3125 (emphasis added).

[75] M. Waelbroeck and A. Frignani, *Commentaire J. Mégret—Le Droit de la CE*, iv—*Concurrence* (Brussels: Université de Bruxelles, 1997), 147.

[76] Point 77 of the report.

[77] A vast body of case law exists on this aspect. See, in particular, Cases C–2/91, *Criminal Proceedings against Wolf W. Meng* [1993] ECR I–5751; C–185/91, *Bundesanstalt für Güterfernverkehr* v. *Gebrüder Reiff GmbH & Co. KG* [1993] ECR I–5801; C–245/91, *Criminal Proceedings against Ohra Schadeverzekeringen NV* [1993] ECR I–5851. For a discussion of these cases, see N. Reich, 'The "November Revolution" of the European Court of Justice: Keck, Meng and Audi Revisited' (1994) 31 *Common Market Law Review*, 459.

[78] By contrast, the simple fact that national legislation has an impact on competition because, for instance, it imposes very strict environmental standards on its own nationals and, thus, penalizes them vis-à-vis their foreign competitors will not cause it to be in breach of Art. 81(1) EC read in conjunction with Arts. 3(1)(g) and 10 EC. In Case C–379/92, *Criminal Proceedings against Matteo Peralta* [1994] ECR I–3453, the ECJ ruled that an Italian law which imposed a prohibition on its domestic vessels against the discharge of tank-flushing liquids into the high seas was not contrary to the above-mentioned provisions. The Court considered that '(the Italian) legislation does not require or foster anti-competitive conduct since the prohibition which it lays down is sufficient in itself. Nor does it reinforce the effect of a pre-existing agreement.' This case makes clear

effect of an environmental agreement concluded by a limited number of undertakings, either by extending to third parties the obligations assumed by the parties to the agreement, or by transforming such obligations into legally binding provisions. As pointed out by one author, '[a] Member State cannot make restrictive agreements banned by Article 81 EC legal by "officializing" them through incorporation or transformation into a legislative measure'.[79] For the same reason, legislation entrusting private undertakings (for example, chemical companies) with the duty to adopt environmental standards that will be binding for a specific sector of industry (for example, the chemical sector) would also be contrary to Articles 3(1)(g), 10, and 81 EC.

The question arises whether this case law does not excessively restrict the freedom of Member States to encourage voluntary initiatives, or to involve industry in the elaboration of environmental regulations. In this regard, some remarks appear appropriate. First, in *Van Eycke*, the ECJ indicated that for a state measure to strengthen the effects of an agreement (for instance, by rendering it binding upon non-participating companies), that measure must literally reproduce the terms of the agreement.[80] Differences, however minor, between the state measure and the agreement will, it seems, rule out application of Article 81(1) EC to the measure.[81] Although this position appears excessively formalistic, it was confirmed by the ECJ in its more recent case law.[82]

Moreover, while it would probably be contrary to Articles 3(1)(g), 10, and 81 EC if a Member State delegates the power to adopt environmental standards binding a whole industry sector to private undertakings, the position adopted by the ECJ in *Reiff, Delta*,[83] and *Spediporto*[84] suggests that these provisions would not prevent a Member State from entrusting committees composed of experts from industry with the duty to implement environmental objectives fixed in legislation.[85] Several conditions would have to be met, however. In particular, members of such committees should not be bound by orders or instructions from the undertaking or the undertakings which proposed them. Also, these decisions should be guided by considerations of public interest and, before becoming effective, be subject to approval by the public authorities.

that what matters is not the impact of environmental legislation on the conditions of competition, but its impact on the behaviour of competitors.

[79] See Vandermeersch, n. 11 above, 95.
[80] Case 267/86, *Pascal Van Eycke* v. *ASPA NV* [1988] ECR 4769.
[81] See Waelbroeck and Frignani, n. 75 above, 151.  [82] See n. 77 above.
[83] Case C–153/93, *Bundesrepublik Deutschland* v. *Delta Schiffahrts- und Speditions-Gesellschaft mbH* [1995] ECR I–2517.
[84] Case C–96/94, *Centro Servizi Spediporto Srl* v. *Spedizioni Marritima del Golfo Srl* [1995] ECR I–2883.
[85] See, e.g., Case C–185/91, n. 77 above, para. 20.

### III. Disciplines Imposed by Article 82 EC on Dominant Undertakings Carrying Out Environmental Tasks

In recent years, laws and regulations requiring that producers or distributors collect and/or recycle the packaging of the products they place on the market (or, in some cases, the products themselves where these have reached the end of their useful lives) have led undertakings to set up waste collection and recycling systems. With a view to achieving economies of scale, such systems are generally organized on a collective basis. Packaging waste collection and recycling schemes, such as DSD in Germany or Eco-emballages in France, will thus have a dominant position on the market for organizing the collection and recycling of packaging waste. The existence of a dominant position is not in itself incompatible with the Treaty. Pursuant to Article 82 EC, only abuses of a dominant position are prohibited. Contrary to Article 81 EC, Article 82 EC does not provide for any exemption. All abusive behaviour is banned.

Article 82 EC provides a series of examples of behaviour that amounts to abuse:

(a) directly or indirectly imposing unfair purchase or selling prices or other unfair trading conditions;
(b) limiting production, markets, or technical development to the prejudice of consumers;
(c) applying different conditions to equivalent transactions, thereby placing some trading parties at a competitive disadvantage;
(d) making the conclusion of contracts subject to acceptance by the other parties of supplementary obligations which, by their nature or according to commercial usage, have no connection with the subject of such contracts.

Waste collection and recycling schemes within a dominant position, such as DSD or Eco-emballages, thus have to refrain from engaging in various forms of behaviour that would amount to abuse of market power under Article 82 EC. For instance, both 'excessive'[86] and 'predatory'[87] pricing would amount to abuse of market power (see paragraph (a) above). Waste undertakings therefore have to ensure that prices are related to costs plus a reasonable profit. Inefficiency, idleness, mismanagement, or refusal to use modern technology could be considered as 'limiting production, markets, or technical development to the prejudice of

---

[86] Case 27/76, *United Brands Company and United Brands Continentaal BV* v. *Commission* [1978] ECR 207, at 251 (holding that to charge an excessive price which had no reasonable relation to the economic value of the product supplied was an abuse, and indicating that an objective means of determining such excess would be a comparison of selling prices with costs of production).

[87] See Case C–62/86, *AKZO Chemie BV* v. *Commission* [1991] ECR I–3359, paras. 69 ff. (holding that prices below variable costs through which an undertaking tries to eliminate a competitor must be considered abusive. Where the price is higher than average variable cost but lower than total cost, abuse may be found when prices are fixed in the context of a plan to eliminate a competitor).

consumers' (see paragraph (b)). Moreover, discriminatory treatment between consumers that is not objectively justified would be contrary to Article 82 EC (see paragraph (c)). Furthermore, 'tying' clauses (for example, clauses that would force consumers that seek access to a collection and recycling scheme to buy recycled materials from that scheme) would be considered as an abuse of market power (see paragraph (d)).[88]

These examples reveal no real tension between environmental protection and competition law. On the contrary, Article 82 EC will prevent behaviour, such as excessive pricing, refusal to use modern technology, or discriminatory treatment, that would be detrimental from the perspective of environmental protection. Access to cheap, efficient, and non-discriminatory waste collection and recycling schemes, or other forms of environmental services, is desirable both from the point of view of competition and environmental protection.

A tension between competition and environmental protection could, however, take place if a dominant supplier would use its market power in order to force suppliers or consumers to improve their environmental performance.[89] A dominant undertaking wishing to improve its environmental performance could, for instance, require its supplier to meet certain environmental criteria relating to the product itself or the way it has been produced. Since Article 82 EC also applies to buying power, it could be argued that this undertaking abuses its market power by making the conclusion of contracts subject to acceptance by the other parties of supplementary obligations which, by their nature or according to commercial usage, have no connection with the subject of such contracts. Yet, with the increasing importance of Integrated Product Policy (IPP) as a quality management tool,[90] it is now widely accepted that the environmental performance of a product is an essential part of its overall quality. Consequently, if an undertaking requires that the products supplied meet high environmental standards, this in effect amounts to requiring high-quality products, behaviour that can hardly be found abusive.[91]

Another interesting question is whether refusal by a collection and recycling system in a dominant position to allow undertakings access to its facilities for the purpose of placing their product on the market, should be considered abuse of a dominant position. An example may be found in *Spa/GDB*.[92] This case concerned the pool of standardized reusable glass bottles set up by the German association of mineral water producers (GDB). In 1989 the Belgian mineral water producer Spa Monopole submitted a formal complaint to the Commission against GDB's refusal to grant access to this pool. The Commission considered that, at the time, the GDB agreement and the ensuing exclusion of foreign water producers did not have an appreciable negative effect on the position of third parties or on intra-Community trade, because

[88] See Case T–30/89, *Hilti AG* v. *Commission* [1991] ECR II–1439.
[89] See Jacobs, n. 11 above, 63.
[90] See European Commission, 'Integrated Product Policy: A Study Analysing National and International Developments with regard to Integrated Product Policy in the Environment Fields and Providing Elements for an EC Policy in this Area', March 1998.
[91] See Jacobs, n. 11 above, 63.          [92] XXIIIrd Competition Report (1993), para. 240.

alternative packaging, such as PVC or one-way glass, had free access to the German market.

In 1992, however, the Commission asked GDB to open its pool to mineral water producers from the rest of the Community. The conditions on the German market had changed considerably. As a result of new German waste management legislation, plastic one-way bottles had to be withdrawn from the market, and one-way glass bottles or other one-way packaging could be used only if a system for their recycling had been set up. In practice, this meant that access to the GDB pool had become essential for foreign producers. In these circumstances, the Commission considered that the GDB agreement:

hindered access by foreign water producers to the German market restricting competition and appreciably affecting inter-State trade within the meaning of Articles (81) and (82) of the EC Treaty. Furthermore, in view of the dominant position of the GDB in the market for mineral water containers, its refusal to grant foreign water producers access to its pool, despite the fact such access was *essential* in order to be able to compete effectively in the mineral water market, constituted an abuse of a dominant position within the meaning of Article (82) of the Treaty.[93]

Following this intervention by the Commission, GDB decided to open its pool to foreign producers of mineral water.

The Commission's reasoning in this case is of great importance because it suggests that when access to a system of collection and recycling of glass bottles controlled by one or several companies in a dominant position (in the 'downstream' market for collection and recycling services) is essential to one of its/their competitors (in the 'upstream' mineral water market), this system must be considered an 'essential facility', access to which must be granted in exchange for adequate compensation.

In recent years, this essential facility doctrine has frequently been used (some might say abused) by the Commission to force bottleneck facility holders to grant competitors access to their infrastructure, services, or products.[94] Examples are particularly abundant in the transport sector.[95] In *European Night Services*[96] and *Bronner*,[97] the Court of First Instance (CFI) and the ECJ followed a more cautious approach. The test for establishing the existence of an essential facility elaborated by the CFI in *European Night Services* is strict. In the ECJ's opinion, facilities should be considered as 'necessary' or 'essential' when 'by reason of their special characteristics—in particular the prohibitive

---

[93] Emphasis added.

[94] For an illustrating discussion of this doctrine, see J. Temple Lang, 'Defining Legitimate Competition: Companies' Duties to Supply Competitors and Access to Essential Facilities' (1994) 18 *Fordham International Law Journal*, 437.

[95] See, e.g., Commission Decison 88/589, *London European/Sabena* [1988] OJ L317/47; Commission Decision 92/213, *British Midland/Aer Lingus* [1992] OJ L96/34; Commission Decision 94/19, *Sea Containers/Stena Sealink* [1994] OJ L15/8; Commission Decision 94/663, *European Night Services* [1994] OJ L259/20.

[96] Joined Cases T–374/94, T–375/94, T–384/94 and T–388/94, *European Night Services and others* v. *Commission* [1998] ECR II–3141.

[97] Case C–7/97, *Oscar Bronner GmbH & Co. KG* v. *Mediaprint Zeitungs- und Zeitschriftenverlag GmbH & Co. AG and others* [1998] ECR I–7791.

cost of and/or time reasonably required for reproducing them—there are *no viable alternatives* available to potential competitors . . . which are thereby *excluded from the market*'.[98]

Application of the essential facilities doctrine will thus be allowed when two conditions are satisfied. First, there must be no viable alternative for the facility.[99] Second, refusal of granting access will exclude competitors from an 'upstream' market (as in *Bronner*, when it was alleged that refusal by a newspaper publisher to grant access to its home-delivery scheme would distort competition on the 'upstream' newspaper market) or a 'downstream' market (as in *European Night Services* where it was alleged that refusal by rail companies to grant access to some rail services would distort competition on the 'downstream' market for transport passengers).[100] It is submitted that there may be circumstances where the essential facilities doctrine, as set out in *European Night Services* and *Bronner*, may find application in the environmental field. As illustrated by *GDB*, this is particularly likely to be the case where operators hold non-duplicable collection and recycling schemes.

Finally, a brief reference should be made to *Diego Calì & Figli*.[101] In this case, the ECJ was asked whether Article 82 EC was applicable to an anti-pollution surveillance activity entrusted to a body governed by private law (Servizi Ecologici Porto di Genova SpA, hereafter 'SEPG') by the public authorities governing the oil port of Genoa. The Court answered in the negative. It considered that:

The anti pollution surveillance for which SEPG was responsible in the oil port of Genoa is a task in the public interest which forms part of the essential functions of the State as regards protection of the environment in maritime areas.

Such surveillance is connected by its nature, its aim and the rules to which it is subject with the exercise of powers relating to the protection of the environment which are typically those of a public authority. It is not of an economic nature justifying the application of the Treaty rules on competition.[102]

The interesting aspect of this case is that it shows that the activities of some organizations in charge of accomplishing environmental duties will not fall within the scope of Article 82 (or other competition provisions) of the Treaty, because they are not of an 'economic' nature. From a policy perspective, it is debatable whether the narrow definition of the concept of economic activity adopted by the ECJ is desirable, in that it allows a series of bodies to escape the discipline imposed by the competition provisions of the Treaty.

---

[98]  Case C–7/97, n. 97 above, para. 209 (emphasis added).
[99]  On this aspect, see also Case C–7/97, n. 97 above, paras. 41 ff. On this case, see L. Hancher, (1999) 30 *Common Market Law Review*, 1289.
[100]  For a fuller discussion, see P. Larouche, *Competition Law and Regulation in European Telecommunications* (Oxford: Hart, 2000).
[101]  Case C–343/95, *Diego Calì & Figli Srl* v. *Servizi Ecologici Porto di Genova SpA (SEPG)* [1997] ECR I–1547.
[102]  Case C–343/95, n. 101 above, paras. 22–3.

## IV. Exclusive Rights in the Environmental Field in Light of Article 86 EC

Increasingly, Member States resort to specialized agencies or undertakings in order to accomplish certain environmental duties, such as the treatment of waste water, the collection and recycling of waste, or the clean-up of polluted sites. These agencies or undertakings often enjoy exclusive rights, granting them a monopoly over certain activities. As already noted, the granting of exclusive rights may be justified for several reasons. In some cases, economies of scale render a single operator more efficient than two or several operators (theory of 'natural monopoly').[103] In other cases, the granting of exclusive rights is justified on the ground that the beneficiary undertaking commits itself to provide public service obligations. It may commit itself, for instance, to offering its services in the entirety of a given territory, including loss-making areas, in a continuous manner, and at an affordable price for all citizens.[104]

The compatibility of exclusive rights with Community law must be examined in the light of Article 86 EC.[105] Article 86(1) EC provides that, in the case of undertakings to which Member States grant exclusive rights, Member States shall neither enact nor maintain in force any measure contrary to the rules contained in the Treaty, in particular to those rules provided for in Article 12 EC and Articles 81 to 89 EC. This provision does not seem to forbid Member States to grant exclusive rights to an undertaking. It prohibits, however, to adopt vis-à-vis these undertakings measures that are incompatible with the Treaty. Thus, a Member State may not adopt regulatory measures requiring or encouraging an undertaking holding exclusive rights to abuse its dominant position on the market.[106]

Article 86(2) EC qualifies the above principle. Pursuant to that provision, undertakings entrusted with the operation of 'services of general economic interest' are subject to the rules of the Treaty only 'in so far as the application of such rules does not obstruct the performance, in law or in fact, of the particular tasks assigned to them'.[107] The objective of this provision is to avoid that an excessively stringent application of the rules of the Treaty (in particular competition provisions) prevents a state monopoly entrusted with services of

---

[103] A 'natural monopoly' is said to exist where a single enterprise is able to provide a good or a service to users in a given area at lower costs than would two or more enterprises. Generally, on the theory of natural monopoly, see W. Sharkey, *The Theory of Natural Monopoly* (Cambridge: Cambridge University Press, 1992).

[104] See D. Geradin, 'The Opening of State Monopolies to Competition: Main Issues of the Liberalization Process' in D. Geradin (ed.), *The Liberalization of State Monopolies in the European Union and Beyond* (The Hague: Kluwer Law International, 2000), 194.

[105] Generally, on Art. 86 EC see Blum and Logue, n. 18 above.

[106] Case 13/77, *SA G.B.-INNO-B.M.* v. *Association des détaillants en tabac (ATAB)* [1977] ECR 2115.

[107] For a discussion of Art. 86(2) EC, see A. Wachsmann and F. Berrod, 'Les Critères de Justification des Monopoles: Un Premier Bilan après l'Affaire Corbeau' (1994) 30 *Revue Trimestrielle de Droit Européen*, 39.

general interest to accomplish its mission.[108] As with all exceptions provided for in the Treaty, Article 86(2) EC is interpreted strictly.

In recent years, the ECJ has produced a rich and complex case law on Article 86 EC.[109] Until recently, the compatibility with the Treaty of exclusive rights granted to undertakings in charge of environmental duties had not been examined by the Court. This lacuna was recently filled by *Dusseldorp*.[110] This case concerned a Dutch undertaking (Dusseldorp) that had applied for authorization to export to Germany two cargoes of oil filters and related waste for processing in that country. However, this application was rejected by the competent minister on the basis of Dutch legislation pursuant to which export of oil filters could not be authorized, unless the processing performed in the foreign country was of a higher quality than that performed by AVR Chemie, an undertaking holding exclusive rights for eliminating through incineration oil filters and other related waste in the Netherlands. Following the rejection of its application, Dusseldorp started legal proceedings before the Dutch *Raad van State* (Council of State), which submitted several questions for a preliminary ruling to the ECJ.

In its judgment, the ECJ considered that, in so far as it held exclusive rights to incinerate dangerous waste on Dutch territory, AVR Chemie had to be regarded as having a dominant position within a substantial part of the common market. The ECJ then observed that 'although merely creating a dominant position is not, in itself, incompatible with Article (82) of the Treaty, a Member State breaches the prohibitions laid down by Article (86) in conjunction with Article (82), if it adopts any law, regulation, or administrative provision which enables an undertaking on which it has conferred exclusive rights to abuse its dominant position'.[111] The ECJ considered that the decision of the Dutch Government prohibiting Dusseldorp exporting its waste was such a measure since, by favouring AVR Chemie in enabling it to process waste intended for processing by a third undertaking, it limited outlets in a manner contrary to Article 86(1) EC in conjunction with Article 82 EC. The ECJ also noted, however, that a measure contrary to Article 82 EC adopted in favour of an undertaking to which the state has granted exclusive rights can be justified under Article 86(2) EC if that measure is *necessary* to enable the undertaking to perform the particular task of general interest assigned to it.

---

[108] For examples of application of Art. 86(2) EC, see Case 13/77, n. 106 above; Case C–320/91, *Criminal Proceedings against Paul Corbeau* [1993] ECR I–2533; Case C–393/92, *Municipality of Almelo and others* v. *NV Energiebedrijf IJsselmij* [1994] ECR I–1477.

[109] For an excellent discussion of this case law, see F. Blum, 'The Recent Case-Law of the European Court of Justice on State Monopolies and Its Implications for Network Industries' (2000) 1 *Journal of Network Industries*, 55.

[110] Case C–203/96, *Chemische Afvalstoffen Dusseldorp BV and others* v. *Minister van Volkshuisvesting, Ruimtelijke Ordening en Milieubeheer* [1998] ECR I–4075. For informative discussions of this case, see P. Nihoul, 'Les Droits Exclusifs en Matière de Déchets au regard du Droit Européen de la Concurrence' (1999) *Aménagement–Environnement*, 16; N. Notaro, (1999) 36 *Common Market Law Review*, 1309.

[111] Case C–203/96, n. 110 above, para. 61.

This judgment provides some useful indications on the compatibility of exclusive rights granted to undertakings to accomplish environmental protection tasks with the Treaty. First, it is noteworthy that what the ECJ declares incompatible with Articles 86(1) and 82 EC is not so much the granting of exclusive rights to an undertaking for the incineration of dangerous waste on the territory of a Member State, as the combination of such exclusive rights with an export ban. Such a prohibition strengthens the dominant position of the undertaking enjoying exclusive rights, and results in the restriction of outlets in breach of Article 82 EC. Second, this judgment provides some useful indications on the conditions of applicability of Article 86(2) EC. The ECJ indicates that, in order for an undertaking holding exclusive rights to benefit from an exemption of the application of certain rules of the Treaty, it must be entrusted with a 'service of general economic interest'. The ECJ also affords a central role to the criterion of 'necessity' in the analysis of a measure in light of Article 86(2) EC. Pursuant to this criterion, which as we have seen is also one of the conditions for application of Article 81(3) EC,[112] the restrictive measure adopted by the state, i.e. the granting of exclusive rights, can only be justified if a less restrictive measure could not also satisfy the result desired.[113] Thus, a Member State that has granted exclusive rights to an undertaking entrusted with environmental duties will have to demonstrate that, absent such rights (i.e. in a competitive regime), the undertaking in question will not be able to provide its service of general economic interest in a satisfactory manner.

*Dusseldorp*, however, leaves some important questions unanswered. First, the judgment leaves open the question whether, independent of any restriction on exportation, exclusive rights to incinerate, or more generally to treat, certain categories of waste are in themselves incompatible with the Treaty. The ECJ case law on this issue is not entirely clear. While in its traditional case law, the Court defended the view that exclusive rights were not *per se* contrary to the Treaty,[114] some of its more recent judgments suggest that in certain circumstances, the mere exercise of an exclusive right can be contrary to the Treaty.[115] Second, the judgment does not clarify whether waste-treatment undertakings, or more generally undertakings entrusted with environmental protection duties, should be considered as discharging a 'service of general economic interest'.

Interestingly, these issues have been addressed recently, and to some extent clarified, by the ECJ in *FFAD*.[116] In that case, a Danish regional court referred

---

[112] See above.

[113] For an illustration of that criterion see Commission Decision 82/731, n. 25 above.

[114] See Cases 155/73, *Criminal Proceedings against Giuseppe Sacchi* [1974] ECR 409; C–311/84, *Centre belge d'études de marché—Télémarketing (CBEM)* v. *SA Compagnie luxembourgeoise de télédiffusion (CLT) and Information publicité Benelux (IPB)* [1985] ECR 3261.

[115] See, in particular, Cases C–41/90, *Klaus Höfner and Fritz Elser* v. *Macrotron GmbH* [1991] ECR I–1979; C–179/90, *Merci convenzionali porto di Genova SpA v Siderurgica Gabrielli SpA* [1991] ECR I–5889.

[116] Case C–209/98, *Entreprenørforeningens Affalds/Miljøsektion (FFAD)* v. *Københavns Kommune* [2000] ECR I–3743. For a good discussion of this case, see N. Notaro, 'European Community Waste Movements: the Copenhagen Waste Case' (2000) *European Environmental Law Review*, 304.

to the ECJ several questions for a preliminary ruling, concerning the compatibility with the EC Treaty of the system for the collection of non-hazardous building waste organized by the municipality of Copenhagen. One such question was whether the exclusive rights granted by the municipality of Copenhagen to a limited number of undertakings to process building waste produced within Copenhagen, thereby excluding other undertakings from processing that waste, was compatible with Article 86 EC in conjunction with Article 82 EC.[117] The rationale for that system was to ensure that the undertakings selected would have sufficient access to building waste destined for recovery, so as to exploit that waste on an economically viable basis.

In its judgment, the ECJ confirmed that there are circumstances where the granting of exclusive rights can in itself be incompatible with Articles 86(1) and 82 EC, independent of any restriction designed to strengthen the effect of such rights. Such a breach of the Treaty would occur 'if the undertaking in question, merely by exercising the exclusive rights granted to it, led to abuse its dominant position or when such rights are liable to create a situation in which that undertaking is led to commit such abuses'.[118] However, the ECJ considered that 'the grant of an exclusive right over part of the national territory for environmental purposes, such as establishing the capacity necessary for the recycling of building waste, does not in itself constitute an abuse of dominant position'.[119] The ECJ provided no indication as to whether there are circumstances in which the granting of exclusive rights to a waste-treatment undertaking could 'lead (this undertaking) to abuse its dominant position' or 'create a situation in which that undertaking is led to commit such abuses'. Previous judgments such as *Höfner*[120] and *Job Centre*[121] suggest, however, that this might be the case when the undertaking enjoying exclusive rights is unable to satisfy demand. In *FFDA*, this situation was not present, since the very objective of granting exclusive rights to a limited number of undertakings was to encourage capacity for waste treatment.

The ECJ also indicates that '[t]he management of particular waste may properly be considered to be capable of forming the subject of a service of general economic interest, particularly when the service is designed to deal with an environmental problem'.[122] The last part of this formula suggests that undertakings entrusted with environmental protection duties (waste management, water treatment, etc.) will generally be considered as providing services

---

[117] One should note that the ECJ makes a rather unusual, and to some extent misleading, use of the concept of 'exclusive rights'. Indeed, it is generally agreed that 'exclusive rights' exist where a single undertaking has been granted the right to carry a certain activity throughout a given territory. See Case C–323/93, n. 18 above. By contrast, the concept of 'special rights' is generally used when the right to carry out a certain activity throughout a territory has been granted to a limited number of undertakings. See Case C–302/94, n. 18 above. See generally Blum and Logue, n. 18 above, 9.

[118] Case C–209/98, n. 116 above, para. 66.          [119] Ibid., para. 68.

[120] Case C–41/90, n. 115 above.

[121] Case C–55/96, non-contentious proceedings by *Job Centre coop. arl.* [1997] ECR I–7119.

[122] Case C–209/98, n. 116 above, para. 75.

of general economic interest and therefore be in a position to benefit from the exemption provided for in this Treaty provision.

Finally, the ECJ tackles the condition of 'necessity', provided for in Article 86(2) EC, ruling that, in order to determine whether Article 86(2) EC could be applied to the three undertakings that had been granted exclusive rights by the Copenhagen Municipality, one had 'to consider whether the exclusive rights granted to the three undertakings is necessary for them to be able to perform the task of general economic interest which has been assigned to them under acceptable economic conditions'. As it had done in previous cases, such as *Corbeau*,[123] the ECJ therefore implies that ensuring the economic viability of the undertakings entrusted with a service of general economic interest is a sufficient justification for the granting of exclusive rights. In its evaluation, the ECJ took into account the fact that the exclusive rights were 'limited in time to the period over which the investments could foreseeably be written off and in space to the land within the boundaries of the municipality'.[124] This suggests that open-ended exclusive rights (i.e. rights that are neither limited in time nor in space) probably do not fulfil the necessity criterion contained in Article 86(2) EC.

## IV. Environmental State Aids in Light of Articles 87 to 89 EC

From a theoretical perspective, state aids is an area in which competition policy and environmental protection policy seem to be in perfect harmony.[125] Competition generally prohibits state aids on the ground they distort the competitive process. Similarly, from the perspective of environmental protection, state subsidies breach the 'polluter-pays principle' pursuant to which the costs of pollution should be borne by the polluters and not by the Community at large.[126]

In practice, however, a tension between competition policy and environmental protection takes place whenever Member States choose to achieve environmental goals by granting subsidies to industry. Member States may, for instance, decide to grant financial aid to undertakings that develop new, cleaner technologies or products. In such cases, the key question is how the Commission should react vis-à-vis such measures. Should the Commission systematically ban the use of environmental aids, or should it take a more flexible approach, allowing such aids in some circumstances? As will be seen, the

---

[123] Case C–320/91, n. 108 above, para. 14.        [124] Case C–209/98, n. 116 above, para. 77.

[125] For an overview of the policy of the Commission with respect to state aid for environmental protection see S. Budlong, 'Article 130r(2) and the Permissibility of State Aids for Environmental Compliance' (1992) 30 *Columbia Journal of Transnational Law*, 431; J. Jans, 'Does the Polluter Really Pay' in Geradin (ed.), n. 11 above, 109; G. Van Calster, 'State Aid for Environmental Protection: Has the EC Shut the Door?' (1998) 3 *Environmental Taxation and Accounting*, 38.

[126] The 'polluter-pays principle' is found in Art. 174 EC. For a discussion of the 'polluter-pays principle' in the European Union context, see K. Vandekerckhove, 'The Polluter Pays Principle in the European Community' in Barav and Wyatt (eds.), n. 5 above, 201.

European Commission has decided to opt for the latter approach, using the discretionary powers entrusted to it by the Treaty to develop guidelines authorizing environmental state aids, provided that some specific criteria are met.[127]

This Section is divided into four parts. First, I will discuss the concept of state aid as defined by the ECJ in order to determine which types of environmental measures fall within the scope of the prohibition contained in Article 87(1) EC. In section B, I will examine the exceptions contained in Article 87(2) and (3) EC. As will be seen, Article 87(3) EC presents several useful bases for justifications of environmental aids. Next, I will review the Commission guidelines on state aids for environmental protection (part C). This Section will end with a discussion of some recent environmental aid cases decided by the Commission (part D).

### A. ARTICLE 87(1) EC: THE PROHIBITION OF STATE AIDS

Article 87(1) EC provides that 'any aid granted by a Member State or through state resources in any form whatsoever which distorts or threatens to distort competition by favouring certain undertakings or the production of certain goods shall, in so far as it affects trade between Member States, be incompatible with the common market'.[128] For an environmental measure to fall within the scope of Article 87(1) EC, it must be demonstrated that it falls within the concept of state aid as defined in Article 87 EC, that it distorts competition, and that it affects intra-Community trade.

### i. *The Concept of State Aid*

For an environmental measure to be a state aid, several conditions must be met. First, the measure in question must confer an *advantage* on one or several undertakings. This excludes from the notion of state aid sums that would be paid by the state to undertakings to compensate them for environmental services rendered to the Community. Thus, in *Waste Oils*, the ECJ considered that the permission given to Member States by Directive 75/439/EEC financially to reward undertakings in charge of collecting and/or eliminating waste oils was not a state aid within the meaning of Article 87 EC, but a form of payment for the services rendered by these undertakings.[129] In contrast, the Commission considered that state subsidy for the decontamination of a

---

[127] This approach complies with economic theory. From an economic perspective, aid regimes can be justified when they are used to correct 'market failures', such as externalities, imperfect information, or imperfect movement of factors of production. For a discussion of this issue, see D. Geradin, 'Quel Contrôle pour Les Aides d'Etat', in *Les Aides d'Etat en Droit Communautaire et en Droit National* (Documents to a seminar, held at Liège, 14–15 May 1998) (Brussels: Bruylant, 1999), 68–71.

[128] For discussions of Art. 87 EC, see L. Hancher, T. Ottervanger, and P. J. Slot, *EC State Aids* (London: Chancery Law Publishing, 1993), 17 ff.; R. D'Sa, *European Community Law on State Aid* (London: Sweet & Maxwell, 1998), paras. 3.001 ff.

[129] Case 240/83, *Procureur de la République v Association de Défense des Brûleurs d'Huiles Usagées (ADBHU)* [1984] ECR 531.

polluted site had the effect of favouring the undertaking that owns the site, except if that undertaking is subsequently bound to repay the state-financed clean-up costs.[130]

Second, the measure must be *imputable to the state,* and involve a direct or indirect *transfer of state resources* to one or several undertakings. Concerning the imputability, the ECJ has made clear that Article 87(1) applies to aid granted not only by central government, but also by regional or local authorities.[131] This provision also applies to aid granted by undertakings in which the state exerts a dominant influence.[132] In contrast, aids granted by EU authorities (LIFE programme, structural funds, etc.) cannot be considered aids within the meaning of Article 87 EC.[133]

As for the notion of state resources, the ECJ requires that the measure forms a pecuniary burden for the state. This burden may take a variety of forms, such as for instance direct subsidies[134] or tax exemptions.[135] By contrast, measures that do not involve pecuniary charges for the state do not fall under the concept of state aid, even if they present an advantage for the undertakings concerned. This would be the case, for instance, in respect of a state measure exempting certain categories of undertakings (for example, chemical companies) from the scope of an environmental legislation (for example, legislation concerning liability for damage caused by waste). In the Community system, such 'regulatory subsidies' must be eliminated through harmonization of environmental standards applied by Member States.[136]

Finally, for a state measure to be considered a state aid, it must *favour one or several undertakings.* This condition of specificity would be fulfilled, for instance, in the case of a state measure exempting from tax undertakings producing clean-up equipment. Such a measure would clearly favour these undertakings to the detriment of foreign competitors. By contrast, nothing would prevent Member States from exempting certain categories of environmentally friendly products from taxation.[137] To the extent that such a measure

---

[130] Commission Decision 1999/272/EC on the Measure Planned by Austria for the Clean-Up of the Kiener Deponie Bachmanning Landfill [1999] OJ L109/51.

[131] Case 78/76, *Steinike & Weinlig* v. *Germany* [1987] ECR 595.

[132] See Cases 67, 68, and 70/85 R, *Kwekerij Gebroeders van der Kooy BV and others* v. *Commission* [1988] ECR 219.

[133] For a survey of the environmental aid regimes granted by the Community, see C. London, 'Les Aides Financières en Faveur de la Protection de l'Environnement' (1994) 20 *Droit et Pratique du Commerce International*, 282.

[134] See, e.g., the aid granted by the Spanish Government to Opel for a project designed to apply new technology to the painting process, so as to reduce pollution; IP/97/437 (published on the Internet at: http://www.europa.eu.int (RAPID database)).

[135] See, e.g., the Dutch aid scheme aimed at stimulating the use of electricity generated by renewable energy-sources, by exempting 'green electricity' from energy tax; IP/98/411 (published on the Internet at: http://www.europa.eu.int (RAPID database)).

[136] On this issue, see D. Geradin, *Trade and Environment—A Comparative Study of EC and US Law* (Cambridge: Cambridge University Press, 1997), 75 ff.

[137] See E. Grabitz and C. Zacker, 'Scope for Action by EC Member States for the Improvement of Environmental Protection under EEC Law: The Example of Environmental Taxes and Subsidies' (1989) 26 *Common Market Law Review*, 423.

applies in a non-discriminatory fashion,[138] it can reach its environmental objective without unduly favouring national industry or production.

### ii. Negative Impact on Competition and Intra-Community Trade

For an environmental measure to fall within the concept of state aid, it must affect the conditions of competition, as well as trade between Member States.

In its application of Article 87 EC, the Commission has generally considered that state aid measures quasi-automatically affect conditions of competition and trade,[139] transforming in practice this conditional provision into a *per se* prohibition.[140] There are, however, some exceptions. For instance, in *RENOVE*, which is examined in greater detail below, the Commission considered that, in so far as it only concerned individual or small and medium-size companies operating locally, a Spanish state subsidy for the purchase of heavy vehicles could not affect trade between Member States and therefore did not fall within the prohibition of Article 87 EC.[141] Such aid could, however, affect intra-Community trade if it was intended for road transport companies entering in competition with companies of other Member States.

It should also be noted that, pursuant to a Communication adopted in 1996, the Commission considers that aids inferior to 100,000 euros in three years do not fall within the scope of Article 87(1) EC (*de minimis* criterion).[142] Environmental aids involving sums inferior to the above amount do not therefore trigger the prohibition established by that provision and do not require notification to the Commission pursuant to the procedure of Article 88(3) EC. The Commission's power to define the scope of Articles 87(1) and 88(3) EC by establishing a *de minimis* rule has sometimes been questioned. However, Article 2 of Regulation (EC) No. 994/98 on the Application of Articles 92 and 93 of the Treaty Establishing the European Community to Certain Categories of Horizontal State Aid, now formally empowers the Commission to declare, by means of a Regulation, certain aids to fall outside the scope of Article 87(1) EC because they do not exceed a certain fixed amount over a given period of time.[143] In its draft Regulation on the application of Articles 87 and 88 EC to *de minimis* aid, the Commission decided to maintain the threshold of 100,000 euros over a three-year period.[144] Adoption of this Regulation will thus not modify the substance of state aid policy vis-à-vis aids of a small amount.

[138] See the French biofuels case, discussed below.

[139] This approach has been criticized by those who would like the Commission to engage in a more detailed analysis of the effects of a measure on competition and intra-Community trade. See S. Bishop, 'The European Commission's Policy towards State Aid: A Role for Rigorous Competitive Analysis' (1997) 18 *European Competition Law Review*, 84.

[140] F. Jenny, 'Competition and State Aid Policy in the European Community' (1994) 18 *Fordham International Law Journal*, 534.

[141] Commission Decision 98/693/EC Concerning the Spanish Plan Renove Industrial System of Aid for the Purchase of Commercial Vehicles [1998] OJ L329/23.

[142] See Commission Notice on the *De Minimis* Rule for State aid [1996] OJ C68/9.

[143] Council Reg. (EC) No. 994/98 on the Application of Arts. 92 and 93 EC to Certain Categories of Horizontal State Aid [1998] OJ L142/1.

[144] See Commission Reg. (EC) No. 69/2001 on the Application of Arts. 87 and 88 EC to *De Minimis* Aid [2001] OJ L10/30.

## B. ARTICLES 87(1) AND (2) EC: THE EXCEPTIONS TO THE PRINCIPLE OF INCOMPATIBILITY

The prohibition contained in Article 87(1) EC is not absolute. State aid affecting competition and intra-Community trade can be exempted on the basis of one of the exceptions contained in the second and third paragraph of Article 87 EC.

We will not discuss the exceptions figuring in Article 87(2) here, since they are of only limited interest as a source of justification for environmental state aids. By contrast, Article 87(3) EC presents several useful bases for the justification of such aids, in particular in paragraphs (b) and (c). Article 87(3)(b) EC allows the Commission to consider as compatible with the common market 'aid to promote the execution of an important project of common European interest'. In *Glaverbel*, the ECJ ruled that the concerted actions of several Member States in order to fight against a common threat, such as pollution of the environment, could be part of that category.[145] In addition, Article 87(3)(c) EC authorizes the Commission to exempt from the prohibition of Article 87(1) EC 'aid to facilitate the development of certain economic activities or of certain economic areas'. As will be seen, it is on this basis that the Commission has exempted the majority of state aids for environmental protection.

When an environmental aid falls within one of the exceptions indicated above, it will not automatically be exempted. Such derogations only apply when the Commission considers, pursuant to its discretionary powers, that it is appropriate that they be applied to the aid project in question. The discretionary powers enjoyed by the Commission pursuant to Article 87 EC led that institution to develop a series of principles, on the basis of which the notified aid regimes will be judged.[146] Among these criteria figure the principles of *necessity*, pursuant to which an aid regime will be justified only if it is necessary to achieve the intended environmental objective,[147] and *proportionality*, pursuant to which environmental aids will be justified only 'when adverse effects on competition are outweighed by the benefits for the environment'.[148]

The application of the principle of proportionality illustrates the extent of the discretionary powers enjoyed by the Commission in the area of state aid. In order to implement this principle, the Commission will indeed have to

[145] Cases 62 and 72/87, *Exécutif régional wallon and SA Glaverbel v. Commission* [1988] ECR 1573.

[146] I do not pretend to be exhaustive here. For a more detailed examination, see M. Merola, 'Introduction à l'Etude des Règles Communautaires en Matières d'Aides d'Etat Aux Entreprises' (1993) *Revue de Droit International Economique*, 298–302.

[147] In the area of state aids, this principle of necessity takes the form of a requirement of a 'compensatory justification' pursuant to which 'aid may only be granted when the Commission can establish that it will contribute to the attainment of the objectives specified in the exemption, which under normal market conditions the recipient firms would not attain by their own actions'. Commission Decision 79/743/EEC on Proposed Netherlands Government Assistance to Increase the Production Capacity of a Cigarette Manufacturer [1979] OJ L217/17.

[148] See point 1.6 of the Commission Guidelines on State Aid for Environmental Protection, n. 21 above.

maintain a balance, inevitably subjective,[149] between the protection of competition and other policy objectives indicated in the second and third paragraph of Article 87 EC.

## C. THE COMMUNITY GUIDELINES ON STATE AID FOR ENVIRONMENTAL PROTECTION

One of the characteristics of state aid law is the adoption by the Commission of 'guidelines'. These guidelines are intended to facilitate the tasks of Member States wishing to grant aids to industry. They articulate the criteria the Commission intends to use to appraise compatibility with the Common Market of state aid regimes granted to achieve a variety of objectives, such as regional integration, environmental protection, research, and development, etc. Whenever a specific aid regime fulfils the criteria set in the guidelines, it will be favourably considered by the Commission.

As already noted, the first Commission guidelines on state aid for environmental protection were adopted in 1974. These guidelines, which were confirmed in 1980[150] and 1986,[151] provided that aid could be authorized mainly to help firms make the investment necessary to achieve certain mandatory minimum standards. The use of aids was considered as a transitional stage, paving the way for the progressive introduction of the polluter-pays principle. This first set of guidelines was, however, replaced in 1994 by new guidelines which continue to allow environmental aids in some circumstances.[152] In the introductory part of these new guidelines, the Commission acknowledges once again the importance of the polluter-pays principle, but it also points to the Community's 5th Environmental Action Programme, which argues that, given the unsatisfactory results of traditional 'command and control' regulatory approaches, recourse should be had to a broader set of instruments, including positive financial incentives (i.e. subsidies) and disincentives (i.e. taxes and levies).[153] For the Commission, the application of state aid rules should reflect the role economic instruments can play in environmental policy.[154]

Unlike the 1974 guidelines, which authorize certain environmental aids on the basis of Article 87(3)(b) EC, the new guidelines use Article 87(3)(c) EC as a justification. Regarding the specific criteria on the basis of which it will appraise environmental aids, the Commission draws a distinction between

[149] On the subjective character of the analysis of proportionality, see D. Geradin and R. Stewardson, 'Trade and Environment: Some Lessons from *Castlemaine Tooheys* (Australia) and *Danish Bottles* (European Community)' (1995) 44 *International and Comparative Law Quarterly*, 66–70.

[150] Tenth Report on Competition Policy (1980), paras. 222–6.

[151] Sixteenth Report on Competition Policy (1986), para. 259.

[152] The validity of these Guidelines, which where to expire on 30 June 2000, was extended by the Commission until 30 Dec. 2000. See Commission Press Release (IP/00/676), published on the Internet at: http://www.europa.eu.int (RAPID database).

[153] Proposal for a Resolution of the Council of the European Communities on a Community Programme of Policy and Action in relation to the Environment and Sustainable Development, COM(92)23 final, 27 Mar. 1992

[154] Point 1.2 of the Guidelines, n. 21 above.

three broad categories of aids: investment aid,[155] horizontal support measures,[156] and operating aid.[157] I will concentrate hereafter on the first and third of these categories, which present most difficulties from a competition perspective, namely investment aid and operating aid.

As far as *investment aids* are concerned,[158] the Commission maintains a distinction between two subcategories: aids designed to help firms adapt to new mandatory standards, and aids to encourage firms to improve on mandatory environmental standards. Regarding the first subcategory, aids can be authorized up to 15 per cent gross of eligible costs for a limited period, and only in respect of plants which have been in operation for at least two years prior to the new standards or obligations entering into force.[159] As regards aids falling within the second subcategory, the level of aid that is authorized is much higher as it can cover up to 30 per cent gross of eligible costs.[160] A similar level of aid is authorized when the investment is made in the absence of mandatory standards.[161] By adopting differentiated levels of admissible aid, the Commission seeks to reward undertakings that decide to make investments to implement standards that go beyond the existing regulatory framework.

As far as *operating aids* are concerned, the Commission is much more careful,[162] as it indicates that it does not normally approve operating aid which relieves firms of costs resulting from the pollution or nuisance they cause. However, the Commission may make an exception to this principle in certain well-defined circumstances. So far, it has done this in the fields of waste management, and relief from environmental taxes. In the field of waste management, the public financing of the additional costs of selective collection and recycling schemes may involve state aid. According to the Commission's guidelines, such aid will be authorized only if businesses are charged in proportion to their use of the system, or the amount of waste they produce. As far as environmental taxes are concerned, temporary relief may be authorized when it is necessary to offset losses in competitiveness, in particular at the international level. The Commission indicates that it will assess operating aid regimes on their merits, and in the light of strict criteria it has developed in the above fields. These are that the aid must only compensate for extra production costs by comparison with traditional costs, and that it should be temporary and in principle digressive, so as to provide an incentive for reducing pollution or introducing more efficient uses of resources more quickly.

---

[155] These measures comprise aid to help firms to adapt their plant to new standards or to encourage them to reach such standards more rapidly; aid to encourage firms to improve on mandatory standards through investments that reduce the level of pollution below what is required by legislation, etc.

[156] These measures comprise aid to encourage research and development of technologies that cause less pollution, provision of technical information, consultancy services, and training about new environmental technologies and practices, etc.

[157] Such measures comprise aid in the form of grants, relief from environmental taxes or charges, and aid for the purchase of environmentally friendly products.

[158] Point 3.2 of the Guidelines, n. 21 above.     [159] Point 3.2.3 of the Guidelines, n. 21 above.

[160] Ibid.          [161] Ibid.          [162] Point 3.4 of the Guidelines, n. 21 above.

It should be noted that there exists some uncertainty over the legal status of these Commission guidelines.[163] As far as horizontal aids are concerned (including environmental aids), in the future these guidelines will be 'solidified' into block exemption regulations adopted pursuant to Article 2 of Regulation (EC) No. 994/98 on the Application of Articles 92 and 93 of the Treaty Establishing the European Community to Certain Categories of Horizontal State Aid.[164] The formal enpowerment of the Commission by Regulation (EC) No. 994/98 to adopt such block exemption regulations will give more legal certainty to the compatibility criteria developed so far in the Commission guidelines.[165] From a procedural perspective, it will also scrap the obligation for Member States to notify the aid regimes that are compatible with the criteria set in the block exemption regulations.

### D.  ILLUSTRATIONS

This part will be devoted to a short discussion of some recent Commission decisions in the field of state aid for environmental protection. Here again, the objective is not to provide an exhaustive account of the Commission's decisional practice in the field, but to provide some illustrations how the Commission applies competition principles to environmental measures.

In *French Biofuels*, the Commission considered incompatible with the common market a French regime which exempted biofuels of agricultural origin from the domestic tax on petroleum products.[166] This measure sought to encourage the production of renewable polluting fuels, as well as to offer new outlets for surplus agricultural products.

The Commission felt that this regime fell within the scope of Article 87(1) EC since it distorted competition by giving an advantage to the categories of biofuels covered by the exemption, as well as the agricultural products used for their production. The Commission also considered that this regime could not be justified on the basis of Article 87(3) EC because it was discriminatory. Since the exemption could only benefit biofuels produced on the basis of *certain* agricultural products, other biofuels produced on the basis of other raw materials could not benefit from the exemption.

Following this Commission Decision, the French Government decided to extend the benefit of the tax exemption to all types of biofuels, independent of the agricultural products used for their production. The compatibility of this

---

[163] On this issue, see A. Evans, *EC Law of State Aid* (Oxford: Clarendon Press, 1997), 408–27.

[164] See n. 143 above. For a discussion of the impact of Council Reg. (EC) No. 994/98 (n. 143 above), see J. P. Kepenne, '(R)évolution dans Le Système Communautaire de Contrôle des Aides d'Etat' (1998/2) 8 *Revue du Marché Unique Européen*, 125.

[165] The Commission has not yet adopted a block exemption regulation for environmental state aids. So far, it has only adopted draft block exemption regulations for training aid and aid to small and medium-sized enterprises. These draft regulations are available on the Commission's website, published on the Internet at: http://www.europa.eu.int/comm/dg04/lawaid/aid.htm.

[166] See Commission Decision. 97/542/EC on Tax Exemptions for Biofuels in France [1997] OJ L222/26.

new regime with competition rules was recognized by the Commission in a second decision.[167]

*Hydrogen Peroxide* concerned an aid granted by the Dutch Government towards the costs of constructing a hydrogen peroxide production plant in Delfzijl, in the province of Groningen.[168] This aid exceeded the maximum level of admissible aid which the Commission had approved in relation to the regional aid scheme applicable to Delfzijl. The Dutch Government argued that the excess aid could be justified on ecological grounds. The region of Delfzijl hosting a conservation area, the mandatory environmental standards in force in the area are indeed especially strict.

In its Decision, the Commission referred to its 1994 guidelines pursuant to which '[a]id for investment that allows significantly higher levels of environmental protection to be attained than those required by mandatory standards may be authorized up to a maximum of 30 per cent gross of eligible costs'. Pursuant to the same guidelines, 'the level of aid actually granted for exceeding standards must be *in proportion* to the improvement of the environment that is achieved and the investment necessary for achieving the improvement'.

The Commission took the view that these conditions were not met in the case at hand. According to the Commission, the Dutch authorities did not produce anything to show that the company in question had complied with Dutch environmental legislation. Neither did they show that the aid was in proportion to the investment or to the extent to which the standards had been exceeded. The Commission added that aids up to the ceiling of 30 per cent gross of the eligible costs only are admitted in cases in which 'the measures being taken go *very substantially* beyond the compulsory standards', something that was not demonstrated in the present case.[169]

*RENOVE* related to a Spanish aid regime involving the granting of loans for the purchase of commercial vehicles, the objective of which was to facilitate the renewal of the commercial vehicle fleet in Spain.[170] In its Decision, the Commission considered that in a road transport market open to competition, this measure could create a distortion of competition between carriers established in Spain, and those who operate in Spain but are based in other Member States. It was therefore deemed contrary to Article 87(1) EC.

In its assessment of the applicability of the exception contained in Article 87(3)(c) EC, the Commission acknowledged the validity of the argument that financial incentives may help to withdraw from the market commercial vehicles with low technical standards with regard to safety and/or the environment. It considered, however, that in order to be compatible with the Common Market, the aid regime must be organized in such a way that 'the eligible costs are strictly confined to the extra investment costs necessary to meet environmental

---

[167] IP/97/285, published on the Internet at: http://www.europa.eu.int (RAPID database).

[168] Commission Decision 98/384/EC on Aid Granted by the Netherlands to a Hydrogen Peroxide Works in Delfzijl [1998] OJ L171/36.

[169] Point 3.2.3 of the Guidelines, n. 21 above.

[170] Commission Decision 98/693/EC, n. 141 above.

objectives by achieving standards higher than those already required by law'. In the case at hand, these conditions were not met, since in the RENOVE system the basis for calculating the subsidy was the price of a new vehicle: no environmental factor was taken into account. The subsidy was proportional to the price of the vehicles and not to their environmental or safety performance.

In *German Eco-Taxes,* the Commission decided to consider compatible with the Treaty the special tax provisions in the ecological tax law for the benefit of certain sectors of the economy, including the manufacturing industry, the agriculture and forestry sectors, and rail transport services.[171] These special provisions reduced the full tax rate for electricity and mineral oil to as little as 20 per cent, thus relieving the said companies from a part of the tax.

The Commission noted that such special tax provisions in the form of reduced tax rates or refunds may qualify as state aid if they intend to favour certain undertakings or sectors of industry. The Commission decided, however, not to raise any objections to the measures notified, since it saw them in line with the Community guidelines on state aid for environmental protection, its past practice with regard to similar schemes in other Member States, and the environmental policy of the Community.

In its assessment, the Commission took into account the fact that, at the time of adoption of the German measures, few other countries had imposed energy taxes, and that therefore the introduction of such taxes could affect the competitive position of German undertakings.[172] The Commission further took into account that the German Government committed itself to renotify the measures for approval after three years. Finally, another factor taken into account by the Commission was that German law was in line with the proposal submitted by the Commission in 1997 for a Council Directive Restructuring the Community Framework for the Taxation of Energy Products.[173]

The above decisions provide helpful indications on the way the Commission applies state aid rules in the environmental field. First, it should be observed that to exempt a state aid regime for environmental reasons, the Commission requires a causal link between the adoption of the measure, and the improvement of the environment. As illustrated by the *RENOVE* decision, a purely hypothetical environmental benefit will not be sufficient to justify a state aid regime restricting competition.

Even if the environmental benefit is clearly established, the Commission refuses to exempt certain forms of restrictions, such as discrimination based on the origins of products (see the *French Biofuels* decision). Such restrictions

---

[171] See IP/99/245. This decision concerned the first phase of the ecological tax reform in Germany. The Commission has recently adopted another positive decision on the second phase of this ecological tax reform. See IP/00/157 (published on the Internet at: http://www.europa.eu.int (RAPID database)).

[172] It should be noted that the Commission has also taken competitiveness factors into account in other decisions: IP/96/1130 (Danish fiscal package on waste water tax); IP/96/1129 (Swedish fiscal measures concerning $CO_2$); IP/96/1129 (Danish environmental taxes package). Published on the Internet at: http://www.europa.eu.int (RAPID database).

[173] Proposal for a Council Directive Restructuring the Community Framework for the Taxation of Energy Products, COM (97)30 final, 12 Mar. 1997.

enter into direct conflict with the core objectives of EC competition law policy. The *Hydrogen Peroxyde* decision also suggests that the Commission intends to apply very rigorously the criteria enounced in its 1994 guidelines. The maximum levels of aid provided for in this document cannot be interpreted in a flexible manner and, further to the proportionality principle, state aid regimes will be justified only if the environmental benefits they provide outweigh their impact on competition.

Finally, the *German Eco-Taxes* decision shows that the Commission is ready to take into account competitiveness factors in its appraisal of state aid regimes. Competitiveness pressures often have a paralysing effect on governments when they make environmental policy choices, and allowing tax exemptions for industrial users may be the only politically acceptable way for national governments to set up an energy taxation scheme.[174] Yet, such exemptions directly contradict the polluter-pays principle, since they usually benefit the largest polluters. They also considerably reduce the effectiveness of the scheme adopted. This strongly supports the adoption of a tax energy scheme at the EC level. Unfortunately, for reasons that go beyond the scope of this chapter, adoption of a strict, environmentally oriented energy taxation regime seems to be an insurmountable task for the EC.

## V. Conclusions

This chapter has endeavoured to provide a general overview of the way the European Commission has dealt with various forms of conflict between environmental measures and competition rules.

From a general perspective, it can be said that the Commission attempted, and largely succeeded, to find a proper balance between environmental considerations, whose importance is reflected in the EC Treaty, and the objectives of competition policy. As the above analysis shows, it would be wrong to say that competition principles have been enforced to the detriment of environmental protection. Conversely, the principle of integration provided for in Article 6 EC has not been interpreted as affording priority to environmental protection over competition policy. Avoiding extreme positions, EC authorities have sought to render environmental protection measures and competition policy principles as compatible as possible.

From a technical perspective, this balancing exercise has generally been pursued by means of a proportionality test (understood in the broad meaning of the term) of environmental protection measures which have a restrictive effect on competition.[175] This test involves the application of four criteria, all of which can be found in a more or less explicit manner in the implementation of the rules applicable to restrictive practices, exclusive rights, and state aids.

---

[174] See D. Esty and D. Geradin, 'Environmental Protection and International Competitiveness: A Conceptual Framework' (1998) 32 *Journal of World Trade*, 5.

[175] See generally W. Van Gerven, 'Principe de Proportionalité, Abus de Droit et Droits Fondamentaux' (1992) 111 *Journal des Tribunaux*, 305.

— The first criterion relates to the *objective* sought by the measure. In practice, it must be demonstrated that the measure serves an environmental
goal. Although environmental protection is not specifically mentioned
in Articles 81(3), 86(2), and 87(3) EC, we have seen that these provisions
can be used to justify environmental protection measures.
— The second criterion requires the presence of a *causal link* between the
measure adopted and the environmental objective. The application of
this criterion seeks to avoid the adoption and subsequent implementation of restrictive measures whose positive impact on the environment
are purely hypothetical.
— The third criterion relates to the *necessity* of the measure. An environmental measure that restricts competition will only be justified provided
the environmental objective cannot be achieved by a less restrictive
measure.
— Finally, there must be a *balance* between the measure and its objective.
The restrictions of competition brought about by the measure must be
proportionate to the environmental benefits of that measure.

The reasoning followed by the Commission in its appraisal of an environmental agreement, an exclusive right, or a state aid regime is thus relatively
coherent. Some authors have, however, noted a significant difference in the
way the Commission analyses environmental agreements and exclusive
rights, on the one hand, and state aids, on the other.[176] While for the first category of measures the Commission has as its sole option to accept or reject the
measure, it enjoys a much greater degree of flexibility for state aids, since it
does not necessarily have to adopt or reject the aid, but can also modify its
level of intensity. These authors are concerned that this difference of treatment
could encourage Member States to pursue environmental objectives through
state subsidies, instead of other, perhaps more efficient, instruments. In this
view, the various tests that are used to assess the compatibility of a measure
with the Treaty must lead to a similar result at the risk of significant distortions
as a result of the choice of policy instruments.

Although important, this observation must nevertheless be qualified.
Indeed, the appraisal by the Commission of an environmental agreement does
not necessarily lead to an approval or a rejection of the measure. As illustrated
by the *VOTOB* and *Oliebranches Faelleråd* decisions, the Commission will
often try to obtain modifications of the agreement, so as to eliminate the
restrictions of competition that are not necessary to achieve the desired environmental objective. Conversely, some environmental aid regimes may be
rejected altogether, because they contain unacceptable forms of discrimination. Whereas it is true that the Commission enjoys a greater degree of freedom
in its control of state aid measures, the rigidity of the control procedures
applied to other environmental measures must not be exaggerated.

---

[176] See, e.g., Gyselen, n. 11 above, 253–4.

# Thirty Years of EC Environmental Law: Perspectives and Prospectives

LUDWIG KRÄMER*

## I. Introduction

Principles of European Community (EC) environmental policy were for the first time formulated in 1971/2,[1] and progressively expanded in the period that followed. During the first fifteen years, EC environmental policy lacked an explicit legal basis in the EC Treaty, but such legal grounding was finally established in 1987, by the Single European Act (SEA),[2] which inserted Articles 130r to 130t EC into the Treaty. These provisions have since been renumbered, and now form Articles 174 to 176 EC. The Treaties of Maastricht[3] and Amsterdam[4] further fine-tuned these environmental provisions, and the Treaty of Nice, which still must be ratified by the fifteen Member States, contains some other—minor—amendments of the environmental chapter in the EC Treaty.

The European Union (EU) does not enjoy the prerogatives of a state; it may act only where it has been expressly so authorized by the Treaty.[5] Any comparison with domestic environmental law in the Member States, or with that the USA is therefore necessarily misleading. In particular, there exists no 'European public opinion', 'European media', or pan-European interest groups pursuing the general interest of the Community.[6] In the area of environmental protection, which is a general interest, the EC's *sui generis* character implies considerable disadvantages. Indeed, 'Community' lawyers hardly exist in the EC. Instead, lawyers still perceive, interpret, and discuss EC environmental law from a national law perspective.

---

* DG Environment, Commission of the European Communities, Professor of Law, University of Bremen, Germany. Opinions expressed are personal to the author.

[1] The first significant political statement is the Communication from the Commission on a Community environmental policy SEC(71)2616. It was followed by a political agreement among Member States on the guiding principles of a Community environmental policy, which was reached at 15 Sept. 1972. Subsequently, this agreement was inserted into the Declaration of the Council and of the Representatives of the Governments of the Member States on the Programme of Action of the European Communities on the Environment (First Community Environmental Action Programme) [1973] OJ C112/1. In Oct. 1972 the Heads of State and Government, which met in Paris, favoured Community measures on the environment, and asked the Community to elaborate a Community environmental action programme, see Commission, *6th General Report* (Luxembourg: Office for Official Publications, 1972), 8.

[2] [1987] OJ L169/1.      [3] [1992] OJ C191/1.      [4] [1997] OJ C340/1.

[5] Art. 5(1) EC: 'The Community shall act within the limits of the powers conferred upon it by this Treaty and of the objectives assigned to it therein.'

[6] Wording derived from Art. 157(2) EC.

This chapter endeavours to provide a balanced assessment of EC environmental law achievements and disappointments.

Having briefly summarized the historical development of primary EC environmental law (Section II), the role played by the EC institutions in this development will be examined (Section III). Section IV focuses on processes, instruments, and principles of EC environmental law. An analysis of substantive EC environmental law is undertaken in Section IV. Crucial issues of implementation are dealt with in Section VI, which simultaneously paves the way for a discussion of the political results of thirty years of EC environmental law in Section VII. Some conclusions are articulated in Section VIII.

## II. Primary EC Environmental Law

The environmental provisions, which were originally inserted in the EC Treaty in 1987, now form Articles 174–6 EC. These provisions establish objectives and principles for EC environmental policy and action, specify decision-making procedures, and allow Member States, after the adoption of Community measures, to maintain or introduce more stringent environmental measures, provided these are compatible with the other provisions of the Treaty, in particular Article 28 EC.

At a more general level, Article 2 EC instructs the Community to promote 'a high level of protection and improvement of the quality of the environment'. Article 3(1) EC provides that EC activities shall include 'a policy in the sphere of the environment', and Article 6 EC continues that 'environmental protection requirements must be integrated into the definition and implementation of the Community policies and activities . . ., in particular with a view to promoting sustainable development'.

The provision of Article 95 EC, found in the chapter on the approximation of laws with a view to establishing an internal market, instructs the Commission to elaborate proposals in the area of the environment that have 'as a base a high level of protection'. After the adoption of a Community measure based on Article 95 EC, Member States may, under certain conditions, maintain or introduce more stringent environmental measures.

Finally, Article 161(2) EC concerns the setting up of a Cohesion Fund with the task to provide financial contributions to projects in the field of the environment. This provision contributes to realizing the objectives of Article 158 EC, which includes the reduction of 'the backwardness of the least favoured regions or islands, including rural areas'.

The structure of the EC Treaty still reflects the preponderance of economic interests, evidenced in particular by the provisions on the internal market, agriculture, competition, and transport. Thus, Article 28 EC contains the principle that (national) barriers to trade which impair the free circulation of goods are prohibited,[7] Article 81 EC stipulates that agreements and concerted practices

---

[7] Art. 28 EC reads: 'Quantitative restrictions on imports and all measures having equivalent effect shall be prohibited between Member States.'

between undertakings are illegal,[8] and Article 87 EC declares that, in principle, state aids are prohibited;[9] Articles 174–6 EC, however, do not contain a prohibition to cause pollution. Rather, these provisions are drafted in a way so as to entrust the protection of the environment to public administration, which may adopt regulatory measures, or provide for incentives to preserve the environment. In contrast to the free-trade provisions, individuals enjoy no participation or enforcement rights.

This has led the Avosetta Group, a recently created group of environmental lawyers in the Community, to suggest that a new provision be inserted into the EC Treaty, which would read:

Subject to imperative reasons of overriding public interests, significantly impairing the environment or human health shall be prohibited.

This provision would hence come to mirror the present Articles 28 and 30 EC, the basic Treaty provisions on the free circulation of goods.

No specific environmental provisions have been inserted into the Treaty establishing the European Coal and Steel Community (ECSC) or the Treaty establishing the European Atomic Energy Community (EURATOM). As regards the EURATOM Treaty in particular, this omission is regrettable, since the policies of this Treaty now hardly take account of the requirement to integrate environmental requirements into nuclear energy policy.

Neither does the Treaty on European Union (TEU) refer to the protection of the environment, except for a marginal reference in its eighth recital,[10] which is striking, because this contrasts with other policies such as the internal market, monetary policy, and the free movement of persons.

When negotiating international Conventions, Protocols, Agreements, or Declarations at international level, the Community, within its sphere of competence, in theory is represented by the Commission, which conducts the negotiations on the basis of a mandate by the Council, and in concertation with a Council working group.[11] In practice, however, Member States are often unwilling to follow these rules, as they do not want to be seen, at international level, as having forfeited their sovereignty. Therefore, they frequently conduct

---

[8] Art. 81(1) EC reads: 'The following shall be prohibitied as incompatible with the common market: all agreements between undertakings, decisions by associations of undertakings and concerted practices which may affect trade between Member States and which have as their object or effect the prevention, restriction or distortion of competition within the common market.'

[9] Art. 91(1) EC reads: 'Save as otherwise provided in this Treaty, any aid granted by a Member State or through State resources in any form whatsoever which distorts or threatens to distort competition by favouring certain undertakings or the production of certain goods shall, insofar as it affects trade between Member States, be incompatible with the common market.'

[10] Treaty on European Union, 8th Recital (Maastricht, 7 Feb. 1992) [1997] OJ C340/145:

Determined to promote economic and social progress for their peoples, taking into account the principle of sustainable development and within the context of the accomplishment of the internal market and of reinforced cohesion and environmental protection, and to implement policies ensuring that advances in economic integration are accompanied by parallel progress in other fields.

[11] See Art. 300 EC.

these negotiations themselves, a problem which goes well beyond the environmental aspects of the Treaty. The idea of progressively transferring national sovereignty to the Community in practice still meets objections from diplomats and foreign policy administrations.

However, the insertion of environmental provisions into the EC Treaty appears to have been successful. The broad formulation of environmental objectives and principles, the integration requirement of Article 6 EC, and the different provisions which formulate the relationship between Member States and the Community give a sufficient legal basis for a coherent and progressive environmental policy at Community level. The question whether the Community has adequately made use of these opportunities, which is a question of policy, rather than law, nevertheless needs to be addressed.

## III. Community Institutions

### A. THE COMMISSION

Over the past thirty years, the Commission changed its environmental bureaucracy only slightly. In 1973 it set up an Environment and Consumer Protection Service, conceived as a horizontal Service placed under one of the Commission's Vice-Presidents which should, in a way similar to the Legal Service, influence policies of all other departments. However, this initiative met the resistance of existing administrative departments, and was therefore soon abandoned.

When Greece acceded to the Community in 1981, the Service was transformed into a Directorate-General. Following the accession of Spain and Portugal, environmental and consumer protection matters were separated in 1989, and two independent Directorate-Generals were formed. At present, the environmental department counts approximately 500 officials, roughly 10 per cent of which are on secondment from national administrations for a maximum period of three years. However, other EC policies such as industry, internal market, energy, regional, agriculture, transport, research, consumer protection, and the legal service, also have to deal with environmental questions, so that the total number of Commission officials working in the area of the environment is considerably higher.

The Commission instituted a Consultative Forum on the Environment and Sustainable Development,[12] and a Scientific Committee for Toxicity, Ecotoxicity and Environment.[13] Both bodies only play a limited role in the decision-making process at Community level. Furthermore, the Commission is supported by the European Environmental Agency, which was set up by the

---

[12] Commission Decision 97/150/EC on the Setting-Up of a European Consultative Forum on the Environment and Sustainable Development [1997] OJ L58/48; the Forum was set up in 1993.

[13] Commission Decision 97/579/EC Setting-Up Scientific Committees in the Field of Consumer Health and Food Safety [1997] OJ L237/18; this Scientific Committee was first set up in 1978

Council,[14] and has the task to collect, process, and distribute information on the environment. The approximately seventy officials of the Agency are too few in number to allow the Agency to assume additional functions, such as relating to monitoring and control. In any event, Member States do not wish to see the Agency develop in this direction. Instead, they set up an informal, more or less intergovernmental network, IMPEL (European Network on the Implementation and Enforcement of Environmental Law), to discuss and promote implementation of Community environmental legislation. Although IMPEL closely cooperates with the Commission, its influence on the latter and on the implementation of Community environmental law remains fairly limited.

Attempts in the early 1980s to set up an environmental fund failed, which find its expression in the present Article 175(4) EC, stipulating that, in general, 'the Member States shall finance . . . the environment policy'. Apart from the Cohesion Fund,[15] the Commission administers a financial instrument, LIFE,[16] which is equipped with about 100 million euros per year, and cofinances pilot and demonstration projects for clean technologies, and nature protection projects.

### B. THE COUNCIL OF MINISTERS

The Council of Ministers (the Council) meets as Environment Council four times per year. In addition, there are two informal Council meetings which discuss more basic problems, and which do not take decisions. This frequency is high compared to other policy areas, which allows, at least in theory, for a close alignment of policy and legal approaches among Member States' governments.

Until 1993, the Council decided unanimously on environmental matters. For environmental issues adopted under Article 100a EC (now Article 95 EC) concerning the establishment of the internal market, majority voting was introduced in 1987. This dichotomy gave rise to frequent discussions as to whether Article 175 EC or Article 95 EC was the appropriate legal basis for environmental measures.[17] In 1993 the TEU introduced majority decisions for the majority of environmental measures adopted under Article 175 EC. This amendment, in conjunction with the Treaty of Amsterdam, largely eliminated any procedural differences between both provisions, thus removing many

---

[14] Council Reg. (EEC) No. 1210/90 on the Establishment of the European Environment Agency and the European Environment Information and Observation Network [1990] OJ L120/1. The Agency started to work only in 1994.

[15] The Cohesion Fund was set up by Council Reg. (EC) 1164/94 Establishing a Cohesion Fund [1994] OJ L130/1; see Council Reg. (EC) 1265/99 Amending Annex II to Reg. No. 1164/94 [1999] OJ L161/62.

[16] European Parliament and Council Reg. (EC) 1655/2000 Concerning the Financial Instrument for the Environment (LIFE) [2000] OJ L192/1. The Fund and its predecessors have existed since 1991.

[17] See Cases C–300/89, *Commission v. Council* [1991] ECR I–2867; C–155/91, *Commission v. Council* [1993] ECR I–939; C–187/93, *European Parliament v. Council* [1994] ECR I–2857.

grounds for litigation. De facto, however, the Council on environmental matters frequently continues to decide unanimously.

Decisions of the Council are prepared by working groups, composed of the environmental *attachés* of Member States' representations with the Community, whom officials from Member States' ministerial departments assist. The Council Presidency, which also chairs the working groups, determines which Commission proposals are discussed in the working groups, and subsequently submitted for a decision by the Council.

Between 1973 and 2000, the Council adopted, in part together with the European Parliament, some 150 environmental directives and regulations, as well as decisions to adhere to international environmental agreements. A similar number of amendments was adopted, in part also by the Commission by virtue of the Comitlogy procedure pursuant to Article 145 EC. The exact number of measures adopted depends on the method of calculation. It is not easy to define what constitutes an environmental measure. For example, it is debatable whether this should include emission standards for cars or airplanes, provisions on chemicals or pesticides, and measures to combat mad cow disease. Similarly, amendments of existing directives may sometimes be of minor technical significance, but in other cases may have considerable political and legal implications.

### C.  THE EUROPEAN PARLIAMENT

The European Parliament (EP), directly elected since 1979, saw its role in the decision-making procedure progressively strengthened. While, originally, it was only to be consulted, it is now partner in the co-decision procedure in almost all environmental decisions. The consultation process only continues to apply in the cases specified in Article 175(2) EC, where the Council decides by unanimity, in the agricultural sector (Article 37(2) EC), and for basic decisions in the transport sector (Article 71(2) EC).

The opinions and positions of the EP in the past were strongly influenced by its progressive Environmental Committee, and it normally called for stronger environmental measures than proposed by the Commission or the Council. Since 1999, the EP, for the first time since 1979, has a conservative majority, and a shift may take place in this regard, although it is too early to categorically confirm this tendency.

The EP once used the prerogative granted to it by Article 192 EC, and formally requested the Commission to submit a proposal for a Directive on Environmental Liability. However, the Commission was of the opinion that its right of initiative for new proposals could not be affected by such a request, and refused. The practical significance of this prerogative therefore remains uncertain.

Strikingly, environmental petitions addressed to the EP pursuant to Article 194 EC, are not administered or monitored by Parliament itself. Rather, the EP asks the Commission to investigate the matter. This might well be the only example of an elected parliament renouncing the use of the instrument of petitions, as a means of autonomous control of any incriminating behaviour.

Parliament also sporadically organizes hearings on environmental matters, but this occurs in a form which all too clearly shows the absence of a European public opinion.

### D. THE ECONOMIC AND SOCIAL COMMITTEE AND THE COMMITTEE OF THE REGIONS

The Economic and Social Committee, and the Committee of the Regions, set up by Articles 257 EC and 263 EC, have advisory tasks, and play a limited role in environmental matters. Their opinions are rarely echoed in the Council or the EP. The Economic and Social Committee regularly supports Commission proposals, while the Committee of the Regions, set up only in 1993, still seems to struggle to adopt a cohesive position as regards environmental questions.

### E. THE EUROPEAN COURT OF JUSTICE

The European Court of Justice (ECJ) and the Court of First Instance (CFI) have delivered judgments in over 200 environmental cases.[18] These judgments often enhance the legal status of the environment, in particular the integration of environmental requirements into other policy areas. For instance, the ECJ ruled that Community environmental directives are binding legal instruments, rather than voluntary guidelines lacking binding force. During the first years of environmental policy, this clearly had been different.

ECJ procedures in environmental matters, on average, take approximately twenty months. However, for infringement procedures under Article 226 EC, the duration of the prejudicial phase should also be taken into account. Consequently, at present the overall average duration of litigation in environmental matters pursuant to Article 226 EC, exceeds five years (68 months).[19]

A penalty payment, first introduced in 1993 after an amendment of Article 228 EC, was only once applied, in a case against Greece for not having taken necessary measures to comply with an earlier ECJ judgment of 1992.[20] This new provision clearly has a deterrent effect, in the sense that Member States will seek to comply with earlier judgments in order to avoid a second ECJ judgment and a penalty payment. The problem of Article 228 EC lies elsewhere, however. Between the formal opening of infringement proceedings and the second judgment pursuant to Article 228 EC, more than nine years usually pass,[21] a time-span which makes this sanction relatively ineffective.

In summary, it may be concluded that all EC institutions by now have adapted to the requirements of the policy area 'environment'. Yet problems for

---

[18] Once more, this number depends on the exact definition of 'environmental case'.

[19] For details, see L. Krämer, 'Die Rechtsprechung der EG-Gerichte zum Umweltschutz 1998 und 1999' (2000) 24 *Europäische Grundrechte Zeitschrift*, 265.

[20] Case C–387/97, *Commission* v. *Greece* [2000] ECR I–5047.

[21] In Case C–387/97, n. 20 above, this period exceeded eleven years (134 months).

individuals to enforce a right to a clean and healthy environment continue to exist. There also remains a gap in the effectiveness of enforcement and monitoring mechanisms for EC environmental law. Finally, reliable Community-wide data and statistics on the environment, which are necessary in order for decisions to be based on sound knowledge and *ex post* impact assessment, are still largely lacking.

## IV. The Framework of EC Environmental Law

### A. LEGAL PRINCIPLES

The EC Treaty contains a number of guiding principles which concern action in the field of the environment. The EC Treaty contains the precautionary principle, the principle of prevention, the principle that environmental damage should be rectified at source, the polluter-pays principle (all in Article 174 EC), and the principle that environmental requirements must be integrated into other Community policies (Article 6 EC). The legal status of these principles, however, remains ambiguous. Although, as early as in 1975, the Council adopted a Recommendation on the polluter-pays principle,[22] and the Commission issued a Communication on the precautionary principle,[23] these merely raised questions on the political relevance of the principles, rather than clarifying their substantive scope. The ECJ justified a Belgian import ban on hazardous waste in 1992, *inter alia*, with reference to the principle that environmental damage should be rectified at source.[24] In 1998 the ECJ declared that the Community export ban for British beef was justified, *inter alia*, by virtue of preventive considerations laid down in Article 174 EC, in conjunction with the integration principle.[25]

It should be noted that the ECJ has consistently held that provisions of Community law could not be interpreted in such a way 'as to give rise to results which are incompatible with the general principles of Community law, and in

---

[22] Council Rec. 75/436/Euratom, ECSC, EEC regarding Cost Allocation and Action by Public Authorities on Environmental Matters [1975] OJ L194/1.

[23] Communication from the Commission on the Precautionary Principle, COM(2000)1, 2 Feb. 2000.

[24] Case C–2/90, *Commission* v. *Belgium* [1992] ECR I–4431, para. 34: 'The principle that environmental damage should as a priority be rectified at source—a principle laid down by Article 130r(2) EEC for action by the Community relating to the environment—means that it is for each region, commune or other local entitiy to take appropriate measures to receive, process and dispose of its own waste.'

[25] Case C–180/96, *United Kingdom* v. *Commission* [1998] ECR I–2265, paras 99–100: Where there is uncertainty as to the existence or extent of risks to human health, the institutions may take protective measures without having to wait until the reality and seriousness of those risks become fully apparent. That approach is borne out by Article 130r(1) of the EEC Treaty, according to which Community policy on the environment is to pursue the objective, *inter alia*, of protecting human health. Article 130r(2) provides that that policy is to be based in particular on the principles that preventive action should be taken and that environmental protection requirements must be integrated into the definition and implementation of other Community policies.

particular with fundamental rights'.[26] It does not seem likely that the ECJ would ever consider the principles of Article 174 EC 'general principles of Community law' in this sense. The environmental principles are not 'general principles of Community law', but rather 'specific principles', which may help support a specific decision or interpretation, but which lack the legal force to justify any decision on their own.[27] They serve as *leitmotifs*, or guidelines for action in environmental matters. This does not rule out that they may progressively acquire a more precise meaning, and develop into proper principles of law.

The political nature of these principles may be demonstrated by the integration principle of Article 6 EC, which refers to 'policies and activities', rather than to individual measures taken in pursuance of such policies. The principle requires the 'greening' of Community policies, by taking into consideration environmental objectives, principles, and concerns. This, however, does not imply that each individual regulation, directive, or decision, which is taken in the context of such policies, must fully respect the objectives and principles of Article 174 EC. Taken to its logical conclusion, such a requirement would mean that numerous measures would have to be declared illegal.

### B. LEGAL INSTRUMENTS

#### i. Environmental Programmes

Environmental policy is unique in that it is the only Community policy sector which, from its inception and throughout its existence, has been based on environmental action programmes. In the absence of an explicit legal competence for environmental action in the EC Treaty in the early 1970s, these programmes were designed to articulate the objectives, principles, and priorities of Community environmental action. Adopted by the Commission, the Council and the Representatives of Member States meeting in Council subsequently approved the general principles of these programmes in the form of a political Resolution, but not the programme as such.[28] Between 1973 and 1993, five such action programmes were adopted at Community level.

With the Maastricht Treaty of 1993, Article 175(3) EC was inserted in the EC Treaty, which provides that 'general action programmes' were to be adopted jointly by the EP and the Council. Community action programmes thereby

---

[26] Joined Cases 97/87, 98/87, and 99/87, *Dow Chemical Ibérica, SA, and others* v. *Commission* [1989] ECR I–3165, para. 9; see also Case C–22/94, *The Irish Farmers Association and others* v. *Minister for Agriculture, Food and Forestry, Ireland and Attorney General* [1997] ECR I–1809, para. 27.

[27] If Community measures in the area of transport or agricultural policy were to be assessed under the principles that environmental damage should be prevented, that the polluter should pay, or that damage should be rectified as source: not many measures would survive such a test.

[28] See e.g. the Resolution of the Council and the Representatives of the Governments of the Member States on a Community Programme of Policy and Action in relation to the Environment and Sustainable Development (5th Environment Action Programme) [1993] OJ C138/1: 'The Council and the Representatives of Member States meeting in Council] approve the general approach and strategy of the programme "Towards sustainability" presented by the Commission '

acquired a more legal character. At the same time, the EP, by virtue of the co-decision procedure of Article 251 EC, for the first time may co-decide on specific actions to be undertaken within the life-span of these action programmes. While, in theory, the Commission remains free to ignore a request for a proposal on a specific directive by the EP and the Council formulated in the decision that adopts an action programme, in practice the pressure to take heed of such a request will be considerable. This is also because the EP and the Council are the budgetary authorities for the Commission, and also possess other means to exercise political pressure on the Commission.

The response of the institutions to the new legal status of action programmes was almost immediate: when the fifth environmental action programme was revised in 1998, the Council, supported by the Commission, fixed objectives and principles, but avoided specific actions.[29] The Commission proposal for a decision to approve the sixth environmental action programme for the years 2001 to 2010 also very carefully avoids any wording which could be interpreted as a commitment, and refers to 'priority areas for action', rather than actions.[30] The political struggle for power between the EP and the Council is decisive in respect of the follow-up of action programmes. This is evidenced by the fact that, in the past, the Commission frequently has not undertaken the actions promised in a programme. Conversely, legislation has been adopted which had not previously been anticipated in an action programme.

## ii. Regulations

According to Article 249 EC, numerous different legal instruments are available for Community action: regulations, directives, decisions, recommendations, and opinions. Environmental law does not reflect much creativity in the use of these instruments, however. Recourse to regulations is essentially limited to either monitoring, control, or other forms of administration,[31] or to transposition of obligations flowing from an international environmental convention.[32] Environmental regulations mostly do not exhaustively regulate a specific subject matter at Community level. Rather, they contain substantive

[29] European Parliament and Council Dec. 2179/98/EC on the Review of the European Community Programme of Policy and Action in relation to the Environment and Sustainable Development 'Towards Sustainability' [1998] OJ L275/1.

[30] Communication from the Commission to the Council, the European Parliament, the Economic and Social Committee, and the Committee of the Regions on the Sixth Environment Action Programme of the European Community 'Environment 2010: Our Future, Our Choice'—The Sixth Environment Action Programme and Proposal for a Decision of the European Parliament and of the Council Laying Down the Community Environment Action Programme 2001–2010, COM(2001)31, 24 Jan. 2001.

[31] Examples are Council Reg. (EEC) No. 880/92 on a Community Eco-Label Award Scheme [1992] OJ L99/1; Council Reg. (EEC) No. 1836/93 Allowing Voluntary Participation by Companies in the Industrial Sector in a Community Eco-Management and Audit System [1993] OJ L168/1.

[32] Examples are Council Reg. (EEC) No. 259/93 on the Supervision and Control of Shipments of Waste within, into and out of the European Community [1993] OJ L30/1; Council Reg. (EC) No. 338/97 on the Protection of Species of Wild Fauna and Flora by Regulating Trade therein [1997] OJ L61/1.

provisions requiring Member States to take action, leaving issues of enforcement to Member States.

### iii. Directives

As regards environmental directives, they are frequently less precise than internal market or agricultural directives. This is partly due to the fact that most directives were based on Article 175 EC, which allows Member States, by virtue of Article 176 EC, to maintain or introduce more stringent environmental measures. In effect, Article 176 EC has spurned legislation reflecting standards lower than those envisaged by Article 176 EC. Member States desiring to introduce or maintain more stringent standards were entitled to do so on the basis of that provision. At the same time, the provision has influenced the content of directives. While Community directives on motor vehicles (i.e. internal market regulation) consist of countless pages, outlining in detail the composition of products, test methods, control mechanisms, etc.,[33] such degree of detail has been avoided in the case of environmental directives. More recently, environmental directives have even failed to fix methods and frequencies of analyses, and other measurement requirements.

Since about a decade, environmental directives, apart from lacking measurement provisions, have more generally developed into framework measures preferring quality standards over emission limits, and increasingly resorted to clean-up or management plans, leaving the final responsibility for their implementation to Member States. This tendency to resort to looser and less precise regulatory techniques is a direct product of a political, largely Anglo-Saxon driven demand for environmental deregulation.

With Directive 94/62/EC on Packaging and Packaging Waste,[34] the Community for the first time applied the so-called 'new approach' in the field environmental legislation. Directive 94/62/EC fixed general requirements for the safety and environmental aspects of packaging. The details were to be elaborated in the shape of technical standards under the authority of the European Committee for Standardization (CEN). Industry largely elaborating these standards itself, the added environmental value of the new approach, in this case, was not visible.

Another important feature of many environmental directives is that, since they address administrations their provisions are not directly applicable. This may lead to considerable application problems at a later stage. At the same time, directives on air quality standards are drafted in such a way that they are hardly enforceable against recalcitrant Member States. Meanwhile, the drafting of directives was made more onerous by virtue of the Anglo-Saxon requirement of prior cost–benefit analyses and risk assessments, because any generally accepted criteria for such assessments as yet are lacking.

[33] European Parliament and Council Dir. 97/24/EC on Certain Components and Characteristics of Two- or Three-Wheel Motor Vehicles [1997] OJ L226/1 has a length of 454 pages in the *Official Journal*.

[34] European Parliament and Council Dir. 94/62/EC on Packaging and Packaging Waste [1994] OJ L365/10.

Directives which introduce economic and financial levies, or similar constraints or incentives, have not yet been developed. Some waste directives contain general provisions in this regard, by allowing Member States to introduce economic instruments (a power they had in any event) but without obliging them to do so. A proposal for a directive on the introduction of an environmental tax on fossil fuels, made in 1992,[35] did not garner the unanimous agreement in the Council necessary under Articles 93 and 175(2) EC. Since then, no further attempts have been undertaken in the sphere of economic instruments.

### iv. Recommendations

Because they are not binding, the Community has not frequently resorted to environmental recommendations. The experience with the Council of Europe and OECD, which have adopted numerous (non-binding) measures without much visible effect, has probably influenced this practice. Similarly, the few Community environmental recommendations that were adopted have had an almost negligible effect.[36]

### v. New Instruments[37]

In the early 1990s environmental agreements were considered a contemporary form of standard setting which, in concertation with economic operators, would allow the realization of environmental objectives quicker and more effectively than 'command- and control-measures', such as legislation.[38] A Commission Communication of 1996 set out the conditions for environmental agreements at Community level.[39] This has not resulted in increased use of such agreements, however. The only significant agreement is the unilateral commitment of car manufacturers to reduce $CO_2$ emissions of new cars, from 2008 onwards, to 140 grammes $CO_2$ per kilometre. The Commission tacitly agreed to abstain from legislating on $CO_2$ emissions from cars, as long as this commitment is honoured.[40] This agreement shows that its main attraction for industry is that it pre-empts binding legislation, rather than any environmental considerations.[41] Constitutionally, the question how agreements

---

[35] [1992] OJ C196/1; amended by COM(95)172, 10 May 1995.

[36] See e.g. Council Rec. 75/436/Euratom, ECSC, EEC (n. 22 above); Council Rec. 79/3/EEC regarding Methods of Evaluating the Cost of Pollution Control to Industry [1979] OJ L5/28; Council Rec. 81/972/EEC concerning the Re-Use of Waste Paper and the Use of Recycled Paper [1981] OJ L355/56.

[37] See generally on this question, J. Golub (ed.), *New Instruments for Environmental Policy in the EU* (London/New York: Routledge, 1998), where these questions are mainly discussed from a policy perspective.

[38] See Fifth Environment Action Programme, n. 28 above.

[39] Communication from the Commission to the Council and the European Parliament on Environmental Agreements, COM(96)561, 27 Nov. 1996.

[40] For details, see L. Krämer, *EC Environmental Law* (London: Sweet & Maxwell, 2000), 214 ff.

[41] Thus, the agreement does not provide for the overall reduction of $CO_2$ emissions from cars; its environmental effects are thus likely to be at least in part outweighed by increased numbers of cars. Furthermore, it is questionable whether car production should really limit itself to this one measure or whether other measures—concerning raw materials, construction plants, etc.—are also necessary to combat the generation of greenhouse gases. Similarly, it may be asked whether the production of cars in the Community that are to be exported outside the Community should not also have reduced $CO_2$ emissions.

can be concluded at Community level which preserve the institutional parti-
cipatory rights of the EP, the Council, the Economic and Social Committee,
and the Committee of the Regions, has not yet been resolved. It is also unclear
how such agreements are to be applied, monitored and enforced in non-
oligopolistic markets. Although Directive 2000/53/EC for the first time stipulates that some of its environmental provisions may be implemented by
agreements at Member State level,[42] the legal aspects of environmental agreements at Community level remain ambiguous. Such agreements seem geared
more towards deregulation, than to the protection of the environment.[43]

Another species of new instruments, tradable pollution permits, have not
yet been developed at Community level. Pursuant to the Kyoto Protocol to the
Convention on Climate Change, which was internationally agreed in 1998, the
Community will have to develop such tradable permits for greenhouse gas
emissions, and for that purpose issued a Green Paper in 2000.[44] Beyond climate issues, such instruments do not appear to be planned.

## C. CITIZENS' INVOLVEMENT

### i. Institutional Questions

Environmental organizations are hardly represented in the Community institutions.[45] The Commission has not provided for a consultative committee of
environmental organizations or any other form ensuring their institutional
representation. Consequently, the influence of vested interest groups on
Community environmental policy and law is considerably bigger than that of
environmental interest groups. Neither is there any institutional representation
of environmental organizations in the European industrial standardization
organizations CEN and CENELEC (European Committee for Electrotechnical
Standardization). The formal argument is that environmental organizations are
free to participate in standardization work. However, since travel and other
costs are borne by participants themselves, this system is not necessarily equitable.[46]

Hearings of interested groups are hardly ever organized by the Commission,
never by the Council and, as noted, sporadically by the EP. The fact that discussions are therefore often essentially unstructured works to the disadvantage of environmental groups.

---

[42] European Parliament and Council Dir. 2000/53/EC on End-of-Life Vehicles [2000] OJ
L269/34.
[43] See on Community and Member States' environmental agreements, J. Verschuuren, 'EC
Environmental Law and Self-Regulation in the Member States: In Search of a Legislative
Framework' (2000) 1 *Yearbook of European Environmental Law*, 103 ff. Verschuuren discusses the
issue from a Dutch perspective.
[44] Commission, Green Paper on Greenhouse Gas Emissions Trading within the European
Union, COM(2000)87, 8 Mar. 2000.
[45] See generally on this question, P. Newell and W. Grant, 'Environmental NGOs and EU
Environmental Law' (2000) 1 *Yearbook of European Environmental Law*, 225 ff.
[46] For the same reason as the statement 'The access to the Ritz Hotel in Paris is open for everybody' is not constructive.

No Community measures exist which require institutional representation of environmental interest groups or individual citizens in the Member States, since this question is left entirely to Member States.

## ii. Legal Issues

A Directive of 1990 grants everybody a right of access to environmental information held by public authorities in Member States.[47] Until recently, a similar right of access to environmental information held by Community institutions had been lacking. However, the Council and the Commission also have adopted measures to provide for access to documents, and Article 255 EC now articulates a right of access to documents for any person residing in the Community, and furthermore provides that before 1 May 2001 specific rules are elaborated on this right.[48]

As regards participation in public decision-making, Directive 85/337/EEC on the Assessment of the Effects of Certain Public and Private Projects on the Environment grants the 'public concerned' a right to express its opinion in environment impact assessment procedures relating to certain public or private projects.[49] A proposal for a directive, which would grant similar rights in respect of environmental plans or programmes, is under discussion at present. Participation rights for measures emanating from Community institutions, in particular the Commission, do not exist, however.

No general legislation has yet been adopted on access to national courts. Directive 90/313/EEC, mentioned above, provides for access to national courts where access to environmental information has been refused. Community provisions grant a right to apply to European courts when the right of access to documents has been refused.[50]

Access to information, participation in public decision-making, and access to the courts in future might be further regulated, as a UN Convention on these matters was opened for signature in 1998 in Aarhus, and signed by the Community.

As regards information on the state of the environment and of the relevant law, the Commission published several reports which, overall, were not always informative. The European Environmental Agency now has the statutory duty to publish a report on the state of the environment every five years.[51] Thus far, two such reports have been published.[52] In addition, numerous environmental

---

[47] Council Dir. 90/313/EEC on the Freedom of Access to Information on the Environment [1990] OJ L158/58.

[48] Council Dec. 93/731/EC on Public Access to Council Documents [1993] OJ L340/43; Commission Dec. 94/90/EC on Public Access to Commission Documents [1994] OJ L46/58. Latest developments are published on the Internet at: http://www.europa.eu.int/comm/secretariat_general/sgc/acc_doc/en/index.htm#2.

[49] Council Dir. 85/337/EEC on the Assessment of the Effects of Certain Public and Private Projects on the Environment [1985] OJ L175/40.

[50] European Parliament and Council Reg. (EC) No. 1049/2001 regarding public access to European Parliament, Council and Commission documents [2001] OJ L145/43.

[51] Article 2(VI) of Council Reg. (EEC) No. 1210/90, n. 14 above; amended by Council Reg. (EC) No. 933/1999 [1999] OJ L117/1.

[52] See European Environment Agency, *Environment in the European Union at the Turn of the Century* (Luxembourg: Office for Official Publications, 1999).

directives and regulations require regular Commission reports regarding their implementation. In reality, however, such reports were produced very unsystematically. An attempt to rationalize and standardize such implementation reports had only limited success.[53] It must be noted that, significantly, these implementation reports are based on data provided by Member States, rather than some independent EU agency.

## V. Sectoral Perspectives

### A. HORIZONTAL QUESTIONS

*i. Products*

The Community has yet to develop a 'green' product policy.[54] Despite the requirement of the EC Treaty that products circulating in the internal market must reflect high environmental standards, free trade considerations often have prevailed.[55]

In particular, the Commission in the past has concentrated on tackling national product-related measures aiming at the protection of the environment but which contained, in its view, a protectionist element. This position in turn was based on the assumption that any national product-related environmental measure constituted a threat to the free circulation of goods. The ECJ has corrected the most obvious excesses in this regard.[56]

EC environmental product regulation has been elaborated in a piecemeal fashion.[57] Some random examples may serve to illustrate this. No attempt has been made to introduce a 'substitution principle' into Community law, requiring the replacement of known harmful substances, whenever less harmful alternatives exist. The use of pesticides and pesticide residues, fertilizers and similar products in agriculture was largely left unregulated from an environmental perspective.[58] As regards cars, although the introduction of the catalytic converter for all *new* cars became mandatory as of 1 January 1993, no measures were introduced for cars already on the market, so that, *de facto*, cars may be equipped with a catalytic converter as late as around 2006. Similarly,

[53] Council Dir. 91/692/EEC Standardizing and Rationalizing Reports on the Implementation of Certain Directives Relating to the Environment [1991] OJ L377/48.

[54] See also H. Temmink, 'From Danish Bottles to Danish Bees: The Dynamics of Free Movement of Goods and Environmental Protection—a Case Law Analysis' (2000) 1 *Yearbook of European Environmental Law*, 61 ff.

[55] See the remarks under Sect. II above.

[56] Cases C–302/86, *Commission* v. *Denmark* [1988] ECR I–4607; C–473/98, *Kemikalieinspektionen* v. *Toolex Alpha AB* [2000] ECR I–5681.

[57] See in particular, Council Dir. 76/769/EEC on Restrictions on the Marketing and Use of Certain Dangerous Substances and Preparations [1976] OJ L262/201, which has been amended about twenty times in an unsystematic way, resulting in numerous derogations, exceptions, transitional periods, etc.

[58] Council Dir. 91/414/EEC concerning the Placing of Plant Protection Products on the Market [1991] OJ L230/1 was adopted after fifteen years of discussion. It provides for uniform standards for the authorization of pesticides, which are still being elaborated.

when asbestos was finally banned from the Community market in 1999, following sixteen years of discussion and a ban at national level in nine Member States,[59] no measure was taken as regards asbestos already on the market. When PCB/PCT products were banned from the Community market in 1985, discussion shifted to the removal of the existing PCB/PCT. After ten years of discussions, Member States were finally granted until 2010 to remove them.[60]

In respect of products containing genetically modified organisms, the Community first adopted legislation in 1990. However, it soon appeared that this directive could not be enforced in view of consumer objections to biotechnology echoed in a number of Member States. In the first half of 2001, much more stringent Community legislation was drafted, aiming to overcome popular objections against this new technology.[61]

As already noted, harmonization of fiscal and financial product-related provisions has not yet occurred, as this requires unanimity in the Council. In this respect, Member States therefore enjoy considerable discretion to adopt legislation, and the Commission constantly seeks to narrow down national autonomy in this field.[62]

As regards exports, it has been decided not to prohibit or restrict the export of products which themselves are prohibited or their use restricted within the Community. Instead, it adopted the international trade principle to allow the export of dangerous chemicals subject to 'prior informed consent' (PIC). Pursuant to this principle, the importing third country must be informed of any risks and the internal Community restrictions. The importing country shall then decide if and what form of import restrictions it wishes to establish.[63] Beyond the chemical sector, no export provisions exist, with the notable exception of the waste sector, which will be examined elsewhere in this chapter.

## ii. Production Processes

EC law contains no provision which, by way of a general principle, obliges installations to have a permit and respect certain emission limits. Rather, legislation applies to certain specific as well as large installations. For example, Directive 76/464/EEC requires permits for installations which discharge certain dangerous substances into water,[64] and Directive 84/360/EEC similarly

---

[59] The Commission did not take action against these Member States. However, prior to 1998, it did not propose to extend such a ban to the whole of the Community.

[60] Council Dir. 96/59/EC on the Disposal of Polychlorinated Biphenyls and Polychlorinated Terphenyls (PCB/PCT) [1996] OJ L243/31.

[61] European Parliament and Council Dir. 2001/18/EC on the Deliberate Release Into the Environment of Genetically Modified Organisms and Repealing Council Dir. 90/220/EEC [2001] OJ L106/1.

[62] See also Communication from the Commission to the European Parliament and the Council: Single Market and Environment, COM(99)263, 8 June 1999.

[63] Council Reg. (EEC) No. 2455/92 concerning the Export and Import of Certain Dangerous Chemicals [1992] OJ L251/13.

[64] Council Dir. 76/464/EC on Pollution Caused by Certain Dangerous Substances Discharged into the Aquatic Environment of the Community [1976] OJ L129/23.

requires prior authorization for industrial installations which discharge certain pollutants into the air.[65]

In the early 1990s, without any prior public debate, it was decided not to adopt harmonized standards for production processes. The basic approach of the Community is now contained in Directive 96/61/EC,[66] the elaboration of which has been influenced considerably by United Kingdom experience. The Directive applies to certain types of installations enumerated in an Annex, which thereby must obtain a permit laying down emission limits which 'shall be based on the best available techniques' (BAT). The notion of BAT includes economic considerations, and the permit has also to take into consideration the specific local conditions of the installation. This approach in practice means that for identical installations, different emission standards may apply, impacting on the competitiveness of the installation, and also on the environmental performance of the products which are produced. Although guidance documents elaborated for different types of installations should mitigate these effects, it is noteworthy that these Best Available Techniques Reference Notes (BREFs) are elaborated with the very active participation of industry. Neither are these documents binding on competent authorities.

Originally, it was anticipated that the scope of Directive 96/61/EC would extend to smaller installations. This approach appears later to have been abandoned, however. Exceptionally, the Community opts to adopt uniform emission limit values at Community level. Such limit values were fixed for large combustion installations,[67] and for waste incinerators.[68]

For installations, very few monitoring requirements exist. The auditing system set up by Regulation (EC) No. 1836/93 allows for the voluntary participation of industries.[69] Installations which process dangerous substances fall within the field of application of Directive 96/82/EC,[70] and waste incinerators[71] must regularly be inspected by the competent national authorities.

No provisions exist, however, concerning the export of production installations to third countries.

---

[65] Council Dir. 84/360/EEC on the Combating of Air Pollution from Industrial Plants [1984] OJ L188/20.

[66] Council Dir. 96/61/EC concerning Integrated Pollution Prevention and Control [1996] OJ L257/26.

[67] Council Dir. 88/609/EEC on the Limitation of Emissions of Certain Pollutants into the Air from Large Combustion Plants [1988] OJ L336/1. This Directive is presently being revised.

[68] European Parliament and Council Dir. 2000/73/EC on the Incineration of Waste [2000] OJ L332/91. This Directive will progressively substitute earlier directives on the incineration of waste: Council Dir. 89/369/EEC on the Prevention of Air Pollution from New Municipal Waste Incineration Plants [1989] OJ L163/32; Council Dir. 89/429/EEC on the Reduction of Air Pollution From Existing Waste-Incineration-Plants [1989] OJ L203/50; Council Dir. 94/67/EC on the Incineration of Hazardous Waste [1994] OJ L365/34.

[69] Council Reg. (EEC) No. 1836/93, n. 31 above.

[70] Art. 18 of Council Dir. 96/82/EC on the Control of Major-Accident Hazards Involving Dangerous Substances [1997] OJ L10/13.

[71] Council Dir. 75/442/EEC on Waste [1975] OJ L194/39; as amended by Council Dir. 91/156/EEC [1991] OJ L78/32 (Art. 13).

### *iii. Other Measures*

Rather than a single Community-wide environmental label, specific labels have been developed for organic food, dangerous chemicals, energy, water and noise of household appliances, genetically modified products, and the separate collection of waste, in addition to a general eco-label.[72] Participation in this eco-label scheme is voluntary, and the label coexists with national eco-labels. The number of products on the Community market which carry the EC eco-label remains relatively small.

More than twenty years of efforts to introduce Community provisions on civil liability for damage caused to the environment thus far have not produced a final outcome. The Commission elaborated a proposal for liability for damage caused by waste,[73] which was not discussed in the Council, as well as a Greenbook,[74] and a White Paper on Environmental Liability.[75] Furthermore, a Directive on Liability for Defective Products applies to defective products, including waste.[76]

No Community provisions are in force regarding criminal sanctions for environmental impairment. For years, it was believed that the EC enjoyed no competence in this field of criminal law, but this assessment has recently changed. A recent proposal for the first time requests Member States to fix criminal sanctions where national law transposing Community environmental law has been breached.[77]

B.   WATER LAW

Community water legislation has not evolved out of a clear concept. Based on the aforementioned framework Directive 76/464/EEC, emission limits for discharges in water were fixed for seventeen dangerous substances, which had been selected on the basis of their toxicity, persistence, and bioaccumulation. However, confronted with UK objections against the emission limits approach, the Community also fixed quality objectives in parallel. Comparative studies were to be carried out in order to decide which approach should be retained as a definite Community solution.

This approach was abruptly overhauled in the first half of the 1990s, when the Commission shifted towards quality objectives and framework provisions. These ideas were provisionally given shape in the Water Framework Directive

---

[72] Council Reg. (EEC) No. 880/92, n. 31 above; amended by European Parliament and Council Reg. (EC) No. 1980/2000 on a Revised Community Eco-Label Award Scheme [2000] OJ L237/1.

[73] [1989] OJ C251/3.

[74] Communication from the Commission to the Council and Parliament and the Economic and Social Committee: Green Paper on Remedying Environmental Damage [1993] OJ C149/2.

[75] Commission: White Paper on Environmental Liability, COM(2000)66, 9 Feb. 2000. See also Betlem and Brans elsewhere in this volume.

[76] Council Dir. 85/374/EEC on the Approximation of the Laws, Regulations and Administrative Provisions of the Member States concerning Liability for Defective Products [1985] OJ L210/29.

[77] See COM(2001)139, 13 Mar. 2001; [2001] OJ C180E/238.

in 2000,[78] which is progressively to be put into operation over the next fifteen years.

As regards earlier measures in this area, the Community traditionally has focused on elaborating quality objectives, which were fixed for surface water, bathing water, fresh fish, and shellfish water. Directive 76/160/EEC on the Quality of Bathing Water[79] enjoyed considerable public attention because of its impact on tourism. The Directive led to considerable investment in combating coastal discharges. Other directives were more difficult to monitor for the Commission, undermining their ultimate efficiency.

Yet, Directive 80/778/EEC on Drinking Water,[80] an 'end-of-the-pipe' directive, fixed maximum concentrations for pollutants in drinking water and required considerable investment for clean-up measures for surface and groundwater, in particular in respect of parameters for heavy metals, pesticides, nitrates, and other chemicals. Attempts from the agricultural and chemical sectors to relax these standards essentially failed.[81]

Directive 91/271/EEC required Member States, for urban agglomerations with more than 5,000 inhabitants, to provide canalization and waste-water treatment installations,[82] which once more necessitated considerable investments in all Member States. Finally, Directive 91/676/EEC intends to protect water against nitrates from agricultural sources.[83] For that purpose, the number of livestock per hectare must be limited in vulnerable zones, which has a considerable impact on agricultural practice, and the implementation of this directive therefore causes controversy in all Member States.

The Community deals with questions of marine pollution mainly by way of regional conventions. These are ratified by some Member States, and the Community also adheres to them. Likewise, the clean-up of international rivers such as the Rhine, Elbe, Danube, and Oder takes place through the cooperation between Member States and third states, rather than autonomous Community activities. Questions of quantitative management of water resources were left practically untouched by the Community.

### C. AIR POLLUTION

The Community has approached air pollution issues rather more systematically than water pollution, partly in response to the widespread phenomenon

---

[78] European Parliament and Council Dir. 2000/60/EC Establishing a Framework for Community Action in the Field of Water Policy [2000] OJ L327/1.

[79] Council Dir. 76/160/EEC concerning the Quality of Bathing Water [1976] OJ L31/1.

[80] Council Dir. 80/778/EEC relating to the Quality of Water Intended for Human Consumption [1980] OJ L229/11.

[81] Council Dir. 98/83/EC on the Quality of Water Intended for Human Consumption [1998] OJ L330/32.

[82] Council Dir. 91/271/EEC concerning Urban Waste-Water Treatment [1991] OJ L135/40; this is the only environmental directive, which requires the construction of installations by Member States.

[83] Council Dir. 91/676/EEC concerning the Protection of Waters against Pollution Caused by Nitrates from Agricultural Sources [1991] OJ L375/1.

of *Waldsterben* in continental Europe. Early progress to tackle pollution by installations systematically[84] gradually slowed down, and were eventually substituted by the Integrated Pollution Prevention and Control (IPPC) approach for bigger installations. For the most common air pollutants, the quality objective approach was pursued, although the quality objectives were hardly monitored or enforced.[85] Later quality directives were drafted in a way which makes them almost unenforceable, and in any event are not yet fully operational.[86]

As regards atmospheric emissions from transport, the Commission, with the support of the Council and the EP, negotiated an 'auto oil programme' with the car and the mineral oil industries, which led to the fixing of emission standards for motor vehicles, and product standards for different types of fuels.[87] To what extent this agreement constitutes the environmental optimum and incites technological improvement remains to be seen. Similarly, the car industry entered into an environmental agreement on $CO_2$ reductions with the Commission.[88]

The Community transposed the provisions of the Montreal Protocol on Substances that Deplete the Ozone Layer into Community law, took the lead in international discussions, and adopted EC-wide legislation which, in several aspects, went beyond international commitments.[89]

Community discussions as regards climate change issues started in the late 1980s. However, this led only to few specific measures regarding the reduction of greenhouse gases. Plans for a directive to reduce $CO_2$-emissions from cars were replaced by an agreement with the car industry.[90] Modest energy conservation measures were adopted in 1993, and supported by measures allowing financial incentives.[91] A monitoring mechanism for greenhouse gases was set

---

[84] Council Dir. 84/360/EEC (n. 65 above), Council Dir. 88/609/EEC (n. 67 above), Council Dir. 89/369/EEC (n. 68 above).

[85] Council Dir. 80/779/EEC on Air Quality Limit Values and Guide Values for Sulphur Dioxide and Suspended Particulates [1980] OJ L229/30; Council Dir. 82/884/EEC on a Limit Value for Lead in the Air [1982] OJ L378/15; Council Dir. 85/203/EEC on Air Quality Standards for Nitrogen Dioxide [1985] OJ L87/1.

[86] Council Dir. 96/62/EC on Ambient Air Quality Assessment and Management [1996] OJ L296/55; Council Dir. 1999/30/EC relating to Limit Values for Sulphur Dioxide, Nitrogen Dioxide and Oxides of Nitrogen, Particulate Matter and Lead in Ambient Air [1999] OJ L163/41.

[87] Council Dir. 1999/32/EC relating to a Reduction in the Sulphur Content of Certain Liquid Fuels and Amending Dir. 93/2/EEC [1999] OJ L121/13.

[88] Further discussed elsewhere in this chapter.

[89] Council Dec. 88/540/EEC concerning the Conclusion of the Vienna Convention for the Protection of the Ozone Layer and the Montreal Protocol on Substances that Deplete the Ozone Layer [1988] OJ L297/8; Council Reg. (EC) No. 3093/94 on Substances that Deplete the Ozone Layer [1994] OJ L333/1. This last Regulation is now replaced by European Parliament and Council Reg. (EC) No. 2037/2000 on Substances that Deplete the Ozone Layer [2000] OJ L244/1.

[90] Further discussed elsewhere in this chapter.

[91] Council Dir. 93/76/EEC to Limit Carbon Dioxide Emissions by Improving Energy Efficiency (SAVE) [1993] OJ L237/28; Council Dec. 96/737/EC concerning a Multiannual Programme for the Promotion of Energy Efficiency in the Community [1996] OJ L335/50; Council Dec. 98/352/EC concerning a Multiannual Programme for the Promotion of Renewable Energy Sources in the Community (Altener II) [1998] OJ L159/53.

up,[92] but the proposal for a tax on fossil fuels could not be adopted.[93] At international level, the Community succeeded to speak with a single voice at the Kyoto meeting, where a Protocol on the reduction of greenhouse gases was agreed, and the reduction for the Community was fixed at 8 per cent. As a follow-up after the Kyoto meeting, Member States agreed in Council, without a corresponding Commission proposal, the relative percentages of reductions for each Member State. This state of affairs perfectly illustrates the tension between Community and national environmental policy.[94]

### D. NOISE

Community noise legislation did not primarily aim to address environmental problems, but stems from internal market considerations. Noise emission standards apply to new products (mainly to means of transport such as cars, motorcycles, aircraft, and trucks), and construction equipment, and were based on their technical feasibility. No standards for products already on the market, and no noise quality standards, for instance in respect of airports, schools, or hospitals, were fixed. A new, more environmentally oriented approach was initiated by the Commission in 1999 and 2000, the impact of which needs to be awaited.

### E. NATURE PROTECTION

The Community imposed a legal requirement for Member States to designate habitats for fauna and flora species and other habitats.[95] Implementation of this requirement, however, has proved problematic. Other conservation measures for birds, endangered fauna and flora species also exist.[96] In an effort to include wild animal welfare into the Community's sphere of competence, and due to public pressure in certain Member States, measures to protect baby seals,[97] whales,[98] and animals caught in leghold traps[99] were also adopted. Although not a member of the International Convention on Trade in Endangered Species (CITES), the Community adopted provisions to transpose,

---

[92] Council Dec. 93/389/EEC for a Monitoring Mechanism of Community $CO_2$ and Other Greenhouse Gas Emissions [1993] OJ L167/31; amended by Council Dec. 1999/296/EC [1999] OJ L117/35.

[93] Further discussed elsewhere in this chapter.  [94] See Krämer, n. 40 above, 225.

[95] Art. 4 of Council Dir. 79/409/EEC on the Conservation of Wild Birds [1979] OJ L103/1; Council Dir. 92/43/EEC on the Conservation of Natural Habitats and of Wild Fauna and Flora [1992] OJ L206/7.

[96] Ibid.

[97] Council Dir. 83/129/EEC concerning the Importation into Member States of Skins of Certain Seal Pups and Products Derived therefrom [1983] OJ L91/30.

[98] Council Reg. (EEC) No. 348/81 on Common Rules for Imports of Whales or Other Cetacean Products [1981] OJ L39/1.

[99] Council Reg. (EEC) No. 3254/91 Prohibiting the Use of Leghold Traps in the Community and the Introduction into the Community of Pelts and Manufactured Goods of Certain Wild Animal Species Originating in Countries which catch them by means of Leghold Traps or Trapping Methods which do not Meet International Humane Trapping Standards [1991] OJ L308/1.

*in toto*, the requirements of the Convention, and occasionally went considerably beyond these requirements.[100]

International efforts to preserve biodiversity were supported by the Community, which did not, however, take specific measures of its own for that purpose.

## F. WASTE MANAGEMENT

Community waste legislation was adopted from the mid-1970s onwards. The EC adopted three types of legislation: horizontal provisions on waste,[101] provisions on hazardous waste,[102] and a regime on the shipment of waste.[103] As for horizontal provisions, Community-wide definitions of 'waste', a general permit requirement and basic substantive requirements for the handling of waste, and Member State waste management plans are now in place. As regards shipment of waste, the Community, following OECD developments, differentiated between shipments for waste recovery, and shipments for waste disposal. While shipments for recovery are controlled according to the hazardousness of waste, Member States are allowed to prohibit shipments for waste disposal altogether. Also, the shipment of hazardous waste to non-OECD countries has been prohibited.[104]

A separate set of rules concerns waste incinerators,[105] landfill installations,[106] and port reception facilities,[107] for which stringent minimum requirements are fixed. Another distinct set of rules concerns deals with individual waste streams such as waste oils,[108] sewage sludge,[109] batteries,[110] packaging waste,[111] and end-of-life vehicles.[112]

The elaboration and implementation of waste legislation was and continues to be marked by tensions between the Community and Member States regarding their respective responsibilities. While disputes over the legal basis for waste legislation have by now been resolved in favour of the application of Article 175 EC, controversies continue in particular as regards the scope for Member States to adopt more specific waste legislation, mainly in those areas where the Community provisions are not sufficiently precise.

---

[100] Council Reg. (EC) No. 338/97, n. 32 above.
[101] Council Dir. 75/442/EEC, as amended by Council Dir. 91/156/EEC; n. 71 above.
[102] Council Dir. 91/689/EEC on Hazardous Waste [1991] OJ L377/20.
[103] Council Reg. (EEC) No. 259/93, n. 32 above.
[104] Council Reg. (EC) No. 120/97 Amending Reg. (EEC) No. 259/93 [1997] OJ L22/14.
[105] See the references cited in n. 68 above.
[106] Council Dir. 1999/31/EC on the Landfill of Waste [1999] OJ L182/1.
[107] European Parliament and Council Dir. 2000/59/EC on Port Reception Facilities for Ship-Generated Waste and Cargo Residues [2000] OJ L332/81.
[108] Council Dir. 75/439/EEC on the Disposal of Waste Oils [1975] OJ L194/23.
[109] Council Dir. 86/278/EEC on the Protection of the Environment, and in particular of the Soil, when Sewage Sludge is Used in Agriculture [1986] OJ L181/6.
[110] Council Dir. 91/157/EEC on Batteries and Accumulators Containing Certain Dangerous Substances [1991] OJ L78/38.
[111] European Parliament and Council Dir. 94/62/EC, n. 34 above.
[112] European Parliament and Council Dir. 2000/53/EC, n. 42 above.

## VI. Implementation

Under Article 175(4) EC, Member States must implement EC environmental policy, which of course includes the implementation of the measures adopted in pursuance of that policy. Under Article 211 EC, it is the Commission's task to ensure that the measures adopted by the Community institutions are properly applied.

Whereas the Commission, during the first decade of EC environmental law, did not closely monitor the practical application of environmental directives, it has progressively made this a priority from 1985 onwards. Cases of non-application were more systematically pursued, applications to the ECJ more frequently made, individuals actively encouraged to file complaints,[113] and breaches of Community law by Member States systematically made public. This policy increased attention in Member States for the implementation, application, and enforcement of environmental legislation. Progress remained slow, however, also because particular administrations were not used to see their administrative practice challenged by an outside body.[114] At present, at any given moment, the Commission monitors about 1,100 cases of presumed breaches of Community environmental law.

In environmental matters, the Commission does not dispose inspectors to check whether the law is actually applied on the ground. Cooperation by Member States is limited for obvious reasons. Almost the only sources of information for the Commission in respect of specific cases are information from private complainants, and replies to questions by national administrations.

Attempts to locate some enforcement monitoring tasks with the European Environment Agency were resisted by Member States, and at present are no longer pursued. No alternative external body was set up to monitor application of the law. This means that the administration which has to elaborate EC environmental law in close collaboration with Member States simultaneously is to pursue the latter under Article 211 EC, and to take formal legal action against them. Indeed, the infringement procedure under Article 226 EC is the only means available to enforce application of Community environmental law against Member States. The use of financial means to exercise pressure on recalcitrant Member States is not foreseen by EC law, and not really accepted as a possibility by the Commission.

The Commission does not systematically ensure that international environmental conventions to which the Community has adhered and which thereby

---

[113] The number of environmental complaints rose from eight in 1983 to 525 in 1989; see Krämer, n. 40 above, 286 (n. 39). At present, there are about 600 environmental complaints per year.

[114] See, on these developments in particular, Eighth Annual Report to the European Parliament on Community Monitoring of the Application of Community Law (1990) [1991] OJ C338/1 (Annex).

become part of Community law,[115] are applied, since there is no monitoring of such international conventions. The situation is different only in cases where the Community has adopted specific legal provisions to transpose provisions of a convention. It is submitted that this is not only a rather serious breach of the Commission's obligations flowing from Article 211 EC, but also an omission which is highly detrimental to the environment.

Apart from this formal side concerning monitoring, several aspects add to the problem of the application of environmental law. The lack of a 'European' public opinion, has already been mentioned. Equally important is the existence of distinct legal cultures in Member States, developed over centuries. Uniform environmental law which originated from Community institutions therefore produces different effects in these different legal cultures, which also has implications for the effectiveness of subsequent implementation. A Member State such as Portugal which, according to its own estimation, did not possess any environmental legislation prior to its accession in 1986, will inevitably take a different position vis-à-vis implementation of an environmental directive from a Member State such as the Netherlands, which disposes a sophisticated and complete system of national environmental law.

Also, while some Member States appear to regard it a point of principle to transpose, implement, and apply EC environmental law timely and correctly, experience shows that other Member States more systematically transpose environmental law too late, and may not invest much effort in applying EC environmental law at local, regional, or even national level.[116] Such differences are also expressions of the value which Member States attach to the protection of the environment, the degree to which a tradition of an 'open society' exists, the value attached to legal rules, and the degree to which Member States are prepared to limit the power of administrations to disregard environmental provisions.

## VII. State of the Environment

The state of the environment provides the ultimate yardstick against which to evaluate the success of the protection of the environment by means of law. In 1999, the European Environment Agency published its report on the state of

---

[115] Art. 300(7) EC: 'Agreements concluded under the conditions set out in this Article shall be binding on the institutions of the Community and on Member States.'

[116] The judgments of the ECJ are rife with examples. For example, in December 2000, the Commission decided to apply a second time to the ECJ, because bathing water in Blackpool (UK) continued to breach the requirements of Council Dir. 76/160/EEC (n. 79 above), despite a first judgment by the ECJ in 1993 (Case C–56/90, *Commission* v. *United Kingdom* [1993] ECR I–4109); in Case C–168/95, *Criminal Proceedings against Luciano Arcaro* [1996] ECR I–4705, the ECJ found that Italy had not transposed the requirement of permits for cadmium discharges from existing industrial installations, about twenty years after the adoption of Council Dir. 76/464/EC (n. 64 above); and by the end of 1996, the ECJ found that Germany had not transposed two water directives from 1978 and 1979 into national law (Case C–298/95, *Commission* v. *Germany* [1996] ECR I–6747).

the European environment,[117] which gave rise to the following assessment of the present situation as shown in Table I.[118]

The chapter which carries this table, and explains the present situation and likely future developments, carries the sober title: 'some progress, but a poor picture overall', and this might well apply more generally to the state of the environment in the EU. The particularly negative evaluation for the natural environment (biodiversity, coastal and marine areas, rural areas, mountain areas, soil degradation) confirms the impression that, despite all our best efforts, nature slowly but progressively withdraws from Western Europe.

The Commission's Sixth Environmental Action Programme observes in this respect:

despite the improvements on some fronts, we continue to face a number of persistent problems. Of particular concern are climate change, the loss of biodiversity and natural habitats, soil loss and degradation, increased waste volumes, the build-up of chemicals in the environment, noise and certain air and water pollutants. We also face a number

*Table I: State of the European environment*

| Environmental issue | Present pressure | Present state and impact |
| --- | --- | --- |
| Greenhouse gases and climate change | 0 | — |
| Ozone depletion | + | — |
| Hazardous substances | 0 | 0 |
| Transboundary air pollution | 0 | 0 |
| Water stress | 0 | 0 |
| Soil degradation | — | — |
| Waste | 0 | — |
| Natural and technologcal hazards | 0 | 0 |
| Genetically modified organisms | 0 | ? |
| Biodiversity | — | 0 |
| Human health | 0 | — |
| Urban areas | 0 | 0 |
| Coastal and Marine Areas | — | — |
| Rural areas | — | — |
| Mountain areas | — | — |

[117] European Environment Agency, n. 52 above.
[118] Ibid. 23; the signs mean: +: positive development; 0: some positive development, but insufficient; —: unfavourable development; ?: uncertain.

of emerging issues such as pollutants that affect the functioning of our hormone systems. Forecasts suggest that, with current policies and socio-economic trends, many of the pressures that give rise to these problems, such as transport, energy use, tourist activities, land-take for infra-structure, etc. will worsen over the coming decade. [119]

## VIII. Conclusion

What, then, has EC law achieved or failed to achieve over the past thirty years? It is obvious that because of the interdependence of EC environmental law and national environmental law, many developments cannot be attributed to one sphere of law or the other. Through cross-fertilization, national developments are sometimes communitarized which, in turn, influence the evolution of law in the Member States. With this proviso, the following observations may be made.

Environmental law has reached constitutional status in the EU. In numerous Member States, there now exist express constitutional provisions pertaining to the constitution which require the protection of the environment. This constitutional development has occurred over the last thirty years, reached the EU in 1987, and continues to influence constitutional developments in Central and Eastern Europe. The positioning of environmental needs at a level equal to human rights or social rights is important. It conveys the message to all stakeholders, including citizens, that the need to protect, preserve, and improve the quality of the environment is of fundamental importance, vital for the state and for society as a whole.

Environmental law in the EU has thus led to the emergence of administrative infrastructures in the Member States. Over the past thirty years, progressively, environmental bureaucracies were set up at Community, state, regional, and local level. Overall, it seems fair to say that environmental administration, policy, and law is most structured, developed, and sophisticated, where economic performance is highest.

Environmental law has now come to regulate all aspects of the environment, from the more classical areas such as water, air, products, noise, nature, and waste, to more intricate areas such as town and country planning, climate change, transport and energy law. Again, the number, substance, and intensity of regulation varies, and the evolution of environmental law, including the 'conquest' of new areas, has not yet come to a halt.

Environmental law has also begun to permeate universities, environmental organizations, lawyers, and courts. While there may exist a general problem in any affluent society to interest the young in anything beyond wealth and leisure, environmental law, human rights law, and legal disciplines linked to modern technology are taken up by young lawyers not merely seeking personal wealth.

---

[119] Sixth Environment Action Programme, n. 30 above, 10.

Environmental law thereby has become a most important tool in the fight against environmental impairment in the EU. Although such impairment continues to exist, public authorities in the EU which now tolerate the impairment of the environment do so at their peril. Enviromental impairment has become socially undesirable behaviour, and environmental law has reached a social status equivalent to human rights law.

European integration was and remains a powerful tool to ensure the spread of environmental laws and know-how well beyond the territorial limits of the EU.

Meanwhile, the enforcement of EC environmental law vis-à-vis Member States remains a task of paramount importance. ECJ judgments against Member States now have become routine, and although often with some delay or even reluctance, Member States normally do comply with these judgments, if only to avoid penalty payments under Article 228 EC. The progress which the EC has achieved with this procedure can only be fully appreciated if it is realized that the USA, Japan, Russia, or any other state are not prepared to accept judgments from foreign courts. It is often argued that the environment knows no frontiers. Yet, when it comes to enforcing (environmental) provisions of international conventions, national sovereignty directly conflicts with the supremacy of the jurisdiction of a foreign court. In this regard, the Community truly is a model for other parts of the world.

Meanwhile, the Community has entrusted the protection of the environment almost exclusively to the administration. It is the administration which takes thousands of administrative decisions on a day-by-day basis, that permit emissions of pollutants into the environment, allows certain substances to be marketed, projects to be realized, or industrial activity to take place. Administrations are also in charge of monitoring application of, and compliance with the law, and may, by taking action or by failing to do so, very substantially affect the environment. In environmental matters, it is often still presumed that the public administration can do no wrong. Administrations serve multiple interests, which are linked to the governing classes, and they are not politically neutral, as the theory of the modern state might suggest. They are inherently conservative, and therefore tend to protect the *status quo*. Since the rise of modern administration, the status quo has felt at liberty to use and abuse the environment.

Similarly, from the start, the EC's administration favoured the free circulation of goods, services, capital, and labour, and only reluctantly and slowly took into consideration environmental imperatives. The Community's administration, which is not particularly accountable or transparent for citizens and environmental groups, often may appear to be little responsive to critique.

Environmental law, of course, is heavily dependent on measurement methods, frequencies of analysis, the location of measurement stations, etc. However, even the contours of principles such as 'sustainable development', 'the polluter shall pay', the 'precautionary principle', or the 'integration requirement' remain so vague that by themselves they do not help solve daily threats to the environment. In particular, these principles must not obscure the technical details related to their implementation. Nobody is opposed to sustainable development or a high level of environmental protection, but when it comes to a ban of cadmium in batteries or lead in the environment, such high principles are all too quickly forgotten. EC environmental law therefore must also remain concerned about details.

Even if Community law is adequately drafted, if the political will is lacking, it becomes extremely difficult to ensure that such legislation is properly applied. Increased recourse to framework legislation will only add to these difficulties. Framework legislation increases inconsistent interpretation and application of such legislation, and thus will contribute to different levels of environmental protection in Member States.

EC environmental legislation should, in the present writer's opinion, over the next years regulate the protection of soil, fix uniform emission standards (air, water, and soil) for the most important industrial installations, ensure the protection of groundwater, provide for serious provisions on energy saving, contain an export ban on nuclear waste to non-OECD countries in the same way as for hazardous waste, and provide for effective rules to promote waste recycling. It should systematically phase out heavy metals and other hazardous substances where less hazardous substitutes are available, provide for an EC-wide ban on night flights, create a public pollution emission register, and apply the provisions of the Aarhus Convention to Community institutions. It must reduce the overall output of greenhouse gases by cars, provide for prices of fuels that reflect environmental costs of exhaust emissions from vehicles, develop a uniform eco-label at Community level, and develop instruments in order to protect nature, biodiversity, and climate more effectively.

'Community environmental law cannot be developed without Community environmental lawyers, however. Placing this law into the hands exclusively of administrations or, worse, vested interest groups, could have disastrous effects on the law, as it could become placebo law.

To be sure, Community environmental law is a success story. A considerable amount of Community legislation discussed in this chapter is truly innovative, and has paved the way to progressive legal standards throughout the EU and beyond.

The environment would be much worse off if there had not been a constant flow of EC environmental provisions. The challenge with which our industrialized society is confronted, is whether we can attach even more importance to the environment. Attempts to find legal answers to environmental challenges must therefore continue, in particular at EC level. Without the political will to improve the EU and global environments, not much will be achieved. And without laws on the statute books, all political arguments about the environment will remain greenspeak.

# The Future Role of Civil Liability for Environmental Damage in the EU

GERRIT BETLEM and EDWARD H. P. BRANS*

## I. Introduction

Early in 2000, the European Commission issued its White Paper on Environmental Liability (White Paper), which is an important step in the legislative process.[1] This long-awaited White Paper outlines the views of the Commission on some of the key elements needed for an effective and practicable EU-wide environmental liability regime. The regime as proposed in the White Paper not only covers damage to persons, goods, and soil pollution, but also damage to nature. However, the latter is limited to natural resources protected under relevant European Community (EC) law. The natural resources concerned are viewed as being of importance for the conservation of biodiversity in the European Union (EU), and are generally considered to be of a special interest and of public value.[2]

In this contribution, we will first examine the proposals by the Commission as laid down in the White Paper, and analyse various specific issues (Section III). A number of these issues will form the basis for a more general discussion as to what are—in our opinion—desirable elements of a future EU-wide liability regime (Section IV). Third, three specific problem areas—mining, GMOs, and oil pollution—are discussed in the light of the regulatory choice between a general environmental liability regime, and sector-specific liability rules. They will also serve to illustrate the interrelationship between civil law remedies, and regulatory control (Section V). Finally, Section VI draws together some concluding remarks. First, a summary will be provided of developments within the EU preceding the publication of the document (Section II).

---

* Gerrit Betlem, senior lecturer, University of Exeter, Exeter, UK; Edward H. P. Brans, lecturer, Free University Amsterdam, Amsterdam, the Netherlands. This article takes account of the case law, literature, and legal documents that were available up to 1 Aug. 2000. Occasionally later developments are noted.

[1] COM(2000)66 final, 9 Feb. 2000. Published at the Internet at: http://www.europa.eu.int/comm/environment/liability.

[2] According to, *inter alia*, the Preamble to Council Dir. 79/409/EEC on the Conservation of Wild Birds [1979] OJ L103/1, and the Preamble to Council Dir. 92/43/EEC on the Conservation of Natural Habitats and of Wild Fauna and Flora [1992] OJ L206/7, the natural resources concerned form part of the Community's common natural heritage. Cf. Case C–252/85, *Commission* v. *France* [1998] ECR I–2234.

## II. Chronology

In order to discuss likely and possible future developments of civil liability for damage to the environment, a brief look at the past may be helpful. We will therefore briefly review the recent history of environmental liability law at the Community level. On the basis of past developments, caution must be expressed about the prospects for the speedy adoption of future legislation. On the other hand, the current political climate differs from that in the 1990s. For example, there exists growing public concern over the environmental consequences of various pollution incidents that have occurred over the years, and the possible impact of releases of genetically modified organisms (GMOs) on public health and the environment. Increased public awareness about environmental matters provides an incentive for regulators to establish rules on environmental liability. The White Paper is an important step in that direction. As will be seen, the Commission is now determined to establish a 'horizontal regime', covering damage to the environment resulting from harmful activities generally, instead of adopting sector-specific liability rules, for example, liability for damage caused by GMOs, or waste.

The first time that harmonization of environmental liability law was mentioned in an EC legislative instrument, was in Article 11(3) of Directive 84/631/EEC,[3] pursuant to which the Council was obliged to regulate the liability for damage caused by waste. Although this obligation dates back to 6 December 1984, legislative progress so far has only resulted in an Amended Proposal for a Council Directive on Civil Liability for Damage caused by Waste.[4] In the mean time, Directive 84/631/EEC has been replaced by Council Regulation (EC) No. 259/93 on the Supervision and Control of Shipments of Waste within, into and out of the European Community.[5] The Regulation does not contain any reference to a regime for the liability of producers of waste, so that liability is governed by the legal systems of the Member States. Nonetheless, this is unlikely to remain so, because this Regulation also implements the Basel Convention, a global regime regulating transboundary waste shipments.[6] Since a supplementary Protocol on liability has been adopted in 1999, it would appear that the EU will eventually also have to give effect to these liability rules, although by July 2000 the EU had not yet signed the Protocol.[7]

---

[3] Council Dir. 84/631/EEC on the Supervision and Control within the European Community of the Transfrontier Shipment of Hazardous Waste [1984] OJ L326/31.

[4] [1991] OJ C192/6; see for an extensive commentary P. von Wilmowsky and G. Roller, *Civil Liability for Waste* (Frankfurt am Main: Peter Lang, 1992).

[5] [1993] OJ L30/1; applicable as of 1 May 1994.

[6] Convention on the Control of Transboundary Movements of Hazardous Wastes and their Disposal (signed at Basel, 22 Mar. 1989), (1989) 28 *International Legal Materials*, 649, and (1989) 1 *Journal of Environmental Law*, 255; see also G. van Calster, 'The Legal Framework for the Regulation of Waste in the EC' (2000) I *Yearbook of European Environmental Law*, 161 and 181.

[7] Protocol on Liability and Compensation for Damage resulting from Transboundary Movements of Hazardous Wastes and their Disposal (signed at Basel, 10 Dec. 1999), published on the Internet at: http://www.basel.int; see generally D. A. French, 'The 1999 Protocol on Liability

Liability clauses have been put forward at various moments in time in several other proposals, such as the Landfill Directive,[8] and the PCB/PCT Disposal Directive.[9] Both directives would have imposed strict liability on the operator for damage and impairment of the environment. These liability clauses were ultimately deleted in favour of one single instrument of general applicability, even though at that stage the final form of such an instrument was unclear. The only Commission initiative adopted prior to the 2000 White Paper was the 1993 Green Paper, which examined, in broad terms, the policy issues involved in formulating an EU-wide environmental liability regime.[10] The Green Paper did not include a proposal for legislation, as its aim was to stimulate debate on the future liability regime, and to collect the views of various interested parties. One of the conclusions of this paper was that '[c]ivil liability is a useful legal instrument for recovering the costs of restoring environmental damage as well as for its prevention and enforcement functions'.[11] However, due to strong opposition of economic operators against a horizontal EU liability regime, and the difference of opinions among Member States, the Green Paper was not followed up by a (draft) directive.

In 1994 the European Parliament (EP) called for legislation in this area, and adopted a resolution calling on the Commission to submit a proposal for a directive on civil liability for environmental damage.[12] In January 1997, the Commission decided, taking into account the need to reply to the resolution, to prepare a White Paper on environmental liability. In the meantime, it commissioned a number of studies on the state of the art in the various domestic legal systems (including the USA), the economic aspects of environmental liability, and the valuation of 'ecological damage'.[13] Interesting is also that the EP recently voted to introduce a liability clause in a directive on the deliberate

and Compensation for Damage Resulting from the Transboundary Movements of Hazardous Wastes and their Disposal' (2000) 8 *Environmental Liability*, 3.

[8] Art. 14 Amended Proposal [1993] OJ C212/33; not included in Council Dir. 1999/31/EC on the Landfill of Waste [1999] OJ L182/1. However, Art. 13d does impose a post-closure monitoring duty on the operator 'without prejudice to any Community and national legislation as regards liability of the waste holder'.

[9] Art. 6(3b) Amended Proposal [1991] OJ C299/15; not included in Council Dir. 96/59/EC on the Disposal of Polychlorinated Biphenyls and Polychlorinated Terphenyls (PCB/PCT) [1996] OJ L243/31.

[10] Communication from the Commission to the Council and the Parliament and the Economic and Social Committee: Green Paper on Remedying Environmental Damage, COM(93)47 final, 14 May 1993.

[11] Green Paper, n. 10 above, 27. On subsequent occasions, the usefulness of environmental liability has been underlined. See e.g. Communication from the Commission, Europe's Environment: What Directions for the Future? The Global Assessment of the European Community Programme of Policy and Action in relation to the Environment and Sustainable Development, COM(99)543, 24 Nov. 1999, 24.

[12] European Parliament Resolution on Preventing and Remedying Environmental Damage [1994] OJ C128/165. See also Opinion of the Economic and Social Committee on the Green Paper [1994] OJ C133/8, para. 2.2.1.

[13] Summaries are published in European Commission, White Paper on Environmental Liability: COM (2000)66 final, 9 Feb. 2000; see also G. Betlem, 'Liability for Damage to the Environment' in A. S. Hartkamp *et al.* (eds.), *Towards a European Civil Code* (The Hague: Kluwer, 1998), 473, 477.

release of genetically modified organisms. However, the Commission opposed adoption of such a regime, and the proposed amendment was rejected in favour of an EU horizontal liability regime.

Significant, too, is a recent parallel development in criminal law, which could have some interesting implications for civil suits (for example, the facilitation of fact finding, and establishing unlawfulness under traditional tort law). Within the framework of the EU's Third Pillar, Title VI of the Treaty on European Union (TEU) on Police and Judicial Cooperation in Criminal Matters, a Danish initiative for a Council Framework Decision has been put forward.[14] According to Article 34(2b) (TEU), framework decisions adopted in this context, like EC directives, are concerned with the harmonization of Member States' laws and regulations but, unlike EC directives, are expressly excluded from producing any direct effect. The proposal is primarily concerned with international cooperation and exchange of information, and allocating jurisdiction to prosecute cross-border pollution. However, it also introduces criminal liability for legal persons. Yet, particularly important for civil law purposes is the fact that in Article 2 (2)(e) Member States are under an obligation—as is proposed—to ensure that 'serious environmental crime is covered by effective compensation rules and rules on environmental rehabilitation under national law'. Interesting also is a proposed amendment by the EP designed to prevent the statute of limitations to constitute a bar to prosecution for crimes 'which may only be detected over a longer period of time'.[15] It would seem to follow that, after adoption, Member States must ensure that latent serious environmental crimes cannot be time-barred (or, that the limitation period does not run without the damage having become manifest), whilst making available their civil liability rules in these situations as an adjunct to criminal suits.

## III. White Paper on Environmental Liability

On 9 February 2000 the Commission published the final version of the White Paper.[16] The document contains the core elements and principles of a horizontal environmental liability directive. The regime, as proposed, is set up as a framework with minimum requirements and standards, and is to be completed over time on the basis of experience with its initial application. The regime outlined has a closed character, as it is linked with relevant EC environmental legislation. It covers two areas: damage caused by activities that bear an inherent risk of causing damage to the environment, and that are subject

---

[14] Initiative of the Kingdom of Denmark with a view to adopting a Council Framework Decision on Combating Serious Environmental Crime [2000] OJ C39/4. This instrument is comparable to the Council of Europe's Convention on the Protection of the Environment through Criminal Law (Strasbourg, 4 Nov. 1998) published on the Internet at: http://www.conventions.coe.int (European Treaty Series 172).

[15] EP Doc. No. A5–0178/2000, Amendment 14 (Art. 2(1)(ba)(new) ).        [16] See n. 1 above.

to EC law, and damage to natural resources, but only in so far as these are protected by EC law. Strict liability applies to damage caused by inherently dangerous activities, and a fault-based liability to damage to (what is termed) biodiversity caused by an activity not listed as dangerous. The regime will not be applied retroactively: environmental damage that was caused in the past is a matter that should be dealt with by Member States.

The Council of Ministers, in a preliminary policy debate on the matter, welcomed the initiative.[17] A majority favoured Community action covering a broad range of types of loss including traditional damage (personal injury and property damage), as well as environmental damage. Like the Commission, the majority of the Council was also in favour of a framework directive, rather than acceding to the 1993 Council of Europe Convention on Environmental Liability.[18] The scope of the Council of Europe Convention was thought to be too wide,[19] and some of its provisions too general to ensure legal certainty. The latter relates in particular to the provisions on liability for damage to natural resources. It was thought that through an EU framework directive, the scope of the future liability regime could be better delineated, and the regime dealing with damage to natural resources better developed.

Given the moderately positive reactions to the White Paper of the Environmental Council, the Committee of the Regions, and the Economic Social Committee, it is not unlikely that, finally, an EU liability directive will be adopted. Commissioner Wallström declared that every effort will be made to present a proposal for a directive before the end of 2001.[20] However, if the current progress is not accelerated, such a timetable seems too optimistic. On the other hand, concerns about the impact of the release of GMOs on the environment and public health may be decisive in establishing a regime relatively speedily. The Commission confirmed its commitment in its proposal for a Sixth Environmental Action Programme 2001–10 'Environment 2010: Our Future, Our Choice'.[21]

---

[17] 2253rd Council Meeting, Environment, Brussels, 30 Mar. 2000, PRES/00/91, published on the Internet at: http://www.europa.eu.int (RAPID database); Agence Europe (2000) 7689 *Bulletin Quotidien Europe*, 7.

[18] Council of Europe Convention: Convention on Civil Liability for Damage resulting from Activities Dangerous to the Environment (Lugano, 21 June 1993) published on the Internet at: http://www.conventions.coe.int (European Treaty Series 150) and (1993) 32 *International Legal Materials*, 1228; signed by Cyprus, Finland, Greece, Iceland, Italy, Liechtenstein, Luxembourg, the Netherlands, and Portugal (but not yet in force).

[19] The concern is that, unlike the White Paper, the 1993 Council of Europe Convention is not limited to the dangerous activities listed, and may also cover activities that are not explicitly designated in the convention as dangerous (Art. 2).

[20] Intervention at EP Plenary Session regarding revision of the GMOs Directive, Strasbourg, 11 Apr. 2000 (SPEECH/00/142); IP/00/374, published on the Internet at: http://www.europa.eu.int (RAPID Database).

[21] Published on the Internet at: http://www.europa.eu.int/comm/environment/newprg; see also the Press Release of 24 Jan. 2001, IP/01/102, published on the Internet at: http://www.europa.eu.int (RAPID Database).

A.  AIMS AND OBJECTIVES OF THE REGIME

The main objectives of the proposed regime are environmental. It is believed that an EC environmental liability regime is an effective way of implementing key principles of EC environmental policy, such as the 'polluter-pays' principle and the 'preventive action' principle of Article 174(2) EC.[22] Its main purpose is to ensure—in accordance with the polluter-pays principle—funding of measures necessary to clean up and restore any environmental damage caused. Moreover, it is expected that the future EU regime will lead to improved compliance with existing Community legislation, and will encourage better implementation of existing and future EC environmental law. It is also expected that it will encourage actors who will become potentially liable to take greater care to avoid damage, and to invest in research and development to prevent further environmental harm.

   Another important argument for an EC regime is that, at present, there are gaps in the environmental liability regimes of most Member States as far as damage to natural resources is concerned. This is especially apparent in cases where damage is caused to natural resources which are not (privately) owned, which makes it difficult to recover damages for this type of harm.[23] There also exists substantial disparity between Member States in respect of liability for soil pollution and the clean-up standards and objectives employed in these cases. So to prevent or correct distortions in competition between Member States, the EU-wide environmental liability regime will also harmonize these clean-up standards and clean-up objectives. Furthermore, since there does not exist at the moment an effective liability instrument for transfrontier environmental damage, the future regime is also expected to solve problems that emerge in such instances.

B.  KEY FEATURES OF THE PROPOSED POSSIBLE REGIMES

*i.  A Two-track Regime*

One of the main features of the liability regime proposed is that its scope of application is closed and limited to EC environmental law. The regime proposed covers damage to persons and goods (traditional damage), and contamination of sites, but only if such damage is caused by dangerous or potentially dangerous activities regulated by EC law. Damage to natural resources such as wildlife, habitats, and ecosystems, is also covered, but only if it concerns natural resources in sites designated by virtue of EU nature

---

[22] White Paper, n. 1 above, para. 3.1. For more details on these principles, see: L. Krämer, *EC Environmental Law* (London: Sweet & Maxwell, 2000), 16–20; N. de Sadeleer, *Les Principes du Pollueur-Payeur, de Prévention et de Précaution. Essai sur la Genèse et la Portée Juridique de Quelques Principes du Droit de l'Environnement* (Brussels: Bruylant/A.U.F., 1999), Part I.

[23] McKenna & Co., *Study of Civil Liability Systems for Remedying Environmental Damage* (unpublished, DG XI document, 1996), 273–303. This is one of the studies commissioned by the European Commission in preparation for the publication of the White Paper. For a summary of the study, see: Annex 1 to the Office for Official Publications' version of the White Paper, n. 13 above.

conservation law. For the application of this part of the proposed regime, it is immaterial whether such damage is caused by a dangerous activity regulated by EC law or an activity that is not covered by EC law, and which is considered a non-dangerous activity. The difference resides in the type of liability that is applicable. The White Paper provides for strict liability for damage caused by dangerous activities regulated by EC law, and fault-based liability for damage caused by so-called 'non-dangerous activities'. In summary, damage to natural resources covered by the proposed regime is recoverable, whether it is caused by a dangerous activity or not. Only the type of liability may vary, depending on the nature of the activity that caused the damage. Tables I and II illustrate how the proposed regime has been designed.

### ii. Dangerous and Non-dangerous Activities

Although strict liability applies to damage caused by EC-regulated dangerous activities, it is not clear precisely what dangerous activities are meant. In the

*Table I: Scheme as proposed in the White Paper*

| Nature of liability | Type of activity | Traditional damage | Damage to biodiversity | Damage threshold | Contaminated sites |
|---|---|---|---|---|---|
| Strict | (Potentially) dangerous and covered by EC law | X | X | Significant for biodiversity damage and contaminated sites | X |
| Fault | All, including non-dangerous activities | | X | Significant damage only | |

*Table II: Heads of damage and types of loss*

| | Nature of liability | Activities | Place of harm | Threshold |
|---|---|---|---|---|
| Traditional damage | Strict | (potentially) dangerous and EC regulated | Anywhere | No threshold |
| Damage to biodiversity | Fault and strict | All (including non-dangerous) | Natura 200 sites only | Significant damage |
| Contaminated sites | Strict | (potentially) dangerous and EC regulated | Anywhere | Significant damage |

White Paper, a mere indication is provided of the activities that are covered, which include those regulated by EC environmental legislation, and relate to or contain discharge or emission limits for hazardous substances into water or air; the transport of dangerous substances; the prevention and control of accidents;[24] the transport, storage, and disposal of hazardous and other waste; and biotechnology. A final list of activities is not available yet but will be developed at a later stage.[25]

Although a wide range of dangerous activities appears to be covered, it is difficult to determine on the basis of the information provided in the White Paper precisely what dangerous activities are falling within the scope of the proposed regime. The legislation referred to basically covers industrial companies, transporters, and other professional parties who produce, use, or transport dangerous substances. It has been suggested that all industrial activities are covered, except for a small category of mostly innocent industrial activities.[26] However, it may be seriously doubted whether this is indeed the case. For instance, it is unclear whether mining sites, such as the one in Spain from which pollutants were released that seriously affected the Doñana national park, are covered. Furthermore, since EC law primarily covers activities for which there exist paramount reasons to regulate them, activities below this 'threshold', but which are potentially dangerous to the environment, may possibly not be covered. It is dubious, for instance, whether an illegal discharge of toxic waste by a private person is covered. Once a private discharge is regulated by any of the above-mentioned categories of EC law, according to the White Paper, it is not a dangerous activity, and will therefore be governed by fault liability.

Evidently, the scope of EC law with regard to activities potentially dangerous to the environment is crucial. This is true not only because it determines the type of liability that applies in a given case, but also because it affects the type of damage that is recoverable under the regime. As noted, the future directive will only cover personal injury, property damage, contamination of sites, and damage to natural resources covered by EC conservation law, if such damage is caused by a dangerous activity regulated by the EC. As to the damage caused by other so-called non-dangerous activities, the scope of regime is limited to natural resources protected under EC law, and does not cover, *inter alia*, the contamination of land or groundwater (see Table II).

*iii. Types of Loss Covered*

The future liability regime will cover traditional damage (personal injury and damage to property) and environmental damage. The White Paper employs

[24] Council Dir. 96/82/EC on the Control of Major-Accidents Hazards involving Dangerous Substances [1997] OJ L10/13; Council Dir. 96/61/EC concerning Integrated Pollution Prevention and Control [1996] OJ L257/26. The latter directive covers specifically listed large industrial installations (approximately 10% of the industrial installations in the EU).
[25] White Paper, n. 1 above, para. 4.2.2.
[26] L. Bergkamp, 'The Commission's White Paper on Environmental Liability: A Weak Case for an EC Strict Liability Regime' (2000) 9 *European Environmental Law Review*, 111.

'environmental damage' as an overarching concept, encompassing two sub-categories: 'damage to biodiversity' (also termed 'natural resource damage') and 'damage in the form of contaminated sites'.[27] The White Paper may give rise to terminological confusion where it distinguishes between traditional and environmental damage. This is true in particular for damage to contaminated sites, which is regarded as environmental damage. Yet, this type of harm always concerns a very traditional head of damage: damage to real property. Land is always owned,[28] which means that since it is already included under material loss, there is no need for its separate inclusion under the notion of environmental damage. More generally, Member State practice shows that it is preferable to regulate the clean-up of contaminated land in a separate instrument, as it primarily concerns public law obligations of owners vis-à-vis public authorities in respect of their private property.

Confusion may also arise because the category of environmental damage covers more than just damage to unowned natural resources. The introduction of a category of environmental damage besides the traditional types of compensatable harm is useful, because damage to unowned natural resources is not recoverable under the national laws of most Member States.[29] Most other forms of damage to the environment are, in principle, covered, or at least could be covered as damage to property, or as pure economic loss. However, there are other reasons to include a separate category of damage, in addition to 'traditional damage'. One is the Commission's intention to develop a regime that also covers damage to certain owned natural resources. The justification for extending the scope of the regime to these resources is that some privately owned natural resources exceed private interests, and are of public value. These natural resources directly or indirectly serve public interests, such as human health or recreation, but may also represent different values to people and nature. A wetland, for instance, provides rearing and feeding habitat for birds and certain wildlife species. It may form a buffer between the water and the upland, support the purification of groundwater, and provide shoreline stabilization benefits.

A difficulty is that these natural resources are subject to property rights, and that harm to such resources is, in principle, recoverable as damage to property. However, since there is no duty for any property owner to file a claim, or to use the recovered sums for restoration, damage to these public natural resources may not be restored. To tackle this problem, the Commission proposes special rules on standing as regards these natural resources. Another reason to distinguish environmental damage from traditional damage, is that damage to natural resources, whether owned or not, is often difficult to quantify because the

---

[27] White Paper, n. 1 above, para 4.2.1.
[28] See Article 5:24 Dutch Civil Code, providing for state ownership of land in the absence of another owner.
[29] Cf. A. Carette, *Herstel van en Vergoeding voor Aantasting aan Niet-Toegeëigende Milieubestanddelen* (Antwerp/Groningen: Intersentia, 1997).

market does not properly represent the value of the natural resources concerned. To address this problem, the Commission has introduced a separate regime for these natural resources.

Hence, in order to distinguish damage to public natural resources from traditional damage, a separate category of damage has been introduced. We support the Commission in its general approach, but the term 'environmental damage' as an overarching term may give rise to confusion. The term is often given a very general meaning in legal literature and legislative documents, encompassing damage caused via the environment as well as to the environment itself. The White Paper also employs the term 'biodiversity damage' to distinguish damage to certain public natural resources from traditional harm. As will be seen, this term may not fulfil its purpose. We therefore suggest the term 'natural resource damage or damage to public natural resources' instead.

The term 'biodiversity damage' also gives rise to confusion because of the Commission's interpretation of the term 'biodiversity', which differs from more authoritative and generally accepted interpretations, such as that provided by the 1992 Convention on Biological Diversity. In this Convention, 'biodiversity' is defined as the number, variety, and variability of all species of plants, animals, and micro-organisms, as well as the ecosystems of which they are part (Article 2).[30] Biodiversity thus is more than just the number of species in a certain area.[31] In fact, there are four levels at which biodiversity is assessed: genetic diversity within a species, the variety of species, functional diversity which refers to the variety of biological functions of ecosystems, and ecological diversity which refers to the variety of types of habitats and ecosystems.[32]

The White Paper proposes to impose liability for damage to 'natural resources that are important [for] the conservation of biological diversity in the Community'.[33] From this quote it appears that the polluter will not be liable for the loss of genetic diversity within a species, the variety among species, or the loss of ecological diversity, but only for the injury to, destruction of, or loss of, natural resources.[34] This is important, since one may wonder whether it is possible to bring about a realistic regime establishing liability for damage to biodiversity as defined in the 1992 Biodiversity Convention at this time. Currently, only limited information about the extent of biodiversity is available,[35] which makes it difficult to determine the extent of biodiversity loss caused by a particular incident. Furthermore, it is probably also rather difficult

---

[30] Rio de Janeiro, 5 June 1992 (1992) 31 *International Legal Materials*, 818, and [1993] OJ L309/3.

[31] J. L. Harper and D. L. Hawksworth, 'Preface' in D. L. Hawksworth (ed.), *Biodiversity: Measurement and Estimation* (London: Chapman & Hall/The Royal Society, 1996), 7–10.

[32] Harper and Hawksworth, n. 30 above, 6; V. H. Heywood (ed.), *Global Biodiversity Assessment* (Cambridge: Cambridge University Press, 1995), 27; B. Thorne-Miller, *The Living Ocean. Understanding and Protecting Biodiversity* (Washington, DC.: Island Press, 1999), 6–7.

[33] White Paper, n. 1 above, 1.

[34] As a matter of fact, in the earlier drafts of the White Paper, the term 'natural resources' was used instead of 'biodiversity'. No clear explanation is given for this change in terminology.

[35] Harper and Hawksworth, n. 30 above, 9–10; R. Perman *et al.*, *Natural Resources & Environmental Economics* (Harlow: Longman, 1999), 47.

to prove that damage has been caused to the variety of species, or the genetic diversity within a species. To be sure, this is more difficult than proving that a certain animal species or habitat has been detrimentally affected by an oil spill or other incident.[36]

It may be possible to incorporate biodiversity considerations into restoration planning activities developed in response to an incident that caused injury to natural resources. Nonetheless, it seems troublesome to hold any party liable for damage to biodiversity, as defined under the above-mentioned Convention.

### iv. What Natural Resources are Covered?

As explained, the proposed regime will not cover all natural resources. The scope of the proposed regime is limited to certain natural resources covered by EC nature conservation law, namely the Wild Birds and Habitats Directives.[37] Both directives are aimed at the preservation, protection, and improvement of natural habitats and of wild flora and fauna, and require the establishment of protection areas.[38] Many Member States are still in the process of classifying these protection areas, for which they use certain objective ornithological and other scientific criteria.[39] The protection areas that are to be designated will together form a European ecological network named *Natura 2000*. It is expected that ultimately approximately 10 per cent of the territory of the EU will be classified as a Natura 2000 site. By April 2000, 2,525 sites had been designated under the Wild Birds Directive (approximately 173,691 $km^2$) and Member States had proposed 10,250 sites for designation under the Habitats Directive (approximately 360,681 $km^2$).[40] Since several sites have been proposed under both directives, either in part or in total; one cannot simply add up the figures. Noteworthy, also, is that some Member States, such as the Netherlands and the UK, have designated substantial portions of their coastal waters as protection areas.

The regime as proposed in the White Paper is limited to natural resources in Natura 2000 areas. Since the Natura 2000 network will ultimately cover only a small percentage (about 10 per cent) of the EU's land, wetlands, and waters, the future regime will have a very limited scope. The main justification for this limitation is probably legal clarity—the natural resources located in these areas are relatively easily identifiable—and related to the fact that Member States are already under an obligation to manage and protect the natural

[36] A. Ascencio and R. Mackenzie, 'Legal Issues Relating to Liability and Compensation for Damage in Relation to the Transboundary Movement of Living Modified Organisms' in K. J. Mulongoy (ed.), *Transboundary Movement of Living Modified Organisms Resulting from Modern Biotechnology: Issues and Opportunities for Policy-Makers* (Geneva: Geneva University Press, 1997), 151.

[37] See n. 2 above.     [38] White paper, n. 1 above, para. 4.5.1.

[39] With regard to the Wild Birds Directive the Inventory of Important Bird Areas is relied on. Cf. Case C–3/96, *Commission* v. *Netherlands* [1998] ECR I–3031, para. 70.

[40] *Natura 2000*, Apr. 2000, 6–7, published on the Internet at: http://www.europa.eu.int/comm/environment/news/natura/indexen.htm. It should be noted that Member States have added new sites to the list of Natura 2000 sites, but these figures had not been incorporated.

resources in these areas, and to take restoration measures if significant harm is caused to the natural resources of Natura 2000 sites.[41]

Damage to natural resources located outside the Natura 2000 sites is thus not covered by the proposed regime, even where the species and habitats concerned are listed in the annexes to the Wild Birds and Habitats Directives, and where both directives require protection of these natural resources. The geographical limitation to Natura 2000 sites is therefore a serious restriction to the scope of the regime.

With others, we reject the limitation to natural resources in Natura 2000 sites because it unduly restricts the scope of the regime.[42] First of all, natural resources outside the Natura 2000 sites and protected under national or EC law, are of no less importance than the natural resources in these areas. Furthermore, even if ultimately 10 per cent of EU territory is designated, it will not necessarily cover all qualifying sites. According to a World Wildlife Fund study, a significant number of sites needing protection are not listed.[43] In addition, it is not even necessary to designate all sites which constitute a relevant habitat under the Habitats and Birds Directives, as is sufficient to list those with high conservation value.[44] Consequently, an environmental liability regime linked with a designation system sits uneasily with the environmental protection obligations under the EC Treaty. It has also been argued that the positive system of the Habitats Directive—only those species and habitats included in a list are protected—is less in keeping with the precautionary principle than the negative system of the Birds Directive, which protects all the species within its scope.[45] The same can therefore be argued in respect of a civil liability regime stated to be a manifestation of the precautionary principle, and that is linked to the Habitats Directive.

Another concern relates to the delay, or even denial, in designating Natura 2000 sites. Two issues give rise to uncertainties, and merit attention. First, will the future regime apply to sites which have not been designated in breach with the directives? Second, what national acts actually constitute designation? Interestingly, regarding the first point, it follows from ECJ case law that some of the obligations of the Wild Birds Directive, notably Article 4(4), requiring Member States to take steps to avoid significant pollution in the Special Protection Area (SPA), apply not only where the sites have been designated, but

---

[41] White Paper, n. 1 above, para. 4.2.

[42] See also Opinion of the Committee of the Regions on the White Paper, CdR 13/2000 (COM–4/031), para. 2.1 and European Environmental Law Association (EELA), *Comments to the European Commission's White Paper on Environmental Liability, COM (2000) 66 final, July 2000* (unpublished), para. 4.2.1.

[43] Agence Europe, (2000) 7741 *Bulletin Quotidien Europe*, 16. See also the Opinion of the Economic and Social Committee on the White Paper on Environmental Liability, CES/2000/803, published on the Internet at: http://www.esc.eu.int, para. 4.1.1.

[44] Cf. Art. 4 of the Wild Birds Directive and Art. 4 of and Annex III to the Habitats Directive. For further details, see: J. Scott, *EC Environmental Law* (Harlow: Longman, 1998), 113–14.

[45] Scott, n. 43 above, 116.

also where they should have been designated.[46] It is true that this specific obligation is no longer in force, as it has been replaced by Article 7 of the Habitats Directive. However, the obligations to prevent deterioration of the habitat and disturbance of species still apply. Failure to take measures to prevent deterioration of habitats, even with respect to sites which should have been designated, may still give rise to an ECJ judgment declaring an infringement of the directive.[47] On the basis of these judgments, it would seem that the future liability regime will also apply to areas not yet designated under the Wild Birds Directive, but in respect of which an obligation to classify the areas concerned exists. This is different for areas to be designated under the Habitats Directive, pursuant to which under Article 4(5) obligations to manage and protect the natural habitats concerned arise only after the area has been included in the list of sites of Community importance. Presumably, therefore, the future regime will not apply to areas not included in the list of sites of Community importance.

Regarding the question as to what constitutes an act of designation, following the ECJ's *Leybucht* judgment,[48] arguably, a freestanding act of designation may not be required. According to the ECJ, it suffices for a site to be afforded a relevant nature protection status under national law. This would be undesirable, given the wide-ranging legal consequences of such a status.[49] This uncertainty also affects proposed liability in the regime, as neither the Wild Birds nor the Habitats Directives prescribe any method of designation.

### v. Valuation and Assessment

One of the primary objectives of the White Paper is to restore damage caused to natural resources in Natura 2000 sites. Therefore it is not surprising that the Commission has placed an emphasis on restoration, and chooses restoration costs as the primary and preferred method to assess damages. In addition to restoration costs, the responsible party will also be held liable for the reasonable cost of assessing damages.[50]

To prevent disproportionate claims, the White Paper proposes that the cost of restoration measures are only recoverable if they are reasonable. This approach is in line with most international civil liability conventions,[51] previous EC

---

[46] Case C–355/90, *Commission* v. *Spain* [1993] ECR I–4221, paras. 22, 57–8; see also Scott, n. 43 above, 110. Confirmed in Case C–166/97, *Commission* v. *France* [1999] ECR I–1719, para. 38 and Case C–96/98, *Commission* v. *France* [1999] ECR I–8531, para. 41.

[47] Case C–96/98, n. 45 above, para. 46.

[48] Case C–55/89, *Commission* v. *Germany* [1991] ECR I–883.

[49] C. Backes, *Juridische bescherming van ecologisch waardevolle gebieden* (Zwolle: W. E. J. Tjeenk Willink, 1993), 304–5. In addition, under the very complex procedure of Art. 7 of the Habitat Directive, certain substantive obligations apply without designation if only after a long period of time. Also, failure to designate sites listed in the Inventory of Important Bird Areas in the EC is actionable in its own right under Art. 226 EC, see Case C–3/96, *Commission* v. *Netherlands* [1998] ECR I–3031.

[50] White Paper, n. 1 above, para. 4.5.1. The White Paper does not use the term 'reasonable' here, but we presume that it is the Commission's intention to permit the recovery of reasonable assessment costs only.

[51] See Art. I(6) of the International Convention on Civil Liability for Oil Pollution Damage (Brussels, 29 Nov. 1969) (1970) 9 *International Legal Materials*, 45, as amended by the Protocol of 1984 (1906) *Tractatenblad* (Dutch Treaty Series), 13 and the Protocol of 1992, IMO Document

proposals for liability directives, and the law of some Member States. To determine whether restoration costs are reasonable, the White Paper proposes to apply a reasonableness test or cost–benefit analysis (CBA). The starting point here is the weighing of the cost of the restoration measures (including assessment costs), against the benefits of these measures. To quantify the benefits of the measures, the Commission proposes abstract methods or economic valuation methods, such as the contingent valuation method (CVM) and the travel cost method.[52] To save on the costs, it is proposed, however, to use in so far as appropriate the benefits transfer method. This is a relatively cheap and time-saving method, because the results of previous valuation studies are used to estimate economic values for changes in environmental goods and services.

With regard to the application of a CBA or a reasonableness test, used to determine whether or not restoration measures are reasonable, it should be noted that the format of a reasonableness test is probably more flexible than a cost–benefit analysis. A reasonableness test often involves the weighing of various factors, including the costs of a restoration plan, the extent to which the restoration plan accelerates natural recovery, and the degree of success of the measures. A CBA is more focused on finding economically efficient solutions, and compares the costs of a certain restoration plan with future benefits in monetary terms. The underlying assumption of a CBA is that optimum economic efficiency is reached where the future benefits—as measured by the abstract models or economic valuation techniques such as CVM—are equal to, or greater than, the costs involved in restoring the natural resources injured.[53] Economic efficiency clearly plays a key role here.

Both methods may be applied to determine whether or not a certain restoration plan is reasonable, but they only provide an indication as to the reasonableness of the costs of a certain restoration plan. They support the decision-making process in restoration planning, but an overall judgement still needs to be made. It could be attempted to introduce a certain standard above which the costs are deemed prima facie disproportionate. However, such a standard would necessarily be arbitrary. Illustrative in this respect is the suggestion of the USA Court of Appeal in the *Ohio* case, to consider the costs of restoration measures unreasonable if they exceed three times the value of the natural resources impacted.[54] Obviously, such a standard is arbitrary. In addition, it requires a full assessment of the value of the damaged natural resources, which is often difficult, costly, and time-consuming.

LEG/CONF 9/15 (the 1992 Civil Liability Convention); Art. 1(1) of the UNECE Convention on Civil Liability for Damage caused during Carriage of Dangerous Goods by Road, Rail and Inland Navigation Vessels (CRTD) (Geneva, 10 Oct. 1989) (1989) 17 *Revue de Droit Uniforme*, 281; Art. 1(6) of the International Convention on Liability and Compensation for Damage in connection with the Carriage of Hazardous and Noxious Substances by Sea (HNS Convention) (1996) 35 *International Legal Materials*, 1415; Art. 2 of the Protocol on Liability and Compensation for Damage resulting from Transboundary Movements of Hazardous Wastes and their Disposal (signed at Basel, 10 Dec. 1999), published on the Internet at: http://www.basel.int.

[52] For a description of these methods, see Perman, n. 34 above.
[53] Perman, n. 34 above, 144–5.       [54] *Ohio* v. *DOI*, 880 F.2d 432, 444 (D.C. Cir. 1989).

We are in favour of using a mix of factors or criteria to determine the reasonableness of proposed restoration measures, cost–benefit considerations being one of them. This is also the approach favoured by the 1997 Vienna Convention on Civil Liability for Nuclear Damage. In this Convention, a number of factors are indicated, including the likely effectiveness of the restoration measures, proportionality and scientific and technical expertise.[55] In the USA factors or criteria are also used to determine whether the cost of implementing a restoration plan is reasonable or not. However, there is one important difference with the Vienna Convention. The US Oil Pollution Act and Comprehensive Environmental Response, Compensation and Liability Act (CERCLA) both require that the extent of interim losses—that is, the loss of natural resource services from the time of the injury until full recovery—is considered under the various restoration options. Therefore, apart from factors such as the technical feasibility of the various restoration options, the likelihood of success of each of these options, the extent to which each option is expected to return the injured resources and services to base-line condition, the cost of implementing the various restoration alternative(s), and the extent of the interim losses under the various options also need to be taken into account. It is striking that the White Paper does not address this type of harm at all.[56] However, this might change in the future Directive—or in the guidelines that accompany the Directive.

Where restoration is impossible for technical or financial reasons, the cost of alternative solutions may be used as a measure of damages. These alternative solutions should be aimed at re-establishing the level of nature conservation and biological diversity embodied in the Natura 2000 network, and may include actions to secure the equivalent of the damaged natural resources.[57] Damages may thus also be assessed on the basis of the cost of, for example, the purchase of land to be re-created as a habitat favourable to the animal species concerned, and that replaces the site irreversibly affected. This is in line with some of the international civil liability conventions more recently drafted, such as the 1993 Council of Europe Convention. Article 2(8) of this Convention provides that, where restoration is not possible, an equivalent site may be developed.

The focus in the White Paper therefore is on restoration or replacement of the natural resources impacted. In that light, it is understandable that monies recovered from an operator must be spent on restoring or replacing the environment (earmarked damages). This is a useful innovation compared with the traditional law of damages, where generally it is left to the plaintiff to decide how to spend the money. A precedent for this approach can be found

---

[55] Art. 2(4)(o) of the 1963 Convention as amended by the Protocol of 12 Sept. 1997 (1997) 36 *International Legal Materials*, 1454.

[56] The issue of the compensation of interim losses is raised, however, in a background study for the White Paper: *Liability for Ecological Damage and Assessment of Ecological Damage* (summary of the paper is published as an Annex to the White Paper (Office of Official Publications version, n. 13 above)).

[57] White Paper, n. 1 above, para. 4.5.1.

in the 1990 German Environmental Liability Act, which in §16(2) *Gesetz über die Umweltshaftung,* includes advance payments for restoration.[58] The 1999 Austrian Nuclear Liability Act, likewise, has adopted this form of earmarked damages.[59]

Finally in this context, the White Paper delimits the notion of natural resource damage further by the introduction of the positive requirement of 'significance'. In keeping with the linkage between natural resource damage and EC nature protection law, only significant damage is actionable.[60] Because the plaintiff must pass this threshold, the uncertainty inherent in this notion will act as a disincentive to bringing an action. It would be more in keeping with the traditional law of damages to introduce a *de minimis* defence (a negative requirement).[61] In this approach, it is up to the defendant to establish negligible damage. Once again, the 1997 Vienna Convention on Civil Liability for Nuclear Damage is an appropriate model, as it refers to the compensation for the restoration costs of impaired environment, 'unless such impairment is insignificant'.[62]

## vi. Defences to Liability

In the White Paper, it is proposed to allow at least the commonly accepted defences.[63] In that respect it is noted that a responsible party should escape liability if it proves that the damage was attributable to: an act of God, contribution to the damage or consent by the plaintiff, and the act or omission of a third party.[64] The White Paper refers also to the 'regulatory compliance' defence, according to which the operator is exempted from liability if he can prove that the damage was caused entirely and exclusively by emissions that were explicitly allowed in a permit. Although, the 'regulatory compliance' defence itself is rejected in the White Paper, the Commission notes that, if the operator can prove that the damage was caused by an authorized release, the courts may decide, on a case-by-case basis, that 'part of the compensation [is] to be borne by the permitting authority'.[65] The Commission justifies its proposal by noting that in these circumstances it would be 'inequitable for the polluter to have to pay the full compensation'.[66] It appears that this rule is

---

[58] In English: B. S. Markesinis, *A Comparative Introduction to the German Law of Torts* (Oxford: Clarendon Press, 1994), 871. See, for a further elaboration, the equivalent of this provision in the Draft Environmental Code, Independent Expert Commission on the Environmental Code, Ministry for the Environment, *Environmental Code: Draft* (Berlin: Duncker & Humblot, 1998).

[59] W. Posch, 'New Developments in the Law of Civil Liability for Nuclear Damage Spearheaded by Austria' (1999) 3 *Environmental Liability,* 82.

[60] White Paper, n. 1 above, p. 16.

[61] European Environmental Law Association, 'Repairing Damage to the Environment—A Community System of Civil Liability' (1994) 2 *Environmental Liability,* 1. See also Opinion of the Committee of the Regions, n. 41 above, para. 2.4.

[62] Art. 1(k) of the 1963 Convention as amended by Protocol of 12 Sept. 1997, n. 54 above.

[63] White Paper, n. 1 above, para. 4.3.          [64] Ibid.          [65] Ibid.

[66] Ibid. Interestingly, the EC Committee of the Regions (COR) rejects this proposal, as it is of the opinion that the party responsible for the damage should pay for the restoration costs, and not the permitting authority. Opinion of the Committee of the Regions, n. 41 above, para. 1.5.

proposed to provide an incentive to the polluter to comply with their permits.[67] In addition, it is expected that this rule will result in increased levels of care by the administration when acting in their statutory capacity in the context of setting permit restrictions or standards.[68] It is not explained how liability is to be shared between public authorities and the operator, and on the basis of what criteria. It has been noted that the courts may take into account, for instance, whether the operator has done everything possible to avoid the damage.[69] This could mean that if the operator knew, on the basis of new technical and scientific knowledge, that the standards attached to the permit were too lenient, it must act in compliance with these new insights, and should not wait for a new or updated permit. Hopefully, the final directive will be more specific here.

The White Paper is not very specific about other defences, such as the 'state of the art' or 'development risk' defence. The 'state of the art' defence is an important defence for economic operators involved in dangerous activities. It makes it possible to escape liability if the defendant proves that the dangerous effects were impossible to foresee, given the state of scientific and technical knowledge in the given field at the time the activity took place.[70] The Commission recognizes the importance of the defence, but no clear position is taken in the White Paper.[71] The reason for this is probably the debate within the EU on the implementation of the precautionary principle, which is incorporated in Article 174(2) of the EC Treaty.[72] Although there exists uncertainty about the precise meaning and scope of the precautionary principle, it is generally understood as justifying measures to prevent environmental impairment, even where there is no full scientific certainty to prove a causal link between emissions or inputs and certain possible effects.[73] The absence of adequate scientific information is therefore not necessarily a sufficient reason to postpone certain measures to prevent environmental harm. Since the 'state of the art' defence enables the defendant to exempt himself from liability if an investigation into the possible dangerous effects of the activity concerned

---

[67] Cf. Green Paper on Remedying Environmental Damage, COM(93)47 def., 14 May 1993, 9; Draft White Paper, version 14.9.1998 (unpublished), para. 7.3.

[68] Ibid.                    [69] White Paper, n. 1 above, para. 4.3.

[70] The defence has proven to be of importance in environmental cases, such as those concerning soil pollution and liability of employers for asbestos-related illnesses of their employees. For more details; G. Betlem, *Civil Liability for Transfrontier Pollution* (London: Graham & Trotman/Martinus Nijhoff, 1993), 455–7.

[71] An earlier version of the White Paper is far more specific here. It notes the 'state of the art' defence should not be allowed because it 'would considerably reduce the benefits of a strict liability approach'. In addition, this is considered the only way to stimulate operators to undertake measures through research and development to minimize risks (version 14.9.1998, n. 66 above, para 6.2).

[72] Communication from the Commission on the Precautionary Principle, COM (2000)1, 2 Feb. 2000 (reproduced in full, elsewhere in this volume).

[73] The precautionary principle is included in many treaties and policy documents, including the 1992 Rio Declaration. For more details, see: D. Freestone and E. Hey (eds.), 'Origins and Development of the Precautionary Principle' in D. Freestone and E. Hey, *The Precautionary Principle and International Law* (The Hague: Kluwer International Law, 1996), 3–15; see also L. Krämer, n. 22 above, 16–17.

would not have produced sufficient information on the dangers, there exists a certain tension between this defence and the precautionary principle. It is difficult to predict what position the Commission will finally request.[74]

Finally, in the context of defences, the White Paper notes that certain procedural aspects such as limitation are relevant.[75] No further examination of the important question of limitation periods is carried out.

### vii.  Burden of Proof of Causation

With regard to the issue of the burden of proof, the White Paper is not specific. The Commission recognizes that an impossible burden of proof would undermine the positive effects of strict liability, but no concrete proposal is included regarding the alleviation of the burden of proof.[76] It is merely indicated that '[t]he Community regime could also contain one or other form of alleviation of the traditional burden of proof, to be more precisely defined at a later stage'.[77] Decisions regarding this issue therefore have been postponed.

Previous versions of the White Paper were more specific on this issue. For instance, in one of the earlier drafts of the White Paper, it was proposed to alleviate the plaintiff's burden of proof with respect to causation by including a rebuttable presumption.[78] According to this proposal, the plaintiff would have to 'prove the damage and indicate its origin and present elements that make causation between the two plausible'.[79] So it seems that it suffices for the plaintiff to prove that a certain substance is capable of causing detrimental effects to the natural resources concerned or to his personal health, and that the defendant is responsible for the exposure to the substance, rather than to show a scientifically proven individual link between the loss and the release of the individual substance. However, in order to prevent defendants from being subjected to unreasonable liabilities, it is further noted that if the plaintiff succeeds in this, the burden of proof would then rest with the defendant who has to prove with a 'prevailing probability' that his activity did not cause the damage.[80] The Commission further noted that it depends on the circumstances of the individual case how this criterion is to be applied.

The proposal was probably inspired by the German Environmental Liability Act of 1990 (*Umwelthaftungsgesetz*), which includes a provision that alleviates the burden of proof (Article 6).[81] However, the German Act is more specific about the circumstances that can be relied upon to establish a presumption that a certain facility has caused the damage, and about the rebuttal of the

---

[74]  See text n. 71 above. Striking is that the 'state of the art' defence was not included in the 1991 Amended Proposal for a Council Directive on Civil Liability for Damage Caused by Waste, COM(91)219 final, 27 June 1991. The defence, however, is included in Council Dir. 85/374/EEC on the Approximation of the Laws, Regulations and Administrative Provisions of the Member States concerning Liability for Defective Products (Product Liability Directive) [1985] OJ L210/29.

[75]  White Paper, n. 1 above, para. 4.3, n. 12.          [76]  White Paper, n. 1 above, para. 4.3.

[77]  Ibid.          [78]  Draft White Paper, n. 66 above, para. 7.1.          [79]  Ibid.          [80]  Ibid.

[81]  Art. 7 *Umwelthaftungsgesetz* is also of interest here, as it creates an alleviation of the burden of proof in the case where several installations could have caused the damage.

presumption of causation. The Commission drew inspiration from other parts of Community law too, such as from the field of sex discrimination law where the burden of proving indirect discrimination is alleviated both by legislation and relevant case law.[82]

Since, with regard to the issue of the burden of proof, no decisions have yet been taken, it remains to be seen what position will ultimately be adopted. However, it should be noted that since a future liability directive would give effect, *inter alia,* to the precautionary principle, scientific certainty should not be required in the context of proof of causation.[83] This is consistent with public authorities taking preventive measures as happened with the ban on the exportation of British beef to reduce the risk of BSE infection and transmission to humans, or in upholding legislation to protect the ozone layer.[84] At the very least as regards damage caused by GMOs, to be covered by the future directive in the absence of a *lex specialis,* courts must be expected to apply and interpret the liability regime in the light of the precautionary principle. This is because these liability rules will be complementary to the regulatory regime of the forthcoming GMO Directive, which, in turn, has been based upon the same principle, and is to be taken into account at the implementation stage.[85] We argue that any rules regarding proof of causation, both of national and Community origin, should be construed in the light of this principle. The significance of the precautionary principle at the level of national law, as a result of the combined effects of (future) directives and Article 174 EC, will thus be comparable to its role as an aid to interpretation at Community level.[86]

---

[82] Council Dir. 97/80/EC on the Burden of Proof in Cases of Discrimination based on Sex [1998] OJ L14/6 (amended by Council Dir. 98/52/EC) on the Extension of Dir. 97/80/EC on the Burden of Proof in Cases of Discrimination based on Sex to the United Kingdom of Great Britain and Northern Ireland [1998] OJ L205/66); for case law, see most recently Case C–226/98, *Birgitte Jørgensen* v. *Foreningen af Speciallæger and Sygesikringens Forhandlingsudvalg* [2000] ECR I–2447.

[83] See de Sadeleer, n. 22 above, 223, citing French case law regarding HIV infection due to blood transfusion; and Communication from the Commission on the Precautionary Principle, n. 71 above, 15.

[84] Respectively regarding BSE: Case C–157/96, *The Queen* v. *Ministry of Agriculture, Fisheries and Food, Commissioners of Customs & Excise, ex p. National Farmers' Union and others* [1998] ECR I–2211, paras. 63–4 and Case C–180/96, *United Kingdom* v. *Commission* [1998] ECR I–2265, paras. 99–100; Case C–284/95, *Safety Hi-Tech Srl* v. *S. & T. Srl* [1998] ECR I–4301. See also Case T–199/96, *Laboratoires pharmaceutiques Bergaderm SA and Jean-Jacques Goupil* v. *Commission* [1998] ECR II–2805, para. 66 (on appeal, the ECJ did not rule on the complaint against this consideration because it was not decisive for the operative part: Case C–352/98P judgment of 4 July 2000, not yet reported, para. 53); Pres. CFI, Case T–70/99, *Alpharma Inc.* v. *Council* [1999] ECR II–2027, para. 153.

[85] Council Common Position (EC) No. 12/2000 with a View to Adopting a Directive of the European Parliament and of the Council on the Deliberate Release into the Environment of Genetically Modified Organisms and Repealing Council Dir. 90/220/EEC [2000] OJ C64/1, recital 8, Art. 1, Art. 4 and Annex II.

[86] Joined Cases C–418/97 and C–419/97, *ARCO Chemie Nederland Ltd* v. *Minister van Volkshuisvesting, Ruimtelijke Ordening en Milieubeheer and Vereniging Dorpsbelang Hees, Stichting Werkgroep Weurt and Vereniging Stedelijk Leefmilieu Nijmegen v Directeur van de dienst Milieu en Water van de provincie Gelderland* [2000] ECR I–4475, paras. 39–40, where the ECJ stipulates that the concept of waste cannot be interpreted restrictively consistent with the principles laid down in Art. 174 EC.

### viii.  Who Will Be Held Liable?

The White Paper recommends channelling liability to the person who exercises control over the activity by which the damage is caused, which will often be the operator.[87] Where the activity is carried out by a company in the form of a legal person, liability will rest on the legal person, and not on the managers or other employees who may have been involved in the activity.[88] This approach is in line with most of the international civil liability conventions, previous EC liability proposals, and the law of some Member States.[89]

Unlike previous drafts of the White Paper, there is no facility designed to anticipate the use of legal persons specifically set up to reduce the liability risk, such as through the development of separate entities with minimal assets. It is further proposed that lenders, such as banks and other financial institutions, should not be held liable for the damage caused by their clients, except where the lender exercises operational control over the company, which is not further defined.[90]

### ix.  Access to Justice: A Two-Tier Approach

In civil liability cases, the right to sue is usually granted only to the party with a legal interest in recovering compensation. Where damage is caused to the flora and fauna in one of the designated protection areas, the question arises which parties have the right to sue. Where damage is caused to a habitat, it is the owner of the land of which the habitat forms a part who has the right to sue. However, under civil law there exists no duty to file a claim or to use the compensation obtained for restoration purposes. Hence, in order to ensure recovery and restoration of damage to the natural resources that are of Community interest, it is necessary to develop an alternative mechanism. A problem also exists if damage is caused to wildlife that uses the habitat for breeding, wintering, or as a staging post during the spring and autumn migration. These natural resources are not owned, which makes damage to these resources difficult to recover via traditional civil liability.

In this respect, the White Paper includes an interesting proposal for access to justice for cases where damage is caused to Natura 2000 sites. The aim of the proposed mechanism is to ensure restoration of damage to the areas and species protected under the Natura 2000 network. The Commission proposes a two-tier approach.[91] Under this approach, the state is empowered to file

---

[87] White Paper, n. 1 above, para. 4.4.          [88] Ibid.

[89] See e.g. the 1999 Protocol to the Basel Convention and 1997 Protocol to the Vienna Convention on Civil Liability for Nuclear Damage. An example of an EC proposal is the 1989 proposal for a Council Directive on Civil Liability for Damage caused by Waste. For a comparative overview of national laws, see McKenna & Co., n. 23 above.

[90] White Paper, n. 1 above, para. 4.4. See further: M. Grant, 'Environmental Liability' in G. Winter, *European Environmental Law* (Aldershot: Dartmouth, 1996), 232–3; European Environmental Law Association, n. 41 above, 14–15.

[91] White Paper, n. 1 above, para. 4.7.

claims against the polluter, and the primary responsible for the restoration and decontamination of the affected area and species concerned. It is further proposed, however, to provide public interest groups with a right to act on a subsidiary basis. Only in cases where public authorities do not act at all—or improperly—will such collective action groups have a right to take action.[92] Public interest groups are thereby only granted an indirect form of access to justice. They must respect an unspecified waiting period, during which the public authorities have the exclusive right to take action, and decide on the necessity of restoration measures, as well as the extent of such measures. There is one exception; in case of urgent situations, public interest groups can ask a court for an injunction in order to prevent significant damage, or to avoid further damage.[93] In these urgent cases they may sue the alleged polluter, and do not have to wait for the state to act. It is noteworthy also, that NGOs may bring a claim for reimbursement of the reasonable costs incurred in the taking of urgent preventive measures.

The proposed regime on access to justice only applies to damage to natural resources in Natura 2000 areas and contaminated sites, and not to personal injury or property damage, and even pure economic loss is possibly excluded.[94]

*Member States*
The European Commission proposes to grant to Member States the primary right to sue if damage is done to the natural resources falling within the scope of the proposed regime. The legal status of the natural resources covered is of little relevance: even with regard to the natural resources that are owned—such as a habitat which forms a part of private land—the state has the right to file a claim against the polluter.

The White Paper does not explain in much detail why the state should be afforded the primary responsibility to act (even with regard to natural resources that are privately owned). It is merely observed that 'the protection of the environment is a public interest', and that the natural resources protected in the Natura 2000 areas are important for the conservation of biodiversity in the Community.[95] In other words, the natural resources concerned are of Community interest, and have—where it concerns natural resources subject to ownership rights—a value that exceeds the interests of a private owner. The approach is consistent with the Wild Birds and Habitats Directives, pursuant to which species and their habitats are protected irrespective of the existence of property rights.

Interestingly, this part of the proposal is comparable with certain aspects of the USA Oil Pollution Act (OPA) and the CERCLA. Under OPA and CERCLA, certain governmental agencies have been appointed as trustees. These trustees act on behalf of the public, and are authorized to assess and recover damages for injuries to certain natural resources. These natural resources

---

[92] Ibid., para. 4.7.1.       [93] Ibid.       [94] White Paper, n. 1 above, para. 4.5.3.
[95] Ibid., para. 4.7.1, p. 2.

include the natural resources that 'belong to, are managed by, held in trust by, appertaining to, or otherwise controlled by' the United States, any state or Indian tribe.[96]

Consequently, if the public authorities have an interest in certain natural resources, these resources are covered, and it is immaterial whether the resources are privately owned or not. When considering the legal obligations for EU Member States with regard to the natural resources in the Natura 2000 areas, a parallel can be drawn with the scope of OPA and CERCLA. The natural resources in Natura 2000 areas are managed and controlled by the public authorities of the various Member States.[97] It can even be argued that these natural resources are held in trust for the benefit of the public (and future generations). From this perspective—and the fact that states are already under a duty to protect, preserve, and manage the natural resources concerned[98]—it is not so surprising that the state is granted the primary right to sue. However, the White Paper does not address the issue who has standing in case the state itself (or another public authority) caused the damage. NGOs are possibly entitled to file claims in these cases, but the White Paper is unclear as to this issue. Hopefully, a clearer position is adopted in the future Directive.

*NGOs*

As noted, the Commission proposes to grant public interest groups a secondary right of standing.[99] Only in cases where public authorities fail to act at all or act improperly will collective action groups have the right to take action. Public interest groups thus must respect a waiting period, during which public authorities have the exclusive right to take action, and decide on the necessity of restoration measures, and the extent of such measures. This rule obviously harbours the risk of delays, frustrating effective action by NGOs. At the very least, any future directive should therefore include a period within which public authorities must act. Failure to act after expiry of this period would then open the doors for NGOs. Alternatively, one could include the requirement that the NGOs first seek redress extrajudicially from the operator itself.[100]

Although the White Paper is not specific, NGOs—exercising their secondary right of action—may raise all types of claims against the potentially liable person, including claims for monetary damages. However, the recovery of

---

[96] 42 U.S.C.A. §9601(16); 33 U.S.C.A. §2701(20).

[97] Obviously, certain natural resources belong to local or central governments.

[98] Currently the EU and its Member States are spending considerable amounts of money to preserve and restore the natural resources concerned. For instance, the EU's budget for financing nature conservation projects in Natura 2000 sites is 450 million euro (LIFE 1996–9).

[99] White Paper, n. 1 above, para. 4.7.1.

[100] Cf. Art. 3:305a(2) Dutch Civil Code. This provision of the Civil Code entitles an NGO with full legal capacity to bring an action in court—other than a damages claim—for the purpose of protecting the interests of other persons, inasmuch as it promotes these interests according to its articles of association. However, NGOs first need to seek redress by way of consultation with the defendant. For further details, see: G. Betlem, 'Environmental Standing for Ecosystems. Going Dutch' (1995) 54 *Cambridge Law Journal*, 160–7.

damages for the injury to, or the loss of, natural resources is subject to limitations regarding the use of the sums obtained: the compensation is only to be used for restoration purposes. From the White Paper, it appears that NGOs may take the measures of reinstatement themselves, provided that the measures are carried out in cooperation with the public authorities.[101]

There is one exception to the rule regarding the compulsory waiting period. For so-called urgent situations, it is proposed to grant NGOs the right to ask a court directly for an injunction in order to prevent significant damage or avoid further damage to the environment. In these circumstances, NGOs may also ask for an injunction ordering the reinstatement of the environment.[102] In addition, NGOs may take action to prevent or limit damage to the natural resources falling within the scope of the proposed regime, and may recover the reasonable cost incurred as a result of taking of these urgent preventive measures, such as of the costs made to clean up oiled birds. It should be noted that such costs are already recoverable in some Member States, and under some of the international civil liability conventions.[103]

Not every NGO will be entitled to file claims. The Commission proposes that only public interest groups that comply with objective qualitative criteria are to be granted standing to sue. No further details are available in the White Paper on what criteria need to be fulfilled. However, parallel to the criteria included in Directive 98/27/EC on Injunctions for the Protection of Consumers' Interests,[104] it may be expected that, in order to be entitled to file claims, NGOs need to be properly constituted according to the law of the Member State, have legal capacity, and have the purpose to protect the environment (as shown by their articles of association).[105] In addition, it may be anticipated that in order to be able to take action in case of a transboundary incident, NGOs willing to take action need to be listed as qualified national entities. Such a list is to be drawn up under the Consumer Injunction Directive, and will be published in the *Official Journal of the EC.*[106] The same system could be used in respect of qualified environmental NGOs.

## Outlook

From the White Paper, and other EC documents such as the Aarhus Convention, which has been signed by the EC, it appears that the EC is currently in the

[101] White Paper, n. 1 above, para. 4.7.3.

[102] Ibid. This proposal is not new, as it was already included in one of the earlier proposals on environmental liability. See Art. 4(b)(iii) Amended proposal for a Council Directive on Civil Liability for Damage Caused by Waste, n. 73 above. Cf. Art. 18(1)(d) of the 1993 Lugano Convention.

[103] *Arrondissementsrechtbank* (District Court) Rotterdam, 15 Mar. 1991, T.M.C. Asser Institute, *Netherlands Yearbook of International Law 1992*, 513 (*Borcea*-case).

[104] European Parliament and Council Dir. 98/27/EC on Injunctions for the Protection of Consumers' Interests [1998] OJ L166/51. For more details, see: G. Betlem and C. Joustra, 'The Draft Consumer Injunctions Directive' (1997) *Consumer Law Journal*, 8–17; G. Betlem, 'Verbodsacties Consumenten' (1998) *Tijdschrift voor Milieu Aansprakelijkheid/Environmental Liability Law Quarterly*, 167–9.

[105] Art. 3 and Art. 4 of European Parliament and Council Dir. 98/27/EC, n. 103 above.

[106] Ibid. Art. 4(2).

process of granting NGOs (and individuals) more extensive rights of legal standing.[107] The aim of these initiatives is to ensure a better rate of implementation and enforcement of Community environmental law.[108] NGOs, as environmental watchdogs, are considered a welcome supplementary power to assist in the protection of the environment.[109]

In our view, granting standing to NGOs and permitting them to file claims for damages is a positive development. However, to what extent are NGOs really capable of playing the role of environmental watchdog? It is not unlikely that the high costs of civil procedures will form an obstacle for NGOs to file claims, and seek monetary compensation for injuries to natural resources covered. Not only is there a risk of losing the case, and being forced to pay the costs of the winning party,[110] in many natural resource damage cases NGOs will have to undertake studies to determine, for example, the extent of the injuries to natural resources. These costs may obviously influence the willingness of NGOs to file claims. To stimulate NGOs to use their right of action, beyond high profile cases, the EC should consider the establishment of a mechanism to compensate NGOs for the costs made in these legal procedures. Various options could be pursued. The EC could establish a fund to assist in civil litigation. It could also expand its current programme that provides NGOs financial assistance for activities that are of Community interest, and that contribute to the implementation of EC law.[111] Another option is to include a specific (and more favourable) cost rule in the future directive.

Apart from the issue of the cost of litigation, barriers to access to justice also limit the opportunities for private enforcement by NGOs. It is therefore difficult to see why the White Paper in §4.5.3 rules out the future elaboration of specific provisions on access to justice, in so far as traditional damage, possibly even including pure economic loss, is concerned. It would seem to follow that the rules on access to justice are only concerned with environmental damage. As the example of an NGO suing a Member State for non-implementation of a directive shows, non-compliance with EC environmental law standards may give rise to a variety of types of loss, environmental and 'traditional' loss in the sense covered by the White Paper. Why should eliminating the barriers to access to justice *a priori* be ruled out, given that litigation will thus be further complicated by making the admissibility of a claim conditional upon the kind of loss at stake?

---

[107] See Communication from the European Commission: Implementing Community Environmental Law, COM(96)500 def., paras. 40–1; Preamble to Dir. 98/27/EC, n. 103 above. See also the Commission Discussion Paper: The Commission and Non-Governmental Organizations: Building a Stronger Partnership, COM(2000)11 final.

[108] Ibid.

[109] COM(96)500 def., para. 37; Council Dec. 97/872/EC on a Community Action Programme Promoting Non-Governmental Organizations Primarily Active in the Field of Environmental Protection [1997] OJ L354/25.

[110] Most EU Member States apply the rule that the loser has to pay the costs of the winner, and will also have to bear his own. See McKenna & Co., n. 23 above, 312–14.

[111] Council Dec. 97/872/EC, n. 108 above.

## IV.  Desirable Elements of an EC Environmental Liability Regime

In addition to the comments and suggestions put forward above in discussing the key features of the proposed regime, this section contains some further proposals for an effective EU-wide regime, which will be based in part on domestic legal experience. Where appropriate, we will briefly refer to developments outside the environmental law sphere, in particular consumer law, with a view to suggesting desirable features of the forthcoming directive. References will be made to examples of Community law impacting on the domestic law of obligations of Member States in so far as these have relevant 'precedent-value' for the Community legislature in preparation of a Framework Directive on Environmental Liability.

### A.  MOTHER DIRECTIVE WITH DAUGHTERS

Just as the CERCLA and the USA Oil Pollution Act are supplemented by secondary statutory instruments, which outline in great detail the determination and assessment of natural resources damages,[112] a future framework directive should be supplemented at a later stage by guidelines on the assessment of natural resource damage.[113] Such guidelines will benefit the public authorities and NGOs in determining the nature and extent of any losses, the assessment of the natural resource damages, the development of reasonable restoration alternatives, and the selection of the most appropriate restoration plan. Such rules may also facilitate uniform application of liability rules within the Member States, and will support courts in applying these new rules and assessing natural resource damages.[114] Interestingly, the Commission recently issued a call for tender for a study on assessment and restoration of natural resource damage. The objectives of the study are to provide guidance to the Commission on how to assess natural resource damages, and to develop criteria for determining whether or not a certain injury exceeds the minimum threshold, and is therefore to be considered significant. Although it is unclear whether it is the Commission's intention to use the result of the study for developing a secondary statutory instrument, it may be used as a step in that direction.[115]

Disregarding the precise form of the instruments involved, the establishment of detailed secondary regulations by the Commission is not new. The Commission has, for instance, developed such regulations for the imposition of a sanction in the form of a lump sum fine or periodic penalty payment against Member States for non-compliance with a judgment of the ECJ in the

---

[112]  43 CFR 11; 15 CFR 990.

[113]  The White Paper refers to a step-by-step approach, n. 1 above, para. 6.

[114]  See also the ERM Economics' Study on economic aspects of liability in Annex 2 to the Office for Official Publications' version White Paper, n. 13 above, 38.

[115]  The follow up to the White Paper is made public on the Commission's website, published on the Internet at: http://europa.eu.int/comm/environment/liability/followup.htm.

context of Article 228(2) EC. Thus, whereas the Treaty merely stipulates that, in the event of non-compliance with a judgment, the ECJ may impose a lump sum or penalty payment, the Commission has formulated rules on the factors determining the calculation of the fines or penalties it would request the ECJ to impose. These factors include the Member States' gross domestic product and voting power, as well as the seriousness and duration of the infringe-ment.[116] The seriousness coefficient includes taking into account the effects of the infringement, such as irreparable damage to the environment.[117]

In so far as the combination of directive and regulation is concerned, the Community legislature may draw inspiration from the current system regard-ing the licensing of the placing on the market of certain high-technology medicinal products. A 1993 Regulation introduces uniform Community-level procedures for the authorization of such medicines, alongside national procedures of the Member States which already had been extensively harmon-ized by directives. It follows that a 'daughter' regulation can supplement any future framework directive.[118]

Finally, in the environment sector itself, the 'parent/child' approach is of course well known. For instance, both with respect to air and water pollution, daughter directives are envisaged laying down emission limit values. However, the Community legislature has not been a very 'productive parent'; only a limited number of substances are covered after years of negotiation.[119]

### B.  TWO COMPLEMENTARY ROLES: ENFORCEMENT IN ADDITION TO COMPENSATION

The White Paper repeatedly refers to the need to facilitate the enforcement of Community environmental law.[120] The Commission notes that there will always be a lack of resources at Community level (centralized enforcement through Article 226 EC) to deal with even the minority of cases of alleged breach of EC environmental law.[121] It is in this context that the Commission is proposing to open up the 'ordinary' tort law regimes, encompassing both new actors (NGOs) and new forms of damage. However, in order to facilitate the enforcement of EC law with civil law remedies before national courts, the Community legislature should not suffice to set the aims and objectives while leaving the instruments (the choice between public and private law

[116] Memorandum on Applying Art. 171 of the EC Treaty [now Art. 228] [1996] OJ C42/6 and Method of Calculating the Penalty Payments provided for pursuant to Art. 171 of the EC Treaty [1997] OJ C36/2.

[117] In its first ruling on this Article—Case C–387/97, *Commission* v. *Greece* judgment of 4 July 2000, not yet reported—the ECJ regarded the guidelines not as binding but as a useful point of ref-erence. It also considered Greece's endangerment of the environment as being particularly serious.

[118] See Council Reg. (EEC) No. 2309/93 laying down Community Procedures for the Authorization and Supervision of Medicinal Products for Human and Veterinary Use and estab-lishing a European Agency for the Evaluation of Medicinal Products [1993] OJ L214/1.

[119] Scott, n. 43 above, 26.        [120] See e.g. White Paper, n. 1 above, para. 1.1, 3.3.

[121] Communication from the European Commission, n. 106 above, paras. 12–15, 25.

instruments),[122] to the Member States. The Community legislature should take harmonization one step further. Obviously, any directive within the meaning of Article 249 EC is only binding as to the result, leaving choice of form and methods to Member States. However, the result of any future Environmental Liability Directive is aimed at not only environmental protection as such, but also the availability of civil law remedies at national level. The freedom of Member States to choose form and methods is therefore restricted to a specific national law instrument (adaptation of the national Civil Code, enacting of separate act of environmental liability, etc.). The directive should therefore pursue an approach comparable to the directives dealing with cultural goods, consumer injunctions, and the Public Procurement Remedies Directive.[123] All these instruments either introduce a specific right of action, or apply standards to the ones already available. For example, in the sphere of cultural goods, Community law creates an independent right of action (besides any rights based on ownership) for the state of the country from which the good in issue has been unlawfully removed before the civil courts of the state where the good is situated. It does therefore not merely provide that the Member States must ensure adequate remedies. Likewise, in a cross-border context, the Consumer Injunctions Directive entitles so-called qualified entities of one state to institute legal proceedings before the courts of another state, without them having to fulfil any requirements of that second state's law, provided they satisfy the criteria of the Directive. The Directive specifically prescribes that the courts of this second state (other than the home state of the entity) must accept this list as sufficient proof of the applicant's capacity to bring proceedings. Again, this directive does more than merely prescribe 'adequate measures' in general. An independent right of action has been created. This is mirrored in Dutch implementation legislation, which has added an additional cause of action for foreign qualified entities to the two existing categories of possible plaintiffs under the Civil Code.[124]

Only if the envisaged Environmental Liability Directive creates new common remedies, or sets standards for existing remedies, will common enforcement within the whole Community be attainable. It is not sufficient that in some Member States NGOs can apply to the civil courts, whereas in others they can, at best, seek judicial review of decisions of the public authorities to act or not to act. Indeed, this is the present situation, which as we noted was deemed inadequate by the Commission in its 1996 Implementation Communication.

[122] White Paper, n. 1 above, para. 6.
[123] Council Dir. 93/7/EEC on the Return of Cultural Objects Unlawfully Removed from the Territory of a Member State [1993] OJ L74/74 and European Parliament and Council Dir. 98/27/EC, n. 103 above; Council Dir. 89/665/EEC on the Coordination of the Laws, Regulations and Administrative Provisions relating to the Application of Review Procedures to the Award of Public Supply and Public Works Contracts [1989] OJ L395/33, regarding civil and/or administrative law.
[124] See Art. 3:305c and Art. 6:240(6) Civil Code, inserted by Act of 25 Apr. 2000, (2000) *Staatsblad* (Dutch Official Journal), 178.

The Council, similarly stressing the role of liability in the enforcement process, notes that there is a need for improving the implementation and enforcement of EC environmental law, and is concerned about the lack of progress in broadening the range of instruments. It is recommending new instruments as a priority and preferred option under the forthcoming 6th action programme.[125] Detailed legislative action of the kind suggested above is needed to prevent private enforcement remaining 'an unfulfilled promise'.[126] In general terms, a choice between two techniques is open to the EC legislature.

It could introduce specific rights of action for the purpose of enforcement along the lines of the USA citizen suits provisions. Typically, these provisions provide that any person may commence a civil action 'against any person (including the United States and any other governmental . . . agency) . . . who is alleged to be in violation of any standard, regulation, condition . . . of the relevant Act.'[127] The plaintiff is entitled to seek any order necessary to correct the violation as well as civil penalties (comparable with periodic penalty payments).

The second option would be to require modification of domestic tort law so as to widen the range of interests protected by tortuous liability, and include the general interest of environmental protection as such, and grant *locus standi* to organizations promoting this goal. Dutch tort law is a case in point, where it is well established that breach of a norm which aims at environmental protection constitutes unlawfulness within the meaning of the relevant Civil Code provision vis-à-vis organizations with a matching purpose.[128] During the 1980s, this non-contractual liability regime has been judicially adapted for enforcement purposes to that effect. Breaches of environmental statutory duties are actionable by environmental protection organizations (NGOs). Community law can and should require this kind of adaptation of the law of obligations throughout the EU. Such a requirement in tort law may be compared with the sphere of contract law, where EC law similarly requires Member States to ensure that contracts concluded electronically have the same effect and validity as 'normal' contracts.[129] By implication, national contract law may have to be modified to attain this result.

[125] 2253rd Council Meeting, Environment, Brussels, 30 Mar. 2000, PRES/00/91, n. 17 above. We cannot help noticing that it was of course mainly the Council that emphasized the application of national liability law rather than developing EC law, see e.g. Common Position (EC) No. 20/97 with a View to adopting a Decision of the European Parliament and of the Council on the Review of the European Community Programme of Policy and Action in Relation to the Environment and Sustainable Development 'Towards Sustainability' [1997] OJ C157/12, Art. 3(1)d: 'encouraging the application of the concept of environmental liability at Member State level.'

[126] H. Somsen, 'The Private Enforcement of Member State Compliance with EC Environmental Law: An Unfulfilled Promise?' (2000) 1 *Yearbook of Eurpean Environmental Law*, 311.

[127] See e.g. CERCLA, 42 U.S.C.9659; see generally W. Wilson, *Making Environmental Laws Work. Law and Policy in the UK and USA* (Oxford: Hart Publishing, 1999).

[128] Betlem, n. 69 above, 317, 375.

[129] Art. 9 of European Parliament and Council Dir. 2000/31/EC on Certain Legal Aspects of Information Society Services, in Particular Electronic Commerce, in the Internal Market (Directive on Electronic Commerce) [2000] OJ L178/1.

A final question concerning enforcement issues is whether the linkage of the future liability regime to existing administrative EC environmental law as proposed by the White Paper is desirable. With or without formal linkages, only a limited number of Community environmental law provisions are of a kind capable of being enforced before the national (civil) courts in any event. In practice, the main categories concern emission limit values, permits, designation of conservation areas, and incorrect implementation of directives.[130] An argument in favour of linking liability and administrative environmental law is legal certainty. A list could be drawn up with instruments of EC environmental law qualifying for enforcement under the liability regime; this approach reflects the Consumer Injunctions Directive.[131] It defines actionable infringements by referring to an annexed list of directives. The disadvantage of this approach, however, is that even a list is likely to leave room for uncertainty. Legal certainty can only be advanced to the extent that the scope of the norm to be enforced itself is clear. Defining waste and determining which birds the Birds Directive covers has proved far from straightforward, for instance.[132]

The preferred option, in our view, is therefore to follow the model of the Product Liability Directive, which does not establish a link with Community product safety law at all. Simply *any* defective product, as defined by the Product Liability Directive itself rather than other administrative product safety rules, is covered. The Product Liability Directive is an autonomous regime. Apart from ensuring seamless enforcement of EC environmental law, such an approach would have the additional benefit of facilitating the enforcement of other environmental law, including that derived from domestic and international law. A consistent approach to enforcement should take into account that Community law does not operate in isolation, but leaves scope for more stringent protection under national law (Article 176 EC), and itself is subject to international obligations. A first step in this direction has been made by the 1998 Aarhus Convention, signed by the EU, which requires contracting parties to ensure that qualified persons have access to justice where private persons or public authorities have contravened provisions of national environmental law.[133]

The importance of this choice should probably not be exaggerated, as most environmental damage will be caused by discharges to water or air, dangerous

---

[130] Somsen, n. 125 above, 337. See also Scott, n. 43 above, 35 pointing out that for hazardous substances, emission standards are to be preferred over quality objectives, in particular from the point of view of enforcement.

[131] European Parliament and Council Dir. 98/27/EC, n. 103 above.

[132] For the former see: Joined Cases C–304/94, C–330/94, C–342/94, and C–224/95, *Criminal proceedings against Euro Tombesi and Adino Tombesi, Roberto Santella, Giovanni Muzi and others, and Anselmo SaviniTombesi* [1997] ECR I–3561 and for the latter Case C–169/89, *Criminal proceedings against Gourmetterie Van den Burg* [1990] ECR I–2143, Case C–149/94, *Criminal proceedings against Didier Vergy* [1996] ECR I–299 and Case C–202/94, *Criminal proceedings against Godefridus van der Feesten* [1996] ECR I–355.

[133] UNECE Convention on Access to Information, Public Participation in Decision-Making and Access to Justice in Environmental Matters (Aarhus, 25 June 1998), published on the Internet at: http://www.unece.org/env/.

substances, or by GMOs. All these activities are covered by the EC legislation set out in §4.2.2 of the White Paper.

Unlike the Green Paper on Liability for Defective Products,[134] the White Paper makes no mention of the issue of limitation periods within which actions must be brought (prescription).[135] Litigation concerning the detrimental effects of hazardous substances—which are likely to constitute the bulk of environmental liability cases—involves complex and time-consuming scientific assessments. Moreover, the harmful impact on man and/or the environment may take years to materialize (latent damage), whereas it may take even longer to establish a causal connection between the exposure to substances and personal or natural resource injuries. Illustrative for personal injury cases are a number of English High Court cases dealing with personal injury resulting from exposure to organophosphates (OHPs). A typical situation is the one involving farmworkers required to 'dip' sheep in baths containing OHPs. The basis of liability was the alleged insufficient protection of health and safety at work by their (former) employer. Even though ultimately successful, one plaintiff's case, despite admission of liability by the ex-employer, involved a lengthy debate on medical causation.[136] Another, however, was struck out on prescription grounds.[137]

Although this case also concerned possible product liability on the ground that the manufacturers had given insufficient warning/instructions, it is noteworthy that these cases were not pleaded on the basis of the English implementing legislation of the Product Liability Directive, because the limitation periods applicable to this cause of action (Article 10 of the Directive) are too short in these scientifically complex cases.[138] Given possible long periods of latency, the ten-year period linked to the date the product was put into circulation may have expired before there is sufficient certainty about the damage. Even where the plaintiff has become aware of the injury, the defect, and the identity of the producer, the relevant three-year period running from this date may be too short to gather sufficient medical evidence.

Unlike in the case of the Product Liability Green Paper, we cannot accept that these relatively short limitation periods are necessary to strike a proper balance between consumer protection and interests of producers. Apparently, shorter prescription periods are regarded as a price worth paying for a strict,

---

[134] COM(99)396 final, 28 July 1999.

[135] It merely notes, in the context of defences, that certain procedural aspects such as limitation are relevant; there is no further discussion, see White Paper, n. 1 above, para. 4.3, n. 12.

[136] *Hill* v. *Tomkins*, judgment of 17 Oct. 1997 (QBD, unreported, cited from Lexis). Most of the four-week trial was taken up with medical expert testimony on causation. See also *Re Human growth Hormone Litigation*, judgment of 19 July 1996 (QBD, unreported, cited from Lexis), involving a 25-day oral hearing.

[137] *Liversidge* v. *Coopers Animal Health Farm Ltd and Another*, judgment of 29 Oct. 1998 (QBD, unreported, cited from Lexis).

[138] Interview with Peter Bright, solicitor, Plymouth, 9 May 2000.

rather than a fault-based liability system.[139] However, as illustrated by the practical problems facing victims of exposure to hazardous substances, one should not see this as a bargaining issue because, in these situations, the three- and the ten-year limitation periods exclude all compensation due to factors outside the control of the victim. Extended periods of limitation taking into account these difficulties should therefore be part of the future regime.[140]

Precisely in view of these difficulties, a proposal to amend the Dutch Civil Code in situations of personal injury resulting from latent damage is pending before the Dutch Parliament.[141] In this proposal, it is suggested to extend the three-year (short stop) period to five, whereas the running of the twenty- or thirty-year (long stop) period following the harmful event is excluded altogether.[142] In addition to these legislative developments, the Dutch Supreme Court recently determined in two asbestos cases, concerning two former employees who suffered from mesothelioma, that under certain conditions the thirty-year limitation period could be circumvented.[143] A somewhat comparable development has taken place in the context of the 1997 Vienna Convention on Civil Liability for Nuclear Damage, where personal injury claims will be prescribed after thirty years, instead of the ten years in the 1963 version.[144]

Finally in this context, reference may be made to Article 7(1) of Council Directive 93/7/EEC of 15 March 1993 on the Return of Cultural Objects Unlawfully Removed from the Territory of a Member State,[145] which takes a thirty-year period as its starting point. An extension of this period applies in the case of certain specially protected cultural goods to seventy-five years, or even longer if (inter)national law so provides. It follows that the national, international, and Community legislatures have been prepared to afford extra weight to the interests of victims in special cases. In order to protect the environment effectively, and to prevent injustice to individuals, careful consideration should be given to regulating limitation periods. In particular, as is shown by Dutch and English case law and the Dutch proposed legislation, extinction of rights to compensation, even before there could have been any sufficiently certain assessment about the occurrence of loss at all, must be avoided. In situations of complex (medical) causation connected with the release of hazardous substances, a ten-year prescription period following this liability-triggering event proved too short. In certain circumstances, the 'right' will have expired even before the loss had occurred (i.e. any loss that can be proven with a sufficient degree of certainty), which clearly is unacceptable.

[139] Green Paper on Liability for Defective Products, COM(99)396, 28 July 1999, 26.

[140] See also, in the context of product liability, the Opinion of the European Parliament's Committee on the Environment, Public Health and Consumer Policy, EP Doc. A5-0061/2000, p. 10.

[141] Amendment of the provisions on the statute of limitations in the Civil Code in cases of latent damage resulting in personal injury or death, *Kamerstukken* (Parliamentary Documents) II, 1999–2000, 26 824.

[142] Parliamentary Documents, n. 140 above.

[143] *Hoge Raad* (Supreme Court) 28 Apr. 2000, (2000) *Rechtspraak van de Week*, 118 (*Van Hese* v. *De Schelde*); *Hoge Raad* (Supreme Court) 28 Apr. 2000, (2000) *Rechtspraak van de Week*, 119 (*Rouwhof* v. *Eternit*).

[144] See n. 54 above, Art. VI.      [145] [1993] OJ L74/74.

## V.  Specific Sectors of Environmental Liability Law

Because of recent incidents, as well as related legislative reform of the regulatory framework, the question of liability for damage to the environment has
come to the fore in connection with three specific sectors: the mining industry, the release of GMOs into the environment, and oil pollution at sea. There
is merit in surveying developments in these sectors, as they highlight public
concern about the issue of environmental liability, and raise the question
whether the legislative process should focus on adopting a general framework
directive (horizontal approach) to the exclusion of any sector-specific liability
rules, or whether these could both be developed in parallel.

### A.  MINE SPILLS

A sector which has recently proved to be capable of causing significant damage
to the environment, but for which no EC rules yet exist, is the mining industry,
and in particular companies extracting minerals such as gold, tin, and other
metals. According to one study, the fact that toxins such as cyanide are used in
the extraction process, generating acid mine water, which is then either stored
in the mines (in particular in abandoned ones), or in above-ground lagoons, is
particularly problematic. Leaks and spillage affect the surrounding environment, and dams which contain the acid water within the lagoons have been
know to give way. One such serious accident occurred in Southern Spain in
1998, affecting the Doñana wetlands, a Natura 2000 site. The study concludes
that an effective legislative framework at EC level on the protection of health
and the environment from mining activities is lacking at present.[146]

A second serious incident, the Baia Mare cyanide spill, took place in
Romania in January 2000, affecting the River Danube in Hungary. In a statement after her fact-finding mission to Romania and Hungary, Commissioner
Wallström announced seven steps that would be taken in order to prevent
such accidents from happening again, including a review and adaptation of
current EC environmental law. She referred in particular to inclusion of mining activities where this is presently not the case or uncertain, and the acceler-
ation of the preparation of legislation on environmental liability.[147] As a first
step, the Commission has adopted a Communication on the broad policy lines
for promoting sustainable development in the mining industry.[148] Priorities

---

[146] V. M. Sol, S. W. M. Peters, and H. Aiking, 'Toxic Waste Storage Sites in EU Countries. A
Preliminary Risk Inventory', IVM Report No. E–99/02, commissioned by WWF; see Agence Europe,
(2000) 7656 *Bulletin Quotidien Europe*, 16. Cf. for a similar lack of regulation the potential release
into the Baltic sea of dioxines and furanes embedded in the sediment of the Kymijoki river in
Finland, Written Question E–2311/99 by Esko Seppänen, 'Environmental disaster in the Kymijoki
river' [2000] OJ C219E/145.

[147] 'Cyanide Pollution Statement by Commissioner Wallström', BIO/00/32, Brussels 18/2/00,
published on the Internet at: http://www.europa.eu.int/comm/environment/press/bio0032.htm

[148] Press release 3 May 2000, 'Commission sets out plans for sustainable development of EU mining industry', IP/00/431, published on the Internet at: http://www.europa.eu.int (RAPID database).

include the prevention of mining accidents, and sound management of waste. No explicit mention is made of operator liability, although it can clearly be relevant in the context of the prevention of incidents. It is worth noting that 'typical' mining damage, i.e. subsidence of the soil, was subjected to strict liability as early as the 1920s by the Dutch courts, applying the general tort law rules of the (old) Civil Code as referred to in the 1810 Mining Act. Within the general context of tort law it was reasoned that the special nature of mining and the serious risks it poses to neighbouring property justifies such a high level of due diligence that any shortcoming by the operator constitutes fault. Familiar issues of environmental litigation already surfaced during this period: the irrelevance of the plea that the operator managed the mine according to usual practice in that line of business (the so-called 'state of the industry'), absence of fault only where the damage would have been completely unforeseeable, and dismissal of the plea that the costs of preventive measures are too high.[149]

Mining incidents may also spur legislative action at the international level. In a UN Environment Programme (UNEP) Report on the Baia Mare–Danube cyanide spill, it is noted that the issue of liability and compensation would have been easier to settle if there had been an international regime. It is therefore recommended that a Liability Protocol be developed to the UN/ECE Convention on the Protection and Use of Transboundary Watercourses and International Lakes and the UN/ECE Convention on Transboundary Effects of Industrial Accidents.[150] The Report notes that the mine had been wrongly classified under Romanian law as not requiring special monitoring. The mine thus operated in compliance with its licence but, being wrongly classified, the conditions of the licence were too lenient. It was doubtful if the operator could be liable under a regime which accepts compliance with a licence as an exoneration of liability.

### B. GMOS

Directive 90/220/EEC constitutes the current legal framework on the regulation of genetically modified organisms (GMOs). It establishes a system of coordinated licensing, where other Member States through the intermediary of the Commission must recognize permits granted by the relevant Member State authority.[151] If other Member States object to the purported licensing, the decision to permit the release of the GMOs is taken at EC level. This regime is considered to be inadequate by the EC legislature, and a proposal for a new directive replacing the current regime is being debated. More stringent

---

[149] Betlem, n. 69 above, 450–2.

[150] UNEP/OCHA, 'Cyanide Spill *at Baia Mare, Romania, Geneva, March 2000*', published on the Internet at: http://www.reliefweb.int/library/documents/baiamare.pdf.

[151] Council Dir. 90/220/EEC on the Deliberate Release into the Environment of Genetically Modified Organisms [1990] OJ L117/15. And see European Commission, 'Facts of GMOs in the EU', MEMO/00/43, published on the Internet at: http://www.europa.eu.int (RAPID database).

requirements are proposed regarding public participation (currently consultation takes place where a Member State considers this appropriate), labelling, and traceability. Indeed, certain Member States (Denmark, France, Greece, Italy, and Luxembourg) are refusing to grant any licences for GMO products/crops under the old regime (*de facto moratorium*), pending the entry into force of new legislation on labelling, traceability, and producer liability.[152] There are no rules on producer liability in the current GMO Directive (although, where applicable, a producer may be liable under the Product Liability Directive).

In April 2000 the European Parliament finalized its involvement in the pending GMO legislation, by adopting several amendments to the Council Common Position. The final text will be shaped in the conciliation procedure of Article 251 EC. The Common Position provides no other guidance as to liability than that the 'Directive shall be without prejudice to national legislation in the field of liability'.[153] The EP decided not to adopt the following amendment:

Those legally responsible for deliberate releases of genetically modified organisms shall have strict civil liability for any damage to human health and the environment caused by the release in question. Before the activities begin, they shall take out sufficient liability insurance to cover such losses as might be occasioned thereby.[154]

It comes perhaps as no surprise that this provision met with opposition, as it includes taking out compulsory insurance without further defining 'damage to the environment' which 'might occur'. At this stage of the legislative process, it is more appropriate to supplement the Product Liability Directive, rather than to introduce a new unspecified GMO-liability. In so far as GMOs are contained in products placed on the market, this regime is currently already applicable, and it does not require producers to take out compulsory insurance. Indeed, some larger producers have opted for self-insurance, either because they can meet their obligations more cheaply this way, or because they are unable to insure their products at reasonable costs.[155] Furthermore, Article 8 of the Product Liability Directive provides for joint and several liability of multiple defendants, with the possibility of recourse or contribution actions against third parties. Additional legislation would then be required to address the limited scope of heads of damages under the Product Liability Directive, the development risk defence, prescription periods and, of course, to cater for

[152] 'Most Member States will not give up moratorium on GMOs until Parliament and Council agree and new complete legal framework is known', Agence Europe, (2000) 7760 *Bulletin Quotidien Europe*, 10.

[153] Council Common Position (EC) No. 12/2000, n. 84 above, recital 16.

[154] See Recommendation for Second Reading, Rapporteur David Bowe, EP Doc. A5–0083/2000; Minutes EP, 12 Apr. 2000, no. 12, PE 289.451; Agence Europe, (2000) 7705 *Bulletin Quotidien Europe*, 14.

[155] C. Hodges, *Product Liability. European Laws and Practice* (London: Sweet & Maxwell, 1999), no. 23–003. Erroneously, the Economic and Social Committee states that compulsory insurance is already regulated for defective products: Opinion of the Economic and Social Committee, n. 42 above, no. 4.6. Cf. the ESC's Opinion on the Green Paper Liability for Defective Products [1999] OJ C117/1, para. 3.8, supporting the current *absence* of compulsory insurance.

damage caused by GMOs not covered by the definition of a product which was placed on the market.[156]

The Commission also opposed a separate GMO-liability clause.[157] A general/horizontal, rather than a sector-specific regime is preferred, partly because it is difficult to justify that one sector should be singled out. However, does this mean that the Commission should be against such rules *ab initio*? There would appear little harm in *starting* to legislate in a limited field. If and when a horizontal directive has been adopted, the specific directive could be simply amended by revoking or modifying the specific regime.

For example, Council Regulation (EC) No. 2027/97 on Air Carrier Liability in the Event of Accidents[158] has been adopted as an interim measure, awaiting review of the relevant international conventions in this field. Apparently, in this case there was no reason to abstain from regulating at EU level. Moreover, there are good reasons, such as the scale and uncertainty of the risks involved, why the GMO-sector can justifiably be 'singled out'. It is recalled that Dutch case law of the 1920s already took the special risks created by certain activities, in this case mining, into account to vary the level of due care required from operators. Similarly, the risks associated with GMOs have prompted certain Member States to refuse all applications for permits.

Finally as regards GMOs, without a specific regime, all GMO liability will be regulated in the context of the future general Environmental Liability Directive. However, if adopted as proposed, the scope of future regime will be limited to Natura 2000 sites, which would be highly inappropriate since GMOs are likely to cause environmental damage primarily elsewhere. We assume that sites with genetically modified crops will—of course—not be situated in or close to Natura 2000 areas. Yet, contrary to the somewhat rosy picture of the White Paper, which presumes that dangerous activities are not to take place in protected areas, a substantial number of Natura 2000 sites, in particular estuaries, may be affected by them, as these sites are surrounded by heavy industry.[159] Damage to unowned natural resources outside the Natura 2000 network, and resulting from the release into the environment of GMOs, would not be compensatable at all because, in the main, domestic

---

[156] See for analyses of GMO liability under English tort law M. L. Wilde, 'The Law of Tort and the "Precautionary Principle": Civil Liability Issues Arising from Trial Plantings of Genetically Modified (GM) Crops' (1998) 6 *Environmental Liability*, 163 and A. J. Waldron, 'Transgenic Torts' (1999) 43 *Journal of Business Law*, 395.

[157] White Paper, n. 1 above, para. 5.5 and see Press Release IP/00/374 of 12 Apr. 2000, published on the Internet at http://www.europa.eu.int (RAPID database).

[158] [1997] OJ L285/1. For further 'updating' see Proposal for a Regulation of the European Parliament and of the Council amending Council Reg. (EC) No. 2027/97 on Air Carrier Liability in the Event of Accidents, COM(2000)340 final, 6 June 2000.

[159] White Paper, n. 1 above, 20; EELA, n. 41 above, no. 4.2.2(b). Moreover, adequate protection of Natura 2000 sites is not necessarily guaranteed: French law allowed waiver of impact assessment for certain projects on the grounds of their low costs, see Case C–256/98, *Commission v France* [2000] ECR I–2487, para. 39. And see e.g. the following newspaper reports about possible GMO-damage elsewhere: 'Monster Salmon Scare for Fish Farmers', *The Guardian*, 12 Apr. 2000 and 'Beekeepers seek GM Halt after Honey Contamination', *The Guardian*, 17 May 2000.

tort law regimes do not cover this kind of loss, apart from limited exceptions in terms of clean-up costs.

### C. OIL POLLUTION: EUROPEAN COMMISSION INITIATIVES

An interesting feature of legislative initiatives in this field is that the Commission does not hesitate to propose fresh EC law where there already exists detailed regulation, as in the case of liability for oil pollution in international conventions.[160] Unlike the 1993 Council of Europe Convention, which completely excludes from its scope damage caused by oil pollution in so far as covered by these instruments (as well as liability for nuclear accidents, it may be added), the Commission in the Safety of the Seaborne Oil Trade Communication regards that regime as insufficient, and seeks to adopt additional, complementary, EC law.[161] These proposals are in response to the oil spill of the tanker *Erika*, causing extensive damage to the coast of Brittany. In keeping with the Commission's stance, the French authorities are contemplating to sue other parties than the one to which liability is channelled under the international regime: the shipowner. They intend to engage the owner of the cargo who is also the charter of the vessel.[162]

Supplementing international regimes, rather than stepping back from any regulation at EC level, is not unprecedented in the context of the harmonization of liability rules. As noted, Council Regulation (EC) No. 2027/97 on Air Carrier Liability in the Event of Accidents is an example.[163] The White Paper itself also envisages the possibility of complementary rules, in that it states that a future regime should 'clarify to which extent there is room for application in those areas already covered by international law'.[164] We would welcome this approach, and recommend that it not be restricted to oil pollution. Other international civil liability regimes, such as the nuclear accidents regime of the Paris and Brussels Conventions,[165] would certainly benefit from complementing legislation, for example extension of limitation periods, as Van Maanen has put it, now 'allows' victims a ten-year period within which to contract cancer or leukaemia.[166] One EU Member State has decided to produce its own 'update'. In 1999 Austria adopted the Atomic Liability Act, which contains a

---

[160] 1969 International Convention on Civil Liability for Oil Pollution Damage, n. 50 above; the 1971 International Convention on the Establishment of an International Fund for Compensation of Oil Pollution Damage, (1971) 11 *International Legal Materials*, 284 and the 1992 Protocols to these conventions, *International Transport Treaties*, Suppl. 17, I–459/476 (Sept. 1993).

[161] COM(2000)142 final, 21 Mar. 2000.

[162] E. H. P. Brans, 'The 1999 *Erika* Oil Spill in France. Can the cargo-owner be held liable for the damage caused?' (2000) 2 *International Law FORUM du Droit International*, 66.

[163] [1997] OJ L285/1.                    [164] White Paper, n. 1 above, para. 4.8.

[165] Convention on Third Party Liability in the Field of Nuclear Energy (signed at Paris, 29 July 1960), (1964) *Tractatenblad* (Dutch Treaty Series), 175 (as amended); Supplementary Convention (signed at Brussels, 31 Jan. 1963), (1963) *Tractatenblad* (Dutch Treaty Series), 176 (as amended).

[166] G. E. van Maanen, 'Wettelijke aansprakelijkheid voor kerncentrales' (1981) 56 *Nederlands Juristenblad*, 286.

number of interesting features, including a presumption of causation and the concept of pure ecological loss.[167]

## VI.  Concluding Remarks

The White Paper is a positive step towards an EC environmental liability regime. Despite the fact that the White Paper is not very specific with regard to some important issues, and that some issues have not been addressed at all,[168] the document contains some very interesting ideas. Especially those concerning *locus standi* for environmental groups, and the measure of damages are most interesting. However, if adopted as proposed, the future regime will have very limited scope.

First of all, with regard to damage to nature, the future regime will only apply to natural resources located in, or forming part of, Natura 2000 sites. The regime will therefore ultimately cover only about 10 per cent of the territory of the EU (unless Member States decide to expand the regime). A majority of the wild flora and fauna and nature habitats are located outside these areas, and will therefore not be covered, even if these natural resources are listed in the annexes to the Habitats and Wild Birds Directives. A positive aspect of the restricted scope is that it will be relatively easy to know what natural resources are covered by the EC regime. Positive is also, that sufficient data are probably available on the state of the environment in these areas, or at least that it is clear for which natural resources such data need to be collected. Although disappointing from an environmental perspective, such clarity will prevent (some) legal controversy over the exact scope of the regime, and the pre-injury condition of the natural resources impacted or destroyed. However, these aspects are overshadowed by the incompatibility of this restriction with the need to cover damage caused by, in particular, GMOs, wherever this may occur, in compliance with the requirements of the precautionary principle. The restriction should therefore be removed.

A second element that provides a serious limitation to the regime is the nature of the liability. It is proposed that, unless the damage is caused by a listed (potentially) dangerous activity, the regime will be covered by fault-based liability. Since proving fault will be difficult in many cases, this will provide an obstacle, and reduces the effectiveness of the regime. However, it is suggested in the White Paper that the Commission might include provisions that will alleviate the burden of proof of causation regarding both strict and fault liability.

---

[167] Posch, n. 58 above.

[168] The White Paper leaves several important matters unresolved. Examples are: the limitation periods for commencement of actions; the apportionment of liability in multi-party cases; and rules regarding the recovery of cost of preventive measures taken in response to threats of damage. Many other issues need to be discussed in this section with greater clarity (see above).

The proposed assessment of damages, which is based on reasonable cost of restoration and the assessment costs, is most appropriate in the light of the objectives of EC nature conservation law. The measure of damages is comparable to most international civil liability conventions, national regimes, and previous EC liability proposals. However, unlike some of the international conventions and previous EC proposals, the White Paper clearly provides that, where restoration is not feasible, the measure of damages is the reasonable cost of alternative solutions. This may include actions to acquire a site close to, or some distance away from, the impacted site, and the costs necessary to re-create the land into a habitat with comparable functions and comparable in size. Other options would be to enhance degraded habitats or to improve the biological value of an area already listed as a Natura 2000 site, but not being in the required condition.

The White Paper does not provide much guidance as to how to measure the extent of the injuries to natural resources, the loss of natural resources services, or how to determine the appropriate scale of the restoration measures. For an efficient liability regime, these and other issues need to be resolved. Without further guidance, it will be difficult (and expensive) for public authorities, NGOs, and others to determine the extent of the loss, and estimate the amount of damages. This might affect the willingness of parties to press claims. In addition, strong guidance might help courts to cope adequately with Natural Research Damage (NRD) cases. As noted earlier, dealing with natural resource damages requires an understanding of biology as well as economics. In order to prevent unpredictable and deviating court decisions, such guidelines may have to be developed.

The proposal on standing for NGOs is a step in the right direction. However, it should be noted that the introduction of a formalized two-tier approach sits uneasily with one of the Commission's earlier proposals in the context of the 1996 Communication on Implementing Community Environmental Law concerning access to justice. Having identified insufficient access to justice by NGOs for enforcement purposes, it proposed—as a first step—a broadening of *locus standi* for NGOs before national courts, without mentioning any primary right of action for the state. Although granting a secondary right of standing for damages claims is understandable, we do not see why NGOs should have to wait for the state to act if they consider pressing claims for injunctions. However, the harmonization of standing rules is a positive development, and must be seen against the backdrop of the enforcement function of liability rules. Having identified the need for law reform in this connection (endorsed by the Council), the Commission should also consider including proposals for adapting tort law in order to facilitate enforcement. Minor adjustments regarding the scope of protected interests and eligible plaintiffs might suffice.

In conclusion, although the White Paper is to some extent a disappointing document because of serious flaws it contains, it is an important step in the development of an EU-wide liability regime. Given that many of the parties involved—including the European Parliament, the Economic and Social

Committee, and the Council of Ministers—have reacted positively to the publication of the White Paper, it has become likely that, finally, such a directive will be adopted. We are optimistic that it will prove possible to establish a balanced and effective liability regime for natural resource damages. For this to be realized, the European Commission will have to adapt parts of its proposal, in particular the limited definition of environmental damage.

# The Role of the European Union in the Formation of International Environmental Law

GERHARD LOIBL*

## I. Introduction

Since its creation, the European Union (EU) has become an important player in international relations. The European Community (EC) and its Member States participate actively in international negotiations. The specific legal nature of the EU raises a number of issues under international law. This chapter will describe and analyse some of the issues, which concern the role of the EU in the formation of international environmental law.[1]

In discussing the contribution of the EU to the formation of international environmental law, international law-making in the strict sense as well as issues pertaining to implementation and compliance of international law have to be considered.

This chapter will set out the legal framework shaping the role of the EU in the formation of international environmental law, but it will also try to analyse the current practice of the EC and its Member States. The examples used are those of the Kyoto Protocol to the UN Framework Convention on Climate Change,[2] and the Cartagena Protocol on Biosafety.[3] Although both Protocols have not yet entered into force, they serve to demonstrate the role of the EU in the formation of international environmental law.

* Professor, University of Vienna, Austria.
[1] In discussing the role of the EU in the formation of international environmental law the term 'international environmental law' is understood in a broad sense, so as to include issues of sustainable development, as used by the UN Environment Programme (UNEP). See UNEP Governing Council Decision 19/1 of 7 Feb. 1997 and the Final Report of the Expert Group Workshop on International Environmental Law aiming at Sustainable Development (UNEP/IEL/WS/3/2 of 4 Oct. 1996). Both documents are published in: UNEP, *Development and Periodic Review of Environmental Law at the United Nations Environment Programme: Programmes, Implementation and Reviews—Compilation of Documents* (Nairobi: UNEP, 1997).

[2] UN Framework Convention on Climate Change (New York, 9 May 1992) published on the Internet at: http://www.unfccc.de/resource/conv/ index.html

[3] Cartagena Protocol on Biosafety to the Convention on Biological Diversity (Montreal, 29 Jan. 2000) (2000) 39 *International Legal Materials*, 1027 ff.

## II.  Competence of the European Union and its Member States to Deal with Environmental Issues

Before discussing the role of the EC and its Member States in international environmental law-making, the legal nature of the EU as 'hybrid conglomerate situated somewhere between a State and an intergovernmental organization'[4] has to be borne in mind. This *sui generis* legal nature has a bearing on the role of the EU in the international environmental area.

The practice of the EU has been to conclude international environmental agreements as 'mixed agreements'.[5] Although the term mixed agreements as such does not exist in the EU Treaty,[6] it has been the practice in a number of areas of international agreements that both the EC and some or all of its Member States become parties individually.[7] Moreover, the concept has been unequivocally accepted by the European Court of Justice (ECJ).[8] The reasons for the need of mixed agreements vary in different areas,[9] and depend on both internal and external factors. Different types of mixed agreements may

---

[4] A. Rosas, 'Mixed Union—Mixed Agreements' in M. Koskenniemi (ed.), *International Law Aspects of the EU* (The Hague: Kluwer Law International, 1998), 125. See on mixed agreements in an EU context also J. H. H. Weiler, 'The External Legal Relations of Non-Unitary Actors: Mixity and the Federal Principle' in J. H. H. Weiler, 'The Constitution of Europe—"Do the New Clothes have an Emperor" and Other Essays on European Integration' (Cambridge: Cambridge University Press, 1999), 130–87.

[5] Mixed Agreements have been defined by Schermers as follows: 'A mixed agreement is any treaty to which an international organization, some or all of its member states and one or more third states are parties, and for the execution of which neither the organization nor its member states have full competence' (H. G. Schermers, 'A Typology of Mixed Agreements' in D. O'Keeffe and H. G.Schermers (eds.), *Mixed Agreements* (Deventer: Kluwer Law and Taxation, 1983), 25–6); see further L. Granvik, 'Incomplete Mixed Environmental Agreements of the Community and the Principle of Bindingness' in Koskenniemi, n. 4 above, 255 ff.

[6] Mixed agreements are foreseen in the Treaty establishing the European Atomic Energy Community (Euratom). Art. 102 Euratom states: 'Agreements or contracts concluded with a third State . . . to which in addition to the Community one or more Member States are parties, shall not enter into force until the Commission has been notified by all the Member States concerned that those agreements or contracts have become applicable in accordance with the provisions of their respective nationals laws.'

[7] This is true both for global environmental agreements, such as the UN Framework Convention on Climate Change (New York, 9 May 1992) (n. 2 above), the Convention for the Protection of the Ozone Layer (Vienna, 22 Mar. 1985) (1987) 26 *International Legal Materials* 1529, the Protocol on Substances that Deplete the Ozone Layer (Montreal, 16 Sept. 1987) (1987) 26 *International Legal Materials* 1550; and regional agreements such as the Convention for the Protection of the Mediterranean Sea against Pollution (Barcelona, 16 Feb. 1976) published on the Internet at: http://sedac.ciesin.org/pidb/texts/ mediterranean.pollution.1976.html; the Convention on Cooperation for the Protection and Sustainable Use of the Danube River (Sofia, 29 June 1994) published on the Internet at: http://www.internationalwaterlaw.org/No-Frames/ Regional Docs/Danube1994.htm; or the Convention on the Protection of the Alps (Salzburg, 7 Nov. 1991) [1996] OJ L 61/32.

[8] See e.g. Opinion 2/91, *Convention No. 170 of the International Labour Organization concerning Safety in the Use of Chemicals at Work* [1993] ECR I–1061.

[9] See I. MacLeod, I. D. Hendry, and S. Hyett (eds.), *The External Relations of the European Communities* (Oxford: Clarendon Press, 1996), 142; D. McGoldrick, *International Relations Law of the EU* (London: Longman, 1997). The book scrutinizes the practice of the EU in different areas, such as environment, transport, or culture.

be distinguished.[10] In the environmental area, the main arguments for mixed agreements are derived from the fact that EC competence is not exclusive, which follows from the provisions in Title XIX of the EC treaty. The competence instead is shared between the EC and its Member States, and consequently both the EU and its Member States have to become parties to these agreements. As will be demonstrated, whether the EC may become a party to an international agreement depends both on EC law and on international law. For example, although the EC has adopted internal legislation implementing the 1973 Convention on International Trade in Endangered Species (CITES), it has not been able to become a party, for CITES so far only permits states as parties.

## A. THE EUROPEAN FRAMEWORK

Before discussing the international activities of the EU in the shape of environmental regulations, the legal framework set up by EU law needs to be summarized. The EC Treaty contains a number of provisions which are relevant in this context, and the provisions of the Treaty on European Union (TEU) have to be taken into consideration too.

### i. The Provisions of the EC Treaty

The provisions of the EC Treaty, which serve as the legal base for the external activities of the EC in environmental matters, are found in Article 3(1)(l) EC, and Title XIX EC. Article 3(1)(l) EC states that the activities of the EC also include 'a policy in the sphere of the environment'. Article 174(1) EC sets out the objectives of this policy, which includes 'promoting measures at the international level to deal with regional or worldwide environmental problems'. The EC hence acknowledges that certain environmental problems cannot be resolved at Community level, but need to be addressed on a broader basis. The need for international cooperation is also underlined by Article 174(4) which reads:

Within their respective spheres of competence, the Community and the Member States shall cooperate with third countries and with the competent international organizations. The arrangements for Community cooperation may be the subject of agreements between the Community and the third parties concerned, which shall be negotiated and concluded in accordance with Article 300. [This] shall be without prejudice to Member States' competence to negotiate in international bodies and to conclude international agreements.

Furthermore, Declaration No. 10, concerning the external competence of the EC, which was annexed to the Treaty of Maastricht, states that 'the principles resulting from the judgment handed down by the Court of Justice in the AETR case' are not affected.[11] Moreover, Article 176 EC providing that protective

---

[10] McGoldrick, n. 9 above, 78 ff.; Rosas, n. 4 above, 128 ff.

[11] Declaration (No.10) on Arts. 109, 130r, and 130y EC reads: 'The Conference considers that the provisions of Article 109 (5), Article 130r (4), second paragraph, and Article 130y do not affect the principles resulting from the judgment handed down by the Court of Justice in the AETR case.'

measures adopted by the Community 'shall not prevent any Member State from maintaining or introducing more stringent protective measures', is relevant in this context too.

The scope of the Community's competence to conclude international environmental agreements on the basis of these provisions has been hotly debated by legal scholars and practitioners.[12] The ECJ has developed a number of principles, which are to be taken as guidance for the EC's participation in international environmental agreements.[13] So far, the practice of the Council has been that the EC participates in international environmental agreements to the extent internal measures have been put in place. This is also reflected in the declarations on competence, which the EC submits on becoming a party to an international environmental agreement, and which invariably define the EU's competence by reference to legislation that had already been adopted within the Community.[14]

By including in the objectives of Community environmental policy the promotion of measures at the international level to deal with regional and worldwide environmental problems, the EC Treaty instructs the EC and its Member States to seek international solutions for global or regional issues. At the same time, these provisions underline that the EC and its Member States must take an active part in international environmental treaty-making.

By virtue of Article 174 EC, the EC enjoys the competence to be active in areas of environmental protection, which, however, is never exclusive. This is in part because Article 176 EC gives Member States the right to set more stringent standards, and thus also to conclude international agreements setting more stringent standards.[15]

### ii. The Provisions of the Treaty on European Union

Since the competence of the EC is not exclusive, and international environmental agreements may also cover areas which remain within Member State competence, the provisions concerning the Common Foreign and Security Policy (CFSP, 'second pillar') contained in Title V of the TEU are significant.

Article 11 TEU states that 'the Union shall define and implement a common foreign and security policy in all areas of foreign and security policy'. This implies that international environmental matters, such as meetings of the

---

[12] See MacLeod *et al.*, n. 9 above, 325 ff.; L. Krämer, *E.C. Treaty and Environmental Law* (London: Sweet & Maxwell,1998), 104 ff.

[13] See M. Fitzmaurice, 'Actors and Factors in the Evolution of Treaty Norms (An Empirical Study)' (1999) 4 *Austrian Review of International and European Law*, 63 ff.; M. Cremona, 'The Doctrine of Exclusivity and the Position of Mixed Agreements in the External Relations of the EU' (1982) 2 *The Oxford Journal of Legal Studies*, 393 ff.

[14] The issue of declarations of competence of the EC is discussed in more detail below.

[15] Therefore, in contrast to other areas of European policy—e.g. external trade relations (Art. 133 EC)—no exclusive competence of the EU is established. Cf. C. Calliess and M. Ruffert (eds.), *Kommentar zum EU-Vertrag und EG-Vertrag* (Neuwied: Luchterhand, 1999), 1560 ff.; Krämer, n. 12 above, 106 ff.; H. von der Groeben, J. Thiesing, and C.-D. Ehlermann (eds.), *Kommentar zum EU-EG-Vertrag Volume 3* (Baden-Baden: Nomos, 1999), 1984; A. Epiney, *Umweltrecht in der Europäischen Union* (Cologne: Heymann, 1997), 79 ff.

bodies of respective international institutions, for example, the Governing Council of the UN Environment Programme or the Conference of the Parties established by various international environmental treaties, fall within the scope of the CFSP. According to Article 19 TEU, 'Member States shall coordinate their action in international organizations and at international conferences. They shall uphold the common positions in such fora.'

Combining the provisions of the first and second pillars, it becomes obvious that close cooperation takes place on the EU level in *all* aspects relating to international environmental matters. This was acknowledged by the ECJ in Opinion 1/94, where it ruled that 'in all aspects of the negotiations, conclusion and implementation of a mixed agreement, the Member States and the Community are required to cooperate and to act in close association'.[16] This judgment closely mirrors current practice in the sphere of the environment.

## III. The Role of the European Community and of its Member States in International Negotiations

### A. THE POLITICAL ROLE OF THE EUROPEAN UNION

In the last decade, the EU has emerged as one of the key players in international environmental negotiations. Integration within the EU—which was accelerated by the Single European Act 1986, the Treaty of Maastricht 1992, and the Treaty of Amsterdam 1997—and the evolution of the Common Foreign and Security Policy,[17] have led to changes in the respective roles of the EC and its Member States on the international level. This evolution has resulted in a more coherent and unified performance of the EU at the international level. In the environmental field in particular, the EC and its Member States have established mechanisms to ensure that the EU speaks with one voice in international relations. This may occur either through the Presidency of the Council or the European Commission, depending whether it is an issue of mixed competence, Member State competence, or Community competence. Although the nature of coordination differs to a certain degree, depending on the subject matter and the practice established over the years, some common features may be noted.

It has become practice that, in international environmental treaty-making, the EU establishes a common stance before a position is taken vis-à-vis the outside world. Thus, prior to reaching a common position, the EU does not express a view on the matter under consideration. Although, this practice has sometimes been criticized as too cumbersome for the purpose of effective

---

[16] Opinion 1/94, *Competence of the Community to Conclude International Agreements concerning Services and the Protection of Intellectual Property* [1994] ECR I–5267.

[17] On the development of European integration see P. Craig and G. de Búrca, *EU Law—Text, Cases and Materials* (Oxford: Oxford University Press, 1998), 3 ff.; C. Thun-Hohenstein and F. Cede, *Europarecht—Das Recht der Europäischen Union unter Besonderer Berücksichtigung der EU-Mitgliedschaft Österreichs* (Vienna: Manz, 1999), 19 ff.

international negotiations, it ensures that the EC and its Member States take a common position.

In other areas of international negotiations, which are not within exclusive Community competence, a different approach is sometimes followed. In such cases, in as far as a common stance has been agreed within the EU, the Presidency will bring this to the attention of the other negotiating parties on behalf of the EU. In areas where no agreement is reached, each Member State expresses its own position after the Presidency has spoken. Different opinions prevailing within the EU will thereby become very obvious to the outside world, which undermines the EU's negotiationing role.

In this context, it is significant to note that the EU is one of the major donors on the international level. As financial issues have become of paramount importance in international environmental negotiations, the EC and its Member States also have increased their role. Certain international negotiations have been possible only thanks to EU sponsorship. For example, the negotiations on the Convention on Persistent Organic Pollutants depended heavily on financial support from the EU.[18]

## B. THE EUROPEAN UNION'S INPUT IN INTERNATIONAL ENVIRONMENTAL NEGOTIATIONS

### i. Preparation of a European Union Position

Within the EU, an extensive system of committees consisting of representatives of Member States and the European Commission has been set up, with responsibility for the preparation and coordination of the EU position in international environmental negotiations. Depending on whether a particular issue falls within the exclusive competence of the EC, the exclusive competence of Member States, or involves shared competence, different approaches are followed.

For international negotiations which fall within exclusive Community competence, the position is elaborated within a committee chaired by the European Commission, and subsequently articulated by the European Commission.[19] For international negotiations in areas of mixed or exclusive Member State competence, a system of working groups or working parties has been established. These groups, which are chaired by the Presidency,[20] do not only meet during the negotiations, but also hold regular meetings in Brussels to elaborate the EU's position.

---

[18] The financial contributions to the so-called 'POPs Club' (UNEP/POPS/INC.5/INF/7, published on the Internet at: http//irptc.unep.ch/pops/POPs_Inc/INC_5/meetdocen.htm), were significant.

[19] An example of such a committee is provided in the context of negotiations on international waste management, in particular the Convention on the Control of Transboundary Movements of Hazardous Waste and their Disposal (Basel, 22 Mar. 1989) (1989) 28 *International Legal Materials*, 657. It should be noted that even in these international environmental agreements, there are certain issues, such as liability or financial resources, which remain within Member States' competence.

[20] Such groups have been set up in the areas of climate change, biological diversity, biological security, persistent organic pollutants, as well as environment and development.

## ii. *The Role of the European Union in International Negotiations*

The mode of participation of the EU in the international negotiating process also depends on the division of competence between the Community and the Member States. Therefore, it is either the European Commission or the Presidency which negotiates on behalf of the EU. The Commission acts by virtue of a 'mandate' obtained from the Council. The Presidency conducts the negotiations on the basis of 'Council Conclusions' setting out the positions for the negotiations, and is assisted by the 'troika' (incoming Presidency and the European Commission).[21] In addition, it has become practice to ask outside experts to deal with specific topics on behalf of the EU. Although not anticipated in EU law, this has proved to be an advantage in the negotiating process.

### C. EXAMPLES OF THE ROLE OF THE EU IN INTERNATIONAL ENVIRONMENTAL NEGOTIATIONS

In this section, the role of the EU in international negotiations will be examined by way of two important examples: the UN Framework on Climate Change and its Kyoto Protocol, and the Cartagena Protocol on Biosafety.

### i. *The UN Framework on Climate Change and the Kyoto Protocol*

The EU has committed itself to taking measures to reduce emissions which affect the global climate. For this purpose, Community legislation has provided measures to reduce emissions of gases with a detrimental effect on the climate. Although at the time of their adoption their main objective might not always have been to fight climate change, they nevertheless have to be seen as initiatives in the area of climate protection.[22]

In the negotiations leading up to the adoption of the Kyoto Protocol,[23] the EU has made great efforts to ensure that the commitments of the Kyoto Protocol would have a positive effect on climate change. Without having to go into any detail about the proposals made by the EU which helped shape the Kyoto Protocol, it is safe to say that during the last few years, the EU has strongly advocated the establishment of mechanisms ensuring compliance with the obligations agreed. This is deemed particularly important in the field of environmental protection, because the traditional means of dispute settlement would become effective only after a violation of an international obligation has occurred, and the environment adversely affected. The idea underpinning such compliance mechanisms is to assist states in securing

---

[21] Art. 18 TEU.

[22] Measures to reduce emissions from motor vehicles initially were aimed at reducing air pollution, rather than preserving the world climate. For EU measures taken to combat air pollution, see Krämer, n. 12 above, 18 ff.; N. Moussis, *Access to EU—Law, Economics, Policies* (Rixensart: European Study Service, 1999), 291 ff.

[23] Protocol to the UN Framework Convention on Climate Change (Kyoto, 10 Dec. 1997) (1998) 37 *International Legal Materials*, 22 ff.

compliance, rather than to punish them. The first such procedures were set up and operationalized under the Montreal Protocol. The case of the Russian Federation and other countries with economies in transition which received advice and assistance in the implementation of their obligations, shows the effectiveness of these instruments.[24] The EU has proposed to establish a similar compliance mechanism early in the negotiations leading up to the Kyoto Protocol. It has been clear from the outset that such a procedure could not be included in the Protocol itself, since the substantive rules needed to be formulated first. Consequently, the Kyoto Protocol stipulates that compliance procedures should be developed in the future. During the Fourth Conference of the Parties (COP4), held in Buenos Aires in 1998, it was discussed which matters needed to be resolved in order to make the Kyoto Protocol work. The EU was the driving force in elevating compliance to a central issue to be resolved at the Sixth Conference of the Parties (COP6), and thus to be included into the 'Buenos Aires Plan of Action'.[25] At the initiative of the EU, a 'joint working group on compliance under SBI (Subsidiary Body for Implementation) and SBSTA (Subsidiary Body for Scientific and Technological Advice)' was set up. Since COP6, the EU has actively participated in the elaboration of a compliance mechanism, and made a number of proposals which form part of the negotiating text.[26]

### ii. The Cartagena Protocol on Biosafety

Another example of the potential role to be played by the EU is provided by the negotiations leading to the adoption of the Cartagena Protocol on Biosafety.[27] The negotiations were based on the so-called Jakarta mandate, adopted at the Second Meeting of the Conference of the Parties to the Convention on Biological Diversity.[28] Originally the EU, in common with other developed countries, had been sceptical about the need for a Protocol to deal with biosafety as demanded

---

[24] J. Werksmann, 'Compliance and Transition: Russia's Non-Compliance Tests and the Ozone Regime' (1996) 56 *Zeitschrift für Ausländisches und Öffentliches Recht*, 750; G. Loibl, 'Compliance with International Environmental Law—The Emerging Regime under the Kyoto Protocol' in W. Benedek, H. Isak, and R. Kicker (eds.), *Development and Developing International and European Law—Essays in Honour of Konrad Ginther on the Occasion of his 65th Birthday* (Frankfurt am Main: Lang, 1999), 263 ff.

[25] Cf. Decision 8/CP.4 Annex II entitled 'Initial List of Work for the Conference of the Parties serving as the meeting of the Parties to the Kyoto Protocol at its first session' (FCCC/CP/1998/16/Add.1, 37; published on the Internet at: http://www.unfccc.int/resource/docs/cop5/01a01.htm).

[26] Cf. the reports of the Conference of the Parties and the subsidiary bodies on the elaboration of the compliance system. See also the compilation documents on the negotiating parties proposals on this matter (published on the Internet at: http://www.unfccc.de).

[27] Cartagena Protocol on Biosafety to the Convention on Biological Diversity (Montreal, 29 Jan. 2000) (2000) 39 *International Legal Materials*, 1027 ff.; cf. P. T. Stoll, 'Controlling the Risks of Genetically Modified Organisms: The Cartagena Protocol on Biosafety and the SPS Agreement' (1999) 10 *Yearbook of International Environmental Law*, 82 ff.

[28] Decision II/5 entitled 'Consideration of the Need for and the Modalities of a Protocol for the Safe Transfer, Handling and Use of Living Modified Organisms' (published on the Internet at: http://vls.law.strath.ac.uk/ conference1999/document_ server/DECISIONII–5.html).

by developing countries. Already during the negotiations on the Convention on Biodiversity in August 1990, developing countries had raised questions concerning biotechnology and biosafety. Some developing countries feared that their territories might be used for 'scientific trials' in the area of biotechnology, others wished to gain access to biotechnology. A compromise between the different positions was finally found in Article 19 of the Convention on Biodiversity.[29] It provides, *inter alia,* for the possible elaboration of a protocol dealing with these concerns.[30]

The Jakarta mandate was agreed only at the Second Conference of the Parties of the Convention on Biodiversity, after the EU developed a positive position on the elaboration of an international agreement concerning biosafety. The main reason for this change in attitude, was the realization that environmental aspects of transboundary transfers of Living Modified Organisms (LMOs)[31] were not regulated in any international agreement. The mandate was intended to close this gap in international law. The terms of reference for the *ad hoc* working group (established by the Jakarta mandate as the negotiating forum for the Protocol) state that the Protocol should set up rules to ensure an adequate level of protection in the field of the safe transfer, handling, and use of LMOs, and their transboundary movements.[32]

Although the EC had already adopted legislation dealing with LMOs, which also applies to LMOs originating from outside the EC,[33] it attached particular importance to the creation of an international framework to deal with LMOs in the interest of human health and environmental protection. Such a regime should depart from the premise that the risks posed by movements of LMOs may be handled effectively only if the necessary information is provided to the countries concerned. Although the EC already had established rules concerning LMOs, and therefore did not strictly need an international instrument to regulate LMOs, it participated actively in the negotiations and pushed the creation of such an instrument. Moreover, public attitude in most European countries as regards LMOs had to be taken into account, which often views

---

[29] Art. 19(3) reads as follows: 'The Parties shall consider the need for and modalities of a protocol setting out appropriate procedures, including, in particular, advance informed agreement, in the field of the safe transfer, handling and use of any living modified organism resulting from biotechnology that may have adverse effect on the conservation and sustainable use of biological diversity.'

[30] The possibility to elaborate a protocol to deal with issues of biosafety was also reaffirmed in Resolution 2 para. 2(c) of the 1992 Nairobi Final Act (1992) 31 *International Legal Materials* 842 ff.

[31] LMOs are defined in Art. 3 of the Cartagena Protocol (n. 3 above) as 'any living organism that possesses a novel combination of genetic material obtained through the use of modern biotechnology'. In this context it should be noted that in EU law the term 'Genetically Modified Organism (GMO)' is used.

[32] Cf. 'terms of reference for the open-ended *ad hoc* working group', set up in an Annex to Decision II/5 (n. 29 above). See also Art. 1 of the Cartagena Protocol (n. 3 above).

[33] Cf. e.g. Council Dir. 90/220/EEC on the Deliberate Release into the Environment of Genetically Modified Organisms [1990] OJ L117/15. For a detailed description of the European legislation concerning LMOs, see R. O'Rourke, *European Food Law* (Bembridge: Palladian Law Publishing, 1998), 121 ff. Cf. also Krämer, n. 12 above, 26.

LMOs as a potential threat to human health and the environment.[34] During the negotiations, the EU took the position that an international agreement should address the global challenges posed by LMOs, and provide the necessary legal response to ensure the protection of human health and the environment.[35] The EU also insisted that the precautionary principle[36] needed to be included into the provisions of the Protocol.[37] Furthermore, it argued that 'all LMOs' should be covered by the Protocol, thus opposing the position of a number of countries that 'LMOs that are intended for direct use as food and feed, or for processing' should be exempted from the international agreement. The inclusion of the precautionary principle into the text of the Protocol,[38] and the application of the Protocol to LMOs that are intended for direct use as food and feed, or for processing[39] prove that the EU succeeded in realizing its objective.

The EU has played an important role, not only by providing substantive input in a number of areas, but also as a bridge-builder between the interests of negotiating parties.

---

[34] In September 1997 in a Eurobarometer Poll, 80% of Europeans considered that biotechnology was useful in detecting hereditary illnesses and for the production of new innovative medicines, but only one in four Europeans would buy genetically modified fruit, even if it tasted better, and less than one in four Europeans considered that current legislation was adequate to control the risks they believed to be associated with modern biotechnology. The risks concerning genetically modified foods/organisms are perceived mainly as issues of food security, food allergies, and antibiotic resistance (O'Rourke, n. 34 above, 122–5). See also R. Paarlberg, 'The Global Food Fight' (2000) 79 *Foreign Affairs*, 24 ff., who points to the different views adopted by the public in Europe and the USA: in Germany 82% of the respondents to a Canadian survey stated that they would be less likely to buy groceries labelled as GM products, whereas in the USA as few as 57% of the respondents expressed similar concerns.

[35] Cf. C. Ford Runge and B. Senauer, 'A Removable Feast' (2000) 79 *Foreign Affairs*, 39 ff.

[36] The precautionary principle is set out in Principle 15 of the Rio Declaration on Environment and Development 1992 (published on the Internet at: http://www.unep.org/unep/rio.htm), and reads as follows: 'In order to protect the environment, the precautionary principle shall be widely applied by States according to their capabilities. Where there are threats of serious or irreversible damage, lack of full scientific certainty shall not be used as a reason for postponing cost-effective measures to prevent environmental degradation.'

[37] See Art. 174(2) EC, which states that the 'Community policy on the environment shall aim at a high level of protection taking into account the diversity of situations in the various regions of the Community. It shall be based [*inter alia*] on the precautionary principle.' Thus, the EU is obliged to apply the precautionary principle in its activities concerning the environment.

[38] See Art. 1, which is entitled 'objective' and reads:

In accordance with the precautionary approach contained in Principle 15 of the Rio Declaration on Environment and Development (n. 37 above), the objective of this Protocol is to contribute to ensuring an adequate level of protection in the field of the safe transfer, handling and use of living modified organisms resulting from modern biotechnology and that may have adverse effects on the conservation and sustainable use of biological diversity, taking into account risks to human health, and specifically focusing on transboundary movements.

Reference to the precautionary approach is also made in Art. 10(6) and in preambular para. 4 of the Cartagena Protocol (n. 3 above).

[39] See in particular Art. 11, entitled 'procedure for living modified organisms intended for direct use as food or feed, or for processing' and Art. 18(2), which deals with the documentation accompanying 'living modified organisms intended for direct use as food or feed, or for processing'.

## IV. General Legal Issues raised by the European Community as a Party to International Negotiations and International Agreements

The *sui generis* legal nature of the EC has led to a number of adjustments to international law provisions, which may be regarded as standard clauses in international environmental agreements.

### A. THE EUROPEAN COMMUNITY AS A PARTY TO INTERNATIONAL AGREEMENTS

The final clauses of international agreements in which the EC participates require adjustment. Whereas, traditionally, international agreements allowed only for states to become party, the creation of the European Economic Community (EEC) and its role as an actor in international relations have led to changes in international law. More specifically, a clause needs to be inserted allowing for a 'Regional Economic Integration Organization' (REIO), such as the EC, to become a party to international agreements. Such clauses have been termed 'REIO-clauses'. Earlier, international environmental agreements lacked such provisions, for example the Convention on International Trade in Endangered Species (CITES) 1973. Such agreements therefore need to be amended in order for the EU to become a party[40] although, as the example of CITES demonstrates, the EC may decide to adopt legislative measures to apply the provisions of CITES even in anticipation of such a change.[41]

A Regional Economic Integration Organization (REIO) is defined as an 'organization constituted by sovereign states of a given region, to which its members have transferred competence in respect to matters governed by this Convention and which has been duly authorized, in accordance with its internal procedures, to sign, ratify, accept, approve, or accede to it'.[42] Although, the EC is not mentioned by name, the definition reflects the legal nature of the EC.

---

[40] In 1983 an amendment to Art. XXI of CITES was adopted, which would accommodate the EC (so-called Gaborone Amendment; see W. Wijnstekers, *The Evolution of CITES* (published on the Internet at: http://www.cites.org/CITES/common/docs/evolution.pdf, 2000), 354 ff.)). According to Art. XVII(3) 'an amendment shall enter into force for the Parties which have accepted it 60 days after two-thirds of the Parties have deposited an instrument of acceptance of the amendment with the Depositary Government'. As of the beginning of January 2001, only 38 of the 81 parties to CITES had expressed the intention to be bound by the Gaborone Amendment (cf. Wijnstekers, above in this note, 349 ff.). Consequently, the amendment has not yet entered into force, and the EU is not yet able to become a party to CITES.

[41] See Krämer, n. 12 above, 28 ff. The author points out that Council Reg. (EEC) No. 3626/82 on the Implementation in the Community of the Convention on International Trade in Endangered Species of Wild Fauna and Flora [1982] OJ L384/1, in 1997 was replaced by Council Reg. (EC) No. 338/97 on the Protection of Species of Wild Fauna and Flora by Regulating Trade therein [1997] OJ L61/1, which went considerably beyond the provisions of both CITES and Council Reg. (EEC) No. 3626/82.

[42] See e.g. Art. 2 of the Convention on Biological Diversity (Rio de Janeiro, 5 June 1992) (1992) 31 *International Legal Materials*, 818, Art. 1 of the UN Convention to Combat Desertification in those Countries Experiencing Serious Drought and/or Desertification, particularly in Africa (Paris, 17 June 1994) (1994) 33 *International Legal Materials*, 1328, Art. 1 of the UN Framework Convention on Climate Change (n. 2 above).

Thus, no other international organization exists which meets the conditions set out in this clause.

Final clauses not only allow a REIO to become party to the agreement, they also deal with the scenario where not all Member States of a REIO become party to the treaty, as well as with the question of shared competences between the REIO and its Member States. Article 24 of the Kyoto Protocol serves as an example.[43] Article 24(1) explicitly lays down that states and REIOs may become party to the Protocol if they are parties to the UN Framework Convention on Climate Change. Article 24(2) deals with the case where not all Member States of a REIO are also parties to the Protocol. It reads:

> Any regional economic integration organization which becomes a Party to this Protocol without any of its member States being a Party shall be bound by all the obligations under this Protocol. In the case of such organizations, one or more of whose member States is a Party to this Protocol, the organization and its member States shall decide on their respective responsibilities for the performance of their obligations under this Protocol. In such cases, the organization and the member States shall not be entitled to exercise rights under the Protocol concurrently.

Similarly, Article 24(3) deals with the situation when the competences of the REIO and its Member States are shared. It provides:

> In their instruments of ratification, acceptance, approval or accession, regional economic integration organizations shall declare the extent of their competence with respect to the matters governed by this Protocol. These organizations shall also inform the Depository, who shall in turn inform the Parties, of any substantial modification in the extent of their competence.

This provision clearly establishes the right of a REIO to become a party to an international agreement, and also deals with issues of competence and compliance. Thus, Article 24(2) implies that when a REIO becomes a party to the international environmental agreement, it has to honour all its obligations, and cannot advance its limited competence as an excuse for failing to fulfil those obligations which are outside its competence.

By implication, a REIO which is unable to fulfil all of its obligations under the treaty would be well advised to become a party to the treaty only once all its Member States concerned have become a party. Alternatively, the internal law of the REIO would need to be adapted in a way to enable it to fulfil all the commitments under the agreement.

In practice, the EC therefore has only become party to international environmental agreements once it was clear that the necessary internal legislation was in place, or that the Member States concerned had become a party to the agreement. The EU has endeavoured to ensure that the EC and the Member States simultaneously sign or deposit their instrument of ratification or acceptance.

---

[43] Similar provisions are found in other international environmental agreements, e.g. Art. 34 of the Convention on Biological Diversity (n. 42 above), or Art. 34 of the UN Convention to Combat Desertification in those Countries Experiencing Serious Drought and/or Desertification, particularly in Africa (n. 42 above).

Third parties are informed on the division of competencies between the REIO and its Member States by means of a declaration.[44] In the past, the EC phrased such declarations (which are required by the respective treaty) rather cautiously, listing the most important internal legal instruments adopted by the EC. This leaves unaffected any future instruments that might be adopted, and could have a bearing on the Community's competence with regard to the treaty in question.

This practice has sometimes been criticized by third parties, which have argued that requirements of legal certainty oppose such declarations. It has to be borne in mind, however, that, due to the continuous evolution of the EC, no final statement regarding the competence of the EC can be made. Neither has EC practice led to serious problems, although in certain cases it has led to delayed negotiations. Since the potential economic and financial impact of the Kyoto Protocol is so considerable, during the negotiations a number of industrialized countries argued that the legal structure of the EU gives it an advantage compared to other industrialized countries.

The specific legal nature of the EU may also have an impact on the substantive provisions of international environmental agreements. The Kyoto Protocol, in Article 4, states that parties may conclude agreements to fulfil their reduction or limitation commitments jointly—so called 'bubble agreements'. Such agreements set out the respective emission levels allocated to each of the parties. Although any of the Annex I parties may conclude such agreements,[45] due to the particular legal nature of a REIO, specific provisions have been included in Article 4 for REIOs concerning the implementation of such agreements, and the allocation of responsibility in case of non-fulfilment. In particular, if parties act jointly in the framework of and together

---

[44] Cf. e.g. the instrument of ratification of the UN Framework Convention on Climate Change by the EU. Annex B of Council Dec. 94/69/EC concerning the Conclusion of the UN Framework Convention on Climate Change [1994] OJ L33/11, contains 'the declaration of competence' pursuant to the provisions of Art. 22(3) of the Convention (cf. Art. 2). This Annex lists the legal instruments which have been adopted by the EU, and which fall within the scope of the Convention. Furthermore, Annex C to the Council Decision contains a 'Declaration by the European Economic Community on the Implementation of the UN Framework Convention on Climate Change' which reads: 'The EU and its Member States declare that the commitment to limit anthropogenic $CO_2$ emissions set out in Article 4(2) of the Convention will be fulfilled in the Community as a whole through action by the Community and its Member States, within the respective competence of each.

'In this perspective, the Community and its Member States reaffirm the objectives set out in the Council conclusions of 29 Oct. 1990, and in particular the objective of stabilization of $CO_2$ emissions by 2000 at the 1990 level in the Community as a whole.

'The European Economic Community and its Member States are elaborating a coherent strategy in order to attain this objective' (see [1994] OJ L33/13–28).

A similar approach has been pursued by the EU in the framework of other international environmental agreements, e.g. the UN Convention to Combat Desertification in those Countries Experiencing Serious Drought and/or Desertification, particularly in Africa 1994 (n. 43 above) ([1998] OJ L83/1) and the ECE-Convention on the Transboundary Effects of Industrial Accidents (Helsinki, 17 Mar. 1992) published on the Internet at: http://sedac.ciesin.org/pidb/texts/industrial.accidents1992.html ([1998] OJ L326/1).

[45] Cf. Art. 4(1) of the Kyoto Protocol (n. 24 above).

with a regional economic integration organization, any alteration in the composition of the organization after the adoption of the Protocol does not affect existing commitments.[46] Furthermore, Article 4 provides that, in the event of failure by the parties to such an agreement to achieve their total combined level of emission reductions, each party to the agreement is responsible for the level of emissions set out in the agreement. In case parties act jointly in the framework of, and together with a regional economic integration organization which is itself a party to the Protocol, each Member State of the regional economic integration organization individually, and together with the regional economic integration organization acting in accordance with Article 24 is, in the event of failure to achieve the total combined level of emission reduction, responsible for its emissions as notified in accordance with this Article.[47]

In summary, the Kyoto Protocol thus contains several provisions which deal specifically with regional economic integration organizations and their Member States. These provisions enable the EU to become a party to the Protocol, and deal with the status of the EC and its Member States as parties to the Protocol.

### B. THE EUROPEAN COMMUNITY AND ITS MEMBER STATES IN INTERNATIONAL INSTITUTIONS ESTABLISHED UNDER THE AUSPICES OF INTERNATIONAL ENVIRONMENTAL AGREEMENTS

The provisions of international environmental agreements and the rules of procedure also reflect the special legal nature of regional economic integration organizations as regards their participation in international environmental agreements. Although the final clauses of international environmental agreements define the role of the EC, more detailed rules clarify the participation of the EC and its Member States in the work of the institutions established by the treaties in question. These provisions follow a similar pattern to those found in Article IX of the Agreement to establish the World Trade Organization (WTO),[48] or Article 18 of the UN Framework Convention on Climate Change. The latter states as follows:

1. Each Party to the Convention shall have one vote, except as provided for in paragraph 2 below.
2. Regional economic integration organizations, in matters within their competence, shall exercise their right to vote with a number of votes equal to the number of their member States that are Parties to the Convention. Such an organization shall not exercise its right to vote if any of its Member States exercises its right, and *vice versa*.

---

[46] Art. 4(4).
[47] Art. 4(6). Cf. G. Loibl, 'Trade and Environment—A Difficult Relationship, New Approaches and Trends: The Kyoto Protocol and Beyond' in G. Hafner, G. Loibl, A. Rest, L. Sucharipa-Behrmann, and K. Zemanek (eds.), *Liber Amicorum Professor Ignaz Seidl-Hohenveldern in honour of his 80th Birthday* (The Hague: Kluwer Law International, 1998), 432 ff.
[48] Art. IX(1) provides explicitly that 'each Member of the WTO shall have one vote. Where the European Communities exercise their right to vote, they shall have a number of votes equal to the number of their members, which are Members of the WTO.'

Similar provisions on the right to vote of the EC and its Member States are found in the Kyoto Protocol 1997,[49] the Convention on Biological Diversity 1992,[50] the United Nations Convention to Combat Desertification 1994,[51] and the Rotterdam Convention on the Prior Informed Consent Procedures for Certain Hazardous Chemicals and Pesticides in International Trade 1998.[52]

In brief, the REIO and its Member States cannot exercise their voting rights simultaneously. It will depend on the declaration of competence, whether on a particular issue the EC or rather the Member States are entitled to exercise the right to vote. These provisions take into account the specific legal nature of the EU, whilst at the same time the EU is not afforded a privileged position in international decision-making.

### C. THE UNITY OF A REGIONAL ECONOMIC INTEGRATION ORGANIZATION FOR THE PURPOSE OF THE APPLICATION OF INTERNATIONAL AGREEMENTS

Issues concerning the unity of a REIO may arise in connection with the application of international environmental agreements. This is true, in particular for international treaties which include specific rules on the movement of goods between the territory of parties to the treaty. Examples include the Convention on International Trade in Endangered Species 1973,[53] the Basel Convention on Transboundary Movement of Hazardous Waste 1989,[54] the Rotterdam Convention on the Prior Informed Consent Procedure for Certain Hazardous Chemicals and Pesticides in International Trade 1997,[55] and the Cartagena Protocol on Biological Safety 2000.[56]

Article XIV (3) of CITES provides that, where customs controls between the Member States of a customs union have been removed and replaced by a common external customs control, or where countries have put a single market in place, the Convention's provisions with regard to the control of permits and certificates cannot be implemented by them as regards movements between the respective Member States. Nevertheless, Resolution Conf. 9.4. (Rev.) repeats the recommendation of Resolution Conf. 5.5, that each Party to the Convention, if a member of a regional trade agreement within the meaning of Article XIV para. 3, include in its annual reports information on trade in specimens of species within the scope of the Convention with other Member States of that regional trade agreement, unless the record-keeping and reporting duties of Article VIII are in direct and irreconcilable conflict with the provisions of the regional agreement.[57] CITES therefore acknowledges the existence of regional trade agreements, but does not take into account the existence of REIOs.

---

[49] Art. 22.        [50] Art. 31.        [51] Art. 32.        [52] Art. 23.        [53] Cf. Wijnstekers, n. 41 above.
[54] Cf. K. Kummer, *International Management of Hazardous Wastes: the Basel Convention and Related Legal Rules* (Oxford: Clarendon Press, 1995); see also Fitzmaurice, n. 13 above, 67 ff.
[55] Cf. K. Kummer, 'Prior Informed Consent for Chemicals in International Trade: The 1998 Rotterdam Convention' (1999) 8 *Review of European Community and International Environmental Law*, 322 ff.
[56] Cf. Stoll, n. 28 above.        [57] Wijnstekers, n. 41 above, 331.

The Basel Convention adopts a still different approach. Article 11(1) provides that 'Parties may enter into bilateral, multilateral and regional agreements or arrangements with Parties or non-Parties, provided that such agreements or arrangements do not derogate from the environmentally sound management of hazardous wastes or other wastes as required by this Convention.' According to Article 11(2) such agreements or arrangements must be notified to the Secretariat. The provisions of the Convention must not affect transboundary movements which take place pursuant to such agreements, provided they are compatible with the environmentally sound management of hazardous wastes and other wastes as required by this Convention. Hence, no specific provision has been included in the Basel Convention to deal with the implications for a REIO and its Member States, beyond the above-mentioned provisions.[58]

Similarly, the Rotterdam Convention does not include any provisions concerning bilateral, multilateral, or regional agreements, customs unions or REIOs, merely referring to REIOs in its final clauses.[59]

This issue whether the provisions of an international agreement also affect movements—for example of LMOs—between the REIO's Member States, or whether they are to be treated as a single 'territory' has also been raised in the negotiations on the Cartagena Protocol. In legal terms, the question may be phrased more precisely as follows: should the EC, when party to a treaty with competence in respect of certain of its provisions, be regarded as a single territory, or do the rules also apply to movements between the territories of its Member States?

In answering this question, the specific provisions concerning REIOs and bilateral, multilateral, and regional agreements have to be taken into account, as well as the declaration of competence made by a REIO when becoming a party to the treaty in question. This is because a declaration of competence defines the division of responsibilities between the REIO and the Member States for the purpose of complying with the treaty provisions. Consequently, if Member States have transferred competence to the REIO, the latter must take the necessary steps as a 'single' party to the treaty. Therefore, rules concerning movement of goods between parties of a treaty only apply to movements of goods across the external borders of the REIO, and not to movements within the territory of the REIO. In addition, the Cartagena Protocol provides that parties may enter into bilateral, regional, and multilateral agreements and arrangements regarding intentional transboundary movements of LMOs which are consistent with the objective of the Protocol, and provided that such agreements and arrangements do not result in a lower level of protection than

---

[58] See Kummer, n. 56 above, 127 ff. The author concludes that internal legislation of the EU concerning hazardous wastes is an 'arrangement' in the sense of Art. 11, which therefore must conform to the fundamental concepts of the Basel Convention (n. 20 above).

[59] See Art. 26(2).

provided for by the Protocol.[60] Internal EC legislation concerning LMOs may be regarded as such an 'agreement and arrangement', and therefore governs transboundary movements between the territories of the Member States.

### D. THE EUROPEAN UNION AND THE IMPLEMENTATION OF INTERNATIONAL AGREEMENTS

In general, international environmental agreements are not self-executing.[61] Therefore, the parties have to take measures on the domestic level to implement the commitments undertaken on the international level. In the context of the EU, this means that, depending on whether a matter falls within the competence of the EC or of its Member States, measures to implement international environmental commitments either need to be taken at European level or Member State level.[62]

Nearly all international environmental agreements contain provisions which oblige the parties to report on measures which have been taken for the implementation of the provisions of the respective treaty, and their effectiveness in meeting the objectives of that treaty.[63] As the EU treats international environmental agreements as mixed agreements, and the necessary implementation measures are both taken by the EC and its Member States, both report on the measures undertaken.

## V. Concluding Remarks

The EU has emerged as a key player in international environmental negotiations. This is not surprising, considering the role some Member States played before they joined the EU. Countries like Austria, Denmark, Finland, Germany, the Netherlands, and Sweden always have strong commitments to protect the domestic environment, and traditionally also played an important role in international environmental negotiations.

The evolution of EC environmental policy, and the clear principle that environmental issues should be addressed at regional and global level, has led to a strong international engagement of the EU in international environmental negotiations. Importantly, coordination mechanisms within the EU ensure a

---

[60] Cf. Art. 14(1). This provision states that parties shall inform each other through the Biosafety Clearing-House of any agreements and arrangements (para. 2). Furthermore, para. 3 states that 'the provisions of this Protocol shall not affect intentional transboundary movements that take place pursuant to such agreements and arrangements as between the parties to those agreements or arrangements'.

[61] Cf. A. Kiss and D. Shelton, *International Environmental Law* (Ardsley-on-Hudson: Transnational Publishers, 1991), 98 ff.

[62] Krämer, n. 12 above, 122 ff.; J. Scott, *EC Environmental Law* (London: Longman, 1998), 24 ff.

[63] Art. 26 of the Convention on Biological Diversity (n. 43 above). Similar 'reporting requirements' are contained in Art. 33 of the Cartagena Protocol (n. 3 above), Art. 12 of the UN Framework Convention on Climate Change (n. 2 above), and Art. 26 of the UN Convention to Combat Desertification in those Countries Experiencing Serious Drought and/or Desertification, particularly in Africa (n. 43 above).

coherent and coordinated appearance in international negotiations, which increase the EU's role as a key player.

The substantive input of the EU in international negotiations is of particular importance. The complexity of the problems to be solved requires considerable resources, which small countries lack. Economy-of-scale gains benefit developing as well as developed countries. The input of the EU therefore tends to be very thorough, since views are the product of an extensive coordination process, in which various alternatives have been considered.

The intensive coordination process of the EU has been criticized, as it inevitably is slow and time-consuming. As the EU has rigidly defined positions, the flexibility needed in international negotiations is absent, leaving little or no room to manoeuvre for the negotiators. International negotiations frequently are slowed down by the need for further EU coordination, in order to adjust positions or to respond to proposals made by other partners. This could lead to situations where the EU is not able to present its position in a speedy way.

Although some of this criticism holds true, the overall role of the EU in international environmental negotiations remains a very positive one. It is a donor of significant expertise to the negotiating process, which is an important impetus for the evolution of international environmental law.

The emergence of the EC and its Member States has also led to a number of changes in the way international environmental agreements are concluded and implemented, and international institutional arrangements have had to be adjusted in order to accommodate the EC and its Member States.

There is every reason to expect that, in the years to come, the EU will consolidate and expand its creative and constructive role in shaping international environmental law.

# Overcoming Deadlock? Enhanced Cooperation and European Environmental Policy after Nice

STEFANI BÄR, INGMAR VON HOMEYER, and ANNEKE KLASING*

## I. Introduction and Background

The Amsterdam Treaty created a new instrument for European integration called Enhanced Cooperation.[1] This procedure allows a group of Member States to take joint action, and use the institutions and procedures of the European Union for this purpose, thereby further developing European integration in a flexible way.

The development towards a more differentiated integration process started as far back as the 1970s. More than in any other field of European policy, the discussion of differentiation within the Community is characterized by a variety of concepts and terms related to various strategies and objectives.[2] A few examples may serve to illustrate the wide spectrum of the discussion: 'variable-geometry Europe', 'multi-speed Europe', or the concept of 'core Europe'.[3] But also the French notion '*Europe à la carte*' or the English 'multi-tier Europe'[4] played a major role in the discussion.[5] There is no agreed understanding of these terms, and the variety of interpretations contributes much to the lack of clarity of the thematic debate. European environmental policy represents a field where application of the provisions on Enhanced Cooperation seems necessary. In fact, European Community (EC) environmental policy is already characterized by a certain degree of flexibility, which is due to the fact

---

\* Stefani Bär is Senior Research Fellow for Ecologic, Centre for International and European Environmental Research, Berlin, Germany. Ingmar von Homeyer and Anneke Klasing are Research Fellows at the same institute.

[1] With the Treaty changes at Nice, the name of the new instrument was amended from Closer Cooperation to Enhanced Cooperation. In this text, 'Enhanced Cooperation' is used in the context of the Amsterdam Treaty as well as in the context of the Nice Treaty.

[2] Cf. in particular A. Stubb, 'A Categorization of Differentiated Integration' (1996) 34 *Journal of Common Market Studies*, 283–95, who identified and categorized 61 different terms in English, French, and German used in this discussion.

[3] W. Schäuble and K. Lamers, 'Manifesto' (1994) 39 *Blätter für Deutsche und Internationale Politik*, 1271–80.

[4] H. Wallace and W. Wallace, *Flying Together in a Larger and More Diverse European Union* (The Hague: Netherlands Scientific Council for Government Policy, 1995).

[5] Proposals submitted by the Member States (cf. A. Duff (ed.), *The Treaty of Amsterdam* (London: Federal Trust, 1997)) and by the institutions, in particular the European Parliament (cf. D. Tsatsos (ed.), *Verstärkte Zusammenarbeit: Flexible Institutionen oder Gefährdung der Integration?* (Baden-Baden: Nomos, 1999)), have to be taken into account as well.

that it has always had to consider various requirements in terms of prevailing ecological conditions and substance. The establishment of permanent exemptions or temporary transition periods within the framework of the EC Treaty or in individual secondary legislation (directives or regulations) meets this necessity of flexible responses to different conditions. Under certain (strict) conditions, EC law, for example, permits that environmentally advanced Member States adopt more stringent product[6] or process standards[7] than required at a Community level. Individual Community measures, such as Directive 88/609/EEC on the Limitation of Emissions of Certain Pollutants into the Air from Large Combustion Plants or the Auto-Oil Programme,[8] include transition periods for individual countries, or other provisions which cater for different needs. Hence, flexible regulation of environmental policy objectives is nothing new at the European level.

The instrument of Enhanced Cooperation, however, has not yet been used. Application seems to be hindered by ambiguities, and strict prerequisites in the clauses of the Treaties. As a consequence of these hindrances, discussions about reforming the new instrument have been on going since the adoption of the Amsterdam Treaty. In June 2000, the European Council in Santa Maria da Feira (Portugal), agreed to put Enhanced Cooperation on the agenda of the Intergovernmental Conference. The revision of this instrument was the only 'new' official issue on the agenda. During the Intergovernmental Conference, Enhanced Cooperation emerged as a key item, because of the link it represented between a conference otherwise devoted to narrow—albeit politically important—changes, and the growing debate on the European Union's future.[9] It seems that discussions on the revision of the enabling clauses of Enhanced Cooperation have been much less controversial than other issues on the agenda.

This chapter first analyses the legal prerequisites of Enhanced Cooperation (Section II), and then identifies fields where it can be applied in EC environmental policy (Section III). This is followed by a brief assessment of the longer-term impact of the application of Enhanced Cooperation on the integration process in the Community (Section IV). Section V serves to draw some conclusions about the value of Enhanced Cooperation for the environmental policy of an enlarged European Union (EU).[10]

[6] At the Community level, environmental product standards are usually adopted on the basis of Art. 95 EC. More stringent national measures must comply with the provisions of Art. 95(4), (5), and (6) EC.

[7] Environmental process standards are usually based on Art. 175 EC. Measures going beyond Community actions must meet the requirements of Art. 176 EC.

[8] European Commission, *The European Auto-Oil Programme: A Report by the Directorate-General for Industry, Energy and Environment, Civil Protection and Nuclear Safety (XI/361/96)* (Brussels: European Commission, 1996).

[9] D. Dinan and S. Vanhoonacker, 'IGC 2000 Watch (Part 2): The Opening Round' (2000) 13 *European Community Studies Association Review*, 1.

[10] The following analysis is based on the study 'Verstärkte Zusammenarbeit im Umweltbereich—Möglichkeiten der Anwendung der in Titel VII EU Vertrag festgelegten Bestimmungen für Flexibilität im Umweltbereich' commissioned by the Austrian Federal Ministry of Environment, Youth and Family Affairs in Sept. 1999; Federal Ministry of Environment, Youth

## II. Legal Prerequisites of Enhanced Cooperation

Numerous requirements which were introduced into the Treaties at the last instance reflect concerns expressed by some Member States within the framework of the Intergovernmental Conference, which resulted in the adoption of the Amsterdam Treaty.[11] Fears focused on a permanent split in the Community, and a division of Member States into two classes, in contrast with the goal of further integration. The functioning of the EU, and the possibility of achieving progress were not to be impeded by one partner's temporary difficulties in keeping pace with other Member States.[12]

### A. STRUCTURE OF ENCHANCED COOPERATION IN THE TREATIES

The provisions on Enhanced Cooperation, which were introduced into both the EU Treaty and the EC Treaty by the Amsterdam Treaty as amended by the Nice Treaty, comprise so-called 'general clauses' and 'special authorization provisions'. The general clauses are laid down in Title VII of the EU Treaty, and are horizontal provisions applicable to all three pillars of the EU. They formulate the conditions which have to be met to establish Enhanced Cooperation in all three pillars. For the first (EC Treaty, Euratom, European Coal and Steel Community (ECSC), Economic and Monetary Union (EMU)) and third pillars (police and judicial cooperation in criminal matters), special authorization clauses are defined. In the field of foreign and security policy, the second pillar, the Nice Treaty introduced Enhanced Cooperation. The new provision concerning foreign and security policy contains conditions which are to be observed as cumulative stipulations, in addition to the general clauses.

The following analysis of the legal prerequisites is limited to the provisions relevant for the adoption of EC environmental legislation.

The procedure for establishing Enhanced Cooperation can be divided into three: the 'normal' legislative procedure, the 'authorization procedure', and the 'implementing procedure'. The procedure actually authorizing Member States to establish Enhanced Cooperation is always preceded by a 'normal' legislative procedure. Only if the 'normal' procedure fails may the process laid down in Articles 43 and 44 of the Treaty on European Union (TEU) and Article 11 EC[13] be initiated to establish Enhanced Cooperation (section B). In this

and Family Affairs, *Enhanced Cooperation in European Environmental Policy after Amsterdam* (Vienna: *Bundesministerium für Umwelt, Jugend und Familie*, 1999 (Band 32/1999)).

[11] P. Hall, 'Verstärkte Zusammenarbeit—Flexibilität' in J. Bergmann and C. Lenz (eds.), *Der Amsterdamer Vertrag—Eine Kommentierung der Neuerungen des EU- und EG-Vertrages* (Cologne: Omnia, 1998), 335.

[12] Cf. joint proposal on closer Cooperation by the German and French Foreign Ministers, Klaus Kinkel and Hervé de Charette, for the Intergovernmental Conference, published on 18 Oct. 1996 in Bonn and Paris. Excerpts in: (1997) 3 *Internationale Politik*, 72.

[13] In the following, the EC Treaty and EU Treaty are cited based on the Treaty of Nice in the version of 10 Mar. 2001.

context, a basic distinction has to be made between the authorization procedure, and the implementation decisions. Within the framework of the former, at least eight Member States are granted the basic authorization for engaging in Enhanced Cooperation (section C). For the authorization, a Commission proposal (section D) and observance of the requirements stipulated in Article 43 TEU (section D) are also necessary. The authorization procedure includes the involvement of the EP, as demanded in Article 11(2) 1 EC (section E). Following this authorization, implementation decisions are taken in accordance with the legislative procedures laid down in the EC Treaty with the difference, however, that only the Member States participating in Enhanced Cooperation (the 'ins') vote on implementation decisions (section F). Subsequent participation of additional Member States remains possible (section H).

The Nice Treaty did not change the general mechanism of Enhanced Cooperation as described above. Treaty changes at Nice[14] primarily concern the four main obstacles which have been identified as hindrances to the practical application of Enhanced Cooperation:[15]

— the ambiguity of the 'last resort principle';
— the difficulty of initiating a quorum of a 'majority of Member States';
— the right of veto for stated reasons of national policy; and
— the strict requirements for the protection of the 'outs'.

The need for revising the authorization conditions was commonly agreed by the delegations during the discussions of the Intergovernmental Conference leading to the Treaty changes in Nice, in order to make the use of *ad hoc* cooperation within the EU's institutional framework more attractive (against other forms of cooperation outside an EU setting).[16]

In the following sections, changes resulting from the Nice Treaty are only explicitly mentioned if they have substantial implications for the application of the provisions on Enhanced Cooperation.

### B.  FAILURE OF THE PROCEDURE

The requirement that a procedure has to fail before initiating the mechanism of Enhanced Cooperation belongs to those provisions which were changed at Nice. Before the Treaty reform, Enhanced Cooperation could only be used 'as a last resort, where the objectives of the . . . Treaties could not be attained by applying the relevant procedures laid down therein'. This provision of the

---

[14] The following analysis of the changes to the instrument of Enhanced Cooperation is based on a study commissioned by the Baltic Environmental Forum; S. Bär, I. von Homeyer, A. Klasing, and R. A. Kraemer, *A Nice Environment for Enlargement? An Analysis of the Treaty of Nice and its Effects on the Environmental Policy of the European Union with a Special View to Enlargement* (Riga: Baltic Environmental Forum, 2001).

[15] European Conference on Closer Cooperation in European Environmental Policy, held on 28 June 2000 in the Permanent Representations of Austria to the European Union.

[16] Conference of the Representatives of the Governments of the Member States, Presidency Note, IGC 2000, Closer Cooperation, CONFER 4761/00, 18 July 2000.

Treaty clearly reflects the view of Member States that Enhanced Cooperation should remain an exception. Thus, the new instrument only serves as *ultima ratio*,[17] as an 'emergency concept'.[18] However, the version of the Treaty before Nice did not clearly define what amounts to such a failure of procedure. The crucial question was whether the withdrawal of a proposal by the Commission also constituted a 'failure', or whether a formal decision from the Council was required in order to prove that a project had failed. Moreover, it was not clear how much time needed to pass in the course of a legislative process, before the procedure could be assumed to have failed, and who was to decide on the existence of such a failure.

Many of the ambiguities mentioned remain unsolved by the Treaty reform. The new version of the Treaty, trying to clarify what is meant by the term 'last resort', refers to a 'reasonable period' within which an objective cannot be attained 'by applying the relevant provisions of the Treaties'. This formulation clearly indicates that the time-aspect of a failure constitutes the decisive factor. How much time is needed and whether a formal statement confirming a failure is required, however, is still unclear. The current wording concerning the last resort principle will therefore remain subject to legal debate, although it is likely to remain a question of political assessment.

This continuing ambiguity, however, does not preclude the application of Enhanced Cooperation in EC environmental policy *per se*. After all, Member States desiring Enhanced Cooperation can request the Council's President to take a vote in the Council at any time.[19] By such a vote, a procedure can be declared to have failed.

In the first pillar, there are three procedural situations in which a 'failure' may occur: (a) unanimity cannot be achieved in the Council;[20] (b) a qualified majority cannot be achieved in the Council;[21] and (c) a legislative proposal fails due to rejection by the European Parliament.

With regard to the first scenario, it was always relatively difficult to achieve agreement in the Council for adopting environmental measures. The increasing number of Member States will make it even more difficult to reach unanimity at a European level in the future.[22] Thus, the instrument of Enhanced Cooperation is suitable in this case. But failure to achieve a qualified majority is also a conceivable case in EC environmental policy, which may therefore call for Enhanced Cooperation. It is possible that Member States are not ready to commit themselves to Community action, but do not object to Enhanced Cooperation by some Member States. The final case, where Enhanced

[17] J. Ukrow, 'Die Fortentwicklung des Rechts der Europäischen Union durch den Vertrag von Amsterdam' (1998) 1 *Zeitschrift für Europarechtliche Studien*, 145.

[18] J. Janning, 'Europa Braucht Verschiedene Geschwindigkeiten' (1997) 20 *Integration*, 287.

[19] According to Art. 7(2) of the Council's Rules of Procedure, the majority of the Member States has to vote in favour of such a decision in the Council.

[20] Unanimity, for example, is required for measures based on Art. 175(2) EC, or on Art. 93 EC, or Art. 152(4) EC.

[21] A qualified majority is required for decisions based on Art. 175(1) and Art. 95(1) EC.

[22] For further details, see Sects. III.A and III.F.

Cooperation is initiated following the rejection of a proposal by the European Parliament (EP), seems rather unlikely in view of its past (constructive) attitude.

At a European level, approximately a hundred legislative procedures are pending in the environmental field—most of them already for more than ten years without a directive or regulation having been adopted.[23] This illustrates the potential importance of Enhanced Cooperation.

### C. REQUEST OF THE MEMBER STATES

Member States wishing to establish Enhanced Cooperation can submit a request to the Commission, which in turn may present a proposal to that effect to the Council.[24] Before the Treaty reforms of Nice, Enhanced Cooperation could only be initiated if a threshold of 'at least a majority of Member States' had been passed.[25] This participation threshold was commonly thought to be too high. The Commission's proposal[26] to lower this quorum to one-third of the Member States was already supported by several Member States at an early stage during the Intergovernmental Conference. The Member States in favour of this modification apparently believed that the basic conditions governing Enhanced Cooperation were sufficiently strict to prevent the instrument from being used too liberally—a development which would lead to excessive fragmentation of the Union.

The reformed Treaty now requires a minimum of eight Member States willing to initiate Enhanced Cooperation.[27] Considering that currently the EU consists of fifteen Member States, the amendment still requires a majority of Member States. However, twenty-one Member States or more will make up the enlarged Union, so that the participation threshold effectively has been considerably lowered. This highlights the intention of the parties of the Intergovernmental Conference to increase flexibility with special regard to the enlarged Union. In a Union of twenty-seven Member States, it will be much easier to find eight like-minded countries to initiate further integration in a special area of European policy.

If the Commission, at the request of a group of eight Member States, decides against submitting a proposal, it has to inform the Member States concerned of this decision, and state its reasons.

---

[23] During the work for the study for the Austrian Ministry for environment (mentioned above), an analysis was carried out concerning legislative procedures pending at a Community level. This analysis showed that some proposals, such as the Modified Proposal for a Council Directive on Water Quality Objectives for Chromium and Limits for Chromium in Waters (COM(88)29, 16 Feb. 1988), and the Amended Proposal for a Council Directive on Civil Liability for Damage Caused by Waste (COM(91)219, 27 June 1991), have been pending for more than ten years without procedural progress having been made.

[24] Art. 11(1) EC.           [25] Art. 43(d) TEU.

[26] European Commission and M. Barnier, IGC 2000, Commission Opinion: Adapting the Institutions to make a success of enlargement, CONFER 4701/00, 1 Feb. 2000.

[27] Art. 43(g) EU.

An open issue concerns the criteria to be used for deciding which Member States are to participate in Enhanced Cooperation, and who may take this decision.[28] This is problematic in a case where a Member State participated in submitting the request for Enhanced Cooperation, and is willing to take part in the Enhanced Cooperation, but is not considered capable of meeting the requirements within the framework of Enhanced Cooperation. If not resolved otherwise, such disputes will have to be submitted to the European Court of Justice (ECJ).

In practice, the identity of Member States interested in engaging in Enhanced Cooperation will vary from case to case, depending on the topic under discussion. In the light of previous experience, it is not possible to identify a core group of environmental leaders who will cooperate closer in numerous cases for the entire environmental field.

### D. CONDITIONS TO PROTECT THE EUROPEAN UNION

Enhanced Cooperation is permitted if 'it is aimed at furthering the objectives of the Union and at protecting and serving its interests'.[29] The reference to the objectives of the Union clarifies that Enhanced Cooperation can only be used as a means to realize accelerated progress by some Member States. This is to preclude explicitly a retrograde step, for example, towards lower standards.[30] Moreover, this provision highlights that the aim of Enhanced Cooperation is not to divide the Union by a series of individualistic decisions, but rather to strengthen it by the exemplary progress by some countries with regard to the objectives and interests of the Union.[31]

The additional requirement of 'reinforcing its [the Union's] process of integration', which was introduced by the Nice Treaty supports this view. The change in name of the new instrument from Closer Cooperation to Enhanced Cooperation similarly serves to downplay the excluding character of Enhanced Cooperation, by placing emphasis on the integrating factor.

Another requirement is that Enhanced Cooperation 'respects the Treaties and the single institutional framework of the Union'.[32] The special emphasis on the observance of the principles and institutional framework of the Union

---

[28] For example, cf. C. Thun-Hohenstein and F. Cede, *Europarecht* (Vienna: Manz, 1995), 126; C. D. Ehlermann, 'Engere Zusammenarbeit nach dem Amsterdamer Vertrag: Ein Neues Verfassungsprinzip?' (1997) 32 *Europarecht*, 373; W. Wessels, 'Verstärkte Zusammenarbeit: Eine Neue Variante Flexibler Integration' in M. Jopp and A. Maurer (eds.), *Die Europäische Union nach Amsterdam* (Bonn: Europa Union, 1998), 203; E. Philippart and G. Edwards, 'The Provisions on Enhanced Cooperation in the Treaty of Amsterdam: The Politics of Flexibility in the European Union' (1999) 37 *Journal of Common Market Studies*, 92.

[29] Art. 43(a) TEU.

[30] In line with the statements of the Committee on Institutional Affairs of the European Parliament in its report on the implementation of the Amsterdam Treaty of 1 July 1998; Rapporteur: Friedhelm Frischenschlager; EP 225.918/fin.

[31] V. Constantinesco, 'Les Clauses de "Coopération Renforcée", le Protocole sur l'Application des Principes de Subsidiarité et de Proportionalité' (1997) 33 *Revue Trimestrielle de Droit Européen*, 49.

[32] Art. 43(b) TEU.

means that Enhanced Cooperation must neither create new institutional structures, nor result in amendments to the Treaties. This is further underlined by the provisions of Article 43(d) TEU, which states that Enhanced Cooperation 'remains within the limits of the powers of the Union or of the European Community and does not cover areas falling within the exclusive competence of the Community'.

Moreover, the provisions adopted within the framework of Enhanced Cooperation must 'respect the *acquis communautaire* and the measures adopted under the other provisions of the said Treaties'.[33] In addition to primary law, the *acquis communautaire* also includes the entire body of secondary law adopted by the institutions of the Union.[34]

Whereas the current version of the Treaty requires Enhanced Cooperation not to 'affect' the *acquis communautaire*, the version after Nice refers to 'respecting' *the acquis communautaire*. According to the wording prior to Nice, Enhanced Cooperation appeared to be stricter than the general principles guiding the relation between national and European legislation. For the adoption of national environmental measures in non-harmonized fields (this is in fields where no Community legislation exists), a general principle requires that primary and secondary European legislation must not be jeopardized.[35] This requirement appears to be less onerous than that which is implied by the use of the term 'restricted'. In fields where environmental legislation on the European level exists (harmonized fields), stricter national environmental measures can be enacted according to the requirements laid down in Articles 95(4), (5), (6), and 176 EC. These provisions contain conditions governing the compatibility of much more stringent national measures with the EC Treaty, EC trade principles, and other specific preconditions, such as the requirement of 'new scientific evidence' (Article 95(5) EC).[36]

The amended wording after Nice suggests that 'respecting' the *acquis communautaire* is a less strict condition than 'affecting' it. On this assumption, the prerequisites for Enhanced Cooperation now seem to be comparable to the requirements for national environmental measures in a non-harmonized area. Provided the other conditions are met, conceivable actions in the framework of Enhanced Cooperation in the field of environment include, in particular:

---

[33] Art. 43(b) TEU.

[34] Primary law comprises the treaties establishing the Community, ranging from the founding treaties, the declarations and protocols adopted thereon to the amendments to the founding treaties (Single European Act, Maastricht Treaty, Amsterdam Treaty). Secondary law is any legislation adopted on the basis of the Treaties by institutions of the Community; cf. F. Emmert, *Europarecht* (Munich: Beck, 1996), 124.

[35] Case 6/64, *Costa* v. *E.N.E.L.* [1964] ECR 1141; Case 11/70, *Internationale Handelsgesellschaft mbH* v. *Einfuhr- und Vorratsstelle für Getreide und Futtermittel* [1970] ECR 1125; Case 106/77, *Aministrazione delle finanze dello Stato* v. *Simmenthal* [1978] ECR 629.

[36] Cf. S. Bär, I. von Homeyer, R. A. Kraemer *et al.*, *Closer Cooperation in European Environmental Policy after Amsterdam: Concise Analysis* (Vienna: Federal Ministry of Environment, Youth and Family Affairs, 1999), sect. 2.4.1.

— the adoption of directives or regulations; and
— the regulation of an entire area not yet harmonized at the European level.

Subject to compliance with the other conditions, Enhanced Cooperation in a harmonized area in environmental policy is basically admissible in order to:

— render an existing European environmental directive more stringent;
— use a new instrument to achieve an objective defined in a harmonization measure.

In sum, it is likely that the amended wording increases the scope of an application of Enhanced Cooperation. In non-harmonized areas, the requirements for Enhanced Cooperation seem to correspond to the ones for national measures. In harmonized areas, the new conditions for Enhanced Cooperation appear to be less strict than the requirements for national measures which are more stringent than Community law, particularly pursuant to Article 95(4) and (5) EC.

As has been observed, concerns that Enhanced Cooperation may undermine the homogeneity of Community law should not be overstated. In fact, Enhanced Cooperation may in some cases contribute to further harmonization. This is particularly true for non-harmonized areas, where Enhanced Cooperation leads to harmonization among participating Member States. As argued in Section III, it seems likely that, once an Enhanced Cooperation has been established, more and more Member States will join. In many cases Enhanced Cooperation may therefore function as a precursor to full harmonization, which includes all Member States. However, even in harmonized areas, Enhanced Cooperation may contribute to increased convergence. This may be the case if more than one Member State employs Enhanced Cooperation as an alternative to national measures pursuant to Article 95(4), (5) EC or Article 176 EC. In this case, it may prevent the emergence of further differentiation as a result of several different national measures. In addition, Enhanced Cooperation is likely to provide other incentives than gradually to achieve full harmonization, as a result of the effects described in Section IV.

### i. Safeguards for the Protection of Minorities

The provisions for protecting the 'outs' include the examination of compliance with the prerequisites by the Commission, as Enhanced Cooperation 'respects the competencies, rights, obligations and interests of those Member States which do not participate therein'[37] and is 'open to all Member States'.[38] 'It shall also be open to them at any time, in accordance with Articles 27e, 40b, and 11a, subject to compliance with the basic decision and with the decisions taken within that framework.'[39] This provision, also known as the 'principle of openness' reflects the intention of the signatories not to create a permanent core Europe, or '*Europe à la carte*', but only to allow a temporary lead, by providing the opportunity for others to catch up with the 'leaders' at a later date.

---

[37] Art. 43(h) TEU.     [38] Art. 43(j) TEU.     [39] Art. 43(b) TEU.

Similar to the conditions for accession to the EU, later participation in a sub-field of Enhanced Cooperation requires that a Member State wishing to participate accepts the basic decision resulting from the relevant authorization, as well as the decisions taken by the 'ins' in the course of their Cooperation. These decisions, so to speak, form the *acquis* of the Enhanced Cooperation in question. The acceding Member State is not able to influence the agreements previously reached, and can only participate in future decisions. The new sentence introduced in Nice ('The Commission and the Member States parties to Enhanced Cooperation shall ensure that as many Member States as possible are encouraged to take part'), implies that participating Member States must shape Enhanced Cooperation in such a way that the participation of further Member States is made permanently possible in practice.

### ii. Prohibition of Discrimination and Distortion of Competition

A particularly important barrier to the practical application of Enhanced Cooperation after its introduction by the Amsterdam Treaty is the prohibition of discrimination and distortion of competition. This means that Enhanced Cooperation must not 'constitute a barrier to or discrimination of trade between the Member States and does not distort competition between them'.[40] The discrimination ban, which also forms the basis of other norms in the EC Treaty (Articles 28, 95, and 176 EC), was intended to allay concerns of Member States that Enhanced Cooperation could be abused as an instrument of covert protectionism.

The Treaty of Nice introduced some amendments to this ban. Whereas formerly 'a restriction of trade' between Member States was prohibited, Enhanced Cooperation may not constitute 'a barrier' to trade according to the new version of the Treaty. An interpretation pursuant to the wording would mean that the requirements for Enhanced Cooperation have been eased. According to the *Collins Dictionary of the English Language*, a restriction is 'something that restricts', whereas to restrict means 'to confine or keep within certain often specified limits or selected bounds'. A barrier is '1. Anything serving to obstruct passage or to maintain separation, such as a fence or gate, 2. Anything that prevents or obstructs passage, access or progress, 3. Anything that separates or hinders union.'[41] This implies that a barrier to trade is something more definite, which poses more of an obstruction than a restriction. The fact that the corresponding clause in Article 95(6) EC, referring to 'disguised restriction', remains unchanged shows that the signatories of the Treaty intended to draw a distinction between the clause often discussed and subject to several ECJ rulings, and the new wording of Enhanced Cooperation. Interpreted in this way, Enhanced Cooperation, permitted only if not constituting a barrier to trade, is easier to realize than if a restriction to trade would have remained the acid test.

---

[40] Art. 34(1)(f) TEU.
[41] P. Hanks (ed.), *Collins Dictionary of the English Language* (London/Glasgow: William Collins Sons & Co., 1984).

However, the discrimination ban remains unchanged after the reforms of Nice. ECJ rulings indicate that the prohibition of discrimination among Member States is closely associated with the principle of proportionality.[42] Discrimination exists if a sovereign entity, in its jurisdiction, treats equivalent situations in a dissimilar way, or dissimilar situations in an equivalent way.[43] Applied to the movement of goods, this means, for example, that domestic manufacturers of goods must not be afforded preferential treatment compared to foreign competitors, in the absence of accepted justifications, in diverging national regulations.[44] Within the framework of Enhanced Cooperation, such discrimination may occur if stricter product standards are introduced in the territory of the 'ins', and products manufactured in the 'outs', which do not comply with these standards, may not be sold in the 'ins'. But unequal treatment is not prohibited *per se*. Using the justifications for discrimination within the framework of Article 28 or Article 95 EC, we assume that unequal treatment is permitted for reasons related to environmental protection provided that the restriction is proportionate.[45] According to the generally accepted definition of proportionality in the field of administrative and constitutional law, an action is proportionate if it is suitable for pursuing the objective envisaged, necessary and reasonable.[46]

With regard to restrictions to trade (in respect of products) caused by measures of Enhanced Cooperation, we therefore can conclude that unequal treatment of products manufactured by the 'ins' and 'outs' may be justified for environmental reasons. The admissibility of a measure to be taken within the framework of Enhanced Cooperation, however, has to be examined on a case-by-case basis.

Furthermore, for the application of Enhanced Cooperation in the field of environmental policy it is also of importance that the measures must not distort competition between Member States.[47] This is another manifestation of Article 81 EC, which states that any 'prevention, restriction or distortion of competition' is prohibited. Simply put, competition is impeded if there is an objectively intensive and sustained negative effect on competition within the common market.[48] Consequently, competition is not distorted merely because environmental measures raise production costs for an industry. Any other interpretation would preclude all measures which affect the economic activities of Member States, and Enhanced Cooperation would become utterly impossible. The latter cannot have been intended, given the objective of Article 43 TEU to create a possibility of further integrating European

---

[42] Case 178/84, *Commission* v. *Germany* [1987] ECR 2301.    [43] Emmert, n. 34 above, 144.

[44] Discrimination against domestic organizations (reverse discrimination), such as the unilateral imposition of the German purity requirements for beer, is still permitted, at least according to past case law.

[45] It is assumed that the exception of Art. 30 EC or the rule of reason in the sense of *Cassis de Dijon* (Case 120/78, *REWE* v. *Bundesmonopolverwaltung für Branntwein* [1979] ECR 649) are applicable.

[46] R. Streintz, *Europarecht* (Heidelberg: C. F. Müller, 1999), 243.    [47] Art. 43(f) TEU.

[48] Ukrow, n. 17 above, 148.

policy.[49] In the light of comparable provisions such as Articles 28 and 30 EC, it is to be assumed that the principle of proportionality also applies to Article 43 (f) TEU. In other words, the distortion of competition has to be balanced against requirements of environmental protection. An interpretation along these lines would mean that only national regulations resulting in a *disproportionate* distortion of competition are not permitted.

In addition to the prohibition of a restriction of trade and the discrimination ban, a new sub-paragraph was introduced which might further restrict practical application in the field of the environment. The clause states that Enhanced Cooperation 'does not undermine the internal market as defined in Article 14(2) of the EC Treaty or the economic and social cohesion established in accordance with Title XVII of the European Commission Treaty'. The internal market, according to Article 14 EC, comprises an area without internal frontiers in which the free movement of goods, persons, services, and capital is ensured.

The new clause restricts the field of application for Enhanced Cooperation. For the environmental sector, in particular, the clause on the internal market is important. It is unclear as to how far the new clause *strictly excludes* practical application of Enhanced Cooperation.[50] The choice of the word 'undermine' indicates that not strictly all actions concerning or affecting the internal market are to be excluded. 'Undermining' implies some substantial implications for the functioning of the internal market. A comparison with the wording of Article 95(6) EC supports this interpretation. According to this clause, Member States may be allowed to introduce or maintain stricter national measures relating to the environment if they 'do not constitute an obstacle to the functioning of the internal market'. This supports the conclusion that certain exceptions are allowed. Enhanced Cooperation should therefore be possible in those cases in which stricter national measures pursuant to Article 95 EC would also be allowed. After the reform by the Treaty of Amsterdam, the field of application of Article 95 EC has increased considerably.[51]

As a preliminary conclusion, it appears that the legal requirements of Enhanced Cooperation in Article 43 TEU do not preclude its applicability in the environmental field. In individual cases, the admissibility of measures will depend mainly on a proportionality test, first by the Commission, and ultimately by the ECJ.

---

[49]  Cf. the corresponding argumentation regarding Art. 95(6) EC, introducing the requirement that national measures must not affect the functioning of the internal market. S. Albin and S. Bär, 'Nationale Alleingänge nach Amsterdam—Der neue Artikel 95 EGV: Fortschritt oder Rückschritt für den Umweltschutz?' (1999) 21 *Natur und Recht*, 185.

[50]  Strict exclusion of Enhanced Cooperation in extensively integrated areas was discussed during the Intergovernmental Conference, Conference of the Representatives of the Governments of the Member States, Presidency Note, IGC 2000, Closer Cooperation, CONFER 4761/00, 18 July 2000.

[51]  S. Bär and S. Albin, 'The "Environmental Guarantee" on the Rise? The Amended Article 95 after the Revision through the Treaty of Amsterdam' (2000) 2 *European Journal of Law Reform*, 119–34. See also H. Sevenster, 'The Environmental Guarantee after Amsterdam: Does the Emperor Have New Clothes?' (2000) 1 *Yearbook of European Environmental Law*, 291–310.

### E. CONSULTATION OF THE EUROPEAN PARLIAMENT

Currently, the EP is only consulted during the procedure establishing Enhanced Cooperation, whereas after the Treaty reform in Nice, if Enhanced Cooperation relates 'to an area covered by the procedure referred to in Article 251, the assent of the European Parliament shall be required'. This implies that there is a legal obligation to take the opinion of the European Parliament into consideration. If the European Parliament disagrees with the proposed Cooperation, action may not be taken. Thus, the process establishing Enhanced Cooperation is subject to the democratic supervision of the Parliament, and corresponds with its power within the framework of the implementation decisions, which have to be adopted in line with the usual legislative procedures, the co-decision procedure in most environmental cases.

### F. DECISIONS IN THE COUNCIL

The decision to establish Enhanced Cooperation must be taken by a qualified majority in the Council. This remained unchanged after the Treaty reform. However, prior to the reforms, Enhanced Cooperation could not have taken place against the expressed will of a Member State, which enjoys the so-called 'quasi-veto'. This right of veto considerably limits the practical use of Enhanced Cooperation. Therefore the second subparagraph of Article 11(2) EC (and the corresponding second subparagraph of Article 40(2) TEU) has now been deleted. As a result, a Member State opposing a planned project of Enhanced Cooperation will lose the right to refer a positive decision on this project agreed by a qualified majority of Member States to the European Council for a unanimous decision. Abolishment of the veto decisively increases the practical use of the new instrument in the field of environmental policy.

At present, the Council of Ministers acting upon a qualified majority can request that the matter be referred to the European Council. After the Treaty reforms in Nice, a single Member State within the Council of Ministers may initiate the referral to the European Council. It seems that the reformers of the Treaty, by easing the referral to a 'higher body', intended to introduce some sort of compensation for the loss of the right of veto. After the matter has been raised before the European Council, the Council of Ministers 'may take a decision in accordance with the provisions of the first subparagraph'. This implies that, once the European Council has discussed the issue, the Council of Ministers again has to decide according to the procedure laid down in Article 11(2)(1) EC. It seems unlikely, however, that the European Council, being obliged to find unanimous consent, will take a decision against the will of a qualified majority of the Member States in the Council of Ministers. The importance, however, resides in the possibility of raising the issue at a higher political level.

### G. LATER PARTICIPATION OF MEMBER STATES

Member States which initially are not involved are entitled to join the 'leaders' at any time. This principle is a manifestation of the principle of openness referred to above.[52] Article 11a EC provides a specific procedure to this effect. If a Member State wishes to become a party to an existing Enhanced Cooperation, it informs the Council and the Commission. Within three months, the Commission submits its opinion to the Council. Within four months, the Commission decides on the request and on any additional arrangements required. This provision is complemented by Article 43b TEU, which states that the new participating Member States have to comply with the basic decision and the implementation decisions already taken. Consequently, when deciding the request, the Commission only has to examine whether the Member State requesting to become a party to the Cooperation meets these requirements, and whether any specific transitional arrangements are required. Since the Commission is interested in the re-establishment of the homogeneity of the legal area, which can only be guaranteed by the involvement of as many additional Member States as possible, it can be assumed that the Commission will generally support participation.

### H. PRELIMINARY CONCLUSION

The application of Enhanced Cooperation is a feasible proposition in the field of European environmental policy. In particular following the reforms agreed in Nice, the new instrument is more than a 'structural principle of the future'.[53]

However, objectives and mechanisms still need to be further elaborated. The actual utilization of the provision will decisively shape the room for manoeuvre for individual Member States, and will show whether the new instrument can develop into a central instrument of integration. National governments, individual politicians, and the urgency of items on the European agenda will determine whether groups of Member States can be formed, which meet the formal requirements of Enhanced Cooperation. At the same time, conflicting interests of Member States not participating must be resolved in such a way that blocking attitudes do not emerge. The problems resulting from the 'quasi-veto' and the old participation requirement were eased by the Treaty changes in Nice. As in other legislative procedures, the Commission will play a major role in decisions on the actual application of Enhanced Cooperation in the first pillar. Above all, its position allows it to interpret the provisions in either a restrictive or a liberal way and, thus, to set the standards for utilization of the new instrument. Several points needing clarification (for example, the question of who decides according to which criteria, or when a 'standard' procedure to adopt a Community measure is deemed to have failed)

---

[52] Cf. Sect. II.D.i (see below).
[53] G. Müller-Brandeck-Bocquet, 'Flexible Integration: Chance für die Europäische Umweltpolitik?' (1997) 20 *Integration*, 302.

were amended as a result of Nice. Final clarification of controversial issues by the ECJ is only to be expected in several years.

Although the new instrument was primarily developed with reference to policies (for example, Schengen, social policy, Economic and Monetary Union), its application to individual acts of secondary law is not precluded. In fact, it will above all be secondary law where potential cases of application will arise, thus resulting in a wide application field in practice.

## III. The Potential for Application in European Environmental Policy

As observed, application of Enhanced Cooperation is tied to a series of requirements. The most important conditions can be summarized as follows:

— legal authorization in the EC Treaty;
— failure of a procedure based on the EC Treaty;
— request by eight Member States;
— qualified majority in Council in favour of the authorization decision;
— no adverse effects on primary and secondary law;
— no undermining of the internal market;
— no discrimination or restrictions of trade or distortion of the conditions for competition.

### A. ENCHANCED COOPERATION AND UNANIMITY

Under certain conditions, the new instrument of Enhanced Cooperation may lead to an easing of the unanimity requirement for certain environmental measures. In particular, in the environmental field, central empowering provisions[54] still require unanimity. This applies in particular to Article 175(2) EC, which stipulates that unanimity is required in Council in the following fields:

— provisions primary of a fiscal nature;
— town and country planning, land use,[55] quantitative management of water resources;
— issues concerning the choice between different energy sources and the general structure of energy supply.

Accession of new Member States will make the requirement of unanimity even more onerous at the European level in the future. Aware of this problem, the agenda of the Intergovernmental Conference of 1996 already included the extension of the co-decision procedure with qualified majority voting in the Council. The Amsterdam amendments to the Treaty were, however, only partly successful in this respect. In particular, measures falling within the scope of Article 175(2) EC still have to be adopted unanimously. Interestingly,

[54] In this context, the most important fields are transport (Art. 71(1) EC), harmonization of legislation (Art. 95(1) EC), social policy in the field of vocational training and youth (Art. 137(2) EC), but also health (Art. 152(4) EC) and consumer protection (Art. 153(4) EC).
[55] With the exception of waste management and measures of a general nature.

the introduction of the instrument of Enhanced Cooperation into the Treaties was seriously considered in the discussions of the Intergovernmental Conference only when it became obvious that a sweeping retreat of the unanimity principle would not be realized. The Nice Treaty introduced only slight changes to Article 175 EC. Therefore, it is anticipated that the failure of the governments to agree on qualified majority voting for all measures in the area of the environment will, within the framework of an enlarged Union, increase deadlock in certain areas of environmental policy.

The establishment of Enhanced Cooperation only requires a qualified majority in the Council. When unanimity cannot be achieved in support of a measure at the Community level, but a qualified majority is possible, at least eight Member States can join forces to initiate Enhanced Cooperation. After the adoption of the authorization decision, however, the countries participating in Enhanced Cooperation have to agree unanimously on the implementation decisions in those areas where the EC Treaty still prescribes unanimity. The requirement of unanimity is thereby transferred to a smaller circle of Member States. Consequently, by virtue of Enhanced Cooperation, deadlock in legislative procedures can be circumvented in the future. This should not divert our attention from the fact that it is also permitted in cases requiring 'only' a qualified majority. There may be situations in which some Member States do not participate themselves in Enhanced Cooperation, but are ready to agree to it.

### B. PRODUCT-RELATED REGULATION

At a national and European level, environmental regulation frequently addresses the environmental properties of goods.[56] Basically, we have to distinguish product regulations in harmonized areas, where secondary law has already been adopted, from regulation in non-harmonized areas.

The legal requirement established by the Treaty to respect the *acquis communautaire* is relatively unproblematic in the context of the establishment of product standards in non-harmonized areas. Enhanced Cooperation in non-harmonized areas has to comply with the principles of the Treaty, in common with national measures. In the field of product regulation, the prohibition of quantitative restrictions or measures having equivalent effect is of particular relevance.[57] Like national measures, measures taken in the context of Enhanced Cooperation violating this prohibition may be justified for environmental reasons.[58]

---

[56] Product standards include all provisions directly regulating the properties of marketable and tradable *products*. This applies to exhaust gas regulations for cars as well as to the ban on certain detergent additives or product-specific restrictions on the utilization of chemical substances, e.g. PCP. See H. Temmink, 'From Danish Bottles to Danish Bees: The Dynamics of Free Movement of Goods and Environmental Protection—a Case Law Analysis' (2000) 1 *Yearbook of European Environmental Law*, 61–102.

[57] Art. 28 EC.

[58] For national regulations, see in particular Cases 8/74, *Procureur du Roi* v. *Benoît and Gustave Dassonville* [1974] ECR 837 and 120/78, *REWE* v. *Bundesmonopolverwaltung für Branntwein* [1979] ECR 649.

between process regulation and the internal market. National process regulation imposes additional burdens on domestic manufacturers, which may raise production costs and, hence, result in a disadvantage for manufacturers for European and international markets.[62] The more intensive competition is in a sector the more difficult it will be for a 'pioneering country' to adopt environmental process regulations at national level. In contrast, environmental laggards tend to be interested in offsetting other, potentially unfavourable production factors, such as market distance or relatively low productivity by lower process standards in order to raise their competitiveness. They are therefore normally not interested in the harmonization of process standards. These conflicting interests usually imply that European minimum standards for production processes cannot be agreed, or are defined in many cases at a low level.

Against this backdrop, Enhanced Cooperation offers environmental leaders the opportunity to set a high standard in the territory of the Member States involved. They can thereby offset part of the negative economic impact which national measures would have. As a result, two different minimum standards would exist which applied to different groups of countries. Since countries not involved in Enhanced Cooperation would not suffer a disadvantage (they would even have an advantage due to the raising of production costs in the high-standard countries), they would probably not oppose Enhanced Cooperation within the framework of the authorization procedure initiated by other Member States. A sufficient number of pioneering states, however, is only likely to be found for the definition of higher process standards if the economic impact of the new standards does not exceed an economically supportable level. In order for this to be the case, all manufacturing countries crucial for the field to be regulated would have to commit themselves to these higher standards.

There is a considerable potential for increased flexibility in the field of process-related regulation in environmental policy.[63] For example, it is conceivable that the standards for large combustion plants could be raised 'unilaterally', or the scope of the existing Directive could be extended within the framework of Enhanced Cooperation if the proposal for a revision[64] should fail at the European level.[65]

A possible test case of Enhanced Cooperation in the environmental field could be provided by the taxation of energy products, which is heavily contested

---

[62] Additional requirements with regard to environmental protection usually raise the costs only in the short term. In the longer term, additional costs are often offset by efficiency gains, renewal of capital stock, and the diversification of the product range.

[63] See also A. Epiney, 'Flexible Integration und Umweltpolitik in der EU—Rechtliche Aspekte' in K. Holzinger and P. Knoepfel (eds.), *Environmental Policy in a European Union of Variable Geometry?: The Challenge of the Next Enlargement* (Basel: Helbing & Lichtenhahn, 2000), 39–64.

[64] Proposal for a Council Directive Amending Directive 88/609/EEC on the Limitation of Emissions of Certain Pollutants into the Air from Large Combustion Plants (COM(98)415 final, 8 July 1998).

[65] Epiney, n. 63 above, also explicitly identifies the field of more extensive emission protection measures as a potential application of Enhanced Cooperation.

at the European level. Although the tax is to be applied to energy *products*, this type of taxation is more in line with the logic of process regulation, since the costs will be incurred in the production process in the countries collecting the tax. The discussion on the Commission's proposal on the harmonization of certain energy products,[66] such as diesel, gas oil, kerosene, or electricity, has lost momentum at the European level, in particular due to the objections of Spain.[67] If the proposed directive were to be put to a vote in the Council, it would seem likely that unanimity, as required by the EC Treaty, would not be achieved. Without explicitly referring to the instrument of Enhanced Cooperation, the Dutch Finance Minister Gerrit Zalm already proposed that this field be regulated only by like-minded Member States.[68] Recently, Environment Commissioner Margot Wallström and Budget Commissioner Michaele Schreyer have called for Enhanced Cooperation to be used to facilitate agreement on an energy tax.[69] If the Member States do not change their opinion, the necessary qualified majority could be achieved for submitting such a request to the Commission. Whether the qualified majority in the Council can be reached would then depend on the concrete wording of the proposal.

In this context, environmental liability could also be mentioned. In this field, Enhanced Cooperation is likely to come about only when a 'standard' legislative procedure has failed at the European level.

### D. MISCELLANEOUS REGULATION

A considerable potential for Enhanced Cooperation seems to exist in fields in which major effects on the internal market are not feared. This relates, on the one hand, to environmental regulation concerning administrative procedures or court proceedings and, on the other hand, to measures in the field of nature conservation and the protection of biodiversity.

In the field of nature conservation and the protection of biodiversity, Enhanced Cooperation could possibly serve as a model, and contribute to the gradual dissemination of successful measures and concepts across Community territory. Hesitant Member States would be faced with the example of the countries participating in Enhanced Cooperation. In the medium to long term, this could influence the general orientation of their own environmental policies.

### E. IMPLEMENTATION OF INTERNATIONAL AGREEMENTS

In addition to the examples mentioned, Member States may use Enhanced Cooperation for the implementation of international agreements.

[66] Proposal for a Council Directive Restructuring the Community Framework for the Taxation of Energy Products COM(97)30, 12 Mar. 1997.
[67] Greece, Portugal, and Ireland also seem to take a negative view of the proposal, *ENDS Daily*, 16 July 1999.
[68] *ENDS Daily*, 13 July 1999.
[69] 'Tax Chief Orders Probe into Treaty Unanimity "Loophole" ' (2001) 7 *European Voice*, 22–8 Feb. 2001.

The protection of Community assets is often regulated outside the Community framework by international agreements. This state of affairs is essentially due to the fact that the group of countries participating in such conventions is not identical to the group of the Member States of the EU. As a result, two problems emerge: geographical incongruity and incongruity in terms of substance. The first problem occurs, for example, in the context of the protection of regional and subregional areas such as the North Sea, the Carpathian Mountains, the Rhine, or the Alps. The second problem arises if not all the Member States are affected by the contents of the international agreement and, hence, do not have reason to accede to it.[70] The forthcoming enlargement eastward will further increase incongruities in terms of geography and substance.

However, there are also cases in which the signatories of international environmental protection agreements commit to a level of protection that is higher than that achievable at the European level. Relevant cases include the Convention on the Conservation of Migratory Species of Wild Animals,[71] the Convention on the Protection of the Marine Environment of the North-East Atlantic,[72] and the Convention on Civil Liability for Damage resulting from Activities Dangerous to the Environment.[73]

The legal requirements laid down in the EC and EU Treaties have to be observed by the Member States concerned when implementing international agreements. In cases where only a few Member States are affected for geographical reasons, it seems to be a fallacy that at least eight Member States have to join forces. In some cases (for example, the protection of the Mediterranean Sea, the Carpathian Mountains, or the Alps) this criterion will be difficult to satisfy. However, implementation of measures within the framework of the Convention on the Protection of the Marine Environment of the North-East Atlantic (OSPAR), may be a suitable case for Enhanced Cooperation, because the Convention has been signed not only by adjoining states, but also by Member States with jurisdiction over rivers flowing into the North-Eastern Atlantic. In all these fields, we have to bear in mind that a procedure at Community level based on the EC Treaty must have failed, before Enhanced Cooperation can be initiated.

If the legal conditions are fulfilled, the instrument of Enhanced Cooperation offers the possibility of accommodating transboundary environmental protection further into the institutional framework of the Community. The main advantage for the Member States involved is that they would be able to use the highly advanced and relatively successful institutional decision-making mechanisms of the EC (for example, the involvement of the Commission, monitoring by the ECJ, Council voting by a qualified majority, etc.) for collective decision-making. In addition, EC environmental policy would no longer

---

[70] International environmental agreements may also specify different requirements to be met by the signatories.

[71] Entry into force in 1983.       [72] The OSPAR Convention became effective on 25 Mar. 1998.

[73] The Convention was adopted in 1993, but has as yet not come into force.

be orientated primarily towards achieving standards that are uniform for the entire EC. Rather, environmental policy would be geared to finding 'tailored' solutions to specific environmental problems, which previously had to be tackled outside the Community framework, or was made subject to relatively low EC environmental standards.

The mechanism of Enhanced Cooperation could also be helpful if the Community intends to participate in international agreements in addition to some of the Member States, while some Member States declare in advance that they do not wish to comply with the associated obligations within the framework of the EC.[74] Provided that the provisions laid down in the EC and EU Treaties are observed, the Community could accede to the international agreement and implement it within the framework of Enhanced Cooperation with some Member States only.

In the context of the ratification and implementation of the Kyoto Protocol by the Member States, a detailed examination of the applicability of Enhanced Cooperation should be considered. Against the background of the accession of ten Central and Eastern European Countries to the EU, differences in reduction commitments of the individual Member States will become even more marked. The kind of measures needed, and the capabilities of the candidate countries to achieve the reduction targets applicable to them, can probably not be compared with those of the majority of the current Member States. Enhanced Cooperation could contribute to ensuring a flexible solution for the implementation of the obligations. But even prior to enlargement, it is conceivable within the framework of EC burden-sharing that some Member States would join to create a legal framework for emissions trading, while others would implement their reduction obligations by national measures. In particular, in the context of the implementation of the Kyoto Protocol, Enhanced Cooperation could be used to create a framework for the further harmonization and an increase of taxes on energy products which, as mentioned above, is currently under debate at the Community level.

On the whole, it may be useful to employ Enhanced Cooperation for the implementation of certain international environmental agreements. It will have to be ascertained on a case-to-case basis whether an international agreement can best be implemented by non-harmonized national measures, Community legislation, or rather by Enhanced Cooperation.

### F. ENHANCED COOPERATION AND EASTERN ENLARGEMENT

As a result of the forthcoming enlargement of the EU,[75] a number of countries will accede to the Community which, in all likelihood, will probably join the

---

[74] Presuming admissibility in international law.

[75] The following sections primarily relate to the accession of the ten Central and Eastern European candidate countries, i.e. Bulgaria, Czech Republic, Estonia, Hungary, Latvia, Lithuania, Poland, Romania, Slovak Republic, and Slovenia.

group of environmental 'laggards'.[76] The following considerations focus on the question how far Enhanced Cooperation can contribute to a new dynamism in European environmental policy in the face of enlargement, or at least to the maintenance of the environmental *status quo.*

First, basic aspects of the problems involved in enlargement with regard to European environmental policy will be briefly presented. The potential environmental impact of Enhanced Cooperation is then examined against this backdrop, using two important factors of influence: reform of the decision-making rules of the Community and differences between groups of candidate countries. Finally, we analyse the questions as to whether new Member States have to join an Enhanced Cooperation already existing at the time of their accession, and which effects enlargement could have on existing cases of Enhanced Cooperation.

### i. Problems of Enlargement

Eastern enlargement constitutes a challenge for environmental progress in the Community. On the one hand, the existing deficit in the practical application and enforcement of EC environmental law may be exacerbated.[77] As the Commission stated in its annual reports on the progress of the candidate countries towards accession,[78] major deficits still exist in the candidate countries, with regard to the formal transposition of EC legislation, and its implementation and enforcement, in particular in the environmental field. Therefore, a limited number of transitional periods will probably be necessary before EC environmental law can be fully applied.[79] On the other hand, there is the risk of an obstruction to further environmental progress following accession because, as mentioned, the number of environmental 'laggards' is likely to increase as a result of enlargement.[80]

The exacerbation of the implementation deficit to some extent depends on the level of protection provided by EC environmental standards. If the level of

[76] Cf. A. Carius, I. von Homeyer, and S. Bär, 'Die Osterweiterung der Europäischen Union—Herausforderung und Chance für eine Gesamteuropäische Umweltpolitik' (1999) 48 *Aus Politik und Zeitgeschichte*, 21–9.

[77] For the implementation deficit of European environmental law, see e.g. European Commission, *Environment Chapter of the 16th Annual Report on Monitoring the Application of Community Law* (1998) (Brussels: European Commission, 1999) ([1999] OJ C354/1); I. von Homeyer, 'Enlarging EU Environmental Policy: the Challenges of Flexibility and Integration' in L. Giorgi, A. Pearman, C. Reynaud, and D. Tsamboulas (eds.), *Project and Policy Evaluation in Transport* (Avebury: Ashgate, forthcoming).

[78] European Commission, *2000 Regular Report from the Commission on the Czech Republic's Progress towards Accession* (Brussels: European Commission, 2000); European Commission, *2000 Regular Report from the Commission on Estionia's Progress towards Accession* (Brussels: European Commission, 2000); European Commission, *2000 Regular Report from the Commission on Hungary's Progress towards Accession* (Brussels: European Commission, 2000); European Commission, *2000 Regular Report from the Commission on Poland's Progress towards Accession* (Brussels: European Commission, 2000); European Commission, *2000 Regular Report from the Commission on Slovenia's Progress towards Accession* (Brussels: European Commission, 2000).

[79] Cf. I. von Homeyer, L. Kempmann, and A. Klasing, 'EU Enlargement: Screening Results in the Environmental Sector' (1999) 11 *Environmental Law Network International (ELNI) Newsletter*, 43–7.

[80] Cf. I. von Homeyer, n. 77.

protection is raised at the European level, an increase in the implementation deficit is to be expected at a national level, and vice versa.[81] Since the candidate countries lack the requisite financial and administrative capacity, and the political will to put high standards of environmental protection into practice,[82] the relationship between the level of regulation and the implementation deficit is probably very pronounced in these countries. This could become an obstacle to further progress in the EC environmental policy. In the course of enlargement, the Community might face the dilemma of either having to lower its level of environmental regulation, or having to accept further implementation deficits. Either option would not only adversely affect environmental protection in the EC, but would also reduce the credibility and legitimacy of EC environmental policy in the long term. A tendency towards the 'renationalization' of European environmental policy could be one of the possible consequences.[83]

Against this backdrop, Enhanced Cooperation may create opportunities for decoupling the connection between implementation deficits and levels of regulation. In addition, Enhanced Cooperation could reduce the growing risk of obstruction of a high level of protection by the increasing number of 'laggards'.

### ii. The Impact of Institutional Reforms

Before the 2000 Intergovernmental Conference was concluded, discussions concerning the impact of Enhanced Cooperation on environmental policy in the context of enlargement involved some uncertainties. This was due to the fact that the effects of Enhanced Cooperation strongly depended on the future institutional decision-making rules in the EU, which were to be adopted by the Intergovernmental Conference. Two outcomes of the Intergovernmental Conference are particularly important for environmental policy. First, Member States failed to agree on introducing qualified majority voting for all environmental measures, in particular, for energy taxes and other measures of a primarily fiscal nature, which are still subject to the unanimity requirement.

Second, modifications of the distribution of votes in the Council and of related rules which were agreed by the Intergovernmental Conference in Nice are likely to be insufficient to counter the negative impact on the efficiency of decision-making of the rising number and diversity of Member States in the wake of enlargement. For example, rather than drastically lowering the threshold for a qualified majority, the Intergovernmental Conference even resulted in a slight increase. Perhaps more importantly, the future distribution of votes among environmental pace-setters and environmental laggards may create problems for European environmental policy, as it seems likely that at least in

---

[81] Cf. A. Jordan, 'The Implementation of EU Environmental Policy: A Policy Problem without a Political Solution?' (1999) 17 *Environment and Planning: Government and Policy*, 84–5.

[82] Cf. Carius, von Homeyer, and Bär, n. 76 above.

[83] I. von Homeyer, A. Carius, and S. Bär, 'The Eastern Enlargement of the European Union and Environmental Policy: Challenges, Expectations, Multiple Speeds and Flexibility' in Holzinger and Knoepfel (eds.), n. 63 above, 141–80.

the first years following accession, many of the new Member States will oppose the adoption of stricter environmental legislation at the EU level.[84] On the one hand, environmental pace-setters among the existing Member States will lose their ability to block decisions when the first candidate countries have joined the Union. On the other hand, existing laggard Member States will most likely be able to form a blocking minority in the future if several accession countries are willing to join their ranks.[85]

Given these problems, and taking into account the relaxation of the conditions for Enhanced Cooperation, this new instrument may not only allow circumventing obstructionism. Enhanced Cooperation also creates the opportunity for environmental pace-setters to pursue measures reflecting a protection level which would be blocked by laggards under the conventional legislative procedure.

### *iii. Differences between Candidate Countries*

As has been noted, application of Enhanced Cooperation will probably only have minor adverse effects on the homogeneity of legislation and the political integration process. With regard to enlargement, this statement, however, has to be qualified. Due to enlargement, it is to be expected that future differences between the Member States, in particular in terms of economic performance, will increase to an extent hitherto unknown.[86] While the economic gap between the present Member States and the so-called 'Luxembourg' candidate countries of the 'first wave' (Estonia, Poland, Slovenia, Czech Republic, Hungary, and Cyprus) still seems to be comparable with the relevant differences which characterized enlargement of the EC towards the South, further accessions—for example, by countries such as Romania or Bulgaria—could involve a new degree of differences. For the field of environmental policy, this would mean that a third group of 'late laggards' could form within the EU after the accession of countries such as Romania or Bulgaria. This group would differ from the laggards in two respects. First, environmental traditions and, in particular, financial and administrative capacities of the countries concerned for the implementation and enforcement of EC environmental legislation would be even more limited than, for example, those of the candidate countries of the first wave. Second, the potential 'late laggards' either do not border on present Member States, or border on other laggard countries. For this reason, very little environmental impetus is to be expected from cross-border cooperation for the group of 'late laggards'.[87]

In this situation, the environmental benefits of Enhanced Cooperation would be doubtful. On the one hand, cooperation aiming at a high level of protection would involve the danger that the 'late laggards' would hardly be able to catch up with the participants of Enhanced Cooperation without foreign or Community assistance within a reasonable period of time. On the other hand,

---

[84] Cf. von Homeyer, n. 77 above.      [85] Bär, von Homeyer, Klasing, and Kraemer, n. 14 above.
[86] Cf. Carius, von Homeyer, and Bär, n. 83 above.
[87] For a detailed discussion, see von Homeyer, n. 77 above.

it might be politically difficult, after accession of the present twelve official candidate countries, to achieve the qualified majority of Member States required for the initiation of Enhanced Cooperation without the involvement of some laggards. Even if a qualified majority could be achieved, it remains doubtful whether Enhanced Cooperation would lead to a level of protection that is significantly higher than one which could have been agreed through the conventional legislative procedure involving qualified majority voting.

In sum, Enhanced Cooperation is an instrument which may help to limit the lowering of the level of protection in the wake of the enlargement of the European Union. Given the restrictive prerequisites for its establishment, and the limits to its benefits, Enhanced Cooperation, however, has to be supplemented by further instruments, in particular flexible provisions in secondary environmental law, and more flexibility in implementation in order to prevent, as far as possible, a reduction of protection levels as consequence of enlargement.[88]

### iv. Enlargement and Existing Cases of Enhanced Cooperation

Accession to the EU requires the candidate countries to transpose the *acquis communautaire*. This raises the question as to whether the candidate countries would be obliged to take over an Enhanced Cooperation which already existed at the time of their accession. Since all Member States are involved in the authorization decision for Enhanced Cooperation, the decision belongs to the *acquis communautaire*. However, this does not mean that the candidate countries would have to participate in Enhanced Cooperation. The view that participation in Enhanced Cooperation would not be necessary to achieve full transposition of the *acquis communautaire* is supported by the fact that not all of the 'old' Member States participate in Enhanced Cooperation. Moreover, the implementation provisions of Enhanced Cooperation, which must also be taken over in case of participation, have not been adopted by all Member States. The new Treaty provisions on Enhanced Cooperation agreed in Nice explicitly state that the implementation decisions do not form part of the *acquis*.

### IV. Impact on the Integration Process

The long-term impact of Enhanced Cooperation on European integration is difficult to assess, as it will significantly depend on factors such as the speed of enlargement. There are, however, signs indicating that Enhanced Cooperation may accelerate the integration process without considerably affecting the

---

[88] For a detailed discussion of this possibility with a view to eastern enlargement, see A. Carius, I. von Homeyer, and S. Bär, *Die Umweltpolitische Dimension der Osterweiterung der Europäischen Union: Herausforderung und Chancen, Endbericht im Auftrag des Rates von Sachverständigen für Umweltfragen* (Berlin: Ecologic, Institute for International and European Environmental Policy, 1999).

homogeneity of the *acquis communautaire,* and without causing permanent divisions among Member States. At the same time, Enhanced Cooperation offers opportunities for supporting a high level of protection in the field of environmental protection. Three factors support this assessment: the 'threat effect' of Enhanced Cooperation, its 'pull effect', and the interests of the European institutions and the 'ins'.

### A. 'THREAT EFFECT' OF ENHANCED COOPERATION

One reason why Enhanced Cooperation may be expected to have only minor effects on the homogeneous legal area, is the fact that its 'threat effect' alone could suffice to ensure that the potential participants achieve satisfactory political results. In this case, the actual application of the instrument would not be necessary. Due to this 'threat effect', the potential participants could succeed, for example, in adopting a higher level of environmental protection in the conventional legislative procedure at the European level.

The 'threat effect' of Enhanced Cooperation consists of various aspects. First, non-participation in Enhanced Cooperation may be linked to loss of political prestige, and might be associated with the status of a 'second-rate' Member State. Moreover, the 'outs' may also have to bear additional political and economic costs. These essentially correspond to the ones which give rise to the 'pull effect' of Enhanced Cooperation discussed next.

Whether Enhanced Cooperation generates a 'threat effect', or whether it exerts a 'pull effect' after its establishment also depends on the concrete circumstances and political interests involved.

### B. 'PULL EFFECT' OF ENHANCED COOPERATION

Enhanced Cooperation may result in economic effects which could prompt manufacturers based in countries not participating in the Cooperation also to comply with the higher level of regulation for their entire production. In this context, important factors include the size of the market of the 'ins',[89] and the extent of additional costs for separate production lines for 'ins' and 'outs'.[90] Moreover, the cost of taking over the higher level of regulation decreases over time because of the depreciation of the initial investment in the development of new technologies. This stimulates the later accession of 'outs'. Apart from these factors, non-participation may also result in additional costs for 'outs', in particular with regard to catching up with technological developments, but the demand of final consumers may also shift towards more environmentally friendly products and production processes corresponding to the level of protection of Enhanced Cooperation.

---

[89] Cf. Sects. III.B–C.

[90] This argument, however, is valid only if the higher standards of the Enhanced Cooperation are equally applied to the 'outs'. The possibility suggested in Sects. III.B and III.C not to apply the higher standards in order to avoid discrimination is not taken into account here.

In addition to economic costs, the 'outs' may have to bear administrative and political costs. By establishing Enhanced Cooperation, the 'ins' create political and administrative constellations, which can subsequently hardly be reversed, since the relevant regulations have already been adopted and applied in practice by a significant number of Member States and the Commission. If, at some point, 'laggards' also wish to raise the level of environmental protection, they will, therefore, have to adopt the regulations of Enhanced Cooperation. The latecomers then face the problem that they cannot modify the type and level of the regulation in whose adoption they were not involved, safe for the authorization decision for Enhanced Cooperation. The consequences may be severe, since the rules of Enhanced Cooperation are geared towards the specific environmental conditions, political interests, administrative traditions, and technological trajectories in the states which established the Enhanced Cooperation in the first place.[91]

These effects result not only in a strong 'threat effect' of Enhanced Cooperation, but also provide an incentive for the 'outs' to join Enhanced Cooperation as soon as possible, since this is the only way to influence the further elaboration of the regulations. It may, however, also create incentives for laggard Member States to block the authorization of an Enhanced Cooperation, even if the establishment of the Enhanced Cooperation implied no direct costs for the laggards.

## C.  INTERESTS OF THE EUROPEAN UNION AND THE 'INS'

The European institutions not dominated by Member States, for example the Commission, the EP, and the ECJ have a strong institutional interest in preventing a sustained split of the Community. Therefore, if the homogeneity of the legal area is at risk due to Enhanced Cooperation, it is to be expected that these institutions will take measures to counter this tendency. For example, the 'outs' could be given assistance, permitting them to catch up with the 'ins' relatively soon. Within the context of its important role in the preparation of the proposal for Enhanced Cooperation, the Commission could try to include measures to that effect.[92] The EP could also use its influence on the authorization and implementation decisions of Enhanced Cooperation. Furthermore, the Commission decides on the participation of additional Member States in Enhanced Cooperation. By a generous interpretation of the requirements, it could mitigate the risk of a split in the Community.

It is to be expected that, in many cases, the 'ins' will also be interested in preventing a permanent split in terms of the level of regulation. This will be the case in particular if the lower level of regulation of the 'outs' gives them a competitive edge. In order to avoid sustained competitive disadvantages, the 'ins'

---

[91]  The interest in avoiding adaptation costs and competition for the position of pacemaker in the Community has already been an important motor of European environmental policy to date. Cf. Héritier, n. 59 above.

[92]  Cf. Ehlermann, n. 28 above, 379.

may well be ready to provide financial assistance to the 'outs', so that they can catch up with the higher level of regulation.

In spite of the complexities outlined above, the overall assessment of Enhanced Cooperation is positive, both with regard to the integration process, and a high level of protection in the environmental field. Enhanced Cooperation seems unlikely to cause erosion of the homogeneous legal area. Enhanced Cooperation could generate a 'threat effect', which may produce positive effects with respect to the level of environmental protection without rendering the actual establishment of Enhanced Cooperation necessary. Moreover, it is to be expected that the number of participants in any instance of Enhanced Cooperation will probably increase quickly due to its pull effect. Finally, there are significant incentives, both for the European institutions and the 'ins', to counter tendencies towards a sustained split, in particular by way of intensified support for the 'outs'. This should also allow the 'outs' to join in Enhanced Cooperation quickly.

## V. Conclusions

Despite the Treaty changes agreed at Nice, which were expected to clarify the ambiguity of many provisions relating to Enhanced Cooperation, the pre-requisites laid down in the Treaty for the implementation of Enhanced Cooperation in many cases require further interpretation. However, this does not undermine the instrument's practical applicability in EC environmental policy. The interpretation of remaining uncertain issues will be decisively influenced by the actors involved, in particular the Commission, the Member States, and the ECJ. The legal requirements permit the application of Enhanced Cooperation not only to entire policies, but also to individual legislative acts which cannot garner the required majority at European level, be it unanimity or qualified majority. Against this backdrop, Enhanced Cooperation particularly provides the opportunity to reduce cases of obstruction in the environmental field.

In environmental policy, potential fields of application for Enhanced Cooperation are product or process standards, regulations in the field of nature conservation and the promotion of biodiversity, horizontal measures and administrative procedures, as well as the implementation of international environmental agreements. The application of Enhanced Cooperation to environmental product standards is restricted, due to the importance of the internal market. Since process regulation has less effect on the internal market, this field of application appears more promising.

The instrument of Enhanced Cooperation offers new opportunities to advance the European integration process. The risk of a sustained split in the level of regulation is limited by the fact that there are numerous incentives for the countries not participating in Enhanced Cooperation to catch up with the 'leaders' relatively soon. At the same time, the European institutions and the participants of Enhanced Cooperation are interested in enabling the 'outs' also to pursue the level of regulation of Enhanced Cooperation.

From the perspective of environmental policy, and the integration process as such, the new instrument of Enhanced Cooperation is, on the whole, a positive tool. In particular with regard to the forthcoming enlargement of the EU, speedy utilization of the new instrument should be considered. Since the agreement of the Member States required for the authorization decision will be more difficult to achieve after the accession of additional countries, the current membership offers a unique opportunity to use Enhanced Cooperation in the further development of environmental policy, thus serving both European integration and the protection of the environment in Europe.

# Enforcing European Environmental Law: Can the European Commission be Held to Account?

RHIANNON WILLIAMS*

## I. Introduction

The European Commission is charged by the EC Treaty[1] with ensuring that the Treaty provisions and measures taken under it are applied. In the area of European Community (EC) environmental law, the Commission largely fulfils this task through the Article 226 procedure. It has been argued that the Commission's structure and method of working is inappropriate and inadequate for the performance of this task.[2] This is because the Commission legitimately performs a number of other, overtly political roles, but there is no formal division between these and its enforcement role. There is, therefore, the potential for political influence at every stage of an investigation or infringement procedure. Although Neil Kinnock, as Personnel Commissioner, is instituting various reforms, none of these is intended to impinge on the enforcement procedures. Indeed, the situation has, if anything, deteriorated. Despite criticism of the internal changes in DG Environment during the past few years,[3] further 'reforms' in recent months have done nothing to assuage concerns. The 'restructuring' of the Waste and Nature Directorates undertaken by British Director-General James Currie have led to suspicions that the two Directorates were perceived as being too zealous in their drafting and pursuit of the enforcement of EC environmental law to remain viable within the primarily political Commission.

The European Union (EU) is founded on four fundamental principles:[4] liberty; democracy; respect for human rights and fundamental freedoms; and the rule of law, principles which are common to Member States. In the light of the application of the principles of democracy and the rule of law, one would expect to see accountability of some sort of the Commission in its role as enforcer. This chapter will examine whether, if the Commission is not performing its enforcement function properly, it can be held to account effectively.

---

* Solicitor with Renouf & Co., European Law Firm, Brussels, and part-time Lecturer at the University of Liège, Belgium.

[1] Art. 211 EC.

[2] R. Williams, 'The European Commission and the Enforcement of Environmental Law: an Invidious Position' (1994) 14 *Yearbook of European Law*, 351.

[3] Ibid.       [4] Art. 6 TEU.

There are three basic areas of EC judicature which can fruitfully be examined. The first is the accountability of the Commission with regard to Article 226 EC proceedings, which will be examined in Section II. The second concerns the accountability of the Commission as an actor and enforcer bound by EC environmental law, which is further investigated in Section III. Section IV concerns access to documents relating to environmental law enforcement through Article 226 EC proceedings.

## II. The Accountability of the Commission with regard to Article 226 EC

A commonly made assumption is that the Commission has absolute discretion as to whether it brings infringement proceedings against a Member State. Cases like *Emrich*[5] and *Star-Fruit*[6] have long established that an individual does not have the right to challenge a Commission decision as to whether or not to bring a Member State before the European Court of Justice (ECJ) under the infringement procedure of Article 226 EC. The Council and individual Member States are most unlikely to try to do so for political reasons. But it is worth recalling the words of Article 211 EC: that the Commission *shall* ensure the application of EC primary and secondary law. In strict law, therefore, the Commission cannot have an absolute discretion, even though at present it does in practice. How might the law be developed in order to ensure that the Commission is effectively bound to comply with its Treaty obligations? One possibility would be the importation of a concept from English administrative law: that of an administration having the discretion to act so long as it does so within the range of reasonable responses. Where the Commission has a discretion to act, that discretion should be exercised, and there must, in an effective democracy, be control of that exercise. One method of redressing the current imbalance would be Treaty reform to enable either the European Parliament (EP), or possibly—to a limited extent—Non-Governmental Organizations (NGOs), to challenge decisions on Article 226 EC proceedings. This is not, sadly, realistically likely.

It is just possible that the ECJ might one day grant standing to an individual or NGO in such a case, if sufficiently grave, in order to ensure (as it is bound to do) that, 'in the interpretation and application of this Treaty the law is observed'.[7] At the moment, there is little prospect of any such development, given the ECJ's decision on the second area to be examined here.

## III. The Accountability of the Commission as an Actor Bound by European Community Law

The Commission is in charge of administering the Community Structural Funds at EC level. Its accountability in doing so will be examined here. Living

---

[5] Case 371/89, *Maria-Theresia Emrich* v. *Commission* [1990] ECR I–1555.
[6] Case 247/87, *Star Fruit Company SA* v. *Commission* [1989] ECR 291.       [7] Art. 220 EC.

in a democracy, we make certain assumptions regarding the accountability of the institutions which govern and represent us, both at national and EC level. For example, that they should be bound by the law, and should be accountable if they breach it.

Those assumptions and Treaty provisions are both made because if the law is not being observed, and if it cannot be enforced, it is worthless. And it is in this light that the case of *Greenpeace* v. *Commission*[8] should be examined. Commonly cited as a case concerning standing, its democratic implications are far greater. The reason why the final judgment in the case is so inadequate would appear to be because it concerns the accountability of the European Commission with regard to its compliance with EC law.

The case arose from the building in Spain of two new power stations. In March 1991 the Commission adopted a Decision granting Spain Structural Funds for the building of the power stations in the Canary Islands. The money was to be paid in four annual tranches between 1991 and 1994. Under the Decision, the Commission could reduce or suspend payment of the monies if an irregularity were shown. In December 1991 the Commission received a complaint alleging that works on one of the power stations were unlawful because there had been no prior environmental impact assessment, contrary to Directive 85/337/EEC on the Assessment of the Effects of Certain Public and Private Projects on the Environment.[9] In November the following year, the Commission received a second complaint, alleging that work had commenced on both power stations without the necessary prior impact assessment. The next month, two environmental assessments were published in Spain. A year later, in December 1993, Greenpeace Spain took legal action, challenging the authorizations granted to the developing company.

Meanwhile, in March 1993, Stichting Greenpeace Council (the Greenpeace of the case) had asked the Director-General of Regional Policies to confirm whether Community Structural Funds had been paid to Spain to fund the power stations, and asking what the timetable was for the release of the funds. He referred them to the Commission's Decision of March 1991. Greenpeace wrote back requesting more information in the light of Article 7 of Regulation (EC) No. 2052/88 on the Structural Funds. This provides that,

Measures financed by the Funds . . . shall be in keeping with the provisions of the Treaties, with the instruments adopted pursuant thereto and with Community policies, including those concerning . . . environmental protection.

The Commission refused to provide this information on the grounds that it concerned the internal decision-making procedures of the Commission.

A meeting of the parties failed to resolve the matter, and, in December 1993, Greenpeace and various private individuals began an action before the Court

---

[8] Case 321/95P, *Stichting Greenpeace Council (Greenpeace International) and others* v. *Commission* [1998] ECR I–1651.

[9] Council Dir. 85/337/EEC on the Assessment of the Effects of Certain Public and Private Projects on the Environment [1985] OJ L175/40.

of First Instance (CFI), seeking the annulment of the Commission's decision to disburse further monies to Spain after the alleged irregularities had been brought to its attention.

The action was brought under Article 230 EC, which provides that any natural or legal person may institute proceedings against a decision addressed to that person or against a decision which, although in the form of a regulation or a decision addressed to another person is of direct and individual concern to the former. Much of the case is about whether the applicants fulfilled that direct and individual concern test.

The Commission argued that the applicants lacked *locus standi*, and the CFI agreed. It examined the question separately with regard to the individual applicants (residents, fishermen, and farmers) and the applicant associations (NGOs).

In a clear exposition of existing case law, the CFI summarized how persons to whom a Decision is not addressed can only claim that it is of direct concern to them if it affects them by reason of certain attributes peculiar to them, or because of factual circumstances which differentiate them from everyone else in such a way that they are distinguished individually in the same way as the person addressed—a test developed through cases involving economic interests. The CFI was invited by the applicants to develop the existing case law on the basis that third-party applicants would otherwise suffer damage because of damage to the environment arising from unlawful conduct by EC institutions.

The CFI held that the relevant criteria held good whether the interests involved were economic or environmental. Harm *per se* could not confer *locus standi* on an applicant, because it could affect a large number of people who could not be determined in advance in such a way as to distinguish them individually: the 'floodgates' argument.

The applicant associations were also denied standing because of case law holding that such groups may not bring actions for annulment where their members cannot do so individually.

The applicants appealed to the ECJ on the grounds that in using this 'closed class' test, which was developed with regard to economic interests, the nature of the environmental concerns in the case had not been taken into account.

They put forward four arguments:

— that this approach creates a legal vacuum in ensuring compliance with EC legislation because, given the nature of environmental interests, there never could be a closed class of applicants;
— national and international law have largely moved towards allowing *locus standi* in such cases;
— environmental protection has been held to be one of the EC's 'essential objectives'; EC environmental legislation can create rights and obligations for individuals, and did so in this case through a combination of Directive 85/337/EEC and the March 1991 Decision; and,
— Article 230 EC should be reinterpreted to allow the standing of *persons* where:

(a) personal detriment will be caused by the illegal conduct of an EC institution; (b) the detriment is caused by the act; and (c) it can be redressed by an ECJ judgment, so as to allow the standing of *environmental associations* where their objectives concern chiefly environmental protection, one or more of their members is directly concerned by the decision, and where their primary objective is environmental protection and they can demonstrate a specific interest in the question at issue.

In other words, Article 230 EC must be interpreted in such a way as to safeguard fundamental environmental interests and protect individual environmental rights effectively.

The ECJ agreed with the reasoning of the CFI, which was unimpeachable in the light of existing case law.

However, in an extraordinarily short and inadequate judgment (ten pages in total, of which nine summarized facts and arguments, and one listed the Findings of the Court), the ECJ then veered off at a tangent. With regard to the special nature of environmental interests, the ECJ stated that it was the decision to *build* the power station which affected the environmental rights of the applicants *under Directive 85/337/EEC* (the CFI had been dealing with their rights under Article 230 EC). In those circumstances, the ECJ held, 'the contested decision, which concerns the EC financing of those power stations, can affect those rights *only indirectly*'.[10]

Money speaks pretty directly, however. If significant funding is being unlawfully released to finance a project, that project will probably go ahead faster than if the allocating authority withholds the cash on the ground that basic legal procedural safeguards have not been complied with. Such action would give affected individuals more time to launch any legal challenge, time during which irremediable damage to the environment could be avoided. That means that the impact on certain rights under EC law of decisions such as that taken by the Commission to continue funding may indeed be direct—whether those rights arise from a directive or from a regulation or from a Treaty provision.

The ECJ then considered what it described as the 'appellants' argument' that if the CFI's judgment were to stand, their rights 'derived from Directive 85/337/EEC would have no effective judicial protection at all'. The extraordinary thing is that there is nothing in the CFI judgment to this effect. The Advocate General's opinion refers to no such argument, and there is no reference to such argument elsewhere in the judgment of the ECJ. Either the ECJ was mistaken, or the point was raised during the oral hearing.

Having made that sudden assertion, the ECJ proceeded:

Although the subject-matter of those proceedings and of the action brought before the CFI is different, both actions are based on the same rights afforded to individuals by Directive 85/337, so that in the circumstances of the present case those rights are fully

---

[10] Emphasis added.

protected by the national courts which may, if need be, refer a question to this Court for a preliminary ruling under Article 177 (now Article 234) of the Treaty.

It then summarily dismissed the appeal.

This judgment is disingenuous in the extreme. The statement that both actions are based on rights afforded under Directive 85/337/EEC is inaccurate.

The action before national courts was indisputably based on rights afforded under the Directive. However, the applicants requested under Article 230 EC that the ECJ annul the Commission's March 1991 Decision on the grounds that it was an EC measure which unlawfully caused them loss. They did not request that it find there had been a breach of Directive 85/337/EEC. Of course, whether there had been such a breach was a necessary link in the fundamental legal argument, which would have followed had standing been granted. But the action regarding the question of standing was based on rights allegedly afforded under Article 230 EC, not the Directive, and warranted serious examination in that light. The CFI, in considering the question of standing, managed to do so in its findings without once mentioning Directive 85/337/EEC. It was not relevant to that issue. The applicants were concerned with their rights under EC Treaty law to hold the Commission to account for any loss-causing unlawful activity.

At paragraph 30 of the CFI judgment, it states that:

In order to establish that they are individually concerned, the applicants submit, primarily, that all individuals who have suffered or will suffer detriment or loss as a result of a Community measure which affects the environment have standing to bring an action under Article 230 EC of the Treaty and, in the alternative, that all individuals who have suffered or potentially will suffer 'particular' detriment or loss as a result of such a measure have that standing.

The CFI then goes on to consider the point without one reference to the question of the applicants' rights under Directive 85/337/EEC.

Moreover, Advocate General Cosmas points out three times[11] in his opinion that the case turns on the interpretation of the fourth paragraph of Article 230 EC. He also considers seriously the appellants' argument that the approach followed by the CFI creates a vacuum in the judicial protection afforded by the EC legal order, where the question arises of the compliance by EC institutions with EC environmental legislation.

Other parties could have brought a case against the Commission without having to jump the standing hurdle. Why did they not do so? The privileged applicants under Article 230 EC, are the Member States, the Council, and the Commission. It would be surprising if the Commission were to prosecute any action against itself. And when it comes to the allocation of Structural Fund monies, a complicated balancing and negotiating exercise will have taken place prior to the agreement on how to share out the cake. No individual Member State is therefore going to be tempted to upset the apple-cart without

[11] Opinion of Advocate General Cosmas of 23 Sept. 1997 in Case C–321/95P, n. 8 above, paras. 2, 18, and 47.

great personal provocation. Besides which, if the Commission is allowed to get away with sloppy and unlawful practice in one Member State, who knows when their own country may benefit equally? The Council is unlikely to act for the same reason. The EP can only act under Article 230 EC to protect its own prerogatives. The Ombudsman has no standing.

With regard to the rights of natural or legal persons, there was no concept of the need for the protection of the environment in the public interest when the EEC Treaty was first ratified. It works on the assumption that the defence of the individual interests of producers, traders, and competitors will promote the general interests of the EC. This is no longer acceptable. As Lord Diplock asserted in the *Fleet St Casuals* case:[12] 'it would in my view be a grave lacuna in our system of public law if a pressure group . . . were prevented by outdated technical issues of *locus standi* from bringing the matter to the attention of the court to vindicate the rule of law and get the unlawful conduct stopped.'

The Advocate General also demolishes the argument of the Commission and the Spanish authorities that the applicants could have secured adequate judicial protection if they had simply relied on seeking redress before the national courts. National courts have no jurisdiction to address the legality of or set aside the financing decision by the Commission.

The Advocate General wrote that, notwithstanding the apparent homogeneity of ECJ judgments, the ECJ does not profess to adhere to an entirely immutable point of view. It has shown that it will ease procedural obstacles where the specific nature of a case requires it in order to afford more comprehensive judicial protection (as it did for standing in *Les Verts*[13] and in *Sofrimport*,[14] where it was found to be possible to have a closed class within an open class).

The Advocate General seized the nettle and invited the ECJ to examine the possibility of 'taking a further step forward' and extending its case law on a point on which 'the need for advancement in the case law is brought into sharp relief': the definition of *individual concern*. He invited the ECJ to find that there could be a closed class of people affected more intensely and with graver consequences by an environmental intervention than the large numbers of persons inevitably affected in a general, objective, and abstract manner.

In the light of these points, it is most disappointing that the ECJ chose to ignore the issue. Perhaps the most charitable interpretation of the judgment would be that the judges were so divided on the point that they could not bring themselves to acknowledge it.

Some hope can at least be seen in the ECJ's apparent *myopia* with regard to the real issue: at least it was not examined and rejected. This leaves open the possibility of standing being granted in a similar case in future without the ECJ losing too much face. The problem is whether the environment or the EC's

---

[12] *R. v. IRC, ex p. National Federation of Self-Employed and Small Businesses Ltd* [1982] AC 617.
[13] Case 294/83, *Parti écologiste 'Les Verts' v. European Parliament* [1986] ECR 1339.
[14] Case C–152/88, *Sofrimport SARL v. Commission* [1990] ECR I–2477.

democratic credibility (as a Community governed by the rule of law) can afford to wait that long.

The ECJ is bound under Article 220 EC to ensure that in the interpretation and application of the Treaty the law is observed. The Commission is bound under Article 211 EC to ensure that the provisions of the Treaty and the measures taken by the institutions pursuant thereto are applied. There is a *lacuna* in EC law of the type to which Lord Diplock was referring in the quotation above. The Commission's role as 'Guardian of the Treaties' is untenable where there is a need to challenge its own decisions. This case deserved better from the ECJ.

Just a glance at recent EC documentation will show that this case does not exist in a vacuum. Not only is there no guarantee that the Commission will not breach Structural Funds rules with impunity again, but there are other areas where it is difficult to see how it could be brought to account. For example, Graham Watson, MEP, recently asked[15] about the following matter: Directive 94/62 EC on Packaging and Packaging Waste provides that, within ten years of its deadline for implementation under national law, a percentage of packaging waste—to be determined by the Council—will be recovered and recycled. At the latest six months before the end of the first five-year phase, the Council must, acting on a proposal from the Commission, fix targets for the second five-year phase. The Commission was asked to explain why it has not yet made a proposal in accordance with its duties under the Directive. The Commission's reply was that:

there are a large number of parties involved in the packaging chain including economic operators, consumers, environmental organizations and authorities with a wide variety of different interests, making it necessary to set up a framework for dialogue in order to ensure a balanced approach. This process is, however, enabling the Commission to evaluate the situation correctly and to develop possible solutions with the aim of making the Directive more effective. Several options have been presented and discussed with those concerned and the Member States, but the measures to be finally proposed by the Commission are still under consideration internally.

If a Member State tried to make such an argument for failing to transpose a directive on time, both the Commission and the ECJ would give it short shrift. Yet, the Commission can get away with such an approach because there is no person or body which is both willing and able to challenge it in court.

The Commission is no stranger to controversy surrounding its granting of Structural Fund monies. Another well-known case in this area is *WWF* v. *Commission*,[16] a case which, like the last, involves Article 7 of the Structural Funds Regulation. Unlike the *Greenpeace* case, however, the main focus of this one is access to documents, the final area of case law upon which this chapter will focus.

---

[15] Written Question E–1103/00 by Paul Lannoye on the Implementation of Directive 94/62/EC on Packaging [2001] OJ C53E/89.

[16] Case T–105/95, *WWF UK (World Wide Fund for Nature)* v. *Commission* [1997] ECR–II 313.

## IV. Access to Documents relating to the Enforcement of Environmental Law

It will be considered here whether there is any good reason why letters of formal notice and reasoned opinions should not be made public under Commission Decision 94/90/EC on public access to Commission documents.[17]

The case law concerning access to Commission documents concerning infringement procedures is not as clear as that considered above. The case law on access to documents in general, which are held by the EC institutions, is currently characterized by a gradual chipping-away at the monolith of with-held documentation in a series of recent cases.

It has been arguable for some time[18] that the Commission's enforcement function suffers from the ease with which political factors may impinge upon, (or—equally damagingly—wrongly be perceived to impinge upon) its integrity. In terms of democratic theory, it is vital for agents of legal enforce-ment to be independent. Examples of the application of this theory in practice crop up frequently. To take just one recent example from the United Kingdom (UK): the Attorney General, Lord Williams of Mostyn, QC, is to scrutinize the prosecuting powers of Customs and Excise, following a recently published report by John Gower, QC, and Sir Anthony Hammond, QC. This proposes that these powers should be brought into line with those of other prosecuting agencies, so as to ensure a clear division between prosecuting and investiga-tory roles. Decisions on prosecutions should be made by lawyers, and not by administrators, stresses the report, and the lawyers concerned must be 'inde-pendent both in reality and perception'.[19] It is of note that the UK, together with every Member State, continues to fail to argue for the application of these principles at EC level, presumably because the present situation is more advantageous. Within the Commission, the relevant decisions are regularly made not only by administrators, but also by career politicians (many of whom have come from and will return to national politics).[20]

To sum up the Commission's infringement procedure very briefly: there are three basic stages of document exchange between the Commission and a Member State before the Commission will apply to the ECJ. When a possible infringement of EC environmental law is brought to the attention of the Commission, acting in its role as guardian of the Treaty, it is initially investi-gated by means of informal letters of inquiry, to which the Member State is under a duty to reply. This is the first stage. If, following these informal exchanges, the Commission believes that an infringement appears to have taken place, it sends the Member State a letter of formal notice setting out why it believes so (the second stage). If the reply to this is deemed inadequate, a Reasoned Opinion is sent (the third stage), and if the reply to this is also

---

[17] [1994] OJ L46/58.   [18] Williams, n. 2 above.   [19] *The Times*, 13 Mar. 2001, 2.
[20] Williams, n. 2 above.

deemed unsatisfactory, the Commission may bring the Member State before the ECJ under Article 226 EC.

In such a situation, which is far from ideal for the reasons set out above, it might be assumed that some form of compensatory balance could be found, for example, via public access to information. It is arguable that if the public is fully informed about the decisions taking place, and the reasons for them, that might provide some counterbalance to a situation where administrators and politicians take decisions which should ideally be taken by independent lawyers charged with enforcement alone. Indeed, Declaration 17 in the Final Act of the Treaty on European Union (TEU) provides that, '[t]he Conference considers that transparency of the decision-making process strengthens the democratic nature of the institutions and the public's confidence in the administration'. It accordingly recommended a report on measures designed to improve public access to the information available to the institutions. This led on to the approval of Decision 94/90/EC on Public Access to Commission Documents.[21]

Under this decision it is provided that, 'The public will have the widest possible access to documents held by the Commission and the Council.' 'Document' is defined as meaning, 'any written text, whatever its medium, which contains existing data and is held by the Commission or Council'. There are two possible categories of grounds for rejecting a request for access to documents. The first is known as the 'mandatory category'. It provides that the institutions *will* refuse access to any document where disclosure could undermine, *inter alia*, 'the protection of the public interest (public security, international relations, monetary stability, court proceedings, inspections, and investigations)'. An institution *may* also refuse access in order to protect its interest in the confidentiality of its proceedings (the 'discretionary category'). An applicant applies to the relevant department of the institution concerned. If the application is rejected, the applicant has one month to make a confirmatory application to the institution, which has a further month in which to reply.

To what extent do the mandatory category's public interest exceptions for Court proceedings and inspections and investigations cover Reasoned Opinions and Letters of Formal Notice?

The Commission has traditionally refused access to all documents associated with investigations and infringement procedures on the grounds that none of them may be made available under the public interest exception. Is this attitude justified? In general, with criminal matters under investigation or prosecution, it is not in the public interest to have access to the documentation in the case, even if the public would be interested. But it is important not blindly to apply the correct answer to that question to all other legal procedural matters. When it comes to actions against Member States for infringement of EC environmental law, it is *our* government which is answerable, and

---

[21] See n. 17 above.

the protection of *our* environment which is at stake. Why should we not know rather more about what is happening than in the average criminal prosecution of individuals? The cases against Member States range from quite complicated ones, involving commercial and other interests, to simple legal issues where a Member State has failed to introduce transposing legislation. At the simpler end of the scale, it is hard to see any justification for withholding a Reasoned Opinion from the public.

It is arguable that the flurry of recent case law on access to documents held by the institutions provides the means to force the Commission to provide access to some Reasoned Opinions at least.

The interpretation of Decision 94/90/EC on Access to Commission Documents was at issue in *WWF* v. *Commission*.[22] WWF had already lost actions brought before the CFI and the ECJ in which it had challenged, firstly, a decision by the Commission not to bring infringement proceedings against Ireland for breach of EC environmental law, and, secondly, the possible wrongful use of Structural Funds by Ireland for the same project (the building of a visitors' centre at Mullaghmore in the Burren National Park).[23] WWF then wrote to the Commission asking for all Commission documents relating to the examination of the project and concerning the internal Commission consideration of whether Structural Funds could be disbursed for it. WWF wrote separately in this regard to DGs Environment and Regional Policies.

DG Environment replied that they would not supply the documents because they fell within the exceptions to the general principle of access, namely: protection of the public interest (with regard to investigations); and the protection of the Commission's interest in the confidentiality of its own proceedings. DG Regional Policies argued solely that they could not provide access because of the need to protect the confidentiality of their own proceedings. Confirmatory applications were made to the Secretary-General and similarly refused.

The applicants appealed to the CFI on the grounds of breach of Decision 94/90/EC. They also applied, under Article 253 EC, for the annulment of the Commission's decision on the ground that it had failed to state its reasons for refusal.

The CFI held that, in respect of the non-mandatory reasons for refusing access, the Commission must balance the interests involved *and* provide reasons for withholding any documents. To the extent to which it fails to do so, its decisions will be annulled. With regard to the mandatory category of exceptions to the principle of access, these must be strictly construed and applied. It also held that the Commission must refuse access to anything in the mandatory category once the relevant circumstances are shown to exist. It held that within this category lay 'documents relating to investigations which may lead

[22] See n. 16 above.
[23] Cases T–461/93, *An Taisce—The National Trust for Ireland and World Wide Fund for Nature* v. *Commission* [1994] ECR II–733 and C–325/94P, *An Taisce—The National Trust for Ireland and World Wide Fund for Nature UK (WWF)* v *Commission* [1996] ECR I–3727.

to an infringement procedure'.[24] For categories of documents at the very least, held the CFI, the Commission must explain why they are related to a possible infringement procedure, give the subject matter, and say if they involve inspections or investigations, though not to the extent that the contents of the documents are disclosed.

Following these general points, the Court found that, with regard to the DG Regional Policies refusal, there had been no genuine balancing of interests because neither letter referred to any such balancing. For the DG Environment refusal, the Court found that there had been no mention of any balancing of interests, which was necessary because the letters had not stated that all the documents concerned the mandatory public interest exception. So WWF won its case. So far, so good. But it was more a victory of form than of content because when WWF repeated its requests of the Commission following the judgment, the Commission now knew how to couch its letters of refusal properly, and did so in such a way which left WWF none the wiser, and without any possibility of further recourse to the ECJ.

The Commission's discretion, held the CFI, is to strike a genuine balance between the interest of the citizen in gaining access to those documents, and its own interest in protecting the confidentiality of its deliberations. With regard to infringement procedures, found the Court, where documents concerning investigations into a possible breach of EC law, potentially leading to the opening of an Article 226 EC procedure are concerned, the Commission can rely on the public interest exception because of the confidentiality which Member States are entitled to expect of the Commission in such circumstances.

This appears to have been interpreted by the Commission to mean that all documents concerning infringement procedures are automatically excepted from the presumption of access to documents. But the important question is: at what level do the 'investigations' stop, and the infringement procedures begin? Before a Letter of Formal Notice, or before a Reasoned Opinion? In addition, did the Court really mean that where a Member State has, for example, failed to transmit any transposing legislation for a given directive by the deadline set, that any letter sent by the Commission about the matter prior to the Member State being brought before the ECJ is going to prejudice the relationship of confidentiality? If so, it would be ridiculous when lists of transposing measures received by the Commission are publicly available from it, and any citizen interested in such matters could easily work out by the deadline for transposition whether a Member State has indeed transmitted to the Commission the necessary legislation.

There is no definition of the public interest *per se* in these cases, but there is something very near a definition in the *WWF* case. The CFI found that the first category (mandatory exceptions) 'effectively protects the interest of third parties or of the general public in cases where disclosure of particular documents

---

[24] Case T–105/95, n. 16 above, para. 63.

by the institution concerned would risk causing harm to persons who could legitimately refuse access to the documents if held in their own possession. On the other hand, in the second category, relating to the internal deliberations of the institution, it is the interest of the institution alone which is at stake.'[25]

The reasoning for the mandatory exceptions category does not appear to provide any reason why Reasoned Opinions or Letters of Formal Notice (Article 226 EC Letters) should not benefit from a presumption that they should be made public, with the proviso that any letter or part of a letter which could cause the harm referred to be held back.

Later cases add more to our understanding of how the Decision should be interpreted. *Netherlands and Van der Wal* v. *Commission*,[26] arose from a Commission Notice on cooperation between national governments and the Commission in applying Articles 81 and 82 EC. A lawyer requested copies of some of the Commission's replies to questions from national courts on competition law, which concerned the cooperation procedure arising from the Commission Notice. The existence of these had been reported in the 24th Competition Policy Report. Following the confirmatory application, the Secretary-General refused access on the grounds that disclosure would undermine the protection of the public interest and the sound administration of justice—it would undermine the cooperation between the Commission and the national courts.

The national courts were able to ask the Commission for three types of information: that of a procedural nature; points of law; and information of a factual nature. The ECJ held that, with documents not specially prepared for the case, the Commission must, for each document, assess whether it falls within the exceptions set out in Decision 94/90/EC. However, legal or economic analysis drafted on the basis of data supplied by a national court is subject to national procedural rules on expert reports, which may preclude their disclosure. In such cases, the Commission must consider whether it can disclose, and if it can, it must then ask a national judge whether it would be an infringement of national law to do so. In other words, legal analyses where the Commission acts as a legal adviser to a national court can be disclosed if all the necessary safeguards are observed. Nothing in this judgment rules out the possibility of disclosure of Reasoned Opinions or Letters of Formal Notice by the Commission.

In *Svenska Journalistförbundet* v. *Council*,[27] the applicant was the Swedish journalists' union. It brought the case to test rights on access to documents about the setting up of Europol. The CFI held that if the Council refuses to grant public access to documents, its statement of reasons must contain—for each category of documents, if not each document concerned—the reasons why those documents fell within the exceptions on the grounds of the public interest and the confidentiality of the Council's proceedings. It pointed out

---

[25] Case T–105/95, n. 16 above, para. 60.
[26] Joined Cases C–174/98P and C–189/98P, *Kingdom of the Netherlands and Gerard van der Wal* v. *Commission* [2000] ECR I–1.
[27] Case T–174/95, *Svenska Journalistförbundet* v. *Council* [1998] ECR II–2289.

that if there is no explanation as to why disclosure would be liable to prejudice a particular aspect of public security, the applicant cannot defend its interests, and the CFI cannot assess which exception is applicable for each document. This is important, held the CFI, because it is necessary to check whether the institution has complied with its duty to make a comparative analysis, seeking to balance the interests of citizens and the confidentiality of the institution's proceedings.

The CFI explained that rules against the misuse of pleadings and evidence reflect a general principle in the due administration of justice: that parties have the right to defend their interests free from all external influences, particularly on the part of members of the public. So if someone is granted access to procedural documents (for example, those of the defence), they can be used only to pursue that party's own case, and not for other purposes such as to invite public criticism of the other party's arguments.

Could such an argument be used to prevent all public access to Reasoned Opinions and Letters of Formal Notice sent to Member States by the Commission? The situations can be sharply distinguished. A compliance action against a Member State has little in common with an action involving private parties, and different considerations arise.

To argue that no access to such documentation should be allowed is to perpetuate the antiquated theory that the relations between the Commission and individual Member States should proceed more in the nature of international than EC law. This approach cannot work if the EC is to develop as a democracy fundamentally based on law, rather than one sadly dependent on political compromise.

In most court cases at national level, the enforcing body is independent of the executive and of politicians, and there is less need for openness to ensure that legal arguments are not being suppressed for political reasons.

Cases against governments are not comparable to those against individuals. Our governments represent us. There is something of a fiduciary duty there. Why should we not know in what respect our representatives are alleged to have broken the law? In a democracy, embarrassment is simply not good enough as a reason for withholding information.

If the issue is in the public domain, especially if it appears there after all investigations have taken place, that cannot influence the Member State's duty to answer any questions from the Commission in that or in any other case—it will remain under a legal duty to do so under Article 10 EC.

On the question of the mandatory exceptions, the CFI in *Svenska* held, on the question of the undermining of the public interest, that an institution must refuse a request for access to documents if they fall within one of the exceptions in this category *once* the relevant circumstances are shown to exist.[28] This echoes the *Carvel* case,[29] which used the phrase, 'where certain circumstances

---

[28] Para. 111.
[29] Case T–194/94, *John Carvel and Guardian Newspapers Ltd* v. *Council* [1995] ECR II–2765, para. 64.

exist'. The ECJ held that the use of the word *could* in the Decision shows that, in order to demonstrate that the disclosure of particular documents could undermine the protection of the public interest, the Council *must* consider, in respect of each requested document, whether disclosure is likely to undermine the public interest.[30] The reasoning behind this case could be transferred to Reasoned Opinions and Letters of Formal Notice, on the grounds that access to them should not be refused because of their nature *per se*.

*Kuijer* v. *Council*,[31] concerns Council Decision 93/731/EC,[32] the equivalent of Commission Decision 94/90/EC. The relevant words are identical to those in Commission Decision 94/90/EC, as both Decisions incorporated the Code of Conduct which the Commission and the Council had jointly adopted on 6 December 1993.[33] The applicant was an academic working in the area of asylum and immigration. He asked for documents concerning the Centre for Information, Reflection and Exchange on Asylum (CIREA). Most of the documents concerned were individually refused on the grounds of the exception concerning international relations. The Council argued that the very detailed information contained in them could endanger EU/bilateral relations with the countries concerned. The applicant argued that the Council was in breach of its duties to provide reasons under Article 7(3) of the Decision and Article 253 EC, which sets out the criteria for a statement of reasons in individual decisions. These, held the ECJ, are to enable interested parties to protect their own interests, and to enable the Community court to exercise its jurisdiction to review a decision. Article 253 EC is breached if it is impossible to ascertain whether the necessary balancing of interests has taken place. In respect of each, it must be considered whether the public interest is likely to be undermined (*Svenska*).[34] Here, although the documents were of differing degrees of sensitivity, the reasons given for each were the same. In addition, the Council had not responded to the points in the confirmatory application which set out why the applicant believed that the Council's fears were unjustified. The Council's decision was therefore annulled.

The applicant also argued that the Council had acted unlawfully because no partial access had been granted. In accordance with the *Hautala* case,[35] it was held that Article 4(1) of Decision 53/731/EC must be interpreted in the light of the principle of the right to information and the principle of proportionality. As the Council was bound in any event to carry out a specific assessment of the risk to the public interest of disclosure, the removal of sensitive passages would not be too great a burden. This case still leaves open the possibility of allowing access to at least some Reasoned Opinions and Letters of Formal Notice.

---

[30] Citing Case T–124/96, *Interporc Im- und Export GmbH* v. *Commission* [1998] ECR II–231 and Case T–83/96, *Gerard van der Wal* v. *Commission* [1998] ECR II–545.
[31] Case T–188/98, *Aldo Kuijer* v. *Council* [2000] ECR II–1959.
[32] Council Decision 93/731/EC on Public Access to Council Documents [1993] OJ L340/43.
[33] [1993] OJ L340/41.      [34] See n. 27 above.
[35] Case T–14/98, *Heidi Hautala* v. *Council,* [1999] ECR II–2489.

Yet another application for the annulment of a decision not to provide access to information was considered in *Bavarian Lager Co.* v. *Commission.*[36] The applicant tried to import German beer for sale in British pubs. It alleged an infringement of EC legislation: that British legislation regarding what could be sold constituted a quantitative restriction on imports, contrary to Article 28 EC.

The Commission began Article 226 EC proceedings against the UK. It sent a Letter of Formal Notice, decided to send a Reasoned Opinion, and made a press statement to that effect. Then the UK announced a proposed amendment to the legislation in question. The Commission suspended the procedure without having sent the Reasoned Opinion. The new legislation came into force, and the Commission closed the file. The applicant requested the Reasoned Opinion. DG Internal Market and Financial Services refused the application, claiming that it fell within the public interest exception. The reasons the Commission gave were that allowing access would:

— harm the administration of justice in the implementation of EC law;
— compromise the treatment of infringements; and
— undermine the climate of mutual confidence necessary for full and frank discussion between the Commission and a Member State with a view to ensuring compliance by that Member State with its Treaty obligations.

The applicant made a confirmatory application. The Secretary-General refused it on the grounds that allowing access could undermine the protection of the public interest, in particular with regard to Commission inspections and investigations. It was argued that there needs to be sincere cooperation and a climate of mutual confidence between the Commission and the Member State, allowing for both to engage in the process of negotiation and compromise in the search for a settlement to a dispute at an early stage.

The CFI held, contrary to the Commission's assertions, that it did not follow from the case law, in particular the *WWF* case, that all documents linked to infringement procedures are covered by the public interest exception. Access to documents may be refused with regard to investigations which may lead to an infringement procedure. It was wrong in fact and in law to classify the document as a Reasoned Opinion. The draft Reasoned Opinion was drawn up after the Commission made the decision to send one. So it was a purely preparatory document. Under a Communication of March 1994,[37] anyone can ask for access to any unpublished Commission document, including preparatory documents and any other explanatory material. In this case, the Article 226 EC procedure was still at the stage of inspection and investigation. The CFI held that a Member State can expect confidentiality from the Commission during investigations which may lead to an infringement procedure. The

---

[36] Case T–309/97, *The Bavarian Lager Company Ltd* v. *Commission* [1999] ECR II–3217.

[37] Communication from the Commission on Improved Access to Documents, [1994] OJ C67/3. This explains the conditions for implementation of Commission Decision 94/90/EC, ECSC, Euratom on Public Access to Commission Documents.

disclosure of documents relating to that stage could undermine the proper conduct of the infringement procedure inasmuch as its purpose could be jeopardized. The purpose is to enable the Member State to comply of its own accord with Treaty requirements or, if appropriate, to justify its position.[38] The safeguarding of that objective warrants the refusal of access to a preparatory document regarding the investigation stage of Article 226 EC procedures.

This ruling is most helpful as it goes much further in clarifying the meaning of 'investigations' in Decision 94/90/EC. Significantly, the CFI refers to the refusal of access to *a* preparatory document being warranted. It does not say *all* preparatory documents. This could be interpreted to mean that the Commission should examine *individually* all preparatory documents in respect of which access has been requested. To return to a point made above: it is difficult to see how access to a Letter of Formal Notice, in a case where no legislation at all has been received for the transposition of a directive, could in any way prejudice the public interest or the purpose of the infringement procedure.

The negative aspect of the judgment is that it appears to rule out the possibility of the public gaining access to most Letters of Formal Notice. The positive and exciting side to the judgment is that it leaves wide open the possibility of arguing that a Reasoned Opinion is not part of the investigations which may lead to an infringement procedure. Which leads on to various questions: *is* a Reasoned Opinion part of the investigations? Is it part of the infringement procedure? It is not part of the court proceedings, though its contents limit the scope of any action before the ECJ which the Commission may choose to bring. Does it stand *sui generis*? Where exactly does the infringement procedure start?

Furthermore, it is indeed possible to argue that there is a public interest in settling matters, and there must therefore be respect for a certain level of confidentiality. However, if all is settled behind closed doors in such cases, many issues which are raised and settled will never be seen by the public. How many interesting points are settled in such a way? And how? The ECJ would necessarily remain the final arbiter on issues of EC law—it is not being argued here that the Commission's opinion would be final—but knowing about the existence of many legal issues would be in the public interest, as would knowing how the Commission and Member States had resolved them. The Commission's ability to compromise would not be challenged because of its discretion as to whether or not to bring Article 226 EC proceedings. Finally, how can it be assessed whether such matters were settled for legal or political reasons? There are compelling reasons there for allowing some form of access to the documents concerned. The law at present fails to protect that side of the public interest.

And once again, not only is the Member State representative of the people, but the Commission's function is paid for out of public money. To deny the public the chance to know what much of their money is spent on, in cases

---

[38] Case C–191/95, *Commission v. Germany* [1998] ECR I–5449.

concerning their environment, and against their elected representatives, is disdainful at best, corrupting at worst.

*Interporc* v. *Commission*[39] is not helpful in this regard. It concerned a spat between Interporc and Germany over the recovery of import duty on beef imports. The Commission supported Germany. Interporc requested access to documents on the matter. In the first *Interporc* case,[40] the CFI held that the Commission's statement of reasons not to provide access to the documents requested was inadequate. It was annulled. Here, the Commission again refused access to the documents on the basis of the public interest exception regarding the proper conduct of court proceedings because all the documents concerned pending legal proceedings. These concerned an action before the CFI for annulment of the Commission's decision that import duty was not refundable. If disclosed, argued the Commission, it would damage the interests of the parties. The CFI held[41] that the objective of Decision 94/90/EC was to make the EC more open. Transparency of the decision-making process strengthens the democratic nature of the institutions and the public's confidence in the administration.[42] The 1993 Code of Conduct produced by the Commission and the Council aimed to allow the public 'the widest possible access to documents' to enable citizens to carry out genuine and efficient monitoring of the exercise of the powers vested in the EC institutions. So far, so good.

The CFI went on to hold that, in view of the aims of the Decision, and the requirement to interpret the exception strictly, 'court proceedings' must be interpreted as meaning that the protection of the public interest precludes the disclosure of the content of documents drawn up by the Commission solely for the purpose of specific court proceedings.

The CFI defined 'documents drawn up by the Commission solely for the purpose of specific court proceedings' as comprising:

— the pleadings or other documents lodged;
— internal documents concerning the investigation of the case before the Court;
— correspondence concerning the case between the Directorate-General concerned and the Commission's Legal Service or a lawyer's office.[43]

The 'purpose of the definition', held the CFI, was to ensure three things: the protection of the work done within the Commission; confidentiality; and the safeguarding of professional privilege for lawyers.

What the CFI meant exactly by the first two subjects listed as being in need of protection is far from clear. The CFI did concede that the exception does not allow the Commission to escape from its obligation to disclose documents drawn up in connection with a purely administrative matter—even if the disclosure of such documents in proceedings before the EC judicature might be

---

[39] Case T–92/98, *Interporc Im- und Export GmbH* v. *Commission* [1999] ECR II–3521.
[40] Case T–124/96, n. 28 above.                     [41] Para. 39.
[42] The reasoning being drawn from a Declaration to the Maastricht Treaty.          [43] Para. 41.

prejudicial to the Commission. Despite this one nod in the direction of democratic accountability, in this case the CFI appears to have lost sight of the meaning of the test of public interest.

Why did it take this approach? It does not follow from the wording of the Code of Conduct that the interpretation has to be so sweeping. As it was held in *Kuijer*—a more recent case—each document must be considered individually to see whether its disclosure would undermine the public interest. That, combined with the strong emphasis in *Svenska* on the meaning of 'could' in Decision 94/90/EC, leads to the conclusion that *Interporc* should in these respects be reinterpreted in the light of the more recent and better-reasoned judgments of the CFI. *Svenska* was cited approvingly in *Kuijer*:

It is also clear from the case law of the Court of First Instance that the Council is obliged to consider, in the case of each document to which access is sought, whether, in the light of the information available to the Council, disclosure is in fact likely to undermine one of the facets of public interest protected by the first category of exceptions.[44]

*Interporc* was not mentioned.

In any event, it would appear that Reasoned Opinions do not fall into the definition of 'documents drawn up by the Commission solely for the purpose of specific court proceedings'. They are drawn up, as the Commission acknowledged in *Bavarian Lager Co.* v. *Commission* (in which access to a draft Reasoned Opinion was unsuccessfully requested), with the ultimate aim of facilitating the 'process of negotiation and compromise in the search for a settlement to a dispute at an early stage'.

Indeed, it is difficult to see why the CFI was of the opinion that all pleadings ought—as has long been the practice for cases heard before the Community courts—automatically to be precluded from disclosure on the grounds of protection of the public interest. In the first place, it would seem logical for them also to be subjected to individual consideration and assessment. Why should it be against the public interest to make publicly available pleadings concerning a simple failure to transpose on time? In the second place, and rather more radically, why should there not be a presumption that all pleadings should be made public unless there are particular circumstances which warrant their confidentiality? Many pleadings for civil cases in the UK are automatically publicly available. The salient contents of pleadings submitted to the CFI and the ECJ are set out in the summary note published in the OJ 'C' series, more information will be provided in the report for the hearing, yet more at the oral hearing, and it will all be duly reported in the case report. What legitimate benefit would the Commission, the Member State, or the public interest lose following the publication of most pleadings concerning the enforcement of environmental law? It is to be hoped that the CFI will reassess this situation and *Interporc* in the light of its more recent judgments, the need for more efficient environmental protection, and the Commission's lack of accountability.

---

[44] Case T–188/98, n. 31 above, para. 37.

*Denkavit* v. *Commission*[45] concerns an application for the annulment of a Commission decision refusing access to a report concerning measures taken to combat swine fever in the Netherlands. The Commission refused access on the grounds of the public interest exception and the commercial secrecy exception. Just the first will be examined here. It was the only one relevant to the reasons given by the Commission for refusing access to Reasoned Opinions, and the CFI did not pronounce judgment on the commercial secrecy argument. The Commission justified its refusal on the grounds of the public interest in two ways. First, it said that it needed to preserve a relationship based on mutual trust with the Netherlands during the inspection period. Second, the Commission claimed that possible court proceedings against the Netherlands might be prejudiced if access to the report were to be granted. The applicant argued that by the time the contested decision was adopted, the investigation had already been closed, so there was no further need for consultation with the Netherlands. In addition, the applicant dismissed the alleged risk to possible court proceedings on the grounds that the Netherlands already had a copy of the report, and it was already publicly known that there were differences of opinion between the Member State and the Commission.

The CFI found that although the document concerned an inspection, that cannot in itself justify the application of the exception involved. It cited *Netherlands and Van der Wal* v. *Commission* as establishing that any exception to the right of access to Commission documents covered by Decision 94/90/EC must be interpreted and applied strictly. However, it found that the Commission could properly form the view that the inspection work which remained to be carried out in the Netherlands required that the report should be withheld in order to 'preserve the climate of mutual trust essential to the smooth conduct of that procedure'.[46] The CFI therefore dismissed the application.

Does a Reasoned Opinion qualify as part of an ongoing investigation? It would seem not, because the Commission bases any application it makes to the ECJ on the Reasoned Opinion. It is a document clarifying the legal issues which the Commission believes to be at stake. It is not a document 'relating to investigations which *may* lead to an infringement procedure',[47] as once a Reasoned Opinion has been issued, the investigations are over. Whether it constitutes the commencement of that infringement procedure or stands *sui generis* is as yet undecided in EC law. This conclusion is supported by the CFI in *Bavarian Lager*, where it finds that, as the Commission had suspended its decision to deliver the Reasoned Opinion, it was 'clear that the procedure under Article 169 of the Treaty was still at the stage of inspection and investigation'.[48] If the CFI had believed that the Reasoned Opinion constituted part of that stage, it would not have needed to make that point.

---

[45] Case T–20/99, *Denkavit Nederland* v. *Commission* judgment of 13 Sept. 2000, not yet reported.
[46] Joined Case C–174/98P and C–189/98P, n. 26 above, para. 49.
[47] Case T–105/95, n. 16 above, para. 63 (emphasis added).
[48] Case T–309/1997, n. 36 above, para. 46.

In *JT's Corporation Ltd* v. *Commission*,[49] the applicant sought the annulment of a Commission decision refusing access to documents. The request for access arose out of a dispute as to post-clearance demands for customs duty. With regard to the requested mission reports and correspondence sent by the Commission to the Government of Bangladesh, the CFI found that the Commission's decision not to allow access to them was vitiated by manifest errors in the application of Decision 94/90/EC. The Commission had, in its decision, given no indication that any examination had taken place as to the possibility of granting partial access. Indeed, the Commission had reasoned by reference to categories of documents and not on the basis of the actual information contained in the documents in question, contrary to *Hautala*.[50] For this reason it was also in infringement of Article 253 EC

On 22 February 2000 the author wrote to the Commission requesting, under Decision 94/90/EC, copies of all Letters of Formal Notice and Reasoned Opinions sent to the UK in the course of procedures for infringement of EC environmental law from January 1995 to the date of the request. The reply from DG Environment, dated 17 March 2000, stated that:

Disclosure of the letters of formal notice and or of the reasoned opinions could undermine the proper conduct of infringement procedures based on Article 226 of the EC Treaty (ex 169) inasmuch as their purpose, which is to enable the Member State to comply of its own accord with the requirements of the Treaty or, if appropriate, to justify its position, could be jeopardised. In the matter of investigation of infringements, sincere cooperation and a climate of mutual confidence between the Commission and the Member State concerned (UK) are required, which allow for both parties to engage in a process of negotiation and compromise with the search for a settlement to a dispute without bringing it before the Court of Justice. The safeguarding of this objective warrants, under the heading of the protection of public interest, the refusal of access to the documents requested.

This was fascinating. First, there appears to be a breach of Decision 94/90/EC in that the Commission has, just as in *JT's Corporation*, reasoned by reference to categories of documents and not on the basis of the actual information contained in the documents in question, contrary to *Hautala*.[51] For this reason it also appears to be in infringement of Article 253 EC.

Second, DG Environment's assertion that the purpose of the Article 226 EC infringement procedure is to enable the Member State to comply with the Treaty of its own accord or to justify its position is striking. Article 226 EC reads:

If the Commission considers that a Member State has failed to fulfil an obligation under this Treaty, it shall deliver a reasoned opinion on the matter after giving the State concerned the opportunity to submit its observations.

If the State concerned does not comply with the opinion within the period laid down by the Commission, the latter may bring the matter before the Court of Justice.

---

[49] Case T–123/99, *JT's Corporation* v. *Commission*, judgment of 12 Oct. 2000, not yet reported.
[50] Case T–14/98, n. 35 above, paras. 87–8.　　　　　[51] Ibid.

The definition in the letter of the purpose of the Article is taken from *Commission* v. *Germany*.[52] The potential referred to does constitute part of the purpose of the Article, but surely not its sole purpose? Article 226 EC appears primarily to have been inserted to enable the Commission to fulfil its duties under Article 211 EC to ensure that Member States comply with EC law. The Commission's ultimate power to bring the matter before the ECJ would be a redundant part of the Article if its sole purpose was to enable the Member State to comply with the EC Treaty of its own accord or to justify its position.

It is of concern that 'cooperation and a climate of mutual confidence between the Commission and Member States' are focused on by DG Environment to the exclusion of the Commission's enforcement role. 'Negotiation' and 'compromise' in searching for a settlement to a dispute without bringing it before the ECJ smack rather worryingly of political, rather than legal priorities. The law and its enforcement should be the Commission's primary aim, not an overriding desire to avoid confrontation in court. Enforcement agencies should enforce, not negotiate and compromise routinely and overridingly in order to avoid embarrassment to a Member State. At the point when a Reasoned Opinion has been sent, the issues have usually come down to differences in the interpretation of laws. If the Commission believes that it is right, it should not be negotiating or compromising at this stage. If the need for negotiation and compromise at the post-Reasoned Opinion stage is meant to refer only to the Member State, it is somewhat difficult to negotiate on one's own, and though a Member State might go on to compromise, why should the public not know about it? If there is a serious disagreement between the Commission and a Member State over a point of law, once the information-gathering stage is over, there is overwhelming public interest in being informed about the issue, for the sake of clarity in the understanding of the law, and its application to the protection of our environment. There is also a legitimate public interest in knowing what an elected representative government and an unelected bureaucracy have been spending their money and time on.

There are good arguments in favour of withholding documentation relating to the investigation part of an infringement procedure, but those given by DG Environment here do not qualify as such. Such a misguided approach by the Commission only lends support to suspicions that compromises on important legal points may be reached for political reasons, and strengthens the need to promote greater transparency of infringement procedures within the Commission.

The author applied on 18 April 2000 for a review of DG Environment's decision. The reply was dated 8 May 2000. Carlo Trojan confirmed the refusal of access 'for the reasons explained' by Georges Kremlis of DG Environment. He stated that this view was:

---

[52] Case C–191/95, n. 38 above, para. 44.

entirely compatible with the judgments of the Court of First Instance in Cases T–105/95 (*WWF-UK* v. *Commission*) and T–309/97 (*Bavarian Lager* v. *Commission)*, which state that the Court considers that the confidentiality which the Member States are entitled to expect of the Commission in such circumstances warrants, under the heading of protection of the public interest, a refusal of access to documents relating to investigations which may lead to an infringement procedure, even where a period of time has elapsed since the closure of the investigation.

The criticisms of Mr Kremlis's letter remain applicable, and as has been argued above, the applicability of the public interest exception to Reasoned Opinions was not judicially determined in the cases cited by Mr Trojan. Therefore, it remains arguable that, having reasoned by reference to categories of documents and not on the basis of the actual information contained in the documents in question, contrary to *Hautala*, paragraphs 87 and 88, the Commission appears to be in infringement of Decision 94/90/EC and Article 253 EC.[53]

This situation could provide the opportunity for an organization concerned with law enforcement or environmental protection, for example, to find a member (if necessary one who could claim legal aid or its equivalent) in order to challenge the Commission's stance in this matter.

## V. Conclusion

The cases considered above demonstrate three areas concerning the enforcement of EC environmental law where the Commission appears at present to be almost entirely unaccountable: the accountability of the Commission with regard to Article 226 EC infringement proceedings; the accountability of the Commission as an actor bound by EC law; and access to documents regarding the enforcement of EC environmental law.

The EC is purportedly based on democratic principles. This claim is void unless those principles are put into effect.

There are at least three possible avenues which might allow for development of the accountability of the Commission: Treaty reform; the development of case law by the ECJ and the CFI; and the application of the Aarhus Convention.[54] This was signed by the EC and fourteen of its Member States in June 1998. On the question of standing, the Convention is much broader than Article 230 EC. It provides for standing in environmental matters 'to challenge the substantive and procedural legality of any decision, act or omission', with certain provisos, for members of the 'public concerned' and either 'having a sufficient interest' or 'maintaining impairment of a right, where the administrative procedural law of a Party requires this as a precondition' where required

[53] See n. 48 above.
[54] The 1998 UNECE Convention on Access to Information, Public Participation in Decision-Making and Access to Justice in Environmental Matters (Aarhus, 25 June 1998), published on the Internet at: http://www.unece.org/env/.

by a party's law. Exceptions to the right of access to information in environmental matters apply where that access would have an adverse effect on the
course of justice, a fair trial, or a public authority's ability to conduct an
enquiry of a criminal or disciplinary nature. Material 'in the course of completion' can be withheld if it is so provided in national law or 'customary practice'.
There are a number of problems concerning the interpretation of the
Convention, in particular the need to clarify a number of its provisions.

The Commission's Legal Service takes the view that all national and EC laws
must be amended to reflect the requirements of the Convention before it can
be ratified by the EC. Given that all the three areas covered by the Convention
are controversial—it is difficult to conceive of three such difficult areas combined in any one other convention—and much of the necessary new legislation will have to go through the co-decision procedure, it has been estimated
by Commission officials that, although the EC formally hopes to be able to
ratify the Convention by 2002 or 2003, it is not likely to be ratified for at least
ten years.

The necessary Treaty reform is highly unlikely because the current position
is advantageous to the Member State governments, who would therefore have
little incentive to change it.

The effective transposition into EC law of the Aarhus Convention is likely to
take years, if not decades.

The best hope for the environment and the democratic credentials of the EC
lies with the ECJ and CFI. Will they be sufficiently bold as to find a way to
ensure that the unelected Commission becomes more accountable, whether
by extending rights of standing or in their interpretation of Decision
94/90/EC? There would remain the question of the time it takes to obtain judgment at the European Courts and then reapply for documents, when the
immediacy of disclosure is often as important as the nature of the disclosure.
It is vital that the Community courts do not focus their considerable skills on
sectoral judgments to such an extent that they lose sight of their main purpose:
to ensure the observance of EC law—whether that be by individuals, organizations, Member States, or the institutions themselves.

To cover all the concerns raised in this article, fundamental reforms and
changes are necessary. It is desirable that some form of discreet control be set
up to examine Commission investigations which are closed prior to an
infringement procedure being begun, to ensure that the understandable urge
to compromise for political reasons is appropriately restrained. Such responsibility could be assigned to an EP body. At the point where investigations
cease and an infringement procedure is under way, it is submitted that the presumption should be that the matter is now very much in the public interest.
Only in specific and individually justified cases should Reasoned Opinions be
withheld from the public.

# CURRENT SURVEY

# Substantive European Community Environmental Law

## I. Atmospheric Pollution

ALEXANDRA GONZALEZ-CALATAYUD*

### A. INTRODUCTION

Atmospheric pollution was an important issue on the EU agenda in 1999. Several significant draft directives, which had not been completed in 1998, were due for adoption, while others required adoption of the corresponding proposals by the Commission. The latter included the draft Directive on Large Combustion Plants, and the draft Directive on National Emission Ceilings. Furthermore, the Council was also to make vital decisions pertaining to its position on issues such as climate change and the integration of the environment into sectoral policies.

Political developments within the EU were paramount in 1999. After months of political tension between the Commission and the European Parliament (EP), the Commission resigned *en masse*, following persistent accusations of nepotism, mismanagement, and fraud, in March 1999. It was not until October 1999, that a new Commission was installed. Additionally, in June 1999, elections were held for the EP.

### B. CLIMATE CHANGE

#### i. Implementation of Kyoto Protocol Obligations

The most controversial topic during the first half of 1999 was undoubtedly the definition of a specific cap for the Kyoto Protocol flexible mechanisms. Ever since the initial negotiations on the Protocol, the EU has promoted the definition of a precise ceiling on the use of these mechanisms to meet greenhouse gas emissions. The EU has consistently expressed its fear that lacking such a specific cap, Parties to the Protocol might attempt to circumvent their

---

* Trainee at the Foundation for International Environmental Law and Development (FIELD), London, UK.

commitment to reduce domestic emissions by means of so-called flexible mechanisms: emissions trading or joint implementation projects with third countries. Agreement had to be reached within the Council of Ministers, on the definition of a specific cap, in order for the EU to have a sufficiently strong basis for negotiations during the meeting of the UNFCCC Subsidiary Bodies (SBI/SBSTA) in Bonn in June 1999. At the last EU Environment Council prior to the Bonn meeting, three proposals for a cap aimed at prevention of possible abuse of these flexible mechanisms were discussed.[1]

The first proposal suggested a formula to calculate the permissible amount of greenhouse gas reductions which each country could achieve through these mechanisms. Figures to be inserted into the equation were left open for discussion, but a limit of 50 per cent seemed most likely.

The second proposal prohibited countries from using the mechanisms to account for more emission reductions than those achieved through domestic efforts and suggested that this should be assessed after the commitment period.

Finally, the third established a proposal threshold for the amount of reduction achieved by these mechanisms, to be determined by the extent of progress made by countries in the implementation of domestic action.

Negotiations on these cap definitions failed, due to conflicts over the effective level of ceilings, and the failure to formulate a detailed calculation formula.[2] The Dutch Government held the most entrenched position, as it opposed all three definitions, due to domestic political commitments.[3]

In view of this failure to reach an agreement, the German Presidency called for a special session of the Environment Council on 18 May 2000, before the round of international talks in Bonn. However, this special session was cancelled, since EU ministers reached an agreement at a meeting of the Environment Ministers in Weimar on 10 May 1999, following a shift in the rigid Dutch position.[4] The compromise allowed for industrialized countries to meet no more than 50 per cent of their greenhouse gas reduction commitments by means of flexibility mechanisms. Once publicized, the proposal was almost instantly attacked from all sides. In addition to the expected opposition of the so-called Umbrella Group—comprising, *inter alia*, the USA and Australia—environmental NGOs accused it of being too weak. Furthermore, the International Energy Agency (IEA) claimed that the compromise proposal would result in a reduction of economic efficiency, and result in vastly differing national trading caps.[5]

Perhaps as a result of this fierce criticism, the EU was content to let its proposal rest during the tenth session of the UNFCCC Subsidiary Bodies in June 1999, delaying serious international debate on the issue. The EU did maintain

---

[1] *ENDS Environment Daily*, 9 Mar. 1999.     [2] *ENDS Environment Daily*, 12 Mar. 1999.
[3] As part of a political deal made on forming the Dutch Government, the parties agreed to call for the Kyoto mechanisms to be allowed to account for a minimum of 50 per cent of a country's target, *ENDS Environment Daily*, 29 Apr. 1999.
[4] Ibid., 10 May 1999.     [5] Ibid., 1 June 1999 and 7 June 1999.

a strong position in the debate over compliance, however, by proposing that compliance processes should operate exclusively through one supervisory body, function through a single set of procedures, and provide for measures that apply gradually.[6] Such a supervisory body should consist of an independent committee of experts from relevant fields. With regard to the consequences of non-compliance, the EU defended the notion of a system that combines 'hard' and 'soft' enforcement measures, in balance with the gravity of the breach and the nature of the underlying obligation. The EU's success in these negotiations gave high hopes for the agreed international workshop on protocol compliance issues, which was organized prior to the fifth Conference of the Parties (COP-5).[7]

In the course of the difficult Council negotiations on a cap definition, the Commission presented its strategy 'Preparing for the Implementation of the Kyoto Protocol'.[8] The report had been requested by the December 1998 Vienna European Council, to form the basis of discussions at their summit in Cologne in June 1999. The Communication focuses on proposals for policies and measures at Community level, rather than national implementation measures.[9] It is very critical about the EU's possibilities to meet its international commitments regarding climate change, stating that 'ambitious negotiating positions must be complemented by concrete actions and tangible results'. If no additional policy measures are taken, total greenhouse gas emissions in the EC are expected to increase by nearly 6 per cent by 2010, as compared to 1990 levels. Since the EU is committed to cut emissions over the same period by 8 per cent, this would leave a 14 per cent gap to be filled. According to the Commission, in order to generate a persistent downward trend in emissions there will have to be a reinforcement of measures. It goes on to review the options available to the EU, and calls for action in all sectors and at all levels. The Commission allocates the lack of progress in this area largely to Member States. It has developed a wide range of policy initiatives at the request of the Council, which are subsequently not further pursued, or left without substance, by the Council. According to the Communication, this is particularly true in respect of the Commission proposal for energy product taxation, which it considers to be one of the most crucial instruments among tax incentives for lowering greenhouse gas emissions. In addition to the general improvement of coordination between various Council formations, the Communication suggests two complementary measures to remedy this situation: first, the impetus of the Cardiff Process for including environmental policy into all relevant policy areas, which should result in an increase of consistency between Council formations; and second, the improvement of the exchange of information, and the monitoring of policies and measures implemented and/or planned, both at

---

[6] See (1999) 12 *Earth Negotiations Bulletin* 110, 11 June 1999.
[7] *ENDS Environment Daily*, 14 June 1999.     [8] COM(1999)230 final, of 19 May 1999.
[9] The national strategies will be subject to a report by the European Environment Agency (EEA), on the basis of Member States' national communications.

national and Community level, as part of the amended Monitoring Decision 1999/296/EC, 26 April 1999.[10]

With regard to the latter, the Communication calls upon all relevant parties to increase efforts to develop the Monitoring Mechanism as an integral part of an EC compliance system. In particular, it calls upon Member States to take advantage of the implementation of the IPPC Directive,[11] which was due in 1999. It also recognizes the importance of effective and ambitious environmental agreements in the reduction of greenhouse gas emissions, and invites industry to conclude more environmental agreements.

Finally, the Communication notes the lack of knowledge in the EU of the so-called flexible mechanisms introduced by the Kyoto Protocol. It urges that there should be an informed debate on the instruments of emissions trading and the project mechanisms within the EC, to be initiated by the publication of a Green Paper on this topic. In respect of emissions trading, the Communication suggests that the EC should set up its own trading system by 2005, in preparation of an international system, which should be operative by 2008. Such an EC system could initially be limited to the largest $CO_2$ emitters, and possibly in only a single sector, later to be expanded to other sectors, and include other gases.

Generally, the reactions from the EP and the Environment Council to the Commission strategy were positive. In its resolution on climate change of 7 October 1999,[12] the EP welcomed the new Commission Communication and requested the Commission to produce detailed proposals for future action. Moreover, it asked to be fully involved in the preparation of international negotiations on climate change, in view of the fact that it would eventually have to ratify the resulting agreements. The Environmental Council's conclusions were adopted on 12 October 1999,[13] welcoming in particular the establishment of a monitoring mechanism. However, it requested that the Commission identify new priorities for various common policies, predominantly on transport, energy, industry, agriculture, and taxation, by 2000. Additionally, the Council plans to establish new measures and timetables in the sectors most responsible for greenhouse gas emissions (energy supply, transport, and industry). The final development in respect of Climate Change, in 1999, was the fifth Conference of the Parties to the UNFCCC (COP-5), from 25 October to 5 November, in Bonn.[14] In its statement released after the Conference, the EU declared itself satisfied with the meeting, which it said 'had established a firm basis for future political decisions'.[15] The EU expressed its commitment to ratify the Kyoto Protocol by April 2002, in time for the tenth

[10] Council Decision 1999/296/EC amending Decision 93/389/EEC for a Monitoring Mechanism of Community $CO_2$ and other Greenhouse Gas Emissions, [1999] OJ L117/35.

[11] Council Dir. 96/61/EC concerning Integrated Pollution Prevention and Control, [1996 ] OJ L257/26.

[12] [10–1999] EC Bulletin, point 1.3.102.

[13] Conclusions of the 2207th Council meeting, Luxembourg, 12 Oct. 1999.

[14] See (1999) 12 *Earth Negotiations Bulletin* 123, 8 Nov. 1999.

[15] *ENDS Environment Daily*, 5 Nov. 1999.

anniversary of the Rio 'Earth Summit'. The EU further submitted a number of proposals on flexible mechanisms, implementation, and Activities Implemented Jointly (AIJ) under the Pilot-phase.[16] However, detailed negotiations moved slowly, and most progress was made in respect of strategies for future negotiations. Some progress was also made with regard to rules for the protocol on limiting emissions. Most countries expressed their determination to achieve a final compromise at COP-6, and a reinforced series of negotiations is expected, prior to the meeting in The Hague, where COP-6 will take place in 2000. Following the appointment of a new Commission in the summer of 1999, several new EU climate change initiatives by the Commission are to be expected in 2000. According to the new EU Environment Commissioner, Margot Wallström, speaking before the EP in October 1999, there could even be a shift in traditional positions of the EU, *inter alia* in respect of emissions trading.[17] Additionally, Wallström predicted the launch of a new 'action programme' on climate change early next year, which would bring together all stakeholders, create synergies, and work towards a consensus on practical steps forward, as well as the publication of a Green Paper on emissions trading within the EU in Spring 2000. Moreover, she pointed out that there needed to be changes in a variety of policies that affect greenhouse gas emissions but which do not fall within environmental policy, such as energy, transport, and industry.[18]

### ii. Renewable Energy

The increased use of electricity from renewable energy sources constitutes an important part of the package of EC measures to reduce the emission of greenhouse gases, as first laid down in the Kyoto Protocol, and eventually in the policy package to meet further commitments. In the EU, renewable energy has been promoted since the early 1990s through the SAVE (Specific Actions for Vigorous Energy Efficiency) and ALTENER (Alternative Energy) Programmes. However, the EU lacks a clear regulatory framework to facilitate a significant increase in renewable generated electricity, and to integrate renewable energy into the new internal electricity market.[19] In 1999 proposals were made for directives on the promotion of electricity from renewable energy sources. Both proposals received criticism from Member States, industry, NGOs, and the DG Energy and the DG Industry.

A first draft proposal was prepared by the Commission in early 1999. This draft intended to require all EU countries to make at least 5 per cent of their electricity renewable, which constitutes a decrease from the 5.44 per cent

---

[16] EU statements agreed in coordination and delivered during COP-5 and SBSTA- and SBI-11 (paper by the Finnish Council Presidency).

[17] *ENDS Environment Daily*, 6 Oct. 1999. Walström indicated a more open approach to emissions trading, stating that 'if based on sound rules, trading would help us deliver the emissions reduction we need in a more cost-effective way'.

[18] Commission Document SPEECH/99/125, 6 Oct. 1999.

[19] The internal electricity market was created pursuant to Dir. 96/92/EC concerning Common Rules for the Internal Market in Electricity, [1997] OJ L27/20.

share of renewables in EU electricity supply in 1995, yet a substantial increase for production in numerous Member States. It also provided for the removal of barriers to access to the electricity grid for renewables, in order to allow smaller generating companies to supply their power to networks more easily.[20] It also contained proposals on harmonizing 'green electricity' policies across Member States, to make national schemes mutually acceptable.

The main point of criticism to this proposal concerned its objective to prevent national renewable energy support schemes from creating trade barriers in the context of the European electricity supply market, which is currently undergoing liberalization. While consensus appears to have been reached in respect of the necessity of a direct price support scheme to promote renewable energy consumption, conflicting opinions exist concerning the most suitable system. Essentially, two categories of direct price support mechanisms were in place within the EU: quota-based systems, and fixed-price systems with purchasing obligations.

First, quota-based systems, operating notably in the UK, Ireland, and the Netherlands, are based on setting the price through competition between renewable generated electricity generators for available support. Two different mechanisms operate within such schemes: green certificates and tendering schemes. These systems have not led to a substantial increase in energy capacity, but rather, according to their supporters, they have imposed a downward pressure on the costs of renewables.[21]

Second, fixed price systems operate mainly in Germany and Spain, and are characterized by a specific set price for renewably generated electricity, which must be paid by electricity companies and distributors to domestic producers of renewably generated electricity. In such schemes, in principle, there is no quota or maximum limit for renewably generated electricity in the Member States, although this limit or quota is set indirectly by the level at which the renewably generated electricity price is set. This system has been the most successful in the EU.

To the dismay of, in particular, the German renewables industry, the Commission proposal clearly favoured the first, competition-based funding schemes. According to the European Wind Energy Association (EWEA), the German Government promptly decided to exert its political power in Brussels by forcing the Commission to abandon plans for such a directive.[22]

The Commission subsequently decided to prepare a working paper outlining different options for the harmonization of renewables support systems, as an alternative.[23] Following review of all possible funding schemes, the Commission concluded that a competitive renewables market could be achieved in the short term by means of a directive, or in the medium term by means of state aid and internal market rules. The former option of a directive received overwhelming political support at a meeting of EU Energy ministers

---

[20] *ENDS Environment Daily*, 10 Dec. 1998.           [21] Ibid.           [22] Ibid., 9 Feb. 1999.
[23] Commission Working Paper concerning possible future action towards a competitive internal market for electricity generated from renewable energy sources (IP/99/224, 13 Apr. 1999).

in May 1999, where the Commission working paper served as a basis for discussions. The Energy ministers formally asked the Commission to submit a concrete proposal for an EU framework on promoting electricity from renewable sources.[24]

Consequently, the Energy DG decided to revise the old draft directive, although its adoption by the Commission would not be possible during 1999. Details emerging from the proposal provoked a renewed outcry from NGOs, in Member States, and within the Commission itself. The draft directive received strong criticism in respect of its failure to establish binding targets for renewable energy production and consumption. Instead, it simply required Member States to set national targets for the share of renewable electricity, specifying only that these targets should be compatible with the overall aim of the EC to double the share of renewable energy by 2012. With regard to competition, at the request of EU Energy ministers, the proposal explicitly permits national governments to choose which measures they find most suitable to promote renewables in their countries. An additional innovation is the 5 per cent ceiling to Member States' freedom to provide financial support to domestic renewable energy producers, followed by a ban on schemes limited to domestic producers only from 2010. Where the amount of renewables production receiving state support in any country surpasses 5 per cent of domestic electricity consumption, the government must open its support scheme to renewable generators in any other Member State that has also passed this threshold.

Finally, the draft introduced an obligation for Member States to create renewable energy certification schemes. A competent body designated by the Member States, independent from industries for generation and distribution of electricity, should issue these certificates. However, adoption of this proposal was postponed until 2000.

Agreement on a budget for the SAVE II (energy efficiency) and ALTENER II (renewable energy) programmes was another important issue on the Community Agenda for 1999 concerning energy. The programmes run from 1998 to 2002 and have become co-decision procedures after the entry into force of the Amsterdam Treaty. A common position had been reached on ALTENER and SAVE in June 1999,[25] but at their second reading the European Parliament (EP) rejected the budget cuts proposed by the Council,[26] which in turn approved the common position. In the complex conciliation talks which followed, the Council offered to increase both programmes' budgets by 1.9 million euros, half of which would be reallocated from the EU Synergy budget.[27] Upon rejection of this proposal by the EP, a second meeting was scheduled, where agreement was finally reached.[28] The agreement entailed

---

[24] *ENDS Environment Daily*, 12 May 1999.

[25] Common Position (EC) ALTENER of 28 June 1999, [1999] OJ C243/47; and Common Position (EC) SAVE of 28 June 1999, [1999] OJ C232/12.

[26] The Council had proposed to cut the SAVE budget from 68.4 to 64 million euros, and the ALTENER budget from 81.1 to 74 million euros.

[27] *ENDS Environment Daily*, 12 Nov. 1999.     [28] The EP approved the joint text on 3 Feb. 2000.

a compromise between the EP and Council positions prior to conciliation, effectively granting SAVE II ALTENER II 66 and 77 million euros, respectively.

Parallel to these negotiations, the Commission launched its 'Campaign for Take-Off' (CTO), a promotion campaign which is intended to coordinate national and EU efforts to trigger private sector funding of large-scale renewable energy projects in four key sectors. The strategy was envisaged in the 1997 White Paper on Renewable Energy Sources[29] and aims at creating a clear and well-defined investment climate. The Commission's role in the campaign will be to provide marketing, promotional, and project development support through ALTENER.

### iii. Energy Efficiency

In Spring 1999 the Energy DG published a policy paper on stand-by energy, in which it urged electronic equipment manufacturers to take immediate action to reduce this type of energy waste. According to the paper, electronic equipment in idle mode accounts for approximately 10 per cent of household electricity use. In line with the projected growth in consumption of electronic appliances, this figure could easily double by 2010. The Commission considers that voluntary agreements with manufacturers would be the most effective method to achieve substantial reduction of this energy loss. In addition, it suggests setting minimum standards for product energy efficiency and the use of product labels in order to encourage sales of the most efficient appliances. Following the suggestion by the Energy DG for the EC to consider participation in the 'Energy Star' system established in the USA, agreement was reached to this end, between the Commission and the US Environmental Protection Agency in 1999.[30] Pursuant to the draft agreement, European manufacturers will be able to qualify for the label, which is to be recognized in Europe. The draft agreement also establishes a joint technical committee made up of representatives of the EPA and the Commission, which is to establish criteria for equipment to qualify for the label. The agreement is expected to be endorsed by the EP and the Council.

### iv. Energy Taxation

In 1997 the Commission presented a proposal for a Council Directive restructuring the Community framework for the taxation of energy products.[31] The draft directive is aimed at determining an overall tax system for the taxation of energy products with a view to improve the functioning of the internal market and to protect the environment. The proposal entails minimum taxation of motor fuels, heating fuels, and electricity, which must be imposed in accordance with certain time-frames. It further contains an exhaustive list of exemptions, relating to, *inter alia*, air and sea navigation. To prevent increases of overall tax burdens in Member States, the draft alternatively suggests that statutory charges on labour are to be reduced.

[29] COM(97)550, [1998] OJ C46/7.        [30] *ENDS Environment Daily*, 15 July 1999.
[31] COM(97)30 final CNS0111, [1997] OJ C139/1.

Due to the sensitive nature of the project, in addition to the fact that all legislation on taxation requires unanimous agreement in the Council, the 'Monti' proposal was shelved almost immediately after publication. It was only by the end of 1998, in view of the importance of this proposal for the achievement of the EU Kyoto Protocol commitments, that finance ministers decided to reinitiate negotiations on this controversial energy tax.

In April 1999, after twenty-seven amendments, the EP approved the Commission's proposal.[32] The amendments were largely concerned with 'greening' the draft, by ruling out certain exemptions to taxation of energy-intensive industries, and by creating new exemptions for activities such as renewable energy production.

Meanwhile, national governments continued to declare themselves in favour or against the proposal, resulting in some surprising positions. France decided to give support to the project and even demanded it to go further, but there was the expected opposition from countries such as Spain.[33] In response to Spanish criticism, the German Government proposed compromise measures, after having desperately tried to save at least one environmental project from failure during their Council presidency. The proposal included concessions to Spain, such as the setting of minimum tax rates for coal or lignite at zero rates and of 'low positive' rates for other fuels, that did not already have an EU minimum rate. However, the German attempts proved futile, as in the following EU Finance Council in May 1999 Spain decided to veto the proposal. Subsequently, the notion of a 'Schengen energy tax' emerged, including only those countries which are in favour of establishing a taxation system on energy products. The European Parliament was the first institution to propose such a system, which would make use of the flexibility clause in the Amsterdam Treaty.[34] The Portuguese Government declared that the proposal on energy product taxation would remain on the agenda during their Council Presidency in the first half of 2000.[35]

### v. $CO_2$ Monitoring Mechanism

One of the most important instruments for the control of the EU Kyoto commitments was amended in 1999. The updated 1998 proposal for a decision amending Council Decision 93/389/EEC[36] was awaiting its second reading by the EP early in 1999. After the second reading,[37] the Decision was adopted on 26 April 1999.[38] Final agreement had been preceded by amendments to the common position,[39] which strengthened the requirements on national

---

[32] [1999] OJ C150/22.    [33] *ENDS Environment Daily*, 13 Apr. 1999 and 5 May 1999.
[34] EP Resolution R5–0059/1999 of 7 Oct. 1999. The Dutch Government was, in fact, the first to unofficially propose this; *ENDS Environment Daily*, 13 July 1999. Cf. Margot Wallström's speech before the EP; *ENDS Environment Daily*, 6 Oct. 1999.
[35] Ibid., 15 Nov. 1999.    [36] COM(98)108 of 2 Mar. 1998, [1998] OJ C 120/22.
[37] EP Resolution R4–0052/1999 of 9 Feb. 1999 (second reading).
[38] Council Decision 1999/296/EC of 26 Apr. 1999, amending Decision 93/389/EEC for a Monitoring Mechanism for Community $CO_2$ and other Greenhouse Gas Emissions, [1999] OJ L117/42.
[39] Common Position 50/98/EC, adopted by the Council on 16 June 1998, [1999] OJ C333/38.

inventories and data reporting, and introduced a consultative committee instead of a regulatory committee as proposed by the Council in the common position. It is expected that this Monitoring Mechanism Committee will play a significant role in the development of a long-term strategy for monitoring mechanisms, including reinforcement of the 'learning' elements of the process for the Commission and the Member States, and flexibility considerations.[40]

### vi. $CO_2$ Emissions from Passenger Cars

In its Communication 'Preparing for the Implementation of the Kyoto Protocol' the Commission declared that the transport sector is the most worrying of all policy sectors, given the expected increase in carbon dioxide ($CO_2$) emissions of 39 per cent between 1999 and 2010.[41] In order to prevent this expectation from becoming a reality, the EU has initiated several strategies, including the 1998 agreement with the European Automotive Manufacturers Association (ACEA), to reduce average emissions from new cars sold in the EU by approximately 25 per cent to 140g $CO_2$/km by 2008.[42]

After the ACEA agreement was signed on 29 June 1998, the Commission initiated similar negotiations with non-ACEA car manufacturers, in particular with Japan Automobile Manufacturers Association (JAMA), and the Korean Automobile Manufacturers Association (KAMA). Since the major US car manufacturers are also represented within ACEA, there was no need to negotiate separate agreements with them. The envisaged agreements should prevent distortion of competition on the European market. On 11 June 1999, after several months of negotiations, an agreement was signed by the Commission and KAMA, followed shortly by the JAMA agreement on 16 September 1999. The content of these agreements is contained in the Commission Communication 'Implementing the Community Strategy to reduce $CO_2$ Emissions from cars: Outcome of the Negotiations with the Japanese and Korean Automobile Industries.'[43]

JAMA committed to place, no later than 2000, models emitting 120g $CO_2$/km or less on the European market, and to meet the target of 140g $CO_2$/km by 2009. JAMA 2003, is to bring its emissions within a target range between 165g and 175g $CO_2$/km, and will review the potential for further reductions in emissions. KAMA will market models emitting no more than 120g $CO_2$/km at the earliest possible date after 2000. Like JAMA, it will achieve a target of 140g $CO_2$/km by 2009, but will not review potential for further reductions in emissions until 2004, when its estimated target range will be 165g to 170g $CO_2$/km.

According to the Commission the difficult economic situations and the higher $CO_2$ levels of JAMA's and KAMA's car fleet called for an extended period

[40] J. Hyvarinen, 'The European Community's Monitoring Mechanism for $CO_2$ and other Greenhouse Gases: the Kyoto Protocol and other Recent Developments' (1999) 8 *Review of European Community & International Environmental Law* 2, 191–7.

[41] See n. 8 above.

[42] Commission Recommendation 1999/125/EC of 5 Feb. 1999, concerning the reduction of carbon dioxide emissions from passenger cars under the ACEA agreement.

[43] COM(1999)446 final, of 14 Sept. 1999. See also Press Release IP/99/922, of 1 Dec. 1999.

for achievement of the target value of 140g $CO_2$/km.[44] In contrast, ACEA must meet an identical target by 2008.

A second element of the European strategy on $CO_2$ emissions from cars is the fuel-economy information scheme,[45] for which the initial proposal was published on 3 September 1998.

The proposal compromised a fuel economy label for all new cars, a fuel economy guide, a poster containing the fuel efficiency and the $CO_2$ emissions of all new cars, and the inclusion of official fuel consumption data in promotional literature.

In its first reading of the proposal, the EP adopted a number of amendments, aimed at improvement of consumer information.[46] Specifically, the EP sought simplification of the information on fuel consumption by making a distinction between consumption in and outside urban areas. Moreover, the EP suggested adding an explanation of the effects of additional options, such as air-conditioning, on fuel consumption and to delete the requirement to provide information on estimated fuel costs, as this would wrongly favour diesel cars.

The amended proposal from the Commission retained part of the EP amendments, but was later altered by the Council, which, in the common position, adopted amendments from Parliament that had earlier not been retained by the Commission.[47] These amendments included deletion of the requirement to indicate average fuel costs, as well as the requirement to indicate $CO_2$ emission data alongside fuel economy data in promotional literature.

The Directive was adopted on 13 December 1999, after a second reading by the Parliament did not result in further proposals of amendments.[48] The Directive entered into force on 18 January 2000.

The last proposal concerning $CO_2$ emissions on the Community agenda in 1999 was the scheme to monitor the average specific emissions of $CO_2$ produced on the territory of the Member States by new cars. The initial proposal, of 12 June 1998,[49] had undergone its first reading by the EP on 17 December 1998, which made it subject to a number of amendments.[50] These included, *inter alia*, the proposal to apply the scheme to light commercial vehicles (LCVs), and to require data on emissions to be grouped by manufacturer. Furthermore, the EP asked for the annual report from the Commission to be submitted to the Council and the EP.

The Council partially accepted Parliament's proposals for amendment in its common position, but failed to take into account parts of the amendment

---

[44] *ENDS Environment Daily*, 25 June 1999.
[45] COM(98)489, of 3 Sept. 1998; [1998] OJ C305/2.     [46] PE R4–0489/1998, [1999] OJ C98/22.
[47] Common Position 17/1999, of 4 May 1999, [1999] OJ C123/1.
[48] EP and Council Dir. 1999/94/EC relating to the Availability of Consumer Information on Fuel Economy and Carbon Dioxide Emissions in Respect of the Marketing of New Passenger Cars, [2000] OJ L12/16.
[49] COM(98)348, of 12 June 1998; [1998] OJ C231/6.
[50] PE R4–0492/1998, of Apr. 1999, [1999] OJ C198/251.

which promoted application of the monitoring scheme to LCVs.[51] The latter was considered unacceptable by the EP, which subsequently insisted on this element in its second reading. It furthermore asked the Commission to incorporate the negotiated agreement with ACEA into a legal framework.

### vii. $CO_2$ from Air Transport

A five-year Community strategy on air transport was initiated in 1999, which addresses, *inter alia*, the reduction of $CO_2$ emissions from the sector, necessary for the EU to meet its commitments to the Kyoto Protocol.[52] Recent studies show that the sector's carbon dioxide emissions annually increase by 3 per cent, which may amount to 15 per cent of global warming in fifty years.[53]

Following several months of debate with the aircraft and engine industries, and the airlines over the level for, and the appropriate instrument to achieve $CO_2$ reductions, the Commission decided to set out the different options in a Green Paper on air transport. The Commission pledged to initiate discussions, early in 2000, towards a voluntary agreement with airlines and aircraft manufacturers to reduce emissions, similar to earlier agreements with car manufacturers. The paper is focused largely financial instruments, by proposing, *inter alia*, three types of environmental levies to tackle emission reductions. First, a surcharge, to be added to flight ticket prices. Second, an *en route* charge based on travel distance, and the average emission per kilometre. Finally, a take-off and landing charge. The EU does not yet commit itself to any of these instruments, but singles out *en route* charges as a promising technique. Ultimately, the EU foresees a global agreement on future charges, with the International Civil Aviation Organization (ICAO), but in the meantime, it is prepared to take unilateral action if no agreement is to be reached at the next ICAO assembly, in 2001.[54]

### viii. Integration into Other Policy Sectors

Throughout 1999 environmental integration has been one of the key initiatives on the Community agenda, with priority for procedural issues in particular establishing clear timetables and indicators. As regards substantive issues, the focus in 1999 was on the adoption of strategies by the Transport, Agriculture, and Energy Council, complemented by the presentation of initial sectoral integration strategies by the Development, Internal Market, and Industry Councils.

The EU summit, in June 1999 in Cologne, reiterated the three main topics of discussion: agricultural and structural policy and, in particular, the trans-sectoral issue of climate change.[55] The relevant Councils were urged explicitly to incorporate climate change in their reports. Furthermore, the Fisheries, Ecofin, and General Affairs Councils were invited to develop an integration

---

[51] Common Position 18/1999, of 4 May 1999, on a Council Dir. establishing a scheme to monitor the average emissions of $CO_2$ from new passenger cars [1999] OJ C123/13.
[52] COM(1999)640, of 1 Dec. 1999. See also press release IP/99/925, of 1 Dec. 1999.
[53] *ENDS Environment Daily*, 2 Dec. 1999.          [54] Ibid., 1 Dec. 1999.
[55] D. Grimeaud, 'The Integration of Environmental Concerns into EC Policies: A Genuine Development?' (2000) 7 *European Environmental Law Review*, 207.

strategy. The Council welcomed the May 1999 Commission working document for the Cologne summit,[56] which criticizes the Council for being too slow responding to legislative proposals by the Commission. The document points in particular to the Commission proposal on energy taxes, as a proposal which is urgently in need of adoption. The Commission also assesses its own efforts towards integration. It acknowledges the weaknesses of the current Green Star system,[57] which it plans to replace by 'new integration strategies', which might operate on the basis of a tools guide including a screening list and a set of appropriate assessment methods.

During the preparations for the Helsinki Council summit in December 1999, the Commission presented two further documents relating to integration. The first document assessed the progress in the different Council formations which had been asked to prepare strategies for environmental integration.[58] The Commission considers such progress to be uneven among the Councils, and is generally critical of the result, in particular where it concerns the adoption of clear timetables for individual measures and objectives, which are still largely lacking.

The second report is a response to the request by the Vienna Council, in 1998, to develop a report on environment and integration indicators.[59] In its report, the Commission formulates a draft system of indicators, but notes that considerable effort is still required to complete the system. It further calls on the Council to confirm its support for the development of the system, and to instruct the different Council formations to accelerate the process of development of sectoral indicators.

At the Helsinki summit in December 1999, the Council agreed on strategies for integration of the environment into agriculture,[60] transport,[61] and energy[62] sectors. Contrary to expectations, the Council did not review these, nor did it urge even greater integration.[63] The Internal Market,[64] Development,[65] and

---

[56] Commission working document, 'The Cologne Report on Environmental Integration: Mainstreaming of Environmental Policy', SEC(99)777.

[57] According to this system, all policies or legislative proposals which were likely to have a significant environmental impact had to carry a green star if they were listed in the Commission Work Programme.

[58] Commission working document, 'From Cardiff to Helsinki and beyond. Report to the European Council on integrating environmental concerns and sustainable development into Community policies', SEC(99)1941.

[59] Commission working document, 'Report on Environment and Integration. Indicators to Helsinki Summit', SEC(99)1942.

[60] 2218th Council meeting—Agriculture—Brussels, 15 Nov. 1999: Strategy on Environmental Integration and Sustainable Development in the Common Agricultural Policy established by the Agriculture Council.

[61] 2204th Council meeting—Transport—Luxembourg, 6 Oct. 1999: Transport and Environment—Report to the European Council in Helsinki.

[62] 2230th Council meeting—Energy—Brussels, 2 Dec. 1999: Strategy for Integrating Environmental Aspects and Sustainable Development into Energy Policy.

[63] See n. 54 above.

[64] 2210th Council meeting—Internal Market—Luxembourg, 28 Oct. 1999: Integration of Environmental Protection and Sustainable Development into Internal Market Policy.

[65] 2215th Council meeting—Development—Brussels, 11 Nov. 1999: Development Council Report including Elements of a Comprehensive Strategy on the Integration of Environment and Sustainable Development into EC Economic and Development Cooperation.

Industry[66] Councils made similar strategies available. Most importantly, the Council asked the Commission to complete these strategies, including a timetable for further measures and a set of indicators for these sectors. It was to submit the completed strategy to the Council by June 2001.[67] Thus, although no additional Sectoral Council reports were requested, the first clear deadline was established. In this sense, the Helsinki Summit may be seen as a turning point within the process.[68]

C. THE AUTO/OIL PROGRAMME

The most important proposals to be discussed in the framework of the Auto/Oil programme were, first, the proposal[69] for a directive amending Council Directive 88/77/EEC[70] on Measures to be taken against the Emission of Gaseous and Particulate Pollutants from Diesel Engines for Use in Vehicles, and second, a proposal[71] for a Directive on the roadside inspection of vehicles circulating in the Community. Discussions on the first proposal were marked by complications with the previous three Auto/Oil dossiers in which strenuous negotiations between the Council and the EP, and even within the institutions themselves, had delayed adoption of the directives by almost two years. In an attempt at conciliation, positions in respect of the proposal on polluting emissions from heavy goods vehicles, were, in general, aimed at a compromise. In March 1999, after the EP's first reading, the Commission submitted an amended proposal for the directive,[72] including ten of the twenty-four EP amendments. The Council, in turn, agreed on a common position in April 1999, in line with the agreement of the Environment Council.[73] At the request of the EP, the Council decided to introduce a second stage of more stringent emission limit values by 2005, followed by a third stage, from October 2008, for additional reduction of the $NO_x$ limit by 43 per cent over the limit set for 2005. The latter date was deemed insufficient by the EP Environment Committee, which demanded stricter $NO_x$ limits to be met by 2006.[74] However, as environment ministers proved unwilling to make a further concession, the requirement was dropped in the EP's second reading.[75] Finally, Directive 1999/96/EC on Measures to be taken against the Emission of Gaseous and Particulate Pollutants from compression ignition engines for use in vehicles, and the

---

[66] 2214th Council meeting—Industry—Brussels, 9 Nov. 1999: Integration of Sustainable Development into EU Industrial Policy.

[67] *Council Press Release*, Presidency Conclusions Helsinki European Council, 10 and 11 Dec. 1999.

[68] M. Unfried, 'The Cardiff Process: The Institutional and Political Challenges of Environmental Integration in the EU' (2000) 9 *Review of European Community & International Environmental Law* 2, 112–19.

[69] COM(97)627, of 3 Dec. 1997, [1997] OJ C173/1.          [70] [1988] OJ L036/33.

[71] COM(98)0117, of 11 Mar. 1998, [1998] OJ C190/10.

[72] COM(1999)89 final, of 11 Mar. 1999.

[73] Common Position 35/1999, of 22 Apr. 1999. See also *ENDS Environment Daily*, 22 Dec. 1998.

[74] PE A5–0043/1999, of 19 Oct. 1999, *rapporteur* B. Lange.

[75] PE R5–0099/1999, of 16 Nov. 1999. See also *ENDS Environment Daily*, 16 Nov. 1999.

emission of gaseous pollutants from positive ignition engines fuelled with natural gas or liquefied petroleum gas for use in vehicles and amending Directive 88/77/EEC, was adopted on 13 December 1999.[76]

The second Auto/Oil Programme proposal under review in 1999 concerned the roadside inspection of vehicles circulating in the Community. In the first EP reading, on 9 February 1999, seventeen amendments were made to the proposal,[77] of which the Commission adopted eleven, rejecting those related to harmonization of certain provisions, such as penalties or training, and to the pass and failure of vehicles on roadside inspection.[78] The Council accepted most of the amendments included in the new Commission proposal, with the exception of the one providing that the Member States must submit their plans for roadside inspections to the Commission prior to implementation.[79] It also made two changes to the proposal. First, it limited the scope of the Directive to inspections on the public highway, except in case of a more elaborate inspection justified on safety grounds. Second, it abandoned the progressive three-step approach for roadworthiness inspection, and replaced this with a less complex and less progressive approach. The result of the second reading by the EP was to be expected in 2000.

### D. ACIDIFICATION

During 1999 several significant developments occurred within the framework of the EC 'acidification strategy', as established by the Commission in 1997.[80] Two 1998 proposals on acidification were pending for adoption in 1999, concerning, first, the reduction of the sulphur content in fuels, and, second, large combustion plants. A third, vital proposal was presented in 1999: a proposal for a directive on national emission ceilings.

The first of the 1998 proposals, a Council directive on the reduction of the sulphur content of certain liquid fuels,[81] had the most advanced *dossier*. The common position of the EP and the Council was awaiting its second reading in 1999. The EP's Environmental Committee had recommended its adoption, save three amendments concerning the time-frame for implementation.[82] The Committee proposed a deadline for implementation of a limit value of 1 per cent for sulphur in heavy oil to be brought forward from 1 January 2003 to 1 January 2001. Moreover, it rejected the Council's derogation to permit Member States which do not contribute significantly to acidification—Spain, Greece, Portugal, and Italy—to continue using heavy fuel oil with a content of 3 per cent. Rather, it considered the initial Commission proposal for a limit of

---

[76] [2000] OJ L44/1.          [77] PE R4–0025/1999, of 20 Jan. 1999.

[78] COM(1999)458 final, of 14 Oct. 1999, [1999] OJ C116/7.

[79] Common position CSL 11287/1999, of 2 Dec. 1999, [2000] OJ C29/1.

[80] COM(97)88 final, Communication to the Council and the EP on a Community strategy to combat acidification.

[81] COM(98)385, of 8 July 1998, [1998] OJ C259/5.

[82] PE A4–0002/1999, of 5 Jan. 1999, [1999] OJ C104/5, *rapporteur* Ms Hautala. See also *ENDS Environment Daily*, 5 Jan. 1999.

2.5 per cent more appropriate. It was decided that the deadline for limiting the sulphur content of gas oil to 0.1 per cent should be moved forward from 2008 to 2004. However, when the assembly had to vote in plenary,[83] it surprisingly decided to reject the three amendments of the Environmental Committee, and accepted the common position agreed by EU environment ministers in June 1998. Finally, Directive 1999/32/EC concerning a Reduction of the Sulphur Content of Certain Liquid Fuels, was adopted on 26 April 1999.[84]

In contrast, negotiations surrounding the proposal for a directive amending Directive 88/609/EEC on the Limitation of Emissions of Certain Pollutants into the Air from Large Combustion Plants were less expedient, not only due to the EP position on the matter, but also due to the rigid positions of the Member States.[85] In its first reading of the Commission proposal, the EP largely endorsed the amendments previously recommended by its Environmental Committee to strengthen the proposed directive.[86]

The most radical proposed amendment was to expand the scope of the directive to include existing installations, whereas the Commission's proposal only covered new plants. The EP argued that, lacking this expansion of the scope, plants built before 1987 would have produced 85 per cent of $SO_2$ emissions by 2010, without being subject to any legislative control by the EU. In turn, the Commission argued that emissions from existing plants would be covered by the forthcoming proposal on national emissions ceilings. The EP also decided to lower emission limit values for $NO_x$ and $SO_2$ of plants licensed on or after 1 January 2000. Additionally, it rejected a proposed derogation for Spanish plants to comply with $SO_2$ emission limit values for new plants. Finally, it demanded the application of stricter standards to existing plants by 2005.[87] Conflict existed within the EP, fed by fears that an overly ambitious directive might have excessive consequences for domestic industry, in particular in respect of German and British coal-operated power stations.

In response to the EP's first reading, the Commission presented an amended proposal, incorporating several EP amendments, none of which, however, included any of the major revisions cited above.[88] Within the Council, Member States were divided along the usual North–South polarization, the Mediterranean countries demanding weaker emission limits, while the Northern countries called for tighter standards.[89] Division also existed in respect of the scope of application of the proposed directive, since Austria and Germany were in favour of extending its scope to existing plants, whereas all other Member Sates were opposed. Even the Council Presidency's proposal to review the Directive in 2004, to decide on the extension of its scope, failed to bring consensus. In fact, Spain raised the issue of the legal basis of the

---

[83] PE R4–0002/1999, of 9 Feb. 1999, OJ C150/18.          [84] [1999] OJ L121/13.

[85] COM(98)415, of 14 Aug. 1998, [1998] OJ C286/6.

[86] PE R4–0121/1999, of 14 Apr. 1999, OJ C219/175. See also recommendations of the Environmental Committee, PE A4–0121/1999, of 17 Mar. 1999, *rapporteur* Ms Oomen-Ruijten.

[87] *ENDS Environment Daily*, 3 Feb. 1999, 22 Mar. 1999, and 14 Apr. 1999.

[88] COM(1999)611 final, of 25 Nov. 1999, [1999] OJ C212/36.

[89] *ENDS Environment Daily*, 16 July 1999.

Directive, claiming that, as it affected energy policy, it would require unanimous voting in the Council. However, this claim was ultimately rejected. In an attempt to achieve compromise, the Finnish Council Presidency submitted a new proposal, at the last meeting of the EU environment Ministers in December 1999. The flexibility clause included in this proposal would give Member States two options to reduce emissions from pre-1987 plants: first, to apply stricter emissions standards to all plants by 2007, or, alternatively, to include them in national emission reduction plans, in the form of a 'bubble' allowing flexibility over individual plants. Discrepancies focused on whether the reduction plan should set binding targets for cuts.[90] Since it was not possible to reach an agreement on this issue, the attainment of a common position by the Council was left for 2000.

The third initiative within the framework of the Commission's acidification strategy, a proposal for a directive on national emission ceilings (NEC) for certain atmospheric pollutants, was submitted by the Commission on 9 June 1999.[91] The proposed ceilings in the draft Directive were significantly more rigid than those suggested in the acidification strategy. One reason for this was that, due to the similarity in origins of acidification and ground-level ozone, the Commission decided to combine both proposals. In fact, two of the acidifying gases—nitrogen oxide and volatile organic compounds—are also key precursors of low-level ozone. Another reason was that the statistics applied to calculate ceilings had changed since 1997. Furthermore, the Commission decided to include the predicted impact of other EC legislation, such as the Auto/Oil Directives, or the proposed Amending Directive on Large Combustion Plants, in its estimates of what 'business as usual' (BAU) would be.[92]

The proposal for a Directive on National Emission Ceilings sets, for the first time, individual limits for each Member State's total emission of four acidifying and eutrophying pollutants and ozone precursors nitrogen oxides ($NO_x$), volatile organic compounds (VOC), sulphur dioxide ($SO_2$), and ammonia ($NH_3$). Member States have the flexibility to assess what action is appropriate in their particular circumstances, in the implementation of national ceilings, which have to be met by 2010 at the latest. Thereby, Member States' primary obligation is to draw up programmes including detailed emission-reduction strategies, proposed policies and measures, and their estimated effect on pollution levels. These programmes must be reported to the Commission before the end of 2002, and will be updated and revised by 2006. Furthermore, Member States are required to compile annual national emission inventories and emission projections for 2010, which must be updated regularly, in order to allow for the Commission to produce publicly available reports, in collaboration with the European Environment Agency (EEA). The Commission will monitor Member States' progress, and report to the EP and the Council in 2004 and in 2008.

[90] *ENDS Environment Daily*, 14 Dec. 1999.     [91] COM(1999)125 final, [2000] OJ C56E/34.
[92] *ENDS Environment Daily*, 11 Jan. 1999.

According to the Commission, by the time Member States have complied with the emission ceilings in 2010, the result will be a 30 per cent reduction in areas subject to soil eutrophication, a 75 per cent decrease in the exposure of humans to ozone pollution, and a significant reduction in the EU land area affected by acidification from 37 million hectares in 1990 to 4.3 million by 2010. Member States were once again divided along the classic North–South line over the proposed emission limits and measures necessary to implement them.[93] Fears of difficulties in meeting stricter targets within the EC, than within the global context—the CLRTAP[94] multi-pollutant multi-effect Protocol—were expressed during an open debate in the Council.[95]

### E. OZONE

Intense efforts were made in 1999 to reach agreement on the 1998 proposal for a new Council Regulation on Substances that Deplete the Ozone Layer,[96] starting with the revision of the initial proposal by the Commission, which adopted the EP amendments in their entirety,[97] apart from the most controversial ones.[98] The latter entailed an earlier phasing-out date of methyl bromide, and the reduction in HCFC production in the EC. The common position of the Council postponed the phase-out date for methyl bromide to 2005, four years later than initially foreseen.[99] At the same time, it established a stricter procedure with respect to eventual derogations for 'critical' uses. The common position also included a 60 per cent cut in the use of methyl bromide by 2001, and a subsequent cut of 75 per cent by 2003 compared with 1991 levels. Regarding the production of HCFCs, the Council accepted the Commission's timetable of 2001, only after inclusion of expanded revision clauses. Contrary to the EP Environmental Committee's rejection, the EP assembly accepted these amendments in order to avoid conflict with Member States.[100] It is ultimately up to the Council to approve the amendments, failing which the interinstitutional conciliation might be invoked. In 1999 the Commission also adopted its annual decisions on import quotas and essential uses. Decision 1999/58/EC[101] allocates import quotas for several types of CFCs, carbon tetrachloride, and methyl bromide, *inter alia*, whereas Decision 1999/59/EC[102] allocates quantities of controlled substances allowed for essential uses in the EC in 1999.

---

[93] *ENDS Environment Daily*, 12 Oct. 1999
[94] Convention on Long-Range Transboundary Air Pollution (CLRTAP), Geneva, 13 Nov. 1979.
[95] 2207th Council meeting, Environment, Luxembourg, 12 Oct. 1999, at 12.
[96] COM(98)398, of 14 Aug. 1998, [1998] OJ C286/6.
[97] PE R4–0465/1998, of 17 Dec. 1998 [1999] OJ C98/22.
[98] COM(1999)67 final, of 11 Feb. 1999, [1999] OJ C83/4.
[99] Common position 5748/3/1999 of 23 Feb. 1999, [1999] OJ C123/28.
[100] PE R5–0155/1999 of 15 Dec. 1999, and recommendation from the Environment Committee A5–0777/1999 of 24 Nov. 1999, *rapporteur* A. Hulthen. See also *ENDS Environment Daily*, 17 Dec. 1999.
[101] [1999] OJ/10.                    [102] [1999] OJ/18.

From 29 November to 3 December 1999, the eleventh meeting of the parties to the Montreal Protocol took place in Beijing.[103] With the EU playing an active role in negotiations, the meeting ended with an agreement to freeze HCFC production at 1989 levels by 2004 in industrialized countries, and at 2016 on a baseline of 2015 in developing countries. The parties also decided to begin phasing-out the right of industrialized countries to export CFCs to developing countries, and to make adjustment controls to methyl bromide. Thus, the EU managed to include into the Protocol most of the current and future EC provisions.

Finally, 1999 saw the adoption of Directive 1999/13/EC on the Limitation of Emissions of Volatile Organic Compounds due to the Use of Organic Solvents in certain Activities and Installations.[104] The Council adopted the draft directive on 11 March 1999, without introducing any further amendments after the EP's second reading in 1998. Member States must transpose the new Directive by April 2001.

### F. AIR QUALITY: DAUGHTER DIRECTIVES

The 1996 Directive on Ambient Air Quality Assessment and Management[105] required the adoption of target values for the substances listed in Annex I, by means of so-called 'daughter directives'. Two of these daughter directives were proposed in 1998, the first concerning benzene and carbon monoxide,[106] the second concerning limit values for sulphur dioxide, oxides of nitrogen, particulate matter, and lead in ambient air.[107] The second reading in the EP of the latter proposal on 13 January 1999 produced eleven amendments,[108] *inter alia* a recommendation to the Commission to grant particular attention to the adoption of alert thresholds, consistent with other pollutants in the Directive, for particulate matters PM10, PM2.5, or particular fractions of particulate matter when it will review the Directive in 2003. Moreover, the EP demanded stricter 'alert thresholds' for which warnings should be issued. Finally, Directive 1999/30/EC relating to Limit Values for Sulphur Dioxide, Nitrogen Dioxide and Oxides of Nitrogen, Particulate Matter and Lead in Ambient Air was adopted without further complications on 22 April 1999.[109] The deadline for transposition by the Member States is 19 June 2001.

Due to the EP elections in June 1999, the proposal for a Directive on Limit Values for Benzene and Carbon Monoxide was not discussed until eleven months after its publication by the Commission, on 2 December 1998. The draft Directive marks an important step in the EC air pollution strategy, as it proposes for the first time air quality limits for a carcinogen: benzene. The

---

[103] See (1999) 19 *Earth Negotiations Bulletin* 6, 6 Dec. 1999. See also *ENDS Environment Daily*, 7 Dec. 1999.
[104] [1999] OJ L85/1.                    [105] Dir. 96/62/EC, [1996] OJ L296/55.
[106] COM(98)59, [1999] OJ C53/8.          [107] COM(97)500, [1998] OJ C9/6.
[108] PE R4–0483/1998 of 1 Jan. 1999, [1999] OJ C104/36, *rapporteur* A. Pollack.
[109] [1999] OJ L163/41.

draft stipulates limits of 5 micrograms/m² for benzene, and of 10 milligrams/m² for carbon monoxide, to be achieved by 2010 and 2005, respectively. The EP's most vital amendment in its first reading concerned the exclusion of a five-year derogation for benzene limit values in areas experiencing severe socio-economic difficulties,[110] which represents a complex challenge to Member States, as they remain divided over the issue of exemptions. At a meeting of the Environment Council for 13 December 1999 in Brussels, it was agreed that the derogation would apply for a period of five years, as in the Commission proposal, excluding an upper air quality limit once a derogation has been granted. Although some Member States argued for more lenient derogation clauses, only Spain voted against the compromise, arguing that its climatic circumstances warranted longer potential exemptions.[111] The proposal now awaits a common position by the Council.

The Commission decided to publish a third proposal for a daughter directive in 1999, relating to ozone in ambient air.[112] The proposal was made more than a year behind schedule, as a result of, *inter alia*, the resignation of the Commission in March 1999. The proposal sets indicative target values for ozone of 120 micrograms/m², based on World Health Organization (WHO) guidelines. The Commission rejected mandatory limit values, and deadlines, on the basis of the transboundary nature of ozone pollution, leaving states with only limited control over pollution levels. Similar to other daughter directives, the proposal requires Member States to test ozone values, and to inform the general public when pollution levels of 180 micrograms/m² are exceeded. The proposal further allows for a number of annual violations, set initially at sixty days, to be reduced to twenty days per year by 2010. The first reading of the proposal in the EP was scheduled for 2000.

## G. INTERNATIONAL DEVELOPMENTS

At the international level, several major developments took place during 1999. The CLRTAP Protocol on Persistent Organic Pollutants (POPs) 1998[113] was the subject of intense negotiations, which resulted in an agreement at the conference in Geneva, in September 1999. The Protocol phases out ten persistent organic pollutants, including, *inter alia*, chemical aldrin, DDT, PCB, chlordane, and endrin. It also envisages two exceptions for DDT and PCBs which could still be used in certain applications. Agreement could not be reached in respect of two other POPs: dioxins and furans, which are by-products of industrial processes. Although the current text of the Protocol states that these should be reduced, some parties including the EU, would prefer to apply 'gradual elimination'. *The next major round of negotiations was to take place in Bonn in 2000.*[114]

---

[110] PE R5–0131/1999 of 2 Dec. 1999, [2000] OJ C194/4, *rapporteur* H. Breyer.
[111] *ENDS Environment Daily*, 13 Dec. 1999.   [112] See n. 89 above.
[113] Åarhus, 24 June 1998.   [114] *ENDS Environment Daily*, 13 Sept. 1999.

Another protocol negotiated in the framework of CLRTAP is the 1999 Protocol to Abate Acidification, Eutropication, and Ground-Level Ozone.[115] It targets similar substances as those contained in the EC's proposal for a Directive on National Emission Ceilings—sulphur dioxide, nitrogen oxides, volatile organic compounds, and ammonia—and establishes national emission limits for these substances for 2010. Ceilings are based on a 'reference-scenario' for expected 2010 emission levels, based on implementation of currently agreed measures only. The Protocol includes technical annexes with guidelines and standards for the various substances. In June 1999 the WHO adopted a Charter on Transport, Health, and Environment, within the framework of a Pan-European meeting of environment and health ministers. The Charter contains action plans with targets to reduce human exposure to pollutants by means of air quality targets. Although the Charter is not legally binding, there is increasing support to convert it to a binding document at the next ministerial conference in 2002.

In November 1999 the Commission announced that it is planning an environmental action programme to combat environmental degradation, *inter alia*, air pollution in northern Europe.[116] The programme is intended to improve coordination between EU and third countries, and will concentrate on the integration of environmental policy into sectoral policies, capacity building, and increased public participation. Among its action proposals are investments in major pollution areas, and a regional programme to combat climate change.

### H. MISCELLANEOUS

The EU also discussed a number of initiatives relating to air pollution in 1999. In respect of waste incineration, a new directive combining EC provisions for burning hazardous and non-hazardous waste was proposed, as anticipated in 1998 it is now awaiting its first reading in the EP.

A common position on a draft Directive concerning Emission of Gaseous Pollutants and Particulate Matters from Agricultural Tractors was also achieved in 1999,[117] with an aim to reduce emissions from agricultural and forest vehicles, applying similar requirements as those applicable to off-road mobile machinery. It would set emission limits for carbon monoxide, oxides of nitrogen, hydrocarbons, and particulates. The EP was satisfied with the proposal, but made a recommendation to the Commission to propose a third phase of emission limits before the end of 2002. The proposal now awaits its second reading by the EP.

---

[115] CLRTAP Protocol to Abate Acidification, Eutrophication and Ground-level Ozone, Gothenburg, 30 Nov. 1999.

[116] *ENDS Environment Daily*, 12 Nov. 1999.

[117] COM(98)472, of 3 Sept. 1998, [1998] OJ C303/9.

316 Alexandra Gonzalez-Calatayud

Despite the tumultuous resignation of the Commission, 1999 was certainly a productive year, in which important directives were adopted, particularly on the topic of acidification, and new initiatives were launched, such as the one on $CO_2$ and air transport. Furthermore, the Commission announced in early 1999 that it would initiate a feasibility study aimed at integration of all major EC air pollution policies into a single comprehensive programme. The 'Clean Air for Europe (CAFE)' study would be based on the notion of a single framework for EC air policy, which would be a very positive development and certainly something to look forward to in 2000. However, despite these encouraging developments, the archetypal behaviour of the Council in respect of many vital proposals, *inter alia*, energy product taxation, blocked progress, and left the EC without the necessary grip to confront the future challenges of atmospheric pollution.

## II. Chemicals and Biotechnology

### A. INTRODUCTION

Major developments have taken place in Europe in relation to the regulation of chemicals, genetic engineering, and plant protection. Since the beginning of 1998, EC chemical law in general has been under dispute, starting with the informal Transport and Environment Council meeting held in Chester, UK, on 24–6 April 1998. This meeting was followed by the evaluation of the main pieces of EC chemical law by the Commission, in addition to other documents of investigation. Moreover, the Commission issued unprecedented recommendations on marketing and use restrictions in the framework of the existing chemicals regime. Additionally, for the first time after the Amsterdam Treaty entered into force, the Commission decided upon several national marketing and use restrictions, notified by Member States. Finally, the ongoing progression of EC chemical law has now given rise to judicial disputes. In 1999 the European Court of Justice (ECJ) was confronted for the first time with the examination of the validity of EC regulatory measures, and those of Member States. A second case was brought before the ECJ in 1999, concerning a national phase-out programme.

In the field of genetics, after the amendment of Directive 90/219/EEC on the Contained Use of Genetically Modified Micro-Organisms (GMMOs),[1] in early 1998,[2] the debate subsequently focused on the deliberate release of genetically modified organisms (GMOs), and the marketing of products which contain them, both in the form of legislation and politics.

No truly significant developments have taken place in respect of the regulation of plant protection products.

### B. LEGISLATION ADOPTED

#### i. Classification, Packaging, and Labelling of Dangerous Preparations

In the field of chemical legislation, the most crucial development is the 'new' Directive 1999/45/EC on Classification, Packaging, and Labelling of Dangerous Preparations.[3] This Directive will substitute Directives 88/379/EEC[4] and 78/631/EEC,[5] concerning the classification, packaging, and labelling of, respectively, dangerous preparations and plant protection products, for the future.[6]

* Head of Division, Ministry for Construction Work and the Environment, Division of Soil Protection and Polluted Areas, Bremen, Germany.
[1] [1990] OJ L117/1.      [2] Dir. 98/81/EC, [1998] OJ L330/13.      [3] [1999] OJ L200/1.
[4] [1988] OJ L187/14; last amended by Dir. 96/65/EC, [1996] OJ L265/15.
[5] [1978] OJ L206/13; last amended by Dir. 92/32/EEC, [1992] OJ L154/1.
[6] Art. 21 and Annex VIII Dir. 1999/45/EC.

Directive 1999/45/EC aims at the protection of the general public, and above all, persons who come into contact with dangerous preparations at work or while conducting a hobby, complemented by the protection of consumers and the environment. The Directive demands specific safeguards for children by virtue of child-resistant fastenings on containers of certain dangerous preparations. With reference to the seventh amendment[7] of Directive 67/548/EEC on the Classification, Packaging, and Labelling of Dangerous Substances,[8] provisions at EC level are adopted by the new Directive 1999/45/EC. This enables the consideration of ecological effects of dangerous substances in classification and labelling, while it also allows for the introduction of an appropriate method for the assessment of ecotoxilogical properties.[9] In the case of a preparation posing a danger to consumers without being dangerous within the meaning of Directive 1999/45/EC, special labelling requirements will have to be observed.[10] Animal experiments are to be avoided so far as reasonably possible. Without prejudice to Directive 91/414/EEC concerning the Placing of Plant Protection Products on the Market (Pesticides Directive),[11] the provisions of Directive 1999/45/EC apply also to the classification, packaging, and labelling of plant protection products.[12] Therefore, the authorization procedure for plant protection products is still in force, and instructions on the use of a product must be provided in addition to the labelling. The Member States are to have transposed the Directive by 30 July 2002.

## ii. Marketing and Use Restriction

Directive 76/769/EEC on Restrictions on the Marketing and Use of Certain Dangerous Substances and Preparations (Marketing and Use Restriction Directive)[13] was adapted to technical progress for the fifth and sixth time, and was amended for the seventeenth time during 1999.

The fifth adaptation[14] concerned the regulation of tin, pentachlorphenol (PCP), and cadmium, and is to be transposed and applied by Member States before 1 September 2000. Organostanic compounds, in particular tributyltin, may not be used for anti-fouling in free associate paints, unless the release is controlled. Moreover, such substances must not be used for anti-fouling of ships shorter than 25 metres, or for ships only used in inland waters of the EC. Sweden and Austria were permitted to apply their stricter regulations on tin and cadmium until the end of 2002. The use of PCP was regulated *more* strictly, once again. Substances and preparations which contain PCP in volume of 0.1 per cent mass and over may not be marketed and used in the future. In fact, this regulation brings about an actual phase-out of the deliberate use of PCP in any substance or preparation. However, the exemption to allow for the use of PCP for certain industrial applications in France, Ireland, Portugal, Spain, and the UK, was prolonged until the end of 2008. By the end of 2002, the EC

---

[7] Dir. 92/32/EEC, [1992] OJ L154/1.                       [8] [1967] OJ L196/1.
[9] Art. 2 II. o, and Art. 7 Dir. 1999/45/EC.        [10] Art. 1 I and Art. 10 Dir. 1999/45/EC.
[11] [1991] OJ L230/1.        [12] Art. 1 IV Dir. 1999/45/EC.        [13] [1976] OJ L262/24.
[14] Dir. 1999/51/EC, [1999] OJ L142/22.

regulation on cadmium should be reassessed, based on the recommendation in the framework of the existing chemical regime.

The sixth adaptation[15] to technical process related to certain types of asbestos, namely chrysotile asbestos. Since less hazardous substitutes are now available for almost all purposes of this substance, its marketing and use was prohibited in 1999. Although some transitional exemptions have remained in force, these must be re-examined by the Scientific Committee on Toxicity, Ecotoxicity, and the Environment by 2008. The directive is to be transposed by Member States before 1 January 2005.[16]

Finally, the seventeenth amendment[17] of the Marketing and Use Restriction Directive included sixteen new substances which are carcinogenic, mutagenic, or toxic on reproduction in the Appendix to points 29, 30, and 31 of Annex I of the Directive, and excludes five such substances under point 29 (carcinogenic substances) as they are listed elsewhere. The amendment follows the adaptation to technical progress of Directive 67/548/EEC (Packaging and Labelling Directive),[18] and should be implemented by Member States before 1 July 2000.[19] In this new Directive, the availability of substitutes was considered to be an argument for restriction and for certain uses. Where alternatives were not available, transition periods were granted. The ban on chrysotile asbestos was justified, in that exposure limits which do not pose any risks to human beings cannot be determined scientifically. The availability of substitutes as a precondition for marketing and use restrictions has essentially been accepted by the ECJ. The transition periods appear to reflect a reasonable balance between the interests of the industries concerned.

### iii. Classification, Packaging, and Labelling of Dangerous Substances

Less significant developments in chemical law in 1999 include three adaptations to technical progress of Directive 67/548/EEC on Classification, Packaging, and Labelling of Dangerous Substances.[20] The first adaptation,[21] entailed the inclusion of several new dangerous substances, while also some methods for the determination of the physico-chemical properties, toxicity, and ecotoxicity were revised. In the second adaptation of the Directive, the Annexes were partly replaced, and partly new phrases were inserted, following new scientific knowledge.[22] The third adaptation permitted Sweden and Austria to apply their domestic provisions until the end of 2000.[23]

### iv. Good Laboratory Practice

Another less significant legal development in the area of chemical law in 1999 concerned an adaptation of Directive 88/320/EEC on the Inspection and Verification of Good Laboratory Practice.[24] The Annex to the 1988 Directive

---

[15] Dir. 1999/77/EC, [1999] OJ L207/18.  [16] Art. 2(1) of Dir. 1999/77/EC.
[17] Dir. 1999/43/EC, [1999] OJ L166/87.  [18] Dir. 96/54/EC, [1996] OJ L248/1.
[19] Art. 3(I) Dir. 1999/43/EC.  [20] [1967] OJ L196/1.  [21] Dir. 98/73/EC, [1998] OJ L305/1.
[22] Dir. 98/98/EC, [1998] OJ L355/1.  [23] Dir. 1999/33/EC, [1999] OJ L199/57.
[24] [1988] OJ L145/35.

was replaced, following an OECD Council decision of 9 March 1995, which amended the Annexes to the Council decision-recommendation on compliance with principles of good laboratory practice.[25]

## v. Existing Substances

For the first time since the establishment of the existing substances regime in 1993,[26] recommendations on risk reduction measures were issued.[27] For three of the four substances assessed, risk reduction measures were recommended, differentiating between measures which concern workers, and those which are intended for consumers.[28] These measures range from use instructions to marketing and use restrictions.[29] The recommendations will have to be considered by the Commission, when amendments are proposed in the framework of the Marketing and Use Restriction Directive, or in the framework of Directive 89/391/EEC on the Introduction of Measures to Encourage Improvements in the Safety and Health of Workers at Work.[30]

## vi. General Product Safety

In the framework of Directive 92/59/EEC on General Product Safety,[31] the Commission has issued a decision adopting measures prohibiting the placing on the market of toys and childcare articles intended to be placed in the mouth by children under 3 years of age, made of soft PVC containing one or more of certain listed substances.[32] Under Article 9 of the General Product Safety Directive, the Commission is allowed, after certain procedural conditions have been fulfilled, to oblige Member States to take temporary measures in order to prohibit the marketing of a product which can pose a serious and immediate threat to the health and safety of consumers. Since the Market and Use Restriction Directive does not contain provisions on phthalates, and Directive 88/378/EEC on the Safety of Toys[33] does not allow for temporary measures, the General Product Safety Directive was chosen for regulatory measures. Denmark, Greece, Austria, Sweden, Finland, Italy, France, and Germany had notified their national measures. Based on the precautionary principle, Member States were required to prohibit the marketing of such toys for three months, until 8 March 2000, although a thorough risk assessment had not yet been conducted. The significance of the decision lies in the fact that it highlights the necessity for temporary measures in order to cope with uncertainties, and to deal with imminent risks following the precautionary principle.

[25] Dir. 1999/12/EC, [1999] OJ L77/22.
[26] Regulation (EEC) No. 793/93 on the Evaluation and Control of the Risks of Existing Substances, [1993] OJ L84/1.
[27] [1999] OJ L292/42.
[28] The substances were 2-(2-butoxyethoxy)ethanol; 2-(2-methoxyethoxy)ethanol; Alkanes, C10-13, chloro; Benzene, C10-13-alkyl derivs. For the latter no risk reduction measure was recommended.
[29] Annex I. [30] [1989] OJ L183/1. [31] [1992] OJ L228/24.
[32] Di-iso-nonyl phthalate (DINP), di(2-ethylhexyl) phthalate (DEHP), dibutyl phthalate (DBP), di-iso-decyl phthalate (DIDP), di-n-octyl phthalate (DNOP), and butylbenzyl phthalate (BBP).
[33] [1988] OJ L187/1.

Neither the existing chemicals regime, nor the Marketing and Use Restriction Directive foresees such a regulatory option, at least not explicitly. Although the General Product Safety Directive allows for temporary measures, this Directive is limited to products.

### vii. Plant Protection Products

No major changes have occurred in respect of Directive 91/414/EEC concerning the Placing of Plant Protection Products on the Market (Pesticides Directive),[34] although the Directive was amended three times[35] to include three new active substances to Annex I.[36] Several Commission decisions in 1999 concerned the completeness of the documents submitted for this procedure.[37]

An amendment was made to Commission Regulation (EEC) No. 3600/92,[38] which regulates the risk assessment of existing plant protection products, to require the Member State designated as *rapporteur* to make available, at specific request or for consultation, certain information in the report to the interesting parties.[39] The rationale for this change is that the information on the active substances should be available as early as possible, in order to facilitate effective risk assessment and management.

C. LEGISLATION IN PROGRESS

### i. Genetically Modified Organisms

The most essential activity in the field of genetic engineering concerns the ongoing process regarding the revised Directive on the Deliberate Release into the Environment of Genetically Modified Organisms (GMO Directive) which repeals Directive 90/220/EEC.[40] In 1998 the Commission had proposed an amendment of the 1990 Directive, aiming to simplify and strengthen its provisions. By the very end of 1999, the legislative process for this proposed Directive had progressed to a Common Position of the Council. Following the Commission proposal on 23 February 1998,[41] the opinion of the economic and social committee,[42] and the first reading by the European Parliament (EP),[43] an amended proposal was presented by the Commission on 25 March 1999.[44] Finally, on 9 December 1999, the Council agreed upon a Common Position.[45] The

---

[34] [1991] OJ L230/1.     [35] [1999] OJ L21/21; [1999] OJ L206/16; [1999] OJ L210/13.

[36] Kresoxim-methyl, spiroxamine, and azimsulfuron.

[37] [1998] OJ L14/31; [1999] OJ L54/21; [1999] OJ L87/15; [1999] OJ L180/49; [1999] OJ L210/22; [1999] OJ L242/29.

[38] Commission Regulation (EEC) No. 3600/92 Laying Down the Detailed Rules for the Implementation of the First Stage of the Programme of Work Referred to in Article 8(2) of Directive 91/414/EEC, concerning the Placing of Plant Protection Products on the Market, [1992] OJ L366/10; last amended by Commission Regulation (EC) No. 1199/97, [1997] OJ L170/19.

[39] Ibid., No. 1972/1999, [1999] OJ L244/41.

[40] [1990] OJ L117/15; last amended by Dir. 97/35/EC, [1997] OJ L169/72.

[41] COM(98)85 final, [1998] OJ C139/1.     [42] [1998] OJ C407/1.     [43] [1999] OJ C150/363.

[44] COM(1999)139 final, [1999] OJ C139/7.

[45] Common Position (EC) No. 12/2000, [2000] OJ C64/1.

general purpose of the Common Position is to provide a regulatory framework, to regulate risks which might result from the deliberate release of GMOs into the environment, and the marketing of products which consist of or contain GMOs. The amendments should allow for simplified, transparent, and effective procedures, with a view to avoid outstretched and onerous proceedings for the applicants. The new provisions still require an environmental risk assessment prior to the release of GMOs into the environment, in addition to a step-by-step approach, for deliberate release as well as for marketing. In particular, resistances against antibiotics must be taken into account. The revised GMO Directive will have to be implemented in close conjunction with other relevant EC secondary legislation, in particular Directive 91/414/EEC concerning the Placing of Plant Protection Products on the Market.[46] The primary amendments to the Directive concern the marketing of GMO products. Following the Common Position, the marketing of GMO products is to face stricter requirements: first, a special environmental risk assessment must be conducted; second, product labelling must indicate the inclusion of GMOs; third, GMO markers must be attached to improve consumer awareness; fourth, retraceability must be guaranteed; and, finally, a monitoring scheme is to be established in all Member States.[47] Furthermore, permission for marketing can only be granted temporarily, for a maximum of ten years. Although the new GMO Directive will not apply to animal and human pharmaceuticals, provisions which regulate these products must at least guarantee an equivalent level of protection in the event they contain GMOs. Finally, Member States are allowed to take additional measures for the control and monitoring of GMO products. In order to avoid discrepancies with the consents based on the former Directive 90/220/EEC, these consents are to be revised within a certain period. The stricter regulatory approach proposed by the Council in its Common Position, with regard to the marketing of GMO products, is clearly a result of factual moratoria established by Member States in the recent past. The safeguard clause of the 1990 Directive,[48] allowing Member States to adopt measures upon Commission consent, remains in force, albeit more restrictively. Under the new provision,[49] assessments must be based on new or additional information, and must also be newly conducted.

### D. POLICY DOCUMENTS

#### i. Reform of Chemical Law

The Commission initiated a debate on reforming EC Chemical Law in 1998. A working paper was issued in November 1998, which contained an evaluation of the four central pieces of EC chemical legislation, and the subsequent adaptations made thereto:

— Directive 67/548/EEC on Classification, Packaging, and Labelling of

---

[46] [1991] OJ L230/1.      [47] Art. 13(II) Common Position.      [48] Art. 16.
[49] Art. 22 of the Common Position.                          [50] [1967] OJ L196/1.

Dangerous Substances;[50]
— Directive 88/379/EEC on Classification, Packaging, and Labelling of Dangerous Preparations;[51]
— Regulation (EEC) No. 793/93 on the Evaluation and Control of the Risks of Existing Substances;[52] and
— Directive 76/769/EEC on Restrictions on the Marketing and Use of Certain Dangerous Substances and Preparations.[53]

The working paper included detailed evaluations of each of these vital pieces of legislation, the conclusions of which were approved by the Council in December 1998.[54] With regard to Directive 67/548/EEC, the main criticism concerned the complicated and time-consuming procedure, the defective implementation of the labelling provisions, and the lack of appropriate risk reduction measures for carcinogenic, teratogenic, and mutagenic substances. The recommendations with regard to Directive 88/379/EEC had by this time already been realized by the new Directive 1999/45/EC.[55] The existing chemicals regime established by Regulation (EEC) No. 793/93 was criticized for its lack of efficiency: risk assessments had taken up to between two and four-and-a-half years, while no risk reduction recommendation had been achieved. As regards Directive 76/769/EEC, it was recommended that new substances be adopted by committee proceedings to facilitate the amendment procedure, and to achieve a higher level of harmonization at EC and international level. Following the precautionary principle, risk reduction measures should also be based on preliminary risk assessments.

In June 1999, the Environment Council decided that the EC chemicals strategy was in need of reform, and thus asked the Commission to deliver official proposals to this end, in the form of a White Book, by the end of 2000. The Council had taken into account the recommendations of the Simplification of Legislation for the Internal Market (SLIM) Team, concerning Directive 67/548/EEC, which were released in May 1999, and the three-yearly report on the implementation of the this Directive.[56] The Council mandated the Commission to consider, *inter alia*, whether primary responsibility should be placed with the chemical industry, the importers, or with the commercial users. Furthermore, the Commission was to consider whether targeted risk assessments should be applied, whether risk reduction measures can be based on certain inherent properties of substances, and whether a cluster approach would be appropriate.

By the end of 1999 the Environment Commissioner, Ms Wallström, presented the concepts at the Stakeholder meeting in Brussels, organized by CEFIC, thus accentuating the mandates by the Council.[57] First, the new

---

[51] [1988] OJ L187/14.        [52] [1993] OJ L84/1.        [53] [1976] OJ L262/24.
[54] EU Bull 12–1998, 83.        [55] See Section B(*i*) above.
[56] Both documents are published on the Internet at: http://europa.eu.int/comm/environment/dansub/home_en.htm.
[57] Ms. Wallström, 'Towards a New Strategy for Chemicals', speech for the CEFIC Stakeholders Dialogue meeting in Brussels, 6 Dec. 1999.

strategy should also be applied to existing chemicals, which is expected to necessitate a supplementary notification system. One option would be to determine a deadline, after which the marketing and use of existing substances is only permissible in the event data has been provided by the industry, which is comparable to the data on new chemicals. Second, Ms Wallström indicated, generally the industry should bear the burden of proof that a certain substance does not pose a risk to humans or to the environment. This proposal is primarily related to existing chemicals, and might allow for a transitional period. Third, not only the producer, but also the professional user should be responsible for safe application, and for the transfer of information to governmental authorities. The significance of this proposal lies in the fact that substances, in many cases, have such a wide range of potential uses that the producer usually does not know all of them. Fourth, Ms Wallström proposed that risk assessments should be limited to problematic uses only, in order to curtail the time for preparing them. It appears that such an adaptation would certainly derogate from the requirement to conduct a comprehensive risk assessment.

## ii. Endocrine Disrupters

On 20 December 1999 the Commission adopted a Communication on a Community Strategy for Endocrine Disrupters: substances which are suspected of interfering with the hormone system of human beings and wild life.[58] The Commission has taken into account the Resolution of October 1998 of the Parliament on the same subject.[59] These substances might cause cancer, behavioural changes, and reproductive abnormalities. In the short term, EC policy, in the form of further research work, is aimed at the identification of the problem of endocrine disruption, its causes, and its consequences. Moreover, the public is to be informed efficiently and, based on international cooperation and coordination, in order that the available knowledge and resources should be used to their fullest. As a matter of priority, Member States are encouraged to apply the existing legislation in full, while new legislative instruments for the long-term future are assessed.

## iii. Report on Seveso Directive

The Commission issued a report in 1999 on Council Directive 82/501/EEC on the Major-Accident Hazards of Certain Industrial Activities (Seveso Directive),[60] particularly on its application between 1994 and 1996. Such three-yearly Commission reports are required by the amended[61] Article 18 of the Seveso Directive. The 1999 report concludes that the Directive has been effectively transposed by Member States, based on the fact that the number of safety reports, examinations of the safety reports, national measures taken, and emergency plans has significantly increased, although the number of establishments has decreased in the same period. However, it is critical of the

---

[58] COM(1999)706.                    [59] [1998] OJ C341/1.                    [60] [1982] OJ L230/1.
[61] Dir. 91/692/EEC Standardizing and Rationalizing reports on the implementation of Certain Directives Relating to the Environment, [1991] OJ L377/48.

lack of uniformity in the definition of 'sites', as this vastly differs between Member States, thereby complicating reasonable assessments. Furthermore, the report indicates that the relative rate of accidents has not decreased in the evaluation period, while pointing to the need for further efforts to reduce the risks of serious accidents in industrial installations. Directive 96/82/EC on the Control of Major-Accident Hazards Involving Dangerous Substances (Seveso II Directive) is intended to address these and other criticisms.[62]

### iv. Hormones and Beef: the WTO

On 13 February 1998 the Dispute Settlement Body of the World Trade Organization (WTO) approved the reports of the WTO Appellate Body, concerning the 'EC-measures on meat and meat products (hormones)'.[63] It demanded that the EC bring its legislation into line with WTO law, in particular with the Agreement on the Application of Sanitary and Phytosanitary Measures (SPS Agreement), within a period of fifteen months, which ended on 13 May 1999. In the Communication to the Council and the EP, the Commission identified and assessed three options for a response,[64] with the ultimate aim of protecting the consumer, balanced with its international obligations. First, the Commission suggested negotiations with the USA to find agreement on appropriate compensation. Second, it proposed a transfer of the definite import prohibition into provisional measures, based on the currently available scientific information in conformity with Article 5(VII) SPS Agreement. Finally, substitution of the import prohibition by labelling requirements could also be an alternative, according to the Commission, thereby enabling the consumer to take conscious decisions. The Commission stressed the advantage of the first two options, in view of the possibility of maintaining current levels of protection, while the third option would entail a conformation of the EC with its international obligations. The Council and the EP have been urged to respond promptly to these options, and ultimately to agree upon an appropriate strategy to address this trade conflict.

### v. Moratorium of Marketing of GMO Products

Since April 1998, as a result of consensus in the relevant committees, no Community-wide consent on the marketing of GMO products based on Directive 90/220/EEC (GMO Directive) was granted. In fact, several national moratoria on the commercial cultivation of genetically modified plants currently exist, *inter alia*, in Denmark, France, Greece, and the UK. Austria and Luxembourg have also issued national prohibitions against BT-raps. Additionally, the new German Government favours a moratorium on genetically modified crops. These moratoria, and the lack of consensus, form the background to the stricter requirements for the placing on the market of GMO products in the revised Directive on the Deliberate Release of Genetically Modified Organisms into the Environment.[65]

[62] [1997] OJ L10/13.          [63] Published on the Internet at: http://www.wto.org.
[64] COM(1999)81 final.          [65] See Section C*(i)* above.

E. CASE LAW

*i. Chemicals*

In a preliminary ruling in the *Nederhoff* case,[66] the ECJ held that a Dutch prohibition on the use of creosote was not inconsistent with, *inter alia*, Directive 76/769/EEC concerning Restrictions on the Marketing and Use of Certain Dangerous Substances and Preparations, as amended by Directive 94/60/EC.[67] The case concerned the question of whether a Member State can adopt more stringent measures for the regulation of the use of creosote than those of the Directive. The ECJ indicated that following Article 1 of the Directive, according to which it applies 'without prejudice to the applications of other relevant Community provisions', the Dutch prohibition on the placing of wooden posts impregnated with creosote in surface water was not in violation of EC chemical law, since Article 10 of the Directive authorizes such measures.

In another preliminary ruling involving chemicals, the *Kemikalienin-spektionen* v. *Toolex Alpha* case,[68] the ECJ was asked to decide whether a Swedish prohibition against the industrial use of trichloroethylene was consistent with Article 30 EC, even if it contravened Article 28 EC. The Swedish regulation had established a complete phase-out of this substance, while exemptions could only be granted in the event that a company could prove its continued investigations for alternative solutions had been fruitless. The burden of proof was placed completely with the applicant. Since one point of discussion in the reform debate is how to allocate the responsibility for providing information about the properties of substances, but also on potentially available substitutes, this ECJ judgment is of great importance for the design of future political and regulatory options, for national and EC authorities alike.

*ii. Genetically Modified Organisms*

In the *Greenpeace* case,[69] submitted for a preliminary ruling by the French *Conseil d'Etat*, the ECJ examined the question whether a Member State, which has received a favourable decision upon its application to the Commission to authorize the placing on the market of a product containing GMOs, may ultimately refuse authorization if in the meantime new information indicating risks has been found. Furthermore, ECJ was to assess the general consequences of irregularities in the national procedure, after a favourable decision is taken by the Commission.

---

[66] Case C–232/97, *L. Nederhoff & Zn.* v. *Dijkgraaf en hoogheemraden van het Hoogheemraadschap Rijnland* [1999] ECR I–6385.

[67] Other relevant legislation included, *inter alia*, Dir. 76/464/EEC on Pollution Caused by Certain Dangerous Substances Discharged into the Aquatic Environment, [1976] OJ L129/23.

[68] Case C–473/98, *Kemikalieninspektionen* v. *Toolex Alpha AB* [2000] ECR-I–5681.

[69] Case C–6/99, *Association Greenpeace France and Others* v. *Ministère de l'Agriculture et de la Pêche and Others* [2000] ECR–I–1651.

### iii.  Plant Protection Products

In case C–306/98,[70] the UK *Queen's Bench Divisional Court* made a reference to the ECJ for a preliminary ruling on the interpretation of the Plant Protection Products Directive. The case concerned in particular the question which requirements are to be observed by Member States in the process of granting a provisional authorization to put plant protection products on the market, which contain substances that are not listed in Annex I.

Two additional actions involving pesticides were brought by the Commission in 1999 against France[71] and Luxembourg.[72] In both actions, the Commission alleged a failure to transpose Directive 96/28/EC adapting to technical progress Council Directive 76/116/EEC relating to Fertilizers.[73] Both cases were removed from the record by order of the Court of First Instance (CFI) in September 1999.[74]

### F. INTERNATIONAL COOPERATION

### i.  Prior Informed Consent

In September 1998 the signing of the Rotterdam Convention on Trade in Certain Hazardous Chemicals and Pesticides, established in EC law the principle of prior informed consent for nationally banned or severely restricted hazardous chemicals or pesticides. Accordingly, the Convention is now transposed in European law by Directive 96/52/EC, and the EC and its Member States are responsible 'within their respective spheres of competence'.[75]

### ii.  Marine Environment

Furthermore, the Commission has proposed adoption by the Council of four decisions by the OSPRAR-Commission,[76] in which all Contracting Parties are represented.[77] The decision by the OSPRAR-Commission is concerned with the transposition of the amended Annex V, which deals with the assignment of certain protected areas in the marine environment.[78] In the EC, the new Annex V will be implemented in the respective frameworks of the Wild Birds Directive[79] and the Habitats Directive.[80] With the second proposal, the decision of the OSPRAR-Commission to revoke the exemptions for France and the UK to dump radioactive waste in the marine environment shall be accepted.[81] The third proposal concerns the adoption of the OSPRAR-decision on the removal of offshore installations which have been shut down.[82] Finally,

---

[70] Case C–306/98, *Queen v. Minister for Agriculture, Fisheries and Food, and Secretary of State for the Environment,* [1998] OJ C299/27.

[71] Case C–31/99, *Commission v. France,* [1999] OJ C086/13.

[72] Case C–32/99, *Commission v. Luxembourg,* [1999] OJ C086/13.

[73] [1996] OJ L140/30.        [74] [1999] OJ C366/24.        [75] [1998] OJ L326/6.

[76] Convention on the Protection of the Marine Environment in the North-East Atlantic, [1998] OJ L104 /1.

[77] [1999] OJ C158/1.        [78] [1999] OJ C158/1.        [79] Dir. 79/409/EEC, [1979] OJ L103/1.

[80] Dir. 92/43/EEC, [1992] OJ L206/7.        [81] [1999] OJ C158/8.        [82] [1999] OJ C158/10.

the fourth decision of the OSPRAR-Commission established emission and discharge limit values for the manufacture of vinyl chloride monomer (VCM), including the manufacture of 1.2-dichloroethane (EDC).[83]

Finally, in 1999 the Council decided to accept the amendment of the Protocol for the Protection of the Mediterranean Sea against Pollution from Land-Based Sources, in the framework of the Barcelona Convention for the Protection of the Mediterranean Sea against Pollution.[84] The Protocol obliges all parties to take all appropriate measures to prevent, abate, combat, and eliminate discharges from any land-based sources such as rivers, coastal establishments, or outfalls. Thereby, the Protocol shall apply to all sources, irrespective of whether they are point or diffuse sources. Priority shall be given to the phase-out of inputs of substances that are toxic, persistent, and liable to bio-accumulate. To this end, the Contracting Parties shall elaborate and implement national or regional action plans containing measures and time-tables. These shall take into account the best available techniques and best environmental practice. Criteria for the definition of these principles are fixed in Annex IV. A list of categories of substances which shall be phased out is contained in Annex I(C). The Protocol is transposed in EC law by a set of directives, *inter alia*, the IPPC-Directive.[85]

## G. MISCELLANEOUS

### i. PCP and Creosote Decisions

For the first time since the entry into force of the new provision allowing for national derogations,[86] Article 95 EC, the Commission issued five decisions on unilateral marketing and use restrictions against chemical substances which were notified by Member States. Four of these decisions concerned national provisions on creosote, a biocide primarily used for the protection of wood, which were already in force in the Netherlands, Germany, Sweden, and Denmark.[87] A Dutch PCP usage restriction, also pre-existing, was the subject of the fifth Commission Decision.[88] In all cases, the national actions went beyond the requirements of Directive 76/769/EEC (Marketing and Use Restriction Directive), and the subsequent amendments thereto. Accordingly, the legal basis for the decisions was Article 95(4) EC, in respect of national measures which are sought to be maintained. The Commission adopted a somewhat uniform method for the review of the national measures by, first, focusing on the facts, in particular relevant EC and domestic legislation,

---

[83] [1999] OJ C158/19.

[84] [1999] OJ L322/18. Convention for the Protection of the Mediterranean Sea against Pollution, [1977] OJ L240/1.

[85] Dir. 96/61/EC concerning Integrated Pollution Prevention and Control, [1996] OJ L257/26.

[86] See H. Sevenster, 'The Environmental Gurarantee after Amsterdam: Does the Emperor have New Clothes?' (1998) 1 *Yearbook of European Environmental Law*, 291–310.

[87] [1999] OJ L329/25 (Netherlands); [1999] OJ L329/43 (Germany); [1999] OJ L329/63 (Sweden); [1999] OJ L329/83 (Denmark).

[88] [1999] OJ L329/15.

followed by a comparison of both. Second, focus shifted to the procedure, followed, finally, by an assessment, primarily in respect of the justification on grounds of major needs. The Commission has developed a clear approach as regards its decisions on national derogations, mirroring the requirements set out by the ECJ in its first PCP-ruling.[89] The decisions are based on detailed examinations of the national provisions and their justification. In respect of creosote, the Commission based its conclusions on the assessment of external consultants, a long-term study of the Frauenhofer Institute on the carcinogenity of creosote, and the evaluation of all arguments presented by the Scientific Committee for Toxicity, Ecotoxicity, and the Environment. Generally, the national derogations in all these cases were held to be justified by health considerations, in view of a new scientific study indicating a potential carcinogenic effect of creosote, even below the exposure limits established by the Marketing and Use Restriction Directive. The environmental justification for the national derogation was only accepted in the single case of the Netherlands, in consideration of the extraordinarily frequent use of wooden posts treated with creosote in Dutch waterways. The Dutch measures restricting the use of PCP were also held to be justified by health and environmental considerations. The Commission managed to issue its decisions within the deadline of six months after the entry into force of the Amsterdam Treaty, as required by Article 95(4) EC. It will probably prove difficult to administer this provision, due to the significant requirements in terms of the substantiation of any decision. In conformity with this provision, the Commission is in fact examining the possibility of an amendment to the Marketing and Use Restriction Directive, in order to harmonize the level of protection guaranteed in the decisions permitting national derogations. In fact, Directive 1999/51/EC[90] has already transferred the stricter national regulations in Germany, Denmark, and the Netherlands, to Community level.

## ii. *Major-Accident Hazards*

Of further importance is certainly Commission Decision 1999/314/EC[91] which entails a questionnaire relating to Directive 96/82/EC on the Control of Major-Accident Hazards Involving Dangerous Substances (Seveso II Directive).[92] In the framework of this Directive, Member States are to report to the Commission every three years. The new questionnaire contains information about the number of so-called upper-tier establishments, about safety reports and emergency plans of the establishments listed, as well as about potential domino effects. Furthermore, in respect of the means of land-use planning employed with respect to upper-tier establishments, reports must be made on the distribution of information to the general public, as well as in how many cases the use of certain establishments was prohibited, or the sites inspected. Where appropriate, the neighbour Member States must also be informed thereof. The questionnaire is intended to improve the exchange of

---

[89] Case C–41/93, *French Republic* v. *Commission* [1994] ECR I–1829.     [90] See n. 14 above.
[91] [1999] OJ L120/43.               [92] [1997] OJ L10/13.

information between Member States and the Commission, as required by Article 19 of the Seveso II Directive.

## H. CONCLUSION

Certainly, European chemical law gained in effectiveness and routine during 1999. This is exemplified by the first recommendations on risk reduction measures under the existing chemical regime, the decisions of the Commission on national actions, and the two Court decisions. Moreover, the reform process has just started, and the proposals of the Commission expressed by Ms Wallström are by all means far-reaching. Although industry has committed itself to present basic information on so-called high-production volume substances, the cooperation between the authorities and industry is in need of further evaluation. Additionally, instruments to oblige industry to make available information about dangerous properties of substances to the general public, as a means to force industry to stop using these substances, will have to be debated more in detail. Comparable measures have already been applied in the USA, and in several Scandinavian countries.

Biotechnology law is also in constant progress, and typically remains subject to political controversy. Following national moratoria on the use of genetically modified crops and plants, the Common Position seeks to reflect necessities of risk management.

# III. Nature Conservation

## CHRIS BACKES*

### A. LEGISLATION ADOPTED

### i. Birds Directive and Habitats Directive

In 1999 no changes were made to Council Directive 79/409/EEC on the Conservation of Wild Birds (Birds Directive),[1] nor were there any proposals to this end. Council Directive 92/43/EEC on the Conservation of Natural Habitats and of Wild Fauna and Flora (Habitats Directive)[2] was also left unaltered. However, in the last days of 1998, the Council approved a change to Annexes II and III of the Bern Convention on the Conservation of European Wildlife and Natural Habitats.[3] In accordance with the parties' decision at the 17th meeting of the Standing Committee, four species were added to Annex II, and twenty-two were added to Annex III. The Council decision observes that two of these species are listed under the Birds Directive and three of them under the Habitats Directive. It provides no information regarding the other twenty-one species, or their conservation status in EC law. One might have expected that, since these twenty-one species appear to fall neither under the Birds Directive nor under the Habitats Directive, a change of (the Annexes to) these Directives would be proposed. However, such action was not taken. In response to a question from a Member of the European Parliament (MEP) regarding this issue the Commission stated that it had recommended that Member States include additional species, not yet covered by the Habitats Directive.[4] However, this does not clarify why the Commission has not recommended that all species listed under the Bern Convention—but not yet covered by the Habitats Directive—should be included. Existing discrepancies between the Annexes to the Bern Convention on the one hand, and the EC directives on nature conservation on the other, are likely to cause problems in practice.

In 1999, again, MEPs filed numerous questions concerning the application and enforcement of the Birds Directive[5] and the Habitats Directive.[6] Many of

---

* Professor, University of Utrecht, Utrecht, the Netherlands
[1] [1979] OJ L103/1.      [2] [1992] OJ L201/7.
[3] Council Decision 98/746/EC concerning the Approval, on behalf of the Community, of Amendments to Appendices II and III to the Berne Convention on the Conservation of European Wildlife and Natural Habitats adopted at the 17th Meeting of the Convention's Standing Committee [1998] OJ L358/114.
[4] Question E-1338/98, [1999] OJ C402/113.
[5] Written Questions No. P-2754/98 on a Sicilian Regional Assembly law on hunting, [1999] OJ C013/158; No. E-1753/98 on trapping of wild birds by the use of liming, [1999] OJ C013/78; No. E-2053/98 on damage to crops by wild geese in Germany, [1999] OJ C013/141; No. P 2186/98 on the wish to 'clarify and modify' the Directive in the interest of hunting, [1999] OJ C013/151; No. E-2099/98 about the number of complaints, infringement procedures, and Court judgments, especially relating to Germany, [1999] OJ C013/148; No. E-3088/98 on the delay of Germany in

[footnote 6 on p.332

these questions, in particular those concerning the Birds Directive, are largely of practical interest, and do not raise legal questions. However, several of these questions are of special interest because the answers provided offer an insight into the Commission's legal interpretation of some of the objectives of that Directive.[7]

Many of the questions concern the protection of sites proposed by Member States to the Commission following Article 4(1) Habitats Directive, in order to draw up the Community list of the Natura 2000 Network, in accordance with Article 4(2). However, the Commission has not yet drawn up such a list. According to Article 4(5) Habitats Directive, from the moment the Commission has published its list, Article 6(2), (3), and (4) will apply to these sites. In the meantime, many plans and projects exist, affecting the proposed sites. In a number of parliamentary questions the Commission is asked to take action to ensure the conservation of those sites. On the one hand, the Commission answers that in this interim situation it is principally the responsibility of Member States to adopt the necessary measures to guarantee a favourable conservation status to the proposed sites.[8] However, the fact that a Member State has proposed a certain site, and the fact that a site inevitably includes several types of natural habitats and (priority) species, renders it very likely that such a site will be accepted for the Natura 2000 Network. Therefore, in the meantime, the conservation of these sites is not only the responsibility

designating enough SPAs, [1999] OJ C135/166; No. E-2565/98 about several infringements of the Directive's provisions by the Lombardy Regional Council, [1999] OJ C135/72; No. E-2154 about the killing of *capercaillies* by poachers in Spain, [1999] OJ C118/34; No. E-2747/98 about 'the scandalous French law' opening hunting seasons for water fowl which violate the provisions of the Birds Directive, [1999] OJ C142/36; No. E-2268/98 about the 'blatant disregard' of France extending the hunting seasons for migratory birds in violation of the Directive; No. E-2177/98 about a draft law of Valencia which allows lime-hunting, [1999] OJ C142/7; No. E-3293/98 about other measures taken by the EC to protect birds on behalf of the Birds Directive, [1999] OJ C182/58; No. E-3006/98 about illegal agricultural practices in the Pego-Oliva marsh (Valencia/Spain), [1999] OJ C142/68; No. E-2382/98 and No. E-3184/98 about the construction of a dam in the Ems (Emssperrwerk, Germany), [1999] OJ C182/6 and [1999] OJ C182/50.
   [6] Written Questions No. E-1291/98 about the construction of a road across Monte Epomo (Ischia, Italy) located within a site of Community interest, [1999] OJ C31/31; No. E- 3196/98 about the order of priority of the reasons justifying derogations according to Art. 6(4), [1999] OJ C142/105; No. E-0787/98 about threat to badgers in connection with combating tuberculosis in the UK, [1999] OJ C31/129; No. E-1338/98 about the differences between the Annexes to the Bern Convention and the Annexes to the Habitats Directive, [1999] OJ C402/113; No. E-2638/98 about the question whether the environmental benefits of rail transport generally can be qualified as consequences of primary importance for the environment, [1999] OJ C118/110; No. E-2272/98 about the upgrading of the Sefton coast road (UK), [1999] OJ C118/49; No. E-3214–98 about a quarry situated in a Greek site, proposed but not yet selected as an SCI, [1999] OJ C135/178; No. E-2868/98 and No. E-2869/98 about how 'significant effect' has to be interpreted in case of upgrading roads, [1999] OJ C142/50; No. E-2657/98 about the enlarging of San Giuseppe Airport at Treviso (Italy), [1999] OJ C142/30; No. E-2282/98 about whether the Commission 'places a higher value on a bear's life than on the life of a human being', [1999] OJ C142/10; No. E-2925/98 about the delay of Greece to implement the Habitats Directive, [1999] OJ C135/137.
   [7] From the answer to question No. E-2099/98 one can infer that a total of 646 complaints reporting infringements of the Birds Directive have been lodged with the Commission until summer 1998.
   [8] See e.g. Written Question No. E-2657/98, n. 6 above.

but also the duty of Member States, under supervision of the Commission.[9] In the author's opinion, this does not necessarily mean that Article 6 is to be applied word-for-word, but rather that the function of all proposed sites within the Natura 2000 Network must, as a result, not be diminished before the decision on the Community list is taken. Although the Commission does not use this legal argument, it evidently derives from Article 10 EC.[10] In other cases, the Commission simply applies Article 6(2), (3), and (4) Habitats Directive to sites proposed by Member States, although the Community list has not yet been published.[11] A similar application does not seem entirely appropriate in the opinion of the author.

In a number of questions, the Commission is asked to take immediate action to stop certain activities, which, in the opinion of the MEPs, will breach the Birds Directive or the Habitats Directive. In these cases, the Commission responds that it has contacted the national authorities and has requested information, or that it has already initiated an infringement procedure. However, infringement procedures involve a lengthy process, and in the Commission's own opinion, it is not empowered to grant interim relief to stop domestic projects in Member States.[12]

One of the parliamentary questions concerns railway projects. The environmental benefits of transport by rail compared with transport on road cannot generally be qualified as 'consequences of primary importance for the environment', which always justify the building of new railtracks. A case-by-case analysis must be undertaken. The requirement that there may be no alternatives to a railway-track adversely affecting the integrity of a protected site means that the applicant must consider alternative routes and show in a convincing manner that they are not feasible.[13] Two other questions arose regarding what can be qualified a 'significant effect': first, does the creation of new sign-posting systems, to encourage traffic to use a particular route, which leads to a significant increase in the usage of a road passing through an SCI imply a significant effect? And, second, does the same hold for the upgrading of a road with the consequence that heavy vehicles may pass through an SCI? The Commission does not truly answer these questions, arguing that only the European Court of Justice (ECJ) can provide a definitive interpretation of the provisions concerned. However, the Commission does provide an implicit answer, by stating that no action automatically requires an assessment within the meaning of Article 6(3) Habitats Directive.

---

[9] See e.g. ibid. No. E-3214/98, [1999] OJ C135/178.
[10] See further Ch. W. Backes, 'Veel Habitat, Weinig Richtlijnen?' in Ch. W. Backes, J. A. W. M. Ponten, and F. Neumann (eds.), *Gemeenten en de Vogel- en Habitatrichtlijn* (The Hague: Boom Juridische Uitgevers, 2000), 17.
[11] See e.g. the answer to Written Question No. E-1291/98, n. 6 above.
[12] Answer to Written Question No. E-2272/98, n. 6 above.
[13] See ibid. No. E-2638/98, n. 6 above.

## ii. CITES Regulation

Following the adoption of an entirely new CITES Regulation in 1997,[14] some further changes were necessary in 1999. The list of those species which may not be brought into the Community required twofold amendment. As a consequence, and in order to prevent a lack of clarity, the existing Regulation (EC) No. 2473/98[15] was replaced in its entirety by the new Regulation (EC) No. 1968/1999 Suspending the Introduction into the Community of Specimens of Certain Species of Wild Fauna and Flora,[16] including a completely revised list.

## iii. Laboratory Animals

On 10 February 1987 the EC signed the European Convention for the Protection of Vertebrate Animals used for Experimental and Other Scientific Purposes. Until recently, this Convention was not approved. However, on 23 March 1998, the Council decided to approve the Convention, while making a reservation in respect of Article 28(1), to relieve the EC of the requirement to provide statistical data.[17] As early as 1986, the provisions of the Convention had already integrally been adopted in Directive 86/609/EEC on the Protection of Animals used for Experimental and Other Scientific Purposes.[18]

### B. LEGISLATION IN PROGRESS

## i. Forest Protection

Council Regulation (EEC) No. 3528/86 on Protection of the Community's Forests against Atmospheric Pollution[19] and Council Regulation (EEC) No. 2158/92 on Protection of the Community's Forests against Fire[20] were annulled by the ECJ, because the Council had chosen the former Article 43 EC (now Article 37 EC) instead of the former Article 130S EC (now Article 175 EC) as their legal basis.[21] However, the Court suspended the effects of its decision in order to enable the Council to adopt two new regulations with the same purpose within a reasonable time. On 9 August 1999 the Commission sent proposals for revised regulations to the Council and the European Parliament (EP).[22]

## ii. OSPAR Convention

The EC is a party to the Convention for the Protection of the Marine Environment of the North-East Atlantic (OSPAR),[23] which entered into force on 25 March 1998. In the first ministerial meeting, held in Sintra (Portugal), of the OSPAR Commission since the entry into force of the Convention in July

[14] Council Reg. (EC) No. 338/97 on the Protection of Species of Wild Fauna and Flora by Regulating Trade Therein, [1997] OJ L61/1.
[15] [1998] OJ L308/18.   [16] [1999] OJ L244/22.   [17] [1999] OJ L222/29.
[18] [1986] OJ L358/1.   [19] [1986] OJ L326/2.   [20] [1992] OJ L217/3.
[21] Joined Cases C–164/97 and C–165/97, *European Parliament* v. *Council* [1999] ECR I–1139.
[22] COM(99)379 final.
[23] Paris, 22 Sept. 1992.

1998, a new Annex V on the Protection and Conservation of the Ecosystems and Biological Diversity of the Maritime Area was adopted. Consequently, on 26 April 1999, the Commission submitted a proposal for the approval of the new Annex V, to the Council.[24] An additional five decisions were adopted by the OSPAR Commission at the Sintra meeting. However, these decisions did not necessitate any changes to EC legislation.[25]

C. CASE LAW

In accordance with previous years, the number of complaints which the Commission lodged against Member States involving environmental law increased in 1999. Moreover, again in line with earlier experiences, more than half of these cases concerned nature conservation law.[26]

### i. Birds Directive

In 1999 there were two important judgments concerning the Birds Directive, both in cases against France. In its *Seine Estuary* ruling of 18 March 1999,[27] the ECJ ruled that France had failed to classify a sufficiently large area of the Seine estuary as a Special Protection Area (SPA), and subsequently had failed to adopt measures to provide an adequate legal regime to protect the sites which it had classified. However, the Court dismissed the Commission's complaint relating to the construction of an industrial plant, arguing that the Commission had not furnished sufficient proof that this part of the Seine estuary was to be qualified as an area of special importance for the birds concerned.

An interesting question in this judgment concerned Article 7 Birds Directive. It has yet to be determined whether this Article merely applies to SPAs which actually have been classified, or that it could also be held to apply to sites that ought to have been classified, on the basis of their 'outstanding importance'. If Article 7 only relates to officially classified SPAs, Article 4(4) Birds Directive would certainly apply to those sites which require classification, but still lack such categorization. However, Article 4(4) Birds Directive creates a very strong protection regime, which does not allow for derogations on economic or social grounds. In this particular case, the industrial plant was situated in a non-classified site. By discussing whether this plant was built and managed in accordance with Article 6(2), (3), and (4) Habitats Directive, the ECJ appears implicitly to have decided that this provision, and hence not Article 4(4) Birds Directive, is applicable to sites that should have been classified, but were not treated accordingly. Thus, the Court seems to suggest that Article 7 Habitats Directive also relates to those sites, although it remains questionable whether it fully appreciated the consequences of its own ruling. The question regarding

[24] COM(99)190 final.                    [25] Ibid.
[26] Seventeenth Annual Report on Monitoring the Application of Community Law (1999), COM(2000) 92 final, 62.
[27] Case C–166/97, *Commission* v. *France* [1999] ECR I–1719.

the scope of Article 7 Habitats Directive was not discussed explicitly. In a subsequent case,[28] however, Advocate General Alber argued that the *Seine Estuary* judgment may not be construed as to hold an extension of the scope of application of Article 7 Habitats Directive. According to the Advocate General, it is evident from the case law that this provision is exclusively applicable to officially classified SPAs. In the author's opinion, this conclusion seems highly debatable. However, the ECJ has decided in conformity with the opinion of the Advocate General: Article 7 only applies to officially classified SPAs.[29]

The second judgment in a case against France concerned the Poitevin marsh.[30] In case C–96/98, France had again failed to classify a sufficient area as an SPA, and had also failed to adopt measures conferring a sufficient legal status to the SPAs which it had classified. The ECJ held that contractual measures, in this case contracts with farmers, are not sufficient given the uncertainty of their duration. Secondly, measures which fail to cover all possible threats to a classified site are not sufficient. Although the site concerned was a wetland, water legislation alone does not offer a sufficient protection regime. Finally, the judgment clearly shows that Article 6 Birds Directive not only contains a duty to provide a sufficient legal regime, but also a duty to achieve sufficient protection in practice. The Court established that in the period 1977–86 there had been an average population of 67,845 wintering ducks, whereas for the period 1987–96, this average amounted to a mere 16,551 ducks. Having established this negative trend, the Court went on to conclude that France had failed in its obligation to take appropriate measures to avoid deterioration of the areas in the Poitevin marsh classified as SPAs.

During 1999, numerous Article 228 EC infringement procedures have been dropped following the adoption of appropriate measures by the Member States concerned. One of these procedures concerns the infamous judgment of 2 August 1993 relating to the Santoña marshes.[31] A second infringement procedure in this case was dismissed after it had been established that significant progress had been made towards restoring the Santoña marshes, and measures had been adopted to prevent future deterioration.

In December 1999 the Commission also withdrew an Article 228 EC procedure against France concerning the transposition of Article 5 Birds Directive, in relation to several species of birds which had been referred to the Court in 1998,[32] after the French Government had adopted the necessary orders at last. In the latter case, the Commission had requested a fine of 105,000 euros per day. The case is exemplary for the effectiveness of the penalty system of (now) Article 228 EC procedures, introduced by the Maastricht Treaty. The ECJ has rarely had to impose such penalties, since Member States tend to bring their

---

[28]  Case C–374/98, *Commission* v. *France* [2000] ECR I–1512.
[29]  Case C–96/98, *Commission* v. *France* [1999] ECR I–8531.
[30]  Case C–372/98, *Commission* v. *France*, judgment of 7 Dec. 2000, not yet reported.
[31]  Case C–355/90, *Commission* v. *Spain* [1993] ECR I–4221.
[32]  Case C–378/98, *Commission* v. *France*, removed from the register on 13 Jan. 2000.

domestic legislation and policy in conformity with Community law as soon as the case against them is referred to the Court for a second time.

Many cases referred to the Court in 1999 concern hunting legislation of several Member States (France, Italy, Finland, and Spain), in particular relating to the duration of the hunting seasons.[33] Foremost, the French hunting rules gave rise to numerous complaints and numerous parliamentary petitions.

### ii. Habitats Directive

There were no ECJ judgments concerning the Habitats Directive within the period covered by this report. However, a number of new actions were initiated by the Commission against, *inter alia*, Germany, France, and Ireland. Most of these actions concern failures by Member States to submit sufficient lists with sites that are most suitable for the conservation of the relevant habitats, in accordance with Article 4(1) Habitats Directive. One of these complaints is especially interesting from a legal perspective. In an action against France, brought by the Commission on 9 June 1999, the Commission stated that the French list adopted in accordance with Article 4(1) Habitats Directive, was inadequate in the light of the requirements set out in this provision in conjunction with Annex III of the Directive. Specifically, the French list made no mention of areas used for military purposes, nor of any habitats of several species listed in Annex I and Annex II, whereas, according to the available scientific data, those habitat types do in fact occur in France. Finally, the French list covered only 2.5 per cent of French territory, whereas a national list of 'outstanding and very interesting sites' covered 13.6 per cent of the identical territory.

It seems appropriate to ask whether such a complaint is well founded in law. According to the somewhat complicated procedure laid down in Articles 4 and 5 Habitats Directive, no Member State can ultimately be forced to bring a certain site under the protection of the Habitats Directive, even if it concerns a site of outstanding importance for the Natura 2000 Network. According to Article 5(3) Habitats Directive, only the Council can decide to bring such sites under the Natura 2000 Network, with the added requirement of unanimity. It is arguable that, since Member States cannot be forced to bring a site under the protection of Article 6, they consequently cannot be found to have drafted an insufficient list. This particular action against France demonstrates that the Commission disagrees with the latter conclusion.

### iii. Forest Protection

In Joined Cases C–164/97 and C–165/97,[34] the ECJ ruled on the validity of Commission Decisions 164/97/EC and 165/97/EC[35] concerning the two previously discussed regulations on the protection of the Community's forests against atmospheric pollution and fire, respectively. According to the Court,

---

[33] See e.g. Case C–38/99, *Commission* v. *France* [2000] ECR I–3549.     [34] See n. 21 above.
[35] See n. 19 and n. 20 above.

both regulations were adopted on an incorrect legal basis. The aims of the Community schemes for the protection of forests against fire and against atmospheric pollution are in part agricultural and in part of a specifically environmental nature. Due to the fact that the procedures for measures based on Articles 37 EC and 175 EC are mutually incompatible, it is clearly not possible to adopt regulations on this dual legal basis. Moreover, there is no indication that, in case of conflict, either Article should take precedence over the other. In this particular case, the consequences for agriculture were held to be incidental to the primary aim of conservation of the Community's natural heritage, in particular forest ecosystems. Thus, Article 175 EC should have been used as the proper legal basis for the measures concerned, and since the Commission had failed to do so, the ECJ annulled both Regulations. However, the Court suspended the effect of the annulments in order to prevent its judgment from substantially undermining the progress in the environmental protection in the Member States.

### D. POLICY DOCUMENTS

#### i. Forest Protection

In its Resolution of 15 December 1998 on a Forestry Strategy for the European Union,[36] the Council stressed the outstanding importance of European forests and asked, *inter alia*, the Commission to undertake a review of measures for the protection of the Community's forests against atmospheric pollution and fire. This EC Council Resolution follows resolutions on the same subject by the Committee of Regions and the EP.[37]

#### ii. Miscellaneous

A final interesting issue which was raised in Written Questions by MEPs to the Commission in 1999, concerned the crucifixion of doves during the Whit Sunday ceremony in Orvieto.[38] In accordance with a religious and cultural tradition in the Italian city of Orivieto, on Whit Sunday a living dove is crucified on a wheel of fireworks and made to run along a wire to the doors of the church. It is not unusual for the dove to be dead, or dying, by the time it arrives at its destination. The condition in which the bird reaches the doors is taken as a good or bad omen for the future of the city. In response to a question concerning possible obligations on the part of the Commission to prevent such mistreatment of animals, Commissioner Fischler simply stated that substantial EC legislation concerning the protection of wild animals, farm animals, and laboratory animals is in place. Additionally, he argued, a protocol to the Treaty of Amsterdam requires the Commission and the Member States to fully consider the welfare requirements of animals in the areas of agriculture, transport, internal market, and research. However, Fischler said in conclusion, this

---

[36]  [1999] OJ C56/1.
[37]  See C. Backes, 'Nature Conservation' (1998) 1 *Yearbook of European Environmental Law*, 397.
[38]  Written Question No. E-1542/98, [1999] OJ C31/53.

protocol stresses that religious rites, cultural traditions, and regional heritage should continue to be respected. Upon closer examination, Commissioner Fischler's answer appears to suggest that any mistreatment of animals may potentially be justified by reference to religious rites and cultural traditions.

### E. INTERNATIONAL COOPERATION

*i. Dolphin Conservation*

At the 35th meeting of the Inter-American Tropical Tuna Commission (IATTC) in 1998, agreement was reached on an 'International Dolphin Conservation Programme'. On 26 April 1999 the Council decided on the signature by the EC to the agreement on this programme.[39] The Commission argued that only by signing the agreement, and by acceding to the IATTC could the Community be guaranteed an active role in the management of this agreement.

[39] Council Decision 1999/337/EC, [1999] OJ L132/1.

# IV. Waste

GEERT VAN CALSTER*

## A. LEGISLATION ADOPTED

### i. Directive on the Landfill of Waste

Council Directive 1999/31/EC on the landfill of waste (Landfill Waste Directive)[1] entered into force on 16 July 1999, and is to be implemented by the Member States before 16 July 2001.

The Directive was hotly debated, and the European Parliament (EP) in particular had taken a tough stance. A Council Common Position,[2] reached in April 1998, included far from all the suggestions made by the EP during the earlier reading of the Commission Proposal.[3] The EP subsequently adopted a report by Member of European Parliament (MEP) Caroline Jackson, rejecting key elements of the Council's Common Position.[4] Essentially, the EP wanted to introduce a clear hierarchy of waste management principles in the text, which would expressly have made landfill the option of last resort. The Council had refrained from making such explicit statements as this would reopen a tense debate between Member States, since different Member States have invested in a variety of waste-management techniques. The key change in the text proposed by the EP was a reduction from the 35 per cent proposed by the Council, to 25 per cent of the total percentage of biodegradable waste that may be dumped in landfills by 2016.

The new Landfill Waste Directive establishes varying duties for three classes of landfills: those for hazardous, non-hazardous, and inert wastes. These duties include in particular the types of waste that may be accepted in the site. Moreover, all landfill sites are subjected to general criteria, laid down in the Annex to the Directive. Member States must submit to the Commission a strategy to ensure—by 17 July 2006—a reduction of biodegradable municipal waste intended for landfill to 75 per cent of the total amount by weight of such waste produced in 1995. By 17 July 2009 this figure must be further reduced to 50 per cent, and by 17 July 2016 to 35 per cent. The figures may be amended by the Council along the way. Those Member States that have put more than 80 per cent of their municipal waste to landfill during 1995, may postpone the

---

* Senior Research Fellow, IMER—Collegium Falconis, KU Leuven, Belgium; Member of the Brussels Bar.

[1] [1999] OJ L182/1.

[2] [1998] OJ C333/15. See for more details concerning the legislative process of Dir. 1999/31/EC G. van Calster, 'Waste', ch. IV of the Current Survey Section (1998) 1 *Yearbook of European Environmental Law*, 401–2.

[3] COM(97)105 final, [1997] OJ C156/10.          [4] Report A4-0028/99.

aforementioned dates for up to four years, provided, however, that the figure of 35 per cent is reached no later than 2019.

The method of landfill is explicitly prohibited for a number of materials, including liquid waste, explosive, corrosive, oxidizing, and flammable waste, hospital and clinical wastes, and tyres. All waste intended for landfill must be treated to ensure that the waste acceptance criteria and procedures specified in the Annex are met. The price charged by the operator must ensure that all his obligations under the Directive can and will be met, including the estimated cost of the closure and the aftercare of the site for a period of at least thirty years. The operator is responsible for such aftercare, while authorities are obliged to maintain a financial security for as long as they deem necessary to guarantee proper aftercare. The Directive does not in itself provide any specific liability regime. National law and/or relevant Community regulations shall therefore apply.

Member States have discretionary powers to declare the main elements of the Directive inapplicable to landfill sites intended for non-hazardous waste, or inert waste with a total capacity of not more than 15,000 tonnes or with an annual intake not exceeding 1,000 tonnes serving islands, where this is the only landfill on the island, and where it is exclusively destined for the disposal of waste generated on the island. However, once the total capacity of such landfill sites has been reached, any new site established on the island must comply with all requirements of the Directive, and is thus not covered by national exemptions. Member States also have this discretionary power in respect of landfill sites intended for non-hazardous or inert waste in isolated settlements if the site is destined for the disposal of wastes generated only by that isolated settlement. All existing landfill sites must meet the requirements of the Directive by 17 July 2009.

*ii. Shipments of Waste—Exports of 'Green List Wastes' to Non-OECD Countries*

After its controversial preparation,[5] Regulation (EC) No. 1420/1999 Establishing Common Rules and Procedures to Apply to Shipments to Certain Non-OECD Countries of Certain Types of Waste[6] was finally adopted by the Council on 29 April 1999. The Regulation concerns so-called 'green list wastes', which are not considered to be hazardous by the relevant OECD and Community waste instruments. Adoption of the Regulation was necessitated by the decision taken within the context of the Basel Convention on the Transboundary Movements of Hazardous Wastes and Their Disposal,[7] to enact a ban on the shipments of hazardous wastes to non-OECD countries, both for recovery and for final disposal.[8]

---

[5] See G. van Calster, n. 2 above, 400.          [6] [1999] OJ L166/6.

[7] Basel, 22 Mar. 1989. See (1989) 28 *International Legal Materials*, 649.

[8] Third Meeting of the Conference of the Parties to the Basel Convention, Geneva, 18–22 Sept. 1995, published on the Internet at: http://www.unep.ch/sbc/cop3-a.html.

The European Commission had originally[9] wanted to continue to enable exports of wastes listed on the EC's 'green list of wastes' of Council Regulation (EC) No. 259/93 on the Supervision and Control of Shipments of Waste within, into, and out of the European Community (Waste Shipments Regulation),[10] which in itself constitutes a direct transposition of OECD provisions on this topic. The OECD and the EC regard these wastes as being intrinsically non-hazardous, and therefore subject to the rules of the traffic of ordinary commercial goods. Part of the Commission's approach was to enable such transport of wastes, even where the non-OECD country concerned had indicated its unwillingness to receive green list wastes. The Commission had proposed to make such shipments subject to the 'red list' procedure, requiring explicit approval for each individual shipment. The new Regulation has altered the latter procedure: in the event that non-OECD countries communicate their general unwillingness to receive green list wastes, those types of waste cannot be exported to these countries. However, where no such explicit indication has been received by the Commission, the red list procedure shall apply. The concerned countries can then evaluate such shipments on a case-by-case basis. The new Regulation is to be read in conjunction with subsequent, regularly updated Commission regulations, listing the replies of non-OECD countries to notify the Commission of their intentions.[11]

### iii. *Shipments of Waste—Amendments to the Green, Amber, and Red Lists of Wastes*

Commission Decision 1999/816/EC of 24 November 1999 adapting, pursuant to Articles 16(1) and 42(3), Annexes II, III, IV, and V to Council Regulation (EEC) No. 259/93 on the Supervision and Control of Shipments of Waste within, into, and out of the European Community[12] holds a modification of the lists of wastes under the Waste Shipments Regulation,[13] in view of modifications adopted at the OECD level.[14]

### B. LEGISLATION IN PROGRESS

### i. *Incineration of Waste*

What started as a proposal to integrate the two existing regimes on the incineration of waste[15] has now, at the instigation of the EP, been redrafted also to integrate Directive 94/67/EC on the Incineration of Hazardous Waste

---

[9] Commission Proposal of 8 Feb. 1995 for a Council Regulation (EC) Establishing Common Rules and Procedures to Apply to Shipments to Certain Non-OECD Countries of Certain Shipments of Waste, COM(94)678 final.

[10] [1993] OJ L30/1.       [11] See e.g. Regulation (EC) No. 1547/1999, [1999] OJ L185/1.

[12] Commission Decision 1999/816/EC, [1999] OJ L316/45.       [13] See n. 10 above.

[14] OECD Council Decision C(98)202.

[15] Proposal of 7 Oct. 1998 for a Council Directive on the Incineration of Waste, COM(98)558 final, [1998] OJ C372/11. The proposal did away with the two existing regimes on the incineration of municipal waste, one for new, and one for old plants. See for more detail: G. van Calster, n. 2 above, 399–402.

(Hazardous Waste Incineration Directive).[16] The amended proposal[17] led to a Council Common Position which was adopted in November 1999. Emission limits for dioxins, acidifying gases, and heavy metals from incineration of non-hazardous wastes will be tightened. Existing emission limits for the incineration of hazardous wastes remain unaltered. Co-incineration plants that burn waste as a fuel in a commercial process are subject to more lenient limits for nitrogen oxides. The text of the amended proposal will be subjected to a 'second reading' by the EP in 2000.

### ii. Packaging and Packaging Waste—Review of Targets

Under the provisions of Directive 94/62/EC on Packaging and Packaging Waste,[18] the Commission is to propose revised targets for recycling and reuse, to be in place before June 2001. In a leaked draft proposal of June 1999, the Commission proposed ambitious recycling and reuse targets, while further discouraging waste incineration, and proposing quantitative obligations to be imposed on Member States to reduce the amount of packaging waste. The rather ambitious proposed new targets are undoubtedly influenced by the interim review of the current regime, which indicates that the targets for reuse, recycling, and recovery are in general met by those Member States to which they apply. For certain materials and in some Member States, the targets included in the Directive have already been exceeded.[19] The leaked draft included a clarification of the definition of 'packaging', and the suggestion that producers should pay for collection schemes. The draft proposal sparked immediate controversy, and it was said it did not reflect the view of the entire environment Directorate-General (DG Environment).

In December 1999, the Commission circulated a new draft proposal, which now includes a downward revision of the overall recycling target. It also introduced differing targets for varying packaging materials. Under this draft proposal, general recovery targets for packaging waste, which already exist under the current Directive, are to be abandoned. The regime would thus focus exclusively on recycling targets. One particularly controversial element of the proposal concerns so-called 'feedstock' recycling of plastics, as opposed to mechanical recycling. The Commission suggests that the former procedure of recycling could only count towards Member States' overall recycling efforts, not towards the specific figure set out for plastics recycling. Member States, industry, and environmental organizations have expressed their concern about the proposals, which are not likely to result in specific legislation before the end of 2000.

### iii. Packaging and Packaging Waste—CEN Standards

In January 1999 the European standardization organization (CEN) issued draft standards for packaging and packaging waste, in line with the Packaging and

---

[16] [1994] OJ L365/34.  [17] COM(1999)330 final, [2000] OJ C150E/1.
[18] [1994] OJ L365/10.
[19] See Commission Report of 19 Nov. 1999 'Interim Report according to Article 6.3(a) of Directive 94/62/EC on Packaging and Packaging Waste', COM(1999)596 final.

Packaging Waste Directive.[20] The Directive includes provisions for the prevention of packaging waste, and obliges Member States to ensure that three years from its entry into force packaging may be placed on the market only if it complies with all the 'essential requirements' laid down by the Directive, including Annex II. Specific EC standards are to be developed to meet these requirements, while pre-existing EC standards which already are in conformity are to be published in the *Official Journal of the European Communities*, along with equivalent national standards.

Annex II of the Directive contains the 'essential requirements on the composition and the reusable and recoverable, including recyclable, nature of packaging'. The Annex consists of vague and general criteria, which nevertheless impose far-reaching conditions, including the requirement that packaging be designed, produced, and commercialized in a manner permitting its reuse or recovery, including recycling, and to minimize its impact on the environment upon disposal.

The Commission mandated CEN to create these standards in 1996.[21] However, the study and standardization efforts were delayed by the comprehensive nature of the requested standards: they should not only meet the requirements of the Directive, but also provide industry with workable solutions. The six drafts which were ultimately adopted include the following standards: first, a truly comprehensive standard, which regroups all others and generally describes procedures for minimizing the effect of packaging on the environment; second, a standard which aims to prevent pollution by a reduction of packaging at source; third, a standard on reuse; fourth, a standard on requirements for packaging recoverable through material recycling; fifth, a standard on requirements for packaging recoverable in the form of energy recovery; and finally, a standard on requirements for packaging recoverable through composting and biodegradation.

All drafts are to be voted upon, and are expected to be adopted during the second half of 2000.

### iv. End-of-Life Vehicles

The proposed legislation on end-of-life vehicles continues to spark controversy, and its ride during 1999 did not get any smoother. In February 1999 the relevant EP Committee adopted a report by MEP Karl-Heinz Florenz[22] on the Commission Proposal for a directive.[23] The EP Committee proposed even more ambitious targets than the Commission had laid down in its proposal, including a proposal to increase the target for reuse and recovery to at least 85 per cent of vehicle weight for vehicles authorized for production before 1 January 2005, and subsequently to at least 95 per cent by 2015. For vehicles

---

[20]  CEN Press Notice of 14 Jan. 1999.
[21]  Commission mandate to CEN of 8 Mar. 1996 for standardization and a study related to packaging and packaging waste.
[22]  Report A4-0051–99.         [23]  COM(97)358 final, [1997] OJ C337/3.

authorized after 1 January 2005, it was proposed that the 95 per cent target should come into force immediately. The Committee report envisaged a possible role for voluntary agreements at the national level, which is atypical given the EP's general mistrust of such agreements.

The Committee proposal was on the agenda of a memorable meeting of the EU environment ministers in June 1999, but last-minute pressure by the German car manufacturers, in particular, prevented the adoption of the Directive. Agreement appeared to have been reached, but the consensus was shattered by the intervention of the German car lobby. It argued that the text imposed an excessively heavy and exclusive burden on industry. This argument persuaded the German Presidency of the Union, which subsequently led to the collapse of the agreement. Technically, there was a clear majority in favour of the text, since Germany was the only opponent. However, the other Member States did not care for a power struggle on the issue, against the will of the Member State whose car industry accounts for 40 per cent of cars currently on European roads. Germany indicated that a compromise was possible, which was to include a practically immediate take-back duty for new vehicles, in combination with strict reuse and recycling limits, and a further postponement of the take-back duty for existing vehicles.[24] In fact, the car lobby had proposed that the take-back duty for existing vehicles be abandoned altogether.

The Commission reacted in fury to the last-minute breakdown of the agreement, accusing Germany of caving in to the short-term benefits of the car industry. In unusually rigid language, representatives of the Commission characterized the events as 'a disgrace'. Finland, next in line for the Union Presidency, said that it wanted to tackle the issue as soon as possible, even prior to the next scheduled meeting of environment ministers, in October 1999. Finally, Member States' representatives reached an agreement in July 1999, with a compromise which only minimally displayed the German concerns. The agreement envisages that as from 2001, car manufacturers will have to cover the cost of taking back all cars sold after that date. Furthermore, as from 2006, they have to take cars back regardless of their selling date, and without being able to charge consumers directly for this service. The text would also force car manufacturers to recycle or reuse 80 per cent of car weight from 2006, raising to 85 per cent within a decade.[25] Further discussion on the proposal involves, *inter alia*, the take-back duty for all existing cars as from 2006, a retroactive element that has attracted the interest of, *inter alia*, the Commission and the EP legal services.

---

[24] 2194th Council meeting, Environment, 24–5 June 1999.
[25] Common position (EC) No. 39/1999 of 29 July 1999 with a View to Adopting a Directive of the European Parliament and of the Council on End-of-Life Vehicles, [1999] OJ C317/19.

*v. Review of Hazardous Waste List—Integration of European Waste Catalogue and Hazardous Waste List*

The Hazardous Waste List of Council Decision 94/904/EC,[26] drawn up in accordance with Directive 91/689/EEC on Hazardous Waste (Hazardous Waste Directive),[27] was undergoing revision in 1999. The EC Hazardous Waste List had to be amended for a variety of reasons. First, the Basel Convention on Transboundary Movement of Hazardous Wastes and their Disposal, has adopted a list of hazardous wastes, which must be integrated into EC law.[28] Second, apart from dangerous waste as laid down by Annexes I and II in conjunction with Annex III of the Directive, Article 1(4) defines as hazardous wastes 'any other waste which is considered by a Member State to display any of the properties listed in Annex III'. Member States have to notify such cases to the Commission, which will review them in accordance with the procedure laid down in Article 18 Directive 75/442/EEC (Waste Framework Directive),[29] with a view to adaptation of the list. This process is now underway, and as part of the review process, the Commission has suggested to integrate the European Waste Catalogue[30] and the Hazardous Waste List into a single list, in order to increase clarity. The compilation of the current list used for the first time the procedure laid down in the Hazardous Waste Directive,[31] whereby Member States are to notify the Commission of those substances which they deem hazardous, and which they want to see included in the list. Following this procedure, Member States have notified some 500 substances for inclusion into in the Hazardous Waste List. Within the context of the so-called Technical Adaptation Committee (TAC), Member State notifications were subsequently discussed, some resulting in inclusion, others in rejection of the requests. The review process is expected to be finalized by the summer of 2000. Significantly, the Hazardous Waste Directive expressly excludes 'domestic waste' from its scope of application. The Commission is still finalizing a proposal to extend the scope of application of the Directive. The text aims to include 'hazardous municipal waste' in the provisions of the Directive. Such waste will have to be collected separately. In a draft proposal, hazardous municipal waste has been defined as not merely waste produced by households but also commercial, industrial, institutional, and other hazardous

[26] Council Decision 94/904/EC of 22 Dec. 1994 Establishing a List of Hazardous Waste Pursuant to Article 1(4) of Council Directive 91/689/EEC on Hazardous Waste, [1994] OJ L356/14.

[27] [1991] OJ L377/20.

[28] This Convention establishes a ban on the export of hazardous waste for recovery to non-OECD countries. In an Annex to the Convention, the Hazardous Waste List (List A) bans the export of wastes containing arsenic, lead, mercury, asbestos, and dozens of other chemicals and substances. The Non-Hazardous Waste List (List B) exempts from the ban those wastes that can be safely recycled or reused, including scrap iron, steel or copper, certain electronic assemblies, non-hazardous chemical catalysts, paper, and textile wastes.

[29] [1975] OJ 194/39.

[30] Commission Decision 94/3/EC of 20 Dec. 1993 Establishing a List of Wastes pursuant to Article 1a of Council Directive 75/442/EEC on Waste, [1994] OJ L5/115.

[31] See n. 27 above.

waste which, because of its nature or composition, is similar to hazardous waste from households. Member States will be obliged to ensure that such waste is collected in separate fractions by professional waste collectors or delivered in separate fractions in specialized collection facilities. The undertakings involved must obtain a registered status with the competent authorities. Producers and holders of hazardous municipal waste will have to be informed of the need to collect this type of waste separately. Products which become or could potentially become hazardous municipal waste will have to be marked or labelled accordingly. The products subject to this requirement will be identified through amending the EC Hazardous Waste List. A formal proposal to this end has not yet been submitted by the Commission, while Member States remain divided on the issue. A significant number of Member States (Austria, the Flemish Region of Belgium, Denmark, Finland, Germany, Luxembourg, the Netherlands, and Sweden) already have systems in place which provide for the separate collection of (part of) the municipal waste stream. Other Member States fear the extra costs which will be imposed on local authorities following adoption of the amendment.

### vi. Port Waste Facilities

The Council has adopted a Common Position on port waste facilities,[32] which was subject to debate in the EP during 1999. The Commission Proposal for a directive complements international rules on the discharge of waste at sea.[33] The proposed regime lays down specific standards covering the requirements for ports and port states to provide adequate reception facilities, including proper waste reception and handling planning, clear notification guidelines, and adequate final treatment. Furthermore, it improves and specifies the obligations of ships to use these facilities. As a general rule, all ships are to deliver their ship-generated waste to a port reception facility, unless there is proof of adequate on-board storage facilities. Finally, the proposal envisages a monitoring regime.

One of the most contested provisions of the proposal is the fee structure which Member States should be allowed to maintain. Germany, in particular, insists that Member States should employ a single fee for the use of port reception facilities, arguing that a fee based on the amount of deposited waste would encourage illegal dumping at sea, to the detriment of all Member States' interests.

[32] Common Position (EC) No. 2/2000 of 8 Nov. 1999 with a View to Adopting a Directive of the European Parliament and the Council on Port Reception Facilities for Ship-Generated Waste and Cargo Residues, [2000] OJ C010/14.

[33] Commission Proposal of 17 July 1998 for a Council Directive on Port Reception Facilities for Ship-Generated Waste and Cargo Residues, COM(98)452 final, [1998] C271/79.

## i. Framework Waste Directive

In case C–365/97,[34] the Commission accused Italy of not having properly implemented Directive 75/442/EEC on Waste (Framework Waste Directive).[35] The bone of contention was the San Rocco valley in the vicinity of Naples, where waste management had shown serious shortcomings, including, *inter alia* continuous dumping of biological and chemical waste in the river basin, and the operation of illegal landfill sites in disused quarries. Urged by the Commission, the Italian Government provided an overview of the environmental and health hazards facing the area, at the beginning of the 1990s. However, by 1996, the Commission had not yet received any governmental plans to remedy the situation, and sent Italy a Reasoned Opinion. It set out that Italy was in breach of, in particular, Article 4 Waste Framework Directive, laying down a general duty for Member States to take the necessary measures to ensure that waste is recovered or disposed of without endangering human health and without using processes or methods which could harm the environment. Italy subsequently communicated a range of measures which were designed to redress the situation, but the Commission found these measures to be largely unsatisfactory.

This case identifies an important development which extends beyond the waste sector: Italy called into question the role of the Commission to seek specific enforcement of a Directive in an altogether tiny area of the Italian state. Therefore, the judgment of the European Court of Justice (ECJ) in this case might have relevance for the enforcement of EC environmental legislation in general. Italy argued that the legal basis of the Commission's actions,[36] restricts its competence to the task of ensuring the correct transposition of Community law into national law, in so far as it concerns Directives. Consequently, Italy argued, the Commission had *in casu* illegitimately stretched its authority by seeking to protect the environment itself. Moreover, it put forward that a condemnation in accordance with Article 226 EC has to relate to a significant part of the territory of the Member State concerned. Thus, according to the Italian arguments, the territorial dimension of the San Rocco valley does not justify proceedings on the basis of Article 226 EC. The ECJ, however, referred to the role of the Commission as the 'guardian of the Treaties',[37] and to settled case law, in which it had underlined the Commission's all-encompassing competence to ensure the proper enforcement by the Member States of primary and secondary Community law. According to the Court, the Commission does not only have the right but indeed the duty to ensure that, where it identifies shortcomings in the proper enforcement of Community law, all necessary measures are taken to ensure cessation of the infringement.

---

[34] Judgment of the Court in Case C–365/97, *Commission* v. *Italy* [1999] ECR I–7773.
[35] See n. 29 above.     [36] Art. 226 EC.     [37] Under Art. 211 EC.

Applied to the facts of the case before it, the Court recalled the general obligation under Article 4 Waste Framework Directive, which, albeit perhaps not sufficiently precise to transfer rights and obligations upon individuals,[38] nevertheless imposes obligations upon Member States which the Commission is obliged to uphold. In view of the Commission's duties as 'guardian of the Treaty', the Court held that the nonconformity of a specific set of facts with the result envisaged by a directive is not in itself sufficient to establish the failure of the Member State to correctly transpose that Directive. However, the Court decided that the persistent nature of such a shortcoming, in particular where this leads to a significant degradation of the environment during a long period of time without intervention on the part of the competent authorities, could indicate that the Member State has exceeded its margin of appreciation granted by the general obligations laid down in Article 4 Waste Framework Directive. In this respect, the extent of the affected territory is irrelevant for the determination of the competence of the Commission. The Court subsequently assessed the proof furnished by the Commission, and concluded that Italy had indeed failed to take the necessary measures to prevent the illegal and/or unsustainable discharge of wastes in the San Rocco valley, and that this amounted to a failure to implement Article 4 of the Directive.

### ii. *Waste Oil Directive*

In case C–102/97,[39] the Commission sought to establish that Germany had failed to implement Directive 75/439/EEC on the Disposal of Waste Oils (Waste Oil Directive).[40] This Directive requires Member States to grant priority to the processing of waste oils by regeneration, as opposed to disposal by combustion or other means:

(1) Where technical, economic and organisational constraints so allow, Member States shall take the measures necessary to give priority to the processing of waste oils by regeneration.
(2) Where waste oils are not regenerated, on account of the constraints mentioned in paragraph 1 above, Member States shall take the measures necessary to ensure that any combustion of waste oils is carried out under environmentally acceptable conditions, in accordance with the provisions of this Directive, provided that such combustion is technically, economically and organisationally feasible.
(3) Where waste oils are neither generated nor burned, on account of the constraints mentioned in paragraphs 1 and 2, Member States shall take the measures necessary to ensure their safe destruction or their controlled storage or tipping.[41]

The dispute *in casu* concerned the hierarchy of waste management principles as laid down in the Community waste regime, the proper way to prioritize those waste management techniques, and the scope of the discretion granted to the Member States in pursuing this hierarchy. Along the lines of Advocate General (AG) Fennelly's summary of the dispute, Germany's reading of Article

---

[38] As held in Case C–236/92, *Comitato di Coordinamento per la Difesa della Cava and others* v. *Regione Lombardia and others* [1994] ECR I–0483.
[39] Case C–102/97, *Commission* v. *Germany* [1999] ECR I–5051.     [40] [1975] OJ L194/23.
[41] Art. 3 Waste Oil Directive.

3 Waste Oil Directive is that the technical, economic, and organizational constraints of each individual Member State provide the benchmark to determine how priority is to be given to processing of waste oils by regeneration in each individual Member State. In contrast, the Commission construed the priority of regeneration as a principle which the Member States can only derogate from by way of exception, on account of the constraints identified in the Directive. Since it regarded these as exceptions, the Commissions emphasized the need for a restrictive interpretation of the 'constraints'.

The ECJ found that Germany attached particular importance to the regeneration of oil in its implementing regulations, in particular because it organizes the separate collection of waste oils, and because it obliges operators to separate oils suitable for recycling. However, the Court observed that the German legislation and regulations do not in any way grant priority to regeneration over other means of processing, by means of compulsory measures or other incentives.

The Court ultimately sided with Germany, in holding that the 'constraints' referred to in Article 3 Waste Oil Directive did not provide for limited exceptions to a rule having general application, but defined the scope and content of a positive obligation to give priority to the processing of waste oils by regeneration. However, the Court emphasized that the definition of the constraints cannot be left to the exclusive discretion of the Member States. It construed the provision relating to constraints as an expression of the principle of proportionality. Germany had failed to take any specific measure to give specific priority to regeneration and thus, in the Court's view, had clearly exceeded its discretion under the Waste Oil Directive.

D. INTERNATIONAL COOPERATION

### i. Basel Protocol on Liability and Compensation for Damage

In December 1999, at their fifth Conference (COP-5), the Parties to the Basel Convention on the Control of Transboundary Movements of Hazardous Wastes and Their Disposal[42] have adopted a Protocol on Liability and Compensation for Damage Resulting from Transboundary Movements of Hazardous Wastes and Their Disposal.[43] The Protocol was the result of protracted negotiations and was centred around a strict liability regime. The following paragraphs provide a brief summary.[44] 'Damage' is defined as: first, loss of life or personal injury; second, loss of or damage to property other than property held by the person liable in accordance with the Protocol; third, loss of income directly deriving from an economic interest in any use of the environment, incurred as result of impairment of the environment, taking into account savings and costs; fourth, the costs of measures of reinstatement of

---

[42] See n. 7 above.     [43] Basel, 10 Dec. 1999.

[44] For a more detailed discussion of the Protocol, see: D. A. French, 'The 1999 Protocol on Liability and Compensation for Damage resulting from the Transboundary Movements of Hazardous Wastes and Their Disposal' (2000) 1 *Environmental Liability*, 3.

the impaired environment, limited to the costs of measures actually taken or to be undertaken; and finally, the costs of preventive measures, including any loss or damage caused by such measures.[45] The former definitions apply in so far as the damage has arisen out of, or results from, hazardous properties of the wastes involved in the transboundary movement and disposal of hazardous wastes and other wastes subject to the Basel Convention.

The Protocol does not cover historic damage.[46] A number of persons are subject to a strict liability regime. The notifier of the shipment is responsible for damage until the disposer has taken possession of the hazardous wastes or other wastes. Subsequently, the disposer is responsible for damage. If the state of export is the notifier, or if no notification has taken place, the exporter is responsible for damage until the disposer has taken possession of the hazardous wastes or other wastes.[47]

Fault-based liability is also imposed by the Protocol: any person is responsible for damage caused or contributed to by his lack of compliance with the provisions implementing the Convention, or by his wrongful intentional, reckless, or negligent acts or omissions.[48]

Claims for compensation are subject to an absolute time limit of ten years, and must be brought within five years from the date on which the claimant knew or ought reasonably to have known of the damage if within the ten years limit.[49]

The Protocol requires ratification by twenty Parties to enable its entry into force.[50]

### E. MISCELLANEOUS

### i. *Packaging and Packaging Waste—German Court Finds Illegality of Quota System*

Adding an interesting twist to the continuing German quota-saga, the *Landgericht Bonn* held that the quota system with respect to refillable beverage packaging, contained in the *Verpackungsverordnung*, is a clear violation of the Packaging and Packaging Waste Directive. The court heard a complaint by the Austrian drinks company *Hermann Pfanner*, that Germany had failed properly to implement the Directive, causing Pfanner's distributors to refuse to continue to retail Pfanner drinks. They felt obliged to do so, since the packaging of the drinks at issue was not refillable, thus reflecting badly on the retailers' overall refill quota. The plaintiff was seeking damages from Germany for the alleged violation of the Packaging and Packaging Waste Directive. The court found against granting damages, but only on the basis of the third of the three conditions laid down in the ECJ case law on the matter: *Francovich*,[51] *Brasserie du Pêcheur and Factortame*,[52] and

---

[45] Art. 2(2)c.　　[46] Art. 3.　　[47] Art. 4.　　[48] Art. 5.　　[49] Art. 13.　　[50] Art. 29.

[51] Judgment of the Court of 19 Nov. 1991 in Joined Cases C–6/90 and C–9/90, *Andrea Francovich and Danila Bonifaci* v. *Italian Republic* [1991] ECR I–5357.

[52] Judgment of the Court of Justice of 5 Mar. 1996 in Joined Cases C–46/93 and C–48/93, *Brasserie du Pêcheur SA* v. *Bundesrepublik Deutschland and The Queen* v. *Secretary of State for Transport, ex parte: Factortame Ltd. and others* [1996] ECR I–1029.

*Dillenkofer*,[53] have firmly established the principle of state liability for loss and damage caused to individuals as a result of breaches of Community law for which the state can be held responsible.[54] The principle of state liability for loss and damage caused to individuals as a result of breaches of Community law for which the state can be held responsible is inherent in the system of the Treaty. In *Francovich, Brasserie du Pêcheur and Factortame*, and *Dillenkofer*, the ECJ held that the conditions under which state liability gives rise to a right to reparation depend on the nature of the breach of Community law. In the case of a breach of Community law attributable to a Member State acting in a field in which it has a wide legislative discretion, the ECJ has held that such a right to reparation must be recognized if three conditions are met: first, the rule of law infringed must be intended to confer rights on individuals; second, the breach must be sufficiently serious; and third, there must be a direct causal link between the breach of the obligation resting on the state and the damage sustained by the injured parties.[55] The German court found against the link of causality. The court's reasoning for finding Germany in breach of the Directive was entirely based on Article 18 of the Directive, which provides that 'Member States shall not impede the placing on the market of their territory of packaging which satisfies the provisions of this Directive.' The *Landgericht* refers to ECJ case law on Article 28 EC, to decide that Article 18 of the Directive grants individuals rights which are sufficiently precise and clear when read in conjunction with the principles underlying the Directive.

The court's findings are not as uncontroversial as the packaging industry would have one believe. It remains uncertain what exactly constitutes 'packaging which satisfies the provisions of this Directive'. The essential requirements defined in Annex I to the Packaging and Packaging Waste Directive do not exactly lay these down with sufficient clarity so as to function as a benchmark in a given case. Moreover, Member States are given some discretion with respect to the methods they employ to achieve the targets laid down in the Directive. Article 5 states, with respect to reuse, that Member States may encourage reuse systems of packaging, which can be reused in an environmentally sound manner, in conformity with the EC Treaty. Article 7 Packaging and Packaging Directive obliges Member States to set up systems to provide for the return and/or collection of used packaging and/or packaging waste from the consumer, other final user, or from the waste stream in order to channel it to the most appropriate waste management alternatives, and for the

[53] Judgment of the Court of 8 Oct. 1996 in Joined Cases C–178/94, C–179/94, C–188/94, C–189/94, and C–190/94, *Erich Dillenkofer et al.* v. *Bundesrepublik Deutschland* [1996] ECR I–4845.

[54] *See, inter alia*, N. Emiliou, 'State Liability Under Community Law: Shedding More Light on the *Francovich* Principle?' (1996) 21 *European Law Review*, 399–411; H. Somsen, 'Case-note *sub* Judgment of the Court of 23 May 1996 in Case C–5/94, *The Queen v Ministry of Agriculture, Fisheries and Food, ex parte Hedley Lomas (Ireland) Ltd*' (1996) 6 *European Environmental Law Review*, 287–293; W. van Gerven, 'Non-contractual Liability of Member States, Community Institutions and Individuals for Breaches of Community Law with a View to a Common Law for Europe' (1994) 1 *Maastricht Journal for European and Comparative Law*, 6–40.

[55] The Court in Joined Cases C–46/93 and C–48/93, notes 47, 51.

reuse or recovery including recycling of the packaging and/or packaging waste collected. The exercise of Member States' discretion is embedded in the EC Treaty's provisions on the Internal Market. Setting out the boundaries of national discretion is a balancing-act which the Commission hesitates to bring before the ECJ, as the *Danish Cans* case and *German Quota* case illustrate. The ease with which the *Landgericht* seemingly concluded a breach of the Directive, based on the language of Article 18 in conjunction with a summary reference to Internal Market principles, is indeed striking. The Commission in turn does not seem intent on bringing an action against Germany before the ECJ over the implementation of the Directive.

### ii. *Packaging and Packaging Waste—Approval of Austrian Stricter National Measures*

In January 1999, in a benchmark Decision, the Commission cleared Austrian regulations in the packaging waste sector.[56] The Packaging and Packaging Waste Directive[57] lays down, *inter alia*, minimum and maximum limits of national recycling per category of packaging waste. The Austrian measures exceeded the maximum limits for a number of product categories, in particular for glass, ceramics, metals, and paper. They generally imposed strict recycling and refilling targets for a number of product groups, in particular beverages. The delay in the Commission Decision—the Austrian measures had been notified at the end of 1995—was caused by the absence of a specific procedure to this end in the Directive. The measures which were notified were supported by statistics from 1994 and 1995, but the Austrian request concerned the packaging regulations generally, including the recycling and recovery targets which stretch until 2001.

The Commission decided that the Austrian measures are in conformity with the conditions set out in the Packaging and Packaging Waste Directive. These conditions include the requirements that: first, the Member State in question must provide appropriate capacities for recycling and recovery, in order to efficiently manage the higher targets; second, the measures must be taken in the interests of a high level of environmental protection and on condition that they avoid distortions of the internal market; third, the measures may not hinder compliance by other Member States with the Directive; and finally, the measures may not constitute an arbitrary means of discrimination or a disguised restriction on trade between Member States. According to the Commission, *in casu*, all conditions of the Directive had been sufficiently fulfilled. There is no doubt that this Decision was facilitated by the absence of controversy, as no Member State claimed that any of the conditions were not fulfilled. The Commission relied heavily on this absence of complaints by other Member States for its affirmative Decision. The case is in sharp contrast

---

[56] Commission Decision 1999/42/EC Confirming the Measures Notified by Austria pursuant to Article 6(6) of Directive 94/62/EC of the European Parliament and of the Council on Packaging and Packaging Waste, [1999] OJ L14/24.

[57] See n. 18 above.

with other, more controversial cases in the packaging sector, including the Danish can saga, discussed in Section E.*iii* below,[58] and the German quota on reusable packaging, discussed in Section C.*ii* above.[59] Of a similar nature were Commission Decision 1999/652/EC[60] concerning Belgian measures to a similar effect, and Commission Decision 1999/823/EC[61] in respect of Dutch measures.

### *iii. Packaging and Packaging Waste—Denmark finally in the ECJ Dock for Can Ban?*

In April 1999 the Commission decided formally to make an application to the ECJ against Denmark, for its ban on the use of metal cans for beverages.[62] The application also covers the Danish ban on the marketing of beverages of domestic origin in non-refillable glass and plastic packaging. Denmark stands accused of not properly implementing the Packaging and Packaging Waste Directive.[63] The 1994 Directive aims to reconcile the free movement of goods with lessening the environmental impact of packaging waste. A number of Member States having adopted legislation in this field, the Commission took the initiative for the current legislation. The Directive includes an Annex with 'essential requirements' which packaging needs to fulfil, *inter alia*, with respect to reusability and recyclability, for it to be marketable. These essential requirements are currently the subject of standardization efforts, as discussed in Section B.*iii* above. The Commission argues that it is possible for metal cans, irrespective of whether aluminium or steel is used for their production, to fulfil the essential requirements for composition and nature of packaging laid down in Packaging and Packaging Waste Directive. It also holds that the Danish provisions infringe the EC Treaty provisions with respect to free movement of goods, which Member States must respect, in accordance with express provisions to that effect in the Directive. Moreover, the Commission considers that the ban on the marketing of beverage of domestic origin in non-refillable glass and plastic packaging infringes the Directive. It indicates that this ban will be assessed in terms of the provisions of the Directive, in which, however, 'Article 28–30 EC-like' language is not absent.[64] This development signals the last stage of a very protracted chain of events, indeed. Ever since the Packaging and Packaging Waste Directive entered into force, Denmark has stood accused of not properly implementing it. However, the Commission has been very reluctant to pursue the case before the ECJ.[65]

---

[58] Case C–246/99, n. 62 below.  [59] Case C–102/97, n. 39 above.
[60] [1999] OJ L257/20.  [61] [1999] OJ L321/19.
[62] Case C–246/99, *Action brought on 1 July 1999 by the Commission against Denmark*, [1999] OJ L246/19.
[63] See n. 18 above.  [64] IP/99/236.  [65] See also G. van Calster, n. 2 above, 407.

# V. Water

MARK STALLWORTHY*

## A. INTRODUCTION

### i. The Status of Community Water Legislation

This chapter offers an overview of legislative developments and judicial rulings in the field of protection of the European Union's aquatic environment, as well as continuing policy initiatives pursued during the year 1999. In this context it is necessary to recall that Community water legislation has a history which antedates specific recognition of environmental protection within the Treaty of Rome. Its genesis lay in the First Environmental Action Programme in 1973, with early measures adopted under former Articles 100 or 235 EC.[1] Its catalyst was an early framework directive aimed at controlling the introduction into water of dangerous substances, through emission limit values supported respectively by prohibitions and mandatory authorizations.[2]

### ii. Quality Standards, Emission Controls, and Zoning

Legislative development since can be approximated into two distinct phases. Initial efforts were directed to the setting of minimum-quality standards for receiving waters. This was marked by a concern for anthropocentric uses of water, and legislation was established for the following areas: drinking water,[3]

---

* Professor, Norwich Law School, University of East Anglia, UK.

[1] Prior to the introduction of the former Art. 130r EC (now Art. 174 EC) into the Treaty, by the Single European Act (SEA) 1987.

[2] Dir. 76/464/EEC on Pollution Caused by Certain Dangerous Substances Discharged into the Aquatic Environment of the Community, [1976] OJ L129/23; subsequently amended by Dir. 90/656/EEC, [1990] OJ L353/59 and Dir. 91/692/EEC, [1991] OJ L377/48. Though extremely slow progress was made, there followed so-called 'daughter directives' setting out limit values and quality objectives, respectively: Dir. 82/176/EEC for Mercury Discharges from the Chlor-Alkali Electrolysis Industry, [1982] OJ L81/29; Dir. 83/513/EEC for Cadmium Discharges, [1983] OJ L291/1, Dir. 84/156/EEC for Mercury Discharges by Other Sectors, [1984] OJ L74/49; Dir. 84/491/EEC for Hexachlorocyclohexane Discharges, [1984] OJ L274/11; and Dir. 86/280/EEC for Discharges of Certain Dangerous Substances included in list I to the Annex to Dir. 76/464/EEC, [1986] OJ L181/16 (as amended by Dir. 88/347/EEC, [1988] OJ L158/35 and Dir. 90/415/EEC, [1990] OJ L219/49).

[3] Dir. 75/440/EEC concerning the Quality Required of Surface Water intended for the Abstraction of Drinking Water, [1975] OJ L194/26, and Dir. 79/869/EEC concerning the Methods of Measurement and Frequencies of Sampling and Analysis of Surface Water intended for the Abstraction of Drinking Water in the Member States, [1979] OJ L271/44. Further quality standards and compliance programmes were added by Dir. 80/778/EEC relating to the Quality of Water intended for Human Consumption, [1980] OJ L229/11, as amended by Dir. 81/858/EEC, [1981] OJ L319/19 (and also by Dir. 90/656/EEC and Dir. 91/692/EEC, n. 2 above).

bathing waters,[4] and water connected with food extraction.[5] A subsequent phase moved towards the control of discharges once again towards, as in the original approach, pollution by dangerous substances. Here, following specific provisions being put in place for groundwater quality,[6] zoning-based approaches were introduced[7] with the intention of targeting particular problem areas and circumstances: namely, sewage treatment impacts upon surface inland and coastal waters;[8] non-point source nitrate pollution impacts on fresh and marine waters; [9] and the operation of large-scale industrial installations.[10] The most recent of these measures, Directive 96/61/EC on Integrated Pollution Prevention and Control (IPPC Directive), expressly calls on the application of cross-media approaches, with the eventual development of prevention-based schemes rather than emissions-based end-of-pipe technology.[11] Another measure in this new generation of Directives, Directive 91/676/EEC concerning the Protection of Waters against Pollution caused by Nitrates from Agricultural Sources,[12] illustrates a recognition of a need to seek integrated approaches to problems in achieving compliance with other Directives, such as Directive 80/778/EEC relating to the Quality of Water intended for Human Consumption.[13]

### B. LEGISLATIVE DEVELOPMENTS

#### i. *A New Framework for Community Water Policy- and Law-Making*

As will be discussed in Section D of this chapter, a proposed Water Framework Directive will subsume much of the earlier legislation, including Directive 80/68/EEC on the Protection of Groundwater against Pollution caused by Certain Dangerous Substances.[14] It is the Commission's intention that the more recent, zoning-based, measures, will progress in tandem with the new Directive.[15]

---

[4] Dir. 76/160/EEC concerning the Quality of Bathing Waters, [1976] OJ L31/1 (also amended, Dir. 90/656/EEC, and Dir. 91/692/EEC, n. 2 above). The sixteenth Commission report on the quality of bathing waters (1998) reported the results of the examination of 13,218 coastal beaches and 6,004 inland bathing areas, with almost 95% (90% in 1997) of coastal bathing areas and 85% (80% in 1997) of inland bathing areas meeting water-quality requirements (25 May 1999).

[5] Dir. 78/659/EEC on the Quality of Fresh Waters needing Protection in order to Support Fish Life, [1978] OJ L222/1, and Dir. 79/923/EEC on the Quality Required of Shellfish Waters, [1979] OJ L281/47 (also amended, Dir. 90/656/EEC, and Dir. 91/692/EEC, n. 2 above).

[6] Dir. 80/68/EEC on the Protection of Groundwater against Pollution caused by Certain Dangerous Substances, [1980] OJ L20/43 (also as amended, Dir. 90/656/EEC, and Dir. 91/692/EEC, n. 2 above).

[7] Following the Frankfurt Ministerial Conference in 1988.

[8] Dir. 91/271/EEC concerning Urban Waste Water Treatment, [1991] OJ L135/40; amended by Dir. 98/15/EC, [1998] OJ L67/29.

[9] Dir. 91/676/EEC concerning the Protection of Waters against Pollution caused by Nitrates from Agricultural Sources, [1991] OJ L375/1, concerned with pollution by chemical fertilizers and livestock manures, requiring non-mandatory codes of good agricultural practice and identification of vulnerable zones for a stricter regime of mandatory codes and action programmes.

[10] Dir. 96/61/EC on Integrated Pollution Prevention and Control, [1996] OJ L257/26.

[11] Ibid., Art. 3 of which looks to 'prevent or solve pollution problems rather than transferring them from one part of the environment to another'.

[12] See n. 9 above.          [13] See n. 3 above.          [14] See n. 6 above.

[15] See Sect. B.*iii* below.

## ii. *Updating and Review of Drinking-Water Laws*

Those Directives concerned with drinking water are to be separately updated. A start has now been made in this respect, with the adoption of Directive 98/83/EC on the Quality of Water intended for Human Consumption.[16] This has the effect of repealing Directive 80/778/EEC relating to the Quality of Water intended for Human Consumption.[17] The new measure will have fully replaced the former by 25 December 2003.[18] Taking account of scientific and technical improvements over the past two decades the measure aims for fuller harmonization of measures for drinking water, through reformed quality assessment criteria and monitoring arrangements.

Before looking at the proposed Framework Directive in Section D, the next section is devoted to a consideration of a key issue which the Commission and the Council now seek to address. This concerns the question of realizing and sustaining the Treaty commitment towards integration of environmental protection priorities into Community legislation generally. Water policy here has a key place in emerging sectoral policies, especially in connection with agriculture.

## iii. *Amending other Directives*

Another Directive to survive the major reform discussed under Section D is Directive 76/160/EEC concerning the Quality of Bathing Waters.[19] Nevertheless, with efforts focused elsewhere, progress towards its envisaged repeal remains slow, and the introduction of more effective pollution controls and updated evaluation criteria still awaits final adoption by the Council.[20] Meanwhile, the process of implementation of Directive 91/271/EEC concerning Urban Waste Water Treatment continues, together with one amending measure thus far, correcting certain national differences in interpretation.[21] The new approaches contained in Directive 91/271/EEC,[22] together with Directive 91/676/EEC concerning the Protection of Waters against Pollution caused by Nitrates from Agricultural Sources,[23] will retain their importance when the draft Framework Directive's coordinated regime of river basin management, with objectives set pursuant to analyses of human impacts and the effects of full implementation of existing legislation, comes on stream.

---

[16] [1998] OJ L330/32.    [17] See n. 3 above.

[18] With a deadline for transposition of 25 Dec. 2000.    [19] See n. 4 above.

[20] See Proposed Dir. concerning the quality of bathing water COM(94)36 final, [1994] OJ C112/3, amended COM(97)585, [1998] OJ C6/9.

[21] See n. 8 above: the Dir. requires secondary treatment for significant discharges and advanced treatment in 'sensitive areas' ('significant' in this context including all inland agglomerations above a 2,000 population). Rules were required to be in place before 1999 for regulation/authorization of disposal, with the phasing-out of dumping of sewage sludge into surface waters. Other deadlines for application of treatment requirements are set for the end of 2000 and 2005, dependent upon size of agglomeration and character of receiving waters.

[22] See Commission report on implementation of Dir. 91/271/EEC concerning Urban Waste Water Treatment, as amended by Dir. 98/15/EC, COM(98)775 final, [1998] OJ L67/29.

[23] See n. 9 above.

## C. INTEGRATION

### i. Foundations: the Status of Environmental Protection within the Treaty

The Commission has recognized the importance of water policy and law-making in the newly emerging context of policy integration. For instance, it has cited the need for integration of national planning policies and Community water policy into agricultural policy as being 'particularly essential', and described the area generally as one 'which illustrates the need to have a coherent and effective coordination of all relevant Community policies'.[24] The current progress of the proposed Framework Directive is a significant expression of this philosophy. Community law-making, founded upon a liberal economic order and the benefits of economic integration, has traditionally accorded the highest value of judicial protection to related legal measures.[25] In contrast, environmental provisions only appeared expressly in the Treaty from 1987.[26] The Amsterdam Treaty has furthered commitment by Community institutions to the principle of integration,[27] by inserting the requirement that environmental protection be integrated into the definition and implementation of Community policies and activities.[28] Article 6 of the amended Treaty, which also includes a commitment to the promotion of sustainable development, is mirrored in the Treaty on European Union (TEU).[29] This benchmark may in due course be available to challenge hitherto dominant economic objectives.[30] Moreover, whilst Article 174 EC is in substantially similar form to the previous version, it contains fuller recognition of national rights to pursue stricter environmental measures.[31]

---

[24]  See Communication on Implementation COM(96)500 final, para. 5(6).

[25]  Categorized as 'pre-emptive norms': see R. Macrory, 'Environmental Citizenship and the Law: Repairing the European Road' (1996) 8 *Journal of Environmental Law* 219, 230–3.

[26]  See n. 1 above: following the revisions agreed at the Amsterdam Council, [1997] OJ C340/173–308, Art. 174 EC has replaced Art. 130r EC (originally in the Single European Act 1986, and later amended by the Treaty on European Union 1993 (TEU)). Moreover, the co-decision procedure under Art. 251 EC has been extended throughout environmental legislation.

[27]  See G. van Galster and K. Deketelaere, 'Amsterdam, the Intergovernmental Conference and Greening of the EU Treaty' (1998) 12 *European Environmental Law Review*, 18. The authors conclude that integration 'has moved to the highest steps of the Community hierarchy'.

[28]  Art. 6 EC mandates the integration of environmental protection requirements into Community policies and activities, with a view to promoting sustainable development; note the introduction of 'environmental correspondents' into each Directorate-General (Commission release IP/97/636).

[29]  The objective of balanced and sustainable development appears in Art. 2 EC.

[30]  Cf. P. Sands, *Principles of International Environmental Law: Part I—Frameworks, Standards and Implementation* (Manchester: Manchester University Press, 1994), 1998–9. The author argues for intergenerational equity, sustainable use, equitable use, and integration into economic and other plans, programmes, and projects to be coextensive elements under international law.

[31]  Art. 174(2) EC confirms that, where appropriate, environmental harmonization measures shall include safeguards allowing national provisional measures for non-economic environmental reasons. Under Art. 95(5) EC, despite previous harmonization, stricter national measures are authorized where there is scientific evidence that these are necessary to resolve problems in individual Member States.

## ii. A Commitment to Integration

Thus a wider imperative is to secure the integration of environmental priorities into the policy process. We are yet to see the fruits of the Fifth Action Programme's changed emphasis towards intervention in target sectors including energy, transport, industry, agriculture, and tourism.[32] The avowed intention is to move beyond previous vertical, or sectoral, approaches to ecological problems, and to encourage the development of a horizontal approach, taking account of all causes of pollution in the area of intervention. This has important implications for the protection of waters, given the vulnerability of the aquatic environment to both point source and diffuse emissions out of the various sectors.

Numerous sectoral proposals have emerged variously from the Commission during 1999.[33] Following a Commission Communication,[34] the Council has accordingly laid foundations for coordinating Community action to integrate environmental concerns into wider policies.[35] Thus in the agricultural sector, the Commission is seeking to pursue the integration of environmental aspects into policy-making, to combat the destruction of eco-systems and related problems caused by intensive use of fertilizers and pesticides, as well as to tackle problems caused by the depletion of water resources, including soil erosion.[36] A Proposal for a Decision on a Community Framework for Cooperation to Promote Sustainable Urban Development has also been produced by the Commission.[37] With problems in enforcement, the Commission is also looking

[32] Programme of policy and action in relation to the environment and sustainable development, 'Towards Sustainability', [1993] OJ C138/1.

[33] The Cardiff Council meeting (June 1998) resolved upon guidelines having four aims: reviewing existing policies and the level of integration into sectoral policies; introducing strategies for action in the above key areas; achieving integration into all activities of Community institutions; and defining priority actions and mechanisms for monitoring implementation; the Vienna and Cologne Council meetings (Dec. 1998 and June 1999) invited those councils with sectoral responsibilities to produce strategies; the process culminated in the presentation to the Helsinki Council meeting (Dec. 1999), as follows: of sectoral reports: transport (6 Oct. 1999), agriculture (16 Nov. 1999), and energy (2 Dec. 1999); and of preliminary draft strategies: internal market (28 Oct. 1999), industry (9 Nov. 1999), and development (11 Nov. 1999).

[34] 'Europe's environment: what directions for the future? global assessment of the Community programme of policy and action in relation to the environment and sustainable development—Towards Sustainability', COM(1999)543 final; a follow-up to a Communication on a partnership for integration: a strategy for integrating the environment into EU policies, COM(98)333 final.

[35] The Helsinki Council has called on the Commission to submit comprehensive strategies in June 2001 (and a proposal for a Sixth Action Programme by the end of 2000).

[36] Communication on directions towards sustainable agriculture, COM(1999)22 final, [1999] OJ C173/68.

[37] COM(1999)557 final; this follows a Communication on sustainable urban development in the EU: a framework for action, COM(98)605 final; the emphasis remains vague but appears to be in pursuance of the Agenda 21 Protocol at the Rio Summit, exhorting awareness raising and sharing of good practice at the local level, with financial support (2000–2004).

to an intensification of efforts to integrate the environment in order to improve both the coherence and the enforcement of legislation.[38]

### iii. Problems in the Delivery of Integrated Environmental Protection

There is, however, a lack as yet of a truly integrated environmental protection regime within the Community's legal order. Policy-making apart, Treaty environmental principles presently appear unlikely to have much impact through the doctrine of direct applicability or effect.[39] Given the need for justiciability under the doctrine of direct effect, the increased commitment to integration under the Amsterdam Treaty may yet founder for lack of precision in the enforcement context. The principle of integration may be included within the notion of 'soft law', and is arguably unlikely to assume more than a marginal role in legal environmental protection mechanisms unless more effective means of enforcement are developed. However, this is no foregone conclusion. For instance, by analogy with the principle of proportionality, the integration principle might be interpreted as requiring the least harmful solution for the environment.[40] There have furthermore been instances of judicial recognition of Treaty principles where legal duties do not impose contrary restrictions.[41] Moreover, opportunities may be accorded to apply even soft law as a matter of interpretation.[42]

Still, in view of constraints on the Commission, discussed further in section F.*iii*, implementation partly depends upon how far Community jurisprudence can accommodate the existence of meaningful rights of individual action. An extension of individual rights would contribute towards a counterbalancing of traditional rights rooted in liberal economic principles and thereby assist in the processes of integration.[43] Whilst a conceptual basis for enforcing public law rights in defence of the general interest remains uncertain, increased

---

[38] Progress report on implementation of the fifth action programme, COM(95)624 final: see n. 32 above. Also, Council Dec. 2179/98/EC of 24 Sept. 1998 concerning the Review of the Community Programme of Policy and Action in relation to the Environment and Sustainable Development, 'Towards Sustainability'. For a discussion of enforcement difficulties see Section F.

[39] See an English Court of Appeal decision where the precautionary principle had been cited as an aid to interpretation of an administrative discretion: *R* v. *Secretary of State for Trade and Industry, ex parte Duddridge* (1995) 5 *Environmental Law Review*, 151; see also N. Haigh, 'The Introduction of the Precautionary Principle into the UK', in T. O'Riordan and J. Cameron (eds.), *Interpreting the Precautionary Principle* (London: Earthscan, 1994), ch. 13.

[40] Cf. Case 240/83, *Procureur de la Republique* v. *Association de Defense des Bruleurs D'huiles Usagees (ADBHU)* [1985] ECR 531, in particular paras. 12–13; Case 302/86, *Commission* v. *Denmark* [1988] ECR 4607; Case C–2/90, *Commission* v. *Belgium* [1992] ECR I–4431.

[41] See the discussion of the principle of subsidiarity (now contained in Art. 5 EC) in the case report for '*R* v. *London Boroughs Transport Committee, ex parte Freight Transport Association*' (1992) 1 *Common Market Law Review*, 5.

[42] See Case C–322/88, *Grimaldi* v. *Fonds des Maladies Professionelles* [1989] ECR–4407. There is some evidence as to the availability of the European Convention on Human Rights to assist in the assertion of environmental rights: e.g., case report for '*Guerra* v. *Italy*' (1999) 11 *Journal of Environmental Law*, 157; see further R. R. Churchill, 'Environmental Rights in Treaties', in A. Boyle and M. Anderson (eds.), *Human Rights Approaches to Environmental Protection* (Oxford: Clarendon Press, 1996), ch. 6.

[43] See G. de Búrca, 'The Language of Rights and European Integration', in J. Shaw and G. More (eds.), *New Legal Dynamics of European Union* (Oxford: Clarendon Press, 1995).

access to justice in domestic courts would enhance the enforcement of directives, and also contribute by the way to the development of the soft law contained in Article 174 EC.[44] There have been some significant cases in the context of Water Directives and this issue is returned to in Section G.

### D. THE PROPOSED WATER FRAMEWORK DIRECTIVE

#### i. The Contribution of Water Policy to Sustainable Development

The Commission has identified environmental protection as one of the EU's fundamental challenges in the light of the continuing degradation of the natural environment.[45] A recitation, as in Section A above, of the veritable stream of Community water legislation, exposes none of the underlying challenges and contradictions of policy-making, especially in this area. Environmental policy-making has generally been described as 'among the most complex in government because it requires policy makers to arrange an extraordinarily diverse array of information into a coherent decision-making process'.[46] The role of water policy must be central to any strategy for sustainable development and balanced resource management.

Whilst Article 174 EC is policy-aspirational, its principles can be seen as translating into legislative forms, such as the precautionary principle through the application of controls notwithstanding (inevitable) scientific uncertainties, and the preventive principle through the application of clean technologies within licensing schemes. However, it has been said that despite

all the technological skills and capital wealth of our own age, the sharing of good-quality water can no longer depend on yet more or better technical fixes. We have to effect a transformation in our economic and social institutions . . . The sustainability of the river basin habitats, on which we and future generations will depend, is still being put in peril.[47]

There are significant obstacles to the achievement of assured quality of the water supply,[48] and foremost among these may sensibly be expressed in terms of sustainability. In this context, the Directive 2000/60/EC (Water Framework Directive),[49] adopted in October 2000, has emerged from the Community's still somewhat inchoate commitment to the concept of sustainability.

---

[44] E Rehbinder, '*Locus Standi*, Community Law and the Case for Harmonisation', in H. Somsen (ed.), *Protecting the European Environment: Enforcing EC Environmental Law* (London: Blackstone Press, 1996), 151–66.

[45] See 'The Commission's Work Programme for 1999: The Policy Priorities', COM(98)604 final, [1998] OJ C366/1.

[46] W. Rosenbaum, *Environmental Politics and Policy* (Washington, DC: CQ Press, 2nd edn. 1991), 13.

[47] D. Kinnersley, *Coming Clean: the Politics of Water and the Environment* (London: Penguin Books, 1994), 210–11.

[48] W. Rosenbaum charts similar difficulties in the USA: see n. 46 above, 194–209.

[49] COM(97)49 final, [1997] OJ C184/20; see amended proposals COM(97)614 final, [1998] OJ C16/14, COM(98)76 final, [1998] OJ C108/94, COM(1999)271 final, [1999] OJ C342E/1, and Common Position (EC) No. 41/1999 of 22 Oct. 1999, [1999] OJ C343/1.

The emergent Directive is likely to be the most significant measure yet in the field of water policy-making and legislation at the EU level. EU water policy had been the subject of a fundamental consultation and review since 1995, partly resulting from pressure from those Member States concerned at the cost of current legislative commitments,[50] and the Commission produced a Communication on EU Water Policy in February 1996.[51] The various types of pollution were identified, including point source, diffuse, and accidental pollution, as well as acidification and eutrophication. A new policy approach was to be based on the Fifth Environment Action Programme,[52] as well as specific Treaty principles such as a high level of environmental protection, the polluter pays, the precautionary principle, the rectification of environmental damage at source, and giving consideration to the distinct environmental conditions in the various territories.[53] The process appears therefore to have been informed by the Treaty objectives of preserving, protecting, and improving the quality of the environment and a prudent and rational utilization of natural resources.[54]

### ii. Objectives for a Sustainable EU Water Policy

The new Directive will therefore seek a common strategy, applying common objectives and principles, as well as common definitions and basic measures, in order to protect EU surface and groundwaters.

In the context of a wider legislative review, the measure has a key role as part of a new generation of Directives, to contain strict criteria in support of harmonized Community strategies to challenge environmental degradation, but otherwise recognizing that responsibility for ensuring compliance lies with individual Member States. The achievement of a greater coherence will be on the basis of a so-called 'combined approach' to water regulation. This will subsume much existing Community legislation,[55] and set up machinery to facilitate greater harmonization in the sector. The proposed Directive applies notions of sustainability in a more integrated way, creating a scheme for management planning for water on a river basin basis. A more comprehensive

---

[50] See e.g. the UK's House of Commons Select Committee on Environment, Transport and the Regions, Second Report, 1997–8, Sewage Treatment and Disposal, received evidence that UK compliance with Dir. 91/271/EEC, n. 8 above, would cost between £6bn and £8bn (para. 212); cf. concerning the Framework Directive, a Report of the House of Lords Select Committee on the European Communities, Eighth Report, 1997–8, Community Water Policy, concluding that 'it would be a pity nevertheless if agreement on the Directive were unduly delayed because of largely speculative arguments about costs' (para. 54).

[51] COM(96)59 final.      [52] See n. 32 above.      [53] Under Art. 174(2) EC.

[54] Art. 174(1) EC.

[55] e.g. the following are to be integrated and extended beyond waters specific to human drinking: Dir. 75/440/EEC, n. 3 above (with related Dir. 79/869/EEC, n. 3 above, concerning the methods of measurement and frequencies of sampling and analysis of surface water intended for the abstraction of drinking water in the member states and Decision 77/795/EEC, [1977] OJ L334/29, on procedure and information exchange); also, Dir. 80/68/EEC, n. 6 above, Dir. 78/659/EEC and Dir. 79/923/EEC, n. 5 above. The draft Dirrctive on the Ecological Quality of Water, [1994] OJ C222/6, had been subject to much criticism, as it appeared to allow Member States responsibility for deciding what 'good ecological quality' amounted to and both to identify sources of pollution and fix objectives accordingly: it is now to be dropped.

regulatory scheme should emerge, in place of the piecemeal approach to sustainability to date,[56] encouraging cross-media approaches as appropriate.[57]

The stated objectives therefore underlying the proposal are the prevention of further deterioration and the protection and enhancement of the quality and quantity of aquatic ecosystems, and to ensure a supply of water in the quantities and qualities needed for sustainable development. It purports to seek a more rational arrangement for the protection and use of water, reduced water treatment costs, increased amenity value of surface waters, and a more coordinated administration of waters. The premises for its sustainable water policy amount to four main objectives: sufficiency of drinking water; sufficiency of water for other economic requirements; protection of the environment; and alleviation of the adverse impact of floods and droughts. Common principles will be established

in order to coordinate Member States' efforts to improve water quantity and quality, to promote sustainable water consumption, to contribute to the control of transboundary pollution problems, to protect ecosystems, in particular aquatic ecosystems, and to safeguard the recreational potential of Community waters.[58]

This expansive approach accordingly extends to the following:

— the protection of all surface waters and groundwaters in their quality and quantity with a proper ecological dimension;
— the control of emissions and discharges by a combined approach;
— the introduction of water pricing policies;
— integrated river basin management across administrative and political borders with coordinated programmes of measures; and
— and strengthened public participation and reporting arrangements.

The regime will seek 'good status' for all groundwaters and surface waters, as a necessary step if the EU is to ensure sustainability of consumption and use. It is to cover water quality and quantity, including surface waters and groundwaters used for drinking water abstraction, and will include assessment of the impact of human activities, including pollution from both point and diffuse sources. Specific objectives, aimed at a high level of environmental protection and a secure supply of high-quality water for human consumption and economic purposes, are as follows:

— the focusing of environmental water policy on water as it flows naturally through river basins towards the sea;
— taking into account the natural interaction between both surface and groundwater, both qualitatively and quantitatively;

---

[56] Though numerous Directives have been informed by notions of sustainability and preventive action: e.g. Dir. 80/68/EEC, n. 6 above, which aimed to protect groundwater against contamination by identified substances.

[57] It will form part of a combined approach, alongside with such measures as Dir. 91/271/EEC, n. 8 above, Dir. 91/676/EEC, n. 9 above, and Dir. 96/61/EC, n. 10 above (though for smaller industries, Dir. 76/464/EEC, n. 2 above, is to be updated as 'a broadly agreed form of control of pollution of small installations': COM(97)49 final, 2).

[58] See draft framework Dir., n. 49 above, recital 19.

— general protection of the aquatic ecology, and designation of 'protected areas' with special requirements as identified in existing EU legislation such as bathing waters, areas intended for drinking-water abstraction, protection of unique and valuable habitats; and

— achieving such good status of all waters (probably by 2010), that is with:

(a) good surface water status to require a rich, balanced, and sustainable ecosystem and that established environmental quality standards for pollutants are respected;

(b) certain pollutants to be identified for cessation or phase-out of discharges, emissions, and losses within a timetable of (probably) twenty years; and

(c) good groundwater status to require that abstractions and alterations to the natural rate of recharge are sustainable in the long term, and that environmental quality standards for pollutants are respected.

### iii. A Combined Approach to Water Regulation

The measure will provide for procedures to ensure transparency and coordination of water policy at the EU level, including emission controls and environmental quality objectives in a so-called 'combined approach'. [59] According to the Commission:

Environmental quality objectives alone are often insufficient to tackle serious pollution problems and can be abused as a 'licence to pollute' up to the defined level. Likewise, a strict emission limit values approach based on BAT (best available techniques) can in some circumstances lead to unnecessary investment without significant benefits to the environment.[60]

This combined approach will be supported by a so-called 'feedback mechanism', to identify where further action is necessary. Cross-sectoral strategies, reflecting the approach to integration generally,[61] will provide a mechanism for improving the dialogue between the policy areas concerned, including agriculture, industry, energy, or regional policy.[62] Such coordination will extend to the following:

— setting and requiring observance of quality standards for surface water abstraction areas;

— creation of a professional network, to compare and contrast working methods and to exchange information and ideas;

— ensuring that water needs are satisfied within the overall water policy, without imposing new obligations in respect of protected areas under existing EU or national legislation; and

---

[59]  A difficulty for the UK had been its traditional resort to schemes based upon receiving waters. An original compromise, allowing the UK to opt for quality objectives approaches in dealing with polluting emissions, has been gradually replaced by preferred emission limits, as for large-scale industrial installations under Dir. 96/61/EC on Integrated Pollution Prevention and Control, [1996] OJ L19/83.

[60]  See Communication, n. 51 above, para 7.1.

[61]  See Sect. C above, in particular n. 33 above.

[62]  e.g. draft Framework Directive, n. 49 above, recital 19.

— management planning for the whole river system, with measures for each river basin within a 'River Basin Management District', to be contained in a River Basin Management Plan, for a six-year implementation period, to be issued in draft for consultation with interested parties a year before adoption, and thereafter updated on a six-yearly basis.

River basins, being the natural geographical and hydrological unit and therefore viewed by the Commission as the best model for water management, are to be central to the whole scheme. To this end, comprehensive management plans and programmes will be required with a view to achieving environmental objectives set through the establishment and implementation of legally binding measures.[63] Member States will be obliged to conform across a broad range of 'tasks', including an analysis of their characteristics and identification of waters to be used for human consumption. Nevertheless Member States and local competent authorities will be the main players in implementing most measures to ensure adequate protection and use of waters. It will depart from a prescriptive emission limit approach, allowing considerable discretion to Member States in matters of designation. The new scheme will be premissed upon the need to recognize individualized conditions, and to encourage the efficient and effective protection of water at a local level, seemingly in accordance with the principle of subsidiarity. The proposal therefore conforms to a recognition of a need for procedures 'allowing the elaboration of solutions tailored to the needs of individual waters'.[64]

The benefits afforded by the proposal appear to be compelling. In the first place, ensuring sustainable water use appears to be the ultimate goal; secondly, a more rational scheme for the protection and use of water, including greater coordination of water administration, should emerge; thirdly, as well as in terms of utility, greater amenity value of surface waters should result; and finally, as the quality of water improves, and sourcing of water supply becomes more efficient, there should be reductions in water treatment costs. The issue of costs is also a real one, especially in the short- and medium-term. Such costs are expected to vary, depending on national and local water status, the extent of previous action, and the need for further actions in order to achieve the Directive's objectives.[65]

### iv. The Measure as an Economic Instrument

The area of environmental taxation, given the prime importance of neutrality of tax measures in international law, is a difficult one for the Community.[66] There is

[63] Ibid., in particular Arts. 3–6, 13.

[64] See D. Freestone and H. Somsen, 'The Impact of Subsidiarity' in J. Holder (ed.), *The Impact of EC Environmental Law in the UK* (New York: Wiley, 1997), 96.

[65] See draft Framework Directive, n. 49 above, explanatory memorandum, economic analysis under para. 4, which emphasizes the need to internalize costs; any analysis must recognize that most costs are likely to result from ongoing demands under legislation already in place.

[66] For a discussion of potential conflicts with GATT/WTO rules, see K. Borgsmidt, 'Eco-taxes in the Framework of Community Law' (1999) 13 *European Environmental Law Review*, 270.

also, problematically for the EU, a close nexus with competitiveness, for environmental taxes and charges impinge 'directly or indirectly, on several areas of Community legislation other than environmental policy, and in particular on competition, single market and taxation policies'.[67] Nevertheless, in defence of such approaches to water resources, it has been said that measures 'towards the measurement and economic pricing of water services mean that economic, financial, environmental (including sustainability) and equity interests are all simultaneously pursued'.[68] The draft Framework Directive, apparently in recognition of this, suggests introducing an economic instrument, through a principle of 'full cost recovery'.[69] In this case, prices affected will be those set for both water supply and waste water collection and treatment, in light of economic analyses for each river basin. It is proposed that under full cost recovery pricing, Member States will be obliged to ensure that by (probably ) 2010 true costs of water supply, as well as treatment of waste water, are integrated into prices charged to water consumers. Social objectives will necessitate to certain derogations, concerning the provision of affordable supplies to households and where conditions are such that water provision is demonstrably more expensive than normal.[70]

Overall, the development is thus a concrete expression of the polluter-pays principle, and the ramifications of this for consumers. It also reflects a wider policy direction on the part of the Commission.[71] In terms of taxation policy, the measure meets wider environmental goals, the 'double dividend' moving tax away from labour to resources.[72] The measure will have the effect of pushing Member States towards resolving these difficult issues, in spite of the complications caused by fears for competitiveness. However, in the UK in this respect, measures proposed by government for introducing charges for polluting emissions to water from point sources and product charges in connection with diffuse pollution caused by known agents have in the meantime stalled.[73]

### v. A New Approach to Control of Dangerous Substance

Finally, the combined approach under the proposal referred to above requires that harmonized water-quality standards and emission controls be elaborated for all dangerous substances, with a priority list identified by early in 2000. The priority list is to be produced on the basis of risk to the aquatic ecosystem and to human health via the aquatic environment. It is anticipated that there will

[67] Commission Communication 'Environmental Taxes and Charges in the Single Market', COM(97)9 final, para. 6.

[68] P. Herrington, 'Pricing Water Properly' in T. O'Riordan (ed.), *Ecotaxation* (London: Earthscan, 1997), 284.

[69] See n. 49 above, esp. recital 32, Arts. 2.33, 12.          [70] See n. 65 above e.g. para. 4.2.3.

[71] See Communication, n. 67 above. See also Amended Proposal for a Council Directive Introducing a Tax on Carbon Dioxide Emissions and Energy, COM(95)172 final; and proposal for a Council Directive Restructuring the Community Framework for the Taxation of Energy Products, COM(97)30 final, [1997] OJ C139/14.

[72] See White Paper 'Growth, Competitiveness, Employment: the Challenges and Ways forward into the 21st Century, COM(93)700. Cf. OECD document 'Environmental Taxes and Green Tax Reform, and Environmental Policies and Employment', 1997.

[73] See Department of Environment, Transport and the Regions, economic instruments for water pollution (Nov. 1997).

be greater progress in prescribing for identified substances than has been the case pursuant to Directive 76/464/EEC on Pollution caused by Certain Dangerous Substances Discharged into the Aquatic Environment of the Community.[74] The exercise is inevitably constrained by exclusions caused by insufficient data, problems in monitoring, and even industry confidentiality, but the draft Framework Directive contains provisions for a six-yearly revision of the list thereafter.[75]

### E.  MARINE POLLUTION

Although the terms of the draft Framework Directive exclude the marine environment, the priorities underlying the measure are also being followed for the North-East Atlantic under the ruling OSPAR Convention.[76] Following consultations within OSPAR, a series of measures are under discussion: including amendments to the Fifth Annex of the Convention requiring further measures for the protection, conservation, and restoration of ecosystems and the biodiversity of the maritime area;[77] the loss of exemptions for France and the UK from the permanent prohibition of dumping at sea of low and intermediate level radioactive substances and waste;[78] prohibitions concerning the dumping and leaving in place of disused offshore installations;[79] and proposed limit values of emissions relating to vinyl chloride monomer and manufacture of suspension PVC.[80]

For the Mediterranean region, the Community acceded to the Barcelona Convention for the Protection of the Mediterranean Sea against Pollution and related Protocol for the Prevention of the Pollution of the Mediterranean Sea from Ships and Aircraft in 1977.[81] Subsequent Council decisions have

[74] See n. 2 above.

[75] There also appears no reason to exclude the possibility of accretions on a case-by-case basis.

[76] See Cooperation Agreement for the Protection of the Coasts and Waters of the North-East Atlantic against Pollution, [1993] OJ L 267/22; also, Dec. 98/249/EC on the Conclusion of the Convention for the Protection of the Marine Environment of the North-East Atlantic, [1998] OJ L104/2. The ruling Paris Convention of 22 September 1992 replaced the Oslo and Paris Conventions of 1972 and 1974 respectively.

[77] Proposal for a Council Decision concerning the Approval, on behalf of the Community, of the New Annex to the Convention for the Protection of the Marine Environment of the North-East Atlantic on the Protection and Conservation of the Ecosystems and Biological Diversity of the Maritime Area, the Corresponding Appendix 3 and the Agreement on the Meaning of Certain Concepts in the New Annex, COM(1999)190 final, [1999] OJ C158/1.

[78] Proposal for a Council Decision concerning the Approval, on behalf of the Community, of OSPAR Decision 98/2 on the Dumping of Radioactive Waste at Sea, COM(1999)190 final, [1999] OJ C158/8.

[79] Proposal for a Council Decision concerning the Approval, on behalf of the Community, of OSPAR Decision 98/3 on the Disposal of Disused Offshore Installations, COM(1999)190 final, [1999] OJ C158/10.

[80] Proposal for a Council Decision concerning the Approval, on behalf of the Community, of OSPAR Decision 98/4 on Emission and Discharge Limit Values for the Manufacture of Vinyl Chloride Monomer, and OSPAR Decision 98/5 on Emission and Discharge Limits in the Vinyl Chloride Sector, COM(1999)190 final, [1999] OJ C158/19. See parameters contained in Dir. 76/464/EEC, Dir. 86/280/EEC, and Dir. 96/61/EC, n. 2 above.

[81] Dec. 77/585/EEC, [1977] OJ L240/1.

addressed pollution in the region by energy-related substances,[82] land-based sources,[83] and dealt with specially protected areas.[84] During 1999 concerns at threats to specially protected areas have resulted in the adoption of a further Protocol.[85] Currently, in the light of the 1995 Barcelona conference, and in order to address particular problems of marine pollution resulting from dumping or incineration by ships and aircraft, the Commission has proposed a Decision on Amendments to the Barcelona Convention.[86] Likewise, there are further proposals concerned to review, respectively, responses to land-based pollution threats, especially the dumping of untreated domestic and industrial waste containing toxic non-degradable substances that are likely to bio-accumulate.[87] In respect of the third major marine area, namely the Baltic, the Community acceded to the Helsinki Convention on the Protection of the Marine Environment of the Baltic Sea Area 1974 in 1994.[88] Amendments to the Convention have also been under discussion and a Decision has been proposed.[89]

Finally, in connection with accidental marine pollution, an action programme is already in place,[90] and a Community task force of experts exists for the purpose of rendering practical assistance. In order to reinforce levels of cooperation and improve response capabilities, a more integrated system is under discussion.[91]

## F. ENFORCEMENT OF EC WATER LEGISLATION THROUGH THE ECJ

### i. *Enforcing Directives: General Issues*

The development of a harmonized environmental law, in respect of water measures as elsewhere, is reliant upon effective transposition and implementation of Community Directives. The rationale for the mechanism of the Directive is that Member States, whilst allowed some freedom as to method, are obliged under Article 249 EC to incorporate required measures into domestic

---

[82] Dec. 81/420/EEC concerning Cooperation in Combating Pollution of the Mediterranean Sea by Oil and other Harmful Substances in the Case of Energy, [1981] OJ L162/4.

[83] Dec. 83/101/EEC for the Protection of the Sea against Pollution from Land-Based Sources, [1983] OJ L67/1.

[84] Dec. 84/132/EEC concerning Specially Protected Areas, [1984] OJ L68/36.

[85] Protocol concerning Specially Protected Areas and Biological Diversity in the Mediterranean, [1999] OJ L322/1.

[86] COM(1999) 29 final; see Parliament's opinion of 14 Apr. 1999 [1999] OJ C219. The measure awaits final adoption by the Council.

[87] Proposal for Decision on improving programmes and measures for protection against pollution from land-based sources and activities, COM(1999) 28 final; see Parliament's opinion, n. 86 above; also awaiting adoption.

[88] Decisions 94/156 and 157 [1994] OJ L73/1,19

[89] Proposal for Decision to approve amendments to annexes to the Convention, COM(1999) 128 final [1999] OJ C176.

[90] Community Action Programme on the control and reduction of pollution caused by hydrocarbons discharged at sea [1978] OJ C162; and a related Community information system [1981] OJ L355, [1986] OJ L77.

[91] Proposal for Decision setting up a Community framework of cooperation in the field of accidental marine pollution, COM(98) 769 final [1999] OJ C25, amended COM(1999) 641 final.

law in order to achieve the contemplated results. In principle, therefore, a directive is not directly applicable, in contrast with legislation in the form of regulations, as also certain Treaty provisions where at least they include appropriate rights and obligations.[92] Nevertheless, Member States are under an obligation under Article 10 EC to do everything to ensure the fulfilment of Community obligations, requiring that all appropriate measures be taken. The requirement to transpose directives into national law under Article 249 EC is guaranteed (at least in principle) by the power of the Commission to bring enforcement proceedings under Article 226 EC.

### ii. The Requirement for Effective Legal Compliance

The European Court of Justice (ECJ) has consistently laid emphasis on the objective nature of the requirement to enact fully binding national law.[93] During 1999, in an enforcement action brought under Directive 91/676/EEC concerning the Protection of Waters against Pollution caused by Nitrates from Agricultural Sources,[94] the Court ruled against Italy for

[a failure] to adopt and communicate to the Commission within the prescribed period the laws, regulations and administrative provisions necessary to implement the Directive, and in particular by failing to comply with the obligation laid down [under that Directive].[95]

It is also unacceptable as a defence to proceedings to argue that national arrangements have resulted in implementation being left in the hands of local or regional authorities.[96]

Likewise, the Court has been unimpressed with assertions that reasonably practicable measures have been taken.[97] The argument, that all practicable steps had been taken, was raised in earlier proceedings against the UK for non-compliance with Directive 75/440/EEC concerning the Quality Required of Surface Water intended for the Abstraction of Drinking Water, on grounds that parameters set for nitrates in designated drinking water had been exceeded.[98]

---

[92]  Case C 26/62, *van Gend en Loos* v. *Nederlandse Administratie der Belastingen* [1963] ECR 1

[93]  See under Dir. 76/464/EEC on pollution caused by certain dangerous substances discharged into the aquatic environment of the community, n. 2 above, Case C–262/95, *Commission* v. *Germany* [1996] ECR I–5729.

[94]  See n. 9 above.

[95]  Case C–195/97, *Commission* v. *Italy*, para. 19; the breach was specifically under Article 3(2), under which Member States are required to designate as vulnerable zones all known areas of land in their territories which drain into waters affected by pollution and waters which could be affected by pollution and to notify the Commission.

[96]  See under Dir. 76/160/EEC concerning the quality of bathing waters, n. 4 above, Case 96/81, *Commission* v. *Netherlands* [1982] ECR 1791; under Dir. 75/440/EEC concerning the quality required of surface water intended for the abstraction of drinking water, n. 3 above, Case 97/81, *Commission* v. *Netherlands* [1982] ECR 1819, and Case C–58/89, *Commission* v. *Germany* [1991] ECR I–4983; under Dir. 91/271/EEC concerning urban waste water treatment, n. 8 above, Case C–297/95, *Commission* v. *Germany* [1996] ECR I–6739; under Dir. 78/659/EEC on the quality of fresh waters needing protection in order to support fish life and Dir. 79/923/EEC on the quality required of shellfish waters, n. 5 above, Case C–298/95, *Commission* v. *Germany* [1996] ECR I–6747.

[97]  Case C–56/90, *Commission* v. *United Kingdom* [1993] ECR I–4109, para. 43, and Case C–92/96, *Commission* v. *Spain* [1998] ECR I–505, para. 28.

[98]  See n. 3 above: Case C–337/89, *Commission* v. *United Kingdom* [1992] ECR I–6103.

The Court held that the obligation was to achieve compliance with the limit values laid down in the Directive and not simply to take all practicable steps.[99] In a 1999 judgment, following proceedings brought by the Commission against Germany under Directive 76/160/EEC concerning the Quality of Bathing Waters,[100] there had been a failure to adopt in due time the steps necessary to ensure that the quality of bathing water conformed to limit values and to meet the prescribed minimum sampling frequency.[101] This was found to be in breach, the Court ruling that it was not sufficient to take all reasonably practicable measures, for the Directive requires that Member States take all necessary measures to ensure that bathing waters conform to the set limit values.

The Court continues to apply a purposive approach to the review of the exercise of discretion, as exemplified in earlier proceedings against the UK concerning the interpretation of the term 'bathing waters' for the purposes of that same Directive.[102] The Commission had there instituted proceedings for non-compliance with mandatory quality values. The Directive affords wide discretion to Member States in the designation of beaches for its purpose.[103] The UK had argued that all practicable steps had been taken, that compliance was not possible, that the duty was conditional, and that due diligence towards the achievement of the standards had been exercised. The Court ruled that it was the state's responsibility to ensure conformity with objective characteristics. The notion of taking all practicable steps afforded no acceptable ground of defence,[104] and reliance outside the formal derogation process on particular national circumstances did not justify breach.[105]

The Court has consistently held that an action under Article 226 EC is objective in nature and that the bringing of such an action before the Court is a matter for the Commission in its entire discretion.[106] In this context, in the proceedings against Germany above, the Court rejected arguments based upon proportionality, though strangely without express allusion to the notion in the judgment. Thus, concerning sampling frequencies and the impact of a single breach in a short bathing season making 100 per cent compliance necessary in practice,[107] the Court ruled that the Directive 'only specifies the minimum frequency of sample-taking, and does not therefore preclude the Member States from increasing the number of samples, thus reducing the

[99] See n. 3 above: Case C–337/89, *Commission* v. *United Kingdom* [1992] ECR I–6103, paras. 24–5.

[100] See n. 4 above: Case C–198/97, *Commission* v. *Germany* [1999] ECR I–3257.

[101] Ibid., Arts. 3, 4(1), and 6(1).                    [102] Case C–56/90, n. 97 above.

[103] On the basis of either specific national authorization or traditional use and non-prohibition.

[104] Ibid., paras. 43–4, although physical impossibility (not there established) was arguably left open.

[105] Ibid., para. 33.

[106] Case C–209/89, *Commission* v. *Italy* [1991] ECR I–1575.

[107] See n. 100 above, para. 29: the Directive otherwise allows for between 5 and 10% of samples to be discounted: see Article 5(1); here, samples were taken every 2 weeks during the 15- to 17-week bathing season, so that a single excessive result would exceed the 10% tolerance limit allowed.

proportion represented by samples not satisfying the conditions laid down'.[108] On the general point, the opinion of Advocate General (AG) Jacobs was that whilst the Commission had 'ample justification in instituting the proceedings', it was in any event

no defence to an action under [the former] Article 169 EC [now Article 226 EC] for a Member State to argue that the infringements which it has committed are minor ones or are not significant.[109]

It should be noted that proportionality was addressed more directly by the Court upon a reference by the English High Court in which the Court pronounced judgment in 1999, and which is further discussed in Section G.[110] There, it was held that:

the Directive contains flexible provisions enabling the Member States to observe the principle of proportionality in the application of the measures which they adopt. It is for the national courts to ensure that that principle is observed.[111]

In the *Germany* case the Court was moreover unwilling to accept arguments as to difficulties in compliance: Germany had pointed to waters having 'a catchment area extending beyond German territory' and thus 'involve absolute physical impossibility within the meaning of the case-law of the Court . . . (and in other areas) aquatic birds were the main cause of the breaches'.[112] Yet the Court ruled that 'even if, under the Directive, the absolute impossibility of fulfilling the obligations arising from the Directive could justify a failure to comply with it, the Federal Republic has not succeeded in proving absolute impossibility in this case'.[113] As to catchment areas extending beyond German territory, the Court was of the view that 'the German Government has not shown that the adoption of measures other than those already taken up to 1994 was physically impossible, in particular, measures taken in collaboration with the neighbouring States'.[114] The claim of a principal cause being the presence of aquatic birds was rejected as a matter of fact, for it had not been shown that

the modernisation of the sanitation equipment . . . was adequate, taking into account the regular, natural fluctuations in the aquatic bird population present there, nor proven that it is not possible to adopt additional measures for the purification of the waters.[115]

It appears that the Court is likely to place strict reliance upon the requirement for objective compliance, even in the face of scientific uncertainty, as in this case in accordance with the results of sampling, presumably on the (somewhat dubious, if clear) basis that this is the most certain way of arriving at a

---

[108] Ibid., para. 36.  [109] Ibid., para. 25.
[110] Case C–293/97, *R* v. *Secretary of State for the Environment, ex parte Standley* [1999] ECR I–1603; see case report in (1999) 9 *Environmental Law Review*, 801.
[111] Ibid., para. 50.
[112] See n. 100 above, para. 30 (and see *Commission* v. *United Kingdom*, n. 97 above, para. 46).
[113] Ibid., para. 41.  [114] Ibid., para. 39.  [115] Ibid., para. 40.

legal solution. The German Government therefore pointed in vain to a 'signi-ficant variance in the methods used to assess the microbiological parameters and that this did not warrant the classification of the bathing waters con-cerned as not conforming to the Directive', it being asserted that

there was no need for purification measures to be taken since no external cause of the departures from the limit values had been identified . . . [and even that] . . . the criteria for analysis set out in the Directive made it impossible to tell whether the total coliform level was a result of the natural environment or caused by waste water polluted by fae-cal matter.[116]

It is unacceptable for Member States simply to rely upon administrative prac-tices to achieve compliance.[117] Moreover, factual compliance is not enough on its own. The Court has held that, in order to secure the full implementation of Directives in law and not only in fact, Member States must establish a specific legal framework.[118] The principle that specific legal arrangements are required in order to achieve compliance has been exemplified in an ECJ judgment in 1999 in enforcement proceedings against the UK.[119] The Commission chal-lenged the lawfulness of UK statutory arrangements, purportedly transposing Directive 80/778/EEC relating to the Quality of Water intended for Human Consumption,[120] whereby for the purpose of ensuring compliance with the Directive the government could accept undertakings from water companies, otherwise in breach as to maximum pesticide concentrations.[121] As a result of the acceptance of these undertakings without statutory specification of con-ditions governing their acceptance, the UK was held to have failed to fulfil its obligations under the Directive.[122] The domestic legislation therefore failed on two counts: first, to offer a specific legal framework; and, second, to specify the matters to be covered by undertakings, such as parameters to be observed in respect of derogations, work programmes to be carried out, time limits, and appropriate provision for information to be given to concerned population groups.[123]

Relying upon an argument as to practicability, the UK Government had sub-mitted that

the water companies are best placed to identify the measures required for compliance with the Directive, and, consequently, that undertakings constitute, for the purpose of attaining the desired result, a more expeditious and efficacious procedure than that of enforcement orders.[124]

The Commission's case was that the failure to specify conditions as to which acceptance would be subject allowed the amendment both of target dates and

---

[116] See n. 100 above, at paras. 12, 15.
[117] See under Dir. 80/68/EEC on the protection of groundwater against pollution caused by cer-tain dangerous substances, n. 6 above, Case C–360/87, *Commission* v. *Italy* [1991] ECR I–0791, and Case C–131/88, *Commission* v. *Germany* [1991] ECR I–0825.
[118] Case C–360/87, *Commission* v. *Italy*, n. 117 above, judgment at para. 13.
[119] Case C–340/96, *Commission* v. *United Kingdom* [1999] ECR I–2023.      [120] See n. 3 above.
[121] Under section 19 Water Industry Act 1991.          [122] See n. 119 above, para. 32.
[123] Ibid., paras. 29–30.                    [124] Ibid., para. 26.

of technical specifications for required works in breach of the requirements of the Directive.[125] It was this factor which weighed most heavily with the Court, the domestic legislation having failed to 'set out a specific legal framework' in authorizing the minister

to accept an undertaking on the sole condition that it contains such measures as it appears to him for the time being to be appropriate for the company to take in order to secure or facilitate compliance with the standards in question.[126]

The UK's plea was clearly linked to the pragmatics of financial constraint. However, it is well established that reasons by reference to 'financial difficulties, which it is for the Member States to overcome by adopting appropriate measures' are insufficient to justify non-compliance with obligations under Directives.[127] The philosophy underlying the Court's approach contrasts with that which was seen in the earlier UK domestic proceedings brought by Friends of the Earth by way of judicial review, challenging the UK's approach to compliance with the same Directive through the acceptance of undertakings.[128] There, the High Court accepted that a defensible distinction existed as between obligations of a primary nature, namely transposition into domestic law, and of a secondary nature, thereby allowing a pragmatic approach for implementation up to enforcement. The new ECJ judgment reflects its earlier stated view that 'the adoption of legal provisions is not in itself sufficient to achieve the objectives sought'.[129]

In a further 1999 judgment arising out of Commission enforcement proceedings, the Court was required to interpret Directive 76/464/EEC on Pollution caused by Certain Dangerous Substances Discharged into the Aquatic Environment of the Community.[130] The Commission asserted that Belgium had failed to fulfil its obligations by not adopting pollution-reduction programmes including quality objectives for water in respect of ninety-nine listed substances. The technical complexity of bringing the Directive fully into force has meant that only a fraction of substances have been legislated for in detail.[131] Various interim approaches had as a result been required, and the Commission argued that remaining substances, whilst properly belonging to List I, must be treated in the same way as the priority substances referred to in List II of the Directive.[132] The Court agreed, holding that:

---

[125] Ibid., paras. 19–22.   [126] Ibid., paras. 30, 28.

[127] Case C–42/89, *Commission* v. *Belgium* [1990] ECR I–2821, para. 24, concerning Dir. 80/778/EEC relating to the Quality of Water intended for Human Consumption, n. 3 above.

[128] *R* v. *Secretary of State for the Environment, ex parte Friends of the Earth* (1994) 3 *Common Market Law Review*, 760 (affirmed in the Court of Appeal).

[129] Case C–337/89, *Commission* v. *United Kingdom*, n. 97 above: see opinion of AG Lenz, para. 43.

[130] See n. 2 above: Case C–207/97, *Commission* v. *Belgium* [1999] ECR I–0275.

[131] Of 132 such substances, only 18 have been the subject of directives laying down emission limit values and quality objectives: see now the proposals under the Framework Directive, discussed in Sect. D.

[132] See n. 130 above, para. 13; the difference lies essentially between measures of prohibition (List I) and reduction (List II).

so long as the Council has not determined emission limit values, there is absolutely no need for more specific legislative provision before the substances in question, which have been identified, are to be treated as List II substances by the Member States. The latter are under an obligation to establish the programmes referred to in Article 7 of the Directive in order to reduce pollution . . . Thus the Directive cannot be regarded as a framework-directive so far as that obligation is concerned.[133]

The Court went on to rule that:

by not adopting pollution reduction programmes including quality objectives for water in respect of the 99 substances listed in the annex to the application, the Kingdom of Belgium has failed to fulfil its obligations under Article 7 of the Directive.[134]

Specifically, national measures had failed to comply with the requirement to

embody a comprehensive and coherent approach, covering the entire national territory of each Member State and providing practical and coordinated arrangements for the reduction of pollution caused by any of the substances in List II which is relevant in the particular context of the Member State concerned, in accordance with the quality objectives fixed by those programmes for the waters affected. They differ, therefore, both from general purification programmes and from bundles of ad hoc measures designed to reduce water pollution. It should be added that the quality objectives fixed by those programmes on the basis of analyses of the waters affected serve as the point of reference for calculating the emission standards specified in the prior authorisations. Moreover, those programmes must be communicated to the Commission in a form which facilitates comparative appraisal and their harmonised implementation in all the Member States.[135]

It is not therefore sufficient for a Member State to rely upon an argument that measures in place set out a programme for compliance of an implicit nature.[136] Such finding reflects the Court's concern, discussed above, that compliance requires that specific legal frameworks be established.

### iii. Continuing Problems of Implementation and Enforcement

The successful delivery of Community environmental priorities is, however, ultimately dependent upon more than a purposive interpretation of Community legislation on the part of the ECJ. For the Community, as the creative force behind environmental policy-making across Member States, the importance of harmonization is as great as in economic fields within the Treaty and securing the implementation of directives is essential to this process. As discussed above, ineffective transposition being a breach of the EC Treaty, the Commission is empowered under Article 226 EC to take enforcement proceedings in the ECJ. However, the Commission faces significant difficulties in carrying out this role. For instance, there is no Treaty provision for an environmental 'police' function,[137] and the Commission, lacking information and

---

[133] See n. 130 above, para. 35; see also Case C–206/96, *Commission* v. *Luxembourg* [1998] ECR I–3401.

[134] Ibid., para. 47.                    [135] Paras. 40–1.                    [136] Ibid., para. 45.

[137] There are few such Community administrative powers or bodies, notably excepting enforcement of Arts. 81 and 82, and Reg. (EEC) No. 4064/89 on Merger Control, concerning cartels, abuse of dominant position, mergers; also, Art. 87, concerning subsidies.

resources,[138] relies heavily upon informal approaches.[139] Despite significant Member States' default in compliance,[140] the Commission's role is necessarily a reactive one, generally following upon complaint by Member States or interested groups. The process is slow and has led to criticisms that action to protect the environment is thereby prejudiced and risks lagging behind the damage which it seeks to prevent.[141] The introduction into the Treaty of the ECJ power to impose a lump sum or penalty payment, should a judgment be referred back for non-compliance, will in the future assist in assuaging these difficulties, although during 1999 no such fines were applied.[142]

Realistically, the capacity for Commission enforcement is unlikely to see any significant increase. Seeking other solutions, the Commission is currently looking to secure more effective national enforcement.[143] The Commission's approach recognizes that implementation demands coordination through a regulatory chain, which it defines as:

the whole process through which legislation is designed, conceived, drafted, adopted, implemented and enforced until its efficiency is assessed. It is a methodological tool allowing for a 'holistic' approach to address instruments of environmental policy.[144]

The Commission has emphasized the importance of maximizing degrees of consultation, coordinated through the Member States, an approach which encourages wide involvement of interests at an early stage in the process.[145] Proposed solutions cover a broad raft of possible measures, including increased transparency, a review of environmental legislation, the preparation of clearer legislative texts, voluntary environmental agreements, economic instruments, and a widening of access to justice in domestic courts.[146]

The problems of implementation and enforcement raise fundamental issues of law-making. More inclusive structures, from an early stage, could lead to greater clarity and transparency, and encourage higher levels of cooperation by both Member States and wider interests. Adequate arrangements for implementation are essential to its efficacy. The commitment to a Directive-led delivery of harmonized measures inevitably carries a structural risk to the achievement of satisfactory implementation. There is also the

---

[138] See L. Krämer, 'Public Interest Litigation and Environmental Matters before the European Courts' (1996) 8 *Journal of Environmental Law*, 1. This is partly mitigated by the establishment of the European Environment Agency (EEA) under Reg. (EEC) No. 1210/90, with the prime objective to provide information on the environment at a Community level to the Commission and Member States; a specific role confirmed in recital 31, Art. 20 for the purposes of the draft framework directive.

[139] See R. Macrory, 'The Enforcement of Community Environmental Laws: Some Critical Issues' (1992) 1 *Common Market Law Review*, 347.

[140] See e.g. (1997) ENDS Report 274, 46–7.

[141] See e.g. G. Stuart, 'Combating Non-compliance with European Community Environmental Directives' (1994) 6 *Environmental Law & Management*, 160.

[142] Now under Art. 228(2) EC; see Commission Memorandum of 5 June 1996, imposition of penalties under the former Art. 171 EC (now Art. 228 EC) on Member States who fail to comply with European Court judgments, [1996] OJ C242/21.

[143] See in particular the Communication on Implementation, n. 24 above.

[144] Ibid., para. 9, Annex I.        [145] Ibid., paras. 51–2.

[146] See also Commission Report to the European Council, 'Better Law-making' COM(97)626 final.

essentially political restriction of defective consideration being given from the first to the implications, especially resource-led, of compliance. In this respect the costs of compliance with water measures can be significant;[147] for instance, estimated compliance costs at stake in a UK case applying Directive 91/271/EEC concerning Urban Waste Water Treatment referred to below, and involving two relatively small city-regions, were approximately £90m.[148]

## G. ACCESS TO JUSTICE IN DOMESTIC COURTS

### i. Opportunities for Individual Enforcement

The existence of a coherent set of rights offers the best opportunity of an effective Community-wide approach to compliance. This has recently been recognized by the English Court of Appeal, which approached the question whether Directive 79/923/EEC on the Quality required of Shellfish Waters was intended to confer rights on individuals 'by acknowledging the significant part played in securing compliance with, and enforcement of, European directives by the granting of rights under directives to individuals'.[149] However, opportunities for individual enforcement of environmental laws, such as those concerned with water quality, are limited by conceptual and procedural difficulties, partly consequent upon the use of the mechanism of the Directive for legislative choice, as well as normative Treaty arrangements which carry doubtful justiciability. Whilst the more traditional economic-related freedoms are appropriate for expression in terms of rights, environmental interests offer a more tenuous basis for rights-assertion by individuals or groups. The administrative bias of environmental directives, classically of a programmatic nature,[150] with obligations on Member States to promote protection measures, operate authorization schemes, and monitor performance, suggests restricted room for individual claims to arise.[151] It is the nature of such Directives that they are likely to be found to be insufficiently clear, precise, and unconditional.[152] This factor is compounded by problems in fixing upon objective standards, further put at risk of foundering at the limits of science.[153]

Nevertheless, the development of the doctrine of direct effect by the Court has considerably enhanced opportunities for private enforcement of Directives within domestic courts. Thus a right may be maintained against the

---

[147] See n. 50 above.

[148] *R* v. *Secretary of State for the Environment, ex p Kingston-upon-Hull City Council and Bristol City Council* (1996) 8 *Journal of Environmental Law*, 336.

[149] See case report '*Bowden* v. *South West Water Services Ltd and others*' (1998) 32 *Common Market Law Review*, 438, 443 (judgment of Court given by Beldam LJ).

[150] Case 380/87, *Enichem Base* v. *Commune di Cinisello Balsamo* [1989] ECR 2491.

[151] L. Kramer, 'The Implementation of Community Environmental Directives within Member States: Some Implications of the Direct Effect Doctrine' (1991) 3 *Journal of Environmental Law*, 39, 42.

[152] Cf. Case C–236/92, *Comitato di Coordinamento per la Difesa della Cava* v. *Regione Lombardia* [1994] ECR I–0483.

[153] M. Shere, 'The Myth of Meaningful Environmental Risk Assessment' (1995) 19 *Harvard Environmental Law Review*, 409.

state, and by extension bodies which can be categorized as emanations of the state, on the basis of the state's default in effective transposition.[154] This extends to a right to an adequate remedy for the breach.[155] However, where the pollution is neither the state nor an emanation of the state, it cannot directly incur an obligation under a directive without more, as the Court has been unwilling to accord the remedy where failure to transpose leads to such a horizontal claim.[156] Moreover, direct effect has developed in areas where the existence of individual rights can most readily be identified, such as in the traditional areas of free movement, financial or employment rights.[157] The doctrine may therefore be unlikely to prove of significant benefit in the search for a clearer rationale underlying environmental rights.[158]

In the context of damage to the quality of waters, though Directives tend to be aimed at putting management programmes into place, direct effect can in principle be supported where there is an intention to create rights and obligations, for 'individuals concerned must in appropriate circumstances be able to rely upon them before the national courts'.[159] AG van Gerven has concluded that as Directive 80/68/EEC on the Protection of Groundwater against Pollution caused by Certain Dangerous Substances was intended to create individual rights and duties,

the full implementation of the Directive must be ensured by sufficiently clear and precise provisions transposing it, so that those persons are made aware of their rights and duties under Community law and the extent to which they may rely upon Community law before the national courts.[160]

Moreover, the Court has ruled that a directive's creation of a specific legal framework should mean that 'persons concerned can ascertain the full extent

---

[154] Case 41/74, *van Duyn* v. *Home Office (No. 2)* [1974] ECR 1337; Case 152/84, *Marshall* v. *Southampton and South-West Area Health Authority (No. 1)* [1988] QB 40; Case C–188/89, *Foster* v. *British Gas plc* [1990] ECR I–3313.

[155] *Marshall* v. *Southampton and South-West Area Health Authority (No. 2)* (1993) 4 *All England Law Reports*, 586.

[156] Case 14/86, *Pretore di Salo* v. *Persons Unknown* [1987] ECR 2545; Case C91/92, *Faccini Dori* v. *Recreb Srl* [1994] ECR I–3325.

[157] Case 148/78, *Pubblico Ministero* v. *Ratti* [1979] ECR 1629; Case 152/84, *Becker* v. *Finanzamt Munster-Innenstadt* [1982] ECR 0053.

[158] There is some, albeit underexplored, potential in the doctrine of indirect effect: see Case 14/83, *von Colson* v. *Land Nordrhein-Westfalen* [1994] ECR 1891: this requires national bodies, including the courts, to interpret domestic law as far as possible so as to accord with the terms of a relevant directive; see Case C–106/89, *Marleasing SA* v. *La Comercial Internacional de Alimentacion SA* [1990] ECR I- 4156; cf. Case C–168/95, *Luciano Arcaro* [1996] ECR I–4705.

[159] Case C–58/89, *Commission* v. *Germany*, n. 96 above, relating to Dir. 75/440/EEC concerning the Quality Required of Surface Water intended for the Abstraction of Drinking Water, n. 3 above. AG Jacobs, para. 33, however appeared to limit availability to the class of persons 'who are engaged in any activity leading directly or indirectly to the discharge of noxious substances into the environment'. See also Case C–237/90, *Commission* v. *Germany* [1992] ECR I–5973, concerning Dir. 80/778/EEC relating to the Quality of Water Intended for Human Consumption, n. 3 above; cf. *R* v. *Secretary of State for the Environment, ex parte Friends of the Earth*, n. 128 above, where the English Court of Appeal was prepared to accept conferment of individual rights upon a public interest group.

[160] Case C–360/87, *Commission* v. *Italy*, n. 117 above, para. 2: although the AG made no reference to health, he advised a purposive interpretation in the context of the Directive being aimed to restrict the discharge of polluting substances.

of their rights, and where appropriate, rely on them before the national courts'.[161]

It is *a fortiori* arguable that individuals can seek enforcement of those water Directives which can be interpreted as intended to protect human health. The Court has referred to the second recital of Directive 75/440 as 'intended to protect public health' and ruled that its surveillance arrangements imply that 'whenever non-compliance with the measures required . . . might endanger the health of persons, those concerned should be able to rely on mandatory rules in order to enforce their rights'.[162] AG van Gerven has opined that such provisions may be

important for third parties (for instance environmental groups or neighbourhood residents) seeking to have the . . . Directive enforced as against the authorities or other individuals.[163]

A similar interpretation may succeed given the express health-related purposes of Directive 76/160/EEC concerning the quality of bathing waters.[164]

Otherwise, it is in the area of procedures that enforcement processes are most likely to succeed, for these seem the most amenable to public law remedies, without the considerable hurdle of establishing damage.[165] However, administrative discretion is typically vested in the governments of Member States, especially in respect of matters of designation or definitional interpretation, and challenges may fail in this light, whether available expressly or recognized as inherent. Still, the ECJ has proved resistant to the idea of absolute discretion.[166] It is notable that the English High Court has followed such an approach in interpreting the obligations arising under Directive 91/271/EEC concerning Urban Waste Water Treatment. There, Harrison J ruled that:

[an] area of water either is or is not an estuary regardless of what it will cost to treat waste water discharged into it . . . [and moreover that] . . . there must be a genuine and rational assessment in each case of what actually constitutes the estuary having regard to all the relevant circumstances relating to the characteristics of the area of water in question and having regard to the purpose of the Directive.[167]

[161] Case C–131/88, *Commission* v. *Germany*, n. 117 above, para. 6: also concerning Dir. 80/68/EEC on the Protection of Groundwater Against Pollution Caused by Certain Dangerous Substances, n. 6 above; see also AG van Gerven's opinion, para. 3.

[162] Case C–58/89, *Commission* v. *Germany*, n. 96 above, para. 14.

[163] See n. 161 above, para. 7.

[164] See the first recital of Dir. 76/160/EEC concerning the Quality of Bathing Waters, n. 4 above, and of Dir. 80/778/EEC relating to the Quality of Water intended for Human Consumption, n. 3 above.

[165] e.g. Dir. 90/313/EEC on Freedom of Access to Environmental Information, Dir. 85/337/EEC on the Assessment of the Effects of Certain Public and Private Projects on the Environment (as amended by Dir. 97/11/EC).

[166] e.g. it adopted such an approach in relation to Dir. 85/337/EEC, n. 165 above, to the effect that there is no discretion to exempt whole classes, without review on the merits: Case C–72/95, *Aannemersbedrijf P K Kraaijevelt BV* v. *Geputeerde Staten van Zuid-Holland* (1997) 9 *Journal of Environmental Law*, 119.

[167] See n. 8 and n. 148 above.

## ii. The Assertion of State Liability

In the light of the restrictions inherent in the doctrine of direct effect, a more recent possibility of securing a remedy concerns state liability for damages in the event of a failure fully to implement a directive in such circumstances, under a principle originally expounded in the *Francovich* case,[168] on the basis of a responsibility to compensate those who suffer as a consequence of that default.[169] The broad application, however, of *Francovich* principles to environmental actions is problematic. For instance, under English law prevalent approaches to entitlement to damages for breach of statutory duty are restrictive, especially as to the question of whether a statute's purpose is to protect a class, as opposed to the general interest.[170] As well as inevitable difficulties caused by a 'potential multiplicity of pollution victims',[171] the nature of the damages award may often be inappropriate, given limitations such as the requirements for harm.[172] A lack of established causation is 'likely to prove insuperable in all but a few cases', [173] unless a reform can be countenanced along the lines of a lower requirement for establishing harm such as a mere association between harm and injury, under the dictates of the precautionary principle.[174]

An instructive illustration of the potential for extension of the *Francovich* doctrine to cases of environmental breach can be seen in decisions of the English High Court[175] and Court of Appeal.[176] *Bowden*, the plaintiff, was a fisherman of mussels from the sea bed, and claimed damages under the *Francovich* principle, having suffered losses as a consequence of actions by the UK authorities in addressing water pollution. Certain waters had been designated under Directive 79/923/EEC on the Quality required of Shellfish Waters[177] as needing protection and improvement in order to support shellfish

---

[168] Case C–6 & 9/90, *Francovich v. Italy* [1991] ECR I–5357.

[169] See further C–5/94, *R v. Ministry of Agriculture, Fisheries and Food, ex parte Hedley Lomas (Ireland) Ltd* [1996] ECR I–2553, para. 24; as also applied to other breaches: C–46/93, *Brasserie du Pecheur SA v. Germany,* Case C–49/93, *R v. Secretary of State for Transport, ex parte Factortame (No. 4)* [1996] ECR I–1029, paras. 55–6; see also C–392/93, *R v. HM Treasury, ex parte British Telecom* [1996] ECR I–1631; Case C–178/94, *Dillenkofer v. Germany* [1996] ECR I–4845, para. 23.

[170] e.g. *X (Minors) v. Bedfordshire CC* [1995] 2 AC 528; see P. Craig, 'Once More unto the Breach: the Community, the State and Damages Liability' (1997) 113 *Law Quarterly Review*, 67.

[171] C. Miller, 'Environmental Rights: European Fact or English Fiction?' (1995) 22 *Journal of Law and Society*, 374, 386; who further suggests that limits on environmental knowledge as a factor may in any event restrict opportunities to those with pre-existing susceptibilities, at 385.

[172] See case (1993) QBD 'Reay and Hope v. British Nuclear Fuels Ltd', and (1994) '*Merlin v. British Nuclear Fuels Ltd.*

[173] C. Hilson, 'Community Rights in Environmental Law: Rhetoric or Reality?' in J. Holder (ed.), *The Impact of EC Environmental Law in the UK* (New York: Wiley, 1997), 68.

[174] See J. Holder, 'The Sellafield litigation and Questions of Causation in Environmental Law' (1994) *Current Legal Problems*, 287, 305; cf. Case C–379/92, *Peralta* [1994] ECR I–3453.

[175] Case report '*Bowden v. South West Water*' (1998) 8 *Environmental Law Review*, 445.

[176] See n. 149 above.

[177] See n. 5 above: the Directive promotes measures to protect waters, including shellfish waters, against pollution for 'the protection of and improvement of the environment' and 'to safeguard certain shellfish populations from various harmful consequences resulting from the discharge of pollutant substances into the sea'.

life and growth and to contribute to the high quality of shellfish directly edible by man.[178] As well as an assertion of breach of statutory duty under domestic principles, the plaintiff claimed under two further directives, Directive 76/160/EEC concerning the Quality of Bathing Waters,[179] and Directive 91/271/EEC concerning Urban Waste Water Treatment.[180]

The first instance judge struck out these claims, including those based on direct rights under the Directives. He ruled that there was nothing in either of the latter two Directives

which could possibly be said to 'entail the grant of rights' to shell-fishermen, or which would enable the content of any such rights to be identified. They are concerned with different subject matter. Of course, improvements in water quality for bathers, and in treatment standards of waste water, may assist other interest groups, but that is not enough to give them a right of action.[181]

The Court of Appeal agreed, ruling that the test must be

whether the provision was adopted in order to protect the interests of the person who claims to be entitled to a right under the directive, and whether the result prescribed entailed the grant of rights to individuals. The content of the rights must be identifiable on the basis of the provisions of the directive and a causal link must exist between the breach of the state's obligations and the loss and damage suffered. [Accordingly, the plaintiff] was not directly affected either as a bather nor were his interests directly affected by waste water; the mere fact that an improvement in water quality assisted other interest groups was not enough to confer a right of action.[182]

However, whilst the appeal court expressly rejected 'so broad a generalization' as a submission that a failure to implement or comply with directives having the objective of environmental protection was a breach of a right given to individuals whose interests might be affected by any directive,[183] the appeal was allowed in respect of Directive 79/923/EEC on the Quality required of Shellfish Waters. The High Court had rejected the challenge on the basis that, even if it were established that there had been a failure to designate the relevant area, that would be a breach of an obligation owed to the public in general and there was nothing to tie such a breach to specific rights of individuals or which would enable the content of such rights to be ascertained. In contrast, the appellate ruling means that it is at least arguable that the Directive was intended to confer a right upon mollusc fishermen such as the plaintiff.[184] The Court emphasized that:

[178] Member States were required to initiate programmes to reduce pollution so that within 6 years the designated areas complied with values set out in the Directive. Subsequently, Dir. 91/492/EEC laid down health conditions for the production and marketing of shellfish intended for immediate human consumption. The implementation of the Directive under the Food Safety (Live Bivalve Molluscs and other Shellfish) Regulations 1992 was the immediate cause of the plaintiff being unable to collect molluscs for direct human consumption: production in this case had been categorized as for marketing only after re-laying over a long period.

[179] See n. 4 above.    [180] See n. 8 above.    [181] See n. 175 above, 461.
[182] See n. 149 above, 442.    [183] Ibid. 443.
[184] The case was heard only on interlocutory motion to strike out, and it should be noted that as a result of the successful appeal the plaintiff is merely able to argue the point at a full hearing.

the recitals make clear that the purpose of the Directive is to safeguard shellfish populations from various harmful consequences. The Directive had in mind that the failure to protect the shellfish populations could result in unequal conditions of competition[185] which suggests that those who collect and market shellfish may have been intended to have a right of reparation if there was a failure to implement the Directive's requirements.[186]

There may be a confusion here with economic rights, but the importance of the judgment is that such a claim is arguable in principle.

### iii. Public Law Challenges

In contrast, a case heard by the ECJ and reported in 1999 offers a good illustration of the surer foundations of classical public law grounds of challenge, albeit in proceedings which were ultimately unsuccessful. The applicant in *Standley* challenged the legality of the UK's transposing measures under the requirements of Directive 91/676/EEC concerning the Protection of Waters against Pollution caused by Nitrates from Agricultural Sources.[187] Effectively it was a challenge by agricultural interests to the legality of the Directive itself in the light of other principles of EC law and arising under the Treaty. This case proceeded by way of reference from the English High Court and was the first case heard by the ECJ arising out of this Directive. The Court held that the Directive requires the identification of surface freshwaters as 'waters affected by pollution', and therefore the designation as 'vulnerable zones' of all known areas of land which drain into those waters and contribute to their pollution, where those waters contain a concentration of nitrates in excess of 50 mg/l and the Member State concerned considers that agricultural sources make 'significant contribution' to that overall concentration of nitrates.[188]

In light of this interpretation, numerous arguments of the applicant had been referred to the Court, on the question at what degree of agricultural source contribution the test may be satisfied. The issue was therefore whether liability might follow, though agricultural sources might of themselves not exceed the limit, it infringes numerous principles: proportionality, the polluter pays, and the fundamental right to property of the farmers concerned, thereby rendering the Directive invalid.[189] The Court ruled against these arguments. As to the principle of proportionality, the Court cited the variety of obligations placed upon Member States to take account of actual conditions in the regions comprising identified vulnerable zones, in drawing up and reviewing action

---

[185]  See n. 5 above: para. 4 of preamble.

[186]  See n. 120 above, 445: see also Case 131/88, Case C–131/88, *Commission* v. *Germany* 1991 ECR I–825, 867, concerning Dir. 80/68/EEC on the Protection of Groundwater against Pollution caused by Certain Dangerous Substances, n. 6 above, where the ECJ stated that the purpose of the Directive was to create rights and obligations for individuals.

[187]  See n. 9 above: Case C–293/97, *R* v. *Secretary of State for the Environment, ex parte Standley*, n. 110 above.

[188]  Ibid., para. 40; see Arts. 2(j), 3(1)(2); a figure in excess of 50 mg/litre is set out in Annex I.

[189]  Ibid., para. 41.

programmes, including responding to changes of circumstance in relation to pollution from both agricultural and other sources.[190] The Court concluded that

the Directive contains flexible provisions enabling the Member States to observe the principle of proportionality in the application of the measures which they adopt. It is for the national courts to ensure that that principle is observed.[191]

Concerning alleged infringement of the polluter-pays principle, the Court held that the Directive does not mean that farmers must take on burdens for the elimination of pollution to which they have not contributed. By reference to the principle of proportionality, Member States must take account of other sources when implementing the Directive and, having regard to the circumstances, must not impose unnecessary costs.[192] The Court further relied upon the requirements of proportionality in the case of a related argument concerning the related Treaty principle under which environmental damage should as a priority be rectified at source. As to whether farmers were required to bear the entire burden of preventing or reducing nitrate pollution of surface freshwaters rather than such nitrate pollution from atmospheric deposition originating principally from industry and transport being prevented or reduced at source, the Court ruled that:

the arguments of the applicants in the main proceedings are indissociable from their arguments relating to breach of the principle of proportionality.[193]

A final submission, that the right to property had been infringed by imposing on farmers the entire responsibility for, and economic burden of, reducing nitrate concentrations, was likewise rejected. The Court has held that although the right to property forms part of the general principles of Community law, it is not an absolute right and must be viewed in relation to its social function.[194] Thus

its exercise may be restricted, provided that those restrictions in fact correspond to objectives of general interest pursued by the Community and do not constitute a disproportionate and intolerable interference, impairing the very substance of the rights guaranteed.[195]

---

[190] Ibid., paras. 46–50: these include Art. 5(3) whereby action programmes for vulnerable zones must take account of available scientific and technical data with reference to the respective nitrogen quantities originating from agricultural and other sources; under Annex III, para. 1(3), mandatory measures under those programmes must take into account the characteristics of each vulnerable zone; under Art. 5(6)–(7), suitable monitoring programmes to assess the effectiveness of the action programmes must be drawn up and implemented, with review and any necessary revisions in the action programmes at least every 4 years; under Art. 4(1)(a) and Annex II, para. A, the codes of good agricultural practice must take account of conditions in the different regions of the Community.

[191] Ibid., para. 50.      [192] Ibid., paras. 51, 52.      [193] Ibid., para. 53.

[194] See further Case 44/79 *Hauer* v. *Land Rheinland-Pfalz* [1979] ECR 3727, para. 23; Case 265/87, *Schräder* v. *Hauptzollamt Gronau* [1989] ECR 2237, para. 15, and Case C–280/93, *Germany* v. *Council* [1994] ECR I–4973, para. 78.

[195] See n. 110 above, para. 54.

Accordingly, the Court held that, subject to the application of the principle of proportionality, any restriction upon the right to property consequent upon mandatory measures contained within action programmes

reflects requirements relating to the protection of public health, and thus pursues an objective of general interest without the substance of the right to property being impaired.[196]

### iv. Applying Purposive Interpretations

During 1999 the ECJ has also given judgment in two further cases which arose out of (once again for the first time) references in the context of Directive 76/464/EEC on Pollution caused by Certain Dangerous Substances Discharged into the Aquatic Environment of the Community.[197] Both references were from the Dutch courts, the first case concerned a point of interpretation of the Directive,[198] specifically as to whether the term 'discharge' extended to precipitation, resulting from a wood preservation process, of contaminated steam on to surface water, and whether the distance from which the steam precipitation occurs is a relevant issue.[199] The responsible authority had rejected a complaint by the applicant, *van Rooij*, against its refusal to adopt measures for the protection of the surface water. The Court found that semantic differences existed across various language translations of the provision, and unsurprisingly ruled that it was necessary to test the interpretation against the purpose of the Directive.[200] It duly held that the Directive applied to discharges of all dangerous substances set out in the annex to the Directive, in whatever state. The Court did not accept that substances set out in the annex were dangerous for the aquatic environment only in the liquid state. Such an interpretation would

run counter to the objective of the directive, which, as may be seen from the first recital in its preamble, is to protect the aquatic environment of the Community from pollution, particularly that caused by certain persistent, toxic and bioaccumulable substances.[201]

A related question, the distance between the surface water and the place of emission of the contaminated steam, resolved itself into a matter of causation, being

relevant only for the purpose of determining whether the pollution of the waters cannot be regarded as foreseeable according to general experience, so that the pollution is not attributable to the person causing the steam.[202]

Moreover, pragmatically, the notion of discharge was

---

[196] Ibid., paras. 55–8.
[197] See n. 2 above; the references were made under what is now Art. 234 EC.
[198] Case C–231/97, *A.M.L. van Rooij and Dagelijks Bestuur van het Waterschap de Dommel*, [1999] ECR I–6355.
[199] See n. 2 above, Art. 1(2)(d).     [200] See n. 198 above, para. 26.
[201] Ibid., paras. 27–9.     [202] Ibid., para. 32.

to be interpreted as covering the emission of contaminated steam which is first pre-cipitated on to land and roofs and then reaches the surface water via a storm water drain. It was immaterial in this respect whether the drain in question belongs to the establishment concerned or to a third party.[203]

An interesting ancillary question arose as to whether pollution by steam first occurring in the atmosphere and later reaching surface water was rather a matter for air pollution controls.[204] Whilst the 1976 Directive under discussion cannot comfortably be put forward as a masterstroke of integration, the Court was clearly unwilling to accept an unnecessary further atomizing of the legislative framework. Accordingly it found that such a possibility was

not capable of precluding a phenomenon such as that at issue in the main proceedings from being classified as a discharge within the meaning of Directive 76/464/EEC, where there is pollution of surface water and that pollution is caused, directly or indir-ectly, by an act attributable to a person.[205]

The second judgment of the Court also followed a reference from the Dutch courts,[206] and once again concerned the term 'discharge' under the 1976 Directive.[207] The Court held that it must refer to *any* act attributable to a per-son by which one of the listed dangerous substances is directly or indirectly introduced into the waters to which the Directive applies.[208] The facts of the case concerned the effective prohibition of the applicant, by refusal of *ex post facto* authorization, from using wooden posts treated with creosote for shoring up watercourse banks.[209] Authorization had been denied in accord-ance with a policy that the emission of PAHs should be combated above all at source,[210] and therefore on the ground that, since it was impossible to avoid PAHs escaping and causing pollution, alternative solutions less harmful to the environment were preferable.

Under the system established by the 1976 Directive to ensure that Community limit values are complied with and in accordance with laid down national emission standards,[211] any discharge is made subject to authorization. According to the Court, the basis of this is that 'the discharge can be attributed to a person from significant sources including multiple and diffuse sources'.[212] The Directive was accordingly concerned with the discharge by man, directly or indirectly, of substances or energy into the aquatic environment, the results of

---

[203] See n. 198 above, para. 36.

[204] See Dir. 84/360/EEC on the Combating of Air Pollution from Industrial Plants, [1984] OJ L188/20.

[205] See n. 198 above, para. 31.

[206] Case C–232/97, *L. Nederhoff v. Dijkgraaf en Hoogheemraden van het Hoogheemraadschap Rijnland* [1999] ECR I–6385.

[207] See n. 2 above, for the purposes of Art. 1(2)(d).          [208] See n. 206 above, para. 37.

[209] Creosote contains polycyclic aromatic hydrocarbons ('PAHs') and belongs to the families and groups of substances mentioned in List I of the Annex to Dir. 76/464/EEC, n. 2 above. Since no limit value had yet been fixed under Art. 6, it accordingly fell within the List II rules.

[210] See n. 206 above, para. 19: it appeared that only if such 'source approach' produced unsatis-factory results would tests be carried out in pursuance of water-quality standards laid down in the relevant water management plan.

[211] See n. 2 above, Arts. 3, 7(2).          [212] See n. 206 above, para. 38.

which cause hazards to human health, harm to living resources and to aquatic ecosystems, damage to amenities, or interference with other legitimate uses of water. Thus 'discharge' must include the placing by a person in surface water of wooden posts treated with creosote. This contrasted with the obligation upon Member States to avoid or eliminate, by specific programmes, pollution from significant sources, including multiple and diffuse sources, contained in the daughter Directive 86/280/EEC concerning Discharges of Certain Dangerous Substances included in List I to the Annex to Directive 76/464.[213] The Court ruled that this could not refer to

> sources of discharges subject to Community limit value rules or national emission standards, that is, cases where the pollution is caused by an act attributable to a person, which are subject to the system established by Directive 76/464/EEC.[214]

In contrast, the latter Directive concerns pollution which 'precisely because of its diffuse nature, cannot be attributed to a person and therefore cannot be the subject of prior authorization'.[215] The latter must be interpreted as excluding the escape of creosote from wooden posts placed in surface water, where the pollution caused by that substance is attributable to a person.

Finally, the Court held that the effect of making the grant of authorization impossible was an acceptable consequence of Directive 76/464 which permits making authorizations for discharge subject to additional requirements not provided for in the Directive in order to protect the aquatic environment against pollution caused by dangerous substances. Accordingly, the imposition of an obligation to investigate or choose alternative solutions which have less impact on the environment constitutes such a requirement. For all that, the Court's interpretation in these latter cases was a purposive one, by reference to the objectives underlying these Directives, the references once again illustrate the importance to governments of Member States of paying close attention to the wording of implementation measures.

### v. *Extending Access to Justice in National Courts*

Increased access to justice is one response to the problems of enforcement discussed in Section F. Indeed, the Commission has referred to interests

> in which there is often not a proprietary stake . . . it has to envisage methods of ensuring its effectiveness other than methods which are adequate in other fields of law.[216]

This would require broader acceptance of standing to protect environmental interests at a Community level. In a case referred to above, AG Jacobs went so far as to state

---

[213] See n. 2 above, Art. 5(1).     [214] See n. 206 above, para. 30.     [215] Ibid., para. 40.
[216] See Communication, n. 24 above, para. 7; see also Council Resolution of 7 Oct. 1997 on the Drafting, Implementation and Enforcement of Community Environmental Law, [1997] OJ C321/1; Council Decision 97/872/EC on a Community Action Programme Promoting Non-Governmental Organizations Primarily Active in the Field of Environmental Protection, [1997] OJ L354/25, making funds available during 1998–2001; and Resolution of Parliament of 14 May 1997 on a Communication from the Commission on Implementing Community Environmental Law, [1997] OJ C167/92.

that the public at large, as well as ecologists and environmental pressure groups, have a general interest in water quality, and indeed in the respect for Community law. It does not however automatically follow that enforceable rights must be made available to them in the national courts.[217]

It seems that a general Community provision would be required, for it is perhaps too radical a step to leave to the judicial process within the ECJ.[218] Such a change would also demand a changed approach to the drafting of environmental Directives, as again referred to in Section F. The impetus toward a wider recognition of rights might come from a citizen action approach,[219] although progress has been made in some Member States, notably in the Netherlands, where the Supreme Court has accepted that an environmental organization has a right to represent diffuse ecological interests in acting against third parties.[220] Yet, even where standing requirements have been relaxed, as for the 'sufficient interest' test under English law,[221] costs remain a severely delimiting factor for individuals and (most) public interest groups. Solutions at a Community level would require that suitable means of allocating public funding support to actions 'in the public interest' be found.[222]

## H. CONCLUSION

The importance of the status of our water, in the light of our reliance upon it to meet multiple human needs, has been a major factor in Community water legislation to date. This, however, is with the exception of resource aspects, which have received little attention. The availability of supply, and a structured awareness of its importance in economic terms, is set to become a main theme of Community water law.

The quality and quantity of water provision have accordingly assumed central significance in Community environmental policy- and law-making. Water issues have been accepted as major factors in securing sustainable development, and are a crucial part of demands at Community level to integrate environmental protection priorities into other policy areas.

An emergent Water Framework Directive will place significant obligations upon Member States. The same can be said for remaining key Directives, such as Directive 91/271/EEC concerning Urban Waste Water Treatment, Directive

---

[217] Case C–58/89, *Commission* v. *Germany*, n. 96 above, para. 34.

[218] Indeed, the Court has in the past explicitly contrasted rights with mere 'general interests': Case C–158/80, *Rewe Handelsgesellschaft Nord mbH* v. *Hauptzollamt Kiel* [1981] ECR 1805.

[219] As in the USA: see *Hallstrom* v. *Tillamook Community* 493 US 20, 23, n.1 (1989); cf. L. Morelli, 'Citizen Suit Enforcement of Environmental Laws in the United States: an Overview' (1997) 5 *Environmental Liability*, 19; M. Greve, 'The Private Enforcement of Environmental Law' (1990) 65 *Tulane Law Review*, 339.

[220] See G. Betlem, 'Standing for Eco-systems—Going Dutch' (1995) 54 *Cambridge Law Journal*, 153, 167–70.

[221] See e.g. *R* v. *H.M. Inspectorate of Pollution, ex p Greenpeace (No. 2)* (1994) 4 *All England Law Reports*, 328.

[222] See Law Commission of England and Wales, *Administrative Law: Judicial Review and Statutory Appeals*, No. 226, 1994, paras. 5.20–2.

91/676/EEC concerning the Protection of Waters against Pollution caused by Nitrates from Agricultural Sources, and Directive 96/61/EC on Integrated Pollution Prevention and Control (IPPC Directive). The new strategic arrangements will require that harmonized approaches can be assured.

The Community, however, continues to face significant problems in ensuring that such improvements are implemented. The general issues discussed above in relation to the role of the Commission, and of private and interest group litigants, will assume greater importance once the new scheme is in place. The political will by and large now exists, although tensions will inevitably persist. For instance, referring once again to Directive 91/676/EEC, the Commission has pointed to the fact that 'the main polluters—farmers—are sensitive to anything which affects the economic viability of their activity',[223] and recent litigation is perhaps an indication of this.[224] On the other hand, the measure itself has been justifiably described as 'as significant advance in Community water policy in that it targets a non-individual and indirect source of pollution'.[225]

Ultimately, the environmental arena is beset with issues of cost, whether arising from past or present socio-economic practices. Political solutions need to take account of the sensitive dilemmas that these issues inevitably generate. Community-led political decisions will furthermore be required in order to determine how far legal solutions along the lines of those discussed above can be utilized in the delivery of legislation which protects water as a fundamental resource.

---

[223] See the Commission's annual survey for 1999, published on the Internet at: http://www.europa.eu.int/scadplu/leg/en.

[224] Case C–293/97, *R* v. *Secretary of State for the Environment, ex parte Standley*, n. 110 above.

[225] R. Macrory, 'European Community Law' (1993) 20 *Ecology Law Quarterly* 1, 119.

# VI. Horizontal Instruments

JONATHAN VERSCHUUREN and JOS JANSSEN*

## A. LEGISLATION IN PROGRESS

### i. Environmental Impact Assessment

During 1999 negotiations between the European Parliament (EP) and the Council on the proposed Directive on Strategic Environmental Assessment, or the Directive on the Assessment of the Effects of Certain Plans and Programmes on the Environment, as it is officially called,[1] resulted in a Common Position adopted by the Council on 30 March 2000.[2] According to the draft, plans and programmes and their modifications subject to preparation and/or adoption by an authority at national, regional, or local level—or those to be prepared by an authority for adoption through a legislative procedure by parliament or government, as required by legislative, regulatory, or administrative provisions—are subject to an environmental assessment (EA) in case they are likely to have significant impact on the environment. Member States can determine whether the potential for such impact exists, on a case-by-case examination or by specifying certain types of plans or programmes which are *prima facie* subject to an EA, or they may adopt a combination of both approaches. Annex II to the draft identifies the criteria to be used in determining the likely significance of the effects, including examination of the characteristics of the plans and programmes, of the environmental effects, and of the relevant area which could be affected. The EA will result in an Environmental Report, which shall be taken into account during the preparation of the plan or programme and before its adoption or submission to the legislative procedure.[3]

### ii. Eco-management and Audit Scheme

On 23 June 1999 an amended proposal for the new Regulation allowing Voluntary Participation by Organizations in a Community Eco-Management and Audit Scheme (EMAS) was published, introducing most of the amendments

---

* Jonathan Verschuuren, Professor, Centre for Legislative Studies, Tilburg University, the Netherlands (Environmental Impact Assessment and Eco-management and Audit Scheme); Jos Janssen, Researcher and Lecturer, University of Nijmegen, the Netherlands (Access to Information).

[1] COM(1999)73 final, [1999] OJ C83/13.

[2] Common Position (EC) No. 25/2000, [2000] OJ C137/11.

[3] See for further details on the proposed Directive on the Assessment of the Effects of Certain Plans and Programmes on the Environment: J. Holder, J. Verschuuren, and J. Janssen, 'Horizontal Instruments', ch. VI of the Current Survey Section (1998) 1 *Yearbook of European Environmental Law*, 417–20.

of the EP into the proposal.[4] The amendments further clarify that EMAS is open to all organizations having environmental impacts. One of the main goals of the new Regulation is to attract more companies to participate in EMAS, and link EMAS even more closely to the international ISO 14001 norm. The introduction of a European version of this international standard known as EN-ISO 14001 has made the latter easier. However, some significant differences between ISO 14001 and EMAS remained.[5] These differences have now been dealt with by deciding that EN-ISO 14001 will be the environmental management system element of EMAS, while some additional elements from the previous EMAS-Regulation were taken to form the audit element of EMAS: compliance with environmental legislation, the improvement of environmental performance, external communication, and employee involvement. In addition, it has explicitly been laid down in the draft that the administrative burden for small and medium-sized enterprises (SMEs) to join EMAS—this being an important objective of the new Regulation—shall not be excessive. At the same time, however, the Commission expressed that SMEs must adhere to identical requirements as all other businesses. On 28 February 2000 the Council unanimously agreed upon the Common Position.[6]

### iii. Access to Information

In respect of the right of access to information in the Member States, the Commission has worked on a proposal to amend Directive 90/313/EEC on the Freedom of Access to Information on the Environment (Environmental Information Directive),[7] the outcome of which is not yet known. Furthermore, the 1998 Aarhus Convention on Access to Information, Public Participation in Decision-Making and Access to Justice in Environmental Matters,[8] which includes several provisions on access to environmental information which also bind the Community institutions has not yet been ratified.[9] A proposal for the necessary 'concluding act' to the Council and the EP is to be made once any necessary amendments have been made to Community legislation in order for it to be in conformity with the Aarhus Convention.[10]

The Commission failed to issue a proposal in 1999 for implementation of Article 255 EC on access to information of the Community institutions, which was expected to be announced after the entry into force of the Amsterdam Treaty.[11] However, a draft regulation was prepared by the Commission, which has not yet been published.[12] The first impression gained from the draft regulation is that it is vastly more restrictive in providing access to information of

---

[4] COM(1999)313 final, [1999] OJ C212E/1.

[5] See for more details; Holder, Verschuuren, and Janssen, n. 3 above, 420.

[6] Common Postition (EC) No. 21/2000, [2000] OJ C128/1.      [7] [1990] OJ L158/56.

[8] Aarhus, 23–5 June 1998.                          [9] COM(98)344 final.

[10] See Written Question No. E–0611/99 by Carlos Pimenta (PPE), and the answer by Commissioner Bjerregaard on 3 May 1999, [1999] OJ C370/99.

[11] See 'Freedom of Information Plan Delayed' (1999) 5 *European Voice* 22.

[12] *Statewatch* published a copy of the draft on the Internet at: http://www.statewatch.org/secreteurope.html.

the Community institutions than the existing rules.[13] For example, all working documents are excluded from its scope until the decision-making process has resulted in the formal adoption of a decision. Moreover, documents obtained by an applicant may not be reproduced without authorization by the institution. If Member States receive requests for access to documents drawn up by one of the institutions, they must apply the general principles and limits laid down in Articles 1, 3, and 4 of the draft regulation. These include a narrow definition of 'documents' and a broad range of exceptions. It remains to be seen how the EP will receive the Commission's eventual proposal, to be adopted by the Council and the EP following Article 255 EC, having regard to Parliament's critical remarks on openness within the EU institutions.[14]

B.  CASE LAW

*i. Environmental Impact Assessment*

During 1999 several important cases on Directive 85/337/EC on the Assessment of the Effects of Certain Public and Private Projects on the Environment (EIA Directive)[15] were decided by the European Court of Justice (ECJ), two of which concern projects listed in Annex II of the Directive. In the first of these cases, a preliminary ruling in *WWF and others* v. *Autonome Provinz Bozen and others*,[16] the ECJ further elaborated its ruling in *Kraaijeveld*.[17] The *WWF* case concerned the restructuring of an airport for which the decision was made by an individual national legislative act, after an environmental impact study had been carried out. This study, however, did not meet the requirements of the EIA Directive. Similar to its position in *Kraaijeveld*, the Court ruled that Articles 4(2) and 2(1) EIA Directive are to be interpreted as not conferring on a Member State the power either to exclude, from the outset and in their entirety, from the environmental impact assessment procedure established by the Directive certain classes of projects falling within Annex II to the Directive, including modifications to those projects, or to exempt from such a procedure a specific project, such as the project of restructuring an airport with a runway shorter than 2,100 metres, as was the case here, either under national legislation or on the basis of an individual examination of that project, unless those classes of projects in their entirety or the specific project could be regarded, on the basis of a comprehensive assessment, as not being likely to have significant effects on the environment.

---

[13]  Council Decision 93/731/EC and Commission Decision 94/90/EC, n. 34 below.

[14]  'Résolution sur la Transparence dans l'Union Europééne' (not available in English) A4-0476/98, [1999] OJ C104/20.

[15]  [1985] OJ L175/40.

[16]  Case C–435/97, [1999] ECR I–5613. See case reports by C. Backes, (2000) 7 *Administratie-frechtelijke Beslissingen* 39, 241–51; M. A. A. Soppe (1999) 5 *Nederlands Tijdschrift voor Europees Recht* 11, 291–6; G. Toggenburg and M. Hofstötter (1999) *European Law Reporter*, 474–5; J. Verschuuren, (1999) 26 *Milieu & Recht* 12, 286–91.

[17]  Case C–72/95, *Aannemersbedrijf P. K. Kraaijeveld BV and Others* v. *Gedeputeerde Staten van Zuid-Holland* [1996] ECR I–5403.

It is for the national court to review whether those authorities correctly assessed, on the basis of the individual examination carried out by the national authorities which resulted in the exclusion of the specific project at issue from the assessment procedure established by the Directive, the significance of the effects of that project on the environment. Any alternative procedure must satisfy the requirements of the EIA Directive. Furthermore, the Court ruled that Article 1(4) of the Directive, excluding military defence projects from the scope of the EIA, is to be interpreted as meaning that an airport which may simultaneously serve civil and military purposes, but whose main purpose is commercial, falls within the scope of the EIA Directive.

The second case in 1999 concerning the EIA Directive was an infringement procedure against Ireland: *Commission* v. *Ireland*.[18] For projects concerning deforestation, land reclamation, or peat extraction, Ireland had set thresholds only taking account of the size of project. However, it had failed to take into account the nature of the projects, and their locations, while *in casu* the projects were located in 'sensitive areas' by nature conservation standards. Thus, Ireland had, in practice, excluded these projects from any EIA-obligations in advance, as long as they did not reach the absolute thresholds which it had set, without looking into the possibility of significant effects on the environment of specific projects. Or, as the Court puts it in its judgment of 21 September 1999: 'Even a small-scale project can have significant effects.'[19] Although Ireland had argued that the Commission did not prove that significant effects on the environment existed *in casu*, the ECJ found this claim unfounded in concluding that:

the alleged infringement has to do with the way in which the Directive has been transposed into Irish law and not with the actual result of the application of the transposing legislation. In order to prove that the transposition of a directive is insufficient or inadequate, it is not necessary to establish the actual effects of the legislation transposing it into national law: it is the wording of the legislation itself which harbours the insufficiencies or defects of transposition.[20]

The Commission, however, gave several examples to indicate the consequences of the Irish approach. For instance, the cumulative effect of land reclamation projects, covered by point 1(d) of Annex II to the EIA Directive, was not taken into account by the relevant Irish legislation. As a consequence, limestone pavement, which is characteristic of the area, has been destroyed, as have vegetation and archaeological remains giving way to pasture. The Commission also mentioned sheep farming as an example, but the Court found that it could not be demonstrated that sheep farming as practised in Ireland constitutes a 'project' within the meaning of Article 1(2) EIA Directive.[21]

---

[18] Case C–392/96, [1999] ECR I–5901. See case reports by Ch. Backes, (2000) 6 *Administratiefrechtelijke Beslissingen* 33, 193–99; M. A. A. Soppe (1999) 5 *Nederlands Tijdschrift voor Europees Recht* 11, 291–6; G. Toggenburg and M. Hofstötter (1999) *European Law Reporter*, 477–8; J. Verschuuren (2000) 27 *Milieu & Recht* 4, 84–9.

[19] Para. 66.          [20] Paras. 58–60.          [21] Para. 81.

According to the Court, Ireland had thus exceeded the limits of its discretion under Articles 2(1) and 4(2) EIA Directive. It held that Ireland should have enabled cumulative effects to be taken into account for the decision on thresholds. Additionally, Ireland should have taken account of factors such as the nature or location of projects, *inter alia*, by setting a number of thresholds corresponding to varying project sizes and applicable by reference to the nature or location of the project. Furthermore, Ireland was found to have infringed Article 2(3) EIA Directive, because national legislation provides for an exemption formula enabling the competent minister to dispense with an impact assessment for a project where he considers this to be warranted by exceptional circumstances. The Commission pointed out that this provision holds a twofold inconsistency with the EIA: first, the minister is not required to consider whether another form of assessment would be appropriate and whether the information collected should be made available to the public; and second, the minister is not required to inform the Commission of his decision. Although this provision has now been amended, the Court did not take this amendment into account, referring to settled case law,[22] holding that amendments to national legislation are irrelevant for the purposes of giving judgment on the subject matter of an action for failure to fulfil obligations if they have not been implemented before the expiry of the period set by the reasoned opinion.

Finally, there was one other case in 1999 on the EIA Directive in which the ECJ gave a judgment. In *Commission* v. *Portugal*[23] Portugal had failed to fulfil its obligations under the EIA Directive. In its national legislation, Portugal had adopted a transitional provision holding that these national laws did not apply to projects for which the consent procedure had been initiated prior to the entry into force of the national law transposing the EIA Directive, but after 3 July 1988: the deadline for transposition of the EIA Directive. Portugal argued that such transitional provisions were necessary to respect the principle of legal certainty, but the Court, in its ruling of 21 January 1999, held that nothing in the Directive could be construed as authorizing the Member States to exempt from the obligation to carry out an environmental impact assessment projects for which the consent procedures were initiated after the expiry of the deadline for transposition. This judgment is completely in line with previous case law, in particular *Bund Naturschutz in Bayern and Others* v. *Freistaat Bayern*.[24]

Many more cases are expected to follow these 1999 judgments, as the Commission on 28 February 2000 announced that it has submitted a reasoned opinion to Germany for its failure to implement the ECJ ruling of 22 October

---

[22] Case C–123/94, *Commission* v. *Greece* [1995] ECR I–1457.
[23] Case C–150/97, [1999] ECR I–0259.
[24] Case C–396/92, [1994] ECR I–3717. See also Case C–431/92, *Commission* v. *Germany* [1995] ECR I–2189, Case C–81/96, *Burgemeester en Wethouders van Haarlemmerliede en Spaarnewoude and Others* v. *Gedeputeerde Staten van Noord-Holland* [1998] ECR I–3923; and Case C–301/95, *Commission* v. *Germany* [1998] ECR I–6135.

1998,[25] while reasoned opinions for failures to transpose Directive 97/11/EC amending the 1985 EIA Directive[26] have been sent to Austria, France, Germany, Greece, Luxembourg, Spain, and the UK.

### ii. Access to Information

The transposition of the Environmental Information Directive[27] by the Member States is not without difficulties, as is indicated by the fact that the Commission continues to receive complaints concerning the nonconformity of national measures implementing the Directive.[28]

According to the Commission, the most common complaints involve refusals by national authorities to respond to requests for information, delays in replies, tendencies of national government departments to adopt excessively broad interpretation of the exceptions to the principle of disclosure, and demands for payment of unreasonably high fees.

In 1999 the ECJ delivered its first ruling following infringement proceedings for failure to comply with the Environmental Information Directive. The action in case-217/97[29] was brought against Germany, which was alleged to have incorrectly transposed the Directive on several points. The Court decided that Germany had failed to fulfil its obligations on three counts:

First, the German *Umweltinformationsgesetz* (*UIG*) excluded all access to information during 'administrative proceedings', whereas Article 3(2) Environmental Information Directive merely provides for an exception for information which is the subject of 'preliminary investigation proceedings'. Previously, the Court held in a preliminary ruling in *Mecklenburg* v. *Kreis Pinneberg-Der Landrat*[30] that an administrative procedure constitutes preliminary investigation proceedings only if it immediately precedes a contentious or quasi-contentious procedure, and arises from the need to obtain proof or to investigate a matter prior to the opening of the actual procedure. As a logical consequence, Germany was held to have breached its obligations under the Directive by excluding administrative proceedings from the right of access to information, contrary to Article 3(2) of the Directive.

Second, the Commission argued that the *UIG* contained no provisions for information to be supplied in part, where it is possible to distinguish between information on items concerning the grounds for refusal as required by Article 3(2) of the Directive. Although the German law did not explicitly lay down this obligation, the German Government contended that it was sufficiently clear from the context of certain provisions of the *UIG*, and from the practice of the competent authorities. The Court admitted that transposing a directive into

---

[25] C–301/95, *Commission* v. *Germany* [1998] ECR I–6135.     [26] [1997] OJ L073/5.
[27] See n. 7 above.
[28] See Environment Chapter of the 'Sixteenth Annual Report on Monitoring the Application of Community Law (1998)', COM(1999)301, 10.
[29] Case–217/97, *Commission* v. *Germany* [1999] ECR I–5087.
[30] Case C–321/96, *Mecklenburg* v. *Kreis Pinneberg—Der Landrat* [1998] ECR I–3809.

national law does not necessarily require the provisions of a directive to be enacted word-for-word in a specific legal provision of national law, and that the general legal context may be sufficient if it actually ensures the full application of the Directive in a clear and precise manner.[31] However, the Court also held that it is necessary for the legal situation to be sufficiently precise and clear to enable the parties concerned to know the full extent of their rights, and where appropriate, to be able to rely on them before the national courts. With regard to the contested German law, the Court held that the duty to supply information on the environment in part was

not guaranteed in a manner sufficiently clear and precise to ensure compliance with the principle of legal certainty and to enable persons who may submit a request for information to know the full extent of their rights.[32]

The Court further explained that the absence of an express provision regarding partial communication may keep applicants seeking information unaware of the fact that the existence of the grounds of refusal set out in Article 3(2), first subparagraph, does not prevent partial communication. In addition, public authorities to whom a request for information is addressed may be dissuaded from granting it. The sole fact that partial communication was mentioned in connection with charges in an annex to the national rules was held insufficient to ensure that those seeking information are aware of the full extent of their rights, and to enable them to rely on them before the national courts.

Finally, the Court was to decide whether the imposition of a charge is compatible with Article 5 Environmental Information Directive if a request for access to information is refused. Although certainly Article 5 allows Member States to make a reasonable charge for supplying information, the Commission was of the opinion that, in the event of a refusal to provide access to information, there is no 'supply of information' within the meaning of the Directive. The Court agreed with the Commission for the following reasons. First, Article 5 permits Member States to make a charge for 'supplying' information, and not for the administrative task connected with a request for information. In addition, the purpose of the Directive, which is to guarantee freedom of access to information on the environment and to avoid any obstacles thereto, precludes any interpretation which is liable to dissuade those wishing to obtain information from making a request to that effect. Furthermore, a charge connected to a refusal to provide information cannot be described as reasonable, since in such a case no information has in fact been supplied within the meaning of Article 5 of the Directive.

Similar judgments of the Court are to be expected since the Commission decided to bring Article 226 EC actions against Belgium, Germany, and Portugal, for failure to comply with the Environmental Information Directive in several respects.[33]

---

[31] See Case 29/84, *Commission* v. *Germany* [1985] ECR 1661, para. 23; and Case 247/85, *Commission* v. *Belgium* [1987] ECR I–3029, para. 9.

[32] Para. 34.　　　　　[33] See Commission press release IP/99/489 of 12 July 1999.

The Court of First Instance (CFI) delivered several judgments on access to information of the Community institutions, which increasingly clarify the scope of Council and Commission rules in this field.[34] Since myriad documents held by the Council and Commission will include information on the environment, it seems useful to refer to some interesting judgments of the CFI on this matter. It should be noted at the outset that a general principle in Community law exists that the public should have the widest possible access to documents held by the Commission and the Council, and that exceptions to that principle must be construed and applied strictly.[35]

Whereas the Environmental Information Directive provides that information held by the public authorities is to be supplied in part where it is possible to separate out the confidential parts, Council Decision 93/731/EC lacks any analogous provisions. Nevertheless, the CFI decided that the Council is obliged to consider partial access to documents. In *Hautala* v. *Council*,[36] a Member of the European Parliament (MEP) applied for access to a report of the Common Foreign and Security Policy (CFSP) Working Group on Conventional Arms Exports. In an application for annulment of the Council's decision to refuse access, the question arose whether the Council is obliged under Article 4(1) of Decision 93/731/EC to consider the granting of partial access instead of refusing access to the required document altogether. The CFI first noted that Decision 93/731/EC does not expressly require the Council to consider whether partial access to documents may be granted, nor expressly prohibits such a possibility.

However, Article 4(1) must be interpreted in the light of the principle of the right to information and the principle of proportionality. With regard to the principle of the right to information it was held in *Netherlands* v. *Council*[37] that the objective of Decision 93/731/EC is to give effect to the principle of the largest possible access for citizens to information, with a view to strengthening the democratic character of the institutions and the trust of the public in the administration. It was added in the current judgment that the principle of proportionality requires that derogations remain within the limits of what is appropriate and necessary for the achievement of the aim. The objective pursued by the Council in refusing access to the contested report was to protect the public interest with regard to international relations, as laid down in Article 4(1) of Decision 93/731/EC. According to the CFI, such a goal may be

[34] See Council Decision 93/730/EC laying down the Code of Conduct of Public Access to Council and Commission Documents, [1993] OJ C340/41, as implemented in Council Decision 93/731/EC on Public Access to Council Documents, [1993] OJ L340/43, and Commission Decision 94/90/ECSC, EC, Euratom, on Public Access to Commission Documents, [1994] OJ L46/58. For a detailed survey of these instruments see: 'Recent Developments on Access to Environmental Information: Transparency in Decision-Making' (1998) 7 *European Environmental Law Review*, 268–76.

[35] See as regards Commission and Council documents respectively Case T–105/95, *WWF UK* v. *Commission* [1997] ECR II–313, para 56; and Case T–174/95, *Svenska Journalistförbundet* v. *Council* [1998] ECR II–2289, para. 66.

[36] Case T–14/98, *Hautala* v. *Council* [1999] ECR II–2489.

[37] Case C–58/94, [1996] ECR I–2169.

achieved even if the Council merely removes, after examination, the passages in the contested report which might harm international relations. In conclusion, the CFI ruled that the Council is obliged to examine whether partial access should be granted to the information not covered by the exceptions.

In two other judgments in 1999, the CFI clarified the rule on authorship, which implies that the Council and Commission rules on access to information are not applicable to documents in their possession of which they are not the author. The first case, *Rothmans International* v. *Commission*,[38] concerned a refusal by the Commission of access to the minutes of the Customs Code Committee, a 'comitology' committee. According to the Commission, comitology committees are entirely distinct from, and independent of, the Commission. The documents in question were consequently not to be seen as Commission documents. However, the CFI held that the Committee cannot be regarded as being 'another Community institution or body' within the meaning of the Code of Conduct adopted by Decision 94/90/EC. To support this position, the CFI produced a list of reasons. The comitology committees have their origin in Article 202 EC, which provides that the Council may confer on the Commission, in the acts which the Council adopts, powers for the implementation of the rules which the Council lays down. These committees established pursuant to the 'comitology' decision are composed of representatives of the Member States and are presided over by a Commission representative.[39] The committees established under that decision assist the Commission in performing the tasks conferred on it. Furthermore, the Commission provides secretarial services for the Committee, in that it draws up the minutes which the Committee adopts. In addition, in common with the other comitology committees, it does not have its own administration, budget, archives, or premises, let alone an individual address. Moreover, the CFI held that the committee is not a natural or legal person, a Member State or any other national or international body not belonging to any of the categories of third-party authors listed in the Code of Conduct. Finally, the CFI stated that refusal of access to the minutes of the numerous comitology committees would amount to placing a considerable restriction on the right of access to documents, which is not compatible with the very objective of the right of access to documents. Therefore, the Commission was not entitled to refuse access to the minutes of the Committee by invoking the rule on authorship. From an environmental law perspective this is an important judgment since comitology committees are numerous in the Community's decision-making process on environmental matters.

In another judgment concerning the authorship rule, the CFI ruled that the Commission had lawfully refused access to documents drawn up by Member States and other documents emanating from Argentine authorities.[40] It should

[38]  Case T–188/97, *Rothmans International BV* v. *Commission* [1999] ECR II–2463.

[39]  Council Decision 87/373/EEC of 13 July 1987 Laying Down the Procedures for the Exercise of Implementing Powers Conferred on the Commission, [1987] OJ L197/33.

[40]  Case T–92/98, *Interporc Im- und Export GmbH* v. *Commission* [1999] ECR II–3521.

be noted that the CFI in both cases ruled that the authorship rule lays down an exception to the general principle of transparency in Decision 94/90/EC and that, therefore, this rule must be construed and applied strictly.[41] However, it is submitted that the authorship rule is not a true exception to the principle of transparency, as it essentially excludes certain information from the scope of application of the Council's and Commission's rules on access to information. In other words, the Council and Commission deem it beyond their competence to give access to documents drawn up by third parties.

The last judgment that should be discussed here concerns the question of access to preparatory Commission documents drawn up in the stage of inspection and investigation in infringement procedures under Article 226 EC.[42] The CFI had held before that access to documents relating to investigations which may lead to an infringement procedure may be refused on grounds of protection of the public interest, even where a period of time has elapsed since the closure of the investigation.[43] However, the CFI in this judgment clarified that not all documents linked to infringement procedures are covered by the exception relating to protection of the public interest. The document at issue was a preparatory document which was never signed by the responsible Commissioner, nor was it sent to the Member State concerned, since the Commission had suspended its decision to deliver a reasoned opinion. Consequently, the procedure was still at the stage of inspection and investigation, during which Member States are entitled to expect confidentiality from the Commission.[44] The CFI held that the disclosure of documents relating to the investigation stage, during the negotiations between the Commission and the Member State concerned, could undermine the proper conduct of the infringement procedure inasmuch as its purpose, which is to enable the Member State to comply of its own accord with the requirements of the EC Treaty or, if appropriate, to justify its position, could be jeopardized.[45] It was decided that the safeguarding of that objective warrants, under the heading of protection of the public interest, the refusal of access to a preparatory document relating to the investigation stage of an infringement procedure. The conclusion to be drawn from this judgment is that documents linked to infringement procedures are not categorically prevented from being disclosed, but rather that each individual Commission document should be assessed for a possible exception to disclosure justified by protection of the public interest.

---

[41] Case T–188/97, n. 38 above, paras. 53–5; and Case T–92/98, n. 40 above, para. 69.
[42] Case T–309/97, *Bavarian Lager Company Ltd* v. *Commission* [1999] ECR II–3217.
[43] Case T–105/95, *WWF UK* v. *Commission* [1997] ECR II–313.          [44] Ibid.
[45] See Case C–191/95 *Commission* v. *Germany* [1998] ECR I–5449.

# VII. Miscellaneous Instruments

DIANE RYLAND*

## A. LEGISLATION ADOPTED

### i. Cohesion Fund

Council Regulation (EC) No. 1264/1999 of 21 June 1999 amends Regulation (EC) No. 1164/94 Establishing a Cohesion Fund.[1] From 1 January 2000, and in accordance with the Regulation's requirements, Spain, Greece, Portugal, and Ireland continue to be eligible under the Cohesion Fund.[2] Total resources of 18 billion euros are made available for commitments in the period 2000–6. This sum is broken down into commitment appropriations of 2.615 billion euros for each of the years 2000–3, 2.515 billion euros each for 2004 and 2005, and 2.510 billion euros for 2006.[3] The indicative allocation of the total resources of the Fund is to be based on precise and objective criteria, principally population, per capita GNP taking account of the improvement in national prosperity attained over the previous period, and surface area. In addition, it will consider other socio-economic factors such as deficiencies in transport infrastructure. Applying those criteria, provision is made for the indicative allocation of the total resources as follows: Spain receives 61–3 per cent of the total, Greece and Portugal are each allocated 16–18 per cent, and Ireland is granted a 2–6 per cent share.[4] The Regulation provides that total annual receipts from the Cohesion Fund, in combination with assistance provided under the Structural Funds, should not exceed 4 per cent of national GDP.[5]

A further Council Regulation (EC) No. 1265/1999 of 21 June 1999 amends Annex II to Regulation (EC) No. 1164/94 Establishing a Cohesion Fund.[6] Accordingly, the concepts of 'project', 'groups of projects', and 'stages of a project', and the criteria for grouping under the Fund are defined.[7] Other amendments concern the provision of the requisite information, including the result of feasibility studies, *ex ante* appraisals, and environmental impact assessments on the part of the beneficiary Member States.[8] Amended provisions cover the basis for commitments of finance under the Fund, form and methodology of payment, technicalities, and financial management generally.[9] A system of improved checks and responsibilities for ensuring sound financial management and the correction of any detected financial irregularities is introduced, effective from 1 January 2000.[10]

---

* Senior Lecturer, University of Lincoln, Lincolnshire, UK.
[1] [1999] OJ L161/57.　　[2] Arts. 2(4) and 6.　　[3] Art. 4(3)–(4).
[4] Art. 5(1)–(2) and Annex I.　　[5] Art. 5(3).　　[6] [1999] OJ L161/62.
[7] Art. A of Annex II.　　[8] Art. B(2) of Annex II.　　[9] Arts. C, D, E, and F of Annex II.
[10] Arts. G and H of Annex II.

## ii. Energy

In its Resolution of 7 December 1998 on Energy Efficiency in the European Community,[11] the Council emphasizes the contribution of efficient use of energy to security of supply, economic competitiveness, and environmental protection. It reaffirms the importance of the further development and implementation of appropriate common and coordinated policies and measures (CCPMs) for the energy-efficient sector, complementary to national policies and measures, and taking into account specific national characteristics and priorities, in order to enable the Community and Member States to achieve their respective commitments under the Kyoto Protocol. The importance of an energy efficiency strategy at Community level, complementary to Member States' policies, receives confirmation, with the Council stressing the necessity for a renewed and strong commitment to the rational use of energy to be made by the Community and Member States. It considers that increased exchange of information and other forms of cooperation between Member States and the Commission on energy efficiency policies, programmes, measures, and results are necessary. The desirability of developing further Community activities in cooperation with Member States, taking into account the principle of subsidiarity, is confirmed in the Resolution. Such activities might, *inter alia*, consist of: first, increased use of combined heat and power (CHP), including district heating and cooling; second, increased emphasis on the building sector, and on energy use by industry and households; third, increased and extended use of labelling, certification, and standardization; fourth, increased dissemination of best-practice information on the application of energy-efficient technologies and techniques; and finally, increased use of negotiated and long-term agreements on energy efficiency on a voluntary basis. The Council notes the Commission's list of possible policy measures which include appropriate energy-fiscal measures, economic incentives, and other similar economic measures to reduce emissions.[12] Ultimately, the Council invites the Commission to formulate, as soon as possible, a proposal for a prioritized action plan for energy efficiency, using as a basis, in particular, the activities considered by the Council in this Resolution.

## iii. Financial Instruments

Several multiannual framework programmes were adopted by the Council in 1999: Council Decision 1999/21/EC, Euratom, of 14 December 1998 Adopting a Multiannual Framework Programme for Actions in the Energy Sector (1998–2002) and Connected Measures,[13] is intended to contribute to the balanced pursuit of the priority objectives of energy policy, namely: security of supply, competitiveness, and protection of the environment. Its objectives are to

---

[11] [1998] OJ C394/1.

[12] Commission Working Document, 'Energy Policy Options corresponding to the Climate Change Challenge: Towards the Definition of a Post-Kyoto Energy Policy Strategy'.

[13] [1999] OJ L7/16.

provide transparency, coherence, and coordination to all of the Community's actions and other measures in the field of energy.[14] The framework programme is to be implemented through six specific programmes of a horizontal or thematic nature, corresponding to the following actions:

— development, in cooperation with Member States, of a programme for regular monitoring of the evolution of the energy markets and trends, so that policy decisions relating to energy can be taken on the basis of a shared analysis;

— reinforcement, within the scope of this framework programme, of international cooperation in the energy field;

— promotion of renewable energy sources;

— encouragement of rational and efficient use of energy resources;

— promotion of the use of environmentally compatible technologies in the solid fuels sector; and

— activities in the nuclear sector relating to safe transport of radioactive materials and also to safeguards and industrial cooperation in order to promote safety in nuclear facilities in countries included in the TACIS programme.

Each specific programme, the duration of which will coincide with the period of application of the framework programme, will set out the arrangements for its implementation.[15] The financial reference amount for the implementation of the framework programme is 170 million euros, of which 68 million euros are allocated for 1998–9.[16]

Council Decision 1999/22/EC of 14 December 1998 Adopting a Multiannual Programme of Studies, Analyses, Forecasts and Other Related Work in the Energy Sector (1998–2002), establishes the ETAP programme.[17] The objectives of this specific programme are:

(a) to establish a shared approach in the Community to studies, analyses, forecasts, and other related work in the energy sector;

(b) to promote coordinated analyses of energy markets and policies at the level of the Community and the Member States;

(c) to analyse and evaluate energy market trends in Europe and the world, *inter alia* in relation to security of supply and competitiveness;

(d) to analyse and evaluate the impact of energy production and use on the environment, including in relation to climate change;

(e) to help identify and transfer the best analysis methods and practices;

(f) to facilitate information networks in the energy field;

(g) to develop an active policy for the dissemination of the results obtained; and

(h) to develop methodologies for monitoring the implementation of the energy framework programme.[18]

---

[14] Art. 1(2)–(3).      [15] Art. 2(1).      [16] Art. 3(1).      [17] [1999] OJ L7/20.
[18] Art. 1(2).

The financial reference amount for the implementation of the ETAP programme is 5 million euros, including 2 million euros for 1998–9, and it is open to participation by the associated Central and Eastern European (CEE) countries and Cyprus.[19]

The Synergy programme, a multiannual programme to promote international cooperation in the energy sector (1998–2002), is established by Council Decision 1999/23/EC of 14 December 1998.[20] Its objectives are to provide assistance to third countries with the definition, formulation, and implementation of energy policy, and to promote industrial cooperation in the energy sector between the EC and third countries.[21] The financial reference amount for the implementation of the Synergy programme is 15 million euros, of which 6 million euros are allocated for 1998–9.[22]

Furthermore, Council Decision 1999/24/EC of 14 December 1998 establishes a multiannual programme of technological actions promoting the clean and efficient use of solid fuels (1998–2002): the Carnot programme.[23] The specific objectives of the Carnot programme are: promote the use of clean and efficient technologies to plants using solid fuels in order to limit emissions, including carbon dioxide emissions, from such use; and to encourage the development of advanced clean solid fuel technologies in order to achieve improved BAT at affordable cost.[24] The financial reference amount for the implementation of the programme is 3 million euros, including 1.2 million euros for the period 1998–9, and it is open to participation by the associated CEE countries and Cyprus.[25]

In its Decision 1999/25/Euratom of 14 December 1998, the Council further establishes a multiannual programme (1998–2002) of actions in the nuclear sector, relating to the safe transport of radioactive materials and to safeguards and industrial cooperation to promote certain aspects of the safety of nuclear installations in the countries currently participating in the TACIS programme: the SURE programme.[26]

The objectives of SURE are: first, to review and, if necessary, harmonize safety practice in the transport of radioactive materials in the Community; second, to help to establish in countries participating in the TACIS programme an effective and reliable system of safeguards through cooperation measures; and third, to promote industrial cooperation and cooperation among regulatory bodies with those countries and the exchange of know-how within the nuclear industry to help them achieve high safety standards that are consistent with internationally recognized principles of nuclear safety for nuclear equipment and installations.[27]

The financial reference amount for the implementation of the SURE programme is 9 million euros, including 3.6 million euros for 1998–9, and it is open to participation by the associated CEE countries and Cyprus.[28]

---

[19] Arts. 2 and 6.      [20] [1999] OJ L7/23.        [21] Art.1(2).            [22] Art. 2.
[23] [1999] OJ L7/28.    [24] Art. 1(2).      [25] Arts. 2 and 9.      [26] [1999] OJ L7/31.
[27] Art. 1(2).          [28] Arts. 2 and 7.

Regulation (EC) No. 1655/1999 of the European Parliament and of the Council of 19 July 1999 amends Regulation (EC) No. 2236/95 Laying Down General Rules for the Granting of Community Financial Aid in the Field of Trans-European Networks.[29] The financial framework for the implementation of this Regulation for the period 2000–6 is 4,600 million euros.[30] The amended provisions introduce, *inter alia*, risk-capital participation for investment funds or comparable financial institutions as a form of Community financial aid, in accordance with Article 4(1)(e) of the Regulation. The facilitation of public–private partnerships is specifically promoted under this multiannual programme, under Articles 4(4) and 5.

In respect of the Community programme for energy efficiency, SAVE II,[31] several Association Council decisions were adopted by the Council in 1999, to establish participation by association countries in this multiannual programme. Participation by the following countries was adopted by the following decisions:

— Poland: Council Decision 1999/12/EC adopting Decision 4/98;[32]
— Czech Republic: Council Decision 1999/16/EC adopting Decision 4/98;[33]
— Bulgaria: Council Decision 1999/113/EC adopting Decision 6/98; [34]
— Romania: Council Decision 1999/248/EC, ECSC, EURATOM adopting Decision 1/1999;[35]
— Lithuania: Council Decision 1999/409/EC, ECSC, EURATOM adopting Decision 2/1999;[36] and
— Hungary: Council Decision 1999/626/EC adopting Decision 2/1999.[37]

Furthermore, the participation of Romania in the financial instrument of the Community in the field of environment was agreed in Association Council Decision 1/98 of 15 September 1998, and subsequently adopted by Council Decision 1999/106/EC.[38]

### iv. Information

The Council has adopted Regulation (EC) No. 933/1999 of 29 April 1999 amending Regulation (EEC) No. 1210/90 on the Establishment of the European Environment Agency and the European Environment Information and Observation Network.[39] The amended provisions reinforce the primary role of the Commission as the provider of objective, reliable, and comparable information on the environment. Replacement provisions amend the tasks of the agency as follows:

---

[29] [1999] OJ L197/1.     [30] Art. 18.
[31] Council Decision 96/737/EC concerning a Multiannual Programme for the Promotion of Energy Efficiency in the Community—SAVE II, [1996] OJ L335/50.
[32] [1999] OJ L6/4.     [33] [1999] OJ L6/14.     [34] [1999] OJ L35/29.
[35] [1999] OJ L96/19.     [36] [1999] OJ L156/27.     [37] [1999] OJ L247/27.
[38] [1999] OJ L35/1.     [39] [1999] OJ L117/1.

— to provide the Community and the Member States with the objective information necessary for framing and implementing sound and effective environmental policies; to that end, in particular, to provide the Commission with the information that it needs to be able to carry out successfully its tasks of identifying, preparing, and evaluating measures and legislation in the field of the environment;[40]

— to assist the monitoring of environmental measures through appropriate support for reporting requirements (including through involvement in the development of questionnaires, the processing of reports from Member States, and the distribution of results), in accordance with its multiannual work-programme and with the aim of coordinating reporting;[41]

— to advise individual Member States, upon their request and where this is consistent with the Agency's annual work-programme, on the development, establishment, and expansion of their systems for the monitoring of environmental measures, provided such activities do not endanger the fulfilment of the other tasks established by this Article. Such advice may also include peer reviews by experts at the specific request of Member States;[42]

— to record, collate, and assess data on the state of the environment, to draw up expert reports on the quality, sensitivity, and pressures on the environment within the territory of the Community, to provide uniform assessment criteria for environmental data to be applied in all Member States, to develop further and maintain a reference centre of information on the environment. The Commission shall use this information in its task of ensuring the implementation of Community legislation on the environment;[43] and

— to publish a report on the state of, trends in, and prospects for the environment every five years, supplemented by indicator reports focusing upon specific issues.[44]

Additionally, the Regulation adds several tasks, by including the obligation to ensure the broad dissemination of reliable and comparable environmental information, in particular on the state of the environment, to the general public and, to this end, promote the use of new telematics technology;[45] to support the Commission in the process of exchange of information on the development of environmental assessment methodologies and best practice;[46] and the obligation to assist the Commission in the diffusion of information on the results of relevant environmental research and in a form which can best assist policy development.[47]

Other amendments concern, *inter alia*, the composition and operation of the Management Board and the Scientific Committee.[48]

---

[40] Art. 2(ii).      [41] Ibid.      [42] Ibid.      [43] Art. 2(iii).      [44] Art. 2(iv).
[45] Art. 2(xi).      [46] Art. 2(xii).      [47] Art. 2(xiii).      [48] Arts. 8 and 10.

Furthermore, the European Parliament (EP) and the Council have adopted Directive 1999/94/EC, of 13 December 1999, on the Availability of Consumer Information on Fuel Economy and $CO_2$ Emissions in Respect of the Marketing of New Passenger Cars.[49]

*v. Instruments*

Council Decision 1999/296/EC of 26 April 1999 amends Decision 93/389/EEC for a Monitoring Mechanism of Community $CO_2$ and Other Greenhouse Gas Emissions, by establishing a mechanism for monitoring all anthropogenic greenhouse gas emissions that are not controlled by the Montreal Protocol on Substances that Deplete the Ozone Layer[50] in the Member States, and by evaluating progress towards meeting commitments in respect of these emissions.[51] Member States are required to devise, publish, and implement national programmes for limiting and/or reducing their anthropogenic emissions by sources and enhancing removals by sinks of all greenhouse gases not controlled by the Montreal Protocol in order to contribute to:

— the stabilization of $CO_2$ emissions by 2000 at 1990 levels in the Community as a whole, assuming that other leading countries undertake commitments along similar lines, and on the understanding that Member States which start from relatively low levels of energy consumption and therefore low emissions measured on a per capita or other appropriate basis are entitled to have $CO_2$ targets and/or strategies corresponding to their economic and social development, while improving the energy efficiency of their economic activities, as agreed at the Council meetings of 29 October 1990, 13 December 1991, and 15 and 16 December 1994;
— the fulfilment of the Community's commitments relating to the limitation and/or reduction of all greenhouse gas emissions not controlled by the Montreal Protocol under the UN Framework Convention on Climate Change and under the Kyoto Protocol; and
— transparent and accurate monitoring of the actual and projected progress of Member States, including the contribution made by Community measures, in meeting any agreed national contributions to the Community's commitments under the UN Framework Convention on Climate Change and the Kyoto Protocol.[52]

*vi. Research and Development Programmes*

Decision 182/1999/EC of the European Parliament and of the Council of 22 December 1998 adopts the fifth multiannual framework programme of the European Community for research, technological development, and demonstration activities (1998–2002).[53] The fifth framework programme comprises four Community activities, the first of which relates to implementation of

---

[49] [2000] OJ L12/16.          [50] Montreal, 1987, last amended: Copenhagen, 23–5 Nov. 1992.
[51] [1999] OJ L117/35.                    [52] Art. 2(1).                    [53] [1999] OJ L26/1.

research, technological development, and demonstration programmes, by way of four themes: first, quality of life and management of living resources; second, user-friendly information society; third, competitive and sustainable growth; and fourth, energy, environment, and sustainable development. The maximum overall amount allocated for Community participation in the fifth framework programme is 13,700 million euros, of which 3,140 million euros are intended for 1998–9, and 10,560 million euros for 2000–2.

Council Decision 1999/167/EC of 25 January 1999 adopts a specific programme for research, technological development, and demonstration on quality of life and management of living resources for the period from 25 January 1999 to 31 December 2002.[54] The amount deemed necessary to carry out this specific programme is 2,413 million euros, broken down into 553 million euros for 1998–9 and 1,860 million euros for 2000–2.[55]

A further Council Decision 1999/168/EC of 25 January 1999 establishes a specific programme for research, technological development, and demonstration on a user-friendly information society for the period 25 January 1999 to 31 December 2002.[56] The amount deemed necessary to carry out this programme is 3,600 million euros, with 857 million euros for 1998–9 and 2,743 million euros for 2000–2.[57] Annex I lists the priority activities under this programme including, *inter alia*, monitoring, forecasting, and decision support; intelligent information systems on air, water, and soil quality, and for monitoring and management of natural resources.

Council Decision 1999/169/EC of 25 January 1999 adopts a specific programme for research, technological development and demonstration on competitive and sustainable growth for the period from 25 January 1999 to 31 December 2002.[58] With 646 million euros for 1998–9, and 2,059 million euros for 2000–2, the total budget for the programme is 2,705 million euros.[59] Annex I identifies, *inter alia*, sustainable mobility, and land transport and marine technologies as key actions under this programme.

Council Decision 1999/170/EC of 25 January 1999 adopts a specific programme for research, technological development, and demonstration on energy, environment, and sustainable development for the period from 25 January 1999 to 31 December 2002.[60] The amount of 2,125 million euros is deemed necessary for carrying out the programme. Of this amount, 446 million euros is for 1998–9, and 1,679 million euros for the period 2000 to 2002.[61] Its Annex I provides an indicative breakdown of the total sum, in respect of the key actions in the fields of the environment and sustainable development, and energy.

Council Decision 1999/171/EC of 25 January 1999 adopts a specific programme on confirming the international role of Community research for the period from 25 January 1999 to 31 December 2002.[62]

---

54 [1999] OJ L64/1.    55 Art. 2(1)–(2).    56 [1999] OJ L64/20.    57 Art. 2(1)–(2).
58 [1999] OJ L64/40.    59 Art. 2(1)–(2).    60 [1999] OJ L64/58.    61 Art. 2(1)–(2).
62 [1999] OJ L64/78.

A further Council Decision 1999/174/EC of 25 January 1999 adopts a specific programme for research and technological development, including demonstration, to be carried out by means of direct actions for the EC by the Joint Research Centre for the period from 25 January 1999 to 31 December 2002.[63]

Council Decision 1999/64/Euratom of 22 December 1998 establishes the Fifth Framework Programme of the European Atomic Energy Community (Euratom) for research and training activities in the field of nuclear energy (1998–2002).[64] Council Decision 1999/175 /Euratom of 25 January 1999 establishes a research and training programme (Euratom) in the field of nuclear energy (25 January 1999 to 31 December 2002).[65] A further Council Decision 1999/176/Euratom of 25 January 1999 adopts a specific programme for research and training to be carried out by the Joint Research Centre by means of direct actions for the European Atomic Energy Community (25 January 1999 to 31 December 2002).[66]

Several Council decisions in 1999 adopt the terms and conditions for the participation of a number of association countries in the fifth framework programme of the EC for research, technological development, and demonstration (1998–2002), as follows:

— Cyprus: Council Decision 1999/460/EC of 20 May 1999 concluding the Additional Protocol to the EEC/Cyprus Association Agreement;[67]
— Estonia: Council Decision 1999/464/EC adopting Decision 2/1999;[68]
— Romania: Council in Decision 1999/620/EC adopting Decision 3/1999;[69]
— Hungary: Council Decision 1999/621/EC adopting Decision 3/1999;[70]
— Slovenia: Council Decision 1999/649/EC adopting Decision 3/1999;[71] and
— Poland: Council Decision 1999/708/EC adopting Decision 4/1999.[72]

### vii. Statistics

The Council has adopted Decision 1999/126/EC of 22 December 1998 on the Community Statistical Programme 1998 to 2002.[73] This Decision, in accordance with Council Regulation (EC) No. 322/97 of 17 February 1997 on Community Statistics,[74] defines the approaches, the main fields, and the objectives of the actions envisaged during this five-year period.[75] The programme is aimed, *inter alia*, at ensuring the continuation of existing statistical support for decisions in current policy areas.[76] In particular, in the EC policy area of Trans-European Networks, work will focus, *inter alia*, on developing a set of statistics on the environmental impact of energy in accordance with the obligations taken on by Member States, within the framework of the post-Kyoto strategy. Focus will also be on telematic networks supporting the

---

[63] [1999] OJ L64/127.  [64] [1999] OJ L26/34.  [65] [1999] OJ L64/142.
[66] [1999] OJ L64/154.  [67] [1999] OJ L180/35.  [68] [1999] OJ L181/24.
[69] [1999] OJ L245/35.  [70] [1999] OJ L245/43.  [71] [1999] OJ L256/73.
[72] [1999] OJ L281/71.  [73] [1999] OJ L42/1.  [74] [1997] OJ L52/1.
[75] Arts. 1 and 3.  [76] Art. 2.

European statistical system on priority areas such as, *inter alia*, the environment. In relation to transport networks, statistics are needed within the framework of a geographical information system to evaluate the environmental impacts of trans-European networks.[77] The main effort in the next five years in the European Community's environmental policy will be: first, to pursue the development of environment statistics with preference given to the existing, available basic data, and improve their dissemination; second, to continue the production and further development of environmental indicators and statistics linking the environment and various sectors of the economy; third, to develop a set of satellite accounts for the environment with which developments in the areas of the economy and the environment can be jointly analysed; and finally, to increase cooperation with the European Environment Agency (EEA). Generally, these objectives will be pursued in partnership with the EEA.[78]

### *viii. Trans-European Energy Networks*

The Commission has adopted a Recommendation of 14 December 1998 concerning the improvement of authorization procedures for trans-European energy networks,[79] in which it recommends that Member States work more closely with each other and, where appropriate, with third countries, in order to speed up the authorization procedures for trans-European energy network projects. Accordingly, the Commission suggests that Member States should simplify such procedures where possible, and provide information at an early stage on the need for a project and on its environmental effects. Finally, it calls upon Member States to assist in the periodic monitoring of the implementation of the Recommendation.

Decision 1741/1999/EC of the European Parliament and of the Council of 29 July 1999 amends Decision 1245/961/EC laying down a series of guidelines for trans-European energy networks.[80] The indicative list of projects of common interest has been updated in line with developments in interconnected energy networks both inside and outside the Community and taking account of the enlargement process and, more generally, the strengthening of energy links with third countries.[81] New projects are also added to the list.[82]

B.  POLICY DOCUMENTS

### *i. Action Programmes*

On 24 November 1999 the Commission issued its Communication 'Europe's Environment: What Directions for the Future? The Global Assessment of the European Community Programme of Policy and Action in Relation to the Environment and Sustainable Development, "Towards Sustainability".'[83] This Communication was a response to a request of the EP and the Council that, at

---

[77] Annex I, Title XII.   [78] Annex I, Title XVI.        [79] [1999] OJ L8/27.
[80] [1999] OJ L207/1.    [81] Art. 1(1) and Annex I.   [82] Art. 1(2) and Annex II.
[83] COM(1999)543, 24 Nov. 1999.

the end of the Fifth Environment Action Programme, the Commission submit an assessment of the implementation of the programme, giving special attention to any revision and updating of objectives and priorities which might be required, and where appropriate, proposing the priority objectives and measures that will be necessary beyond 2000.[84] The Global Assessment Communication indicates that progress has been made in putting into place new and improved instruments to protect the environment and the quality of life. The state of the environment overall, however, remains a cause for concern. The guiding principles of the programme are still valid, but are in need of translation into more effective action by all stakeholders. The Communication invites comments on the development of the Sixth Environment Action Programme.

In a Communication on 'Air Transport and the Environment' of 1 December 1999, the Commission outlined an action programme in order to achieve sustainable development by integrating environmental concerns into sectoral policies in the field of air transport.[85]

### ii. Cohesion Fund

According to the Commission Communication 'Cohesion and Transport' of 14 January 1999,[86] environmental protection is a common objective of transport and cohesion. The environment is recognized as a factor in the attraction of new investment to the regions, and as a source of new opportunities via, *inter alia*, the development of clean technologies.

The Communication indicates that Community transport policy has increasingly emphasized sustainable mobility, which is consistent with the general objective of cohesion. It would appear that road traffic volumes for both passengers and freight have greatly increased in the last twenty-five years, that they are continuing to do so, and that this has been a major source of pollution. Rail, inland waterways, and maritime transport tend to have relatively lower levels of emissions, while emissions from air transport are growing along with demand. It is suggested, therefore, that limiting the environmental impacts could be assisted by a modal shift towards more environmentally friendly forms of transport, which will require a combination of different policy measures. A particular priority, however, is to make the most effective use of existing capacities throughout the transport system. Ultimately, developing a transport network that supports the cohesion of the EU, with special emphasis on remote and peripheral regions, will remain a priority for the Structural and Cohesion Funds, and for the trans-European network budget line.

Furthermore, the Commission, in its Communication 'Structural Funds and their Coordination with the Cohesion Fund', of 1 July 1999,[87] issued guidelines for programmes in the period 2000–6.

---

[84] Art. 1 Decision 2179/98/EC on the Review of the European Community Programme of Policy and Action in Relation to the Environment and Sustainable Development Towards Sustainability [1998] OJ L275/1.

[85] COM(1999)640 final.      [86] COM(98)806 final.      [87] COM(1999)344 final.

### iii. Energy

A Communication of the Commission 'Preparing for Implementation of the Kyoto Protocol' of 19 May 1999,[88] concentrates on what Member States and the Community must do in order to curb current trends in greenhouse gas emissions, and in order to achieve the Kyoto target of an overall 8 per cent reduction of greenhouse gas emissions compared to 1990 levels by the end of the commitment period 2008–12. The Commission is of the opinion that the main responsibility for taking adequate policies and measures lies with the Member States, and that Community measures should merely complement national initiatives. The Commission urges the Ecofin Council to adopt as a priority the proposal for a directive on an energy product tax. Further, Member States should develop other appropriate fiscal incentives to improve energy efficiency and to reduce greenhouse gas emissions. Also, the Commission recognizes that effective and ambitious environmental agreements may act as a basis for important emission reductions in specific industrial sectors. The Communication gives an overview of Community progress on proposals for common and coordinated policies and measures. Reliable and pro-active monitoring and verification systems are stated to be the key to the assessment of progress.

### iv. Instruments

In a further Communication, 'Single Market and Environment' of 8 June 1999,[89] the Commission refers to the tensions which exist between the functioning of the single market and the implementation of environment policy, when these two policies ought to be mutually supportive. The Commission describes how the Community principles in relation to the free movement of goods and environmental policy could be applied in the assessment of national environmental measures in such a way as to ensure the effective achievement of both Community objectives. The Commission identifies other single market policy areas in which closer integration with environmental policy should be reached, namely: instruments of economic policy, standardization, public procurement, financial reporting, eco-labelling, transport, and energy. The Communication concludes that further measures are necessary and suggests initiatives to be undertaken by the Commission for the purpose of integrating the single market and the environment. These include, *inter alia*: updating the existing Commission database on environmental taxes and charges used in the internal market; developing the role of EU-wide environmental agreements; developing, in close cooperation with the relevant national authorities, the role and contribution of the Community eco-label with respect to the single market.

---

[88] COM(1999)230 final.        [89] COM(1999)263 final.

## C. INTERNATIONAL COOPERATION

The Council has adopted Decision 1999/37/EC of 26 November 1998 on the Position to be taken by the European Community on the Rules concerning the Conduct of the Conciliation of Transit Disputes to be Adopted by the Energy Charter Conference.[90]

In its Decision 1999/819/Euratom of 16 November 1999, the Commission approves the accession to the 1994 Convention on Nuclear Safety by the European Atomic Energy Community (Euratom).[91]

In the Communication, 'Integrating Environment and Sustainable Development into Economic and Development Cooperation Policy' of 20 October 1999,[92] the Commission presents a strategy in support of developing countries' efforts to address environmental problems. Emphasis is placed, *inter alia*, on global environmental issues, links between poverty and the environment, on the need both for integrating environmental concerns into other policies, and increased dialogue on sustainable development.

## D. MISCELLANEOUS

### i. The Cohesion Fund

The Commission issued its Annual Report of the Cohesion Fund for 1998 on 15 October 1999.[93] The Cohesion Fund had a total budget for commitments of 2,870.7 million euros in 1998, and this sum was fully committed in the year. Environmental projects received 53.5 per cent of total commitment appropriations in 1998, as opposed to 46.5 per cent awarded to transport in the same year.[94] The share of the transport budget going to roads was reduced in 1998. The Fund is continuing to support the trans-European network projects adopted by the Essen Council in 1994. In 1998 the Fund continued to concentrate on the water sector, namely the abstraction and distribution of drinking water, and waste-water treatment. The Cohesion Fund also initiated and distributed the results of a major study to demonstrate the environmental dimension of the transport and environmental projects it assists. The Commission, in 1998, entrusted the *ex post* evaluation programme, which will run until the end of 2000 for the present generation of Fund projects, and in the course of which about 120 projects will be evaluated, to an outside assessor. The first results of *ex post* evaluation became available in the autumn of 1998. The Commission is of the opinion that it is too early to draw general conclusions, while indicating that in the medium term results should have a positive impact on project assessment and on the quality of project preparation.

---

[90] [1999] OJ L11/37.     [91] [1999] OJ L318/20.     [92] COM(1999)499 final.
[93] COM(1999)483 final. Cohesion Fund projects with a cost of more than fifty million euros are listed in [1999] OJ C201/6.
[94] Between 1993 and 1998, transport accounted for 49.9% of commitments and the environment sector for 50.1%.

The process of monitoring and following up decisions from earlier years continued to gain in importance over the appraisal and approval of new applications. The Monitoring Committees in the four beneficiary countries, including special committees set up to monitor particularly important and large complex projects, met on ten occasions in 1998. Greece received 516.4 million euros in assistance from the Cohesion Fund in 1998, with 209.8 million euros (40.6 per cent) going to environmental projects and 306.6 million euros (59.4 per cent) to transport infrastructure. Spain received 1,575.1 million euros in assistance from the Cohesion Fund in 1998. Environmental projects in Spain received 871.1 million euros (55.3 per cent of the total) and transport received 704 million euros (44.7 per cent). Assistance from the Cohesion Fund to Ireland, in 1998, amounted to 258.5 million euros. Of that sum, 142.1 million euros (55 per cent of the total) went to environmental projects and 116.4 million euros (45 per cent) to transport infrastructure. Portugal received 518.1 million euros in assistance from the Cohesion Fund in 1998, with 303.8 million euros (58.6 per cent of the total) going to environmental projects and 214.3 million euros (41.4 per cent) to transport infrastructure.

Greece submitted the update of the convergence programme, for 1998–2001, in September 1998. The primary objective of the convergence programme is the fulfilment by Greece of the conditions allowing for full participation in the Euro area from 1 January 2001. On 3 May 1998 the Council decided that Spain, Ireland, and Portugal, respectively, had fulfilled the conditions to adopt the single currency on 1 January 1999. In March 1998 examination of the Greek general government deficit for 1997 resulted in a figure of 4 per cent of GDP, while in Spain a figure of 2.6 per cent of GDP was established, and the Portuguese general government deficit for 1997 resulted in a figure of 2.5 per cent of GDP. As a result of this assessment, the Commission was able to continue to approve part-financing from the Cohesion Fund for new projects. Ireland was not held to be in an excessive deficit position. On 1 May 1998 the Council decided that Spain and Portugal were no longer in excessive deficit,[95] while a further examination in autumn 1998 was required for Greece, in view of its excessive general government deficit in 1997. The Council had recommended an annual general government deficit target for Greece in 1998 of 2.4 per cent of GDP, in line with the convergence programme. The Commission's autumn 1998 forecast estimated the general government budget deficit for 1998 at 2.4 per cent of GDP. As a result, the Commission was able to continue to provide financial assistance for new projects and stages of projects in Greece.

### ii. Financial Instruments

The Commission had adopted a Report on 4 December 1998[96] on the implementation of LIFE under Article 14 of the Financial Instrument for the Environment (LIFE) Regulation EC No. 1404/96.[97] In 1998 finance totalling

---

[95] Council Decisions of 1 May, [1998] OJ L139.          [96] COM(98)721.
[97] [1996] OJ L181/1.

101.3 million euros was granted. Of that sum, 48 million euros financed eighty-five nature conservation schemes, 48.6 million euros funded 115 environmental schemes, and 4.7 million euros provided assistance to sixteen schemes in certain third countries.

### iii. Implementation

On 9 July 1999 the Commission presented its 'Sixteenth Annual Report on Monitoring the Application of Community Law (1998)'.[98] Generally, in 1998, the Commission undertook a reform of its internal rules for operating infringement proceedings to improve speed, transparency, and relations with complainants. In monitoring the implementation of Community environmental law, in 1998, the Commission referred fifteen cases against Member States to the ECJ, and issued 118 original or supplementary reasoned opinions, of which four concerned Article 228 EC. A referral under Article 228 EC, with an application for a daily penalty payment of 105,500 euros, was made on 16 October 1998 against France, in respect of the Wild Birds Directive.[99]

The problems highlighted in previous annual reports with the implementation of environmental law remain, namely: the difficulties encountered in the transposition and application of environmental law, failure to notify initial and subsequent national implementing measures, and the limited monitoring ability of the Commission. The causes of delays in the transposition of directives comprise: internal institutional and administrative structures of Member States, techniques, specific difficulties in particularly sensitive areas (chemicals, biotechnology), and possible lack of coordination between representatives of the Member States, who negotiate the directives, and the national implementing bodies. Regarding the conformity of national measures implementing Community law, infringement proceedings are underway in all areas of environmental legislation, and against all Member States. The number of complaints alleging infringements, after falling for two successive years, increased in 1998. One in every two complaints was concerned with nature conservation, and one in every four with environmental impact. Waste-related problems were raised in one in ten cases, as were those relating to air pollution and water pollution. On 11 December 1998, the Commission adopted Communication 'The review clause: environmental and health standards four years after the accession of Austria, Finland and Sweden to the European Union',[100] in which it consolidates the process of strengthening environmental and health standards.

In its State and Outlook Report entitled 'Environment in the EU at the turn of the century',[101] the European Environment Agency (EEA) concludes that the general environmental quality in the EU is not recovering significantly. There

[98] COM(1999)301 final, [1999] OJ C354/1.
[99] Case C–374/98, *Commission* v. *French Republic*, [2000] ECR I–1374.
[100] COM(98)745 final.
[101] Published on the Internet at: http://www.themes.eea.eu.int/showpage.php/improvement/information?pg=40330.

have been significant cuts in ozone-depleting substances, and progress has occurred in river quality and acidification/transboundary air pollution. The situation is getting worse regarding waste.

Emerging trends of non-sustainable development are evident in the sectors of transport, energy, agriculture, household consumption, and tourism. One consequence is a rise in emissions of the main greenhouse gas: $CO_2$. Emissions and discharges of heavy metals and hazardous chemicals are expected to increase. The EEA report refers to the difficulty of assessing the effect of chemicals such as dioxin and genetically modified organisms in food.

The EEA further issued its Annual Report for 1998,[102] which indicates an increase in use of the EEA's European Reference Centre, which makes environmental information available on the Internet. A new multiannual work programme for 1999–2003 has been adopted. It is the EEA's mission, during that period, to support sustainable development and to help to achieve significant and measurable improvement in the European environment. The aim is to achieve this through the provision of timely, targeted, relevant, and reliable information to policy-making agents, and to the public.

### iv. Research and Development

On 25 June 1999 the Commission issued its 'Annual Report of the Research and Technological Development Activities of the European Union (1999)'.[103]

### v. State Aid

The Commission decided to extend until 30 June 2000, the applicability of the Community guidelines on state aid for environmental protection, which initially were to expire on 31 December 1999.[104]

### vi. Statistics

A first set of environmental pressure indicators for the EU has been published in a document entitled 'Towards environmental pressure indicators for the EU'.[105]

### vii. Trans-European Networks

The Annual Report for 1998 on trans-European networks was presented by the Commission on 15 September 1999.[106]

---

[102] The Court of Auditors has presented its Report on the financial statements of the EEA for the financial year ended 31 Dec. 1998 together with the EEA's replies, see [1999] OJ C372/7.

[103] COM(1999)284 final.                                          [104] [2000] OJ C14/8.

[105] Published on the Internet at: http://www.europa.eu.int/en/comm/eurostat/compres/en/7599/6807599a.htm.

[106] COM(1999)410 final.

# VIII.  Case Law of the European Court of Justice

## KIERAN ST. C. BRADLEY*

### A. INTRODUCTION

Although perhaps less abundant than in some previous years, the judgments delivered in 1999 allow the Court-watcher a good overview of the state of the Community's environmental law, and in particular the perennial problems of transposition, implementation, and enforcement. Some of these at least must be considered inevitable in a Community of autonomous legal systems. The United Kingdom drinking water case,[1] for example, arose from a clash of regulatory cultures, and the defendant Member State's penchant for non-interventionist solutions, even self-regulation where appropriate. In these circumstances, the Court can only insist on strict compliance with the terms and scheme of the Community measure, even where the obligation infringed might, to the layman, appear rather formal in character, such as the establishment of pollution reduction programmes when the Member State claims to have achieved full implementation of the environmental objective at issue. It must also tread a thin line between the rights of defence of the Member States, and the concomitant obligation on the Commission to prove every element of its case without the benefit of presumptions, and the duty of the Member State in effect to provide the evidence of its own wrongdoing. The Court was given the opportunity during the year of affirming, in response to Italy's bluster,[2] the conformity with the Treaty of the Commission's pursuing specific infringements of protective norms, though the matter was not seriously in doubt, and indeed is a feature of most areas of environmental protection enforcement.

The decided cases also illustrate that, despite the variety of the problems raised and solutions adopted in each of the areas of environmental regulation, there are a number of common features and/or cross-pollination in legal analysis. Thus, for example, complaints by individuals, either to the Commission or the responsible national authorities, are an essential trigger for direct or indirect Community judicial supervisory mechanisms in areas as diverse as environmental impact assessment, bird protection, the enforcement of restrictions on the discharge of dangerous substances into the aquatic environment, and the maintenance of the quality of water intended for human consumption. The

* Former Distinguished Lecturer on European Law, Harvard (Spring 2000), USA; former *Référendaire* at the European Court of Justice, Luxembourg. The views expressed are personal, and may not be attributed to any Community institution or member thereof. Only the current numbering of the EC Treaty Articles is used throughout; [ ] indicates that the original reference was to the pre-Amsterdam Treaty numbering.
[1]  Case C–340/96, *Commission* v. *United Kingdom* [1999] ECR I–2023.
[2]  Case C–365/97, *Commission* v. *Italy* [1999] ECR I–7773.

right of Member States to resort to habitats protection to protect an endangered species of fauna, at the risk of creating obstacles to intra-Community trade, was justified in a judgment by reference to the Birds Directive.[3] In holding that bio-diversity was an interest within the meaning of Article [30] EC justifying national measures, the Court could equally have referred in this context to its case law on the definition of subspecies and the protection of genetic purity, though curiously it did not cite this expressly. Infringement actions in some of these areas also suffer from the fact that deterioration of environmental conditions may occur progressively over a long period of time, rendering proof of responsibility rather difficult in some cases. Equally, the content of Member State's legal obligations may have been modified. The problems of diverse sources of pollution, and of the relationship between quality objectives and emission limit values, are also common to a number of the areas of environmental protection examined by the Court during 1999. It also affirmed the duty of Member States to ensure strict respect for the general protective norms of environmental legislation which reflect the fundamental principles of the Community's environmental policy such as prevention or precaution, even in the absence of more specific provisions on a given topic.

### B.  DANGEROUS SUBSTANCES

The difficulties the Member States' experience in drawing up programmes to reduce pollution from batteries and accumulators under Article 6 of Directive 91/157/EEC on Batteries and Accumulators Containing Certain Dangerous Substances,[4] stands in marked contrast to their apparent willingness to take other measures to this end. In infringement proceedings against Belgium, for example, the defendant Member State sought to rely on a voluntary agreement concluded with battery manufacturers, a code of good practice to reduce the amount of mercury in electric batteries, and a fund which had been set up to ensure the collection and recycling of spent batteries.[5] The Court underlined first that the Commission depended on the notification of national measures in particular to evaluate 'whether the measures envisaged . . . actually contribute to implementing the programmes designed to attain the objectives of the Directive'. The Directive envisages a precise timetable, and the fact that a Member State may have achieved positive results early in some areas does not absolve it of the obligations under Article 6. Belgium was found not to have drawn up the necessary programmes, and the measures it sought to rely on either lacked a precise timetable and provision for regular review and updating (the agreements and code of practice) or were not shown to have the potential to replace proper programmes (recycling fund).

   The Court reached similar conclusions in the infringement proceedings against France.[6] It did not accept the defendant Member State's view that

---

[3]  Case C–67/97, Criminal proceedings against *Ditlev Bluhme* [1999] ECR I–8033.
[4]  [1991] OJ L78/38.       [5]  Case C–347/97, *Commission* v. *Belgium* [1999] ECR I–0309.
[6]  Case C–178/98, *Commission* v. *France* [1999] ECR I–4853.

the objectives of Article 6 had all been achieved by its substitute measures: cooperation with market operators, recycling of batteries supported by an environment and energy management agency, and the establishment of an agency to manage the collection and disposal of accumulators. Again, the absence of a precise timetable proved fatal, and the measures were dubbed 'no more than a series of legislative provisions or *ad hoc* measures which do not possess the characteristics of an organized and coordinated system of objectives such as to make it possible to regard them as programmes within the meaning of Article 6'. Greece's efforts to show compliance with this provision, rather than merely to show willing, were equally unsuccessful.[7]

## C. NATURE CONSERVATION

### i. Wild Birds Directive

France was required to explain its failure, in two remarkably similar cases, to classify sufficiently large special protection areas (SPAs) for wild birds under Article 4 of Directive 79/409/EEC on the Conservation of Wild Birds (Wild Birds Directive),[8] and for failing to provide a proper legal protection regime, respectively in the Seine Estuary[9] and the Poitevin Marsh.[10] On each occasion, the Court had no difficulty in finding against France as regard the geographical extent of the SPA. In the Seine Estuary, France had classified less than 20 per cent of the area recognized by the French authorities themselves as being of ornithological interest, while in the Marais Poitevin, the figure was closer to 33 per cent. The Court reached its conclusion in each case on the existence of an infringement partly on the basis of the results of a 1994 study by the French authorities identifying the '*zones importantes pour la conservation des oiseaux*' or '*ZICOs*', though it expressly acknowledged in *Seine Estuary* that 'the mere fact that [a] site . . . was included in the inventory of *ZICOs* does not prove that it ought to have been classified as an SPA'.[11] In neither case did the Court consider it necessary to address the question of the area which France was required to classify in order to comply with its obligations under Article 4(1) Wild Birds Directive, limiting its finding to the 'common ground' that the particular area was of ornithological importance and that an insufficient area had been classified. The Court's non-committal approach leaves open the extent of the infringement, which may be a rather difficult issue in any proceedings under Article 228(2) EC seeking the imposition of a lump sum or periodic payment for non-compliance with a judgment.[12]

---

[7] Case C–215/98, *Commission* v. *Greece* [1999] ECR I–4913.     [8] [1979] OJ L103/1.

[9] Case C–166/97, *Commission* v. *France* [1999] ECR I–1719.

[10] Case C–96/98, *Commission* v. *France* [1999] ECR I–8531.

[11] AG Fennelly had noted that 'Member States should be encouraged to arrange for comprehensive surveys of their national territories with a view to carrying out their duty of classification under the Directive. It would be counter-productive, in my view, to treat every area identified as suitable for the protection of wild birds as automatically requiring classification' (para. 19).

[12] The first such action, concerning non-implementation of two waste directives, was decided in 2000 (Case C–387/97, *Commission* v. *Greece* [2000] ECR I–5047, Opinion of AG Ruiz-Jarabo Colomer).

The Court was, on the other hand, rather more forthcoming on the question of the minimum protection requirements for SPAs. Article 4(1) and (2) Birds Directive 'requires the Member States to provide SPAs with a legal protection regime that is capable, in particular, of ensuring both the survival and reproduction of [endangered] bird species . . . and the breeding, moulting and wintering of migratory species'. The only legal protection for the Seine Estuary SPA derived from the fact that the land was state-owned and a maritime game reserve, which the Court found 'incapable of providing adequate protection'. As regards the Marais Poitevin SPAs, France had relied on the application of the 1992 Law on Water and of certain agri-environmental measures. The former related only to water management and was not such as to ensure the protection required under the Directive—and, in any case, not all the territory in question constituted wetlands—while the latter were 'voluntary and purely hortatory in nature in relation to farmers working holdings in the Poitevin Marsh'. The Court largely upheld the Commission's complaint that France had allowed wild bird habitats in the SPAs on the Marsh to deteriorate, relying by way of evidence on the reasoned opinion, the French response thereto and various maps placed on the case-file, and on figures showing that the average populations of wintering ducks had fallen dramatically in the decade from 1987.[13] The French defence that the deterioration was due to the common agricultural policy, which it claimed discouraged agricultural activity compatible with conservation requirements, was dismissed on the ground that any such consistency 'could not authorize a Member State to avoid its obligations under that Directive'. Though also upholding the Commission's claim that France had allowed the deterioration of areas which were suitable for classification as SPAs, the Court was careful to identify the areas concerned, rather than accept the more global approach of the Commission, as some of the areas had already been placed under cultivation before the Wild Birds Directive had entered into force.

In each of these cases, the Commission had alleged that one small portion of an SPA which was presently being used for economic purposes (a titanogypsum plant and a motorway, respectively) had been either improperly excluded from classification, or declassified. In *Seine Estuary*, the Commission had failed to show that the site in question was suitable for classification as an SPA, or that France had failed in its duty to avoid pollution or deterioration of the local habitat. Exceptionally, the defendant Member State was able to rely on scientific studies to prove its case. In *Poitevin Marsh*, the French Government had explained that the inclusion in the notified area of a road-shaped 300-metre strip running through an SPA was the result of a mistake. On the basis of a careful examination of such evidence as could be gleaned from the case-file, the Advocate General had noted that the Commission had been informed of the designation of the SPA, including the 300-metre strip, in July 1993, which was then confirmed by a letter of September 1993 in response to

---

[13] The Court did not address the issue of whether such a fall could conceivably be due to conditions in other areas inhabited or visited by the ducks.

the Commission's letter of formal notice.[14] Indeed, the strip was still included in a 1998 map of the SPA, helpfully provided to the Court by the French Government. For its part the Court found that the designation as an SPA had only taken place in November 1993, after the decree declaring the motorway construction on the strip to be of public utility and concluded that 'it is evident . . . that the strip of land . . . was mistakenly referred to as forming part of the Marais Poitevin *intérieur* SPA at the time the SPA was notified'.

### ii. Danish Bees

Though rather particular on its facts, the preliminary ruling in *Bluhme*[15] raised a number of important questions of principle concerning the possibility for Member States to pursue environmental objectives even where these may clash with other Treaty goals. The accused in the main proceedings had been prosecuted for keeping bees other than those of the subspecies *Apis mellifera mellifera* (Læso brown bee) on Læso, a small Danish island where bee-keeping is one of the major sources of income.[16] In his defence, he argued *inter alia* that the Danish provisions prohibiting such activity were in breach of Article [28] EC. The Court agreed that the national legislation was a measure having an effect equivalent to a quantitative restriction on the importation of bees from other Member States. In line with established case law, this conclusion was not affected by the limited territorial application of the prohibition. Equally, as the legislation 'concerns the intrinsic characteristics of the bees', it could not be considered a 'selling arrangement' *à la Keck*.[17] The Court did, however, go on to hold that 'measures to preserve an indigenous animal population with distinct characteristics contribute to the maintenance of biodiversity by ensuring the survival of the population concerned', and that this corresponded to the protection of the life of the animal concerned within the meaning of Article [30] EC. Moreover, despite the exceptional character of Article [30] EC, the notion of 'population' was not to be interpreted restrictively: 'it is immaterial whether the object of protection is a separate subspecies, a distinct strain within any given species or merely a local colony, so long as the populations in question have characteristics distinguishing them from others and are therefore judged worthy of protection',[18] the judgement in each case being made, presumably, by the Member State. In the light of the Wild Birds and Habitats Directives and the Rio Convention on Biodiversity,[19]

[14] The AG noted the 'surprising fact' which had emerged at the hearing, that the designation of SPAs by France took the form of a simple letter from the administration to the Commission (para. 31).

[15] Case C–67/97, see n. 3 above.

[16] The island is 114 km² in area and has a population of some 2,350.

[17] Joined Cases C–267/91 and C–268/91, *Criminal proceedings against Bernard Keck and Daniel Mithouard* [1993] ECR I–6097.

[18] The sweeping terms of the Court's ruling may reflect its view in Case C–202/94, *Criminal proceedings against Godefridus Van der Feesten* [1996] ECR I–0355, where, in the context of the Wild Birds Directive, it had noted that 'the concept of subspecies is not based on distinguishing criteria which are as strict and objective as those defining species *inter se*' (para. 15).

[19] Dir. 79/409/EEC, n. 8 above, Dir. 92/43/EEC on the Conserrvation of Natural Habitats and of Wild Fauna and Flora [1992] OJ L206/7, and Dec. 93/626/EEC concerning the conclusion of the Convention of Biological Diversity [1993] OJ L309/1.

the Court went on to find that the establishment of SPAs for threatened species was a recognized method of biodiversity conservation. Though the matter had been hotly contested by the defendant, on the grounds that the bees on Læsø were already a mixture of different bee strains, and that the Læsø brown bee was found in many parts of the world and was not threatened with eradication, the Court concluded that 'the threat of the disappearance of the Læsø brown bee . . . is . . . undoubtedly genuine in the event of mating with golden bees by reason of the recessive nature of the genes of the brown bee', and hence that the national measure was justified under Article [30] EC.

### D. WASTE

The range and virulence of Italy's defence in the *San Rocco Valley* case[20] could be said to be inversely related to its strength in legal terms. The proceedings nonetheless threw up a large number of useful points of interest both generally and more specifically in the environmental law context. Amongst the grounds it relied on to contest the admissibility of the action, Italy argued that the Commission's application did not correspond exactly to the reasoned opinion, as the latter cited only Directive 75/442/EEC on Waste,[21] while the former also referred to the provisions of that Directive as amended by Directive 91/156/EEC on Waste (Waste Directive).[22] Recalling that the existence of an infringement must be assessed in the light of the Community legislation in force at the expiry of the compliance period set in the reasoned opinion, the Court held 'that the claims as stated in the application cannot in principle be extended beyond the infringements alleged in the operative part of the reasoned opinion and in the letter of formal notice'. The 1991 Directive strengthened the 1975 Directive,[23] and the majority of the provisions of the earlier measure remain applicable under the amended Directive. The action was therefore deemed admissible but only 'inasmuch as it concerns obligations arising under the amended Directive which were already applicable under Directive 75/442/EEC'. On the merits, Italy argued *in limine* that the Commission was seeking to afford direct protection to the environment, rather than a review of the transposition into Italian law of the Directive. A concrete example of infringement of the Directive could not, in its view, be relied upon to show a breach of Article 4 Waste Directive, which lays down the principal substantive obligation on Member States to ensure the safe clean disposal of waste. Furthermore, the Commission may only use infringement proceedings in respect of 'a significant part of the national territory'. The Court noted the Commission's duty as guardian of the Treaty and confirmed that this

---

[20] Case C–365/97, see n. 2 above.        [21] [1975] OJ L194/39.

[22] [1991] OJ L78/32. The Court noted that the provisions of the former had been replaced by those of the latter. The Council's failure to repeal the earlier measure undermines the attainment of its much vaunted objective of clarity in legislation.

[23] See Joined Cases C–58/95, C–75/95, C–112/95, C–119/95, C–123/95, C–135/95, C–140/95, C–141/95, C–154/95, C–157/95, *Criminal proceedings against Sandro Gallotti and others* [1996] ECR I–4345.

institution may take infringement proceedings in a specific case. The general character of the obligations under Article 4 Waste Directive, and its lack of direct effect, did not undermine the Commission's approach in this case: '[while] that provision does not specify the actual content of the measures which must be taken . . . it is nonetheless true that it is binding on the Member States as to the objective to be achieved.' A factual situation not in conformity with the requirements of Article 4 which persists and leads to a significant deterioration in the environment without any action by the national authorities could therefore be relied upon as an indication that a Member State has exceeded its discretion under that provision.

On the question of the burden of proof, here of pollution by the systematic discharge of waste other than by waste waters, the Court reiterated that the Commission must prove that a given obligation has not been fulfilled. In the present case, the evidence had been supplied by various departments of the Italian administration, and had not been denied by Italy. The Court added that 'it is primarily for the national authorities to conduct the necessary on-the-spot investigations in a spirit of genuine cooperation and mindful of each Member State's duty . . . to facilitate attainment of the general task of the Commission' *qua* guardian of the Treaty. The Commission's principal complaint alleging that the discharge of waste into the San Rocco valley was an infringement of Article 4 Waste Directive was therefore upheld, along with one of its subsidiary claims alleging a breach of Article 8 Waste Directive, in respect of the operation of an illegal tip.

The Court was invited to distinguish between the 'temporary storage' of waste and 'storage pending collection' in *Lirussi and Bizarro*.[24] The accused in the main proceedings were each charged with keeping dangerous waste in the period after expiry of the necessary authorization (Lirussi) or before the authorization was in force and in a greater quantity than specified therein (Bizzaro). Though the prosecuting authority was minded to consider the incident in each case as being temporary storage and hence exempt from any authorization requirement, the national court sought guidance on the matter from the Court. On a simple reading of the relevant points in the Annexes to the 1975 Waste Directive, the Court held that temporary storage must be distinguished from storage pending collection. While the latter was classified as one of the operations leading to the disposal or recovery of waste, temporary storage was expressly excluded from this category. Temporary storage is classified as the first operation in the management of waste. It therefore precedes a management operation, and constitutes a preparatory operation to one of the recovery or disposal operations. The governments which had submitted observations and the Commission were *ad idem* in considering that temporary storage is not in principle subject to the substantive provisions of the Directive, and in particular Article 4, though the Commission was careful to argue that the notion of 'temporary storage' should, as a derogation to a rule

---

[24] Joined Cases C–175/98, *Criminal proceedings against Paolo Lirussi* and C–177/98, *Criminal proceedings against Francesca Bizzaro* [1999] ECR I–6881.

which sought the achievement of a fundamental objective, be interpreted strictly.

The Court took a distinctly less accommodating line. Article 4 seeks to implement the principles of precaution and prevention. The Community and the Member States are therefore obliged to prevent, reduce, and as far as possible eliminate from the outset, sources of pollution or nuisance by the adoption of measures which are able to eradicate known risks. In so far as the temporary storage of waste may cause significant environmental damage, Article 4 is applicable. Though companies carrying out this activity may be dispensed from the obligation to register or to obtain a permit, all storage operations and waste management operations are subject to respect for the precautionary principle and that of preventive action, and in particular those which arise from Articles 4 and 8 Waste Directive.

The very conditional character of the obligation imposed on the Member States by Article 3 of Directive 75/439/EEC on the Disposal of Waste Oils,[25] as amended by Directive 87/101/EEC (Waste Oils Directive),[26] was at the heart of the dispute between Germany and the Commission in which the Court gave judgment on 9 September 1999.[27] According to this provision, in the processing of waste oils, the Member States are to give priority, in order, to regeneration, combustion, and safe destruction, in each of the first two cases subject to 'technical, economic, and organizational constraints'. The Commission contended that the relevant national provisions only gave recycling parity with thermal processing, while Germany relied on a variety of factors which, it claimed, constituted constraints which justified the conformity of its provisions with the Waste Oils Directive.

The Court started by noting that no national provision expressly laid down priority for regeneration, and that the general legal context was not sufficient here to ensure full application of the Directive. It rejected the Commission's view that the provision on technical, economic, and organizational constraints should be considered a derogation, and hence interpreted strictly. The expression rather defined the scope and content of Member States' obligation to give regeneration priority. Equally, it rejected the German Government's suggestion that the definition of such constraints was within the exclusive discretion of the Member States. Interpretation by the Member States alone would mean that priority for regeneration 'would depend entirely on the goodwill of the Member State concerned, which could thus render the obligation imposed on it worthless'. Instead, the Court interpreted the provision as an expression of proportionality, defining the outer limit of the obligation in question, which was 'to take measures appropriate and proportionate to the objective of giving priority to the processing of waste oils by regeneration'. A Member State could not therefore abstain from the adoption of any measure whatsoever, as this would result in the maintenance of the *status quo*, and

---

[25] [1975] OJ L194/23.    [26] [1987] OJ L 42/43.
[27] Case C–102/97, *Commission* v. *Germany* [1999] ECR I–5051.

deprive Article 3 of the Waste Oils Directive of any practical meaning. The various constraints upon which Germany had relied were examined and found to be insufficient to justify its failure to adopt specific measures giving regeneration priority. Though unwilling to indicate what measures the defendant Member State could have taken, the Court was firmly of the view that there were a number of measures which could have contributed to the attainment of this goal.

E. WATER

### i. Drinking Water

In its infringement proceedings against the UK[28] for failing properly to enforce the Directive 80/778/EEC relating to the Quality of Water Intended for Human Consumption (Drinking Water Directive),[29] the Commission sought to bring this sometimes troublesome Member State, in terms of its approach to environmental protection,[30] back into the fold of Community orthodoxy. Under the relevant national provisions, the Secretary of State for the Environment is empowered to make an enforcement order against a water company which does not comply with the Directive's purity requirements. However, the Secretary may refrain from doing so where the company gives an undertaking to take all appropriate steps for securing or facilitating compliance with the standards. The UK argued in particular that the water companies are best placed to identify the measures which are necessary for compliance, and that such undertakings constitute 'a more expeditious and efficacious procedure than that of enforcement orders', a view which had apparently been accepted by the national courts. The relaxed UK approach to the transposition of the Directive did not wash with the Court, which began by recalling its dictum, regularly used in the environmental context, that 'Member States must, in order to secure the full implementation of directives in law and not only in fact, establish a specific legal framework in the area in question.' As the UK Water Industry Act 1991 had failed to specify the matters to be covered by the undertakings, a specific legal framework was missing. The Commission's previous acceptance of the system of undertakings was deemed irrelevant, as the Commission can in no circumstances authorize practices which are contrary to Community law. A second complaint, regarding the absence of a legal remedy for individuals in circumstances when the undertaking system is applied, was rejected as inadmissible, as the Commission had failed to raise it in the pre-litigation procedure. The Court nonetheless gave a broad hint that, but for this technicality, it would have upheld the second complaint too.

---

[28] Case C–340/96, see n. 1 above.      [29] [1980] OJ L229/11.
[30] See the classic exposé by D. Taylor, G. Diprose, and M. Duffy, 'EC Environmental Policy and the Control of Water Pollution: the Implementation of Directive 76/464' (1986) 24 *Journal of Common Market Studies*, 225.

## ii. Bathing Water

Germany's failure to comply with Directive 76/160/EEC concerning the Quality of Bathing Water (Bathing Water Directive)[31] was condemned in June 1999, despite a wide-ranging series of defence arguments, including reliance on the principle of proportionality as a justification for not taking costly purification measures.[32] The Court opened by noting wryly that 'the fact that [certain areas had] lost their status as bathing areas or that remedial measures have been taken does not cure the infringement', and by holding that even if the limit values were exceeded only once in a given season, that would also be sufficient to constitute an infringement. It next clarified the extent of Member States' duties under the Bathing Water Directive: 'it is not sufficient to take all reasonably practicable measures: the Directive requires the Member States to take all necessary measures to ensure that bathing waters conform to the limit values set therein ... [and] therefore requires the Member States to ensure that certain results are achieved.' For bathing spots whose catchment area extends beyond its territory, Germany had not shown the 'absolute impossibility' of taking remedial measures, including measures in collaboration with other Member States. Nor had it shown that the presence of aquatic birds made purification physically impossible in other sites. The Court did, however, acknowledge that the Commission could not find an infringement on the part of that state in respect of areas which had been incorrectly classified in its database.

## iii. Discharge of Dangerous Substances into the Aquatic Environment

The transposition of Directive 76/464/EEC on Pollution Caused by Certain Dangerous Substances Discharged into the Aquatic Environment of the Community (Dangerous Substances Directive)[33] is a regular source of litigation between the Commission and the Member States. The year 1999 was no exception in this regard. In answering the charge that it had failed to adopt pollution reduction programmes under Article 7 in respect of the ninety-nine List I substances for which the Council has (still) not determined limit values and which are hence still on List II, Belgium argued that the list had no legal value, and that the ensemble of its legislative provisions constituted a programme for the purposes of the Directive.[34] The Court interpreted the first argument as being whether the particular ninety-nine substances belong to the families of substances in List I, and whether more specific legislation was required before they could be treated as List II substances. In view of their undisputed scientific classification, the substances did belong to List I, but the Court held that more specific legislative rules, such as specific directives, were required to fix their emission limit values and to eliminate the associated pollution. The obligation to treat them as List II substances pending any such measures, however, and to draw up the requisite programmes, arose directly

---

[31] [1976] OJ L31/1.     [32] Case C–198/97, *Commission* v. *Germany* [1999] ECR I–3257.
[33] [1976] OJ L129/23.    [34] Case C–207/97, *Commission* v. *Belgium* [1999] ECR I–0275.

from the Directive, as the Court had previously held in *Commission* v. *Luxembourg*.[35] The Court was no more sympathetic to Belgium's alternative defence argument regarding the sufficiency of its substitute measures. Article 7 programmes must be specific, in the sense that they must embody a comprehensive and coherent approach, covering the entire national territory of each Member State and providing practical and coordinated arrangements for the reduction of pollution caused by any of the substances in List II which is relevant in the particular context of the Member State concerned, in accordance with the quality objectives fixed by those programmes for the waters affected. They differ, therefore, both from general purification programmes and from bundles of *ad hoc* measures designed to reduce water pollution. The Belgian measures were found to fall short of these requirements in a number of respects.

The Commission's complaint against Germany,[36] also for failing to define programmes under Article 7 Dangerous Substances Directive, allowed the Court to clarify a number of significant issues, in particular the relationship between quality objectives and emission standards in this context.[37] In essence, Germany argued that it was not obliged to define quality objectives as it had, by laying down a system of prior authorizations for discharges of those substances and setting emission standards which reflect the relevant limit values, adopted more stringent measures, as it was permitted to do under Article 10 Dangerous Substances Directive. In its view, ensuring observance of the limit values results in the full implementation of the Directive, rendering nugatory the establishment of programmes under Article 7 and the definition of quality objectives. The Court did not agree. It held that Article 7 programmes 'are necessary because where the Council has not laid down limit values for emissions of List I substances, they constitute the sole means of verifying that the Member States have adopted measures under the Directive to combat water pollution'. It is on the basis of the comparison between national programmes that the Commission can coordinate their implementation and take any necessary legislative initiatives in this regard. The obligation to establish quality objectives for List II substances is imposed by Article 7(3) Dangerous Substances Directive. While a Member State may obtain a derogation in respect of limit values, it may not do so as regards quality objectives, and, in any case, only programmes including quality objectives can cover pollution by substances emanating from diffuse sources. Nor was the fixing of limit values in itself sufficient to ensure the elimination of water pollution or necessarily a more stringent instrument than Article 7 programmes. The improvement in fact of water quality in Germany through the application of limit values was not shown to have been any different from the result which could have been

---

[35]  Case C–206/96, *Commission* v. *Luxembourg* [1998] ECR I–3401.

[36]  Case C–184/97, *Commission* v. *Germany* [1999] ECR I–7837.

[37]  Apart from D. Taylor *et al.*, n. 27 above, see J. Coadou, *La quantification de la pollution dans le droit de l'environnement: valeurs limites d'émission et objectifs de qualité* (Luxembourg: EIPA, 2000).

achieved through the carrying out of such programmes. The Court was not prepared to accept that the relevant German legislation could be considered a programme within the meaning of the Directive, in absence of quality objectives or the requisite comprehensive and coherent approach to the reduction of pollution adapted to the Member State in question, notwithstanding the alleged absence of water pollution: 'the obligation on Member States to draw up programmes including quality objectives is conditioned not by a finding of actual water pollution by List II substances . . . but by discharges of those substances into the aquatic environment.' It also rejected Germany's contention that the infringement alleged was a consequence of the Commission's failure to propose uniform emission limit values for the Community, and that the Commission was therefore not acting in good faith. The Directive itself determined Member States' obligations in the absence of such limit values, and these were not affected by any failure on the part of the Commission.

In *Nederhoff*,[38] the Court had to rule on the relationship between, and the respective scope of, the 1976 Dangerous Substances Directive and Directive 86/280/EEC on Limit Values and Quality Objectives for Discharges of Certain Dangerous Substances included in List I of the Annex to Directive 76/464/EEC,[39] which implemented the 1976 Directive in some respects and imposed a number of supplementary obligations on the Member States. In particular, Article 5(1) of the 1986 Directive requires the Member States to draw up specific programmes 'to avoid or eliminate pollution from significant sources of [certain dangerous] substances including multiple and diffuse sources other than sources of discharges subject to Community limit values or national emission standards'. Under Dutch law, the applicant in the main proceedings was refused authorization to use posts impregnated with creosote in shoring up embankments, as the creosote would seep into and pollute the water. He argued that the national authorities were entitled to adopt more stringent measures than those laid down in the Dangerous Substances Directive, but could not impose an authorization requirement in respect of sources of pollution other than those caused by discharges into the aquatic environment. He also contended that the policy of the national authorities rendered the grant of an authorization so difficult as to constitute a prohibition on such discharges, in breach of Article 3 Dangerous Substances Directive.

The Court first interpreted the term 'discharge' as used in Article 1(2)(d) of the Directive, whose meaning depended in turn on that of the definition of 'pollution' in Article 1(2)(e). In the light of that comparison the Court held that: 'the term "discharge" . . . must be understood as referring to any act attributable to a person by which one of the dangerous substances listed in List I or List II of the Annex to the Directive is directly or indirectly introduced into the waters to which the Directive applies.' Pollution from significant sources as

---

[38] Case C–232/97, *Nederhoff & Zn. v. Dijkgraaf en Hoogheemraden van het Hoogheemraadschap Rijnland* [1999] ECR I–6385.
[39] [1986] OJ L181/16.

used in Article 5(1) of Directive 86/280/EEC, on the other hand, refers to pollution which cannot be attributed to any person, and no authorization requirement could therefore apply. The Court went on to explain that Community law had set up different systems for these two types of pollution, an authorization system where the pollution derives from an attributable act, that is, a discharge, and a system of pollution reduction/elimination programmes where the pollution derives from multiple and diffuse sources. In answer to the remaining questions, the Court held that the escape of creosote was to be considered a 'discharge' for the purposes of the Dangerous Substances Directive, and that the Directive allowed the Member States to impose additional authorization requirements—here an obligation to investigate alternative solutions which have less impact on the environment—to those it laid down, including requirements which render the grant of an authorization to discharge List I substances practically impossible.

The concept of 'discharge' was also at issue in the *Van Rooij* case,[40] on which the Court gave judgment on the same day as in *Nederhoff*, though in this case the applicant in the main proceedings was relying on the Dangerous Substances Directive to challenge the authorized activities of a third party, *in casu* a company engaged in the business of treating wood. In the course of a wood impregnation process, Mr Van Rooij's neighbour released steam which precipitated onto surface water via a storm water drain, and in particular into a ditch near the Van Rooij property. Mr Van Rooij complained that the ditch was polluted by arsenic, copper, and chrome from the steam, and requested the competent authority to take action against the polluter. On the question of whether the emission of contaminated steam was a 'discharge' for the purposes of the Directive, the French Government was of the view that this concept only covered discharges of liquid substances into another liquid environment, and did not apply to steam. The Court noted that certain of the language versions of the Directive could be taken as implying that the substance discharged must be in the liquid or solid state, though the majority of the language versions did not. Such a narrow interpretation would, however, 'run counter to the objective of the Directive, which . . . is to protect the aquatic environment of the Community from pollution', and the Court therefore concluded that it applies to all discharges of the dangerous substances listed, whatever their state. It also rejected the rather sophistical French view that pollution by steam in these circumstances should be considered atmospheric pollution, and held that the distance between the surface water and the place of the emission of the contaminated steam was only relevant in the attribution of responsibility for the polluting act. The fact that the storm drain did not belong to the polluter was considered immaterial.

---

[40] Case C–231/97, *A. M. L. Van Rooij* v. *Dagelijks bestuur van het waterschap de Dommel* [1999] ECR I–6355.

*iv. Nitrate Pollution*

The preliminary ruling in *Standley*[41] raised the problem of diffuse sources of
water pollution and the division of powers between the Member States and the
Community in regard to combating such pollution. In the main proceedings,
a number of farmers in England, supported by the National Farmers Union,
had argued that Directive 91/676/EEC concerning the Protection of Waters
against Pollution Caused by Nitrates from Agricultural Sources (Nitrates
Directive)[42] only required action by the Member States to counteract the discharge of nitrates where the threshold of 50 mg/l in the surface water was
directly or indirectly attributable to agricultural sources of pollution, and that
the Member States were therefore obliged to identify the sources of the nitrates
which cause the threshold to be exceeded. On a proper construction of
Nitrates Directive, the Court held that a Member State is to identify the waters
affected by pollution by the simple application of the threshold, without being
required to determine what proportion of that pollution is attributable to agricultural activities. The approach proposed by the applicants 'would lead to the
exclusion from the scope of the Directive of numerous cases where agricultural sources make a significant contribution to the pollution, a result which
would be contrary to the Directive's spirit and purpose'. The fact that a
Member State may designate its entire territory as a nitrate-vulnerable zone
allows it to establish action programmes even where agricultural pollution
does not cause the nitrate concentration to exceed 50 mg/l. Furthermore, the
cross-reference to Directive 75/440/EEC concerning the Quality Required of
Surface Water intended for the Abstraction of Drinking Water in the Member
States (Surface Water Directive)[43] shows that the level of the maximum concentration had been determined on public health grounds, as nitrate pollution
is harmful to human health irrespective of its source. The Court was careful to
point out that the Nitrate Directive itself only applied to circumstances where
the agricultural nitrate discharges made a significant contribution to the pollution level, but did not preclude a Member State's applying its provisions to
other circumstances. Nor did the Directive provide precise criteria for establishing in a given case whether agricultural nitrate discharge made a significant contribution or not; this was a matter within the discretion of the Member
States. That the Directive could therefore be applied differently by the Member
States was not incompatible with its purpose, which was held to be 'to create
the instruments needed in order to ensure that waters in the Community are
protected against pollution caused by nitrates from agricultural sources'
rather than to harmonize national legislative provisions. The applicants had
also argued that Member State action where the threshold had been exceeded
because of non-agricultural nitrate pollution gave rise to disproportionate
burdens on farmers, infringed the principles that the polluter pays and that

[41] Case C–293/97, *The Queen* v. *Secretary of State for the Environment and Minister of
Agriculture, Fisheries and Food, ex p. Standley and others* [1999] ECR I–2603.
[42] [1991] OJ L375/1.                          [43] [1975] OJ L194/26.

pollution should be rectified at source, and undermined their property rights by imposing on them the entire economic burden for reducing nitrate pollution. Once again, the Court relied on the detailed provisions of the Directive to conclude that the proportionality principle had been respected as demonstrated, for example, by the requirement that the Member State take account of scientific and technical data on the source of the pollution and of the local environmental conditions, the characteristics of the vulnerable zone concerned, and any change of factual circumstance regarding the source of the pollution. In the context of the Directive, the polluter-pays principle and the rectification at source principle were melded with the principle of proportionality, while the acknowledged restrictions on farmers' property rights were, in the Court's view, justified on grounds of public health, 'an objective of general interest [pursued] without the substance of the right to property being impaired'.

Italy had been condemned earlier in 1999 for failing to identify the waters which were, or could be, affected by nitrate pollution in breach of the same Directive.[44] The Court agreed with the Commission that the obligation to identify vulnerable zones preceded in time the adoption of action programmes.

F. HORIZONTAL INSTRUMENTS

### *i. Environmental Impact Assessment*

It may have taken the Commission almost a decade to get a ruling on Ireland's transposition of Directive 85/337/EEC on the Assessment of the Effects of Certain Public and Private Projects on the Environment (EIA Directive),[45] but its persistence was rewarded.[46] In the result, the only point really argued by the defendant Member State with any conviction was the compatibility with Article 4(2) of the EIA Directive of the thresholds fixed by the applicable national legislation for projects involving intensive farming of uncultivated land or semi-natural areas, deforestation, land reclamation, and peat extraction.

As a preliminary point, Ireland contested the reliance by the Commission on individual complaints which were still under investigation and which had not been mentioned in the reasoned opinion. It also contended that the Commission had failed to demonstrate that the thresholds had actually been misused. The Court held, however, that, as the alleged infringement was of incorrect transposition, 'it is not necessary to establish the actual effects of the [transposition] legislation . . . it is the wording of the legislation itself which harbours the insufficiencies or defects of transposition'. A requirement to show harmful effects would run counter to the principle of prevention on which the Community's environmental policy is based, and the Commission

---

[44] Case C–195/97, *Commission v. Italy* [1999] ECR I–1169.     [45] [1985] OJ L175/40.
[46] Case C–392/96, *Commission v. Ireland* [1999] ECR I–5901.

was therefore entitled to rely on evidence gleaned from complaints which had not yet been investigated.[47]

On the principal question, the Court recalled its judgment in *Kraaijeveld*[48] to the effect that the Member State's discretion to establish criteria or thresholds for Annex II projects was limited by the underlying obligation of Article 2(1) to ensure that projects likely to have significant effects on the environment are subject to an assessment. A Member State could not therefore set criteria or thresholds based solely on the size of the project without taking their nature and location into consideration:

[even] a small-scale project can have significant effects on the environment if it is in a location where the [listed] environmental factors . . . are sensitive to the slightest alteration . . . a project is likely to have significant effects where, by reason of its nature, there is a risk that it will cause a substantial or irreversible change in those environmental factors, irrespective of its size.

The Court rejected Ireland's claim that it was unnecessary to assess projects involving deforestation, land reclamation, and peat extraction, as the areas concerned were protected under other legislation, notably the Habitats Directive.[49] It also upheld the Commission's complaint that the Irish provisions did not take account of the cumulative effect of projects. No project for peat extraction, for example, had ever been subject to an assessment, despite the mechanization and intensification of the process 'resulting in the unremitting loss of areas of bog of nature conservation importance'. The same was true of land reclamation projects in the Burren. The only crumb of comfort for Ireland was the Court's finding that the Commission had not shown that sheep farming as practised there constituted a project within the meaning of the Directive.[50]

The practice of excluding entire classes of Annex II projects was also condemned in *WWF v. Bozen*,[51] decided a week before the former case against Ireland. This dispute arose from the omission of the Italian authorities to carry out an impact assessment on a project, which had been approved by a law of the Autonomous Province, to transform a military airfield near Bolzano into a commercial airport. On the principal question of the exclusion of classes of projects, the Court relied on existing case law to the effect that the criteria and thresholds did not allow exemption in advance of entire classes of projects 'unless all projects excluded could, when viewed as a whole, be regarded as not being likely to have significant effects on the environment'. On the other hand, the Court held that Member States were entitled to determine whether or not

[47] In fact, the Court cited a number of examples of such harmful effects (see paras. 78 and 80).
[48] Case C–72/95, *Aannemersbedryj P. K. Kraaijeveld BV and others* v. *Gedeputeerde Staten van Zuid-Holland* [1996] ECR I–5403; see also Case C–301/95, *Commission* v. *Germany* [1998] ECR I–6135.
[49] Dir. 92/43/EEC, see n. 19 above.
[50] Ireland had argued that 'it would be absurd to suggest that a farmer is obliged to seek prior consent whenever he wants to increase the number of sheep able to graze on a piece of land'.
[51] Case C–435/97, *World Wildlife Fund (WWF) and others* v. *Autonome Provinz Bozen and others* [1999] ECR I–5613.

a project required an assessment on the basis of an individual evaluation thereof, rather than by fixing criteria or threshold, though once again such an individual evaluation was subject to the overriding obligations arising from Article 2(1). In such circumstances, it fell to the national court to review the authorities' decision on the significance of the effects of the project on the environment. Similarly, while recognizing that Member States enjoy a certain discretion as to the procedure they use for impact assessment, the Court was adamant that any alternative procedure respect the requirements laid down in Articles 3 and 5 to 10 of the Directive. The national authorities sought to rely on the exceptions in respect of 'projects serving national defence purposes' and projects whose details are set out in national legislation allowed by Article 1(4) and (5), respectively. The Court pointed out that, as an exception, the military exclusion must be interpreted restrictively; the restructuring project was not one which served principally military purposes, even if the airport could also be used for such purposes. The exception allowed by Article 1(5) only applied 'where the details of the project [are] adopted by a specific legislative act', rather than in a separate administrative measure, and 'where the objectives of the Directive, including that of supplying information, [are] achieved through the legislative process'. In responding to a question on the enforcement by national courts of the obligations arising for Member States, from Articles 4(2) and 2(1), the Court repeated its statement in *Kraaijeveld*[52] that:

if [Member State] discretion [under Article 4(2)] has been exceeded and the national provisions must therefore be set aside on that account, it is for the authorities of the Member State . . . to take all the general or particular measures necessary to ensure that projects are examined in order to determine whether they are likely to have significant effects on the environment and, if so, to ensure that they are subject to an impact assessment.

Portugal was condemned for failing to apply its 1990 implementing provisions to projects in respect of which the approval procedure was already under way on the date from which its obligation to apply the Directive came into effect, 3 July 1988.[53] The defendant Member State was not allowed to rely on either the rule against retrospective legislation, as the developers had acquired no vested interest in projects not yet approved, or on the paucity of applications concerned.

### ii. Access to Environmental Information

The Court's judgment in Case C–217/97[54] completed the job started in *Mecklenburg*[55] in 1998, of clarifying the extent to which Germany had failed to transpose Directive 90/313/EEC on the Freedom of Access to Information on the Environment.[56] The Commission's charge that Germany had excluded its

---

[52] See n. 48 above.    [53] Case C–150/97, *Commission* v. *Portugal* [1999] ECR I–0259.
[54] Case C–217/97, *Commission* v. *Germany* [1999] ECR I–5087.
[55] Case C–321/96, *Wilhelm Mecklenburg* v. *Kreis Pinneberg* [1998] ECR I–3809; see K. Bradley, 'Case Law of the European Court of Justice' ch. VIII of the Current Survey Section (1998) 1 *Yearbook of European Environmental Law*, 441 and 453.
[56] [1990] OJ L158/56.

courts from the authorities which were obliged to supply such information was rejected, as the Commission had failed to prove that the courts come within the scope of such authorities as defined in Articles 2(b) and 3(2) of the Directive. The excessive scope of the exclusion in German law for 'administrative proceedings' had, on the other hand, already been established in *Mecklenburg,* and was not contested in this case. Germany's failure clearly to provide for the partial supply of information was condemned as not permitting potential applicants to know the full extent of their rights, and to rely on them in the national courts. On the most contentious issue, the interpretation of the expression used in Article 5, 'reasonable cost' for supplying information, the Court adopted a particularly nuanced approach. Noting that 'the purpose of the Directive is to confer a right on individuals . . . without his or her having to prove an interest', it held that the Directive 'does not authorize Member States to pass on to those seeking information the entire amount of the costs, in particular indirect ones, actually incurred for the State budget in conducting an information search'. The cost must therefore be 'reasonable' from the perspective of the applicant rather than necessarily from that of the state, which may be two very different things. However, once again, the Commission failed as it had not established that the German legislation did not properly transpose Article 5. The question of possible breaches of this provision in practice was not before the Court in these proceedings. Finally, the Court held that Germany was not entitled to impose a charge in respect of an application where no information had been supplied.

### G. MISCELLANEOUS

#### i. The Legal Basis of Environmental Legislation

The Court's judgment in the *Forestry Protection* cases[57] provides a useful overview of the state of the case law on the choice of the legal basis for normative measures which have both an environmental element and elements from other areas of regulation which has given rise to such problems in the past.[58] The European Parliament (EP) had challenged the decision of the Council to base on Article [37] EC alone two regulations concerning the protection of forests against, respectively, atmospheric pollution and fire. In its view, the measures were specifically concerned with the environment, and were only marginally concerned with agricultural production. The Council contended that the regulations were part of its forestry strategy and hence concerned agricultural structures, and that agricultural provisions enjoy priority over those concerning the establishment of the internal market. For its part, the Commission, intervening in support of the Council, argued that trees were

---

[57] Joined Cases C–164/97 and 165/97, *European Parliament* v. *Council* [1999] ECR I–1139.
[58] In its didactic enthusiasm, the Court cited the Plant Protection Products Directive as a measure which must be based on Art. 175 EC (para. 15), rather overlooking the fact that the Directive in question was in fact based on Art. 37 EC.

agricultural products, though the Council had expressly conceded that this was not the case.

The Court started by observing that the aims of the measures were partly agricultural, as protecting the productive potential of agricultural, and partly specifically environmental, as their primary objective is 'to maintain and monitor forest ecosystems'. It rejected the view that agricultural policy provisions had any priority over those on environmental policy, and concluded that any consequences the measures had on the functioning of agriculture were merely 'incidental to the primary aim of . . . the protection of forests'. A brief examination of the customs nomenclature was sufficient to reject the Commission's slightly far-fetched attempt to classify trees as 'agricultural products'.

## ii. Ecological Taxes

The compatibility with the Community's excise duty rules of a national environmental protection tax on domestic commercial aviation was examined in *Braathens*.[59] Directive 92/81/EEC on the Harmonization of the Structures of Excise Duties on Mineral Oils[60] required Member States to exempt from such duty fuel oils used in commercial aviation. A 1988 Swedish law charged a tax on domestic commercial flights, the amount of which depended partly on the basis of the amount of fuel consumed, and partly on the amount of hydrocarbons and nitric oxide emitted, in each case in accordance with averages calculated on the basis of data produced by the civil aviation authority. The Swedish tax authorities argued that as the tax was designed to protect the environment and was charged, not directly on fuel consumption, but on polluting emissions, the excise duty provisions were inapplicable. The Court did not accept this rather subtle, not to say sophistical, argument:

there is a direct and inseverable link between fuel consumption and polluting substances . . . emitted in the course of such consumption, so that the tax at issue . . . must be regarded as [being] levied on consumption of the fuel itself.

## iii. Public Health Derogations from Community Rules

The right of a Member State to rely upon the failure of an institution to comply with its Treaty obligations to defeat the direct effect of an unimplemented provision of a public health Directive was at issue in *Kortas*.[61] The Court was asked to clarify whether the possibility for a Member State to obtain a derogation under Article 95(4) EC could defeat such direct effect, where the Commission had simply failed to reply to Sweden's request for authorization to apply its national legislation. Under the heading of admissibility, the Court dealt in a single sentence with the issue—much debated at the time of the Single European Act (SEA)—whether the benefit of the derogation was restricted to a Member State which had voted against the harmonizing measure:

---

[59] Case C–346/97, *Braathens Severige AB* v. *Riksstatteverket* [1999] ECR I–3419.
[60] [1992] OJ L 316/12.
[61] Case C–319/97, *Criminal Proceedings against Antoine Kortas* [1999] ECR I–3143.

there is nothing in the wording of Article [95(4) EC] to suggest that a State which had joined the European Union after the adoption of a particular directive may not rely on that provision vis-à-vis that Directive.

On the principal question, the Court held that unimplemented provisions of directives may have direct effect if unconditional and sufficiently precise:

[it] is not decisive . . . that its legal basis allows a Member State to apply to the Commission for a derogation from its implementation . . . [the] general potential for a directive to have direct effect is wholly unrelated to its legal basis, depending instead on [its] intrinsic characteristics.

Nor does this provision allow a Member State to apply national provisions before a derogation has been accorded. The Court was unwilling to interpret into the EC Treaty any particular deadline for the Commission to act, and found support for this view in the express stipulation of a six-month deadline in accordance with Article 95(6) EC, inserted by the Treaty of Amsterdam, though recognizing that the Commission is under a duty to act diligently and 'examine as quickly as possible the provisions of national law submitted to it'. The evident failings of the Commission in this regard could not be allowed to affect the rights of individuals under the Directive. Though heavily criticized at the time of its adoption by some commentators,[62] this derogation continues to play a rather limited role in Community law.

The practical difficulties and cost to the public of preventing the illegal use of a veterinary pharmaceutical product, and need to protect consumer confidence, were held to be sufficient to justify a near-total Community ban on its use, despite its proven therapeutic qualities in *Boehringer Ingelheim Vetmedica*.[63] The Court of First Instance (CFI) was not convinced that the establishment of controls would be sufficient to prevent misuse of the product, clenbuterol, by unscrupulous farmers.

---

[62] In particular P. Pescatore, Some Critical Remarks on the 'Single European Act' pp 9–10 (1987) 24 *Common Market Law Review* 9.

[63] Joined Cases T–125/96 and T–152/96, *Boehringer Ingelheim Vetmedica GmbH and others* v. *Council and Commission* [1999] ECR II–3427.

# Environmental Law in the Member States

## I. Austria

KARL WEBER*

### A. INTRODUCTION

In 1999 there were no far-reaching reforms or developments in Austrian environmental law. The reforms and developments that *did* occur were partly inspired or even necessitated by European Community (EC) environmental law. Furthermore, they were inspired by cautious efforts to improve environmental standards without burdening the economy with the costs thereof. Although 1999 was not truly a period of stagnation, eagerness to reform was nevertheless low, in particular at the federal level. More successful reforms were undertaken by the individual *Länder* (states), and within the public administration. In short, 1999 may be characterized as a phase of observation regarding the effectiveness of earlier reform initiatives. The same may be said in respect of the case law of the Constitutional Court and the Administrative Court, which had to review the practical implications of such earlier reforms.

The development of Austrian environmental law is typically frustrated by the somewhat antiquated and complex political and legislative structure under the Austrian Constitution. A proper understanding of the developments in Austrian environmental law, in part influenced by EC environmental legislation, therefore requires some general knowledge of the Austrian constitutional system, and its political framework.[1] The most significant obstacle to the progress in efficiency in environmental legislation and policy is the rather obscure, and extremely complicated system of allocation of competences in the federal structure.[2] This system was established under the 1867 Constitutional Law of the Austro-Hungarian Monarchy: the 'December-Constitution'.[3] It is based on the historical structure of the ministries of the central royal government, and their relationship with the autonomous authorities in the states which have the legal status of provinces. Following the

---

* Professor, University of Innsbruck, Innsbruck, Austria.
[1] See also K. Weber, 'Austria' (1998) 1 *Yearbook of European Environmental Law*, 459.

[2] See e.g. P. Pernthaler, *Raumordnung und Verfassung*, vol. 3 (Vienna: Braumüller-Universitätsverlag, 1990), 513–50; P. Pernthaler, *Kompetenzverteilung in der Krise* (Vienna: Braumüller-Universitätsverlag, 1989); M. Kind, *Umweltschutz durch Verfassungsrecht* (Vienna-New York: Springer-Verlag, 1994), 9–163; K. Weber, 'Public Environmental Law in Austria' in R. Seerden and M. Heldeweg (eds.), *Comparative Environmental Law in Europe: An Introduction to Public Environmental Law in the EU Member-States* (Antwerp-Apeldoorn: MAKLU, 1996), 8–11.

[3] RGBl 1867/141–5.

confirmation of this problematic system in the Federal Constitution of 1920, the system for allocation of competences has been reformed approximately ninety times.[4] Until fifteen years ago, environmental protection had not yet been clearly defined as a state function. Therefore, the topic was not addressed in the system for the allocation of competences.

Competences are formulated mostly as 'matters', which appear to have little in common with the current understanding of state functions, making environmental protection a *Querschnittsmaterie* ('cross-section-matter'), falling within the scope of several areas of competences exercised by the *Bund* Federation and by the *Länder* (states).

The system for the allocation of competences is characterized by a combination of the enumeration method and the provision of general clauses. The competence of the Federation is founded upon the Federal Constitution, whereas the competences of the states is based on the general clauses of Article 15 sub 1 B-VG.[5]

The Austrian Constitutional Court interprets the provisions of the Federal Constitution by referring to the allocation of competences according to a historical method of interpretation: the *Versteinerungstheorie.*[6] The notion of 'allocating competences' is thus deemed currently to have the same meaning as it had at the time it was inserted in the Federal Constitution. The majority of competences date back to times when environmental protection was not a specific topic of legislation.

The characterization of environmental protection as a cross-section matter may be explained by the following: specific measures of environmental protection form part of different spheres of competences, *inter alia*, water laws, trade and industry regulations, traffic laws, etc. Specific modern targets of environmental policy, including climate change environmental impact assessment (EIA), air pollution, soil protection, and the ecological transformation of agriculture, are typically covered by several competences of the Federation and the states, rather than a single competence. Therefore, under the existing Constitution and the current federal policy, the translation of modern notions of environmental policy, *inter alia*, of EC law, into Austrian legislation is rather complicated. Due to the traditionally weak position of the states in terms of allocated competence,[7] they are very reluctant to cede

---

[4] See J. Werndl, *Die Kompetenzverteilung zwischen Bund und Ländern: Ihre Ausgangslage, Entwicklung und Bedeutungsverschiebung auf der Grundlage des Bundes-Verfassungsgesetzes von 1920* (Vienna: Braumüller-Universitätsverlag, 1984), 115–21.

[5] Art. 15 sub 1 B-VG reads: 'In so far as a matter is not expressly transferred by the Federal Constitution to the legislation or execution of the Federation, it remains in the independent competence of the *Länder*.'

[6] See B. C. Funk, *Das System der bundesstaatlichen Kompetenzverteilung im Lichte der Verfassungsrechtsprechung* (Vienna: Braumüller-Universitätsverlag, 1980), 69–77; P. Pernthaler, *Kompetenzverteilung in der Krise*, n. 2 above, 79–83; E. Wiederin, 'Anmerkungen zur Versteinerungstheorie', in H. Haller, C. Kopetzki, and R. Novak *et al.* (eds.), *Staat und Recht: Festschrift für Günther Winkler* (Vienna-New York: Springer-Verlag, 1997), 1231–72.

[7] See A. Gamper, 'Österreich—Das Paradoxon des zentralistischen Bundesstaates', in *Europäisches Zentrum für Föderalismus-Forschung Tübingen: Jahrbuch des Föderalismus 2000* (Baden-Baden: Nomos Verlagsgesellschaft, 2000), 251–65.

competences. Although Article 15a B-VG includes an authorization for the conclusion of federal treaties between the Federation and the states, because of the requirement to transform such treaties into separate legal acts of the Federation and the states, very little use has been made of this system in the field of environmental protection.[8]

Allocation problems also exist within the sphere of the Federation, since the allocation of competences to the ministries follows the federal allocation of competences. Consequently, many modern environmental protection measures fall within the scope of the competences of various ministries, leading to many coordination problems. In fact, this is not a problem specific to the Constitution, but rather of the political system in general. In the last fifty years there have always been coalition governments, with the exception of two legislative periods.[9] The political parties of these coalition governments divide the ministries according to the priorities of party politics. The consequence is a noticeable 'resort-egoism', which is particularly evident in the lack of cooperation between ministries of different 'colours', forming a significant obstacle to reform.

During 1998 and 1999, Austria was governed by the 'grand coalition' between the Social Democratic Party (SPÖ) and the Conservative Peoples Party (ÖVP), which held a two-thirds majority, creating the opportunity for reform of the federal constitution. However, given the states' veto-power in constitutional reforms concerning their competence, negotiations are not only required between the coalition parties, but also between the Federation and the states.[10] Given the strong influence of party politics in Austrian federalism,[11] political problems between coalition partners have traditionally blocked necessary reforms in the allocation of competence in these matters.[12]

In 1999 no progress was made towards the overdue general reform of the Federal Constitution,[13] including a fundamental reform of the allocation of competences by formulating competence in terms of state functions.

The most vital part of Austrian environmental legislation consists of administrative law, forming a dense and complex network of heterogeneous rules of

[8] See K. Weber, 'Umweltschutz im Spannungsfeld von Bundes- und Landesrecht', in S. Morscher, P. Pernthaler, and N. Wimmer (eds.), *Recht als Aufgabe und Verantwortung: Festschrift Hans R. Klecatsky zum 70. Geburtstag* (Vienna: Manzsche Verlags- und Universitätsbuchhandlung, 1990), 282–4.

[9] See A. Pelinka, *Austria: Out of the Shadow of the Past* (Boulder-Oxford: Westview Press, 1998), 23–30; W. C. Müller, 'Regierung und Kabinettsystem', in H. Dachs, P. Gerlich, and H. Gottweis *et al.* (eds.), *Handbuch des politischen Systems Österreichs* (Vienna: Manzsche Verlags- und Universitätsbuchhandlung, 1997), 123.

[10] Art. 44 sub 2 B-VG.

[11] See K. R. Luther, 'Bund-Länder-Beziehungen: Formal- und Realverfassung', in Dachs, Gerlich, and Gottweis *et al.* (eds.), n. 9 above, 816–26.

[12] See Institut für Föderalismusforschung, *24. Bericht über die Lage des Föderalismus in Österreich, 1999* (Vienna: Braumüller Universitätsverlag, 2000).

[13] See P. Pernthaler and P. Bundschuh, *Hat die Österreichische Bundesstaatsreform noch eine Zukunft?*, *Sozialwissenschaftliche Studienarbeit Nr. 114* (Vienna: Sozialwissenschaftliche Arbeitsgemeinschaft, 1998); P. Pernthaler (ed.), *Materialien zur Bundesstaatsreform* (Innsbruck: Institut für Föderalismusforschung, 1998).

the Federation and the states. Therefore, to provide a systematic description of Austrian environmental law would be a very difficult task.[14] The origin of these complexities lies in the constitutional principle of the strictly binding public administration. According to Article 18 sub 1 B-VG, the entire public administration may be exercised only on the basis of the law. The existence of a formally enacted law is a *conditio sine qua non* for any authoritative act. Moreover, the Constitutional Court consistently demands precisely determined laws. Given the necessarily dynamic nature of environmental legislation, they require regular amendments, even if these amendments merely address issues of a modest importance. According to the Austrian Constitution, legislation in the form of rules and principles is virtually impossible,[15] although some relief is granted by Article 18 sub 2 B-VG, which provides that the public administration may issue *Verordnungen* (general orders), on the basis and within the limits of existing laws. These general orders form a significant part of the Austrian environmental regulation, in particular in the area of transposition of EC secondary laws. In addition to their reference to existing laws, general orders also require a certain standard of casuistry, to form the basis of administrative acts. The constitutional system is strictly supervised by the Constitutional Court and the Administrative Court. These Supreme Courts tolerate some relaxation in the rule that the public administration is strictly bound by law in the areas of planning law, and in some parts of business law.[16]

The most important political reason for the very modest developments in Austrian environmental law in 1999 was the fact that this was a year of political elections, involving the elections for the *Nationalrat* (federal parliament) and for some *Landtage* (state parliament). The federal parliamentary elections of 3 October 1999 came long before its regular term, and the political campaigns brought legislation to a standstill by summertime. Only such laws as were absolutely necessary were passed by the parliament after the summer, not including environmental protection. In addition, this was also only a minor theme in the political campaigns, with the exception of the 'Green' Party. Issues such as the employment outlook, the enlargement of the EU, the future of the pension system, budgetary economics, questions of immigration, and other economic-orientated themes dominated the election campaign, while similarly, in the scale of priorities of the Austrian voters, concern about the sustained protection of environment was not pronounced. Moreover, the existing trend of industry defending itself against expensive measures of environmental protection increased significantly as compared to previous years.

---

[14] In fact, there is no truly comprehensive academic publication on Austrian environmental law. Cf. M. Kind, *Umweltrecht* (Vienna: Verlag Österreich, 1999), which is, respectfully, merely a compilation of selected environmental legal acts.

[15] See B. C. Funk, 'Regeln und Prinzipien in Teilsystemen des Rechts, dargestellt am Beispiel des Staats- und Verwaltungsrechts', in B. Schilcher, P. Koller, and B. C. Funk (eds.), *Regeln, Prinzipien und Elemente im System des Rechts* (Vienna: Verlag Österreich, 2000), 259–66.

[16] See K. Korinek and M. Holoubek, *Grundlagen Staatlicher Privatwirtschaftsverwaltung* (Graz: Leykam Verlag, 1993), 59–85.

The mainstream in the political discussion argued that measures of environmental protection, including ecological reform of the tax system, could only be realized through EC legislation, or at least on the basis of harmonization with other EC Member States.

In addition to these problems, some other characteristics of the Austrian political system may present obstacles to the development of environmental policy. A good example is the so-called *Sozialpartnerschaft* (social partnership) in Austrian politics, whereby all important political decisions are taken in harmony with the government, employers' associations, trade unions, and the agricultural associations.[17] In this system, economic interests are the main themes, whereas the environment is left without any lobby. While it is true that non-governmental organizations (NGOs) act self-confidently and successfully in individual projects, on the whole they fail to provide effective opposition to the system of coordinated and organized economic interests.

### B. AIR POLLUTION

Article 10 sub 1 n 12 B-VG divides the competence for air pollution into two special (sub)competences. The general competence delegates the power to lay down regulations on air pollution to the Federation, complemented by special 'smog alarm powers'.[18] When air pollution has reached critical values, the Federation is empowered to take all necessary measures to reduce it.[19] The states, in turn, are empowered to lay down regulations on air pollution in so far as they concern private heating systems. Prior to this division of competences, which came into force in 1990, air cleaning was within the general competence of the states,[20] while the Federation was only authorized to lay down regulations on air pollution within its areas of special competence, *inter alia*, industrial affairs, motor transport, mining, and forestry. As a consequence of this splintering of competences, the law on air pollution was also splintered, creating a complex system, which still exists.[21] The laws of the states were partially transformed into laws of the Federation, in so far as they did not concern private heating systems. The law on air pollution of the Federation has not yet been codified, and remains fragmented over many different provisions in different laws and general orders (*Verordnungen*), mostly concerning definitions of critical values.

---

[17] See E. Talos, 'Kooperation—Konzentrierung—politische Regulierung', in Dachs, Gerlich, and Gottweis *et al.* (eds.), n. 9 above, 432–51.

[18] See S. Schwarzer, *Die neuen Luftreinhaltungskompetenzen des Bundes, Österreichische Zeitschrift für Wirtschaftsrecht* (Vienna: ÖZW, 1989), 47–54.

[19] See B. C. Funk, 'Die Zuständigkeit des Bundes zur Abwehr von gefährlichen Umweltbelastungen. Verfassungsrechtliche Konstruktionsschwächen im Umweltrecht' (1986) 11 *Zeitschrift für Verwaltung*, 525–35; H. P. Rill, 'Der "Immissionsgrenzwerte"-Kompetenztatbestand in Art. 10 Abs 1 Z 12 B-VG idF der B-VGN 1983 BGBl 175' (1984) 9 *Zeitschrift für Verwaltung*, 225–39.

[20] Art. 15 sub 1 B-VG.

[21] See S. Schwarzer, *Österreichisches Luftreinhaltungsrecht* (Vienna: Orac Wirtschaftsverlag, 1987).

The 1997 Emission Protection Law-Air (IG-L)[22] provided the basis for a comprehensive planning of emission protections. The Measurement-Concept-Emission-Protection-Law-Air (*Messkonzept IG-L*),[23] which is a general order (*Verordnung*), lays down the necessary measuring practices. In 1999 no concrete acts were adopted, although the authorities were preparing a comprehensive plan to this end. Evidently, the law on air protection is still fragmented. A large number of general orders, according to plant, for improving the quality of the air remains in force. In 1999 this number was raised by another general order, concerning combustion engines,[24] laid down in accordance with sections 69 and 71 *Gewerbeordnung*.[25] The order transposes into the Austrian legal order Directive 97/68/EC on Measures against the Emission of Gaseous and Particulate Pollutants from Internal Combustion Engines to be installed in Non-Road Mobile Machinery,[26] and lays down detailed rules on type standardization and type approval of combustion engines intended for the installation in mobile engines and equipment. Exempted from this regulation are combustion engines for military and motor vehicles. This general order constitutes one more piece in the puzzle of the law of industrial air pollution.

The air cleaning law of the states lays down regulations to reduce emissions from private heating systems. The states negotiated treaties to coordinate technical standards. The last adaptation was made by an amendment to the states' treaty on protection from small heating systems.[27] Consequently, the states adapted their laws and general orders.

The most significant reform of the air pollution law of the states is the heating law of Carinthia.[28] It implements Directive 78/170/EEC,[29] Directive 92/42/EEC,[30] and Directive 93/76/EEC.[31] This law is part of Austria's efforts in climate policy by improving the protection against air pollution and the reduction of energy use. It entered into force in part on 1 October 1998, and in part on 25 May 1999. The law lays down regulations for the approval of (private) heating systems, including strict limit values for emissions and efficiency. For the future, the state's government is authorized to amend the limit values on the basis of new scientific data. Private heating systems are to be monitored periodically. Furthermore, building laws and general acts on building techniques may support such efforts in reducing the supply of heating. The general acts in building techniques (*Bautechnikverordnungen*) of the states make

---

[22] *Immissionsschutzgesetz-Luft*, BGBl I 1997/115.

[23] *Verordnung über das Messkonzept zum Immissionsschutzgesetz-Luft*, BGBl II 1998/358.

[24] *Verbrennungsmotorenverordnung*, BGBl II 1999/185, see (1999) 6 *Recht der Umwelt* 4, 166.

[25] BGBl 1994/194, last amended by BGBl I 1999/59.          [26] [1998] OJ L059/1.

[27] *Ländervereinbarung über Schutzmassnahmen betreffend Kleinfeuerungen*. See (1995) 2 *Recht der Umwelt*, 148 and 195; (1998) 5 *Recht der Umwelt*, 205.

[28] *Kärntner Heizungsanlagengesetz*, LGBl 1998/63.

[29] Dir. 78/170/EEC on the Performance of Heat Generators for Space Heating and the Production of Hot-Water in New or Existing Non-Industrial Buildings and on the Insulation of Heat and Domestic Hot-Water Distribution in New Non-Industrial Buildings, [1978] OJ L052/32.

[30] Dir. 92/42/EEC on Efficiency Requirements for New Hot-Water Boilers Fired with Liquid or Gaseous Fuels, [1992] OJ L167/17.

[31] Dir. 93/76/EEC to Limit Carbon Dioxide Emissions by Improving Energy Efficiency (SAVE), [1993] OJ L 237/28.

increasing demands on building and insulation materials, Upper Austria[32] tightening the demands in the direction of ecological building methods. Additionally, subsidies for buildings (*Wohnbauförderung*) increasingly demand reductions in energy consumption and reductions in the emissions of heating systems.[33] The guidelines of these subsidies are reformed continuously.[34]

### C. BIOTECHNOLOGY

The *Genmaisverbotsverordnung*[35] prohibits the marketing of a special sort of genetically modified corn, which was registered in France and permitted by the European Commission. Application of the available exceptions to this prohibition depends upon a guarantee that no cultivation will take place in the open air.

### D. CHEMICALS

The *Chemikaliengesetz*[36] regulates the production and distribution of poisonous chemicals. In March 1999 a general order on the prohibition of poisonous chemicals entered into force,[37] prohibiting certain carcinogenic substances, and substances affecting the genotype or human reproduction. A new general order lays down regulations on the registration of poisonous chemicals introduced for the first time, without being registered in Austria.[38] Furthermore, a general order on informing authorities about highly poisonous or corrosive substances entered into force,[39] providing that undertakers must inform the federal Environmental Office (*Umweltbundesamt*) of the first time these substances are put into circulation. The *Umweltbundesamt* subsequently passes this information on to the *Vergiftungszentrale* in the federal Institute of Health Affairs (*Bundesinstitut für Gesundheitswesen*). These requirements are supplemented by special duties regarding information on intoxication.

### E. NATURE CONSERVATION

The states' nature conservation laws are based on the general clause of Article 15 sub 1 B-VG, and lay down regulations for the protection of the landscape, wild animals, and plants, and the basis of their ecological existence.[40] In 1999 only the nature conservation law of Upper Austria changed more than

---

[32] *Oberösterreichische Bautechnikverordnung*, LGBl 1999/59.

[33] See H. Abele, M. Cerveny, S. Schleicher, and K. Weber (eds.), *Reform der Wohnbauförderung* (Vienna: Service Fachverlag, 2000).

[34] The guidelines are not published in official bulletins.     [35] BGBl II 1999/175.

[36] BGBl I 1997/53.

[37] *Verordnung über das Verbot gefährlicher Chemikalien*, BGBl II 1998/461.

[38] *Giftliste-Meldeverordnung*, BGBl II 1999/129.

[39] *Gift-Informationsverordnung*, BGBl II 1999/137.

[40] See P. Bussjäger, *Die Naturschutzkompetenzen der Österreichischen Bundesländer* (Vienna: Braumüller-Universitätsverlag, 1995), 46–110.

marginally.[41] The requirement for permits and denouncements were vastly changed in 1999, as on the basis of experience with the administration of the law, new categories of permits were laid down, *inter alia*, for quarries for the exploitation of broken stone. Yet, aspects of nature conservation are still not covered by the laws regulating mining activities.[42] However, during the last few years, in Upper Austria, quarries exploitation has been booming, leading to state legislation efforts to gain control over this development by reforming the relevant nature conservation law.

In Upper Austria, a general act on non-sited plants[43] regulates the release of genetically modified plants, defined as non-sited plants. All non-sited plants may be planted outside buildings only with a permit issued by the state government. Following EC legislation, it may be impossible to avoid the release of genetically modified plants generally through nature conservation laws.

The nature conservation law of Salzburg has been amended several times during the last few years, and was announced in 1999 as *Naturschutzgesetz 1999*,[44] being one of the most progressive nature conservation laws in Austria. Serious disturbances of the environment are only permitted under the act, in so far as a public interest is connected to the disturbance *and* in so far as additional compensation measures are adopted.

### F. WASTE

As a result of the allocation of competence in the Federal Constitution, legislation on the administration of dangerous waste is the responsibility of the Federation, whereas non-dangerous waste is regulated by the states.[45] The federal *Abfallwirtschaftsgesetz* 1990[46] was reformed by the end of 1998.[47] Many regulations changed by incorporating the experiences of the administration. The amendment introduces new definitions of problematical substances (*Problemstoff*), of the owner of waste, and of the collector of waste, and the clarifications of the previously confusing definitions of waste, as given by the Administrative Court, have now been incorporated in the law. The regulation of waste mandataries (*Abfallbeauftragte*) in enterprises was clarified and simplified, while the regulation of liability was relaxed.

The provisions on the transport of waste and of the exploitation of dumps for harmless waste have become less bureaucratic. The relevant amendment laid down a prohibition on the incineration of dangerous waste outside permitted installations. Furthermore, it is forbidden to mix different categories of substances. In some states the waste laws were reformed.[48] The provisions on the collection of waste, of garbage, and of waste treatment have been adapted to practical demands.

[41] *Oberösterreich*: LGBl 1999/35; *Tirol*: LGBl 1999/8.
[42] *Mineralrohstoffgesetz*, BGBl I 1999/38.
[43] *Standortfremde Pflanzenverordnung*; LGBl 1999/47.     [44] *Salzburg*: LGBl 1999/73.
[45] Art. 10(1) Z 12 B-VG.                                    [46] BGBl 1990/325.
[47] BGBl 1998/151. See K. Weber, 'Austrian' (1998) 1 *Yearbook of European Environmental Law*, 461.
[48] *Kärnten:* LGBl 1999/14; *Salzburg*: LGBl 1999/35.

## G. WATER

An amendment of the *Wasserrechtsgesetz*[49] changed this law in several ways. In respect of the protection of groundwater, the amendment laid down general restrictions and prohibitions on the pouring of certain substances or sludge into the water. The minister of agriculture and environment is empowered to lay down a general order for permitting installations, whereby recourse to best available technologies can be permanently guaranteed.

Voralberg introduced a new state water law: the *Wasserversorgungsgesetz*,[50] which charges the communities with the task of taking precautions for water supply installations according to modern sanitary, hygienic, technical, and economic requirements, and according to the target of a sustained preservation of the drinking water supply.

An amendment to the Styrian Drain Law (*Steiermärkisches Kanalgesetz*) entered into force on 1 November 1998.[51] It holds that the drainage system must be organized according to ecological concerns. The state government may lay down general orders for sewage disposal planning.

## H. HORIZONTAL INSTRUMENTS

### i. Eco-label

Austrian law currently provides no legal basis for the award of eco-labels. Public and private institutions and organizations award eco-labels to persons and companies for activities in environmental protection. Eco-labels are not a priority within the environmental policy of the Federation.[52] The minister of environmental protection[53] awards certificates of honour to ecologically beneficial enterprises. Similar to eco-labels is the association of climate protection (*Klimaschutzbündnis*), which is open to communities that reach certain standards of climate policy, as *Klimaschutzgemeinden*. In cooperation with the states, local governments, private sponsors, and tourist organizations may award the *Umweltgütesiegel* to hotels and restaurants.

### ii. Access to Information

The *Umweltinformationsgesetz 1993*[54] implemented Directive 90/313/EEC on the Freedom of Access to Information on the Environment.[55] Its aim is to ensure free access to information on the environment for the general public. It includes data gathered by administrative authorities and lays down the duty to make information available, and the procedures to this end.

---

[49] BGBl I 1999/155.   [50] *Vorarlberg:* LGBl 1999/3.

[51] *Steiermärkisches Kanalgesetz*; LGBl 1998/82.

[52] See G. Schuster (ed.), *Das Österreichische Umweltzeichen* (Vienna: Österreichische Staatsdruckerei, 1992); B. Schwar, *Umweltzeichen und betrieblicher Umweltschutz* (Vienna: Verlag Österreich, 1999).

[53] *Bundesminister für Land- und Forstwirtschaft, Umwelt und Wasserwirtschaft.*

[54] BGBl 1993/495; see J. Hofmann, *Das Recht auf Umweltinformation* (Vienna: Wiener Universitätsverlag, 1995).

[55] [1990] OJ L158/56.

An amendment to the *Umweltinformationsgesetz* extends the range of authorities having such duties to inform.[56] Henceforth, police authorities (*Organe des öffentlichen Sicherheitsdienstes*) also incur such duties, in so far as they are charged with environmental tasks.

The replacement of the system of charging flat-rate fees for information where its dissemination incurs higher costs is not part of the amendment,[57] but plans exist for a system of flat-rate fees for all information. The relevant authorities are required to provide the requested information within eight weeks. The amendment replaces former exceptions from this period.

The states also have environmental information laws, albeit of varying quality. The laws of some states still do not completely transpose Directive 90/313/EEC on the Freedom of Access to Information on the Environment.[58] Styria, one of these states, laid down provisions on environmental information in the *Umweltschutzgesetz*,[59] making information available to the public in so far as it concerns the state's administration. In the case of information on waste, one can request information from the *Unabhängige Verwaltungssenat* (UVS). The state's government is to establish a catalogue of environmental data.

### iii. IPPC

Efforts to implement Directive 96/61/EC on Integrated Pollution Prevention and Control (IPPC Directive)[60] have so far not been successful. Small reforms were made by the *Gewerbeordnung*:[61] Some installations may now be applied for in a simplified procedure.[62] The failure to implement the IPPC Directive occurred as a result of differences of opinion within the coalition government, although there were some parliamentary initiatives in 1999.[63] The governing parties SPÖ and ÖVP agreed upon the fundamental characteristics of a uniform law concerning installations, but failed to agree on the detail relating to questions of sole responsibility and voluntary self-control by enterprises; the value limits for emissions; the concept of 'best-available techniques',[64] etc.

### iv. EIA

Discussions about a reform of the procedure for environmental impact assessment (EIA)[65] excited large differences of opinion in the coalition government during 1999. Although the parties agreed that a simplified procedure for EIA should be introduced, in addition to the ordinary procedure for the assessment of environmental effects, the lack of consensus on the details constituted

[56] BGBl I 1999/137.
[57] See K. Weber, 'Austria' (1999) 1 *Yearbook of European Environmental Law*, 462.
[58] [1990] OJ L158/56.    [59] *Steiermark*: LGBl 1999/15.    [60] [1996] OJ L257/26.
[61] BGBl I 1997/63.    [62] BGBl II 1998/265, 1999/19.
[63] See E. Schäfer, *Umwelt- und Anlagenrecht: Exposé für eine Kodifikation* (Vienna: Verlag Österreich, 2000), 37–45.
[64] Art. 2 n 11 IPPC-Directive, n. 43 above.
[65] *Umweltverträglichkeitsprüfungsgesetz*, BGBl 1993/697, 1996/773 (UVP-G); see W. Bergthaler, K. Weber, and J. Wimmer, *Die Umweltverträglichkeitsprüfung. Handbuch für Juristen und Sachverständige* (Vienna: Manzsche Verlags- und Universitätsbuchhandlung, 1998).

an obstacle to the adoption of a decision. The trade associations tried to use the reforms for softening the strict regulations of the UVP-G, while the SPÖ and the opposition parties demanded at least the maintenance of current standards. Ultimately, the project faltered.

## I. MISCELLANEOUS

### i. Eco-taxes

During 1999 ecological tax reform was not a theme of governmental policy. Although the 'Green' Party had fiercely demanded ecological tax reform, they were unsuccessful in their opposition. In addition, the discussion on ecological tax reform in Germany contributed to exclusion of this theme from the election campaign. The states of Salzburg, Tirol, and Vorarlberg introduced 'nature protection taxes' (*Naturschutzabgaben*) under their nature conservation laws.[66] For the exploitation of natural resources, *inter alia*, broken stone, water for energy installations, artificial snow, or the construction of ski-pistes, the operators must pay taxes. The revenues are used towards nature conservation projects.

### ii. Energy Policy

In 1999 most of the Austrian states introduced energy laws to implement the 1998 *Elektrizitätswirtschaftsorganisationsgesetz* (ElWOG).[67] Similar to the federal ElWOG, the energy laws of the states are primarily economic laws, rather than environmental protection laws.

Also in 1999 the states continued their efforts to reduce energy consumption, through the renovation of old buildings.[68] The practice of granting subsidies was improved while general acts on building techniques established the details to support such efforts in reducing energy consumption.

[66] See K. Weber, 'Entwicklungstendenzen und Trends im österreichischen Naturschutzrecht' (2000) 122 *Juristische Blätter* 12.

[67] BGBl I 1998/143, *Burgenland*: LGBl 1999/7; *Kärnten*: LGBl 1999/5; *Niederösterreich*: LGBl 7800-0; *Oberösterreich*: LGBl 1999/20; *Salzburg*: LGBl 1999/75; *Tirol*: LGBl 1999/9; *Vorarlberg*: LGBl 1999/6; *Wien*: LGBl 1999/37; see D. Pauger and H. Pichler, *Das Österreichische Elektrizitätsrecht* (Graz: Leykam Verlag, 2000).

[68] See M. Cerveny, 'Anreize für den Klimaschutz in der Wohnbauförderung der Bundesländer', in Abele, Cerveny, Schleicher, and Weber (eds.), n. 33 above, 63–72.

## II. Belgium

KURT DEKETELAERE and JAN VANHEULE*

### A. AIR POLLUTION

#### i. Brussels Capital Region

A Brussels Ordinance of 25 March 1999 regulates the quality of air in the region, by means of a programme with specific measures for the improvement of air quality.[1] It determines quality objectives in order to reduce or exclude harmful effects on the health of mankind and the environment. To this end, it prescribes, first, air quality assessment based on a range of methods and criteria, second, adequate information with respect to air quality and to ensure that people are informed, and finally, maintenance of air quality, in conformity with the quality standards set out in the Ordinance, and lacking such conformity, improvement thereof.

Existing legislation in this area has been elaborated and completed as follows during 1999.

A Royal decree of 3 February 1999[2] concerns the protection of the atmosphere against emissions of gases and particles by mobile machines not intended for road use, transposing into Belgian law Directive 97/68/EC on Measures against the Emission of Gaseous and Particulate Pollutants from Internal Combustion Engines to be Installed in Non-Road Mobile Machinery.[3] A decision of the Walloon Government of 25 March 1999 amends a decision of 9 December 1993 on air pollution caused by incineration of household waste.[4] A decision of the Brussels Regional Government amends the Royal decree of 29 December 1988 on the prevention and reduction of air pollution by asbestos, adding certain categories of works to the decree.[5] A Walloon decree of 17 December 1998[6] ratifies, for the Walloon region the CLRTAP[7] Protocol on the Control of Emissions of Nitrogen Oxides, which was adopted in Sofia on 31 October 1998. Two decisions of the Brussels Capital Government of 14 October 1999 amend the decision of the Brussels Government of 31 May 1991 concerning the reduction of air pollution caused by both existing and new installations for the combustion of household waste.[8]

* Kurt Deketelaere, Professor, Director Institute for Environmental and Energy Law, University of Leuven, Belgium. The author would like to thank Jan Vanheule, Research Associate, Institute for Environmental and Energy Law, University of Leuven.
[1] *Moniteur Belge*, 24 June 1999.      [2] Ibid., 31 Mar. 1999.      [3] [1998] OJ L59/1.
[4] *Moniteur Belge*, 21 Apr. 1999.      [5] Ibid., 9 July 1999.      [6] Ibid., 7 Jan. 1999.
[7] Convention on Long-Range Transboundary Air Pollution (CLRTAP), Geneva, 13 Nov. 1979.
[8] *Moniteur Belge*, 28 Oct. 1999.

B. CHEMICALS

*i. Federal Government*

A Law of 28 January 1999 regulates the quality of chemical substances in light of safety of workers at the workplace, by prescribing standards for the well-being of workers, to the suppliers of such substances. However, its Article 2 states that the law is neither intended to protect consumers, nor the environment.[9]

In respect of existing legislation, the following developments took place in 1999. A Royal decision of 14 December 1998 amends the Royal decree of 24 May 1982 on the placing on the market of substances that can be dangerous for man or the environment.[10] Following a European Court of Justice (ECJ) ruling, this decree transposed into Belgian, the most recent amendments and adaptations to technical progress of Directive 67/548/EEC on the Classification, Packaging and Labelling of Dangerous Substances.[11] The Royal decree of 11 January 1993 on dangerous preparations is amended by a Royal decree of 15 January 1999, transposing Directive 96/54/EC[12] Directive and 97/69/EC,[13] again adapting Directive 67/548/EEC.[14] A Royal decree of 9 February 1999 amends the Royal Decree of 16 April 1996 determining the duty on the collection and recycling of batteries, for the purpose of environmental taxes, which is currently set at 5BFr. per battery.[15] A decision of the Brussels Regional Government of 21 January 1999 establishes conditions for the exploitation of fuel stations, with particular attention to the protection of soil and groundwater.[16] An erratum to the annex of the *Moniteur Belge* of 17 December 1998, regarding classification and marketing of dangerous substances, was published on 19 May 1999.[17] A decision of the Walloon Government of 25 March 1999 contains provisions on the management and identification of PCBs and PCTs.[18] A decision of the Brussels Government of 4 March 1999 regulates the use of hexachlorine ethane.[19] A Royal decree of 1 July 1999 regulates the appointment of, and professional qualifications for, safety advisers for the transport of dangerous substances by road, railway, or internal waters.[20] A Royal decree of 7 December 1999 regulates the filling, distribution, and the labelling of bottles with fluid petrol.[21]

C. NATURE CONSERVATION

*i. Federal Government*

Following Flemish regional legislation to this effect,[22] a Federal law of 10 May 1999 gives legal force to the Protocol to amend the Convention on Wetlands of

---

9 *Moniteur Belge*, 14 Apr. 1999.     10 Ibid., 16 Jan. 1999.     11 [1967] OJ L196/1.
12 [1996] OJ L248/1.     13 [1997] OJ L343/19.
14 [1967] OJ B196/1; *Moniteur Belge*, 24 Feb. 1999.     15 Ibid., 27 Feb. 1999.
16 Ibid., 24 Mar. 1999.     17 Ibid., 19 May 1999.     18 Ibid., 22 May 1999.
19 Ibid., 24 June 1999.     20 Ibid., 13 July 1999.     21 Ibid., 29 Dec. 1999.
22 Flemish Region Decree of 14 July 1998, *Moniteur Belge*, 22 Aug. 1998.

International Importance, particularly Waterfowl Habitats,[23] and the amendments to the Convention adopted in Regina on 28 May 1987.[24]

### ii. Flemish Region

In case 18/99[25] of 10 February 1999, the *Arbitragehof* was asked to rule on the validity of certain provisions of the Flemish decree on nature conservation. An association of Flemish landowners had alleged that the existence of a prohibition on the use of pesticides in areas covered by the ecological network established under that Decree, constitutes a violation of the constitutional principle of equality, notwithstanding the existence of certain explicit exceptions to the prohibition. The court concluded, however, that in this case the distinction between land in general, and land for agricultural use was reasonable.

### iii. Walloon Region

Case 92/99[26] of 15 July 1999 concerned Article 59 of the law on nature conservation as implemented by the Walloon decree of 11 April 1984. A lower court judge referred to the *Arbitragehof* the question whether Article 59(2) and (3) were in conformity with the current regional competence in criminal matters. These provisions concern the probatory force of an official report, and the search of a house by a magistrate's order. The *Arbitragehof* ruled that the Walloon Region Government had exceeded its competence in this matter, since the competence to regulate the probatory force of official reports, and the search of a house by a magistrate's order, were only granted to the regions and communities by the 1993 State Reform. A Decision of the Flemish Government of 18 December 1998 amends the Royal decree of 9 September 1981 on the protection of birds in the Flemish Region.[27] It amends, *inter alia*, some provisions relating to the hunting and catching of wild birds. The Ministerial decree of 14 September 1981, executing the Royal decree, is amended by a Ministerial decree of 9 February 1999.[28] The decision of the Walloon Government of 2 April 1998 organizing the hunting examination was amended by a decision of 23 December 1998.[29] A number of nature reserves have been created in the Brussels Capital Region by a decision of 10 December 1998.[30] A decision of the Flemish Government of 1 December 1998 lists the conditions under which hunting areas can be combined, in order to become larger management areas, and the conditions under which this may be allowed.[31] Two errata to the decision, the first of which was still not correct, have been published.[32] A circular letter of the Flemish ministry of 10 November 1999 concerns, *inter alia*, landscape conservation, as regulated by the decision of the Flemish Government of 23 July 1998, implementing the decree on nature conservation and the natural environment of 21 October 1997.[33] The territory of some regional forest areas was amended by several

---

[23] Paris, 3 Dec. 1982.  [24] *Moniteur Belge*, 3 Sept. 1999.  [25] Ibid., 26 Feb. 1999.
[26] Ibid., 7 Sept. 1999.  [27] Ibid., 20 Jan. 1999.  [28] Ibid., 20 Feb. 1999.
[29] Ibid., 28 Jan. 1999.  [30] Ibid., 30 Jan. 1999.  [31] Ibid., 12 Feb. 1999.
[32] Ibid., 20 Feb. 1999 and 6 Mar. 1999.  [33] Ibid., 17 Feb. 1999.

decisions of the Walloon regional government of 4 February 1999.[34] A Walloon decree of 25 February 1999 amends the decree of 16 July 1985 on nature parks, amending, *inter alia,* the list of authorities with competency to create a nature park, and some provisions on the park management committee.[35] A decision of the Flemish Government of 9 March 1999 amends the decision of 22 July 1993 on access to, and occasional use of forests.[36] The Walloon Government has adopted several decisions establishing, or enlarging nature reserves in the region.[37] A decision of the Flemish environment minister establishes a nature reserve at the river Yser.[38] A Flemish ministerial decision of 2 March 1999 contains the planned course of action for the drafting of plans for nature conservation areas established in the Flemish decree on nature conservation of 21 October 1997.[39] A decision of the Flemish Government of 11 May 1999 holds minor amendments to the decision of 8 December 1998 on the recognition of regional landscapes.[40] A decision of the Walloon Government of 3 June 1999 protects a number of species of mollusks.[41] A ministerial decision of 3 September 1999 demarcates the expanding zones of recognized nature reserves. Chapter V of the decree on nature conservation and the natural environment establishes the basis for a territory-oriented policy, and provides for the creation of different categories of territories. These territories are to be placed within the Flemish Ecological Network, the Integral Network for Acquisition and Support, and various nature reserves.[42] A decision of 29 June 1999 of the Flemish Government establishes conditions for the recognition of nature reserves and nature associations controlling territories, and regulates subsidy policy.[43] Following two Royal decisions of 21 April 1999, several Belgian Federal woods and forests have been transferred to the jurisdiction of the Walloon Region.[44] A decision of the Flemish Government of 26 November 1999 determines the rules concerning compensation for deforestation, or withdrawal of the prohibition on deforestation.[45] A decision of the Walloon Government of 14 December 1999 amends the decision of 14 July 1994 concerning the protection of birds in the Walloon region.[46]

*iv. Noise*

A Walloon decree of 1 April 1999, amending the law of 18 July 1973 on tackling noise pollution, deals with noise levels in the vicinity of airports.[47] Article 1 of the decree empowers the Walloon Regional Government to take measures to protect the population against noise pollution.[48]

---

[34] *Moniteur Belge,* 26 Feb. 1999.        [35] Ibid., 6 Mar. 1999.        [36] Ibid., 20 Mar. 1999.
[37] Ibid., 8 Apr. 1999.        [38] Ibid., 9 Apr. 1999.        [39] Ibid., 26 May 1999.
[40] Ibid., 24 June 1999.        [41] Ibid., 17 July 1999.        [42] Ibid., 17 Sept. 1999.
[43] Ibid., 21 Sept. 1999.        [44] Ibid., 17 Sept. 1999.        [45] Ibid., 11 Dec. 1999.
[46] Ibid., 31 Dec. 1999.
[47] Ibid., 10 July 1999 for other decisions relating to airport noise levels.
[48] Ibid., 28 Apr. 1999.

## v. Nuclear Accidents

A law of 5 June 1998 gives legal force to the Convention on the early notification of a nuclear accident, Vienna, 26 September 1986.[49]

The law on budgetary and other provisions of 15 January 1999 contains a chapter on the Federal Agency for Nuclear Control, amending the law of 15 April 1994. A number of goods, rights, and obligations of the state are transferred to the agency.[50]

## vi. Product Norms

A Royal decree of 25 March 1999 contains product norms for packaging materials, and more specifically regulates the maximum content of lead, cadmium, mercury, and chromium in those materials.[51]

## vii. Spatial Planning, Construction, and Town Planning

(a) Federal Government
A Royal decree of 3 May 1999 regulates temporary or mobile construction sites. It contains provisions on the coordination, safety, and organization of construction sites.[52]

(b) Flemish Region
A new Flemish decree on spatial planning was adopted on 18 May 1999. It regulates administrative organization, planning procedures, the organization of construction permits, transparency obligations, and enforcement measures.[53]

(c) Walloon Region
A Walloon decree of 1 April 1999 deals with the conservation and management of the regional historical patrimony. It amends Book III of the Walloon Code of Spatial Planning, Town Planning and Patrimony.[54] A number of subsidies are created in the Walloon Region for the construction, renovation, and demolition of private houses, by several decisions of the Walloon Government of 21 January 1999. Other measures concerning, *inter alia*, social housing, are contained in a series of decisions of 11 February 1999.[55]

(d) Brussels Capital Region
A Brussels ordinance of 10 December 1999 amends the ordinance of 29 August 1991 on the organization of spatial planning.[56] Existing legislation in this area has been completed and elaborated as follows. A decision of the Walloon Government of 23 December 1998 contains a minor amendment to the decision of the Walloon Government of 19 March 1998, determining which applications for building permits, parcelling permits, and planning certificates must be subject to a public inquiry.[57] A ministerial decree of 27

---

[49] Ibid., 11 Dec. 1999.  [50] Ibid., 26 Jan. 1999.  [51] Ibid., 1 Apr. 1999.
[52] Ibid., 11 May 1999.  [53] Ibid., 8 June 1999.  [54] Ibid., 22 May 1999.
[55] Ibid., 25 Feb. 1999; ibid., 12 Mar. 1999.  [56] Ibid., 30 Dec. 1999.
[57] Ibid., 20 Jan. 1999.

December 1998 complements—in pursuance of Article 447 of the Walloon Code on spatial planning—the lists of municipalities whose territory is subject to the general regulation on construction in rural areas.[58] A decision of the Flemish Government of 18 December 1998 revokes the Royal decree of 6 April 1967 establishing an advisory commission on certain aspects of spatial planning and construction in the coastal strip.[59] A decision of the Flemish Government of 8 December 1998 regulates the recognition of 'regional landscapes', which must promote, *inter alia*, education, recreation, and conservation.[60] The annex to the decision of the Walloon Government of 2 April 1998, on industrial areas of regional importance, is amended by a decision of 11 February 1999.[61] A decision of the Walloon Government of 29 April 1999 contains the scale and data prescribed for the drafting of graphical plans under the Walloon code of spatial planning, town planning, and patrimony.[62] A decision of the Flemish Government of 16 March 1999 amends Articles 2 and 3 of the Royal decree of 16 December 1971 establishing the works and actions that are exempted from the intervention of an architect, the requirement for a building permit, or the opinion of the authorized official.[63] Several articles of the Walloon decree of 27 November 1997 amending the code of spatial planning, town planning, and patrimony, have been amended by a decree of 6 May 1999.[64] A decision of the Walloon Government of 6 May 1999 regulates competence of civil servants of the Institute for the Walloon Patrimony.[65] A decision of the Walloon Regional Government of 20 May 1999 lists the technical and architectural norms with which buildings listed in Article 414 of the Walloon code must comply.[66] A decision of the Brussels Regional Government of 3 June 1999 gives force to Titles I–VII of the regional town-planning regulation, for that region. It wants to establish a modern set of rules for town planning and construction.[67] A number of regional plans for Wallonia were published in the *Moniteur Belge* of 13 July 1999. A decision of the Walloon Government of 10 June 1999 replaces Articles 279–83 of the Walloon code on spatial planning, town planning, and patrimony. The new provisions establish conditions under which natural persons, associations of natural persons, or moral persons may be recognized, in respect of layout, revision, or amendment of spatial planning instruments.[68] A decision of the Walloon Government of 27 May 1999 approves the spatial plan for Wallonia.[69] A Flemish decree of 28 September 1999 delays the date of the entry into force of the Flemish decree of 18 May 1999 on spatial planning, construction, and town planning, until 1 May 2000.[70] For the Brussels Region, an ordinance was adopted on 20 May 1999, amending the ordinance of 29 August 1991 on the organization of spatial planning, amending the procedure for layout and modification of specialized plans.[71] A decision of 9 July 1999 of the Brussels

---

[58] *Moniteur Belge*, 26 Jan. 1999.   [59] Ibid., 28 Jan. 1999.   [60] Ibid., 12 Feb. 1999.
[61] Ibid., 6 Mar. 1999.   [62] Ibid., 28 May 1999.   [63] Ibid., 28 May 1999.
[64] Ibid., 22 June 1999.   [65] Ibid., 24 June 1999.   [66] Ibid., 3 July 1999.
[67] Ibid., 9 July 1999.   [68] Ibid., 3 Sept. 1999.   [69] Ibid., 21 Sept. 1999.
[70] Ibid., 30 Sept. 1999.   [71] Ibid., 25 Sept. 1999.

Government amends its decision of 23 November 1993 to lay down the forms for the receipt of the request for licences and attestations with regard to spatial planning and environmental protection.[72]

## D. SOIL

### i. Flemish Region

A decision of the Flemish Government amends the decision of 4 March 1997, adding some sites to the list of historically contaminated sites which must be cleaned up, and removing other sites from the list.[73] An erratum was added to the decision of the Flemish Government of 4 March 1997, listing the contaminated soils which require clean-up, following Article Article 30(2) of the decree of 27 February 1995 on soil clean-up.[74] A decision of the Flemish Government lists the clean-up actions to be initiated or continued by the Flemish Waste Company, in or during 1999.[75]

## E. WASTE

### i. Federal Government

By a decision of the Interregional Packaging Commission of 31 March 1999, the non-profit organization VAL-I-PAC has been recognized as an authority in respect of packaging waste,[76] while another decision, of 23 December 1998, recognizes FOST Plus as an organization for packaging waste.[77]

### ii. Flemish Region

On 19 January 1999, an environmental policy agreement regarding scrap cars was concluded between the Flemish Government and a number of representative organizations representing the automobile sector. It deals with prevention, collection, processing, and recycling of waste. Several other organizations adhered to the agreement on 13 April 1999.[78] An environmental policy agreement concerning paper has been concluded between the Flemish Region and the associations representing certain large paper-producing sectors, *inter alia*, the Belgian Direct Marketing Union, the Federation of Belgian Graphics Companies, the Belgian Federation of Distribution Companies, and the Association of Graphic Enterprises. For the initial duration of five years, the agreement is intended to prevent the excessive use of paper, and to achieve certain specific recycling percentages. It obliges paper producers to accept paper waste resulting from their publications.[79] The Federation of Belgian Graphics Companies does not accept this for its members,[80] and therefore has decided not to sign the agreement.[81]

---

[72] Ibid., 28 Oct. 1999.  [73] Ibid., 14 Sept. 1999.  [74] Ibid., 30 Sept. 1999.
[75] Ibid., 14 Oct. 1999.  [76] Ibid., 9 June 1999.  [77] Ibid., 27 Mar. 1999.
[78] Ibid., 19 May 1999.  [79] Ibid., 10 Feb. 1999.  [80] Ibid., 30 Sept. 1999.
[81] Ibid., 3 Apr. 1999.

### iii. Walloon Region

A decision of the Walloon Government of 1 April 1999 established the plan of the centres for technical burial of waste, listing the sites that can be used for this type of waste disposal. These sites are reserved for residential and non-hazardous waste, in addition to inert waste and waste from dredging rivers.[82] A decision of the Walloon Government of 10 June 1999 regulates the organization of the Walloon Office for Waste.[83]

### iv. Brussels Capital Region

A new ordinance of 22 April 1999 concerning the prevention and the management of waste paper and/or cardboard products was adopted for the Brussels Region. Chapter I determines the general principles and objectives of the new regulation. One of the main objectives is to further qualitative and quantitative preventive action by consumers, waste-producing taxpayers, companies, and public authorities. Another important objective is to stimulate the recycling of paper and cardboard products. It is a general principle of the ordinance to hold producers of paper and cardboard products responsible. In Chapter III, the principle of preventive action is elaborated. Chapter IV establishes an Intervention Fund for financing selective collection and environmental education. Article 10 of the ordinance empowers the Brussels Region to sign agreements with taxpayers with regard to the objectives of the ordinance, while Chapter VI determines administrative sanctions for violations of the ordinance.[84]

A decision of the Walloon Government of 23 December 1998 contains minor amendments to the decision of 14 November 1991 on the collection of tax on waste in the Walloon Region.[85] Procedural rules for the taxation of waste are contained in a decision of the Walloon Government of 23 December 1998.[86] Lists of authorized waste collectors for the Walloon Region, and for the Flemish Region, have been published. A decision of the Walloon Government of 20 May 1999 contains a list of substances which, in the context of the 1996 Waste Decree, have to be considered as products.[87] A decision of the Walloon Government of 20 May 1999 amends the decision of 30 April 1998 on subsidies for the prevention of waste by subordinate administrations.[88] The plan for the management of packaging waste in the Flemish Region was adopted by a decision of the Flemish Government of 8 June 1999.[89] A decision of 10 June 1999 of the Walloon Government amends the Decision of 30 November 1995 concerning the control of substances which are removed from the bed and banks of watercourses, and sheets of dredging operations.[90] Some Flemish authorizations to use waste as a secondary raw material have been published.[91] A circular letter of the ministry of the Walloon Region identifies the technical officer

---

[82] *Moniteur Belge*, 13 July 1999.         [83] Ibid., 17 July 1999.         [84] Ibid., 14 Oct. 1999.
[85] Ibid., 28 Jan. 1999.         [86] Ibid., 13 Feb. 1999.         [87] Ibid., 18 June 1999.
[88] Ibid., 1 July 1999.         [89] Ibid., 27 July 1999.         [90] Ibid., 9 Sept. 1999.
[91] Ibid., 12,23,25 and 31 Mar. 19999, and 1 Oct. 1999.

mentioned in the decision of the Walloon Government of 30 November 1995, concerning the management of substances removed from the beds and the banks of watercourses, and water surfaces by means of dredging operations.[92] A Ministerial decision of the Brussels Region of 20 December 1999 contains a plan for the removal of PCBs and PCTs.[93]

F. WATER

### i. Federal Government

A law of 18 June 1998 gives legal force to the UN Convention on the Law of the Sea (UNCLOS),[94] and the agreement relating to the implementation of Part XI of UNCLOS.[95]

A law of 20 January 1999 regulates the protection of the marine environment in marine territories under Belgian jurisdiction, while corresponding amendments to the Code of Civil Procedure regarding jurisdiction are contained in a law of 28 February 1999.[96] This comprehensive law applies to the marine environment the prevention and precaution principles, along with the principle that the polluter pays (strict liability), and provides that, in so far as possible, the damaged environment should be repaired. Attention is also afforded to sustainability.[97]

### ii. Flemish Region

The Flemish decree of 22 December 1999 concerning budgets for the year 2000 introduces a new tax on groundwater.[98] A Flemish decree of 18 May 1999 containing various provisions with regard to the budget of 1999 amends the Flemish decree of 28 June 1985 on environmental permits. Representatives of advising public authorities may not vote in the event an appeal procedure is initiated by them. The decree also adds a new exemption from water tax,[99] in favour of taxpayers with a family member who is legally declared a minor for a longer period than is *strictu sensu* foreseen, and who receives a specific disability allowance. Finally, this decree amends the Flemish decree of 13 June 1990 concerning forests.[100]

### iii. Walloon Region

Following on the Walloon decree of 15 April 1999 with regard to the circular watercourse, and the founding of the *Société publique de gestion de l'eau*, a Committee of experts and a Committee for the management of water have been founded, whose activities are regulated by two decisions of the Walloon Government of 3 June 1999. The task of the Committee of experts is to advise the board of the *Société publique de gestion de l'eau* with regard to technical

---

[92] Ibid., 5 Oct. 1999.          [93] Ibid., 31 Dec. 1999.
[94] Montego Bay, 10 Dec. 1982.          [95] *Moniteur Belge*, 16 Sept. 1999.
[96] Ibid., 16 Sept. 1999.          [97] Ibid., 12 Mar. 1999.          [98] Ibid., 30 Dec. 1999.
[99] Law of 26 Mar. 1971 on the protection of surface waters against pollution.
[100] *Moniteur Belge*, 30 Sept. 1999.

problems concerning water control, including the circular watercourse. The Committee on water control is an autonomous public institution whose primary task is to ensure that the price of water is based on the general interest, and the water policy of the region.[101] A Walloon decree of 15 April 1999 regulates recycling of water, and establishes a Public Society for Water Management. It contains provisions on pricing, public service, and organizational issues relating to the society.[102] A decision of the Walloon Government of 29 April 1999 regulates wastewater from dentist cabinets.[103] A decision of the Walloon Government of 29 April 1999 introduces a subsidy for the establishment of an individual purification system.[104]

### iv. Brussels Capital Region

A decision of the Brussels Government regulates the protection of water against contamination by nitrates from agricultural sources, transposing into Brussels Regional law Directive 91/676/EEC concerning the Protection of Waters against Pollution Caused by Nitrates from Agricultural Sources.[105] It provides for the creation of nitrate-vulnerable zones, and contains a code of sound agricultural practice.[106] Existing legislation in this area has been elaborated and completed as follows.

A decision of the Walloon Government of 17 December 1998 applies some provisions of the decree of 11 October 1985 on restoring damage caused by the extraction of groundwater.[107] A decision of the Flemish Government of 8 December 1998 identifies the surface waters which may be used for the production of drinking water, bathing water, fish water, and shellfish water.[108] A law of 10 August 1998[109] gives legal force to the 1992 Protocol[110] to the 1969 International Convention on Civil Liability for Oil Pollution Damage.[111] A decision of the Walloon Government of 25 February 1999[112] transposes the relevant provisions of Directive 98/15/EC, amending Table 2 of Annex I to Council Directive 91/271/EEC on Urban Waste-Water Treatment.[113]

### H. MISCELLANEOUS

A decision of the Walloon Government of 11 March 1999 regulates subsidies for environmentally friendly agriculture.[114] A Royal decree of 13 January 1999 determines the amount and method of payment of the costs and duties relating to the EC eco-label, in order to achieve complete implementation.[115] A series of amendments to the decision of the Flemish Government of 1 June 1995, containing general and sectoral provisions on environmental hygiene, are contained in a decision of 19 January 1999.[116] A decision of the Flemish Government of 15 June 1999 amends the decision of 6 February 1991 on the

[101] *Moniteur Belge*, 9 Sept. 1999.   [102] Ibid., 22 June 1999.   [103] Ibid., 23 June 1999.
[104] Ibid., 26 June 1999.   [105] [1991] OJ L375/1.   [106] *Moniteur Belge*, 29 Jan. 1999.
[107] Ibid., 28 Jan. 1999.   [108] Ibid., 29 Jan. 1999.   [109] Ibid., 16 Mar. 1999.
[110] London, 27 Nov. 1992.   [111] Brussels, 29 Nov. 1969.   [112] Ibid., 27 Mar. 1999.
[113] [1998] OJ L67/29.   [114] *Moniteur Belge*, 31 Mar. 1999.
[115] Ibid., 13 Jan. 1999.   [116] Ibid., 31 Mar. 1999.

regulation of environmental permits (VLAREM I) and the decision of 1 June 1995, containing general and sectoral provisions on environmental permits (VLAREM II).[117] Two Royal decrees of 23 December 1999 determine the Belgian contribution to, first, the trust fund for the budget of the UN Framework Convention on Climate Change,[118] and second, to the trust fund for the budget of the Convention on Biological Diversity.[119] Finally, a Royal decree of 24 November 1999[120] determines the Belgian contribution to the trust fund for the budget of the Basel Convention on the Control of Transboundary Movements of Hazardous Wastes and their Disposal.[121] A decision of the Brussels Regional Government of 14 January 1999 amends the decision of 23 November 1993 on the intervention of the Brussels Institute for Environmental Management in the application procedure for an environmental certificate or permit, and replaces the annexes thereto.[122] A decision of the Flemish Government of 9 February 1999 contains additional provisions on the application of Article 15(4)–(5) of the decree of 23 January 1991 on the protection of the environment against contamination by manure. It contains provisions on digital inventories of certain areas, and rules on manuring.[123] The European Commission has notified the Flemish Government that it has initiated the procedure in Article 93(2) EC in respect of aid paid to farmers pursuant to the 1991 decree on manure.[124] A decision of the Flemish Government amends the Royal decision of 28 February 1977 on hunting authorizations and hunting permits, whereby the hunting examination certificates of the Walloon Region and of the Flemish Region are combined.[125]

A law of 21 December 1998 regulates product norms for the promotion of sustainable production, and consumption partners, and the protection of the environment and public health. To this end, the federal government is granted a variety of measures, *inter alia*, to regulate, suspend, or prohibit market introduction of certain products, to regulate product composition and packaging, to promote recyclable products, and to categorize products according to their impact on humans and the environment.[126] A decision of the Brussels Government of 20 May 1999 replaces its decision of 23 November 1993, concerning supervision of fulfilment of the environmental provisions. The latter decision is not revoked by the Brussels ordinance of 25 March 1999 on environmental crimes, yet this ordinance empowers the Brussels Government to appoint competent authorities for the supervision of fulfillment of environmental provisions. To avoid any confusion on the applicability of the new regulation, the Brussels Government enacted a new decision, based on the ordinance.[127] A ministerial decision of 9 July 1999 amends annex III of the Royal decision of 3 May 1994 concerning the fighting of noxious organisms for vegetables and vegetable products.[128] A decision of the Walloon Government

---

[117] Ibid., 4 Sept. 1999.      [118] New York, 9 May 1992.      [119] Rio de Janeiro, 5 June 1992.
[120] *Moniteur Belge*, 8 Sept. 1999.      [121] Basel, 22 Mar. 1989.
[122] *Moniteur Belge*, 26 Mar. 1999.      [123] Ibid., 26 Feb. 1999.      [124] Ibid., 5 Mar. 1999.
[125] Ibid., 11 Sept. 1999.      [126] Ibid., 11 Feb. 1999.      [127] Ibid., 22 Oct. 1999.
[128] Ibid., 12 Oct. 1999.

of 4 March 1999 seeks to reduce and prevent environmental pollution from asbestos, amending earlier legislation on waste water, waste, landfills, and workers' protection.[129] A circular letter clarifies the definition and treatment of circuits for races and test-drives with motor vehicles, as contained in the Flemish regulation of environmental permits (VLAREM I), adopted by a decision of the Flemish Government of 26 June 1996.[130] A Royal decree of 8 February 1999 regulates the classification and marketing of natural mineral water and spring water.[131] A decision of the Flemish Government implements certain articles of the decree of 23 January 1991 on manure, and amends earlier decisions implementing the decree, by introducing formulae for the calculation of nutrient balances.[132] A decision of the Flemish Government of 13 April 1999[133] concerns subsidies for certain agricultural production methods, and the conclusion of management agreements following Regulation (EEC) 2078/92 on Agricultural Production Methods Compatible with the Requirements of the Protection of the Environment and the Maintenance of the Countryside.[134] A Walloon decree on environmental permits of 11 March 1999 establishes revised regulation of environmental permits, in respect of, *inter alia*, categories, procedure, and sanctions.[135] A decision of the Walloon Government of 4 March 1999 amends the general regulation on labour protection, adding specific provisions on the installation and exploitation of fuel stations. It deals with the construction and installation of tanks, fire prevention, control, and environmental issues concerning air, water, noise, and soil.[136]

The Brussels Capital Region has adopted an ordinance on environmental crimes, with procedural provisions concerning investigation and punishment of environmental crimes.[137] A decision of the Brussels Regional Government establishes a standardized form for installations of category III, as defined in the ordinance on environmental permits of 5 June 1997.[138] A law of 6 May 1999 is intended to promote the establishment of civil societies, grouping forest exploitations.[139] A law of 22 April 1999 identifies the limits, legal status, and the status of living and non-living resources in the Belgian Exclusive Economic Zone (EEZ) in the North Sea, including provisions on environmental protection, artificial islands, and customs and immigration issues.[140] A Decision of the Walloon Government of 27 May 1999 concerns the drafting and financing of municipal environmental plans and plans, for the promotion of nature.[141]

Many articles of the Flemish forest decree of 13 June 1990 have been amended by a Flemish decree of 18 May 1999.[142]

---

[129] *Moniteur Belge*, 8 Apr. 1999.
[132] Ibid., 8 May 1999.
[135] *Moniteur Belge*, 8 June 1999.
[138] Ibid., 2 July 1999.
[141] Ibid., 14 July 1999.

[130] Ibid., 17 Apr. 1999.
[133] Ibid., 26 May 1999.
[136] Ibid., 11 June 1999.
[139] Ibid., 7 July 1999.
[142] Ibid., 23 July 1999.

[131] Ibid., 23 Apr. 1999.
[134] [1992] OJ L215/85.
[137] Ibid., 24 June 1999.
[140] Ibid., 10 July 1999.

# III. Denmark

PETER PAGH\*

## A. AIR POLLUTION

In 1999 the majority of efforts to prevent air pollution were focused on $CO_2$-emissions. In addition to increasing green taxes and direct and indirect subsidies for sustainable energy sources (windmills, solar energy), the Danish parliament supplemented the implementation of Directive 96/92/EC on Common Rules for the Internal Market in Electricity[1] with a new instrument to reduce $CO_2$-emission: emission trading. By Act No. 376 of 2 June 1999 on $CO_2$-quotas for electricity production,[2] Denmark has made new efforts to comply with the Climate Convention and the Kyoto Protocol. The legislator decided that the $CO_2$-emission from electricity production must be limited to 23 million tonnes in the year 2000, and to 20 million tonnes by 2003. Based on the total quotas each power plant is granted a yearly quota, based on the emission in the period 1994–8. The quota for each power plant can either be transferred (traded) to other power plants, or saved for future emission (saving quotas). If the quota or parts of the quota is traded, the contract is subject to approval by the minister of environment and energy. Saved emission quotas must also be notified and approved by the energy agency.

## B. NATURE CONSERVATION

Early 1999, the Danish minister of environment decided to reintroduce beavers into two areas of Jutland, which form part of areas designated under the Habitats Directive[3] and the Birds Directive.[4] The beaver became extinct in Denmark approximately 1000–2500 years ago. However, the ministry argues that the beaver is not dangerous to people and might in fact improve Danish nature. The ministerial decision was challenged by various environmental organizations, and was brought before the nature conservation appeal board. In the ruling of the Appeal Board in September 1999, the plan for reintroduction was rejected for one area, but accepted for the other, under certain conditions. Following this decision, in October 1999, twenty beavers were released in the latter area, but the decision has now been challenged by the Danish anglers association in the High Court. The association claims that the reintroduction constitutes a violation of obligations under the Bern Convention and Article 22 of the Habitat Directive, regarding the reintroduction of species. Furthermore, it would be in breach of Articles 6 and 7 of the Habitat Directive,

---

\* Professor, University of Copenhagen, Copenhagen, Denmark.
[1] [1997] OJ L027/20.     [2] By Act No. 376, 2 June 1999.     [3] [1992] OJ L206/7.
[4] [1979] OJ L103/1.

since no impact assessment has been undertaken to determine how the reintroduction of the beavers might affect birds and other protected species in the
area.

C. WASTE

As in other Member States, legislation on waste has been a cause for substantial legal uncertainty as well as many legal disputes in Denmark. With the
exception of transboundary shipments of waste, in Denmark it is the 275 local
councils which are designated as the competent authorities in matters relating
to waste. Each local council has its own waste law and waste plan, for which
they are individually responsible. Most of the local councils perform the collection, treatment, incineration, and recovery of waste in their region. The
holder of the waste is obligated to join the council's collection scheme, under
Statutory Order No. 299 of 30 April 1997.[5] The application of this provision to
industrial and building waste for recovery remains rather ambiguous.
Furthermore, not only does the definition of waste in the Framework Directive
generate substantial legal doubts, the definition of recovery and its legal implications also generate legal battlefields, since the Danish environmental protection agency does not recognize the use of waste as fuel as a recovery
operation, but rather defines it as disposal.

Similar to other Member States, Denmark has experienced substantial problems regarding the issue of end-of-line-vehicles. None of the waste regimes
established by the local councils have proved sufficient to solve this problem,
and partly destroyed vehicles are now found on roadsides, parking places, and
even in forests. In an attempt to overcome this serious problem, three legislative initiatives were introduced in 1999. The first was Act No. 372 of 2 June
1999[6] on environmental fees and the compensation for scrapping and disposal of vehicles, whereby the holder of the vehicle is urged to transfer the
vehicle to a licensed operator. Second, by Act No. 273 of 2 June 1999 amending
the Environmental Protection Act, the minister of environment and energy
was authorized to establish a comprehensive licensing and authorization
scheme for such operators. Third, Statutory Order No. 860 of 29 November
1999[7] instituted a new instrument requiring registration of any natural or legal
person commercially involved in disposal and recovery activities, including
the separation of specific parts of end-of-life vehicles.

D. WATER

The focus of Danish water law in 1999 has been on implementing the water
action plan. Under the Environmental Protection Act, the minister of environment and energy submitted Statutory Order No. 501 of 21 June 1999 on permits to release wastewater, [8] whereby each local council is obliged to adopt a

---

[5]  Statutory Order No. 299, 30 Apr. 1997.       [6]  Act No. 372, 2 June 1999.
[7]  Statutory Order No. 860, 29 Nov. 1999.       [8]  Statutory Order No. 501, 21 June 1999.

wastewater treatment plan, which will define which localities are or will be covered by public sewerage or private sewerage. The local municipal councils are granted discretion to oblige landowners to be connected, at their own expense, to the public sewerage system owned by the local council. The new order is intended to implement Directive 80/68/EEC on the Protection of Groundwater against Pollution Caused by Certain Dangerous Substances[9] and Directive 91/271/EEC on Urban Waste-Water Treatment.[10] However, it is doubtful whether the order complies with EC regulations regarding the definition of best-available technology (BAT), since it defines BAT as: 'the technique, which technically can be used and is economically achievable for the operator in question.'

### E. HORIZONTAL INSTRUMENTS

### i. Environmental Impact Assessment

In 1999, the Danish Government formally published the two-year-old ratification of the Espoo Convention on Environmental Impact Assessment (EIA) in a Transboundary Context; no further efforts have been taken to implement the Convention. Denmark has implemented Directive 85/337/EEC on the Assessment of the Effects of Certain Public and Private Projects on the Environment (EIA Directive)[11] in a piecemeal manner. Initially, the Danish Government assumed that EIA was required merely for Annex I projects, and that it would be sufficient to implement the EIA-requirements into the Physical Planning Act.[12] This act was to be supplemented by a statutory order regarding traffic projects on the marine territory, granting the minister of traffic discretion to decide which investigatory measures should be taken and whether a public hearing was necessary. After criticism from the Commission, implementation was expanded in 1994, to include screening of Annex II projects on land, and since 1996, extraction of raw materials offshore.

During 1999 several cases have highlighted other substantial weaknesses in the Danish implementation of the EIA Directive. First, the screening criteria are often related only to the size of the project, without regard to specific characteristics and the location of the projects, as required by the ECJ.[13] While the nature protection board of appeal, in general, has accepted the criteria, the position now seems to have been overruled by the Danish Supreme Court in *Danish Biking Association* v. *Council of Roskilde*.[14] This case concerned the question whether a road connection between two main roads resulting in an increase in traffic should be subject to an EIA. In another case, on the temporary dumping of 80,000 tonnes of contaminated soil, the Appeal Board also found that an EIA was not required, but after complaints to the Commission and a compliance letter, the Danish Government acknowledged that such dumping must, in the future, be subject to an EIA. After the Danish parliament,

[9] [1980] OJ L020/43.     [10] [1991] OJ L135/40.     [11] [1985] OJ L175/40.
[12] Act No. 563, 30 June 1997.     [13] Case C–392/96, *Commission* v. *Ireland* [1999] ECR 5901.
[14] *Danish Biking Association* v. *Council of Roskilde*, 8 Feb. 2000, UfR 2000.1103.

by Act No. 368 of 2 of June 1999 on amendments to the Physical Planning Act, implemented Directive 97/11/EC[15] amending the EIA Directive, two months after the deadline, the problem with the screening criteria was solved by the new Statutory Order No. 428 of 2 June 1999 on supplementary rules to the Physical Planning Act, albeit only to the extent that projects are covered by this act.

Still, Danish implementation seems to present at least three additional problems. First, the derogation clause for projects adopted in Article 1(5) EIA Directive is subject of a dispute in a case pending with the eastern higher court, regarding Act No. 477 of 24 June 1992 on Öresund City. This case concerns plans to establish a major new city on open land, in the vicinity of the Danish capital, Copenhagen, and close to a bird protection area. One of the issues arising in the dispute is whether the Act concerned complies with the ruling of the ECJ in the *Bozen* case.[16]

Second, problems with Danish EIA-implementation arise due to the fact that the competent authorities under the Physical Planning Act are the regional councils, which only enjoy jurisdiction within their own regions. In a previous ruling on a power plant and its infrastructure, the nature protection Board of Appeal concluded that environmental impact and alternatives outside the region should not be included in the assessment.[17] Although challenged in many other cases, this position was upheld by the Board of Appeal until October 1999, when it changed its position in a higher eastern court case, regarding another power plant (*Avedöreværket*), which is still pending.

Finally, a dispute regarding expansion of Esbjerg Harbour, one of the biggest harbours in Denmark several hundred metres from a bird protection area, shed light on another weakness in Danish implementation. Not only had the project not been made subject to an EIA-procedure or investigations on the implications for the bird protection area, infringement of the EIA-requirements had not been sanctioned. Thus, it appears that under Danish implementing legislation, such infringements are allowed if they occur with traffic installations in the marine territory. Complaints on the project, as well as on the missing enforcement mechanism, have been sent to the Commission, which is currently investigating the questions.

## ii. IPPC

In May 1999, in order to implement Directive 96/61/EC on Integrated Pollution Prevention and Control (IPPC Directive)[18] and Directive 96/82/EC on the Control of Major Accident Hazards involving Dangerous Substances (Seveso Directive),[19] the Danish parliament adopted Act No. 369 of 2 June 1999 on amendments to the Environmental Protection Act.[20] Based on this new Act, the ministry of environment and energy submitted Statutory Order No. 807 of 25 October 1999 on the licensing of listed plants.[21] This provision includes

---

[15] [1997] OJ L073/5.      [16] [1999] I-ECR 5613.      [17] Nordjyllandsvärket, KFE 1994.208.

[18] [1996] OJ L257/26.      [19] [1997] OJ L010/13.      [20] Act No. 369, 2 June 1999.

[21] Statutory Order No. 807, 25 Oct. 1999.

certain substantial changes in the licensing of heavy polluting plants, including mandatory revision and an obligation for local authorities to monitor and, if necessary, revise the licence conditions, in order to prevent substantial risks caused by unforeseen pollution. However, one important emission from heavy polluting plants is not covered by the Danish implementation: the release of waste water through public sewerage pipelines to public sewerage works is not covered by the IPPC permit. Permits are required for such releases, but this permit scheme is separate, and not in any respect integrated in the IPPC permit scheme, nor is it subject to public participation, as required under Article 15 IPPC Directive.

The new provisions do not identify the party responsible for complying with the conditions in the IPPC permit, whereas this question has generated substantial problems in the enforcement of the permit. The existing Environmental Protection Act does not clarify this either, save that it defines the plant itself as the holder of the permit. In a highly controversial case, *Proms Kemiske Fabrikker*,[22] on contamination caused by a chemical plant, the eastern higher court overruled the lower court judgment and found that the present owner was criminally liable for deposits of waste caused by the previous owner. However, this ruling was based on the fact that, because of family relations as well as the involvement of the present owner in the former company, the present owner could be considered partly identical to the previous owner.

### F. MISCELLANEOUS

#### i. Contaminated Land

In May 1999, after years of debate on liability for contaminated land, and many cases in which the courts have overruled administrative decisions and practices of the Danish environmental protection agency, the Danish parliament adopted a new Act No. 370 of 2 June 1999 on contaminated land.[23] The Act introduces a comprehensive new regime for all types of contaminated land, irrespective of the cause or time of contamination. It does, however, exclude contamination caused by (ordinary) farming. The new regime is based on three pillars: first, public responsibilities; second, administrative liability; and finally, control of the treatment of contaminated soil.

The words 'public responsibilities' imply that the regional councils are under the obligation to map the contamination of all land. This registration is divided into two categories: potentially contaminated sites on the one hand, and highly probably contaminated sites on the other. The distinction between registration of these two categories relates to the priority of public scrutiny. In terms of legal implications for the landowner or in terms of the actual use of the site, the distinction has no practical effect. The limitations on the landowner are identical, irrespective of whether the site is placed in the first or

---

[22] *Prosecuter v. H.C. Prom Kemi ApS under bankruptcy*, Higher Court, 30 Nov. 1999.
[23] Act No. 370, 2 June 1999.

the second category. If the site is used for housing, kindergartens, public parks, or other 'sensitive uses', a permit is required for any physical change on the ground or for any change in respect of use. The same requirement exists in the event that the contamination of the site should create a threat to drinking-water supplies or significant drinking-water resources. If the contamination creates a 'substantial hazardous risk' to the actual use of land or to drinking-water interests, it is the obligation of the regional councils to take precautionary measures and, if necessary, to clean up the contamination. For 'non-sensitive' sites, the level of public scrutiny, monitoring, and clean-up activities of the regional councils depend on the priorities and finance.

Not only clean-up actions are subject to a permit scheme. Any movement of soil from registered land or from newly discovered contaminated sites is subject to a supplementary approval scheme, which governs where and how the contaminated soil must be moved.

Administrative liability under the Act can be divided into three parts. Regarding recent contamination of land (one year after the entry into force of the Act), a new administrative liability regime for the polluter applies, based on administrative orders. If commercial or public activities or installations are the cause of the contamination, the polluter is subject to an administrative order based on strict liability. Otherwise, administrative orders require negligence. The obligation for the polluter does not include compensation for damage caused by the pollution, but rather an obligation to restore the contaminated site to the condition in which it was prior to the pollution. However, the scope of this regime is limited to contamination occurring after 1 January 2001. Evidently, the Act leaves room for discussion on the question of whether it is the polluter who is required to clean up, in the event that the pollution has been caused on a site which is contaminated by prior (non-recent) pollution.

Scrutinization and monitoring of contamination are subject to a largely identical regime, albeit that the scope is expanded. First, administrative authorities are entitled to require monitoring even when pollution is caused by third parties. Second, the regime may be partly retroactive, since the polluter can be required to monitor, even if the pollution has been caused before the entry into force of the new Act, provided that the pollution was caused before 1992. However, the retroactive section of this part of the Act remains somewhat unclear. When parliament adopted the Act, it was presumed by the environmental protection agency that the similar provision on monitoring requirements in the Environmental Protection Act granted authorities the right to order monitoring of past pollution. However, this presumption was held to be incorrect by the Danish supreme court, one month after the Contaminated Soil Act was adopted, in *Shell Denmark* v. *The Environmental Protection Agency*.[24] Although this case concerned the monitoring provision of the Environmental Protection Act, the presupposed link between both provi-

---

[24] *Shell Denmark* v. *The Environmental Protection Agency*, UfR 1999.1600.

sions necessitated an amendment to the Contaminated Soil Act, prior to its entry into force.[25]

Contamination caused by mineral oil tanks with a capacity under 6,000 litres, used for the heating of private houses, is subject to a separate regime. The owner of the oil tank is strictly liable for monitoring and clean up of contamination, yet only if the contamination is discovered after 1 March 2000. While no mandatory insurance exists for other pollution, such is the case for owners of oil tanks, in order to cover these costs up to approximately 270,000 euros. This insurance obligation is, due to negotiations with the environmental protection agency, covered by an agreement between all relevant oil companies and Top-Danmark A/S, one of the major insurance companies in Denmark. The insurance fee is paid by the oil companies on the condition that the oil tanks are operated with oil from one of these companies. The Danish parliament presumed that the agreement had to be notified to and confirmed by the Commission under Article 81 EC, given its impact on competition. However, the Commission was not notified, yet the agreement has been confirmed for a three-year period by the Danish competition agency. The administrative liability regime under the new Act resides under public law and does not have any impact on the rights of citizens to claim damages. Generally, citizens suffering damages or injuries from pollution rely on negligence, unless the damage is caused by registered heavy polluting plants. The Act has been in force since 1 January 2000. Its practical effects are as yet unknown, but it has already been criticized for being too complicated and for generating more legal work than environmental clean-ups.

### iii. Access to Environmental Information

Following the Århus-Convention on Access to Environmental Information, Public Participation in Decision-Making and Access to Justice in Environmental Matters,[26] a public hearing was held in September 1999. The minister of environment and energy presented in parliament a complex array of amendments to existing environmental legislation to implement the Åarhus Convention. The draft legislation is expected to be adopted by the Danish parliament in Spring 2000. However, the draft did not (yet) include any provisions on citizens' access to enforcement or legal remedies, including injunctive relief.[27]

---

[25] Act No. 1109, 29 Dec. 1999.     [26] Århus, 23–5 June 1998.

[27] The drafted legislation and comments have been published on the Internet at: www.mst.dk.

# IV. Finland

PEKKA VIHERVUORI*

## A. INTRODUCTION

Two important reforms concerning environmental law—the new *Ympäristön-suojelulaki* (Environmental Protection Act)[1] and the new Planning and Building Act,[2] both with subsequent amendments of related legislation—were finalized during 1999, although they will not enter into force until 2000. With respect to connections to European environmental law, the Environmental Protection Act (EPA) is undoubtedly more significant.

As regards the remaining fields of environmental law, the hundreds of appeals lodged against the national proposal to the EC Natura 2000 Network are still pending with the Supreme Administrative Court.[3] No other major developments in Finnish environmental law in 1999 can be reported.

Therefore, the following report will be exclusively concerned with the introduction into Finnish law of this comprehensive Environmental Protection Act.

## B. THE NEW ENVIRONMENTAL PROTECTION ACT

### i. Background

The reform in general is motivated by two considerations: first, the domestic need to create a uniform permit system for all kinds of emissions, discharges, nuisances, and pollution risks grew more and more pressing; and second, Council Directive 96/61/EC concerning Integrated Pollution Prevention and Control (IPPC Directive),[4] necessitated such a reform at least in respect of major industrial installations.

The multidimensional Finnish environmental permit system, which is the core of legislation and administration on the protection of the environment, has traditionally been sectoral and incoherent. Since 1992 this has been true only in part, in so far as it concerns the great procedural and substantive watershed between water protection on the one hand and all the other aspects and environmental media on the other. The substantively separate permit systems for air pollution prevention, waste, public health, and neighbourhood nuisances law have been combined into a single permit procedure following the entry into force of the 1991 Environmental Permit Procedure Act, in 1992.[5] The remaining dualism was augmented by the fact that the procedures laid down by the Environmental Permit Procedure Act were managed by general environmental authorities (either the Regional Environmental Centres or the

---

* Professor, Justice at the Supreme Administrative Court, Helsinki, Finland.
[1] Official Legislation Journal No. 86/2000. In Swedish: *Miljöskyddslagen*.
[2] See P. Vihervuori, 'Finland' (1998) 1 *Yearbook of European Environmental Law*, 481.
[3] Ibid. 477.      [4] [1996] OJ L257/26.      [5] Official Legislation Journal No. 735/1991.

municipal Environmental Authorities, depending on the nature and size of the activity or installation), but permits regarding emissions, discharges, and effluents to waters fell within the jurisdiction of independent special courts of justice: the Water Courts. However, in procedures before these Water Courts, the administrative environmental authorities also had legal standing. In all cases it was possible to appeal against a permit decision with administrative courts, and ultimately to the Supreme Administrative Court. The role of the administrative courts has been important also in respect of substantive and technical protection aspects, because the powers of the courts include, where applicable and feasible in practice, direct reform of administrative permit decisions and the conditions attached thereto.

During the early stages of the legislative process, the possibility of maintaining a partly sectoral system was considered. It was noted that, by virtue of Article 7 IPPC Directive, a system with a single permit authority for one application was not obligatory, in so far as certain procedural and substantive requirements were met. However, for several reasons, the option of separate Water Courts as sectoral permitting authorities was rejected.[6]

After years of legislative drafting and public debate, the present reform was introduced in parliament on 24 September 1999, and passed in relatively little time, certainly considering its unusually broad scope. No serious political discrepancies emerged. Although the parliamentary proceedings were concluded on 10 December 1999, ratification by the president could not take place until 4 February 2000, for technical reasons. The new legislation entered into force on 1 March 2000. Due to the scale and complexity of the task—twenty-seven new or amending Acts, including those of the very extensive Water Act—a special Act on the versatile transitional arrangements was also enacted. The previous Air Pollution Prevention Act, the Noise Abatement Act, and the Environmental Permit Procedure Act were completely repealed, and the scope of application of, *inter alia*, the Water Act, the Public Health Act, and the Waste Act were significantly reduced.

The reform was, *inter alia*, affected by the fact that section 20 of the Constitution Act of Finland[7] identifies a duty for the government to strive to ensure for its citizens the right to a healthy environment and the opportunity to influence decision-making concerning the environment. Here it is relevant to note the role of environmental permit systems as frameworks for participation and means of horizontal legal protection of affected individuals and their properties.

## ii. Main Features of the Reform

The reform is very profound in several respects. It not only integrates the various permit systems into a single procedure, but also introduces important changes in the legislative structure. The borderline between courts and administration is altered and the Water Courts are abolished. A new category

---

[6] On the discussion, see P. Vihervuori, n. 2 above, 479.
[7] Official Legislation Journal No. 731/1999.

of permit authorities, the Environmental Permit Offices, is established to replace the Water Courts. A reform of this extent and significance will inevitably be problematic in several respects. Consequently, a sufficient consensus could not be achieved until the end of the twentieth century. The reform was prepared on various occasions throughout the 1990s.

The core of the new legislation consists of the Environmental Protection Act (EPA), being the first codification of Finnish pollution prevention law. Its 118 sections include all the principal starting points of the IPPC Directive and EC environmental law in general. The detailed provisions required by the various directives are mostly included in decrees based on the EPA. Officially, the EPA has been declared to implement, which in most cases means reimplementation, completely or partially a total of thirty-eight EC environmental directives, while the number is even greater in practice. In addition, the EPA encompasses complementary provisions to one EC Regulation.

The scope of application of the EPA covers in principle all activities that cause or might cause 'pollution of the environment', a very extensive notion defined in Section 3 EPA. Moreover, the Act is applicable to any waste-producing activity, and to all reuse or management of waste. However, there are certain general exceptions, such as discharges caused by the normal use of vessels, for which separate legislation exists. The general principles listed by Section 4 EPA include prevention of negative impacts and reducing harm, precaution and care, best available techniques, best environmental practice, and the polluter-pays principle. The specific judicial relevance of these principles depends mostly on other provisions of the EPA. There is also a general duty for all operators to be aware of the impacts and risks, and the ways to reduce these, in Section 5 EPA. General provisions on location, applicable to all activities involving a risk of pollution, are laid down in Section 6 EPA.

In addition to the permit system, the EPA encompasses directly applicable provisions (or authorizations with respect to decrees) on a variety of items with relevance to the environment. These include environmental requirements of diffuse sources of pollution, as well as those of certain products, substances, and machines. A notification system is established for several specific purposes, rather than permits. One of the novelties of the Act is the establishment of Municipal Environmental Regulations: a complementary, albeit voluntary, instrument of environmental guidance at the municipal level.

The integrated provisions on permitting and the general contents of a permit decision are applicable to a wide range of activities, and also to environmental impacts and risks. Installations requiring a permit range from, *inter alia*, industries of various types to agricultural installations, fish farms, fur farms, landfills, airports, motor circuits, quarries, harbours, bus depots, municipal sewers, and shooting ranges. In practice, a uniform system of decision-making was created for all categories of permit-requiring activities, irrespective of whether they are covered by the IPPC Directive. The legislative alternative according to which only IPPC-level applications would have been integrated was rejected at an early stage in the legislative process. The new system is nevertheless adjustable in many respects, which is exemplified by the three different types of permit authorities described below.[8]

In many cases, the legislative solutions are more or less new creations, in particular where existing sectoral provisions had diverged, and could no longer be adopted as such. However, one can see the provisions' origins in domestic sectoral laws on occasion, in particular where the provisions only apply, for natural reasons, to certain environmental media and related impacts. The provisions on the obligations of the permit holder in respect of fisheries management are identical to those in the Water Act, which remains applicable to various water management and construction projects.

In the new integrated permit system, all conditions are in principle based on the same general provisions of the EPA, irrespective of whether it concerns air pollution, water pollution, nuisance, etc. Naturally, certain differences exist depending on the type of emission and the actual environmental media. Hence, a difference exists in respect of the relevance of the decrees between water pollution norms and all other norms.[9]

The permit requirements were previously stipulated in very disparate ways by the existing sectoral legislation. In respect of water the general notion of 'pollution of a water body' was most crucial, since any discharge or other activity causing a mere risk of pollution required a permit, according to the Water Act.[10] Here 'pollution' included all kinds of harm to private or public interests, which made the scope rather wide. It should be mentioned that this arrangement, in combination with the largely private ownership of waters and the compensation system discussed below, is related to the role of the permit system as a safeguard of the private property interests of the affected parties. Besides the general clause, certain listed activities and discharges also required a Water Act permit, yet this was largely a formal legislative insert in line with EC water directives. In most cases, no actual change was required, or in fact enacted. Furthermore, regarding nuisance to neighbourhood properties, a general clause based on the notion of 'continuous, unreasonable nuisance' created the necessity to obtain an environmental permit. In the fields of air pollution prevention and public health protection, the permit requirement was based on specified lists of activities and installations. Generally, the totality of the various ways of stipulating permit requirements resulted in a significantly broader scope of the activities and installations requiring permits as compared to the IPPC Directive. Approximately the same general scope was adopted in the EPA as previously was the case in domestic law. Not surprisingly, the notion of 'pollution of a water body' and that of 'continuous, unreasonable nuisance' continued also to be relevant, as will be explained below.

In the drafting of the new legislation, the previous means of defining the necessity to obtain a permit created a technical problem, given the objective

---

[8] See Sect. B*v.* below.                    [9] See Sect. B*iii.* below.
[10] The clause was called 'ban on pollution', although no absolute ban was at stake, as the norm in fact defined the case-by-case threshold concerning the necessity of a permit.

of a uniform permit system. Nonetheless, existing differences were still considered relevant inasmuch as a certain dualism was preserved within the system for environmental permits in the EPA. First, the need for a permit is established by an exhaustive list laid down in the main decree: the Environmental Protection Decree,[11] under Section 28 EPA. Second, again under Section 28 EPA, and irrespective of the former list, a permit is necessary for, *inter alia*:

— any activity that could potentially cause pollution of surface water,[12] territorial seas included;[13]
— any activity that could potentially cause unreasonable nuisance to neighbouring properties, as defined in the Neighbourhood Relations Act;[14] and
— any installation-scale or professional reuse or management of waste.

No general ban on polluting surface waters has been included. Discharges to surface waters or public sewers may, by decree, be declared to require permits, irrespective of any specific risk of pollution. Similarly, a discharge to the sea may, by decree, be declared to require a permit when so prescribed by international agreements.

A permit is also required for activities with existing permits, in the event of an increase in the emissions or the effects thereof, or if any other essential change is made, except in such cases where the change does not increase the environmental impacts or risks, and where there is no need to review the permit due to the change. As may be seen, the opposing needs of efficient control on the one hand, and flexibility on the other, have both had an impact on the provision.

As regards existing activities based on older sectoral permits, a new integrated permit is required by 2003, 2004, or 2005, as specified in the Environmental Protection Decree, only when prescribed by the IPPC Directive or, for air polluting activities, when required by earlier legislative measures. In case of an evident failure to meet these requirements, the authorities may also demand a permit application in other circumstances. Essentially, if any change is made to the previously permitted activity, a new permit is required.

No general ban on the pollution of surface waters has been preserved in the technical, permit-requiring sense similar to the Water Act. Nevertheless, there are four absolute bans on polluting or dumping in the EPA.[15] Of these bans, the

[11] Official Legislation Journal No. 169/2000.
[12] The scope of the notion is similar to the earlier clause in the Water Act. There are certain systematic exceptions in the field of watercourse management and construction to the polluting effects, to which the EPA is partly applicable within the permit procedure of the remaining Water Act.
[13] Traditionally, Finnish water law treats sea areas (i.e. the Finnish parts of the Baltic Sea) as bodies of surface water. The same holds for the EPA, Sect. 3(1)(6).
[14] See the new Sect. 17 of the Neighbourhood Relations Act; Official Legislation Journal No. 90/2000.
[15] Sects. 7–9.

ban on polluting groundwater, the ban on polluting international seas or territorial waters of another country, and the ban on dumping waste in Finnish territorial seas, originate in the Water Act, while the ban on polluting soil originates in the Waste Act. The previously separate regimes of groundwater pollution prevention and soil pollution prevention have now been combined, enabled by the new integrated approach. Chapter 12 of the EPA concerns permits and coercive measures with respect to the reinstatement of polluted soils and groundwater. One administrative decision may now combine injunction-type and permit-type ingredients.[16]

Pursuant to Finnish practice, administrative discretion concerning environmental permits is highly judicial, regarding the permit itself and its various conditions. Identical rules apply to the permit authority as to the appellate courts. Another important characteristic is that the affected subjects are treated as parties to the proceedings, a state of affairs that naturally requires maximum publicity regarding the project at stake. With respect to earlier law and practice, the provisions on access to information and public participation in Article 15 of the IPPC Directive have not caused any changes in the Finnish approach.[17]

### iii. Key Provisions on Environmental Permits

The core of the permit system, and of the EPA in general, is perhaps most visible in Sections 41 and 42, by virtue of which the specific conditions of the (geographic) area have also been recognized. An Environmental Permit shall be granted, if the activity in question meets the requirements set forth in this Act, the Waste Act, and the decrees adopted by virtue of the Acts.

The permit authority shall examine the statements in respect of the application given by authorities and remarks made by individuals, as well as the requirements for a permit. The authority shall also in other respects pay attention to what has been provided to safeguard public and private interests. In the decision attention shall moreover be paid to what has been provided in the Nature Conservation Act or by virtue of it.[18]

For granting a permit, it is required that the activity, when the conditions laid down in the same decision and the location of the activity are taken into account, will not, as such or together with other activities, cause:

— risks to health;
— significant other pollution of the environment or risk thereof;
— a consequence forbidden by sections 7–9 of this Act;
— deterioration of specific natural conditions or hazard to water supply or another important opportunity of use in the area impacted by the activity;
— unreasonable nuisance as provided in section 17(1) of the Neighbourhood Relations Act.

---

[16] Sects. 75–80.
[17] The relevant procedural provisions are included in Ch. 6, Sects. 35–40 EPA.
[18] Sect. 41.

No activity shall be located in contradiction to a Town Plan. In the locating of the activity, section 6 of this Act shall also be observed.[19]

Any person undertaking an activity involving utilization of waste or waste management shall have access to sufficient expertise, taking into consideration the quality and quantity of the activity.

According to Section 50 EPA, any binding obligation laid down in a national plan or programme for environmental protection that is based on EC law shall be observed in the permit decisions. Moreover, attention shall be paid to certain plans according to the Waste Act, and to the national programmes already mentioned in so far as binding obligations are not at stake.

Of further significance is Section 43 EPA, concerning permit conditions. In fact, the permit itself and the imposing of conditions are two strongly intertwined issues. Consequently, Sections 41, 42, and 43 EPA may only be understood on the basis of mutual interaction. Section 43 reads:

A permit shall contain necessary conditions:

(1) on the emissions, on the prevention and other restrictions thereof, and on the location of the emission site;

(2) on wastes and on the reducing of waste originating and of the harmful properties of waste;

(3) on measures in cases of malfunction and in other exceptional situations;

(4) on measures to be taken after the activity has been closed down, such as reinstatement and prevention of emissions;

(5) on other measures in order to prevent, reduce or research pollution, risk thereof or harm caused by it.

If conditions based on paragraph (1) above were, due to the nature of the activity in question, not able sufficiently to prevent or reduce the environmental harm, the permit may, except for industrial activity or energy production, contain necessary conditions on allowed quantities of production, on fodder being used in production, or on energy produced.

When laying down conditions, the nature of the activity, the properties of the impacted area, the total impact of the activity, the importance of the measures to prevent pollution in respect to the totality of the environment, and the technical and economical possibilities in carrying out these measures shall be taken into account. The conditions on preventing and reducing emissions shall be based on best available techniques.[20] Moreover, the efficiency of energy use,[21] as well as preparation for the prevention of accidents[22] shall be paid attention to.

Provisions on more specific types of permit conditions, the applicability of which depends upon the specific case, are included in Sections 45–9 EPA, concerning, *inter alia*, fisheries management, wastes and waste management, monitoring and surveillance of the emissions and their impacts by the permit holder, including publicity and the participation of the interested subjects, discharges of industrial waste water to public sewers, and the construction of sewer pipes in water bodies.

---

[19] Sect. 42.      [20] Cf. Art. 3(1) IPPC Dir.      [21] Cf. ibid., para. d.      [22] Cf. ibid., para. e.

The previous, largely EC-based sectoral decrees including detailed numeric norms on various emissions and discharges remain in force unchanged, at least for the time being. One problem of fundamental importance emerged, however: traditionally, technical requirements regarding various discharges and effluents to waters have been decided on a case-by-case basis, by comparing all the relevant public and private interests and the natural conditions of each receiving body of water. This approach resulted, in practice, prior to the implementation of the EU water protection directives in Finland, in a significantly high level of protection. When the (partly out-of-date) Directives had to be implemented starting early in 1994, as a result of the Agreement on the European Economic Area (EEA),[23] they were taken mainly as a formality or a checklist, and in most cases the respective decrees merely repeated the EC minimum requirements. Only on rare occasions did they have practical importance, such as in the case of the removal of nitrates from municipal effluents, in order to observe the requirements of the relevant Directive[24] and the respective decree.[25] In the field of air pollution prevention the situation was different. The technical norms laid down in the relevant decrees, meeting the requirements of the EC Directives, were applied by the permit authority as general minimum standards. More stringent conditions deviating from them were allowed, and required, only on grounds specified by law.

Section 51 EPA now stipulates the relationship between permit conditions, and general minimum requirements of a specified nature laid down by decree. Permit conditions may be more stringent than the respective general minimum standards in three situations:

— in order to meet the requirements for granting a permit, to eliminate an absolute obstacle to a permit, such as risk to health according to Section 51, by laying down a more stringent condition;
— in order to safeguard an environmental quality standard required by another decree;
— for the protection of waters.

Regarding agricultural activities, a more stringent condition based on the protection of waters may only be laid down in order to prevent a threat of specific pollution of the environment.

Section 51 is particularly significant in the field of water protection, where the primary starting point continues to be individual discretion, now based on Sections 42 and 43 EPA. Of course, it must always be ensured that the minimum requirements in the relevant decrees are met. Formal environmental standards are not common thus far. According to Article 10 IPPC Directive, an environmental quality standard—based on EC law—may require additional measures which are stricter than those achievable by the use of best available

---

[23] Finland became a Member State of the EC on 1 Jan. 1995.
[24] Dir. 91/271/EEC on Urban Waste Water Treatment, [1991] OJ L135/40.
[25] Official Legislation Journal No. 365/1994.

techniques (BAT).[26] In so far as the BAT level has been specified by general technical minimum requirements in a decree, Section 51 EPA is applicable, *inter alia*, for safeguarding the relevant quality standard. However, it will also be possible to reject a complete permit application, notwithstanding compliance with the BAT requirements or any other minimum requirements in a decree if, for example, any of the obstacles laid down in Section 42 EPA could not be eliminated by using a permit condition.

According to Section 52, a permit is issued either for the time being or for a limited period of time. However, a permit without any time limitation shall normally be updated at a later stage, as stipulated by Section 55.[27] Sections 57–9, in turn, include provisions on the expiry of permits, on the manner in which a valid permit may be altered later on, in addition to the updating procedure of Section 52, and on the repealing of permits at a later date.

### iv. Compensation

The provisions regarding compensations for environmental damage in Finland have been closely connected to the permit procedures in so far as water pollution is concerned. This development has contributed to domestic problems in creating an integrated permit system. It was the duty of the former Water Courts to decide *ex officio* on compensation for (future) damages to, *inter alia*, owners of water areas or of shore lands, in principle as a part of a permit for discharge of wastewater. In practice, however, the—often annual—compensation was mostly decided upon at a later date. With respect to air or soil pollution or noise, no such connection existed, thus initiation of a lawsuit for compensation rather depended upon each individual victim. In these cases, the ordinary courts had competence, and the Environmental Damages Act was applied.[28]

Even the new integrated permit system did not succeed in completely eliminating this dualism. According to Sections 66–74 EPA, compensation for damage caused by pollution of surface waters[29] is decided upon by the permit authority, and still *ex officio*. However, contrary to previous practice, the substantive regulation is now to be found in the Environmental Damages Act instead of in the Water Act. It remains to be seen how a private law liability system fits into the new context. In practice, the changes are believed by some to be insignificant. This solution implies some differentiation in the environmental permit procedures and decisions, depending on the respective environmental media.

---

[26] See Art. 2(7) and Art. 10 IPPC Directive.     [27] Cf. Art. 13 IPPC Directive.

[28] Official Legislation Journal No. 737/1994. See e.g. P. Vihervuori, 'Environmental Law in Finland: a. The Environmental Law system' in N. S. J. Koeman (ed.), *Environmental Law in Europe* (London: Kluwer Law International, 1999), 177–94.

[29] As pollution of groundwater continues to be completely forbidden (Sect. 8 EPA), no permits resulting in the same consequence are possible.

### v. Procedural Aspects

Permit applications, and all other permit-related cases such as amendments, pursuant to the EPA are dealt with by the competent environmental permit authority, of which there are three categories. The most significant projects, mainly consisting of projects of IPPC or EIA level, belong with the new Environmental Permit Offices, the 'middle class' with the Regional Environmental Centres, and all remaining applications belong with the respective municipal Environmental Authorities. The Environmental Protection Decree contains detailed lists of activities for the division of competence between these three categories.

The three collegiate Environmental Permit Offices resemble in many respects the previous three Water Courts. Their independence has been accentuated by several legislative measures, a state of affairs that partly results from the fact that the new offices also deal with all the applications pursuant to the Water Act, including permits and other judicial or administratively sensitive issues. Moreover, the procedural rules of the EPA have been elaborated in such a way that most compensation issues in practice are to be dealt with by the offices. The composition of an Environmental Permit Office consists of a lawyer as chair and two members with technical or ecological expertise.

Appeals against the decisions made by any of the permit authorities are lodged with the Regional Administrative Court in Vaasa, the decisions of which are in turn subject to appeal before the Supreme Administrative Court. The Regional Administrative Court in Vaasa specializes in environmental and water cases, and the *quorum* in these cases includes a permanent engineer and/or ecologist members.

The new provisions on appellate procedures have been developed on the basis of the partly divergent appellate provisions of the 1991 Environmental Permit Procedure Act and of the Water Act. Simultaneously with the EPA, the appellate provisions of the remaining Water Act have been amended on the same basis, to avoid unnecessary discrepancies. The necessity of these measures has been accentuated by the fact that certain projects, such as fish farms of various types, may require a permit both under the EPA and under the Water Act. In such cases only one application is required and one permit decision is issued, *in casu* by the Environmental Permit Office, although both Acts are applicable. The procedures in all stages, appellate procedures included, nevertheless observe the Water Act. Following the EPA and the Water Act, all appeals are lodged with the Regional Administrative Court in Vaasa and subsequently with the Supreme Administrative Court.

Appeals against a decision under the EPA may be lodged by a variety of subjects listed in Section 97 EPA, including: first, all those whose rights or interests may be concerned; second, associations and foundations with a task to protect the environment, health, or nature, or the promotion of amenity of an inhabited area provided that the project impacts within their geographical area of activities; third, the municipality where the project of the applicant takes place, and other municipalities whose territories are (to be) impacted upon by the project; fourth, the Regional Environmental Centre, the municipal Environmental Authority of the municipality where the project takes place, and the municipal Environmental Authority of other municipalities whose territories are impacted upon by the project; and finally, other authorities charged with supervision and representation of specific public interests, for example the fisheries authorities. In this respect, the main amendment is that *locus standi* has been extended to the environmental organizations.

The same administrative authorities and appellate courts also deal with injunctions and other forms of administrative coercion. An injured or otherwise interested party, or an association or foundation as defined in section 97(2) EPA, as discussed above, is entitled to ask for a decision on administrative coercion which may contain injunctive bans and orders on the activity itself or on reinstatement. In practice, this mechanism, as it is subject to review by administrative courts, is highly significant for the relationships of private parties *inter se*, for example for the legal protection of affected individuals and properties. The courts of general jurisdiction have no competence in this area.

### vi. Miscellaneous

The inclusion of provisions on measures against climate change was one of the most politically controversial issues during the preparation of the EPA. Ultimately, no specific provisions on this topic were included. However, according to the statements in the Bill, the scope of application of the EPA can be extended at a later date, with an inclusion of necessary provisions on the abatement of climate change in so far as would be required by future international obligations. It is, however, one of the explicit aims of the EPA to abate climate changes and to otherwise support sustainable development.[30] In fact, several parts of the EPA are directly connected to these issues, since the emissions stipulated by the EPA also include greenhouse gases such as methane, nitrous oxide, and CFC substances. Measures for protecting the ozone layer based on international obligations were stipulated by the former Air Pollution Prevention Act, and are similarly included in provisions of the EPA. Moreover, the deterioration of the ozone layer is one of many types of pollution of the environment defined by Section 3 EPA.

Pursuant to Section 110 EPA, environmental impacts in other countries are equally relevant as similar impacts in Finland, without prejudice to bilateral treaties. However, pollution of the territorial waters or economic zones of another state is completely prohibited by Section 9 EPA.

Sections 111–13 EPA have enabled joint implementation of environmental protection measures, especially those of international air pollution prevention obligations, and have adjusted the permit system accordingly. Systematically, joint implementation is always based on an exception from specified requirements laid down by decree granted beforehand to the

---

[30] Sect. 1(7).

applicant of an environmental permit by the ministry of the environment. It is required, *inter alia*, that the operator take protection measures elsewhere in Finland or in another country, for example a Central of Eastern European (CEE) country, in such a way that the total emissions within the arrangement or their combined impact are essentially reduced. This precondition means in practice that joint implementation is not on the whole applicable to the protection of most waters, *inter alia*, excluding the Baltic Sea, but is rather limited to air pollution prevention of certain types. No measures shall be made in conflict with any of Finland's international obligations, and all requirements of, *inter alia*, EC law shall be observed. If the negative impact of the activity varies according to the location of the impacted areas, it is also required that emissions to the territory of Finland are always reduced. An application for an exception may be made public pursuant to section 112 EPA. This procedure takes place separately from the permit procedures for each of the separate activities involved with the project. An exception establishing a joint implementation may later be amended or abolished on the grounds specified in Section 113. According to a statement in the EPA Bill, the necessary implementation of future legislation will take place irrespective of any arrangement on joint implementation, without making the Finnish Government liable for any economic loss suffered by interested parties.

# V. France

MICHEL PRIEUR*

## A. INTRODUCTION

Although the participation of the Green Party (ecologists) in the coalition government with the Socialist Party, since 1997, has certainly resulted in several developments in certain restricted areas of French environmental law, as a result of continuing political conflict within the coalition in respect of environmental issues, particularly nuclear policy, no major breakthroughs were accomplished in 1999.

## B. INSTITUTIONAL REFORMS

Traditionally, the ministry of environment has been dominated by engineers, rather than lawyers. A ministerial order of 4 March 1999 identifies a new legal assistance manager, who is to coordinate legal advice within the ministry, and to supervise the implementation of EC legislation in the French legal order. The general state budget for 2000 adopted by parliament at the end of 1999, shows a significant increase in the budget for the ministry of environment,[1] yet the number of civil servants remains low. In total, the ministry has 2,760 employees, of which 1,245 operate the environmental regional directorates.

## C. ECO-TAXATION

Law No. 98-1266[2] of 30 December 1998 holds a significant reform, by the creation of an eco-taxation called *Taxe Générale sur les Activités Polluantes* (TGAP), which has been said to entail a reversal of the general environmental taxation system.[3] In fact, the system revises and combines a set of five existing taxation schemes for air pollution, noise, and wastes, which, prior to 1999, had been directly paid and allocated to the environmental agency ADEME. Since 1999 these taxes have been collected by the Treasury, and are included in the general state budget without any specific designation. Following Law No. 98–1178[4] of 30 December 1998, the TGAP will be allocated to the special fund for social security in 2000, and will be used to compensate the reduction of social charges for employers. Meanwhile, the TGAP eco-tax has been extended to cover new products, *inter alia*, washing powder with phosphate, gravel, and chemical powders for agricultural purpose.

---

* Professor, University of Limoges; France. Director of CRIDEAU (CNRS-INRA).
[1] Four billion francs, i.e. 0.3% of the state budget.
[2] *Journal Officiel*, No. 303 of 31 Dec. 1999, 20171.
[3] R. Herzog, 'TGAP a reversal in the environmental taxation?' (1999) 47 *Droit et Ville*, 103–31.
[4] *Journal Officiel*, No. 303 of 31 Dec. 1998, 20178.

D. INTEGRATION OF ENVIRONMENT IN OTHER POLICIES

In 1999 two major laws were adopted to implement Principle 4 of the Rio Declaration on Environment and Development,[5] in respect of integration of environment concerns into other policy sectors. Law No. 99-533[6] of 25 June 1999 on land planning and sustainable development of the territory, amends the 1995 Law on land planning.[7] Among the new national land-planning programmes, which the 1999 Law establishes, is the 'Collective services scheme on rural and natural areas', which entails a long-term programme, of twenty years. The scheme is intended to ensure proper management of the quality of the environment and of the landscape, by identifying natural areas to protect or to manage in an ecologically sound manner, thereby having legal effect on the various regional land-planning instruments.

The second law implementing Principle 4 of the Rio Declaration is Law No. 99-574[8] of 9 July 1999 on agriculture, which provides that agricultural policy must take into account environmental concerns, in order to attain sustainable development. The integration objective in this new legislation is, *inter alia*, pursued by means of a new type of voluntary agreement between the state and the agricultural exploitants, referred to as a 'territorial contract of exploitation'. In this contract, specific provisions are to guarantee the protection of biological diversity, water, soil, nature, and landscape. In respect of genetically modified organisms (GMOs), Article 91 of this law establishes 'bio-vigilance': a general system of control and supervision.

E. NOISE

In pursuit of more effective control and regulation schemes for noise emissions in the vicinity of airports, Law No. 99-588[9] of 12 July 1999 establishes a control authority for airport noise. This new independent administrative body consists of eight inspectors, whose task is to determine noise levels within a certain range from airports, and to verify that all relevant standards are adhered to. Violations of noise emission limits may result in administrative sanctions, applied by the control authority.

F. WASTE

*i. Radioactive Waste*

In 1999 a primary project for depleted uranium deposits in several sites in France was cancelled by the Administrative Court and, subsequently, by the *Conseil d'Etat*,[10] following insufficient security studies and environmental impact assessments. The question remains whether depleted uranium is to be considered a waste.

---

[5] Rio de Janeiro, 13 June 1992.       [6] *Journal Officiel*, No. 148 of 29 June 1999, 9515.
[7] Ibid., No. 31 of 5 Feb. 1995, 1973.       [8] Ibid., No. 244 of 20 Oct. 1999, 15647.
[9] Ibid., No. 160 of 13 July 1999, 10400.       [10] *CE*, 7 July 1999, *Cogema*.

A Decree of 3 August 1999 provides for a laboratory installation in Bure, Moselle region, to test underground deposits of high-level radioactive waste in clay soils in this region in eastern France. A second installation site is envisaged for 2000, in respect of granite areas. A consultation process has been initiated for fifteen sites in Brittany, and in the Massif Central, but following the 1991 law on radioactive waste, only parliament may decide upon the definitive site of deposit, by 2006.

### G. MISCELLANEOUS

#### i. Liability for Mining Damages

Following cases involving serious pollution of former mining sites, Law No. 99-245[11] of 30 March 1999 creates a new procedure of control for closed mines, with specific impact statements on the environment, mainly in respect of hydrologic concerns. This law establishes an objective liability system, by virtue of which the former mine exploitant, or alternatively the state, is held liable for damages.

#### ii. Liability for Defective Products

Throughout 1999 several commentators have raised serious doubts in respect of Law No. 98–389[12] of 19 May 1998, which implements into the French legal order Council Directive 85/374/EEC on Liability for Defective Products.[13] Some controversy exists regarding its success in transposing the Directive, and regarding its apparent lack of practical impact on French environmental law.[14]

---

[11] *Journal Officiel*, No. 76 of 31 Mar. 1999, 4767.    [12] Ibid., No. 117 of 21 May 1998, 7744.
[13] [1985] OJ L210/29.
[14] See e.g. M. P. Camproux-Duffrìne, 'La loi du 19 Mai 1998 sur la responsibilité du fait des produits défectueux et la protection de les environment' (1999) 2 *Revue Juridique l'Environment*, 189–207.

# VI. Germany

### MICHAEL RODI*

#### A. INTRODUCTION

Similar to 1998, the developments in German environmental law in 1999 were dominated by the introduction of Ecological Tax Reform, and the drafting of a comprehensive General Environmental Code (UGB).[1]

The Law on the Start of the Ecological Tax Reform[2] entered into force on 1 April 1999, containing, in Article 1, the new Electricity Tax Act and, in Article 2, an amendment to the Mineral Oil Tax Act, increasing the taxation on fuels and heating oils. The Law is intended to discourage energy consumption by increasing energy taxes while, at the same time, lowering the cost of labour by reducing social security contributions.[3] The current government, a coalition between the Social Democrats and the Green Party, is continuing its efforts in this direction with the Law on the Continuation of the Ecological Tax Reform,[4] which was passed in the German *Bundestag* on 11 November 1999 and entered into force on 1 January 2000. Work on an Environmental Code has come to a halt, following questions regarding its constitutionality.[5] The Code was intended to implement Directive 96/61/EC concerning Integrated Pollution Prevention and Control (IPPC Directive),[6] and Directive 97/11/EC amending Directive 85/337/EEC on the Assessment of the Effects of Certain Public and Private Projects on the Environment (EIA Directive).[7] The current interruption in the drafting process of the unified Environmental Code is problematic, as the deadlines for the implementation of these Directives passed on 30 October 1999 and 15 March 1999, respectively. The ministry for environment has now expressed its intent to implement the Directives by two separate laws.[8]

Abandoning the production and use of nuclear energy is one of the primary objectives of the current government,[9] and although negotiations between the government and the operating companies of the nuclear power plants, on the

---

* Professor of Law, University of Greifswald, Greifswald, Germany.

[1] See Ministry for the Environment, Nature Conservation and Nuclear Safety of the Federal Republic of Germany (ed.), *Environmental Code* (*Umweltgesetzbuch-UGB*), draft prepared by the Independent Expert Commission, Berlin, 1998. See also M. Rodi, 'Germany' (1998) 1 *Yearbook of European Environmental Law*, 487.

[2] *Gesetz zum Einstieg in die Ökologische Steuerreform*, BGBl. 1999 I 378.

[3] M. Rodi, 'Ecological Tax Reform in Germany' (2000) 54 *Bulletin for International Fiscal Documentation*, 486.

[4] *Gesetz zur Fortführung der Ökologischen Steuerreform*, BGBl. 1999 I 2432.

[5] Press release of the Ministry for Environment, Conservation and Power Plant Safety (*Ministerium für Umwelt, Naturschutz und Reaktorsicherheit*) 139/99, of 2 Sept. 1999; See also e.g. A. Wasielewski, 'Stand der Umsetzung der UVP-Änderungs- und der IVU-Richtlinie' (2000) 1 *Neue Zeitschrift für Verwaltungsrecht*, 19.

[6] [1996] OJ L257/26.      [7] [1997] OJ L73/5.      [8] See A. Wasielewski, n. 5 above.

[9] See Coalition Agreement between the Social Democratic Party of Germany and Bündnis 90/ Die Grünen, 20 Oct. 1998, 16.

terms for abolition of nuclear power failed in 1999, these negotiations are to be continued during 2000. Questions concerning the constitutionality of this 'green' objective, and the legal means to achieve it, remain still unanswered.[10]

## B. NATURE CONSERVATION

According to Article 3 of Directive 92/43/EEC on the Conservation of Natural Habitats and of Wild Fauna and Flora (Habitats Directive),[11] a coherent European ecological network called Natura 2000 is to be set up. This network will consist of Special Areas of Conservation that have been designated as reserves by the Member States, based on the Habitats Directive and Directive 79/409/EEC on the Conservation of Wild Birds (Birds Directive).[12] The dead-lines for designating these special areas of conservation, however, passed without a complete registration of all areas worthy of protection in Germany.[13] Consequently, the question was raised as to how these areas can be protected prior to their official designation as special areas of conservation. In one of its decisions in 1998,[14] the Federal Administrative Court approved the possibility of *de facto* protection areas, following similar rulings by the ECJ.[15] In 1999 the courts were confronted with two issues concerning such *de facto* protection areas: first, what requirements must be met for an area to be considered a *de facto* protection areas, and second, what are the terms of protection for these areas.[16] In response to the former question, the Higher Administrative Court of Nordrhein-Westfalen, following the ECJ precedents,[17] held that some discretion exists in setting up requirements for reserves, except in cases where the ornithological relevance of an area is already evident.[18] An important indication that special relevance exists in this sense is the inclusion of an area on the 1989 Inventory of the International Birds Association (IBA).[19]

While the Administrative Court of Schleswig followed the precedents of the ECJ, it ruled in the cited case[20] that an area intended for a future waste-disposal plant did not belong to the area included on the 1989 IBA inventory.

---

[10] See M. Rodi, 'Grundlagen und Entwicklungslinien des Atomrechts' (2000) 1 *Neue Juristische Wochenschrift*, 7; M. Böhm, 'Der Ausstieg aus der Kernenergienutzung' (1999) 12 *Natur und Recht*, 661.

[11] [1992] OJ L206/7.          [12] [1979] OJ L103/1.

[13] Art. 4(2) Habitats Directive suggests 5% of the total area of each Member State. See also A. Schink, 'Die Verträglichkeitsprüfung nach der FFH-Richtlinie' (1999) 11–12 *Umwelt- und Planungsrecht*, 417.

[14] Bundesverwaltungsgericht, Case 4 C 11.96, (1998) 11 *Natur und Recht*, 649.

[15] Case C–355/90, *Commission* v. *Spain* [1993] ECR I–4221, and Case C–44/95, *Regina* v. *Secretary State for the Environment, ex p. Royal Society for the Protection of Birds* [1996] ECR I–3805.

[16] H. W. Rengeling, 'Umsetzungsdefizite der FFH-Richtlinie in Deutschland?' (1999) 8 *Umwelt und Planungsrecht*, 284.

[17] See n. 15 above.

[18] Oberverwaltungsgericht Nordrhein-Westfalen, Case 20 B 1464/98.AK (2000) 13 *Natur und Recht*, 165.

[19] Case C–3/96, *Commission* v. *Netherlands* [1998] ECR I–3031. See also J. Verschuuren, 'Netherlands', in this volume.

[20] Verwaltungsgericht Schleswig, Case 12 A 230/95, (1999) 12 *Natur und Recht*, 714.

The Administrative Court of Stade ruled[21] that the provisions of the Habitats Directive and the Wild Birds Directive can be extended to include areas that are in the immediate vicinity of an area already protected under the regulation of the Wild Birds Directive, which are, in potential, worthy of protection according to Article 4(2) Wild Birds Directive.

Concerning the level of protection for *de facto* protection areas, uncertainty exists as to whether the requirements of Article 4(4) Wild Birds Directive, or the lower level of protection of Articles 6(3) and (4) of the Habitats Directive are to be applied.[22] So far, the Federal Administrative Court has left this question unanswered.[23] The Higher Administrative Court of Nordrhein-Westfalen, however, decided in favour of the application of Articles 6(3) and (4) of the Habitats Directive.[24]

In 1998 the Federal Administrative Court approved the existence of 'potential areas of protection' under the Habitats Directive. [25] Essentially, although the courts appear willing to consider this concept, so far, they have refrained from identifying the actual requirements for such 'potential' reserves.[26]

### C. WASTE

In the field of waste law, problems repeatedly occur regarding the definition of 'waste', which is of great importance as the waste holder's legal responsibilities depend on whether an object can be regarded as waste. For example, certain responsibilities for holders based on Regulation (EEC) No. 259/93 on the Supervision and Control of Shipments of Waste within, into and out of the EC (Waste Shipment Regulation)[27] apply to anyone seeking to ship waste abroad, *inter alia*, a duty to notify authorities and obtain their approval for the transboundary shipment of waste.

The definition of waste under Directive 75/442/EEC on Waste (Waste Framework Directive)[28] is, according to a decision of the Federal Administrative Court,[29] identical to the German term used in the Waste Management and Product Recycling Act,[30] including the provisions of Annex I, defining as waste all those things 'which the waste holder discards or intends or is required to discard'.

'To discard' in the legal sense of the term means to dispose of or to recover a certain object, and through the process of recovery, the object is no longer considered waste. Yet, according to the decision mentioned above, sorting out

---

[21] Verwaltungsgericht Stade, Case 2 A 772/97, (1999) 12 *Natur und Recht*, 411.
[22] H. W. Rengeling, n. 16 above, 286.     [23] Bundesverwaltungsgericht, n. 14 above, 651.
[24] Oberverwaltungsgericht Nordrhein-Westfalen, n. 18 above. A similar approach is suggested by H. W. Rengeling, n. 16 above, 286; and A. Schink, n. 13 above, 421.
[25] Bundesverwaltungsgericht, Case 4 A 9.97, (1998) 7 *Umwelt und Planungsrecht*, 384.
[26] H. W. Rengeling, n. 16 above, 284.
[27] [1993] OJ L30/1, last amended by Regulation (EC) No. 120/97, [1997] OJ L22/14.
[28] See Art. 1(a) Dir. 75/442/EEC on Waste, [1975] OJ L194/47; last amended by Dir. 91/156/EEC, [1991] OJ L78/32.
[29] Bundesverwaltungsgericht, Case 7 C 31/97, (1999) 12 *Gewerbearchiv*, 261.
[30] Kreislaufwirtschafts- und Abfallgesetz (KrW-/AbfG), BGBl. 1994, I 2705.

used clothes in order to use them for the production of cardboard is not considered recovery. The clothes are then still considered as waste and the intention to ship them abroad must therefore be notified.[31]

This distinction between waste for disposal and waste for recovery is equally important as the definition of 'waste', since the distinction leads to different rights and duties for the person who ships the waste, and for the competent authorities, under the Waste Shipment Regulation.[32] As regards the decision-making competence of the authorities, the Administrative Court of Appeal of Mannheim[33] held that, although the authorities have the right to object to transboundary shipments of waste for recovery, their permission is not required for such shipments.[34]

In German waste law the issue of whether waste has to be disposed privately by industry, i.e. waste for recovery, or by public authorities, i.e. waste for disposal, depends upon the above-mentioned distinction.[35] Germany's higher courts are currently dealing with specific questions concerning this distinction, for example the classification of mixed wastes.[36]

In German law, there is an obligation to leave particularly hazardous waste, so-called 'waste requiring strict supervision', to the public authorities responsible for waste disposal.[37] While in the past, these obligations were regulated by means of special state ordinances, at present there is increasing doubt about whether these ordinances are compatible with German and EC law.[38] The Federal Administrative Court, for example, was required to rule on a case involving a duty established by an ordinance to hand over waste to public authorities. In this case, the waste holder was required to hand over his waste to an incineration plant located in Hamburg, although he had intended to use a cheaper facility in Belgium. In a reference for a preliminary ruling, the Federal Administrative Court[39] asked the ECJ on 29 July 1999 for a decision as to whether the duty to hand over waste to public authorities, and the export ban on the affected waste, are compatible with EC waste law, especially Article 4(3)(a)(i) of the Waste Shipment Regulation and the EC treaty provisions on the free movement of goods.

[31] See Art. 17(I) and (III) of the Waste Shipment Regulation, in connection with n. 27 above, Commission Decision 94/575/EC from 20 July 1994, concerning the establishment of a control system for the shipment of certain wastes into certain non-OECD countries, [1994] OJ L220/15.
[32] See Arts. 3 and 6 ff.
[33] Verwaltungsgerichtshof Mannheim, Case 10 S 3242/98, (1999) 12 *Natur und Recht*, 456.
[34] See Arts. 7 and 8 Waste Shipment Regulation.
[35] See para. 13 I 2 of the Waste Management and Product Recycling Act; see also Dolde and Vetter, 'Beseitigung und Verwertung nach dem KrW-/AbfG' (1999) 18 *Neue Zeitschrift für Verwaltungsrecht*, 21.
[36] See e.g. Verwaltungsgerichtshof Baden-Württemberg, (2000) 12 *Umwelt- und Planungsrecht*, 39; Verwaltungsgerichtshof München (1999) 12 *Natur und Recht*, 585; Verwaltungsgerichtshof Baden-Württemberg (1999) *Die Öffentliche Verwaltung*, 830; Oberverwaltungsgericht Koblenz (1999) 18 *Neue Zeitschrift für Verwaltungsrecht*, 679 and 682.
[37] See para. 13 IV of the Waste Management and Product Recycling Act.
[38] M. Beckmann, book review on 'R. Breuer: Die Zulässigkeit landesrechtlicher Andienungs- und Überlassungspflichten' (1999) 7 *Deutsches Verwaltungsblatt*, 145.
[39] Bundesverwaltungsgericht, Case 7 CN 2/98, (1999) 18 *Neue Zeitschrift für Verwaltungsrecht*, 1228.

D. HORIZONTAL INSTRUMENTS

*i. EIA*

In an infringement proceeding against Germany,[40] the ECJ ruled that Germany had violated its obligation under the EC Treaty by, first, making the Environmental Impact Assessment Act (EIA Act)[41] effective only after the deadline for the implementation of the EIA-Directive[42] had passed, second, by failing to inform the Commission of its measures for the implementation of the Directive, and finally, by granting block-exemptions to types of projects listed in Annex II EIA Directive. The court's decisions on the EIA Act primarily concern projects for which an EIA was not carried out, although this was required by law. There is a tendency to regard the lack of an EIA as acceptable in so far as ecological concerns have otherwise been taken into account in the plans for the project.

In this respect, the Federal Administrative Court has indicated that the lack of an EIA which is legally required does not necessarily render the result of the entire decision-making process unlawful.[43] In this judgment, the court applied this to the planning of roads, based on a development plan under the Urban Development Law, which was originally developed for the Law on Planning Major Roads, holding that the lack of an EIA in the planning of a road is relevant only in so far as it led to a different result in the decision-making process.

The Administrative Court of Appeal of Baden-Württemberg also ruled that the lack of an EIA in the process of setting up a regional planning chart concerning high-tension lines was not relevant.[44] In this case, the EIA had not taken place due to the existence of a temporary state arrangement, whereby an EIA was unnecessary if the creation of a regional planning chart had already been initiated before the EIA Directive had been implemented. However, according to the court, this did not mean that EC law had been violated, as *in casu* the application for the execution of the regional planning chart had been filed before the deadline for the implementation of the EIA Directive had passed on 3 July 1998.

*ii. Access to Information*

The Act on Information on the Environment (UIG),[45] which entered into force in 1994, gave rise to two questions for the German courts to clarify: first, the definition or scope of 'information on the environment' under paragraph 3 II UIG, which the ECJ tends to interpret rather liberally.[46] The Federal Administrative Court, for example, ruled that a claim could be filed on information concerning

[40] Case C–301/95, *Commission* v. *Germany* [1998] ECR I–6135. See also case report in (1999) 7 *Deutsches Verwaltungsblatt*, 232.

[41] *Gesetz über die Umweltverträglichkeitsprüfung*, BGBl. 1990 I 205.   [42] See n. 7 above.

[43] Bundesverwaltungsgericht, Case 4 BN 27/98, (1999) 18 *Neue Zeitschrift für Verwaltungsrecht*, 989, refering to other decisions on the same topic.

[44] Verwaltungsgerichtshof Baden-Württemberg, Case 10 S 1406/98, (2000) 13 *Natur und Recht*, 455.

[45] *Umweltinformationsgesetz* (UIG), BGBl. 1994 I 1490.

[46] See e.g. Case C–321/96, *Mecklenburg* v. *Kreis Pinneberg* [1998] ECR I–3809.

financial aid provided by authorities for a production method having a positive effect on the environment, irrespective of whether this effect was direct or indirect.[47] The Higher Administrative Court of Schleswig[48] includes subjective estimates and evaluations in the term 'information' in so far as some kind of relationship exists with environmental protection; that is, if direct environmental improvement is the primary goal of these estimates and evaluations.

Second, uncertainty exists as to the scope of reasons leading to an exemption from the obligation to provide information, under paragraph 7 UIG. Following ECJ case law on this topic,[49] courts tend to hesitate, in difficult cases, to acknowledge the existence of such reasons. The Higher Administrative Court of Schleswig, for example, stated in its previously discussed decision,[50] that only the deliberation itself, and not its basis, nor its results, are protected under the 'confidentiality of deliberations of authorities' under paragraph 7 No. 1, 3 alt. UIG. In contrast, the Federal Administrative Court ruled in a case concerning the scope of the exception laid down in paragraph 7 I No. 2, 1 and 2 alt. UIG,[51] that during the course of a court procedure or a preliminary criminal procedure, no requests can be made for information on the environment in so far as this concerns the procedure. According to this decision, a request for information has to be denied regardless of whether an authority received the data during the course of the procedure or before the procedure was initiated.

During an infringement proceeding against Germany, the ECJ expressed its opinion on paragraph 7 I No. 2 UIG,[52] which denies requests for information during administrative procedures. The ECJ held that this provision violates Article 3(2) of Directive 90/313/EEC on the Freedom of Access to Information on the Environment,[53] as this merely exempts preliminary investigation proceedings from a request for information.

E. MISCELLANEOUS

*i. Soil Protection*

On 1 March 1999 the new Federal Soil Protection Act entered into force,[54] introducing protective regulation for this so-called 'third medium',[55] which is expected to tackle the insufficiencies of existing soil protection laws. The Act is also expected to stimulate standardization of state regulations, thereby tackling problems concerned with contaminated soil.[56]

---

[47] Bundesverwaltungsgericht, Case 7 C 21/98, (1999) 18 *Neue Zeitschrift für Verwaltungsrecht*, 1220.

[48] Oberverwaltungsgericht Schleswig, Case 4 L 139/98, (1998) 11 *Natur und Recht*, 667.

[49] See n. 46 above.				[50] See n. 47 above.

[51] Bundesverwaltungsgericht, Case 7 C 32/98, (2000) 13 *Natur und Recht*, 215.

[52] Case C–217/97, *Commission* v. *Germany* [1999] ECR I–5087. See also case report in (2000) 13 *Natur und Recht*, 26.

[53] [1990] OJ L158/56.

[54] *Bundes- Bodenschutzgesetz*, BGBl. 1999 I, 502; concerning the federal power to pass a law according to that matter, see the first decision at the first instance made by the Verwaltungsgericht Frankfurt am Main (1999) 12 *Natur und Recht*, 711.

[55] R. Wolf, 'Bodenfunktionen, Bodenschutz und Naturschutz' (1999) 10 *Natur und Recht*, 545.

[56] See also F. J. Peine, 'Das Bundes-Bodenschutzgesetz' (1999) 3 *Natur und Recht*, 121.

# VII. Greece

JOANNA KOUFAKIS*

## A. AIR POLLUTION

Three major European Community (EC) Directives in the field of air protection law were implemented by Greece in 1999.

First, by Joint Ministerial Decree D13E/9321[1] of the ministers of national economy and economics, Greece transposed into national law European Parliament and Council Directive 97/68/EC on Measures against the Emissions of Gaseous and Particulate Pollutants from Internal Combustion Engines to be installed in Non-Road Mobile Machinery.[2]

Second, Joint Ministerial Decree 5535/459[3] transposed into national law Commission Directive 98/77/EC Adapting to Technical Progress Council Directive 70/220/EEC on Measures to be Taken against Air Pollution by Emissions from Motor Vehicles.[4] Third, on 8 April 1999, the ministers of economics, the environment, physical planning and public works, and transport, adopted a Joint Decree[5] concerning the procedure and the supporting documents needed in order for a motor vehicle to be qualified as 'non-polluting', based on the emission requirements laid down by Directives 88/76/EEC, 89/548/EEC, 91/441/EEC, and 94/12 /EC on Measures to be Taken against Air Pollution by Emissions from Motor Vehicles.[6]

## B. BIOTECHNOLOGY

Joint Ministerial Decree 12924/1369[7] amending Decree 88740/1883/1995,[8] transposed into national law Commission Directive 97/35/EC Adapting to Technical Progress for the Second Time Council Directive 90/220/EEC on the Deliberate Release into the Environment of Genetically Modified Organisms.[9]

## C. CHEMICALS

In the field of chemical regulation, 1999 saw many transpositions of EC Directives in Greece, on a variety of topics.

---

* Advocate, Member of the Athens Bar Association, the Greek Ombudsman, Quality of Life Department.

[1] *Official Gazette,* Vol. B., No. 1218, Nov. 1998.    [2] [1998] OJ L059/1.
[3] *Official Gazette,* Vol. B, No. 370, Apr. 1999.    [4] [1998] OJ L286/34.
[5] Joint Decree 44203/2137/1999, *Official Gazette,* Vol. B, No. 338, Apr. 1999. *Official Gazette,* Vol. B, No. 290, Apr. 1999.
[6] [1988] OJ L036/88; [1989] OJ L226/89; [1991] OJ L242/91; and [1994] OJ L100/94.
[7] *Official Gazette,* Vol. B, No. 1071, June 1999.    [8] Ibid., Vol. B No. 1008, Dec. 1995.
[9] [1997] OJ L169/72.

## *i. Biological Agents at Work*

On 2 February 1999 Presidential Decree 15/99[10] amending Decree 186/95, was adopted to transpose into national law Commission Directives 97/59/EC and 97/65/EC, Adapting for the (respectively) Second and Third Time to Technical Progress Council Directive 90/679/EEC on the Protection of Workers from Risks Related to Exposure to Biological Agents at Work.[11]

On 13 May 1999 Presidential Decree 90/99[12] amending Presidential Decree 307/86, was adopted to comply with the requirements of Commission Directives 91/322/EEC and 96/94/EC, concerning the Protection of Workers from Risks Related to Exposure to Chemical, Physical and Biological Agents at Work.[13]

## *ii. Dangerous Substances and Preparations*

Joint Ministerial Decree 93/1999[14] amending Decree 445/83 was adopted to comply with the requirements of European Parliament and Council Directive 97/56/EC amending for the Sixteenth Time Council Directive 76/769/EEC on Restrictions on the Marketing and Use of Certain Dangerous Substances and Preparations.[15] The Directive was to have been implemented by the Member States by 4 December 1998. In addition, Joint Ministerial Decree 537/98[16] was adopted to comply with Commission Directive 97/64/EC Adapting to Technical Progress, for the Fourth Time, Annex I to Directive 76/769/EEC on Restrictions on the Marketing and Use of Certain Dangerous Substances and Preparations.[17]

## *iii. Classification, Packaging, and Labelling of Dangerous Substances*

Joint Ministerial Decrees 482/98[18] and 511/98[19] of the ministers of national economy and economics were adopted to transpose into national law Commission Directives 96/56/EC[20] and 97/69/EC[21] respectively, both amending Directive 67/548/EEC on the Classification, Packaging and Labelling of Dangerous Substances,[22] following a Reasoned Opinion by the Commission, in December 1998, for Greece's failure to adopt legislation implementing these Directives.[23]

## *iv. Plant Protection Products*

On 4 May 1999 the ministry of the environment, physical planning and public works submitted a draft Presidential Decree to the competent department of the Council of State for further elaboration on the transposition into national

[10] *Official Gazette*, Vol. A, No. 9 , Feb. 1999.
[11] [1997] OJ L282/33; and [1997] OJ L335/17.
[12] *Official Gazette*, Vol. A, No. 94, May 1999.
[13] [1991] OJ L177/22; and [1996] OJ L338/86.
[14] *Official Gazette*, Vol. B, No. 814 , May 1999.
[15] [1997] OJ L333/1.
[16] *Official Gazette*, Vol. B, No. 156, Feb. 1999.
[17] [1997] OJ L315/13.
[18] *Official Gazette*, Vol. B, No. 1316 , Dec. 1998.
[19] Ibid., Vol. B, No. 168, Feb. 1999.
[20] [1996] OJ L236/35.
[21] [1997] OJ L343/19.    [22] [1967] OJ L196/1.
[23] Press Release IP/98/1093, Dec. 1998.

law of the Council Directive 97/73/EC on the Placing of Plant Protection Products on the Market.[24]

*v. PCB Directive*

The aim of Council Directive 96/59/EC on the Disposal of Polychlorinated Biphenyls (PCBs) and Polychlorinated Terphenyls (PCTs)[25] is to streamline the legislation of the Member States on the decontamination or disposal of equipment containing PCBs/PCTs and/or the disposal of used PCBs/PCTs, in order to eliminate them completely on the basis of the provisions of the Directive. Although the Directive was to be implemented by the Member States by 16 March 1998, Greece has yet to adopt legislative measures to transpose it into national law. Consequently, in July 1999, the European Commission decided to make an application to the European Court of Justice (ECJ) against Greece for failure to adopt and communicate the necessary implementing legislation for the Directive.[26]

*vi. PVC Products*

In January 1999, the ministers of development and public health, having regard to Council Directive 92/59/EEC of 29 June 1992 on General Product Safety,[27] which has been transposed into national law by Ministerial Decree F1-503/1995,[28] adopted a prohibition on the use of soft PVC containing certain phthalates for products in the market of childcare articles and toys intended to be placed in the mouth of children of less than 3 years of age. According to the provisions of the Decree,[29] these measures will be reconsidered in the framework of the latest development and technical progress concerning replacement of phthalates on the EC level.

*vii. Shipment of Dangerous and Polluting Goods*

Presidential Decree 3/199[30] amending Decree 174/1998 has been adopted to comply with Commission Directive 97/26/EC amending Directive 93/75/EEC concerning Minimum Requirements for Vessels Bound for or Leaving Community Ports and Carrying Dangerous or Polluting Goods.[31] On 29 September 1999 a Presidential Decree[32] was adopted to comply with Council Directive 95/50/EC on Uniform Procedures for Checks on the Transport of Dangerous Goods by Road.[33] Presidential Decree 104/99[34] transposed into national law Directive 94/55/EC concerning the Transport of Dangerous Goods by Road.[35]

---

[24] [1997] OJ L353/26.     [25] [1996] OJ L243/31.     [26] Press Release, IP/99/513, July 1999.

[27] [1992] OJ L228/24.          [28] *Official Gazette*, Vol. B, No. 98, Feb. 1995.

[29] Ibid., Vol. B, No. 77, Feb. 1999.     [30] *Official Gazette*, Vol. A, No. 2 , Jan. 1999.

[31] [1997] OJ L158/40.

[32] Presidential Decree 256, *Official Gazette*, Vol. A, No. 209, Oct. 1999.

[33] [1995] OJ L249/35.          [34] *Official Gazette*, Vol. A, No. 113, June 1999.

[35] [1994] OJ L319/7.

### D. NATURE CONSERVATION

By Joint Ministerial Decree 1289[36] Greece transposed into national law Council Directive 92/43/EEC[37] on the Conservation of Natural Habitats and Wild Fauna and Flora, which was to have been implemented by the Member States by 21 May 1994.

On 31 March 1999 the ministers of national economy and agriculture adopted a Joint Ministerial Decree[38] concerning trade in endangered species of wild fauna and flora. This Decree contains the implementing measures necessary to give effect to Council Regulation (EC) No. 338/1997 on the Protection of Species of Wild Fauna and Flora by Regulating Trade therein.[39] Ministerial Decree 331739/1999[40] of the Minister of Agriculture concerns the keeping of records by companies involved with trade of species of wild fauna and flora.

By Law No 2719[41] Greece ratified the International Convention on the Conservation of Migratory Species of Wild Animals,[42] as amended by the Conference of the Parties in 1997. The Convention entered into force in Greece on 1 October 1999.[43]

### E. WASTE

#### i. Hazardous Waste Incineration

On 8 March 1999 the ministers of environment, physical planning and public works, economics and national economy adopted Joint Ministerial Decree 2487/455[44] transposing into national law Council Directive 94/67/EC on the Incineration of Hazardous Waste,[45] whereas the deadline for transposition was actually 31 December 1996.

#### ii. Implementation of Waste legislation

Member States are required under EC law to provide reports concerning the implementation of EC waste legislation. The reports for the period 1995–7 were due by the end of September 1998, but Greece failed to provide the relevant report to the Commission.

In addition to this requirement, Member States are obliged to draw up, within the framework of Regulation (EEC) No. 259/93 on the Supervision and Control of Shipments of Waste within, into and out of the Community,[46] a similar report before the end of each calendar year, and send it to the Secretariat of the Basel Convention on the Control of Transboundary Movements of Hazardous Wastes and Their Disposal,[47] in addition to sending

---

[36] *Official Gazette,* Vol. B, No. 1289, Dec. 1998.      [37] [1992] OJ L 206/7.
[38] Joint Ministerial Decree 331794/1999, *Official Gazette,* Vol. B, No. 281, Mar. 1999.
[39] [1997] OJ L061/1.      [40] *Official Gazette,* Vol. B, No. 194 , Mar. 1999.
[41] Ibid., Vol. A, No. 106, May 1999.      [42] Bonn, 23 June 1979.
[43] Announcement of the Ministry of External Relations F. 0546/21/AS 696/M.2898/1999, *Official Gazette,* Vol. A, No. 200, Sept. 1999.
[44] *Official Gazette,* Vol. B, No. 196 , Mar. 1999.      [45] [1994] OJ L365/34.
[46] [1993] OJ L030/1.      [47] Basel, 22 Mar. 1989.

a copy to the Commission. Greece also failed to comply with this second requirement, which led the Commission to notify a Letter of Formal Notice to Greece for failing to provide the relevant reports.[48]

### iii. Packaging and Packaging Waste Directives

Greece has yet to adopt legislative measures to transpose into national law European Parliament and Council Directive 94/62/EC on Packaging and Packaging Waste,[49] although this Directive was to be implemented by Member States by 30 June 1996. However, the competent Ministries prepared a draft law which was set for submission to the Greek parliament in 2000.

### iv. Waste Management Plans

The European Commission decided to make an application to the ECJ against Greece for its failure to adopt and communicate to the Commission waste management plans complying with the Directive 91/156/EEC (Framework Waste Directive),[50] Directive 91/689/EEC (Hazardous Waste Directive),[51] and Directive 94/62/EC (Packaging Waste Directive).[52] Although Greece had provided information on waste management within its territory, it had not yet transmitted any documents that could be considered waste management plans for the purposes of the Directives mentioned above.[53]

#### F. WATER

### i. Drinking Water

In June 1999 the ministers of the environment, physical planning and public works and public health, having regard to the framework Law for the Environment 1650/86, the provisions of Decree A5/288/1986 transposing Council Directive 80/778/EEC on drinking water,[54] and the provisions of Directive 94/10/EC laying down the procedure for the provision of information in the field of technical standards and regulations, as transposed into the national law by Presidential Decree 48/96, adopted a Decree[55] concerning the quality of bottled drinking water.

### ii. Nitrates from Agricultural Sources

On 22 July 1999 Joint Ministerial Decree 19652/1906[56] was adopted, identifying those waters that have been affected by pollution, and those waters that could be affected by pollution according to Article 3 of Council Directive 91/676/EEC concerning the Protection of Waters against Pollution Caused by Nitrates from Agricultural Sources.[57] The Decree, amending Ministerial Decree 16190/1335/1997,[58] which transposed into national law the Directive,

---

[48] Press Release, IP/99/521, July 1999.     [49] [1994] OJ L365/10.     [50] [1991] OJ L078/32.
[51] [1991] OJ L377/20.     [52] See n. 49 above.     [53] Press Release, IP/99/487, July 1999.
[54] *Official Gazette,* Vol. B, No. 379, 1986.
[55] Joint Decree No. 1263/1999, *Official Gazette,* Vol. B, No. 1070, June 1999.
[56] Ibid., Vol. B, No. 1575, Aug. 1999.     [57] [1991[ OJ L375/1.
[58] *Official Gazette,* Vol. B, No. 519, 1997.

aims at the effective protection of the environment, on the one hand, by identifying waters affected and waters that could be affected by pollution from areas of land which are designated as vulnerable zones, and on the other, by simplifying the procedure of Article 5 of the previous Decree, concerning the action programmes, in accordance with Article 5 of the Directive.

### iii. Oil Pollution

In February 1999 the minister of commercial navigation, having regard the provisions of Law 2252, by which Greece ratified the 1990 International Convention on Oil Pollution Preparedness, Response and Cooperation,[59] and Presidential Decree 206/87 transposing into national law the Council Directive 83/189/EEC,[60] to comply with the requirements of Directives 88/182/EEC[61] and 94/10/EC[62] amending Directive 83/189/EEC Laying Down the Procedure for the Provision of Information in the Field of Technical Standards and Regulations, adopted a Decree concerning the terms and conditions for the acceptance of floating locks in the Greek marine waters in cases of oil pollution.[63]

### iv. Port State Control

On 2 February 1999 Presidential Decree 16/99[64] was adopted, transposing into national law Council Directive 98/25/EC[65] and Commission Directive 98/42/EC,[66] both amending Directive 95/21/EC concerning the Enforcement, in Respect of Shipping using Community Ports and Sailing in the Waters under the Jurisdiction of the Member States, of International Standards for Ship Safety Pollution Prevention and Shipboard Living and Working Condition.[67]

### v. Urban Waste Water

By Joint Ministerial Decree 19661/1982/1999,[68] Greece transposed into national law Commission Directive 98/15/EC which amends Table 2 of Annex I to Council Directive 91/271/EEC concerning Urban Waste-Water Treatment.[69] The Decree, in conformity with Article 5 of Directive 91/271/EEC, identified sensitive waters, in catchments of which urban waste waters must be subject of more stringent treatment than secondary treatment.

In March 1996 Greece was condemned by the ECJ for not transposing into national law Council Directive 91/271/EEC concerning Urban Waste-Water Treatment.[70] In 1997 the Greek Government adopted a Decree[71] which the Commission found unsatisfactory to this end.[72] By this new legislation transposing Commission Directive 98/15/EC, Greece has attempted once again to meet the requirements set by Council Directive 91/271/EEC.

---

[59] *Official Gazette*, Vol. A, No. 102, Nov. 1994.     [60] [1983] OJ L109/26.
[61] [1988] OJ L081/75.     [62] [1994] OJ L100/30.
[63] *Official Gazette*, Vol. B, No. 76, Feb. 1999.
[64] Ibid., Vol. A, No. 9, Feb. 1999.     [65] [1998] OJ 133/20.     [66] [1998] OJ L184/40.
[67] [1995]OJ L157/1.     [68] *Official Gazette*, Vol. B, No. 1811, Sept. 1999.
[69] [1998] OJ L067/29.     [70] [1991] OJ L135/40.
[71] Joint Ministerial Decree No. 5673/400/1997.     [72] Press Release IP/99/507, July 1999.

## G. HORIZONTAL INSTRUMENTS

### i. Eco-audit

At the end of 1998 a Ministerial Decree[73] was adopted taking the necessary measures for the application of Regulation (EEC) No. 1836/93 Allowing Voluntary Participation by Companies in the Industrial Sector in a Community Eco-Management and Audit Scheme (EMAS).[74] In January 1999 Ministerial Decree 33910/1999 approved the composition of the EMAS Committee as a competent body for the operation of the scheme. On 4 February 1999 the EMAS Committee approved the first registration.

## H. MISCELLANEOUS

### i. Agricultural Production Methods

In July 1999 the ministers of national economy and agriculture adopted a Decree[75] concerning programmes for the management and exploitation of agricultural land in the framework of Council Regulation (EEC) No. 2078/92 on Agricultural Production Methods, compatible with the Requirements of the Protection of the Environment and the Maintenance of the Countryside.[76]

### ii. Energy

In July 1999 the ministers of national economy, development and the environment, physical planning and public works, having regard to Law 2476/1997,[77] by which Greece ratified the Final Act of the European Energy Charter Conference, the European Energy Charter, and the Energy Charter Protocol on Energy Efficiency and Related Environmental Aspects, Council Directive 93/76/EEC to Limit Carbon Dioxide Emissions by Improving Energy Efficiency (SAVE)[78] and Joint Ministerial Decree 21475/4707/1998,[79] which transposed into national law the SAVE Directive, adopted a Regulation[80] concerning the procedures, requirements, and directions for the conduct of energy inspections.

### iii. Electrical Equipment

Joint Ministerial Decree 44203/2137[81] amending Decree 2923/161/1986, has been adopted to comply with Commission Directive 97/53/EC Adapting to Technical Progress Council Directive 79/176/EEC concerning Electrical Equipment for Use in Potentially Explosive Atmospheres Employing Certain Types of Protection.[82]

---

[73] *Official Gazette*, Vol. B, No. 1177, Nov. 1998.
[74] [1993] OJ L168/1.
[75] *Official Gazette*, Vol. B, No. 1515, July 1999.
[76] [1992] OJ L102/19.
[77] *Official Gazette*, Vol. A, No. 58, Apr. 1997.
[78] [1993] OJ L237/28.
[79] *Official Journal*, Vol. B, No. 880, Aug. 1998.
[80] Joint Ministerial Decree D6/B/11038/1999, *Official Gazette*, Vol. B, No. 1526, July 1999.
[81] Ibid., Vol. B, No. 290, Apr. 1999.
[82] [1997] OJ L257/27.

*iv. Foodstuffs*

By Joint Ministerial Decree 412/99[83] of the ministers of national economy and economics, Greece transposed into national law European Parliament and Council Directive 98/72/EC amending Directive 95/2/EC on Food Additives other than Colours and Sweeteners.[84]

Joint Ministerial Decree A2E/5392[85] amending Decree Y3E/4243/97 has been adopted to comply with Commission Directive 98/36/EC amending Directive 96/5/EC on Processed Cereal-Based Foods and Baby Foods for Infants and Young Children.[86] On 16 June 1999 the ministers of national economy and agriculture adopted a Decree[87] amending Annex II of Ministerial Decree 290341/88,[88] to comply with the requirements of Commission Directive 98/82/EC amending the Annexes to Council Directives 86/362/EEC, 86/363/EEC and 90/462/EEC of the Fixing of Maximum Levels for Pesticides Residues in and on Cereals, Foodstuffs of Animal Origin and Certain Products of Plant Origin, including Fruit and Vegetables respectively.[89]

---

[83] *Official Gazette*, Vol. B, No. 1964, Nov. 1999.     [84] [1998] OJ L295/18.
[85] *Official Gazette*, Vol. B, No. 28, Jan. 1999.      [86] [1998] OJ L167/23.
[87] Joint Ministerial Decree 97252, *Official Gazette*, Vol. B, No. 1240, June 1999.
[88] Ibid., Vol. B, No. 560, July 1999.           [89] [1998] OJ L290/25.

# VIII. Ireland

YVONNE SCANNELL*

## A. AIR POLLUTION

The Environmental Protection Agency Act 1992 (Ambient Air Quality Assessment and Management) Regulations 1999[1] give effect to Articles 2, 3, 5, and 11(1)(d) of Directive 96/62/EC on Ambient Air Quality Assessment and Management (Ambient Air Directive).[2] The European Communities (Motor Vehicle Type Approval) (No. 2) Regulations 1999[3] give effect to and Commission Directives 98/90/EEC and 1999/7/EEC, concerning the type approval of motor vehicles, trailers, and their components.[4] The European Communities (Agricultural and Forestry Vehicles Type Approval) Regulations 1999[5] give effect to Commission Directives 98/38/EC, 98/40/EC, and 98/89/EC concerning the type approval for agricultural or forestry tractors.[6]

The Air Pollution Act 1987 (Environmental Specifications for Petrol and Diesel Fuels) Regulations 1999[7] prescribe environmental specifications for petrol and diesel fuels marketed on or after 1 January 2000 and 1 January 2005, subject to provisions for existing residues in storage tanks and other limited circumstances.

The European Communities (Control of Emission of Gaseous and Particulate Pollutants from Non-road Mobile Machinery) Regulations 1999[8] set out requirements for the type approval of certain types of non-road mobile machinery in accordance with the requirements of Directive 97/68/EEC,[9] and prohibit the placing on the market of machines which do not comply with the Directive after 15 December 1999.

## B. CHEMICALS

### i. Plant Protection Products

The European Communities (Introduction of Organisms Harmful to Plants or Plant Products) (Prohibition) (Amendment) (No. 2) Regulations 1999[10] implement the provisions of Commission Directive 98/100/EC Recognizing Protected Zones Exposed to Particular Plant Health Risks in the Community.[11]

The European Communities (Introduction of Organisms Harmful to Plants or Plant Products) (Prohibition) (Amendment) (No. 2) Regulations 1999[12] protect against the introduction and spread of harmful organisms by implementing

---

* Professor, Trinity College Law School; Arthur Cox Solicitors, Dublin, Ireland.
[1] SI 1999/28.  [2] [1996] OJ L296/55.  [3] SI 1999/183.
[4] [1998] OJ L337/29; and [1999] OJ L040/36.  [5] SI 1999/99.
[6] [1998] OJ L170/13; [1998] OJ L171/28; and [1998] OJ L322/40.  [7] SI 1999/407.
[8] SI 1999/396.  [9] [1998] OJ L059/1.  [10] SI 1999/53.  [11] [1998] OJ L351/35.
[12] SI 1999/227.

Directive 98/57/EC and Commission Directive 1999/53/EC amending Annex III of Council Directive 77/93/EC.[13] The European Communities (Introduction of Organisms Harmful to Plants or Plant Products) (Prohibition) (Prohibition) (Temporary Provisions) Regulations 1999[14] implement Commission Decisions 95/506/EC and 98/738/EC,[15] and prohibit the import of Dutch potatoes which do not meet the requirements of Directive 95/506/EC[16] in relation to brown rot disease. The European Communities (Introduction of Organisms Harmful to Plants or Plant Products) (Prohibition) (Amendment) (No. 3) Regulations 1999[17] implement the provisions of Commission Directive 1999/84/EC amending Directive 92/76/EEC,[18] extending the period of recognition of the EU protective measures against beef necrotic yellow-vein virus. The European Communities (Authorization, Placing on the Market and Control of Plant Protection Products) (Amendment) Regulations 1999[19] give effect to Commission Directive 98/47/EC including an active substance (azoxystrobin) in Annex 1 to Council Directive 91/414/EEC concerning the Placing of Plant Protection Products on the Market.[20] The European Communities (Authorisation, Placing on the Market, Use and Control of Plant Protection Products) (Amendment) (No. 2) Regulations 1999[21] give effect to Commission Directive 97/73/EC and 1999/1/EC which amend Annex 1 to Council Directive 91/414/EEC.[22] The European Communities (Authorization, Placing on the Market, Use and Control of Plant Protection Products) (Amendment) (No. 3) Regulations 1999[23] give effect to Commission Directives 1999/73/EC and 1999/80/EC, amending Annex 1 to Council Directive 91/414/EEC.[24]

### ii. *Classification, Packaging, and Labelling of Dangerous Substances*

The European Communities (Classification, Packaging, Labelling, and Notification of Dangerous Substances (Amendment) Regulations 1999[25] amend the 1994 Regulations by amending Annexes 1 and V of Directive 67/548/EEC.[26]

### C. NATURE CONSERVATION

The European Communities (Conservation of Wild Birds) (Amendment) Regulations 1999[27] add ten additional sites to the list of Special Protection Areas (SPAs) for wild birds, in accordance with Article 4 of Directive 79/409/EEC on the Conservation of Wild Birds (Wild Birds Directive).[28] Many controls exist with respect to developments affecting these sites.

Nature conservation law is one of the hottest areas of environmental law for the immediate future. This area of law provides fertile grounds for litigation, in particular where public sector development is concerned.

---

[13] [1998] OJ L235/1; and [1999] OJ L142/29.  [14] SI 1999/38.
[15] [1995] OJ L291/48; and [1998] OJ L354/62.  [16] [1995] OJ L291/48.  [17] SI 1999/354.
[18] [1999] OJ L273/11.  [19] SI 1999/182.  [20] [1998] OJ L191/50.  [21] SI 1999/198.
[22] [1997] OJ L353/26; and [1999] OJ L021/21.  [23] SI 1999/356.
[24] [1999] OJ L206/16; and [1999] OJ L210/13.  [25] SI 1999/363.  [26] [1967] OJ L196/1.
[27] SI 1999/131.  [28] [1979] OJ L103/1.

An example of such litigation in Ireland is the High Court case *Dubsky* v. *Drogheda Port Company*,[29] which constituted the final stage of a drama which had begun in an earlier High Court case on 10 September 1999. The plaintiff in the case, a respected Irish environmentalist, sought an interlocutory injunction restraining Drogheda Port from carrying out further dredging works and directing it to open sluices so that water drained off from the foreshore could be reintroduced, and food could be provided for migratory winter birds in two SPAs which hosted a priority species under Directive 92/43/EEC on the Conservation of Natural Habitats and of Wild Fauna and Flora (Habitats Directive).[30] Part of the area had also been identified as a 'Candidate Site' for designation as a Special Area of Conservation (SAC) under the Habitats Directive. Drogheda Port was licensed to carry out the dredging in the area, under the condition that it would provide compensatory feeding for wild birds whose normal habitats on the Stagreenan Polder would be disturbed by the land reclamation works, which it intended to do by removing an infestation of spartina grass from an area of the foreshore adjacent to the area being reclaimed. Spartina grass inhibits access by birds to food in the mudflats on which it grows. Removing it provides access to food underneath, but this has to be done in a delicate manner, or the food and the habitats may be destroyed, as the plaintiff in this case feared *in casu*. Justice O'Sullivan in the High Court agreed with the plaintiff, and on 10 September 1999 ordered the Port to apply proper methods within five weeks, under the supervision of a wildlife expert.

However, the Port did not comply with this timeframe, and the plaintiff consequently brought a second action against it with the High Court, in view of the imminent arrival of migratory birds to the area. In this case, with Justice Kelly presiding, the orders for proper compliance with the earlier High Court order and the reopening of the sluice gates were refused on 22 October 1999. Plaintiff appealed this decision to the Supreme Court, which on 17 November 1999 overturned the High Court judgment, but refused to order the reopening of the sluice gates.

The case was referred back to the High Court, with Justice O'Sullivan again presiding. Plaintiff repeated her argument that the compensatory measures proposed by the Port in its Environmental Impact Statement (EIS) were defective, and that alternative measures which she proposed would be better. The High Court dismissed this argument stating that once a licence is granted, it is not open to the court to modify its terms. The court held that its role is to ensure that the licence terms are complied with, although Justice O'Sullivan later admitted to some reservations as to the suitability of the measures proposed in the EIS, holding that some breaches of his order were more technical than substantial because the lack of alternative food for the birds was caused, not by non-compliance with the court order or the undertakings in the EIS, but by the 'limitations in the philosophy' in the EIS. The court restrained the Port from carrying out further work until they complied

[29] *Dubsky* v. *Drogheda Port Company*, High Court, 22 Feb. 2000.       [30] [1992] OJ L206/7.

with the terms of the original order, and had prepared a timeframe for providing a properly defined area of feeding grounds for the birds.

This case is an interesting example of wildlife protection being achieved not by directly relying on wildlife legislation, but rather by enforcing a licence granted for development on the foreshore. Yet, it raises concerns about the wisdom, if not the legality, of enforcing undertakings in an EIS accompanying an application for an environmental authorization which are subsequently found unsuitable for achieving their objectives. This is a danger which arises when regulatory authorities, and sometimes environmentalists, insist that proposals to mitigate or compensate for environmental damage in EISs must be complied with to the letter. Licences and planning permissions frequently condition developers to comply with measures to mitigate predicted environmental effects as proposed in their EISs. This is undesirable in principle because measures proposed in EISs cannot take account of the practical situations which occur when a development is being carried out. If they are not good enough to ensure habitat protection, sufficient flexibility should be given to developers to allow them to take alternative measures when experience shows that the originally proposed measures are inadequate. Developers are not at liberty to do this when they are obliged to comply with inappropriately rigid conditions in authorizations. Nor, according to Justice O'Sullivan in this case, are the courts free to modify terms in authorizations.

Article 4(4) Wild Birds, as amended by Article 6 Habitats Directive, requires Member States to take 'appropriate steps' to avoid significant deterioration of natural habitats and disturbances of protected species in SPAs. Strict requirements in environmental authorizations to comply with mitigatory proposals in an EIS are not always 'appropriate measures'. Regulatory authorities should therefore consider whether expecting or conditioning developers to adhere rigidly to proposals in EISs constitutes appropriate measures. In extreme cases, it may be that the courts in fact have powers to modify conditions in authorizations in order to ensure compliance with Article 6 Habitats Directive.

Nature conservation was also at issue in *Murphy* v. *Wicklow County Council*.[31] The court dismissed an appeal against a High Court decision on 19 March 1999. Murphy had sought to prevent the widening of the N11 through the Glen of the Downs on various grounds. A Nature Reserve Order designating lands in the Glen of the Downs provided that 'any part thereof which is a public road' was not included in the nature reserve. Murphy alleged that widening the road constituted a breach of the order and that this was illegal unless or until the order was revoked or amended, arguing that the words 'any part thereof which is a public road' could only mean the public road as it was when the order was enacted in 1980. Defendants argued that the words of the statutory instrument must be construed as to mean a public road which may *at any time* be built through the reserve, including any future road or widening the existing road. Consequently, they contended that an amendment of the 1980

---

[31] *Murphy* v. *Wicklow County Council*, Supreme Court, 2 Dec. 1999.

order was unnecessary for road widening. The Supreme Court, reversing the High Court on this issue, held that the order did not have to be amended to enable the proposed road widening but that it might be 'advisable' to redefine that area excluded from the order to avoid ambiguity created by the words 'a public roadway' in the order.[32] The High Court had held that the plaintiff in the 'exceptional' circumstances of the case had *locus standi* to enforce the Wildlife Act 1976. This finding was not appealed. Although this writer considers that the courts have been somewhat too generous in according *locus standi* to third parties in some environmental cases, it is submitted that important issues on how public authorities carry out their statutory functions were raised in this case and that the decision to grant *locus standi* was justified by these. The history of the transfer of the ownership of the lands involved and other examples of administrative inertia graphically described in the High Court judgment are indicative of a culture which should not be tolerated in public authorities. The pubic interest was surely served in exposing this.

### D. WASTE

The European Communities (Processing of Mammalian and Animal Waste) (Amendment) Regulations 1999[33] set higher standard for treating these wastes prior to disposal in order to protect human health and the environment. The Litter Pollution Regulations 1999[34] revoke earlier regulations and provide for better controls over litter pollution, including on-the-spot fines.

### E. WATER

#### i. Marine Pollution

The Sea Pollution (Amendment) Act 1999 amended the 1991 Act, in order to give effect to the International Convention on Oil Pollution Preparedness, Response and Cooperation.[35] The Act was came into force by virtue of the Sea Pollution (Amendment) Act 1999 (Commencement) Order 1999 on 1 September 1999.[36]

The European Communities (Minimum Requirements for Vessels Carrying Dangerous or Polluting Goods) (Amendment) Regulations 1999[37] give effect to Commission Directive 98/74/EC amending Council Directive 93/75/EEC concerning the Minimum Requirements for Vessels Bound for or Leaving Community Ports and Carrying Dangerous or Polluting Goods,[38] and amend the earlier European Communities (Minimum Requirements for Vessels Carrying Dangerous or Polluting Goods) Regulations 1995.[39]

---

[32] Justice Denham, in a separate judgment, interpreted the order literally and more convincingly as excluding *any* public road. She held that the use of the indefinite 'a' public road, as distinct from 'the' public road in the order, meant that *any* widened public road that is wider than the 1980 road is excluded from the order.

[33] SI 1999/200.     [34] SI 1999/359.     [35] London, 30 Nov. 1990.     [36] SI 1999/18.

[37] SI 1999/96.     [38] [1998] OJ L276/7.     [39] SI 1995/229.

The European Communities (Marine Equipment) (Amendment) Regulations 1999[40] give effect to Commission Directive 98/85/EC which amends Council Directive 96/98/EC on Marine Equipment.[41]

The Oil Pollution of the Sea (Civil Liability and Compensation (Annual Returns and Contributions) Regulations 1999[42] made under the Oil Pollution of the Sea (Civil Liability and Compensation) Act 1988 require persons receiving more than 150,000 tonnes of crude or fuel oil each year to make an annual return to the Minister for the Marine and pay *pro-rata* financial contributions to the International Oil Pollution Compensation Fund 1992.

### ii. Groundwater

The protection of Groundwater Regulations 1999[43] made under the Environmental Protection Agency (EPA) Act 1992 give effect to Council Directive 80/68/EEC on the Protection of Groundwater against Pollution Caused by Certain Dangerous Substances.[44] Environmental standards are prescribed for certain substances. Sanitary authorities must now obtain a licence from the EPA for discharging certain dangerous substances to groundwater unless the activity to which the licence relates is subject to licensing under the Environmental Protection Agency Act 1992 or the Waste Management Act 1996.[45] The Regulations now ensure that an independent regulatory authority controls their discharges. The procedures governing the licence application and decision-making procedures are similar to those applicable to applications for licences made under the Local Government (Water Pollution) Acts 1977–90.

### iii. Drinking Water

The European Communities (Quality of Water Intended for Human Consumption) (Amendment) Regulations 1999[46] give further effect to Directive 80/778/EEC relating to the Quality of Water for Human Consumption (Drinking Water Directive).[47] The Regulations require that the public be warned when the quality of water in public and private supplies does not meet the standards in the European Communities (Quality of Water Intended for Human Consumption) Regulations 1998, and that action programmes for improving the inferior water quality be prepared as soon as practicable. Implementation of the Drinking Water Directive had previously been considered defective in so far as it had excluded private water supplies from statutory requirements. The new Regulations were intended to tackle these insufficiencies.

### iiv. Urban Waste Water

The Environmental Protection Agency Act 1992 (Urban Waste-Water Treatment) (Amendment) Regulations 1999 clarify certain monitoring requirements for

---

[40] SI 1999/112.     [41] [1998] OJ L315/14.     [42] SI 1999/16.     [43] SI 1999/41.
[44] [1980] OJ L020/43.
[45] Sanitary authorities are exempted from the requirement to obtain a licence for discharges to waters under section 4 of the Local Government (Water Pollution) Act 1977.
[46] SI 1999/350.     [47] [1980] OJ L229/11.

phosphorus and nitrogen and give effect to EC Directive 98/15/EC amending Council Directive 91/271/EEC with Respect to Certain Requirements Established in Annex I thereof.[48]

The Local Government Act 1994 (By-Laws) Regulations 1999[49] extend and improve the owners of local authorities to make by-laws under the Local Government Act 1994 in relation to agricultural activities.

The Local Government (Water Pollution) (Amendment) Regulations 1999[50] amend Part VI of the Local Government (Water Pollution) Regulations 1992. They require applicants for licences to discharge effluents to aquifers to submit the results of prior investigation (the contents of which are prescribed), unless the applicant can satisfy the local authority concerned that the harmful substance in the trade or sewage effluent is present in such small quantities and concentration as to obviate present or future danger of deterioration in the quality of the water in the aquifer to which the discharge is to be made. Quality standards are set for discharges. Certain conditions must be attached if a licence is granted for a discharge to an aquifer and the licence must be reviewed at intervals of not more than four years. These standards must also be applied by the Bord Paella (the Planning Appeals Board) in dealing with water pollution licences and by the EPA, carrying out its functions under the Environmental Protection Agency Act 1992 and the Waste Management Act 1996. Furthermore, the local authorities are to apply these standards in carrying out their functions under the Waste Management Act 1996, unless special circumstances exist.

### F. HORIZONTAL INSTRUMENTS

#### i. EIA

The European Communities (Environmental Impact Assessment) (Amendment) Regulations 1999[51] extensively amend a number of earlier EIA Regulations and various Acts.[52] The Regulations were necessary to give effect to Directive 97/11/EC amending Directive 85/337/EEC on the Assessment of the Effects of Certain Public and Private Projects on the Environment (EIA Directive).[53] Important amendments include the obligation of regulatory authorities to determine the scope of environmental impact statements on request, the provision of better procedures for notifying other Member States when a project is likely to have significant effects on their environments, specification of the information to be provided in EISs, and thresholds for requiring EISs for projects listed in Annex II in the Directive. They also ensure that projects located in environmentally sensitive locations and habitats classified under the Habitats Directive are

---

[48] [1998] OJ L067/29.     [49] SI 1999/78.     [50] SI 1999/42.     [51] SI 1999/93.
[52] *Inter alia*, the Local Government (Planning and Development) Acts 1963–98, the Foreshore Act 1933, the Arterial Drainage Act 1945, the Harbours Act 1946, the Petroleum and Other Mineral Act 1960, the Gas Act 1960, the Roads Act 1993, the Transport (Dublin Light Rail) Act 1996, the Dublin Docklands Development Act 1997, and the Fisheries (Amendment) Act 1997.
[53] [1997] OJ L073/5.

subjected to EIA. The latter amendments were designed to ensure full compliance with Community Law. Associated Regulations made under the Local Government (Planning and Development) Act 1963 were also amended

Case C–392/96, *Commission* v. *Ireland*,[54] judgment of 21 September 1999, is one of the most significant decisions of the ECJ on EIA. Ireland chose to implement the Directive by requiring EIA for all projects listed in Annex II thereof once they reached a certain threshold level set out in Part 11 of the First Schedule to the 1989 Regulations. In addition, discretion was granted to planning authorities to require EIA below those thresholds if they consider that the development is likely to have significant effects on the environment. Yet no provision was made for requiring EIA for projects below these thresholds, consisting of the land reclamation and afforestation. These activities were exempted under section 4 of the Local Government (Planning and Development) Act 1963, unless they exceeded specified thresholds which related solely to their size. Consequently, EIA could not be made obligatory for these projects. The Irish implementation measures were impugned by the ECJ, holding that, although Article 4(2) EIA Directive confers a discretion on Member States to specify types of projects which are to be subject to EIA and to establish the criteria or thresholds applicable, the limits of that discretion are circumscribed by Article 2(1) EIA Directive, which requires that projects 'likely to have significant effects on the environment, by virtue of their nature, size or location' require EIA, rather than merely by virtue of its *size*. The ECJ further held that Ireland had exceeded the limits of its discretion under Articles 2(1) and 4(2) EIA Directive by setting thresholds for afforestation and land reclamation without also ensuring that the objective of EIA legislation will not be circumvented by the splitting of projects.

The discretion given to Member States in Article 4(2) EIA Directive in deciding which Annex II projects should be subjected to EIA has been examined by the ECJ in a number of cases. The court has consistently held that the Directive is not to be construed narrowly and that Member States may not set thresholds for projects which are so high that most, if not all, projects of that kind will automatically be exempt from EIA.[55] It has also decided that Member States may not exempt whole classes of projects from assessment in advance.[56]

The vigilance of the Irish courts in upholding EC environmental law manifested itself again in a High Court case concerning the EIA Directive: the *O'Nuallain* v. *Dublin Corporation*.[57] The case concerned a proposal by Dublin Corporation to erect a Millennium Monument in the most important historic street in Dublin: O'Connell Street. The sculptural feature consisted of a 400-feet-high metallic spire which would be visible from many locations and which would exceed the height of all other structures in the vicinity. The decision to

[54] Case C–392/96, *Commission* v. *Ireland* [1999] ECR I–5901.
[55] Case C–72/95, *Aannemersbedrijf Kraaijeveld BV and Others* v. *Gedeputeerde Staten van Zuid-Holland* [1996] ECR I–5403.
[56] Case C–133/94, *Commission* v. *Belgium* [1996] ECR I–2323.
[57] *O'Nuallain* v. *Dublin Corporation*, High Court, 2 June 1999.

erect this was adopted by Managerial order after compliance with the provisions of Part X of the Local Government (Planning and Development) Regulations 1994, which regulate local authorities carrying out developments in their own areas. In respect of a possible EIS requirement, it had been decided that the project should be pursued under Part X of the 1994 Regulations, rather than Part 1X, and that it was not subject to EIA under Part I or Part II of the First Schedule to the European Communities (Environmental Impact Assessment) Regulations 1989, thus relieving it of the EIS requirement. The High Court[58] held that since the project entailed 'infrastructural and, in particular, . . . urban development', it fell within the scope of Annex II EIA Directive and the Irish implementing Regulations thereto. Furthermore, it indicated that the Minister for the Environment, rather than a local authority, is exclusively empowered to decide upon the EIA requirement under the former provisions. An argument that EIA is only required when an *adverse* environmental impact could be predicted was dismissed as being a delimitation of the EIA Directive which the court, following a decision of the European Court of Justice (ECJ) in *Kraaijeveld*,[59] held could not be construed narrowly as it holds 'a wide scope and a broad purpose'. Consequently, although the project fell well below the threshold for Part II, section 10 developments set in the 1989 EIA Regulations implementing the Directive, it was a project likely to have, and intended to have, 'significant' effects on the environment, leading the court to require an EIS on the basis of an EIA.

At first blush, this decision appears to be excessively *'communitaire'* since, after all, an independent jury for an art feature selected the proposal after a public open competition. It is reasonable to assume that the authors of the designs submitted and the jury which selected the winning project were qualified (and indeed more qualified than members of the general public) to ensure the aesthetic quality of the monument and that it would cause no adverse environmental impacts. On reflection, however, compliance with EIA procedures *formally* ensures that *all* relevant impacts of the proposed structure are considered and that all citizens have an opportunity to comment on an aesthetic proposal which, if erected, will have a very real impact on the most important street in the country and perspectives from many other locations.

### ii. IPPC

An interesting case in respect of Integrated Pollution Prevention Control (IPPC) in 1999 was the Supreme Court case *Ni H-Eili* v. *Environmental Protection Agency and Roche Ireland*.[60] This case concerned an application for judicial review challenging the validity of a revised Integrated Pollution Control (IPC) licence granted by the Environmental Protection Agency (EPA) for a hazardous waste incinerator at a pharmaceutical plant owned by Syntex in Clareclastle, County Clare. Roche had bought the plant by the time the proceedings were heard in the Supreme Court. The incinerator was necessary

---

[58] Justice Smyth.    [59] See n. 55 above.
[60] *Ni H-Eili* v. *Environmental Protection Agency and Roche Ireland*, Supreme Court, 30 July 1999.

to enable Roche to meet BATNEEC standards for the production of pharmaceuticals. It was designed to ensure, *inter alia*, a reduction of at least 90 per cent in the amount of volatile organic substances emitted from the plant. Plaintiff was concerned that the incinerator would emit dioxins. The Environmental Impact Statement (EIS) submitted with the planning application and the IPC licence application for the project had indicated that the emissions of dioxins would not cause significant environmental pollution.[61]

Plaintiff alleged, first, that the decision to permit the incinerator was unreasonable due to the lack of medical evidence to support the contention that the project would not have a negative impact on human health.[62] Essentially, the court held that the EPA did not act unreasonably in concluding that human health would not be endangered by the dioxin emissions of the project.

Second, the plaintiff alleged that the decision was invalid as a result of the non-compliance with various regulations requiring a description of the plant and technology to be used because the design and details of the incinerator had not been provided. The court described this argument as 'misconceived', and consequently did not really address the issue. It concluded that the EPA was justified in its acceptance of the plans for the project.

The third and final argument concerned the alleged breach by the EPA of its statutory duty to provide reasons for its decision.[63] Essentially, the court was asked to decide whether authorities are required to present *all* their motivations and considerations, rather than the most relevant ones, thereby touching upon the quality control function on administrative decision-making. Environmental regulatory authorities in Ireland are not noted for giving such exhaustive reasoned decisions. The scope of the *O'Keeffe* test which is similar to the English test in *Wednesbury Corporation* v. *Ministry and Housing and Local Government*[64] is such that if this function is not taken seriously, the rule of law may be undermined in administrative decision-making. In dealing with this argument, the Supreme Court drew a distinction, the merits of which are questionable, between the adequacy of reasons given for a proposed determination and the adequacy of reasons given for the final decision made after dealing with objections to the proposed determination. It considered that the former was primarily relevant to the applicant since conditions imposed constitute intrusions on his industrial enterprise. Applying *O'Keeffe* v. *An Bord Pleanala*,[65] the court held that the EPA could rely on the entire document constituting the proposed determination which includes a combination of reasons given for its decision and the conditions and the reasons given for those

---

[61] The maximum amounts which could be emitted under the license ($0.1\text{ng/m}^3$—in the order of 1% of background level) would not increase ground level concentrations of dioxins above background levels.

[62] In particular, no studies had been carried out to establish the levels of dioxins in *human beings* in the neighbourhood of the plant. Evidence had been provided of ambient dioxin levels in the environment ($0.001\text{ng/m}^3$) and of the impact of the proposed incinerator on these ($0. + 00003\text{ng/m}^3$).

[63] Art. 28 Environmental Protection Agency (EPA) Act (Licensing) Regulations 1995.

[64] (1965) 3 *All England Law Reports* 371.          [65] (1993) 1 *Irish Law Review* 39.

conditions. However, the court considered that the EPA's obligation is different when giving its final decision. In this case, the court held that the EPA was obliged to give the reasons for overruling objections or rejecting submissions made to the Agency during the objection procedure stating that:

Those who have gone to the trouble and expense of formulating and presenting serious objections on a matter of intense public interest are entitled to obtain an explanation as to why their submissions are rejected.

In this respect, the court held, approving the High Court decision in *O'Donoghue* v. *An Bord Pleanala*,[66] that the duty to give reasons could not be satisfied by recourse to an 'uninformative if technically correct formula' and that the decision should indicate that the decision-maker had 'addressed its mind to the substantive issue', which justified its decision. In *O'Donoghue*, the High Court held that formulaic reasons given by An Bord Pleanala in planning appeals such that it considered 'the application accorded with the proper planning and development of the area' would not be sufficient. By analogy, one can safely assume that formulaic reasons for conditions given by the EPA such as 'in the interests of environmental protection' are not sufficient. The court held, citing a statement in the House of Lords decision in *Bolton Metropolitan District Council & Others* v. *Secretary of State for the Environment*, that reasons given must be 'proper, intelligible and adequate'.[67] Essentially, the court held that the reasons for the Agency's decision were contained in the inspector's report and that it was not necessary on grounds of practicability 'in the circumstances of this case', being a complex and contentious one, to repeat those reasons in the minutes of the EPA's Board meeting. Accordingly, *in casu*, the Court found sufficient compliance with the statutory requirement.

The Court did not sanction this method of giving reasons for decisions in *all* cases because it held that the Environmental Protection Agency Act (Licensing) Regulations 1995 anticipated that the record of the Agency's decision would itself explain 'shortly and simply' why objections were rejected. It stated that reasons for a decision should be readily available without the need for excessive research or inquiry.

The *Ni h-Eili* case sets out extensive guidelines on the duty of administrative authorities to give adequate reasons for their decisions. The judicial deference granted to administrative decisions since *O'Keeffe* is somewhat balanced by the stringency of this obligation. One may anticipate future judicial reviews based, not on the argument of the unreasonableness of administrative decisions, but on failures to justify them properly. The eventual outcome may be a marked improvement in the quality of decisions, although it is regrettable that the burden of the costs of this improvement will fall partly on applicants for various regulatory authorizations.

---

[66] (1991) *Irish Law Reports Monthly* 750, at 757.     [67] (1995) *JPL* 1043.

### D. MISCELLANOUS

*i. Noise*

The Air Aviation Authority (Noise Certification and Limitation) (Amendment) Order 1999[68] amends the Air Aviation Authority (Noise Certification and Limitation) Order 1984 1999[69] by incorporating noise standards in the latest edition of Annex 16, Chapters 2 and 3 of the Chicago Convention.

*ii. Motorway Schemes*

Under section 55A of the Roads Act 1993, inserted by section 6 of the Roads (Amendment) Act 1998, leave to apply for judicial review of motorway schemes is subject to the same procedures as leave to apply for judicial review of decisions on planning applications under section 19 of the Local Government (Planning and Development) Act 1992. Applicants must first apply for leave to apply and must show 'substantial' grounds before it will be granted. No appeal against the High Court decision can be taken without a certificate that a point of law of exceptional public importance is involved which it is desirable in the public interest that the Supreme Court should consider.

In case *Jackson Way Properties Ltd* v. *Minister for the Environment and Others*,[70] the applicant applied for leave to apply for judicial review challenging the validity of an order made by the minister. The order had approved a motorway scheme, and was contested on the grounds that, *inter alia,* in assessing an EIS for the motorway, the minister did not take account of a change in the zoning of land (from agricultural industrial use) which occurred *after* the inquiry into the proposed scheme and *before* the minister made the order confirming the scheme. A proposal to zone the land industrial had been published prior to the inquiry, and had been considered by the inspector. The High Court held that this was not a 'substantial' or even an arguable ground. It also held that the test for 'substantial' was the same under planning legislation and roads legislation, but that the definition of 'substantial grounds may in practice be applied rather differently where a vast public scheme for a motorway is involved as distinct from an individual planning permission'. The court did not indicate what these might be.

---

[68] SI 1999/421.                              [69] SI 1984/131.
[70] *Jackson Way Properties Ltd* v. *Minister for the Environment and Others*, High Court, 2 July 1999.

# IX. Italy

FRANCESCO FRANCIONI and MASSIMILIANO MONTINI*

## A. AIR POLLUTION

Legislative Decree No. 351 of 4 August 1999,[1] which implemented in Italy Directive 96/62/EC on Ambient Air Quality Assessment and Management (Ambient Air Directive),[2] defines new reference criteria for the evaluation and management of ambient air quality, defined as outdoor air in the troposphere, excluding workplaces. The Decree modifies the legislation presently in force in Italy on air quality and envisages the progressive abrogation of Decree No. 203/88[3] and its implementing regulations. The new decree introduces new prescriptions on the periodic evaluation and management of air quality, with particular reference to air quality in bigger cities. Regional authorities are required to undertake periodic evaluations of the air quality in their respective territories every five years, starting with a preliminary evaluation within three months from the entry into force of the new decree. On the basis of the results of these evaluations a specific action plan for the management of air quality within each region must be drafted. Such plans must contain measures for the improvement of air quality in those areas where the maximum concentration limit values for certain pollutants are exceeded, and maintenance actions for the areas in which the level of pollutants is below the limit values.

Pursuant to the power of delegation conferred by Law No. 413/1997,[4] the ministry of environment, in cooperation with the ministry of health, issued Decree No. 163 on 21 April 1999.[5] This Decree established environmental and sanitary criteria to be relied upon by the mayors of major Italian cities for the adoption of measures for limiting vehicular circulation when the concentration of certain pollutants in the air reaches dangerous levels. The Decree (also called the *Benzene Decree*) calls upon the mayors to initiate a preliminary evaluation of the quality of air in major cities, within one month from its entry into force. Subsequently, they are to produce annual reports, on the basis of which the mayors with the technical support of the competent ARPA (Regional Authority for the Protection of the Environment) and ASL (Local Health Authority), may determine temporary or periodic limitations to vehicular circulation to achieve a reduction of the concentration of certain pollutants in the air.

In order to contribute to an improvement of the quality of air, the ministry of environment issued Decree No. 76 of 20 January 1999,[6] including a requirement

---

* Both Professor and Researcher, University of Siena, Siena, Italy.
[1] *Gazzetta Ufficiale della Republica Italiana* (*G.U.R.I.*) No. 241 of 13 Oct. 1999.
[2] [1996] OJ L296/55.  [3] *G.U.R.I.* No. 241 of 13 Oct. 1999.
[4] *G.U.R.I.* No. 282 of 3 Dec. 1997.  [5] *G.U.R.I.* No. 135 of 11 June 1999.
[6] *G.U.R.I.* No. 73 of 29 Mar. 1999.

for vapour recovery units at petrol refuelling pumps by 30 September 1999 in bigger cities and by 30 June 2000 nationwide.

## B. NATURE CONSERVATION

On the basis of framework law No. 394/1991,[7] a substantial number of new parks and protected areas have been created. Of particular relevance is the institution of the marine protected areas of Portofino (in the Liguria Region)[8] and Capo Carbonara (in the Sardinia Region).[9] Additionally, a new National Park of the Cinque Terre (in the Liguria Region)[10] has been created, pursuant to this framework law.

In October 1999, the government, acting upon delegation powers conferred by parliament, issued the long-awaited 'Single Act on Cultural and Environmental Heritage',[11] with the specific aim of coordinating and rationalizing all existing legislation regarding this field. The Single Act constitutes a systematic text collecting all the provisions applicable to the management and conservation of cultural and environmental heritage.

## C. WASTE

There have been repeated pleas for the exclusion from the scope of the framework legislation on waste[12] of substances that remain at the end of an industrial process, but are capable of reutilization as such in the same industrial process, or in another, without being subject to any waste recovery activity. To tackle this problem, the ministry of environment issued an explanatory document in 1999.[13] However, not all problems and doubts have been resolved by this *circolare*, and parliament is working on a new Act, which should provide an authoritative definition of the notions of 'waste' and 'action of discarding', with the aim of excluding from the scope of the legislation on waste most substances capable of economic reutilization without the need of any waste recovery operation.

On 8 July 1999 CONAI, the super-consortium empowered by Law No. 22/1997 of 5 February 1997,[14] with the task of coordinating the reuse, recycling, and recovery of waste and packaging materials nationwide, signed an agreement with the Association of the Italian Municipalities (ANCI). The agreement enumerates the costs to be paid by the CONAI to the municipalities for the collection of steel, aluminium, paper, wood, and plastic.[15] No agreement was reached

---

[7] *G.U.R.I.* No. 292 of 13 Dec. 1991.

[8] Decree of the Ministry of Environment of 26 Apr. 1999; *G.U.R.I.* No. 131 of 7 June 1999.

[9] Decree of the Ministry of Environment of 3 Aug. 1999; *G.U.R.I.* No. 229 of 29 Sept. 1999.

[10] Decree of the President of the Republic of 6 Oct. 1999; *G.U.R.I.* No. 295 of 17 Dec. 1999.

[11] Legislative Decree No. 490 of 29 Oct. 1999; Ordinary Supplement No. 227/L to G.U.R.I. No. 302 of 27 Dec. 1999.                                          [12] Decree No.22/1997; n. 14 below.

[13] *Circolare* of the Ministry of Environment of 28 June 1999, published on the Internet at: www.minambiente.it.

[14] *G.U.R.I.* No. 38 of 15 Feb. 1997.

[15] Agreement between CONAI and ANCI, published on the Internet at: www.conai.it.

for the costs incurred by the municipalities for the collection of glass. Instead, the payable amount was determined by a ministerial decree, a month later.[16]

With the adoption of Legislative Decree No. 209 of 22 May 1999,[17] which implements Directive 96/59/EC on the Disposal of Polychlorinated Biphenyls and Polychlorinated Terphenyls (PCB/PCT Directive),[18] a specific regulation on the disposal of items containing used PCBs/PCTs, has finally been issued. Following the Decree, all PCB-containing items will need to be registered with the competent authorities by 31 December 2000, to be progressively disposed of by means of burning in controlled incineration plants. The incineration technique must be in conformity with the provisions of Directive 94/67/EC on the Incineration of Hazardous Waste,[19] which has not yet been implemented into Italian law

Article 5(6) of Decree No. 22/1997[20] had initially set 1 January 2000 as the deadline for the disposal of waste in landfills, with the exception of certain specific categories of waste identified by ministerial decrees. However, as this proved to be an unrealistic goal, the deadline was subsequently shifted to the date of implementation in Italy of Directive 99/31/EC on the Landfill of Waste,[21] by Article 1 of Law No. 500[22] of 30 December 1999.

Legislative Decree No. 471/1999 of 25 October 1999[23] finally gave the long-awaited full effect to Article 17 of Decree No. 22/1997 on soil sanitation.[24] The new decree specifies the concentration limit values for certain pollutants in soil, superficial water, and groundwater, for two different categories of (end) use of the site: first, residential and green areas, and second, commercial and industrial areas. It also supplements the provisions of Article 17 of Law 22/1997, laying down procedures for the drafting of clean-up and reinstatement projects, including approval by the competent administrative authorities. Additionally, it makes a clear distinction between the different types of operations that should be selected to clean up a contaminated site, depending upon the quality and quantity of pollutants present at the site, with regard to BATNEEC.

Decree No. 246/1999[25] of 24 May 1999 introduces a new regulation for underground storage tanks (USTs) aimed at the prevention of accidental spills from USTs which may pollute soil, superficial water, and groundwater. The regulation sets norms for the construction, installation, operation, and maintenance of USTs. Pursuant to the new regulation, before a new UST may become operational, authorization must be obtained and registered by the municipality. Existing USTs must be registered within eighteen months from the entry into force of the Decree. Furthermore, a timetable is given for their periodic maintenance. USTs which are deemed unsuitable for further operation must be

[16] Decree of the Ministry of Environment of 4 Aug. 1999; *G.U.R.I.* No. 191 of 16 Aug. 1999.
[17] *G.U.R.I.* No. 151 of 30 June 1999.      [18] [1996] OJ L243/31.
[19] [1994] OJ L365/34.          [20] See n. 14 above.          [21] [1999] OJ L182/1.
[22] *G.U.R.I.* No. 305 of 30 Dec. 1999.
[23] Ordinary Supplement No. 218/L to *G.U.R.I.* No. 293 of 15 Dec. 1999.
[24] See n. 14 above.          [25] *G.U.R.I.* No.176 of 29 July 1999.

decommissioned in conformity with requirements of the Decree. In the event that clean-up and reinstatement of the site is required, this will occur on the basis of the general provision on clean-up, Article 17 of Decree No. 22/1997.

### D. WATER

In 1999 new framework legislation on the protection of water from pollution, on water quality and on waste-water discharge was adopted by Legislative Decree No. 152/1999[26] of 11 May 1999. The Decree implements Directives 91/271/EEC on Urban Waste-Water Treatment[27] and Directive 91/676/EEC on Protection of Waters against Pollution Caused by Nitrates from Agricultural Sources,[28] but also anticipates an 'integrated approach' to water management, presently under discussion at EC level. Generally speaking, the new Decree provides norms for the protection of quality of watercourses, marine and groundwater by means of reducing the pollution and providing for the gradual cleaning up of contaminated water sources. Along with general criteria for the classification of national waters, the Decree identifies certain 'sensitive' and 'vulnerable' areas. Annex 5 establishes limit values applicable to waste-water discharges in Italy. Regional authorities may provide for their own specific limit values, to be applied on their territories, albeit that they may not lower the national standards set for certain dangerous substances listed in Table 3 of Annex 5. All water discharges require prior authorization. Competence to issue industrial waste-water discharge permits rests with the provinces, unless the emission is discharged into a public sewer, in which case the permit is issued by the municipality. Permits remain valid for four years and may be renewed. If the request is correctly filed with the competent authority before the expiry date, the permit will remain valid while the province decides upon its renewal. Permits for discharges including dangerous substances must be expressly granted. Any violation of Decree No. 152/1999 which causes contamination of waters, soil, subsoil, or other natural resources, creates a personal responsibility to cover the costs of clean-up and reinstatement operations, in conformity with Article 17 of Decree No. 22/1997.

### E. HORIZONTAL INSTRUMENTS

*i. Eco-Audit*

The number of Italian sites with EMAS certification reached twenty-one at the end of 1999. In general, it may be observed that most Italian companies which seek environmental certification prefer to obtain the ISO14000 certification rather than the EMAS, probably due to the higher costs and heavier administrative load of the EMAS procedures.

---

[26] Ordinary Supplement No. 101/L to *G.U.R.I.* No. 124 of 29 May 1999.
[27] [1991] OJ L135/40.                              [28] [1991] OJ L375/1.

## ii. *EIA and IPPC*

By means of Legislative Decree No. 372 of 4 August 1999,[29] Italy has partially implemented Directive 96/61/EC concerning Integrated Pollution Prevention and Control (IPPC Directive).[30] The implementation of the Directive is limited to the existing plants. For new plants, the matter is still under discussion in parliament in the form of a new framework Act, which should provide comprehensive joint discipline for EIA and IPPC in Italy. For the moment, Decree No. 372/99[31] provides for the introduction of an integrated environmental authorization for the existing plants listed in Annex I (chemical plants and other industrial activities with a main impact on the environment). This integrated environmental authorization, valid for five years, will replace all existing environmental authorizations which were required previously to operate a plant. Plants subject to the IPPC regulation will be subject to existing binding limit values for polluting emissions prescribed by law. Additionally, they must attain the environmental quality standards listed in the authorization, which are determined also with regard to the environmental conditions of the plants' surrounding environment.

## iii. *SEVESO II*

Legislative Decree No. 334 of 17 August 1999[32] transposed into Italian law Directive 96/82/EC (SEVESO II Directive)[33] on the Control of Major-Accident Hazards Involving Dangerous Substances, amending Directive 82/501/EEC on the Major-Accident Hazards of Certain Industrial Activities (SEVESO Directive).[34] Generally speaking, the new Directive is characterized by a more rigorous approach to the identification of the duties of private companies with respect to safety measures and information procedures towards public authorities and local communities. The new Decree abolishes the distinction between plants using more dangerous and less dangerous substances, and imposes on all plants dealing with hazardous substances the same duty of notification. This notification must contain a safety report with all relevant information on the activities carried out within the plant, the dangerous substances used or produced, the security measures adopted, and the emergency plan in the event of an accident. The new notification requirement, pursuant to Decree No. 334/1999,[35] has to be made within 180 days from the beginning of construction, for new plants, and within one year from the entry into force of the new Decree for existing plants. The new Decree aims at promoting a stronger role for local public authorities and more relevant local community involvement with the management of the area surrounding the industrial plant. In this respect, the Decree introduces new provisions about the local community's involvement, consultation, and acknowledgement in the case of accidents or significant risk.

---

[29] *G.U.R.I.* No. 252 of 26 Oct. 1999.       [30] [1996] OJ L257/26.
[31] *G.U.R.I.* No. 252 of 26 Oct. 1999.
[32] Ordinary Supplement No. 177/L to *G.U.R.I.* No. 228 of 28 Sept. 1999.
[33] [1996] OJ L010/13.       [34] [1982] OJ L230/1.       [35] *G.U.R.I.* No. 228 of 28 Sept. 1999.

F. MISCELLANEOUS

### i. Taxation and Subsidies

In order to foster and develop biological agriculture in Italy, Law No. 488 of 23 December 1999 (*Budget Law for year 2000*),[36] sets up a 'fund for biological and quality agriculture'. The fund will be financed by a tax of 0.5 per cent levied on the turnover of producers and importers of certain phytosanitary products, as well as on foodstuffs containing animal products and animal proteins. In order to achieve its objective, the fund will contribute to the development of agriculture with a lower impact on the environment, and to the production of foodstuffs aimed at preventing the more common plant diseases, to the promotion of consumer information programmes on biological agriculture, and to the elaboration and use of codes of good practice in agriculture.

As from 2001, a minimum of 2 per cent of all energy products or imports placed on the market must originate from renewable sources, following Article 11 of Legislation Decree No. 79 of 16 March 1999.[37] Energy producers or importers that fail to meet this requirement will have to compensate this by purchasing from other companies with higher production of energy from renewable sources, 'green certificates', up to the equivalent of 2 per cent of their total output.

The ministry of environment has adopted ecological incentives in order to achieve the greenhouse gases emissions reduction target laid down by the Kyoto Protocol. For this purpose, the ministry has set out a plan involving the introduction and use of energy-saving items and equipment in households, industry, and the tertiary sector. Moreover, a new set of economic incentives for the acquisition of new catalysed cars is currently being planned by the ministries of industry, in cooperation with the ministries of environment and finance, in order to reach a higher percentage of catalytic cars in circulation when at the end of 2001 lead-containing petrol will be definitively banned, pursuant to EC standards. In addition, the ministry of environment has recently proposed the introduction of economic incentives for companies which obtain the EMAS certification or deliver products that obtain the eco-label or more generally invest in 'green' technologies.

---

[36] Ordinary Supplement No. 227/L to *G.U.R.I.* No. 302 of 27 Dec. 1999.

[37] *G.U.R.I.* No. 75 of 31 Mar. 1999, supplemented by the implementing provisions of Decree of the ministry of environment of 11 Nov. 1999; *G.U.R.I.* No. 292 of 14 Dec. 1999.

# X. The Netherlands

JONATHAN VERSCHUUREN*

## A. INTRODUCTION

The following chapter will cover the developments in Dutch environmental law influenced by environmental law of the European Community (EC), as they occurred between January and December 1999. This period saw relatively little activity on the part of the Dutch legislator in this area. The only major amendments of Dutch environmental law concerned the implementation of Directive 96/82/EC 1996 on the Control of Major-Accident Hazards Involving Dangerous Substances (Seveso II Directive)[1] and the implementation of Directive 97/11/EC amending Directive 85/337/EEC on the Assessment of the Effects of Certain Public and Private Projects on the Environment (EIA Directive).[2]

However, the lack of legislative developments is largely compensated by the considerable amount of interesting case law concerning Dutch implementation matters, which was passed in 1999.

## B. AIR POLLUTION

In 1999 an environmental agreement on energy efficiency was concluded between the minister of housing, spatial planning and the environment, the minister of economic affairs, and several business organizations. In the agreement 'Convenant Benchmarking Energy-Efficiency' business has committed itself to achieve a 60–130 peta-joule reduction of energy consumption by 2012, corresponding to a $CO_2$ emission reduction of 5–9 million tons. In turn, the ministers agreed not to impose an energy tax for businesses that have signed the agreement, and to refrain from imposing additional direct regulation to reduce $CO_2$ emissions for these businesses. Whether the agreement is in conformity with the rules of the Commission, laid down in its 1996 Communication to the Council and the European Parliament on Environmental Agreements, remains uncertain.[3] Problems may also arise with respect to Articles 81 and 87 EC.[4]

In a letter to parliament dated 2 June 1999, the minister of housing, spatial planning and the environment announced his desire to introduce a system of emissions trading to combat the emissions of $SO_2$, $CO_2$, and $NO_x$. However, the minister indicates that the relevant EC legislation, in particular Directive 96/61/EC on Integrated Pollution Prevention and Control (IPPC Directive),[5]

---

* Professor, Centre for Legislative Studies, Tilburg University, Tilburg, The Netherlands.
[1] [1997] OJ L010/13.          [2] [1997] OJ L073/5.          [3] COM(96)561 final.
[4] J. H. G. van den Broek, J. Niezen, 'Convenant Benchmarking Energy-Efficiency' (1999) 6 *Milieu & Recht*, 152–9.
[5] [1996] OJ L257/26.

does not allow for the introduction of such emissions trading systems, but rather imposes a duty on Member States to integrate all environmental aspects into a single permit. In addition, EC competition legislation also prohibits the introduction of emissions trading in the Netherlands. Nonetheless, the minister announced that an experiment to introduce $CO_2$ emissions trading is to be further examined, indicating that such an experiment should ideally be pursued in a European context.[6]

In order to implement Directive 98/70/EC relating to the Quality of Petrol and Diesel Fuels and Amending Council Directive 93/12/EEC (Fuel Quality Directive),[7] a new decree on Quality Standards for Fuels for Road Traffic was adopted on the basis of Article 13 Air Pollution Act.[8] This new Decree replaces the Decree on Leaded Petrol and also amends the existing Decree on Sulphur Content of Fuels. The Netherlands has not opted for the possibility of temporarily postponing implementation, under Article 3(3) Fuel Quality Directive. According to the minister, this was not necessary since Dutch oil refineries should have no difficulties in supplying fuels that meet the quality standards of the Directive.

C. CHEMICALS

Several Statutes were changed in order fully to implement Directive 96/82/EC on the Control of Major-Accident Hazards Involving Dangerous Substances (Seveso II Directive).[9] Amendments were made to the Environmental Protection Act, the Working Conditions Act, several Decrees on chemicals regulation,[10] and the Disasters and Major-Accidents Act, including the introduction of provisions to ensure that information on Emergency Plans can be obtained easily by the public. Furthermore, as a result of the amendments, the municipal authorities are now empowered to shut down installations that do not provide the necessary information on safety measures. The amended provisions entered into force on 19 July 1999.[11]

In March 1999 a new Decree on Cadmium was adopted on the basis of the Chemical Substances Act.[12] The Decree contains new rules on the use of cadmium in products and brings Dutch legislation in conformity with Council Directive 76/769/EEC on Restrictions on the Marketing and Use of Certain Dangerous Substances and Preparations.[13] The new Decree puts an end to

[6] Parliamentary Documents II, 1998–9, 26 578, Nos. 1–2.   [7] [1998] OJ L350/58.
[8] *Bulletin of Acts and Decrees 1999*, No. 566.   [9] [1997] OJ L010/13.
[10] See i.e. the Decree on Major Accident Risks (*Bulletin of Acts and Decrees 1999*, 234), Decree on Emergency Plans for Installations (Bulletin of Acts and Decrees 1999, 237) and the Disasters and Major Accidents Information Decree (Bulletin of Acts and Decrees 1999, 238). Amendments to the Environmental Protection Act, the Working Conditions Act, and the Disasters and Major Accidents Act was made by Act of 25 Feb. 1999 (*Bulletin of Acts and Decrees 1999*, 122).
[11] *Bulletin of Acts and Decrees 1999*, 305; For an overview of Dutch legislation implementing the Directive, see S. D. M. de Leeuw and A. H. Swart-Bodrij, 'Het Besluit Risico's Zware Ongevallen 1999 en de gevolgen voor de Wm-vergunningverlening' (1999) 6 *Milieu & Recht*, 146–51.
[12] *Bulletin of Acts and Decrees 1999*, 149.   [13] [1976] OJ L262/201.

the Dutch practice of consistently maintaining stricter rules for the use of cadmium, applying the former Article 100a(4) EC (now Article 95(4) EC).

A very informative review of EC legislation on substances and the Dutch legislation to implement such legislation was published in early 1999.[14] The author, Den Breejen, concludes that the relevant EC and Dutch legislation similarly offer a fairly complete system of rules to systematically control the risks involved with the thousands of dangerous substances that currently exist. Den Breejen also warns the Dutch legislator that any gaps in the legislation can only be tackled at the EC level.

### D. NATURE CONSERVATION

### i. Habitats Directive

Numerous Dutch cases came before the Council of State in 1999 concerning Directive 92/43/EEC on the Conservation of Natural Habitats and of Wild Fauna and Flora (Habitats Directive),[15] of which the case between the Hamster Foundation and the Provincial Executive of Limburg was the most publicized.[16] The case concerned the development of a transboundary industrial area between the Dutch city of Heerlen and the German city of Aachen. In this area, two species listed in Annex IV Habitats Directive, the badger and the hamster, occurred in the wild. While deciding on the development of the area, the competent authorities had not considered the consequences of the development plans for the habitats of both species. These consequences were in particular severe for the hamster population, as the area constituted the habitat of the last population of hamsters in the Netherlands. As a result of the development activities in the area, this species is now considered to be extinct in the Netherlands. After a long series of judicial reviews, the Administrative Law Division of the Council of State finally decided in October 1999 that, although a final decision on the compatibility of the Dutch Nature Protection Act with the Habitats Directive could not be given until early 2000, the development plans should not have been approved by the authorities, following indications of possible incompatibilities with the Habitats Directive and the Berne Convention on the Conservation of European Wildlife and Natural Habitats 1979.[17]

In several other cases, the Dutch Council of State has indicated that the provisions of the Habitats Directive concerning Special Areas of Conservation will

---

[14] A. den Breejen, 'Het stoffenbeleid: integraal, wetenschappelijk en Europees' (1999) 1 *Milieu & Recht*, 2–9.

[15] [1992] OJ L206/7.

[16] Administrative Law Division of the Council of State, *Hamster Vereniging en anderen* v. *Provinciale Staten van Limburg*, 26 Oct. 1999, (1999) *Jurisprudentie Milieurecht* 165 (annotation Woldendorp), (2000) *Administratiefrechtelijke Beslissingen* 23 (annotation Backes) See for an overview of all the procedures prior to this decision: H. E. Woldendorp, 'De Habitatrichtlijn (Richtlijn 92/43/EEG)' (1999) *Jurisprudentie Milieurecht* 165, 651–60.

[17] Berne, 19 Sept. 1979.

not have direct effect until a list of sites of Community importance has been published, further to Article 4(2) Habitats Directive.[18]

## ii. Wild Birds Directive

Similar uncertainty remains as to which areas are to be designated as Special Protection Areas (SPAs) on the basis of Directive 79/409/EEC on the Conservation of Wild Birds (Wild Birds Directive).[19] As a consequence of the ruling of the European Court of Justice (ECJ) in Case C–3/96,[20] many additional areas in the Netherlands are now to be designated as SPAs. In its judgment, the ECJ referred to the 1989 inventory of the International Birds Association (IBA), indicating that the Netherlands did not designate all areas that are of ornithological importance. However, prior to the ruling, in 1994, a new inventory was published by the IBA, introducing even more areas of particular ornithological importance, to which the ECJ, surprisingly, did not refer. Therefore, to date, it remains uncertain whether the 1989 inventory or the 1994 inventory is to be followed in designating SPAs. Interestingly, in a case concerning the development of a large-scale site of wind generators, the Administrative Law Division of the Council of State tested the development plans directly against the Wild Birds Directive, and concluded that since the area was not listed on the IBA 1994 inventory there was no reason to annul the decision to develop the site.[21] This case seems to indicate that the Dutch Council of State has decided to take the most recent inventory as a guideline for the designation of SPAs. Nevertheless, the issue remains controversial, and the designation of each individual site typically sparks fierce debate. In 1999, a list of fifty-seven new areas was drafted, giving rise to a total number of 5,000 official objections, which are currently under review by the ministry of housing, spatial planning and the environment.

In January 2000 the European Commission decided to submit an Article 228 EC Reasoned Opinion to the Netherlands concerning its failure to implement the ECJ ruling in case C–3/96.[22]

The Wild Birds Directive played a major role in the public and political debate concerning the application of a Dutch oil company to drill for gas in the Waddensea, in an area designated as a SPA. The precautionary principle, in particular, was a primary topic in the discussion, which eventually led the minister of housing, spatial planning and the environment to refuse to deny the requested permit for drilling activities in the Waddensea.[23]

---

[18] See e.g. Administrative Law Division of the Council of State, *Vereniging Milieudefensie* v. *Gemeenteraad van Ambt Delden*, 29 Jan. 1999, (1999) *Tijdschrift voor Milieu en Recht* 53 (annotation Backes), (1999) *Administratiefrechtelijke Beslissingen* 286 (annotation Verschuuren), and Administrative Law Division of the Council of State, *Wadden Vereniging en anderen* v. *Provinciale Staten van Friesland*, 8 June 1999, (2000) *Administratiefrechtelijke Beslissingen* 14 (annotation Backes).

[19] [1979] OJ L103/1.      [20] Case C–3/96, *Commission* v. *the Netherlands* [1998] ECR I–1031.
[21] See case *Wadden Vereniging*, n. 18 above.          [22] See n. 20 above.
[23] W. Brussaard, 'De Waddenzee als bron van recht' (1999) 9 *Milieu & Recht*, 207.

An interesting judgment of the Dutch Supreme Court in a case concerning the Wild Birds Directive was the *Red-Fronted Canaries* case.[24] The case entailed the prosecution of a person who bought five red-fronted canaries from a German trader, and offered these for resale in the Netherlands. The accused argued in his defence, first, that the Dutch legislation on the trading of birds was not compatible with the Wild Birds Directive, and second, that the Dutch legislation imposed unjustified trade restrictions in violation of Article 28 EC. In response to the first argument, the Supreme Court concluded that the red-fronted canary was not covered by the Wild Birds Directive. It subsequently examined, further to the second argument, whether Article 30 EC could be applied to justify the Dutch import restrictions. The Court concluded that, although trade in the red-fronted canary is not prohibited in Germany, Dutch legislation still may restrict this species from being imported from other Member States, because the EC and its Member States have ratified the 1979 Berne Convention,[25] which, unlike the Directive, does list this bird as a protected species. This may indeed be a valid reason to apply Article 30 EC to justify a measure, in particular in view of the ECJ judgment in Case C–67/97 *(Ditlev Bluhme)*,[26] of merely twelve days earlier, in which the Court included the protection of biodiversity as a justification within the scope of Article 30 EC. In another case, concerning squirrels, the Dutch Council of State had concluded that the prohibition on keeping a certain species of squirrels did not conflict with Article 28 EC. However, some doubts exist as to the accuracy of this judgment, in view of standing ECJ case law.[27]

E. WASTE

### i. Dusseldorp

In 1999 the Council of State gave a final decision in the *Dusseldorp* case,[28] following the ECJ judgment in Case C–203/96 *(Dusseldorp)*.[29] It concluded that the policy of applying the principles of self-sufficiency and proximity not only to the shipment of waste for disposal, but also for recovery, is not valid under EC law, and that the exclusive rights conferred upon AVR Chemie, as the sole end-processor for the incineration of hazardous wastes in a high-performance rotary furnace were contrary to Article 34 EC.[30]

[24] Supreme Court, *Red-Fronted Canaries*, 15 Dec. 1998, (1999) *Tijdschrift voor Milieu en Recht* 25 (annotation Jans).

[25] See n. 17 above.

[26] Case C–67/97, *Criminal Proceedings against Ditlev Bluhme* [1998] ECR I–8033.

[27] Administrative Law Division of the Council of State, *Vereniging van liefhebbers van Exotische Zoogdieren* v. *Ministerie van Landbouw, Natuurbeheer en Visserij*, 18 June 1998, (1999) *Tijdschrift voor Milieu en Recht* 12 (annotation Jans).

[28] Administrative Law Division of the Council of State, *Chemische Afvalstoffen Dusseldorp BV and Others* v. *Ministerie van Volkshuisvesting, Ruimtelijke Ordening en Milieubeheer*, 28 Jan. 1999, (1999) *Tijdschrift voor Milieu en Recht* 74 (annotation Jans).

[29] Case C–203/96, *Chemische Afvalstoffen Dusseldorp BV and Others* v. *Ministerie van Volkshuisvesting, Ruimtelijke Ordening en Milieubeheer* [1998] ECR I–4075.

[30] See P. J. Leefmans, 'Provinciaal afvaltransport: een zuiver binnenlandse aangelegenheid?' (1999) 5 *Nederlands Tijdschrift voor Europees Recht*, 129–31.

### ii. Waste Shipment Regulation

In a series of new cases, the Council of State had to give further rulings on the compatibility of provincial export restrictions on waste with Regulation (EEC) No. 259/93 on the Supervision and Control of Shipments of Waste within, into and out of the European Community (Waste Shipment Regulation).[31] The Court ruled that a system of regional export restrictions for wastes for disposal operations based on the principles of self-sufficiency and proximity is in accordance with the Waste Shipment Regulation. In fact, it explicitly stated that the judgments of the ECJ in case C–363/93 (*Lancry*)[32] and in Joined Cases C–485/93 and C–486/93 (*Simitzi*)[33] do not provide arguments to rule otherwise.[34]

### iii. Batteries

In 1999 a draft for the amendment of the Decree on the Recovery of Batteries was published.[35] These amendments are necessary to implement Commission Directive 98/101/EC Adapting to Technical Progress Council Directive 91/157/EEC on Batteries and Accumulators Containing Certain Dangerous Substances.[36]

### iv. Other Wastes

Two Dutch cases concerning preliminary questions on the definition of waste were pending before the ECJ in 1999: Joined Cases C–418/97 and C–419/97.[37] Essentially, the Court is asked to clarify whether the fact that a certain substance is subject to disposal operations and to operations which may lead to recovery, under Annexes IIA and IIB of Directive 75/442/EEC on Waste (Waste Framework Directive),[38] makes them 'waste'. On 8 June 1999 Advocate General (AG) Alber delivered his opinion on this question, stating that the mere fact that a certain substance is subject to a treatment listed in Annex IIB, for example being used mainly as fuel, does not necessarily imply that it is always 'waste' as laid down in the Directive. However, when this treatment leads to 'recovery' of the said substance, this is certainly a strong indication that it con-

---

[31] [1993] OJ L030/1.

[32] Case C–363/93, *René Lancry SA* v. *Direction Générale des Souanes and Société Dindar Confort*, [1994] ECR I–3957.

[33] Joined Cases C–485/93 and C–486/93, *Maria Simitzi* v. *Dimos Kos* [1995] ECR I–2655.

[34] Administrative Law Division of the Council of State, *Van Vliet Recycling* v. *Provinciale Staten van Utrecht*, 24 Dec. 1998, (1999) *Tijdschrift voor Milieu en Recht* 50, and of the same date: *V. Vcon* v. *Provinciale Staten van Noord-Holland* (1999) *Tijdschrift voor Milieu en Recht* 51, and *Koks Nilo Milieu* v. *Provinciale Staten van Noord-Holland* (1999) *Tijdschrift voor Milieu en Recht* 52 (annotations by Addink).

[35] *Government Gazette 1999*, No. 246.          [36] [1999] OJ L001/1.

[37] Joined Cases C–418/97 and C–419/97, *ARCO Chemie Nederland Ltd.* v. *Ministerie van Volkshuisvesting, Ruimtelijke Ordening en Milieubeheer (C–418/97) and Vereniging Dorpsbelang Hees, Stichting Werkgroep Weurt+ and Vereniging Stedelijk Leefmilieu Nijmegen* v. *Directeur van de dienst Milieu en Water van de Provincie Gelderland* (C–419/97) [2000] ECR I–4475.

[38] [1975] OJ L194/39.

cerns 'disposal of waste'. Moreover, according to AG Alber, it is necessary to examine whether or not inherent risks are involved with the substances in question that make it necessary to recover the substances. Also, the substance in question may have lost the characteristics of waste because it no longer imposes a bigger danger for the environment than raw materials.

F. WATER

## i. Discharges

Two important judgments were given by the ECJ in 1999 on the definition of 'discharge' under Directive 76/464/EEC on Pollution Caused by Certain Dangerous Substances Discharged into the Aquatic Environment of the Community,[39] in relation to the definition in the Dutch legislation on the protection of surface waters.

In Case C–231/97 (*Van Rooij*),[40] the ECJ ruled that the emission of contaminated steam which is precipitated on to surface water, both directly and indirectly,[41] falls within the definition of 'discharge' under Article 1(2)(d) of the Directive. The distance between those waters and the place of emission of the contaminated steam is relevant only for the purpose of determining whether the pollution of the waters may be regarded as foreseeable according to general experience, so that the pollution is not attributable to the person producing the steam.

In Case C–232/97 (*Nederhoff*),[42] the ECJ ruled that the escape of creosote from wooden posts placed in surface waters, where the pollution caused by that substance is attributable to a person, also falls within the definition of 'discharge' of the Directive. When the pollution is not attributable to a person, but rather is caused by multiple and diffuse sources referred to in Article 5(1) of Council Directive 86/280/EEC,[43] it cannot be considered to fall within definition of 'discharge' of Directive 76/464/EEC.

These two judgments bear consequences for the Dutch legislation on the protection of surface waters. First, several sources that were considered to be diffuse and were not dealt with in individual licences, for example placing creosote-treated posts in surface waters, now must be made subject to the duty to apply for a permit under the Pollution of Surface Waters Act. Secondly, the permits that have been issued on the basis of the Environmental Management Act, concerning air quality, and the permits issued on the basis of the Pollution of Surface Waters Act, concerning discharges to surface waters,

[39] [1976] OJ L129/23.

[40] Case C–231/97, *A. M. L. van Rooij v. Dagelijks Bestuur van het waterschap de Dommel* [1999] ECR I–6355.

[41] Via land and roofs, and via a storm water drain.

[42] Case C–231/97, *L. Nederhoff & Zn. v. Dijkgraaf en hoogheemraden van het Hoogheemraadschap Rijnland* [1999] ECR I–6385.

[43] Dir. 86/280/EEC on Limit Values and Quality Objectives for Discharges of Certain Dangerous Substances included in List I of the Annex to Directive 76/464/EEC, [1986] OJ L181/16.

must now be more coordinated, or even completely integrated, as a consequence of these judgments.[44]

### *iii. Nitrates*

During 1999 the 'battle' between farmers and the minister of agriculture, nature management and fisheries on the implementation of Directive 91/676/EEC concerning the Protection of Waters against Pollution Caused by Nitrates from Agricultural Sources,[45] continued with vigour. The central instrument to implement this Directive: the Act on Reorganization of Livestock Industry, was considered, in several preliminary decisions, to be unlawful because it contains provisions limiting the number of animals that farmers keep and therefore is thought to be an infringement of Article 1, Protocol No. 1, of the European Convention for Human Rights.[46] These decisions were praised by some,[47] and criticized by others,[48] the latter pointing in particular to case law of the ECJ,[49] in so far as the Court had held that the exercise of the right to property may be restricted, provided that those restrictions in fact correspond to objectives of general interest pursued by the Community and do not constitute a disproportionate and intolerable interference, impairing the very substance of the rights guaranteed. While a final decision by the Supreme Court is still awaited, environmental non-governmental organizations (NGOs) have now also taken their positions on the 'battlefield'. Several NGOs have sued the Dutch state for taking insufficient measures to comply with Directive 91/676/EEC. On 24 November 1999 the District Court of The Hague declared the Dutch policy on nitrates from agricultural sources to be unlawful. It issued a Court order for the state to ensure that the targets set out in the Directive will be met by 2002.[50]

### *iv. Bathing Water*

The Decree on Quality Objectives and Measurements for Surface Waters was amended in December 1999, following a Reasoned Opinion by the

[44] H. F. M. W. van Rijswick, 'De consequenties van een ruime uitleg van het begrip lozing uit richtlijn 76/464' (1999) 12 *Milieu & Recht*, 291–6.

[45] [1991] OJ L375/1.

[46] District Court, The Hague, *Nederlandse Vakbond Varkenshouders* v. *Staat der Nederlanden*, 23 Dec. 1998, (1999) *Tijdschrift voor Milieu en Recht* 28, and President of the District Court The Hague, *Nederlandse Vakbond Varkenshouders* v. *Staat der Nederlanden*, 23 Feb. 1999, (1999) *Tijdschrift voor Milieu en Recht* 29 (annotation by Hoitink), later followed by Higher Court, The Hague, *Staat der Nederlanden* v. *Nederlandse Vakbond Varkenshouders*, 10 June 1999, (1999) *Agrarische Rechtspraak* 4977.

[47] L. P. J. Mertens, 'Voor wat hoort wat' (1999) 2 *Agrarisch Recht*, 58–9. For a more comprehensive review of the European legal aspects of the Reorganisation Act, see G. J. M. de Jager, 'Wet herstructurering varkenshouderij Europeesrechtelijk gezien' (1999) 2 *Agrarisch Recht*, 60–78.

[48] J. E. Hoitink and Ch. W. Backes, 'Eigendom van "milieuvervuilingsrechten"' (1999) 37 *Nederlands Juristenblad*, 1759–63.

[49] Case C–293/97, *The Queen* v. *Secretary of State for the Environment and Ministry of Agriculture, Fisheries and Food, ex parte H. A. Standley and Others and D. G. D. Metson and Others* (*Standley*) [1999] ECR I–2603, which also concerned Dir. 91/676/EEC.

[50] District Court, The Hague, *Stichting Waterpakt en anderen* v. *Staat der Nederlanden*, 23 Nov. 1999, (2000) *Tijdschrift voor Milieu en Recht* 23 (annotation Jans and Verschuuren).

Commission concerning the Dutch failure properly to implement Directive 76/160/EEC concerning the Quality of Bathing Water.[51] Some of the emission standards which were not in conformity with the quality standards of the Directive have now been amended,[52] in addition to several provisions of the Decree on Hygiene and Safety in Swimming Pools.[53]

## G. HORIZONTAL INSTRUMENTS

### i. EIA

The revision of the Environmental Management Act and the Decree on Environmental Impact Assessment were completed in 1999.[54] The amendments had become necessary as a consequence of Directive 97/11/EC amending Directive 85/337/EEC on the Assessment of the Effects of Certain Public and Private Projects on the Environment (EIA Directive).[55] In the Environmental Management Act, the conditions that must be taken into account by the competent authorities in the case-by-case examination of whether an EIA has to be made, have been specified. Also included in the new legislation is a special procedure for the examination of activities or projects that have transboundary environmental effects. The Decree on Environmental Impact Assessment has been subject to substantial revision. Amendments include the addition of new categories of activities, and the alteration of existing thresholds and criteria, increasing the number of activities subject to EIA. Furthermore, certain specified activities no longer require a case-by-case examination by the competent authority, in order to subject them to an EIA procedure.

Case law on the EIA Directive is still abundant. In many of the cases decided in 1999, prior to the entry into force of the amended legislation, as discussed above, the Council of State tested decisions directly against the EIA Directive, leaving national legislation out of consideration due to its incompatibility with EC law, as a consequence of the ECJ ruling in the *Kraaijeveld* Case.[56] Some interesting cases concerned large-scale bio-industry (so-called Annex II projects)[57] on lands bordering protected areas of the Waddensea. In one case, the President of the Council of State concluded that the fact that an installation for livestock farming is located near an area that has been designated an SPA under the Wild Birds Directive,[58] constitutes a sufficient reason to seriously consider termination of the project if an EIA procedure has not been initiated.[59]

---

[51] [1976] OJ 031/1.      [52] *Bulletin of Acts and Decrees 1999*, No. 565.      [53] Ibid., No. 581.
[54] Ibid., 208 (Act of 29 Apr. 1999), and ibid., 224 (Decree of 7 May 1999).
[55] [1997] OJ L073/5.
[56] Case C–72/95, *Aannemersbedrijf P. K. Kraaieveld BV and Others* v. *Gedeputeerde Staten van Zuid Holland* [1996] ECR I–5403. For further details see J. Verschuuren, 'The Netherlands' (1998) 1 *Yearbook of European Environmental Law*, 513. See also e.g. Administrative Law Division of the Council of State, *M. L. Nieuwhuizen en anderen* v. *Gemeenteraad van Steenbergen*, 30 Mar. 1999, (1999) *Tijdschrift voor Milieu en Recht* 66 (Annotation Verschuuren).
[57] Annex II EIA Directive.      [58] See n. 19 above.
[59] President of the Administrative Law Division of the Council of State, *W. Pool en anderen* v. *Gemeenteraad van Delfzijl*, 13 July 1999, (1999) *Tijdschrift voor Milieu en Recht* 114 (annotation Verschuuren).

Although they did not concern Dutch legislation, the recent ECJ rulings in Cases C–392/96[60] and C–435/97,[61] once again raised questions about the Dutch EIA Regulation, in particular concerning the manner in which the Dutch Council of State determines some cases. It has become increasingly difficult to uphold the Council's case law allowing a variety of related activities in a small area to be considered separately, when considering the question as to whether the activity has a significant effect on the environment.[62]

### ii. IPPC

The IPPC Directive[63] was implemented in the Netherlands by some minor amendments to the Decree on Installations and Permits in 1997. In 1999 some additional changes were made to the Execution-Decree on the Pollution of National Waters, in order to fully implement the IPPC Directive.[64] These changes relate, in particular, to the data to be included in the application for a permit on the basis of the Surface Waters Act, in line with Article 6 IPPC Directive, and to provisions on transboundary effects, in line with Article 17 IPPC Directive.

There is growing doubt among authors as to whether the Environmental Management Act and the Surface Waters Act are truly in conformity with the Directive,[65] with particular attention for the question of how the so-called 'alara-principle', which forms the basis for provisions in permits according to the EMA ('alara' stands for 'as low as reasonably achievable'), relates to the principle of 'Best Available Techniques' (BAT).[66] Furthermore, serious doubts exist as to whether the definition of 'installation' under the IPPC Directive, is identical to the definition under the EMA.[67] Finally, concerns have been expressed as to whether the fact that a permit on the basis of the Surface Waters Act has not been integrated into the EMA permit would make it contrary to the provisions of the IPPC Directive.[68] The first case law on these and other questions can be expected in 2000 and will be awaited anxiously by many.

---

[60] Case C–392/96, *Commission* v. *Ireland* [1999] ECR I–5901.

[61] Case C–435/97, *World Wildlife Fund (WWF) and Others* v. *Autonome Provinz Bozen and Others* [1999] ECR I–5613.

[62] M. A. A. Soppe, 'Wederom verduidelijking contouren m.e.r.-richtlijn; Nederlandse M.E.R.-regeling opnieuw ter discussie?' (1999) 11 *Nederlands Tijdschrift voor Europees Recht*, 291–6. See also the annotation by C. Backes for Case C–392/96, *Commission* v. *Ireland* (2000) *Administratiefrechtelijke Beslissingen* 33.

[63] See n. 5 above.                    [64] *Bulletin of Acts and Decrees 1999*, No. 397.

[65] P. C. Gilhuis, 'IPPC nu ernst' (1999) 12 *Milieu & Recht*, 283.

[66] R. A. J. van Gestel and J. M. Verschuuren, 'Alara: minimumregel of beginsel met aspiraties?' (2000) 3 *Milieu & Recht*.

[67] Cf. R. Uylenburg, 'De stolpvergunning' (1999) 11 *Milieu & Recht*, 267; H. E. Woldendorp and P. C. M. Heinen, 'Het begrip inrichting in de Wet milieubeheer' (1999) 5 *Bouwrecht*, 376.

[68] M. van Rijswick, 'De IPPC-Richtlijn en de Nederlandse 'integrale' vergunning' (1998) 14 *Het Waterschap*, 561–8.

# XI. Portugal

PEDRO MACHADO*

## A. INTRODUCTION

The intensive legislative activity that occurred in Portugal during 1999 was largely dominated by efforts to implement EC environmental Directives. This confirms a growing tendency for Portuguese environmental policy to reflect the needs and demands of EC law. At the margins, the Portuguese legislator was also motivated by autonomous environmental concerns, which were either raised nationally or locally. Although this activity has been residual in the context of legislative activity in the environmental domain, the specific issue of co-incineration has been a central issue on the 1999 environmental agenda, for it became an arena of litigation between the environmental actors engaged therein. Moreover, it has revealed the shortcomings of the existing environmental impact assessment procedure to cope with environmental issues which are imbued with uncertainty.

The number of reported infringements by the Portuguese Republic of its EC environmental obligations in 1999 has significantly diminished, compared with the previous year. Yet, case law of the European Court of Justice (ECJ) denotes, once more, the insufficiencies of the Portuguese legal framework for environmental impact assessment, thereby rendering even more evident the inadequacy of environmental decision-making procedures. Domestically, Portuguese environmental legislation was not free of criticism either, as two Constitutional Court rulings may exemplify. Both cases concern vital elements of the Portuguese environmental legal order: first, the competence of courts, other than the administrative tribunals, to preside in environmental cases involving public interest litigation, and secondly, the balance between individual property rights and public concerns of environmental protection.

## B. AIR POLLUTION

Decree-Law 276/99 of 23 July 1999 transposed Council Directive 96/62/EC on Ambient Air Quality Assessment and Management.[1] In addition to its implementing purpose, the scope of this new legislation is to provide guidelines on the policy of air quality management, following general provisions on air quality protection of the 1987 Basic Law on Environment.[2]

Following several improvements in air quality protection legislation, another significant transposition of EC legislation was accomplished by Decree-Law 432/99 of 25 October 1999, transposing Directive 97/68/EC on

---

* Ph.D. Researcher, European University Institute, Florence, Italy.
[1] [1996] OJ L296/55.          [2] Law 11/87 of 7 Apr. 1987.

Measures against the Emission of Gaseous and Particulate Pollutants from Internal Combustion Engines to be Installed in Non-Road Mobile Machinery.[3]

C. NATURE CONSERVATION

In respect of nature conservation, concerns have grown regarding the lack of implementation, by Portugal, of Directive 79/409/EEC on the Conservation of Wild Birds (Wild Birds Directive)[4] and Directive 92/43//EEC on the Conservation of Natural Habitats and of Wild Fauna and Flora (Habitats Directive).[5] Finally, in 1999, to this end, Decree-Law 140/99 of 24 April 1999 was approved and subsequently regulated by Decree-Law 384-B/99 of 23 September 1999. The primary objective of both measures is enhancement of procedural effectiveness and transparency of environmental decision-making processes, in order to fulfil adequately the obligations under the Natura 2000 programme.

D. WASTE

The legislative developments in the waste sector were largely dominated by the transposition of two vital EC Directives concerning waste. The first of these Directives was Council Directive 96/59/EC on the Disposal of Polychlorinated Biphenyls (PCBs) and Polychlorinated Terphenyls (PCTs),[6] which was transposed in Portugal by Decree-Law 277/99 of 23 July 1999. Following the *telos* of the PCB/PCT Directive, the Law established the rules under which a complete ban on the use of these chemicals is to be achieved, complemented by the decontamination or disposal of all equipment containing PCBs/PTCs.

The second waste Directive to be transposed in 1999 was Council Directive 96/23/EC on Measures to Monitor Certain Substances and Residues thereof in Live Animals and Products.[7] It was implemented in Portugal by Decree-Law 148/99 of 4 May 1999, which also transposed Commission Decisions 97/747/EC[8] and 98/179/EC.[9] The former concerns the fixing of levels and frequencies of sampling provided by Council Directive, while the latter lays down detailed rules on official sampling for the monitoring of certain substances and residues thereof in live animals and animal products.

E. WATER

Decree-Law 68/99 of 11 March 1999 modified Decree-Law 235/97 of 3 September 1997, which originally had transposed Council Directive 91/676/EEC on the Protection of Waters against Pollution Caused by Nitrates from Agricultural Sources (Nitrates Directive).[10] The amendments made by the 1999

---

3  [1998] OJ L59/1.            4  [1979] OJ L103/1.            5  [1992] OJ L206/7.
6  [1996] OJ L243/31.          7  [1996] OJ L125/10.           8  [1997] OJ L303/12.
9  [1998] OJ L65/31.          10  [1991] OJ L375/1.

Law were intended to clarify certain normative provisions of its predecessor, in order to fulfil fully the obligations of the Directive.

Furthermore, Decree-Law 431/99 of 22 October 1999 was adopted, transposing Council Directive 82/176/EEC on Limit Values and Quality Objectives of Mercury Discharges by the Chlor-Alkali Electrolysis Industry.[11] Although this Directive had already been given legal force in Portugal by Decree (*Portaria*) 1033/93 of 15 October 1993, the posterior enactment of legislation in the realm of the hydric domain,[12] establishment of rules, criteria, and quality objectives to protect the aquatic environment, and, generally to improve the quality of waters,[13] required the establishment of a comprehensive legal framework.

F. HORIZONTAL INSTRUMENTS

*i. Environmental Impact Assessment*

The controversial environmental impact assessment procedure for the 1997 co-incineration programme in Portugal remains one of the most crucial and problematic issues, if not the most sensitive and turbulent one, on the Portuguese environmental agenda for 1999. Council of Ministers Resolution 98/97 of 25 June 1997 on a management strategy for industrial waste listed co-incineration in cement plants as the preferred treatment of industrial hazardous waste. This strategy was complemented with the transposition of Council Directive 94/67/EC on the Incineration of Hazardous Waste,[14] by Decree-Law 273/98 of 2 September 1998,[15] which established the legal framework under which the incineration of hazardous waste should be pursued, with a view to prevent the externalities associated with it. Yet, despite the existence of a similar regulatory framework the governmental co-incineration strategy also required an environmental impact (EIA) procedure, as a result of the transposition of Council Directive 85/337/EEC on the Assessment of the Effects of Certain Public and Private Projects on the Environment (EIA Directive).[16] In order to facilitate a ministerial decision concerning the location of two co-incineration systems in cement facilities, in accordance with the co-incineration programme, an environmental impact study was carried out in 1998. In spite of prevailing criticism and distrust voiced by the local population during the public consultation process, later that same year, in addition to the uncertainties associated with the air pollution impacts,[17] and the insufficiencies of the environmental impact assessment procedure highlighted by the National Council for the Environment and Sustainable Development in its recommendations,[18] the ministerial decision to locate the

---

[11] [1982] OJ L81/29.  [12] Decree-Law 46/94 of 22 Feb. 1994.
[13] Decree-Law 236/98 of 1 Aug. 1998. For a more detailed review of this legislation, see L. C. Pitta, 'Portugal' (1998) 1 *Yearbook of European Environmental Law*, at 516–17.
[14] [1994] OJ L365/34.   [15] See Pitta (n. 13 above), at 516.   [16] [1985] OJ L175/40.
[17] See Ministério do Ambiente (Lisbon, 1998) *Projectos de eliminação de resíduos industriais pelo sector cimenteiro. Parecer da Comissão de Avaliação de Impacte Ambiental*, 39.
[18] See CNADS—Conselho Nacional do Ambiente e do Desenvolvimento Sustentável (Lisbon, 1998) *Parecer sobre o processo da co-incineração de resíduos industriais*, 9–14.

two co-incinerators was adopted on 28 December 1998.[19] This controversial decision immediately raised fierce reactions from the local population and from environmental organizations. It was against this backdrop of intense social conflict marking the co-incineration decision-making procedure, that parliament issued its Resolution (*Resolução da Assembleia da República*) 6/99 of 6 February 1999. This Resolution approved a deliberation in which, *inter alia*, the suspension of the co-incineration process was recommended, and the revocation of the decisions already taken on the location of the co-incineration was requested. However, the most significant legislative development in this matter was the adoption of Law 20/99 of 15 April 1999, which compelled the government to formulate, within the present legislature, a revised strategy for the management of industrial waste. Logically, it suspended the earlier Decree-Law 273/98. Finally, the Law envisaged an independent scientific commission, to provide reports and advice on the treatment of hazardous industrial waste, which was subsequently established by Decree-Law 120/99, and Decree-Law 121/99, of 16 April 1999, as the 'Independent Scientific Commission for the Environmental Control and Surveillance of Co-Incineration'. The independent commission's findings in respect of the environmental impact of the co-incineration system on the relevant two locations are to determine the future of the co-incineration programme. Moreover, Decree-Law 121/99 also revoked the previous suspension by Law 20/99, of Decree-Law 273/98, for such a suspension constituted an infringement of Portugal's obligation under Council Directive 94/67/EC.

While 1999 brought no conclusion to this controversial issue, but merely expectations for the upcoming report of the Independent Scientific Commission, the complex decision-making process of co-incineration of hazardous industrial waste and the EIA procedure it requires, has certainly revealed the shortcomings of the existing framework for EIA, to provide an adequate and effective forum for discussion on controversial dilemmas, and thereby establish an efficient, institutional framework for scientific expertise and public participation. Nonetheless, the ongoing controversy surrounding the issue of EIA has served to awaken parliament to environmental concerns. In fact, following the adoption of the 1987 Basic Law on Environment,[20] parliament has been confined to a rather secondary role in environmental matters. Since then, Portuguese environmental policy has largely been defined by the ministers, particularly as a result of the growing amount of EC environmental legislation. In contrast, in respect of the EIA in the co-incineration strategy, parliament assumed an active role, through the adoption of legislative acts whose significance was the establishment of rules to arbitrate existing litigation. This will unequivocally stand as a rare moment of parliamentary proactivism in environmental matters in Portugal.

---

[19] See Minister for the Environment Decision (*Despacho*) of 28 Dec. 1998.
[20] See n. 2 above.

G. CASE LAW

In contrast with 1998, when several EC environmental Law infringements by Portugal were ruled upon,[21] during 1999 the European Court of Justice (ECJ) issued only one judgment declaring that Portugal had failed to fulfil its obligations. In Case C–150/97,[22] the Commission filed a complaint concerning Article 11(2) of Decree-Law 186/90, which transposes the EIA Directive. This Law does not apply to projects for which the approval procedure had already been initiated prior to its entry into force. Conversely, the Directive under Articles 2(1) and 12(1), shall apply whenever it is necessary to take a decision concerning a consent application as from the end of the deadline for its transposition into Member States' legal orders. Rejecting the arguments of the Portuguese Republic relating to the principle of legal certainty, the ECJ ruled that nothing in the Directive authorizes Member States to exempt certain projects under similar conditions.[23] Having declared that Portugal had failed to fulfil its obligations under the Directive, the ECJ highlighted once more the insufficiencies and inadequacies of Portuguese legislation on EIA. As a result of the arguments of the Portuguese Republic in the case, the misperceptions in view of transposition of the EIA Directive became manifest, particularly in respect of the excessive reliance on the principle of legal certainty, which ran contrary to the environmental interests embedded in the Directive. Ultimately, Portugal demonstrated an excessively formalistic attachment to principles such as that of legal certainty, thereby plainly distorting the scope and purpose of the EIA Directive.

In 1999 the Constitutional Court had the opportunity to issue several decisions on environmental matters, two of which are particularly significant, in the realm of the diffuse control of the constitutionality of norms.

First, Case (*Acórdão*) 458/99 of 13 July 1999[24] concerned the constitutionality of the norms of the 1987 Basic Law on Environment,[25] which, by Article 45(1)-2, attributes competence to the common courts to preside in environmental cases. Consequently, administrative courts have no jurisdiction in environmental litigation. Given the public interest in such litigation, the constitutional question under assessment concerned compliance of the competence attributed to the common jurisdiction in environmental matters, with the reserve of competence recognized for the administrative courts under the Constitution to judge litigation addressing the defence of a public interest.[26] In its decision, the Constitutional Court tended towards a less restrictive interpretation denying that the norm constitutes an absolute reserve of jurisdiction in favour of the administrative courts. The Court thereby confirmed the competence of common courts in matters involving a public interest, particularly protection of the environment.

---

[21] See Pitta, n. 13 above, 516–517.
[22] Case C–150/97, *Commission* v *Portuguese Republic* [1999] ECR I–259.
[23] Para. 19 of the judgment.
[24] See *Diário da República*, II Série, No. 55 of 6 Mar. 2000, 4454.     [25] See n. 2 above.
[26] Art. 214(3) of the Portuguese Constitution.

Secondly, Case 639/99 of 23 November 1999[27] concerned the alleged unconstitutionality of several provisions of Decree-Law 327/90 of 22 October 1999,
which intended to regulate the use, occupation, and transformation of burned
soils. The Law had introduced a prohibition to use burned soils for purposes
other than forestry, over a period of ten years. The Constitutional Court denied
claims of unconstitutionality on the basis of the principles of equality, impar-
tiality, justice, and proportionality, and went on to consider the temporary
restriction of exclusive ownership rights to be reasonable, fair, and proportionate in the light of the environment concerns at stake. Consequently, the
exercise of those property rights must necessarily bend when confronted with
the pursuit of the environmental public interest, and thus the Provisions of
Decree-Law 327/90 were not held to be unconstitutional.

[27]  See *Diário da República*, II Série, No. 70, 23 Mar. 2000, 5514.

# XII. Spain

CARMEN PLAZA MARTÍN*

## A. INTRODUCTION

In 1999, in order to comply with EC and international environmental law, the Spanish state introduced new legislation in the areas of waste, chemicals, air, and access to environmental information. In the fields of nature conservation and water, new legal instruments or significant amendments were necessary in order to implement or improve domestic legislation, unrelated to EC law. Several Autonomous Communities have also exercised their normative powers in order to supplement state basic environmental law on waste, environmental impact assessment, water, and nature conservation. The most important judgment in 1999 came from the Spanish Supreme Court, which applied Directive 92/43/EEC on the Conservation of Natural Habitats and of Wild Fauna and Flora (Habitats Directive)[1] so as to annul part of the Royal Decree which transposed it into Spanish law.

## B. AIR POLLUTION

On 28 October 1999, following the required approval by parliament, Spain ratified the amendment to the 1987 Montreal Protocol on Substances that Deplete the Ozone Layer,[2] as approved at the ninth meeting of the Parties, in 1997.[3] No other substantial legal measure was adopted in the field of air protection in 1999. However, it should be noted that Directive 96/62/EC on Ambient Air Quality Assessment and Management (Ambient Air Directive),[4] which was to be implemented by 21 May 1998, has not yet been transposed into Spanish law, whereas the European Commission has initiated an infringement procedure pursuant to Article 229 EC.[5]

## C. NATURE CONSERVATION

In 1999 the government adopted delegated legislation to implement the provisions relating to National Parks management of Act 4/1989 on the conservation of natural habitats and wild fauna and flora.[6] First, Article 22 *quáter* of Act

---

* Professor, Universidad Complutense, Madrid, Spain.
[1] [1992] OJ L206/7.     [2] Montreal, 16 Sept. 1987.
[3] *Instrumento de Aceptación de España de la Enmienda del Protocolo de Montreal de 16 de septiembre de 1987, aprobada por la novena reunión de las Partes el 17 de septiembre de 1997, Boletín Oficial del Estado (BOE)* No. 259, 28 Oct. 1999, 37714.
[4] [1996] OJ L296/55.
[5] See Sixteenth Report on Monitoring the Application of Community Law (1998), COM(1999) 301 final, [1999] OJ C354/1.
[6] *BOE* No. 181, 20 July 1989.

4/1989, as amended by Act 41/1997,[7] envisaged the grant of public aid to those villages that have a National Park within their territory, as certain forms of economic development were at odds with the conservation of these protected areas. This was eventually implemented by Royal Decree 940/1999, establishing a comprehensive legal framework for the grant of such aids with the aim of promoting sustainable development of the population in the vicinity of a National Park.[8] Second, Article 22 *bis* of Act 4/1989, as amended by Act 41/1997,[9] provided that a management plan (*Plan Director de Parques Nacionales*) would be the main legal instrument to regulate the National Parks Network (*Red de Parques Nacionales*).[10] Such a plan was approved on 26 November 1999 by state Royal Decree 1803/1999.[11] For a seven-year period, it fixes the goals for conservation, research, public use, and education of the National Park Network, in addition to the common activities programme for the National Parks. Moreover, it establishes common aims in the field of international cooperation and for cooperation of the state administration with other regional or local public authorities, and regulates the sources for financing National Parks. For the first time, this Management Plan provides the state administration with essential instruments to ensure coherent and efficient management of the National Park Network.

As regards the protection of some special natural areas, two developments in 1999 were of particular interest. First, Law 3/1999[12] designated a new National Park: Sierra Nevada, in Andalusia. This ecosystem of Mediterranean high mountains brings the number of National Parks in Spain to twelve. Second, new clean-up works are in progress to protect one of the most emblematic National Parks: Doñana, which was affected by a spill of toxic waste from a mine in 1998. In March 1999 Royal Decree-Law 7/1999 was passed, approving and declaring of public interest the works for water regeneration comprised in *Project Doñana 2005*,[13] which aims to ensure the hydraulic balance and water quality in the Doñana Marshes.[14] It allows the

---

[7] *Ley 41/1997 por la que se modifica la Ley 4/1989, de 27 de marzo, de Conservación de los Espacios Naturales y de la Flora y Fauna Silvestres, BOE No. 266, 6 Nov. 1997, 32179.*

[8] *Real Decreto 940/1999 por el que se aprueba el Reglamento sobre la determinación y concesión de subvenciones públicas en las áreas de influencia socioeconómica de los Parques Nacionales, BOE No. 145, 18 June 1999, 23390.*

[9] *Ley 41/1997 por la que se modifica la Ley 4/1989, de 27 de marzo, de Conservación de los espacios naturales y de la flora y fauna silvestres, BOE No. 266, 6 Nov. 1997, 32179.*

[10] Currently, the National Park Network comprises twelve National Parks, which are representative of the distinct ecosystems of the Iberian Peninsula.

[11] *Real Decreto 1803/1999 por el que se aprueba el plan director de la red de parques nacionales, BOE No. 29, 13 Dec. 1999, 429332.*

[12] *Ley 3/1999, de 11.1.1999, por la que se crea el Parque Nacional de Sierra Nevada, BOE No. 11, 13 Nov. 1999, 1512.* According to Law 4/1989, parliament is empowered to declare a nature protected area as a National Park.

[13] *Real Decreto-Ley 7/1999, de 23.4.1999, por el que se aprueba y declara de interés general las obras de regeneración hídrica incluidas en el conjunto de actuaciones Doñana 2005, BOE No. 98, 24 Apr. 1999, 152111.*

[14] In response to the spill of toxic waste from the Aznalcollar mine, which occurred on 25 Apr. 1998, an emergency plan to clean up the polluted area was devised by the government on 22 May 1998. During 1998, the most urgent tasks were accomplished: cleansing of acid waters, the

government to develop several new public works to achieve this aim. Meanwhile, the criminal case brought by the state, non-governmental organizations (NGOs), and other individuals against the multinational company that owns the mine has been progressing slowly.[15]

Within the realm of the legislative initiatives of the Autonomous Communities, the Castille-La Mancha Act 9/1999 on nature conservation[16] implements the basic national legislation on nature conservation,[17] establishing additional protective norms as well as regulating the executive powers of the regional government. *Inter alia*, it has created a new category of conservation area: the 'Sensitive Areas'. Designations will apply to the special protection bird areas established by Directive 79/409/EEC on the Conservation of Wild Birds (Wild Birds Directive),[18] and to the special areas of conservation envisaged by Directive 92/43/EEC on the Conservation of Natural Habitats and of Wild Fauna and Flora (Habitats Directive).[19]

Finally, the Supreme Court judgment delivered on 15 March 1999 is an important step in the judicial application of EC environmental law in Spain.[20] In this case, the Supreme Court declared void Article 13(2) of Royal Decree 1997/1995,[21] transposing Article 16 Habitats Directive, as the Decree provision was held to be a defective transposition Directive provision. According to Article 16 of the Directive, Member States may derogate in certain cases from the protective measures established in Articles 12, 13, 14, and 15, provided that 'there is no satisfactory alternative'. Although Article 13(1) Royal Decree 1997/1995 literally transposed Article 16(1) Habitats Directive, it did not copy the derogation provision. In contrast, Article 13(2), the Decree stated that 'the Autonomous Communities may allow, under strictly supervised conditions, on a selective basis and to a limited extent, the taking or keeping of certain specimens of the species listed in Annex IV in limited numbers specified by the Autonomous Communities'. This derogation was not, however, subject to the

---

removal of toxic mud, and provisional public works to prevent temporarily polluted waters from the Guardiamar river from entering the National Park. In July 1998, once the most urgent clean-up works were in progress, the management body of Doñana National Park approved the *Project Doñana 2005*.

[15] For an account of the activities carried out by the government after the Aznalcollar spill see ministerio de medio ambiente, *Balance de actuaciones en torno al accidente de las minas de Aznalcollar*, 23 Apr. 1999, published on the internet at: http://www.mma.es. A critical assessment of the development of criminal proceedings against the mine owners was published on the Internet at: http://www.nodo50.org/ecologistas/ayuda/home.htm.

[16] *Ley de Castilla-La Mancha 9/1999 de conservación de la naturaleza, BOE* No. 179, 28 July 1999, 28086.

[17] Act 4/1989, n. 6 above, and Royal Decree 1997/1995, of 7 Dec. 1995, establishing measures to protect biodiversity by the conservation of the natural habitats and of the fauna and flora, *BOE* No. 310, 28 Dec. 1995.

[18] [1979] OJ L103/1.                              [19] [1992] OJ L206/50.

[20] Supreme Court judgment of 15 Mar. 1999 (*Sentencia* del *Tribunal Supremo, Repertorio de Jurisprudencia Aranzadi* 1999/2141).

[21] *Real Decreto 1997/1995, por el que se establece medidas para contribuir a garantizar la biodiversidad mediante la conservación de los hábitats naturales y de la fauna y flora silvestres, BOE* No. 310, 28 Dec. 1995, 37310.

condition that there should be 'no satisfactory alternative' to these measures. Therefore it did not constitute correct transposition of Article 16(1)e Habitats Directive.

D. WASTE

*i. PCBs/PCTs*

The state has adopted several legal measures on waste management and industrial hazards in order to transpose EC law into Spanish basic legislation. First, in August 1999, Royal Decree 1378/1999[22] transposed into Spanish basic environmental law Directive 96/59/EC on the Disposal of Polychlorinated Biphenyls and Polychlorinated Terphenyls (PCB/PCT Directive).[23] Since the deadline for implementation was 16 March 1998, the Commission has issued a complaint against Spain for failing to take sufficient measures within the prescribed timeframe.[24] Within the framework established by the 1998 Waste Act,[25] this Royal Decree establishes a new regime to achieve the controlled disposal of PCBs, including disposal of equipment containing PCBs, or decontamination of equipment containing PCBs. It prohibits the separation of PCBs from other substances for the purpose of reusing the PCBs and the topping-up of transformers with PCBs. Furthermore, the Decree identifies the conditions to handle and store PCBs, used PCBs, and equipment containing PCBs, with all the necessary precautions to avoid the risk of fire. It also regulates the conditions to eliminate PCBs and equipment containing PCBs, and the duties of undertakings engaged in the decontamination and/or the disposal of PCBs. In accordance with Article 3 of the PCB/PCT Directive, the deadline for realization of the decontamination or controlled disposal is set at 2010. Under the Decree, the following are within the powers of Autonomous Communities: first, to compile inventories of equipment with PCBs, although they must submit summaries of such inventories to the ministry of environment annually, in order to furnish the Commission with the information required by Article 4 of the Directive. Second, to verify that transformers decontamination and maintenance are carried out in accordance with the requirements established by Royal Decree 1378/1999. Third, to license and grant permits to undertakings engaged in the decontamination and/or the disposal of PCBs, used PCBs and/or equipment containing PCBs. Finally, to draft plans for the decontamination and disposal of PCBs inventoried equipment and the PCBs contained therein.

It is for the state to draw up a National Plan for the decontamination and disposal of PCBs, based on the Autonomous Communities' plans, to be passed by 2002.

---

[22] *Real Decreto 1378/1999, de 27.8.1999, sobre medidas para la eliminación y gestión de los policlorobifenilos, policloroterfenilos y aparatos que los contengan, BOE* No. 206, 28 Aug. 1999.
[23] [1996] OJ L243/31.          [24] See Sixteenth Annual Report (1998), n. 5 above, 62.
[25] *Ley 10/1998 de Residuos, BOE* No. 96, 22 Apr. 1998, 13372.

*ii. SEVESO II*

Third, in the field of industrial risk management, Council Directive 96/82/EC on the Control of Major-Accident Hazards involving Dangerous Substances (SEVESO II Directive)[26] was transposed into Spanish law by Royal Decree 1254/1999[27] of 16 July 1999, almost five months after the deadline for implementation. The government adopted this delegated legislation on the basis of Act 2/1985 on civil protection,[28] and Act 21/1992 on industry.[29] Following the innovations introduced by the aforementioned SEVESO II Directive in this field, Royal Decree 1254/1999 has simplified and broadened the scope of the national legislation which transposed the prior Directive 82/501/EEC (SEVESO Directive).[30] In the new system the list of affected industrial establishments has been replaced by a list of named substances, exclusively. Moreover, the latter has been considerably reduced and is now accompanied by a list of categories of substances, including substances considered dangerous for the environment. Also, new obligations for operators and competent authorities are included with regard to accident prevention and limitation of the consequences of major-accidents. Additionally, the new system includes measures to prevent, and to ensure an adequate reaction in the case of industrial accidents capable of causing transboundary effects, taking into due account the UN Convention on Transboundary Effects of Industrial Accidents, which Spain ratified on 16 May 1997. Moreover, in Annex IV it reproduces Commission Decision 98/433/EC of 26 June 1998 on Harmonized Criteria for Dispensations according to Article 9 of Council Directive 96/82/EC on the Control of Major-Accident Hazards involving Dangerous Substances.[31] In accordance with the distribution of powers enshrined in the Constitution, Royal Decree 1254/1999 specifies which duties are to be performed by the state, the Autonomous Communities, and the local public authorities. Generally, it is for the Autonomous Communities to perform most tasks related to the administrative implementation of the Royal Decree, *inter alia*, licensing, planning, monitoring, reporting, and enforcing. At state level, the home affairs ministry is to ensure compliance with the information and notification duties vis-à-vis the Commission and the other Member States, as required by the Directive. It must also guarantee the constant coordination and supply of information, as well as the management and assessment of information related to the application of this Royal Decree.

---

[26] [1997] OJ L10/13.
[27] *Real Decreto 1254/1999 sobre medidas de control de los riesgos inherentes a los accidentes graves en los que intervengan sustancias peligrosas, BOE* No. 172, 20 July 1999, 27167.
[28] *Ley 2/1985 de Protección civil, BOE* No. 22, 25 Jan. 1985, 2092.
[29] *Ley 21/1992 de Industria, BOE* No. 176, 26 July 1992.     [30] [1982] OJ L230/1.
[31] [1998] OJ L192/19.

*iii. Miscellaneous*

A ministerial order of 21 October 1999[32] implemented Commission Decision 1999/177/EC of 8 February 1999 Establishing the Conditions for a Derogation for Plastic Crates and Plastic Pallets in relation to Heavy Metal Concentration Levels Established by Directive 94/62/EC on Packaging and Packaging Waste.[33]

Furthermore, a new Act on waste was passed in the Canary Autonomous Community: Act 1/1999 implements in the Canary Islands the relevant Spanish basic state legislation and Community legislation on waste.[34]

E. WATER

The most significant development in Spanish water law in 1999 was the amendment of the 1985 Water Act.[35] This Act had established a new legal regime for freshwaters taking due account of the distribution of powers between the state and the Autonomous Communities enshrined in the 1978 Constitution.[36] Although in theory the 1985 Water Act represented an innovative and coherent legal framework for the rational and sustainable management and quality of freshwaters, its practical implementation was not fully satisfactory.[37] In fact, the National Water Plan, which was foreseen to be one of its cornerstones, has not been approved yet. More than a decade elapsed before the different river basin plans were approved. Compliance with the waste-water dumping water tax has been extremely poor, and water quality control has also been deficient as is acknowledged in *Libro Blanco del Aqua* published by the ministry of environment.[38] Moreover, it has been argued that sufficient mechanisms were lacking to address prolonged droughts and to secure the proper quantity and quality of water.[39] After several years of political debate, Act 46/1999, amending Law 29/1985, was finally passed on December 1999.[40] The new Water Act regulates the use of new technologies to

---

[32] *Orden de 21 de octubre de 1999 por la que se establecen las condiciones para la no aplicación de los niveles de concentración de metales pesados establecidos en el artículo 13 de la Ley 11/1997, de 24 de abril, de Envases y Residuos de Envases, a las cajas y paletas de plástico reutilizables que se utilicen en una cadena cerrada y controlada, BOE No. 265, 5 Nov. 1999, 38762.*

[33] [1999] OJ L56/47.

[34] *Ley de la Presidencia del Gobierno de Canarias 1/1999, de 29 de enero, reguladora de residuos,* BOE No. 46, 23 Feb. 1999, 7471.

[35] *Ley 29/1985 de Aguas,* BOE No. 189, 8 Aug. 1985, 25123.

[36] It placed both surface and underground water in the public domain as state property, and established a system of administrative water rights. It also assigned a central role to water resources planning and introduced one of the first examples of eco-taxes: a tax for waste-water dumping, the revenue of which was to be invested in the protection and improvement of river basins.

[37] See C. Plaza, 'Spain' (1998) 1 *Yearbook of European Environmental Law,* 523.

[38] See MIMAM, *Libro Blanco del Agua* 1998, 549, and 263.

[39] See the *Exposición de Motivos* (State of Reasons) of Law 46/1999, para. 3.

[40] *Ley 46/1999, de 13 de diciembre, de modificación de la Ley 29/1985, de 2 de agosto, de Aguas,* BOE No. 298, 14 Dec. 1999, 43100.

increase the freshwater available for human consumption by means of, *inter alia*, desalination and water reuse. It amends certain provisions relating to the working regime of the state water public authorities (*Confederaciones Hidrográficas*) in order to reinforce coordination, public participation, and shared liability among the different public and private actors involved in water management. Furthermore, it strengthens the integration of environmental requirements into water management planning, while it regulates 'ecological flows' in river basins, thereby limiting water consumption in order to protect the aquatic environment. Additionally, the Act strengthens the waste-water dumping provisions. The most significant and controversial measures introduced by the 1999 Water Act, however, are to allow more flexibility in the permit system for the use of water, and to reinforce taxation for water uses, in order to foster the efficient use of water. It finally opened the possibility of transferring water rights, thus, the change of ownership and the use of market mechanisms, albeit still subject to certain legal conditions and to the administrative approval of the transfer of rights. It also introduced a new regime of taxation for use of goods and premises belonging to the public (water) domain, and for waste-water dumping. This fixes new methods to calculate the levy payable and the procedure for collecting those levies.

The Autonomous Community of Catalonia has also amended its water regulation.[41] A critical assessment of the legislation passed since 1981[42] led to the enactment of a new law on the regulation, management, and taxation of water resources in July 1999.[43] Law 6/1999 reorganizes the principles and powers of the Catalonian water authorities, the Catalonian Water Agency, and the local authorities, and reforms the water planning regime and the system of water taxation. Its main goal is to promote water management efficiency by means of techniques for water saving and reuse.

### F. HORIZONTAL INSTRUMENTS

#### i. Access to Environmental Information

Spanish legislation concerning access to environmental information has undergone several modifications in order to improve compliance with EC law, some of which were triggered by infringement procedures against Spain brought by the Commission.

On 1 October 1999 the Spanish Council of Ministers adopted an agreement on informing the general public about health protection measures to be

---

[41] In accordance with Arts. 149.1.22 and 149.1.23 of the Spanish Constitution, and Arts. 9, 10, and 11 of the Statute of Autonomy of Catalonia 1979, this Autonomous Community is empowered to regulate and manage water resources which do not run through other Spanish Autonomous Communities, and to adopt environmental legislation. See C. Plaza, 'Spain' (1998) 1 *Yearbook of European Environmental Law*, 523.

[42] The first law enacted was *Ley 5/1981 sobre desarrollo legislativo en materia de evacuación y tratamiento de aguas residuales*, BOE No. 121, 4 July 1981.

[43] *Ley de la Presidencia de la Generalitat de Catalunya 6/1999, de 12.7.1999, sobre Ordenación, Gestión y Tributación del Agua*, BOE No. 190, 10 Aug. 1999, 29468.

applied, and steps to be taken, in the event of a radiological emergency.[44] It amends a former agreement adopted in 1993 to transpose Directive 89/618/EURATOM on Informing the General Public about Health Protection Measures to be Applied and Steps to be Taken in the Event of a Radiological Emergency[45] into the Spanish legal order. The statement of reasons in the 1999 Agreement explains why the Commission held the 1993 Agreement to be an incorrect transposition of the Directive, which resulted in an infringement procedure pursuant to Article 141 EURATOM. Following the Commission's Reasoned Opinion of 9 December 1998,[46] the Spanish Government modified the 1993 agreement widening the scope of public information to comply with the Directive.[47]

The Commission brought an action against Spain concerning several alleged failures in the Spanish transposition of Directive 90/313/EEC on the Freedom of Access to Information on the Environment (Environmental Information Directive).[48] According to the Commission, Act 38/1995[49] transposing the Directive into the state basic legislation was not in conformity with Community law on several points. These related to matters such as excluded categories of information, and the reasonable cost that might be charged for providing access to information.[50] Against this background, Spain introduced the following amendments in Act 38/1995 by Act 55/1999 of 20 December 1999:[51] first, it reworded Article 3(1)e to express clearly that public authorities may refuse access to information concerning files whose contents concern judicial procedures or administrative sanctions, whether resolved in the past or still in progress. Furthermore, it makes explicit that only preliminary inquiries which are in progress shall be covered by this exception to the right to information. However, Article 3(1)e as it was phrased by Act 38/1995 seemed to include any preliminary inquiry, irrespective of whether it eventually led to contentious or quasi-contentious proceedings. Therefore, it did not fully conform with Article 3(2), third indent of the Environmental Information Directive, as it has been interpreted in standing case law of the ECJ.[52] Second, it amended Article 4(1) of Act 38/1995. This provision established that public

---

[44] It was published by order of the Ministry of Presidency subsecretary. See *Resolución de 20 de octubre de 1999, de la Subsecretaría, por la que se dispone la publicación del Acuerdo del Consejo de ministros de 1 de octubre de 1999, relativo a la información del público sobre medidas de protección sanitaria aplicables y sobre el comportamiento a seguir en caso de emergencia radiológica, BOE* No. 253, 22 Oct. 1999.

[45] [1999] OJ L357/31.          [46] See Sixteenth Annual Report (1998), n. 5 above, 164.

[47] The 1999 Agreement expressly states that the Reasoned Opinion was one of the main reasons to modify the 1993 Agreement.

[48] [1990] OJ L158/56.

[49] *Ley 38/1995 sobre el derecho de acceso a la información en materia de medio ambiente, BOE* No. 297, 13 Nov. 1995, 35708.

[50] See Sixteenth Annual Report (1998), n. 5 above, 46.

[51] *Ley 55/1999, de 29 de diciembre, de Medidas fiscales, administrativas y de orden social, BOE* No. 312, 30 Dec. 1999, 46095.

[52] For the interpretation of the term 'preliminary investigation procedure', used by Art. 3(2) of the Directive, see Case C–321/96, *Wilhelm Mecklenburg* v. *Kreis Pinneberg—Der Landrat* [1998] ECR I–3809, and Case C–217/97, *Commission* v. *Germany* [1999] ECR I–5087.

authorities had to reply to any request for information within a two-month period, but that if no answer was issued after the deadline it was to be presumed that the request had been refused. Nevertheless, any refusal, whether express or tacit, could be directly challenged before the contentious administrative courts. Thus, there was no need to pursue any previous administrative proceedings. Act 55/1999 suppressed the figure of tacit refusal to provide information, although in fact this does not establish an obligation on public authorities to give an express answer. Furthermore, it also subjected the resolutions of public authorities in this field to the general system of administrative review, which has to be exhausted in order to have access to judicial review.[53] Finally, Article 5 of Act 38/1995 established that access to information could give rise to the payment of a 'public fee' agreed by the public administration that has to provide the information. Therefore, it did not expressly restrict the charge for supplying information at a 'reasonable cost', as Article 5 of the Directive requires. Act 55/1999 has modified this article so as to make an explicit reference to the Directive's concept of 'reasonable costs'. How this is to be defined will be determined in each particular case, according to a general regulation on public prices and charges.

Although the deadline for implementation was 30 October 1999, Spain has not taken any action in respect of transposition of Directive 96/82/EC on Integrated Pollution Prevention and Control (IPPC Directive).[54] By the end of 1999 Catalonia alone had passed legal measures to implement the IPPC Directive in time, while the state had not yet adopted any legal measures.[55]

### ii. Environmental Impact Assessment

Finally, in the field of environmental impact assessment, Spain failed once more to implement Council Directive 97/11/EC amending Directive 85/337/EEC on the Assessment of the Effects of Certain Public and Private Projects on the Environment (EIA Directive)[56] within the prescribed timeframe. Although the ministry of environment had made tremendous efforts to draft a bill transposing the EIA Directive into the basic legislation of the state, the government did not introduce any such bill in parliament during 1999, and thus, the deadline of 14 February 1999 passed without any Spanish action having been taken. However, Autonomous Communities such as Castille-La Mancha in 1999 did pass new legislation on environmental impact assessment. The Castille-La Mancha Act 5/1999 on environmental impact

[53] The general system of administrative proceedings is regulated in Act 30/1992 regarding the legal regime of public administrations and on the common administrative procedure (*BOE* No. 258, 27 Nov. 1992) as amended by Act 4/1999 (BOE No. 12, 14 Jan. 1999, 1739).

[54] [1996] OJ L257/26.

[55] Catalonia Act 3/1998 on the integral action of environmental administration was further implemented by delegated legislation in 1999 (see *Decreto 136/1999, de 18 de mayo, por el que se aprueba el Reglamento general de desarrollo de la Ley 3/1998, de 27 de febrero, de la intervención integral de la administración ambiental, y se adaptan sus anexos, Diario Oficial de la Generalitat de Cataluña*, No 2894, 21 May 1999).

[56] [1997] OJ L73/5.

assessment[57] not only transposes the EIA Directive into the legal order of this Autonomous Community, but also regulates the assessment of certain plans and programmes on the environment. Thus, it anticipates the Commission proposal for a directive on the assessment of certain plans and programmes on the environment, relating to strategic environmental assessment.[58]

---

[57] *Ley de la Presidencia de la Junta de Comunidades de Castilla-la Mancha 5/1999, de 8 de abril, sobre Evaluación de impacto ambiental, BOE* No. 124, 25 May 1999, 19617.

[58] COM(96)511 final, [1996] OJ C109/14.

# XIII. Sweden

ANNIKA NILSSON*

## A. INTRODUCTION

The Environmental Code, the main Swedish statute on environmental issues, entered into force on 1 January 1999.[1] The Code does not entail entirely new legislation, as it is largely based on previously existing provisions.[2] It establishes some general rules of consideration which, in principle, apply to any activity which may potentially cause harm to human health or the environment. Several issues, such as nature conservation, environmentally hazardous activity, remediation of polluted sites, water undertakings, genetically modified organisms, chemicals, and waste are, in addition to the general rules of concern, subject to more specific regulation. The Code also includes provisions on environmental impact assessment (EIA) and environmental quality standards. Furthermore, it regulates procedural, administrative, criminal and some civil law issues, such as tortuous liability, concerned with the protection of the environment. Apart from some minor elements of civil law, Swedish environmental law can generally be characterized as administrative law.

The primary objective of the Environmental Code was to make environmental legislation more easily accessible and predictable, rather than to create a stricter environmental protection scheme, although some improvements to this end have nevertheless been undertaken. Efforts to improve Swedish implementation of EC environmental law have had significant success during 1999, in many areas, although still some concerns remain.

Although the Environmental Code is truly comprehensive, still several issues of significance to the implementation of EC environmental law have not been included. Some striking examples of statutes with relevance for the environment which were left outside the new Code are the Forestry Act,[3] the Hunting Act,[4] the Fisheries Act,[5] the Roads Act,[6] the Minerals Act,[7] and the Planning and Building Act.[8]

## B. CHEMICALS

The Act on Measures to Control Major-Accident Hazards Involving Dangerous Substances entered into force on 1 July 1999,[9] implementing into the Swedish

---

* Lecturer, Lund University, Lund, Sweden.
[1] *Svenska Fozfattningssamling* (*SFS*) (1998: 808). See also on the new Code: S. Rubenson, 'Sweden' (1998) 1 *Yearbook of European Environmental Law*, 527.
[2] *Inter alia* the 1964 Nature Conservancy Act, the 1969 Environmental Protection Act, the 1982 Health Protection Act, the 1985 Chemical Products Act, and the 1983 Water Act.
[3] *SFS* (1979: 429).    [4] Ibid. (1987: 259).    [5] Ibid. (1993: 787).    [6] Ibid. (1971: 948).
[7] Ibid. (1991: 45).    [8] Ibid. (1987: 10).    [9] Ibid. (1999: 381).

legal order Directive 96/82/EC on the Control of Major-Accident Hazards Involving Dangerous Substances (SEVESO II Directive).[10] By adopting this Act, the Swedish Parliament did more than simply comply with its obligation to transpose the Directive; it also responded to serious concerns regarding the existing regulation of chemicals, following a massive chemical accident in the Halland Ridge.[11] Prior to the entry into force of the new Act, the handling of substantial amounts of chemicals was largely left unregulated, unless it concerned a certain type of operation requiring a permit or a notification to a supervisory authority. Following the Act, operators must take measures to prevent the risk of major chemical accidents. In the event that a chemical accident should nonetheless occur, the operator is to limit the consequences for human health and the environment in so far as possible. For certain types of operations and for the handling of certain amounts of chemicals, a notification of the activity must be made to the competent authorities. Concerning those types of operations that are covered by the Act, the Swedish Government may establish a permit requirement, even if no such requirement is laid down in the Environmental Code. Operators shall adopt action plans for the prevention of serious chemical accidents, and may also be required to submit security reports informing the supervisory authorities of important facts concerning the operation and the risks connected thereto. Local authorities shall inform all persons running the risk of being affected by a serious chemical accident in their region, and shall educate them on how to handle such situations. Additionally, persons from outside the region shall have access to similar information, upon their request.

### C. NATURE CONSERVATION

Part of the Swedish legislation on the protection of species and habitats is found in chapters 7 and 8 of the Environmental Code.[12] However, several important issues including forestry, hunting, and fishery are not included in the Code, and are regulated by, respectively, the Forestry Act,[13] the Hunting Act,[14] and the Fisheries Act.[15]

Chapter 7 of the Environmental Code regulates several types of conservation areas. It serves as the legal basis for the government to designate Special Protection Areas (SPAs) and Natura 2000 areas in accordance with the Directive 1979/409/EEC on the Conservation of Wild Birds (Wild Birds Directive)[16] and Directive 1992/43/EEC on the Conservation of Natural Habitats and of Wild Fauna and Flora (Habitats Directive).[17] These designations in line with the EC Directives as such have no legal consequences under national law, since the management of SPAs and Natura 2000 areas is regulated by existing national territory protection provisions, *inter alia*, in chapter 7 of the Environmental Code.

---

[10] [1997] OJ L10/13.  [11] For further details, see Sect. E.*i*.  [12] See n. 1 above.
[13] See n. 3 above.  [14] See n. 4 above.  [15] See n. 5 above.
[16] [1979] OJ L103/1.  [17] [1992] OJ L206/7.

National Parks may be designated in sites owned by the state, for the purpose of preserving a larger area of a special type of landscape as unspoiled countryside, or in order to prevent changes in the landscape. The Environmental Protection Agency (EPA) shall issue directions for the management National Parks, in addition to guidelines to limit to the use of land and water.

The objective of a Nature Reserve may be to preserve biodiversity, to attend and preserve valuable nature, to provide for outdoor life, to protect or remedy valuable nature or habitats for protected species, or to re-create such areas. Nature Reserves may also be designated on privately owned land, in addition to state property. In the event of a Reserve being created in a privately owned site, and that it runs adjacent to privately owned land, the proprietors of those sites may have to accept quite far-reaching restrictions on the use of their land, and conditions for the management of the area. If privately owned land is taken, or if restrictions cause severe hindrance to the current use of the land, the landowner is entitled to compensation. Furthermore, it is not possible for the state to oblige landowners to perform or pay for active measures for the management of these areas. Such measures are always to be performed on behalf and at the expense of the competent authorities, or ultimately the Government.

Biotype Protection Areas (BPA) are areas that are rare and threatened in the landscape, and may serve as a habitat for certain threatened species. Examples of such areas are alleys, stonewalls, and small wetlands in agricultural areas. Within a BPA, any activity that might potentially cause damage to the area is generally prohibited. The dimensions of BPAs are typically rather modest, and the protection strategies pursued therein are generally intended not to cause disproportionate hindrance to the current use of land in the surrounding area. Most BPAs are situated in farmlands or forests, cultivated in traditional or an otherwise careful manner. Restrictions on 'normal operation or rationalization' of farming or forestry, *inter alia*, the practice of tearing down stonewalls and logging activity, normally give rise to a right to compensation on the part of the landowner.

Natura 2000 sites or SPAs are typically protected by designating them as Fauna or Flora Protection Areas under the Environmental Code, to which certain hunting and fishing restrictions apply, in addition to a regulated right of entry for, *inter alia*, the landowner. Aside from these specific restrictions, however, no further restrictions may be established in such areas.

Chapter 8 of the Environmental Code is aimed at the protection and preservation of specimens of threatened species. It contains a general prohibition against damaging specimens. Planting of exotic species and trade therein is restricted, while hunting and fishing of species is regulated by, respectively, the Hunting Act[18] and the Fisheries Act.[19]

---

[18] See n. 4 above.    [19] See n. 5 above.

Swedish implementation of the Wild Birds Directive and the Habitats Directive is not free from controversy, as several environmental lawyers and organizations have expressed their concerns, while also the European Commission has submitted criticism in respect of the insufficiency of the transposing provisions in Swedish environmental legislation.[20] Most of the controversy concerns the insufficiency of the authorities' economic resources to provide compensation to landowners.

Important areas may not be designated as SPAs or Natura 2000 sites due to this lack of resources. An additional problem is the somewhat limited competence on the part of the authorities to prevent deterioration of protected areas from operations located outside the area. The general rules do not principally exclude the location of new operations in vulnerable areas. If the permit authority accepts such a location, as it is generally required to do if there are no suitable alternatives, its competence to prescribe more stringent precautionary measures, on the grounds that the area is ecologically vulnerable, is limited. The Commission has emphasized that the relevant Swedish legislation does not ensure proper assessment of all plans and projects likely to significantly affect SPAs or Natura 2000 sites.

### D.  WASTE

#### i.  Packaging and Packaging Waste

The policy for packaging and packaging waste in Sweden is, in so far as possible, intended to place the responsibility for waste management on the producer, including for, *inter alia*, paper, tyres, and cars. In 1997 the government adopted an ordinance on packaging and packaging waste,[21] in order to reduce the amount of packaging waste and to promote reuse and recycling of packaging. The ordinance was amended at the end of 1998,[22] and again at the beginning of 1999.[23] By the (amended) Ordinance, Directive 94/62/EC on Packaging and Packaging Waste (Packaging and Packaging Waste Directive)[24] is implemented in Swedish law. The Swedish statute is more stringent than the Directive with regard to the levels of recovery and recycling. Most types of packaging are to be recovered up to 65–70 per cent, and the target for recycling is similarly high. With regard to aluminium packaging for beverages and certain types of bottles, the recovery and recycling target is set at 90 per cent by the ordinance. Producers are responsible for providing information to consumers and for organizing functional recovery systems. Furthermore, producers are to submit reports to the Swedish Environmental Protection Agency on the effectiveness of the recovery and recycling activities. Local authorities may

---

[20]  Concerning the Wild Birds Directive, the EU Commission has made an application to the ECJ concerning 'outstanding weaknesses in the Swedish legislation, notwithstanding progress made in 1999', while concerning the Habitats Directive, the Commission has notified a Reasoned Opinion to Sweden: IP/00/1007 of 13 Sept. 2000.

[21]  Ordinance (1997: 185).          [22]  Ordinance (1998: 949).          [23]  Ordinance (1999: 190).

[24]  [1994] OJ L365/10.

prescribe that the producers must also report to the municipal cleansing authority. Municipal waste management plans are to contain a separate section on packaging and packaging waste, concerned with the prevention of the production of packaging waste and the promotion of recycling. The latter provisions are, it appears, principally intended to be implemented by means of 'self-regulation' of the actors involved.

## ii. Waste Tax

As part of the political and legal objective to reduce the disposal of waste by landfill, a tax on waste has been introduced in Sweden,[25] to be paid by the operators of waste-disposal sites. As a result of this tax, waste deposition, in particular by means of landfill, is expected to become vastly more expensive, which should serve as an incentive for waste producers to investigate more environmentally sound alternatives, such as recycling. Although the tax applies to most types of waste, including domestic waste and industrial waste, some types of waste from specific trade sectors are exempted.

### E. HORIZONTAL INSTRUMENTS

## i. EIA

Although Directive 85/337/EEC on the Assessment of the Effects of Certain Public and Private Projects on the Environment (EIA Directive)[26] should have been implemented into Swedish law as early as in 1993, prior to the entry into force of the Environmental Code in 1999, the wording of the Directive had not been clearly transposed into domestic legislation. Certainly, the obligation to assess the possible effects on human health and the environment of a proposed project was prescribed in several individual statutes, *inter alia*, the Act on Management of Land and Water Areas,[27] the Environmental Protection Act,[28] and the Roads Act.[29] In fact, the obligation existing under Swedish law to make an environmental assessment prior to the Environmental Code was, arguably, more comprehensive than the provisions of the Directive, as it applied to every operation regulated under each individual statute, irrespective of its size or its potential impacts on human health and the environment.[30] However, somewhat surprisingly, some major projects and operations, for example the construction of new railroads, were not subject to an environmental assessment. The consequences of this apparent omission became strikingly obvious following attempts to construct a railroad tunnel through the Halland Ridge, in the south of Sweden, which resulted in a major chemical disaster. The project was initiated in 1993, without any prior assessment of the possible effects and the environmental impact of the operation. Consequently, the area has been subjected to continuous and substantial

[25] *SFS* (1999: 673).   [26] [1985] OJ L175/40.   [27] *SFS* (1987: 12).
[28] Ibid. (1969: 387).   [29] See n. 6 above.
[30] Although the assessment of small and harmless operations was, typically, of a rather modest nature.

damage to the environment, including severe decreases in the groundwater levels and a chemical catastrophe leading to numerous deaths among local cattle and fish, illnesses among workers, and severely poisoned freshwater wells. Meanwhile, these paramount effects have been the result of merely a fraction of the planned activities in the area: to date, only 5.5 km of the 17 km-long railroads have been constructed.

Generally, the insufficiency of the existing Swedish provisions on EIA was caused by its rather vague language concerning the requirements of the assessments. The Act on Management of Land and Water Areas,[31] which was the primary statute with regard to EIA prior to the introduction of the new Environmental Code, simply required that an assessment make possible a comprehensive review of the project's impact on the environment, human health, and the management of land and water areas. Similar wording was used in other statutes on this issue. In the 1991 ordinance on environmental impact assessment,[32] reference was made to the Espoo Convention on Environmental Impact Assessment in a Transboundary Context,[33] in so far as that all assessments should contain reasoned accounts of, where appropriate, alternative locations, alternative methods, and a description of the consequences of termination of the project. Notwithstanding these provisions, Swedish environmental law has traditionally been rather non-descriptive concerning the issue of EIA content requirements. The ministry of environment considered it inappropriate to regulate the EIA content in detail, noting that the government found it more appropriate to prescribe the results to be achieved by the process.[34]

Subsequent regulatory attempts for EIA have been subject to widespread criticism in Sweden, due to the evidently insufficient implementation of the EIA Directive as a result of severe deficiencies in the practice of assessments. In respect of the latter, the Swedish National Audit Office has indicated that, *inter alia*, it is common in Sweden for consultations between parties with opposing interests to be initiated too late in the process, that the control and supervision of the assessments is often insufficient, that vital environmental aspects are often not granted proper consideration in the decision, and finally, that the listing of alternatives is missing or insufficient.[35]

With the adoption of the new Environmental Code, the government has finally introduced a more detailed EIA regime, whereby assessments are not only obligatory under the permit procedure of the Environmental Code, but also under the provisions of several other statutes, such as the Railway Construction Act.[36] Generally, the Swedish regime is now firmly in line with the EIA Directive, although some minor yet interesting differences remain.

According to the Environmental Code, the EIA procedure is to be initiated at an early stage of the planning of a permit-requiring project. To this end, timely consultations are to be undertaken with the private parties concerned and

---

[31] See n. 27 above.          [32] Ordinance (1991: 738) on environmental impact assessment.
[33] Espoo, 1991; (1991) 30 *International Legal Materials*, 800.          [34] Bill (1990/91: 90), 187.
[35] Rihszevisionsvezhet (RRV) (1996: 29), in particular at 115.          [36] *SFS* (1995: 1649).

with the County Administrative Board and, upon which the latter shall submit a report on the possible impacts on the environment of the project. If significant problems are to be expected, an EIA is to be undertaken without further delay. In line with the EIA Directive, the government may subject certain types of projects to EIA generally, without prior consultations. The content of EIA procedures is laid down in the Code and in more detail in a separate ordinance.[37] These provisions largely correspond with the EIA Directive, although in the Swedish provisions more emphasis is placed upon the consultation process and the transparency and openness of the process, as not only the competent authorities and the parties concerned may participate, but also the interested general public. The permit authority is ultimately to decide upon the sufficiency of an EIA, taking into account the results of the consultations.

Given the novelty of the Environmental Code, it is not yet possible to reach any conclusion on the practical implications on EIA in Sweden. Yet, as the report from the Swedish National Audit Office indicates, previous deficiencies in the process were most probably not only the result of the vagueness of the relevant legislation, but also of heavily ingrained routines of the courts and the administrative authorities.

### ii. IPPC

Sweden will have no difficulties in conforming with most of the provisions of Directive 96/61/EC concerning Integrated Pollution Prevention and Control (IPPC Directive).[38] In Sweden, following the adoption of the Environmental Protection Act in 1969,[39] all operators of projects and activities that can be classified as 'environmentally hazardous' are required to exercise precaution. The concept of 'environmentally hazardous activity' is quite comprehensive, covering any activity causing pollution to air, water, or land; noise hindrance; light hindrance; vibrations; or other disturbances. A permit requirement is in place for several types of environmentally hazardous activities. The introduction of the new Environmental Code has provided a more integrated approach, as it provides for application of identical rules of consideration to these types of operations, as to other types of activities regulated under the Code. Notwithstanding this progressive policy on IPPC, some ambiguities remain in the Swedish implementation of the IPPC Directive. The concept of 'best possible techniques' in the Environmental Code is currently a topic of discussion in Sweden, as it is somewhat unclear whether this should be interpreted as corresponding to the concept of 'best available techniques' in the IPPC Directive. Since the wording of the preparatory works of the Code had followed the wording of the Directive quite closely, and no statement was made to indicate or imply an intended deviation,[40] it is an open question as to why the legislator ultimately chose to use different wording in the statute.

Discussion also exists as to whether Article 10 of the IPPC Directive is fully implemented by the Environmental Code. It is questionable whether it would

---

[37] Ordinance (1998: 905) on environmental impact assessment.     [38] [1997] OJ L257/26.
[39] See n. 23 above.     [40] Bill (1997/98: 45 II), 16.

be possible to demand stricter conditions than those which follow from 'best possible techniques', if necessary for the proper maintenance of environmental quality standards. This question is analysed in more detail below in Section F.i.

## i. Environmental Quality Standards

Prior to the introduction of the Environmental Code, Swedish legislation was significantly insufficient with regard to EC regulations on environmental quality standards. The difficulties and insufficiencies of the previous regime may be illustrated by two striking examples: the regulation of air quality standards and bathing-water quality standards.

First, air quality standards were provided for in section 14(a) of the 1982 Health Protection Act,[41] holding that limit values should be established for nitrogen dioxide, sulphur dioxide, suspended particles, and lead. The Swedish Environmental Protection Agency (EPA) subsequently established limit values for nitrogen dioxide, sulphur dioxide, and suspended particles in 1993.[42] Although the EPA had also required the emissions of these substances to be measured, this obligation would not apply until the limit values were presumed to be transgressed. Since neither the operators nor the competent authorities were under any obligation to take action in the event that the limit values were exceeded, no deterring sanctions existed under the previous regime, making it impossible to enforce the normative provisions on this issue. The primary statute on emissions, the Environmental Protection Act, laid down an obligation to take precautionary measures for several types of operations. However, this obligation was limited to what could be achieved by means of the 'best possible techniques', considering the costs involved, and the expected benefits to the environment. The Act did not give grounds for the possibility of prohibiting an operation, denying a permit, or repealing an existing permit on the grounds that air or water limit values were not complied with. Additionally, although the Health Protection Act provided the supervisory authorities with the competence to demand precautionary measures, such demands could not go beyond what was prescribed in the permit under the Environmental Protection Act.

Bathing-water quality standards were previously established by section 8 of the Health Protection Act,[43] on the basis of which the EPA laid down limit values for the quality of the bathing water, and the measurement thereof.[44] Yet, most operations with a potential to cause deterioration of the quality of bathing waters fell within the scope of the Environmental Protection Act, with the limitations described above.

[41] *SFS* (1982: 1080). Further measures were laid down in section 9(b) in ordinance (1983: 616) on health protection.
[42] *Sveriges Naturvärdverhs Forfattningssamling* (*SNSF*) (1993: 10, 11, and 12). The provisions were later amended by Ordinance (1998: 897).
[43] Further measures were laid down in sect. 9(c) of ordinance (1983: 616) on health protection.
[44] *SNSF* (1996: 6).

It may be concluded from these two examples that the former regime of environmental quality standards was in urgent need of reform. Following the adoption of the Environmental Code, environmental quality standards may be issued if they are necessary for the durable protection of the environment and human health. Standards may apply nationally or regionally, and may also be established in respect of disturbances without serious or evident risks for human health or the environment. Standards may be based on, *inter alia*, the amount of substances in the soil, water, or air; the level of noise, vibrations, radiation, or similar nuisances; the height or torrent of water; and the existence in water of certain indicator organisms for assessment of the water quality. The government shall allocate the responsibility for the measurement of such control, along with procedures for the methods of control and for the presentation of the results thereof. Thus, the legal basis to establish environmental quality standards appears to be—at least—in conformity with the EC legislation on this topic, given rather extensive regulation under Swedish law. However, given the novelty of this type of legal instrument in Swedish law, it is not yet possible to predict the frequency of its application.

Although the Environmental Code certainly constitutes an improvement on existing regulation on environmental quality standards, some questions still remain. For example, while it is provided that authorities shall ensure compliance with the standards in their policy and practice of granting permits, supervising, planning, and general regulatory activity, it is not completely clear to what extent the authorities are empowered to impose restrictions on individuals pursuant to these provisions. According to Chapter 16 of the Code, a new permit cannot be granted if a quality standard is transgressed, unless the operator contributes to a significant reduction of nuisance from other activities. Also, the balancing according to Chapter 2, section 7 of the Code, must not be executed in such a way as to transgress quality standards, but it remains uncertain what this implies exactly. Is it possible to demand measures that go beyond best possible techniques, including consideration of sound business economics? Or is the provision merely such that, when environmental quality standards are infringed, the benefits for the environment shall be assumed to outweigh the costs of precautionary measures that are considered reasonable *within* the balancing concept? Furthermore, the provisions of review of permits in Chapter 24 of the Code provide legal grounds for review if the activity contributes to the transgression of a quality standard, yet, this review is very limited, as it may not result in such stringent conditions as to significantly hinder or completely disable the continued operation or activity. An additional problem is that several activities that may influence the quality of the environment, *inter alia* land-, sea-, and air-traffic and transport, are not regulated in the Environmental Code, nor in any other statute dealing with this issue in an appropriate way. Consequently, it remains ambiguous whether environmental quality standards can be upheld entirely.

In the event that an environmental quality standard is likely to be infringed, an action programme would be adopted which may include any activity that has an impact on the standard. The action programme would identify the relevant standards, prescribe the appropriate enforcement measures, their respective time-limits, and the final deadline for accomplishment of the standards. Furthermore, it would identify the responsible authorities, who must ensure maintenance of the quality standard by means of supervision, review of existing permits, and by adopting general regulations.

# XIV. United Kingdom

TIM JEWELL*

## A. AIR POLLUTION

A gradual process of formalization in air quality controls has continued in the United Kingdom during 1999, with the publication of a review, and revised draft, of the *National Air Quality Strategy*,[1] and the promulgation of proposed revisions to the limited number of statutory air quality standards.[2] The strategy is intended to set out objectives for the management of ambient air quality until 2005, focusing on the eight air pollutants considered to have the greatest impact on human health. As such, it is the principal vehicle for giving effect to obligations being imposed under Council Directive 96/62/EC on Ambient Air Quality Assessment and Management (Ambient Air Directive).[3] Yet, the strategy relies for its implementation on a raft of legal and other instruments operated on a devolved and rather haphazard basis. General obligations on regulators to 'have regard to' the strategy in the exercise of their functions,[4] for example, provide a tenuous link between strategic policy and its implementation, and whilst performance of local authorities—which have important, increasing air quality management powers—has been the subject of particular recent criticism.[5]

## B. NATURE CONSERVATION

The fact that UK conservation policy is maturing unusually rapidly provided fragile reassurance last year for those seeking the modernization of UK conservation law. A government-sponsored review of conservation legislation has now resulted in proposals being put to parliament, but there have been mixed messages from the courts in interpreting UK measures giving effect to key EC conservation obligations, and continuing controversy over genetically modified organisms.

The Countryside and Rights of Way Bill[6] is intended to give greater coercive edge to the site designation framework—the principal legal means of

---

* Director of the Centre for Environmental Law, University of Southampton, Southampton, UK.

[1] *Report on the Review of the National Air Quality Strategy*, Department of the Environment, Transport and the Regions (DETR), Jan. 1999; *The Air Quality Strategy for England, Scotland, Wales and Northern Ireland*, DETR Consultation Paper, 25 Aug. 1999.

[2] *Air Quality (England) Regs. 2000*, DETR Consultation Paper, 25 Oct. 1999.

[3] [1996] OJ L296/55.

[4] e.g., on the Environment Agency under Environment Act 1995, s. 80(1).

[5] *Local Authority Progress in Implementing the Local Air Pollution Control Regime: Action Plan and Response*, DETR, Oct. 1998; see (1999) 11 *Environmental Law & Management* 35.

[6] House of Commons Bill 78EN, Session 1999–2000. See also *SSSIs: Better Protection and Management. The Government's Framework for Action—Outcome of the Consultation Exercise*, DETR, 2 Aug. 1999.

implementing in England and Wales Directive 79/409/EEC on the Conservation of Wild Birds (Wilds Birds Directive)[7] and Directive 92/43/EEC on the
Conservation of Natural Habitats and of Wild Fauna and Flora (Habitats
Directive)[8]. The Bill includes new powers by which conservation agencies
could prohibit landowners and occupiers from causing damage to designated
sites and require neglect to be remedied, along with higher penalties,
improved powers to act against third parties, and a statutory duty on certain
public bodies to secure the positive management of sites. In Scotland, any corresponding reform would fall to the Scottish parliament.[9] In the meantime,
there have also been some notable cases of local planning authorities acting
robustly in modifying existing development consents where their implementation would be inconsistent with subsequently imposed obligations under
the Habitats Directive.[10]

More problematic is the important decision of the Scottish Court of Session
concerning the designation, and authorization of development adjacent to
land which was both a special protection area (SPA) under the Birds Directive
and a special area of conservation (SAC) under the Habitats Directive.[11]
Although the Court accepted that decisions of the European Court of Justice
(ECJ) require the boundaries of an SPA to be defined by reference to ornithological criteria alone, it did not consider that identifying a site and defining its
boundaries were entirely distinct processes.[12] As, in the Court's judgment,
delineating boundaries is an integral part of defining a site, there is an element
of discretion involved in the whole process. As a matter of discretion, therefore, this could lead to linked or contiguous habitats or species populations
being excluded from the SAC or SPA itself. The Court also concluded that existing land uses (in this case, skiing) were rightly considered to be relevant to the
scientific basis for designation, rather than irrelevant economic or recreational factors. The Court's implicit acceptance that WWF-UK had standing to
challenge the designation and authorization decisions may be welcome, but
the apparent dilution of the RSPB principle is less so. The implications, environmentally and for the remainder of the UK, remain unclear.

The decision of the English High Court that the UK has not properly transposed the Habitats Directive in a different respect is more environmentally
benign.[13] The relevant implementing regulations were held to be inadequate
in applying only to the 12-mile limit of UK territorial waters, rather than the
maximum 200-mile limit of the UK continental shelf.[14] The breadth of factors

---

[7]  [1979] OJ L103/1.              [8]  [1992] OJ L206/7.              [9]  Scotland Act 1998.
[10]  e.g., Decision GOSE/104/4/Kent/1, 9 Nov. 1998; noted at (1999) 51 *Environmental Law
Bulletin* 34.
[11]  *WWF-UK Ltd* v. *Secretary of State for Scotland, Scottish Natural Heritage and Highland
Council* 1998 GWD 37–1936; (1999) Environmental Law Reports 632.
[12]  e.g., Case C–44/95, *The Queen* v. *Secretary of State for the Environment, ex p. Royal Society for
the Protection of Birds* [1996] ECR I–3085; Case C–3/96, *Commission* v. *Netherlands,* [1998]
ECR–3031.
[13]  *The Queen* v. *Secretary of State for Trade & Industry, ex p. Greenpeace Ltd* (1999) 5 Nov. 1999.
[14]  Conservation (Natural Habitats) Regs. 1994, SI 1994/2716.

considered by the Court is particularly striking: the desirability of protecting certain coral species, despite their omission from the Directive; unchallenged evidence that oil exploration would be harmful to cetaceans, listed in Annex IV of the Directive as being of Community interest and in need of strict protection; and the parallel application beyond 12 miles of Directive 85/337/EEC on the Assessment of the Effects of Certain Public and Private Projects on the Environment (EIA Directive).[15] The Court was equally certain that the Directive has direct effect.

Prospective developments have received attention too, particularly in the Commission's proposal for revised legislation aimed at stricter and more transparent control of the release of genetically modified organisms.[16] The broad thrust of those proposals has been welcomed, although complex problems remain in industrial demands for certainty in defining when an end-product is considered to be safe, aspects of competition between agro-chemical/seed companies, the ability of UK policy and regulatory structures to reconcile scientific developments with conservation policy, and continuing high levels of public concern.[17]

C. WASTE

### i. Waste Policy and the Landfill Directive

The site-specific waste regulatory system established in the UK in 1990 was only complemented in 1995 by an obligation on central government to prepare a national waste strategy.[18] The emphasis in 1990 was upon 'reining-in' a badly performing waste management industry, and on closing the worst gaps in the waste production and disposal chain, rather than on setting long-term targets for waste reduction, reuse and recovery, or recycling. With the regulatory foundations now laid, and in light of the obligations imposed by the long-delayed Directive 99/31/EC on the Landfill of Waste (Landfill Directive),[19] UK waste policy has begun to develop at a more rapid pace. This has not been as swift or effective as many would wish, however—not least the House of Commons Select Committee on the Environment.[20] Yet, 1999 saw the publication of a draft waste strategy, which prepares the way for the implementation of the

---

[15] [1985] OJ L175/40.

[16] *EC Regulation of Genetic Modification in Agriculture*, House of Lords Select Committee on the European Communities, Second Report, Session 1998–9 (HL Paper 11).

[17] See Pontin (1999) 11 *Environmental Law & Management* 145, commenting on *Genetically Modified Organisms and the Environment: Co-ordination of Government Policy*, House of Commons Select Committee on Environmental Audit, Fifth Report, Session 1998–9 (HC Paper 384).

[18] Environment Act 1995, s. 92.   [19] [1999] OJ L182.

[20] 'It is important to stress . . . our profound disappointment, on the basis of the evidence we have received, that waste management in this country is still characterised by inertia, careless administration and ad hoc, rather than science-based, decisions. Lip-service alone, in far too many instances, has been paid to the principles of reducing waste and diverting it from disposal. Central Government has lacked the commitment, and local government the resources, to put a sustainable waste management strategy into practice.': *Sustainable Waste Management*, Sixth Report, Session 1997–8 (HC Paper 484), para. 17.

Landfill Directive.[21] As landfill accounts for some 90 per cent of waste disposal in England and Wales, the importance of this should not be underestimated.[22]

In general, the British Government's view is that the landfill standards introduced by the Directive will not be much greater than those currently applied. A shift to other forms of disposal—incineration in particular—is anticipated, but the most difficulty will be in achieving targets for the reduction of biodegradable municipal waste. The issue in much of the UK is therefore not so much *how* to landfill as *when* to do so. New instruments to limit landfill are therefore under consideration, including prohibitions or limitations on disposal of biodegradable wastes to landfill, and extension of the landfill tax.[23] Yet real problems remain in translating the general targets set by the new policy into the waste management planning and regulation systems, where competencies have been largely devolved. The legal complexity of coordinating this Directive with Directive 96/61/EC on Integrated Pollution Prevention and Control (IPPC Directive)[24] is also a continuing concern.

### ii. Regulatory Developments

Although the UK has generally adopted a pragmatic approach to the definition of waste, based on the notion that to 'discard' a substance or object it must fall out of the commercial cycle or chain of utility,[25] the British Courts have once again been concerned to interpret 'waste' in the light of recent decisions of the ECJ.[26] It is notable that the purposive approach adopted in the *Greenpeace* decision[27] has also informed the conclusion that scrap metals are potentially waste: where it is simply reused without a recovery operation it is not waste; where a recovery operation is applied then it is.[28] Thus, the ability to reuse scrap is not determinative of its legal character, but rather depends on whether its recovery or recycling requires further operations which themselves may create risks to the environment or to public health.

More controversial is the lacuna created by the insolvency of a licensed company. In normal circumstances, a waste management licence cannot be surrendered without the agreement of the regulator, the Environment Agency. The post-closure stability or condition of a site can therefore be secured, at the expense of the licensee. Despite earlier decisions to the contrary, the Court of

---

[21] *A Way with Waste: Draft Waste Strategy for England and Wales*, DETR, June 1999. The *National Waste Strategy: Scotland*, was published in Dec. 1999.

[22] *Sustainable Landfill*, House of Lords Select Committee on the European Communities, Seventeenth Report, Session 1997–8 (HL Paper 83).

[23] *Limiting Landfill*, DETR Consultation Paper, Oct. 1999.

[24] [1996] OJ L257/26, considered further below.

[25] *Waste Management—The Duty of Care—A Code of Practice*, Department of the Environment, Mar. 1996, para. (x).

[26] e.g., Case C–304/94, *Criminal Proceedings against Euro Tombesi and Adino Tombesi* [1997] ECR I-3561, and Case C–129-96, *Inter-Environment Wallonie ASBL* v. *Region Wallone* [1997] ECR I–7411.

[27] See n. 13 and associated text, above.

[28] *Mayer Parry Recycling Ltd* v. *Environment Agency* (1999) Environmental Law Reports 489.

Appeal has now held that insolvency is an exception to this rule:[29] an administrator can effectively disown a waste management licence, creating 'orphan' sites and residual environmental problems.

D. WATER

Water remains the most litigated environmental medium in the UK, a fact explained in part by the influence of EC measures on UK water law. Although those seeking to rely on Community-based rights have recently enjoyed only limited success, the British Government seems set to enjoy even less.

In one of the first *Francovich*-type claims in UK pollution law,[30] a shellfish fisherman has established through an interlocutory appeal that Directive 79/923/EEC on the Quality Required of Shellfish Waters (Shellfish Directive)[31] does entail a grant of rights to him as a fisherman.[32] The Court concluded that as a purpose of the Directive is to protect shellfish populations, and a failure to do so could result in unequal conditions of competition, the claimant was within the class of those collecting and marketing shellfish that may have been intended to have a right of reparation if the Directive were not correctly implemented. Although potentially significant, this decision should not be misunderstood: it does not grant such a remedy, it merely does not rule it out as unarguable.

A challenge to UK measures transposing Directive 91/676/EEC concerning the protection of waters against pollution caused by nitrates from agricultural sources[33] has, however, soundly failed in the ECJ.[34] That decision confirms the broad discretion of Member States to define waters requiring protection, and the arrangements to provide it, while rejecting creative arguments based on both polluter-pays and prevention-at-source ideas. The government itself seems less likely to survive unscathed from two further prospective actions by the Commission concerning its alleged failure to implement Directive 80/68/EEC on Protection of Groundwater against Pollution Caused by Certain Dangerous Substances (Groundwater Directive)[35] and Directive 76/160/EEC Concerning Quality of Bathing Water (Bathing Water Directive)[36]—again.[37]

---

[29] *Official Receiver as Liquidator of Celtic Extraction Ltd & Bluestone Chemicals Ltd* v. *Environment Agency* (1999) 295 ENDS Report 47.

[30] Joined Cases C–6/90 and C–9/90, *Andrea Francovich and Danila Bonifaci and others* v. *Italy* [1991] ECR I–5357; Macrory, (1999) 288 ENDS Report 55.

[31] [1979] OJ L281/47.

[32] *Bowden* v. *South-West Water Services Ltd*, (1999) Environmental Law Reports 438.

[33] [1991] OJ L375/1.

[34] Case C–293/97, *The Queen* v. *Secretary of State for the Environment and Ministry of Agriculture, Fisheries and Food, ex p. H. A. Standley and others* [1999] ECR–I2603; (1999) Environmental Law Reports 801.

[35] [1979] OJ L20/43.     [36] [1976] OJ L31/1.

[37] Case C–56/90, *Commission* v. *United Kingdom* [1993] ECR I–4109.

### E. HORIZONTAL INSTRUMENTS

*i. IPPC*

As anticipated,[38] the superimposition of the IPPC Directive onto an already complex integrated pollution control (IPC) system has proved to be controversial. This is partly because what is now the Pollution Prevention and Control Act 1999 seeks both to give effect in England and Wales to the distinctive features of the Directive, and to modify existing practices in the light of experience with IPC itself. Yet it is the legal approach to implementation, in particular the scope of the delegation proposed, that provoked a parliamentary committee to produce a report on the government's proposals that was virtually unprecedented in its criticism.[39] As a consequence, the powers delegated to the Secretary of State have been truncated, but the brevity of the Act continues to belie its importance. Extremely detailed regulations are therefore to be made to elaborate on the broad statements of objectives found in the Act,[40] with a rolling programme of implementation planned between October 1999 and 2007. Without the regulations it is difficult to comment on the many practical challenges to be overcome if successful implementation is to be achieved. Amongst the most obvious, however, will be the role of local authorities—including cities and districts—in exercising integrated controls for the first time.

*ii. EIA*

It is probably a coincidence that the introduction of new regulations to give effect to the revised EIA Directive[41] has corresponded with a distinct heightening of judicial expectations that both the spirit and the detail of those regulations will be complied with. Early decisions of the British courts on the implementation of the Directive shared the pragmatic approach taken by successive UK governments: that approximate, or 'substantial', substantive compliance[42] was normally sufficient even in the absence of formal compliance. Ambivalence as to the Directive's supposed direct effect was also apparent.[43] The last year has seen more demanding—some would say formalistic— conclusions.

---

[38] T. Jewell, 'United Kingdom' (2000) 1 *Yearbook of European Environmental Law*, 536.

[39] House of Lords Select Committee on Delegated Powers and Deregulation, Third Report, Session 1998–9 (HL Paper 12) and Ninth Report (HL Paper 40); noted at (1999) 11 *Environmental Law & Management* 87.

[40] *Fourth Consultation Paper on the Implementation of the IPPC Directive*, DETR, Aug. 1999.

[41] [1985] OJ L175/40, as amended by Council Directive 97/11/EC, [1997] OJ L173/5; Town and Country Planning (Environmental Impact Assessment) (England and Wales) Regs. 1999, SI 1999/293.

[42] e.g., *Twyford Parish Council* v. *Secretary of State for the Environment and Secretary of State for Transport* (1992) 4 *Journal of Environmental Law* 273.

[43] *Wychavon District Council* v. *Secretary of State for the Environment and Velcourt* (1994) Environmental Law Reports 239.

The starting point is that the implicit acceptance of the Court of Appeal that the Directive has direct effect has been confirmed by the House of Lords.[44] The same decision broadened the application of the Directive in the UK by extending the types of 'development consent' to which it applies beyond the most common form of planning permission. An obligation to carry out an EIA therefore will arise where a decision is a 'new and free-standing consideration of the issues', rather than merely detailed regulation after environmental concerns have been considered in granting the principal consent. This case concerned an unusual statutory system for reassessing the impacts of old mineral workings, but similar problems arise elsewhere. One example is where permission for development in principle is given, followed either by consideration of further details or an additional (say, pollution) licensing process. A growing tendency to require close compliance with the Directive at an early stage is apparent in such cases also.[45] In all cases, delegation of an authority's power to determine the need for an EIA must now be done formally.[46]

### iii. Access to Information

The effectiveness of Council Directive 90/313/EEC on Freedom of Access to Information on the Environment[47] has received an important boost in a High Court decision on the UK implementing regulations.[48] The regulations have been subject to little litigation, perhaps partly because of their breadth, but not surprisingly it is the confidentiality exceptions to disclosure that have received most attention. Certain conclusions can now be drawn, including: whether information is subject to the regulations is a matter of fact reviewable by the court; in refusing access, sufficient reasons for any refusal must be given to enable a person to ascertain whether refusal is well founded in fact and law, or whether it is susceptible to challenge; the mere fact that information is contained in a commercial document is not determinative of whether it is 'environmental information' or not, or of its confidentiality; and the derogations in general are to be read in a strict and proportionate way. A later decision that contaminated land data informing a research report prepared for a local authority are merely 'speculative preliminary thinking' rather than 'information' to which the regulations apply, is less convincing.[49]

---

[44] *The Queen* v. *North Yorkshire County Council, ex p. Brown* (1998) Environmental Law Reports 385 (Court of Appeal); (1999) *Journal of Planning & Environment Law* 616 (House of Lords). Confirmed in the approach of the High Court in *The Queen* v. *Oldham Metropolitan Borough Council and Pugmanor Properties Ltd, ex p. Foster* (1999) 30 July.

[45] *The Queen* v. *Rochdale Metropolitan Borough Council, ex p. Tew* (1999) 7 May; (1999) 57 *Environmental Law Bulletin* 12.

[46] *The Queen* v. *St Edmundsbury Borough Council, ex p. Walton* (1999) *Journal of Planning & Environment Law* 805.

[47] [1990] OJ L158/56.

[48] Environmental Information Regs. 1992, SI 1992/3240, as amended by SI 1998/1447; *The Queen* v. *Secretary of State for the Environment, Transport and the Regions and Midland Expressway Ltd, ex p. Alliance against the Birmingham Relief Road* (1999) *Journal of Planning & Environment Law* 231.

[49] *Maile* v. *Wigan Metropolitan Borough Council* (1999) 294 ENDS Report 55.

### F. MISCELLANEOUS

Two other issues have been prominent in UK environmental law in 1999, although their relationship with express Community obligations is less obvious: environmental standards in general, and the operation of the landfill tax.

### i. Environmental Standards

The Royal Commission on Environmental Pollution has published a substantial report on environmental standards, which is likely to inform policy and legal developments in the next ten years.[50] Apparently motivated by the Royal Commission's concern at widespread confusion and misunderstanding about the purpose and mechanisms of environmental regulation, the report is intended to 'identify a more consistent and robust basis for setting environmental standards for environmental protection, in the broadest sense'.[51] It does so with mixed success, but nevertheless provides an invaluable insight into the hurdles to be overcome if environmental law in the UK and elsewhere is to become more effective.

### ii. Environmental Taxes

The landfill tax meanwhile remains the most prominent direct economic instrument for environmental protection adopted in the UK.[52] A report of its operation has, however, revealed disagreement as to its effectiveness, and its future evolution.[53] The unusual sight of parliament suggesting a significant increase in a tax contrary to the view of a cautious government,[54] has been accompanied by growing concern at alleged abuses of the landfill tax credits scheme, which is intended to divert resources into environmental improvements rather than to provide subsidized public relations gains for taxpayers. Modest reforms have been made, and the tax is set to increase.[55] More significant progress has been made in developing a levy on the business use of energy, to contribute to a planned reduction in greenhouse emissions of 12.5 per cent by 2010. This is now intended to be in place from April 2001, but in the meantime a voluntary reporting scheme has been established.[56]

---

[50] *Setting Environmental Standards*, Twenty-first Report, Cm. 4053; noted at (1999) 11 *Environmental Law & Management* 31.

[51] Ibid., para. 1.3.

[52] Finance Act 1996, ss. 39–41; Landfill Tax Regs. 1996, SI 1996/1527.

[53] *The Operation of the Landfill Tax*, House of Commons Select Committee on Environment, Transport and Regional Affairs, Session 1998–9 (HC Paper 150).

[54] Cm. 4461, 20 Oct. 1999.

[55] e.g., Landfill Tax (Amendment) Regs. 1999, SI 1999/3270; Landfill Tax (Site Restoration and Quarries) Order 1999, SI 1999/2075. A staged increase is planned from the present £10 per tonne to £15 per tonne by 2004.

[56] The Rt. Hon. Gordon Brown MP, Chancellor of the Exchequer, *Official Report*, HC Debates, 9 Mar. 1999, Col. 181; *Guidelines for Company Reporting on Greenhouse Gas Emissions*, DETR, 22 June 1999.

# XV. Central and Eastern European Countries

MARIE SOVEROSKI*

## A. INTRODUCTION

The focus of the Central and Eastern European (CEE) countries in the area of environmental law and policy in 1999 was on continuing to prepare for the obligations of European Union (EU) membership. The environmental area has long been considered one likely to pose some of the most serious problems for the candidate countries, based on their reputation as heavily polluted states, with limited financial resources to undertake such measures as are necessary to meet EU environmental standards. While this image of countries suffering from urban and industrial blight is only part of the picture—Poland and Romania, for example, have some of the largest areas of unaltered natural habitat left on the continent—there is no denying that the Communist policy of developing heavy industry, based on political considerations and often disregarding negative environmental consequences, has left behind a legacy of degradation. Furthermore, access to resources and technology, which would have allowed modernization of facilities in order to control or reduce pollution, was often curtailed under the former Communist regime, due to trade restrictions.

## B. EU MEMBERSHIP NEGOTIATIONS

Environment is one of thirty-one chapters of the *acquis communautaire* (*acquis*), which form the framework of negotiations between the applicant states and the EU. The degree to which these negotiations have proceeded has, in large part, been dictated by whether the country was originally placed in the 'first wave' or 'second wave' of applicants. The European Commission issued its opinion on the applications for membership of the CEE countries in July 1997,[1] and in December of that year, in Luxembourg, the Council went along with the Commission's recommendations and agreed to formally open negotiations with Cyprus and five CEE countries: the Czech Republic, Estonia, Hungary, Poland, and Slovenia. These first wave countries have been referred to as the 'Luxembourg Group'. The other five CEE countries, Bulgaria, Latvia, Lithuania, Romania, and Slovakia, were told negotiations could begin when

* Senior Lecturer, European Institute of Public Administration, European Centre for Lawyers and Judges, Luxembourg.
[1] Commission of the European Communities, 'Summary and conclusions of the opinions of the Commission concerning the Applications for Membership to the European Union presented by the Candidate Countries', DOC/97/8, Brussels, 15 July 1997.

they had made sufficient progress in satisfying the 'Copenhagen criteria'.[2] Negotiations began with the Luxembourg Group in March 1998. The EU Council, at the Helsinki Summit in December 1999, decided to extend negotiations to include the remaining group of CEE countries, in addition to Malta— now referred to as the 'Helsinki Group'. Bilateral negotiations formally commenced in March 2000.

As the first phase of the negotiations proceeds, the national legislation of the applicant states is screened to determine how well it matches with the obligations of the *acquis*. Screening of the environmental chapter with the Luxembourg Group was completed in January and February 1999, while screening with the Helsinki Group extended further into the year.[3] Based on the results of the screening, the candidate countries determine their negotiating positions, put down in the form of position papers, which indicate the country's own assessment of whether it is, or will be, ready to take on the *acquis* at the time of accession, or whether it will need derogations in particular areas.[4] Only the countries in the Luxembourg Group were formally requested to present position papers, which were all presented in 1999. While it was planned that on 4 November 1999, the Member State ambassadors and the chief negotiators would meet to open negotiations on the chapter on environment, talks were postponed until the round held on 7 December 1999, to recommence under the Finnish Presidency.[5]

C. DEROGATIONS REQUESTED BY CANDIDATE COUNTRIES

Without exception, the five CEE countries in the Luxembourg Group have requested derogations with regard to the environmental *acquis*. According to the many proclamations made on the EU side, permanent derogations are out of the question, limiting negotiations to temporary derogations only. An indication of the areas in which the candidate countries have asked for derogation, or the transition periods which they have requested, are as follows:[6]

---

[2] The European Council, in Copenhagen, in June 1993, identified three basic criteria which the applicant states would need to meet before they would be considered ready for membership: first, political criteria (stable democracy, rule of law, and respect for human rights); second, economic criteria (functioning market economy and the ability to cope with competitive pressures); and third, administrative criteria (ability to adhere to the goals of the EU).

[3] Published on the Internet at: http://www.euractiv.com/cgi-bin/eura/cgint.exe, Enlargement/Environment/Dossier outline.

[4] These assessments were based on a potential date for accession of 1 Jan. 2003 , which was subsequently adjusted to 1 Jan. 2004, while no date for the actual accession has been set.

[5] *Agence Europe, Bulletin Quotidien Europe* No. 7609, 'Fifteen and six applicants of "first group" open negotiations on tricky environmental chapter', 13 July 1999.

[6] Due to the nature of negotiations, in certain cases, such as with Hungary, the position of the candidate country has not been publicized. Furthermore, since these positions are in a constant state of transition, the positions presented will not necessarily be identical to those upon which negotiations will be conducted. In addition to the sources cited, information in this section has been acquired on the basis of informal discussions the author has had with individuals involved in the negotiation process.

### i. Czech Republic

The Czech Republic indicated that it will need derogations in the following areas: waste-water treatment and waste management, the content of nitrates in water, protection of water for human consumption, nature protection, and industrial pollution and risk management.[7] Specifically, it has asked for derogations until 2005 in respect of:

— Directive 79/409/EEC on the Conservation of Wild Birds (Wild Birds Directive);[8]
— Directive 92/43/EEC on the Conservation of Natural Habitats and of Wild Fauna and Flora (Habitats Directive);[9]
— and the Directive 94/62/EC on Packaging and Packaging Waste (Packaging and Packaging Waste Directive).[10]

In the area of water management, it has indicated that derogations may be necessary until 2006 in respect of Directive 91/676/EEC Concerning the Protection of Waters against Pollution Caused by Nitrates from Agricultural Sources (Nitrates from Agricultural Sources Directive);[11] and until 2008 to 2010 for compliance with Directive 91/271/EEC concerning Urban Waste-Water Treatment (Urban Waste-Water Directive),[12] which was to have been implemented in the EU Member States by 1 January 2006. Finally, it has asked for a derogation until 2012 with regard to Directive 96/61/EEC concerning Integrated Pollution Prevention and Control (IPPC Directive),[13] which has an implementation deadline of 30 September 2007.[14]

### ii. Estonia

Estonia requested transition periods for compliance with the following Directives:

— until 2004–7 for Directive 94/63/EC on the Control of Volatile Organic Compounds (VOC) Emissions Resulting from the Storage of Petrol and its Distribution from the Terminals to Service Stations (Volatile Organic Compounds Directive);[15]
— until 2006 for Directive 80/68/EEC on the Protection of Ground Water against Pollution Caused by Certain Dangerous Substances (Ground Water Directive);[16]
— until 2006 for Directive 76/464/EEC on Pollution Caused by Certain Dangerous Substances Discharged into the Aquatic Environment of the

---

[7] *Uniting Europe*, No. 62, 19 July 1999, 'Czech Republic seeks Derogation on Opening of Gas and Electiricty Market', 5–6.

[8] [1979] OJ L103/1.        [9] [1992] OJ L206/7.        [10] [1994] OJ L365/10.
[11] [1991] OJ L375/1.        [12] [1991] OJ L135/40.        [13] [1996] OJ L275/26.

[14] *Ecologic Berlin*, 'compilation table of screening results', in EU-Enlargement and Environmental Protection', 2. Special edn. of *EU-Rundschreiben*, edited by Deutscher Naturschutzring, Feb. 1999 (hereinafter *Ecologic Berlin*).

[15] [1994] OJ L365/24.        [16] [1980] OJ L020/43.

Community (Discharge of Dangerous Substances into Surface Water Directive);[17]
— until 2008 for the Nitrates from Agricultural Sources Directive;
— until 2010 for the Urban Waste Water Directive;
— until 2013 for Directive 98/83/EC on the Quality of Water Intended for Human Consumption (Drinking Water Directive).[18]

It also indicated that it may require transition periods for compliance with the Wild Birds Directive and the Habitats Directive. Finally, Estonia indicated a need for derogations with regard to hunting of certain species which are common on its territory, including bear, lynx, beaver, and wolf.[19]

### iii. Hungary

Hungary indicated it will need the following derogations:[20]

— until 2007 for the Ground Water Directive;
— until 2009 for the Dangerous Substances Discharged into the Aquatic Environment Directive; and
— until 2015 for the Urban Waste-Water Directive.

It has also suggested that it may need derogations for the IPPC Directive, Directive 96/82/EC 1996 on the Control of Major-Accident Hazards Involving Dangerous Substances (Seveso II Directive),[21] and the Packaging and Packaging Waste Directive, with some questions also raised about Directive 75/439/EEC on the Disposal of Waste Oils.[22]

### iv. Poland

The derogations that Poland has are the following:[23]

— until 2005 for Regulation (EC) No. 3093/94 on Substances that Deplete the Ozone Layer (Ozone Depleting Substances Regulation);[24]
— until 2005 for the Waste Oil Directive;
— until 2007 for the Packaging and Packaging Waste Directive;
— until 2009 for Directive 93/12/EEC relating to the Sulphur Contents of Certain Liquid Fuels (Fuel Quality Directive);
— until 2009 for the Volatile Organic Compounds Directive;
— until 2010 for the IPPC Directive;
— until 2010 for Directive 75/440/EEC concerning the Quality of Required of Surface Water Intended for the Abstraction of Drinking Water in the Member States (Surface Water for Drinking Water Directive);[25]

---

[17] [1976] OJ L129/23.          [18] [1998] OJ L330/32.
[19] *Uniting Europe*, No. 65, 6 Sept. 1999, 'Estonian Position Papers on Four More Chapters of the Acquis', 3–4, and *Ecologic Berlin*, n. 14 above.
[20] Ibid.          [21] [1997] OJ L010/13.          [22] [1975] OJ L194/23.
[23] *Uniting Europe*, No. 71, 18 Oct. 1999, 'Warsaw seeks derogation on environmental "acquis", while start of accession talks delayed', 4, and *Ecologic Berlin*, n. 14 above.
[24] [1994] OJ L333/1.          [25] [1975] OJ L194/26.

— until 2010 for the Nitrates Directive;
— until 2012 for Directive 75/442/EEC on Waste (Waste Framework Directive);[26]
— until 2012 for Directive 91/689/EEC on Hazardous Waste (Hazardous Waste Directive);[27]
— until 2012 for Regulation (EEC) No. 259/93 on the Supervision and Control of Shipments of Waste within, into and out of the European Community (Waste Shipment Regulation); and[28]
— until 2015 for the Urban Waste-Water Directive.

*v. Slovenia*

Slovenia has requested an extension transition period for the compliance with:

— until 2004–5 for Directive 86/278/EEC on the Protection of the Environment, and in Particular of the Soil, when Sewage Sludge is used in Agriculture (Agricultural Sewage Sludge Directive);
— until 2004–5 for the Fuel Quality Directive;
— until 2007 for the Packaging and Packaging Waste Directive;
— until 2011 for the IPPC Directive; and
— until 2015 for the Waste-Water Treatment Directive.

Slovenia also indicated a need for time to adjust to nature protection, in particular with regard to the species and habitats which currently only exist in this country.[29]

As indicated, these dates and requests for derogations reflect the positions of the candidate countries. The Commission, in turn, has indicated its belief that in many cases longer transition periods will be needed than those presented by the candidate countries, and that problems are also likely to arise with respect to the implementation within the set timeframes.[30] In other cases, *inter alia*, with regard to the Habitats and Wild Bird Directives, the Commission has already indicated its position that derogations should not be considered. In many cases, studies are yet to be concluded to determine the state of affairs more concretely before any final positions can be established. In most areas the Commission has asked for further information, and is undertaking technical consultations to assist the candidate states in preparing revised position papers. Many issues concern definitions, for example, the question of whether an installation is to be considered 'new' under Directive 88/609/EEC on the Limitation of Emissions of Certain Pollutants into the Air from Large Combustion Plants (Large Combustion Plants Directive):[31] should this be from the current point in time, or rather from the date of accession?[32]

---

[26] [1975] OJ L194/39.    [27] [1991] OJ L337/20.    [28] [1993] OJ L030/1.
[29] *Uniting Europe*, No. 64, 2 Aug. 1999, 'Slovenia Presents More Position Papers for Accession Talks', 2–3, and *Ecologic Berlin*, n. 14 above.
[30] Ibid.    [31] [1988] OJ L336/1.
[32] Based on information gathered by the author in several informal discussions.

### D. COMMISSION ASSESSMENT OF PREPAREDNESS FOR MEMBERSHIP

Outside of the context of EU accession negotiations, the Commission has presented its own assessment of the status of the candidate countries, in its second annual update of its opinion on the preparedness of the applicant states for EU membership, issued on 13 October 1999.[33] These second 'Regular Reports', being updates from the assessment of the first Regular Reports of November 1998, encapsulated the achievements of these countries for much of 1999. In the area of environmental policy, the Regular Reports reviewed, *inter alia*, the level of approximation of these countries to the environmental *acquis communautaire*; whether a national environmental policy had been adopted; whether institutional and administrative capacity existed to enforce the law; and whether principles such as integration of environmental policy into other policy areas were considered.

#### i. General Environmental Legislation and Estimation of Costs

In general, the Commission looked for a national environmental policy, and a plan that accurately and realistically assessed the requirements and costs of application of the *acquis*, including a 'directive-by-directive' assessment of the costs, and a strategy on how to proceed.

While Bulgaria had developed a strategic plan for implementation of the *acquis*, the Commission judged that this plan was not yet operational, nor did it contain the costs estimate the Commission had asked for.

With regard to the Czech Republic, the Commission bluntly stated that Czech legislation 'remains insufficiently aligned in many important areas' and concluded that '(no) major legislative progress has been made', despite governmental approval of an updated State Environmental Policy in April 1999. However, the policy did take integration of environmental policy into account, and the Czech Republic had made preliminary estimates as to financial costs.

While Estonia adopted some significant framework laws and a National Environmental Action Plan which addressed integration, the plan did not address the directive-by-directive estimation of costs and the Commission considered pursuit of the plan, and transposition of the remainder of the *acquis*, needed to be speeded up.

In the case of Hungary, the Commission characterized its National Environmental Protection programme for 1998, including investment plans for the years 1998–2002, as 'ambitious', although, in contrast, it characterized the Hungarian progress in fulfilling this programme in 1999 as 'limited'. Hungary had adopted what the Commission called a 'very thorough and

---

[33] The Commission issued reports on the progress of each of the candidate countries preparing for accession: Bulgaria, COM(1999)501 final, hereinafter *Bulgaria*; Czech Republic, COM(1999)503 final, hereinafter *Czech Republic*; Estonia, COM(1999)504 final., hereinafter *Estonia*; Hungary, COM(1999)505 final, hereinafter *Hungary*; Latvia, COM(1999)506 final, hereinafter *Latvia*; Lithuania, COM(1999)507 final, hereinafter *Lithuania*; Poland, COM(1999)509 final, hereinafter *Poland*; Romania, COM(1999)510 final, hereinafter *Romania*; Slovakia, COM(1999)511 final, hereinafter *Slovakia*; Slovenia, COM(1999)512 final, hereinafter *Slovenia*.

comprehensive plan' for transposition, and had included implementation costs and investment strategies in the National Programme for the Adoption of the a*cquis*. However, the Commission pointed out that, in order for the programme to be effective, allocations must be reflected in the annual budget.

Alignment by Latvia to the *acquis* was considered to have progressed satisfactorily and its National Environmental Policy Plan and National Environmental Action Programme, addressing integration, were positively received. Latvia had provided what was probably the most satisfactory estimates of costs in this area, detailing anticipated costs for both public and private investments, and taking into account possible financing by international financial institutions.

Lithuania also received a positive assessment from the Commission for its October 1998 Strategy for Approximation in the Environment Sector, which showed a good understanding of the administrative and financial obligations involved, and addressed the issue of integration of environmental policy.

Poland and Romania had no national plans for environmental policy development, nor did they have strong approximation programmes, and the Commission consequently assessed their progress towards alignment as slow, although Poland claimed that it had nonetheless managed to achieve a moderate level of alignment, as compared to Romania's low level. Poland was told that a financial plan, with a breakdown on the basis of specific directives, still needed to be developed, spreading the costs of alignment 'across a realistic time period'. Romania was also said to be lacking a financial plan of anticipated implementation costs, on a directive-by-directive basis.

Slovakia, like Hungary, was considered to have been far more ambitious than effective in its environmental planning, and was considered not yet to have developed a comprehensive strategic approach towards implementation, particularly with regard to financial planning.

Although it had a detailed legislative programme, there were no financial plans to ensure implementation of this legislation.

Slovenia had adopted approximately twenty legal acts in the fields of water protection, air protection, waste management, and nature protection, since the Commission's assessment in 1998, and its parliament had adopted, in September 1999, a ten-year National Environmental Action Programme, including, *inter alia*, the principle of integration. While Slovenia has estimated overall alignment costs, this has not been done on a directive-by-directive basis.[34]

## ii. Air Pollution

Bulgaria established a national air monitoring system, following regulations adopted in 1998 to transpose aspects of the *acquis* concerning air and noise.

---

[34] Ibid.: Bulgaria, 48–9. *Czech Republic*, 49–50. *Estonia*, 45 and 47. *Hungary*, 47 and 49. *Latvia*, 47 and 48. *Lithuania*, 46–7. *Poland*, 48. *Romania*, 52. *Slovakia*, 48–9. *Slovenia*, 49–50.

Although the Czech Republic was deemed to have achieved 'considerable' reductions in emission levels, it still needed to do a great deal of work to comply with the *acquis* in this area. Legislation on noise emissions was singled out as an area for concern.

Estonia and Latvia were considered quite advanced with regard to approximation in this area. Estonia's Ambient Air Protection Act and implementing regulations, controlling air quality limit values; methodologies used to specify emission; and the issuing of permits, entered into force in 1999, transposing part of the Air Quality Framework Directive. Further progress was made on aligning national legislation to the Volatile Organic Compounds Directive with regard to new installations, and a Pollution Charges Act, adopted in 1999, laying down charges for emissions into the air. Latvia's legislation was considered to be fully in line with the *acquis* with respect to the Air Framework Directive and the Directives on Ozone-Depleting Substances and Volatile Organic Compounds for new installations. In addition, it had adopted two regulations on fuel quality standards, transposing the Fuel Quality Directive.

Poland and Hungary were considered to have made 'no particular progress' in transposing the *acquis* on air quality. Of particular concern to the Commission, in the case of Hungary, was its failure to comply with the directive on the quality of ambient air, and the related Directives on Ozone-Depleting Substances and Non-Road Mobile Machinery. The requirement to identify zones of heavily concentrated pollution had not been met, and the Commission questioned the Hungarian institutional capacity for monitoring and data exchange.

Lithuania adopted regulations in 1999 on maximum permissible concentrations of air pollutants in residential areas, which partially met the requirement of the *acquis*, and had adopted regulations on the import and export of ozone-depleting substances. Although it had adopted a strategy for approximation in the sector of air in 1998, the Commission indicated the need for a framework law and other legislation to transpose limit values and monitoring requirements, in addition to a more detailed action plan.

Romania was told to accelerate the elaboration of a framework law on air quality and to develop costs assessments and investment plans.

Slovakia was considered to have made 'important progress' in this area, with amendments to two Slovakian laws transposing EC legislation on emissions of certain pollutants from large installations, entering into force in early 1999.

The approximation efforts of Slovenia focused on adopting a decree on volatile organic compounds, and a decision concerning exchange of information and data. Several amendments had also been made to the decree on the quality of liquid fuels, with a law clearing the way for the ratification of the International Convention on the Safe Handling of Fuels being passed.[35]

---

[35] The Commission issued reports on the progress of each of the candidate countries preparing for accession: *Bulgaria*, 48. *Czech Republic*, 49. *Estonia*, 46. *Hungary*, 48. *Latvia*, 48. *Lithuania*, 47–8. *Poland*, 49. *Romania*, 52–3. *Slovakia*, 49. *Slovenia*, 50.

*iii. Nature Conservation*

In Bulgaria, a new law on protected areas and a national strategy for bio-diversity were adopted in 1999. The directorates charged with managing the country's national parks were reinforced with additional staff, while new administrative rules were adopted, and efforts were increased to ensure inter-action with other ministries. However, further alignment with the *acquis* in the area of nature protection was considered necessary by the Commission. Gaps remain in the transposition by the Czech Republic of the Habitats and Wild Birds Directives.

Adoption in Estonia of the Protection and Use of Wild Fauna Act partially met the requirements on trade of protected species, although it lacked provisions on sanctions in case of illegal trade. While a national Forest Act, and implementing regulations, were adopted, work to transpose the Wild Birds and Habitat Directives was considered to be progressing too slowly.

On the other hand, Hungary was considered to have arranged for the protection of an 'important part' of its territory through the Law on Nature Protection and various related statutes. Hungary is also an active member of the Convention on International Trade in Endangered Species of Wild Fauna and Flora (CITES),[36] although progress in 1999 in this area was limited to the adoption of certain implementing measures of the *acquis* on protected animal species.

While Latvia adopted regulations on international trade in endangered species in April 1999, in part complying with EC nature conservation legislation, the Commission identified 'significant delays' in the transposition of the Habitats and Wild Birds Directives, and pronounced the need to strengthen the implementation authorities.

In June 1999 the Seimas in Lithuania passed the Law on Wild Flora. However, according to the Commission, 'major gaps' remain with regard to the criteria and classification for protected areas. Furthermore, amendments are necessary to the hunting rules, and provisions are still required to bring legislation controlling trade on endangered species into line with the *acquis* in this area.

While Slovakia certainly achieved some progress with the adoption of two decrees on nature protection, the Commission considered that there was an 'urgent need' to pursue the scientific work required to implement the Habitats and Wild Birds Directives.

Slovenia was considered to have made 'important progress' by adopting the Nature Conservation Act in June 1999, which was designed to protect the natural environment and to preserve biodiversity. It was based not only on the requirements of the relevant EC Directives, but also on international conventions and regional development policy objectives.[37]

[36] Washington, 3 Mar. 1973.
[37] n. 33 above: *Bulgaria*, 49. *Czech Republic*, p. 50. *Estonia*, 46. *Hungary*, p. 49. *Latvia*, p. 49. *Lithuania*, 48. *Slovakia*, 49. *Slovenia*, 50. The Regular Reports for Poland and Romania did not address this issue.

*iv. Waste*

Bulgaria was considered to have made progress in transposition and implementation in the waste sector, particularly at the local level. It adopted regulations establishing requirements for the sites of waste treatment facilities and other conditions for waste treatment, as well as reporting requirements for waste management and procedures for permitting transit transportation of wastes. A classification scheme for waste was also adopted.

The Czech Republic adopted legislation on returnable products and packaging, but made no progress in establishing a framework to deal with packaging and packaging waste, nor in respect of waste and hazardous waste in general.

In Estonia, legislation transposing the EC Waste Framework Directive had already been adopted to a large degree. Other legislation had introduced requirements of permits for waste generation, a system of waste classification and labelling of hazardous waste, and management of waste oils. However, the Commission noted that Estonia's limited administrative capacity and financial resources raised serious doubts as to its implementation capacity.

Although Hungary stated in its environmental strategy that waste management policy was a high priority, no progress on approximation was considered to have been achieved in 1998. In fact, the Commission stated that 'waste represents the weakest sector in Hungary, as the entirety of the corresponding *acquis* needs to be transposed'. However, it noted that significant efforts were made with regard to implementation due to the drafting of ten new regional landfills.

With the adoption of one law and two regulations on municipal waste, Latvia came largely in line with most requirements of the Waste Framework Directive. Latvia has a national programme for waste management and is building a network of disposal sites, including plans for an incineration facility for hazardous waste. It must still establish specific collection systems for different waste streams.

In May 1999 Lithuania adopted its National Waste Management Strategy and Action Plan, which complies with the main requirements of the *acquis*, although administrative strengthening and reform, and 'major efforts' in terms of transposition, were still considered to be necessary, particularly for compliance with the Landfill Directive.

Poland partially transposed the Framework Directives on Waste and Hazardous Waste, while Romania was considered to have made only limited progress to this end. In the latter country, the March 1999 adoption of the European Waste Catalogue and a list of what is considered to be hazardous waste were the only legislative initiatives noted by the Commission.

Adoption of waste management framework legislation in Slovakia had already harmonized the country's legislation to a certain degree, including the priorities for prevention and recycling, and reduction of landfills. The country was considered to have a functioning system of waste management authorities and waste management planning. However, the Commission indicated the remaining need for legislation on product policy and producer responsibility, and legislation on landfilling and separate waste streams, *inter alia*, batteries and packaging.

Slovenia adopted legislation on the management of waste oils and on import, export, and transit of wastes.[38]

### *v. Water*

Generally, the level of water quality in the CEE countries has been an area of particular concern, due to the serious level of pollution in much of the surface waters, in addition to concerns about the high costs of compliance in this area.

In Bulgaria, a framework Water Act was adopted in July 1999, establishing a national programme for the construction of waste-water treatment plants, which covered the period of 1998–2002. However, the Commission considered the programme to lack 'procedural clarity'.

In the case of the Czech Republic, the Commission stated that it 'urgently needed' proper framework water legislation, although some legislation aligning water quality parameters, and integrating the polluter-pays principle had in fact been adopted.

While Estonia had adopted a framework law, it was considered to have major gaps, and in need of 'considerable efforts', including strengthening of the administrative structures and reforms of the water companies. However, adoption of the Public Water Supply and Sewerage Act aligns Estonian legislation to the requirements of the Urban Waste-Water Directive. Furthermore, the Estonian Environmental Monitoring Act not only fulfils obligations of the Directive on Access to Environmental Information, but also requirements with regard to monitoring in the area of water quality.

In the case of Hungary, virtually the complete *acquis* in this area remains to be transposed, and the country needs to complete an assessment of the implications of the Drinking Water Directive. However, Hungary was given some credit by the Commision for 'important implementation steps' taken in the area of urban waste-water treatment, including capacity enlargement; technological upgrading; sewerage development; and construction of mechanical treatment facilities. Efforts to produce a timetable and schedule for the transposition of the Waste-Water Treatment Directive were initiated.

Latvia was considered to be progressing with its approximation, having adopted legislation on bathing waters in line with the *acquis*, while its legislation on drinking water was considered to represent 'substantial progress'. However, despite the completion of waste-water facilities in five cities in 1998, the Commission indicated that 'major gaps' had remained in this area.

Lithuania had adopted a strategy for approximation in this sector, which included the adoption of the Hygienic Norm on Drinking Water Act. This latter law fulfils most parameters, values, and monitoring requirements of the

---

[38] n. 33 above: *Bulgaria*, 48. *Czech Republic*, 49. *Estonia*, 45. *Hungary*, 48. *Latvia*, 48. *Lithuania*, 47. *Poland*, 49. *Romania*, 52. *Slovakia*, 48. *Slovenia*, 50.

*acquis*, and established an implementation timetable for improving compliance, although major gaps still remain. Both Latvia and Lithuania were considered to have administrative structures which need to be restructured and strengthened.

The progress noted for Poland in this area was limited to the partial transposition of the requirements of the Urban Waste-Water Directive and Nitrates from Agricultural Sources Directive, through ministerial regulations.

The Commission considered it imperative that Romania prepare an implementation and investment programme in the field of water management, as the country faces very serious problems in this area. The need to complete transposition was also considered to be urgent.

Like Hungary, Slovakia was considered to be in a situation where virtually all the *acquis* in the field of water law remained to be transposed. It will need to develop an implementation programme and complete an assessment of the implications of the Drinking Water Directive. In Slovenia, although the country had adopted a number of laws concerning emissions of substances in the discharge of waste-water from certain sectors of industry, the lack of proper framework legislation was pointed to as an area for concern.[39]

### vi. IPPC and Seveso II

Bulgaria was considered to have made 'little progress' in transposing legislation establishing limits for hazardous substances emissions into the air, notwithstanding its National Plan for the limitation of emissions from combustion plants.

The Commission considered that the Czech Republic needed to make significant administrative and investment efforts with regard to IPPC.

Estonia adopted two governmental regulations to meet the requirements of the Seveso II Directive on major-accident hazards, and had now transposed legislation meeting all the requirements on new large combustion plants, although it was considered that 'greater efforts' remain necessary in respect of transposition of EC legislation and administrative strengthening to tackle major industrial accidents.

Hungary was praised for its virtually complete compliance with the *acquis* in this area, as it had adopted almost all of the required legislation, including a law on catastrophes of June 1999, which fulfils the requirements of the Seveso II Directive. Hungary was also commended for being an early signatory to the UN/ECE Convention on Industrial Accidents, making it the first of the candidate countries to ratify it.

Latvia was said to be aligning itself with regard to industrial pollution, risk management control, and major industrial accidents. It had introduced, *inter alia*, large combustion plant provisions for new installations.

---

[39] The Commission issued reports on the progress of each of the candidate countries preparing for accession: *Bulgaria*, 49. *Czech Republic*, 49. *Estonia*, 45. *Hungary*, 47. *Latvia*, 48. *Lithuania*, 47. *Poland*, 49. *Romania*, 52–3. *Slovakia*, 48. *Slovenia*, 49.

Lithuania was still considered to have a great deal to do in respect of IPPC and risk management regulation, while Romania and Slovakia were said to have made no progress at all in this area.

Although Poland had achieved partial compliance with regard to the Large Combustion Plants Directive, the Commission felt it appropriate to place particular emphasis on transposition of the IPPC and Seveso II Directives.

Slovenia was told to exert greater efforts in order to meet its own timetable for compliance with regard to industrial risk management.[40]

### vii. Access to Information and Environmental Impact Assessment

In the area of Access to Information on the environment, Bulgaria, the Czech Republic, Estonia, Latvia, Lithuania, Poland, Romania, and Slovenia all made progress towards meeting the EC standards, by signing the Arhus Convention on Access to Information, Public Participation and Access to Justice in Environmental Matters, on 25 June 1998.[41] Slovakia had adopted an Act on Access to Environmental Information, while Latvia had adopted a general law on Access to Information, which meets some of the requirements of the EC Directive. Hungarian legislation was already largely in compliance with the Access to Environmental Information Directive.

With regard to the Environmental Impact Assessment (EIA) Directive, Bulgaria adopted a regulation on environmental impact assessment in 1998, although it does not fully comply with the EIA Directive. The Czech Republic, Lithuania, Poland, and Slovakia, were all told that they need to speed up work on meeting the requirements of the EIA Directive. The Commission also indicated that Hungary needed to make 'more effort', in particular with regard to expanding the range of projects requiring assessment. While Latvia adopted regulations in 1999 to implement its 1998 law on EIA, it needs to further align its legislation towards the EIA Directive requirements. The same applied to Estonia. Latvia established an EIA Bureau, but the Commission considered that its staff requires further training before it can be truly effective.[42]

### viii. Nuclear Energy

Much concern has been expressed over nuclear power in the CEE countries. Of particular concern are eight nuclear power units in Bulgaria (four units at Kozloduy), Lithuania (two units at Ignalina), and Slovakia (two units at Bohunice), which are not considered to be upgradeable to a safe level. Concerns were of such a nature that the Commission recommended in its

---

[40] Ibid.: *Bulgaria*, 49. *Czech Republic*, 49. *Estonia*, 45. *Hungary*, 47–8. *Latvia*, 48. *Lithuania*, 47. *Poland*, 49. *Romania*, 52. *Slovakia*, 49. *Slovenia*, 50–1.

[41] Arhus, 23–5 June 1998. Press Release ECE/ENV/98/15, 25 June 1998, '35 countries and the Europan Community sign the new UN/ECE Convention on Public Participation.'

[42] Ibid.: *Bulgaria*, 48. *Czech Republic*, 49. *Estonia*, 45. *Hungary*, 47. *Latvia*, 47–8. *Lithuania*, 47. *Poland*, 49. *Slovakia*, 48. The Regular Reports for Romania and Slovenia did not address the EIA Directive. The candidate countries were reminded that compliance with the EIA Directive is particularly important 'as the relevant legal provisions will be applied for all projects financed by the Community.'

*Marie Soveroski*

1999 Regular Report, that negotiations with Bulgaria would only be commenced on condition that an acceptable date for the closure of the Kozloduy
units would be established, although the European Council, at the Helsinki
Summit, did not agree to impose such a condition. After fierce debate, the
Bulgarian Foreign Minister, Nadezhda Mihailova, and the EU Commissioner
for Enlargement, Günter Verheugen, signed a Memorandum of Understanding
on 29 November 1999, removing the proposed condition on the opening of
accession negotiations, connected to an agreement to close the Bulgarian
Kozloduy Units 1 and 2 in 2003.[43] Dates for closure of Units 3 and 4 would be
decided upon by Bulgaria at the time of upgrading its national energy policy,
in 2002. Also after much discussion, Slovakia decided upon closure dates for
Unit 1 of its Bohunice power station in 2006, and for Unit 2 in 2008.[44] While
Austria had indicated, in 1999, that it might not approve enlargement until
agreement on earlier closure of nuclear plants in the CEE countries was
agreed,[45] it later indicated that while it still considered the closure dates proposed by Slovakia to be too late, this would no longer be an issue on the basis
of which it would veto enlargement.[46] On 8 September 1999 the Lithuanian
Government agreed on a plan to decommission Unit 1 of the Ignalina nuclear
plant by 2005, followed by complete closure of all units by 2009. The Seimas
approved the declaration on 5 October, conditional upon receiving foreign
assistance to help cover the costs of, and adjustments to, closure.[47]

Although these 'Chernoybl type' reactors provided the most visible source of
concerns in the area of nuclear energy, general issues of nuclear safety and
waste were also addressed in 1999. Lithuania adopted a Law on Civil
Protection, providing for the legal and organizational structures needed in the
event of emergencies. The law included new provisions for the protection of
the population in the case of an accident at Ignalina, with reinforced emergency planning in the districts immediately surrounding the plant. In January
1999 the Seimas approved a law on Radiation Safety, establishing a Radiation
Safety Centre with responsibility for supervisory and control functions. The
Seimas also passed a law on the management of radioactive waste in May
1999.[48]

The government of the Czech Republic, and the State Office for Nuclear
Safety, adopted thirteen decrees implementing the national Atomic Act of July
1997. Estonia also adopted and amended legislation concerning protection
against radiation, and the safety of workers, including requirements for
continued monitoring of workers after they have left the employment of
nuclear facilities. While Latvia has adopted legislation meeting some of the EC
requirements with regard to safe transportation of radioactive substances, the

---

[43] *RFE/RL Newsline,* Vol. 3, No. 231, 30 Nov. 1999.     [44] Ibid., No. 229, 24 Nov. 1999.
[45] Simon, Taylor, 'Vienna gets tough with applicant states over nuclear closure plans', *European Voice,* 8–14 July 1994.
[46] *Uniting Europe,* No. 76, 22 Nov. 1999, 'Greenpeace urges earlier closure of "potential Chernobyls" in the candidate countries', 7–8.
[47] *Bulletin Quotidien Europe (Agence Europe),* No. 7569, 9 Oct. 1999.
[48] n. 33 above: *Lithuania,* 47.

Commission considered that its compliance with regard to medical exposures and protection of outside workers 'represents a challenge', and its administrative structure in this area generally needs to be upgraded. In the case of Hungary, the Commission claimed that progress in 1999 was limited to aligning national legislation on radioactive contamination of foodstuffs, while the main components of the *acquis* still need to be transposed. The Commission determined that no concrete progress took place in Poland and Slovakia in 1999 in the fields of nuclear safety and radiation protection.[49]

Issues of disposal of nuclear waste are particularly problematic in the CEE countries, as many of the nuclear facilities were built in the anticipation that the problem of waste would be tackled within the comprehensive structure of the Soviet Union (USSR), arrangements which are generally no longer possible. The Commission emphasized the need to deal with issues associated with the management of spent fuel and radioactive waste at Kozloduy NPP and the BAS research reactor in Bulgaria, where it considered that management of radioactive materials represents a 'serious threat' to public health. Waste from the Paks NPP in Hungary was also mentioned, while the Commission noted that in Slovenia the problem is being addressed with plans for the construction of storage facilities for low and intermediate level radioactive waste and spent fuel from the Krsko Nuclear Power Plant waste. Pollution from uranium mining is also of concern, with the Commission calling, in particular, for close monitoring of such facilities in Bulgaria, the Czech Republic, and Romania.[50]

An additional, and often forgotten legacy of the Soviet era is the large number of nuclear research facilities which were built under the Communist regimes. The Commission highlighted concern about storage of nuclear waste at the Paldiski nuclear training centre, and the nuclear facilities at Paldiski and Sillimae in Estonia, and management of spent fuel at the Magurele research reactor in Romania. It further welcomed the programme adopted for the decommissioning of the nuclear research reactor in Salaspils in Estonia.[51]

Slovenia and Romania ratified, in February and June 1999, respectively, the Convention on the Safety of the Spent Fuel Management and on the Safety of Radioactive Waste Management, which was opened for signature on 29 September 1997. Bulgaria, the Czech Republic, Hungary, Lithuania, Poland, and Slovakia are also signatories, although Estonia and Latvia have not yet signed.

### viii. International Cooperation

In other areas of international concern, Romania and Slovakia signed the 1997 Kyoto Protocol to the UN Framework Convention on Climate Change (UNFCCC)[52] in January and February 1999, respectively. The other applicant states were already signatories to this.[53] Estonia, Bulgaria, and Slovakia ratified

---

[49] Ibid. *Czech Republic*, 50. *Estonia*, 46. *Hungary*, 49. *Latvia*, 48. *Poland*, 49. *Slovakia*, 49.
[50] Ibid. *Bulgaria*, 49, *Czech Republic*, 50. *Hungary*, 49. *Romania*, 53. *Slovenia*, 47.
[51] Ibid. *Estonia*, 46 and 48. *Romania*, 53.          [52] Kyoto, 10 Dec. 1997.

the London[54] and Copenhagen[55] Amendments to the 1987 Montreal Protocol on Substances that Deplete the Ozone Layer,[56] in January, April, and May 1999, respectively. The other CEE countries have already accepted or acceded to the amendments, with the exception of Romania, which has only acceded to the London Amendment. In December 1999 Poland ratified the 1997 Montreal Amendments to the Montreal Convention, followed by Hungary in July, and Bulgaria and Slovenia in November 1999, when the Czech Republic and Slovakia approved the amendment. Estonia also approved procedures to control production, use, import, and export of ozone-depleting substances (ODS), and approved a government programme for the phasing out of ODS.[57] In Slovakia, a decree implementing the Act for the Protection of the Ozone Layer came into force in 1999.[58]

### ix. Miscellaneous[59]

In addition to the developments discussed above, on a sectoral basis, the Commission made overall assessments of areas of particular environmental concern in each applicant state.

Bulgaria was told to focus its efforts on pursuing further alignment in the areas of water quality, industrial pollution, noise, and chemicals, and to work on its implementation capacity. The Commission felt that the Bulgarian ministry of environment and water lacked adequate staffing and needed to be restructured. Furthermore, it indicated that the primary problem in the environmental sector was a lack of large-scale investments which should be tackled by sectoral investment strategies, focusing on what can be financed under Special Pre-Accession Instruments (ISPA): one of the EU's pre-accession aid programmes designed to finance infrastructure and environmental projects along the lines of the cohesion and structural funds available to EU Member States.

In general, the Czech Republic was considered to have made very limited progress in transposing the environmental *acquis*, particularly in the water and waste sectors. Plans to improve the administrative capacity and to assess directive-specific financing requirements were lacking, and 'strong efforts' with respect to IPPC were deemed necessary by the Commission, in particular concerning considerations of administrative and investment issues.

Estonia was considered to have a high level of formal compliance with regard to legislation on air, waste, and chemicals. It's legal framework concerning the evaluation and control of the risks of existing chemical substances, is firmly in place, the government having adopted regulations on packaging and labelling, classification, and notification, while its regulation on import

---

[53] The Ratification status of the UNFCCC is published on the Internet at: http://www.unfccc.de/resource/convkp.html.

[54] London, 27–9 June 1990.      [55] Copenhagen, 23–5 Nov. 1992.

[56] Montreal, 10 Dec. 1987.      [57] n. 33 above, *Estonia*, 46.      [58] Ibid., *Slovakia*, 49.

[59] Ibid. *Bulgaria*, 48–49. *Czech Republic*, 49–50. *Estonia*, 46–47. *Hungary*, 47–9. *Latvia*, 48–9. *Lithuania*, 47–8. *Poland*, 49. *Romania*, 52. *Slovakia*, 49. *Slovenia*, 50.

and export is already largely in compliance with the *acquis* in this area. However, despite the adoption of the Act on the Deliberate Release of Genetically Modified Organisms (GMOs), many vital parts of the nature protection and GMO *acquis* still need to be implemented in Estonia. Administrative structures must be strengthened, in particular in the areas of water, waste management, chemicals, GMOs, and nature protection.

Hungary was given a rather mixed assessment by the Commission. It was considered to be in line with the *acquis* on the lead content of petrol, but not yet in compliance with regard to the protection and reduction of environmental pollution caused by asbestos. It had adopted mandatory standards on the noise of lawnmowers and household appliances, but not for construction plant equipment. The establishment of an Institute for Chemical Safety, and the upgrading of the laboratory capacity in the Institute for Environmental Management, has met with criticism in the area of chemicals. While a collection and processing system for waste oils and a collection system for used batteries was established, according to the Commission, 'substantial efforts' are still needed in the areas of waste and waste management, water, and air quality. An inter-ministerial committee was established (with representatives of the ministries of environment, agriculture, transport, and others), which developed concrete guidelines for the integration of environmental protection requirements into other policy areas.

In general, approximation in Latvia was considered to be 'progressing satisfactorily', although further attention is needed in the sectors of water, nature protection, and industrial pollution. Sector-specific approximation strategies have been completed in 1999. Latvia adopted a basic law on chemicals, which came into force in January 1999, and partially met the *acquis* requirements on packaging and labelling, although 'further efforts' are needed on import and export regulation. The Commission indicated that particular attention must be granted to administrative structures dealing with GMOs.

The Commission felt that Lithuania should focus its efforts in the area of air and water pollution and the transposition of the IPPC Directive. While 'some steps' had been taken to introduce eco-management and audit standards, more work was needed on the regulation of GMOs, including the establishing of appropriate authorization and enforcement institutions. Furthermore, a great deal still remains to be done in the area of industrial accident and risk management.

Poland established implementation and monitoring time schedules in the NPAA, but progress was considered to be limited, and the legislative basis for monitoring weak. However, the Commission noted that evaluation of progress in Poland must take into account the major reform of Poland's territorial organization, which had recently been undertaken. This modified the enforcement framework with respect to the new regions (*voivodshops*) and counties (*poviats*), in particular with respect to permitting and control. A further consideration is that major efforts have been made towards the adoption of a framework Act of Environment Protection, and related legislation, which is

still in the drafting stage. More specific legislation, targeted at various requirements of the *acquis*, has thus not yet been completed.

Romania was criticized for its lack of a comprehensive policy, and its failure
to make progress in the area of water and waste management, IPPC, air quality protection, chemicals, and GMOs. An inter-ministerial committee was
established in 1998, including representatives from the ministries of environment, industry, agriculture, transport, and physical planning, to pursue integration of environmental protection requirements into other sectoral policies.
However, the Commission considered these developments too premature to
evaluate the practical impact of the committee.

In assessing Slovakia's environmental legislation in general, the Commission
held that adoption of framework legislation in the fields of water, air, waste, and
radiation protection was called for, while also indicating the need for the
strengthening of institutions to transpose and implement the EC *acquis*.
Slovakia was considered to have made no progress in adopting legislation to
comply with the EC law in the areas of noise, chemicals, and GMOs, and the
Commission expressed a need for a 'comprehensive and realistic' approximation and environmental investment strategy on the part of Slovakia.

Slovenia was deemed to have a high level of formal compliance in such sectors as water protection, nature protection, and waste management, but
'greater efforts' were needed on industrial risk management, chemicals, and
GMOs if Slovenia's own timetable for compliance is to be met. The adoption of
the Slovenian Law on Chemicals, in April 1999, responded to the *acquis*
requirements in the areas of health and environment, albeit far from exhaustively. Institutional implementation and enforcement capacity in Slovenia is
weak, according to the Commission, although it noted some progress with
regard to environmental inspections, and an increase in the number of staff of
the ministry of environment and physical planning. Unlike many of the other
candidate countries, Slovenia was deemed by the Commission to be more
realistically able to mobilize the necessary resources to meet the costs of compliance, including on waste water, IPPC, and large combustion plants.

### E. CONCLUSIONS

As is the case in most EU Member States, in the CEE countries development
of environmental policies and the legal framework for their pursuit and
enforcement has largely been dominated by the requirements of the *acquis
communautaire*. The process of screening national legislation and preparing
position papers for EU accession negotiations has succeeded in focusing
national efforts, and has ensured that a detailed evaluation of EC environmental law and national capacity has now been undertaken. Concerns
expressed by current Member States have played a significant role in the
development of the EU's negotiating positions, while the Commission served
as a crucial element in the process, facilitating the evaluation of the state of
environmental law and policy in the candidate countries, including reviews

of their respective implementation and enforcement capacity. The candidates have thus had their legislation and political agendas vastly dictated by these considerations, although questions of cost and capacity have more often than not tempered environmental protection efforts in these countries.

# REVIEWS OF BOOKS

## Lessons from America: Environmental Law in US Law Journals

JOANNE SCOTT*

### I. Introduction

It may seem perverse in a Section of a Yearbook dedicated to *book* reviews in the area of European environmental law to include an overview of recent publications in US law journals. However, such is the dominance of the law review tradition in the USA that major law review articles continue to substitute for the monograph, the preferred publishing vehicle of the European academic. The richness of papers in US journals during the last year or so attests to this (see Annex I for a sample of papers in US journals likely to be of interest to scholars of European environmental law).

There is a staggering, and at times overwhelming, range of law journals published in the USA. Nonetheless, the age of the Internet has rendered this body of material more accessible. For the environmental lawyer two sites will provide particularly convenient kick off points. The first: http://www.usc.edu/dept/law-lib/legal/journals.html (see Annex II) lists major law journals, and in many instances full text or abstracts are available online. The second: http://lawschools.findlaw.com/journals/environmental.html (see Annex III)) is dedicated to environmental journals. Given difficulties in obtaining such materials in Europe, access to tables of contents and article abstracts, and in some cases full texts, is invaluable.

Particularly striking in the last eighteen months is the range and quality of papers examining the question of choice of instrument for environmental protection and, more specifically, the issue of emissions trading. The following five examples illustrate the important contribution that US scholarship can make to debates in Europe, both in theoretical and in empirical terms. Particularly noteworthy is the manner in which the dominance of economics discourse is being challenged by institutionalist approaches, and by recourse to notions of 'environmental justice' and international equity.

* Lecturer of Law, University of Cambridge, UK.

A.  J. B. Wiener, 'Global Environmental Regulation: Instrument Choice in Legal
   Context' (1999) 108 *Yale Law Journal* 677–800

This paper is concerned with what the author calls the 'olympics of instruments choice', with the contest taking shape at the international as opposed to
the domestic level. He seeks to demonstrate the manner in which the specific
characteristics of national and international legal frameworks might impact
upon choice of instrument for environmental protection. Wiener reaches a
broad conclusion: instrument choice cannot be universal, but must rather be
approached in a manner which is contextual and contingent. This is because
of his argument that underlying legal institutions matter to the issue of instrument choice, and that the economics of instrument choice are embedded in,
and contingent upon, the underlying legal system. Thus, '[i]n short, the law
and economics of regulation cannot be all economics; legal institutions matter'. Application of this broad conclusion leads Wiener to examine the international legal context and to assess optimal instrument choice in the light of
this. He focuses upon two features which distinguish the international legal
setting from the domestic legal setting: voting rules and implementation
structures. By the former he is alluding to the manner in which the 'voting rule'
becomes less coercive as we move from a domestic to an international setting,
with participation being based on voluntary assent in international law. Thus,
what the author labels 'participation efficiency' (securing participation at the
least cost) is presented as a crucial factor influencing instrument choice. By
implementation structures the author is referring to the contrast between
unitary and federal models within states, and the 'jurisdictional' model which
is characteristic of the international sphere. In a jurisdictional structure regulatory instruments cannot be imposed directly on sources, but must be implemented through 'subsidiary political jurisdictions—nation-states'. According
to Wiener both voting rules and implementation structures are such at the
international level to generate a strong preference for tradable allowances,
thus reversing the 'standard presumption in favour of taxes in the academic
literature, precisely because of the difference in voting rules and implementation structures obtaining at the global level'. Important to this conclusion is
his argument that under a voluntary assent voting rules, 'beneficiaries of
global environmental protection must attract non-beneficiary sources to
participate', thus necessitating side payments by the beneficiaries to non-
beneficiaries. On this basis Wiener endorses a rebuttable presumption in
favour of a 'cap-and-pay' system of tradable allowances, taking the form of
quantity-based tradable allowances with in-built side payments. 'Market-
based global environmental law could add a new global property law dimension to the world economy—a "green currency"—that could transform
international financial flows towards financing environmentally friendly
development in poorer countries. By bringing market economics to global
environmental protection and bringing environmental protection to global
economic markets, market-based international environmental law could help

heal the rift between environment and development, north and south, environment and trade.'

B. D. M. Driesen, 'Choosing Environmental Instruments in a Transnational Context' (2000) 27 *Ecology Law Quarterly* 1

Driesen, like Wiener above, is concerned with instrument choice in a transnational setting, and with the issue of participation in international environmental regimes. However, unlike Wiener he rejects a rationalistic, cost–benefit, conception of why nations participate in and obey international law, arguing that cost considerations are merely one factor influencing the participation decisions of states. He situates his analysis in the tradition of transnational legal process associated most famously with the work of Harold Koh. He characterizes this as a horizontal model of international legal process in that it looks inside the state, and at the identity and role of actors therein, in shaping domestic preferences on the international stage. Driesen takes institutions seriously and conceives institutions broadly to encompass ideas, values, and beliefs, as well as rules and structures. He points in particular to the important role played by countries' 'perceptions of the equity of proposed international agreements', arguing that 'adoption of an instrument that countries perceive as inequitable can detract from efforts to encourage effective international participation in an international agreement'. Consequently, 'a serious even-handed comparative analysis of countries' actual perceptions of instruments' equitable properties must be part of instrument choice'.

More generally, Driesen's paper may be considered a critical rejoinder to that of Wiener above. He rejects Wiener's conclusions regarding the 'participation efficiency' of tradable allowances. 'Because international allowance trading relies upon international transactions in implementation, it will generate a need for voluntary assent to more international rules than one would need under value pluralism. It increases the chances of a failure to reach agreement and may encourage defections or implementation failures.' By pluralism, Driesen is referring here to methodological pluralism of the kind which permits states to 'tailor its instrument choice to its culture and its sources of environmental harm'. Both Wiener and Driesen seek, in their own ways, to assert the place of law and politics in the choice of instrument debate; a debate so often dominated by economic discourse. Each does so by reference to institutionalism in one guise or another, placing emphasis upon different institutions, and consequently arriving at very different conclusions.

C. L. N. Chinn, 'Can the Market Be Fair and Efficient? An Environmental Justice Critique of Emissions Trading' (1999) 26 *Ecology Law Quarterly* 80

This paper examines the environmental justice dimension of emissions trading, and is concerned with the distributive consequences of such programmes in terms of the allocation of environmental burdens and benefits. It explores the potential for emissions trading to relocate pollution from one community to another in such a way that offends the principle of environmental justice, this being understood as 'the fair treatment of people of all races, income, and culture with respect to the development, implementation and enforcement of environmental laws, regulations and policies'. The paper incorporates a case study of the South Coast Air Quality Management District (SCAQMD), highlighting the deficiencies in data collection regarding the distributional impacts of emissions trading. Occasion for discussion of the environmental justice dimension of emissions trading arises as a result of an administrative complaint submitted by 'Communities for a Better Environment' (CBE) on the basis of Title VI of the Civil Rights Act 1965. Section 601 of Title VI states that '[n]o person in the United States shall, on the ground of race, colour or national origin, be excluded from participation in, be denied the benefits of, or be subjected to discrimination under any program or activity receiving Federal financial assistance'. The nature and legal basis of this claim, and ensuing events and consequences, are explored in detail in this article. It notes that CBE is challenging 'the use of mobile source emissions trading rules . . . in Los Angeles that allow oil companies' marine terminals to buy emissions credits rather than install pollution abatement technology. . . . CBE alleges that allowing air pollution from scrapped vehicles to be relocated to these marine terminals causes toxic hot spots . . . that disproportionately impact the surrounding Latino communities in the San Pedro/Wilmington area of Los Angeles.' Analysis concludes that emissions trading 'can result in disparate impacts to communities under certain circumstances', and the author explores a series of less discriminatory alternatives to existing emissions trading schemes operating within a market framework.

D. R. T. Drury *et al.*, 'Pollution Trading and Environmental Injustice. Los Angeles' Failed Experiment in Air Quality Policy' (1999) 9 *Duke Environmental Law and Policy Forum* 231

This paper offers a more openly polemical critique of emissions trading in the Los Angeles area, seeking to expose the 'immorality, injustice, and ineffectiveness of pollution trading'. As with the previous paper it highlights the challenge which emissions trading raises from an environmental justice perspective, placing as it does 'a disproportionate burden of the region's air pollution on low-income communities, a majority of which are ethnic and racial minorities'. However, the paper goes further making more general claims as to the ineffectiveness of emissions trading. Not only, it is claimed, do such programmes not significantly reduce air pollution, they do not spur technological innovation as is so often claimed, they lead to a decrease in public participation in environmental decision-making, and increase difficulties associated with monitoring and enforcement of emissions reductions. However, the paper is not entirely apocalyptic. While recognizing the serious empirical and theoretical difficulties which emissions trading present, the authors put forward a proposal for domestic, urban pollution trading programmes which seek to 'avoid the pit-falls associated with the Los Angeles pollution trading experiments'. In addition the authors seek to identify the implications of the Los Angeles experiment for the international arena in the context of climate change. In terms of the former the authors propose that regulators:

— prohibit trading in toxic substances;
— prohibit trading into overburdened communities;
— assess and prevent toxic hot-spots and discriminatory impacts;
— prohibit trading out of reasonably available control technology requirements;
— prohibit cross-pollutant trading;
— allow affected communities to review and comment on proposed trade;
— ban inter-source trading (e.g. trading from stationary to mobile source);
— prohibit hot air credits that result from over-allocating the baseline.

While the proposals are rather schematic in their presentation this paper, like the previous one, invites integration of a justice/rights dimension into emissions trading schemes. Particularly interesting for the European Union is the emphasis placed upon public participation in emissions trading, and the challenges this presents in transnational setting.

E. J. R. Nash, 'Too Much Market? Conflict between Tradable Pollution Allowances and the "Polluter Pays" Principle' (2000) 24 *Harvard Environmental Law Review* 465

This paper, like Wiener's above, adopts a favourable perspective on emissions trading, concluding, following analysis, that 'tradable pollution allowance regimes may not be as inconsistent with the polluter pays principle as they facially appear'. Nash's conclusions in this respect have important implications for policy-makers, at least for those who accept the law and economics premises upon which his analysis rests. Particularly significant in this sense is his predictable conclusion that the 'grandfathering' of pollution 'leads to government subsidies and increases the incentive to keep in service older, less efficient plants. . . . [and that] to the extent possible, tradable pollution permit regimes should be structured with auction-based rather than grandfathered allocations.' Nash acknowledges the political difficulties associated with this and proposes a number of compromise solutions such as, for example, the imposition of a time limit on the longevity of permits, thus at any rate reducing the scale of the subsidy. This issue of allocation is discussed in Part V of the paper. This Section as a whole is devoted to outlining the potential inconsistencies between the polluter-pays principle and a tradable pollution allowance regime. Important here is the hot-spot phenomenon highlighted by the previous two papers. Emissions purchased in one area may be transferred to another locality in which the same quantity of output will result in a higher degree of environmental harm. Thus, where trading in pollutants which cause harm of a local nature, policy-makers 'could allocate tradable allowances based on environmental damage rather than emissions of the regulated pollutant'. A number of options are explored in this respect. Throughout the paper Nash is careful to highlight circumstances in which command and control regulation offends the polluter-pays principle. Nonetheless, in his conclusion he pins his colours very clearly to the mast. Even if some inconsistencies between polluter pays and emissions trading may be 'unavoidable and at some level irreducible', such regimes should be favoured as they have the virtue of cost-efficiency. Indeed, it may be appropriate to prefer them even where the inconsistencies which emissions trading programmes exhibit are more exaggerated than those which characterize command and control approaches; at least, Nash seems to suggest, where command and control is not politically feasible but trading schemes more so. What remains unclear is where the polluter-pays principle stands in the hierarchy of values to be respected by a given environmental protection regime, and in what circumstances and on the basis of what considerations, this principle may be sacrificed or compromised in the name of a higher good.

### Annex 1: Sample of Papers in US journals Published in 1999–July 2000

M. D Adler and E. A. Posner, 'Rethinking Cost–Benefit Analysis' (1999) 109(2) *Yale Law Journal*, 165

H. Elliot, 'Standing and *Steel and Co.* v. *Citizens for a Better Environment*' (1999) 26(4) *Ecology Law Quarterly*

D. C. Esty, 'Towards Optimal Environmental Governance' (1999) 74(6) *New York University Law Review*, 1495

D. Farber, 'Taking Slippage Seriously: Non-Compliance and Creative Compliance in Environmental Law' (1999) 23(2) *Harvard Environmental Law Review*, 297

D. J. Fiorino, 'Rethinking Environmental Regulation: Perspectives on Law and Governance' (1999) 23(2) *Harvard Environmental Law Review*, 441

R. Gupta, 'Indigenous People and the International Environmental Community: Accommodating Claims through a Cooperative Legal Process' (1999) 74(6) *New York University Law Review*, 1741

B. A. Harsh, 'Consumerism and Environmental Policy: Moving Past Consumer Culture' (1999) 26(3) *Ecology Law Quarterly*, 543

S. Kuhn, 'Expanding Public Participation is Essential to Environmental Justice and the Decision Making Process' (1999) 25(4) *Ecology Law Quarterly*, 647

T. Kuran and C. R. Sunstein, 'Availability Cascades and Risk Regulation' (1999) 51(4) *Stanford Law Review*, 683

M. McCloskey, 'The Emperor Has no Clothes: The Conundrum of Sustainable Development' (1999) IX(2) *Duke Environmental Law and Policy Forum*, 153

D. L. Markall, 'The Role of Deterrence-Based Enforcement in a "Reinvented" State/Federal Relationship: The Divide between Theory and Reality' (2000) 24(1) *Harvard Environmental Law Review*, 1

M. Montesinos, 'It May be Silly, but It's an Answer: The Need to Accept Contingent Valuation Methodology in Natural Resource Damage Assessments' (1999) 26(1) *Ecology Law Quarterly*, 75

C. A. O'Neill, 'Variable Justice: Environmental Standards, Contaminated Fish, and "Acceptable Risk" to Native Peoples' (2000) 19(1) *Stanford Environmental Law Journal*, 3

Z. Plater, 'Environmental Law and Three Economies: Navigating a Sprawling Field of Study, Practice and Societal Governance in which Everything is Connected to Everything Else' (1999) 23(2) *Harvard Environmental Law Review*, 359

R. Revesz, 'Environmental Regulation: Cost–Benefit Analysis, and the Discounting of Human Lives' (1999) 99(4) *Columbia Law Review*, 941

J. B. Ruhl, 'The Co-Evolution of Sustainable Development and Environmental Justice: Cooperation, then Competition, Then Conflict' (1999) XI(2) *Duke Environmental Law and Policy Forum*, 161

M. R. Schultz, 'Standing and *Bennett* v. *Spear*' (1999) 29 *Ecology Law Quarterly*

A. E. Simon, 'Valuing Public Participation' (1995) 25(4) *Ecology Law Quarterly*, 757

H. A. Span, 'Of TEAs and Takings: Compensation for Confiscated Tradeable Environmental Allowances' (2000) 109(8) *Yale Law Journal*, 1983

C. C. Steincamp, 'Citizenship: A Discussion of Environmental Citizen Suits' (1999) 39(1) *Washburn Law Journal*, 72

C. R. Sunstein, 'Standing for Animals (with Notes on Animal Rights' (2000) 47(5) *University of California Law Review*, 1333

P. S. Weiland, 'Federal and State Pre-emption of Environmental Law: A Critical Analysis' (2000) 24(1) *Harvard Environmental Law Review*, 237

N. Yost, 'Environmental Regulation—Are there Better Ways' (1999) 25(4) *Ecology Law Quarterly*

R. O. Zerbe Jr. and L. J. Graham, 'The Role of Rights in Benefit Cost Methodology: The Example of Salmon and Hydroelectric Dams' (1999) 74(3) *University of Washington Law Review*, 763

### Annex II: US Law Journals (General not including International Law)

*Alabama Law Review*
*American University Law Review*
*Brooklyn Law Review*
*Buffalo Law Review*
*California Law Review* (University of California, Berkeley)

*Cardozo Law Review*
*Chicago-Kent Law Review*
*Columbia Law Review*
*Connecticut Law Review*
*Cornell Law Review*
*Detroit College of Law at Michigan State University Law Review*
*Duke Law Journal*
*Emory Law Journal*
*Florida State University Law Review*
*Georgia Law Review*
*Gonzaga Law Review*
*Harvard Law Review*
*Hastings Law Journal*
*Hofstra Law Review*
*Indiana Law Journal*
*Kentucky Law Journal*
*Mercer Law Review*
*Michigan Law Review*
*New England Law Review*
*New York University Law Review*
*North Carolina Law Review*
*Ohio State Law Journal*
*Oklahoma City University Law Review*
*Regent University Law Review*
*Rutgers Law Journal*
*Rutgers Law Record*
*San Diego Law Review*
*Seattle University Law Review*
*Southern California Law Review*
*Southern Illinois University Law Journal*
*Stanford Law Review*
*Stetson Law Review*
*Tulane Law Review*
*UC Davis Law Review*
*UCLA Law Review*
*University of Kansas Law Review*
*University of Pittsburgh Law Review*
*Wake Forest Law Review*
*Washburn Law Journal*
*Washington & Lee Law Review*
*Washington Law Review*
*Washington University Law Quarterly*
*West Virginia Law Review*
*Willamette Law Review*
*Yale Law Journal*

## Annex III: US Environmental Law Journals

*Buffalo Environmental Law Journal*, State University of New York
*Colorado Journal of International Environmental Law and Policy*, University of
  Colorado
*Columbia Journal of Environmental Law*, Columbia University
*Dickinson Journal of Environmental Law & Policy*, Dickinson School of Law
*Drake Journal of Agriculture Law*, Drake University
*Duke Environmental Law and Policy Forum*, Duke University
*Ecology Law Quarterly*, Boalt Hall
*Electronic Green Journal*, University of Idaho Library
*Energy Law Journal and ABA Year in Review*, University of Tulsa
*Environmental Law* (Lewis & Clark)
*Environmental Law Journal*, Touro College
*Environmental Law Society Newsletter*, DePaul University
*Environmental Lawyer*, George Washington University and the ABA
*Fordham Environmental Law Journal*, Fordam
*Georgetown International Environmental Law Review*, Georgetown University
*Great Plains Natural Resources Journal*, University of South Dakota School of Law
*Harvard Environmental Law Review*, Harvard Law School
*Hastings West-Northwest Journal of Environmental Law and Policy*, University
  of California, Hastings
*Journal of Environmental Law and Litigation*, University of Oregon
*Journal of Land Use and Environmental Law*, Florida State University
*Journal of Natural Resources & Environmental Law*, University of Kentucky
*Land & Water Law Review*, University of Wyoming
*Missouri Environmental Law and Policy Review*, University of Missouri
*Natural Resources Journal*, University of New Mexico
*NYU Environmental Law Journal*
*Ocean and Coastal Law Journal*, University of Maine
*Pace Environmental Law Review*, Pace University
*Pace Interactive Earth Law Journal*, Pace University
*Public Land & Resources Law Review*, University of Montana School of Law
*Real Property, Probate and Trust Journal*, University of South Carolina and the
  ABA
*RISK: Health, Safety & Environment*, Franklin Pierce Law Center
*South Carolina Environmental Law Journal*, University of South Carolina
*Stanford Environmental Law Journal*, Stanford University
*Tulane Environmental Law Journal*, Tulane University
*UCLA Journal of Environmental Law & Policy*, UCLA
*Urban Lawyer*, American Bar Association
*The Vermont Journal of the Environment*, Vermont Law School
*Villanova Environmental Law Journal*, Villanova University
*Washington University Journal of Urban and Contemporary Law*, Washington
  University

*Water Law Review*, University of Denver College of Law.
*William and Mary Environmental Law and Policy Review*, William and Mary.

## II. Book Reviews

*Environmental Policy in the European Union*, Anthony Zito, Macmillan,
    London: 1999, 240 pp., £42.50 hb. ISBN 0333722140

If this were just another book arguing that liberal intergovernmentalism and
neo-functionalism are too simplistic to understand and explain the European
policy-making process, we could put it on the shelf with a whole series of other
books recently published. Fortunately, Zito's detailed empirical study on
the creation of three central European environmental policies offers some
important insights into the conditions under which ideas and policy
entrepreneurs matter to the process and the outcome of European policy-
making. Thus, the book not only enhances our understanding of European
policy-making, but also contributes to the rich literature on transnational networks and the role of ideational factors in international and European politics.
The findings of the book are all the more interesting because Zito avoids the
usual selection bias on the dependent variable by presenting cases of both failure and success of what he calls entrepreneurial policy-making.

Transboundary air pollution, the carbon/energy tax, and hazardous waste
are critical cases for testing the influence of ideas and policy entrepreneurs in
bringing about policy change. All three policies have been extremely controversial among the Member States due to the high costs involved and, hence,
would lead us to expect policy outcomes close to the lowest common denominator. In all three cases, Zito finds entrepreneurial coalitions at work trying to
move policy actors beyond the *status quo* by persuading them to redefine their
interests in the light of a new policy idea (problem-solving). Yet, 'the three
cases reveal that lowest common denominator bargaining among interests
prevails most often' (at 168). At the same time, the empirical study offers evidence for the influence of policy entrepreneurs, particularly in the case of hazardous waste shipment. In his conclusions, Zito presents a set of inductively
gained hypotheses, identifying conditions under which entrepreneurial
decision-making may succeed over lowest common denominator bargaining
as the 'default mode' of EU policy-making. He distinguishes between three
types of factors influencing the success of policy entrepreneurs promoting
new policy ideas in bringing about policy change.

The first factor concerns the institutional context which defines the access
and the influence of policy entrepreneurs at the various stages of the EU
policy-making process. Zito's study confirms a proposition developed in the
transnational relations literature whereby the higher the number of veto
points, the better the chances of access for policy entrepreneurs, but also the
higher the need for an extended number of allies (winning coalition). Thus,
access and influence are inversely related (T. Risse-Kappen (ed.), *Bringing
Transnational Relations Back In* (Cambridge: Cambridge University Press

1995)). Institutional factors, such as the use of majority voting and the role of the European Parliament, are crucial in this respect. Policy entrepreneurs may manipulate these factors by framing policy issues in such a way that they become subject to a particular set of institutional rules, which the policy entrepreneurs deem most favourable. The dominance of policy entrepreneurs at the problem-definition, agenda-setting, and policy-formulation stage is also in line with the general literature. But Zito identifies an institutional venue for policy entrepreneurs to advocate their ideas, which is often overlooked. International organizations, such as the Organization for Economic Cooperation and Development (OECD) or the UN Environment Programme (UNEP), can serve as a source of policy ideas as well as a separate institutional arena, in which European Union (EU) actors may discuss new policy ideas outside the 'interest wedded' context of European institutions.

The second factor identified is the ideational context, in which policy entrepreneurs succeed in incorporating new policy ideas into the process. Zito's conclusion that the less policy ideas challenge the interests and identities of actors, the higher their chances for acceptance, corroborates the 'resonance' hypotheses put forward by constructivist approaches in international relations. It may also explain why successfully incorporated ideas are not necessarily 'heavily instilled with scientific knowledge and understanding of causal linkages' (at 176). Rather than concluding that the power of scientific ideas and knowledge in overcoming the logic of interest-based bargaining may be overrated (at 28), one could also argue that in each of the three cases, the scientific ideas lacked the support of a *united* epistemic community. Knowledge is only power if it is consensual rather than contested, particularly in situations of uncertainty. Zito himself identifies the coherence of the entrepreneurial coalition as crucial to its success (at 119). Finally, epistemic communities are only one type of entrepreneurial coalition which are knowledge based. Principled issue-networks or advocacy coalitions present an alternative type that is value based (M. Keck and K. Sikkink, *Activists Beyond Borders* (Ithaca NY: Cornell University Press, 1998). A clear conceptual distinction between the two types would have also helped in avoiding the confusion between entrepreneurial coalitions and mere interest coalitions in some of the case studies. It is not always clear to what extent actors (Member States, members of the Commission) strive to build or join coalitions in order to advocate new policy ideas rather than merely to promote their own interests. A last factor, which Zito identified as influencing the success and failure of policy ideas, is pressure to change due to policy failure, environmental crisis, or uncertainty.

A third factor identified by Zito is the interest context, which policy entrepreneurs confront when advocating new ideas. Their efforts are more successful in the event that no major societal or economic interests perceive the policy change accompanied by the idea as imposing specific costs on them. Likewise, environmental non-environmental organizations (NGOs) are less supportive if they have difficulties in identifying the general policy implications of the policy change. Such cost–benefit calculations could also explain why interests in European policy-making may be defined along sectoral rather than merely national lines, splitting individual Member States between different ministries (for example, economics *versus* environment) as well as the Commission between different Directorate-Generals (for example, D-G Fiscal Matters *versus* D-G Environment), a development which is particularly visible in the carbon/energy tax case.

Zito presents his approach of entrepreneurial decision-making as a modification of, rather than an alternative to, liberal intergovernmentalism (LIG). But certain elements of the two approaches seem hardly compatible. Zito argues that the influence of policy entrepreneurs depends on their persuasive skills to convince the Member States to redefine their interests enabling solutions beyond the lowest common denominator (at 37). Unfortunately, the case studies present only weak evidence on persuasive processes. Yet, the assumption is hardly reconcilable with the rationalist grounding of LIG, where actors have a set of fixed and ordered preferences which they strive to maximize on the basis of cost–benefit calculation. The same applies to the prevalence of sectoral over nationally defined interests, which Zito finds in some of his case studies and which is the result of Member States not behaving like unitary actors. Liberal *inter*governmentalism has great difficulties in coming to terms with the importance of *trans*governmental relations in European policy-making. Finally, while Zito accepts intergovernmental lowest-common-denominator bargaining as the default mode of European policy-making, he presents some striking evidence where entrepreneurial coalitions made an impact both on the process and on the outcome of European environmental policy-making. Unlike LIG, Zito's approach can accommodate the existence of two different decision modes, these being based on distinct logics of action (self-interested bargaining and collective problem-solving). Moreover, he specifies conditions under which entrepreneurial decision-making is likely to prevail over interest-based bargaining. Thus, Zito's book not only presents three interesting case studies on the role of policy entrepreneurs and ideas in European environmental policy-making. It also contributes to the attempt to overcome the ongoing and rather futile controversy between the two major paradigms of European integration, liberal intergovernmentalism and neo-functionalism, which are anyway too general to theorize about European 'every-day' decision-making.

TANJA A. BÖRZEL
European University Institute
Florence

*New Instruments for Environmental Policy in the EU*, edited by Jonathan Golub, Routledge, London, 1998, 270 pp., £60.00 hb. ISBN 0415156963

In its overall assessment of the results of the fifth Environmental Action Programme, the Commission notes, *inter alia,* the lack of success in trying to broaden the range of instruments of EC environmental policy. *New Instruments for Environmental Policy in the EU* offers a reference work for the ongoing debate in this area.

The book kicks off with an introduction by its editor. The introduction outlines the debate in the European Community (EC), and offers a summary of the pros and cons of green taxes and subsidies; voluntary agreements; eco-audits; eco-labels; and tradable permits. The book has the added value that its editor is not a lawyer. This enables the reader of the introductory chapter to catch up on some of the prevailing ideas among political scientists, such as democratic accountability as one means of testing the effectiveness of new instruments in environmental policy, or the broader theme of corporate good governance and the role of industry and non-governmental organizations (NGOs). The editor, perhaps overcautiously, avoids judging the 'new' instruments according to the three criteria which are generally put forward to assess their effectiveness: first, how well do they curtail pollution to levels consistent with sustainable development; second, do they realize savings in compliance costs; and third, to what extent do they enhance the legitimacy of environmental policy-making. The contributions written by representatives of NGOs in particular, build upon these three criteria and are refreshingly frank in pointing out benefits, and identifying perceived disadvantages.

The editor's references to political science offers a broader picture than that to which the average lawyer is accustomed, and this reviewer for one is looking forward to more papers by political scientists on the subject.

The book consists of two parts. The first part covers the use of new instruments in the UK, Germany, the Netherlands, Belgium, Spain, and Italy. Each contribution is clear and topical, and the authors have not refrained from adding their personal views as to how these instruments actually work, and what ought to be improved. One could argue about the choice of the Member States selected. Whilst one cannot cover each and every Member State in every book written on the subject, it is a pity that none of the Nordic countries, for instance, is included.

The second part reviews the use of new instruments at the EC level, covering negotiated agreements, eco-labels, environmental taxes and charges, and the European Eco-Management and Audit Scheme (EMAS). All these areas have been subject to recent developments, such as the changes to EMAS and the Eco-Label Regulation (Regulation (EC) No. 880/92), finalized in 2000; the actual negotiation of EC-wide agreements in the car sector; the revised guidelines for state aid in the environmental sector; and recent case law of the European Court of Justice (ECJ) with respect to national taxation (Article 90 EC, case C–213/96 [1998] ECR I–177, *Proceedings against Outokompu Oy* in particular). With respect to eco-taxation and voluntary agreements, the analysis of recent policy documents (both from the Commission and from the Council), and the continuing deadlock with respect to Community-wide energy taxes, suggest that whilst the development of EU-wide agreements and taxation remains on the agenda, the use of such instruments at the national level will remain more important in practice. It is therefore a pity that the relevant chapter of the book does not offer more detailed insights into the legal obstacles to such developments, in particular the Treaty provisions on free movement of goods, taxation, and competition law. These provisions are identified, but not truly analysed. This may not be surprising, given that the authors concerned are Commission officials and perhaps did not wish to burn their fingers; it is nevertheless a disappointment.

Refreshingly, the authors' analysis is, on the whole, neutral and objective. The commentators do not to display the kind of naïve belief that emerged in some circles at the end of the 1980s, when new instruments were hailed as the one and only way forward to tackle environmental problems in the EU. This commentator would suggest that many of the perceived advantages of new instruments (speed, transparency, tailor-made, etc.) can be equally well achieved by corrections to traditional command-and-control regulation. The book is, on the whole, non-biased, which is most definitely refreshing.

As noted, the fate of new instruments in environmental policy in the EU will, to a large degree, be determined by their use at national level, and by Commission and ECJ practice in assessing their compatibility with core Treaty provisions. The insights offered by *New Instruments for Environmental Policy in the EU* into national and EC experiences are thus timely.

GEERT VAN CALSTER
IMER—*Collegium Falconis*
K.U. Leuven

*Cross-Border Transactions and Environmental Law*, edited by Mark Brumwell, Butterworths, London, 1999, 386 pp., £110 hb. ISBN 0 406 89590 2

That 'this book is by practitioners for practitioners' is one of the lead themes in Mark Brumwell's introduction, but it would seem that the book's appeal surpasses that mission statement. The book most certainly will prove a very useful tool to practitioners, but this reviewer would subscribe to it being good reading for academics and government officials as well.

*Cross-Border Transactions and Environmental Law* provides a guide to the basics of environmental law in fifteen jurisdictions: Germany, the UK, the Netherlands, Belgium, Sweden, Spain, Austria, France, Portugal, and Greece; the USA, Australia, Switzerland, Israel, and Norway. Inspired by a need perceived in environmental practice in commercial law firms, each chapter identifies core provisions with respect to the environmental issues of business transactions (in particular Mergers and Acquisitions (M&As) and real estate) and the contractual terms to apportion risk. The chapters each comprise more or less twenty pages. Thus, they do not of course purport to be comprehensive. They all follow the same structure: introduction (outlining the core structure of the country's environmental law); outline of environmental law relevant to M&As (not surprisingly, often with preponderant weight for land contamination issues; otherwise summarizing statutory provisions which determine permit regulations); particular environmental issues relevant to transactions (mostly focusing on determination of liability (including of the lender), warranty and indemnity terms); managing environmental issues in transactions (typically considerations which enable the reader to draft a checklist, do's and don'ts as it were).

Whilst the editor does offer a comparative chapter, comparative analysis is not the main thrust of the book. It provides the lead firm in the transaction at issue with a fair introduction to the environmental law of the countries concerned. This undoubtedly will enable it to ask the right questions of all national lawyers involved; it may also facilitate transaction timing for instance.

The contributions are of a consistently high quality, and one can only imagine the amount of editorial work that must have gone into achieving such a streamlined work. Some of the national contributions do disappoint when it comes to the 'Managing environmental issues in transactions' heading; the checklist sometimes does not amount to much more than an essential due diligence list. This is, however, more the exception than the rule, and, at any rate, may prove very instructive for the practice-challenged reader.

The selection of the countries seems determined by mainstream practice, but may nevertheless be unsatisfactory. It is unclear why, among the EU Member States, Denmark, Finland, Ireland, Italy, and Luxembourg are not included, especially if Australia, Israel, and Norway are selected among the non-EU Member States. Likewise, it seems a pity that none of the candidate countries for EU enlargement is included. This may have to be considered in a future edition. Whilst most contributors do pay some attention to town and planning law, the reviewer's impression was that this element of transactions does deserve more attention. This is especially so given that most commercial practices typically include a combined environment/real estate practice. The book includes a comprehensive index, and a table of statutes and other relevant EC legislation, but hardly any references to literature. It may also be worthwhile to consider a list, per country, of Internet-based resources, for a next edition. The book is, as its title suggests, geared towards cross-border transactions, and it emphasizes the need for the practitioners' introduction into the national environmental laws of the individual countries. The editor quite rightly emphasizes the consistent importance of national law and procedure, notwithstanding the influence of EC environmental law for some of the selected countries. However, non-European readers may be well advised not to dismiss EC environmental law altogether. The majority of EC environmental law is implemented via national regulations which the chapters concerned summarize satisfactorily. Nevertheless, as academics and practitioners alike will be aware, it may be crucial to know the EC origin of the national regulation, so as to be able better to appreciate the true impact of some of the national provisions concerned. Moreover, all contributions would seem to underestimate the impact which less commercially obvious EC environmental law may have on commercial transactions such as the Directive on the Conservation of Wild Birds ([1998] OJ L103/1), and the Directive on the Conservation of Natural Habitats and of Wild Fauna and Flora, ([1992] OJ L206/1) the Natura 2000 programme, and the Council Directive on the Assessment of the Effects of Certain Public and Private Projects on the Environment ([1985] OJ L175/40). Whilst allowing 'marketing licence', one would have to make a counterclaim against the assertion that 'no [book on international environmental law and on EU environmental law] looks at the national law which applies in each jurisdiction and the way in which international and EU regimes are applied nationally'. *Comparative Environmental Law in Europe* springs to mind (R. Seerden and M. Heldeweg (eds.), (Antwerp: Maklu, 1996)). I would say that these books together may prove a fruitful pair, the reviewed book being geared towards practice, *Comparative Environmental Law in Europe* being more academically oriented.

It is a great frustration that the enforcement of EC environmental law is hampered by its diverse implementation in the Member States. *Cross-Border Transactions and Environmental Law* provides an ample tool to soften readers' difficulties with that diversity. Its consistent, structured approach is a remarkable achievement, as is the persistently high quality of each individual contribution. Non-EU Member States are not just thrown in as a bonus; they are definitely added value to the book, since these jurisdiction are included in a growing number of transactions. This book is highly recommended for practitioners and, I would urge, for academics.

GEERT VAN CALSTER
IMER—*Collegium Falconis*
K.U. Leuven

*Living with Nature: Environmental Politics as Cultural Discourse* by Frank Fischer and Maarten Hajer. Oxford University Press, Oxford, 1999, viii + 269 pp., £16.99. ISBN 019829509X

For a subdiscipline that makes repeated claims to 'interdisciplinarity', very little academic environmental law writing considers the assumptions behind its starting point. Almost all writing assumes the presence of a Nature–Culture dichotomy within which one is exclusive of the other. Rooted in the Kantian distinction between phenomena and noumena, this construction inevitably leads to the environment being something that can only be impinged upon. The bland universality and alterity of the concept lead to its being used as a rhetorical device to legitimate whatever totalizing prescription the author invoking it has in mind.

Yet there is a tradition, with sociologists and critical geographers as its current foremost advocates, which goes back to Marx and has more intellectual mileage. This asserts that material practices, such as trade, consumption, and industrialization, have over time 'made' the Nature that we currently understand. Less materialist analyses note how conceptions of Nature are linked to perceptions of time, place, and identity, with the consequence that particular visions of Nature are privileged over others. These two forms of analysis differ from each other, but consider that social and ecological relations are so implicated with one another and inform each other to such an extent that it makes little sense to disentangle one from the other.

I had high hopes in reading Fischer and Hajer that this collection of essays edited by two of the leading scholars would develop the debate. The Introduction is information, some of the pieces excellent (notably all those in the second Section) and there is a great bibliography, yet, I am afraid, this collection only brought two cheers.

A major disappointment, as it is increasingly with a number of edited works, is that beyond a brief Introduction, neither of the editors felt the work sufficiently important to contribute a chapter of their own. A further was that three of the ten chapters, nearly a third of the book, had been published elsewhere—in two cases some time before.

Another disappointment was the structure of the book. It was divided by the editors into three headings. These were the natural environment as a cultural construct, 'cultural discourse' in environmental expertise and policy-making, and environmental justice and culture difference. Yet, because the term 'culture' is used so loosely and, at times, so contradictorily across the book, it is difficult finding themes that cross these headings.

In a review such as this it is difficult to do justice to the ten articles contained in the book. To give a reader a flavour of the book, the reviewer has selected one article from each heading.

The first, in perhaps the weakest section of the book, is an article by Sachs in which he tries to deconstruct the three discourses that he claims permeate sustainable development. There is, first, the contest perspective. This conceives of how to accommodate concern for Nature with concerns for economic efficiency and accumulation. Within such a discourse Nature is transformed into a resource whose yield has to be sustained. Alongside this has developed an astronaut's perspective. This sees the globe as a single biosystem which must be managed. Sachs is critical of the totalizing qualities of these discourses and their insensitivities to local socio-economic conditions and modes of organization. He posits therefore a third perspective, that of the 'home perspective'. This is concerned with protection of local life-worlds from overdevelopment. For Sachs this is the most promising form of 'cultural politics' suggested by sustainable development, as it suggests self-limitation and self-examination as the solution to the ecological crisis.

The difficulty with this argument is that whilst the 'cultural ecology' model (the home perspective) that Sachs suggests here has proved to be a powerful weapon in exposing the totalitarian elements in 'sustainable development', he is on less sure ground when meandering off this ground. His argument is essentially a 'strawman' one. It suffers from creating 'ideal types' so that scientific and market conceptions of ecology are reified and idealized in a manner which glosses over their internal tensions and possibilities—so important to his theory—for reflexive self-learning. Indeed, his 'home perspective' is also an ideal type. It ignores how a feature of the sustainable development debate has resulted in individuals increasingly taking multi-scalar perspectives, so that nuclear accidents in Japan are placed alongside location of waste disposal facilities in the neighbourhood, which are inherently unstable and will vary over time. He ultimately falls back therefore on the old Nature–Culture dichotomy by suggesting Nature as a controlling force for 'ecologically disruptive' processes, irrespective of the fact that the social disruption this will entail is not so dissimilar to that critiqued in the other two perspectives.

A piece that cannot be accused of continuing the Nature–Culture dichotomy is the simply outstanding case study done by Keulartz on the Nature Development Project in the Netherlands. The case study considers projects put forward by a variety of environmental non-governmental organizations to turn part of the Dutch landscape back to its primeval, 'original' state. This concept of 'holistic Nature Development' had a strong impact on the establishment by the Netherlands of a National Network of Important Ecosystems. Keulartz, impressively, shows not only the highly selective use of scientific information but also how this language was used to empower and include certain groups whilst excluding certain others. He concludes with a plea for 'evolutionary ecology', which does not see Nature as something that is static but as something that evolves in a dialectic with Society. This produces not only risks but also opportunities.

There is, finally, a fine piece by Harvey on the 'Environment of Justice'. Harvey starts from his standard position of how all environmental conflicts are also social conflicts. He notes that environmental risks have traditionally been distributed in such a way that they impact most heavily upon the disadvantaged in society. He notes that whilst the discourse of ecological modernization has a radical edge by requiring attention to be paid to the question of environmental hazards, its prognoses are to legitimize greater industrial domination by placing industry and 'hi-tech science' as trustees for the global management of the 'fragile health of planet earth'. His suggestion of environmental justice is one that starts from the inequalities in exposure to health and is suspicious of all discourses that have contributed to this asymmetry—be it scientization or naturalistic arguments that belittle human needs. For environmental and social justice are largely co-terminous. There is much in this that has resonance, but Harvey's heavy Marxist heritage does leave one wondering what for him is specifically the 'environmental problematic'. As with many writers of his ilk, terms such as 'social justice' are left worryingly vague. Yet it is surely well known by now, through exposure by writers such as Arendt and communist mismanagement, that the globalizing nature of the 'social' has along with that of the 'economy' been possibly the central tool for the legitimization of individual injustices.

From the above, it will seem that there is only a qualified 'Yes' from this reviewer to this book. It is a 'Yes' however. For all its unevenness and lapses into vagueness, it is a source of argument and ideas. In that, there is an intellectual excitement present. And for that it deserves some credit.

DAMIAN CHALMERS
London School of Economics
London

*Protecting Public Health and the Environment: Implementing the Precautionary Principle*, edited by Carolyn Raffensperger and Joel Tickner. Island Press, Washington, 1999, 384 pp., $30,00. ISBN 1559636882

*Protecting Public Health and the Environment* is a timely publication for EC environmental lawyers. As the Court of Justice moves towards juridifying the Treaty environmental principles, and the Commission issues its paper on the precautionary principle (COM(2000)1), there is a danger that the principle may be diluted in the process of implementation. Raffensperger and Tickner's consistently well-argued collection, though not primarily concerned with European developments, seeks to outline viable applications of the precautionary principle that do not dull its radical edge. It is also timely in its engagement with broader legal concerns over the role of 'sound science' and the limits of a technocratic approach to regulation.

The origins of the precautionary principle and its prolific acceptance, particularly in international legal documents, are identified but the focus of the book is very much on the next stage; that of implementing a meta-concept into detailed procedures and provisions of law and policy. Whilst, as with any edited collection, there are a range of issues and approaches, there is a strong central theme, the need to save the precautionary principle from being subsumed into the discipline of risk assessment. A number of the contributors argue that this engineering-based methodology, with its emphasis on prediction on the basis of laboratory testable parameters, is wholly unsuited for decision-making on matters of the natural environment. They insist that the precautionary principle involves different demands on science, and different attitudes towards science from policy-makers and lawyers, involving the acknowledgement of inherent uncertainty, greater openness as to the moral/political content of scientific judgements, and more inclusive interdisciplinary dialogue. Readers may be interested in comparing the arguments presented here with those in the European Commission's communication, which puts the precautionary principle firmly within the ambit of risk management and cost–benefit analysis.

Whilst the contributors do not present the principle as a panacea for public health and environmental ills, they do not disguise the deep-seated changes to entrenched attitudes that a full-bloodied implementation of the principle would involve. In particular, if decision-making in the face of uncertainty is seen as a political rather than science-based activity, then there are implications for democratic involvement in policy and regulatory fields.

The book is divided into four parts. The first provides theoretical analyses of the implications of the principle for law, policy, and science and reflects on some European (principally Swedish) attempts to adhere to the principle. The second part looks at the way in which law and science are incorporated into decision-making. It contains analyses of the way in which scientific evidence can influence both civil liability cases and governmental regulation, and interesting arguments on modifying the burden of proof and imposing general legal duties for those who initiate potentially harmful activities. Part three describes practical approaches towards implementing precaution. Through a diverse, but surprisingly cohesive, series of chapters ranging from corporate disclosure and financial bonds to nature conservation in Scotland and water quality in the Great Lakes, the tools of environmental precaution and decision-making in the face of uncertainty are examined. The final part consists of case studies of the precautionary principle in action, written by those at the sharp end of applying the principle, such as farmers, doctors, and policy analysts.

A case study from a litigator would have made a useful addition to the final part, and generally the focus of the book is towards policy-making rather than regulation or adjudication. As a truly interdisciplinary book, however, it demonstrates that environmental policy cannot be understood without considering its interpenetration with the law (and science, social policy, political governance, etc.).

Raffensperger and Tickner deserve credit for their editing. Books comprising collections of conference papers do, on occasion, seem to be rather thrown together, with little attempt at stylistic consistency, development of common themes, or evidence of amendment in the light of conference outcomes. This is not the case here. The indexing and bibliographies are exemplary and, with the small exception of some overlap and repetition in the early chapters, this collection manages to combine a potentially daunting range of disciplines by a diverse cohort of contributors, into a coherent, well-organized, and eminently readable book.

There is interesting material here for European environmental lawyers specializing in a wide range of issues; agri-environmental measures, environmental assessment, access to information, pollution control, products policy, water quality, trade and environment, regulatory theory, would be a far from exhaustive list. It is well worth seeking out.

MICHAEL G. DOHERTY

University of Central Lancashire

*Environmental Regulations and Corporate Strategy: A NAFTA Perspective* by Alan Rugman, John Kirton, and Julie Soloway. Oxford University Press, Oxford, 1999, xi + 258 pp., £45.00. ISBN 019829588X

When the North American Free Trade Association (NAFTA) was under consideration in the USA, environmentalists worried that industry threats to move to

Mexico's weaker regulatory regime would cause a regulatory race to the bottom. These predictions were unfounded, according to Rugman, Kirton, and Soloway. On the contrary, they report, there are no known cases of industry moving to Mexico to take advantage of weaker environmental regulation (at 197). Indeed, they say, NAFTA is 'producing an environmental regulatory push to the top rather than race to the bottom' (at 220). Based on 230 interviews with business leaders, government officials, and others, their conclusions about NAFTA are on the whole quite optimistic.

After its first five years, the NAFTA regime works. It is enhancing competitiveness in environmentally enhancing ways. It assures access to the North American economy and helps firms capture global market by opening regulations that help raise access to the global market place. . . . Individual firms within North America have an unrecognized benefit in the environmental regime of NAFTA, which provides a successful architecture for future expansion in global markets (at 239–40).

These optimistic conclusions are, however, accompanied by serious—but seemingly quite ambivalent—concerns about 'environmental protectionism'. The authors seem not to have fully resolved in their own minds the extent of this threat or the ability of NAFTA to control the use of environmental regulations to protect local industry. Thus, early in the book, they say that NAFTA trade rules are ineffective and 'do not pose much of a threat to the abuse of environmental measures' (at 33). Similarly, based on case studies, they find environmental protectionism to be rampant: 'the frequency of protectionist benefits from such regulations and the presence of coalitions of domestic firms and environmental groups supporting them point to how widespread and severe environmental regulatory protectionism can be' (at 52). But later, the authors tell us that '[t]here have been relatively few cases taken to NAFTA's three trade and investment dispute settlement panels, as the very credibility of the NAFTA dispute settlement process appears to have deterred unfair actions from taking place in the first place' (at 196). The upshot is that the effectiveness of NAFTA in countering environmental protectionism is unclear.

Connections between environmentalism and protectionism are hard to assess in part because of the complex dynamics of environmental trade disputes. The authors' discussion of the Methylcyclopentadienyl Manganese Tricarbonyl (MMT) dispute is particularly enlightening in this regard. MMT is a manganese-based fuel additive for gasoline, whose pollution control implications and health effects are sharply contested. The Canadian Government banned all trade in MMT. The ban resulted from pressure by a coalition of three groups: environmentalists, farmers (because MMT competes with ethanol, a gasoline additive derived from grain), and the automobile industry (which wanted uniform fuel standards across North America to simplify design of emission controls) (at 145–50). The economics of the ban are too unclear to make this an obvious case of protectionism, given the strong support of the auto industry for the ban. Yet the coalition between Canadian farmers and environmentalists does illustrate the potential alliance between environmentalism and protectionism. At least from the trade point of view, however, the story seems to have a happy ending. The sole world producer of MMT was unable to enlist the support of the US Government (at 152), but did succeed in obtaining support from three Canadian provincial governments involved in petroleum production or refining (at 153). The producer then filed an action under NAFTA chapter 11, seeking $251 million in damages (at 152). Ultimately, the case was settled, largely in the producer's favour, with the Canadian Government agreeing to pay $19 million in damages and retract the ban. Thus, in the end, the NAFTA regime seems to have been successful in promoting trade.

The difficulty of formulating firm conclusions about the effectiveness of NAFTA's trade regime is illustrated by two divergent statements only a few pages apart. In the passage quoted at the beginning of this review, the authors applaud NAFTA as 'enhancing competitiveness in environmentally enhancing ways'. But a few pages earlier, they tell us that emerging environmental regulation 'severely compromises the competitiveness of most firms having to operate under new business conditions' (at 217).

In short, this book raises as many questions as it answers about the risk of protectionist environmental regulation and the effectiveness of NAFTA in combating that risk. But for those who have worried that free trade would cause an environmental race to the bottom, the book's message should be quite reassuring.

DANIEL FARBER
University of Minnesota

*Environmental Law in the United Kingdom and Belgium from a Comparative Perspective*, edited by Kurt Deketelaere and Michael Faure. Kluwer, Dordrecht, 1999, 328 pp., $135 hb. ISBN 904198210

How considerable are the differences in environmental legislation between the legal systems of two Member States of the European Union (EU)—being based on Common law and Civil law respectively? This is the question tackled in *Environmental Law in the United Kingdom and Belgium from a Comparative Perspective* (see above).

This book contains a collection of essays on key issues relating to environmental legislation in Belgium and the UK, previously presented at a conference bringing together scholars from the Universities of Leuven, Maastricht, Aberdeen, and Liverpool de Montfort. The book has been put together with the aim of comparing the legal systems of Belgium and the UK with a view to learning how these systems might mutually inform and enrich each other. The editors hope to provide practical information about environmental legislation relevant to academics as well as to practitioners dealing with environmental law in the aforementioned countries.

The publication is divided into four parts, each containing a contribution from a UK as well as a Belgian perspective. The book thereby covers a compilation of key issues in national environmental legislation.

In the first part, Brian Jones and Gaëtan Verhoosel consider environmental competencies. While Jones focuses mainly on the formulation of fundamental theoretical questions concerning the distribution of environmental competencies in the UK, and thereby stays on 'fairly general and non-jurisdictionally specific' grounds (at 37), Gaëtan Verhoosel takes a thorough, straightforward, and pragmatic approach to environmental competencies in Belgium.

In the second part of the book, the law governing environmental and building licences and permits is set out by Clíona Kimber and Marc Boes, respectively. Clíona Kimber mainly concentrates on an overview of the British permitting and licensing system with regard to pollution control, and compares the approach taken to that under Belgian law. These solutions are further elaborated in Boes's contribution on Belgian building and environmental permits. After a general introduction to the legal nature of permits in general, equal emphasis is put on a rather plain description of the system of building permits and the system applicable to environmental permits.

The national systems on environmental liability are then discussed by Brian Jones and Michael Faure in the third part of the book. The two authors take different definitions of environmental liability as their starting points. Michel Faure limits his contribution to the concept of civil liability, while Jones takes a much wider meaning of that same concept. Professor Jones puts a lot of emphasis upon elaborating his concept of environmental liability, whereas the Belgian contribution concentrates on questions of material environmental liability.

Finally, the issue of environmental policy instruments such as environmental taxes, subsidies, policy agreements, and other instruments is explained by Clíona Kimber and Kurt Deketelaere in the fourth and last part of the book. In contrast to the rather conventional system of regulations in the UK, described by Clíona Kimber, Deketelaere paints an image of a rather experimental and innovative Belgian system of environmental regulations.

The individual contributions are stimulating and are liable to provoke further study of the subjects treated. Each contribution is clearly embedded in the Common or Civil law legal tradition. There are moments when reference to the determining characteristics of these two distinctive legal systems might have been useful.

While the contributions are interesting individually, the collection of papers does not succeed in conveying a comprehensive and structured comparison of the two legal systems in question. The juxtaposed articles largely fail to complement each other in the absence of a similar format, pronounced references, or communication between them. A comparison both by means of 'broad brush strokes and in finer detail', as indicated in the introduction to the book, is therefore difficult to achieve. This deficiency gives the book a visibly fragmented appearance. Unfortunately the merits of individual articles fail to compensate for this fragmentation which might have been avoided by more careful editing.

The concluding remarks by Eric W. Orts, visiting professor in the framework of the Fullbright programme, providing an American perspective on Belgian and UK environmental law, are an invigorating contribution to this book. The external perspective allows a final broad comparison of the two legal systems in the context of their national peculiarities. Yet this synthesis of the different contributions to the book should not merely be construed as an afterthought. A more thorough and concerted comparison and analysis of the various contributions would have done more justice to the individual contributions and would have considerably raised the profile of this publication.

ISABEL HENDRIX
FIELD, School of African and Oriental Studies
London

*Justice to Future Generations and the Environment* by Hendrik Ph. Visser 't Hooft. Kluwer, Dordrecht, 1999, 180 pp., £63.00 hb. ISBN 0792357566

The central question of environmental ethics is why, from a moral perspective, should we protect the environment? The answer given by this book is unapologetically anthropocentric in its reply: we must do so because we owe a duty to future generations of humans. Visser't Hooft places this moral duty within a Rawlsian theory of justice. Central to his argument is Rawls's first principle of justice, which states that each person is to have an equal right to the most extensive basic liberty compatible with a similar liberty for others. According to Visser't Hooft, future generations have an equal right to environmental resources because these are an essential prerequisite to the enjoyment of liberty. This principle of justice is said to enjoy 'regulative primacy', allowing of no trade-offs with other social aims.

The question that the author then poses is whether our subjective experience supports or limits this uncompromising position of objective ethics. While subjective feelings or motives typically conflict with our objective moral duties, Visser't Hooft claims that our personal motives in relation to the environment and future generations are more likely to be supportive of the ethical point of view. The essence of his argument is that we like to believe that our conception of the good life (whether in terms of research, monuments, or the natural environment) will have a future. But his argument goes beyond mere psychology: he also puts forward this continuity thesis as a moral theory of value that supports the theory of justice. This of course raises problems for liberal political theories such as Rawls's, which tend to promote the right over the good and which favour neutrality between different conceptions of the good. After all, as Visser't Hooft himself notes, environmental policies inevitably discriminate between such conceptions (for example, favouring cycling over car-driving). One way of resolving this problem in liberal terms is to argue that while the protection of *critical* natural capital is a necessary prerequisite for the exercise of *any* conception of the good, for the state to protect less crucial environmental resources conflicts with the neutrality principle. This is not, however, the line taken by Visser't Hooft, who claims that we should be passing on our current conception of the environmental good—both critical and non-critical—to future generations. His point—which is a fair one—is that we should assume that future generations will share our vision of the non-critical environment. However, in making this point, he fails to make it clear whether he has thereby shifted from a liberal to a communitarian position—the latter seeing no role for neutrality and seeing the right and the good as essentially one and the same.

While individual motivation may support the objective standpoint of justice in the way suggested by Visser't Hooft, it is a shame that he does not pay more attention to the structural factors that are equally likely to undermine it. He mentions the 'temporal myopia' which is a feature of capitalist societies, but appears to overlook the devastating impact that this might have on his argument. Certainly, we all have a longing for environmental posterity, but whether it is likely to be achieved via a short-termist economic system with an inbuilt need for economic growth remains debatable.

For a work of analytical jurisprudence, the book is perhaps not as clearly structured and tightly argued as one might have expected. Visser't Hooft's copious discussion of other theorists does not help in this regard: in a number of places, such discussion (and quotation) serves to hamper rather than to further the author's own argument. In content terms, analytical jurisprudence is very much what the book is about: despite the author's claims to the contrary, those looking for much in the way of practical policy details are likely to come away disappointed. The book would also have benefited from a more careful editorial eye: the apostrophe is misplaced enough times in words like 'doesn't' to become irritating; and particularly for an academic work, the author's use of the exclamation mark is, in my view, excessive. Weaknesses aside, some of the individual parts of the book are extremely enlightening and it provides a useful way in to the debate about future generations and the environment.

CHRIS HILSON
University of Reading
Reading

*Global Business Regulation* by John Braithwaite and Peter Drahos. Cambridge University Press, Cambridge, 2000. xvii + 704 pp., £19.95. ISBN 0521784999

When given this book to review, the first reaction of the present reviewer was whether he could manage to get through such a huge treatise in time for the editors of this yearbook! However, the effort of doing so was well worth it. Here is a book which, though not without some flaws, actually offers what it sets out to promise: a widely researched and interestingly argued thesis on the nature and development of global business regulation. It leaves the reader with a feeling that she/he has been exposed to a challenging alternative approach regarding the conceptualization of the problems associated with the topic and with a programme of action which reflects the concerns of the engaged scholars who produced it. It is a work to be argued with, disagreed with, but not discarded.

So to the content of this work. It is divided into three Parts: Part I offers an introduction to the methodology of the book, which will form the main focus of the review below. The one major criticism of this book lies with the construction of Part I. While it offers an overview of the analytical methodology of the work, this is done with, perhaps, too much thought for the non-technical reader. The result is that some of the wealth of analysis present in Part III of the book is not fully shown. Indeed, there is a degree of oversimplification of the concepts and methodologies employed with the result that one might draw the false conclusion that this is a rather superficial work. However, this is a criticism of technique and should not detract from the otherwise high quality of the latter parts of this work.

Part II deals with case studies from which the empirical material for the work is drawn. These include a chapter each on: property and contract (which includes intellectual property issues), financial regulation, corporations and securities, trade and competition, labour standards, the environment, nuclear energy, telecommunications, drugs, food, sea transport, road transport, and air transport. Inevitably, in so ambitious a work, some of these chapters do not do justice to their subject matter. In particular, chapter 10 on trade and competition, subsumes within it discussion of the very important topic of investor and investment promotion and protection, and the wider topic of the regulation of multinational enterprises through codes of corporate conduct. These matters are so central to the development of global business regulation that they should have been dealt with in a chapter of their own. On the other hand, chapters 7, on property and contract, and 9 on corporations and securities, offer a valuable historical account of the development of the basic legal building blocks from which all contemporary business regulation, whether national or global, derives. One could point, with ease, to other industries and sectors that are not featured here. Furthermore, insurance is mentioned in chapter 7 but not in its own right as a separate study. However, to expect the book to cover all major international industries is simply to expect too much. On the other hand, it requires the reader to be wary of making generalizations on the basis of the evidence here presented. There is some risk of this in Part III of the work, but the authors are well aware of the danger and do not invite the reader to take their conclusions as axiomatic, merely as supported by the evidence here presented. They are prepared to be told that they have committed errors, but assert that these will be insufficient in number to invalidate their conclusions (at 13).

Part III is the analytical heart of this work. It presents the following thesis. The growth of global business regulation has a long history, that can, in respect of certain legal concepts, be traced back to classical times (see chapter 7). The key to understanding why current types of business regulation exist lies not in realist theories of international relations (at 481), which focus on the inter-actions of nation states in the international system, nor in structural theories of sociology, with their emphasis on aggregated power between groups of actors (at 581), although this approach contributes to and complements the approach taken by the authors. Rather, the authors develop a more complex methodology that allows us to see the full range of interactions that contribute to the development of global regulatory norms and practices. They begin with a typology of significant actors (see chapter 20). These include: the nation state, which has hitherto been the most important actor but is now being decentred; intergovernmental organizations, whose influence varies accord-ing to how the dominant powers—the USA in particular—perceive them (on which see further chapter 24); business itself through lobbying efforts; indi-viduals who have significant personal influence arising from their positions as leaders of corporations or industries, or as leading intellectuals or activists; non-governmental organizations (NGOs) and mass publics as repositories of popular views on matters germane to business regulation; and epistemic communities of experts who, through their interactions *inter se* and with other types of actors, can create dialogues from which policies, and policy consen-sus, can emerge.

Secondly, the authors stress the importance of contests of principles between actors as the basis for the evolution of international business regu-lation (chapter 21). Here the most strengthened principle is seen to be that of transparency, while national sovereignty is seen to be the most declining. The most important historical contest has been between reciprocity and most-favoured-nation/national treatment principles. Equally contests have occurred in relation to strategic trade and deregulation. Although the latter is seen, rhetorically, as the most important principle by states, it is in practice opposed and contained by strategic trade concerns, in that while states may argue for liberalization and deregulation they will hold out for exceptions in relation to industries in which they have a major interest. The main contest stressed by the authors, which forms the basis of the policy agenda ad-vocated in the final chapter (chapter 26), is that between the lowest cost location for business and that of ratcheting up regulatory standards. In con-cluding this part of their discussion, the authors distinguish between the tra-ditional concept of the 'rule of law', with its seemingly impartial emphasis on individual autonomy of action in the context of rules enacted by a neutral state, and what they term the 'rule of principles', which informs the reality of international business regulation through the continuing contest between competing principles upon which the conduct of such business should be based. They do so to avoid the false objectivity of 'rule of law' analysis, point-ing out that this doctrine, when applied in the international business sphere, is used as an instrumental tool for the furtherance of a liberal version of free-dom (at 531).

Thirdly, the mechanisms of globalization are considered (chapter 22). These include: military coercion, which the authors were surprised to find had a significant influence, mainly as a result of the war aims of the victorious allies in the Second World War, which included the building of a more liberal international economic order; economic coercion and rewards, which were used as a last resort if reciprocal negotiations failed; capacity building and, finally, modelling, which is seen as the most important mechanism. It rests on 'observational learning with a symbolic content, not just the simple response mimicry implied by the term "imitation" ' (at 580). It is based on, 'conceptions of action portrayed by words and images' (ibid.). Its main function is to spread specific types of regulatory regimes by reason of their use as 'models' for wider adoption. This can occur through coercion, as in the case of the spread of Western notions of property, contract, and legal order through the process of colonialism, or it can occur through webs of dialogue and persuasion (on which see chapter 23).

On the basis of these building blocks the authors conclude that the development of international business regulation has been led by the hegemonic USA, spurred on by the lobbying of its leading corporations, whose influence can be seen most pervasively in those fields where they are the dominant actors, as, for example, in intellectual property. At times this analysis hints at a degree of institutionalized corruption, as where an anonymous US trade official suggests that the USA is a 'client state' of big business and that, 'the President likes it when business leaders get the trade agenda they want because they then reward him with support for his next campaign' (at 219). The authors also emphasize, in several places, the disempowerment of the UN Conference on Trade and Development (UNCTAD), the only intergovernmental organization specifically set up to champion the interests of developing countries in the economic sphere (at 67–8, 194–5, 486, 505–6, and 566). This is explained by reference to the concept of 'forum shifting' whereby the USA, as the most powerful state, could move certain issues out of the UN Conference on Trade and Development (UNCTAD), which had a built-in developing country majority given its one-country–one vote system, to new bodies where it could wield more influence. Thus, intellectual property went to the World Trade Organization (WTO) (at 566), while competition issues went to WTO and to the Organization for Economic Cooperation and Development (OECD) (at 567), and sea transport Liner Codes went to a new organization led by the USA, the Consultative Shipping Group (at 567).

From this the authors mistakenly conclude that UNCTAD is an irrelevant organization and they omit to mention it in Table 20.1, which lists the most influential actors in the globalization of regulation. UNCTAD continues to wield influence through the 'dialogic webs' in which it participates. It has, for example, consultative status on both the Trade and Competition and the Trade and Investment Working Groups in the WTO. Furthermore, in the field of investment issues, UNCTAD has continued to organize meetings, workshops, and seminars involving government officials, business, NGOs, and members of relevant epistemic communities over many years. What has gone is a direct negotiating mandate for a UN Code of Conduct on Transnational Corporations (the Draft Code). However, if, as the authors assert, the most important method of furthering new policies on international business regulation is not the making of rules as such, but the production of models for engagement in a process of persuasion through webs of influence, UNCTAD may well be on the way to a revival. Given the greater consciousness of developing country concerns after the failure of the Multilateral Agreement on Investment (MAI) in the OECD—a case of forum-shifting by the USA that went spectacularly wrong, and which is not given sufficient coverage in this book (perhaps due to production delays?)—and after the failure of the Seattle Ministerial in 1999, as a result of bungled consensus building before the meeting by the USA and the WTO itself, the role of UNCTAD may well be of increasing significance as the 'OECD for developing countries' (authors' description at 195). Even the defunct Draft Code has continuing influence as a 'model' for a socially responsible international investment regime. Why else would the WTO Working Group on Trade and Investment have asked UNCTAD to produce a study of the Draft Code and the OECD Guidelines for Multinational Enterprises in 1998 as part of its programme for studying the development of multilateral investment rules? Furthermore, UNCTAD has produced numerous publications, including the widely respected annual *World Investment Report*, on the questions that occupy the agendas of concerned NGOs, including the social responsibility of transnational corporations and competition as a technique for regulating international business, a matter the authors address in their closing chapter. The main criticism from NGOs has been that UNCTAD is not radical enough, which may be seen as a hangover from the attacks made against this body in the past. It must remain cautious and relatively free from interest group capture if it is to regain its status. This may well be an effect of forum shifting that needs further analysis and which is not touched upon by the authors.

Finally, the book concludes with a chapter on policy for civil society groups. This begins by reviewing more utopian schemes for civil society influence, such as a Second Assembly for the UN. However, the thrust of the chapter is elsewhere. Conscious of the fact that the picture they present may be rather cynical (at 220), the authors end by showing how concerned NGOs can shift the debate away from industry-specific concerns towards a more socially responsive agenda from the perspective of what they term 'popular sovereignty which, they feel, still remains a powerful source of opinion even where national and parliamentary sovereignties may be weakened by globalization' (see chapter 26). This may be especially true where national groups, working together to influence international agendas before international bodies, might have more influence than those same groups working individually in national political contexts, where independent national sovereignty may be weak. The prescription is centred on consumer groups and advocates a two-pronged approach: first, action to improve regulatory standards in areas of concern to consumers, such as product safety or pollution controls, and, secondly, to call for stronger competition control over corporate monopolization of economic power. These are not seen as exclusive and other agendas, such as environmental protection or human rights are also mentioned. Furthermore, alliances may be struck with governments and business on specific issues, especially where the latter can be persuaded that a raising of regulatory standards is in their interests as it enhances product quality, or that increased competition is a good for all to further.

Paradoxically, the authors see UNCTAD as an important lobbying site in this process (at 621). Indeed, they feel that linking the raising of regulatory standards with enhanced competition regulation is a way to avoid the fate of the UN Centre for Transnational Corporations (UNCTC) which was, they say, wound up as a result of US pressure following the collapse of negotiations of the Draft Code (at 193). In fact the UNCTC was not wound up. It was moved to Geneva where UNCTAD took over responsibility for it. It was then redesignated. Its successor is the Division on Investment, Technology and Enterprise Development (DITE), the body responsible for much of the work outlined above. It is a body that NGOs may well find useful to lobby, alongside the more obvious targets such as the WTO or OECD, whose apparent strength as intergovernmental organizations seems, to this reviewer, to have been overstated by the authors.

In all, this book promises a great deal. It gets better as one ploughs through its voluminous pages. There is much here to draw upon: specific facts from the industry sectors and issue areas covered in Part II, an analytical model that owes much to the social action programmes and strategies followed, in the recent past, by the feminist and environmental movements and, to a lesser extent, by the consumer movement, and an aspiration that through the process of dialogue, persuasion, and conflicts of principles, based on the use of oppositional regulatory models, a more democratically formed system of international business regulation will emerge. However, one is left with the feeling that this approach assumes so much that is absent in many of the countries engaged in the process of economic globalization. In particular, the effectiveness of the 'modelling' principle of action must surely depend on: a relatively good level of general education so that such devices might be properly appreciated and discussed; access to relevant information for sophisticated discussion to be possible; access to the media for the dissemination of oppositional ideas offered by what the authors acknowledge are weak actors; a liberal and tolerant political order that sees some benefit in pluralism on the question of global economic ordering and, finally, educational institutions, such as research institutes and universities, and NGOs that are sufficiently free and unbiased so that they can become credible sources of alternative policy-making. Such conditions may only exist in the Western liberal democracies, and even here this may be doubted. The protesters on the streets of Seattle were out there not because they were stupid, neocommunist stooges, but because they felt no other means of empowerment. This book suggests that

NGOs with the right policy agenda can fill the democratic void. Perhaps all they will do is paper it over?

PETER MUCHLINSKI
Queen Mary and Westfield College
University of London
London

*Smart Regulation: Designing Environmental Policy* by Neil Gunningham and Peter Grabosky (with Darren Sinclair). Oxford University Press, Oxford, 1998. xx + 494 pp., £45.00 hb. ISBN 0198268572

A long time ago I remember reading a little book by Neil Gunningham about pollution and the law (*Pollution, Social Interest and the Law* (Martin Robinson, 1974)). Rooted in social theory, its basic theme was that much pollution goes unpunished because powerful industrial interests are able to dominate legislative policy-making. The message seemed to be: to reflect properly the social interest in the environment, a tough command-and-control system ought to be imposed on polluters. Is this—I ask myself—the same Neil Gunningham who is the lead author of an excellent and substantial new monograph on environmental regulations and in which it is argued 'there are compelling reasons of efficiency, effectiveness and political acceptability for preferring the *least* interventionist combinations [of regulation] that will work' (my italics)?

Perhaps theory has moved on; or the world has moved on, or writers on environmental law, such as Professor Gunningham, have moved on ... Whatever may be the explanation, the new book is a most welcome addition to the Oxford Socio-Legal series. It provides one of the most rounded and thought-provoking analyses of regulation that has emerged in recent years.

Its avowed aim is to show how environmental regulation can be redesigned to operate optimally (which here refers to the assumed core goals of protection, thus including considerations of equity and fairness). Its strength lies in its forward-looking approach. Its authors argue that the typical methodology which painstakingly examines serially the strengths and weaknesses of single, existing instruments of environmental protection have become sterile. A more promising, and necessarily more innovative, methodology is required which both has regard to developing new administrative and commercial devices and involves a mix of, or synergy between, them and more conventional legal instruments. The authors also distance themselves from the ideological struggle between the ecologist camp and the deregulationist camp: an open pragmatic perspective, they contend is more fruitful.

Nor does the discussion become too abstract or theoretical. Although there is an illuminating overview of different strategies in the first part of the book—and this helpfully concentrates on education, information, and economic instruments alongside conventional command-and-control regulation—the next part (some 240 pages) is devoted to intensive studies of pollution control in two specific sectors, the chemical and agricultural industries. What emerges from the first of these, rapidly changing, fields of operation is that increasingly non-traditional and largely industry-designed, rather than government-imposed, standards and techniques are proving to be the most successful. The story from the agricultural sector is less encouraging, but in essence the message is the same: the problems of overcoming deeply entrenched attitudes, perverse incentive structures, and high monitoring costs can, it is argued, be successfully overcome only by innovative methods.

The themes are drawn together and re-orchestrated in the overlong (77 pages) concluding chapter. Here the authors highlight what are, for them, the essential ingredients of 'smart' environmental regulation, notably: appropriate processes which systematically consider the problems and range of instruments capable of generating solutions; and appropriate principles which are likely to involve low degrees of state intervention, effective participation by third parties, and, most important of all, a mixture of the available instruments. An investigation of what good instruments can usefully complement what other instruments occupies a good third of this final chapter. It is a highly original, and extremely valuable discussion but should, perhaps, have come earlier in the exposition.

It might seem churlish to end a review of this outstanding book by drawing attention to matters which are not sufficiently addressed within its 450 pages. The applicability of the novel instruments to small enterprises is not given adequate attention. Large firms may be the major polluters, but much pollution results from less significant actors and it is far from clear that they are (or would be) as responsive to the new instruments and techniques as much of the discussion implies. Secondly, there is an increasingly international dimension to environmental protection. This involves not merely the problematic phenomenon of transboundary pollution. It also concerns the interaction between the different regulatory systems in different jurisdictions and the extent to which competition between the latter leads to a 'race to the bottom'. While there is no lack of literature on this subject, it has rarely ventured into the complementarity of old and novel instruments which is such a valuable feature of this book. Finally—and this is to complete the circle—has Professor Gunningham totally forgotten his 1974 book? No doubt it is naïve to accept unqualifiedly the public choice story that most regulation is demanded by, and benefits, those who are regulated; but it is equally naïve to dismiss it completely. The institutional or the constitutional means of constraining the opportunistic manipulation of regulatory means to personal ends still requires to be considered.

All this is intended not as a criticism. The ideas which abound in this volume are rich indeed, and additional dimensions can be provided by others, working on the foundations so successfully laid by Gunningham *et al.*

ANTHONY OGUS
University of Manchester
Manchester

*Intellectual Property Rights, Trade and Biodiversity* by Graham Dutfield. Earthscan, London, 2000. 238 pp., £35.00. ISBN 1853836923

Dutfield's work constitutes an original and thorough overview of the intricate web of links between intellectual property, trade, and environmental studies focusing in particular on issues of biodiversity. The book is 238 pages long. The main text is 131 pages. A further 61 pages (Appendix 5, pp. 157–218) are dedicated to a useful and comprehensive annotated bibliography; each reference incorporates keywords and a short abstract. This is a methodical way of organizing information that could be 'lost' in long endnotes. The main text includes references to this bibliography and notes at the end of each chapter. Dutfield has compiled a much longer annotated bibliography with the support of the World Wide Fund for Nature International; without assuming that his selection for this shorter version is based on qualitative criteria we can still use it as a strong starting point for exploring this area. The remaining appendices include statements and recommendations from various organizations and a list of Neem-related patents. These patents, issued by the USPTO in the period between 1985 and 1998, were for inventions based on the Neem-tree that used public domain traditional knowledge as a springboard. Interspersed throughout the book are seven case studies, six tables, and seven 'boxes' of information illustrating particular points.

The first four chapters of the book (at 1–40) constitute an introduction to, and review of, the problems as perceived by Dutfield. Plant genetic resources for agriculture are essential to the development of agriculture and have the potential for contributing in an awe-inspiring way to human welfare and global wealth. Albeit, the primary interaction, and potential source of conflict, is described at p. 2: 'Most of the seed companies best able to add value to the germplasm are located in the North. However, since most of the world's biodiversity-rich countries are developing countries located in the tropics, one might assume that these nations are in a strong position to benefit substantially by trading in crop genetic resources . . . In fact this is far from the case. With pharmaceuticals, biodiversity-rich countries may be in a slightly stronger position to dictate favourable terms of access to genetic resources. With plant genetic resources for the seed industry, the bargaining positions of individual biodiversity-rich developing countries are generally weak and the benefit sharing possibilities are less promising.' Dutfield suggests that there are six main reasons for this: difficulties in apportioning the benefits; interdependence, in relation to genetic resources between countries; the fact that 'a great deal of germplasm is held in *ex situ* collections'; the commercial realities in crop breeding that tend to exclude exotic landraces and wild varieties from breeding programmes; the lack of relevant scientific and technological means in developing countries; and, finally, the fact that biodiversity-rich developing countries may still have to import crop germplasm from agro-biodeversity-rich countries that have cultivated certain major food crops for very long periods of time. In reviewing the development of intellectual property in developed economies Dutfield highlights some recent trends (broadening the scope of existing rights, creating *sui-generis* rights, and a process of 'standardization of the basic features' of intellectual property rights, at p. 9) and the role and imbalances of intellectual property in international trade. He then looks at the international regulatory regime, briefly at the Trade Related aspects of Intellectual Property Rights (TRIPs) Agreement and the UPOV Convention (the International Convention for the Protection of New Varieties and Plants) and, in greater detail, at the CBD Convention (the Convention on Biological Diversity) concentrating on some of the most relevant Articles.

From the perspective of an intellectual property lawyer, the descriptions of intellectual property rights are sometimes partial. A trade mark for example is defined, at p. 25, in the context of TRIPs, as a 'marketing tool that is often used to support a company's claim that its products or services are authentic or distinctive compared with similar products or services from another trading entity'. However, it is the distinctive capacity of the sign that transforms it to a trade mark, a communicator that deserves protection because it enables consumers to choose; only then the sign can be used as a 'marketing tool', whatever 'marketing' means. Perhaps, a more analytical discussion on the nature and scope of intellectual property rights would help the reader understand better the most important parts of Dutfield's work that follow this introductory general overview. For example, on the function of names a very interesting comment is made at pp. 65–6 where it is noted that local communities object when patent claims include names of their own folk varieties, 'especially when these communities depend on exporting these varieties to countries where such a patent is held'. At p. 70, Dutfield makes the point that trade marks and geographical indications may be appropriate forms of protecting products based on traditional knowledge even if they cannot protect the knowledge as such. These questions are also explored in chapter 6.

Chapter 5 is where Dutfield delineates the fundamental issue: is there conflict or synergy between intellectual property rights and biodiversity? There are two key questions. First, whether intellectual property encourages the spread of monocultural agriculture. And second, at p. 44, whether 'the increasing production and sale of seed-agrochemical "packages" (such as transgenic crops sold with pesticides and/or herbicides for which they have built-in resistance) [is] harmful to biodiversity? And if so are Intellectual Property Rights (IPRs) an inducement for companies to produce these kinds of "package"? In other words, is this an IPR issue?' Dutfield shows that there is no clear answer that can be given to such questions. Intellectual property rights must not be seen in isolation, 'the evidence so far indicates that IPRs are at most one of several factors that together cause biodiversity erosion', at p. 55. However, these issues are so sensitive and fundamental, both in a social and environmental context, that there is an incessant need for further research and studies. This is further illustrated by Dutfield's examination of plant variety rights and consideration of relevant transfer of technology issues. Of great interest is his discussion on the parallels between intellectual property and traditional knowledge, in particular his critique of the position of Stenson and Gray that 'moral entitlement theories do not justify indigenous peoples' intellectual property rights over their knowledge', at p. 62. Dutfield is drawing an analogy between the taking of indigenous peoples' knowledge and obtaining patents for inventions based upon this knowledge with the doctrine of *terra nullius,* setting that sparsely populated wilderness is vacant prior to colonization. 'According to such a view, open access is the rule for land, traditional know-ledge and resources, whereas enclosure is the rule as soon as these are proved to have economic value', at p. 63. He establishes that there is a valid argument in that if indigenous peoples are required to accept the existence of the patent system then their own knowledge-related regimes should be respected by others, pointing to the fact that in some jurisdictions (including the USA and Japan) undocumented traditional knowledge held abroad is not considered part of the prior art. Further, patents with broad claims may, mistakenly, cover non-original subject matter. This is a weakness of the patent system that can-not be easily challenged by impoverished or isolated community groups. But informed ignorance not only undermines the patent system itself but also fails to take into account the fact that we are all destined to live together and co-operate.

Chapters 6, 7, 8, and 9 constitute essential reading for intellectual property lawyers and anyone who wants to comprehend the challenge that biodiversity issues impose on intellectual property regimes. Dutfield identifies the solu-tions provided currently and in many cases suggests a way forward. At the end, the reader, irrespective of whether she/he agrees with the suggestions of the author, is left with a much clearer picture. Chapter 6 is an attempt to reconcile the CBD with TRIPs. Chapter 7 gives an overview of international develop-ments that passes through intellectual property and biodiversity. Chapter 8 presents examples of governmental and regional initiatives. And chapter 9 looks at non-governmental initiatives and proposals.

Chapter 10 concludes this work by focusing on unresolved questions and providing recommendations. Dutfield accepts that it is unclear how far intel-lectual property affects biodiversity but stresses that we may not have the time to wait for conclusive evidence before acting in order to achieve the ultimate goal, that is 'environmentally sound IPRs'. Indeed, international developments in this area, sometimes running in parallel and at other times diverging or in conflict, show that there is an urgent need for a global, open, informed, and clear debate. Dutfield provides a valid and valuable contribution to this debate.

SPYROS M. MANIATIS
Queen Mary and Westfield College
London

# DOCUMENTS

LUDWIG KRÄMER*

## I. Summaries of Communications, Green Papers, and White Papers

### A. COMMISSION COMMUNICATION ON SUSTAINABLE URBAN DEVELOPMENT IN THE EUROPEAN UNION: A FRAMEWORK FOR ACTION[1]

The Communication develops a four-tiered framework for action:

(1) strengthening economic prosperity and employment. This tier will address urban programming more explicitly with the Structural Fund as its main instrument. Inter-urban cooperation and attractive urban transport will be promoted, and employment policies in agglomerations addressed;

(2) to promote social inclusion and regeneration in urban areas, cooperation against social discrimination and social exclusion. Action for urban regeneration, and an exchange of know-how are suggsted;

(3) protecting and improving the urban environment requires that European Community (EC) legislation is better implemented, further legislation on air, water, noise, and waste will be developed, pollution control improved, the environmental impact of urban transport reduced, and energy managed more effciently. Climate-change measures should be developed, the application of the eco-audit-schemes promoted, and financial support and know-how exchange increased;

(4) good urban governance and local empowerment includes, *inter alia*, the prevention of urban crime, improved information supply, and a raising of awareness. An annex details the challenges for European towns and cities.

The Communication does not propose a financial programme or any other form of support. It proposes to observe, with a group of experts, progress in the implementation of the proposed actions, which are mainly to be implemented by local, regional, and national authorities.

---

* European Commission, DG Environment; Professor of Law, University of Bremen, Germany. Documents published between 1/10/1998 and 31/12/2000. Opinions expressed are personal to the author.
[1] COM(98)605, 28 Oct. 1998.

### B. COMMISSION COMMUNICATION ON THE COMMON TRANSPORT POLICY. SUSTAINABLE MOBILITY: PERSPECTIVES FOR THE FUTURE[2]

Although the word 'sustainable' appears in the title, the Communication does not in any way define the notion. The Communication is structured in seven sections dealing with, respectively, a framework for sustainable mobility, future developments, improving efficiency and competitiveness, improving quality, improving effectiveness, longer-term perspectives, and finally, conclusions.

The environment is only marginally accommodated in these sections. Section IV observes that the development of transport systems must not be at the expense of the environment, and recalls that environmental requirements shall be integrated into the common transport policy. Some specific actions are mentioned, such as a future communication on air transport and the environment,[3] a directive on waste reception facilities in ports, and the Communication on Heavy Goods Vehicles.[4] Section VI notes that, in future, it will be necessary to assess more globally to what extent existing policy measures will bring the transport sector in line with environmental objectives. Alpine transport is mentioned as an area which will have to be addressed in order to find a replacement for the present ecopoint system, which comes to an end in 2003.

### C. COMMISSION COMMUNICATION ON DIRECTIONS TOWARDS SUSTAINABLE AGRICULTURE[5]

The Communication is divided into five parts. A short introduction (1) is followed by two lengthy sections on farming and the environment (2) and policy reforms (3). Section (4) deals very summarily with the need for agri-environmental indicators and section (5) consists of a short conclusion.

The introduction places the Communication in the general context of the common agricultural policy (CAP), and in particular its latest reform, which forms part of Agenda 2000.[6] In this regard it states that:

[this reform], in addition to adjustments of market regimes to the conditions facing farming in the new century, . . . . would develop a coherent integrated rural development policy as a second pillar of the CAP, largely financed from the guarantee section of the EAGFF. . . . The essence of the environmental elements of the proposals is that farmers should observe a minimum level of environmental practice as part-and-parcel of the support regimes, but that any additional environmental service, beyond the basic level, should be paid for by society through the agri-environment programmes.

---

[2] COM(98)716, 1 Dec. 1998.

[3] This Communication is summarized elsewhere in the Documents Section of this volume.

[4] See the report on that Communication in (2000) 1 *Yearbook of European Environmental Law*, 563–4.

[5] COM(99)22, 27 Jan. 1999.

[6] See Commission, Agenda 2000—For a Stronger and Wider Union COM(97)2000, 15 July 1997.

Section (2) details the environmental problems caused by intensification, specialization, and marginalization in agriculture, sketches the development in organic farming, and pays attention to the impact of farming on water, soil, climate change, biodiversity, and landscape. The figures which are mentioned show that: use of fertilizer in farming has risen from 5 million tonnes in 1950 (nutrients) to currently 16 million tonnes; use of pesticide shows a similar trend, with about 300,000 tonnes per annum in 1996. Organic farms increased in number from 35,476 in 1993 to 93,830 in 1997, although this still only accounts for about 1 per cent of all agricultural holdings. Soil erosion, which is also a result of unsustainable agricultural practices, is increasing. At present, about 115 million hectares suffer from water erosion, and 42 million hectares from wind erosion. About 20 per cent of agricultural land is currently covered by agri-environmental measures,[7] which means that the target of the 5th Environmental Action Programme (15 per cent by 2000) was exceeded, although five Member States account for 86 per cent of the area.

While pursuing the production of food, fibre, and fuel for subsistence or for profit, farmers have in fact provided environmental, social, and amenity benefits for free. Farmers have historically and to a large extent unwittingly been responsible for the development and stewardship of the landscape. This observation introduces section (3), the discussion of policy reforms. The Communication describes the challenge to reach a sustainable agriculture as follows:

The international pressures on domestic markets, resulting from increased productivity and a slower increase or even a long-term decline in consumption in some key sectors (notably cereals and beef), have led to the conclusion that farming must become more efficient and respond better to consumer demands. In the international context, Europe needs to be in a position to take advantage in the expected growth in global consumer demand for many products, such as cereals, beef, value-added milk products. To respond to these challenges, farmers will have to assess their practices carefully, and further optimise their use of factors of production. However, in order to ensure that the necessary reorientation of the CAP and European agriculture does not lead to an environmentally damaging intensification of production and abandonment of marginal land, policies are required to develop EU agriculture on a sustainable path, ensuring an environmentally sound, economically viable, and socially acceptable European model of agriculture.

The underlying philosophy is made explicit in the introduction to the Communication: 'wherever society desires that farmers deliver an environmental service beyond this base-line level, this service should be specifically purchased through the agri-environment measures.' The Communication does not clarify, what the 'base-line level' is, but links it to 'good agricultural practice', without specifying this term either.

---

[7] 'The agri-environment programmes offer payments to farmers who, on a voluntary and contractual basis, provide environmental services to protect the environment and maintain the countryside.'

The Communication then examines how, under this system, Member States can provide for appropriate environmental measures, and suggests to link these measures to 'payments granted directly to farmers'. These payments are obviously to be made by Member States which thus have to link environmental measures and financial support to farmers. Similar solutions are suggested in common market organizations. The Communication also suggests an increase in agri-environment measures and their financing, rural development measures, compensation allowances in less favoured areas, and examines ways to financially support sustainable forestry.

The conclusion once more is that farmers should be paid for any environmental service which goes beyond the basic level of good agricultural practice, which thus may be the principal message conveyed by the Communication.

### D. COMMISSION COMMUNICATION ON THE SINGLE MARKET AND THE ENVIRONMENT[8]

The Communication seeks to contribute to making the two policies—open markets and environmental protection—'mutually supportive and reinforcing, whilst at the same time developing positive synergies between them'. The Communication thus revolves around the integration requirement of Article 6 EC. After having presented the relevant provisions and principles of the EC Treaty, the Communication describes different product-related policies, such as standardization, public procurement, or transport. An annex provides some examples of environmental aspects of the free movement of goods.

The Communication will not be analysed here, as it is reproduced in full elsewhere in this volume. In the present writer's opinion, however, the Communication is clearly written with an emphasis on the internal market, promoting the free circulation of goods rather than the protection of the environment. Some presentations appear ambiguous, in particular those on waste and packaging waste, standardization, public procurement, and vehicles.

At p. 24 of the Communication, the Commission considers Swedish legislation to ban trichlorethylene disproportionate and incompatible with the EC Treaty. In the meantime, the ECJ decided differently, and accepted that the Swedish legislation strikes an appropriate balance between the need to protect the environment and the free circulation of goods.[9] This example shows that the opinions expressed in the Communication are not necessarily legally authoritative.

### E. COMMISSION COMMUNICATION ON FISHERIES MANAGEMENT AND NATURE CONSERVATION IN THE MARINE ENVIRONMENT[10]

The Communication is an expression of the integration requirement for environmental policy, laid down in Article 6 EC. It stresses that overexploitation of

---

[8]  COM(99)263, 8 June 1999
[9]  Case C–473/98, *Kemikalieinspektionen* v. *Toolex Alpha AB* [2000] ECR I–5681.
[10]  COM(99)363, 14 July 1999.

fish continues seriously to affect Community fisheries, and results in excessive pressure on marine ecosystems. Scientific experts have now recommended rapid reductions of exploitation levels of up to 40 per cent, in particular for cod, haddock, hake, plaice, and herring. The primary cause of overexploitation is excess catch capacity.

Section (2) explores interactions between fisheries and marine ecosystems, and the consequences thereof. Section (3) describes the legal context of EC legislation and international aspects. Section (5) defines the Community objectives which are:

— the reduction of pressure caused by fisheries, which means that the number of vessels and their effectiveness must be reduced;
— the conservation of the marine environment, including the protection of habitats, marine animal species, and space/time limits on fisheries activities;
— the integrated management of coastal zones;
— improved vocational training, information, consultation, and research.

Section (6) discusses the strategy to be adopted in international fora. The conclusion summarizes the main points of the Communication.

### F. COMMISSION COMMUNICATION ON IMPLEMENTING THE COMMUNITY STRATEGY TO REDUCE CO$_2$ EMISSIONS FROM CARS: OUTCOME OF THE NEGOTIATIONS WITH THE JAPANESE AND KOREAN AUTOMOBILE INDUSTRIES[11]

In the previous volume of the *Yearbook*, the environmental agreement on CO$_2$ reductions with the European car industry was discussed at some length.[12] The present Communication reports on the outcome of the negotiations with the Japanese and Korean car industries with a view to concluding a similar agreement with them.[13] The Communication considers that the agreements with these industries are equivalent to the one made with European car manufacturers, although it draws attention to some differences. The target value of CO$_2$ emissions per car of 140g CO$_2$/km will be met in 2009, one year later than the European car industry. The intermediate target for Japanese car manufacturers is 165–75 g CO$_2$/km, to be reached by 2003. The intermediate target for Korean car manufacturers is to be reached in 2004 only. Furthermore, the European car industry committed itself to put models of 120 g CO$_2$/km on the European market no later than by 2000, while Korean car manufacturers commit themselves to make every effort to introduce such cars 'as soon as possible'.

---

[11] COM(99)446, 14 Sept. 1999.    [12] See n. 4 above, 565.

[13] See also Commission Rec. 2000/303/EC on the Reduction of CO$_2$ Emissions from Passengers Cars (KAMA) [2000] OJ L100/55, with the Korean car manufacturers; and Commission Rec. 2000/304/EC on the Reduction of CO$_2$ Emissions from Passengers Cars (JAMA) [2000] OJ L100/57, with the Japanese car manufacturers.

The Communication notes that the commitments need to be formally notified under the competition provision of Article 81 EC. In the previous Communication, it was merely stated that this might be necessary. Both agreements contain, in common with the previous agreement with the European car industry, a clause which effectively pre-empts legislation on car emissions:

As long as its commitments (see below) are being honoured, JAMA(KAMA) is assuming that this Commitment provides a complete and sufficient substitute for all new regulatory measures to limit fuel consumption or $CO_2$ emissions, and for any additional fiscal measures in pursuit of the $CO_2$ objectives of this Commitment. Any fiscal measures, including their added value to this Commitment, will be taken into account in the monitoring procedure and their potential effects will be assessed in good faith.

The structure of the car industry worldwide means that no free-rider problems are anticipated: the agreement is made with the Japanese and the Korean car manufacturers associations 'and has the support of all its members'. The Japanese agreement puts it more bluntly: 'who sell cars in the EU market.' Problems of new car manufacturers, not a member of the association, entering the market do not exist. However, this issue does demonstrate the problem of making an environmental agreement concerning, for instance, electrical and electronic goods, where there are 18,000 producers within the EC itself.

G. COMMISSION WORKING PAPER: THE COLOGNE REPORT ON
ENVIRONMENTAL INTEGRATION. MAINSTREAMING OF
ENVIRONMENTAL POLICY.[14] COMMISSION WORKING DOCUMENT:
FROM CARDIFF TO HELSINKI AND BEYOND. REPORT TO THE EUROPEAN
COUNCIL ON INTEGRATING ENVIRONMENTAL CONCERNS AND
SUSTAINABLE DEVELOPMENT INTO COMMUNITY POLICIES[15]

The Council of Heads of State and Government in Cardiff (June 1998) had asked the Commission and the Council to focus on integration, and to develop indicators to help monitor progress and make issues of integration more transparent for citizens. All relevant sections of the Council were asked to develop integration strategies with the Energy, Transport, and Agriculture Councils starting the process.

Two reports were prepared for the meetings of Heads of State and Government in Cologne (June 1999) and Helsinki (December 1999) which analysed progress in the integration of environmental requirements into other Community policies.

The Cologne Report is merely three pages long. It announces that the Commission is to develop 'sets of indicators' for assessing the integration of environmental concerns into transport, energy, and agricultural policies. This is linked to the decision that the Commission will abandon its Green Star System, which identified those actions at EC level with a significant impact on the environment. The report attributes its failure to 'its narrow scope and difficulties in attributing the green stars due to the limited information on the

---

[14] SEC(99)777, 26 May 1999.        [15] SEC(99)1941, 24 Nov. 1999.

environmental impact'. Significantly, however, the original concept was just the opposite: a green star in the Commission's work programme meant that the environmental impact of the measure had to be assessed before it was to be adopted by the Commission. A more plausible explanation for abandoning the system may reside in the reluctance of the Commission's administration to carry out these environmental impact assessments. The report proposes the replacement of the green stars by 'new integration strategies' which 'might operate on the basis of a tools guide including a screening list and a set of appropriate assessment methods'. The exact meaning of this ambiguous phrase remains unclear.

As regards climate change, the Commission considers that structural changes are necessary, especially in the transport and energy sectors. The Commission asserts it has made proposals in this area, but that the Council has been 'too slow' in adopting them. For agriculture, rural development with the promotion of environmental protection as its core is to become the second pillar of the Common Agricultural Policy.[16] For the Community structural funds, the report claims that 'new regulations (which were adopted in 1999 and extend till 2007) offer a host of tools for a better integration of the environmental dimension into regional and cohesion policy'. It would be up to Member States to ensure that integration is effectively taken care of in the framework of actual implementation. The report also touches upon issues of environment and employment as well as international issues ('it would be desirable that the WTO becomes more responsive to environmental concerns').

The annex to the report carries the title: 'review of the integration progress since 1997: "some examples" of successful integration.' The title is somewhat misleading since the mere publication of communications or reports cannot be presented as an example of successful integration.

The Helsinki Report is just five pages long. After an introduction, it outlines the 'Cardiff process', and describes the different integration reports. As regards transport strategy, the Commission recognizes that 'it will be necessary to define more clearly what sustainable transport actually means, and to develop long-term environmental targets for the sector'. Nothing substantive is said about energy questions. In the agricultural section, the Commission reiterates[17] that 'farmers have to bear the compliance costs of observing "good agricultural practice" including the respect of mandatory environmental legislation. More ambitious environmental objectives above this reference level can be pursued through payments to farmers for environmental services.' In the industry sector, work towards the development of an integration strategy is continued. Again, there is a need to develop clear policy targets. Internal market policy will try to achieve a balance between the free movement of goods and environmental protection, and will concentrate on the free move-

---

[16] The integration of environmental policy in the CAP is also dealt with in COM(99)22, summarized elsewhere in the Documents Section of this volume.
[17] Ibid.

ment of goods, standardization, and public procurement. In its conclusion, the report acknowledges that progress as regards integration of the environment is 'clearly uneven' and that, in particular, 'clear timetables for individual measures as well as objectives are largely absent which makes the monitoring of progress difficult'. The Commission undertakes to submit a new progress report in the Summer of 2001.

An annex to the report gives a more detailed analysis of the various integration strategies and reports by the Council.

### H. COMMISSION COMMUNICATION ON FOREST AND DEVELOPMENT: THE EC APPROACH[18]

The Communication defines the EC objectives in forest development cooperation, identifies areas for dialogue and assistance, and sets out actions to achieve these objectives. It confirms the EC's commitment to 'sustainable and social development, while fostering environmental protection'. This wording implies that 'sustainable development' does not, in itself, in the eyes of the Commission, include environmental aspects, an interpretation which is further supported by the wording used in the EC Treaty.

After a short introduction (1), section (2) describes the state of forestry in developing countries, and the diverging vested interests which affect sustainable forest management. The Commission indicates that the dilemma 'environmental conservation *versus* development' continues to exist and should be solved, it is submitted, 'through improved valuation of the non-tangible conservation benefits of forest management'. Section (3) enumerates international commitments in respect of (tropical) forest management. Section (4) deals with European Community action. It notes that:

The underlying concept [of EC policy] is that natural resource management, including forest use, is linked to sustainable socio-economic development. Forests cannot be sacrificed for development of other sectors, and the stage of development determines the framework for the treatment of forests. There may be conversion of forests, based on rational land-use planning, and harvest levels for overmature timber may exceed increment in the short run, as long as overall forest sustainability is maintained.

Section (5) describes the EC objectives based on Article 177 EC,[19] and suggests ways to achieve these (section (6) ), proposing a number of guidelines for financial and other assistance. Section (7) enumerates a number of operational principles, and section (8) concludes with some ideas intended to guide the EC aid programmes in the years to come. Overall, the Communication is mainly destined to guide development aid of the Community—and hopefully also that of Member States.

---

[18] COM(99)554, 4 Nov. 1999.
[19] Art. 177 EC: '1. Community policy in the sphere of development cooperation, which shall be complementary to the policies pursued by the Member States, shall foster: the sustainable economic and social development of the developing countries, and more particularly the most disadvantaged among them; the smooth and gradual integration of the developing countries into the world economy; the campaign against poverty in the developing countries.'

### I. COMMISSION COMMUNICATION ON AIR TRANSPORT AND THE ENVIRONMENT: TOWARDS MEETING THE CHALLENGES OF SUSTAINABLE DEVELOPMENT[20]

The Communication deals with the policy challenges in six parts, goals and strategies (1), improving technical standards and related rules (2), strengthening market incentives to improve environmental performance (3), assisting airports (4), stimulating technological improvement (5), and some conclusions and future monitoring (6). In the annexes, statistical data are provided, and the problem of air transport and climate change is discussed.

The Communication analyses various possibilities to improve the environmental performance of air transport. It does not indicate, by which means sustainable transport can be realized in the light of the rapid increase in the volume of air transport. Many measures which could be taken in theory are conditional upon developments at global level.

The Communication indicates that within the EC, about 15 per cent of the population is affected by aircraft noise, and that the last significant revision of noise stringency rules at international level dates back to 1977 which 'simply no longer represents state of the art engine and aircraft design technology'. The Communication pleads for serious attempts to adopt the more stringent noise levels agreed at the ICAO Conference in 2001. Should the Conference fail to agree more stringent standards, 'the Commission may have to propose European requirements, in close cooperation with other industrialized regions'.

As regards atmospheric emissions from airplanes, the Communication quotes estimates that $CO_2$ emissions will grow at 3 per cent annually between 1990 and 2015. It suggests to support work at international level aiming at more stringent standards for smoke, HC, CO, and $NO_x$. Significantly, $CO_2$ is excluded from this list. In fact, international work on $CO_2$ reduction from airplanes has not even started. The Communication does not clarify what the EC will do in case international work fails, or advances too slowly.

As regards air traffic delays and airspace congestion, the Communication states that the situation in Europe 'steadily deteriorated in 1998 and 1999' and approximately 350,000 flight hours are lost annually. As a remedy, it is suggested to give continued technical and organizational support to the bodies responsible.

The paper further pays attention to the taxation of kerosene, and detects clear political and environmental advantages of such a tax on all routes departing from Community airports. However, due to existing multilateral and bilateral commitments, such an approach cannot be decided unilaterally, but depends on 'progress in international fora'.

Environmental charges could be imposed on air transport, and the Communication sets out different options. It favours the introduction of such

[20] COM(99)640, 1 Dec. 1999

charges and prudently suggests their introduction by the EC should the ICAO Conference 2001 not be able to reach consensus in this regard.

Emission trading is briefly discussed, without leading to any conclusions. It is proposed to 'offset the environmental impact of industry growth by investments in carbon sinks (forestation etc.)', again, however, without further detail. The possibility to introduce environmental management schemes pursuant to Regulation (EC) No. 1836/93 and the conclusion of environmental agreements on $CO_2$ emissions are also considered.

Finally, the Communication discusses ways to assist airports in reducing noise levels, and priorities for further research in the sphere of air transport and the environment.

### J. COMMISSION COMMUNICATION ON A COMMUNITY STRATEGY FOR ENDOCRINE DISRUPTERS—A RANGE OF SUBSTANCES SUSPECTED OF INTERFERING WITH THE HORMONE SYSTEMS OF HUMANS AND WILDLIFE[21]

Endocrine disruption is a mechanism whose effects relate to the endocrine system, that is, development, growth, reproduction and behaviour of human beings and wildlife. There is growing concern about a range of substances which are suspected of interfering with the endocrine system—so-called 'endocrine disruptors.

The Communication consists of seven sections. In an introduction (1) the actual discussion on endocrine disruption is briefly explained. Section (2) states the objectives of the Communication which are 'to identify the problem of endocrine disruption, its causes and consequences' and 'to identify appropriate policy action on the basis of the precautionary principle in order to respond quickly and effectively to the problem, thereby alleviating public concern'. Section (3) examines the nature of endocrine disruptors, their effects and sources of exposure. There are two classes of substances which can cause endocrine disruption: 'natural' hormones such as oestrogen, progesterone, and testosteron, and man-made substances which include synthetically produced hormones and man-made chemicals designed for uses in industry. This last group comprises 'thousands of new and existing man-made chemicals . . . and which . . . may have unforeseen adverse or synergistic effects'.

The Communication cites documented examples of effects of endocrine disruptors on humans and wildlife. Section (4) addresses the need for further research, for international coordination, and communication with the public. Section (5) stresses the need for policy action, in particular the need to identify the substances under suspicion, and to collect independent scientific advice. Existing EC legislation on chemicals, including pesticides, may have to be adapted in order to address better specific problems of endocrine disruptors.

Section (6) develops a strategy for short-term, medium-term, and long-term action. For the short term, the Communication suggests establishing a priority list of substances for further evaluation. Subsequently, monitoring

---

[21] COM(99)706, 17 Dec. 1999.

programmes to estimate exposure to and effects of the substances on the list must be established. Special action may be necessary for specific types of consumer use. Exchange of information, data collection, and appropriate information for the public will also be necessary. In the medium term, endocrine disruptors will have to be identified and assessed, substitutes to be found, voluntary initiatives for phase-out of substances promoted, and research intensified. In the long term, EC legislation will have to be adapted in order to address the specific problems caused by endocrine disruptors. The conclusion (7) constitutes a résumé of the previous chapter.

A comprehensive annex lists and briefly describes EC legislation which deals with risk assessment and risk management.

The Communication indeed gives rise to 'general cause for concern'. It can only be hoped that the Communication is transformed into concrete action as quickly as possible.

### K. COMMISSION WHITE PAPER ON FOOD SAFETY[22]

The White Paper in the introduction underlines that Community food policy must aim at high food safety standards for consumers. 'The production and consumption of food is central to any society, and has economic, social and, in many cases, environmental consequences. . . . In addition, the state and quality of the environment, in particular the eco-systems, may affect different stages of the food chain. Environment policy therefore plays an important role in ensuring safe food for consumers.' Section (2) summarizes the principles of food safety. The general approach is that of a comprehensive, integrated approach, which requires that the role of all stakeholders in the food chain is clearly defined, that feed and fodder are traceable, that food policy is based on risk analysis and recurs, where appropriate, to the precautionary principle. Section (3) identifies as essential elements of food policy information-gathering and analysis—including monitoring and surveillance of data, and the establishment of alert systems—as well as collection of scientific advice.

The central message of the White Paper is found in Section (4): 'The Commission envisages the establishment of an independent European Food Safety Authority, with particular responsibilities for both risk assessment and communication on food safety issues.' The Commission believes that such an authority can restore consumer confidence and retain it. The objective of the future Authority's risk assessment is to generate scientific advice. It is not envisaged to transfer regulatory powers to the Authority. There are three objections against such an approach: dilution of democratic accountability, necessity to retain the functions of regulation and control in the hands of the Commission, and legal obstacles, under the provisions of the present Treaty, to transfer regulatory powers to the Authority. The Authority would therefore have the task to prepare and provide scientific advice, collect and analyse

---

[22] COM(99)719, 12 Jan. 2000.

information, to monitor and control developments which touch on food safety issues, and to communicate its findings to all interested parties. Its legal personality should be separate from the EC institutions. Particular attention must be given to the independence of the Authority. As regards regulatory aspects, section (5) refers to, in particular, a general food law, a new legal framework for animal feed, a proposal on novel food, a coordinated and holistic approach towards hygiene, the possibility of taking emergency measures and, generally, a streamlining and simplifying of the decision-making process at Community level. Section (6) deals with controls, which will be the subject of a 'comprehensive piece of legislation'. Section (7) raises the problem of consumer information on risk communication, labelling, and advertising, and on the nutritional value of food. Section (8) details the increasingly important role of international regimes, in particular the activities of the World Trade Organization and the *Codex Alimentarius*. The paper concludes (9) that 'greater transparency at all levels of Food Safety is the golden thread throughout the whole White Paper, and it will contribute fundamentally to enhancing consumer confidence'.

An annex proposes an action plan on food safety. It will have to be seen, whether the announced measures will be adopted *sufficiently speedily* to restore consumer confidence in the EC. Alternatively, consumers will continue to rely on national governments to guarantee food safety.

### L. COMMISSION COMMUNICATION ON INDICATORS FOR THE INTEGRATION OF ENVIRONMENTAL CONCERNS INTO THE COMMON AGRICULTURAL POLICY[23]

Section (1) sketches the policy context for agri-environmental indicators, and explains that the request for such indicators originates from the European Council in Vienna (December 1998). In particular, it repeats the principle from earlier documents that farmers should respect general requirements as regards environmental care without specific payment. 'This means that all farmers should follow compulsory laws in relation to pesticide use, to fertilizer application, water use, and, where appropriate, national or regional guidelines on good farming practice. However, where society asks farmers to pursue environmental objectives beyond good farming practice, and the farmer incurs a cost or forgoes income as a result, then society must expect to pay for that environmental service.' The Communication submits that this approach is based on the polluter-pays principle. It is silent on the protection of landscapes, habitats and biodiversity, quality of air, water and soil, however. Many of these assets need protection, but in respect of many of these, no regulation exists. For instance, there are practically no rules which regulate the quantity of fertilizers to be used.

Sections (2) and (3) examine the development of indicators for agriculture and rural policies. It reports that, within the OECD, thirteen indicator subject

---

[23] COM(2000)20, 26 Jan. 2000.

areas have been identified which has led to some thirty actual indicators for short-term development, and more than twenty indicators for the medium–long term. Other bodies, such as Eurostat and the European Environment Agency have also worked in this area. The Communication clarifies, in section (4), what further steps are necessary to develop the indicators into an effective instrument for monitoring and evaluating agricultural policy and action. A full set of indicators does not yet exist. Their quality will depend on the statistics available. In that respect, careful assessment of existing data is needed as well as collection of further data. Indicators may improve communication, and make agricultural policy more transparent. In particular, a restricted list of headline indicators would be useful; although such a list may not fully reflect the complexities of agriculture, it could transmit information on broad trends.

## M. COMMISSION COMMUNICATION ON THE PRECAUTIONARY PRINCIPLE[24]

This short Communication—seventeen pages plus three pages of annexes—is reproduced in full elsewere in this volume. The paper seeks to provide 'general guidance' and, at the same time, aims to avoid 'unwarranted recourse to the precautionary principle'.

Where the Communication refers, in annex I, to the case law of the ECJ, it omits to discuss that in the BSE cases the ECJ referred to the principle of preventive action, and not to the precautionary principle.[25] There is no guidance on the difference between prevention and precaution. The 'prevention principle' is not discussed at all.

The Communication largely refers to specific, *ad hoc* decisions, as examples of the application of the precautionary principle. However, the principle of precaution also is relevant, for instance, whether to return to nuclear energy, or to admit genetically modified products on the market. Such long-term policy orientations, examples of which can be found in agricultural, or transport, energy, or regional policy, are not really capable of being submitted to the criteria suggested in the Communication. These criteria include proportionality, non-discrimination, consistency, benefits and costs of action or lack of action, and scientific developments.

The Commuication does not discuss, whether the notion 'precaution' used in the Rio Declaration 1992 is identical or equivalent to the notion as used by the Community—or by Member States such as Denmark, Germany, or Sweden. It would appear that these notions are different, however.

The Communication states that 'each Member of the WTO has the independent right to determine the level of environmental or health protection they consider appropriate. Consequently a member may apply measures, including measures based on the precautionary principle, which lead to a

---

[24] COM(2000)1, 2 Feb. 2000.
[25] Cases C–157/96, *R. v. Ministry of Agriculture* [1998] ECR I–2211; C–180/96 *United Kingdom* v. *Commission* [1998] ECR I–2265.

higher level of protection than that provided for in the relevant international standards or recommendations.' It is not obvious that public international law recognizes this statement as correct.

The Communication further states that 'the Commission considers that, following the example set by other members of the WTO, the Community is entitled to prescribe the level of protection, notably as regards the environment and human, animal, and plant health, which it considers appropriate'. Again, this statement it is not uncontroversial. It is doubtful whether, in the absence of EC legislation, the Commission also interprets Article 28 EC so that Members may fix the level of protection for the environment which they consider appropriate. If this is the case, however, an explicit corresponding statement in this sense would have been desirable. If this is *not* the case arguments for such a difference in approach would have been useful.

There therefore remains room for discussion on the precautionary principle and its legal importance in EC environmental law, as well as in public international law.

### N. COMMISSION WHITE PAPER ON ENVIRONMENTAL LIABILITY[26]

In 1986, following the Sandoz accident in Basel (Switzerland), the Council asked the Commission to consider whether it was appropriate to introduce a system of environmental liability at EC level. In 1993 the Commission submitted a Greenbook on Environmental Liability.[27] The EP, having organized a hearing on the issue, asked for the elaboration of an EC directive.[28] The Commission, confronted with reluctance from Member States to see environmental liability issues regulated at Community level, preferred to issue a White Paper.

The White Paper is structured in eight sections. A first section describes the activities which preceded the preparation of the White Paper. Section (2) tries to answer the question what environmental liability is. Section (3) presents the case for an EC environmental liability regime, and its expected effects, while section (4) outlines the general features of an EC liability regime. Section (5) discusses the different options for Community action: accession to the Lugano Convention, a regime for transboundary damage only, a recommendation, a directive, and systems of liability for different sectors (biotechnology, waste). Section (6) raises questions of subsidiarity and proportionality, followed by section (7) on the economic impact of an EC system. Finally, section (8) draws some conclusions, one of which is of particular interest here:

The Commission considers as the most appropriate option that of a Community Framework Directive on Environmental Liability, providing for strict liability—with

---

[26] COM(2000)66, 9 Feb. 2000.

[27] Communication from the Commission to the Council and Parliament and the Economic and Social Committee: Green Paper on Remedying Environmental Damage COM(93)17, 14 May 1993.

[28] Resolution of the European Parliament on Preventing and Remedying Environmental Damage [1994] OJ C128/165.

defences—with respect to traditional damage (namely damage to health and property) and environmental damage (contamination of sites and damage to biodiversity in Natura 2000 areas) caused by EC-regulated dangerous activities and fault-based liability for damage to such biodiversity caused by non-dangerous activities.

The paper is reproduced in full elsewhere in this volume.

### O. COMMISSION GREEN PAPER ON GREENHOUSE GAS EMISSIONS TRADING WITHIN THE EUROPEAN UNION[29]

The Green Paper is intended to be 'the start of a consultation process which will allow all stakeholders, both governmental and non-governmental, to give their opinions on how the EU should strike the right balance in the use of emissions trading'. It readily admits that it was the Kyoto Protocol, which was adopted in December 1997 by the Third Conference of the Parties to the UN Framework Convention on Climate Change, which has put emissions trading on the agenda of the European Community. This Protocol provides in its Article 17 that there should be, as of 2008, international trading of greenhouse gas emissions. Under the Protocol, the European Community committed itself to reducing its emissions of six greenhouse gases by 8 per cent during the period 2008 to 2012, in comparison with levels in 1990.

The Green Paper defines emissions trading as 'a scheme whereby companies are allocated allowances for their emissions of greenhouse gases according to the overall environmental ambitions of their government, which they can trade subsequently with each other' and goes on to explain its mechanism. The total of the allowances allocated represents the overall limit on emissions that is permitted. It explains how Member States agreed on how to redistribute the 8 per cent reduction among themselves ('burden-sharing'), and states that the Commission envisages to set up an EC-wide trading system by 2005 in order to be better prepared for the start of the international system. Such a system is best limited to some greenhouse gases and emission sources.

The Green Paper points out that Community-wide trading by energy producers and energy intensive industry could save about 1.7 billion euro per year. It then discusses the different options for such a scheme, with more or less active roles for Member States and the Community. The biggest challenge is to get the trading system started, and to decide which sectors and sources should be covered initially. Options include an agreed EC scheme where Member States could, if they so wish, opt in with all economic sectors or with only some. Another possibility would be to set up an EC system but to allow Member States to opt out, either completely or for certain sectors. Problems would be caused by the enlargement of the Community.

The Green Paper does not give answers to the different problems raised, but invites answers to a number of sceptically formulated questions as regards the system to be set up.

---

[29] COM(2000)87, 8 Feb. 2000.

In the last three sections, the paper discusses policy options related to the initial allocation of emission allowances (7), synergy with other policies and measures (8), and options concerning compliance and enforcement. All three sections conclude with a series of questions to which answers from interested groups are invited.

As regards the initial allocation, it will be a delicate task to fix an equitable burden for the sectors concerned, compared to those sectors that are not affected. Also, it might be more expensive to reach an 8 per cent reduction of emissions in transport than in other sectors. Problems are also caused by the way in which allocations are distributed among different companies, whether such allocations should, initially be auctioned or granted free of cost, and how the problem of new entrants to the market should be approached. As regards the relationship with other measures, the problem of existing regulation needs to be discussed, including the function of environmental agreements and the relationship with energy taxation. As for enforcement, the Paper states that 'for any emission trading system to work, adequate enforcement of the rules in relation to participating companies is a foremost necessity'.

An annex provides a short economic analysis of emission trading within the EC.

P.  COMMUNICATION FROM THE COMMISSION ON INTEGRATING ENVIRONMENT AND SUSTAINABLE DEVELOPMENT INTO ECONOMIC AND DEVELOPMENT COOPERATION POLICY—ELEMENTS OF A COMPREHENSIVE STRATEGY[30]

The Communication outlines a strategy to ensure that the natural environment is a key element in the European Union's support to developing countries. Seven sections describe the background to sustainable development[31] (2), the necessity of policy coherence in promoting sustainable development (3), challenges and opportunities for environmental integration (4), obligations under existing multilateral agreements and processes (5), the possibilities to integrate environmental concerns into the programming and project cycle (6), advancing and evaluating the integrating process (7), and some conclusions.

The Commission concedes that the environmental impact of EC policies on developing countries have not yet been systematically analysed and undertakes to continue studies on the environmental impact of its trade policies. It proclaims that environmental sustainability needs to be taken into account systematically in formulating economic and social policies in developing countries. World Trade Organization Rounds need to take heed of environmental considerations.[32] This does not prevent multilateral environment

[30] COM(2000)264, 18 May 2000.
[31] The section gives a new description of 'sustainable development': 'Development is sustainable when it is economically efficient, politically democratic and pluralistic, socially equitable and environmentally sound.'
[32] 'It is necessary to maintain the right of WTO members to take precautionary action to protect human health, safety and the environment while at the same time avoiding unjustified or disproportionate restrictions' (section 4).

agreements from being developed further. The EC will try to use its full weight during these negotiations. Between 1990 and 1995, about 8.5 per cent of all funds committed were dedicated to environmental projects or environmental components of other projects, which is 'modest compared to the overall flows of EC aid'. To improve this situation, better programming in developing countries and the EC is necessary. Environmental integration into programmes has the objective to identify and avoid harmful direct and indirect environmental impacts of cooperation programmes and to recognize and use opportunities for enhancing environmental conditions. At present, environmental assessment procedures are already mandatory for programmes and projects in EC economic and development cooperation, but improvements remain necessary.

The paper concludes by stating that the responsibility for 'identifying and responding to environmental issues and for integrating environmental considerations into policies lies primarily with developing countries themselves'. The EC can support such efforts, but the three key elements 'are political commitment to environmental integration at each level of the hierarchy, formalizing the integration process in organizational structures, and sound management of the overall quality of the integration process. The Commission undertakes to examine to what extent organizational aspects can be improved in the near future, with a view to better integrate the environment.' Furthermore, it will explore the consequences of obtaining certification—for instance by ISO 14001 or the EC Eco-Management and Audit Scheme—for the environmental integration process.

## II. Summaries of Reports

### A. COMMISSION REPORT ON THE OPERATION OF DIRECTIVE 67/548/EEC, DIRECTIVE 88/379/EEC, REGULATION (EC) NO. 793/93, AND DIRECTIVE 76/769/EEC[33]

This Commission Working Paper was produced for the Environment Council at the end of 1998, which had an examination of the state of chemicals legislation within the Community on its agenda. The report starts by describing in detail the content of the four legal instruments mentioned in the title. Under 'findings', it states that there is a 'need to use the current instruments more efficiently and implement as well as enforce them more rigorously and consistently, . . . to streamline the instruments and develop them in order to take account of new emerging problems'. For each of the four instruments the practical operation is examined and assessed. The findings are summarized in the report, and elaborated in detail in four comprehensive annexes.

In line with the working paper character of this publication, there is no conclusion on a new approach to the problem of chemical substances and

---

[33] SEC(1998)1986, 18 Nov. 1998.

preparations. However, it should be noted that this Paper, and the subsequent discussions in the Council and within the Commission, led to the elaboration of a Commission White Paper on a 'Strategy for a Future Chemicals Policy',[34] which was submitted to the other EC institutions in early 2001. This White Paper is likely to form the basis for discussion at Community level for years to come, and will hopefully lead to a more efficient policy on the effects of chemicals in the environment.

### B. COMMISSION REPORT UNDER ARTICLE 14 OF REGULATION (EC) NO. 1404/96 (LIFE)[35]

LIFE is a Community environmental financial instrument, which co-finances pilot and demonstration projects aimed at the conservation of nature. This report is a follow-up to the 1997 report which was reviewed in the previous volume.[36] The report summarily details the expenditures of the LIFE fund during the years 1992 to 1998. Separate information is provided about LIFE-Nature, which concerns nature conservation actions, LIFE-Environment, which co-finances demonstration actions involving industry and local communities, and LIFE-Third Countries, which supports collaborative action involving third countries bordering the Mediterranean and Baltic Seas. Between 1992 and 1998, 8,502 proposals for projects were received. 1,275 projects were co-financed, at a total cost of 643 million euro. The overall expenses in 1998 were 101.3 million euro. 48 million euro was earmarked for 85 LIFE-Nature projects. The report does not specify the identity of the Member States which benefited from these funds. As regards the entire period from 1992 to 1998, most of the 271 million euro went to Spain (54.4 million euro), France (32.2 million euro), Germany (30.2 million euro), Italy (29.6 million euro), and Greece (18.9 million euro).

LIFE-Environment was supported with 48.6 million euro in 1998 (326 million euro between 1992 and 1998). 115 projects were financially supported. The Member States which received the most substantial financial support in 1998 were the UK, Germany, France, Italy, and Spain. The details for the period 1992–8 overall are Germany (45.1 million euro), France (43.4 million euro), UK (41.5 million euro), Italy (38.9 million euro), and Spain (26.9 million euro). In both cases, therefore, the five biggest Member States of the EC obtained the biggest share.

The actions funded by LIFE-Environment between 1992 and 1997—it is not clear why 1998 is not included—mostly concerned clean technologies and modifying industrial production processes (23 per cent), followed by water management (18 per cent), regional planning in rural areas and coastal areas (17 per cent), waste management treatment (15 per cent), regional planning in urban areas (14 per cent), training, promoting awareness, and environmental management (8 per cent), and soil protection and treatment (4 per cent). The report gives some examples of benefits obtained from the projects.

[34] COM(2001)88, 27 Feb. 2001.       [35] COM(98)721, 4 Dec. 1998.       [36] See n. 4 above, 567.

As regards LIFE-Third Countries, in 1998 4.7 million euro was devoted to projects on technical assistance and demonstration projects on sustainable development and nature conservation. It is interesting to note that, between 1992 and 1998, 25.5 million euro was spent in the Mediterranean Region and 7.5 million euro in the Baltic Region. The countries which received most support were Russia, Turkey, Albania, Cyprus, and Syria.

The report is devoted largely to an external evaluation of LIFE, which is now mainly of historical value, as in the meantime a new Regulation has been adopted, covering the period 2000–4. The overall amount made available for that period is 640 million euro.[37]

C. COMMISSION COMMUNICATION ON THE REVIEW CLAUSE.
ENVIRONMENTAL AND HEALTH STANDARDS FOUR YEARS AFTER
THE ACCESSION OF AUSTRIA, FINLAND, AND SWEDEN TO THE
EUROPEAN UNION[38]

When Austria, Finland, and Sweden became members of the European Union on 1 January 1995 by virtue of the Accession Treaty,[39] they had to take over the *acquis communautaire*, i.e. secondary Community legislation. These countries argued that their environmental and health standards were, at least in part, more protective than EC standards and they were unwilling to lower these standards. The Accession Treaty provided for special provisions in the field of the environment and health that allowed the three countries to maintain certain national provisions for a period of four years. The European Union on its part committed itself to review the relevant EC legislation in question within four years.

The present Communication reports on the outcome of the review and other developments that took place between 1995 and 1998.

The report describes the different provisions which the three Member States had been allowed to maintain, and then details the results achieved. As regards Directive 67/548/EEC on the Classification, Packaging and Labelling of Dangerous Substances, solutions were found for differences in classification and labelling of substances. Austria agreed to replace symbols of a crossed-out dustbin and toilet bowl by a text after a transitional period. More stringent rules in the accession countries for PCP, tin compounds, and cadmium were adopted by the Community. No solution, however, could be found for cadmium in fertilizers, where EC law contains no limit value. The transition period was therefore prolonged until the end of 2001.[40] The general ban on

---

[37] European Parliament and Council Reg. (EC) No. 1655/2000 concerning the Financial Instrument for the Environment (LIFE) [2000] OJ L192/1.

[38] COM(98)745, 11 Dec. 1998.

[39] Treaty concerning the Accession of the Kingdom of Norway, the Republic of Austria, the Republic of Finland, the Kingdom of Sweden to the European Union [1994] OJ C241/9. Norway did not become a member of the European Union due to the results of a referendum.

[40] European Parliament and Council Dir. 98/97/EC amending Dir. 76/116/EEC on the Approximation of the Laws of the Member States Relating to Fertilizers, as Regards the Marketing in Austria, Finland, and in Sweden of Fertilizers Containing Cadmium [1999] OJ L18/60.

mercury in batteries was adopted by the Community. The EC limit value for benzene in petrol, which was 5 per cent, was tightened to 1 per cent. Austria, which had a limit value of 3 per cent, therefore also adapted its provisions. The Austrian limit value of 0.1 per cent of sulphur in gasoil will be adopted by the EC as of 1 January 2008. Until then, Austria is allowed to maintain its value.

The Communication considers the review process 'an important achievement in EC environment policy'.

### D. COMMISSION'S SECOND REPORT ON THE APPLICATION IN THE MEMBER STATES OF DIRECTIVE 92/3/EURATOM OF 3 FEBRUARY 1992 ON THE SUPERVISION AND CONTROL OF SHIPMENTS OF RADIOACTIVE WASTE BETWEEN MEMBER STATES AND IN AND OUT OF THE COMMUNITY ('SHIPMENT REPORT')[41] AND COMMISSION COMMUNICATION AND FOURTH REPORT ON THE PRESENT SITUATION AND PROSPECTS FOR RADIOACTIVE WASTE MANAGEMENT IN THE EUROPEAN UNION ('RADIOACTIVE WASTE MANAGEMENT REPORT')[42]

The Radioactive Waste Management Report counts 120 pages. It is based on information furnished by Member States, and reflects a positive attitude vis-à-vis nuclear industry and radioactive waste. The report points out an important difference in terminology with regard to non-nuclear waste. While under EC waste legislation, recyclable or recoverable waste remains waste, radioactive recyclable waste does not constitute, in Community terminology, waste. Section (2) deals with sources, categories, and quantities of radioactive waste in the EU. Radioactive waste results mainly from the generation of nuclear electricity, including decommissioning, the operation of research reactors, the use of radiation and radioactive material in medicine, agriculture, industry, and research, and the processing of material containing natural radionuclides. The report is not very clear on how much radioactive waste is generated from each of these activities. Section (2.1) refers to section (6.3) which is, however, silent on this question.

Section (3) describes, for each Member State, the policy and practice of radioactive waste management and anticipates future developments. The predicted generation of radioactive waste in the European Union is about 50,000 m³ per year. Decommissioning of an average nuclear power plant would generate about 10,000 m³ of radioactive waste. However, the report assures that 'decommissioning is, in most cases, delayed for decades'. Nonetheless (at 99) it is conceded that within the EC, 114 plants are in various stages of decommissioning. The report does not detail problems or environmental effects of the handling of radioactive waste, but limits itself to reproduce Member States' information. Until 1994, a total of 1,640,000 m³ radioactive waste has been disposed, either by ocean disposal (until 1982), by surface and shallow disposal, or by deep geological disposal.

Section 4 describes safety aspects, section 5 financial aspects, section 6 miscellaneous issues, and section 7 interaction with the public and social issues.

---

[41] COM(98)778, 22 Dec. 1998.          [42] COM(98)799, 11 Jan. 1999.

The report contains a number of tables which are for an expert audience, and again based on Member States' information. The Shipment Report was preceded, in 1995, by a first report on the implementation of Directive 92/3 Euratom. This second report includes information covering the period 1994–5, and which originates exclusively from Member States. The report lists national legislation which transposes the Directive into national law, but does not specify, whether the transposition is complete and correct. Since more generally, the report limits itself to reproducing Member States' information, the term 'Commission report' may appear somewhat inaccurate.

During 1994–5, sixty authorizations for transfrontier shipments were granted, mainly by Sweden (20), Germany (19), Belgium (14), and France (4). Four applications were refused. Only two exports to third countries (South Africa and Japan) were signalled. As regards shipments of nuclear waste within their territory, Member States only had to provide certain specific information. The report specifies for only some Member States how many shipments were made.[43] According to the figures, by far most shipments took place in the UK, 2,740 in 1994 and 917 in 1995.

Environmental issues are left almost untouched in these reports and on reading it one acquires the impression that no such environmental problems or public concerns exist within the Community. The fact that, in France, more than 1,000 ordinary landfills containing radioactive waste in different quantities were found, is not mentioned. And ongoing concern about the increased incidence of leukemia in areas close to nuclear installations is dealt with only in general terms, which does little justice to the weight of these concerns.[44]

In sum, the integration of environmental requirements into radioactive waste management still appears in its infancy.

### E. COMMISSION REPORT ON THE IMPLEMENTATION OF COUNCIL DIRECTIVE 91/271/EEC OF 21 MAY 1991 CONCERNING URBAN WASTE-WATER TREATMENT[45]

According to Article 17 of Directive 91/271 EEC on Urban Waste Water[46] the Commission should have been informed of Member States' programme

---

[43] See e.g. the information from France (at p. 28) and Germany (at p. 26): France: 'Radioactive waste shipments on the French territory involved in 1994 approximately 1,300 road vehicles and 300 railway wagons, with an approximate volume of 23,000 cubic metres. In 1995 approximately 626 road vehicles and 410 railway wagons, with an approximate volume of 17,500 cubic metres.' Germany: 'In 1994/95, the following shipments took place to interim facilities and to the disposal facility: Gorleben, shipments 1994: 35; shipments 1995: 26; Mitterteich: shipments 1994: 25; shipments 1995: 21; Morsleben: shipments 1994: 90; shipments 1995: 259: In 1994/95 less than two hundred shipments of radioactive waste from industry and nuclear medicine to the collection points took place.'

[44] See n. 44 above, 75: 'Reports of increased numbers of leukemia cases in areas surrounding some nuclear installations provoke great concern amongst the general public, in spite of independent investigations which conclude that there is no proof of a link between reports of higher doses of radiation in these areas and the incidence of leukemia.'

[45] COM(98)775, 15 Jan. 1999.

[46] Council Dir. 91/271/EEC concerning Urban Waste-Water Treatment [1991] OJ L135/40.

to implement the Directive by 30 June 1994. However, 'because of delays attributable to a number of Member States, it was only now that the Commission was able to publish this first report', which describes the position on 15 July 1998.

Section (4) describes in detail the progress of the implementation of the Directive. Instead of secondary waste-water treatment which is the rule, Member States may provide for primary treatment in less sensitive regions. Only the UK and Portugal have made use of this possibility. Section (6) notes that the Directive is applicable to 17,351 agglomerations with more than 2,000 inhabitants.[47] The increased number of treatment installations will lead to an increase of sewage sludge from 5.5 million tonnes in 1992 to 8.3 million tonnes in 2005 which will raise new problems in respect of the destination of that sludge.

The overall investment planned by Member States between 1993 and 2005 in order to comply with the Directive is 130 billion euro, of which 53 per cent is for collecting systems, and 47 per cent for treatment plants. Almost half of this investment (49 per cent) will be made in Germany. The report calculates that this means, on average, an amount of 0.43 euro per $m^3$ of water consumed.

The Commission concludes from this report that Member States appear to be determined to implement Directive 91/271 EEC, and that a revision of the Directive is not necessary. Only Belgium—for Brussels, and Italy—for Milano, have indicated that they could not meet the deadlines laid down by the Directive. It can only be hoped that this optimism will be prove to be justified.

F. COMMISSION STAFF WORKING PAPER: FIRST ANNUAL SURVEY ON THE IMPLEMENTATION AND ENFORCEMENT OF COMMUNITY ENVIRONMENTAL LAW (OCTOBER 1996 TO DECEMBER 1997);[48] SECOND ANNUAL SURVEY ON THE IMPLEMENTATION AND ENFORCEMENT OF COMMUNITY ENVIRONMENTAL LAW (JANUARY 1998 TO DECEMBER 1999)[49]

In 1996 the Commission issued a Communication on Implementing Community Environmental Law,[50] in which it announced that some information on environmental implementation and enforcement, in particular on questions of policy and procedure, could usefully be provided in an annual survey. The present reports are a follow-up of that announcement.

The reports are structured in six (First Survey) and seven (Second Survey) sections. They report on developments since the 1996 Communication such as specific horizontal actions at Community level (in particular on the activity of IMPEL, the European Union Network of Implementation and Enforcement of

[47] Italian agglomerations are not included in these figures, as Italy had, at the time when the report was adopted, not yet transposed the Directive into national law; see Case C–302/95, *Commission* v. *Italy* [1996] ECR I–6765.
[48] SEC(99)592, 27 Apr. 1999.          [49] SEC(2000)1219, 13 July 2000.
[50] COM(96)500, 22 Oct. 1996.

Environmental Law), national legislation transposing EC directives, and the Commission's reports on the monitoring of application of Community law. Section (2) details, *inter alia*, the Commission's efforts to promote knowledge of Community environmental law (magistrates' training, teaching EC environmental law at universities) and, in the Second Survey, the efforts to introduce a Community recommendation on minimum standards for environmental inspectors in Member States. The information on IMPEL in both reports is interesting, as publications on IMPEL are rare. IMPEL is an informal network which deals with legal policy and implementation on the one hand, and inspection, practical application, and enforcement issues, on the other. Member State and Commission officials participate in the network, which meets in plenary meetings twice a year. It has a number of *ad hoc* Working Groups and a Secretariat which is intergovernmental, but hosted by the Commission. In 1997 the Commission financed IMPEL activities for the sum of 437,346 euro, and in 1998 for 383,000 euro. Member States' financial contribution to the network is not specified in the reports.

IMPEL work produced the following results:

— a comparison of technical standards and pollution control technology for various facilities;
— exchange of information and comparison on the permit systems for installations;
— comparison of enforcement arrangements;
— exchange of programmes for inspectors;
— publication of a report on the monitoring and enforcement mechanisms for the shipment of hazardous waste.

The reports describe in detail the activities of the different groups. The remaining sections of the reports are of limited interest.[51] The overall conclusion, to the effect that the 'achievements to date are considerable and have already resulted in tangible improvements at all stages of the regulatory chain' in the First Survey is not further substantiated. The Second Survey is less blue-eyed. Future surveys should strive to be more critical and less self-applauding on IMPEL and Commission activities.

### G.  COMMISSION REPORTS ON THE QUALITY OF BATHING WATER IN THE 1998[52] AND 1999[53] BATHING SEASONS

As in previous years,[54] the reports consist of an atlas of the measuring results for all fifteen Member States, and an explanatory report. The data is based on information from Member States, but the reports add that the 'Commission does not receive the actual analysis results, the so-called "raw" data'.

---

[51] See also the reproduction of the environmental chapter of the Commission's 16th Report on monitoring application of Community law (1999) elsewhere in this volume.
[52] (Luxembourg 1999) EUR 18831.          [53] (Luxembourg 2000) EUR 19505.
[54] See n. 4 above, 570, as regards the report on the bathing season 1997.

Compared to the 1997 bathing season, the number of coastal bathing waters has slightly increased in 1998, up to 13,128 bathing waters. In 1999 the number fell considerably to 11,435 due to the fact that France had failed to send any data due to a strike. Compliance rates with the mandatory values of Directive 76/160/EEC on Bathing Waters rose from 93.3 (1997) to 94.6 (1998) and then to 95.6 (1999). The report states with satisfaction that the compliance figures have not ceased to improve since 1993.

The number of freshwater zones fell from 6,180 in 1997 to 6,004 in 1998, although the United Kingdom for the first time identified nine freshwater zones in 1998 and monitored them. Some Member States considerably reduced the number of freshwater zones which were covered by the Directive.[55] The report implies that the majority of the zones withdrawn did not comply with the Directive's requirements in 1997. However, it is not clear whether bathing continued to be allowed in these zones or not.

In 1999 the number of freshwater zones was 4,376, again mainly because France had not sent results. However, in 1998, France had 1,553 freshwater zones, so that even if this figure had been included in 1999, the total number of freshwater zones would have fallen. The biggest reduction in number took place in Sweden, from 462 to 412 freshwater zones. The 1999 Report points out that most of the freshwater zones deleted did not comply with the Directive's requirements in 1998.

Of all freshwater zones, 86.5 per cent complied, in 1998, with the mandatory requirements of Directive 76/160/EEC. These figures conceal considerable differences. The compliance rate in Spain, for example, is only 73.0 per cent, and even this figure excludes the 56 per cent of thirty-nine bathing waters which were deleted in 1998 because they did not comply with the Directive's requirements in 1997. In 1999 the compliance rate rose to 90.2 per cent. Again, Spain ranks bottom with a compliance rate of 76.5 per cent.

It is questionable whether the reports really inform the tourist about the quality of bathing water in potential holiday resorts. The Directive may not be sufficiently precise for that. The reports announce a revision of the Directive, a proposal of which is already planned for 2001.

The reference to the 1992 Edinburgh Council, popularly known as the 'Deregulation Council', does not necessarily bode well for the precision of the future Directive.

### H. COMMISSION'S SIXTEENTH[56] AND SEVENTEENTH[57] ANNUAL REPORTS ON MONITORING THE APPLICATION OF COMMUNITY LAW

Reports on monitoring the application of Community law have been published on an annual basis since 1983.[58] For our purposes only environmental

---

[55] Thus, Germany withdrew 100 and added 33 freshwater zones; Spain withdrew 39 and added 3 freshwater zones; Sweden withdrew 84 and added 24 freshwater zones.

[56] COM(99)301, 9 July 1999 [1999] OJ C354/1.

[57] COM(2000)92, 23 June 2000, [2001] OJ C30/1.

[58] See also n. 4 above, 571 concerning comments on the 15th Report.

aspects need to be highlighted. The 16th Report reproduces a table of cases for 1997 and 1998 in which the Commission decided to apply to the ECJ, under Article 228 EC, and ask for a penalty payment. Of the fourteen decisions, eight concern environmental matters. However, by the end of 2000, the Court had only passed one judgment in an environmental case,[59] most other cases having been terminated after Member States complied with EC environmental requirements. In 1999 no single environmental case was submitted to the ECJ under Article 228 EC.

On 31 December 1998 there were eighty-two judgments from the ECJ which had not been implemented by Member States; of these thirty-one concerned the environment. The most frequently named Member States in environmental matters were Belgium, Spain, and Portugal (five cases each). On 31 December 1999, there were seventy-six judgments which had not been complied with, of which thirty in environmental matters; Germany and Portugal had five listed cases each.

The 16th Report categorizes failures to transpose environmental directives into cases of non-communication, nonconformity of national measures, and cases of incorrect application of directives. This harms the transparency of the presentation, and makes comparisons with previous reports almost impossible. Furthermore, the distinction between these three forms of faulty application is everything but clear cut. The 17th report changes the format again: for cases of nonconformity and incorrect application of directives, only the number of the Directive in question, the number of the infringement case, and the Member State are identified. The subject matter of the case is not clarified in the report.

The published data in both reports illustrates the general delay in transposing environmental directives into national law. Transposition within the timespan fixed in directives is the exception rather than the rule. As regards instances of nonconformity, Directive 91/676/EEC on Nitrates in Water, 85/337/EEC on Environmental Impact Assessment, 90/313/EEC on Access to Environmental Information, and 79/409/EEC on the Protection of Birds rank top in the 16th Report. The 17th Report no longer allows such an examination. As for incorrect application, the 16th Report again shows that Directive 79/409/EEC causes most problems, followed by Directive 76/464/EEC on the Discharge of Dangerous Substances to Water, Directive 75/442/EEC on Waste, and Directive 92/43/EEC on Habitats.

According to the statistics in the annexes to both reports, the Commission started formal infringement procedures under Article 226 EEC as shown in Table V.

Except for the non-communication of national measures, it is not specified in which stage of the procedure—letter of formal notice, reasoned opinion, application to the Court—each case is. Why the figures for incorrect application have almost doubled from one year to the other is not explained either, which somewhat undermines the value of this part of the report.

---

[59] Case C–387/97, *Commission* v. *Greece* [2000] ECR I–5047.

*Table V.  Infringement procedures under Article 226 EEC*

|  | 16th Report | 17th Report |
| --- | --- | --- |
| Non-communication of national measures | 71 | 61 |
| Nonconformity of national measures | 61 | 83 |
| Incorrect application of measures | 97 | 178 |

As regards complaints, both reports state that almost 50 per cent of all complaints is concerned with nature conservation, and slightly less than 25 per cent with environment impact assessments of projects. Complaints on water, air, or waste take up 10 per cent of all complaints.

Generally, the complexity of the data presented and the numerous changes of the form of presentation do not really favour transparency, and therefore do not incite further research on implementation issues.

### I. COMMUNICATION FROM THE COMMISSION ON EUROPE'S ENVIRONMENT: WHAT DIRECTIONS FOR THE FUTURE? THE GLOBAL ASSESSMENT OF THE EUROPEAN COMMUNITY ACTION PROGRAMME OF POLICY AND ACTION IN RELATION TO THE ENVIRONMENTAL AND SUSTAINABLE DEVELOPMENT 'TOWARDS SUSTAINABILITY'[60]

The Paper is the Commission's response to a request from the Council and the EP to evaluate the impact of the Fifth Community Environmental Action Programme.

The overall conclusion is not positive:

Despite some improvements . . . the state of the environment overall remains a cause for concern and pressures on the environment are predicted to grow even further in some areas. . . . Although the 5th Programme raised awareness . . ., less progress has been made overall in changing economic and societal trends which are harmful to the environment. The commitment by other sectors and by Member States to the Programme is partial, and the patterns of production and consumption in our countries prevent us from achieving a clean and safe environment and protecting the world's natural resources. The outlook is that new environmental standards will not keep pace with the growing demand for example for transport, consumer goods or tourism. The perspectives are particularly bleak for climate change if trends in the main energy-consuming sectors cannot be reversed. . . . [The 5th Programme's] principles are still valid, but the analysis in this Communication indicates that they have to be put into practice more fully . . . without a reinforced integration of environmental concerns into economic sectors to address the origins of environmental problems and without a stronger involvement and commitment by citizens and stakeholders, our development will remain environmentally unsustainable overall.

---

[60] COM(99)543, 24 Nov. 1999.

The evaluation of the seven environmental priorities of the 5th Programme[61] leads to the observation that, in respect of climate change, there is a broad consensus on the need to take urgent action. The measures taken had 'little impact'; the voluntary agreement with the car industry should contribute to curbing $CO_2$ emissions in the next decade. Industry emissions predict a 15 per cent fall by 2010, but the projections for transport are for 'continuing strong growth'.

On acidification and air quality, there were 'improvements in reducing acidification and the levels of some air pollutants, particularly $SO_2$ and lead'. Several measures proposed or adopted will have to be implemented in the future and a new, more integrative strategy on air pollution will need to be developed. On nature protection, the identification and protection of fauna and flora sites 'is far behind the original deadlines agreed' and remains a future priority. As regards biodiversity, its requirements need to be integrated into other policies, in particular agricultural policy.

Water quality has improved, due to progress in the implementation of the Directive on Urban Waste Water. Nitrate concentrations have shown little change since 1980, and pesticide and nitrate inputs from agriculture are still high. It remains a priority to implement existing provisions.

Little changes have occurred in urban environmental questions, where mostly awareness-raising initiatives were taken. Similar conclusions apply to coastal zones, where few actions were taken, even though 85 per cent of coasts are at risk. As regards waste issues, waste generation continues to grow and 'Waste prevention measures have not stabilized production of waste, nor its hazardousness.' And, while 65 per cent of waste went to landfill in 1990, the figure rose to 66 per cent in 1995. The Paper is reproduced in full elewhere in this volume.

### J. REPORT ON THE IMPLEMENTATION OF DIRECTIVE 82/501/EEC ON MAJOR-ACCIDENT HAZARDS OF CERTAIN INDUSTRIAL ACTIVITIES (1994–6)[62]

This report is the second which the Commission submitted on the application of the so-called Seveso Directive (82/501/EEC). A first report was published in 1988.[63]

The present report is based on voluntary information which Member States transmitted to the Commission. The report therefore does not discuss practical application of the Directive, but lists, in a standardized form, aspects of the Directive's transposition. This includes a summary of the most relevant national provisions, competent authorities, the number of sites or activities falling under the scope of the Directive, the existence of on-site and off-site emergency plans, inspections, information of the public, and the number of

---

[61] Climate change, acidification, biodiversity, water, urban environment, coastal zones, and waste.

[62] [1999] OJ C291/1.

[63] Commission Report on the Application in the Member States of Dir. 82/501/EEC on the Major Accident Hazards of Certain Industrial Activities COM(88)261, 18 May 1988.

accidents notified, etc. Inconsistencies or contradictions are left unexplained. For instance, in France, there are 392 sites covered by Article 5 of the Directive, 698 activities were exercised, and 720 safety reports produced. Yet, there existed only 370 on-site and 227 off-site emergency plans and the public living in the neighbourhood was informed of the hazards and the measures to take in case of emergency in 252 cases. The report does not explain the inconsistencies in these numbers, and what the Commission did to remedy the situation.

The reader is informed that, on average, the time-span between any accident and the Commission's information is one year, even though the Directive requires that the Commission should be informed 'as soon as possible'. No details are given on the ninety-two serious accidents which occurred during the period covered by the report.

The Commission's remarks on the information supplied by Member States are mirror national observations so that it becomes difficult to consider this report truly a 'Commission Report'. Directive 82/501/EEC in the meantime has been replaced by Directive 96/82/EEC[64] which entered into effect in February 1999. The Commission observes that it had not yet received any transposing measure from any Member State.

### K.  COMMISSION REPORT ON THE IMPLEMENTATION OF COMMUNITY WASTE LEGISLATION FOR THE PERIOD 1995–7[65] REPORT ON THE FIRST STANDARDIZED REPORTS FROM MEMBER STATES (WATER) FOR THE PERIOD 1993–5[66]

Directive 91/692/EEC seeks to rationalize and standardize the reports which Member States must submit as regards the implementation of various environmental directives. On the basis of questionnaires, that have been developed jointly by the Commission and Member States, the Member States must submit a report on implementation in sectors such as water, air, and waste, etc. every three years. In smaller Member States in particular, all these national reports are drafted by one and the same official. Therefore, it was decided to require national reports in the water sector for the first three-year period in water in 1996 (thus covering 1993–5), for air in 1997 (covering 1994–6), and waste in 1998 (covering 1995–7). The Commission's consolidated reports were to be published with a delay of one year. For water this was to be in 1997, for air in 1998, and for waste in 1999. The two reports discussed here are the first under Directive 91/692/EEC. As yet, there is no report on the air sector.

As regards these delays, the water report points out that Member States' reports frequently arrived as late as 1997, and even then were often incomplete. In respect of the different questionnaires, the water report indicates, per Member State, how many questions were answered. Luxembourg and Portugal did not answer at all; Spain failed to return six, Ireland four, and Greece and Italy three questionnaires. The waste report notes that Greece,

---

[64] Council Dir. 96/82/EC on the Control of Major Accident Hazards Involving Dangerous Substances [1997] OJ L10/13.
[65] COM(99)752, 10 Jan. 2000.				[66] Luxembourg 2000.

Italy, and Spain did not send any of the four reports requested and Portugal did not reply to three of the four questionnaires. What is truly remarkable is the lack of reporting from the Cohesion-Fund Member States (Spain, Portugal, Greece, Ireland).

Both reports are structured so as to reflect the different directives for which Member States have transmitted information. In this sense, the reports are not really consolidated. The substantive part of the water report provides hardly any significant information on drinking water. The Commission announces that it will, in future, publish a special report on drinking water but this does not answer the need for information regarding present, existing requirements. The reader does not learn where water problems exist, where investments were made or would have to be made, etc. The water report shows considerable omissions in reporting and as many omissions to comply with the requirements of EC law. The return rate of the questionnaires—about 50 per cent—is disappointing and the quality and usefulness of those answers are generally low. The water report concludes that the application of Directive 91/692/EEC to water was an obvious failure, and indicates a number of causes.

While the water report had to cover eight directives, the waste report only had to cover four. It underlines, by way of a general conclusion, that only five Member States had transposed the definition of 'waste' and four the definition of 'hazardous waste' correctly into national law. Furthermore, it points to considerable differences between Member States as to issues of application. For instance, recycling rates for domestic waste vary between zero and 44 per cent. Denmark and Luxembourg incinerate 56 per cent of their domestic waste, whereas Greece and Ireland do not incinerate any such waste. Recycling waste oils does not have priority over incineration in most Member States, in marked contradiction to the requirements of Directive 75/439/EEC. Attention is further devoted to waste management planning, waste statistics, records, and the control of waste management. The report concludes that application is not yet satisfactory, and suggests some possible reasons. It notes that:

the reports are mainly based on contributions from Member States themselves. This obviously limits the possibility to identify omission of applications or weaknesses and lacunas of existing Community waste legislation.

### L. COMMISSION REPORT ON THE APPLICATION OF DIRECTIVE 79/409/EEC ON THE CONSERVATION OF WILD BIRDS—UPDATE FOR 1993–5 BASED ON INFORMATION SUPPLIED BY THE MEMBER STATES ON THE APPLICATION OF NATIONAL MEASURES ADOPTED PURSUANT TO THE DIRECTIVE[67]

This report is the third report which the Commission published pursuant to Article 12(2) of Directive 79/409/EEC[68] which instructs the Commission to

[67] COM(2000)180, 29 Mar. 2000.
[68] See Commission, *Information sur l'Application de la Directive 79/409* (Luxembourg: Office for Official Publications, 1990); Second Report on the Application of Directive 79/409/EEC on the Conservation of Wild Birds COM(93)572, 24 Nov. 1993.

publish such a report every three years. No attempt is made to explain why seven years have passed since the last report, or why data for 1993 to 1995 are published in 2000 only. Obviously, these data now have little more than academic value.

Section (2) discusses the conservation status of species. It expressly refers to a study by BirdLife, a private organization, which is deemed 'the best scientific information currently available'. The study identifies 514 species of birds regularly observed in Europe. Altogether, 319 species (62 per cent) have a conservation status that is considered to be generally satisfactory. The rest, i.e. 195 species or 38 per cent, have an unsatisfactory status, either because these species are showing a marked decline or because they have a (sometimes very) limited distribution. Almost 25 per cent of species regularly observed in Europe have undergone a substantial decline in numbers over the last twenty years. The intensification of agriculture is the main cause for the 42 per cent decline in species. Another important factor is the destruction of habitats.

Section (3) discusses the preservation of habitats in the light of Articles 3 and 4 of Directive 79/409/EEC. Under the Directive, Member States had to designate Special Protection Areas by 1981. Between 1993 and 1995, 148 new Special Protection Areas were designated (increase of 8.5 per cent of the total area), and in total 1,247 such areas were designated by the end of 1995. The report indicates that by 1995 only five Member States had designated more than half (!) of the important bird areas within their territory. Major efforts are still needed in most Member States.

Section (4) raises the highly emotional issues of hunting, capture, killing, and sale. However, the reports limits itself to indicate changes in national legislation, and the number of derogations granted by Member States. Section (5) discusses Articles 10 to 14 of Directive 79/409/EEC and reports on research undertaken by Member States.

There is no conclusion attached to the report which, in any event, limits itself too frequently to reproducing the information transmitted by Member States.

## M.  COMMISSION'S EIGHTH SURVEY ON STATE AID IN THE EUROPEAN UNION[69]

This survey covers state aid given by Member States to economic sectors, as defined under Article 87 EC, in the period between 1994 and 1998, and distinguishes aid to manufacturing, agriculture, fisheries, coalmining, transport, financial services tourism, and employment. The overall average annual national aid in the EC between 1996 and 1996 was 93 billion euro (the average 1994 to 1996 was 106 billion euro), a very impressive statistic in the light of the notion of 'fair competition'. Thirty-five per cent of this sum goes to manufacturing sector (33 billion euro). The survey provides no information on the amounts spent on environmental aids, except for the manufacturing sector.

[69]  COM(2000)205, 11 Apr. 2000.

Between 1996 and 1998, a total of 604.35 million euro in environmental aid was given to the manufacturing industry (0.65 per cent of the total aid to that sector). The most substantial aid was granted by Denmark (232.52 million euro, which is 15.11 per cent of the total state aid for the manufacturing sector granted by that Member State), followed by Germany (118.19 million euro/0.41 per cent), Netherlands (69.47 million euro/2.73 per cent), Austria (49.79 million euro/ 2.19 per cent), and Sweden (46.00 million euro/2.52 per cent). No state aid for environmental purposes was granted by Ireland and Portugal, which are both Cohesion Fund-countries. And for a significant number of Member States, environmental aid amounted to less than 1 per cent of the total state aid given to the manufacturing sector: Belgium (0.19 per cent), Germany (0.41 per cent), Greece (0.01 per cent), Spain (0.31), Finland (0.26 per cent), France (0.20), Italy (0.12 per cent) and the UK (0.05 per cent).

Annex III provides useful information on the different EC 'State aid' funds. The Community average annual 'state aid' (expenditure between 1996 and 1998) was 61 billion euro; more than two-thirds of which went to the agricultural sector.

In view of all these figures, the environment really is the *parent pauvre*.

## N. COMMISSION REPORT ON EXPERIENCE GAINED IN THE APPLICATION OF COUNCIL DIRECTIVE 90/313/EEC OF 7 JUNE 1990, ON FREEDOM OF ACCESS TO INFORMATION ON THE ENVIRONMENT[70]

Under Article 8 of Directive 90/313/EEC, the Commission should have submitted this report in 1996. Although no explanation is given for this delay the report indicates that only one Member State had submitted a national report by the end of 1996. Yet it also appears that Member States were only asked in July 1996 to send in these reports.

The report provides a summary of the Commission's experience with monitoring application of Directive 90/313/EEC in Member States, about which it received 156 complaints. This part is followed by a summary of proceedings before the ECJ, a description of the Aarhus Convention on Access to Environmental Information, Public Participation in Environmental Decision-Making and Access to Justice, and conclusions which describe 'problem areas' of the Directive. Annex A reproduces the titles of national legislation transposing Directive 90/313/EEC, Annex B consists of a summary of reports by Member States on the transposition of the Directive, and Annex C contains a report of a private Dutch environmental organization on a workshop concerning the application of Directive 90/313/EEC.

The report rarely analyses the different problems in detail. It does deal with the use of exceptions by administrations in order to refuse, in full or in part, access to information, and the fees charged for this information service. The latter seems to be a particular problem in Germany, where considerable fees are charged which may deter persons to request information. Whether the

---

[70] COM(2000)400, 29 June 2000.

arguments on 'problem areas' and the recommendations of the Dutch environmental organization for a review of Directive 90/313/EEC are supported by
factual evidence remains unclear.

In the meantime, the Commission has made a proposal for revising
Directive 90/313/EEC.[71]

### O. COURT OF AUDITORS' SPECIAL REPORT 14/2000 ON 'GREENING THE CAP' WITH THE COMMISSION'S REPLIES[72]

As this report emanates from an independent body, it may be expected to give
a 'neutral' assessment of the Common Agricultural Policy (CAP), and at the
same time it reveals the Commission's opinion on the different points raised.
The data submitted allow the reader to form an informed opinion of his own.

The report deals with environmental shortcomings of changes made to the
common organizations of the markets (COMs) for arable crops and livestock by
the 1992 reform of the CAP. Furthermore, it considers problems encountered in
achieving the environmental benefits by means of the new 'accompanying
measures' (Regulation (EC) No. 2078/92 and Regulation (EC) No. 2080/92). The
third part is formed by the Commission's reactions to the Court's findings.

As regards the environmental impact of the common organizations of the
market, the report mentions that Article 10(5) of Regulation (EC) No. 1765/92
requires that Member States shall take the necessary measures to remind
farmers of the need to respect existing environmental legislation. However, the
Commission has not followed up this requirement, and some Member States
appear not to have taken any measures. For arable crops, the 1992 reform of
the CAP reduced institutional prices and introduced area-based direct payments. This served the environmental aim of reducing incentives through CAP
measures for intensive production using large amounts of agro-chemicals.
This intention, however, was counterbalanced by other factors, such as high
prices in the world market for cereals, and the devaluation of some national
currencies against the euro. Consequently, farmers had no real incentive to
reduce the use of such fertilizers. The use of pesticides stagnated too, and even
slightly increased. Only in Member States where national initiatives were
taken to reduce use of pesticides (Denmark, Finland, Netherlands, Sweden),
such as the introduction of taxes, pesticide use declined. Lack of incentives
can also be found in the fields of water use and maize production, as farmers
were paid higher compensatory payments for irrigated farmland than for non-
irrigated farmland, and in maize production simply because it attracts higher
compensatory payments than other cereals. Maize production is concentrated in the south of Europe where water resources are scarce, and nitrate pollution problems are growing, yet maize production requires more water and
agro-chemicals than the cereals which it replaces.

---

[71] Commission Proposal for a European Parliament and Council Directive on Public Access to
Environmental Information COM(2000)402, 29 June 2000; [2000] OJ C337/156.
[72] Adopted on 6 July 2000; [2000] OJ C353/1.

The set-aside of land has a high environmental potential and was to be realized by all Member States. However, Member States have not always followed up these policies and regulations, and the Commission has not effectively monitored their application.

In the beef sector, the reform of the CAP aimed at the increase of extensive production, by introducing strict stocking limits, thus limiting the number of animals per hectare. However, in practice Community rules allow a farmer to keep as many animals as he wishes, provided he limits his claim to the eligible number. Also, derogations in legislation and other possibilities to bypass this objective of the CAP had the effect that the practical impact of the stocking density has been limited.

In the sheep sector, the establishment of the COM in 1980 led to a substantial increase in livestock (from 81 to 113 million animals). The reform stabilized livestock, however, on too high a level, which led to overgrazing in parts of Greece, Ireland, and the UK. For both beef and sheep, Member States were free to impose environmental restrictions on farmers, and to withhold aid in cases where farmers did not comply with such measures. However, only Greece and the UK have introduced such measures.

Finally, the report considers it a major weakness of post-reform Community policy that it has not addressed the serious environmental problems arising from intensive livestock production in Europe.[73] The overall conclusion in this section is that environmental considerations have been integrated into these parts of CAP only to a limited extent. It had been anticipated that the reform would diminish the pressure of agricultural activities on the environment, and in particular reduce the use of pesticides and nutrients in the crop sector and a reduction of emissions—methane, ammonia, nitrates—especially from animal farming. In reality, however, the reform made little difference.

The accompanying measures, introduced in 1992, were aid for the adoption of environment-friendly farming practices, afforestation of agricultural land and early retirement of farmers. However, the Commission omitted to conduct an analysis of the most important environmental needs before launching the implementation of these measures, which made it impossible to guide Member States. The Commission adopted implementation measures for Regulation (EC) No. 2078/92 as late as 1996, and for Regulation (EC) No. 2080/92 no such measures were introduced. The report concludes that as a result, these agri-environment measures had very little effect in converting intensive practices to extensive farming, and that the afforestation measures in many cases stimulated the planting of species which are profitable, but whose environmental impact is negative, especially with respect to biodiversity and landscape. In some countries, a high proportion of aid was used to fund the construction of forest roads. The overall conclusion of the Court is severe: 'with the 1992 reform, the Community may have succeeded in "greening" its CAP but

---

[73] See also the quotation in para. 26 of the report: 'a modern (relatively small) farm of 40 hectares with a dairy herd of 50 cows and a 50-sow-pig herd has a potential pollution load equivalent to that of a village of 1000 inhabitants.'

not necessarily its agriculture.' The Commission's reply conveys two messages. 'Firstly, [that] with the Agenda 2000 Reform the instruments are in place to achieve environmental integration.' This conclusion goes so far as to suggest that on the legislative level, integration of environmental concerns into the CAP is becoming a reality. Second, the Commission agrees that it is important to develop and target the agri-environment programmes and measures to ensure delivery of real and quantified environmental benefits.

### P. COMMISSION COMMUNICATION: BRINGING OUR NEEDS AND RESPONSIBILITIES TOGETHER: INTEGRATING ENVIRONMENTAL ISSUES WITH ECONOMIC POLICY[74]

This Communication is another contribution to the definition of a Community strategy to improve integration of the environmental and economic dimensions of sustainable development. It explains why this integration is inadequate (section 2) and discusses the problem of market-based instruments versus 'traditional' regulation (section 3). The Communication then addresses growth and environment, competitiveness and the environment, and the distribution of resources and social stability (section 4), before raising the problem, how integration may be measured (section 5). Here the possibility to develop indicators—as regards the use and effectiveness of economic instruments, environmentally harmful measures and policies, the 'value' of the environment, and environmental industries—are discussed in rather general terms. The conclusions (section 6) suggests the following measures:

— adoption of a transparent, gradual, credible approach to environmental integration, based on efficient target-setting;
— integration of environmental issues with economic policy, which is consistent with the future European Council strategy on sustainable development;
— an examination of the environmental impacts of economic activity and regulation should be integrated into the process of multilateral surveillance of structural reform, as should be the way environmental policies impact on the economic reform process (level of regulation, functioning of markets);
— the Broad Economic Policy Guidelines should fully incorporate the objectives of environmental integration, making use of a reliable set of indicators to be developed;
— reviews of the quality and sustainability of public finances should take particular account of the contribution of taxation and expenditure policies to environmental integration, and should contain an assessment of the efficiency of economic instruments in achieving their environmental objectives;

---

[74] COM(2000)576, 20 Sept. 2000.

— improved integration of environmental issues into economic policy should make increased use of an appropriate mix of market-based instruments and regulation; this should include the removal of subsidies which are harmful to the environment, and should take account of analyses by the Commission and other bodies of the environmental and economic effectiveness of market-based instruments.

### Q. COMMISSION COMMUNICATION ON INTEGRATED COASTAL ZONE MANAGEMENT: A STRATEGY FOR EUROPE[75]

The Communication presents a series of conclusions and recommendations that constitute an EU Strategy for such zones. It first enumerates the challenge of managing coastal zones, then presents the findings of a Community demonstration programme for coastal zones and develops a so-called 'strategy'. The latter consists of the promotion of coastal zone management activity within Member States and regions (A), the suggestion that EU policies be compatible with such management (B), the promotion of dialogue (C), the development of best management practices (D), the generating of information and knowledge about the coastal zone (E), the diffusion of information and raising of public awareness (F), and implementation measures (G).

The Communication admits that the principles which it develops for coastal zone management 'are not specific to the coast, but rather are fundamental components of good governance'. This remark suggests that the Communication also has the implicit objective to enable regional authorities, in particular in the Mediterranean region, to learn from the know-how developed in the Communication. Financial assistance from the EC might be given for management programmes or projects which follow the orientations indicated in the Communication in the future. Whether the Communication at present is of help to a coastal region in Greece or in Portugal remains doubtful.

### R. COMMISSION COMMUNICATION: A REVIEW OF THE AUTO-OIL II PROGRAMME[76]

The report analyses the Auto-Oil Programme I and explains the background to Programme II (section 2). It then explains the approach under Programme II (section 3), and provides the key results (4). Related legislative proposals are examined in section (5), and finally, some conclusions are drawn in section (6).

The Auto-Oil I Programme was set up in 1992 to provide the analytical foundation for the setting of vehicle emission and fuel quality standards for the year 2000 and beyond. It is a product of meetings between the Commission, the European car industry, and the oil-refining industry. One of the declared objectives was to find the most cost-effective solutions—i.e. to find legislative provisions which accommodated industry. The programme was concluded in 1996, and led to Directives on Emissions from Light-Duty Vehicles (Directive

---

[75] COM(2000)547, 27 Sept. 2000.　　[76] COM(2000)626, 5 Oct. 2000.

98/69/EC) and Fuel Quality (Directive 98/70/EC). The Auto-Oil II Programme was launched in 1997 in order to fix new standards for 2005 and beyond. The present report gives an overview of the results of these discussions.

After having explained the working methods, the report explains the expected emission and air quality results. In road transport, despite the increase in transport, emissions of all pollutants, except $CO_2$, are expected to fall to less than 20 per cent of their 1995 levels. $CO_2$ emissions are expected to rise until 2005 and then to stabilize. Calculations on urban air quality make the report anticipate a big improvement in urban air quality by 2010, although the statements in respect of particulate matter and tropospheric ozone are much less precise. Based on different models predicting the development of air quality, the report indicates what might be the most cost-effective measures including fiscal instruments, on vehicle technology, fuel quality, inspection and maintenance, non-technical measures. As for vehicle technology measures, only a summary of the discussions is reproduced, which is hardly informative.[77] Similar observations apply to fuel quality, where some cost estimations are provided, and also to inspection and maintenance measures.

Section (5) reports on the intentions as regards the update of existing Community legislation on car emission standards, fuel quality, and technical requirements for cars. The conclusions are the most interesting part of the report. They contain 'lessons learnt from Auto-Oil II' which is deemed an important contribution towards a more open, rational, and systematic approach to environmental policy-making. The report underlines the innovative character of that process, in particular:

— the involvement of a wide range of stakeholders;
— the wide range of potential measures contemplated;
— in having ensured, 'through the intensive stakeholder dialogue and involvement of dedicated experts, . . . that its findings are based on the best available scientific information'. The cost-effectiveness of measures is hence underlined on several occasions.

The report briefly discusses measures to be taken in the transport sector, and the future of air quality policy. As to the last point, it clarifies that the reduction in $CO_2$ emissions is not likely to run parallel to the reduction of other air pollutants, and seems to postulate that $CO_2$ reduction is not the same as the reduction of pollution.

The report deserves attention, as it illustrates how far the participation of the car and the mineral oil industry, the principal stakeholders which participated in the Auto-Oil II Programme, in the elaboration and orientation of EC air pollution policy effectively goes. One would have expected that this participation, as well as that of other groups—environmental organizations, environmental departments of Member States, organizations campaigning for

---

[77] As an example, the last phrase of this section may be quoted: 'Whereas the simulated effects often exceeded the potential of EU-wide measures, impacts and costs very much depend on the scope of the application and the situation of the local network and fleet.'

alternative energies, etc.—be better documented, but the report is silent on that. Also, it is not made clear to what extent alternatives to private road transport and to fossil fuels were discussed in a strategic fashion. Finally, as the Auto-Oil Programme is so often presented as a model for modern environmental law-making, it would have been desirable to learn more about the possibility of such a discussion in areas where no oligopolistic market situation exists.

### S. COMMISSION REPORT UNDER COUNCIL DECISION 1999/296/EC FOR A MONITORING MECHANISM OF COMMUNITY GREENHOUSE GAS EMISSIONS[78]

The Report assesses progress towards fulfilling the emission commitments for six greenhouse gases ($CO_2$, $CH_4$, $N_2O$, HFC, PFC, and $SF_6$) under the Climate Change Convention and the Kyoto Protocol. The Convention was aimed at the stabilization of greenhouse gases at 1990 levels, while the Kyoto Protocol set a target of 8 per cent reduction of the 1990 levels for the European Union. It covers data up to the end of 1998, as well as emission projections up to 2010, the mid-point of the Kyoto Protocol's first commitment period (2008 to 2012).

The report first formulates some conclusions (2), informs on the EC monitoring mechanism (3), and Member States' compliance with the reporting requirements (4). Section (5) assesses actual progress and section (6) evaluates projected progress.

As regards actual progress, the total greenhouse gases were 4,150 megatonnes (Mt) $CO_2$ equivalent[79] in 1990. They fell by 104 Mt or 2.5 per cent by the end of 1998. About 82 per cent of all emissions are $CO_2$ emissions. $CH_4$ and $N_2O$ account for about 9 per cent each. Within the different Member States, greenhouse gas emissions increased, with the exception of Germany, Luxembourg, and the UK. The reduction in Germany was due to the economic restructuring in the new Länder, and in the UK due to changes from coal to gas for electricity generation. In Ireland, Portugal, and Spain the increase was more than 20 per cent.

Fossil fuel energy consumption is the main driving force behind $CO_2$ emissions. Reliance on fossil fuels within the Community was 79 per cent in 1997; nuclear energy accounts for about 15 per cent and renewable energy for 6 per cent. The $CO_2$ emissions originate mainly from the energy sector (32 per cent), transport (24 per cent which constitutes an increase of 15.3 per cent over 1990 levels), small combustion (20 per cent), and manufacturing industry (18 per cent).

$CH_4$ emissions were, in 1998, 16.5 per cent below 1990 levels. They mainly stem from agriculture (49 per cent), waste (30 per cent), and fuels (17 per cent). $N_2O$ emissions were, in 1998, about 10 per cent below 1990 levels. They are

---

[78] COM(2000)749, 22 Nov. 2000.

[79] Greenhouse gases have a different greenhouse warming potential ($CO_2$: 1; $CH_4$: 24.5; $N_2O$: 320; HFC: 11.700; PFC 6.500–9.200; $SF_6$: 23.900). In order to compare the total emissions, values are indicated according to $CO_2$ equivalents.

generated from agriculture (61 per cent) and industrial processes (20 per cent). $N_2O$ emissions also come from catalytic converters. As regards the other three greenhouse gases, their emission is estimated between 37 and 70 Mt $CO_2$ equivalent.

As regards the projected development until 2010, the report indicates that $CO_2$ emissions are expected to increase by 97 Mt (2.9 per cent), whereas $CH_4$ emissions will fall by 129 Mt $CO_2$ equivalent, and $N_2O$ by 61 Mt $CO_2$ equivalent. For the other three gases an increase of 37 Mt $CO_2$ equivalent is expected, although the data are somewhat speculative. This means that, overall, there is a 6.6 per cent gap between the expected results and the Community obligations. The report discusses a number of additional measures which Member States should consider undertaking, and which might mitigate greenhouse gas emissions.

## III. Documents

### A. COMMUNICATION FROM THE COMMISSION—EUROPE'S ENVIRONMENT: WHAT DIRECTIONS FOR THE FUTURE? THE GLOBAL ASSESSMENT OF THE EUROPEAN COMMUNITY PROGRAMME OF POLICY AND ACTION IN RELATION TO THE ENVIRONMENT AND SUSTAINABLE DEVELOPMENT, 'TOWARDS SUSTAINABILITY', COM(1999)543 FINAL

### 1. Preface

The Fifth Environmental Action Programme was produced as the Community's main response to the 1992 Rio Earth Summit which called on the international community to develop new policies as outlined in Agenda 21, to take our society towards a sustainable pattern of development. The Programme was to start this process within the Community identifying objectives which required action at Community, national, and local levels. Central to the Programme was the recognition that environmental legislation in itself is not sufficient to improve the environment. Developments in areas that create environmental pressures, such as transport, energy, or agriculture often outweigh the benefits of new regulations. Economic activities therefore have to take better account of environmental objectives in addition to a strengthening of environmental policy. This requires commitment by societal stakeholders and citizens as well as by the Member States and regional and local authorities. A broader range of instruments should provide information, incentives, and support with a view to influencing decisions which affect the environment. In order to focus action, the Fifth Programme identified a number of environmental priority themes and objectives up to the year 2000, and pointed to five key sectors with an important impact on the environment and to which particular attention should be given in terms of integrating environmental concerns.

As the period covered by the Fifth Action Programme is coming to an end, the Commission is now presenting a Global Assessment on the implementation and success of this programme in response to a request from the Council and the European Parliament.[1] It does so also with the intention to launch a debate with the other Institutions, stakeholders, and citizens on the priorities for a Sixth Programme to be put forward in 2000.

*The main results of this Global Assessment*
This Global Assessment shows that the Community has made progress in putting into place new and improved instruments to protect the environment and ensure the safety and quality of the life of European citizens. This includes the better targeting of measures through scientific and economic studies and stakeholder dialogue as well as new market-based and financial instruments. Community policies have brought about, for example, a reduction in transboundary air pollution, a better water quality, and the phase-out of ozone-depleting substances, and will lead to further improvements over the next few years. At the same time, the implementation of EC environmental law in the Member States is not as good as it should be and the Commission will have to continue exercising its powers in this respect.

Despite some improvements, however, the state of the environment overall remains a cause for concern and pressures on the environment are predicted to grow even further in some areas, as highlighted in the European Environment Agency's recent state-of the-environment report.

Although the Fifth Programme raised awareness of the need for stakeholders, citizens, and decision-makers in other sectors to actively pursue environmental objectives, less progress has been made overall in changing economic and societal trends which are harmful to the environment. The commitment by other sectors and by Member States to the Programme is partial, and the patterns of production and consumption in our countries prevent us from achieving a clean and safe environment and protecting the world's natural resources. The outlook is that new environmental standards will not keep pace with the growing demand, for example, for transport, consumer goods, or tourism. The perspectives are particularly bleak for climate change if trends in the main energy-consuming sectors cannot be reversed. At the same time, it is increasingly clear that damages to the environment have costs to society as a whole, and conversely that environmental action can generate benefits in the form of economic growth, employment, and competitiveness.

In the last decade, along with economic globalization, the international nature of environmental problems has become clear. The EU has taken the leadership in the quest for common international action, for instance, on reducing emissions of greenhouse gases, combating ozone depletion, or protecting the Planet's biodiversity.

---

[1] Article 1 of the Decision No. 2179/98/EC of the European Parliament and of the Council of 24 September 1998 on the review of the European Community programme of policy and action in relation to the environment and sustainable development 'Towards sustainability'.

## The way forward

The future of environment policy has therefore to be seen in this wider context, where environmental, social, and economic objectives are pursued in a coordinated and mutually compatible way. Sustainable development, now enshrined as an objective in the Treaty of the European Union, should aim at the welfare of present and future generations both in European and world-wide in terms of economic prosperity, social justice, and security, and high environmental standards and the sound management of our natural resource base. The Fifth Environment Action Programme first signposted the way to a policy approach based on this concept. Its principles are still valid, but the analysis in this Communication indicates that they have to be put into practice more fully.

A Sixth Environment Action Programme should in the first place address the shortcomings in the implementation of the Fifth Programme as well as new issues which have emerged since then. Based on its analysis, this Global Assessment suggests a number of orientations for future environmental policy in order to provide a basis for a debate. The Sixth Programme will also need to be seen in the broader context of an enlarged European Union, taking account of the specific issues in the candidate countries. The full implementation of the environmental *acquis* remains another urgent priority.

However, without a reinforced integration of environmental concerns into economic sectors to address the origins of environmental problems and without a stronger involvement and commitment by citizens and stakeholders, our development will remain environmentally unsustainable overall despite new environmental measures. The current momentum for integration, following the mandates of the Cardiff and subsequent European Councils, therefore needs to be maintained and translated into concrete decisions and new instruments to promote integration should be put into place. Better information and citizens' involvement in environmental decisions as well as more accountability for actions which might harm the environment should be pursued as other priority objectives. The effective application of the polluter-pays principle and the full internalization of environmental costs on to polluters remains a critical process. A Sixth Environmental Action Programme should be one pillar in an overall Community strategy for sustainable development addressing environmental, economic, and social objectives in a mutually reinforcing way.

Opinions and contributions to the debate on the Sixth Action Programme will be welcome. Send them to: European Commission, Environment DG (B1-6EAP), Rue de la Loi 200, B-1049 Brussels by 14 April 2000. Or by e-mail to: new-env-prg@cec.eu.int; or via the Environment DG's website at: http://europa.eu.int/comm/environment/newprg/index.htm.

## Introduction

The Fifth Environmental Action Programme was prepared in parallel to the 1992 Rio Conference and the launch of Agenda 21. It constituted the

Community's first commitment to sustainable development. It can be seen in terms of five objectives:

(1) strategies for seven environmental priority issues (climate change, acidification, biodiversity, water, urban environment, coastal zones, and waste) and for the management of risks and accidents;
(2) target sectors into which environmental concerns should be integrated (industry, energy, transport, agriculture, and tourism);
(3) broadening the range of instruments;
(4) information, transparency of approach, and development of the concept of shared responsibility;
(5) the international dimension reflecting global issues and the Rio Conference.

Some environmental targets were set[2] but in general there was a lack of quantifiable targets and monitoring mechanisms. The Commission, in its review of the Plan in 1996, confirmed these priorities and proposed a new priority on implementation of existing measures.

In 1998 the European Parliament and the Council adopted a Decision on the review of the Fifth Environment Action Programme. It reiterated the commitment of the Community to its general approach and strategy and called for increased efforts in their implementation. The Decision also committed the Commission to submit a global assessment of the implementation of the Programme, giving special attention to any revision and updating of objectives and priorities which may be required, and accompanied, where appropriate, by proposals for the priority objectives and measures that will be necessary beyond the year 2000. This Communication is the first step in the Commission's response to this request. It will be followed by a proposal for a Sixth Environmental Action Programme next year. Besides evaluating the success of the Fifth Programme, it seeks to launch a debate on the overall approach for our policy on the environment and sustainable development with a view to preparing the new Programme.

The recent 'Eurobarometer' study of the opinions and attitudes of European citizens shows that the degradation of the environment is a high concern along with violence, poverty, health, and unemployment. 70 per cent believe that urgent action is needed. This echoes the analysis in this report that further efforts are needed for a clean and safe environment ensuring a high quality of life and for a sustainable management of our global resources.

---

[2] See Commission Staff Working Paper (reference) 'Key developments in the implementation of the Fifth Environment Action Programme'. It includes the key objectives and targets established in the Fifth Environment Action Programme and its review data from the European Environment Agency's report on the state of the environment and examples of EU environmental legislation or actions.

## 2. Overall Assessment of the Fifth Programme

The Programme set out an ambitious vision for sustainable development, leading to its incorporation in the Amsterdam Treaty and to the process of integration, which was highlighted by the Cardiff European Council in 1998. However, practical progress towards sustainable development has been rather limited, mainly because there was no clear recognition of commitment from Member States and stakeholders and little ownership by other sectors of the Programme. Nevertheless, the Fifth Programme has stimulated action at EU level that has led to environmental improvements.

## 3. Evaluation of the Seven Environmental Priorities and of Risk Management

Overall, the lack of targets, indicators, and monitoring mechanisms makes it difficult to make a full evaluation of the Fifth Programme. It is also clear that it will take time for many of the actions initiated by the Fifth Programme to yield results. Even so, on the basis of the European Environment Agency's comprehensive evaluation of the state and outlook of the environment, it is possible to identify the main trends that are emerging and the driving forces behind them. The Agency's recent report, 'Environment in the European Union at the Turn of the Century' illustrates that the quality of Europe's environment has improved in some areas, notably in the phasing out of ozone-depleting substances, acidification, trans-boundary air pollution, and water quality. But it points out that serious problems remain and looking beyond the year 2000, the environment faces a number of major and, in some case, new challenges. This situation calls for a reflection on which new measures should be taken at Community level over the next few years. Against this background, this Communication identifies a number of possible avenues for further action in order to provide the platform for a debate, without necessarily being exhaustive and without prejudging future Commission proposals.

### 3.1. Climate change

*Current situation and trends*
There is a broad consensus on the need to take urgent action on climate change. Climate change is potentially the most serious environmental problem we are facing with far-reaching ecological, health, and economic consequences (e.g. flooding of low-lying areas due to rise of sea levels, changes in weather patterns with implications for agriculture, extreme weather events). Estimates are that $CO_2$ emissions need to fall by at least 35 per cent by 2010 if long-term temperature increases are to be limited to 1.5 by 2100. The Kyoto Protocol commits the Community to decrease its greenhouse gas emissions by 8 per cent between

1990 and 2008–12. However, without further measures, forecasts are that the Community will not achieve this objective. While emissions have fallen in the UK and Germany between 1990 and 1996, this has been due to one-off structural changes and the underlying trends are of growing emissions of $CO_2$.

*Measures taken*
While a number of Community measures have been agreed to promote energy efficiency and conservation and renewable energy sources (e.g. ALTENER and SAVE programmes), these have received less funding than originally proposed and have had little impact faced with the scale of the problem. Progress has not been achieved with the proposed directive introducing a tax on $CO_2$ emissions or the amended proposal for an energy products tax.

The recent voluntary agreement reached with the European car industry should contribute to curbing $CO_2$ emissions from individual cars over the next decade.

The trends in sectors such as industry indicate a growing uptake of energy-efficient technologies with a predicted 15 per cent fall in industrial $CO_2$ emissions by 2010. The projections for transport, however, are for continuing strong growth in emissions which are likely to prejudice the achievement of the Kyoto targets.

*Possible orientations for the future*
The Member States have yet to present convincing plans for the achievement of their individual targets agreed within the framework of the Community strategy for meeting the Kyoto commitment. Consideration will be needed for the development and implementation of new emission reduction measures, including integrating climate objectives into other policies.

The development of an emissions trading system within the EU may be advisable to promote cost-efficient emission reduction measures.

### 3.2. Acidification and air quality

*Current situation and trends*
The Fifth Programme period has seen improvements in reducing acidification and the levels of some air pollutants, particularly $SO_2$ and lead. The levels of $NO_2$ and particulates remain high and the levels of ground-level ozone continue to be regularly exceeded in and around major cities during the Summer.

The improvements which have taken place are largely a result of a steady decline in emissions over the last decade. By 1995 emissions of $SO_2$, $NO_x$ and non-methane VOCs were down by about 39, 9, and 12 per cent respectively on 1990 levels. Further substantial improvements in air quality and reductions of acid deposition are expected to take place in the period up until 2010.

The importance of transport emissions of $NO_x$ and VOCs which were dominant in the past has started to decline since 1990. Thus, by 1999, non-methane VOC and $NO_x$ emissions are projected to be down by over 20 per cent on 1990 levels and in 2010 by as much as 70–80 pr cent in spite of the continued growth in traffic.

*Measures taken*

The Air Quality Framework Directive, approved in 1996, provides a basis for tackling remaining air quality problems. A first daughter directive defining limit values for $SO_2$, $NO_2$, particulates, and lead was adopted in April 1999. Proposals on CO and benzene and on ozone are under discussion in the Council and Parliament.

Measures adopted so far to reduce emissions include vehicle emission and fuel quality directives within the Auto-Oil I exercise, directives on solvent emissions from industry, sulphur emissions from heavy fuel oil, and the Integrated Pollution Prevention and Control (IPPC) Directive for industrial emissions. The implementation of these measures will lead to further progressive improvement of air quality over the next decade. It is, however, likely that particulates will remain a problem over much of the Union and that there will continue to be widespread exceedances of WHO guidelines for ozone.

A proposal to set national emission ceilings which compared with 1990 would reduce acid deposition everywhere in the Community by at least 50 per cent and simultaneously reduce exposure to ozone, and a proposal to revise the Large Combustion Plant Directive are currently under discussion in the European Parliament and Council. Implementation of this joint acidification and ozone strategy will be a priority in the next period. The strategy will also reduce ammonia emissions and hence reduce soil eutrophication.

*Possible orientations for the future*

The priority for the next period will be implementation of already approved measures and those currently under discussion. The complexity of air quality issues and range of polluting sources means that a more integrated strategy should be developed to review air quality standards and ensure they are met in the most cost-effective way.

The main remaining challenges appear to be meeting standards for particulate matter in many cities and ensuring coherence between Community targets on ozone, acidification, and soil eutrophication and the emissions of the pollutants concerned, and to develop cost-effective measures to permit further improvements, including flexible instruments. These policy areas will require further review.

### 3.3. Nature protection and biodiversity

*Current situation and trends*

The nature and biodiversity of the Community continues to be under threat from loss of land to urban development and road-building and the ongoing intensification of agriculture. Threats also arise from the marginalization or abandonment of farming activities, pollution, and the introduction of alien species.

*Measures taken*

Attention during the Fifth Programme period has mainly been on the implementation of the previously approved Birds and Habitats Directives, this latter directive providing the framework for the creation of the Natura 2000 network. Implementation of this Directive should ensure the protection of the best of the remaining natural habitats in Europe. While progress has been made in most Member States towards the identification of sites, this is far behind the original deadlines agreed. The long-term protection of these sites requires the adoption of management regimes and considerable efforts are still required for their establishment and implementation.

The adoption of the Community's Biodiversity Strategy in 1998 has been important in recognizing the need for sensitivity to biodiversity issues in other policy areas. This strategy foresees action plans for biodiversity in a number of key policy areas.

Agricultural policy is particularly important to nature and biodiversity. The agri-environment measures introduced in the 1992 CAP reform and the broadening of measures resulting in environmental gain included in the 1999 reform of the Common Agricultural Policy (CAP) have and will in future provide the potentiality for contributing positively to nature protection, both within the Natura 2000 network and in the wider countryside.

*Possible orientations for the future*

The priority for the future will be the full implementation of the Birds and Habitats Directives and to achieve significant progress with the integration of biodiversity concerns into other policies. The preparation of ambitious action plans under the Biodiversity Strategy should be an important element of the approach.

Full exploitation at the national level of the opportunities created by the new CAP regime and Structural Funds will be of importance. In order to ensure the preservation of high nature value landscapes, the continuation of farming in areas at risk of marginalization and abandonment and the increased uptake of agricultural practices more compatible with environmental protection and enhancement is desirable.

### 3.4. Water

*Current situation and trends*

The period of the Fifth Programme has seen improvement in water quality due to progress in implementation of the Urban Waste-Water Directive (1991). In particular, there has been a significant decrease in the number of heavily polluted rivers due to reductions in point source discharges such as phosphorous, with emissions showing reductions of typically 30–60 per cent since the mid-1980s, organic matter discharges fell by 50–80 per cent over the last fifteen years.

However, nitrate concentrations in EU rivers have shown little change since 1980. EU maximum admissible concentrations of nitrate in groundwater are frequently exceeded. This is contributing to the eutrophication of coastal waters. Nitrate input from agriculture is still high due to poor application of the Nitrate Directive. Groundwater concentrations of certain pesticides also frequently exceed EU maximum admissible concentrations.

In addition, there remains a problem in the use and allocation of water. This is generally attributable to inappropriate pricing, which often amounts to subsidy to some users.

*Measures taken*
The key achievements in the Fifth Programme in respect to water management have been:

(a) the passing of the Integrated Pollution Prevention and Control (IPPC) Directive in 1996, which provides a more comprehensive framework for the control of polluting emissions of all kinds from large industrial plants.
(b) the proposal, currently being discussed in Council and Parliament, for a Water Framework Directive. This Directive seeks to achieve good status for all waters, groundwaters, and surface waters, within a set deadline, and to apply an integrated planning approach to protecting all waters, addressing both quantity and quality issues. It brings together elements from a range of individual measures based on a combined approach of emission controls and quality objectives. It also aims at the reduction of pollutants, listing priority substances. The measure is complemented by a number of existing directives aimed at controlling specific sources of polluting substances—the Urban Waste-Water Directive, the IPPC Directive or limits for specific substances, e.g. the Nitrates Directive. Sustainable levels of water abstraction and use will need to be assured by developing a range of instruments, such as water-pricing.

*Possible orientations for the future*
The approval of this proposal will provide the basis for achieving substantial future improvements in the full range of water quality problems that the Community continues to experience.

The priority now is implementation. This imposes a responsibility on national, regional, and local authorities in the Member States to take the necessary steps to ensure policies are carried out.

### 3.5. Urban environment

*Current situation and trends*
Some 70 per cent of our population live in urban areas, which take up some 25 per cent of land in the EU. This inevitably means both that urban populations face a concentration of environmental problems and that the decisions of

urban authorities and inhabitants are significant driving forces behind environmental pressures. This can be illustrated by the following trends:

— 32 per cent of our population are exposed to high levels of traffic noise.
— Air pollution remains a significant source of health problems and WHO thresholds are frequently exceeded.
— Population of urban areas is expected to increase by more than 4 per cent between 1995 and 2010 and urban sprawl continues.
— Urban waste has increased in volume.
— Seasonal water shortages are common in southern European cities.
— Energy consumption by transport and energy has risen steadily over the last twenty years and further increases are anticipated.

*Measures taken*
The Fifth Action Programme recognized that in addition to the indirect effects of specific environmental legislation, the role of Community policy in this area is to encourage local authorities to tackle the problems and to assist them in working towards sustainability. However, no specific targets or monitoring mechanisms were defined. The European Sustainable Cities & Towns Campaign was established in 1994 to support local authorities and it has operated constructively since. In 1998 the Commission published the Communication 'Sustainable Urban Development in the European Union—A Framework for Action'. The adoption of this Communication, which includes concrete commitments on the part of the European Commission, represents important progress towards a more integrated and strategic approach to urban issues.

*Possible orientations for the future*
The Commission is now in the process of implementing the Communication. The Commission could continue to support and facilitate in particular awareness-raising initiatives and activities relating to local sustainability and Agenda 21.

### 3.6. Coastal zones

Many coastal zones are densely populated and under intense pressure from urban development, industry, transport, and tourism. These activities also impact heavily on the quality of the marine environment. At the same time, coastal areas contain an important part of Europe's natural and cultural heritage.

The Community has during the Fifth Programme period undertaken an Integrated Coastal Zone Management Demonstration Programme to show ways to address coastal zone issues. The question is how this Programme should be followed up.

There continues to be need for urgency for action in this area since 85 per cent of coasts are at risk from different pressures, and in particular they are suffering from increasing urbanization.

### 3.7. Waste

*Current situation and trends*

The problems of waste in the EU are still growing faster, due to consumption patterns, than the implementation of measures to control and prevent them.

Waste-prevention measures have not stabilized production of waste nor its hazardousness. Reported municipal waste produced in OECD Europe was 1.305 million tonnes in 1995, or 420 kg/yr per person. The EU average per capita is 370 kg/yr.

The recycling of certain waste fractions has been successful in a number of EU Member States. In the EU and Norway, recycling of paper and paperboard increased from 40 per cent in 1990 to 49 per cent in 1996. Recycling of glass increased from 43 per cent in 1990 to 55 per cent in 1996.

However, recycling of glass and paper have not increased sufficiently quickly to reduce overall generation for these waste streams, so that total glass disposal, for example, rose by 12 per cent. Furthermore, the amount of plastic waste has considerably increased (about 4 per cent per year) but there has been no corresponding increase in plastic recycling.

Total waste, incinerated or land filled, has risen. Landfilling is still the most common treatment method, despite progress in recovery and recycling. Sixty-six per cent of municipal waste went to landfill in 1995, compared to 65 per cent in 1990.

*Measures taken*

During the period of the Fifth Programme the implementation of the Packaging Directive has helped in making progress in recycling of packaging waste, but progress in waste prevention clearly remains to be achieved. The adoption of the Landfill Directive when implemented will contribute to both reducing the environmental impact of landfilling and encourage waste prevention and recycling options.

The Commission has also advanced work on priority waste streams seeking to apply the principles of prevention, material recycling, and producer responsibility, which are recognized as priority approaches in the Community strategy for waste management. Progress has, however, been slower than expected, particularly due to the opposition of product manufacturers to producer-responsibility schemes. The proposal on end-of-life vehicles is expected to be adopted in 2000.

*Possible orientations for the future*

Priority in the future will need to be given to promoting an active product policy in order to make products recyclable from their design phase as well as further preventing waste generation. For major waste streams specific measures will continue to be required (e.g. durable goods, biodegradable waste, packaging waste, hazardous waste such as batteries). The implementation and enforcement at the local level of waste-management strategies will remain a priority. The reduction of the hazard involved and in particular the toxicity of the material sent for waste disposal also remain priorities.

### 3.8. Risk management: Industrial accidents

*Current situation and trends*
From 1984 to 1999 over 300 accidents were reported. In 1997 thirty-seven major industrial hazard accidents were reported in the EU, the highest annual total since records began. More positively, despite incidents like the *Sea Empress*, oil spills from tankers are declining.

*Measures taken*
During the period of the Fifth Action Programme, the Seveso II Directive was completed, requiring industrial operators to show that they have taken full precautions against major accidents. As part of the Directive, the MARS and SPIRS databases were introduced to assist decision-making related to risk management.

*Possible orientations for the future*
For the future, full implementation of Seveso II remains a challenge. However, this legislation only applies to high-risk establishments. Our society and the environment as a whole are sensitive to the threat of accidents and, in the longer term, an integrated approach to assuring protection of persons, environment, and property, including cultural heritage, would be desirable.

### 3.9. Risk management: Nuclear safety and radiation protection

*Current situation and trends*
Nuclear generation accounts for some 34 per cent of electricity production in the EU. In general, the risk of nuclear accidents has declined, but concerns remain about the safety of some reactors in Central and Eastern Europe and the ex-Soviet Union.

Human health is at the centre of the integrated approach on which radiation protection is based. EU standards are regularly updated according to scientific progress.

*Actions taken*
In the period of the Fifth Programme, legislation on safety standards for health protection from ionizing radiation and movements of radioactive substances have been approved. The most important acts relate to a revision of the Directive on Basic Safety Standards for the protection of exposed workers and the public from the dangers of ionizing radiation, and the revision of the Directive on health protection of individuals in relation to medical exposure to ionizing radiation. In addition, a number of regulations have been adopted

relating to the conditions of radioactive contamination governing imports into the EU of agricultural products originating in third countries following the accident at Chernobyl nuclear power station. A regulation on the administrative arrangements for the movement of radioactive substances has been adopted as has a Directive on the administrative arrangements for the shipment of radioactive waste. A number of technical guides, communications, and recommendations on implementation of legislation have been issued.

*Possible orientations for the future*
The Community has no competence in the safety of nuclear installations but supports cooperation between Member States. Ageing nuclear installations, the economic effects of liberalization of the electricity industry, and a steadily increasing number of decommissioning projects require intensifying this cooperation. The unresolved issue of long-term storage or disposal of high-level radioactive waste will require continued special attention.

In Central and Eastern Europe and the newly independent States, priority should be given to encouraging improvements in the safety regimes. With the ex-Soviet Union, especially in north-west Russia, cooperation is essential to help solve the major environmental problems arising from previously poor management practices for spent nuclear fuel and radioactive waste.

### 3.10. Risk management: Civil protection and environmental emergencies

Natural disasters such as earthquakes or landslides have potentially large-scale effects both in terms of fatalities and economic impact. The European Environment Agency quotes studies that suggest economic losses from floods and landslides in the period 1990–6 were 400 per cent greater than during the preceding decade.

Human activity, such as unsuitable land use that causes flooding and land-slides, is both increasing risk and making people more vulnerable to natural disasters. The Community's role in preparing for such events is largely subsidiary to that of the Member States. However, the Community supports the cooperation between national bodies on civil protection and marine pollution.

For the future, priority in this area should be given to the implementation of the recently adopted legal basis for civil protection to allow for long-term planning and management.

### 4. Emerging Concerns

Since the Fifth Environmental Action Programme was adopted, certain issues have increased in urgency and new problems have emerged which at the time received less attention but are now a cause for concern to citizens or have been identified as requiring special action in the light of the state of the environment. The Community should consider whether and/or how to respond to these concerns, where necessary applying the precautionary principle.

## 4.1. Chemicals

Despite some success of control measures in reducing some emissions and concentrations of persistent organic pollutants and heavy metals, there remain some 75 per cent of large-volume chemicals about which there is insufficient knowledge of the potential impact on nature and on human health. At the same time, the chemical industry is expected to increase its output significantly over the next few years.

The Commission intends to present a strategy to speed up the system for reviewing the ever-growing quantities of chemicals, and to look at whether and how there could be control over the volumes and toxicity of chemicals, particularly where there are recognized harmful effects.

## 4.2. Genetically modified organisms (GMOs)

GMO technology has the potential for providing significant benefit to our society. However, there has been growing concern in recent years as to the impact of this new technology on both the environment and human health.

The control of both experimental and commercial deliberate release of GMOs is covered by legislation that provides a common approval system for the whole EU. Preparations are underway to strengthen the legislation in response to the concerns of citizens. This will provide for more substantial monitoring of potential impacts.

## 4.3. Soil

Degradation and loss of soil in particular through erosion, contamination, sealing (building, roads, etc.) and changes in its structure is worryingly high. Soil loss through human activity is some 10–50 times higher than through natural erosion.

There is a need to identify the relationship between Community policies and intervention and soil problems to enable a decision on the development of a coherent approach at Community level. It is also necessary to integrate soil management objectives, in particular objectives of the UN Convention to Combat Desertification into our policies.

### 4.4. Efficient use and management of resources

Natural resources need to be used and managed more efficiently both to conserve non-renewable resources and to reduce the amount of waste. The concept of 'factor ten' expresses the longer-term goal of a tenfold reduction in absolute resource use in the industrialized countries and a more equitable sharing of resources across the world. Should the Community take up this target as a focus for orienting policy in this area? How could the Community promote more eco-efficient production and consumption patterns, reducing material use, energy consumption, and emissions whilst maintaining levels of products and services? In this context, an Integrated Product Policy should address the entire life-cycle of production and consumption, and be based on a mix of instruments, such as labelling and eco-design, links to the Community's Environmental Management and Audit Scheme (EMAS), greening of public procurement and product standards, and product-related taxes, thus addressing the whole product chain including the production, use, distribution, consumption, and waste phase of products. An Integrated Product Policy should provide a framework that incorporates all relevant stakeholders in the development of a specific strategy in an individual product area.

## 5. Improvement and Implementation of Environmental Legislation

### 5.1. Improved legislation

Under the Fifth Programme, legislation has been reinforced in several key areas, for example, with the Air Quality Framework Directive, the Integrated Pollution Prevention and Control (IPPC) Directive, and the Habitats Directive.

The way in which legislative proposals are developed has also improved. First, with better analysis of the environmental issues and the economic and cost–benefit implications. This has helped us to identify the costs to society of environmental damage and to ensure we commit adequate time and resources to tackling environmental problems. At the same time, we have improved the cost-effectiveness of our policies. Several recent initiatives (the Acidification Strategy, Auto-Oil, and the current elaboration of national emission ceiling for certain air pollutants) were subject to such a process. Further efforts will be needed in areas like waste and water and in strengthening the methodology and data aspects, as well as in translating R&D results into policies. Areas of uncertainty need to be properly identified and measures taken to remedy the deficiency of data. The analysis of environmental proposals should also identify the 'winner' and 'loser' of the initiative in question.

Secondly, legislative proposals now aim at better consultation and involvement of stakeholders. Initiatives such as the Water Framework Directive, the

IPPC Directive, and Auto-Oil show that it is possible and positive to involve the relevant actors and sectors in finding solutions to environmental problems. The Auto-Oil Programme in particular has identified important win-win actions required at national and local level to improve air quality in cooperation with the industries concerned.

Thirdly, the Community has increasingly responded to the call for greater subsidiarity, by developing more framework directives that set objectives, but give Member States the flexibility to implement the measures as they require. But, in the implementation phase, it will be important to ensure that this flexibility is not used in ways that prejudice the achievement of the objectives set.

## 5.2. Implementation and enforcement

Under the Fifth Action Programme, increased attention has been given to implementation and enforcement of environmental legislation. The Communication on the state of implementation, published by the Commission in 1996, showed however that implementation of Community law on the environment was often unsatisfactory. In 1998 the Commission registered some 600 suspected breaches of EC environmental law, based on complaints from the public, parliamentary questions, and petitions and cases detected by the Commission. Of the 123 cases for which an application was lodged with the Court in 1998, forty-nine concerned the environment.

The main reasons for this currently unsatisfactory situation are to be found in the legal and technical complexity of the legislation and the difficulty in balancing the interests of the stakeholders concerned. In some cases, environmental legislation relates to general interests in which there is not always a proprietary interest. There is also a shortage of qualified staff and resources for the complex function of inspection and enforcement at national and local levels. Finally, there is a lack of dissuasive, effective, and proportionate sanctions in Member States when measures are not properly implemented.

Efforts have been made to ensure that all relevant actors and sectors are involved in the legislative process, including the IMPEL network of environmental law inspectors. The Commission has proposed the development of Community-wide minimum criteria for the carrying out of environmental inspection tasks by Member State authorities.

In considering future policy we have to remind ourselves that the first step for improving the environment on the ground is the full implementation of what has been adopted already. This will require reinforced efforts. Implementing the *acquis* will require even more effort from the candidate countries for the Enlargement of the European Union. Realizing the objectives of the measures adopted already therefore remains one task in any future environmental strategy and a firm commitment to it by all (present and future) Member States is necessary. It is critical not least for the credibility of Community environmental policy as a whole.

The Commission for its part will continue to exercise its powers in ensuring the correct and timely implementation of Community law, and to improve the information provided to the public on Community policies and their implementation through, e.g. the annual report on monitoring the application of Community law and the Annual survey on the implementation and enforcement of Community Environmental Law. The effectiveness of environment policy should be regularly assessed and remedial measures taken if required. This requires an efficient monitoring system to ensure that the legislation is properly implemented and the Reporting Directive (91/692) needs revising and strengthening to allow this.

## 6. Progress in Broadening the Range of Instruments

### 6.1. Market-based instruments

Widening the portfolio of policy instruments for achieving our environmental objectives was a main pillar of the Fifth Programme. Market-based instruments include taxes, charges, environmental incentive payments, refundable deposit schemes, permit trading systems, eco-labelling schemes, and environmental agreements, etc. They aim at encouraging producers and consumers, via price and information signals in the marketplace, to adopt practices or make choices that take into account the environmental cost of the production and consumption of goods. The important practical issue is to identify when such instruments are likely to be more efficient and effective than other types of policy measures or, alternatively, to identify when they can be an effective supplement to other instruments.

Environmental taxes will, for instance, often be the most efficient way of applying the polluter-pays principle, through the direct internalization of the environmental costs.

At the Member State level, the last five years have seen the implementation of many new measures although some Member States are clearly more active than others. Most importantly, there is growing evidence that these measures do yield the desired effects (for instance, the link between the fall in lead emissions and the introduction of a tax differential between leaded and non-leaded petrol).

At the Community level, many of the Directives issued by the Commission allow for tax incentives to encourage early implementation (such as those on vehicle emissions and fuel quality). However, the adoption of EU-wide measures, such as a $CO_2$ tax or an energy products tax, has been disappointing. The institutional set-up (need for unanimous agreement in the ECOFIN Council) has prevented any real progress.

The introduction of the EU eco-labelling scheme together with the Eco-Management and Audit Scheme (EMAS) were also new initiatives aimed at influencing producer and consumer behaviour through market mechanisms.

The uptake of EMAS by EU manufacturing industry has been encouraging and, although difficult to quantify in precise terms, has almost certainly contributed to reduced emissions and risks for the environment. The EMAS regulation is now being revised and extended to other sectors of business such as the service and retail sectors.

## 6.2. Financial instruments

Since 1993 actions to promote economic and social cohesion under the Structural Funds have had a stronger link to the environment, including the introduction of strategic environment impact assessment of programmes. More funding has been devoted in the 1993–9 period to environmental investments. The Cohesion Fund has provided an increasing share of its total amount to environmental projects (equivalent to 49.1 per cent).

LIFE, the only programme completely devoted to the environment, has produced many examples of innovative technologies, good practice, and integration at local levels.

Development banks have begun to incorporate environmental criteria into their lending operations. However, progress with private banks and insurers in providing 'green' financial products, green housekeeping, or increased environmental risk assessment is still fairly limited.

Subsidies can have significant impacts on the environment, either positive or negative. Even if they are not deliberately established with the intention of harming the environment, they are often introduced without taking the environmental consequences into account. For example, it is estimated that if energy subsidies were removed in Western Europe + Japan, $CO_2$ emissions in the OECD would be reduced by 13 per cent over the baseline scenario by 2005.

On the other hand, progress has been made, notably in the reform of the Common Agricultural Policy under Agenda 2000. There has been a shift away from product subsidies to income support that is linked, in part, to the adoption of environment-friendly agricultural practices. In addition, agri-environment programmes offer payments to farmers that provide environmental services.

Overall, the experience of the last few years shows that there is potential to direct funding, directly and indirectly, towards environmental benefits. But further progress must be made, in particular for energy and transport subsidies to ensure environmental criteria are fully integrated into EU funding criteria (e.g. for the structural funds).

## 6.3. Research and development

Research and development, through successive EU framework programmes, offers the possibility to address both the scientific, technological, and socio-economic dimensions of the environment.

The Fifth Framework Programme covers subjects such as the Management and Quality of Water, Global Change, Climate and Biodiversity, Marine Ecosystems, City of Tomorrow, Generic Research on Natural Hazards, and Earth Observation. It provides more than 2 billion euros for collaborative environmental research under the programme 'Energy, Environment and Sustainable Development' over the period 1999–2002.

Research results provide operational information for decision-making and for developing environmental policy. The Community's research programmes have the added benefit of promoting the involvement of scientists in environmental issues. Through the many networks set up in transnational research projects, it helps to build consensus among scientists who feed decision-making at the national, European, and international level.

## 6.4. Spatial instruments

Although land-use planning is mainly the responsibility of Member States, a number of key initiatives at EU level of a strategic nature provide scope for developing a more integrated approach. This is the case with the European Spatial Development Perspective, which is intended to promote cooperation between Member States in pursuit of sustainable development through a more balanced spatial use of EU territory. This new generation of land-use instruments can assist cooperation between Member States and between regions and local authorities providing a reference framework on issues such as urban and rural development, the management of sensitive areas or in sectors like transport policy.

## 7. International Issues

Approximately one-third of Community environmental policy aims to implement legally binding international commitments. The EU plays a major role at the negotiating table, and in pushing the implementation of agreements on global issues (e.g. ozone layer, climate change, biodiversity), regional issues (acidification, waste, and water), and all issues relating to hazardous products, such as chemicals or radio-active substances. Research action, supported under the Fourth and Fifth Framework Programmes, provides an important support to these international activities. The EU has also been instrumental in developing many of the international processes that provide guidance to governments on how to develop their environmental policy. This includes an active follow-up to the Rio Declaration and Agenda 21 and supporting activities through the UN Environment Programme.

However, the EU could be more visible and should more systematically use its full economic and political weight and strengthen the coherence between different policies. Trade remains an area of concern, where progress must be made on reconciling the objective of growth in trade with environmental objectives. This is the general approach already adopted by the Community in view of the next WTO round. Climate change is a global problem that can only be solved through concerted efforts at international level. The EU should maintain its leadership in the international negotiations over the next years.

## 8. Overall Progress towards Sustainable Development

The Fifth Environment Action Programme sought to initiate the Community's path towards sustainable development. As this global assessment confirms, however, many environmental trends are not sustainable and the quality of life of citizens continues to be affected, despite progress made in environmental legislation and (although to a lesser extent) in broadening the range of instruments. On the one hand, economic growth, better communications, and transport contribute to an improved quality of life. On the other hand, however, the growth and nature of human activities, expressed through growing consumption of products and services, also means increased use of natural resources and increasing pressures on the environment. Environmental policy has had some success in combating the effects of these pressures, for example, in encouraging cleaner fuel or in reducing or preventing industrial discharges into rivers, the air, and ultimately the sea. However, according to current predictions, it will not be able to keep pace with or account for the increasing aggregate demand for road transport, electricity, house- or road-building, etc. Growth in these areas simply outweighs the improvements attained by better technology and stricter environmental controls. An analysis of the causes of environmental problems confirms the areas of particular concern that were highlighted by the Fifth Programme: road transport, energy production and use, tourism, the production and consumption of consumer goods, and intensive agriculture.

There are a number of issues which highlight in a particular way the need for addressing the environment together with the economic and social dimensions.

*Climate change*
The 'business-as-usual' scenario predicts that the European Union will fail to reach its Kyoto commitment to cut greenhouse gas emissions by 8 per cent by 2008–12 and instead increase its emissions over the coming years. The problem is being aggravated by the fact that the Kyoto targets are only a first step towards achieving the ultimate goal of stabilizing concentrations of these gases.

In this light, current trends, for example in the transport sector, are clearly not in line with the Community's climate change commitments. For transport, which accounts for about a quarter of total $CO_2$ emissions, the Commission has forecast an increase in $CO_2$ by close to 40 per cent between 1990 and 2010 under current conditions.[3] More fuel-efficient cars as a result of the

[3] Communication on Transport and $CO_2$—Developing a Community Approach, COM(1998) 204 final.

Except in industry, where $CO_2$ emissions are projected to decline by 15 per cent between 1990 and 2010, no sector is expected to actually contribute to the EU's Kyoto target under 'business-as-usual' as emissions remain stable.

Community's strategy to reduce $CO_2$ emissions from cars will not be sufficient to outweigh the effect of traffic growth.

Besides focusing on promising individual emission-reduction measures, a strategy to prevent climate change, therefore has to make climate change considerations part of the decisions in a broad range of other sectors— besides energy and transport particularly industry, agriculture, and households. Higher energy efficiency, the increased use of renewable energy sources, and ultimately a decrease in demand for energy and transport will have to be achieved. This can only be done in a framework going far beyond environmental policy and changing societal development patterns, taking into account the environmental, economic, and social impacts. At the same time, the potential costs of climate change to our economy are enormous and actions to improve the energy efficiency of our society will yield immediate economic benefits in terms of reduced wastage and technological progress.

*Globalization and increased pressure on limited natural resources*
Globalization offers opportunities for higher environmental standards worldwide, but at the same time is likely to increase the consumption of resources. Increased trade and higher levels of wealth of developing countries should lead to an improvement of environmental standards in those countries as emerging urbanized middle classes raise awareness and demand for sustainable development and a better environment. The more rapid transfer of information between countries and the transfer of better and less polluting technologies should reduce pressures on the environment.

On the negative side, increased levels of trade are likely to put further pressure on the environment through the increased level of transport and the increased demand for cheaper raw materials and goods supplied by developing countries as trade barriers come down. Final consumption by society as a whole is expected to rise by 50 per cent by 2010 as the high-level consumption patterns of the West spread to large sections of the global population. Increasing population and forecasts of rising GDP per capita (a 40 per cent increase between 1990 and 2010 and a 140 per cent by 2050) may also have an impact on global $CO_2$ emissions, which are forecast to rise by a factor of three by 2050.

This sharpens the need for developed countries to reduce the use of resources to more sustainable levels to allow the developing world a fair share in global resources.

*Citizens' health and quality of life*
While progress has been made in improving ambient quality, the state of Europe's environment continues to affect public health and the quality of life of citizens. Air pollution is associated with hospitalizations and extra deaths in the EU every year. Noise exposure disturbs sleep, affects childrens' cognitive development, and may lead to psychosomatic illnesses. The Commission has estimated that the external costs of air pollution and noise from traffic amount

to 0.6 per cent of GDP.[4] These effects deprive Europeans of the safe and clean environment which they deserve. In addition, they represent an economic cost to society in the form of health care and reduced productivity. The BSE crisis illustrates the potential social costs of unsustainable agricultural practices.

The external economic costs caused by a lack of environmental controls and unsustainable patterns of production and consumption demonstrate the inefficiency of an unsustainable development path and how it affects European citizens. They underline the case for an overall strategy bringing together the environmental, economic, and social dimensions and the promotion of the polluter-pays principle, wherever possible.

Climate change, the legitimate expectations of developing countries for a fair share of the world's limited resources, and the costs to citizens and society of 'non-environment' all call for an environmentally more sustainable development path for the EU while meeting our economic and social aspirations. They illustrate the need for addressing environmental problems through changes in different economic sectors and the broader economic and social benefits which would accrue from such a broader approach. The trends highlighted in this Communication, however, show that we are not on track in ensuring sustainable development. Further environmental policy measures under a Sixth Environmental Action Programme can be expected to go some way in remedying environmental problems. However, given the societal trends underlying environmental pressures, more environmental legislation alone will not be sufficient.

## 9. Building on the Principles of the Fifth Programme

This global assessment of the Fifth Environment Action Programme confirms that the Community has made progress in developing its environmental policy and that this is starting to lead to improvements in the environment in certain areas. Progress towards sustainability has clearly been limited and the Fifth Programme has not achieved its objectives. While there is growing awareness of the importance of integrating environmental objectives into other policies, often in response to the search for more flexible and cost-effective ways of achieving solutions, this approach and the new range of instruments it relies upon, is still poorly developed in many sectors. The underlying trends in many economic sectors and their continuing link with environmental impacts gives cause for concern.

Against this background, the Commission believes that the main principles of the Fifth Environmental Programme remain valid and that we should build on them with further action. The starting point for progressing the Community's policy for protecting and improving the environment is the need to learn from the successes and address the shortcomings in putting the Fifth Programme

---

[4] Green Paper 'Towards Fair and Efficient Pricing in Transport', COM(95) 691 final.

into practice. Besides the implementation and where needed the strengthening of existing measures and the development of new measures to address emerging problems under a Sixth Environment Action Programme, reinforced integration of environmental concerns into other policies and the stronger involvement of citizens and stakeholders in the process aiming at commitment and responsibility are the keys towards sustainable development.

In essence, what we have to achieve is a decoupling of the negative impacts on the environment and the consumption of natural resources from economic growth. Decoupling means economic growth while keeping the environment intact by a more efficient use of resources and higher environmental standards. By enhancing the eco-efficiency of our patterns of production and consumption, we will reduce the footprint of our society on this planet, thereby safeguarding the aspirations of developing countries and both the present and future generations.

### 9.1. Integration—addressing the environmental implications of sector policies

The Fifth Action Programme recognized the key role of the economic sectors in driving environmental change. Since June 1998 the European Council has given new impetus to the process of integrating the environment into other policies by requesting different formations of the Council to report on environmental integration and prepare environmental strategies. The reports and strategies by six Council formations will be examined by the Helsinki European Council at the end of 1999. They are seen as critical to achieving a more structured approach to sectoral contributions to solving environmental problems. The Commission's Working Paper to the Helsinki Summit contributes to this review and suggests further actions for the future. At the same time, they are steps in an ongoing process which necessitates:

— a strong political commitment to integration;
— strengthening of the institutional arrangements; and
— sound management of the overall quality of the process.

More specifically, the likelihood that integration strategies succeed increases if they include:

— objectives, that are quantified as far as possible, and measures;
— European, national, regional, and local components; and
— indicators for monitoring progress and evaluating the effectiveness of policies.

Integration is a process of better understanding the links and the different interests and trade-offs involved in trying to reach a consensus among actors. It is therefore a challenge of modernization of administrations as it implies a new and open management culture and practices, more dialogue, and transparency. A number of tools and skills promote such a new culture:

— Research and development, via the Fifth Framework Programme and the exploitation of results of previous Programmes, can contribute to improved knowledge. Research can provide decision-makers with information on the impact of socio-economic activities on the environment and on the best alternatives for the adaptation of policies.

— Strategic environmental assessment (SEA) is a tool to ensure that relevant and timely information is available to the decision-makers and that the stakeholders and the general public are informed and consulted in the decision-making process, and improves the quality of decision-making at all levels.

— Economic evaluation helps in understanding the hidden environmental costs of actions as well as identifying the most cost-effective options for achieving the different objectives.

— Indicators, both in the form of environmental headline indicators measuring environmental pressures and in the form of integration indicators for individual sectors, help policy-makers by providing factual information that show trends over time. They aim to provide the information basis for more integrated policy decisions within particular sectors and across sectors, ensuring that main environmental concerns are covered by a coordinated policy.

— Tools such as EMAS, once extended to all economic sectors and public authorities, will be an incentive for adapting administrative structures and management.

Agenda 2000 was a positive step that shows how environmental, economic, and social goals can be put into practice in the framework of agriculture, enlargement, and regional policy. It will now depend on the Member States to take up the opportunities offered by Agenda 2000.

The Community will have to push ahead in its efforts in making the environment part of decisions in all policy areas and at European, Member States, regional, and local levels if it is to meet its environmental objectives and live up to citizens' expectations.

### 9.2. Involvement of citizens and stakeholders

An important element of the Fifth Programme, with its emphasis on integration and working in partnership with the economic sectors, was the concept of shared responsibility. Integration will not work without stakeholders taking ownership and citizens being enabled by sound information to participate. While European citizens' concern about the degradation of the environment is high, many people have a restricted view of what they can do to protect the environment and few have confidence in the public information and in the efficiency of public policy. Insufficient ownership on the part of stakeholders is one of the sources of the limited success of the Fifth Action Programme.

The Community has provided itself already with instruments setting incentives for stakeholders to take their responsibilities. These include the eco-auditing scheme (EMAS), eco-labelling, environmental agreements satisfying a clear set of criteria, the LIFE instrument, and support for activities to promote the exchange of experience and best practice (e.g. Sustainable Cities Campaign). An effort has to be undertaken to ensure that full use is made of these instruments. A system of liability for environmental damage would complement this toolbox and promote a higher level of accountability. A liability regime would help ensure that polluters pay for environmental damage. It would contribute to a better implementation of the precautionary principle and the prevention of environmental problems. Factoring the environmental costs of human and economic activities into market prices in line with the polluter-pays principle through fiscal and other economic instruments would be a critical step forward.

Experience shows us that when citizens act, policies start to change for the better. If we want to change behaviour, citizens should be well informed and empowered.

Information needs to be recognized—more than ever before—as a tool enabling citizens to make sound choices on the basis of their own ethical considerations and corresponding to their overall high level of environmental concern. Providing up-to-date information on the state of the environment and on alternative behavioural options must be central components of future policy.

Better access to information, citizens' participation in the political process, and access to justice in environmental matters will give citizens an increased stake in their environment and promote a sound environmental policy. The Amsterdam Treaty (Article 255) grants citizens the right of access to the documents of the European institutions. This now has to be translated into the rules of the Institutions by May 2001. The 1998 Aarhus Convention (UN/ECE Convention on Access to Information, Public Participation in Decision-Making, and Access to Justice in Environmental Matters) will, once ratified, play an important role in 'democratizing' environmental management. This, in turn, will lead to a more informed and open debate between all the stakeholders on the possible solutions to environmental problems. Finally, indicators that measure the performance of policies and progress are a practical tool for ensuring transparency and critical public review.

Relatedly, education and training on environment should be supported more through Community programmes such as Socrates and Leonardo da Vinci.

## 10. Conclusions: From Environment to Sustainable Development, the Next Steps

The assessment of the Fifth Environmental Action Programme shows that we have made progress on environmental legislation but only modest successes in the integration of the environment into other policy areas. The general approach of the programme remains valid, though, and forms the starting point for future policy. The main challenges we face are linked to unsustainable patterns of consumption and production, which:

— erode the quality of the environment;
— generate health and safety concerns;
— waste resources; and
— give rise to new and potentially damaging climatic conditions.

Today, the Union is far from achieving its broader objective of sustainable development as reflected in the Amsterdam Treaty. The task now facing us is how we can give substance to this commitment. In essence it requires a change in the way we define economic, social, and environmental objectives so that they become complementary and jointly contribute to sustainability. Progress will depend not only on action at Community level but also to a large extent on the willingness of Member States to take up their responsibilities.

A strategic approach to sustainable development could consist of a set of guiding principles and objectives backed up by action plans that address the different economic, social, and environmental aspects. A Sixth Environment Action Programme would be one of the pillars of the strategy, addressing key environmental priorities alongside the strategies of the main economic sectors and delivering the environmental policy measures which are essential for sustainability. The new Programme would set general objectives that will need to be translated into quantifiable targets to steer the development of both environmental measures and the strategies in the economic sectors. The environmental priorities for the Sixth Action Programme have to be seen in the broader context of an enlarged EU and one challenge will be for the EU to develop an environmental strategy for the enlargement process.

A broad-ranging debate involving all interests will be a critical element of the preparation of the Sixth Programme. This document aims at providing a platform for that debate on the overall approach and the priorities to be included in the new programme.

B. WHITE PAPER ON ENVIRONMENTAL LIABILITY, COM(2000)66 FINAL

## Introduction

These days, we are confronted with cases of severe damage to the environment resulting from human acts. The recent incident with the *Erika* resulted in a large contamination of the French coast and the suffering and painful death of several hundred thousands sea birds and other animals. This was by far not the first case of an oil spill at sea with terrible consequences for the environment. Some years ago a catastrophe of a different kind happened near the Doñana nature reserve, in the south of Spain, when the breach of a dam containing a large amount of toxic water caused enormous harm to the surrounding environment, including innumerable protected birds. These and other similar events raise the question of who should pay for the costs involved in the clean-up of the pollution and the restoration of the damage. Should the bill for this be paid by society at large, in other words, the taxpayer, or should it be the polluter who has to pay, in cases where he can be identified?

Also in relation to genetically modified products, there is serious public concern that these may affect our health, or may have negative effects on the environment. This concern results in a call for liability of responsible parties.

One way to ensure that better caution will be applied to avoid the occurrence of damage to the environment is indeed to impose liability on the party responsible for an activity that bears risks of causing such damage. This means that, when such an activity really results in damage, the party in control of the activity (the operator), who is the actual polluter, has to pay the costs of repair.

This White Paper sets out the structure for a future EC environmental liability regime that aims at implementing this polluter-pays principle. It describes the key elements needed for making such a regime effective and practicable.

The proposed regime should not only cover damage to persons and goods and contamination of sites, but also damage to nature, especially to those natural resources that are important from a point of view of the conservation of biological diversity in the community (namely the areas and species protected under the Natura 2000 network). So far, environmental liability regimes in EU Member States do not yet deal with that.

Liability for damage to nature is a prerequisite for making economic actors feel responsible for the possible negative effects of their operations on the environment as such. So far, operators seem to feel such responsibility for other people's health or property—for which environmental liability already exists, in different forms, at the national level—rather than for the environment. They tend to consider the environment 'a public good' for which society as a whole should be responsible, rather than an individual actor who happened to cause damage to it. Liability is a certain way of making people realize that they are also responsible for possible consequences of their acts with regard to nature. This expected change of attitude should result in an increased level of prevention and precaution.

## Executive Summary

This White Paper explores various ways to shape an EC-wide environmental liability regime, in order to improve application of the environmental principles in the EC Treaty and implementation of EC environmental law, and to ensure adequate restoration of the environment. The background includes a Commission Green Paper in 1993, a Joint Hearing with the European Parliament that year, a Parliament Resolution asking for an EC directive and an Opinion of the Economic and Social Committee in 1994, and a Commission decision in January 1997 to produce a White Paper. Several Member States have expressed support for Community action in this field, including some recent comments on the need to address liability relating to genetically modified organisms (GMOs). Interested parties have been consulted throughout the White Paper's preparation.

Environmental liability makes the causer of environmental damage (the polluter) pay for remedying the damage that he has caused. Liability is only effective where polluters can be identified, damage is quantifiable, and a causal connection can be shown. It is therefore not suitable for diffuse pollution from numerous sources. Reasons for introducing an EC liability regime include improved implementation of key environmental principles (polluter pays, prevention, and precaution) and of existing EC environmental laws, the need to ensure decontamination and restoration of the environment, better integration of environment into other policy areas, and improved functioning of the internal market. Liability should enhance incentives for more responsible behaviour by firms and thus exert a preventive effect, although much will depend on the context and details of the regime.

Possible main features of a Community regime are outlined, including: no retroactivity (application to future damage only); coverage of both environmental damage (site contamination and damage to biodiversity) and traditional damage (harm to health and property); a closed scope of application linked with EC environmental legislation: contaminated sites and traditional damage to be covered only if caused by an EC-regulated hazardous or potentially hazardous activity; damage to biodiversity only if protected under the Natura 2000 network; strict liability for damage caused by inherently dangerous activities; fault-based liability for damage to biodiversity caused by a non-dangerous activity;[5] commonly accepted defences, some alleviation of the plaintiffs' burden of proof and some equitable relief for defendants; liability focused on the operator in control of the activity which caused the damage; criteria for assessing and dealing with the different types of damage; an obligation to spend compensation paid by the polluter on environmental restoration; an approach to enhanced access to justice in environmental damage cases; coordination with international conventions; financial security for potential liabilities, working with the markets.

Different options for Community action are presented and assessed: Community accession to the Council of Europe's Lugano Convention; a regime covering only transboundary damage; a Community recommendation to guide Member State action; a Community directive; and a sectoral regime focusing on biotechnology. Arguments for and against each option are given, with a Community directive seen as the most coherent. A Community initiative in this field is justified in terms of subsidiarity and proportionality, on grounds including the insufficiency of separate Member State regimes to address all aspects of environmental damage, the integrating effect of

---

[5] See a schematic view of the possible scope of the regime in the annex to this summary.

common enforcement through EC law and the flexibility of an EC framework regime which fixes objectives and results, while leaving to Member States the ways and instruments to achieve these. The impact of an EC liability regime on the EU industry's external competitiveness is likely to be limited. Evidence on existing liability regimes was reviewed and does suggest that their impact on national industry's competitiveness has not been disproportionate. The effects on SMEs and financial services and the important question of insurability of core elements of the regime are dealt with. Effectiveness of any legal liability regime requires a workable financial security system based on transparency and legal certainty with respect to liability. The regime should be shaped in such a way as to minimize transaction costs.

The White Paper concludes that the most appropriate option would be a framework directive providing for strict liability for damage caused by EC-regulated dangerous activities, with defences, covering both traditional and environmental damage, and fault-based liability for damage to biodiversity caused by non-dangerous activities. The details of such a directive should be further elaborated in the light of consultations. The EU institutions and interested parties are invited to discuss the White Paper and to submit comments by 1 July 2000.

## 1. Introduction

### 1.1. The aim of this White Paper

According to Article 174(2) of the EC Treaty:

Community policy on the environment shall be . . . based on the precautionary principle and on the principles that preventive action should be taken, that environmental damage should as a priority be rectified at source and that the polluter should pay.

The purpose of this White Paper is to explore how the polluter-pays principle can best serve these aims of Community environmental policy, keeping in mind that avoiding environmental damage is the main aim of this policy.

Against this background, the Paper explores how a Community regime on environmental liability can best be shaped in order to improve the application of the environmental principles of the EC Treaty and to ensure restoration of damage to the environment. The White Paper also explores how an EC environmental liability regime can help to improve the implementation of Community environmental law, and examines the possible economic effects of such Community action.

### 1.2. The structure of the White Paper

After an introductory part containing some background information and explaining the aim of environmental liability in sections 1 and 2, the White

Paper presents the case for an EC regime in section 3. Section 4 contains some possible features of a Community regime and section 5 considers and compares different options for such a regime. Whereas section 6 considers the issue from the perspective of subsidiarity and proportionality, section 7 examines the economic impact of an EC environmental liability regime. Section 8, finally, draws a conclusion and sets out the next steps in this matter.

## 1.3. Background and institutional context

### 1.3.1. *The Green Paper on Remedying Environmental Damage*

In May 1993 the Commission published its Green Paper on Remedying Environmental Damage.[2] Over 100 comments were submitted from Member States, industry, environment groups, and other interested parties, followed up by continuous consultations. A Joint Public Hearing was held by the Parliament and the Commission in November 1993.

### 1.3.2. *The position of the European Parliament*

In April 1994 the European Parliament adopted a Resolution, calling on the Commission to submit 'a proposal for a directive on civil liability in respect of (future) environmental damage'.[3] In that Resolution, the Parliament applied for the first time Article 192(2) (ex-Article 138b(2) EC Treaty, which enables it to ask the Commission to submit legislative proposals. Since then, the issue of environmental liability has been raised by the Parliament on several occasions, such as the Commission's annual working programmes, in parliamentary questions, and in letters to the Commission.

   In its Questionnaire to the candidate Commissioners in view of their Hearings, the Parliament again raised this question and expressed once more its view that Community legislation in this field is urgently needed. It stressed in particular the need to insert liability provisions in existing Community legislation in the field of biotechnology.

### 1.3.3. *The Opinion of the Economic and Social Committee*

A detailed Opinion on the Green Paper was issued by the Economic and Social Committee on 23 February 1994, which supported EC action on liability for environmental damage, suggesting that this could take the form of a framework directive on the basis of Treaty Articles 174 and 175 (ex-Articles 130r and 130s).[4]

### 1.3.4. *Commission's decision for a White Paper*

Following an orientation debate on 29 January 1997, the Commission decided, taking into account the need to reply to the Resolution from the European

---

[2] Communication of 14 May 1993 (COM(93)47 final) presented to the Council, the Parliament, and the Economic and Social Committee.
   [3] Resolution of 20 Apr. 1994 (OJ C 128/165).
   [4] ESC Opinion of 23 Apr. 1994 (CES 226/94).

Parliament of 1994 asking for Community action, that a White Paper on environmental liability should be prepared.[5]

### 1.3.5. Member States' positions

A number of Member States have expressed, informally or formally, a favourable opinion with respect to Community action in the field of environmental liability in general (Austria, Belgium, Finland, Greece, Luxembourg, the Netherlands, Portugal, and Sweden). Several Member States are known to be awaiting the Commission's proposals before embarking on national legislation in this field, especially with respect to liability for damage to biodiversity. Furthermore, Austria, Belgium, Finland, Germany, the Netherlands, Spain, and Sweden have recently declared in Council that they welcome the Commission's intention, in the context of the forthcoming White Paper on liability, to assess the question of liability for environmental damage linked to the deliberate release and placing on the market of GMOs. The UK has recently called upon the Commission as a matter of priority to consider the feasibility of and possible criteria for a liability regime or regimes to cover the release and marketing of GMOs. The positions of the other Member States are not yet clear.

### 1.3.6. The consultation process

During the process of preparing the White Paper, consultations have been held with independent experts from the Member States, with national experts from the Member States, and with interested parties, many of whom have also sent written comments in relation to informal working papers that they received in the course of the process. The views expressed were quite different, among other things with respect to the need for Community action. A summary report of the comments from interested parties is available on request.

## 2. What Is Environmental Liability?

### 2.1. The aim of environmental liability

*Environmental liability aims at making the causer of environmental damage (the polluter) pay for remedying the damage that he has caused.*

Environmental regulation lays down norms and procedures aimed at preserving the environment. Without liability, failure to comply with existing norms and procedures may merely result in administrative or penal sanctions. However, if liability is added to regulation, potential polluters also face the prospect of having to pay for restoration or compensation for the damage they caused.

---

[5] Four studies have been conducted for the purpose of the preparation of an EC policy in this area. Summaries of these studies are available to the public.

## 2.2. The types of environmental damage for which liability is suited

Not all forms of environmental damage can be remedied through liability. For the latter to be effective:

- there needs to be one (or more) identifiable actors (polluters),
- the damage needs to be concrete and quantifiable, and
- a causal link needs to be established between the damage and the identified polluter(s).

Therefore, liability can be applied, for instance, in cases where damage results from industrial accidents or from gradual pollution caused by hazardous substances or waste coming into the environment from identifiable sources.

However, liability is not a suitable instrument for dealing with pollution of a widespread, diffuse character, where it is impossible to link the negative environmental effects with the activities of certain individual actors. Examples are effects of climate change brought about by $CO_2$ and other emissions, forests dying as a result of acid rain, and air pollution caused by traffic.

### 3. The Case for an EC Environmental Liability Regime and its Expected Effects

#### 3.1. Implementing the key environmental principles of the EC Treaty

Environmental liability is a way of implementing the main principles of environmental policy enshrined in the EC Treaty (Article 174(2) ), above all the polluter-pays principle. If this principle is not applied to covering the costs of restoration of environmental damage, either the environment remains unrestored or the state, and ultimately the taxpayer, has to pay for it. Therefore, a first objective is making the polluter liable for the damage he has caused. If polluters need to pay for damage caused, they will cut back pollution up to the point where the marginal cost of abatement exceeds the compensation avoided. Thus, environmental liability results in prevention of damage and in internalization of environmental costs.[6] Liability may also lead to the application of more precautions, resulting in avoidance of risk and damage, as well as it may encourage investment in R & D for improving knowledge and technologies.

#### 3.2. Ensuring decontamination and restoration of the environment

In order to make the polluter-pays principle really operational, Member States should ensure effective decontamination and restoration or replacement of

---

[6] Internalization of environmental costs means that the costs of preventing and restoring environmental pollution will be paid directly by the parties responsible for the damage rather than being financed by society in general.

the environment in cases where there is a liable polluter, by making sure that the compensation which he has to pay will be properly and effectively used to this effect.

### 3.3. Boosting the implementation of EC environmental legislation

If liability exerts the preventive effect described earlier and restoration is ensured when damage does occur, it should also improve compliance with EC environmental legislation. Therefore, the link between the provisions of the EC liability regime and existing environmental legislation is of great importance. Whereas most Member States have introduced national laws that deal with strict liability for damage caused by activities that are dangerous to the environment in one way or another, these laws are very different in scope and often do not cover in a consistent way all damage caused by activities that are known to bear a hazard for the environment. Moreover, these liability regimes are only operational with respect to damage to human health or property, or contaminated sites. Generally, they are not applied to damage to natural resources. It is therefore important that an EC environmental liability regime should also cover damage afflicted upon natural resources, at least those that are already protected by EC law, namely under the Wild Birds and Habitats Directives, in the designated areas of the Natura 2000 network.[7] Member States should ensure the restoration of damage to these protected natural resources in any event, also in cases where a liability regime could not be applied (for instance, if the polluter cannot be identified), since this is an obligation under the Habitats Directive. The preventive effects of liability should have a 'boosting' effect in an enlarged Union, thus facilitating the implementation of environmental rules by new Member States.

### 3.4. Bringing about better integration

The Treaty of Amsterdam introduced in Article 6 of the EC Treaty the principle that environmental protection requirements must be integrated into the definition and implementation of other Community policies and activities. An EC environmental liability regime covering all Community-regulated activities bearing a risk for the environment (see 4.2.2 for activities to be covered) will bring about a better integration of environmental considerations in the different sectors concerned through the internalization of environmental costs.

---

[7] Council Directives 79/409/EEC on the conservation of wild birds, OJ L103, p. 1, and 92/43/EEC on the conservation of natural habitats and wild fauna and flora, OJ L206, p. 7.

### 3.5. Improving the functioning of the internal market

Even if the main objectives of a Community regime are of an environmental nature, it may also contribute to creating a level playing field in the internal market. This is important since most of EU trade takes place within the internal market, i.e. intra-EU trade is more significant than extra-EU trade for Member States, and therefore differences in the legal framework and costs faced by companies in the internal market matter more than differences vis-à-vis third countries.

Currently, the existence of any problem of competition in the internal market caused by differences in Member States' environmental liability approaches is still unclear. This may be because national environmental liability systems in the EU are relatively new and have yet to become totally operational.

However, most existing Member States' environmental liability regimes do not cover damage to biodiversity. The economic impact of the latter could conceivably be significantly higher than the impact resulting from existing national liability laws and reach thresholds where concerns about the competitiveness of firms established in one Member State would advise the national authorities to wait for an EU initiative and refrain from imposing unilaterally liability for biodiversity. If so, this would justify EU action also on the grounds of ensuring a level playing field in the internal market.

The considerations above suggest that an EU liability regime should also be designed with a view to minimizing possible impacts on the EU industry's external competitiveness[8]—an issue which is discussed specifically in section 7. This is one reason for applying a step-by-step approach when introducing a Community regime (see also section 6).

### 3.6. Expected effects

It follows from what is said in paragraph 3.1 on implementing the polluter pays, the preventive and precautionary principles, that it is expected that liability creates incentives for more responsible behaviour by firms. However, a number of conditions need to be met for this effect to happen. For instance, experience with the US Superfund legislation (liability for cleaning up contaminated sites) shows the need to avoid loopholes for circumventing liability by transferring hazardous activities to thinly capitalized firms which become insolvent in the event of significant damage. If firms can cover themselves against liability risk by way of insurance, they will not tend to resort to this perverse route. Availability of financial security, such as insurance, is therefore important to

---

[8] It should be pointed out in this regard that in the framework of environmental liability legislation, which applies also to natural resource damage, the USA applies border-adjusted taxes for the most sensitive sectors, i.e. the oil and chemical industries.

ensure that liability is environmentally effective, a concern that is discussed in section 4.9. Effectiveness of any legal liability regime requires a workable financial security system, which means that financial security is available for the core elements constituting the regime. Moreover, the effectiveness of liability for environmental damage (as opposed to traditional damage) depends on the capacity of administrative and judicial authorities to treat cases expeditiously, as well as proper means of access to justice available to the public.

The overall effect of liability is therefore a function of the broader context and specific design of the liability scheme.

## 4. Possible Features of an EC Environmental Liability Regime

This section provides a description of the possible main features of a Community regime. All or some of these elements will have to be taken into account depending on the option for further action that is chosen (see section 5).

### 4.1. No retroactivity

For reasons of legal certainty and legitimate expectations, the EC regime should only work prospectively. Damage that becomes known after entry into force of the EC regime should be covered, unless the act or omission that resulted in the damage has taken place before entry into force of the EC regime. It should be left to the Member States to deal with pollution from the past. They could establish funding mechanisms to deal with existing contaminated sites or damage to biodiversity in a way which would best fit their national situation, taking into account elements like the number of such sites, the nature of the pollution, and the costs of clean-up or restoration. In order to apply the principle of non-retroactivity in a harmonized way, a definition of 'past pollution' will need to be given at a later stage.

Some transaction costs associated with litigation concerning the cut-off point between what is to be considered past pollution and pollution covered by the regime are to be expected. However, a retroactive system would have significantly higher economic impacts.

### 4.2. The scope of the regime

The scope of the regime has to be approached from two different angles: first, the types of damage to be covered, and second, the activities, resulting in such damage, to be covered. The following subparagraphs set out how this could be dealt with.

### 4.2.1. *Damage to be covered*

Environmental damage

As the regime concerns *environmental liability,* environmental damage should be covered. This is not as self-evident as it may seem: several national laws called 'environmental liability law' (or similar names) deal with traditional types of damage, such as personal injury, or property damage, rather than with environmental damage as such. Damage is covered by such laws if it is caused by activities that are considered dangerous for the environment, or if the damage is caused by effects that result in (traditional) damage via the environment (for instance: pollution of air or water). Examples of such legislation are the German Environmental Liability Act of 1990 and the Danish Compensation for Environmental Damage Act of 1994. In some other national laws, impairment of the environment is also covered, next to traditional damage, but hardly any further rules are given to specify this notion.

In this White Paper, two different types of damage are brought together under the heading *'environmental damage',* both of which should be covered under a Community regime, namely: (*a*) *Damage to biodiversity* and (*b*) *Damage in the form of contamination of sites*

Most Member States have not yet started to explicitly cover biodiversity damage under their environmental liability regimes. However, all Member States have laws or programmes in place to deal with liability for contaminated sites. They are mostly administrative laws aiming at cleaning up polluted sites at the cost of the polluter (and/or others).

Traditional damage

To be coherent, it is important to cover also traditional damage, such as damage to health or property, if it is caused by a dangerous activity as defined under the scope, since in many cases traditional damage and environmental damage result from the same event. Covering only environmental damage under the EC regime while leaving liability for traditional damage entirely to the Member States might result in inequitable results (for instance no or fewer remedies for health damage than for environmental damage caused by one and the same incident). Moreover, human health—an important policy objective in its own right—is an interest closely connected with environmental protection: Article 174(1) of the EC Treaty states that Community policy on the environment shall contribute to pursuit (among other things) of the objective of protecting human health.

### 4.2.2. *Activities to be covered*

The objective of nearly all national environmental liability regimes is to cover activities[9] that bear an inherent risk of causing damage. Many of such activities are currently regulated by Community environmental legislation, or

---

[9] Dealing with substances that bear such an inherent risk is also referred to, in this Paper, as (dangerous) activities.

Community legislation that has an environmental objective along with other objectives.

A coherent framework for the liability regime needs to be linked with the relevant EC legislation on protection of the environment. In addition to ensuring restoration of the environment where this is currently not possible, the liability regime would therefore also provide extra incentives for a correct observation of national laws implementing Community environmental legislation. An infringement of such legislation would not only result in administrative or penal sanctions, but also, if damage results from it, in an obligation on the causer (polluter) to restore the damage or pay compensation for the lost value of the injured asset. This approach of a closed scope, linked with existing EC legislation, moreover has the advantage of ensuring an optimal legal certainty.

The activities to be covered, with respect to health or property damage and contaminated sites, could be those regulated in the following categories of EC legislation: legislation which contains discharge or emission limits for hazardous substances into water or air, legislation dealing with dangerous substances and preparations with a view (also) to protecting the environment, legislation with the objective to prevent and control risks of accidents and pollution, namely the IPPC Directive and the revised Seveso II Directive, legislation on the production, handling, treatment, recovery, recycling, reduction, storage, transport, transfrontier shipment and disposal of hazardous and other waste, legislation in the field of biotechnology, and legislation in the field of transport of dangerous substances. In the further shaping of an EC initiative, the scope of activities will need to be defined with more precision, for instance by setting up a list of all the pieces of relevant EC legislation with which the liability regime should be linked. Moreover, some of these activities, such as activities with respect to genetically modified organisms (GMOs), are not dangerous *per se*, but have the potential, in certain circumstances, to cause health damage or significant environmental damage. This could be the case, for example, in the event of an escape from a high-level containment facility or from unforeseen results of a deliberate release. For this reason it is considered appropriate for such activities to come within the scope of a Community-wide liability regime. In these cases, the precise definition of the regime, for instance the defences to be allowed, might not be the same for all activities related to GMOs, but may have to be differentiated according to the relevant legislation and the activities concerned.

An important factor to be taken into account with respect to biodiversity damage is the existence of specific Community legislation to conserve biodiversity, namely the Wild Birds Directive and the Habitats Directive. These Directives establish a regime, to be implemented through the Natura 2000 network, of special protection of natural resources, namely those important for the conservation of biodiversity. They contain, among other things, requirements that significant damage to protected natural resources should be restored. These obligations are addressed to the Member States. The environmental liability regime would provide the tool to make the polluter pay for the restoration of such damage. Since the objective of the two Directives is the protection of natural resources concerned, *irrespective of the activity that causes damage to them,* and since such resources are vulnerable and can therefore also rather easily be damaged by other than inherently dangerous activities, a liability regime applicable to biodiversity damage should also cover other than dangerous activities which cause significant damage in protected Natura 2000 areas. However, the type of liability in this case should be different from the liability applicable to damage caused by dangerous activities, as is explained in 4.3.

## 4.3. The type of liability, the defences to be allowed, and the burden of proof

Strict liability means that fault of the actor need not be established, only the fact that the act (or the omission) caused the damage. At first sight, fault-based liability[10] may seem more economically efficient than strict liability, since incentives towards abatement costs do not exceed the benefits from reduced emissions. However, recent national and international environmental liability regimes tend to be based on the principle of strict liability, because of the assumption that environmental objectives are better reached that way. One reason for this is that it is very difficult for plaintiffs to establish fault of the defendant in environmental liability cases. Another reason is the view that someone who is carrying out an inherently hazardous activity should bear the risk if damage is caused by it, rather than the victim or society at large. These reasons argue in favour of an EC regime based, as a general rule, on strict liability. As mentioned in 4.2.2, damage to biodiversity should be covered by liability, whether it is caused by a dangerous activity or not. It is proposed, however, to apply fault-based instead of strict liability to such damage *if it is caused by a non-dangerous activity.* Activities carried out in conformity with measures implementing the Wild Birds and Habitats Directives which aim at safeguarding biodiversity would not give rise to liability of the person carrying out the activity, other than for fault. Such activities can, for instance, take place under an agri-environmental contract in accordance with the Council Regulation on support for rural development.[11] The state will be responsible for restoration or compensation of biodiversity damage caused by a non-dangerous activity, in case fault of the causer cannot be established.

In the framework of an environmental liability regime, consistency should be ensured with other Community policies and measures implementing these policies.

The effectiveness of a liability regime depends not only on the basic character of the regime but also on such elements as the allowed defences and the

---

[10] Fault-based liability applies when an operator has acted wrongly intentionally, by negligence, or by insufficient care. Such an act (or omission) may involve non-compliance with legal rules or with the conditions of a permit, or may occur in any other form.

[11] Council Reg. EC No. 1257/99 (OJ L160, p. 80).

division of the burden of proof. The positive effects of strict liability should therefore not be undermined by allowing too many defences, or by an impossible burden of proof on the plaintiff.

*Defences*

Commonly accepted defences should be allowed, such as Act of God (*force majeure*), contribution to the damage or consent by the plaintiff, and intervention by a third party (an example of the latter defence is the case that an operator caused damage by an activity that he conducted following a compulsory order given by a public authority).[12]

Several interested parties, in particular economic operators, have expressed the view that a defence in relation to damage caused by releases authorized through EC regulations, for state of the art and/or for development risk should also be allowed. For economic reasons they need predictability regarding their liabilities to third parties, but the occurrence and extent of these liabilities are subject to ongoing developments in any event (e.g. changes in legislation and case law, medical progress, etc.). Defences like the ones mentioned here are normally not allowed by existing national environmental liability regimes of EU Member States. When deciding on these defences, all relevant impacts should be considered, among others possible effects on SMEs (see also section 7).

*Burden of proof*

In environmental cases, it may be more difficult for a plaintiff and easier for a defendant to establish facts concerning the causal link (or the absence of it) between an activity carried out by the defendant and the damage. Therefore, provisions exist in several national environmental liability regimes to alleviate the burden of proof concerning fault or causation in favour of the plaintiff. The Community regime could also contain one or other form of alleviation of the traditional burden of proof, to be more precisely defined at a later stage.

*Application of equity*

Circumstances might occur which would make it inequitable for the polluter to have to pay the full compensation for the damage caused by him. Some room might be granted to the court (or any other competent body, e.g. an arbiter) to decide—for instance, in cases where the operator who caused the damage can prove that this damage was entirely and exclusively caused by emissions that were explicitly allowed by his permit—that part of the compensation should be borne by the permitting authority, instead of the polluter. Further criteria would need to be defined for such a provision, for instance that the liable operator had done everything possible to avoid the damage.

---

[12] Certain procedural aspects can also be relevant with a view to contesting liability, such as the lack of jurisdiction of the court seized or questions of limitation.

### 4.4. Who should be liable?

The person (or persons) who exercise control of an activity (covered by the definition of the scope) by which the damage is caused (namely the operator) should be the liable party under an EC environmental liability regime.[13] Where the activity is carried out by a company in the form of a legal person, liability will rest on the legal person and not on the managers (decision makers) or other employees who may have been involved in the activity. Lenders not exercising operational control should not be liable.

### 4.5. Criteria for different types of damage

Different approaches are indicated to deal with the different types of damage. For biodiversity damage, liability rules and criteria do not exist to any meaningful extent, so therefore they need to be developed. With respect to liability for contaminated sites, national laws and systems exist, but they are quite different. Traditional damage should be dealt with in a coherent way in relation to the other, environmental, forms of damage, which can only be achieved if the fundamental rules are the same for each type of damage.

#### 4.5.1. Biodiversity damage

Since this area is not generally covered by Member State liability rules, an EC liability regime could make a start with covering this kind of damage within the limits of existing Community biodiversity legislation.

• Which biodiversity damage should be covered?

Damage to biodiversity, which is protected in Natura 2000 areas, based on the Habitats and the Wild Birds Directives, should be covered. Such damage could take the form of damage to habitats, wildlife, or species of plants, as defined in the annexes to the directives concerned.

• When should damage to biodiversity be covered?

There should be a *minimum threshold* for triggering the regime: *only significant damage* should be covered. Criteria for this should be derived, in the first place, from the interpretation of this notion in the context of the Habitats Directive.[14]

• How to value biodiversity damage and ensure restoration at reasonable cost?

---

[13] However, Member States could make other parties liable also, on the basis of Art. 176 EC Treaty.
[14] A Commission services document on the interpretation of this and other notions in the context of Art. 6 Habitats Directive will be published shortly.

Economic valuation of biodiversity damage is of particular importance for cases where damage is irreparable. But if restoration of damage is feasible, there also have to be valuation criteria for the damaged natural resource, in order to avoid disproportionate costs of restoration. A cost–benefit or reasonableness test will have to be undertaken in each separate case. The starting point for such a test, for cases where restoration is feasible, should be the *restoration costs* (including the costs of assessing the damage). For valuing the benefits of the natural resource,[15] a system needs to be elaborated for which inspiration could be gathered from certain systems that exist or are being developed at the regional level (e.g. Andalusia, Hessen).

If restoration is technically not or only partially possible, the valuation of the natural resource has to be based on the costs of alternative solutions, aiming at the establishment of natural resources equivalent to the destroyed natural resources, in order to re-establish the level of nature conservation and biological diversity embodied in the Natura 2000 network.

Valuation of natural resources may be more or less expensive, depending on the method used. Economic valuation methods, such as contingent valuation, travel cost, and other forms of revealed preference techniques that necessitate surveys involving a large number of people can be expensive if carried out in every case. The use of 'benefits transfer' techniques can, however, significantly reduce the cost. The development of benefit transfer data bases, such as the Environmental Valuation Resource Inventory (EVRJ), which contain relevant valuation material, is particularly important. These databases can be used to provide a context to the problem and as a source of directly comparable valuation.

• How to ensure a minimum level of restoration?

Restoration should aim at the return to the state of the natural resource before the damage occurred. To estimate this state, historical data and reference data (the normal characteristics of the natural resource concerned) could be used. Replication of the quality and quantity of the natural resources will mostly not be possible, or only at extreme cost. Therefore the aim should rather be to bring the damaged resources back to a comparable condition, considering also factors such as the function and the presumed future use of the damaged resources.

• The impact of damage to biodiversity on costs of prevention and restoration.

Biodiversity damage, in the sense of this White Paper, may only occur in areas protected under the Habitats and Wild Birds Directives which, once the Natura 2000 network is established, is expected to cover up to around 10 per cent of the EC territory. In these areas only environmentally friendly activities may be carried out. This means that the bulk of environmental damage to

---

[15] For instance, the presence of the middle spotted woodpecker (see cover page), a protected species under the Wild Birds Directive.

these areas may only be caused by plants operating dangerous activities in neighbouring areas. But these plants are already covered by the other pillars of the proposed regime which address damage in the form of traditional damage and contamination of sites. It follows that the only additional cost for these activities due to biodiversity coverage is the one related to prevention of damage to, and restoration of, biodiversity according to the criteria foreseen in the White Paper.

Given that, as said, dangerous activities are not supposed to operate in protected areas, biodiversity damage occurring there will only exceptionally be caused by IPPC industries or large plants for which costs and competitiveness are a critical issue. Hence, the impact of liability for biodiversity damage will be minimal for these industries. On the other hand, the kind of environmentally friendly activities allowed to operate in the protected areas are, by its very nature, likely to internalize cheaply the desired levels of prevention and restoration.

### 4.5.2. Contaminated sites

Most Member States have special laws or programmes to deal with clean up of contaminated sites, both old and new. The Community regime should aim at implementing the environmental principles (polluter pays, prevention, and precaution) for new contamination and at a certain level of harmonization with respect to clean-up standards and clean-up objectives. For contaminated sites, the dangerous activities approach would apply and the regime would be triggered only if the contamination is significant. Contaminated sites include the soil, surface water, and groundwater. Where an area protected under the biodiversity legislation is part of a contaminated site, the regime for biodiversity damage would apply to that area, in addition to the regime for contaminated sites. This might mean that restoration of the natural resource has to be carried out after decontamination of the site.

- Clean-up standards

These are standards to evaluate and decide *whether clean up of a contaminated site is necessary.* As with biodiversity, only significant damage should be covered. The main qualitative criterion for this will be: does the contamination lead to a serious threat to man and the environment?

- Clean-up objectives

These should define the *quality of soil and water at the site to be maintained or restored.* The main objective should be: removal of any serious threat to man and environment. Acceptable thresholds would be determined according to best available techniques under economically and technically viable conditions (as under the IPPC Directive). Another objective should be to make the soil *fit for actual and plausible future use* of the land. These qualitative objectives should where possible be combined with quantified numerical standards indicating the soil and water quality to be achieved. If clean up is not feasible for economic or technical reasons, full or partial containment might be a possibility.

The definition of traditional damage, namely personal and property damage and possibly economic loss, will remain under the Member States' jurisdiction. All the elements of the regime dealt with in this Paper should, however, also be applied to traditional damage, with the exception of the specific rules on access to justice (4.7) and the specific criteria for restoration and valuation of environmental damage (4.5.1 and 4.5.2). For traditional damage, the EC regime should not introduce a notion of 'significant damage'.

*4.5.4. The relation with the Product Liability Directive[16]*

The Product Liability Directive deals with damage to persons and goods (i.e. traditional damage) caused by a defective product, but it does not cover environmental damage. Overlaps between the two liability regimes cannot be excluded in the field of traditional damage. This could be the case, for example, when damage is caused by a product containing dangerous substances which results in it being a defective product due to a higher presence of chemical substances than allowed under EC environmental legislation. In such a case, the Product Liability Directive prevails as the legislation applicable when compensation is sought for traditional damage.[17]

## 4.6. Ensuring effective decontamination and restoration of the environment

An obligation common to biodiversity damage and contamination of sites should be that damages or compensation paid by the polluter for restoration or clean-up have to be effectively spent for that purpose. If restoration of the damage is not or only partially possible for technical or economic (cost–benefit) reasons, compensation mounting to the value of the unrestored damage should be spent on comparable projects of restoring or improving protected natural resources. Determination of comparable projects by the competent authorities should depend on a thorough analysis of the environmental benefits gained.

## 4.7. Access to justice

The case of damage to the environment is different from the case of traditional damage, where victims have the right to raise a claim with competent admin-

[16] Council Dir. 85/374/EEC on the approximation of the laws, regulations, and administrative provisions of the Member States concerning liability for defective products [1900] OJ L307/54, amended by Dir. 99/34/EC; [1999] OJ L 283/20.
[17] The Commission has recently published a Green Paper on product liability, to gather information on the actual application of the Directive and in order to initiate a debate about the possible need for a substantial revision of the Directive.

istrative or judicial bodies to safeguard their private interests. Since the protection of the environment is a public interest, the state (including other parts of the polity) has the first responsibility to act if the environment is or threatens to be damaged. However, there are limits to the availability of public resources for this, and there is a growing acknowledgement that the public at large should feel responsible for the environment and should under circumstances be able to act on its behalf. The Commission has referred to the need for such an enhanced access to justice in its Communication to the Council and Parliament on 'Implementing Community Environmental Law'.[18]

An important legal instrument in this field is the Århus Convention.[19] It includes specific provisions on access to justice that form a basis for different actions by individuals and public interest groups. These actions include: to challenge a decision of a public authority before a court of law or another independent and impartial body established by law (the right of administrative and judicial review), to ask for adequate and effective remedies, including injunctions, and to challenge acts and omissions by private persons and public authorities which contravene environmental law.[20] An EC environmental liability regime could contribute to the implementation of the Convention in Community law, along the following lines.

### 4.7.1. 'Two-tier approach': the state should be responsible in the first place

Member States should be under a duty to ensure restoration of biodiversity damage and decontamination in the first place (*first tier*), by using the compensation or damages paid by the polluter. Public interest groups promoting environmental protection (and meeting relevant requirements under national law) shall be deemed to have an interest in environmental decision-making.[21] In general, public interest groups should get the right to act on a subsidiary basis, i.e. only if the state does not act at all or does not act properly (*second tier*). This approach should apply to administrative and judicial review and to claims against the polluter.

### 4.7.2. Urgent cases (injunctions, costs of preventive action)

In urgent cases, interest groups should have the right to ask the court for an injunction directly in order to make the (potential) polluter act or abstain

---

[18] COM(96)500 final. 'Better access to courts for non-governmental organisations and individuals would have a number of helpful effects in relation to the implementation of Community environmental law. First, it will make it more likely that, where necessary, individual cases concerning problems of implementation of Community law are resolved in accordance with the requirements of Community law. Second, and probably more important, it will have a general effect of improving practical application and enforcement of Community environmental law, since potentially liable actors will tend to comply with its requirements in order to avoid the greater likelihood of litigation' (p. 12).

[19] UN/ECE Convention on Access to Information, Public Participation in Decision-Making and Access to Justice in Environmental Matters, that has been adopted and signed, also by the Community, at the Fourth Ministerial Conference in Århus (Denmark), 23–5 June 1998.

[20] Article 9 Århus Convention.      [21] Article 2(5) Århus Convention.

from action, to prevent significant damage or avoid further damage to the environment. They should be allowed, for this purpose, to sue the alleged polluter, without going to the state first. Injunctive relief could aim at the prohibition of a damaging activity or at ordering the operator to prevent damage before or after an incident, or at making him take measures of reinstatement. It is up to the court to decide if an injunction is justified.

The possibility to bring claims for reimbursement of reasonable costs incurred in taking urgent preventive measures (i.e. to avoid damage or further damage) should be granted, in a first instance, to interest groups, without them having to request action by a public authority first.

### 4.7.3. *Ensuring sufficient expertise and avoiding unnecessary costs*

Only interest groups complying with objective qualitative criteria should be able to take action against the state or the polluter. Restoration of the environment should be carried out in cooperation with public authorities and in an optimal and cost-effective way. The availability of specific expertise and the involvement of independent and recognized experts and scientists can play a fundamental role.

Since costs will inevitably be involved in making use of rights of access to justice, it would be worthwhile to explore how *out-of-court solutions,* such as arbitration or mediation, could be used in this context. Such solutions aim at saving time and costs.

## 4.8. The relation with international conventions

There are a growing number of international conventions and protocols dealing with (environmental) liability in several fields. There is, for instance, a long-standing body of conventions and protocols concerning damage caused by nuclear activities, as well as in the field of oil pollution at sea. A more recent convention deals with damage caused by maritime transport of hazardous and noxious substances; Member States are currently considering its possible ratification. All these conventions are based on a strict but limited liability, and the concept of a second tier of compensation. In the case of oil pollution, the second tier is a fund, fed jointly by the contributing oil companies in the importing states, which compensates—also up to a certain limit—liabilities exceeding the shipowner's liability. In light of recent marine pollution accidents, it should be considered whether the international regime should be complemented by EC measures. The Commission will prepare a Communication on oil tanker safety (June 2000) examining, *inter alia,* the need for a complementary EC regime on liability for oil spills. Different options in this regard will be examined, taking into account the specific character of the sector. More in general, a future EC regime on environmental liability would have to clarify to which extent there is room for application in those areas that are already covered by international law.

## 4.9. Financial security

Insurability is important to ensure that the goals of an environmental liability regime are reached.

Strict liability has been found to prompt spin-offs or delegation of risky production activities from larger firms to smaller ones in the hope of circumventing liability. These smaller firms, which often lack the resources to have risk management systems as effective as their larger counterparts, often become responsible for a higher share of damage than their size would predict. When they cause damage, they are also less likely to have the financial resources to pay for redressing the damage. Insurance availability reduces the risks companies are exposed to (by transferring part of them to insurers). They should therefore also be less inclined to try to circumvent liability.[22]

Insurance availability for environmental risks, and in particular for natural resource damage, is likely to develop gradually. As long as there are not more widely accepted measurement techniques to quantify environmental dam age, the amount of the liability will be difficult to predict. However, the calculation of risk-related tariffs is important for the fulfilment of liabilities under insurance contracts and insurance companies are required to establish adequate technical provisions at all times. Developing qualitative and reliable quantitative criteria for recognition and measurement of environmental damage will improve the financial security available for the liability regime and contribute to its viability, but this will not occur overnight and is likely to remain expensive. This justifies a cautious approach in setting up the liability regime.

Capping liability for natural resource damages is likely to improve the chances of early development of the insurance market in this field, though it would erode the effective application of the polluter-pays principle.

When looking at the insurance market—insurance being one of the possible ways of having financial security, alongside, among others, bank guarantees, internal reserves, or sector-wise pooling systems—it appears that coverage of environmental damage risks is still relatively undeveloped, but there is clear progress being made in parts of the financial markets specializing in this area. One example is the development of new types of insurance policies for the coverage of costs involved in the clean-up of contaminated sites, for instance in the Netherlands.

The insurability of environmental risks is essential for financial security, but depends considerably on the legal certainty and transparency provided by the liability regime. The environmental liability regimes of nearly all Member States, however, have not made financial security a legal requirement. Where this

---

[22] On the other hand, a company that is able to insure against the damages it can potentially cause to natural resources still has an interest in behaving responsibly. This is so because, to get an insurance policy, a company normally has to go through an environmental audit, is often required to have an effective risk management system and, if insurance payments are required, must frequently shoulder part of the bill.

has been done, for instance in the German Environmental Liability Law, the implementation of the provision concerned has run into difficulties, which have so far prevented the necessary implementing decree from being established.

The concerns of the financial sectors are one reason for the step-by-step approach mentioned in this Paper (see section 6). The closed scope of dangerous activities, the limitation to those natural resources which are already protected by existing Community law, and the limitation to significant damage are all aspects which contribute to making the risks arising from the regime better calculable and manageable. Moreover, *the EC regime should not impose an obligation to have financial security* in order to allow the necessary flexibility as long as experience with the new regime still has to be gathered. The provision of financial security by the insurance and banking sectors for the risks resulting from the regime should take place on a voluntary basis. The Commission intends to continue discussions with these sectors in order to stimulate the further development of specific financial guarantee instruments.

## 5. Different Options for Community Action

A range of different options and instruments have been considered in the course of the process of developing an approach to environmental liability. The main ones are described in this section, as well as their advantages and disadvantages.

### 5.1. Community accession to the Lugano Convention

The Council of Europe Convention on civil liability for damage resulting from activities dangerous for the environment was established in 1993. The Commission and all Member States participated in the negotiations. The Convention contains a regime for environmental liability that covers all types of damage (both traditional damage such as personal injury and property damage and impairment of the environment as such), when caused by a dangerous activity. Dangerous activities in the field of dangerous substances, biotechnology, and waste are further defined. The scope is open in the sense that other activities than the ones explicitly referred to may also be classified as dangerous. A summary on the history, contents, and signatories of this Convention is available to the public.

Community accession to this Convention would have the advantage of being in accordance with the subsidiarity principle at international level (new EC legislation should not be established in so far as the matter concerned can be dealt with by Community accession to an existing international Convention). Moreover, the Convention has a comprehensive coverage (all types of damage resulting from dangerous activities) and a wide and open scope, which has the merit of presenting a coherent system and of treating operators of all dangerous activities in the same way. Six Member States[23] have signed the Convention whereas some others may be considering doing so.

Several Member States[24] have already prepared legislation to implement the Convention, or are in the process of preparing ratification. However, some other Member States[25] do not intend to sign or ratify it. The Convention is also open to accession by Central and Eastern European countries, even by countries which are not members of the Council of Europe, so that it could have an important international spread. Accession by the Community could encourage other countries to accede.

Comparing the regime of the Lugano Convention with the environmental liability regimes of the Member States, a general impression is that the Convention goes further than most Member States in some respects (namely in that it explicitly covers environmental damage as such). Its open scope of dangerous activities also goes further than several Member States which have regimes with a closed and more limited scope. These Member States, and most of industry, feel that the scope of Lugano is too wide and gives too little legal certainty and that its definitions, especially in the field of environmental damage, are too vague. The Convention does cover such damage, but in a rather unspecific way. For instance, it does not require restoration nor does it give criteria for restoration or economic valuation of such damage. Thus, if accession to the Convention was envisaged, an EC Act would be needed to supplement the Lugano regime in order to bring more clarity and precision to this new area where liability is concerned.

### 5.2. A regime for transboundary damage only

Member States are increasingly aware of damage caused across their boundaries, not least because of public sensitivity to pollution originating from another country. Awareness of transboundary problems is likely to increase further as the implementation of the Habitats Directive and Natura 2000 progress and it is found that many protected areas straddle borders between Member States. Even if both pollution and immediate damage to one of these areas are within one Member State, the damage may have implications for other Member States as well, for instance by damaging the integrity of a species or a habitat as a whole. Pollution of rivers or lakes also often has a transboundary dimension.

The main argument used in favour of a 'transboundary only' regime is that, on subsidiarity grounds, there are insufficient arguments for applying a liability regime to problems within one Member State, but that transboundary problems are indeed better dealt with at EC level. Disadvantages are that a system that addresses only transboundary problems would leave a serious gap where

[23] Finland, Greece, Italy, Luxembourg, the Netherlands, and Portugal.
[24] Austria, Finland, Greece, the Netherlands, Portugal.    [25] Denmark, Germany, UK.

liability for biodiversity damage is concerned, since this is not yet covered at all by most Member States. The important objective of strengthening the application of Community environmental legislation could not be reached by a regime which would not cover most of the potential infractions of such legislation, namely all those taking place within one Member State. A 'transboundary only' system would also lead to subjects being treated completely differently within one Member State, since some, who happen to be involved in a case of transboundary damage, could be liable under the EC 'transboundary only' regime, whereas others, who are conducting the same activity in the same country and causing similar damage, could walk free if the national regime happened not to cover such a case. This might even call into question the legitimacy of such a regime under the principle of equal treatment as developed in the case law of the European Court of Justice.

### 5.3.  Member States action guided by a Community recommendation

This option, for instance a recommendation linked with existing Community legislation relevant in this field, might have the support of those who are not convinced of the need for a legally binding instrument. They might feel, for instance, that there is insufficient evidence for Member State laws not being adequate enough for dealing with the relevant environmental problems. A recommendation, being a non-binding instrument without enforcement mechanisms, would bring less cost for operators but also less benefit for the environment, among other things in cases of transboundary damage inside the Community, than a binding instrument. Similar arguments would apply to the use of environmental (voluntary) agreements in this context.

### 5.4.  A Community directive

The main differences between a Community directive and Community accession to the Lugano Convention are that the scope of Community action can be better delimited and the regime for biodiversity damage can be better elaborated, in accordance with the relevant Community legislation. Both differences result in more legal certainty than provided by Lugano. It should be noted that, even if the Community does not accede to the Lugano Convention, the latter can provide an important source of inspiration for a future Community directive. As far as the application of a liability regime to non-EU Member States is concerned, it is clear that a Community directive on environmental liability would be taken into account in the enlargement process of the applicant countries, whereas the situation in these countries with respect to environmental liability would also be examined.

Comparing this type of Community action with the more limited and non-binding options described in 5.2 and 5.3, the former is the option with higher added value in terms of a better implementation of the EU environmental principles and law, and of effective restoration of the environment.

## 5.5. Liability sector-wise, namely in the area of biotechnology

On several occasions the European Parliament has asked the Commission to insert liability provisions into existing directives in the field of biotechnology. The option mentioned in 5.4 could be pursued by proposing more focused liability provisions applicable to specific sectors (e.g. biotechnology), instead of a horizontal approach, covering all (potentially) hazardous activities in an equal way.

A horizontal approach has the advantage of providing the general framework in a single act. Provided that the activities covered pose similar environmental risks and raise comparable economic issues, this approach would not only be more consistent but also more efficient. A sector-wise approach would not ensure a coherent system or an equal application of the polluter-pays, preventive, and precautionary principles to activities that are comparable in the sense that they pose a risk to man and the environment. Moreover, the objective of better implementation of all relevant pieces of Community environmental legislation would not be reached if liability provisions were introduced only in one specific area of legislation. Finally, it would be difficult to explain to a sector why it should be singled out for being subject to liability provisions, different from other sectors posing similar risks. For all these reasons, a horizontal environmental liability regime is to be preferred.

## 6. Subsidiarity and Proportionality

The EC Treaty requires Community policy on the environment to contribute to preserving, protecting, and improving the quality of the environment, and to protecting human health (Article 174(1)). This policy must also aim at a high level of protection, taking into account the diversity of situations in the various regions of the Community. *It shall be based* on the precautionary principle and on the principle that preventive action should be taken, that environmental damage should as a priority be rectified at source and that the polluter should pay (Article 174(2)). All these principles, which are, according to the wording of the Treaty (see italics) binding for the EC institutions, are currently not being implemented in an optimal way throughout the Community. One reason for this is that there is a gap in most Member States' liability regimes as far as biodiversity damage is concerned. (See in this context also section 3.)

Moreover, national legislation cannot effectively cover issues of trans-boundary environmental damage within the Community, which may affect, among others, watercourses and habitats, many of which straddle frontiers.

Therefore, an EC-wide regime is necessary in order to avoid inadequate solutions to transfrontier damage.

Member States apply different instruments to implement their environmental liability rules. Some rely more on administrative or public law whereas others use civil law to a larger extent. They all use a mixture of both. *An EC regime should aim at fixing the objectives and results, but the Member States should choose the ways and instruments to achieve these.*

In accordance also with the subsidiarity and proportionality principles, an EC regime—to be based on Article 175 of the Treaty—could be a framework regime containing essential minimum requirements, to be completed over time with other elements which might appear necessary on the basis of the experience gathered with its application during the initial period (step-by-step approach).

In case the instrument for establishing the regime were to be a directive, a coherent application of the system throughout the Community will be ensured through the Commission's monitoring of EC law and the case law of the European Court of Justice.

### 7. The Overall Economic Impact of Environmental Liability at EC Level

An EC regime along the lines of the White Paper would differ in significant respects from existing regimes. Therefore, past experience is insufficient to support any strong views on the overall economic impact of the EC regime, including its external competitiveness impact. The Commission will continue its research in this area and launch further studies on the economic and environmental impact of environmental liability. The findings of these studies will be profoundly assessed and given due weight in the preparation of the Commission's future initiatives in this field. However, at this point evidence on existing liability regimes offers a useful general analytical framework.

Available evidence on the overall impact of environmental regulation on industry competitiveness suggests that no significant negative impact is discernible. There is also available data on the impact of environmental liability regimes. The annual total clean-up costs, though excluding nature resource damage costs, of the retroactive[26] US Superfund represent some 5 per cent of the total amount spent each year in the USA to comply with all federal environmental regulations. No overall figures are available on costs with natural resource damages for the US Superfund. For what concerns the environmental liability regimes in place in Member States, available evidence suggests they have not led to any significant competitiveness problems.

While we are unsure about the effects on external competitiveness of an EC liability regime, it must be taken into consideration that most OECD countries

---

[26] The White Paper argues against retroactive liability that, all else the same, has higher cost impacts.

have environmental liability legislation of some kind. Therefore, an EU environmental liability regime will not amount to the adoption by the EU of a unilateral standard of environment protection.[27]

This does not mean that the international competitiveness of EU industry, and in particular of export-oriented industries and of sectors facing significant competition from imports, should not be safeguarded by all means possible. There are ways to offset potential external competitiveness problems that might be raised by differences in liability standards at international level compatible with world trade rules.

As to SMEs, they often cause more environmental damage than what their size would predict, possibly due to a lack of resources. From this perspective they might experience a more substantial impact. Undesirable side effects such as an increase in the share of damage caused by SMEs could be mitigated by more targeted use of national or EC support mechanisms aimed at facilitating adoption by SMEs of cleaner processes.

The proposed approach to liability protects economic operators in the *financial sector* from liability unless they have operational responsibilities. Undesirable negative impacts on this sector are therefore unlikely. Provided legal certainty with respect to liability and transparency are assured, the impact, in particular on the insurance sector, should be positive over time, as experience is gained with the working of the regime and new markets for insurance products emerge.

The effect of environmental liability on employment is also a relevant issue. Available research on the overall impact of environmental regulation suggests that, while jobs in particular industries may rise or fall, total employment will not be systematically affected.[28]

While there are no available empirical studies on the specific impact of environmental liability on employment, it is clear that there might be some negative impacts as enterprises shift from more environmentally damaging activities and processes to cleaner ones. However, this impact is likely to be counterbalanced. The economic essence of liability is that it provides incentives to increased levels of prevention. It is therefore to be expected that employment in industries providing and using clean technologies and related services will benefit from environmental liability. As insurance for natural resource damage develops, more jobs should also be created in this sector.

The key concept here is sustainable development taking into account in a balanced way, the economic, social, and environmental dimensions.

---

[27] In this context, it is relevant to note that most problems of competitiveness and delocalization present themselves among developed countries rather than between developing and developed ones (a conclusion that is confirmed in the recent WTO study on trade and environment, *Special Studies, 'Trade and the Environment', WTO 1999*). Then, since most OECD countries already have environmental liability legislation of some kind, the impact on external competitiveness of an EC liability regime is likely to be limited.

[28] See e.g. the benchmark study 'Jobs, Competitiveness and Environmental Regulation: *What Are the Real Issues?*', R. Repetto, World Resources Institute, March 1995.

Finally, it must be recalled that the use of policy instruments often generates costs even if they yield a net benefit. Minimization of costs associated with predetermined goals is therefore necessary to pursue.

In the case of liability, transaction costs, i.e. the costs of reaching and enforcing rules, is a matter of specific consideration. Three cases can be mentioned in this respect. First, the case of the USA, where litigation is admittedly more widespread than in Europe, and where liability laws have entailed high transaction costs, mainly legal fees, to the tune of 20 per cent of total enforcement and compensation costs. Secondly, for the strict environmental liability systems in the Member States, there is no evidence that they have given rise to an increase of claims or transaction costs. Finally, there is the experience in the Community with the introduction of the Product Liability Directive (see footnote 9). A study report on the first period of application of this Directive did not find any significant increase in the number or pattern of claims. It can be concluded from this that, when shaping the features of an environmental liability regime, it is important to look at the reasons for the differences in transaction costs between the different systems, and to avoid features that would in particular contribute to such costs.

Rules concerning direct access to justice by parties other than public authorities should also be assessed in this light. The application of out-of-court solutions could be beneficial in this context. Also clean-up and restoration standards should be assessed in the light of the costs they would be likely to generate.

In order to be able to deal with historic pollution and other forms of pollution for which liability would not be a suitable instrument, for instance in case of diffuse damage, or in cases where the polluter cannot be identified, Member States could use—as some already do—other instruments, such as impact fees levied on polluting activities, or funds established at national or regional level.

## 8. Conclusion

This White Paper has sought to assess different options for Community action in the field of environmental liability. On the basis of the analysis set out in this Paper, the Commission considers as the most appropriate option that of a Community framework directive on environmental liability, providing for strict liability—with defences—with respect to traditional damage (namely damage to health and property) and environmental damage (contamination of sites and damage to biodiversity in Natura 2000 areas) caused by EC regulated dangerous activities, and fault-based liability for damage to such biodiversity caused by non-dangerous activities. This approach would provide the most effective means of implementing the environmental principles of the EC Treaty, in particular the polluter-pays principle.

The details of such a framework directive should be further elaborated in the light of the consultations to be held.

The Commission invites the European Parliament, the Council, the Economic and Social Committee and the Committee of the Regions as well as interested parties to discuss and comment on the White Paper. Comments can be sent to the Commission, to the following address: Directorate-General for Environment, Nuclear Safety and Civil Protection Legal Affairs Unit (DG XI.B.3), Rue de la Loi 200, 1049 Brussels, or sent by e-mail to *Carla.DEVRIES@cec.eu.int or Charlotta.COLLIANDER@cec.eu.int* before 1 July 2000.

ANNEX: Possible scope of an EC environmental liability regime

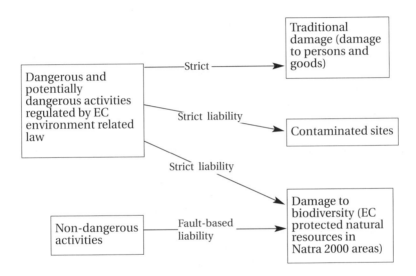

C. COMMUNICATION FROM THE COMMISSION ON THE PRECAUTIONARY PRINCIPLE. COM(2000) 1 FINAL

### Summary

1.   The issue of when and how to use the precautionary principle, both within the European Union and internationally, is giving rise to much debate, and to mixed, and sometimes contradictory views. Thus, decision-makers are constantly faced with the dilemma of balancing the freedom and rights of individuals, industry, and organizations with the need to reduce the risk of adverse effects to the environment, human, animal, or plant health. Therefore, finding the correct balance so that the proportionate, non-discriminatory, transparent, and coherent actions can be taken, requires a structured decision-making process with detailed scientific and other objective information.
    2.   The Communication's fourfold aim is to:

- outline the Commission's approach to using the precautionary principle,
- establish Commission guidelines for applying it,

- build a common understanding of how to assess, appraise, manage, and communicate risks that science is not yet able to evaluate fully, and
- avoid unwarranted recourse to the precautionary principle, as a disguised form of protectionism.

It also seeks to provide an input to the ongoing debate on this issue, both within the Community and internationally.

3. The precautionary principle is not defined in the Treaty, which prescribes it only once—to protect the environment. But in practice, its scope is much wider, and specifically where preliminary objective scientific evaluation indicates that there are reasonable grounds for concern that the potentially dangerous effects on the environment, human, animal, or plant health may be inconsistent with the high level of protection chosen for the Community.

The Commission considers that the Community, like other WTO members, has the right to establish the level of protection—particularly of the environment, human, animal, and plant health—that it deems appropriate. Applying the precautionary principle is a key tenet of its policy, and the choices it makes to this end will continue to affect the views it defends internationally, on how this principle should be applied.

4. The precautionary principle should be considered within a structured approach to the analysis of risk which comprises three elements: risk assessment, risk management, and risk communication. The precautionary principle is particularly relevant to the management of risk.

The precautionary principle, which is essentially used by decision-makers in the management of risk, should not be confused with the element of caution that scientists apply in their assessment of scientific data.

Recourse to the precautionary principle presupposes that potentially dangerous effects deriving from a phenomenon, product, or process have been identified, and that scientific evaluation does not allow the risk to be determined with sufficient certainty.

The implementation of an approach based on the precautionary principle should start with a scientific evaluation, as complete as possible, and where possible, identifying at each stage the degree of scientific uncertainty.

5. Decision-makers need to be aware of the degree of uncertainty attached to the results of the evaluation of the available scientific information. Judging what is an 'acceptable' level of risk for society is an eminently *political* responsibility. Decision-makers faced with an unacceptable risk, scientific uncertainty, and public concerns have a duty to find answers. Therefore, all these factors have to be taken into consideration.

In some cases, the right answer may be not to act or at least not to introduce a binding legal measure. A wide range of initiatives is available in the case of action, going from a legally binding measure to a research project or a recommendation.

The decision-making procedure should be transparent and should involve as early as possible and to the extent reasonably possible all interested parties.

6. Where action is deemed necessary, measures based on the precautionary principle should be, *inter alia:*

* *proportional* to the chosen level of protection,
* *non-discriminatory* in their application,
* *consistent* with similar measures already taken,
* *based on an examination of the potential benefits and costs* of action or lack of action (including, where appropriate and feasible, an economic cost–benefit analysis),
* *subject to review,* in the light of new scientific data, and
* *capable of assigning responsibility for producing the scientific evidence* necessary for a more comprehensive risk assessment.

*Proportionality* means tailoring measures to the chosen level of protection. Risk can rarely be reduced to zero, but incomplete risk assessments may greatly reduce the range of options open to risk managers. A total ban may not be a proportional response to a potential risk in all cases. However, in certain cases, it is the sole possible response to a given risk.

*Non-discrimination* means that comparable situations should not be treated differently, and that different situations should not be treated in the same way, unless there are objective grounds for doing so.

*Consistency* means that measures should be of comparable scope and nature to those already taken in equivalent areas in which all scientific data are available.

*Examining costs and benefits* entails comparing the overall cost to the Community of action and lack of action, in both the short and long term. This is not simply an economic cost–benefit analysis: its scope is much broader, and includes non-economic considerations, such as the efficacy of possible options and their acceptability to the public. In the conduct of such an examination, account should be taken of the general principle and the case law of the Court that the protection of health takes precedence over economic considerations.

*Subject to review* in the light of new scientific data means measures based on the precautionary principle should be maintained so long as scientific information is incomplete or inconclusive, and the risk is still considered too high to be imposed on society, in view of the chosen level of protection. Measures should be periodically reviewed in the light of scientific progress, and amended as necessary.

*Assigning responsibility for producing scientific evidence* is already a common consequence of these measures. Countries that impose a prior approval (marketing authorization) requirement on products that they deem dangerous a priori reverse the burden of proving injury, by treating them as dangerous unless and until businesses do the scientific work necessary to demonstrate that they are safe.

Where there is no prior authorization procedure, it may be up to the user or to public authorities to demonstrate the nature of a danger and the level of risk of a product or process. In such cases, a specific precautionary measure might be taken to place the burden of proof upon the producer, manufacturer, or importer, but this cannot be made a general rule.

## 1. Introduction

A number of recent events has shown that public opinion is becoming increasingly aware of the potential risks to which the population or their environment are potentially exposed.

Enormous advances in communications technology have fostered this growing sensitivity to the emergence of new risks, before scientific research has been able to fully illuminate the problems. Decision-makers have to take account of the fears generated by these perceptions and to put in place preventive measures to eliminate the risk or at least reduce it to the minimum acceptable level. On 13 April 1999 the Council adopted a resolution urging the Commission *inter alia*

to be in the future even more determined to be guided by the precautionary principle in preparing proposals for legislation and in its other consumer-related activities and develop as priority clear and effective guidelines for the application of this principle.

This Communication is part of the Commission's response.

The dimension of the precautionary principle goes beyond the problems associated with a short- or medium-term approach to risks. It also concerns the longer run and the well-being of future generations.

A decision to take measures without waiting until all the necessary scientific knowledge is available is clearly a precaution-based approach.

Decision-makers are constantly faced with the dilemma of balancing the freedoms and rights of individuals, industry, and organizations with the need to reduce or eliminate the risk of adverse effects to the environment or to health.

Finding the correct balance so that proportionate, non-discriminatory, transparent, and coherent decisions can be arrived at, which at the same time provide the chosen level of protection, requires a structured decision-making process with detailed scientific and other objective information. This structure is provided by the three elements of risk analysis: the assessment of risk, the choice of risk management strategy, and the communication of the risk.

Any assessment of risk that is made should be based on the existing body of scientific and statistical data. Most decisions are taken where there is sufficient information available for appropriate preventive measures to be taken, but in other circumstances these data may be wanting in some respects.

Whether or not to invoke the precautionary principle is a decision exercised where scientific information is insufficient, inconclusive, or uncertain and where there are indications that the possible effects on the environment, or human, animal, or plant health may be potentially dangerous and inconsistent with the chosen level of protection.

## 2. The Goals of this Communication

The aim of this Communication is to inform all interested parties, in particular the European Parliament the Council and Member States of the manner in which the Commission applies or intends to apply the precautionary principle when faced with taking decisions relating to the containment of risk. However, this general Communication does not claim to be the final word—rather, the idea is to provide input to the ongoing debate both at Community and international level.

This Communication seeks to establish a common understanding of the factors leading to recourse to the precautionary principle and its place in decision-making, and to establish guidelines for its application based on reasoned and coherent principles.

The guidelines outlined in this Communication are only intended to serve as general guidance and in no way to modify or affect the provisions of the Treaty or secondary Community legislation.

Another objective is to avoid unwarranted recourse to the precautionary principle, which in certain cases could serve as a justification for disguised protectionism. Accordingly the development of international guidelines could facilitate the achievement of this end. The Commission also wishes to stress in this Communication that, far from being a way of evading obligations arising from the WTO Agreements, the envisaged use of the precautionary principle complies with these obligations.

It is also necessary to clarify a misunderstanding as regards the distinction between reliance on the precautionary principle and the search for zero risk, which in reality is rarely to be found. The search for a high level of health and safety and environmental and consumer protection belongs in the framework of the single market, which is a cornerstone of the Community.

The Community has already relied on the precautionary principle. Abundant experience has been gained over many years in the environmental field, where many measures have been inspired by the precautionary principle, such as measures to protect the ozone layer or concerning climate change.

## 3. The Precautionary Principle in the European Union

The Community has consistently endeavoured to achieve a high level of protection, among others in environment and human, animal, or plant health. In most cases, measures making it possible to achieve this high level of protection can be determined on a satisfactory scientific basis. However, when there are reasonable grounds for concern that potential hazards may affect the environment or human, animal, or plant health, and when at the same time the available data preclude a detailed risk evaluation, the precautionary principle has been politically accepted as a risk management strategy in several fields.

To understand fully the use of the precautionary principle in the European Union, it is necessary to examine the legislative texts, the case law of the Court of Justice and the Court of First Instance, and the policy approaches that have emerged.

### Legal texts

The analysis starts with the legal texts which explicitly or implicitly refer to the precautionary principle (Annex I, Ref. 1).

At Community level the only explicit reference to the precautionary principle is to be found in the environment title of the EC Treaty, and more specifically Article 174. However, one cannot conclude from this that the principle applies only to the environment (Annex I, Refs. 2 and 3). Although the principle is adumbrated in the Treaty, it is not defined there.

Like other general notions contained in the legislation, such as subsidiarity or proportionality, it is for the decision-makers and ultimately the courts to flesh out the principle. In other words, the scope of the precautionary principle also depends on trends in case law, which to some degree are influenced by prevailing social and political values.

However, it would be wrong to conclude that the absence of a definition has to lead to legal uncertainty. The Community authorities' practical experience with the precautionary principle and its judicial review make it possible to get an ever-better handle on the precautionary principle.

### Case law

The Court of Justice of the European Communities and the Court of First Instance have already had occasion to review the application of the precautionary principle in cases they have adjudicated and hence to develop case law in this area (see Annex I, Refs. 5, 6, and 7).

### Policy orientations

Policy orientations were set out by the Commission in the Green Paper on the General Principles of Food Safety and the Communication of 30 April 1997 on Consumer Health and Food Safety, by Parliament in its Resolution of 10 March 1998 concerning the Green Paper, by the Council in its Resolution of 13 April 1999, and by the Joint Parliamentary Committee of the EEA (European Economic Area) in its Resolution of 16 March 1999 (Annex I, Refs. 8–12).

Hence the Commission considers that the precautionary principle is a general one which should in particular be taken into consideration in the fields of environmental protection and human, animal, and plant health.

*Although the precautionary principle is not explicitly mentioned in the Treaty except in the environmental field, its scope is far wider and covers those specific circumstances where scientific evidence is insufficient, inconclusive, or uncertain and there are indications through preliminary objective scientific evaluation that there are reasonable grounds for concern that the potentially dangerous effects on the environment, human, animal, or plant health may be inconsistent with the chosen level of protection.*

### 4. The Precautionary Principle in International Law

At international level, the precautionary principle was first recognized in the World Charter for Nature, adopted by the UN General Assembly in 1982. It was subsequently incorporated into various international conventions on the protection of the environment (cf. Annex II).

This principle was enshrined at the 1992 Rio Conference on the Environment and Development, during which the Rio Declaration was adopted, whose principle 15 states that:

in order to protect the environment, the precautionary approach shall be widely applied by States according to their capability. Where there are threats of serious or irreversible damage, lack of full scientific certainty shall not be used as a reason for postponing cost-effective measures to prevent environmental degradation.

Besides, the UN Framework Convention on Climate Change and the Convention of Biological Diversity both refer to the precautionary principle. Recently, on 28 January 2000, at the Conference of the Parties to the Convention on Biological Diversity, the Protocol on Biosafety concerning the safe transfer, handling, and use of living modified organisms resulting from modern biotechnology confirmed the key function of the precautionary principle (see Annex II).

Hence this principle has been progressively consolidated in international environmental law, and so it has since become a full-fledged and general principle of international law.

The WTO agreements confirm this observation. The preamble to the WTO Agreement highlights the ever-closer links between international trade and environmental protection.[1] A consistent approach means that the precautionary principle must be taken into account in these agreements, notably in the Agreement on Sanitary and Phytosanitary Measures (SPS) and in the Agreement on Technical Barriers to Trade (TBT), to ensure that this general principle is duly enforced in this legal order.

Hence, each Member of the WTO has the independent right to determine the level of environmental or health protection they consider appropriate. Consequently a member may apply measures, including measures based on

---

[1] The parties to this agreement . . . recognizing that their relations in the field of trade and economic endeavour should be conducted with a view to raising standards of living, ensuring full employment and a large and steadily growing volume of real income and effective demand, and expanding the production of trade in goods and services, while allowing for the optimal use of the world's resources in accordance with the objective of sustainable development, seeking both to protect and preserve the environment and to enhance the means for doing to in a manner consistent with their respective needs and concerns at different levels of economic development.

the precautionary principle, which lead to a higher level of protection than that provided for in the relevant international standards or recommendations.

The Agreement on the Application of Sanitary and Phytosanitary Measures (SPS Agreement) clearly sanctions the use of the precautionary principle, although the term itself is not explicitly used. Although the general rule is that all sanitary and phytosanitary measures must be based on scientific principles and that they should not be maintained without adequate scientific evidence, a derogation from these principles is provided for in Article 5 (7) which stipulates that:

in cases where relevant scientific evidence is insufficient, a Member may provisionally adopt sanitary or phytosanitary measures on the basis of available pertinent information, including that from the relevant international organizations as well as from sanitary or phytosanitary measures applied by other Members. In such circumstances, Members shall seek to obtain the additional information necessary for a more objective assessment of risk and review the sanitary or phytosanitary measure accordingly within a reasonable period of time.

Hence, according to the SPS Agreement, measures adopted in application of a precautionary principle when the scientific data are inadequate, are provisional and imply that efforts be undertaken to elicit or generate the necessary scientific data. It is important to stress that the provisional nature is not bound up with a time limit but with the development of scientific knowledge.

The use of the term 'more objective assessment of risk' in Article 5.7 infers that a precautionary measure may be based on a less objective appraisal but must nevertheless include an evaluation of risk.

The concept of risk assessment in the SPS leaves leeway for interpretation of what could be used as a basis for a precautionary approach. The risk assessment on which a measure is based may include non-quantifiable data of a factual or qualitative nature and is not uniquely confined to purely quantitative scientific data. This interpretation has been confirmed by the WTO's Appellate body in the case of growth hormones, which rejected the panel's initial interpretation that the risk assessment had to be quantitative and had to establish a minimum degree of risk.

The principles enshrined in Article 5.7 of the SPS must be respected in the field of sanitary and phytosanitary measures; however, because of the specific nature of other areas, such as the environment, it may be that somewhat different principles will have to be applied.

International guidelines are being considered in relation to the application of the Precautionary Principle in Codex Alimentarius. Such guidance in this, and other sectors, could pave the way to a harmonized approach by the WTO Members, to drawing up health or environment protection measures, while avoiding the misuse of the precautionary principle which could otherwise lead to unjustifiable barriers to trade.

In the light of these observations, the Commission considers that, following the example set by other Members of the WTO, the Community is entitled to prescribe the level of protection, notably as regards the environment and human, animal, and plant health, which it considers appropriate. In this context, the Community must respect Articles 6, 95, 152, and 174 of the Treaty. To this end, reliance on the precautionary principle constitutes an essential plank of its policy. It is clear that the choices made will affect its positions at international and notably multilateral level, as regards recourse to the precautionary principle.

Bearing in mind the very origins of the precautionary principle and its growing role in international law, and notably in the agreements of the World Trade Organization, this principle must be duly addressed at international level in the various areas in which it is likely to be of relevance.

Following the example set by the other members of the WTO, the Commission considers that the Community is entitled to prescribe the level of protection, notably as regards environmental protection and human, animal, and plant health, that it considers appropriate. Recourse to the precautionary principle is a central plank of Community policy. The choices made to this end will continue to influence its positions at international level, and notably at multinational level, as regards the precautionary principle.

### 5. The Constituent Parts of the Precautionary Principle

An analysis of the precautionary principle reveals two quite distinct aspects: (i) *the political decision to act or not to act as such*, which is linked to the *factors triggering* recourse to the precautionary principle; (ii) in the affirmative, *how to act, i.e. the measures* resulting from application of the precautionary principle.

There is a controversy as to the role of scientific uncertainty in risk analysis, and notably as to whether it belongs under risk assessment or risk management. This controversy springs from a confusion between a prudential approach and application of the precautionary principle. These two aspects are complementary but should not be confounded.

The prudential approach is part of risk assessment policy which is determined before any risk assessment takes place and which is based on the elements described in 5.1.3; it is therefore an integral part of the scientific opinion delivered by the risk evaluators.

On the other hand, application of the precautionary principle is part of risk management, when scientific uncertainty precludes a full assessment of the risk and when decision-makers consider that the chosen level of environmental protection or of human, animal, and plant health may be in jeopardy.

The Commission considers that measures applying the precautionary principle belong in the general framework of risk analysis, and in particular risk management.

## 5.1. Factors triggering recourse to the precautionary principle

The precautionary principle is relevant only in the event of a potential risk, even if this risk cannot be fully demonstrated or quantified or its effects determined because of the insufficiency or inclusive nature of the scientific data.

It should, however, be noted that the precautionary principle can in no circumstances be used to justify the adoption of arbitrary decisions.

### 5.1.1. Identification of potentially negative effects

Before the precautionary principle is invoked, the scientific data relevant to the risks must first be evaluated. However, one factor logically and chronologically precedes the decision to act, namely identification of the potentially negative effects of a phenomenon. To understand these effects more thoroughly it is necessary to conduct a scientific examination. The decision to conduct this examination without awaiting additional information is bound up with a less theoretical and more concrete perception of the risk.

### 5.1.2. Scientific evaluation

A scientific evaluation of the potential adverse effects should be undertaken based on the available data when considering whether measures are necessary to protect the environment, human, animal, or plant health. An assessment of risk should be considered where feasible when deciding whether or not to invoke the precautionary principle. This requires reliable scientific data and logical reasoning, leading to a conclusion which expresses the possibility of occurrence and the severity of a hazard's impact on the environment, or health of a given population including the extent of possible damage, persistency, reversibility, and delayed effect. However, it is not possible in all cases to complete a comprehensive assessment of risk, but all effort should be made to evaluate the available scientific information.

Where possible, a report should be made which indicates the assessment of the existing knowledge and the available information, providing the views of the scientists on the reliability of the assessment as well as on the remaining uncertainties. If necessary, it should also contain the identification of topics for further scientific research.

Risk assessment consists of four components—namely hazard identification, hazard characterization, appraisal of exposure, and risk characterization (Annex III). The limits of scientific knowledge may affect each of these components, influencing the overall level of attendant uncertainty and ultimately affecting the foundation for protective or preventive action. An attempt to complete these four steps should be performed before decision to act is taken.

### 5.1.3. Scientific uncertainty

Scientific uncertainty results usually from five characteristics of the scientific method: the variable chosen, the measurements made, the samples drawn, the models used, and the causal relationship employed. Scientific uncertainty may also arise from a controversy on existing data or lack of some relevant data. Uncertainty may relate to qualitative or quantitative elements of the analysis.

A more abstract and generalized approach preferred by some scientists is to separate all uncertainties into three categories of Bias, Randomness, and True Variability. Some other experts categorize uncertainty in terms of estimation of confidence interval of the probability of occurrence and of the severity of the hazard's impact.

This issue is very complex and the Commission launched a project 'Technological Risk and the Management of Uncertainty' conducted under the auspices of the European Scientific Technology Observatory. The four ESTO reports will be published shortly and will give a comprehensive description of scientific uncertainty.

Risk evaluators accommodate these uncertainty factors by incorporating prudential aspects such as:

— relying on animal models to establish potential effects in man;
— using body weight ranges to make interspecies comparisons;
— adopting a safety factor in evaluating an acceptable daily intake to account for intra- and inter-species variability; the magnitude of this factor depends on the degree of uncertainty of the available data;
— not adopting an acceptable daily intake for substances recognized as genotoxic or carcinogenic; and
— adopting the 'ALARA' (as low as reasonably achievable) level as a basis for certain toxic contaminants.

Risk managers should be fully aware of these uncertainty factors when they adopt measures based on the scientific opinion delivered by the evaluators.

However, in some situations the scientific data are not sufficient to allow one to apply these prudential aspects in practice, i.e. in cases in which extrapolations cannot be made because of the absence of parameter modelling and where cause–effect relationships are suspected but have not been demonstrated. It is in situations like these that decision-makers face the dilemma of having to act or not to act.

*Recourse to the precautionary principle presupposes:*

— *identification of potentially negative effects resulting from a phenomenon, product, or procedure;*
— *a scientific evaluation of the risk which because of the insufficiency of the data, their inconclusive or imprecise nature, makes it impossible to determine with sufficient certainty the risk in question.*

## 5.2. Measures resulting from reliance on the precautionary principle

### 5.2.1. The decision whether or not to act

In the kind of situation described above—sometimes under varying degrees of pressure from public opinion—decision-makers have to respond. However, responding does not necessarily mean that measures always have to be adopted. The decision to do nothing may be a response in its own right.

*The appropriate response in a given situation is thus the result of an eminently political decision, a function of the risk level that is 'acceptable' to the society on which the risk is imposed.*

### 5.2.2. Nature of the action ultimately taken

The nature of the decision influences the type of control that can be carried out. Recourse to the precautionary principle does not necessarily mean adopting final instruments designed to produce legal effects that are open to judicial review. There is a whole range of actions available to decision-makers under the head of the precautionary principle. The decision to fund a research programme or even the decision to inform the public about the possible adverse effects of a product or procedure may themselves be inspired by the precautionary principle.

It is for the Court of Justice to pronounce on the legality of any measures taken by the Community institutions. The Court has consistently held that when the Commission or any other Community institution has broad discretionary powers, notably as regards the nature and scope of the measures it adopts, review by the Court must be limited to examining whether the institution committed a manifest error or misuse of power or manifestly exceeded the limits of its powers of appraisal.

Hence the measures may not be of an arbitrary nature.

*Recourse to the precautionary principle does not necessarily mean adopting final instruments designed to produce legal effects, which are subject to judicial review.*

## 6. Guidelines for Applying the Precautionary Principle

### 6.1. Implementation

When decision-makers become aware of a risk to the environment or human, animal, or plant health that in the event of non-action may have serious consequences, the question of appropriate protective measures arise. Decision-makers have to obtain, through a structured approach, a scientific evaluation, as complete as possible, of the risk to the environment, or health, in order to select the most appropriate course of action.

The determination of appropriate action including measures based on the

precautionary principle should start with a scientific evaluation and, if necessary, the decision to commission scientists to perform an as objective and
complete as possible scientific evaluation. It will cast light on the existing
objective evidence, the gaps in knowledge, and the scientific uncertainties.

*The implementation of an approach based on the precautionary principle*
*should start with a scientific evaluation, as complete as possible, and where pos-*
*sible, identifying at each stage the degree of scientific uncertainty.*

## 6.2. The triggering factor

Once the scientific evaluation has been performed as well as possible, it may
provide a basis for triggering a decision to invoke the precautionary principle. The conclusions of this evaluation should show that the desired level of
protection for the environment or a population group could be jeopardized.
The conclusions should also include an assessment of the scientific uncertainties and a description of the hypotheses used to compensate for the lack
of the scientific or statistical data. An assessment of the potential consequences of inaction should be considered and may be used as a trigger by
the decision-makers. The decision to wait or not to wait for new scientific
data before considering possible measures should be taken by the decision-
makers with a maximum of transparency. The absence of scientific proof of
the existence of a cause–effect relationship, a quantifiable dose–response
relationship, or a quantitative evaluation of the probability of the emergence
of adverse effects following exposure should not be used to justify inaction.
Even if scientific advice is supported only by a minority fraction of the scientific community, due account should be taken of their views, provided the
credibility and reputation of this fraction are recognized.[2]

The Commission has confirmed its wish to rely on procedures as transparent
as possible and to involve all interested parties at the earliest possible stage.[3]
This will assist decision-makers in taking legitimate measures which are likely
to achieve the society's chosen level of health or environmental protection

*An assessment of the potential consequences of inaction and of the uncertain-*
*ties of the scientific evaluation should be considered by decision-makers when*
*determining whether to trigger action based on the precautionary principle.*

*All interested parties should be involved to the fullest extent possible in the*
*study of various risk management options that may be envisaged once*
*the results of the scientific evaluation and/or risk assessment are available and*
*the procedure be as transparent as possible.*

[2] Cf. the WTO Appellate Body report on hormones, para. 124: 'In some cases, the very existence
of divergent views presented by qualified scientists who have investigated the particular issue at
hand, may indicate a state of scientific uncertainty.'

[3] A considerable effort has already been made notably as regards public health and the environment. As regards the latter, the Community and the Member States have demonstrated the
importance they attach to access to information and justice by signing the Århus Convention of
June 1998.

### 6.3.  The general principles of application

The general principles are not limited to application of the precautionary principle. They apply to all risk management measures. An approach inspired by the precautionary principle does not exempt one from applying wherever possible these criteria, which are generally used when a complete risk assessment is at hand.

Thus reliance on the precautionary principle is no excuse for derogating from the general principles of risk management.

These general principles include:

— proportionality,
— non-discrimination,
— consistency,
— examination of the benefits and costs of action or lack of action, and
— examination of scientific developments.

### 6.3.1.  *Proportionality*

The measures envisaged must make it possible to achieve the appropriate level of protection. Measures based on the precautionary principle must not be disproportionate to the desired level of protection and must not aim at zero risk, something which rarely exists. However, in certain cases, an incomplete assessment of the risk may considerably limit the number of options available to the risk managers.

In some cases a total ban may not be a proportional response to a potential risk. In other cases, it may be the sole possible response to a potential risk.

Risk reduction measures should include less restrictive alternatives which make it possible to achieve an equivalent level of protection, such as appropriate treatment, reduction of exposure, tightening of controls, adoption of provisional limits, recommendations for populations at risk, etc. One should also consider replacing the products or procedures concerned by safer products or procedures.

The risk reduction measure should not be limited to immediate risks where the proportionality of the action is easier to assess. It is in situations in which the adverse effects do not emerge until long after exposure that the cause–effect relationships are more difficult to prove scientifically and that—for this reason—the precautionary principle often has to be invoked. In this case the potential long-term effects must be taken into account in evaluating the proportionality of measures in the form of rapid action to limit or eliminate a risk whose effects will not surface until ten or twenty years later or will affect future generations. This applies in particular to effects on the ecosystem. Risks that are carried forward into the future cannot be eliminated or reduced except at the time of exposure, that is to say immediately.

*Measures should be proportional to the desired level of protection.*

### 6.3.2. Non-discrimination

The principle of non-discrimination means that comparable situations should not be treated differently and that different situations should not be treated in the same way, unless there are objective grounds for doing so.

Measures taken under the precautionary principle should be designed to achieve an equivalent level of protection without invoking the geographical origin or the nature of the production process to apply different treatments in an arbitrary manner.

*Measures should not be discriminatory in their application.*

### 6.3.3. Consistency

Measures should be consistent with the measures already adopted in similar circumstances or using similar approaches. Risk evaluations include a series of factors to be taken into account to ensure that they are as thorough as possible. The goal here is to identify and characterize the hazards, notably by establishing a relationship between the dose and the effect and assessing the exposure of the target population or the environment. If the absence of certain scientific data makes it impossible to characterize the risk, taking into account the uncertainties inherent to the evaluation, the measures taken under the precautionary principle should be comparable in nature and scope with measures already taken in equivalent areas in which all the scientific data are available.

*Measures should be consistent with the measures already adopted in similar circumstances or using similar approaches.*

### 6.3.4. Examination of the benefits and costs of action and lack of action

A comparison must be made between the most likely positive or negative consequences of the envisaged action and those of inaction in terms of the overall cost to the Community, both in the long and short term. The measures envisaged must produce an overall advantage as regards reducing risks to an acceptable level.

Examination of the pros and cons cannot be reduced to an economic cost–benefit analysis. It is wider in scope and includes non-economic considerations.

However, examination of the pros and cons should include an economic cost–benefit analysis where this is appropriate and possible.

Besides, other analysis methods, such as those concerning the efficacy of possible options and their acceptability to the public may also have to be taken into account. A society may be willing to pay a higher cost to protect an interest, such as the environment or health, to which it attaches priority.

The Commission affirms, in accordance with the case law of the Court that requirements linked to the protection of public health should undoubtedly be given greater weight than economic considerations.

*The measures adopted presuppose examination of the benefits and costs of action and lack of action. This examination should include an economic cost–*

*benefit analysis when this is appropriate and feasible. However, other analysis methods, such as those concerning efficacy and the socio-economic impact of the various options, may also be relevant. Besides the decision-maker may, in certain circumstances, be guided by non-economic considerations such as the protection of health.*

### 6.3.5. *Examination of scientific developments*

The measures should be maintained as long as the scientific data are inadequate, imprecise, or inconclusive and as long as the risk is considered too high to be imposed on society. The measures may have to be modified or abolished by a particular deadline, in the light of new scientific findings. However, this is not always linked to the time factor, but to the development of scientific knowledge.

Besides, scientific research should be carried out with a view to obtaining a more advanced or more complete scientific assessment. In this context, the measures should be subjected to regular scientific monitoring, so that they can be re-evaluated in the light of new scientific information.

The Agreement on Sanitary and Phytosanitary Measures (SPS) provides that measures adopted in the context of inadequate scientific evidence must respect certain conditions. Hence these conditions concern only the scope of the SPS Agreement, but the specific nature of certain sectors, such as the environment, may mean that somewhat different principles have to be applied.

Article 5(7) of the SPS agreement includes certain specific rules:

- The measures must be of a provisional nature pending the availability of more reliable scientific data. However, this provisional nature is linked to the development of scientific knowledge rather than to a time factor.
- Research must be carried out to elicit the additional scientific data required for a more objective assessment of the risk.
- The measures must be periodically reviewed to take account of new scientific data. The results of scientific research should make it possible to complete the risk evaluation and if necessary to review the measures on the basis of the conclusions.
- Hence the reasonable period envisaged in the SPS Agreement includes the time needed for completion of the necessary scientific work and, besides, the time needed for performance of a risk evaluation based on the conclusions of this scientific work. It should not be possible to invoke budgetary constraints or political priorities to justify excessive delays in obtaining results, re-evaluating the risk, or amending the provisional measures.

Research could also be conducted for the improvement of the methodologies and instruments for assessing risk, including greater integration of all pertinent factors (e.g. socio-economic information, technological perspectives).

*The measures, although provisional, shall be maintained as long as the scientific data remain incomplete, imprecise, or inconclusive and as long as the risk is considered too high to be imposed on society.*

*Maintenance of the measures depends on the development of scientific knowledge, in the light of which they should be re-evaluated. This means that scientific research shall be continued with a view to obtaining more complete data.*

*Measures based on the precautionary principle shall be re-examined and if necessary modified depending on the results of the scientific research and the follow-up of their impact.*

## 6.4. The burden of proof

- Community rules and those of many third countries enshrine the principle of prior approval (positive list) before placing on the market certain products, such as drugs, pesticides, or food additives. This is one way of applying the precautionary principle, by shifting responsibility for producing scientific evidence. This applies in particular to substances deemed a priori hazardous or which are potentially hazardous at a certain level of absorption. In this case the legislator, by way of precaution, has clearly reversed the burden of proof by requiring that the substances be deemed hazardous until proven otherwise. Hence it is up to the business community to carry out the scientific work needed to evaluate the risk. As long as the human health risk cannot be evaluated with sufficient certainty, the legislator is not legally entitled to authorize use of the substance, unless exceptionally for test purposes.
- In other cases, where such a prior approval procedure does not exist, it may be for the user, a private individual, a consumer association, citizens, or the public authorities to demonstrate the nature of a danger and the level of risk posed by a product or process. Action taken under the head of the precautionary principle must in certain cases include a clause reversing the burden of proof and placing it on the producer, manufacturer, or importer, but such an obligation cannot be systematically entertained as a general principle. This possibility should be examined on a case-by-case basis when a measure is adopted under the precautionary principle, pending supplementary scientific data, so as to give professionals who have an economic interest in the production and/or marketing of the procedure or product in question the opportunity to finance the necessary research on a voluntary basis.

*Measures based on the precautionary principle may assign responsibility for producing the scientific evidence necessary for a comprehensive risk evaluation.*

## 7. Conclusion

This Communication of a general scope sets out the Commission's position as regards recourse to the precautionary principle. The Communication reflects the Commission's desire for transparency and dialogue with all stakeholders.

At the same time it provides concrete guidance for applying the precautionary principle.

The Commission wishes to reaffirm the crucial importance it attaches to the distinction between the decision to act or not to act, which is of an eminently political nature, and the measures resulting from recourse to the precautionary principle, which must comply with the general principles applicable to all risk management measures. The Commission also considers that every decision must be preceded by an examination of all the available scientific data and, if possible, a risk evaluation that is as objective and comprehensive as possible. A decision to invoke the precautionary principle does not mean that the measures will be adopted on an arbitrary or discriminatory basis.

This Communication should also contribute to reaffirming the Community's position at international level, where the precautionary principle is receiving increasing attention. However, the Commission wishes to stress that this Communication is not meant to be the last word; rather, it should be seen as the point of departure for a broader study of the conditions in which risks should be assessed, appraised, managed, and communicated.

## Annex I: Legal and Other Bases for EC Decisions on Precautionary Measures

### The Legislative Texts

Ref. 1
The EC Treaty, incorporating provisions already introduced by the Maastricht Treaty of 1992, and more specifically Article 174 thereof, states:

2. Community policy on the environment shall aim at a high level of protection taking into account the diversity of situations in the various regions of the Community. It shall be based on the precautionary principle and on the principles that preventive action should be taken, that environmental damage should as a priority be rectified at source and that the polluter should pay . . .
3. In preparing its policy on the environment, the Community shall take account of:
— available scientific and technical data, [and]
— the potential benefits and costs of action or lack of action.

Ref. 2
Article 6 of the EC Treaty provides that 'environmental protection require-ments must be integrated into the definition and implementation of the Community policies and activities referred to in Article 3, in particular with a view to promoting sustainable development'.

Ref. 3
Hence, Article 95(3) of the EC Treaty provides that: 'The Commission, in its proposals envisaged in paragraph 1 concerning health, safety, environmental protection and consumer protection, will take as a base a high level of protec-tion, taking account in particular of any new development based on scientific facts. Within their respective powers, the European Parliament and the Council will also seek to achieve this objective.'

Ref. 4
The first paragraph of Article 152 of the EC Treaty provides that: 'A high level of human health protection shall be ensured in the definition and implementa-tion of all Community policies and activities.'

### Case Law

Ref. 5
In its judgment on the validity of the Commission's decision banning the exportation of beef from the UK to reduce the risk of BSE transmission (judg-ments of 5 May 1998, cases C–57/96 and C–80/96), the Court held:
    'Where there is uncertainty as to the existence or extent of risks to human health, the institutions may take protective measures without having to wait until the reality and seriousness of those risks become fully apparent' (Grounds 63). The next section fleshes out the Court's reasoning: 'That approach is borne out by Article 130r(1) of the EC Treaty, according to which Community policy on the environment is to pursue the objective inter alia of protecting human health. Article 130r(2) provides that that policy is to aim at

a high level of protection and is to be based in particular on the principles that preventive action should be taken and that environmental protection requirements must be integrated into the definition and implementation of other Community policies' (Grounds 64).

### Ref. 6
In another judgment concerning protection of consumer health (judgment of 16 July 1998, Case T–199/96), the Court of First Instance cites the above passage from the BSE judgment (see Grounds 66 and 67).

### Ref. 7
Recently, in the Order of 30 June 1999 (Case T–70/99), the President of the Court of First Instance confirmed the positions expressed in the above-mentioned judgments. Note that this judgment contains an explicit reference to the precautionary principle and affirms that 'requirements linked to the protection of public health should undoubtedly be given greater weight that economic considerations'.

## Policy Orientations

### Ref. 8
In its Communication of 30 April 1997 on consumer health and food safety (COM(97) 183 final), the Commission states: 'the Commission will be guided in its risk analysis by the precautionary principle, in cases where the scientific basis is insufficient or some uncertainty exists.'

### Ref. 9
In its Green Paper on the General Principles of Food Law in the European Union of 30 April 1997 (COM(97) 176 final), the Commission reiterates this point:

The Treaty requires the Community to contribute to the maintenance of a high level of protection of public health, the environment and consumers. In order to ensure a high level of protection and coherence, protective measures should be based on risk assessment, taking into account all relevant risk factors, including technological aspects, the best available scientific evidence and the availability of inspection sampling and testing methods. Where a full risk assessment is not possible, measures should be based on the precautionary principle.

### Ref. 10
In its Resolution of 10 March 1998 on the Green Paper, the European Parliament states:

European food law is based on the principle of preventive protection of consumer health;
stresses that policy in this area must be founded on a scientifically based risk analysis supplemented, where necessary, by appropriate risk management based on the precautionary principle; [and]
invites the Commission to anticipate possible challenges to Community food law by WTO bodies by requesting the scientific committees to present a full set of arguments based on the precautionary principle.

Ref. 11
The Joint Parliamentary Committee of the EEA (European Economic Area), adopted a Resolution on Food Safety in the EEA on 16 March 1999. In this connection, on the one hand, it 'emphasizes the importance of application of the precautionary principle' (point 5) and, on the other, 'reaffirms the over-riding need for a precautionary approach within the EEA to the assessment and evaluation of applications for the marketing of GMOs intended to enter the food chain' (point 13).

Ref. 12
On 13 April 1999 the Council adopted a Resolution urging the Commission, *inter alia*, 'to be in the future even more determined to be guided by the precautionary principle in preparing proposals for legislation and in its other consumer-related activities and develop as a priority clear and effective guidelines for the application of this principle'.

## Annex II: The Precautionary Principle in International Law

### The Environment

Although applied more broadly, the precautionary principle has been developed primarily in the context of environmental policy.

Hence, the Ministerial Declaration of the Second International Conference on the Protection of the North Sea (1987) states that 'in order to protect the North Sea from possibly damaging effects of the most dangerous substances, a precautionary approach is necessary which may require action to control inputs of such substances even before a causal link has been established by absolutely clear scientific evidence'. A new Ministerial Declaration was delivered at the Third International Conference on the Protection of the North Sea (1990). It fleshes out the earlier declaration, stating that 'the participants . . . will continue to apply the precautionary principle, that is to take action to avoid potentially damaging impacts of substances that are persistent, toxic and liable to bioaccumulate even where there is no scientific evidence to prove a causal link between emissions and effects'.

The precautionary principle was explicitly recognized during the UN Conference on Environment and Development (UNCED) in Rio de Janeiro 1992 and included in the so-called Rio Declaration. Since then the precautionary principle has been implemented in various environmental instruments, and in particular in global climate change, ozone-depleting substances, and biodiversity conservation.

The precautionary principle is listed as Principle 15 of the Rio Declaration among the principles of general rights and obligations of national authorities:

In order to protect the environment, the precautionary approach should be widely applied by States according to their capabilities. Where there are threats of serious or irreversible damage, lack of full scientific certainty shall not be used as a reason for postponing cost-effective measures to prevent environmental gradation.

Principle 15 is reproduced in similar wording in:

1. The preamble of the Convention of Biological Diversity (1992):

. . . Noting also that where there is a threat of significant reduction or loss of biological diversity, lack of full scientific certainty should not be used as a reason for postponing measures to avoid or minimize such a threat . . .

2. In Article 3 (Principles) of the Convention of Climate Change (1992):

. . . The Parties should take precautionary measures to anticipate, prevent, or minimize the causes of climate change and mitigate its adverse effects. Where there are threats of serious or irreversible damage, lack of full scientific certainty should not be used as a reason for postponing such measures, taking into account that policies and measures to deal with climate change should be cost-effective so as to ensure global benefits at the lowest possible cost. To achieve this, such policies and measures should take into account different socio-economic contexts, be comprehensive, cover all relevant sources, sinks and reservoirs of greenhouse gases and adaptation, and comprise all economic sectors. Efforts to address climate change may be carried out cooperatively by interested Parties.

In the Paris Convention for the protection of the marine environment of the north-east Atlantic (September 1992), the precautionary principle is defined as the principle

by virtue of which preventive measures are to be taken when there are reasonable grounds for concern that substances or energy introduced, directly or indirectly, into the marine environment may bring about hazards to human health, harm living resources and marine ecosystems, damage amenities or interfere with other legitimate uses of the sea, even when there is no conclusive evidence of a causal relationship between the inputs and the effects.

Recently, on 28 January 2000, at the Conference of the Parties to the Convention on Biological Diversity, the Protocol on Biosafety concerning the safe transfer, handling, and use of living modified organisms resulting from modern biotechnology confirmed the key function of the precautionary principle. In fact, Article 10, para. 6 states:

Lack of scientific certainty due to insufficient relevant scientific information and knowledge regarding the extent of the potential adverse effects of a living modified organism on the conservation and sustainable use of biological diversity in the Party of import, taking also into account risks to human health, shall not prevent that Party from taking a decision, as appropriate, with regard to the import of living modified organism in question as referred to in paragraph 3 above, in order to avoid or minimize such potential adverse effects.

Besides, the preamble to the WTO Agreement highlights the ever closer links between international trade and environmental protection.

**The WTO/SPS Agreement**
Although the term, 'Precautionary Principle' is not explicitly used in the WTO Agreement on the Application of Sanitary and Phytosanitary Measures (SPS), the Appellate Body on EC measures concerning meat and meat products (Hormones) (AB1997-4, para. 124) states that it finds reflection in Article 5.7 of this Agreement. Article 5.7 reads:

In cases where relevant scientific evidence is insufficient, a Member may provisionally adopt sanitary or phytosanitary measures on the basis of available scientific information, including that from the relevant international organizations as well as from sanitary and phytosanitary measures applied by other Members. In such circumstances, Members shall seek to obtain the additional information necessary for a more objective assessment of risk and review the sanitary or phytosanitary measure accordingly within a reasonable period of time.

The Appellate Body on Hormones (para. 124) recognizes 'that there is no need to assume that Article 5.7 exhausts the relevance of a precautionary principle'. Moreover, Members have the 'right to establish their own level of sanitary protection, which level may be higher (i.e. more cautious) than that implied in existing international standards, guidelines and recommendations'.

Furthermore, it accepts that 'responsible, representative governments commonly act from perspectives of prudence and precaution where risks of irreversible, e.g. life-terminating, damage to human health are concerned'. The Appellate Body on Japan-Measures affecting agricultural products (AB-1998-8, para. 89) clarifies the four requirements which must be met in order to adopt and maintain provisional SPS measures. A Member may provisionally adopt an SPS measure if this measure is: (1) imposed in respect of a situation where 'relevant scientific information is insufficient'; and (2) adopted 'on the basis of available pertinent information'.

Such a provisional measure may not be maintained unless the Member which adopted the measure: (1) 'seek(s) to obtain the additional information necessary for a more objective risk assessment'; and (2) 'review(s) the . . . measure accordingly within a reasonable period of time'.

These four requirements are clearly cumulative and are equally important for the purpose of determining consistency with the provision of Article 5.7. Whenever one of these four requirements is not met, the measure at issue is inconsistent with Article 5.7. As to what constitutes a 'reasonable period of time' to review the measure, the Appellate Body points out (para. 93), that this has to be established on a case-by-case basis and depends on the specific circumstances of each case, including the difficulty of obtaining the additional information necessary for the review *and* the characteristics of the provisional SPS measure.

## Annex III: The Four Components of Risk Assessment

An attempt to complete as far as possible these four components should be performed before action is taken.

Hazard identification means identifying the biological, chemical, or physical agents that may have adverse effects. A new substance or biological agent may reveal itself through its effects on the population (illness or death), or on the environment and it may be possible to describe the actual or potential effects on the population or environment before the cause is identified beyond doubt.

Hazard characterization consists of determining, in quantitative and/or qualitative terms, the nature and severity of the adverse effects associated with the causal agents or activity. It is at this stage that a relationship between the amount of the hazardous substance and the effect has to be established. However, the relationship is sometimes difficult or impossible to prove, for instance because the causal link has not been established beyond doubt.

Appraisal of exposure consists of quantitatively or qualitatively evaluating the probability of exposure to the agent under study. Apart from information on the agents themselves (source, distribution, concentrations, characteristics, etc.), there is a need for data on the probability of contamination or exposure of the population or environment to the hazard.

Risk characterization corresponds to the qualitative and/or quantitative estimation, taking account of inherent uncertainties, of the probability, of the frequency and severity of the known or potential adverse environmental, or health effects liable to occur. It is established on the basis of the three preceding and closely depends on the uncertainties, variations, working hypotheses, and conjectures made at each stage of the process. When the available data are inadequate or non-conclusive, a prudent and cautious approach to environmental protection, health, or safety could be to opt for the worst-case hypothesis. When such hypotheses are accumulated, this will lead to an exaggeration of the real risk but gives a certain assurance that it will not be underestimated.

# Index